D1994997

HISTORY
OF
WYOMING
COUNTY, N.Y.

Upper and Middle Falls and Portage Bridge.

Grave of Mary Jemison Section of T

INDIAN COUNCIL HOUSE, GLEN IRIS.

1841.

HISTORY

OF

WYOMING

COUNTY, N.Y.

WITH

Illustrations, Biographical Sketches

AND

PORTRAITS OF SOME PIONEERS AND PROMINENT RESIDENTS

Compiled and Published by Frederick W. Beers & Co.

With a New Introduction by Cindy Amrhein

excelsior editions

1880.

Originally published in 1880 by F. W. Beers and Company

Cover Image: Map of Wyoming County, New York: from actual surveys. Philadelphia: N.S. Brown, 1853. Library of Congress Geography and Map Division Washington, D.C. 20540-4650.

Published by State University of New York Press, Albany

Printed in the United States of America

Excelsior Editions is an imprint of State University of New York Press
For information, contact State University of New York Press, Albany, NY
www.sunypress.edu

Library of Congress Cataloging-in-Publication Data

Names: Amrhein, Cindy, writer of introduction. | F.W. Beers & Co., author.
Title: History of Wyoming County, N.Y. : with illustrations, biographical sketches and portraits of some pioneers and prominent residents / with a new introduction by Cindy Amrhein.
Description: Albany : State University of New York Press, [2022] | Series: Excelsior editions | Originally published: F.W. Beers and Company, 1880. | Includes bibliographical references and index.
Identifiers: LCCN 2021050895 | ISBN 9781438487830 (hardcover) | ISBN 9781438487847 (ebook) | ISBN 9781438487823 (paperback)
Subjects: LCSH: Wyoming County (N.Y.)—History. | Wyoming County (N.Y.)—Biography.
Classification: LCC F127.W9 H6 2022 | DDC 974.7/93—dc23/eng/20211025 LC record available at https://lccn.loc.gov/2021050895

10 9 8 7 6 5 4 3 2 1

Contents.

CHAPTER IX.

CHAPTER X.

CHAPTER XI.

CHAPTER XII.

CHAPTER XIII.

CHAPTER XIV.

CHAPTER XV.

CHAPTER XVI.

GENERAL COUNTY HISTORY.

CHAPTER I.

CHAPTER II.

CHAPTER III.

CHAPTER IV.

CHAPTER V.

CHAPTER VI.

CHAPTER VII.

CHAPTER VIII.

CHAPTER IX.

CHAPTER X.

CHAPTER XI.

CHAPTER XII.

CHAPTER XIII.

CHAPTER XIV.

CHAPTER XV.

CHAPTER XVI.

CHAPTER XVII.

CHAPTER XVIII.

CHAPTER XIX.

CHAPTER XX.

CHAPTER XXI.

CHAPTER XXII.

CHAPTER XXIII.

CHAPTER XXIV.

CHAPTER XXV.

CHAPTER XXVI.

CHAPTER XXVII.

CHAPTER XXVIII.

CHAPTER XXIX.

CHAPTER XXX.

TOWN AND VILLAGE HISTORIES.

THE TOWN OF ARCADE.

THE TOWN OF ATTICA.

THE TOWN OF BENNINGTON.

THE TOWN OF CASTILE.

BIOGRAPHIES.

ILLUSTRATIONS.

PORTRAITS.

New Introduction.

THE CREATION OF WYOMING COUNTY

CINDY AMRHEIN, WYOMING COUNTY HISTORIAN

F. W. Beers and Co., the creator of this book, was a successful publisher in the late 1800s and early 1900s. Fredrick W. Beers came from a family of cartographers and publishers. They produced atlases and local histories for counties in several different states, one of them being New York. Most of these county atlases and histories were published by subscription. A spokesman for the company would come to a county and stay several weeks to sell the idea, collect information, and bring surveyors (if necessary), whereby citizens would subscribe to the publication of the book or atlas. County histories were a good seller, as it gave the towns an opportunity to highlight their accomplishments as well as their prominent citizens. The well-to-do were of course enticed to subscribe, and if they paid a bit extra, they could have a short family biography at the end of their town's chapter or have a lithograph included of their homestead.

Wyoming County was no different than any other county in the state. It took pride in its history and eagerly provided the information to the F. W. Beers spokesman. When enough facts and subscriptions were collected, the book would go to press. Their representative would return, often the following summer, with books in tow, collect any funds yet due, and deliver the publication. Because information was gathered directly from the towns, schools, churches, and citizens of the period in which they were published, these books prove to be an invaluable reference still today. Its reprinting will be a benefit to researchers. Aside from originals in collections or from booksellers, there are no hard copies readily available for the public to purchase.

There was one thing in our history book, however, that was not easily verified at the time F. W. Beers set out to compile the work: how our county got its name. I am often asked, "Who named this county?" or "Why did they decide to call it Wyoming?" or some question to that effect. I have heard a lot of conjecture over the years. Some say it was the idea of one of our first county judges, Hon. John B. Skinner from Middlebury. It was also his idea, it is said, to name the village where he lived in Middlebury, Wyoming Village. But the village was named years before our county split from Genesee—almost fifty years earlier, in fact. I found no personal papers, diaries, or government documents that directly discuss any occasion or meeting spelling out the details. Which leads to another often-asked question, "Whose idea was it to split off?" Only the basic wording that names our towns and on what date they were formed have been found in the state legislative acts; but there are no details as to the how, why, or who's idea it was to split from Genesee County.

The answers were found in newspapers from 1841 that laid out in detail the whole affair. It wasn't as cut and dry as first thought. Quite a bit of debate went into it and not everyone was happy about any sort of change. The people who were to remain part of Genesee County were at odds with the idea. In the discussion of the split came the debate, that if the counties were to separate, where would both county seats lie? It was quite a controversy, and fortunately, a heated political topic made for good news. The colorful nitty-gritty accounts in the local newspaper offered much more meat than the wording of the legislative acts.

At a meeting held on January 8, 1841, a resolution was adopted, which, in part, read:

> Whereas, strong and repeated exertions have for a long time been made, by the Southern part of the County of Genesee, to obtain a more central location of the Public Buildings of said county; And whereas, the Commissioners appointed by the last Legislature for the purpose of fixing a site for the new county buildings, in their action, have wholly overlooked or disregarded the wishes and interests of a large portion of said county, in continuing the site at Batavia, and thus dispelled the cherished hope that the vexed question of the division of "Old Genesee" would be put forever at rest, by a central location; And whereas also the southern half of said county contains an equal population with the northern part, and quite sufficient to form a respectable county of itself. [1]

The resolution further noted that the location of Batavia as the county seat disregarded the convenience and interest of the southern towns. If they could not decide on a central location, then the county of Genesee should be split in half. The southern towns of what would become the new county were concerned over the possibility of other towns from Cattaraugus or Allegany counties being tossed into the mix, which was part of the option to the split. The decision was about far more than a division of land. How would a split affect the current leaders come election time? If the new county was combined with outside towns, would the concerns of those towns overshadow the needs of the former Genesee people in this newly created county? Adding towns from other counties to the newly created county could change senate and assembly districts and political party control. The committee that devised the resolution was leaning toward a more central county seat, as opposed to an outright split, unless it was the only answer to satisfy the citizens—primarily the voters.

Even daily living had to be a concern. In 1802, when Genesee County was formed, it was almost all of western New York. The population was sparse, with people living closer to Batavia, but this was not the case in the county as

---

1 *Perry Democrat*, January 28, 1841

it existed in 1841. Communities had spread southward after the War of 1812. Batavia was too close to the northern border and quite a distance to travel if you lived in the county's southern towns. Round trip would be an all-day affair or possibly require an overnight stay. Two working days or more away from farm or business just to record a deed was not practical. Imagine the inconvenience to serve on jury duty for a complicated trial?

A case could certainly be made for either point of view: move the county seat or split the county. Regardless of which camp one was in, the population was growing, and an answer was needed. The committee resolved to meet again in the town of Orangeville, and they would forward the decision to the assemblymen representing the county of Genesee.

Perry Democrat, February 4, 1841

> Division of the County.—We have been informed, on the authority of a letter from a member of the House of Assembly, that it is the impression in the House, that Genesee will be divided in the centre. If this should turn out to be correct, the next scramble will be for the new county seat. So, good people, turn this subject over in your minds in season, it is worth a thought. Warsaw? Orangeville? Wethersfield? or where?

This same newspaper article included a letter that came to the committee from David Scott (Genesee assemblyman, Whig Party) of Albany, dated March 17, explaining the different aspect of the bill that was presented. One option was to combine the towns of Bennington, Attica, Middlebury, Covington, Sheldon, Warsaw, Orangeville, Perry, Java, Wethersfield, Gainesville, Castile, and China to form the county of Marshall, with the county seat to be determined later.[2] Scott felt a provision should be included to submit to the voters at a special election as to whether they prefer a central location for the existing county or a central split through the middle. He was of the mind, as he had made clear, that he was opposed to any split. However, it was clear to him that to relocate the county buildings was not feasible, nor was having men who resided further away to relocate to Batavia if they held office. It was quite a jumbled mess really.

For whatever reason, the bill contained only the choice to leave it whole or split and add other towns. Scott pointed out in his letter that there didn't seem to be the option to just split Genesee. He pointed out, "No application for a division of Genesee alone has been presented but for the central division, any division connected with other counties is reported by the Attorney-General as unconstitutional. Therefore, any division of the Senatorial Districts must be made at the time of their formation or not at all." Another thing to consider

2 Five years later, towns from other counties would be added to Wyoming. Pike was formed from part of Nunda (then in Allegany County, now Livingston) in 1818; Eagle was taken from Pike in 1823 and a part of Pike (and Portage in Livingston County) to Genesee Falls in 1846 when they were added to Wyoming County. China would be renamed Arcade in 1866.

was that Genesee had already begun plans for the construction of their new courthouse made of limestone.[3] Despite David Scott's personal opinions, he felt it was up to the will of the people to decide whether to form a new county and asked the local postmasters to collect the opinions of the neighborhoods and forward them to him at once.

In the March 23rd issue of the *Perry Democrat*, it was reported that it was their view that the county of Genesee should indeed be split. To leave it whole and centralize the county seat was not going to happen, in their opinion: "It is idle to think of getting the county seat away from Batavia, and the people of the South and West will scarcely consent to continue under existing inconveniences."

Ultimately there were two choices, and neither involved leaving the county whole. The only two options in the bill were to (1) split and put the new county seat of Marshall at either Orangeville or Warsaw or (2) leave the county of Genesee whole but move the county seat to Alexander, Bethany, Middlebury, or Attica. In essence, it forced the decision to split. If the county seat of Genesee was to remain at Batavia, there was no other choice. The naming of the new county would go through several changes, beginning with Marshall before it ended up with Wyoming.

They had already prepared if the bill before the assembly passed for the division. The board of supervisors for the county of Genesee would meet at the courthouse in Batavia on the second Tuesday in June and form two separate boards. Felix Tracy of Livingston, David Hurd of Niagara, and Squire S. Case of Erie were chosen to be the commissioners to decide where the buildings of the new county of Marshall would be located. Funds were already set aside by the comptroller for the construction. They were to meet on the first Tuesday of July at the inn at Orangeville Center.[4]

Perry Democrat, April 22, 1841

> Mr. Brownson gave notice of a bill several days ago to provide for the division of Genesee county, and to create the new county of Tonawanda from the southern portion. The bill has not yet been acted on. So many schemes have been proposed for settling this vexed question, and subsequently abandoned, that we shall put faith in none of the present current reports until we see decisive action by the legislature. It is now very generally believed, on the authority of letters from Albany, that the county will be divided in the centre before the close of the present session.

The "Genesee County Bill" came before the assembly on April 27, 1841. The split was heavily debated, with various provisions struck or amended. In the end there were sixty-six ayes and seventeen nays for the split. The bill was then completed with amendments.

3 This courthouse still stands on Main Street in Batavia and is part of the Genesee County Courthouse Historic District.

4 *Perry Democrat*, April 1, 1841.

Now the equally debated name for the new county had to be settled. Marshall had originally been chosen in honor of United States Supreme Court Justice Hon. John Marshall, the respected and well-known constitutional lawyer and historian. Seth C. Hawley of Erie County moved to have the name changed from Marshall to Wyoming. Isaac Stoddard, Genesee County, said Wyoming was originally his choice too but his constituents, who would be in the new county, did not approve. They felt there may be confusion due to its association with Pennsylvania. If not Wyoming then Harrison, after William H. Harrison who was just elected president in 1840. L. Hubbel put it to his collogues whether it would really be an honor to name a little county after them.[5] William McMurray of New York County liked the name Wyoming. If it were up to him, he would strike from the map such exotic names as Rome and Geneva and substitute them with noble Indian names, as they were "once undisputed lords of the new world, who were now fast fading from the face of the earth, to perpetuate, as far as possible those old Indian names." Another said if not Wyoming then "Scott of military glory," meaning General Winfield Scott who was said to be a brilliant strategist during the War of 1812. David C. Scott agreed with the choice of Wyoming. He was also on the Committee on Indian Affairs and would be one of the residents of the new county. He felt it was a pleasant name to speak and easy to write. Besides, there was already a village there with the name and, all things considered, it would be the best choice.[6]

> *Perry Democrat*, May 13, 1841
>
> Division of the County *The Attica Democrat*, of Thursday last, thus discourseth on this subject:
>
> "A bill has passed the Assembly for a central division of this county. The new county is to be called Wyoming. The bill is in direct opposition to the wishes of nine tenths of the citizens of the country."
>
> Well, neighbors, we have long since told you, that you would play with that firebrand till you burned your fingers. We hope you begin to appreciate our fatherly advice, so often tendered you gratis! You, you Attica folks we mean, have made as much noise about 'central location' as anybody we have heard on the subject, in the vain hope of getting a location in your village; and see what you have got for your pains. You ought to have known that there was as much chance of screwing alms from a miser, as of removing the buildings from the Batavians, and that continued agitation could only result in division, much to your disadvantage.

With the bill passing the assembly, it moved to the Senate on May 13, where it passed. *An Act to Divide the County of Genesee and Erect the County of Wyoming* became a reality on May 19, 1841. As with this entire process, the

5 I found no L. Hubbel serving in the assembly in 1841. There was, however, an Assemblyman William S. Hubbell of Steuben County.

6 *Perry Democrat*, May 6, 1841.

county seat was another point of contention. Orangeville and Wethersfield were options, and the *Perry Democrat*, of course, was all for Perry pointing out its trade and manufacturing establishments, its closeness to the Genesee Valley canal, and access to Silver Lake as well as its agricultural success. As expected, Warsaw already claimed it and so the seat was established.[7]

Although it was most likely Middlebury's judge John B. Skinner who named the village of Wyoming, we now know it was Seth C. Hawley of Erie County who moved to amend the bill to substitute Wyoming for Marshall as the name of the new county. Assemblyman David C. Scott was right: it is a pleasant name to speak.[8]

7 *Perry Democrat*, May 27, 1841.

8 For more information on Wyoming County history, the office of the Wyoming County historian has been printing a quarterly periodical called *Historical Wyoming* since 1947. It is available by subscription and in over a dozen stores throughout Wyoming County.

Introductory.

The history of events which have transpired in one's own neighborhood is the most interesting of all history. There is a fascination in the recital of past occurrences, and that fascination is heightened by the fact of their having occurred on familiar ground. The river which flows through a region is invested with an interest beyond what its beauty inspires when it is remembered as an ancient landmark, or as the route of the ancient warrior's trail and the later commercial thoroughfare; when it is known that for centuries it has affected the course of events along its banks—has determined the location of the Indian's village or the white man's city. The valley through which it flows has an interest beyond that which its beauty and fertility lend when it is known to have been the scene of sanguinary conflicts, the retreat of vanquished warriors, or the abiding place of historic characters. The road that has been traveled unthinkingly for years is invested with a new interest when it is learned that it was once an Indian trail. The field where one has harvested but grain or fruit for many a season brings forth a crop of associations and ideas when it is known that it was the scene of one of those battles in which the land was redeemed from savagery, and the character of its civilization determined. The people will look with a heightened and more intelligent interest upon ancient buildings in their midst, already venerated by them they hardly know why, when they read the authentic record of events with which these monuments of the past are associated.

Although the region of which these pages treat is not known to have been the theater of bloody strife among its ancient inhabitants, and although it has only an incidental Revolutionary history, yet the annals of its settlement, of the experiences of its early settlers and its development into its present beautiful and prosperous condition, cannot fail to possess a charm for its present inhabitants, and to strengthen the patriotism which consists not alone in the love of one's country, but also of one's own locality.

Heretofore it has only been possible for the student, with abundant leisure and with ready access to government documents and comprehensive libraries, to trace the written history of his own county by patient and persevering research; but this leisure and these facilities are accessible to but few of those who are intelligently interested in this history, and there are many unwritten facts to be preserved from the failing memories of old residents who will soon carry them to the grave, and others to be gleaned from those best informed concerning present important institutions and interests.

This service of compilation and research, which very few can undertake for themselves, the publishers of this work have endeavored to perform; and though some mistakes may doubtless be found among such a multitude of details in spite of the care exercised, yet the publishers confidently present this result of many months' labor as a true narrative of the events in the history of this county which were of sufficient importance to merit such record.

Events are the offspring of events that have preceded, and the parents of those which follow them. They constitute such an intricate net-work that the history of even so limited a region as a county has its ramifications in remote times and distant regions, and cannot be justly written without transcending the county limits for many essential facts; hence the necessity for such an outline as has been presented of the State history.

To avoid circumlocution, present geographical names are often used in the following pages where the events narrated occurred long before these names had an existence.

In addition to original sources of information, the following works have been consulted in the preparation of this volume: A. W. Young's Histories of Warsaw and of Chautauqua County; Turner's Histories of the Holland Purchase and of Phelps and Gorham's Purchase; Stone's Lives of Brant and Red Jacket; Morgan's League of the Iroquois; Parkman's The Jesuits in North America; Merril's History of the Twenty-fourth Independent Battery; files of the *Western New Yorker*, etc.

Those possessing desirable information have uniformly been kind and courteous in imparting it, and have thus facilitated the preparation of the work. Especial acknowledgments are due to Hon. Augustus Frank and Hon. William P. Letchworth for valuable aid and encouragement; also to Miss Elizabeth Young, for permission to use the works and manuscripts of her father, the late A. W. Young; to David E. E. Mix, of Batavia, for the use of the Holland Land Company's ledgers; to C. A. Hull, clerk of Genesee county, for assistance in his office; and to Charles J. Gardner, clerk of Wyoming county, and his deputy, Mr. Quackenbush, for many acts of kindness. The editors of the various journals in the county have been uniformly courteous and obliging, and to them thanks are due, as well as to the pastors of churches and the secretaries of other organizations.

The following gentlemen are the authors of the histories of their respective towns: Hon. Hugh T. Brooks, Covington; Hon. A. B. Rose and Prof. D. W. Smith, Castile; A. P. Sherrill, Pike; Colonel G. G. Prey, Eagle; B. F. Bristol, Prof. Edson J. Quigley and Augustus Harrington, Gainesville; and Hon. Lucius Peck, Arcade.

Acknowledgments for good offices are also due to the Hon. Wolcott J. Humphrey, General Linus W. Thayer, the Hon. Samuel Tewksbury, Captain A. B. Lawrence, Ephraim Brainard, Colonel J. O. McClure, Lloyd A. Hayward, Esq., C. W. Bailey, Esq., Marvin Wood, Anson Elmer, Amos Otis, Mrs. James McElroy, Simeon Hodges, S. N. Naramore, Captain William S. Agett and James Tolles. The gentleman last named, one of the most prominent pioneers of the town of Bennington, kept a most full and interesting record of noteworthy events, which furnished a large portion of the history of that town in the following pages. We should also mention among those who rendered valuable assistance Ephraim Wheeler, Harvey Merrell (since deceased) and Harvey Stone, of Orangeville; Richard L. Charles, Mrs. Daniel Wolcott and John J. Doolittle, of Wethersfield; and Squire Lockwood, Justus Blakely, Mrs. Moses Twiss and John Eddy, of Java.

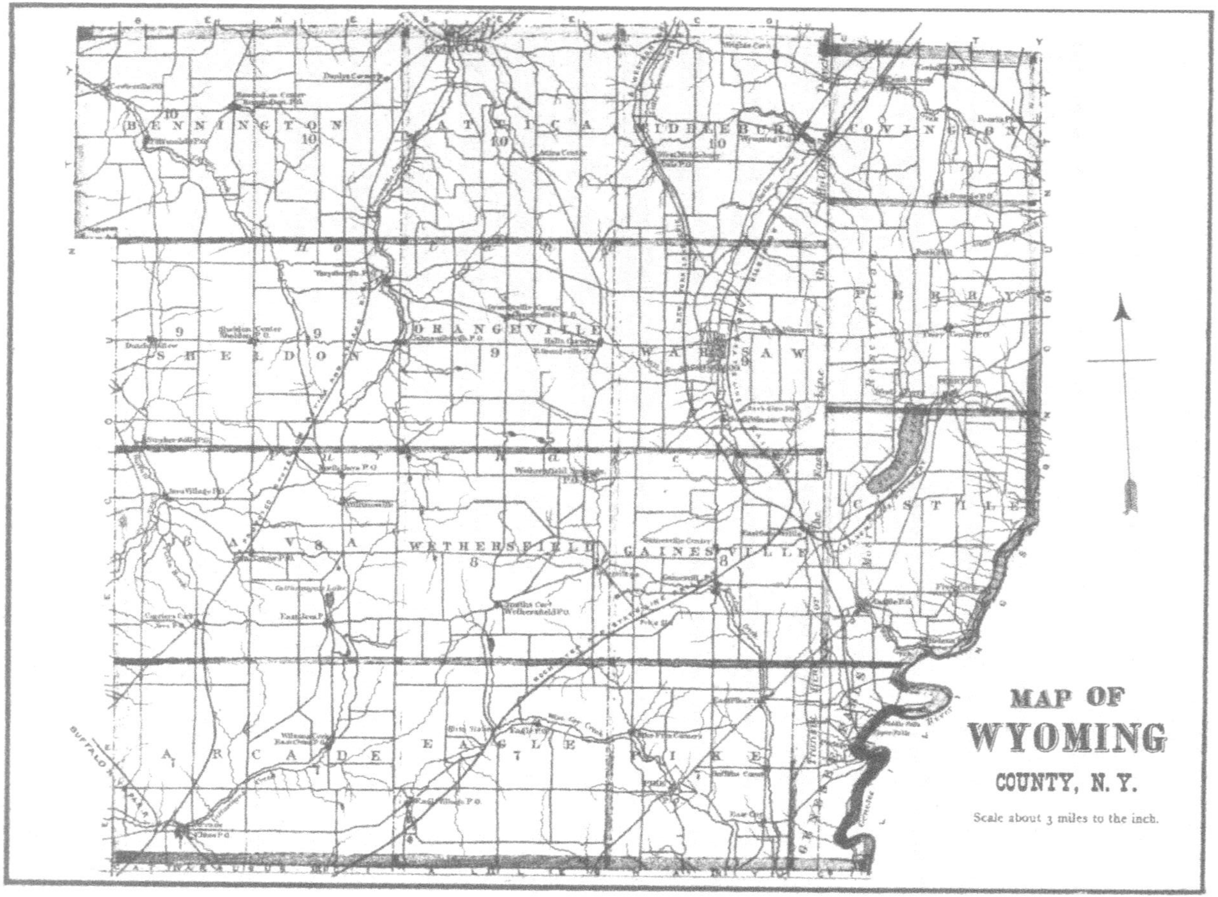
MAP OF
WYOMING
COUNTY, N. Y.
Scale about 3 miles to the inch.
BENNINGTON
ATTICA
MIDDLEBURY
COVINGTON
ORANGEVILLE
WARSAW
PERRY
SHELDON
JAVA
WETHERSFIELD
GAINESVILLE
CASTILE
ARCADE
EAGLE
PIKE
BUFFALO N. Y. & P. R. R.

HISTORICAL PLAN OF THE STATE OF NEW YORK
SHOWING THE DATES AT WHICH THE COUNTIES WERE ORGANIZED AND FROM WHAT FORMED.
DOMINION OF CANADA
LAKE ONTARIO
L. ERIE
PENNSYLVANIA
VERMONT
NEW HAMPSHIRE
MASSACHUSETTS
CONNECTICUT
RHODE ISLAND
NEW JERSEY
LONG ISLAND SOUND
ATLANTIC OCEAN
ST. LAWRENCE
FRANKLIN
CLINTON
ONEIDA
FULTON
SARATOGA
WAYNE
GENESEE
ONTARIO
WYOMING
LIVINGSTON
TOMPKINS
CORTLAND
SCHUYLER
CHEMUNG
TIOGA
CATTARAUGUS
STEUBEN
GREENE
ALBANY
ORANGE
PUTNAM
SUFFOLK
WARREN
McKEAN
POTTER
BRADFORD
SUSQUEHANNA
WAYNE
PIKE
SUSSEX
PASSAIC
LINCOLN
WELLAND
NORTHUMBERLAND
HASTINGS
PRINCE EDWARD
LENOX & ADDINGTON
FRONTENAC
LEEDS
DURHAM
ONTARIO
YORK
ADDISON
ORANGE
RUTLAND
WINDSOR
WINDHAM
BENNINGTON
CALEDONIA
CHITTENDEN
LAMOILLE
WASHINGTON
SULLIVAN
MERRIMAC
CONCORD
CHESHIRE
HILLSBOROUGH
BELKNAP
BERKSHIRE
FRANKLIN
HAMPSHIRE
HAMPDEN
WORCESTER
LITCHFIELD
HARTFORD
TOLLAND
WINDHAM
NEW LONDON
MIDDLESEX
NEW HAVEN
FAIRFIELD
KENT
PROVIDENCE

Outline History of The State of New York.

CHAPTER I.

THE AMERICAN ABORIGINES—CHARACTERISTICS AND CUSTOMS OF THE FIVE NATIONS OF NEW YORK.

THE American continent, in its natural features, presents a striking and diversified display of resources and grandeurs. Bounded by oceans; indented with numerous gulfs and bays; intersected and drained by large rivers; embracing lakes equal in extent to seas, it affords every facility for commerce; while its fertile valleys and extensive plains are admirably adapted to agricultural pursuits, and its rocks are stored with minerals of inestimable value. The magnificence of mountain scenery, the dashing flood and deafening roar of Niagara, the subterranean labyrinths of Mammoth Cave, are features of nature which fill the beholder with wonder and amazement. To what people were these resources offered and these grandeurs presented in the dim ages of the past? With only the shadowy and uncertain light of tradition, little else than speculation can furnish anything like a beginning to the history of the aborigines of America. The ruins of cities and pyramids in Mexico and Central America, and the numerous mounds so common in the valley of the Mississippi, are monuments which point to a people more skilled in arts and farther advanced in civilization than the Indian, found in occupancy when the first Europeans landed. Some of these mounds appear to have been erected for burial places, and others for defense. The remains of fortifications present evidence of mechanical skill, and no little display of the knowledge of engineering. Metallic implements of ingenious design and superior finish, and finely wrought pottery, glazed and colored, equal to the best specimens of modern manufacture, have been found, showing a higher degree of mechanical skill than the Indian has ever been known to possess. Some of these remains have been found twenty feet or more below the surface, showing that they must have lain there for centuries. All the investigations of the antiquarian to discover by what people these mounds were erected have ended in uncertainty. If these are the relics of a lost people, as many believe they are, it seems somewhat probable that they were from Egypt. Their pyramids and skill in the arts, together with the fact that human bodies have been found preserved somewhat similar to Egyptian mummies, support this theory. At an early age the Egyptians, who were noted for their skill in navigation, sailed around Africa, and made many other voyages, in some of which they may have reached America. Aristotle, Plato and other ancient writers appear to have been aware of an extensive body of land in the West, speaking of it as an island, greater than Europe or Africa. It is also supposed that the Egyptians may have reached America through Asia. It is related that an Asiatic people emigrated to Egypt and conquered the Mizraimites, who were then in possession; and that they became distinguished for their arts, built cities and erected gigantic pyramids, which still remain as evidence of their skill and power. The Mizraimites, smarting under their tyranny, rose against them, and after a long struggle succeeded in driving them out of the land. They retreated to the northeast, leaving mounds and walls as far as Siberia as traces of their passage, and, it is thought, crossed Behring's strait, and eventually settled in the Mississippi valley and Mexico.

Leaving conjecture, in regard to the earliest inhabitants of this continent, it is enough to say that the pioneer explorers of our State found dwelling on its soil a race of savages whom English speaking people have universally called Indians since the American aborigines were first met with in the West Indies. New York was occupied by five confederate tribes of these savages, originally named by the English the Five Nations, by the French the *Iroquois*, and by themselves *Konoshioni*—the "cabin builders"—and *Hendenosaunee*–the "people of the long house." The "long house" formed by the Iroquois confederacy extended east and west through the central portion of the State, having at its eastern portal the Mohawks and at its western the Senecas; while between them dwelt the Oneidas, Onondagas and Cayugas, and after 1714 a sixth nation, the Tuscaroras, southeast of Oneida lake.

While we need not share the enthusiasm of some writers, who have competed for the discovery of the most admirable qualities in the Indians of New York, it is yet impossible to regard without interest these primitive inhabitants of our State. It is needless to dwell minutely on their personal appearance, as their muscular forms, reddish brown and beardless faces, black eyes and coarse, straight black hair, are more or less familiar to the present generation. The derivation of the race is still matter of speculation among curious scholars, and the origin of the league of the Iroquois is but little better understood. "Research into conflicting tradition" led Mr. Brodhead to adopt 1539 as the date of that event, and to conclude that the ancestors of the Five Nations, before settling in New York, were driven from Canada by the Adirondacs. One of their own traditions of their origin represented that in the beginning *Tharonhyjagon*, the "Holder of the Heavens," evoked them from beneath a mountain near the falls of the Oswego river (which have nothing like a mountain within thirty miles of them); that they journeyed to their final dwelling places by way of that river and its tributary waters; and that they adopted their league at the suggestion of the wise men of the central tribe, the Onondagas, after experiencing the miseries of hostility among themselves and defeat by enemies from abroad.

While such myths but illustrate the ignorance which has always prevailed as to the origin of the Iroquois and their federal compact, the features of their national character and domestic and public polity, some of which made them undeniably superior to the other savages of North America, have been pretty well ascertained. They lived in huts made of bark fastened by withes to a framework of poles, many families usually crowding into one cabin; permanent villages were stockaded with two rows of posts crossed over a log lying between them, and thus fortified were called castles. They clothed themselves scantily in the skins of wild beasts; and fed on the game brought down by the flint-tipped arrows of the men, who would do no servile labor until too old for war and the chase, and on the corn, beans and pumpkins, or squashes, cultivated by the women. Beasts and reptiles indiscriminately were game to them, and their cookery was of the nastiest description. They had a childish fondness for gaudy ornaments and fabrics, and for showy ceremonies and formalities. Polygamy existed among them, and the marriage agreement was annulled at pleasure, the household goods being divided between the man and woman, and the children accompanying the latter.

The shadow of government existing among the tribes was administered by their chiefs, some of whom, as among certain civilized people, held their position by inheritance, and others by conspicuous force of character. Their jurisdiction did not extend to the punishment of crime, which was left to private vengeance rather than committed to public authority. In the matter of religion these savages believed in a Good Spirit and a happy immortality, but worshiped the devil, with heathenish mummeries and incantations.

One of the most notable of the social arrangements of the Iroquois was the division of each nation into clans, distinguished by symbolic devices which have been called "totems," which they painted upon their cabins and their persons, and in their later history affixed to the deeds of the lands given up by them to the whites. The totems were the same in each of the Five Nations, and the bearer of any one of them was entitled to hospitality from those of his totemic division in any other tribe. The chief clans, as distinguished by their symbols, were those of the Tortoise, the Wolf, the Bear and the Beaver; and the devices of the minor ones were the Deer, Potato, Great and Little Plovers and Eagle.

In their universal fondness for war and their methods of conducting it the Iroquois betrayed their essential savagery. They fought with bows, spears and stone hatchets, and shielded themselves with tough leather; but eagerly obtained rifles, knives and steel tomahawks from the Dutch traders on becoming acquainted with such weapons. They attacked by surprise and ambuscade, and whenever possible fought under cover. They took the scalps of their fallen enemies for trophies, and usually put their captives to death with fiendish tortures, in the unflinching endurance of which was displayed the highest degree of the stoicism which was a marked feature of the Indian character. Hostilities might be suspended at the demand of the women without discredit to the braves who had been carrying them on.

It was in three respects that the Iroquois chiefly showed their mental superiority over the savage tribes surrounding them, namely: the original organization of their league; the boldness of conception with which they pushed their victorious campaigns almost to the eastern and southern limits of the United States and throughout the Mississippi valley; and the cultivation of oratory and its display in their deliberative assemblies. Their confederation united them but loosely and for a few general purposes. There was no authoritative central government, and common action was taken only upon a unanimous vote of the tribes represented in the great council, which sat with the Onondagas, in which each tribe must also speak with unanimous voice. The military advantages of the associated action of the Five Nations are obvious. By their united weight they overcame all opposition until confronted by the superior discipline and armament of the white man, and made their common name a terror to the other native tribes throughout the greater portion of the United States. Their dominance is thus eloquently pictured in Street's "Frontenac":

"The fierce Adirondacs had fled from their wrath,
The Hurons been swept from their merciless path;
Around, the Ottawas, like leaves, had been strewn,
And the lake of the Eries struck silent and lone,
The Lenape, lords once of valley and hill,
Made women, bent low at their conquerors' will.
By the far Mississippi the Illini shrank
When the trail of the TORTOISE was seen on the bank;
On the hills of New England the Pequod turned pale
When the howl of the WOLF swelled at night on the gale;
And the Cherokee shook in his green, smiling bowers
When the foot of the BEAR stamped his carpet of flowers."

The relative superiority of the Mohawks among the Iroquois, except in point of numbers, is a fact attested by abundant historical authority, including the following passage by Mr. Brodhead:

"Of all the confederated nations the Mohawks were the bravest and fiercest. No hunter warriors on the North American continent ever filled a higher measure of heroism and military renown. Their very name was a synonym for blood. From their propinquity to the Dutch settlements, and their superior martial exploits, the name of this nation was frequently applied, by way of eminence, to the whole Iroquois confederation; among all the nations of which the Mohawks were held in the highest veneration. Standing at the eastern door of the 'long house,' the Mohawk warriors were the chief agents in carrying to the sea the conquests of the Iroquois. Far across the hills of Massachusetts, and through the valley of the Connecticut, the dreaded name of Mohawk enforced an absolute submission; and their annual envoys collected tribute and dictated laws with all the arbitrary authority of Roman proconsuls."

After the advent of the whites opposing interests among them appealed to the Iroquois with distracting influences which finally ruined their famous league and drove them from their ancient hunting grounds.

Though the Indians are generally credited with taciturnity, their deliberations in council were monuments of verbosity. It was in their parleys with the whites in early times that they made the long-winded speeches, which, as interpreted by the civilized reporters, have laid the foundation of their oratorical reputation. Their language was extremely figurative, their speeches often consisting largely of a search for picturesque conceits to express the simplest ideas.

It has been customary with recent writers on the Indians to ascribe to them many and lofty excellencies and abilities, and to begin by deprecating the alleged disposition to do them injustice and to ignore their claims to respect and admiration. If such a disposition ever existed, the tide of opinion has of late certainly been flowing the other way, and it may be time for the ebb. There seems to have been something like statesmanship in the formation of the league of the Iroquois, albeit the expedient was the simplest possible, and the object success in savage warfare; also in the means by which the league was strengthened, including the complicated system of family and tribal relationship; but has not the glory of this barbarian union been exaggerated? For example, must we believe all we read of Indian oratory? Not satisfied with the eloquent periods ascribed to the red speech-makers, their eulogists remind us that we have only white men's versions of what the orators said, and assume that the speeches suffered by the interpretation. But it is possible that they gained. The interpreters, it is said, were often illiterate men; but they were in all cases less so than the orators, and in many cases they must be admitted to have been quite adequate to the task. One of the most famous of Indian orations is the address of Garangula, *alias* La Grande Gueule—Big Mouth, as Mr. Parkman translates it—to De La Barre in the conference at the mouth of Salmon river, in Oswego county; "but this," says Mr. Clinton, in his celebrated eulogy of the Iroquois, "was interpreted by Monsieur Le Moine, a French Jesuit, and recorded on the spot by Baron La Hontan, men of enlightened and cultivated minds." The man who translated it from the French must have been a scholar, and it is not likely that the speech suffered in his hands. Mr. Parkman makes a very suggestive remark on Big Mouth: "Doubtless as he stood in full dress before the governor and the officers, his head plumed, his face painted, his figure draped in a colored blanket and his feet decked with embroidered moccasons, he was a picturesque and striking object; he was less so as he squatted almost naked by his lodge fire, with a piece of board laid across his lap, chopping rank tobacco with a scalping knife to fill his pipe, and entertaining the grinning circle with grotesque stories and obscene jests." Fondness for speechmaking does not necessarily argue eloquence, and it is not easy to believe in a phenomenal development of true oratory in a race of savages, who were primarily warriors, in a skulking and brutal fashion, and whose home life, if we may use the expression, was, generation after generation alike, contentedly passed in idleness and squalor. On the whole we may say that, questionable as may have been some of the white man's dealings with the Iroquois, the expulsion from their ancient territory of that people, with their doubtful virtues and indubitable barbarity, was an exceedingly good riddance.

CHAPTER II.

EXPLORATION AND SETTLEMENT ON THE ATLANTIC COAST AND THE HUDSON RIVER.

THE discovery of America was the most important event of modern times. For the honor of this discovery several claims have been presented. Welsh historians have awarded it to Modoc, a prince of Wales, who went to sea in the twelfth century, and discovered land far to the west, to which he made several voyages, but who, with all his crew, was finally lost. This claim is founded on tradition, however, and unsubstantiated.

The Norwegians claim discovery and settlement on stronger evidence. Eric emigrated from Iceland to Greenland in 986 and founded a settlement. Leif, a son of Eric, embarked with a crew of men in the year 1000 on a voyage of discovery. He sailed to the southwest and discovered land; voyaging along the coast he finally entered a bay, where he remained through the winter, calling the region Vinland.

In 1007 Thorfinn sailed from Greenland to Vinland. An account of this voyage is still extant. Other voyages were made, and the Antiquarian Society, after a careful examination of all the evidence, including the geography of the country described in these voyages, do not hesitate to locate this Vinland at the head of Narragansett Bay, in Rhode Island.

These discoveries, however, were so ineffectual that nothing was known in Europe of land beyond the ocean until 1492, when Christopher Columbus, believing that India might be reached by sailing westward, was, at his urgent solicitation, dispatched on a voyage of discovery by Ferdinand and Isabella, king and queen of Spain. He sailed from Palos, and after stopping at the Canaries struck out upon the hitherto unknown sea, discovering first one of the Bahama islands; then proceeding toward the south he discovered Cuba and Hayti, and returned to Spain, thus opening a highway over the trackless Atlantic. He made other voyages, and in 1498 discovered the continent near the mouth of the Orinoco river. The discovery of land in the west promised large profits, and excited maritime enterprise throughout Europe. Henry VII. commissioned John Cabot, a Venetian, in 1497, to sail on a voyage of discovery, and take possession of new lands in the name of England. Sailing westward, in company with his son Sebastian, he discovered Newfoundland, and while off the coast of Labrador saw the main-land of North America. The next year Sebastian set sail to discover a northwest passage to China. The frozen regions at the north compelled him to change his course, and sailing toward the south he visited various points along the coast as far as Albemarle sound, taking possession of the whole region for the crown of England. John Verazzani, a Florentine in the service of Francis I., of France, arrived on the coast of North Carolina in 1524, and sailed south as far as Georgia. Turning north, he explored the coast to about 41° north latitude, and entered a harbor, which, from his description, is believed to have been New York Bay, where he remained about fifteen days, and it is supposed that his crew were the first Europeans that landed on the soil of New York. He proceeded north as far as Labrador, giving to the whole country the name of New France, which was afterward confined to Canada.

Henry Hudson, an English navigator, having failed in two expeditions to discover a passage to the East Indies, for a company of London merchants, by sailing westward, offered his services in 1609 to the Dutch East India Company of Holland, which was formed the preceding year for traffic and colonization. He left Amsterdam on the 4th of April with a small ship and a crew of about twenty English and Dutch sailors, and arrived on the American coast near Portland, in Maine, whence he proceeded south along the shore to the entrance of Chesapeake Bay. From this point he returned northward, discovered and entered Delaware Bay, and on the 3d of September anchored at Sandy Hook. From here he proceeded up New York Bay, sending his boats to the Jersey shore and receiving on board the natives, who came in great numbers to traffic. On the 12th he entered the river which bears his name, and ascended it to a point a little above where the city of Hudson now stands, having been frequently visited on the way by the Indians, who came to traffic, bringing maize, tobacco and other products native to the country. To them he imparted a knowledge of the effects of rum, to the drinking of which in later years they became greatly addicted. Not considering it safe to proceed further with his ship, he sent a boat with a part of his crew to explore the river higher up. It is supposed that they went a little above Albany. On the 23d he commenced to descend the river. When a little below the Highlands, the Indians made several attempts to attack his crew, who, in repulsing their attacks, shot ten or twelve of their number. Descending into the bay he immediately sailed for Europe. The following year he made a voyage for the discovery of a northwest passage to India, and discovered and entered the bay which bears his name. Continuing his search too long, he was compelled to remain through the winter. In the spring part of his crew mutinied, put him in a boat, together with his son and seven others, and left them to perish. In 1607 Samuel Champlain, a French navigator, ascended the St. Lawrence river, exploring its tributaries; and on the 4th of July discovered the lake which bears his name. Hence three nations,

Holland, France and England, founding their titles upon discovery, claimed ownership in a region a part of which lies within the State of New York.

The accounts given by Hudson of his discoveries stimulated the Dutch to avail themselves of the advantages that might be gained by trading with the Indians, and accordingly in the following year another vessel was sent out to engage in the fur trade on the banks of the river he had discovered. In 1612 two more vessels were fitted out by Hendrick Christiansen and Adrian Block, which were soon followed by others. The fur trade proving successful, Christiansen was appointed agent of the traffic, and Manhattan Island made the chief depot. He erected a small fort and a few rude buildings at the southern extremity of the island, calling the place New Amsterdam. The island was covered with giant forest trees and dense thickets, which served as hiding places for reptiles and wild beasts. In 1714 the States General granted a charter to the merchants engaged in these expeditions, conferring the exclusive right of trade in this new territory, between the 40th and 45th parallels of north latitude, for four years, and giving the name of New Netherlands to the whole region. The trade flourished, and had become so profitable at the expiration of the charter that the States General refused to renew it, giving instead a special license for its temporary continuance.

In the meantime the surrounding country was being explored. Adrian Block had passed up the East river, Long Island sound and Connecticut river, and into the bays and along the islands eastward to Cape Cod. Cornelissen Jacobsen May had explored the southern coast of Long Island and southward to Delaware Bay, while Hendrick Christiansen had ascended the Hudson river to Castle Island, a few miles below Albany, where he had established a trading post and erected a small fort. This fort was so much damaged by a flood that it was removed to the Normans-kill, a little below. Here a council was held between the chiefs and warriors of the Five Nations and the representatives of the New Netherlands, and a treaty of peace and alliance was formed.

In 1620 James I. granted to Ferdinando Gorges and his commercial associates all the land between the fortieth and forty-eighth degrees of north latitude, and extending from ocean to ocean. Captain Dermer, in the service of Gorges, appeared at Manhattan, and laid claim to all the territory occupied by the Dutch. The English ambassador at the Dutch capital had been instructed to remonstrate against Dutch intrusion, but it seems his remonstrance was without effect; for in 1621 the States General granted a new charter to the Dutch West India Company, an armed mercantile association, giving them exclusive jurisdiction over the province of New Netherlands for twenty years, with power to appoint governors, subject to the approval of the States; to colonize the territory and administer justice. The executive management was intrusted to a board of directors, distributed through five separate chambers in the city of Holland. The charge of the province had been assigned to the Amsterdam chamber, which sent out a vessel in 1623, under the direction of Captain May and Adrien Joriszen Tienpont, with thirty families for colonization. A portion of these settled on the Connecticut river, and others as far up the Hudson as the present city of Albany, where they built Fort Orange. A fort was also erected on the Delaware river; near Gloucester, and called Fort Nassau. Their number was shortly after augmented by other accessions, and colonization fairly commenced. In May, 1626, Peter Minuit arrived in New Netherlands as director-general or governor of the province. He purchased the whole of Manhattan Island of the Indians for trinkets of the value of $24. Friendly courtesies were then exchanged with the Plymouth colony, and a brisk and profitable trade in furs was carried on.

CHAPTER III.

THE DUTCH REGIME IN NEW YORK—RIVAL CLAIMS OF THE ENGLISH—THE LATTER PREVAIL.

TO encourage immigration, in 1629 an ordinance was adopted granting to any member of the company who within four years should plant a colony of fifty persons, upwards of fifteen years old, the privilege of selecting a tract of land sixteen miles in length, on any navigable stream, and inland as far as he should choose, with the title of patroon, denoting something lordly in rank and means. The patroons on their part were to buy of the Indians the right to the land selected, maintain a minister and school-master, and pay duty on trade carried on by them; but the company reserved the exclusive right to the fur trade, which was becoming extensive and attracting dealers from the banks of the St. Lawrence. Several availed themselves of this privilege, among whom were Michael Pauw and Killian Van Rensselaer, the former securing Staten Island and a large tract on the Jersey shore, and the latter a large tract on the Hudson river, now the counties of Albany and Rensselaer. Although the patroons were excluded in their charter by the company from participating in the fur trade, their interference brought on a controversy, and Minuit, who it was thought favored their pretensions, was recalled. The vessel in which he sailed was detained by the English authorities at Plymouth, on the charge that he had traded and obtained her cargo in territory subject to England, and thus the respective claims of the English and Dutch to the title of New Netherlands were again called in question. The Dutch relied on the discoveries made by Hudson, and their immediate occupation, ratified by charter; and the English on the prior discovery by Cabot and the grant of James I., covering the territory. No final settlement being obtained, the question was deferred; and in April, 1633, Wouter Van Twiller arrived at New Amsterdam as the new director-general, bringing with him Everardus Bogardus, a clergyman, Adam Roelandsen, the first school-master to the colony, and a small military force, with which he subsequently made considerable display. Soon after assuming the government, he directed Jacob Van Corlaer to purchase a tract of land of the Indians on the Connecticut river, near the present city of Hartford. The English colonies earnestly remonstrated against this invasion of their territory, but without effect. The Plymouth colony secured a tract of the Indians at Windsor, and sent Lieutenant William Holmes with a force to take possession and commence a settlement. Van Corlaer being unable to oppose them with any effect, Van Twiller sent a force of soldiers to disperse them. The courage of the Dutch commander forsook him on perceiving that they were prepared to meet him, and he refrained from trying to dislodge them. Better success, however, attended him in an expedition against the Virginia colonists. A band of these, under the lead of George Holmes, had taken possession of Fort Nassau on the Delaware river. Van Twiller immediately sent a force there, which captured and brought them as prisoners to Fort Amsterdam. During his administration Jacob Eelkins, who had formerly been an agent for the company at Fort Orange, arrived at Manhattan as supercargo of an English vessel engaged in the fur trade. Van Twiller refused to let him proceed without a license from the company, which Eelkins declined to present, but claiming a right to trade with the Indians as an Englishman, to whom the territory belonged, he proceeded up the river to Fort Orange, in defiance of the governor, and commenced trading with them. Van Twiller, in great indignation, dispatched a force after him, and bringing his vessel back, sent it out to sea. He was so mindful of his own interest that he became the wealthiest land-owner in the province. Vehemently passionate, he became involved in a bitter quarrel with Bogardus, the clergyman, and with Van Dinklagen, a member of his council. The latter had very justly complained of his rapacity, for which he sent him a prisoner to Holland, on a charge of contumacy. His corruption and incompetency to govern becoming apparent, he was recalled, and William Kieft, in 1638, succeeded him in the government of the colony.

The company in the following year obtained a new charter, limiting the patroons to four miles on the rivers and eight inland. Other efforts were made to encourage immigration. Settlements were extending in all directions, and the province was rapidly filling with inhabitants. The governor, however, instead of proving useful in promoting the prosperity of the colony with the opportunities presented, became involved in difficulties with the English settlements and the neighboring Indian tribes, which finally brought the colony to the verge of extirpation. By injudicious management and cruelty to the Indians, they were incited to revenge and relentless war on the whites. A robbery having been committed, a tribe of Indians, though innocent, were suspected; and Kieft sent an armed force against them, killing several of their number and destroying their property. The Indians retaliated for this unprovoked attack by murdering some settlers and burning their buildings. The chiefs refused to give satisfaction for these outrages, and Kieft resolved on a war against them. An Indian, whose uncle had been killed by the whites a number of years before, vowed revenge, and killed a Dutchman at Manhattan. Kieft sent a force against his tribe, with orders to exterminate them. Seeing their danger, they sued for peace. Before the terms of a treary had been agreed upon, a warrior, who had been made drunk and then robbed by the whites, upon recovering his senses killed two of the Dutch. Just at this time the river Indians, in a conflict with the Mohawks, were compelled to take refuge on the Hudson opposite Manhattan, and solicit protection from their enemies; but instead of it being granted, a party under the sanction of Kieft, and against the remonstrance of the best citizens, went over to massacre them. This wicked and inhuman outrage was perpetrated at midnight, and nearly a hundred of these helpless and unsuspecting fugitives were murdered, or driven into the river to perish. A desperate and bloody war was the result. The neighboring tribes joined to avenge this outrage. The dwellings of the settlers were burned, their fields desolated, and themselves shot by their lurking foes. Their settlements were attacked in every direction, and terror, despair and death prevailed. Captain John Underhill, who had gained some notoriety in Indian warfare, was appointed to command the forces of the colonists. He finally succeeded in bringing the Indians to submission, and in 1645 a treaty of peace was concluded. An earnest appeal was made for the recall of Kieft, who had been the cause of this calamitous war. The request was favorably received, and Peter Stuyvesant, who was appointed to succeed him, took charge of the government May 11th, 1647. He had been in the service of the company as director-general of Curacoa. The controversy between the Dutch and English settlements still continuing, arbitrators were appointed to adjust their claims. The eastern part of Long Island was assigned to the English. A line was specified for the boundary between the Connecticut and New Netherland colonies, but it was unsatisfactory to the Dutch. In 1652 a municipal government was established for Manhattan, consisting of a revenue agent, to be appointed by the company, and two burgomasters and five inferior magistrates, to be elected by the people, and to have jurisdiction in capital cases. The Swedes since the early part of Kieft's administration had been enroaching upon the Dutch territory on the Delaware; and Stuyvesant, by order of the company, went against them with an armed force, recaptured the forts, and resumed possession of the territory. While on this expedition, one of the Indians having been shot by a settler, the savages appeared at Manhattan in canoes, killed the offender, and crossing to the Jersey shore and Staten Island, began killing other settlers and destroying their property. Stuyvesant returned and by conciliatory measures restored peace.

In 1664 Charles II. of England, regardless of the claims of the Dutch to New Netherlands, granted to his brother, Duke of York and Albany, afterward James II., the whole country from the Connecticut to the Delaware, including the entire Dutch possessions. A fleet was sent out by the duke under Colonel Richard Nichols, to enforce his claim and take possession of the Dutch settlements. Arriving in the bay he demanded a surrender, which Stuyvesant at first indignantly refused; but because of the unwillingness of the colonists to fight in his defense and of their insisting upon capitulation, together with the favorable nature of the terms offered, he was induced to yield, and on the 3d of September, 1664, the province was surrendered, and the government of the colony passed into the hands of the English. The names New Netherlands and New Amsterdam were changed to New York, and Fort Orange to Albany. It is supposed that at this time the province contained about six thousand inhabitants. Soon after the surrender the Duke conveyed to Lord Berkley and Sir George Carteret what now constitutes the State of New Jersey, over which a separate proprietary government was established. In 1682 William Penn purchased the settlements on the Delaware, which were annexed to Pennsylvania. Nichols, who became governor, devoted much time to confirming grants under the Dutch government by issuing new ones, and thus making a heavy expense to the land-owners. He changed the form of the municipal government of New York June 12th, 1666, by granting a city charter, placing the executive power in the hands of a mayor, aldermen and sheriff, all to be appointed by the governor. An invasion from Holland had been feared, and preparations for defense had incurred an increase of taxation, of which the colony greatly complained, in consequence of which Nichols resigned his office in 1668, and Colonel Francis Lovelace was appointed to succeed him. Holland being involved in a war with England, an opportunity was presented for the Dutch to regain their lost possessions in America, and for that purpose they sent out a squadron, which anchored at Staten Island July 30th, 1673. The fort at New York was in charge of Captain John Manning, who treacherously surrendered without making any effort to resist. The city was again in possession of the Dutch, and Captain Anthony Clove in command of the province. Manning was afterward tried and convicted by court-martial of cowardice and treachery, and adjudged to have his sword broken over his head in front of the city hall, and to be incapacitated from holding any office. Under Clove the Dutch claims to the province were reasserted, and preparations made for a vigorous defense in case of an attempt on the part of the English for its recapture; but by the provisions of a peace concluded February 9th, 1674, the province reverted to the English. To silence all controversy respecting his claims, the Duke of York obtained a new patent from the King to confirm the one granted in 1664, and commissioned Major Edmund Andros as governor. His arbitrary course made his administration very unpopular. He endeavored to extend his jurisdiction to the Connecticut river, but his claims were stoutly resisted by the people of that province, and he finally concluded to abandon the design. He quarreled with and disputed the right of Philip Carteret, who administered the government of East Jersey, arresting and bringing him prisoner to New York. For this act the proprietors of the New Jersey government preferred charges against him, which he was summoned to England to answer. He returned to continue his oppressions, but the resistance of the people against him was so strong that he was recalled, and Thomas Dongan appointed as his successor, who arrived August 27th, 1683. Through the influence of William Penn he was instructed to organize a popular assembly, and accordingly, soon after his arrival, issued orders for the choosing of representatives. This, the first Colonial Assembly of New York, was convened October 17th, 1683, and consisted of a council of ten and seventeen representatives. A charter of liberties was framed, vesting the supreme legislative power in the governor and council and the people in general assembly; conferring the right of suffrage on the freeholders without restraint; providing that no freeman should suffer but by judgment of his peers, and that all trials should be by a jury of twelve men. The imposition of any tax without the consent of the assembly was prohibited. Martial law was not to exist, and neither soldiers nor seamen were to be quartered on the inhabitants against their will. The province was divided into counties, and the representatives were apportioned according to the population.

CHAPTER IV.

FRENCH AND INDIAN WARS—DISSENSIONS IN THE COLONIAL GOVERNMENT—EXECUTION OF LEISLER.

AT the time Champlain ascended the St. Lawrence, he found the Algonquins at war with the Iroquois, and by an alliance of his forces with the former he enabled them, by the use of fire-arms (hitherto unknown to them), to gain a victory over their enemies. In consequence of this alliance a bitter hostility was created on the part of the Iroquois toward the French. The latter, however, were successful in gaining the confidence and friendship of the other tribes with whom they came in contact. Through the influence of their missionaries, the traders were enabled to establish their posts among them at pleasure, and navigate the lakes and rivers. Although the artful Jesuit missionaries had persistently endeavored to win back the friendship of the Iroquois, they effected but little until New York fell into the hands of the English. Since their trade and intimacy with the Dutch they had availed themselves of fire-arms, renewed their warfare upon the Algonquins with success, repelled the invasions of the French, and, in turn, attacking them, swept over their settlements with fire and tomahawk, carrying consternation in their path even to the gates of Quebec. In 1666 the French and Adirondacs successfully invaded the country of the Mohawks, but the year following a peace was concluded, chiefly through the agency of the English colonial government, acting in obedience to the instructions of the Duke of York, to whom the colony had been granted, and who, in his bigoted and blind attachment to the Church of Rome, was desirous of securing a peace between the French and the Iroquois, with a view of handing the latter over as converts to the church.

Trade, after this peace, was profitably prosecuted by both the French and English; but the French, through their artful Catholic missionaries, were gaining a decided advantage. Through the instigation of these wily priests, hostilities had been committed on the frontier settlements of Maryland and Virginia by the Five Nations. To adjust this difficulty, a council of the chiefs met the governors of Virginia and New York at Albany, in 1684. At this council the difficulties with Virginia were amicably settled, and Governor Dongan succeeded in completely gaining the friendship of the Five Nations. While these conferences were in progress, a messenger arrived from De la Barre, governor of Canada, complaining of the Senecas for their hostilities against the Miamis and other western tribes, with whom the French were allied, whereby their trade was interrupted. This message was communicated to the Indian chiefs, and served to confirm their resolutions of friendship for the English, and revive their slumbering hatred of the French. Immediately on the return of the messenger, De la Barre, meditating the destruction of the Five Nations, proceeded with an army of French and Indians to Lake Ontario. The French Catholics had procured a letter from the Duke of York to Governor Dongan, instructing him to lay no obstacle in the way of the invaders; but Dongan, regardless of this command, apprised the Indians of their designs and also promised to assist them. Owing to sickness in his army, De la Barre was unable to encounter his foes, and found it necessary to conclude his campaign by offering terms of peace, which were haughtily accepted, and he was allowed to depart. He was succeeded in the following year by the Marquis de Denonville, who, with a reinforcement of troops, was sent over to repair the disgrace of De la Barre. In 1687, to prevent the interruption of trade with the Miamis, the country of the Senecas was invaded. The French, through the agency of their missionary to the Onondagas, enticed the Iroquois chiefs into their power, under pretense of making a treaty, and then seized and sent them, with others they had taken prisoners, to France, where they were consigned to the galleys. The Seneca country was overrun without serious resistance, and a fort erected at the mouth of the Niagara river. A peace was finally proposed through the interposition of Governor Dongan, who was for compelling the French to apply to him in the affairs of the Five Nations, but its conditions were rejected by the French. The Five Nations, maddened by this refusal and by the outrages committed upon them, flew to arms, and with twelve hundred warriors descended upon the French settlements with such terrible vengeance that the terms that had been offered for peace were accepted, and the whole region south of the great lakes abandoned by the French.

The Duke of York, on his accession to the throne of England in 1685, under the title of James II., directed Governor Dongan to encourage the Catholic priests who came to reside with the Five Nations, ostensibly for advancing the

Popish cause, but really to gain them over to the French interests. Governor Dongan, although a Catholic, was apprehensive of the insidious designs of the French, and effectually resisted this policy, thereby displeasing his bigoted master. James also instructed Governor Dongan to allow no printing press to be established in the colony, and discouraged representative government. Catholics were appointed to fill all the offices, and Dongan, who, in his endeavors to protect the true interest of the province by opposing the Catholic missionaries, became obnoxious to the King, was recalled, and Francis Nicholson, the deputy of Sir Edmund Andros, who had been commissioned governor of both New England and New York, assumed temporary charge of the government in August, 1688. The revolution in England, resulting in the abdication of James II., and the accession of William and Mary, caused the authority of Nicholson under the dethroned king to be questioned. On one side it was claimed that the government in England did not affect affairs in the province, and that Nicholson's authority was unimpaired till the will of the new monarch was known; on the other side, that the government, extending to the colonies, was overthrown, and as no one was invested with authority in the provinces, it reverted to the people, who might appoint a person to exercise control until one had been commissioned by the ruling power. The advocates of the former of these views were mostly the wealthy and aristocratic, while the mass of the people favored the latter. The government was vested in a committee of safety, who took possession of the fort at New York, and entrusted the exercise of authority to Jacob Leisler, the popular leader, Nicholson in the meantime having returned to England. Leisler sent a statement of what had been done to King William, and dispatched Milborne, his son-in-law, to Albany with an armed force, to secure the recognition of his authority, sanction to which had been refused. A letter from the English ministry arrived, directed to Francis Nicholson, or in his absence to such person as for the time being might be in charge of the government, directing him to take chief command of the province, and to call to his aid such as he deemed proper. Leisler, considering it addressed to himself, assumed command, and appointed a council of advisers. The revolution in England which placed William and Mary upon the throne was followed by a war between England and France, and the colonies were of course involved in the conflict. Count Frontenac, who had succeeded Denonville as governor of Canada, made an effort to detach the Five Nations from the English interest. He sent a secret expedition against Schenectady, which attacked that city, near midnight, on the 8th of February, 1690, and a frightful massacre of the inhabitants ensued. The peril of Albany from such deadly attacks induced its inhabitants to submit to the authority of Leisler. Expeditions were fitted out against the French and Indians, and a fleet sent out for the reduction of Quebec, but all proved unsuccessful. In March, 1691, Henry Sloughter arrived as governor, having been commissioned by the King in 1689. His coming was heralded by Richard

Ingoldsby, who, without proper credentials, demanded the surrender of the fort at New York. This Leisler very properly refused, but consented to defer to Sloughter when he should arrive. Sloughter on his arrival sent Ingoldsby with verbal directions for the surrender of the fort, but Leisler still refused, and asked for an interview with the governor. The next day he complied, but this imprudent hesitation was seized upon by his enemies, who arrested him and his son-in-law on the charge of treason. They were tried by a special committee and condemned to suffer death. Governor Sloughter hesitated to execute this sentence, but their enemies, anxious for their execution, and failing in all attempts to procure his signature, availed themselves of his known intemperate habits, invited him to a banquet, persuaded him to sign the death warrant while intoxicated, and before he recovered from his debauch the prisoner was executed.

During the agitations attending this foul judicial murder, the Indians, from neglect, became dissatisfied toward the English, insomuch that they sent an embassy of peace to Count Frontenac; to counteract this a council with the Five Nations was held at Albany, and the covenant chain renewed. In order to maintain this advantage, Major Schuyler, in whom the Five Nations had great confidence, led them in an invasion of Canada, and signally defeated the French. The intemperate habits of Sloughter brought on a severe illness, from which he died on the 23d of July, 1691, thus ending a weak and turbulent administration. Upon the death of Sloughter the chief command was committed to Richard Ingoldsby, to the exclucion of Joseph Dudley, who, but for his absence, would have had the right to preside, and upon whom, the government devolved; and as Dudley, upon his return, did not contest the authority of Ingoldsby, the latter governed until the arrival of Benjamin Fletcher, with a commission as governor, in August, 1692. He was a man of small ability and violent temper, active and avaricious, but prudently took Major Schuyler into his counsel, and was guided by his opinions in Indian affairs. His administration was so successful the first year that he received large supplies from the Assembly. The unamiable traits of his character were soon exhibited, however, and during most of his administration he was engaged in controversies with the Assembly, principally in regard to appropriations for his expenses, for which he made extravagant demands. He was bigotedly attached to the Episcopal form of church government, and encouraged English churches and schools in place of Dutch. He procured an act from the Assembly, the provisions of which, though admitting of a more liberal construction, he interpreted as a recognition of the Episcopal instead of the Dutch church, and under this act Trinity Church was organized. A printing press was established in New York city in 1693, by William Bradford, who was employed by the city to print the corporation laws.

CHAPTER V.

COUNT FRONTENAC'S CAMPAIGNS—PIRACY—MISGOVERNMENT OF NEW YORK—FRENCH FRONTIER POSTS.

IN 1693 Count Frontenac set out from Montreal with an army of French and Indians, and invaded the Mohawk country, capturing their castles, killing some of the tribe, and taking about three hundred prisoners. Schuyler, with militia of Albany, hastened to the assistance of Mohawks, and pursued the enemy in their retreat, retaking about fifty prisoners. In 1696 Count Frontenac made another effort for the subjugation of the Five Nations. With an army of regular troops and Indians under his command he ascended the St. Lawrence to Cadaraqui, now Kingston; then, crossing to Oswego, made a descent upon the Onondagas, who, apprised of his coming, set fire to and deserted their principal towns. On retracing his march he found his progress obstructed by the Onondagas, and incursions into Canada by the Five Nations were again renewed. In the following year the war between France and England was terminated by the peace of Ryswick, and these barbarous hostilities ceased.

During the late war piracy had prevailed, and was believed to be encouraged by the governments, for the annoyance of the commerce of their respective enemies. Merchant vessels were destroyed within sight of the harbor of New York, the commercial depot of the pirates, some of whom had sailed from there, having a good understanding with Fletcher and other officers. The extinction of piracy was loudly demanded, and the English government found it necessary to resort to vigorous measures for this end; and consequently, in 1695 Fletcher was recalled, and Richard, Earl of Bellomont, appointed in his place, with instructions for the suppression of this evil. The Earl of Bellomont, whose commission included the governments of Massachusetts and New Hampshire as well as New York, did not arrive until May, 1698. Before leaving England, an armed vessel was fitted out by Bellomont and others, and placed under the command of Captain William Kidd, who sailed from England in 1696, and after cruising for a while turned pirate himself, and became the most bold and daring of the ocean marauders. He returned to New York with his booty and concealed portions of it on Long Island. He was subsequently arrested in Boston, by order of the governor, on a charge of piracy, sent to England for trial, and there convicted and executed. Bellomont favored the Democratic or Leislerian party, and the new Assembly in 1699 being also Democratic, an act was passed by which the families of Leisler and Milborne were reinstated in their possessions. Bellomont died in 1701, and John Nanfan, the lieutenant-governor, upon whom the government devolved, succeeded him until the arrival, in 1702, of Lord Cornbury, who was appointed by King William as a reward for his desertion of James II., in whose army he had been an officer. His administration was chiefly distinguished for its intolerance, and he received the unenviable distinction of being the worst governor under the English regime. With savage bigotry he sought to establish the Church of England by imprisoning dissenting clergymen, and prohibiting them from exercising their functions without his special license, and he even robbed one clergyman of his house and glebe. With insatiable rapacity he plundered the public treasury, and opposed every measure of the people for the security of their rights. Destitute of gratitude, licentious and base, he completed the universal contempt in which he was held by appearing in public dressed in women's clothes. As he had become an object of abhorrence, the Queen, through the pressure of popular sentiment, felt compelled to revoke his commission. As soon as he was deposed he was thrown into prison by his creditors, where he remained until the death of his father, when he became Earl of Clarendon. Upon the death of King William his commission was renewed by the Queen, who at the same time gave him the chief command of New Jersey, the government of which the proprietor had surrendered into her hands. He was succeeded December 18th, 1708, by Lord Lovelace, who died on the 5th of May following, leaving the government in the hands of Lieutenant-Governor Ingoldsby, whose administration is only remarkable for an unsuccessful expedition, under Colonel Nicholson, for the reduction of Canada. This failure was chiefly due to the mismanagement of Ingoldsby, who was consequently removed April 10th, 1710, and Gerardus Beekman, the oldest member of the council, exercised the authority of governor till June 14th, when Robert Hunter arrived with a commission as governor. This year Colonel Schuyler went to England to urge the importance of subduing Canada, taking with him the chiefs of the Five Nations, who were highly gratified with their voyage and reception.

The ensuing year another expedition for the reduction of Canada was undertaken. Four thousand troops were raised in the colonies under Colonel Nicholson, to join an English fleet and land force before Quebec. Arriving in the St. Lawrence, many of the ships were wrecked, and about a thousand soldiers lost, which put an end to the campaign. Nicholson, who had proceeded as far as Lake George, on hearing this news returned, and the expedition proved an entire failure. It had entailed a heavy debt upon the province, in consequence of which the governor's influence was somewhat impaired, he having entered into it with much zeal. His request for a permanent appropriation for the government was refused by the Assembly, which brought him into several unhappy contests with that body. In March, 1713, the war between England and France terminated by the treaty of Utrecht, in which the English supremacy over the Five Nations was conceded by the French, and an end put to the inflicton of Indian hostilities. The Five Nations being relieved from hostilities with the

French, engaged in conflict with the Indians at the south. The Tuscaroras, a tribe kindred to the Iroquois, residing in North Carolina, having been greatly reduced by a war with the whites, and being unable to resist their encroachment, removed to the north and joined the confederacy. They settled near Lake Oneida, among the Five Nations, and the confederates were thenceforward called the Six Nations. Hunter remained at the head of the government until 1719, when, his health failing, he returned to England. His intercourse with the Assembly was agreeable during the latter part of his administration, and his attachment to the interest of the colony made his departure regretted.

The government devolved upon Peter Schuyler, the oldest member of the council, who successfully administered affairs until the arrival of William Burnet, September 17th, 1720. A trading post was commenced at Oswego in 1722, by Governor Burnet, in order to engross the trade of the Six Nations, and with the farther design of following it up on the lakes to the westward, to obtain the trade of the more remote tribes. A congress of several colonies was held at Albany to meet the Six Nations, whereby the chain of friendship was strengthened, and trade with remote tribes promoted. The establishment of this post at Oswego was highly displeasing to the French, and in order to intercept the trade from the upper lakes they obtained consent of the Iroquois, through the influence of the Jesuits, to rebuild their trading-house and fort at Niagara, and also decided to erect a chain of military posts to the Ohio river, so as to cut off and confine the English trade. Though not without opposition, they succeeded in erecting their fort at Niagara. Although some of the members of the Six Nations were opposed to this invasion by the French, it succeeded through the disaffection of a party of merchants and others interested in the French trading policy, who, since the peace of Utrecht, had carried on a good trade with Montreal, through the aid of Indian carriers, and were opposed to the governor's policy. The Assembly was also strongly tinctured with the spirit of opposition, and refused a renewal of supplies except for short periods. This body was dissolved in 1727, but the next was quite as stubborn, and it was likewise dissolved, and the governor could only erect a small military defense for the post at Oswego, which, to his credit and the colony's shame, was at his own expense. On the accession of George II., Burnet was, through the efforts of his enemies, transferred to the government of Massachusetts, and John Montgomery appointed to succeed him. He entered upon his duties April 15th, 1728. His short administration is not distinguished for any important event. In 1729 the King, against the wishes of the best citizens of the colony, repealed the act prohibiting the trade in Indian goods between Albany and Montreal. A line was surveyed and agreed upon between Connecticut and New York in 1731. The establishment of this partition gave to New York a tract of land formerly on the Connecticut side, called from its figure the "Oblong," as an equivalent for lands near the sound, surrendered to Connecticut.

Montgomery died July 1st, 1731, and was succeeded by Rip Van Dam, whose administration was unfortunately signalized by the erection of a fort at Crown Point by the French, without resistance from the acting governor.

The arrival of Colonel William Cosby, August 1st, 1732, finished his administration, and began one rendered memorable for its arbitrary proceedings and tumult, rather than for striking or important events. Among the first of Cosby's acts was a demand that Rip Van Dam, his predecessor, should divide equally with him the emoluments of the office before his arrival. Van Dam assented, on the condition that Cosby should reciprocate by an equal division of the perquisites received by him from the colonies since his appointment and before coming to this country. This demand on the part of Van Dam was sustained by the people generally, but Cosby, despotic and avaricious, refused, and commenced a suit against Van Dam for half of his salary. As the governor by virtue of his office was chancellor, and two of the judges his personal friends, the counsel for defense took exception against the jurisdiction of the court. The exception was overruled by the judges in the interest of Cosby, even against the opinion of Chief Justice Morris, who was immediately removed from his office and Colonel Cosby's claim ordered paid. The indignation of the people at such arbitrary proceedings found vent in squibs and ballads, aimed at the aristocracy, and placing some of the members of the legislature in a ludicrous position. The *New York Weekly Journal*, edited by John P. Zenger, in defending Van Dam, published some severe criticisms on the government, arraigning the officials for assumed arbitrary power and perverting their official stations to purposes of private emolument. These papers were ordered to be burnt by the common hangman, and Zenger was arrested and imprisoned on a criminal charge for publishing a seditious libel against the government. When the trial came on, the publication was admitted, and proof offered for its justification, which were objected to by the attorney-general, on the ground that in a criminal proceeding for the publication of libelous matter, the truth of the facts alleged was not proper to be admitted in evidence, and he was sustained by the court, Andrew Hamilton, the counsel for the defense, resisted this decision of the court, and insisted that the jury was the judges of both the facts and the law, and it was for them to interpose between arbitrary violations of law and justice and their intended victim. The jury, after a short deliberation, gave a unanimous verdict of acquittal. Cosby, although repulsed by this verdict, persistently continued to make himself odious to the people by other arbitrary measures. A few days before his death he convened his council in his bed-chamber, and suspended Van Dam, the senior member thereof, upon whom the government would have devolved upon his decease. He died March 10th, 1736. The council convened immediately after his death, and George Clark, next senior counsellor, was declared president, and assumed the authority of governor. The suspension of Van Dam was declared illegal by a powerful party in his favor, and a struggle ensued between him and Clark for the office, both exercising authority until October 30th, when Clarke received a commission from England to act as lieutenant-governor. He sought to conciliate those hostile to him, and to keep in favor with the aristocratic party at the same time, he dissolved the Assembly that had continued in existence for many years, and a new one was elected, which, to his chagrin and regret, was in sympathy with the popular party, and at its session could not be prevailed upon to grant a revenue for a longer period than one year, establishing a precedent that subsequent Assemblies did not depart from.

CHAPTER VI.

THF ALLEGED PLOT TO BURN NEW YORK—FRENCH AND INDIAN HOSTILITIES—THE CONTEST FOR THE OHIO VALLEY.

IN 1741, several fires having occurred in New York, suspicions were awakened that a conspiracy had been formed for the destruction of the city. It was not long before it was charged upon the negro slaves, who at that time constituted about one-fifth of the population. Universal consternation seized upon the inhabitants, and a general panic ensued, in which reason and common sense were scarcely entertained. Rewards were offered for the arrest and conviction of the offenders, and a full pardon tendered to any of their number who would reveal their knowledge of the conspiracy. A weak negro girl, named Mary Burton, a servant in a low boarding house, after much importunity and full promise of pardon, implicated several negroes, by confessing to have heard them talking privately about burning the city. They were arrested and executed on this slender testimony. Others, among them several whites, were implicated by her, and suffered the same fate. Other informers appeared, arrests became numerous, and the popular fury and delusion did not subside until Mary Burton, the chief informer, after frequent examinations, began to touch characters above suspicion and known to be innocent. Then, as reason began to return, the delusion passed away, but not until one hundred and fifty-four negroes and twenty-four whites had been committed to prison, and nearly forty of these unfortunates executed. In the commencement of his administration Clarke had succeeded in conciliating both parties to a considerable extent, but managed before its close to lose the confidence of both, insomuch that his retirement, on the arrival of his successor, Admiral George Clinton, September 23d, 1743, was but little regretted. Favorable accounts of Clinton's talent and liberality had been proclaimed, and he was received with demonstrations of universal satisfaction. The election of a new Assembly was ordered, and a spirit of harmony so far prevailed that he concurred in all its measures.

In March, 1744, war was declared between England and France, and measures were taken for the conquest of Canada. The colonies of New York and New England united in an expedition, to co-operate with a fleet under

Commodore Warren, for an attack on the French fortress at Louisburg, on Cape Breton Island, which capitulated in June, 1745. The country north of Albany was seriously molested by attacks from the Indians and French. The fort at Crown Point with a force sufficient to enable its commander to send out detachments to destroy the English settlements. The settlement at Saratoga was burned, and nearly all the inhabitants either killed or taken prisoners. This was followed by an attack on the village of Hoosick. The fort at that place was commanded by Colonel Hawks, who was compelled to surrender, thus leaving the settlements, all the way to Albany, open to the enemy; but measures were speedily adopted for putting the frontier in a state of defense. In 1746 an expedition against Canada was resolved upon by the English government. The colonies, with the promise of assistance from England, entered into the design with much zeal. New York raised sixteen hundred men for the forces directed upon Crown Point and Montreal. England failed to furnish the promised assistance, and the expedition proved unsuccessful. Peace was concluded at Aix la Chapelle in 1748. Hostilities ceased, and the colony enjoyed a short period of tranquility. The harmony between the Assembly and the governor did not long continue, for, in 1745, an open disagreement occurred, and almost constant bickerings followed. In 1748 Clinton sent a message to the Assembly, demanding an appropriation for the support of the government for five years. The Assembly, justly regarding it as a direct attempt to render the crown independent of the people, indignantly refused; and after a few weeks' contention, the governor prorogued that body, and by successive prorogations prevented it from sitting for nearly two years, until the affairs of the colony were in an alarming condition for want of funds. His reiterated demands for a permanent revenue met with persistent refusal. Opposed and embarrassed by political factions, he tendered his resignation, after an administration of ten years, and was succeeded October 10th, 1753, by Sir Danvers Osborne. The new governor immediately informed the council that his instructions were to maintain the royal prerogative and demand a permanent support for the government. He was told by the members present that the Assembly would never submit to the demand, and appeared greatly depressed, the loss of his wife a short time before having already thrown him into a melancholy state of mind, bordering on insanity. Knowing the difficulties that his predecessor had experienced, and being charged with instructions still more stringent, he saw in the tempest before him a prospect which so worked upon his morbid mind that the next morning he was found dead, having hung himself at his lodgings. On his death, James de Lancey, by virtue of his commission as lieutenant-governor, assumed the administration of the government. He had formerly been a leader in the aristocratic party, but recently had opposed the demands of the crown, and consequently had become highly popular. Striving to retain his popularity by favoring the representatives in measures advantageous to the colony, while holding his office at the will of the English government, and being compelled by the instructions of his predecessor to convince the ministry that he was zealous to promote the interest of the crown, his task was peculiarly difficult; but it was performed with a shrewdness and skill creditable to his ability as a statesman.

By the treaty of Aix la Chapelle, the boundary between the French and English colonies was left as indefinite as before, and consequently those lands which both claimed the right to possess were still in dispute. The French had established their trading posts, missionary stations and fortifications from Canada to the Gulf of Mexico, and were vigorously pursuing their designs for the extension of their power and dominions. The English Ohio Company, formed for settlement and trade with the Indians, obtained in 1749, a grant from the British government of an extensive tract of land on the Ohio river.

When the Assembly met in the spring of 1754, Governor De Lancey, in his message to that body, called their attention to the recent encroachments of the French, and to a request by Virginia for aid from the colony of New York. The Assembly voted only a thousand pounds for aid, and to bear its share in erecting forts along the frontier.

By victories in western Pennsylvania in 1754 the French were left in undisputed possession of the entire region west of the Alleghanies. The necessity of concerted action on the part of the English colonies to resist their aggressions had now become obvious, but unworthy sectional feelings often prevented harmony of action for a general defense. The Six Nations were also becoming alienated from the English by the influence of French emissaries. The English ministry, aware of this critical state of affairs, had advised a convention of delegates from all the colonial assemblies, to secure the continued friendship and alliance of the Six Nations, and to unite their efforts in the common defense. In accordance with this recommendation, a convention of delegates from the colonies of New York, Massachusetts, New Hampshire, Connecticut, Pennsylvania and Maryland, was held at Albany in June, 1754. The chiefs of the Six Nations were in attendance, and the proceedings were opened by a speech to the Indians from Governor De Lancey, who had been chosen president of the convention. A treaty with the Six Nations was renewed, and they departed, apparently satisfied. While this treaty was being negotiated, at the suggestion of the Massachusetts delegates, a plan for the union of the colonies was taken into consideration. The suggestion was favorably received, and a committee, consisting of one member from each colony, was appointed to draft plans for this purpose. The fertile mind of Benjamin Franklin had conceived the necessity of union, and before leaving home he had prepared a plan, which was adopted. It was similar in many of its features to our Federal Constitution, framed many years afterward. The provincial assemblies, considering it too much of an encroachment on their liberties, rejected it, and it was rejected by the English government because it gave too much power to the people.

CHAPTER VII.

THE RESULT OF FOUR ENGLISH EXPEDITIONS AGAINST THE FRENCH—MONTCALM'S SUCCESSFUL CAMPAIGNS.

THOUGH England and France were nominally at peace, the frontier was desolated by savage hordes let loose upon the settlements by the French. While the English ministry were hesitating, the Duke of Cumberland, who at that time was captain-general of the armies of Great Britain, sent over, early in 1755, General Braddock, with a detachment from the army in Ireland. Braddock, soon after his arrival, met the colonial governors in a conference at Alexandria, to devise measures for repelling the encroachments of the French. Four separate expeditions were there resolved upon: the first against Nova Scotia; the second, under Braddock himself, for the recovery of the Ohio valiey; the third against Fort Niagara, and the fourth against Crown Point, on Lake Champlain. The first resulted in the complete reduction of Nova Scotia. The second and most important, under Braddock, from which much had been expected, was, through the folly of that officer, disastrous in the extreme. Washington had repeatedly urged the necessity of sending scouts in advance, but Braddock, obstinate and imperious, would listen to no warnings of danger from Indian ambuscades. When within a few miles of Fort Duquesne, the army was surprised by the lurking foe, and only saved from total destruction by the bravery of Washington, who, upon the fall of Braddock, assumed command, and conducted a retreat, but not until more than half the force had been sacrificed. The expedition against Fort Niagara, under General Shirley, governor of Massachusetts, was also unsuccessful. His troops hearing of Braddock's defeat, soon after leaving Albany, were so disheartened that many of them deserted. At Oswego he was detained by having to wait for the completion of boats. When these were completed, he was further detained by heavy storms and other casualties, until the lateness of the season rendered it imprudent to proceed. Leaving a garrison at Oswego, under Colonel Mercer, he led the residue of his army to Albany, and returned to Massachusetts.

The expedition against Crown Point was entrusted to General Johnson. The greater part of the troops were sent forward under General Lyman, of Connecticut, to the head of boat navigation on the Hudson, which, being the nearest point on the river to Lake Champlain, was called the carrying place, where they erected a fortification, which was afterward called Fort Edward. Here they were joined late in August by Johnson, who, advancing with the main body of the army to the head of Lake George, established a camp, and began to make some arrangements for an attack on Crown Point, but apparently was in no hurry to prosecute the enterprise. Meanwhile Dieskau, the French commander, was approaching by way of Lake Champlain, with the intention of surprising Fort Edward, cutting off Johnson's retreat, and capturing his army; but being misled by his guides, he found himself on the way to Johnson's camp on Lake George. Abandoning his first intention of attacking Fort Edward, he continued his advance on Lake George. Johnson, learning that the French were advancing to the Hudson, sent out Colonel Williams with a thousand troops, and Sachem Hendrick with two hundred Indians, to intercept them and aid Fort Edward. They had advanced only a few miles when they fell into an ambuscade, in which both Williams and Hendrick were slain, and the force hurriedly retreated, closely pursued by the enemy until they reached the camp, when the Canadian militia and Indians, who were in the advance, perceiving the artillery they would have to confront, skulked into the surrounding woods, and left the regulars to begin the attack, thereby giving the English time to recover from the confusion into which they had been thrown, and undoubtedly saving them from defeat. A severe struggle ensued, in which the French at length began to give way, upon observing which the English leaped over their breastworks and dispersed them in all directions. The French leader, Dieskau, was severely wounded and taken prisoner. Johnson was wounded in the commencement of the action and retired from the field, and the whole battle was directed by General Lyman, who proposed and urged a vigorous continuation of efforts by following up the routed enemy, preventing their escape down Lake Champlain, and attacking Ticonderoga and Crown Point; but Johnson, through fear or some other cause, not eaily explained, withheld his consent, and allowed the French to intrench themselves at Ticonderoga, while he spent the residue of the autumn erecting Fort William Henry, on the site of his camp. On the approach of winter he garrisoned it, disbanded the remainder of his army and returned to Albany.

On the 3d of September, 1755, Sir Charles Hardy arrived in New York as governor. He was an admiral, and unacquainted with civil affairs. Being conscious of his deficiencies in executive ability, he soon surrendered all but nominal duties into the hands of De Lancey, and in 1757 resigned the government and returned to his former profession, and De Lancey again became governor. At a meeting of the provincial governors, held at Albany in December, the plan discussed for the campaign of 1756 consisted of movements against Fort Niagara with six thousand men, Fort Duquesne with three thousand, Crown Point with ten thousand, and two thousand were to advance on the French settlements on the Chaudiere, and onward to Quebec. At this time (1756) the population of the province of New York was 96,775. In March, De Levy, with three thousand French troops from Montreal, penetrated the forests to the Oneida portage, took and destroyed the fort at that point and returned to Canada with the garrison as prisoners. Although active hostilities had been carried on for two years in the colonies, the English ministry did not arouse from their imbecility enough to issue a formal declaration of war against France until the 17th of May, 1756. Lord Loudoun was appointed commander-in-chief and governor of Virginia, and General Abercrombie was placed second in command. General Winslow, who had been intrusted with the expedition against Crown Point, finding that he had not sufficient force for the undertaking, waited for reinforcements from England. Late in June Abercrombie arrived with troops, but at the same time blighted any hopes that might have arisen regarding a vigorous prosecution of the war, by showing his contempt for the provincials in announcing that the regular officers were to be over those of the same rank in the provincial service. On this announcement all harmony for a united effort was dispelled. The men began to desert, and some of the officers declared they should throw up their commissions if the obnoxious rule was enforced. This difficulty was finally adjusted by an agreement that the regulars should remain to do garrison duty, while the provincials should advance under their own officers against the enemy. Then, instead of making any effort for the relief of Oswego, which was in danger, Abercrombie ordered his troops to be quartered on the citizens of Albany.

De Villiers had encamped with 800 Frenchmen at the mouth of Sandy creek, on Lake Ontario, whence he could send out detachments to infest the water passes leading to the Oswego fort, and intercept supplies or reinforcements on the way thither. Colonel Bradstreet, however, succeeded in throwing some provisions into the fort. On his return he fell in with a party of De Villiers's men in ambush, and gained a decisive victory over them. Hearing that a large force was already on its way to attack Oswego, he hastened to Albany and informed Abercrombie of the contemplated attack and the necessity of immediate reinforcements. But it was all in vain, as the general could not be induced to move before the arrival of Lord Loudoun. It was nearly August before Loudoun made his appearance, and affairs were not improved by this event. Instead of making an immediate effort to avert the threatened blow at Oswego, he began slowly to make preparations for a descent on Ticonderoga and Crown Point. Reinforcements were sent to forts Edward and William Henry. This procrastination proved fatal, for the opportunity of relieving Oswego was now lost. The Marquis de Montcalm, successor of Dieskau, had cut off communication with Albany, and on the 12th of August opened his artillery on Fort Ontario, nearly opposite Oswego. The fire was returned by the garrison till their ammunition was exhausted, when, spiking their guns, they retreated across the river to Fort Oswego. Montcalm immediately occupied the deserted fort and turned such guns as were yet serviceable against Fort Oswego. Colonel Mercer was killed, and a formidable breach effected in the walls. Montcalm was making preparations for storming the intrenchments when, seeing that the defense was no longer practicable, the garrison surrendered themselves prisoners of war. By this affair sixteen hundred men, one hundred cannon, a large quantity of provisions and stores, and the vessels in the harbor, all fell into the hands of the victors, and were safely conveyed to Montreal. Montcalm demolished the forts, much to the satisfaction of the Six Nations, who afterward sent a delegation from each castle to make peace with the governor of Canada. The French sent their emissaries among them, who now succeeded in seducing them from the English interests.

The fall of Oswego did not awaken the energies of Lord Loudoun—if it can be said that he possessed any—but on the contrary he abandoned all offensive operations that had been contemplated, and contented himself with doing nothing. Having wasted the season in shameful idleness, he on his arrival in the city of New York billeted a part of his force for free winter quarters on the citizens, regardless of the remonstrance of the authorities against this invasion of their rights. Overawed by his profane threats, the colonists found themselves obliged to support the British soldiers, who had done nothing in their behalf. In June of the following year he made an ineffectual effort to capture Louisburg. Before leaving New York he rendered himself still more detestable to the colonists by laying an embargo upon the seaports from Massachusetts to Virginia, and impressing four hundred men from the city of New York alone. He went to Halifax, where he was largely reinforced, but instead of making any advance upon Louisburg contented himself with drilling his troops in mock battles, till the complaints of his inactivity became so numerous that he finally gave orders to embark for that place. Almost as soon as the orders were given, receiving intelligence that Louisburg had been reinforced, and that the French fleet contained one more vessel than his, he countermanded his orders and came back to New York, having accomplished nothing.

While Loudoun was thus trifling, Montcalm, watchful of his movements, proceeded with a large force of French and Indians against Fort William Henry, then in command of Colonel Monroe with about twenty-two hundred men. General Webb, the English commander in that quarter, was at Fort Edward with a force of four thousand men. Montcalm landed with his men and artillery at a point about two miles from Fort William Henry, where he was entirely sheltered from its guns; beleagured its garrison, and sent a summons to Monroe to surrender, which he defiantly disregarded, confident of being relieved by Webb. The French then opened fire on the fort, which was spiritedly returned by the garrison. Expresses were sent to Webb imploring aid, but that coward remained inactive, terrified at the distant roar of artillery. Finally, after repeated solicitations, he allowed Generals Johnson and Putnam, with his rangers, to march to the aid of Monroe; but they had proceeded only a few miles when he recalled them, and sent a letter to Monroe, advising him to surrender. This letter was intercepted by Montcalm, who forwarded it to Monroe, requesting him to follow Webb's advice and save further loss of life. Still the intrepid colonel held out, until his ammunition was nearly exhausted, part of his guns disabled, and all hopes of assistance abandoned, and under these discouraging circumstances he was forced to capitulate on the 9th of August, and the sixth day of the siege. By the terms of surrender the garrison was allowed to leave the fort with all the honors of war, and furnished with an escort to Fort Edward. On the next morning, when they began their march, the Indians, who had spent the night in debauch, began an indiscriminate massacre and robbery of the English troops. Despite the efforts of Montcalm, many of the disarmed and defenseless soldiers were slain, and only a thousand reached Fort Edward. Fort William Henry was demolished. General Webb, paralyzed with terror, prepared to retreat, although reinforced until his army was more than double that of the enemy.

CHAPTER VIII.

EXTINCTION OF FRENCH POWER IN AMERICA—THE NEW YORK JUDICIARY—THE NEW HAMPSHIRE GRANTS.

BY these repeated failures the spirit of the English ministry in meeting the exigencies of the occasion was aroused, and William Pitt, a very able statesman, was intrusted with the management of affairs. His accession gave a new impulse to the national energies, and the campaign for 1758 opened under more favorable auspices. Three formidable expeditions were projected for this year, against Louisburg, Ticonderoga and Fort Duquesne, respectively. Admiral Boscawen, with twenty ships of the line and fifteen frigates, together with twelve thousand men under General Amherst, arrived before Louisburg on the 3d day of June, and entered vigorously upon the siege of that fortress, and on the 26th of July the French commander, finding farther opposition useless, surrendered at discretion. The army destined for the reduction of Ticonderoga and Crown Point, under General Abercrombie, consisting of nine thousand provincials and seven thousand regulars with a fine train of artillery, assembled at the head of Lake George, where it embarked on the 5th of July for the fortress of Ticonderoga, which was held by Montcalm with about four thousand men. The troops landed the next day and began their march, necessarily leaving their artillery behind until the bridges, which had been destroyed by the enemy, could be rebuilt. It was the purpose of Abercrombie to hasten forward and carry Ticonderoga by storm, before reinforcements which were expected could arrive. The advance party fell in with a body of the enemy, and Lord Howe, the second in command and the soul of the expedition, was killed. The loss of Howe was severely felt, and the incompetent Abercrombie, uncertain what course to pursue, fell back to the landing place. Colonel Bradstreet advanced, rebuilt the bridges and took possession of some saw-mills destroyed by the enemy about two miles from Ticonderoga, to which place Abercrombie advanced with his army, and sent forward an engineer with a party of rangers to reconnoitre. They reported that the works could be easily taken. Stark, who led the rangers, thought differently, and so advised Abercrombie; but he rejected his advice and ordered an attack without artillery, which, after a desperate struggle, was repulsed with the loss of nearly two thousand men. With the great force still at his command Abercrombie, instead of bringing up his artillery to bombard the French works, sounded a retreat, and, unpursued by the enemy, returned to the head of Lake George and sent his artillery and stores to Albany.

Colonel Bradstreet, anxious to do something to retrieve the disgrace of this shameful retreat, asked to lead an expedition against Fort Frontenac, which, with the entire fleet on Lake Ontario, surrendered on the 26th of August.

The expedition against Fort Duquesne succeeded through the energy of George Washington. On his approach the French set fire to the fort and fled. On the 25th Washington took possession of the ruins, and changed the name from Duquesne to Pittsburg.

Although Louisburg and Fort Duquesne had been retaken, still there could be no security for the frontier so long as Fort Niagara and the posts on Lake Champlain were held by the French, nor even while Canada remained unsubjugated. Accordingly, adequate preparations were made for the campaign of 1759. Abercrombie was superseded in the command of the expedition against Ticonderoga and Crown Point by General Amherst. General Wolfe was directed to ascend the St. Lawrence to Quebec, and General Prideaux was to take Fort Niagara and proceed to Montreal. He was joined by General Johnson at Oswego, from which point he sailed for Fort Niagara, leaving Haldimand with a force at Oswego. The latter was soon after attacked by a body of French and Indians, but succeeded in repulsing them. On the 7th of July Prideaux appeared before Niagara, but soon after the siege began he was killed by the premature bursting of a shell. Johnson succeeded to the command, and the siege continued without cessation. On the 24th a force of nearly three thousand French and Indian troops made an effort to raise the siege. A sharp conflict ensued, in which the relieving force was defeated, and the next day the garrison surrendered.

General Amherst, with a force of nearly twelve thousand men, arrived at Ticonderoga on the 22nd of July, and in four days thereafter the garrison abandoned the post and withdrew to Crown Point, which also was abandoned on the approach of Amherst.

The strength of Quebec was well known, and General Wolfe left Louisburg under convoy of a large fleet with eight thousand regulars to capture it. A fierce battle occurred before the city, which was held by the Marquis de Montcalm. Both Wolfe and Montcalm were slain; the French army was defeated, and on the 18th of September five days after, Quebec was surrendered to the English.

General Amherst appeared before Montreal on the 6th of September, 1760. De Vaudreuil, the Canadian governor-general, despairing of a successful defense, capitulated on the 8th. As the result of this campaign, Canada, with all her dependencies, fell into the hands of the English, and hostilities between the colonies of the two nationalities ceased. Peace, however, was not concluded between England and France until February 10th, 1763, when France ceded to England all her possessions in Canada.

On the 30th of July, 1760, Governor De Lancey suddenly died, and Cadwallader Colden took charge of the government, being president of the council. In August, 1761, he received his commission as lieutenant-governor. The death of De Lancey left the seat of chief-justice vacant, and the remaining judges, having doubted their ability to issue processes since the death of King George II., under whom they had held their old commissions, urged Colden to appoint a successor. Colden requested the Colonial Secretary of State to nominate a chief-justice, and he not only nominated but appointed Benjamin Pratt, a lawyer from Boston, to hold the position at the pleasure of the King, instead of during good behavior, as formerly. The people, regarding this as an encroachment on their rights and liberties, vigorously protested, and the remaining judges even refused to act longer unless they could hold their commissions during good behavior. When the Assembly met, Colden requested that the salary of the chief-justice should be increased, but that body not only refused to increase it, but refused to provide for it unless the judges' commissions secured them their seats during good behavior. The chief-justice having served some time without a salary, the income of the royal quit-rents of the province was appropriated to his compensation.

General Robert Monkton was appointed governor of New York, and assumed the reins of government in October, 1761, but left on the 13th of the following month to command an expedition against Martinique, leaving the administration of affairs again in the hands of Colden. In 1763 the boundary line between New York and New Hampshire became a subject of much controversy. The disputed territory was the tract of land between the Connecticut river and Lake Champlain, comprising what is now known as the State of Vermont. The patent granted to the Duke of York in 1664 included all the land west of the Connecticut river to the Delaware Bay. Controversies had arisen, growing out of the indefinite character of their respective charters, between the province of New York and those of Connecticut and Massachusetts relative to their boundaries, which had been adjusted by negotiation and compromise. The line agreed upon was to extend north and south twenty miles east of the Hudson river. New Hampshire, regardless of justice or title, insisted upon having the same western boundary. Against this claim New York vigorously protested, but the protests were unheeded, and the governor of New Hampshire continued to issue grants until, in 1763, one hundred and thirty-eight townships had been granted. Alarmed at this encroachment, and in order to stop these proceedings, Governor Colden, in December, 1763, issued a proclamation claiming jurisdiction to the Connecticut river under the patent granted to the Duke of York, and commanded the sheriff of Albany county to return the names of all persons who by virtue of the New Hampshire grants had taken possession of lands west of the Connecticut river. This was followed by a counter proclamation from the governor of New Hampshire, declaring that the grant to the Duke of York was obsolete, and that his own grantees should be protected in the possession of their lands. Through the Board of Trade the disputed question was referred to the crown, and in 1764 a decision was obtained pronouncing the Connecticut river the boundary between the provinces of New York and New Hampshire. Upon this decision the government of New York declared the grants from the governor of New Hampshire illegal, and insisted that the grantees should surrender or re-purchase the lands upon which they had settled. To this unjust demand the greater part refused to accede, and the governor of New York thereupon granted their lands to others, who brought ejectment suits against the former occupants and obtained judgment at the courts of Albany. All attempts, however, of the executive officers to enforce these judgments met with a spirited resistance, and led to continual hostilities between the settlers and the government of New York.

CHAPTER IX.

APPROACH OF THE REVOLUTION—NEW YORK'S PATRIOTIC ATTITUDE—THE FIRST BATTLE FOUGHT IN 1770.

THE representative assemblies of the provinces had occasionally remonstrated against the various acts of Parliament which tended to abridge their liberties, and the regulation of the Board of Trade by which their manufactures and commerce were injuriously affected; yet their attachment to the mother country and regard for her institutions had not to any considerable extent been weakened. But now the borders of the Revolutionary struggle were reached; the time had arrived when unquestioned submission to the exactions of an arbitrary power had ceased to be considered a virtue, and knowing the value of their liberties, the colonies firmly asserted their rights. They were heavily burdened by the expenses of the late war, for which they had liberally contributed, materially aiding in procuring for the English government a vast and valuable accession of territory; yet their generous support of the power and dignity of the realm the British ministry regarded as only the exercise of a duty, and before the smoke had fairly drifted away from the battle grounds began to devise plans for taxing them to raise a revenue without their consent. The first measure which aroused the colonists to a lively sense of their danger was the issuing of writs of assistance, which the English ministry had determined to force upon them. These were, in effect, search warrants, whereby custom-house officers were enabled the better to collect the revenues by breaking open houses or stores that were suspected of containing contraband goods. This exercise of arbitrary power created indignation and alarm, and the colonists resolved to resist it. Public meetings were held, and remonstrances sent to Parliament, but without effect. The ministry were determined to derive a revenue from the colonies, either by import duties or direct taxes, vigorously levied and collected, and the writs were granted; but the feelings of the people were such that the custom-house officers never attempted to carry their new powers into execution.

In 1764 George Grenville, then at the head of the English ministry, submitted to the House of Commons a proposition for raising a revenue by the sale of stamps to the colonists, at the same time assuring the colonial agents that he would not press its immediate adoption, but leave the plan open for consideration. When intelligence reached the colonists that such an act was meditated by the ministry, discontent was everywhere visible. The provincial assemblies strenuously refused to recognize the right of Parliament to tax them without their consent, and asserted the sole right to tax themselves. They passed resolutions of remonstrance, and clearly demonstrated that taxation without representation in Parliament was unjust and tyrannical; but, in contemptuous disregard of all respectful remonstrances and petitions, the Stamp Act was passed in March, 1765. By its provisions no legal or commercial documents were valid unless written or printed on stamped paper, upon which a price was set, according to the nature of the instrument, payable to officers appointed by the crown. The passage of this act created feelings of resentment throughout the colonies, accompanied by a determination to resist or evade its enforcement. The people of New York were among the most bitter in their opposition to the measure. An association styling itself the Sons of Liberty held meetings to discuss plans for resistance. The obnoxious act was reprinted and paraded about the streets of New York city, bearing the inscription, "The Folly of England and Ruin of America." A committee was appointed by the New York Assembly in October, 1764, to correspond with the several colonial assemblies, with a view to resisting the oppressive measures of Parliament. They suggested to the several colonies the holding of a convention, to remonstrate against the violation of their liberties. This suggestion was heartily responded to, and delegates were appointed, who convened in the city of New York on the 7th of October, 1765. This body continued in session two weeks, and adopted a declaration of rights, a petition to the King, and a memorial to Parliament, in which the principles by which the colonies were governed through the Revolution were clearly foreshadowed.

The Stamp Act was to take effect on the first day of November. As the appointed time drew near the excitement increased, and when the day had finally arrived flags floated at half mast, bells were tolled as on funeral occasions, and many other manifestations of public sorrow and discontent were made. The stamped paper, which had previously arrived, had been deposited in the fort for safe keeping, under the direction of Governor Colden, who had taken the oath to execute the Stamp Act; but McEvers, who had been appointed by the crown to manage its distribution and sale, seeing the manifestations of popular indignation, resigned. In the evening the Sons of Liberty appeared before the fort and demanded the stamped paper. On being refused, they repaired to the Commons, where they hung Governor Colden in effigy, and returned to the fort with his image. Not being admitted at the gate, they broke into Colden's stable, and brought out his carriage, placed the effigy in it, paraded the streets, and returned to the fort, where it was again hung. They then made a bonfire and burned the carriage and its accompaniments. A party proceeded to the house of Major James, an artillery officer who had rendered himself particularly obnoxious, destroyed the furniture, and carried off the colors of the Royal Artillery regiment. The next day Colden announced that he should not issue any of the stamped paper while he remained in office, but leave it to his successor, who was already on his way from England. But the Sons of Liberty, not satisfied with this assurance, insisted that the stamped paper should be delivered into their hands, and threatened to take it by force if it was not. The Common Council, alarmed at their ungovernable fury, requested that the paper might be deposited in the City Hall, which was done, and a guaranty given for its safe keeping. In the meantime, at a meeting called by the citizens, a committee was appointed to correspond with the merchants of the several colonies, inviting them to enter into an agreement not to import certain goods from England, which suggestion was promptly acted upon, and the trade with England almost ceased.

When the new governor, Sir Henry Moore, arrived, he was disposed to carry the Stamp Act into execution, but the unanimous advice of his council, together with the unmistakable character of public sentiment, soon convinced him of the folly of such an attempt. The Sons of Liberty seized ten boxes of stamped paper, on the arrival of a vessel containing it, conveyed it to the ship-yards and it was consumed in a bonfire. The Stamp Act was so odious to the colonies, and their opposition to it was so effective, that it was repealed on the 18th of March, 1766; but immediately on its repeal a bill was passed declaring the absolute right of Parliament "to tax the colonies in all cases whatsoever." The repeal, however, was not owing to any appeals from the colonists, for Parliament would not receive the petitions of the Colonial Congress, because that body had not been summoned to meet by it; but it was because of the influence of London merchants, whose trade was seriously affected by the non-importation agreement. Notwithstanding the declaratory act that accompanied the repeal the news was hailed with a delirium of delight, and the city was in a blaze of illumination in honor of the event. On the King's birthday, which occurred soon afterward, the New Yorkers assembled, and with enthusiastic manifestations of loyalty erected a liberty-pole, inscribed to the King, Pitt, and Liberty. The Assembly met in June, and the governor requested its compliance with the demands of the ministry in relation to furnishing supplies for the troops stationed in New York city. Some controversy ensued upon the subject, and only a partial compliance could be obtained from the Assembly.

The sounds of rejoicing which followed the repeal of the Stamp Act had hardly passed away before the ministry by its unjust acts again awakened the murmurs of discontent, and the declaratory act began to loom up and dampen all the hopes of the colonists. The partial provision of the Assembly for supporting the troops was distasteful to the Sons of Liberty, who well knew the soldiers were sent to enforce the abridgement of American liberties, and on their arrival did not disguise their feelings. Animosities arose between them, and the soldiers, believing that it was owing to the Sons of Liberty that the Assembly had not been more liberal in furnishing them with supplies, retaliated by cutting down the citizens' flagstaff. The next day, while the citizens were replacing it, they were assaulted by the troops, and several of them wounded. The officers were indifferent to this conduct of their men, and other outrages were committed. The Assembly met again in November, when the governor placed before it the instructions of the ministry, requesting that immediate provision for the troops should be made; but their outrageous conduct had so disgusted the legislators that they refused to comply, and were severely censured by the crown. Parliament declared the legislative powers of the Assembly annulled, and forbade the governor and council to give their assent to any act passed by that body until unqualified compliance with the demands of the government had been obtained.

In June, 1767, a bill was passed by Parliament imposing a duty on tea, glass, lead, paper, and printers' colors, imported into the colonies. This act was shortly followed by another re-organizing the colonial custom-house system, and establishing a board of revenue commissioners. When intelligence of these acts reached the colonies the excitement was renewed, and the non-importation agreement revived. The colonists saw that Parliament intended to tax them in some way, and declared that taxes on trade for a revenue were as much a violation of their rights as any other taxes. In 1768 the Assembly of Massachusetts addressed a circular to the other colonies referring to the acts of Parliament, and soliciting their co-operation in maintaining the common liberties. This so offended the ministry that a letter was sent from the secretary of State to the several colonial governors, forbidding their assemblies to correspond with that of Massachusetts. When the Assembly of New York was convened the governor placed the document before it, and requested their obedience to its mandates. The Assembly unhesitatingly refused; declared its right to correspond with any other of the legislatures; denounced the infringements upon its rights by Parliament; and was dissolved by the governor. The people sustained their representatives, and when a new Assembly convened in April 1769, it was found that but very little change had been effected by the election.

The death of Sir Henry Moore occurred on the 11th of September, 1769. His mild and prudent course in avoiding controversy as far as possible had endeared him to the colony, and his death was much lamented. By that event the government again devolved upon Cadwallader Colden. The English merchants, suffering from the non-importation agreement, had joined their petitions with those of the colonists for the repeal of the obnoxious custom-house act, and a circular letter assured the people of the colonies that at the next session of Parliament a proposition would be made to abolish the duties on all articles except tea. This attempt at conciliation was far from satisfactory; for the right of taxation was not relinquished, and the principle was the same whether applied to one article or many. A bill was introduced in the New York Assembly in November for issuing colonial bills of credit to the amount of

£120,000, to loan out as a means of revenue. The project at first met with favor from the popular party, but when it was followed by an appropriation to support the British troops in the colony, to be taken out of the interest arising from the loan, a revulsion of feeling at once took place. Shortly after handbills were circulated charging the Assembly with betraying the inhabitants of the colony, and advising the people to meet on a certain day and express their sentiments upon the subject. Accordingly, a large concourse of people gathered, and emphatically denounced the action of the Assembly. That body passed resolutions declaring the handbills libelous, and offering a reward for the detection of their authors. John Lamb, who had presided over the popular meeting, was arrested and brought before the House, but was soon after discharged.

Animosities continued between the Sons of Liberty and the soldiers. Now that their supplies were granted the latter no longer held themselves in check from motives of policy, and on the evening of the 13th of January, 1769, renewed their attack on the flagpole of the citizens. The latter hastily gathered for its defense, whereupon they desisted. Their failure in this attempt, together with the derisive jeers of the citizens, so enraged them that they charged upon a group of people in front of a tavern which was a favorite resort of the Sons of Liberty, drove them in and destroyed the windows and furniture. On the evening of the 16th they cut down the flagstaff, sawed it in pieces, and piled the fragments before the battered hotel. On the following morning several thousands of the citizens assembled at the scene of the outrage, and passed resolutions censuring the riotous proceedings of the soldiers, and recommending that whenever found in the street after roll-call they should be dealt with as enemies to the peace of the city. The next day placards were found posted up, ridiculing the resolutions and daring the citizens to execute them. During the day the Sons of Liberty caught two or three soldiers in the act of putting up these bills, and arrested them. While conducting them to the mayor's office the citizens were attacked by a party of twenty soldiers, armed with cutlasses, and a skirmish ensued—the citizens defending themselves with clubs. The soldiers were forced back to Golden Hill, as John street, between Cliff street and Burling Slip, was then called. Here they were re-inforced, and made a furious charge on the citizens, most of whom were entirely unarmed. The latter stoutly resisted until a party of officers appeared on the scene and ordered the troops back to their barracks. Several of the citizens were severely wounded, some of whom had not participated in the skirmish. Several affrays occurred on the following day, in which the soldiers were generally worsted. The mayor issued a proclamation forbidding them to leave the barracks unless accompanied by a non-commissioned officer, and order was restored.

Thus terminated the first conflict in which blood was shed in the cause of American independence. It is usually asserted that at Lexington was the first battle fought; but the actual beginning of the combat, so doubtful in its progress, and so glorious in its results, was the battle of Golden Hill, on the 18th of January, 1770, at least five years earlier. The Sons of Liberty purchased grounds and erected another pole, which stood until the occupation of the city by the British forces in 1776.

CHAPTER X.

LANDING TEA PREVENTED—CONGRESSIONAL ACTION—THE BATTLE OF LEXINGTON—CANADA INVADED.

IN October Lord Dunmore arrived in New York and superseded Colden in the government of the province. Meanwhile the duties had been removed from all articles except tea, and the non-importation agreement was restricted to that article. The new governor brought the news of the royal approval of the act authorizing the emission of colonial bills of credit. This strengthened the spirit of loyalty, and affairs went on more smoothly. On the 8th of July, 1771, William Tryon was commissioned as governor in place of Lord Dunmore, who was transferred to the government of Virginia. By a recent order of the crown the governor's salary was to be paid from the revenue, thus rendering the executive independent of the people. The East India Company were suffering severely from the non-importation agreement in regard to tea, and in 1773 urgently petitioned the British government to abolish the duty levied upon that article in the colonies, offering to submit to double that duty as an exportation tariff. This would increase the amount of revenue twofold, but the party in power, deluded by false views of national honor, would not in the least relinquish its declared right to tax the colonies. It preferred to favor the East India Company by a special act allowing them to ship their tea to the colonies free of export duty, which would enable them to sell it at a lower rate than in England. By this act the ministers imagined they had outwitted the colonists, and that this appeal to their pockets would end their resistance. Ships were laden with tea and consignees appointed in the colonies to receive it, with the expectation that this new act would secure its ready sale. When information of this arrangement reached the colonies their indignation was deeply aroused. The Sons of Liberty rallied and resolved that the obnoxious article should not be landed under any pretense. The tea commissioners appointed for New York resigned in view of such decided demonstrations of resistance.

Expecting a consignment of tea would soon reach the city the citizens held a mass meeting, and regardless of the efforts of Governor Tryon to secure its reception, emphatically resolved that it should not be landed. The expected vessel was delayed and did not make its appearance until April, 1774. When it arrived off Sandy Hook the pilot, acting under the instructions of the vigilance committee, refused to bring the ship any nearer the city. Captain Lockyer, the commander, under escort of the committee, was allowed to come up and consult with the consignee, but the latter refused to receive the cargo, and advised the captain to return to England immediately. Meanwhile Captain Chambers, of New York, professing to be a patriot, arrived in the harbor. His vessel was boarded by the committee, and upon being questioned he denied having any contraband goods; but on being informed by the committee that with the evidence they had to the contrary they should search his ship, he admitted that there was tea on board which he had brought out on a private venture. The hatches were forced open and the chests brought on deck and given air and water. The next morning Captain Lockyer was conducted by the committee to his ship, together with Chambers, his companion in the tea trade, and they were sent on an outward voyage.

The New Hampshire grants continued a source of serious contention. The civil officers were opposed by force in their efforts to enforce the judgments obtained in the ejectment suits, and the New York Assembly passed an act declaring resistance to be felony. A proclamation was issued by Governor Tryon offering a reward for the apprehension of Ethan Allen and other conspicuous offenders. This was followed by a burlesque proclamation from the proscribed, affirming their determination to resist and offering a reward for the arrest of the governor of New York. In the spring of 1775, at the time appointed for the session of court in the disputed territory, the settlers took possession of the court-house and prevented the New York officers from entering. The officers thereupon collected a force, and being again refused admittance fired into the house, killing one of the occupants and wounding several others. Some of the officers were arrested by the enraged inhabitants and lodged in jail, and matters appeared to be approaching a crisis; but the battle of Lexington occurring at this juncture, active hostilities between Great Britain and the colonies began and caused a cessation of these difficulties.

A cargo of tea had arrived in Boston harbor considerably earlier than in New York, and the Bostonians resolved that it should not be landed. The vessels containing the obnoxious article were boarded and the chests emptied into the water. The ministry, enraged at this spirited resistance, determined to subjugate the colonies. Various measures were determined upon which were ruinous to the liberties of the American people; among them was the celebrated "Boston Port Bill," closing the harbor and destroying the trade of the city to punish the citizens for having destroyed the tea. The people everywhere were awakened to a lively sympathy with Boston, seeing by its treatment what was in store for them. A brisk correspondence was carried on between Boston and New York through the agency of committees appointed for that purpose. Public meetings were held for the consideration of their common grievances, and among the measures devised and recommended were the restoration of the non-importation agreement and the convening of a colonial congress. On the 5th of September, 1774, this congress met at Philadelphia and adopted a declaration of rights, setting forth wherein those rights had been violated; agreed on a petition to the King for the removal of their grievances and also on an appeal to the people of Great Britain and Canada; and then adjourned to meet again in May of the following year. The Assembly of New York was the only colonial assembly that withheld its approval of the proceedings of this congress. It, however, addressed a remonstrance to Parliament, which was treated as all others had been, with disdain. The Assembly adjourned on the 3d of April, 1775, and was never again convened. Its refusal to appoint delegates to the Continental Congress gave great dissatisfaction, and a provincial convention of county representatives was called by the people to perform that duty.

At midnight on the 18th of April, 1775, General Gage sent a detachment of British regulars from Boston to destroy the military stores collected by the Americans at Concord, Massachusetts. The expedition was conducted with great secrecy, but the troops were discovered and the people warned of their coming. On reaching Lexington the following morning they found the militia assembled on the green. The latter, disregarding a command to disperse, were fired upon and several of them were killed. The British troops proceeded to Concord, but the inhabitants, having been apprised of their design, had concealed the greater part of their stores, and the British troops on their return were severely harassed by the militia who had gathered from the neighboring towns.

When intelligence of this event reached New York the excitement was intense. The affair was in fact the signal for a general rush to arms throughout the colonies. The Sons of Liberty took possession of the arms at the arsenal in New York city and distributed them among the people. At the suggestion of the Committee of Observation a provincial government for the city was formed, consisting of one hundred of the principal citizens, who were to control affairs until Congress should otherwise order. The British troops at New York having been ordered to Boston, the provisional government allowed them to depart on condition that they should take nothing but their own arms with them. Regardless of this stipulation they attempted to carry off some military stores belonging to the city, but were defeated in their designs by Colonel Marinus Willett with a party of the Sons of Liberty, who confronted them and succeeded in retaking the property and replacing it in the fort.

While the patriots were flocking toward Boston the Connecticut Assembly was in session, and several of its members agreed upon a plan to seize the cannon and military stores at Ticonderoga and Crown Point for the use of the patriot army. They appointed a committee to repair to the frontier and raise an expedition, under Colonel Ethan Allen, to surprise and capture the posts named. A force of two hundred and seventy men was soon collected, and marched by night under Colonels Allen and Benedict Arnold to a point on Lake Champlain opposite Ticonderoga. They had but few boats, and when day began to dawn only the officers and eighty-three men had crossed. Fearful that delay would be hazardous, Allen resolved to make an attack before the rear division had crossed, and marched at the head of his men directly to the sally port.

The sentinel snapped his musket at him and retreated to the parade with the patriots close at his heels. The garrison were aroused and taken prisoners. Colonel Allen went directly to the apartments of the commander and demanded and obtained a surrender of the fort "in the name of the Great Jehovah, and the Continental Congress." Crown Point was taken without resistance two days afterward, and the command of Lake Champlain was thus secured.

The Continental Congress reassembled and organized on the 10th of May, the same day that Colonel Allen captured Ticonderoga, and proceeded at once to raise and equip an army for the defense of the colonies. New York was ordered to raise three thousand men as her proportion. The population of the province during the preceding year had increased to 182,251. George Washington was commissioned commander-in-chief of the American forces. A provincial congress of New York, convened on the 22nd of May, authorized the raising of troops, encouraged the manufacture of gunpowder and muskets in the province, and projected fortifications at King's Bridge and the Hudson passes in the Highlands.

Captain Lamb was ordered to remove the cannon from the battery at the foot of the city to a place of greater security. On the evening of August 23d he proceeded to the execution of the order. The captain of the British war-ship "Asia," being informed of the intended movement, sent a barge filled with men to watch it. A shot was fired from the barge into the American force, which was immediately answered by a volley, killing one of the crew and wounding several others. The "Asia" then opened a cannonade upon the city, doing considerable damage to the buildings in the vicinity of the battery, but the patriots were undismayed, and in the face of the cannonade deliberately removed every gun. Governor Tryon returned from England in June and strenuously exerted himself to promote the royal cause. Finding that his position was growing more and more unsatisfactory, and having fears for his personal safety, he abandoned the city and took refuge on board a British sloop of war.

The Continental Congress directed General Schuyler to collect an armament at Ticonderoga, and put the post in a state of defense, preparatory to an expedition against Canada. The forces under Generals Schuyler and Montgomery appeared before St. John's in September. General Schuyler was compelled by ill health to relinquish the command to General Montgomery and return to Ticonderoga. The fort at Chambly, twelve miles below, was captured on the 19th of October by a detachment of the American force, aided by friendly Canadians. The spoils taken at Chambly materially aided in carrying on with vigor the siege of St. John's, which after several unsuccessful assaults and numerous mishaps was on the 3d of November compelled to surrender. General Montgomery moved forward to Montreal, which was taken without resistance. Later in the month Montgomery and Benedict Arnold assaulted Quebec, but the former was killed and the colonial force repulsed and soon after driven out of Canada.

CHAPTER XI.

HOSTILITIES TRANSFERRED TO NEW YORK—THE BATTLE OF LONG ISLAND—BURGOYNE'S CAMPAIGN.

IN March, Washington, having compelled General Howe to evacuate Boston, and apprehensive that New York would be the next point of attack, made immediate preparations for putting that city in a posture of defense. General Lee, with twelve hundred men, was ordered forward from Connecticut. The captain of the British man-of-war "Asia" had threatened to cannonade the city if "rebel troops" were permitted to enter it. It was the stronghold of loyalty to the crown and disaffection to the patriot cause, and the committee of safety in their timidity protested against Lee's entrance, but threats and protests were unavailing. Lee came, and the tories either fled or ceased to oppose the cause of the patriots. Sir Henry Clinton, who had been sent over on a secret expedition, appeared off Sandy Hook at nearly the same time that General Lee entered the city, but finding it in possession of the American troops, proceeded south to attack Charleston. Washington hastened forward from Boston, and on the 14th of April arrived at New York and established his headquarters in the city. General Howe went to Halifax on leaving Boston, but about the 1st of July appeared off Sandy Hook, and shortly after landed on Staten Island. He was soon after joined by his brother Admiral Howe, with a force of British regulars and Hessian hirelings, and also by Clinton and Parker on their return from an unsuccessful attack on Charleston, making all together a combined force of nearly thirty thousand men. Howe was here visited by Governor Tryon, who had planned to capture General Washington, blow up the magazine, and secure the passes to the city. The mayor also was in the conspiracy, and was receiving money from Tryon to bribe the Americans. Two of Washington's guards yielded to the temptations of the enemy, but the third, who could not be bribed, exposed the plot. The Provincial Congress of New York, seeing the hostile demonstrations toward the city, adjourned to White Plains, where it convened on the 9th of July, and passed resolutions heartily endorsing the action of the Continental Congress and approving of the Declaration of Independence.

The plan of the campaign on the part of the British army near New York was to take possession of the city and the islands in its vicinity, and to ascend the Hudson, while Carlton should move down from Canada, and thus separate the Eastern from the other States. Two ships succeeded in passing the batteries and ascended the Hudson to furnish the tories of Westchester with arms, but all their attempts to land were frustrated and they returned.

On the 22nd of August a British force of ten thousand men, with forty pieces of cannon, landed on the south side of Long Island, in the vicinity of New Utrecht, and advanced in three divisions upon the Americans stationed in and about Brooklyn. The Hessians, under De Heister, formed the center. The left, along New York Bay, was commanded by General Grant, and the right, which led in the action, was commanded by Clinton and Cornwallis. While Grant and De Heister were diverting the Americans on the left and center, the division on the right was to make a circuitous march and fall upon their rear. This division left the Flatlands on the night of the 26th, and guided by a tory occupied the Bedford and Jamaica passes before General Sullivan, who commanded in that quarter, was aware of the movement. While this advantage was being gained Grant was making a movement toward Brooklyn, and early in the morning came into collision with the Americans under Stirling on the site of Greenwood Cemetery, when an engagement took place without material advantage to either side. De Heister advanced and kept up a cannonade on the works at the Flatbush Pass. In the meantime, Clinton had gained a position in the rear of the continental army and commenced to attack them. De Heister then pressed forward, and Sullivan, perceiving the peril of his army, attempted to retreat, but it was too late. They were met by Clinton's forces and driven back upon the Hessians. Some forced their way through the ranks and reached the fortifications, but after a desperate struggle and great loss of life Sullivan himself and the greater part of the left wing of the American army were taken prisoners. Cornwallis hastened to cut off the division under Stirling, who was not yet aware of the situation. A part of his force succeeded in crossing Gowanus creek in safety, but many were drowned or taken prisoners. Stirling himself was captured and a decisive victory gained by the British. About five thousand men were engaged on the side of the Americans, of whom five hundred were killed or wounded and eleven hundred were taken prisoners. These were confined in loathsome prison-ships on the East river, where they suffered indescribable privations and hardships. Fortunately for the Americans, Howe did not dare to attempt an assault upon their fortifications in Brooklyn, but encamped about a third of a mile distant, and waited for the support of the fleet.

On the 28th, the day after the battle, the British began to cannonade the intrenchments. At night a heavy fog settled over the battlefield, which remained all the following day. When night had added its darkness to the mist which had obstructed the vision of the hostile parties throughout the day, Washington, with the remainder of the troops on Long Island, silently crossed the East river in safety to New York. The British forces took possession of the American works and prepared to attack New York. Washington knew that with his dispirited and undisciplined army he could not successfully oppose them, and decided to evacuate the city. On the 15th of September Howe landed with about four thousand men under cover of his fleet at Kip's Bay, on the east side of Manhattan Island, near what is now the foot of Thirty-fourth street. Two brigades of militia, stationed for defense in that quarter, were panic-stricken and retreated disgracefully despite all the efforts of their officers to rally them. Putnam, who had charge of one column of the army, was compelled to leave in great haste, and narrowly escaped being captured. The Americans retreated to Harlem, and the British took possession of New York and held it until the close of the war.

The next day an advance party of the British were attacked, and after a severe skirmish driven back with considerable loss. Howe, perceiving that the Americans were strongly intrenched upon Harlem Heights, determined to gain their rear, cut off their communication with the north and east, and hem them in. He sent a part of his fleet up the Hudson, and transferred the main body of his army in boats to Westchester county, landing them at Throgg's Neck. When Washington saw this movement he sent a detachment to oppose their landing. All the passes were well guarded, and a detachment was intrenched at White Plains. The main army advanced in that direction and intrenched upon the hills from Fordham to White Plains. On the 28th of October the enemy came up and attacked General McDougal, on Chatterton's Hill. McDougal, after an obstinate resistance, was forced to fall back to intrenchments above White Plains. While Howe was preparing to storm their encampment at this place, Washington withdrew, unobserved by the enemy, to North Castle, where strong breastworks had been erected, and awaited an attack; but Howe, not deeming it prudent to assail him in so strong a position, retreated toward New York, preparatory to the contemplated reduction of Fort Washington, which was soon environed by the British forces. It was gallantly defended by Colonel Magaw until he was overpowered by a superior force and compelled to surrender. Fort Lee, on the opposite side of the Hudson, was abandoned on the approach of the enemy, and Washington, who had crossed the Hudson, retreated through New Jersey to the opposite side of the Delaware river, closely pursued by the enemy. On the night of the 25th of December he recrossed the river and gained an important victory at Trenton, and shortly afterward another at Princeton, and then went into winter quarters at Morristown.

General Gates, who had been appointed to the command of the northern forces, apprehensive that General Carlton would follow up his success in Canada and attempt to capture Crown Point and Ticonderoga, abandoned the former and concentrated his forces at the latter. A small squadron was formed and placed upon Lake Champlain, under the command of Arnold, in August. Carlton constructed a fleet at St. John's. Arnold sailed down the lake, but, being ignorant of the strength of the armament preparing against him, fell back to Valcour's Island. On the 11th of October the British fleet passed around the east side of the island and took up a position south of the American squadron. An action began about noon and continued until night. One of the schooners in Arnold's fleet was disabled, and burned to prevent it from falling into the hands of the enemy. The British force was greatly superior, and as another engagement would have been extremely hazardous it was deemed advisable to return to Crown Point. The night was exceedingly dark, and the Americans succeeded in sailing through the British fleet unobserved, although the latter had been stationed in a line across the lake in anticipation of such a movement. On reaching Schuyler's Island, ten miles distant from the British fleet, they stopped to make some repairs, and on being discovered at daylight, were pursued by the enemy. On the 13th the British ships, three in number, came up with and attacked the "Washington," which, after a heroic defense, was compelled to surrender, and her commander and all his men were taken prisoners. The whole force was now concentrated in an attack upon the "Congress," which maintained the unequal contest with unflinching resolution for four or five hours, till it was reduced to a complete wreck. Arnold then ran the craft into a creek and burned it, together with the rest of his boats, and marching to Crown Point, where the remainder of the fleet was stationed, sailed for Ticonderga. General Carlton took possession of Crown Point and threatened Ticonderoga, but, abandoning his design, he prudently withdrew to Canada.

The Provincial Congress, which had assembled at White Plains on the 9th of July and approved the Declaration of Independence, appointed a committee to draw up and report a constitution. The occupation of New York city and part of Westchester county by the British greatly disturbed the labors of the convention, and finally, in February, they repaired to Kingston, where the draft of a constitution was prepared by John Jay, and adopted on the 21st of April, 1777. George Clinton was elected governor under the new constitution, and took the oath of office on the 31st of July following.

The principal object of the British in the campaign of 1777 was to carry out their cherished design of separating the Eastern from the Southern colonies, by controlling the Hudson river and Lake Champlain. The most prominent feature of the plan was the advance of an army from Canada, under Lieutenant-General Burgoyne, who had superseded General Carlton. It was intended that Burgoyne should force his way down the Hudson as far as Albany, while Sir Henry Clinton was to proceed up the river and join him, and thus a free communication between New York and Canada would be established, and the colonies separated. In order to distract the attention of the Americans, and the more completely subdue the Western border, Colonel St. Leger was to ascend the St. Lawrence with a detachment of regulars, accompanied by Sir John Johnson with a regiment of loyalists and a large body of Indians. From Oswego the expedition was to penetrate the country to Fort Schuyler, on the site of Rome, and after its capture sweep the Mohawk valley and join Burgoyne at Albany. Burgoyne arrived in Canada early in March. Unavoidable difficulties having greatly embarrassed his first movements, it was past the middle of June before his army was assembled at Cumberland Point, on Lake Champlain. The main army, of more than seven thousand men, appeared before Crown Point, and occupied that post on the 30th of June. Having issued a proclamation, intended to terrify the inhabitants into submission, Burgoyne prepared to invest Ticonderoga, then in command of General St. Clair. On the east shore of Lake Champlain, on Mount Independence, there was a star-fort, so connected with Ticonderoga, on the west side of the lake, by a floating bridge, as to obstruct the passage of vessels up the lake. For want of a sufficient force to man all its defenses the outworks toward Lake George were abandoned on the approach of Burgoyne. A detachment of the enemy, under General Fraser, took Mount Hope, and thereby cut off St. Clair's communication with Lake George; and at the same time the abandoned works of the Americans, more to the right, were occupied by General Phillips. On the south side of the outlet of Lake George, and opposite Mount Independence, is a lofty eminence, then known as Sugar-loaf Hill, which was found to completely command the works both at Ticonderoga and Fort Independence. A battery was planted on its summit by the British during the night, and St. Clair, on perceiving his critical situation, at once called a council of war, by which it was unanimously decided that immediate evacuation of Fort Ticonderoga was the only chance of saving the army. During the ensuing night such military stores and provisions as could be removed, together with the sick and disabled troops, were embarked on batteaux, and sent up the lake to Skenesborough, as Whitehall was then called, under convoy of five armed galleys and a detachment of six hundred men under Colonel Long, while the main body of the army was to cross the lake and proceed to the same point by land. The garrison passed over the floating bridge to Mount Independence about two hours before daylight, and would probably have made their retreat undiscovered had not the house of the commander at Fort Independence been set on fire just at this time. This unfortunate occurrence threw the Americans into disorder, for the light of the conflagration revealed their movements to the British, who made immediate preparations for pursuit. St. Clair's force made a disorderly retreat to Hubbardton. On the following morning General Fraser came up, with his brigade, and commenced an attack. The conflict was for some time fierce and bloody. The Americans had almost surrounded the left wing of the British when General Riedesel came up with reinforcements, and St. Clair made a precipitate retreat. The boats which conveyed the military stores and the detachment of Colonel Long reached Skenesborough safely, but Burgoyne in a few hours broke through the boom and bridge at Ticonderoga, on which the Americans had placed much reliance, and with his fleet rapidly pursued them; and while they were landing at Skenesborough three regiments disembarked at South Bay with the intention of gaining the road to Fort Edward, and cutting off their retreat. On the approach of the British gunboats Colonel Long's men destroyed three of their galleys and several buildings, and escaped capture by a rapid flight to Fort Anne. Two days after the battle at Hubbardton St. Clair retreated to Fort Edward. Burgoyne was joined at Skenesborough by the detachments of Fraser and Riedesel, and prepared to push forward to the Hudson. Lieutenant-Colonel Hill was sent forward to Fort Anne to intercept such as might retreat to that post, and to watch the movements of the Americans. This post was guarded by Colonel Long, with about five hundred men, mostly convalescents. Hill's force exceeded this number. Colonel Long did not wait for an attack, but marched out to give battle, and gained a decided advantage; but their ammunition giving out, the patriots were obliged to give way; and aware of their inability to hold the fort against General Phillips, who was approaching with reinforcements, set fire to it, and fell back on Fort Edward.

CHAPTER XII.

THE BATTLE OF BENNINGTON—FAILURE OF ST. LEGER'S MOVEMENT—BURGOYNE'S DEFEATS AND SURRENDER.

BURGOYNE remained at Skenesborough nearly three weeks, while detachments were building bridges and repairing the road to Fort Anne. This delay greatly diminished his supplies, and on arriving at Fort Anne he sent a detachment under Colonel Baum to surprise and capture a quantity of stores which he had heard was collected at Bennington, and with the expectation of receiving material aid from the loyalists in that quarter. General Schuyler had not sufficient force to defend Fort Edward, and throwing all the obstructions possible in Burgoyne's way from there to Fort Anne retreated down the valley of the Hudson. Colonel Baum on his march to Bennington reached Cambridge on the 13th of August. The American General Stark in the meantime had repaired to Bennington, and was collecting the militia to join his brigade in opposing any invasion in that direction. Hearing that a party of Indians were at Cambridge, he detached Colonel Gregg to attack them; and shortly after, learning that a large body of the enemy was in their rear marching on Bennington, he moved immediately to the support of Gregg. After going about five miles he met him retreating, and Colonel Baum not more than a mile in the rear. Stark at once disposed his army for battle, and Baum, perceiving its strength, began to intrench and sent to Burgoyne for reinforcements. The next day some skirmishing took place, and on the following day, August 16th, Stark arranged his army for an attack. Two detachments were sent to flank the enemy while another was attracting their attention in front. As soon as the attack on the enemy's flank began the main body pressed forward, and after two hours' fierce conflict gained a decisive victory. The remnant of Colonel Baum's force in its flight was met by Colonel Breyman with reinforcements, who pressed forward with the combined force to regain the abandoned intrenchments. Stark was also reinforced, and the conflict was renewed with vigor. The enemy at length giving way, were pursued until darkness came to their rescue and enabled them with their thinned and broken ranks to escape to the main army. Colonel Baum was mortally wounded and taken prisoner. The total loss of the enemy was, in killed, wounded and prisoners, nine hundred and thirty-four, and all their artillery and military stores. Up to this time all had gone well with the boastful Briton, and his path had been illuminated with victory; but with the failure of this expedition his glory began to wane and his sky to grow dark and threatening, where hitherto it had been bright and serene.

While these events had been taking place with the main division, the expedition under Colonel St. Leger had invested Fort Schuyler (earlier and even now more commonly called Fort Stanwix), on the site of Rome. A movement of the Mohawk valley militia to its relief was arrested by the bloody battle of Oriskany, but while most of the besiegers were engaged in this conflict their camp was sacked by the garrison; and learning that a more formidable provincial force was on its way to raise the siege of the fort, which had held out tenaciously, St. Leger abandoned his undertaking and returned to Canada.

Schuyler, with his army, marched down the Hudson to Stillwater, and finally to the mouth of the Mohawk, still keeping his headquarters at Stillwater and exerting all his energies for the augmentation of his force, preparatory to a conflict with Burgoyne. On the 19th of August, at the instigation of his enemies, he was very unjustly superseded by General Gates. On the 8th of September the American army advanced to Bemis Heights, above Stillwater, which had been fortified under the superintendence of Kosciusko. The British detachment sent to Bennington, instead of bringing back any plunder had lost largely of what they already had, as well as most of the force, and Burgoyne had hardly recovered from this unexpected shock when the news was brought him of the defeat of St. Leger at Fort Schuyler. These disasters had a very depressing effect upon his army, and the Indians and loyalists began to desert, while the Americans were greatly inspirited. In view of these difficulties the British commander deemed it expedient to halt at Fort Edward. Stores having been brought forward from the posts on Lake Champlain, he proceeded down the Hudson, and on the 18th of September encamped at Wilbur's Basin, two miles from the American position, and prepared for battle, and the next day advanced to the attack in three divisions. General Riedesel commanded the left column, which with the heavy artillery moved down a road along the margin of the river. The center was commanded by Burgoyne in person, and the left by General Fraser. The front and flanks of both the center and right were covered by Indians, tories and Canadians. The American right, which was the main body of their army, was commanded by Gates, and the left by General Arnold. Colonel Morgan was detached from Arnold's division, and encountering the Canadians and Indians in the advance drove them back; but they being reinforced the contest resulted in both parties finally falling within their respective lines. The action became general, and the combined forces of Burgoyne and Fraser were engaged with Arnold's division. Arnold called upon Gates for reinforcements, but they were refused and he, resolving to do what he could with the force at his command, continued the contest with the most obstinate and determined resolution, both armies alternately advancing and retreating without a decisive victory for either. The conflict did not cease until the shades of night fell upon the combatants. The Americans then retired to their encampment unpursued by the enemy. The British forces bivouacked on the field of battle. The total loss of the former was three hundred and nineteen, and that of the latter more than five hundred. Few actions have been more remarkable for determined bravery on both sides than this. The number of the British in the engagement was about three thousand, and that of the Americans five hundred less. Both parties claimed the victory. The object of the British was to advance and gain ground, which they failed to do; while it was not the intention of the Americans to advance, but to maintain their position, which they accomplished, and it is therefore not difficult to determine on which side the advantage lay. Though the British remained in possession of the battlefield through the night, they retired to their camp in the morning without advancing to renew the conflict. General Gates, in his report of the battle, said nothing of Arnold or his division, to whom all the honor was due. He was jealous of the reputation that officer had earned, and of his growing popularity with the army, and carried his meanness so far as to take from him the command of his division. Both parties strengthened their positions after the battle, but no general engagement took place for upward of three weeks.

Burgoyne saw with painful anxiety that the American forces were rapidly increasing, while his own were daily diminishing by the desertion of his Indian allies. His provisions began to fail, and the vigilance of the Americans not only prevented any supplies reaching him, but deprived him of all communication with Sir Henry Clinton for assistance. At length he was obliged to put his troops on short allowance, and hearing nothing from Clinton, who was to make a diversion in his favor, becamed seriously alarmed. Amid the thickening peril he found himself reduced to the alternative of fighting or retreating. The latter was not only inglorious but difficult, and he resolved to make a reconnoisance in force, for the twofold purpose of ascertaining definitely the position of the enemy, and of collecting forage to supply his camp, of which it was in pressing need. On the 7th of October he, at the head of fifteen hundred men and accompanied by Generals Riedesel, Phillips and Fraser, advanced toward the left wing of the American position. The movement was seasonably perceived by the Americans, and the enemy were repulsed and driven back to their lines by Morgan, who, at his own suggestion, was dispatched by a circuitous route to gain the right of the British, and fall upon the flanking party of Fraser at the same time an attack was to be made on the left of the British. General Poor advanced toward an eminence upon which were stationed the British grenadiers and the artillery of Ackland and Williams. He had given his men orders not to fire until after the first discharge of the British guns, and they moved onward toward the frowning battery in awful silence until a sudden volley of grapeshot and musket balls made havoc among the branches of the trees, scarcely a shot taking effect upon the advancing column. At this signal Poor's men sprang forward and delivered their fire, and opening to the right and left pressed furiously upon the enemy's flanks and gained the top of the hill, where the struggle became fierce and obstinate in the extreme. One cannon was taken and retaken five successive times, finally remaining in the hands of the Americans, when

Colonel Cilly turned it upon the retreating enemy, and fired it with their own ammunition. Williams and Ackland were both taken prisoners, the latter being severely wounded; and the grenadiers fled in confusion, leaving the field in possession of the Americans, thickly strewn with their dead and wounded.

As soon as the action was begun at this point Morgan's command rushed down like an avalanche from the ridge skirting the flanking party of Fraser, and assailed them with such a destructive fire that they were hastily driven back to their lines. Then, by a rapid movement, he fell upon the right flank of the British with such impetuosity as to throw them into confusion, and Major Dearborn, coming up at this critical moment, completed their discomfiture. The right and left of the British lines were thus broken, but the center had remained firm. General Arnold, who had so unjustly been deprived of his command, had been watching the progress of the battle in great excitement, and now mounted his horse and started for the battle field. Gates sent Major Armstrong to order him back, but Arnold, suspecting his errand, was quickly beyond his reach, and exposed to such perils that the messenger was not anxious to follow him. Placing himself at the head of the men he formerly commanded, he rushed like an unchained tiger upon the British center, which soon began to give way under his furious assault. General Fraser, who was commanding on the right, seeing the center in such a critical situation, brought up reinforcements, and by his courage and skill restored order. He soon fell mortally wounded; dismay seized the British soldiers, and a panic spread all along the line, which was increased by the appearance of General Ten Broeck with a reinforcement of New York militia. Burgoyne, finding himself unable to keep up the sinking courage of his men, abandoned his artillery and ordered a retreat, and the whole force fell back precipitately to their intrenchments. The Americans pursued them, and scarcely were they within their fortifications when, under a terrific shower of grape and musket balls, Arnold assaulted them from right to left, forcing the outworks, and driving the enemy to the interior of their camp. Here he was overtaken by Major Armstrong, who delivered to him Gates's order to return to camp, fearing that "he might do some rash thing." He returned, but not until he had achieved a glorious victory, and put his life in great peril without a command, while Gates had remained in camp, receiving the honors that justly belonged to others. Night came on and the conflict ceased; before dawn Burgoyne abandoned his encampment, now rendered untenable, and the Americans early in the morning took possession of it.

Burgoyne, who in the beginning of the campaign had boastfully exclaimed in general orders, "Britons never retreat," now found that there was no alternative for him but retreat, and when night came on again he began his retrograde movement, in the midst of a drenching rain. This had been anticipated, and General Fellows, previous to the action on the 7th instant, had been sent with a detachment to take a position opposite Saratoga Ford, on the east side of the Hudson. Another detachment, of two thousand men, was now sent to occupy the heights beyond Saratoga, to prevent Burgoyne's retreat upon Fort Edward; and still another was stationed at the ford above. On the evening of the 9th

Burgoyne halted for the night at Fish creek. The main portion of his army forded the creek and encamped on the opposite bank, while he, with a brigade as a guard, passed the night merrily with some companions in a house belonging to General Schuyler. This delay lost him his army. Finding the ford across the Hudson strongly guarded by the detachment under Fellows, he concluded to continue his retreat up the river to Fort Edward. He sent forward a party to repair the bridges, and a detachment to take possession of the fort; but finding the Americans stationed in force upon the heights, they fell back to the main army. In the afternoon of the 10th General Gates came up, with the bulk of the American army, in pursuit, and occupied the high ground on the south side of Fish creek, opposite the enemy's encampment. The detachment sent forward to Fort Edward led General Gates to believe the rumor that the main army of Burgoyne had retreated, and he resolved to fall upon what he supposed was the rear guard. Burgoyne was aware of Gates's error, and hoping to profit by it concealed his troops for the purpose of falling upon the Americans as soon as a favorable opportunity should be afforded. Early the next morning, and in a thick fog, which both parties considered favorable to their respective designs, the army of Gates advanced. Morgan was ordered to cross the creek and begin the action, and at once fell in with the British pickets, who fired upon him and killed several of his party. His reception led him to believe that the rumor of the enemy's retreat was false; that the main body of Burgoyne's force was still near, and that the position of his own corps was critical. Another brigade had already crossed and captured a picket-guard, and another was about to follow when a deserter from the enemy came in, reporting that the entire British army was at hand, and prepared for battle, which statement was shortly after confirmed by the capture of a reconnoitering party. As the fog cleared away and exposed the position of both armies, a retreat was deemed advisable by the detachments that had crossed the creek. As soon as they turned about the British, who were watching their movements and awaiting their advance, opened fire upon them, but they made their retreat with the loss of only a few men.

Burgoyne was now completely environed. On the opposite bank of the Hudson Fellows was entrenched, with heavy batteries to open on him if he should attempt to cross the river. Fort Edward was held by an American force of two thousand men. On the south and west the main body of the Americans was posted, while small detachments were in all directions watching his every movement, and continually harassing his outposts. His provisions were almost exhausted, and none could be obtained, and it was extremely hazardous to attempt to get water from the river or creek. There was no place of safety for the sick and wounded, and the women and children, as well as soldiers and officers, were constantly exposed to the cannon balls that were flying about the encampment. On the 12th he held a consultation with his generals, and it was decided to retreat that night, but the returning scouts brought such discouraging intelligence that the movement was postponed till morning. During the night the Americans crossed the river on rafts, and erected a battery on Burgoyne's left flank. Retreat was now hopeless. The next morning a general council was called, when it was unanimously decided to open negotiations with General Gates for an honorable surrender. This conclusion was hastened by the passage of a cannon ball across the table at which Burgoyne and other generals were seated. The negotiations were not completed until the 16th, when the terms of his surrender were agreed upon, and were to be signed by the commander on the following morning. During the night a tory succeeded in reaching the British camp from down the river, who reported that Clinton had taken the forts on the Hudson and ascended the river as far as Esopus. This news so excited Burgoyne's hopes that he resolved not to sign the articles of capitulation, and to gain time he wrote Gates that he had been informed that a part of his army had been sent toward Albany, which, if true, should be considered a breach of faith, and that he could not give his signature until convinced that the strength of the Americans had not been misrepresented. He was informed by Gates that his army was as strong as it had been before these negotiations took place, and unless the articles were signed immediately he should open fire upon him. Burgoyne thereupon reluctantly signed the articles of capitulation.

The surrender of Burgoyne was of the utmost importance to the Americans in their struggle for independence. The preponderance of success up to this time had been on the side of the British. The reverses on Long Island and at New York in the previous year, together with the recent defeats in Pennsylvania, had darkened the military horizon with thick clouds of doubt and dismay. All eyes were now anxiously watching the army of the north, which had also been forced to relinquish Ticonderoga and Fort Edward at the commencement of the campaign, and shaded the prospect of successful resistance in that direction. The news of a complete victory filled the patriots with joy and hope, and appalled the tories, who now began to tremble.

CHAPTER XIII.

CLINTON'S HUDSON RIVER CAMPAIGN—FRANCE RECOGNIZES THE UNITED STATES—WARS WITH THE INDIANS.

WHEN Burgoyne first perceived the difficulties gathering around him, he urged Sir Henry Clinton to hasten the expedition up the Hudson to join him, but Clinton was obliged to wait for the arrival of reinforcements, and it was the 4th of October before he was ready to move. The first object to be accomplished was the reduction of Forts Montgomery and Clinton in the Highlands. These had been constructed to prevent the ships of the enemy from ascending the river, and each was indefensible in its rear, and feebly garrisoned. Clinton landed first at Verplanck's Point, and dropped down with a part of his force to Stony Point, where he landed, and marched toward the forts. These were commanded by Governor George Clinton and his brother James. Governor Clinton, on learning that the enemy were moving up the river, sent out a scouting party to watch their movements, and from them he first learned of their having landed at Stony Point. A small force was then sent out by him, which met the advance guard of the British about three miles out. Shots were exchanged, and the Americans retreated to the forts. Governor Clinton then sent out a stronger detachment to oppose the enemy's advance, and as this was soon engaged in a sharp conflict, another was sent to its assistance. They were pressed back by a superior force, but not until the enemy had met with considerable loss. Upon nearing the forts the British were divided into two columns, and made a simultaneous assault upon them. After an incessant fire for several hours the British general demanded an instant and unconditional surrender. The proposition was rejected, and the conflict continued until evening, when part of the besieged fought their way out. Governor Clinton made his escape, and likewise his brother, though wounded. Fort Constitution was abandoned on the approach of the British, which gave them command of the river. A detachment under Vaughn and Wallace landed without much opposition and burned Kingston. On hearing of the disastrous termination of Burgoyne's campaign the expedition returned to New York.

It was obvious that France had no sympathy with Great Britain, but looked upon the revolt of her colonies with secret satisfaction, and earnestly desired their separation from England. By the war which closed in 1763 she had been compelled to relinquish her extensive possessions in North America, and she rejoiced to have an opportunity to assist in the infliction of a like dismemberment of territory upon Great Britain. The commissioners of the court of Versailles from the revolted colonies, although not always openly countenanced, were by no means discouraged, and aid was frequently extended to the Americans in a clandestine manner. When intelligence of the capture of Burgoyne reached France her vacillating policy ended, and, casting off all disguise, she entered into a treaty of alliance with, and on the 6th of February, 1778, acknowledged the independence of the United States. This event made the patriots almost certain of ultimate success.

The Indians and tories who had been dispersed at Fort Schuyler were meditating mischief, and making preparations through the winter of 1777–8 to invade the Mohawk valley. Brant, the Indian chief who had prepared the ambuscade at Oriskany, was foremost in these threatening movements. Sir John Johnson and Colonel John Butler were also active in enlisting tory refugees. A council was called by the Revolutionary authorities, to secure, if possible, the neutrality of the Indians. It met at Johnstown in March. None of the Senecas, the most powerful of the Six Nations, were present, and but few of the Mohawks. General La Fayette, who was to command a proposed expedition against Canada, attended the council. His attention was called to the exposed condition of the settlements, and he directed the building and strengthening of fortifications for their protection. The first hostile movement of Brant was the destruction of the small settlement of Springfield at the head of Otsego lake. On the 2nd of July an engagement occurred on the upper branch of the Cobleskill between an Indian force of four hundred and fifty and fifty-two Americans. The latter were overpowered. The Indians burned the dwellings, and slaughtered the cattle and horses they could not take with them. The settlers generally were continually harassed by marauding parties of Indians during the summer, but on the approach of winter Brant withdrew with his forces toward Niagara, and hostilities apparently ceased. On his way to Niagara he was met by Walter Butler, a fugitive from justice. He had been arrested as a spy and condemned to death, but had been reprieved through the intercession of friends, sent to Albany, and confined in prison, from which he made his escape. He joined his father, Colonel John Butler, at Niagara, and obtained command of two hundred tories to unite with Brant in an incursion into the Mohawk valley. Upon meeting Brant he prevailed upon him to return and attack the settlement of Cherry Valley. Colonel Alden, who was in command of the fort at that place, received information of the intended attack, but treated it with unconcern. He refused to permit the settlers to move into the fort, believing it to be a false alarm. He, however, assured them that he would keep scouts on the look-out to guard against surprise, and he did send them, but they fell into the hands of the savages, who extorted from them all necessary information respecting the situation. On the morning of the 11th of November the enemy entered the settlement under cover of a thick and misty atmosphere, and began an indiscriminate slaughter of men, women, and children. The house of Mr. Wells, of which Colonel Alden was an inmate, was surrounded and the whole of the family brutally massacred. The colonel, in attempting to escape, was tomahawked and scalped. Thirty-two of the inhabitants, mostly women and children, and sixteen soldiers of the garrison, were slain in the most horrible manner. The whole settlement was plundered, and every house burned. Nearly forty prisoners were taken, and conducted down the valley to encamp for the night, promiscuously huddled together, some of them half naked, without shelter, and with no resting-place but the cold ground. The next day, finding the women and children cumbersome, the captors sent most of them back. The infamous Butler was not only the author of this savage expedition, but he was the director of all the cruelty practiced. With the destruction of this settlement hostilities ceased along the frontier until the following spring. Through the winter Brant and his colleagues were making preparations for a renewal of their incursions, and necessity seemed to demand the infliction of severe punishment upon the savages who threatened to desolate the border settlements. Accordingly on the 18th of April, 1779, Colonel Van Schaick was sent out with a force from Fort Schuyler to make a descent upon the Onondagas. The expedition had approached to within a few miles of their villages and castle before their occupants were aware of the expedition against them. The Indians fled to the woods, leaving everything behind them, even to their arms. Their villages, three in number, consisting of about fifty houses, were burned, and their provisions and cattle destroyed. The council house, or castle, was spared from the flames, but a swivel found in it was rendered useless. Thirty-three of the Indians were taken prisoners and twelve killed. The expedition then returned to Fort Schuyler, arriving on the 24th, having accomplished its object in six days, without the loss of a man. While this short campaign was in progress, the lower section of the Mohawk was visited at different points by scalping parties, and the settlements menaced with the fate of Cherry Valley. The Onondagas, fired with indignation at the destruction of their villages, retaliated by a descent upon the settlement at Cobleskill, and more than twenty of the militia were killed in defending it. The settlement at Minisink being unprotected, Brant resolved to ravage it. On the night of the 19th of July, at the head of a party of Indians, and tories disguised as savages, he silently approached the town, and had set fire to several houses before the inhabitants were aroused to the danger of their situation. All who could sought safety in flight, leaving everything to the invaders, who plundered and destroyed all their property, and retired to Grassy Brook, where Brant had left the main body of his warriors. When intelligence of this outrage reached Goshen, Doctor Tusten, colonel of the local militia, ordered them to meet him at Minisink, and one hundred and forty-nine responded to the call. A council was held, and it was resolved to pursue the invaders. Colonel Tusten was opposed to such a hazardous undertaking with so small a force, but he was overruled, and the line of march taken up. The next morning the pursuers were joined by Colonel Hathorn, with a small reinforcement. On coming to the place where the Indians had encamped the previous night, it was obvious from the number of camp-fires that the force was much larger than had been expected, and the leading officers advised return rather than pursuit, but their rash associates were determined to proceed. Soon after Captain Tyler, who was with a scouting party, was shot by a hidden foe, but this circumstance, although it gave the company some alarm, did not check the pursuit. When the party reached a hill overlooking the Delaware, they saw the enemy marching toward the fording place near the mouth of the Lackawaxen. Hathorn determined to intercept them, and arranged his men accordingly. Hills intervened between the opposing forces and they soon lost sight of each other. Brant was watching the movements of the whites, and anticipating their design turned as soon as they were lost to view, and throwing his whole force in their rear, formed an ambuscade. Not finding the enemy where they had expected, Hathorn's men were greatly perplexed, and retracing their steps discovered the Indians in an unexpected quarter and greatly superior in numbers. The latter managed to cut off from the main body of Hathorn's troops about one-third of the entire force in the commencement of the skirmish. From the summit of a hill the militia maintained the unequal conflict until their ammunition was exhausted, and then attempted to retreat but only thirty succeeded in making their escape from their merciless enemies. When the retreat began there were seventeen of the wounded behind a ledge of rocks under the care of Doctor

Tusten, and in this helpless condition they were ruthlessly murdered, together with the doctor, by the Indians.

But a fearful retribution was at hand, and soon fell on the Indians with destructive force. In the spring it was determined to send a large expedition into the Indian country, and so severely chastise the savages and their tory allies as to discourage them from renewing their depredations upon the settlements. General Sullivan was placed in the chief command of this expedition, the plan of which was a combined movement in two divisions: one from Pennsylvania, to ascend the Susquehanna, under Sullivan himself, and the other from the north, under General James Clinton. The two divisions were to unite at Tioga. On the 17th of June General Clinton commenced the transportation of his boats across the country from Canajoharie to Otsego lake, and proceeded to its outlet, where he awaited orders from Sullivan. While there he built a dam to confine the water within the lake, hoping by its sudden removal to render the navigation of the river more certain in case of a long drought. This not only facilitated the transportation of his boats upon the river, but it caused an overflow of its banks and destroyed the corn-fields belonging to the Indians, who, being ignorant of the cause of their loss, were greatly astonished and alarmed. General Clinton formed a junction with Sullivan at Tioga on the 22nd of August, and the combined force moved cautiously up the Tioga and Chemung. On the 29th the enemy were discovered occupying an advantageous position near the present city of Elmira. The light infantry in the advance formed for battle, and while waiting for the main body to come up skirmishing was carried on with small parties of Indians, who would sally out from their works, fire, and retreat, and make the woods echo with their hideous war-whoops. The Indians occupied a hill on the right, and Sullivan ordered Poor with his brigade to flank them, while the main body of the army attacked them in front. As Poor began to ascend the hill he was fiercely opposed by the savages under Brant and the tories under Sir John Johnson. It was some hours before the latter began slowly to give way. Having gained the summit of the hill Poor moved against the enemy's left flank, which he soon carried, and perceiving that they would be surrounded they abandoned their works and made a precipitate retreat. Sullivan's army encamped upon the battle field that night, and the next day the wounded were sent back, together with the heavy artillery, and the march was resumed toward Catharine's Town, where the expedition arrived on the 2nd of September. The following day the place was destroyed, together with the corn-fields and orchards. The Indians fled before the invaders, who continued their work of destruction, pillaging the villages of their enemies and thus depriving them of all means of subsistence. On the 7th Sullivan's army reached Kanadaseagea, the capital of the Senecas. This they destroyed, as well as all the smaller villages on their way to the Genesee river, which was reached and crossed on the 14th. The Genesee castle was doomed to meet the fate of the rest, and the whole surrounding country, together with the town, which comprised 120 houses, was swept as with the besom of destruction. On the 16th the expedition recrossed the Genesee river, and retracing their steps arrived at Tioga, the starting point, on the 3d of October. The Indians, although subjected to great suffering, were not wholly crushed by these severe losses. Their numerical force was but slightly reduced, and they retaliated upon the frontier settlements with savage vengeance whenever a favorable opportunity offered.

CHAPTER XIV.

ARNOLD'S TREASON—CLOSE OF THE REVOLUTION—ADOPTION OF THE CONSTITUTION—INTERNAL IMPROVEMENTS.

EARLY in June of 1779 Sir Henry Clinton conducted an expedition up the Hudson, and attacked two small forts, one at Stony Point, on the west side of the river, and the other at Verplank's Point, nearly opposite. The former had only about forty men to defend it, and they retreated on the approach of the British; but the latter, with its garrison of seventy men, resisted, and was captured. Washington much regretted the loss of these posts, and although they had been enlarged and strengthened after the British took possession of them he resolved to make an effort to regain them. Stony Point was surprised on the night of the 15th of July following, and after a short and fierce conflict the garrison, of more than five hundred men, together with the cannon and military stores, were captured, and the works demolished and abandoned.

In the spring of 1780 Brant was again upon the warpath, and with a band of Indians and tories destroyed Harpersfield in April. It was his design to attack the upper fort of Schoharie, but on his way he captured Captain Harper, who represented to him that the fort had lately been reinforced, and he returned to Niagara with his prisoners. Sir John Johnson, with a force of five hundred tories and Indians, very unexpectedly appeared at Johnstown on the night of May 21st, and the next day swept the country between that neighborhood and the Mohawk. Several persons were murdered, others taken prisoners, and all buildings not belonging to the tories were burned. On the following afternoon the party retreated toward Canada. On the 21st of August Canajoharie and the adjacent settlements were attacked by Brant, at the head of a large body of Indians and tories, who did even more damage than Johnson's party.

General Benedict Arnold, wounded at the last battle with Burgoyne, and unable to take any active position, was appointed military governor of Philadelphia in the spring of 1778. Feeling the importance of his station, and fond of making a show, he began living in such an extravagant manner as to become pecuniarily embarrassed; and rather than retrench, and live within his income, he resorted to a system of fraud which brought him into unpleasant relations with the citizens of Philadelphia. By order of Congress he was tried before a court-martial, and sentenced to the mildest form of punishment—simply a reprimand from the commander-in-chief. He appeared to acquiesce in the sentence, but his pride was wounded and he thirsted for revenge. While in Philadelphia he had married the daughter of a tory residing in that place. She was accustomed to receive the attentions of British officers during their occupancy of the city, and through her intimacy with Major Andre a correspondence had been initiated between him and Arnold, by which means the latter's treacherous schemes were developed, and culminated in a most infamous treason. Still he was loud in his professions of patriotism and attachment to his country's cause, and pretended to be anxious to again join his companions in the field. He solicited the command of West Point, then the most important post in the possession of the Americans. Washington had assigned him to the command of the left wing of the army, but upon his repeated and earnest request the command of West Point was given him instead, on the 3d of August, 1780. He established his headquarters on the opposite side of the river, at the house of Colonel Beverly Robinson, whose property had been confiscated on account of his espousal of the British cause. Arnold well knew that Sir Henry Clinton would richly reward him for being instrumental in placing West Point in his hands, and hinted as much to Major Andre, between whom and himself letters passed in disguised hand-writing and over fictitious signatures. In order to settle the terms of this infamous treachery it became necessary for Sir Henry Clinton to send Major Andre for a personal interview with Arnold, not only to agree upon the conditions of his contemplated surrender but to guard against a counterplot. Major Andre sailed up the Hudson on board of the "Vulture," and a meeting was finally effected. Near the village of Haverstraw resided Joshua H. Smith, who was duped by Arnold to assist in carrying out his designs. It was he who brought Major Andre on shore, where Arnold was awaiting him, and concealed in a thicket they plotted the ruin of the patriot cause from about midnight until day began to dawn, and then repaired to Smith's house to complete their plans. Arnold was to receive ten thousand pounds and the office of brigadier-general in the British army, while West Point was to be given up on the approach of the English fleet. Major Andre was supplied with papers explaining the military condition of the fort, which were concealed in his stockings; while a pass was given him under the name of John Anderson. In the morning a cannonade was opened upon the "Vulture," and she was obliged to fall farther down the river, which reminded Andre of the fact that he was within the American lines. Smith's fears were so much aroused that he refused to convey him by boat to the "Vulture," but offered to accompany him a considerable distance by a land route. They crossed the river and proceeded toward White Plains. Near Pines Bridge they parted, and Andre continued his journey alone. When near Tarrytown he was stopped by three militiamen, who were watching for stragglers from the British lines. From what they said to him he was led to believe they were loyalists, whereupon he avowed himself a British officer, but upon discovering his mistake he presented Arnold's pass, and endeavored to explain his previous statements; they insisted upon searching him, and he was forced to submit, and the important papers were found. His liberal offers of money if they would release him were of no avail, and he was conducted to the nearest military post.

On the same morning that Washington arrived at Arnold's head-quarters from Hartford, where he had been to confer with some French officers, Arnold received intelligence of Andre's arrest, and hastening to his barge made his escape to the "Vulture." He was apprised that Washington would soon be at his quarters, and left orders to inform him that he had gone over to West Point, and would soon return. Washington arrived shortly after, and crossing over to West Point found, to his surprise, that Arnold had not been there. After spending some time in examining the works he returned, when the papers which had been found upon Andre were placed in his hands and the whole conspiracy revealed. An immediate pursuit to overtake the traitor was made, but it was too late to prevent his escape. Unfortunate Andre was tried by a court of fourteen generals, convicted of being a spy, sentenced, and executed. Arnold wreaked his malice on the Americans by devastating different parts of the country during the war. After its close, he went to England, where he was shunned and despised by all honorable men.

On the 15th of October, 1780, a large party of tories and Indians, under Sir John Johnson and Brant, invaded the Mohawk valley by way of Schoharie creek, destroying the settlements on the way to Fort Hunter, and thence up the Mohawk on both sides. As soon as intelligence of this invasion reached Albany General Van Rensselaer marched against them with a body of militia. Colonel Brown was stationed at Fort Paris, and receiving orders from Van Rensselaer to attack the enemy promptly obeyed, but his small force was dispersed, and himself and forty of his men slain. Van Rensselaer, after great delay, attacked and routed the invaders, who fled and succeeded in making their escape to Canada. The Mohawk valley continued to be devastated by the savage foe. On the 9th of July, 1781, Currytown was attacked by a party of more than three hundred Indians, commanded by a tory named Doxstader. They were pursued by Colonel Willett, and in a battle forty of their number were slain and the others routed. On the 24th of October Major Ross and Walter Butler, at the head of nearly a thousand men, consisting of British regulars, Indians and tories, made a sudden descent into the Mohawk valley and began a work of plunder and devastation. They were met by Colonels Willett and Rowley near Johnstown, and a sharp engagement ensued, lasting till dark, when the enemy fled. They were pursued, and at Canada creek another skirmish took place, wherein the cruel and infamous Butler was slain. Upon his fall their whole force fled in the utmost confusion. This was the final invasion of the Mohawk valley, and their flight the closing scene in one of the most terrible warfares on record.

While menacing an attack on New York, Washington carefully withdrew from the Hudson to attack Cornwallis in his devastating march through the

South, and was far on his way to Virginia before Sir Henry Clinton was aware of the movement. Cornwallis was besieged at Yorktown, and compelled to surrender his whole army on the 19th of October, 1781. This virtually closed the war. Sir Guy Carlton was sent to take the command of the British forces in place of Sir Henry Clinton, with directions to open negotiations for peace. A provisional treaty was signed on the 30th of November, 1782, and a definitive treaty, recognizing the independence of the United States, was concluded at Paris September 3d, 1783. On the 25th of November the British troops took their final departure from the city of New York, and on the same day Washington entered it with his army, amid the joyous, acclamations of the emancipated people. Never, perhaps, was peace more welcome, for the long war had been a terrible ordeal for the patriots, and we who are living in peace and plenty, so far removed by the wheels of time from that eventful period, are not likely to properly estimate their endurance of great and continued sufferings, nor fully appreciate the liberties they obtained at so great a sacrifice, and bequeathed to succeeding generations.

The United States having been recognized as an independent nation, it was early perceived that the powers conferred upon Congress by the Articles of Confederation were in many essential respects inadequate to the objects of an effective national government. The States had been leagued together for a particular purpose, but retained their individual sovereignty, and Congress had no power to compel them to obey its mandates. The people were losing their regard for the authority of Congress; its recommendations for the liquidation of the debts incurred by the war were not promptly complied with, and financial and commercial affairs were falling into serious derangement. Each State being independent of the others in the confederacy, jealousies would naturally arise, and without concerted action on the part of the States it was almost impossible to collect revenue. In view of these increasing evils the leading minds of the country desired a closer union of the States under a general government. A convention was held at Annapolis in September, 1786, to take into consideration the establishment of a general tariff on imports and a uniform system of commercial regulations. Commissioners were present, however, from only five States, among which was New York, represented by Alexander Hamilton. They recommended the calling of a convention of delegates from the several States in May following, and transmitted a report of their conclusions to Congress. Their recommendations were adopted by Congress, and that body deemed it expedient that the delegates should be instructed to revise the Articles of Confederation and report to Congress and the several State Legislatures such amendments and provisions as should seem adequate to the exigencies of the government. All the States except Rhode Island were represented in the convention, which was held at Philadelphia. Believing that the Articles of Confederation were so defective as to be wholly inadequate to the wants of the country, the delegates went to work to form a new constitution. Its plan was generally approved, but there were many in the convention who looked upon the preservation of State sovereignty as pre-eminently essential, and regarded the proposed change in this particular as an infringement of State rights. The delegates from New York upon their appointment had been restricted to the revision of the existing Articles of Confederation; and when the convention decided to provide a new constitution they, with the exception of Alexander Hamilton, withdrew. That body then proceeded to form a constitution, which was adopted and submitted to the several States for approval, the assent of nine being required for its ratification. A spirited contest ensued in the State of New York between its advocates and opponents, the latter being in the ascendancy; but having been adopted by the requisite number of States, it was ratified in convention by the State of New York by a close vote on the 26th of July, 1788, but with the recommendation of several amendments which, however, were not adopted. The city of New York was chosen for the seat of the federal government, and George Washington was elected President.

The difficulties relative to the New Hampshire grants still continued. A convention of the people in that disputed territory in 1777 declared it an independent State, and petitioned Congress for admission into the confederacy. New York thereupon sought the interposition of Congress in her behalf, and that body recognized her claims; but the people interested in the New Hampshire grants were determined to maintain their independence, and during the following year organized a State government. This revived the discord, which had remained inactive since the breaking out of the war, and so great was the hatred of the New Hampshire people toward the State of New York, that rather than be subject to her jurisdiction they chose to return to their allegiance to Great Britain, and were secretly negotiating with the British to become a colony under the crown; but before the conspiracy was fully matured it was interrupted by the capture of Cornwallis. Hostile feelings continued after the war, but in 1790 the difficulties were amicably adjusted. New York, on receiving a stipulated sum for the extinction of land claims, relinquished her jurisdiction, and in the following year the disputed territory was admitted into the Union, under the name of Vermont.

Large tracts of wild land were in possession of the State of New York at the termination of the war. In 1786 the State granted two tracts to Massachusetts, to satisfy certain antiquated claims of that State; but retained her sovereignty over the ceded territory. The largest of these tracts, known as the Genesee country, embraced the western part of the State, and was designated by a line running south from Sodus Bay on Lake Ontario to Pennsylvania. The other embraced a portion of the present counties of Tioga and Broome. Land commissioners of the State, a few years later, authorized by an act of the Legislature, disposed of large tracts of land in the northern part of the State for very small considerations. The largest and most important of these was that granted to Alexander Macomb, containing upward of three and a half millions of acres, at about eighteen pence per acre.

In 1791 the Legislature ordered an exploration and survey to ascertain the most eligible method of removing obstructions from the Mohawk and Hudson rivers, with a view to improving their navigation by the construction of canals.

The following year two companies were incorporated, styled the Northern and Western Inland Lock Navigation Companies, for the purpose of facilitating navigation by connecting by canals Lake Ontario with the Mohawk and Lake Champlain with the Hudson.

Governor Clinton in 1795 having declined to be a candidate for re-election, John Jay was chosen as his successor. The State was now rapidly gaining in population, and in 1800 had nearly six hundred thousand inhabitants. By an act of the Legislature a convention was called to amend the State Constitution in regard to the appointment of members of the Legislature. This body convened in 1801, chose Colonel Aaron Burr to preside over it, and fixed the number of Assemblymen at 100. In 1801 George Clinton was again elected to the governorship, which office he held until 1804, when he was chosen Vice-President of the United States, and Morgan Lewis was appointed his successor. At this time Aaron Burr was holding the office of Vice-President, and failing to receive the nomination for re-election was nominated by his friends for the office of governor of New York. Mortified and chagrined at his defeat, he sought revenge upon those who had been the most prominent and influential in causing it. He regarded the influence of Alexander Hamilton as having contributed largely to his failure, and in his desperation at his blighted political prospects determined to wreak his vengeance upon him. An excuse was presented by Hamilton's expressing political views antagonistic to his own, which having been reported to him in a distorted form he chose to consider as personal, and challenged him. The challenge was accepted and the duel fought, Hamilton falling mortally wounded at the first exchange of shots. His deplorable death produced a gloomy feeling throughout the country, as his brilliant talents and unexceptionable character had won for him the esteem of the whole community. After this occurrence Burr visited the Western States and engaged in treasonable schemes for detaching them from their present political associations, to form, in conjunction with Mexico, a separate government. He was arrested and tried for treason, but escaped conviction for want of sufficient proof. All confidence in his integrity, however, was lost, and the remainder of his life was passed in comparative obscurity. In 1807 Daniel D. Tompkins was elected to succeed Morgan Lewis as governor of New York. In this year Robert Fulton completed the "Clermont," the first boat that ever succeeded in steam navigation. It was launched in Jersey City, and made its trial trip up the Hudson to Albany.

Great Britain and France being at war, the former by a series of "Orders in Council" prohibited vessels of neutral nations from trading with France or her allies, and in retaliation Napoleon proclaimed the notable Berlin and Milan decrees, forbidding all trade with England and her colonies. The effects of these ordinances were very injurious to American commerce; and in consequence thereof Congress, on the 23d of September, 1807, laid an embargo on all vessels in the harbors of the United States, which bore heavily on the mercantile interests of the country, and excited considerable opposition.

CHAPTER XV.

CAUSES OF THE LAST WAR WITH GREAT BRITAIN—EXPEDITIONS AGAINST CANADA—BORDER HOSTILITIES.

THE country was now rapidly drifting into another conflict with Great Britain. The aggressions of the British had for several years been a subject of great anxiety and bitter animosity, which continually increased. Although the United States maintained a strict neutrality while the Napoleonic wars were raging between Great Britain and France, their rights as a neutral nation were disregarded. The embargo laid by Congress upon the shipping in American ports was found so injurious to commercial interests that it was repealed, and a non-intercourse act passed in its place. In April, 1809, the English ambassador at Washington opened negotiations for the adjustment of the existing difficulties, and consented to the withdrawal of the obnoxious "Orders in Council" so far as respected the United States, on condition that they should repeal the act prohibiting intercourse with Great Britain. Upon this basis an agreement was effected, when the President issued a proclamation declaring that as it had been officially communicated to the United States that the "Orders in Council" would be repealed on the 10th of June, trade might be resumed with Great Britain after that date. As soon as intelligence of this agreement on the part of their ambassador reached the English government, the latter refused to ratify it on the ground that he had exceeded his instructions, and immediately recalled him. The proclamation of the President was then revoked, and the two governments resumed their former relations. In addition to other injuries and encroachments upon the rights of the United States as neutrals, the English government claimed the right to search American vessels, and authorized its officers to examine their crews, seize all whom they chose to regard as British subjects, and force them into their service. All remonstrances were unavailing. The English officers in enforcing this right of search committed great outrages, and the practice became so obnoxious as to demand some decided measures for its suppression. Under these circumstances there appeared to be no alternative but war, and Congress having authorized it, war was declared against Great Britain on the 19th of June, 1812. The measure, however, was far from being universally sustained. The Federal party, then in the minority, opposed it, and their political opinions being apparently stronger than their patriotism, they loudly denounced it. It was also but feebly sustained by a portion of the Democratic party, not on political grounds, but from the belief that the country was unprepared for war. New York and New England were most prominent in their opposition, and if they did not directly aid the enemy their conduct was discouraging and injurious to those who were periling their lives in their country's cause.

The Americans, deeming it expedient to invade Canada, directed their attention at once toward that point, and measures were taken to collect forces along the northern frontier of New York, and westward to Michigan. They were distributed in three divisions. The eastern rendezvoused in the vicinity of Plattsburg, on the western shore of Lake Champlain. The central was under the command of General Stephen Van Rensselaer, who made his head-quarters at Lewiston, on the Niagara river; and the northwestern division assembled at Detroit. In connection with these armaments a naval force was fitted up on the lakes, the command of which was assigned to Commodore Chauncey. In July a small British fleet made an attack upon Sackett's Harbor, on Lake Ontario, which was defended by Lieutenant Woolsey, who, from a battery arranged on the shore, so disabled the hostile fleet that it withdrew. In October an attack on Ogdensburg by a British fleet was repulsed by General Brown. In the same month Lieutenant Elliott, by a bold movement, captured at the foot of Lake Erie the British vessel "Caledonia," laden with a valuable cargo of furs, while she lay in fancied security, protected by the guns of a British fort.

After the inglorious surrender of General Hull at Detroit, the next offensive movement on the part of the Americans was assigned to the central division, which was eager to offset Hull's disgrace by a brilliant achievement. An attack on the heights of Queenston was decided on, and was made October 13th, 1812. With inadequate means of transportation about a thousand men were transferred to the Canadian bank of the Niagara, drove the British from their batteries, and took the heights. General Brock rallied the enemy and attempted to recapture the position, but was mortally wounded and his force repulsed. The Americans, however, were unable to hold their ground against the British reinforcements which were brought up, having no implements for fortification; and the militia who had not yet crossed the river became panic-stricken on seeing some of the wounded brought over, and refused to go to the aid of their outnumbered comrades. The latter were therefore overwhelmed and forced to surrender, after having about sixty killed and a hundred wounded.

Nothing save a little skirmishing occurred in this quarter during the remainder of the year. The disgrace which had fallen upon the American arms on land this year was alleviated to a considerable extent, however, by their splendid triumphs on the water. Soon after the new year had been ushered in, the sanguinary conflict at Frenchtown, on the Raisin river, took place, resulting in the surrender of the American forces. The prisoners taken on this occasion were left to be tortured by the barbarous Indians under Proctor, the infamous British commander, in direct violation of his pledge for their safety. Several persons in St. Lawrence county were arrested by the British authorities and confined in Canada on charges of desertion. On February 7th, 1813, Captain Forsyth, the commander of the post at Ogdensburg, crossed to the Canadian shore with a small force, and captured about fifty prisoners, and some military stores. In retaliation Colonel McDonnell, on the 22nd of the same month, crossed the river with a considerable force, and attacked Ogdensburg. Only a feeble garrison was stationed there for its protection; but this, with the aid of the citizens, defended the town gallantly, although they were finally obliged to abandon it to the invaders. A large quantity of military stores came into the enemy's possession, several vessels were destroyed, and considerable damage was done to the property of the citizens.

General Dearborn had been entrusted with the command of the central division, and on the 25th of April detached a force of seventeen hundred men, under General Pike, for a descent upon Toronto, then known as York. They embarked at Sackett's Harbor on board the squadron of Commodore Chauncey, and landed on the 27th in the vicinity of York in the face of a spirited fire from the enemy, whom they soon drove back. The British before leaving their fortifications had laid a train of combustible matter, and connecting it with their magazine thus plotted the destruction of the invaders. The scheme was in part successful, for the Americans took the redoubts as they advanced, and when within about fifty rods of the barracks the explosion took place. General Pike was mortally wounded, and about two hundred of his followers either killed or injured. The troops were appalled at this disaster; but at the order of their dying commander they sprang forward and captured a part of the retreating enemy, and drove the remainder from the field. After the capture of Toronto the squadron returned, and preparations were made for an attack upon Fort George, on the Niagara river, near Lake Ontario. A descent was made upon this point on the 27th of May, and although meeting a stout resistance was in the end successful. On the landing of the troops Colonel Scott advanced to attack an advantageous position held by the enemy, and after a sharp conflict succeeded in dislodging them. General Vincent, the British commander, in alarm, ordered the evacuation of the remaining posts on the Niagara frontier, and on retreating from Fort George caused the magazine to be blown up. The greater part of the garrison made their escape, but nearly four hundred regulars and five hundred militia were made prisoners. General Vincent retreated with the view of taking a position on Burlington Heights, and was followed by a detachment of the Americans; but the British turned and attacked their pursuers in the night, and succeeded in capturing their generals, and further pursuit was abandoned. Colonel Boerstler was detached with a force of about six hundred men to dislodge a body of the enemy stationed at Beaver Dam, about seventeen miles from Fort George. Arriving in the vicinity of that place he was attacked by a body of Indians in ambush, who kept up a conflict in their skulking manner until the arrival of a reinforcement of British troops. The British officer then sent a summons to the colonel to surrender, at the same time magnifying the number of his troops. Colonel Boerstler believing that he had a superior force to contend with, and unable to obtain a reinforcement, surrendered his detachment as prisoners of war.

During these offensive operations on the part of the Americans, like expeditions were undertaken by the British. The force at Sackett's Harbor having been reduced to aid the expedition along the Niagara river, and the fleet of Commodore Chauncey being at Fort George, Sir George Prevost made an attempt to take the former post. On the 29th of May he appeared before the place with a force of about one thousand men. It had been left in command of Colonel Backus, who, aided by General Brown, so successfully resisted the onslaught that the enemy, after sustaining considerable loss, withdrew. This affair was followed by considerable skirmishing along the New York side of Lake Ontario, and on the 11th of July Colonel Bishop made an attack upon the village of Black Rock, on the east side of the Niagara river. In this conflict the British force was repulsed with considerable loss, and their leader mortally wounded.

Meanwhile Commodore Perry was preparing to dispute the control of Lake Erie with the enemy. The Americans had no efficient force upon that lake, and Perry, by unremitting exertions, built and equipped a fleet of nine vessels. Of these the "Lawrence" and the "Niagara" each carried twenty guns, and the whole fleet but fifty-four. The British fleet, under Commodore Barclay, consisted of six vessels, carrying sixty-three guns. On the 10th of September the British commander approached the American fleet with his vessels arrayed in battle order, and Perry at once prepared for action. With his flag-ship, the "Lawrence," he advanced to meet the enemy, and maintained an unequal conflict until his ship was reduced to a complete wreck, and nearly all of her crew either killed or wounded. At this juncture, and when the enemy had a fair prospect of obtaining a brilliant victory, Captain Elliot, commander of the "Niagara," who had perceived the crippled and unmanageable condition of the "Lawrence," moved forward to her aid, and Perry, although exposed to a continuous fire from the enemy, sprang into a boat and proceeded to the "Niagara," to which he transferred his flag. The action was then renewed with great vigor by the remainder of the American squadron. They passed fearlessly among the enemy's ships, dealing such a destructive fire upon them that the whole fleet soon surrendered.

This important and brilliant victory was followed by one under General Harrison, commander of the northwestern division, who on the 5th of October defeated General Proctor at the battle of the Thames. By these victories the territory of Michigan, which had been so ingloriously surrendered by General Hull at the commencement of the war, was regained. Late in the autumn of this year an unsuccessful attempt was made to invade Canada, under the direction of General Wilkinson, who had succeeded Dearborn in the chief command of the northern army. The American Generals Izard and Hampton were repulsed near the border in Franklin county. General Wilkinson descended the St. Lawrence, and on the 19th of November, at Chrystler's Farm, near Williamsburg, an indecisive engagement took place, the Americans retreating to their boats and abandoning further opertions.

The forces on the Niagara frontier had been so much reduced that they were inadequate for its defense after the British were reinforced by General Drummond. General McClure, finding he would be obliged to abandon Fort George, removed his military stores, and unnecessarily inflicted great distress upon the citizens of the villages of Queenston and Newark, reducing the latter place to ashes. The British soon after retaliated by a series of cruel barbarities along the Niagara frontier. On the 19th of December a successful attack was made upon Fort Niagara, and a large share of the garrison, together with the hospital patients, were put to death without mercy. General Rial, with a detachment of Royal Scots and a large body of Indians, crossed the river, plundered and burned Lewiston, and inflicted barbarous cruelties upon the defenseless inhabitants. Youngstown, Manchester, Schlosser and the Indian village of Tuscarora were devastated in the same manner. On the 30th of this month an engagement took place near the village of Black Rock, between General Rial's force and the militia, resulting in the repulse of the latter under General Hall. The villages of Black Rock and Buffalo were abandoned by the Americans, and speedily destroyed by the invaders.

In February, 1814, General Wilkinson dispatched a part of his army to Sackett's Harbor, and removed from French Mills to Plattsburg. The British had collected a strong force at La Colle Mills, on the Sorel, and General Wilkinson resolved to dislodge them. On the 30th of March he crossed the frontier and commenced the attack, but was repulsed and withdrew with his force to Plattsburg. In consequence of this failure he was removed from his command, General Izard succeeding him.

The military stores deposited at Oswego Falls attracted the attention of the British, and with the view of capturing them a British squadron appeared before Oswego. As soon as it was discovered information was sent to Captain Woolsey of the navy, and the militia gathered under Colonel Mitchell and gave the enemy such a spirited reception from a battery prepared on the shore that boats approaching found it prudent to return to their ships. The fleet advanced, and the American force of only about three hundred defended their positions for several hours. A landing was finally effected, and the little band, having maintained their ground as long as it was possible against a vastly superior force, withdrew toward the Falls to defend the stores, destroying the bridges in their rear. The British disabled the ordnance of the fort, and on learning that the bridges had been destroyed returned to Kingston. It was deemed prudent, however, to remove the stores thus preserved to Sackett's Harbor, and Captain Woolsey, aided by a body of riflemen and Indians, set out for the accomplishment of this object. The British admiral was apprised of the movement, and learning their destination through the treachery of a boatman, dispatched a force to intercept them. On the approach of the enemy Captain Woolsey's force put into Sandy Creek, and Major Appling was landed with his troops, which he concealed in ambush. The enemy followed and landed a detachment to pursue them. The British having ascended the bank of the creek to the place of concealment of Major Appling's men, the latter arose and opened such a destructive fire upon them that they fell back in confusion and left Captain Woolsey's expedition to proceed to its destination without further molestation.

On the 3d of July, 1814, Fort Erie, on the west bank of the Niagara, where it leaves Lake Erie, was surrendered to an American force of 3,500 under General Brown, who then moved on to Chippewa. Here they met and defeated the enemy in a general action, the latter retreating to Fort George, at the mouth of the river. The Americans pursued as far as Queenston Heights, whence they returned to Chippewa.

On the 25th General Scott's brigade, while reconnoitering in force, encountered the entire British army advantageously posted, and the battle of Lundy's Lane occurred. The brigade of General Ripley came to the relief of Scott's when the latter had maintained the engagement into the evening, and after the brilliant capture of a British battery the enemy gave up the field. The losses were exceedingly severe on both sides.

The next day the Americans broke up their camp and retired to Fort Erie unmolested. Here they immediately proceeded to strengthen their defenses. On the 4th of August the enemy, having been reinforced, appeared and invested the fort, then commanded by General Gaines. On the 7th they opened fire upon the American lines, and before dawn on the 15th a combined and furious assault was commenced. In their attack upon the left of the American lines the enemy were repulsed four times with heavy loss, and on the right they met with no better success. In the center the conflict was desperate in the extreme, and the enemy finally succeeded in gaining possession of the bastion, but their advance was suddenly checked by its explosion, and the combat shortly after ended in their defeat at every point. They retreated to their camp with broken columns, having sustained a loss of nearly a thousand men. The Americans continued to strengthen their defenses, and both armies were reinforced. General Brown, having recovered from his wounds, resumed command, and finding the enemy were intent on prosecuting the siege, determined to make a sortie to dislodge them and destroy their works. The British force consisted of three brigades, each of which, in its turn, was stationed at the batteries, while the others remained at their encampment about two miles distant. The object in making the sortie was to defeat the brigade on duty before it could be reinforced. On the 17th of September the sortie was made, and resulted in the capture of the British batteries and the destruction of their fortifications. A few days afterward General Drummond left his encampment before the fort, and returned to Chippewa. No further offensive operations were carried on in this quarter, and a few weeks later the fort was demolished and the troops withdrawn to the New York shore.

While this siege was in progress, hostile movements of greater magnitude were being made in other sections of the country. The British army had been strongly reinforced during the summer; the city of Washington had been captured and the public buildings destroyed, and the entire coast was held in a state of blockade by their fleet. They contemplated a dismemberment of the Union by obtaining possession of Lake Champlain and the Hudson from the north, and capturing the city of New York; believing that a division of the republic would thus be accomplished and a separate peace concluded with the Eastern States, whose discontent and opposition to the war were manifest. The people were now fully aroused, and measures were immediately taken for the defense of New York. Its fortifications were strengthened and strongly garrisoned. The invasion of New York by the way of Lake Champlain was entrusted to General Prevost with about fourteen thousand veteran troops from Wellington's army, and the aid of a strong fleet carrying ninety guns. To oppose this formidable armament General Macomb, at Plattsburg, had only fifteen hundred regular troops and about three thousand militia, hastily collected and undisciplined. Commodore McDonough, by almost incredible exertions, had in a short time constructed a fleet carrying sixty-six guns. General Izard had transferred a large portion of the troops from this quarter to the Niagara frontier. Knowing the weakness of the American force at Plattsburg, General Prevost hastily organized and put his army in motion before the fleet was ready for co-operation, and on the 6th of September his advance reached Beekmanstown, where their progress was disputed by a body of militia and a few regulars, who, however, soon retreated toward Plattsburg, and tearing up the bridge over the Saranac entered their entrenched camp. The British advanced, and having taken possession of some buildings near the river attempted to cross; but they were met with a shower of hot shot which proved so annoying that they contented themselves with preparing for an assault upon the fortifications. On the morning of the 11th the British fleet under Commodore Downie was seen advancing in line of battle, to engage the American ships at anchor in the bay off Plattsburg. A fierce and determined conflict followed, and in less than three hours the whole British fleet, excepting a part of the galleys, which had made their escape, surrendered. Simultaneously with the naval engagement General Prevost opened his batteries on the American lines, and attempted to force a passage of the Saranac at three different points, but at each place his troops were repulsed with great loss. On the surrender of the fleet, in sight of both armies, further efforts to cross the river were abandoned. When night came on General Prevost, in great alarm, made a precipitate retreat from the town, leaving behind his sick and wounded, together with a large quantity of military stores. This expedition was the last undertaken for the invasion of this frontier, and its signal defeat materially aided in bringing the war to a close. On the 24th of December a treaty of peace was concluded at Ghent, but before the welcome news had reached our shores the British met with another disastrous defeat at New Orleans.

CHAPTER XVI.

THE ERIE CANAL AND RAILROAD—THE STATE ADMINISTRATION—NEW YORK IN THE CIVIL WAR.

THE construction of the Erie and Champlain canals, which had been projected just at the breaking out of the war, had been virtually abandoned by the repeal of the act authorizing the commissioners to borrow funds for the prosecution of the work. But on the termination of the war the policy was revived, and the attention of the people was again called to this great undertaking. The difficulties of the enterprise, however, were formidable. The late war had drawn heavily upon the State treasury. The preliminary measures for the construction of the canals had already been attended with considerable expense, and the people were loth to engage in an enterprise which they plainly foresaw would be so insatiable in its demands upon the public treasury. They were therefore slow to encourage additional legislation for its prosecution, but through the untiring energy and perseverance of De Witt Clinton an act prepared by him was passed in April, 1817, authorizing the construction of the work. Governor Tompkins, having been elected Vice-President of the United States, resigned his office as governor; and in April De Witt Clinton, the ardent and zealous advocate of the system of internal improvement, was elected to succeed him. On the 4th of July, 1817, the Erie Canal was commenced at Rome, and in October, 1817, that portion of it between Utica and Rome was opened to navigation.

In 1821 an act was passed by the Legislature authorizing a convention to be called to revise the State constitution. This convention met at Albany, and after a lengthy session adopted a constitution, which was subsequently ratified by the people, and under its provisions the State was governed for a quarter of a century. By the new constitution the time of holding the State elections was changed from April to November, and the officers elected were to enter upon their official duties on the 1st of January. Joseph C. Yates was elected governor in 1822, and was succeeded in 1824 by De Witt Clinton. The Erie Canal having been completed, the first flotilla of canal boats left Buffalo for New York on the 26th of October, 1825. Intelligence of its departure was communicated to New York in one hour and twenty minutes by the discharge of cannon stationed at points within hearing distances of each other along the entire route. The occasion was celebrated with great rejoicing throughout the State.

The first State charter for the construction of a railroad was granted in 1826. The points to be connected were Albany and Schenectady, and the road was completed in 1831. Although the road was but rudely constructed, the advantages of this new mode of transportation were so obvious that railroads were soon after projected in various parts of the State.

On the evening of February 11th, 1828, Governor Clinton suddenly expired. This unexpected and sad event was deeply lamented throughout the community. Amid discouragements of every kind, and of a magnitude that would have filled ordinary men with dismay, he had persevered with unflagging energy, and accomplished measures which in succeeding years proved eminently beneficial to the best interests of the State. On the death of Clinton, Nathaniel Pitcher, then lieutenant-governor, succeeded to the governorship for the remainder of the term, and in November Martin Van Buren was elected to succeed him. In March following Van Buren was appointed to an office in President Jackson's cabinet, and resigned the governorship, which devolved upon Enos T. Throop, who was elected to the office at the succeeding election in 1830.

In February, 1832, the State Agricultural Society was formed at a convention of its friends in Albany, but received no support from the State until it was reorganized in 1841 and measures were adopted for raising funds and holding annual fairs. In April, 1832, an act was passed chartering a company to construct the New York and Erie Railway, and four years later the comptroller was directed to issue State bonds to the amount of $3,000,000 to aid the enterprise. In November, 1832, William L. Marcy was elected to succeed Throop as governor of the State. In 1833 a legislative act was passed authorizing the construction of the Chenango Canal, connecting the Erie Canal at Utica with the Susquehanna river at Binghamton. In April, 1835, the Legislature passed an act by which the schools in the State were to be provided with libraries. Near the close of this year a great conflagration occurred in New York city, consuming property to the amount of eighteen millions of dollars.

In 1838 William H. Seward was elected governor of the State, and in 1842 was succeeded by William C. Bouck. After the death of the patroon Stephen Van Rensselaer, disturbances arose in Rensselaer, Albany, and other counties from the tenants refusing to fulfill the obligation of their leases, which in 1844 assumed serious aspects. The tenants organized and arrayed themselves in opposition to the enforcement of legal proceedings, and outrages were often committed upon executive officers in the discharge of their duties. Many of the tenants on the Van Rensselaer manor were seriously aggrieved by the demands of their landlords under the provisions of ancient leases, which for a long time had been suspended and the revival and enforcement of which threatened to ruin them. Silas Wright was elected governor in November, 1844, and on assuming the duties of chief magistrate in January following called the attention of the Legislature to these anti-rent outrages, which continued to increase. Stringent laws were passed for the punishment of offenders; but the excitement still prevailed, and lawless acts were committed by members of an organization of anti-renters disguised as Indians. These occurred so frequently that it became necessary to order out the military to suppress the insurrection. In 1846 the Legislature passed laws to abolish "distress for rents," and facilitate legal remedies by extending the time for a "re-entry" on lands for its non-payment, and during the ensuing year those who had participated in these outrages were pardoned by a proclamation.

Through the energy and genius of Professor Morse the magnetic telegraph was added to our list of public facilities for intercommunication, and as early as 1845 various lines were in process of construction through the country. A constitutional convention having been called, met at Albany on the 1st of June, 1846, and continued in session upward of four months. The amendments to the State constitution adopted by that body were ratified by the people in November, and John Young was elected governor of the State.

The annexation of Texas to the Union led to hostilities between Mexico and the United States, and on the 11th of May, 1846, Congress declared that by the acts of the Mexicans war existed between the two nations. The Americans were victorious in all important engagements with the Mexican army, and the part taken by the troops from the State of New York was conspicuous and highly creditable to their valor. Peace was concluded on the 2nd of February, 1848. In November of the same year Hamilton Fish was elected governor.

By the census of 1850 it was found that the population of the State amounted to upward of three millions, being an increase of two and a half millions in half a century. In November of this year Washington Hunt was elected to succeed Hamilton Fish as governor of the State. He was a candidate for re-election in 1852, but was defeated by Horatio Seymour. In 1854 an amendment was made to the State constitution requiring the appropriation of an annual sum during a term of four years for the enlargement of the Erie and the completion of other canals in the State. In November of the same year Myron H. Clark was elected governor. In 1855 the State contained about three thousand miles of railroad, constructed at an aggregate cost of $125,000,000. In 1856 John A. King was elected governor, and at the expiration of his term was succeeded in 1858 by Edwin D. Morgan.

A list of the governors of New York, in a single paragraph, with the dates of their election, will be found convenient for reference. From the organization of the State government in 1777, governors have been elected as follows:

In 1777, 1792 and the four intervening elections, and in 1801, George Clinton; 1795 and 1798, John Jay; 1804, Morgan Lewis; 1807, 1810, 1813 and 1816, Daniel D. Tompkins; 1817 (Tompkins having been elected Vice-President), 1820, 1824 and 1826, De Witt Clinton; 1822, Joseph C. Yates; 1828, Martin Van Buren; 1830, Enos T. Throop; 1832, 1834, 1836, William L. Marcy; 1838, 1840, William H. Seward; 1842, William C. Bouck; 1844, Silas Wright; 1846, John Young; 1848, Hamilton Fish; 1850, Washington Hunt; 1852, 1852, Horatio Seymour; 1854, Myron H. Clark; 1856, John A. King; 1858, 1860, Edwin D. Morgan; 1864, 1866, Reuben E. Fenton; 1868, 1870, John T. Hoffman; 1872, John A. Dix; 1874, Samuel J. Tilden; 1876, Lucius Robinson.

The recognition of slavery in the Territories belonging to the United States having been earnestly combatted for several years, the difficulty finally terminated in a gigantic civil war. On the election of Abraham Lincoln to the

Presidency in 1860, upon principles of avowed hostility to the extension of slavery, and the failure to effect a compromise by which slavery should be recognized or tolerated in any portion of the Territories, the Southern States resolved to secede from the Union and organize a separate government. The capture by the Confederates of Fort Sumter was the first overt act of the Rebellion, and upon its occurrence, in April, 1861, active hostilities were begun, and before the close of the year one hundred and fifteen regiments had been put into the field by the State of New York. In July, 1863, during the execution of the draft ordered by an act of Congress for recruiting the Union army, a terrible riot occurred in the city of New York. The police were unable to check its progress, and for several days the city was convulsed and overwhelmed with tumult, rapine and murder. The outbreak was finally quelled by the interposition of the military, but not until a large amount of property had been destroyed and a considerable number of lives lost. The war was prolonged until the spring of 1865, when it terminated with the complete success of the Union cause, and peace has since prevailed.

By the census of 1875 the State was found to contain 4,705,000 inhabitants. Within a period of two and a half centuries this immense population had accumulated, and from the almost pathless wilderness, in the beginning trodden only by wild beasts and savages, it has by industry and enterprise removed the primeval forests, reared large and numerous cities, and constructed vast and magnificent public works, which conspicuously appear in all parts what is justly termed the "Empire State." With the full enjoyment of peace, it continues to advance with accelerated and rapid strides, in accord with its proud and becoming motto, "Excelsior."

The History of Wyoming County.

CHAPTER I.

RELICS AND THEORIES OF THE EARLIEST INHABITANTS OF WESTERN NEW YORK.

THE historian of the former inhabitants of any country or region is confronted at the outset by various difficulties. The question arises who and what were the progenitors of these inhabitants? and who were their ancestors? and so on. There exist in this country, and to some extent in western New York, evidences of its former occupancy by a people whose customs were, in some respects, different from those of the Indians who were found here near the close of the fifteenth century. These evidences consist of the sepulchral and other mounds or tumuli in the West and South, and of the defensive works which are found in this region. Of the people who constructed these mounds and forts no tradition was preserved by the pre-Columbian Indians, and in and around them many relics have been found concerning the former use of which even the ingenuity of archaeologists has failed to form a conjecture.

The opinion has been held that these people were not the progenitors of the present race of Indians, but that they were expelled from the country or exterminated by those from whom these Indians descended. The correctness of this opinion is doubted by many modern ethnologists, who insist that gradual changes in the surroundings of a people, extending through indefinite periods of time, are sufficient to account for those things which have been regarded as evidences of a distinct race of people. They insist, too, that in the absence of recorded history it is not strange that in the lapse of time many of the customs, the significance of the monuments and works, and even the existence of a people should pass into oblivion among their descendants.

It is not necessary, and it would be improper, to discuss this question here. These mementos of the long ago exist, and as archaeologists become more skilled in searching after them more are discovered, notwithstanding the fact that time, the ax and the plow tend constantly to obliterate the traces of their existence.

In recent times individuals, associations and public institutions have become impressed with the importance of preserving these relics of bygone ages, and with commendable zeal they are engaged in collecting them in cabinets and museums, where they may be preserved and studied in future. The national museum at Washington contains many thousands of these relics, and the cabinets of historical societies are constantly being enriched by accessions of them. Recently Mr. W. P. Letchworth, of Glen Iris, near Portage, has at his own expense established such a museum.

Want of space prevents even a catalogue of all the works that have been discovered in western New York, of the origin and builders of which there exists not even a tradition. Probably many others have been leveled by the plow, and forgotten, if their character was ever known, and perhaps still others, the relics of periods antecedent to these, have been obliterated by time.

There are regions the peculiar topography of which renders them well adapted to the wants of people, and which at the same time does much toward shaping and molding the character of that people. Western and central New York appear to have long been the habitat of a wild, independent and warlike race, and the physical features of the region are adapted to the wants of just such a people as the works and relics found in it indicate, and as were represented by its inhabitants at the time of its settlement by Europeans.

Of these ancient works, one of the most interesting in western New York is in the town of Genesee Falls, in this county, on the Genesee river, three miles above Portageville. It is on a large farm owned by Messrs. T. Dunn and H. T. Mills, on lot 107 of the Cotringer tract. It is called Fort Hill, because of its location on the top of a hill that rises from near the middle of the valley, which is here about a mile in width.

Although this is evidently a drift hill, there are reasons for the belief that in some past period it was the eastern extremity of a spur that extended from the hills on the western boundary of the valley; and that its connection with these hills was severed by the action of the current, which, after breaking through, carried away, little by little, the whole of this spur, except this solitary hill and the short spur of about the same height which still projects from these hills half a mile west from it. When the evidences of past mutations which everywhere present themselves in this valley are considered, it will not be deemed incredible that in the lapse of immense time this spur may have been deposited there; then, by the action of the current which beat against its base, doubled back and swept around to the east of it, been cut through, and afterward, as before stated, washed away by the shifting stream till only this hill and the distant headland remained. The river now runs half a mile east from the hill, but it is known that in 1820 it washed its southeastern base, and evidences of comparatively recent erosive action are plainly visible there. Along its southwestern base a former river bed is easily traceable where the stream passes west of the hill. From the plain on the north side the hill rises to a height of 60 or 70 feet, and from the south about 90. The sides are so steep as to render ascent extremely difficult, except at its eastern and western extremities, where narrow points or "hog backs" extend northeasterly and northwesterly, which afford easier access to its summit.

The top is quite level, and includes an area of about three-quarters of an acre. It is surrounded at the brow of the hill by a mural embankment, which is now about two feet in height. This wall encloses, or rather enclosed, a surface which had the form of the cut surface of a pear divided longitudinally; its base lying toward the east, and its long axis running about twelve degrees south from east. When the river had its course along the southeast base of the hill it undermined or washed away a portion of this base, and a part of the wall, with some of the surface which it included, "slid" away. Elsewhere the continuity of the wall is unbroken, except at the eastern and western "hog backs," where there are sallyports or passageways. A ditch once surrounded the work just without the embankment, but where the sides of the hill have worn away scarcely a trade of this ditch can be seen. It is very distinct where it crosses the eastern and western points of the hill. A short distance east from the center of this work is a depression which marks the site of a former cache, or place of concealment or storage. By some who have visited and described this work this has been spoken of as a well for supplying water. A moment's reflection, however, will convince any one that without a reversal of the law of gravity a supply of water at the top of an isolated hill like this is impossible. A few trees are standing within this embankment, and they are not of a large size. Their growth is said by those who have known them for sixty years to be scarcely perceptible. Such is the present appearance of this work.

At the time of the settlement of this valley an artificial mound rose from the plain some thirty rods north from the hill. This mound was circular, with a diameter at its base of about sixteen yards, and a height of six yards. In 1870, with the consent of the proprietors, Messrs. O. H. Marshall and W. C. Bryant, of Buffalo, and W. P. Letchworth made a thorough examination of this work by excavating trenches across it through the center at right angles, and carefully noting everything that was disclosed. Ashes and charcoal, with fragments of bones, doubtless human, so much decayed as to indicate great antiquity, were found. Partial and careless examinations had before resulted in the discovery of a few stone implements and ornaments. It was a burial mound.

Several "bone pits," which contained very large quantities of human ossements, have been found in the vicinity. The significance of these will be at once recognized when the custom which prevailed among the ancient Indians, of periodically gathering and depositing the bones of their kindred, is remembered. This is admirably described by Parkman in his "Jesuits of North America," under the caption "Feast of the Dead." In the vicinity are several burial places of more modern Indians.

Relics in abundance have been unearthed by the plow in different localities in the neighborhood of this work. Some of these relics belonged to what archaeologists term the paleolithic, or ancient stone age; while others were of more recent origin. The places where they were found thickly strewn were ancient camping grounds or villages; and could investigations have been made by competent archaeologists before they were disturbed by the plough, many of the hut sites might have been pointed out.

Of course different opinions are entertained of this and other similar works, in accordance with the views which are held concerning the ancient inhabitants of the country. That it was a defensive work, strong both by reason of its character and its well chosen site, of course no one will doubt. It appears probable that it was used as a defensive stronghold during a long succession of generations; and that many villages sprang up and decayed in the valley, and perhaps on the hills in its vicinity.

Concerning the antiquity of the work there is room for great diversity of opinion. By reason of the unstable character of the valley around it no inference of great age can be drawn from appearances there. The character of the work itself is such as it might assume in a few, and retain during many centuries. Reasonable conclusions may, however, be drawn concerning its possible age from what has been learned of other similar works in western New York, the appearances and surroundings of which afford more nearly definite information concerning their antiquity.

Near Medina, Orleans county, N. Y., there exist the remains of an ancient fortification similar in many respects, though more extensive and elaborate than this. The walls or embankments of that fortification do not have so much the appearance of great age as the embankment at Fort Hill shows; yet evidences in and around that work indicate that from eight to twelve centuries have passed since it ceased to be used, and the period of its occupancy, though not definitely indicated, was fully as great. The embankments in both these works were better preserved than in any other in this region. That of Fort Hill probably had a height of four or five feet, and though no traces of palisades are now to be seen, they probably surmounted this wall, as well as those of similar works where remains of them can be found. It is also probable that in this work, as in others, excavations would disclose accumulations of stones of a few pounds weight, for hurling at assaulting foes.

Concerning this and other ancient works in this country, or their uses, none of the post-Columbian Indians seem to have had the slightest tradition. This fact is regarded by some as evidence of their great antiquity; and by others of their construction by a race antecedent to the ancestors of the present Indians. Though these works probably have great antiquity, and though they *may* have been constructed by a race now extinct, the absence of tradition concerning them is not to be regarded as evidence of either.

The following, from the pen of Dr. Myron H. Mills, of Mt. Morris, illustrates the facility with which historic events pass into oblivion among the Indians:

"Mt. Morris was called among the Indians Sanungewage, after an early settler, a 'white man' (the late Major-General William A. Mills), whose Indian name was Sanungewa. * * Those who were youths and young men when the Seneca tribe moved from the Genesee river in 1825 still call the village by the

Indian name and have well preserved recollections of the 'white man' after whom it was named. But upon conversing with the *young* Indians at the present day about Sanungewa, the Indian's 'great white friend,' or Sanungewage, the village named after him, they will look strangely at each other, and smile or laugh in one's face, not comprehending what is said to them. They will at the first opportunity ask the older Indians what it means. In fifty years more the traditions both of Sanungewa and Sanungewage, the village named after him, will be entirely lost."

CHAPTER II.

NUMBERS AND LOCATION OF THE SENECAS—THEIR RELIGIOUS BELIEFS.

THE first settlements in western New York were made subsequent to the year 1640. At that time the region was inhabited by a people who termed themselves *Ho-de-no-sau-nee*, or People of the Long House. By the southern Indians they were called Massowamacs; by the Dutch, Maquaas, and by the French, Iroquois, by which designation they have since usually been known.

Charlevoix says of the word Iroquois: "It is formed of the word *hiro*, or *hero*, which signifies 'I have said,' and by which these savages always ended their speeches, as the Latins did theirs by *dixi*; and of *koue*, which is a cry of melancholy when its pronunciation is prolonged, and of joy when it is pronounced short."

Nothing is known of the history of the Iroquois previous to the settlement of the country by the whites. According to their traditions, they once occupied a region north from the St. Lawrence, were they were weak in numbers and subject to the Algonquins, who occupied the country further north from that river. Having been vanquished in a war with the Adirondacks, they fled from the country, and came by way of the St. Lawrence and Lake Ontario to the Oswego river, through which they entered central New York. As nearly as can be learned from their traditions, they lived together for a time near Seneca river. As they increased, however, they sought new territory, scattering east and west through the State.

The brief sketch of the Iroquois confederation which has been given on pages 20 through 24 will enable the reader to comprehend the character of the Senecas, who inhabited western New York, and the elements of that strength which rendered them a terror to the savage nations north, west and south from them, and a serious obstacle in the way of the ambitious projects of the French in Canada.

The original habitat of the Senecas was between Cayuga lake and the Genesee river. They termed themselves *Nun-da-wa-o-no*, or "People of the Great Hill." They knew nothing of the name Seneca, except as applied to them by outsiders. As with other Indian proper names the spelling for a long time varied; the nation being often called in old documents the Sinnekes, and given some sixty other names, mostly similar. The later classical form of the word is certainly an improvement, in spite of its coincidence with the name of the ancient philosopher. Though the same name is applied to this division of "the Romans of the new world" that was great among the Romans of the seven hills, it is pleasant to be able to consider it a slight modification of a native word, and not an instance of the stupid wholesale application of classic titles in the geography of western New York. The French sometimes called the Senecas Tsonnontouans or Sonnonthouans.

One of the first allusions to the nation by Europeans occurs in a Jesuit "relation" dated 1644–45, and is as follows: "Toward the termination of the great lake called Ontario is located the most numerous of the Five Nations, named the Senecas, which contains full twelve hundred men, in two or three villages of which it is composed." In 1677 Wentworth Greenhalgh passed through the "long house" of the Iroquois from end to end and made a detailed report of his journey and observations, from which the following is extracted:

"The Senecas have four towns, viz., Canagora, Tiotohatton, Canoenada and Keint-he. Canagora and Tiotohatton lye within 30 miles of ye Lake ffrontenacque [Ontario], and ye other two ly about four or five miles apiece to ye southward of those. They have abundance of corne; none of their towns are stockadoed.

"Canagorah lyes on the top of a great hill [Boughton hill, near Victor, Ontario county], and in that, as well as in the bignesse, much like Onondago, containing 150 houses, northwestward of Caiouga 72 miles. Here ye Indians were very desirous to see us ride our horses [probably the first they ever saw], wch wee did; they made great feasts and dancing. * * *

"Tiotohatton lyes on the brincke or edge of a hill; has not much cleared ground; is near the river Tiotohatton, wch signifies bending. It lies to the westward of Canagorah about 30 miles, containing about 120 houses, being ye largest of all the houses wee saw, ye ordinary being 50 *a* 60 feet long, with 12 *a* 13 fires in one house. They have good store of corne, growing about a mile to the Northward of the town.

"Being at this place the 17th of June, there came 50 prisners from the southwestward. They were of two nations, some whereof have few guns; the others none at all. One nation is about 10 days' journey from any Christian and trade only with one great house, not far from the sea, and the other trade only, as they say, with a black people. This day of them were burnt two women, and a man and a child killed with a stone. All night we heard a great noyse as if ye houses had all fallen, butt itt was onely ye Inhabitants driving away ye ghosts of ye murthered.

"The 18th going to Canagorah we overtook ye prisoners; when the soudiers saw us they stopped each his prisoner and made him sing, and cutt off their fingers and slasht their bodies with a knife, and when they had sung each man confessed how many men in his time he had killed. Thatt day att Canagorah there were most cruelly burnt four men, four women and one boy. The cruelty lasted aboutt seven hours. When they were almost dead letting them loose to the mercy of ye boys, and taking the hearts of such as were dead to feast on.

"Canoenada lyes about four miles to ye Southward of Canagorah, conteynes about 30 houses well furnished with corne.

"Keint-he lyes about four or five miles to ye Southward of Tiotohatton; contayns about 24 houses well furnished with corne.

"The Senecqucs are counted to bee in all aboutt 1,000 fighting men."

In 1684 Father Lamberville, dissauding La Barre from attacking the Senecas, gave the number of their warriors at 1,500. In 1698 there was made an official census of the Five Nations, in which it was reported that the "Sinnikes" had dwindled to 600 from 1,300, their number in 1689. In 1763 Sir William Johnson estimated the men of the nation as numbering 1,050, and mentioned that it had "several villages, beginning about 50 m. from Cayuga, and from thence to Chenussio [Geneseo], the largest, about 70 m. from Niagara, with others thence to the Ohio." In 1770 he reported that there were 1,000 of the Seneca warriors. The fighting strength of this nation was generally equal to that of all the other Iroquois. This was stated by Governor Tyron to be the case in 1774, when, on the excellent authority of Sir William Johnson, he reported the total number of Iroquois warriors at 2,000.

A tradition of the Senecas says that at the time of their greatest prosperity a census of the nation was taken "by placing a kernel of white flint corn for each Seneca in a corn husk basket, which, from the description of its size, would hold ten or twelve quarts. Taking the smallest size, and making the estimate accordingly, will give the number of Senecas alone at 17,760."

When the Senecas were first known to the whites their villages were scattered from Seneca lake half way to the Niagara. In 1669, when La Salle made his first visit to their country, their four principal villages were from ten to twenty miles south of the falls of the Genesee, and to the eastward of that river. Mention is made of cabins of the Senecas on the Niagara in 1678 and 1736. General Amherst, writing in 1763, mentions the Kanadaseegy and Canadaraggo castles, the former of which, more commonly spelled Kanadaseaga, stood on the site of Geneva. These are presumably the villages which Sir William Johnson, in his enumeration of the Indians in 1763, calls Kandasero and Kanadaragey, and mentions as being in the English interest, while the rest of the nation was hostile. There were, in Sir William's time, two castles of the tribe at Chenussio (Geneseo), once their western outpost, and a village called Chenondonah stood on the west bank of the Genesee, some fifteen miles from its mouth.

Previous to the settlement of this country by the whites, the roads over which the Indians passed in going from village to village, or from one region to another on hunting excursions or hostile expeditions, were termed trails.

These consisted of paths, sometimes from twelve to eighteen inches in width, and often they were worn to a depth of from six to twelve inches, according to the character of the soil. These trails connected village with village, and many of the main ones ran along the sides of rivers, in or near the valleys of which these villages sprang up. The same trails were probably used during centuries; for the routes were determined, as were the locations of the villages, by a sort of natural selection, and the habits and customs of the Indians were not such as to effect changes that would in their turn require changes in these locations. An inspection of a map on which these trails are traced will show that they very nearly coincided with the present main avenues of travel through the State.

A main trail extended from the site of Albany to that of Buffalo, over almost the same route subsequently followed by the main turnpike, and later, generally, by the Central railroad. From this trails branched, traversing valleys, skirting lakes, and connecting with the main trails.

From the site of Rochester two trails ran through the Genesee valley—one on each side of the river—through the villages along the valley as far as Caneadea, the last of the Seneca villages in it. Thence it extended south and west to the *O-hee-yo*, or "beautiful river," as the Senecas termed the Allegheny. It was one of the routes from the main trail which passed through Rochester and Avon (Canawagus), to the Allegheny river and the southwest.

There were, of course, other trails which led from place to place in various directions, the traces and memory of which are now obliterated; but those of which mention has been made were some of the main thoroughfares over which the Indians had traveled, singly or in long files, probably during many centuries.

Along the southern shore of Lake Erie, west of the Senecas, dwelt the powerful "Eries or Cat nation," as the French for an unknown reason called them. About 1654 or 1655 they fell victims to the conquering Iroquois. Tradition says that the immediate occasion of the war in which the Iroquois exterminated the Eries was the defeat of the latter by the former in a series of athletic games. The Eries, having learned with alarm of the confederation of the Five Nations, proposed, as a test of the power of the new alliance, that a hundred of the Seneca braves should contest with as many of their own for a suitable prize in the native game of ball. The challenge was twice declined, but on its third presentation the eagerness of the young warriors overcame the caution of their elders, and it was accepted. The flower of the Five Nations presented themselves. After a desperate struggle the match was won by the picked men of the Iroquois. The Eries, burning to retrieve their reputation as athletes, thereupon challenged their adversaries to a foot race in which ten of each party should compete. The young Iroquois assented, and were again the victors. Smarting with mortification from their double defeat, the Eries in desperation dared the champions of the Five Nations to a last and more serious contest, namely, a wrestling match, ten on each side, in which the vanquished should be slain by the victors. The first of the Eries was thrown by his Seneca antagonist, and on the refusal of the latter to dispatch his fallen adversary, the Erie chief himself brained him. Thrice was this scene of butchery repeated, when the rage of the defeated nation had risen to such a pitch that the Iroquois, to avoid a battle, for which they were not prepared, withdrew and returned to their homes.

The result convinced the Eries that the Iroquois nations had made common cause, and their only hope lay in destroying the Senecas, by a sudden blow, before they could be supported by their confederates. Their purpose to do so was frustrated by a Seneca woman, a captive among the Eries, who escaped to her kindred in time to warn them of their danger. The Iroquois rallied and marched out to meet the invaders. They encountered near the foot of Honeyoye lake, and after a fierce conflict the Eries were routed and almost annihilated. A remnant which escaped attacked the Senecas years after, near Buffalo, but were defeated. Such is the attempt of tradition to account for the extinction of the most powerful native foe that ever crossed the path of the all-conquering Iroquois.

It is remarked in the life of Mary Jemison that "perhaps no people were more exact observers of religious duties than those Indians among the Senecas who were denominated pagans, in contradistinction from those who, from having renounced some of their former superstitious notions, have obtained the name of Christians. They believed in a Great Good Spirit, whom they called in the Seneca language *Nau-wah-ne-u*, as the creator of the world and of every good thing; that he made man and all inoffensive animals, that he supplied men with the comforts of life, and that he was particularly partial to the Indians, who, they said, were his particular people. They also believed that he was pleased in giving them [the Indians] good gifts, and that he was highly gratified with their good conduct; that he abhorred their vices, and that he was willing to punish them for their bad conduct, not only in this world, but in a future state of existence. His residence, they supposed, lay at a great distance from them, in a country that was perfectly pleasant, where plenty abounded even to profusion. * * * To this king they addressed prayers, offered sacrifices, gave thanks for favors, and performed many acts of devotion and reverence.

"They also believed that this king had a brother, less powerful than himself, and who was his opposite in every particular; that he made and sent them diseases, bad weather and bad crops, and made and supported witches; that he owned a large country adjoining his brother's, with whom he was continually at variance. His fields were unproductive, the weather cloudy, destructive frosts frequent, game scarce and not easily taken, streams muddy and unpeopled with fish, ravenous beasts numerous, reptiles of poisonous teeth lay in the traveler's path, and hunger, nakedness and general misery were felt by those who unfortunately became his tenants. He took great pleasure in afflicting Indians here, and after their death received all those into his dreary dominions who in their lifetime had been so vile as to be rejected by *Nau-wah-ne-u*, under whose eyes some of them continued in an uncomfortable state forever. To this source of evil they offered oblations, to abate his vengeance and render him propitious. * * * In each year they had five feasts [six according to Morgan; the third was the strawberry festival], or stated times for assembling in their tribes and giving thanks to *Nau-wah-ne-u* for the blessings they had received from his kind, liberal and provident hand, and to solicit a continuance of such favors. * * * When the green corn became fit for use they held their third or green corn feast, which was usually attended with great interest, and at which a good portion of the time was spent in singing and dancing and otherwise manifesting their joy, and expressing their thankfulness for the addition to their diet of an article of food which is to-day held in such high estimation by the whole civilized world of mankind."

A gentleman residing at Caneadea, in Allegany county, who once witnessed a green corn dance or feast at the upper Caneadea village, in which several hundred Indians from the Buffalo, Tonawanda, Cattaraugus and Big Tree reservations participated, says: "The succotash was made in six five-pail brass kettles, and the whole once full served for one meal. Twelve or fourteen deer were killed, and the venison, cut up in pieces of a pound or more in weight, was thrown in with the green corn and beans, and without a particle of salt all boiled together; and when sufficiently cooked the kettles were surrounded and each one helped him or herself, eating out of the kettles with wooden spoons, some with iron ones and some, provided with bowls or other dishes, would take out their portions and then retire, giving others, not so well provided, a chance immediately about the kettles. This feast passed off without any disturbance, no quarrel or unpleasantness marring the general good feeling and high degree of enjoyment of all who participated in it. The next year the Caneadea Indians visited some other tribe upon the occurrence of this feast, and thus it passed around."

The fourth feast was celebrated after corn harvest, and the fifth at the time of the old moon in the last of January or first of February. For the last mentioned two white dogs were slaughtered and fantastically painted and decorated for sacrifice. The masters of ceremonies, who were hideously gotten up in masks and smeared with dirt, going about among the cabins, collected and concentrated in themselves the last year's sins and guilt of the tribe. On the eighth or ninth day of the proceedings they transferred the accumulation of iniquity to one of their number, and he by a peculiar sleight of hand or magic worked it out of himself into the bodies of the white dogs. The dogs were then burnt, and in the smoke of the sacrificial fire, flavored with the offerings of tobacco, passed away the year's sins of the tribe. The meeting was made the occasion of deliberations on the administration of tribal affairs, and was closed with a feast of succotash and a peace dance.

It was said by pioneers who had been present at the ceremony of burning the dog at what was formerly called by the settlers "Indian Town," but which was afterward known as the lower Caneadea village, or Wiscoy, in Allegany county: "The settlers used to collect in large numbers on such occasions, coming, some of them, many miles to witness it, and when well behaved were kindly received and well treated. But their solemnities having been, upon some occasions, made the subject of considerable levity, they became quite wary when whites were present, and sometimes even refused to proceed with their customary observances and rites until they had withdrawn. All who were present and witnessed the ceremony were expected to contribute something in the way of tobacco or trinkets, and in case of refusal their situation would be made quite uncomfortable by showering upon them live coals and ashes."

Judge A. B. Rose, of Castile, in this county, gives the following account of their ceremonies at a funeral:

"About the year 1818, and when the Indians lived at Gardow and along the Genesee river above and below there, I was present at one of their funerals, that of a boy about fourteen or fifteen years of age. The dead body in its Indian dress was laid on an elevation in one of their houses, where were seated a circle of Indian females, including the mother and female relatives, all silent; when one of their circle raised her head and delivered a short address of two or three minutes, reciting the expectations and hopes of the deceased boy's parents and relations that he would become a brave and successful warrior and bring joy and gladness to his parents; but, alas, their hopes were now blasted. Then she (the speaker), followed by all the circle, would drop their heads and cover their faces with their blankets, and all unite in a loud, shrill, mournful, ringing, plaintive moan for one or two minutes, when they would cease and raise their heads, and another one would recite the boy's agility in the race, his skill with the bow, and his promising traits, when all as before would unite in the moan. And thus the time was occupied until some Indians came in with a rude box, and while putting in the boy and his trinkets I noticed some things that excited my curiosity; an opening was cut near the head in the side of the box, and near the lid, of about seven inches in length and one and one-quarter in width. I inquired of one with whom I was acquainted what it meant, and he said the opening was for the spirit of the boy to escape, and the cakes which they put in the box were for the spirit to subsist on during its long journey to the spirit land of his fathers; and that they would build fires over his grave at night to give light to the spirit during its long, dark voyage. When the body was thus prepared they carried it to the grave, and the Indian females followed in single file, keeping up their plaintive moan until the burial was completed."

CHAPTER III.

"THE WHITE WOMAN," DEHEWAMIS OR MARY JEMISON—HER FAMILY AND POSSESSIONS.

DEHEWAMIS, or Mary Jemison, who was commonly known as "the white woman," was a resident of the Genesee valley during seventy-two years, fifty-two of which she passed at Gardeau Flats, in the town of Castile, Wyoming county.

In 1824 her biography, dictated by herself, was first published. In 1877 Hon. William P. Letchworth, of Glen Iris, republished the work, which had long been out of print. From this, by his kind permission, and from the recollections of those who knew her, the following sketch of her life is gleaned:

She was the third of a family of five children, and was born during the voyage of her parents from Ireland to Philadelphia. Her father was Thomas Jemison, and her mother's maiden name was Jane Irwin. After their arrival in this country they settled at Marsh Creek, on the then frontier of Pennsylvania, and engaged in agricultural pursuits. There they were prosperous and happy, till, in the spring of 1755, the entire family, with another consisting of a woman and three children, were captured by a party of six Shawnese Indians and four Frenchmen. They were taken two days' travel into the wilderness, when Mary and a boy of the other family were separated from the rest, who she afterward learned were inhumanly murdered. They journeyed westward till they came to Fort Du Quesne (Pittsburg), where she was given to two Seneca women, who adopted her in place of a lost brother, according to their custom, which required that either a prisoner or a scalp should be given to the nearest relative of the one lost.

She was taken some eighty miles down the Ohio river to a Seneca town, in the vicinity of which she remained with her adopted sisters four years, during which time she was married to a Delaware Indian named Sheninjee, and gave birth to two children; a girl, that died soon after its birth, and a son, which she named after her father, Thomas Jemison. She was treated with uniform kindness by the Indians, and was as happy as the recollection of her separation from her family would permit. She was young, her spirit was elastic, and she readily learned to adapt herself to her changed circumstances, and to love her friends, by whom she was kindly treated. Her husband and her infant son were additional ties which bound her to the wild life into which she had been adopted, and at that time her desire to leave the forest and return to civilized life was nearly extinguished. She did not look upon the life of an Indian woman as that of a drudge. She said: "Notwithstanding the Indian women have all the fuel and bread to procure, and the cooking to perform, their task is probably not harder than that of white women, who have those articles provided for them; and their cares certainly are not half as numerous nor as great." She always spoke in high terms of the Indian character, when uncontaminated by intercourse or contact with the whites. She stated:

"The use of ardent spirits among the Indians, and a majority of the attempts which have been made to civilize them by the white people, have constantly made them worse and worse; increased their vices and robbed them of many of their virtues; and will ultimately produce their extermination. I have seen, in a number of instances, the effects of education upon some of our Indians, who were taken when young from their families and placed at school before they had opportunities to contract many Indian habits, and there kept till they arrived to manhood; but I have never seen one of these but was an Indian in every respect after he returned. Indians must and will be Indians, in spite of all the means that can be used to instruct them in the arts and sciences.

"Notwithstanding all that has been said against the Indians in consequence of their cruelties to their enemies—cruelties that I have witnessed and had abundant proof of—it is a fact that they are naturally kind, tender, and peaceable toward their friends, and strictly honest; and that those cruelties have been practiced only upon their enemies according to their idea of justice."

In the autumn of 1759, she, with her two Indian brothers, came to Genisneyo, where it was arranged that her husband, Sheninjee, should join her the next spring. She made the journey on foot, bringing her infant, then nine months old, on her back. They halted a day for rest at Caneadea, and came to Little Beard's Town, then a large Seneca village, near where Cuylerville is now located. There she met her Indian mother and sisters and took up her abode. Sheninjee did not join her the next spring, and during the summer she learned that he died in Ohio soon after she left.

At the time of her arrival the French and Indian war was still in progress, and the Senecas, who were the allies of the former, were constantly on the war path. She remembered the ambush and dispersion of the detachment of English that went to attack Fort Schlosser, and the return to Little Beard's Town of the Indians with two white captives, whom they tortured to death. She also remembered the massacre at Devil's Hole, in which the Senecas from Little Beard's Town participated. After the close of the war she had her option to remain with the Indians or return to the whites; but she uniformly chose the former. At one time her abduction and delivery to the whites was attempted, in order to secure a bounty that had been offered for the return of white captives; but she eluded capture and kept herself secreted till the danger passed.

About the year 1763 she was again married, to a Seneca warrior named Hiokatoo. She bore him four daughters and two sons, whom she named, after her relatives, John, Jesse, Jane, Nancy, Betsey, and Polly. Of the daughters, Jane died in 1795 or 1796, aged about fifteen years. The others married and reared families, and many of their descendants still reside on the Indian reservations.

Dehewamis continued to reside at Little Beard's Town till 1779. Of the condition of the Senecas during the interval between the close of the French and Indian war and the breaking out of the Revolution, she spoke in the highest terms. It must be remembered that this was long before any settlements had been made by the whites. She said of them: "No people can live more happy than the Indians did in times of peace, before the introduction of spirituous liquors among them. Their lives were a continual round of pleasures. Their wants were few, and easily satisfied, and their cares were only for to-day, the bounds of their calculation for future comfort not extending to the incalculable uncertainties of to-morrow. If peace ever dwelt with men it was in former times in the recess from war among what are termed barbarians. The moral character of the Indians was (if I may be allowed the expression) uncontaminated. Their fidelity was perfect, and became proverbial. They were strictly honest, they despised deception and falsehood, and chastity was held in high veneration; and a violation of it was considered sacrilege. They were temperate in their desires, moderate in their passions, and candid and honorable in the expression of their sentiments on every subject of importance."

The Seneca Indians during the war of the Revolution were the allies of the English, as is well known. After the massacres at Cherry Valley and Wyoming, in which it was believed they bore a conspicuous part, the well known expedition of General Sullivan was sent against them to destroy their towns and devastate their country. On the approach of the army toward Little Beard's Town some of the Indians fled to the neighboring woods, and others, with the women and children, went across Wyoming county to Catawba creek, which empties into Tonawanda creek at Varysburg. On their return to their village they found everything destroyed. Resolved to care for herself, Dehewamis, with her five children, went up the river till she arrived at Gardeau Flats, where she hired to two negroes, fugitive slaves, who had a cabin and a field of corn there, to husk corn on shares.

The name of these flats is usually spelt Gardeau; but it is pronounced Gardow. It is given by Morgan Ga-da-o, and is defined by him "bank in front." An old settler in Perry, Mr. Otis, says he was informed by the Indians that it means a "cross hill," or a hill projecting from another; and that it was given to these flats because a spur, evidently an old slide, projects across the valley at the northern boundary of the flats. Mrs. Jemison said of it: "My land derived its name—Gardeau—from a hill that is within its limits, which is called in the Seneca language Kautam. Kautam, when interpreted, signifies up and down, or down and up, and is applied to a hill that you ascend and descend in passing, or to a valley." The valley where these flats lie is entered from the north by ascending and descending the spur of a hill spoken of, hence the appropriateness of the name. The fact, however, that the Seneca language has no labials renders it doubtful whether she was correctly understood in the pronunciation of this word.

By her labor she succeeded in procuring sufficient corn to sustain her family during the severe winter which followed, and she continued to reside on these flats during fifty-two of the fifty-four remaining years of her life. The negroes with whom she found refuge left the flats two or three years later.

Not long after the close of the Revolution her brother proposed that if it was her choice she should abandon her Indian life and return to the whites. Her eldest son, Thomas, urged her to do this, and offered to accompany her and assist her on the journey; but the chiefs refused to let him go because he gave promise of becoming an eminent warrior or counsellor. To quote her own language: "The chiefs refusing to let him go was one reason for my resolving to stay; but another, more powerful, if possible, was that I had a large family of Indian children, and that if I should be so fortunate as to find my relations they would despise them, if not myself, and treat them as enemies, or at least with a degree of cold indifference, which I thought I could not endure.

"Accordingly, after I had duly considered the matter, I told my brother that it was my choice to stay and spend the remainder of my days with my Indian friends, and live with my family as I had hitherto done. He appeared well pleased with my resolution, and informed me that as that was my choice I should have a piece of land that I could call my own, where I could live unmolested, and have something at my decease to leave for the benefit of my children."

She heard no more concerning the land till the time of the council of Big Tree, in 1797, when Farmer's Brother sent for her to attend the council, informed her that her brother had spoken to him concerning the land, and requested her to choose and describe it. Said she: "I accordingly told him of the place of beginning, and then went round a tract that I judged would be sufficient for my purpose (knowing that it would include the Gardeau Flats), by stating certain bounds with which I was acquainted."

A survey was made of this tract in 1798 by Augustus Porter, and the following is a copy of his field notes, recorded on the back of a map belonging to Michael Brooks, and now in the possession of Norman Seymour, of Mount Morris:

> "Beginn at the point of high rocks; thence east one mile 79.48 to an oak post in the old path marked N. E. C. of R.; a white oak tree 24 inch diamet. s. 14 e. 49 links; another white oak tree 14 inch diameter n. 72 e. 29 links; a white oak 14 inch marked with a blaze 3 noches n. 87 w. 19 links; thence south 372.04 to a white ash post marked S. E. C. of R.; a s. maple 24 inch a blaze 3 noches n. 87 w. 38 links; a beach 12 inches a blaze 3 noches n. 30 e. 34 links; thence west 481.88 (at 355.32 it intercepts with steep rock w. side Gen. River); thence north 372 chains 4 links; thence east 322.40 to place of beginning; containing 17,929 acres and 137 rods.
>
> "By A. Porter, Sept. 14, 1798."

The grant of this reservation was violently opposed by the Indian demagogue Red Jacket but was made notwithstanding this opposition. After the white woman became the owner of these flats she adopted the practice of letting her land to be tilled on shares by white people, and thus she was enabled to live in what she termed comparative ease. When, however, it is known, as is stated on the authority of old residents, that one of her easy tasks was to carry from a saw-mill in Perry, five miles distant, sufficient boards for a house; and that she accomplished this by lashing together a few at a time with bark strings and suspending them across her back with a strap of the same material, passed over the top of her head after the Indian fashion, her easy life will be appreciated.

On this reservation she lived in quietness which was seldom broken except by domestic afflictions, which were severe. Of her three sons, Thomas, John and Jesse, John became the murderer first of Thomas, and afterward of Jesse; and he was afterward killed by other Indians at Squawkie hill. Thomas, it will be remembered, was the son of her first husband, Sheninjee; and he was the one she brought on her back from Ohio. He was of a mild, peaceble disposition except when under the influence of liquor; then of course reason was disenthroned in him, and, in her words, he conducted himself "like a wild or crazy man, without regard to relatives, decency or propriety."

On the first of July, 1811, in a fit of intoxication, he engaged, as he had frequently done before, in a quarrel with John, at the house of their mother, in the course of which the latter seized him by his hair, dragged him out at the door, and killed him with a blow of his tomahawk. The matter was investigated by the chiefs of his tribe, and John was acquitted, Thomas having been regarded as the first aggressor. Thomas was fifty-two years old at the time of his murder. He left a family, of whom one, a son named Jacob Jemison, was educated in part at Dartmouth College. He afterward passed through a regular course of medical studies and became an assistant surgeon in the United States Navy. He died on board his ship in the Mediterranean squadron about 1850, when about forty years old. In November of the same year Dehewamis's last husband, Hiokatoo, died of consumption.

The bad character which the murder of Thomas gave John caused him to be shunned, and this soured his disposition. In the month of May, 1812, while both, with George Shongo, their brother-in-law, were at work for Robert Whaley, of Castile, a drunken quarrel occurred, in which John killed Jesse by stabbing him. He was twenty-seven or twenty-eight years of age when killed.

John was killed, as before stated, at Squawkie hill by two Indians, named Doctor and Jack. He was fifty-four years of age when killed, and left two wives and nine children. After the lapse of a few weeks Jack, one of the murderers, poisoned himself by eating muskrat root. Doctor, the other assassin, died of consumption in 1819.

In 1811 negotiations commenced between Jellis Clute and Micha Brooks and Dehewamis, for the purchase of a part of her reservation. A special act of naturalization was passed by the Legislature in 1817 to enable her to convey this land, and the transaction was finally consummated in the winter of 1822 and 1823. By this she conveyed all her reservation, except two miles square and a lot for Thomas Clute. The following is a description of that which she retained:

"The tract which I reserved for myself begins at the great slide, thence running west one mile, thence north two miles, thence east about a mile to the river, and thence running southerly up the river, and bounding on the west bank to the place of beginning. In consideration of the before mentioned sale to Messrs. Gibson, Brooks and Clute, among other things they bound themselves, their heirs, assigns, etc., to pay to me, my heirs or successors, three hundred dollars a year forever."

She finally determined to leave Gardeau Flats and join the Indians of the tribe on the reservation at Buffalo. She therefore received a commutation of her annuity, sold her remaining two square miles, and, with her daughters, their husbands and children, removed from Gardeau in 1831. She made her residence on Buffalo Flats, where she resided till her death, September 9th, 1833, at the age of about ninety-one years. She was buried at the cemetery near the Seneca mission church, and a marble slab, with an appropriate inscription, erected at her grave.

Forty years passed after her burial at that place, and the stone that marked her grave had been almost entirely chipped away to furnish mementoes of the woman who had figured so strangely in the early history of the region. Through the cemetery had also been surveyed a street, which, when opened, would pass over this grave. It was therefore determined to remove her remains from the grave that had thus been desecrated, and which was likely soon to be obliterated, and deposit them where such desecrations would not be likely to occur. This determination on the part of some of her descendants was seconded and supported by some philanthropic and benevolent citizens of Buffalo, who were deeply interested in all that pertained to pioneer and Indian history. In March, 1874, these remains were carefully disinterred by an undertaker, under the direction of her grandson Dr. James Shongo, and placed in a tasteful black walnut coffin. It is noteworthy that "near the center of the grave was found a peculiarly shaped porcelain dish, containing what may have been when placed there articles of food. In the dish was a wooden spoon greatly decayed. * * * These were doubtless provided by her Indian relatives to supply her with food while journeying to the Indians' happy hunting grounds."

The coffin, containing everything that was found in her grave, was taken to the council-house grounds at Genesee Falls, where, after brief and appropriate religious services in the old council-house, it was placed in a stone sarcophagus, sealed with cement, and interred. A black walnut tree was planted near the foot of the grave by her grandson Thomas Jemison, son of the babe she brought on her back from Ohio. The seed was borne by the tree that shaded her grave at Buffalo. The grave is curbed with stones that were once used as rude headstones in the Indian cemetery at Gardeau. They had been plowed up and afterwards used to construct a road culvert. Mr. Letchworth and Dr. Shongo were permitted to remove them from this culvert and bring them here, to place around the grave of her who had perhaps assisted to plant them at the heads of the desecrated graves of her kindred. The grave within this curbing is covered with flowers, the seeds of which were furnished by Dr. Shongo. What is left of the old headstone is planted at the head of the grave. Near this stands a marble monument—a square block some six feet in height—on one face of which is copied the inscription which was originally engraved on her tombstone. Upon this pedestal is to be placed a bronze statue of Mary Jemison, in her Indian costume, bearing on her back a babe, just as she came to the Genesee valley. Here, on the banks of the Genesee, to the murmur of which she listened during seventy-two years of her eventful life, repose her honored remains.

It is proper here to state on the authority of the well-informed investigator of Indian history William C. Bryant, Esq., of Buffalo, that the generally accepted orthography and signification of "the name conferred upon the captive by the two gentle Indian women who adopted her as their sister" is incorrect. He says: "The name should be written Deh-ge-wa-nus, and means, literally, the two falling voices. The Indians in pronouncing the name make a circular or undulating sweep of the hand downwards, to emphasize the idea of a prolonged or dying cadence."

The tragical death of her three sons has been spoken of. The fourth wife of the oldest, Thomas, was the daughter of Sally, a Seneca squaw, by an English trapper and fur-trader. Sally was afterward one of the wives of "Indian Allen." His son Thomas, or Buffalo Tom, as he was familiarly called, who died in 1878, was an influential man in the Seneca nation, and was highly esteemed for his many virtues by all who knew him.

Of her daughters, Mary married an Indian named Billy Green, Betsey married John Green, and Polly, the youngest, married George Shongo. All lived with or near her while she remained at Gardeau, and had large families of children. Her descendants on the different reservations are numerous.

Her second husband, Hiokatoo, to whom she was married about 1763, and who was the father of six of her children, was born on the banks of the Susquehanna in 1708. His mother was sister to the mother of the worthy chief Farmer's Brother. From his youth he was a warrior, and though kind in his domestic relations, he was endowed with all the cruelty and bloodthirstiness of a savage, and always boasted exultingly of the many barbarities and cruel tortures he had inflicted on captive foes. From his youth down to the close of the Revolution he was engaged in all the wars of the Senecas, often leading hostile expeditions. He was second in command in an expedition that went against Cherry Valley and other frontier settlements, and was said to have been engaged in the massacre of Wyoming. It is said that after the commencement of the Revolutionary war he was engaged in seventeen campaigns, and during the French and Indian war he was in every battle that was fought on the Susquehanna and Ohio. Of his martial pride, which he entertained to the last, his wife said:

"I have frequently heard him repeat the history of his life from his childhood, and when he came to that part which related to his actions, his bravery, and war; when he spoke of the ambush, the combat, the spoiling of his enemies, and the sacrifice of his victims, his nerves seemed strung with youthful ardor, the warmth of the able warrior seemed to animate his frame, and to produce the heated gestures which he had practiced in middle age. He was a man of tender feelings to his friends, ready and willing to assist them in distress; yet as a warrior, his cruelties to his enemies were perhaps unparalleled, and will not admit of a word of palliation."

CHAPTER IV.

THE NOTORIOUS "INDIAN ALLEN"—PROMINENT CHARACTERS AMONG THE SENECAS.

EBENEZER ALLAN, commonly called Allen, or oftener Indian Allen, first came to Gardeau Flats toward the close of the Revolutionary war, and made his home at Mary Jemison's house, hunting with her son Thomas. He remained and worked her land till after the peace of 1783. His first noteworthy exploit here was to arouse the jealousy of a white man, whose wife was a Nanticoke squaw. He next took a belt of wampum to an American officer at a military post as a token of a desire for peace on the part of the Indians—which he was not authorized to do, and which did not correctly represent them. The Indians were exasperated at this and resolved to punish him, and for that purpose pursued him. He fled, but afterward returned, and was fed and secreted by the kind hearted Mary during some days at several times. He was watched for and tracked like a wild beast, and was once taken, but made his escape and returned. He kept hid during two weeks at one time in a small cave or hole in the rocks in a gulf near the flats, whence he emerged at night to find the food which she left for him at a place agreed on, and to milk a cow and drink the milk from his hat.

He afterward engaged in business at Mt. Morris, built a grist-mill and a saw-mill at Genesee Falls (now Rochester), and engaged in many schemes of speculation. He resided for a time at the mouth of Oatka creek, which was first named from him Allen's creek.

History rarely records a blacker character than his. He was a swindler, a polygamist, an adulterer and a foul murderer. He was a tory in the Revolution; and Mary Jemison said she had often heard him relate this transaction:

"At one time, when he was scouting with the Indians, he entered a house very early in the morning, where he found a man, his wife and one child in bed. The man instantly sprang on the floor, for the purpose of defending himself and little family; but Allen dispatched him with one blow. He then cut off his head and threw it, bleeding, into the bed with the terrified woman; took the little infant from its mother's breast, dashed its head against the jamb, and left the unhappy widow and mother to mourn alone over her murdered family. It has been said by some, that, after he had killed the child, he opened the fire, and buried it under the coals and embers; but of that I am not certain. I have often heard him speak of that transaction with a great degree of sorrow, and as the foulest crime he ever committed, one for which I have no doubt he repented."

Some years since Mr. J. S. Minard, of Hume, Allegany county, published some reminiscences of Caneadea reservation and the Indians who lived there. This reservation was but a short distance from this county, and many of the Indians spoken of were well known to old settlers here. For that reason a few extracts are given:

"Prominent among the Caneadea Indians was the old chief and warrior Shongo, who lived near the residence of the late George Parker. Mr. Parker's flats were called 'Shongo flats,' and a brook which makes into the river near by still retains his name. He it was whom Major Van Campen wounded at the battle of Newtown, now Elmira, if I remember rightly; and with whom he had an interesting interview many years after, at Angelica, when, by mutual relation of the events, personal encounters, etc., in that memorable action, they renewed an old acquaintance begun under quite different circumstances. Shongo is remembered by many of the early settlers as a man of advanced age, sound judgment, good personal appearance and extensive influence with his people.

"A son of his—George Shongo—married a daughter of Mary Jemison (*De-he-wa-mis*), and afterward lived at Gardeau. Mrs. Sarah Ingham says Shongo used frequently to call at their house, and when inclined to conversation, which was generally the case after imbibing a few drinks of *snick-e-i*, would relate his war exploits, tell of being in the battle of Saratoga under Burgoyne, show the various wounds received in battle—four ball holes in one arm, and various sword cuts, etc.

"Shongo was one of the last to remove from the reservation. He was very loth to go, claiming that he never consented to the sale, that the whole transaction on the part of the whites was a fraud; and it was only after repeated importunities on the part of the whites, through Dr. Dwight, of Moscow, who was agent for several of the proprietors of the reservation, and a deposit in the hands of M. W. Miner, Esq., to be paid to him when he should be prepared to go, that he was induced to leave.

"Hudson was another very influential Indian. He was gifted with rare oratorical powers, and was a sort of preacher or exhorter among them. Mr. Charles M. Mills informs me that he has heard him address the assembled Indians upon the occasion of the annual ceremony of burning the dog and remission of sins, when scarcely a dry eye could be seen in the whole assembly. Various others of the early settlers corroborate Mr. Mills's account of the remarkable effect of Hudson's eloquence.

"Hudson at one time lived upon the site of the residence of Andrew S. Bennet, Esq. I have been informed that he was educated at Dartmouth College, and there is good reason for believing it. It is certain that quite a number of young Indians were educated there under the presidency of Dr. Wheelock. Joseph Brant was one of them, and I presume Hudson was another."

[Turner says of Hudson: "He had been a leading 'brave' in the southern Indian wars waged by the Senecas, and afterward in the English and French wars. Hon. George Woods, a prominent citizen of Bedford, Pennsylvania, became a prisoner with the Indians, on the Ohio or the Allegheny. Hudson procured his release after he had been condemned and tied to a stake. In after years they met, and the judge treated him with much kindness, making him a present of a fine house and lot at Bedford, which he never occupied, but he used to pride himself upon its possession and the manner in which he came by it."]

"Washington was the name of another Indian family of some note and influence. 'Old Wayne Washington,' *alias* John Mohawk, the father, died at something over a hundred years of age, and was buried on the farm of Delos Benjamin, only a few rods to the rear of his dwelling. I saw the sunken grave only last summer.

"He it was to whom Van Campen on a certain occasion 'lent his hatchet'—in other words, having dispatched all the rest of his captors, sent him away with a tomahawk sticking in the back of his neck; many with whom I have conversed remember seeing the scar.

"He had sons, Jim and 'Young Wayne Washington,' as he was called, and a daughter, Polly, still remembered by the early settlers as quite a character in those days. One of the boys was said to be the best runner on the reservation. Loren Houghton remembers his running a race on a bet of fifty or sixty dollars, some four miles and turn around the sign post at Radley's tavern and back, coming out victor.

"Long Beard, named in contradistinction to Little Beard, of greater note as a warrior and chieftain (both names, I suppose, having a literal significance and personal application), from whom the rapids in the Genesee river known as 'Long Beard's Riff' take their name, lived upon the farm of James C. Smith, and was quite a farmer for an Indian, raising some grain and keeping cattle, horses and sheep. *Ska-no-boy* lived with him, and was quite a notorious character. *Ska no* in Indian signifies gift—gift boy, or given boy. He was given to the Caneadea Indians by some other tribe, and adopted. He lived with Long Beard, who, I have been told, was at one time a chief; and perhaps was at the time *Ska-no* was given. *Ska-no-boy* was well built, tall, stout, athletic—physically perfection itself, but morally destitute of principle and honor, and as a result incurred the enmity of most of the Indians as well as the whites of the reservation.

"A little incident of *Ska-no-boy*: He, like most of the Indians, loved the 'fire water' of the white man, and had a charge of twenty shillings scored up against him on one of the beams in Ingham's log tavern. One day he presented himself with an otter skin, the finest specimen ever seen in these parts, which Mr. Ingham took and canceled the debt. But poor *Ska-no* had better paid the debt in some other way. He had stolen the otter skin from the trap of another Indian, was detected, and shortly after apprehended by a party of two or three of them and very severely punished.

"He was at one time lodged in jail at Angelica, for insulting a woman somewhere in the neighborhood of 'Oak Hill,' near Colonel Williams's, which was then a part of this county. I mention this for the reason that I have seen it stated that Indians were peculiarly exempt from such conduct.

"Copperhead, a very old Indian, who died a few years since in Careadea, John Shanks, who still occasionally returns to the 'scenes of his childhood,' *Sun-ge-wa*, or Big Kettle, the Trimsharps, Sharpshins, Bear Hunter, Kingee, Elk Hunter, Chickens (so called from his diminutive stature), Joe Daw, Jackson, Powderhom, George Jakes, and *Chick-nit* were Indians of lesser note remembered by our pioneers.

"The marriage contract they regarded with the utmost solemnity. I have been told that divorces were very unusual. There were some exceptions, however, to this general rule. I have been told of two instances where the marital obligations were not respected on the part of the wife, or squaw, and in each case the husband poisoned himself. Young Elk Hunter was one, and was found dead, having eaten of the cicuta, or poison hemlock, and repaired to the woods. He lived near where Reynolds's tavern is located, on the Wiscoy. The other was one of the Kingees.

"One of the Trimsharps—Tom, I believe—was once at the house of Mr. Joel Cooper, one of the early settlers on the reservation, where, among other things thought of and talked of, the subject of marriage came up. Mr. Cooper had several sons, none of them as yet married. Turning to one of them, the Indian said, 'You young, me no young; why you no get you squaw?' and endeavored to persuade him to marry, promising, in case he would agree to it, to bring him a squaw next time he should come out. To this young Cooper assented, of course, and thought no more of it. But judge of his surprise when, in a few days, 'Old Tom' reappeared with a charming young squaw by his side, whom he had brought all the way from Tonawanda to become his bride. This was a stumper for the young man; when he was joking the Indian had been in earnest, and he was reduced to the alternative of marrying the squaw or backing out of his bargain. He chose to repudiate.

"An anecdote is related of an Indian, who, in 1823 or 1824, was frozen to death on the road from Cold Creek to Caneadea, while in a state of beastly intoxication. When found the Indians gathered around him in considerable numbers, and held a sort of impromptu coroner's inquest over the body, discussing the cause of death. After due deliberation they came to the unanimous conclusion that he came to his death by reason of the water that was in the whisky that he drank having frozen in him."

CHAPTER V.

THE TITLE TO THE SOIL OF WESTERN NEW YORK—PHELPS AND GORHAM'S PURCHASE—MORRIS'S RESERVE.

NO topic better deserves a chapter of local history than the ownership of the soil at early periods, on which the present titles rest; and this is the proper point for a statement on this subject with relation to Wyoming county.

"A memorial prepared by the Commissioners of Trade and Plantations in 1697, relating to the right of the crown of Great Britain to sovereignty over the Five Nations of Indians bordering upon the province of New York," recites that those nations had "by many acknowledgments, submissions, leagues and agreements been united to or depended on that colony"; that they, "being the most warlike in those parts of the world, held all their neighboring Indians in a manner of tributary subjection"; that in prospect of an invasion of their territory in 1684 by De la Barre, governor of Canada, Governor Dongan of New York warned that French official "that those Indians are the King of England's subjects, and also sent the then Duke of York's [to whom the province had been granted by the crown] arms to be set up in every one of the Indians' castles, as far as Oneygra [Niagara], which was accordingly done and Mons. De la Barre retired."

Governor Tryon, in 1774, in a "report on the province of New York," said:

"The boundaries of the province of New York are derived from two sources:—first, the grants from King Charles the Second to his brother James, Duke of York; * * * secondly, from the submission and subjection of the Five Nations to the crown of England. * * * It is uncertain to this day to what extent the Five Nations carried their claim to the westward and northward, but there is no doubt that it went to the north beyond the 45th degree of latitude, and westward to Lake Huron, their beaver hunting country being bounded to the west by that lake; which country the Five Nations, by treaty with the governor of this province at Albany, in 1701, surrendered to the crown, to be protected and defended for them."

Such was the foundation of the English claim to sovereignty over the territory of the Iroquois. They themselves never recognized the claim in the sense in which it was put forth, and the French always denied and scoffed at it; but the British government had the power to maintain it, and up to the Revolution continued to assert it.

The encroachment of the whites upon the territory of the Iroquois gave the latter great uneasiness, to allay which a very numerously attended council was held with them at Fort Stanwix (Rome) in 1768, to agree on a line beyond which settlements should not be permitted. The line decided upon in the State of New York "ran along the eastern border of Broome and Chenango counties, and thence northwestward to a point seven miles west of Rome."

The close of the Revolution left the hostile Iroquois unprovided for by their British employers and at the mercy of the United States. Conquered after waging a long, bloody and destructive warfare against the patriots of New York, they had forfeited their territory and would have had little cause of complaint had they been dispossessed. The government, however, thought it wise to deal generously with them; and in a council held on the site of Rome in 1784 recognized their continued ownership of the land between the line agreed on at the same place sixteen years before, and one beginning at Lake Ontario four miles east of the Niagara river, running southward parallel with the river to Buffalo creek, thence still southward to the Pennsylvania line and following that to the Ohio river. All of New York west of this second line seems also to have been subsequently conceded to the Indians except a mile strip along the Niagara.

Every reader of English colonial history knows how ignorantly or carelessly grants of American territory were made by the crown to individuals and companies, the same tracts being in some instances given at different times to different parties, laying the foundation of conflicting claims. Thus the province of New York, when granted to the Duke of York in 1664, covered part of Massachusetts as defined by the charter given to the Plymouth Company in 1620. The territory of both provinces under their charters also extended indefinitely westward; but New York, in 1781, and Massachusetts, four years later, relinquished to the United States their claims beyond the present western boundary of this State, and Massachusetts contented herself with claiming that portion of New York west of the meridian which now forms the eastern line of Ontario and Steuben counties—some 19,000 square miles, New York of course also asserted jurisdiction and ownership of this vast tract.

The dispute was compromised by a convention of commissioners from the two States, held at Hartford in December, 1786. It was agreed that the sovereignty of the disputed region should remain with New York, and the ownership with Massachusetts, subject to the Indian proprietorship, which had been recognized by the general government. "That is to say, the Indians could hold the land as long as they pleased, but were only allowed to sell to the State of Massachusetts or her assigns." The meridian bounding the Massachusetts claim on the east was called the "pre-emption line," because it was decided to allow that State the right of pre-emption, or first purchase, of the land west of it. There was one exception: New York retained the ownership as well as the sovereignty of a strip a mile wide along the Niagara river.

In 1788 the State of Massachusetts sold to Oliver Phelps and Nathaniel Gorham, two of its citizens, and to others for whom they acted, its pre-emption right to western New York for $1,000,000, to be paid in three annual installments, in certain securities of the State, which were then worth about one-fifth of their face. The next thing with these gentlemen was to complete the title by buying the Indian interest. For this purpose Phelps held a council with the Iroquois at Buffalo early in July, 1788, and bought, for $5,000 down and a perpetual annuity of $500, about 2,600,000 acres, bounded on the east by the pre-emption line. Part of the western boundary was a meridian from Pennsylvania to the junction of Canaseraga creek with the Genesee river (being the line forming the western boundary of the eastern tier of towns in Allegany county). Thence northward the line followed the course of the Genesee "to a point two miles north of Canawagus village; thence running due west twelve miles; thence running northwardly so as to be twelve miles distant from the western bounds of said river, to the shores of Lake Ontario." The tract thus defined constituted the famous "Phelps and Gorham's Purchase."

In securing their vast estate Phelps, Gorham and company encountered the opposition of a set of land sharks who also had a covetous eye upon this magnificent domain. These were the capitalists forming the New York and Genesee Land Company, engineered by one John Livingston; and its branch the Niagara-Genesee Company, headed by Colonel John Butler, and consisting almost entirely of Canadians. As we have seen, the Indians were barred from selling their lands except to Massachusetts or her assigns. Butler, Livingston and their associates proposed to get possession of them by a long lease; hence they are spoken of as the "lessee companies." Chiefly through the influence of Butler they obtained from part of the Iroquois chiefs and sachems a nine-hundred-and-ninety-nine years' lease of most of their territory for $20,000, and an annual rent of $2,000. Their scheme fell through, the Legislatures of New York and Massachusetts declaring a lease of that length equivalent to a purchase, and as such null and void. Butler, however, profited by the purchase of Phelps and Gorham. He was one of the three to whom the Indians referred the question of the price they should charge those gentlemen, and is said to have had 20,000 acres placed at his disposal by the purchasers in consideration of the advice he gave the confiding red men. The "lessees" continued their intrigues until they succeeded, in 1793, in getting from the Legislature a grant of one hundred square miles east of the pre-emption line, instead of obtaining twenty thousand miles and founding a new State, as there is reason to suppose the Niagara-Genesee Company, at least, intended, with the cooperation of the Senecas, whom Butler and other Canadian officials were always embittering against the people of New York.

Before Phelps and Gorham had half paid for the entire pre-emption right they had bought from Massachusetts, the securities of that State, in consequence of the adoption of the Federal Constitution, had risen nearly to par; and finding that they should be unable to fulfill their contract they induced the State to resume its right to the portion of its original New York claim which they had not yet bought of the Indians, and release them from their contract as to that part, leaving on their hands the tract since called Phelps and Gorham's

Purchase, and bounded as above described. This agreement was reached on the 10th of March, 1791.

Two days later Robert Morris, the illustrious financier, whose services were of such vital importance to the nation during the Revolution, contracted with Massachusetts for the pre-emption right to all of New York west of Phelps and Gorham's Purchase. About this time he also bought 1,264,000 acres of Phelps and Gorham (paying £30,000 in New York currency), which he soon sold to three English gentlemen, Sir William Pultney, John Hornby and Patrick Colquhoun, for £35,000 sterling. It was only after much difficulty and delay that Mr. Morris completed his title to the tract of which he had purchased the pre-emption right from Massachusetts. It was necessary to buy out the interest of the Indians, and this was accomplished by a council at Geneseo in September, 1797, when he was enabled to purchase all of the State west of Phelps and Gorham's Purchase, except that the Indians retained eleven reservations, amounting to about three hundred and thirty-eight square miles; among them the Gardeau reservation, elsewhere spoken of, a part of which was included in the present town of Castile.

It was by his speeches in the councils affecting the title to the lands of western New York that the Seneca chief Red Jacket came into prominence. He figures in history as a crafty demagogue, vain, ambitious and dishonest; a coward in war and a sot in peace; chiefly noted for his harangues against parting with the lands of the Seneca nation, and the bitterness he usually manifested against the power by whose grace alone the nation had any lands after the Revolution.

The conveyance from Massachusetts to Mr. Morris was made May 11th, 1791, by five deeds. The first covered the land between Phelps and Gorham's Purchase and a line beginning twelve miles west of theirs on the Pennsylvania border and running due north to Lake Ontario. The next three embraced as many sixteen-mile strips crossing the State north and south, and the fifth what remained to the westward of these.

The tract covered by the first mentioned deed was what has been called "Morris's Reserve," from the fact that he retained the disposition of this section in his own hands when he subsequently sold all west of it. It included in Wyoming county the eastern tier of towns. He sold the reserve in large tracts, though small as compared with his purchase. Its western boundary, separating it from the Holland Purchase, was the "east transit" line, so called because it was run with a transit instrument in connection with astronomical observations, the variation of the magnetic needle disqualifying the surveyor's compass for running a meridian line. It is called the "east" transit to distinguish it from a similarly surveyed meridian passing through Lockport, which is called the "west" transit. The laying down of this line was a slow and laborious operation. It involved nothing less than felling a strip of timber three or four rods wide most of the way across the State, to give unobstructed range to the miniature telescope of the transit. This required, beside three surveyors, a considerable force of axmen. On most of the line all hands camped where night overtook them in the unbroken wilderness. All of the summer and autumn of 1798 was consumed in running the first eighty miles of the transit meridian, there being about thirteen miles remaining undone on the 22nd of November.

The surveyor in charge of this work was Joseph Ellicott. He was born in Bucks county, Pennsylvania, in 1756. In 1770 the family removed to Maryland and founded Ellicott's Mills on the Patapsco river. Joseph was taught surveying by his brother Andrew, who was afterward surveyor-general of the United States and professor of mathematics at West Point. He assisted the latter in laying out the city of Washington, and in 1791 surveyed the boundary line between the State of Georgia and the Creek Indian lands. The remaining years of his business career were chiefly spent in the service of the Holland Land Company, so called. His intimate connection, in this capacity, with the history of western New York is thus summed up by the historian of the Holland Purchase:

"No man has ever, perhaps, been so closely identified with the history of any region as he is with the history of the Holland Purchase. He was not only the land agent, superintending from the start surveys and settlement, exercising locally a one-man power and influence; but for a long period he was far more than this. In all the early years of settlement, especially in all things having reference to the organization of towns, counties, erection of public buildings, the laying out of roads, the establishment of post-offices—in all that related to the convenience and prosperity of the region over which his agency extended—he occupied a prominent position, a close identity, that few if any patrons of new settlements have ever attained."

CHAPTER VI.

THE HOLLAND PURCHASE AND PURCHASERS—POLICY OF THE HOLLAND LAND COMPANY.

DECEMBER 24th, 1792, Robert Morris deeded to Herman Leroy and John Linklaen one and a half million acres of his lands west of the east transit line. On the 27th of the following February, he gave a deed for a million of acres to these gentlemen and Gerrit Boon. July 20th, 1793, he conveyed to the same three parties eight hundred thousand acres; and on the same day to Herman Leroy, William Bayard and Matthew Clarkson, three hundred thousand acres. These gentlemen purchased this vast tract as trustees for a number of rich merchants of Amsterdam, Holland, who have been commonly spoken of as the Holland Company, and the Holland Land Company; though there was no corporation with either of those titles. The immense estate acquired by them, being all of New York west of the east transit line except the

Indian reservations and the State mile strip along the Niagara, constituted the Holland Purchase.

The purchasers bought through the above-named citizens of New York because they themselves, as foreigners, could not at the time legally hold real property in the State. The Legislature of 1798, however, changed this regulation, and the trustees thereupon turned over the property to the actual owners; all but three hundred thousand acres being transferred to Wilhelm Willink, Nicholas Van Staphorst, Pieter Van Eighen, Hendrick Vallenhoven, and Rutger Jan Schimmelpennick. The remainder went to Wilhelm Willink, Jan Willink, Wilhelm Willink, jr., and Jan Willink, jr. Two years after, Jan Gabriel Van Staphorst, Roelif Van Staphorst, Roelif Van Staphorst, jr., Cornelius Vallenhoven and Hendrick Seye also acquired an interest in the tract.

When the Indian title to the Holland Purchase had been extinguished by Mr. Morris in 1797, measures were immediately taken for the survey of the tract, so that it might be put in market, sold and settled. Operations were directed from Philadelphia by Theophilus Cazenove, who was the first general agent of the Hollanders. He appointed Joseph Ellicott chief surveyor, and in the autumn of 1797 he and Augustus Porter, Mr. Morris's surveyor, as a step toward ascertaining the actual area of the purchase, made a tour of its lake and river front. The running of the east transit line in the next year by Mr. Ellicott, as already related, was another step in the survey of the Holland Purchase; and at the same time eleven other surveyors, each with his corps of axmen, chainmen, etc., went to work at different points running the lines of ranges, townships and reservations. "All through the purchase the deer were startled from their hiding places, and the wolves were driven growling from their lairs, by bands of men with compasses and theodolites, chains and flags; while the red occupants looked sullenly on at the rapid parceling out of their broad and fair domain."

The division of the land began on the plan which had been followed in Phelps and Gorham's Purchase, namely, the laying off of six-mile strips, reaching from Pennsylvania to Lake Ontario, called ranges, and numbered from east to west, and dividing them by east and west lines into regular townships, numbered from south to north. Each township was to be subdivided into sixteen mile-and-a-half squares called sections; and each of these into twelve lots three-fourths of a mile by one-fourth, containing one hundred and twenty acres apiece. After twenty-four townships had been surveyed on this plan, the subdivision was judged unnecessarily minute, and was so much so as to be often ill adapted to the surface of the ground; and thereafter the mile-and-a-half squares composing a township were each divided into four three-quarter-mile squares of three hundred and sixty acres apiece, which were sold off in quantities to suit purchasers; quite commonly going off in one-hundred-and-twenty-acre lots, as originally planned.

The price at first charged for the company's lands was $2.75 per acre, one-tenth to be paid down. The proprietors found it very difficult to obtain this ten per cent, advance payment. It was extremely desirable to secure settlers for the tract, for every pioneer who located made the country more attractive to those who might be contemplating a similar movement. Lands could be had very cheap in parts of the State nearer the centers of population and also in Ohio, while farms in Canada were offered by the British government at sixpence per acre. The competition among owners of large tracts was thus so strong that the proprietors of the Holland Purchase often waived all advance payment by actual settlers, and subsequently reduced the price to an average of $2 per acre. Even so their lands at first went off but slowly. The rate of sales, however, constantly increased. In 1801 there were 40; in 1802, 56; in 1803, 230; in 1804, 300; in 1805, 415; in 1806, 524; in 1807, 607; in 1808, 612; in 1809, 1,160.

No detailed account will be given here of the settlement of this part of the State. The pioneer experiences of the settlers of different towns belong to the annals of those towns; but a few remarks will give such a glimpse of the progress of settlement as may properly be taken at this point. A tourist who visited western New York in 1792 gives the following:

"Many times did I break out in an enthusiastic frenzy, anticipating the probable situation of this wilderness twenty years hence. All that reason can ask may be obtained by the industrious hand; the only danger to be feared is that luxuries will flow too cheap. After I had reached the Genesee river curiosity led me on to Niagara, ninety miles—not one house or white man the whole way. The only direction I had was an Indian path, which sometimes was doubtful. The first day I rode fifty miles through swarms of mosquitoes, gnats, etc., beyond all description. At eight o'clock in the evening I reached an Indian town called Tonnoraunto, it contains many hundreds of savages, who live in very tolerable houses, which they make of timber and cover with bark. By signs I made them understand me, and for a little money they cut me limbs and bushes sufficient to erect a booth, under which I slept very quietly on the grass. The next day I pursued my journey, nine miles of which lay through a very deep swamp. With some difficulty I got through, and about sundown arrived at the fort of Niagara."

An interesting exhibit of the state of business in western New York in 1804 is afforded in "a description of the Genesee country," by Robert Monroe. From it the following is extracted:

"Trade is yet in its infancy, and has much increased within a few years. Grain is sent in considerable quantities from Seneca lake and the Conhocton, Canisteo, Cowanesque and Tioga rivers to markets on Susquehanna river, and flour, potash and other produce to Albany; and a considerable quantity of grain has for some years past been exported by sleighs in winter to the west of Albany. Whiskey is distilled in considerable quantities, and mostly consumed in the country, and is also exported to Canada and to Susquehanna. The produce of the country is received by storekeepers in payment for goods, and, with horses and cattle, is paid for land. Several thousand bushels of grain have been purchased in the winter beginning this year, 1804, for money at Newtown [Elmira], and at the mills near Cayuga lake. Hemp is raised on Genesee river and carried to Albany. Droves of cattle and horses are sent to different markets, and a considerable number of cattle and other provisions are used at the markets of Canadarqua [Canandaigua] and Geneva, at Niagara, and by settlers emigrating into the country. Cattle commonly sell for money at a good price, and as this country is very favorable for raising them they will probably become the principal article for market; many being of opinion that the raising of stock is more profitable as well as easier than any mode of farming. The following is a list of prices of articles and the rate of wages since January, 1801:

"Wheat, from 62 cents to $1 a bushel; corn, from 37 to 50 cents a bushel; rye, from 50 cents to 62 cents a bushel; hay, from $6 to $12 a ton; butter and cheese, from 10 to 16 cents a pound; a yoke of oxen, $50 to $80; milk cows, from $16 to $25; cattle for driving, $3 to $4 a hundred pounds; a pair of good working horses, $100 to $125; sheep, from $2 to $4; pork, fresh killed, in winter, $4 to $6 a hundred, and salted, in spring, $8 to $10; whiskey, from 50 to 75 cents a gallon; salt, $1 a bushel, weighing 56 pounds; field ashes, 4 to 9 cents a bushel;—600 bushels may be manufactured into a ton of pot or pearl ash, which has been sold at market at $125 to $150, and some persons, by saving their ashes or by manufacturing them, have nearly cleared the cost of improving land; the wages of a laborer, $10 to $15 a month and board; a suit of clothes made at $4 to $5; a pair of shoes, $1.75 to $2.50. Store goods are sold at very moderate prices, the expense of carriage from Albany to New York being about $2 a hundred weight."

The Holland Land Company's policy in selling their lands at a high price and giving long credits has often been criticised, both in its bearing on the company's interests and those of the settlers on these lands.

It has been insisted that a lower cash price would have brought to this region a different class of settlers, having money with which to pay for their lands, and that the relations between the company and the settlers would have terminated sooner, and that the difficulties which arose between them would have been averted. It has been held that this policy caused western New York to be settled by a poorer class of emigrants, and that the development of its resources was thus many years retarded; that easy terms of payment tended to encourage laxity and indolence among the settlers, and that more active and energetic pioneers went beyond the Holland Purchase, where lands could be purchased much cheaper for ready cash or shorter credits.

To this it has been replied that though the settlers in western New York were in many cases poor young men, a larger proportion of them possessed that energy and self-reliance which fitted them for successfully grappling with and surmounting the difficulties and obstacles which they encountered in the untamed wilderness where they sought to make their homes, than of those who had been reared in the midst of comforts and luxuries which they did not create, who were not inured to hardships and privations, and whose energies stern necessity had never called forth.

It has also been stated that though the company gave longer credits, thus enabling a poorer class of immigrants to procure homes and lay the foundations of future independence, it is not true that the average price at which the lands were sold was greater than that charged by the government. It is unknown to many that the price of government lands in the States west of New York was at that time $2 per acre. No one could purchase less than a quarter section (160 acres). An immediate payment of $80 was required, and an annual payment of $80 thereafter, and the land was forfeited if the whole were not paid within five years. In the depression which succeeded the war of 1812 the lands of many settlers were forfeited, and though Congress passed acts for the relief of such, many lost their lands.

According to the books of the company the settlers were very dilatory in making their payments, and many without doubt forfeited their claims. Many others, after remaining some time on the lands which they had purchased, sold their "betterments" and went elsewhere. The process of "natural selection" was not in the end detrimental to the country.

It must be remembered that many of the settlers upon the Holland Land Company's land were poor young men, who, from their scanty wages, had saved a sum barely sufficient to purchase teams, defray the expenses of their journey hither, and make small payments on their purchases. They had then to encounter the stern realities of pioneer life. The heavy timber which grew on their lands was to be cut and cleared away, with little help beyond that of their brave and hopeful young wives. When their farms came to produce a small surplus beyond their domestic wants, this found no market except among new settlers.

In an address delivered by him, Hon. Augustus Frank said: "From 1810 to 1820 the population increased very rapidly, particularly after the war with Great Britain had closed. The year war was declared, 1812, was 'a complete damper to all sales of new land,' and it was said that 'more settlers went out than came into the Genesee county.' The call for volunteers was promptly responded to in all this region of western New York. Companies of infantry and cavalry were raised and went forward. Many took active part in the war, and the loss of life by sickness and in battle was large. In 1812 the country about us was comparatively sparsely settled. The male inhabitants were mostly farmers, who had but a little time before 'taken' up their lands. Few had paid for them. They had to leave their families and their farms, not only to vindicate their country's honor, but to defend their own firesides. The war was just along their own borders. It was a severe trial, but the pioneers of this region were made of stern stuff, and battled for their country as they battled but a few years previous to clear the forests, and make homes for themselves and their families. But few of the soldiers of 1812 are left to tell us of their trials during the war of that and the succeeding years. Even those at home, and the families of those in service, had their severe troubles. Many of you have heard of the fright at times occasioned by the rumor of 'the coming of the British and Indians.' After the burning of Buffalo, particularly, this whole section was terrified. Turner says: 'The citizens commenced their flight soon after the repulse of our troops at Black Rock; but few lingered until after daylight. After putting in requisition all the available means of conveyance, even to the last yoke of oxen and sled, many of the women and children were under.the necessity of fleeing on foot, wading in the snow. From the start upon the frontier the first and second day, the throngs were constantly increasing by addition of families along the roads, that would hastily pile a few of their household goods upon sleighs, horse and hand sleds, and join in the flight. Entire backwoods neighborhoods were deserted, hundreds of log cabins were desolate, and the signs and sounds of life were mostly the deserted cattle and sheep, lowing and bleating, famishing for the lack of fodder there were none left to deal out to them.'

"Many of you remember hearing these incidents and some of you, perhaps, remember the facts. The war ended in 1815, and the tide of emigration again set in for the Genesee country, and from that date until 1820 the increase of population was large, coming particularly from the New England States."

On the return of peace a surplus of labor, which the current prices of produce would not remunerate, flooded the land. The heavy duties which had been imposed on imports for the support of the war had stimulated domestic manufactures. On the removal of these imports the country was flooded with foreign goods. Manufacturing industries became stagnant, the country was depleted of specie, and the currency greatly depreciated. Under such circumstances it was not wonderful that the company's clerks were not fatigued by entering credit in the books, or that the early snows of winter showed the tracks of many naked little feet.

The families of these settlers were clad in cloth which the industry of their wives produced; for the wheel and the loom constituted a part of the furniture of nearly every house, and "black salts," extracted from the ashes into which the forests were burned, were almost their only resource for money with which to pay taxes and purchase a few indispensable supplies. The completion of the Erie Canal in 1825 ameliorated to some extent the condition of these settlers, but still the land debts of many weighed heavily on them.

CHAPTER VII.

RELATIONS BETWEEN THE HOLLAND COMPANY AND THE SETTLERS—LAND OFFICE WARS.

IN their dealings with the early settlers the agents of the Holland Land Company often displayed great kindness and generosity. An instance of this was seen in a neighboring county, where an area of a few hundred acres was covered with excellent pine timber. This land they refused, during many years, to sell. Applicants were uniformly told that it was not in market; and when the agents were informed that the settlers were stealing the timber they replied, "They ought not to do that," or "We must see to them." One applicant, on being refused, said to the agent, "If you won't sell me any of this land I shall be compelled to steal timber there." "I hope you will steal no more than you want," replied the agent, laughingly. It was afterwards learned that this land had been withheld from market that settlers might procure from it timber for their buildings, and the only prosecution for trespass on this land which was ever instituted was in the case of a man who attempted to cut and carry away timber for sale.

Another instance of liberality was the donation of land to religious societies. In a note in his History of the Holland Purchase, Mr. Turner says: "In the fall of 1820 Mr. Busti was visiting the land office in Batavia; the Rev. Mr. R. [Rawson, of Barre, Orleans county] of the Presbyterian sect called on Mr. Busti and insisted on a donation of land for each society of his persuasion then formed on the Holland Purchase. Mr. Busti treated the reverend gentleman with due courtesy, but showed no disposition to grant his request. Mr. R., encouraged by Mr. Busti's politeness, persevered in his solicitations day after day, until Mr. Busti's patience was almost exhausted, and what finally brought that subject to a crisis was Mr. R.'s following Mr. Busti out of the land office when he was going to take tea at Mr. Ellicott's, and making a fresh attack on him in the piazza. Mr. Busti was evidently vexed, and in reply said: 'Yes, Mr. R., I will give a tract of one hundred acres to a religious society in every town on the Purchase, and this is *finis.*' 'But,' said Mr. R, 'you will give it all to the Presbyterians, will you not? If you do not expressly so decide the sectarians will be claiming it, and *we* shall receive very little benefit from it.' 'Sectarians, no!' was Mr. Busti's hasty reply. 'I abhor sectarians; they ought not to have any of it; and to save contention I will give it to the first religious society in every town.' Mr. Busti hastened to his tea, and Mr. R. home (about sixteen miles distant) to start runners during the night, or the next morning, to rally the Presbyterians in the several towns in his vicinity to apply first and thereby secure the land to themselves.

"The land office was soon flooded with petitions for land from societies organized according to law, and empowered to hold real estate, and those who were not; one of which was presented to Mr. Busti, before he left, directed to 'General Poll Busti'; on which he insisted it could not be from a religious society, for all religious societies read their Bibles, and know that *p o* double *l* does not spell Paul. Amidst this chaos of applications it was thought not best to be precipitant in granting those donations, the whole responsibility now resting upon Mr. Ellicott to comply with this vague promise of Mr. Busti; therefore conveyances of the 'gospel land' were not executed for some space of time, notwithstanding the clamor of petitioners for deeds of our land; during which time the matter was taken into consideration and systematized, so far as such an operation could be. Pains was taken to ascertain the merits of each application, and finally a tract or tracts of land, not exceeding one hundred acres in all, was granted, free of expense, to one or more religious societies regularly organized according to law in each town on the purchase where the company had land undisposed of, which embraced every town then organized on the purchase, except Bethany, Genesee county, and Sheldon, Wyoming county; the donors always being allowed to select out of the unsold farming land of each town. In some towns it was all given to one society, in others to two or more societies separately, and in a few towns to four different societies of different sects—twenty-five acres to each."

Though at first the policy of the company toward the settlers was very generous and lenient, as time went on the relations between them came to be less cordial. Evidence of the disposition on the part of the company to assist the settlers in making their payments was seen in the offer to receive cattle, and in some instances grain, on their contracts. Credits of this kind appear on the old books in the office at Batavia. To those greatly in arrears the offer was made to deduct a portion of the money due in case of prompt payment. This was looked upon by those who had met their payments as a sort of premium on the slackness of their thriftless neighbors.

Another measure adopted was that of charging, at the end of ten years, where but little had been paid, "increase of purchase money," or a sum added to what was due. This addition was sometimes greater than the original purchase price. As an example of this, one man in this county in 1806 purchased 728 acres, at $2 per acre, $1,456, on which he paid $10. In 1816 he was charged "to increase," $1,648—a total of $3,104. He was not able to pay this, and the land was sold to other parties. Another owed $615, and he was charged "to increase," $642; making $1,257, at which price the land was sold to others. This was regarded by the settlers as a charge for improvements which they had made, and it gave great umbrage.

It has been stated that the members of the Holland Land Company were compelled to make their original purchases through trustees, because of their alien disabilities. Not only were these disabilities removed by an act of the Legislature, but the company was exempted from taxation. The opinion came to prevail that this discrimination in favor of a foreign company was unjust, and that this company, which had grown rich under the protection of the State that had favored them above its own citizens, should contribute something toward the expenses of the government of that State. It was held that the Erie Canal, in the construction of which the company had not aided, had enhanced the value of their property to the amount of some millions; and that the realization of this, and the value of the securities which the company held, were involved in the stability of laws toward the support of which that company contributed nothing. With this feeling prevalent, the Legislature was asked to pass an act repealing this exemption, and such an act was passed in 1833.

Pending the passage of this act the threat was made by one who represented the interest of the company, that if it passed "it might be worse for the settlers." After the act was passed the company, through their agents, served notices on delinquents that they must either pay or "satisfactorily arrange" their indebtedness, or vacate their premises within a specified time (two months). This measure was regarded as a retaliation on the settlers, and it intensified their hostility toward the company. Articles were published in the newspapers, meetings were held, and measures for resistance were discussed. About this time the company sold their interest in portions of the purchase, and the new proprietors announced their policy to be an advance of from one to three dollars per acre on lands the articles for which had expired or should expire with arrearages due on them. The settlers deemed this advance on the prices of their lands unreasonable, and in Chautauqua county their indignation found vent on the 6th of February, 1836, in the demolition of the land office and burning of the books, records, etc., by a mob of about two hundred and fifty men.

The excitement did not terminate with the demolition of the land office at Mayville. Encouraged, probably, by the success of the raid on that office, the malcontents prepared for an assault upon the one at Batavia. Mr. Evans, who held the keys and was apprised of the meditated attack, took the precaution to send all the books and valuable papers to Rochester, beyond the reach of danger. No hostile movement having been made, for several weeks, the books and papers were brought back to Batavia about the 12th of May; however, it was reported that a large mob from the southeast part of Genesee and Erie counties was gathering, determined to march to this place, and to tear down the land office, and the jail, in which two of their friends were confined.

The land office was accordingly stored with arms and ammunition. It was occupied by fifty men when, in the morning of the 14th, the hostile party arrived, some 700 strong, more than half of whom carried firearms. They proceeded to the land office, but were afraid to attack it; and on the arrival of Sheriff Townsend with 120 men, armed with muskets, they dispersed. Their movement, however, and the prevalence of a hostile spirit represented by it, created so much alarm that the Batavia people procured cannon for their defense, and built and garrisoned two block-houses covering the land office. Apprehending another hostile visitation, they induced Governor Marcy to issue a proclamation, by which they were provided with additional artillery and ammunition.

On being informed that Captain Norris, of a military company in Bennington, had said that he with his company and gun—a brass three-pounder—were ready at a moment's notice to turn out and attack Batavia, the governor directed that Captain Norris be ordered to deliver the gun to the keeper of the arsenal at Batavia forthwith. To this order he at first demurred; but fearing the consequence of disobedience, he finally obeyed. These precautionary measures effectually extinguished all hopes on the part of the malcontents of obtaining a redress of their grievances by a resort to lawless violence, and allayed the fears of the people of Batavia.

CHAPTER VIII.

PIONEERS FROM NEW ENGLAND; HOW THEY CAME, SETTLED AND THRIVED.

THE settlement of the region which includes the present county of Wyoming commenced at about the beginning of the present century. Previous to the war of the Revolution the tide of emigration had begun to set westward from the New England States, but during that war it was arrested; for the emissaries of the enemy sought constantly to arouse and foster a spirit of hostility among the natives, and no one would seek a home in a region where "the merciless Indian savage" might at any time bring destruction on feeble settlements, in accordance with his "known rule of warfare." After the close of this war, and the return of the Revolutionary patriots to their homes, the tide again set in this direction, and at the commencement of this century its foremost wave had reached this region.

The hardy, active and ambitious sons and daughters of the New Englanders left their paternal roofs, and sought homes in the untamed wilderness of what was then the west. They were not the effeminate sons and languid daughters of wealthy parents, who had been reared in the lap of luxury. From their infancy they had, by precept and example, been taught the industry and economy which had enabled their fathers to thrive among the rocks and hills of their native country. Some of them started alone, with knapsacks on their backs, rifles on their shoulders, and axes in their hands. Thus accoutred, they bade adieu for a time to the loved ones at home and turned their faces westward, to seek their future homes and fortunes in the wilderness.

For a time they followed the trail of various emigrants, but sooner or later they abandoned this, left the borders of civilization, and struck into the forest. Having selected suitable locations and secured their titles, they commenced their preparations for the future. Shanties for temporary shelter were constructed, clearings were begun, and preparations made for the erection of rude log houses for the shelter of those whom they were to bring with them on their return the next year. While this work was in progress, these solitary laborers procured what supplies they required, beyond the game they killed, from the nearest settlements, several miles away. Their nearest neighbors were those who were making similar preparations at points one or a few miles distant; and with these they occasionally exchanged visits—to talk of home and to discuss their plans for the future, to anticipate the pleasure which they would derive from such visits the next year, when they would be accompanied by the partners who were to share their fortunes and their privations.

At times they "changed works" in order to accomplish some of their various tasks with greater facility, and occasionally they clubbed together and hired from a distant settler a yoke of oxen with which to draw to their building sites the logs which they had cut for their houses, and to "log up" the timber which they desired to burn on their clearings. Thus passed their first summer in the wilderness. By night they lay in their shanties on their beds of hemlock boughs and dreamed of the homes they had left, or of the future homes which their fancies pictured; or, in their waking intervals, listened to the distant howling of the wolf and the nearer hooting of the owl. Day after day they toiled on sustained and cheered by their hopes of future happiness with their chosen companions and children in the midst of the surroundings which they were creating.

By early autumn their rude houses were erected and partially prepared for their reception on their return. Small areas had been burned off, and here they "brushed in" the wheat which they had brought on their backs from some distant settlement. Larger areas had been cut over and made ready for burning and planting next spring. When these preparations were completed they concealed their axes and few other implements, shouldered their rifles, and with light hearts turned their faces again towards their paternal mansions. Thus terminated the first summer with many a pioneer in the wild woods upon the hills of the Holland Purchase.

In due time he arrived among the scenes of his childhood and wended his way to the old home where parents, brothers and sisters welcomed him warmly, and listened with eager attention to the story of his experience in the wilderness. He received a still more hearty welcome from another, who during his long absence had not ceased to think of him by day and dream of him by night. She listened to the recital of his doings with a deeper interest; for to her and him they were matters of equal importance.

A wedding soon occurred, and the last winter of the pair in their native State was a season of busy preparation for removal to their western home, interspersed with social gatherings and merry-makings among the scenes and companions of their childhood. They sat down to their last Thanksgiving dinner with their parents, brothers and sisters; attended their last Christmas and New Year's festivals with their former playmates and school-fellows, and on the approach of spring bade all these scenes and friends a tearful adieu, and departed for their new home, followed by the good wishes of their friends, and the benedictions and prayers of their parents.

Their outfit consisted of a yoke of oxen and a canvas-covered wagon, loaded with a few utensils and necessary articles of household furniture. They brought with them a cow or two and a few sheep, the latter to serve as the nucleus of a flock, which, if spared by the wolves, was to furnish wool for their future clothing. Thus equipped they pursued their toilsome journey till at length the last settlement was reached. There they left their wagon and went forward with their animals, carrying sufficient blankets to make them comfortable for a night. As they went, they cleared a path among the trees, over which the husband soon brought their wagon and stores, and they entered at once upon the realities of pioneer life.

Their house was made tenable by the few preparations which pioneers found necessary for their comfort. A small spot was prepared for the garden seeds which they had brought, their corn-field was burned off and planted in due season, and a larger area prepared for other wheat and corn-fields. In this the labor of the husband was brightened by the presence and encouraging smiles, and sometimes by the assistance, of his young wife. In their solitude they were sustained by their buoyant hopes of the future, and they ever afterward referred to this summer as the happiest period of their lives.

Their wheat-field gave good returns; a few acres which they cleared and planted with corn yielded abundantly, and early in the winter they secured a sufficient supply of venison. Their wheat and corn were ground in a "pioneer mill"—a mortar hollowed in a stump or in the end of a log. A hovel had been constructed of logs and roofed with brush or straw, for the protection of their animals against the inclemency of the weather and the attacks of wild beasts. No hay was provided for the cattle, but from day to day trees were cut off ground that was to be cleared the next summer, and they lived on the browse which these afforded. A couple of pigs and a few fowls were fed each morning at the door of the house with corn from the wife's folded apron. Thus passed their first winter in the woods. The sound of the husband's ax echoed through the forest during the day, and the wife plied "her evening care" in the cheerful glow of the "blazing hearth" at night. Their simple fare and active exercise in the open air gave them robust health, and though their surroundings were quite different from those in the midst of which they had been reared, this was the home which they had made for themselves, and they were happy in the enjoyment of it. During the summer other settlers had come in, some singly, others in companies with their families; and neighbors were more numerous and less distant, and the monotony of their life was varied by occasional exchanges of evening visits among these. This social intercourse among the pioneers had none of the bad features which characterized that of later times. There were among them no conventionalities, no unmeaning expressions of civility, no unkind criticisms of each other's dress or surroundings, no rivalries and jealousies, and no hypocritical manifestations of interest in each other's welfare. Each rejoiced with his neighbor in his prosperity, or sympathized with him in his adversity. These visits were anticipated with pleasure and remembered without regret.

Another summer and winter passed, and changes indicative of increasing prosperity were visible. The clearing had been enlarged, and a portion of it fenced; a stick chimney, plastered with mud, filled the hole in the roof; glass had taken the place of greased paper in the window; a plank door swung on wooden hinges where formerly hung the blanket, and some flowering shrubbery was growing at the side of it. A more capacious and comfortable stable had been erected for the animals, and a "worm" fence appeared around the house and garden; a log bridge had been built across the stream which ran near the house. Near the edge of the clearing the crackling fire was consuming the logs that the men of a logging bee were piling together for that purpose. The corn, potatoes, pumpkins, etc., which had been planted among the stumps, had attained sufficient growth to be visible from some distance. A calf frolicked at the side of its dam, and a litter of grunting young porkers asserted their right to "life, liberty," etc. Everything wore an air of thrift. The solitude of the wife was enlivened by the prattle of her first born. Emigrants had continued to come, and what was a pioneer residence had become part of a frontier settlement.

The tide of immigration—the first wave of which had borne them hither—continued with increasing flow. Settlers came more rapidly, the smoke from their hearths curled upward at shorter intervals, and clearings encroached more and more on the surrounding wilderness. The hissing and rushing of the whirlwinds of flame was oftener heard, as the trees that had been felled and had become dry were consumed. Small fields of waving corn and here and there a verdant meadow were to be seen. The music of numerous cow-bells was heard by day, and "drowsy tinklings lulled the distant folds," where sheep were herded to protect them from the wolves at night. The merry laughter and shouts of children might be heard as they frolicked in the woods. The frontier settlement was fast becoming a rural neighborhood.

Twenty years rolled by and brought with them still greater changes. The old house was only the wing of a new one, that had been built of squared logs, covered with a shingled roof, lighted by glazed windows, and closed by a paneled door. A lawn appeared in front, tastefully ornamented with flowers, and fruit trees were growing on the former site of the garden. An apiary stood at the margin of the lawn, which was bounded by a straight fence; a commodious framed barn had been built, and where the forest once stood were fields of waving grain. Beyond the grove of sugar maples could be seen the log schoolhouse, where

"In her noisy mansion, skill'd to rule,
The comely mistress taught her little school."

The stream that ran by was spanned by a newer bridge, and the ding-donging of a saw-mill that had been built on its bank could be heard in the distance. Their first born—now grown to be a young man—drove toward the barn with a load of hay drawn by horses, instead of the oxen that for years had constituted their only team. At the well, which still had its primitive sweep, stood a somewhat portly matron who turned to look with matronly pride at her son as he drove the team along. A middle aged man was walking down the road that came from the mill. It was he who came twenty-three years since with his knapsack, rifle and ax and built his shanty in the howling wilderness. The woman at the well was the young wife who came with him a year later. Their industry and economy had been rewarded. They had acquired an honorable competence. But their sky had not always been unclouded. They had followed the remains of two of their children to the grave.

Another interval of twenty years has passed. An elegant mansion stands on the site of the old log cabin, and all its surroundings show that it is the abode of wealth and refinement. The stream passes under a stone arch, the old saw-mill has gone to decay, the sugar orchard is no longer to be seen, and only on the distant hills are patches of forest visible. Spacious fields and elegant farm houses are seen on the extended landscape. A train of cars speeds over the plain, and the tall spire of a church points skyward from among the houses of a village near by. A gray haired man is busy with the cattle in the barnyard.

A portly woman sits by the stove knitting, while some of the grandchildren are playing on the floor, and others are engaged in various kinds of work.

These old people are the ones who left their New England homes more than forty years since and came to this spot. They have deeded their farm to their eldest son and taken the usual life lease. Another of their children has been added to the group in the cemetery, one has settled in an adjoining town, and two have gone to seek their fortunes in the West.

CHAPTER IX.

THE CONDITION OF THE PIONEERS—THEIR WAYS AND MEANS OF LIVING.

THREE quarters of a century have passed since the first settlement of this region, and changing circumstances have brought with them such changes in many of the customs of the people, that one of the present generation can form only an imperfect conception of what some of those customs were.

People are usually slow to adopt those modifications in their customs which changes in their environments render desirable, or even almost necessitate. Like the Welshman who persisted in balancing the wheat in one end of his bag by a stone in the other because his father did so, they follow the beaten track which their ancestors pursued, and often only turn from it when changed circumstances actually compel them to do so.

The march of improvement and the progress of invention make slow advances, except in those cases where necessity compels people to follow the one, or loudly calls for the other.

The rude implements and appliances that were in use "when the country was new" were inventions which grew out of the necessities of the times, and were adapted to the circumstances in which people found themselves. Time wore on, and those circumstances gave place to others. Inventions followed these changes; but in many cases, as in those of the cast iron plough, the grain-cradle and the horse-rake, the inventors only lived to see their improved implements scoffed at and derided. Thus have people always done, and thus they will to a greater or less extent continue to do. As in the physical world, however, one condition is evolved from another by the slow process of natural selection, so in these cases the fittest are in the end the survivors.

The first settlers in this region came when the primitive forest was growing, not only here but in the country through which they had passed for many miles. The first roads, which were simply widened Indian trails, were then barely passable. Of course they could bring with them only those articles of household furniture or those agricultural implements that were indispensable.

The first work of the pioneer was to prepare a house, or dwelling-place for his family. There were no mills for the manufacture of lumber, and the first houses were necessarily built of logs fastened by notching at the corners. They were usually from fifteen to eighteen feet-square, and about seven feet in height, or high enough to just clear the head of a tall man. Often no floor was at first laid. A fire-place was prepared at one end by erecting a back of stones, laid in mud instead of mortar, and a hole was left in the bark or slab roof for the escape of the smoke. A chimney of sticks plastered with mud was afterward erected in this aperture. A space of a width suitable for a door was cut out on one side, and this was closed first by hanging in it a blanket, and afterward by a door made with split plank and hung on wooden hinges. This door was fastened by a wooden latch, which could be raised from the outside by a string, which passed through a hole above it. When the latch string was "pulled in" the door was effectually fastened. The expression used of a hospitable man—"his latch-string is always out"—had its origin from this primitive method of fastening a log house door. A hole was usually cut in each side of this house to let in light, and when glazed sash could not be procured greased paper was used to keep out the blasts and snows of autumn and winter.

Holes were bored at the proper height in the logs at one corner of the room, and into these the ends of poles were fitted, the opposite ends, where they crossed, being supported by a crotch, or a block of the proper height. Across these poles others was laid, and these were covered by a thick matress of hemlock boughs, over which blankets were spread. Thus were "Genesee bedsteads" constructed; and on such a bed many a pioneer couple reposed as sweetly as though "sunk in beds of down." In the absence of chairs, rude seats were made with an ax and auger by boring holes and inserting legs in "puncheons," or planks split from basswood logs and hewn smooth on one side. Tables were often made in the same way, and after a time a floor was constructed of these "puncheons," with a bare space in lieu of a hearth about the fire place. A few necessary pieces of crockery, or sometimes wooden trenchers, were kept on rude shelves, till, after a few years, lumber could be procured of which to make a cupboard.

A dinner pot, a dish kettle, a tea kettle, a frying pan, and a bake kettle constituted the entire stock of iron ware. The bake kettle—a utensil that is now never seen—was a shallow vessel with legs some six inches in length, so that it could be set over coals on the hearth. It had a cover with edges turned up so that coals could be heaped on it. This was used at first for all the baking of many a pioneer family. The fire-place had, instead of the iron crane with which it was afterwards furnished, a transverse pole called a lug pole, laid across two others so that it could be moved backward and forward at a sufficient height to prevent burning. On this, "trammels," or hooks so constructed that their length could be adjusted, where hung.

This room, thus furnished, served all the purposes of kitchen, drawing room, sitting room, parlor, and bed room; and not unfrequently workshop also, for temporary benches were erected, and sleds, ox yokes, and many other farming utensils were made and repaired there during stormy days or evenings. The light for such evening work was furnished by the blazing fire, or sometimes by a "slut," which was made by placing a rag for a wick in a dish of "coon's oil," or the fat of some other wild animal.

Here also, as time went on, were heard the raking of the hand cards and the wirr of the spinning wheel; for in those days the cloth for both the summer and winter clothing of the family was homemade, and all the technicalities of the process, from picking the wool to "taking out the piece," were as familiar to every member of the family as any household word.

At first, before the establishment of cloth dressing mills, the dyeing or coloring, even of all the woolen cloth, was done by the pioneer wives; and after clotheries made their appearance, everything except "fulled cloth" was colored at home. The properties and the proper method of compounding for different colors, of Nicaragua or Nic. wood, log wood, fustic, indigo, madder, copperas, alum, vitriol, etc., as well as all the various indigenous barks and plants, were known to every housewife. The old dye tub, which is still remembered by the older inhabitants, had its place at the side of every hearth, where it was frequently used as a seat for children in cases of emergency, or when the increase of the family was more rapid than that of chairs. Peter Parley (Mr. Goodrich) calls it "the institution of the dye tub, which, when the night had waned and the family had retired, frequently became the anxious seat of the lover, who was permitted to carry on his courtship, the object of his addresses sitting demurely in the opposite corner."

The flax brake, swingling knife and board, and hatchel are never seen now; and one of the present generation would be utterly unable to guess their uses were they shown to him. Then the pulling and rotting and all the details of dressing flax were known to every child; and the process of spinning the flax and tow, weaving and bleaching the different qualities of cloth, and making the thread for all the family sewing, was a part of the education of every girl. Then cotton cloth was only to a slight extent manufactured in this country, and it was practically beyond the reach of most farmers. Woolen goods, other than those of domestic manufacture, were seldom seen. A "broadcloth coat" was an evidence either of unpardonable vanity or of unusual prosperity.

It is hardly necessary to speak of the ordinary food of the first settlers, such as hasty pudding, Johnny cakes, or corn pones, the meal for which was ground in a pioneer mill or wooden mortar; or of the dainties, such as shortcakes, mixed with the lye of cob ashes and baked in ashes on the hearth, that were set before company. The simple and substantial diet of the people then was adopted because circumstances would permit no other. They were too poor to pamper their children with sweetmeats, or to stimulate them with tea and coffee; and the incidental result was a degree of robust health such as the children in later times do not acquire.

It must not be inferred that all the settlers in this region were subjected to severe privations. The kind of fare spoken of was not looked upon as hard, for it was the best the country then afforded. There were instances where people were compelled to go into the woods and gather leeks for a dinner; but these were perhaps as rare as are cases of extreme destitution now. The condition of the country was such that these habits and methods of living were necessary, and they were not regarded as hardships.

The agriculture of those times, if agriculture it may be termed, was such as is never seen now. Very few at the present day have witnessed the process of preparing the virgin soil for the first crop. The timber was often girdled in advance, so that when felled, as it often was, in what were termed wind rows, much of it would burn as it lay, being partially or wholly dried, by kindling the fire at the windward end of these rows. After the first burn some of the remaining fragments were "niggered" into pieces that could be easily moved, and the whole was drawn together with oxen and "logged up" for the final burning. Many in the neighborhood usually joined in this work, and the "logging bees" were at the same time occasions when work was done and social intercourse enjoyed. When the burning was completed and the ashes collected the ground was sometimes made ready for the seed by harrowing with a three cornered harrow, which was often hewed from a crotched tree, with either large wooden pins set at intervals, or very large and strong iron teeth. Such a harrow was drawn over the ground among the stumps to fit the soil for its first crop when the roots were not sufficiently decayed to permit the use of a plow. In using this primitive harrow in these clearings the driver found it necessary to keep always at a respectful distance, for it often bounded from side to side in a manner not compatible with safety at close quarters. In cases where plowing could be done the old bull plow was used. This was an uncouth implement, with wrought iron share and a wooden moldboard, such as is now scarcely ever seen even among relics of the past. In rare cases a wooden plow, hewn out of a crotched tree, was used.

The wheat sown or corn planted in ground prepared in this rude way often gave good returns, such was the fertility of the soil before it was exhausted by repeated cropping. When the crop was grown and ripened, it was cut with sickles, a handful at a time. Sickles may occasionally be seen at the present day; but there are few who ever saw them used. For harvesting grain among the stumps of the first clearings the sickle was best adapted of all instruments, and no other was known; but when these stumps had decayed, and the grain cradle had been introduced, many looked on it as a pernicious invention, by the use of which more than sufficient grain would be wasted to pay for the labor of harvesting, and some insisted that more could be harvested in the same time with the sickle—so strongly are people attached to old customs.

The grain was first threshed with the flail on the ground, and partially separated from the chaff by pouring it from a height in the wind and afterwards dextrously manipulating it in a "corn fan," a description of which would be quite difficult. For many years after barns were erected on all farms the flail and the feet of horses were the only threshing machines, but fanning-mills superseded the old corn fan.

Hay was cut with the old fashioned scythe, which has changed but very little, and the hand rake only was used to gather it. Among the stumps and stones in early times these were the most available tools, but their use continued long after improved implements were available, and after such implements had been invented.

In those days the conveyance most in use was the ox-cart. It was made available for almost everything, from hauling manure to going to meeting, or to balls and weddings. Its use was thus universal because it was, like the other tools spoken of, adapted to existing conditions. The rough and stumpy roads almost forbade the use of four-wheeled conveyances.

It seems hardly necessary to call attention to the wagons, ploughs, harrows, threshing-machines, harvesters, mowers, wheel-rakes, etc., etc., of the present day, and contrast them with the awkward and uncouth implements of former times; but if this is done the adaptation of these to their existing circumstances should be remembered, and the additional fact should be borne in mind that the improved tools of the present day would not then have been available.

During some years after the first settlement of this region trade was carried on in a manner quite different from the way in which it is now conducted. Now all produce has a cash market and a cash value; and all the necessaries or superfluities that are purchased are reckoned according to the same standard. Then there was not sufficient money in the country to be made the medium of exchange, and trade was carried on almost wholly by what was termed barter. About the only article that sold for cash was the crude potash, or black salts, manufactured from the ashes into which the forests were burned. By reason of this nearly exclusive exchange trade, mercantile establishments were quite unlike those of the present time. Then, every store was a sort of commercial microcosm. In it was kept everything that the inhabitants required. As one who lived in those times says: "Every merchant kept dry goods, groceries, crockery, glassware, hardware, dye stuffs, iron, nails, paints, oil, window-glass, school books, stationery, rum, brandy, gin, whiskey, drugs and medicines, ending with a string of etceteras, or every other article usually kept in a country store. Things were sometimes curiously grouped; as, for example, silks and iron, laces and fish, pins and crowbars, pork and tea, molasses and tar, cotton yam and log chains, wheel heads and hoes, cards and pitchforks, scythes and fur hats." In exchange for these, the pioneer merchant received almost every article of country produce. Coarse grain was converted into spirits at his distillery, or that of some one in the vicinity, for distilleries sprung up early. Pork was "packed," feathers, butter, cheese, etc., etc., were received in exchange for goods and sent, at first by teams, sometimes over bad roads, to Albany, where they were exchanged for the goods which these teams brought back; and so the barter trade was kept up. This expensive method of transportation necessarily rendered the price of goods high, and that of produce low; and this condition of things continued up to the time of the completion of the Erie Canal, which, by affording better facilities for transportation, cheapened merchandise and enhanced the price of produce.

Gradually, since that time, has trade changed till it has reached a cash basis, and along with this change has come another important one—the "division of business." Now dry goods, groceries, hardware, books, drugs, liquors, etc., etc., are separate branches of business; and produce dealing is separated from all of them.

A no less marked contrast is to be seen in the manufactures of those times and the present. Then almost every article and utensil that was used was either "homemade," or manufactured at the shops which sprung up to supply the wants of the early settlers. Then, as has been stated, the cloth in which every one was clad was of domestic manufacture. The spinning wheel and the loom were portions of the furniture of almost every house, and clothieries, or wool carding and cloth dressing establishments, were as common as grist-mills. Almost every hamlet had its tailor's shop, where the knight of the shears cut the clothing for the people of the vicinity, and, to avoid the responsibility of misfits, warranted "to fit if properly made up." This clothing was made up by tailoresses, or, as the tailors sometimes termed them, "she tailors." The trade of a tailoress was reckoned a very good one; for she received for her skilled labor two shillings (as currency was then talked) per day; while the price of housework help was six shillings per week.

Shoemakers' shops were abundant also, though there were itinerant shoemakers who "whipped the cat," as going from house to house with their "kits" was termed. After the establishment of tanneries, the people were in the habit of having the hides of their slaughtered animals tanned on shares, and the leather thus obtained was worked up by these circulating disciples of St. Crispin.

The ubiquitous tailor shop has entirely disappeared, and only here and there is to be seen a solitary cobbler's sign. Every village has its shoe stores, and the descendants of Abraham vie with each other in supplying the gentiles with clothing "ferry sheap."

Very early it was a portion of the business of every blacksmith to make the nails that were required where wooden pins could not be used. Now an old fashioned wrought nail is a curious relic of the past; and even the rivets, bolts, and horse shoe nails that were formerly made upon every anvil are now made by machinery, and furnished more cheaply than they can be hammered out by the vulcans or their apprentices.

So of almost everything. Where joiners formerly took lumber "in the rough" and did all the work of building a house, now houses are almost, like Byron's critics, "ready made"; for little is required but to put together the parts that are made by machinery.

The wheelbarrows, carts and wagons, and even the cradles and coffins, that were formerly made in the shops that sprang up when the country was first settled are now made by machinery, and sold at rates far lower than those at which handmade work can be afforded; and the old hand manufactories have gone to decay or degenerated into simple repair shops.

The question has often arisen whether the invention of labor saving machinery, which has led to this centralization and cheapening of manufactures, has been beneficial or otherwise to the country. It is claimed by many that these inventions are detrimental to the best interests of the country, because, though they cheapen manufactured articles to consumers, they throw out of employment and reduce to poverty large numbers of skilled artisans.

To this it is answered that the utilization of natural forces always adds to the wealth of a country; and that those who are thus deprived of employment are in the end benefited, because they are driven into more profitable avenues of industry, raised above their former condition, and made partakers of the increased general prosperity.

In early times, wild animals, especially bears and wolves, were great sources of annoyance. It is not known that any person ever became a victim to the rapacity of these animals, but many cases are recorded of terrible frights. Many swine that were permitted to roam and feed in the woods were destroyed by bears, and great care was necessary to protect sheep against the wolves. For years the slumbers of people were interrupted and night was made hideous by the howling of the latter.

The record of the proceedings of the first board of supervisors of Genesee county, of which Wyoming then (1805) constituted a part, contains the following:

"The board, after considering the necessity and utility of destroying wolves, passed a vote to allow a bounty of five dollars apiece for the scalp and ears of each wolf taken and killed in the county aforesaid since its organization."

The board of 1804 "resolved that certificates given to Indians for wolf scalps shall be certified in the presence of a white person of suitable age, who shall attest the same."

The price paid for the scalps of wolves in different years ranged from $5 to $45 per head for grown ones, and from $2 to $20 for whelps. Between 1803 and 1821, when the payment of bounties was discontinued, an aggregate of $6,782 was paid for 793 wolves and 8 panthers. It was thought that the large bounties offered here induced people to capture wolves elsewhere, bring them into this county and kill them, and obtain the price of their scalps; and this may have led to a discontinuance of the bounties.

Subsequent to 1821 these animals were occasionally seen, and slight depredations were sometimes committed by them; but they have long since ceased to visit this region.

CHAPTER X.

EARLY SCHOOLS—THE ORIGIN OF TEACHERS' INSTITUTES—CHARACTER OF THE PIONEERS.

IT must not be supposed that while the pioneers who settled the hills and valleys of "the Genesee country" were busy reclaiming the wilderness, and surrounding themselves with domestic comforts, they forgot to plant the seeds of those institutions in the midst of which they had been reared, and which by New Englanders and their descendants are considered of paramount importance. As soon as a sufficient number of children could be gathered the school-house made its first appearance, rude at first like the primitive houses of the settlers, but adapted to the circumstances of the people in those times.

Pioneer school-houses, like pioneer dwellings, were usually log structures, and were warmed in winter from fire-places similar to those in these dwellings. The desks were slanting shelves of slabs or boards, supported by long pins driven into auger holes in the logs, with the ends sustained by braces from the logs below. In front of these were benches made of split and hewed slabs, or, where there were saw-mills in the vicinity, of sawed slabs. These were for the "big scholars." A row of similar benches stood in front of these, on which the smaller ones sat.

The course of instruction was limited to reading, spelling, writing, arithmetic, and sometimes geography and grammar. The text books then in use were quite different from those of the present time. Among the primary books in use were the United States Speller, the first reading-lesson in which was:

"My son, do no ill,
Go not in the way of bad men,
For bad men go to the pit;
O, my son! run not in the way of sin."

followed by "Fear God and honor the king"; and Webster's Spelling-book, in which the first exercise was:.

"No man may put off the law of God;
My joy is in his law all the day."

At the same time that they taught the children reading they inculcated morality, and even loyalty. The whole science of orthography was taught in three or four pages of the "fore part of the spelling book." Morse's, and afterward Woodbridge's, Geography (if any), telling very briefly what was known of the earth, were used; and Dilworth's, Pike's and Daboll's Arithmetics, with their condensed rules and no demonstrations, and in which if the "single rule of three" was reached in one term it was considered remarkable progress. The Columbian Orator, American Preceptor and English Reader were the reading books in use, and Lindley Murray's Grammar was studied by some. The practice with this last was to first commit to memory the "coarse print," then "go through" and learn the "fine print," and when these tasks were accomplished the pupil knew, if possible, less of grammar than when he commenced. These books were well adapted to the capacities of those who had mastered the branches of which they treated, but not to those of beginners. The curriculum of study in those days was, with many, limited to reading, writing and cyphering.

Schools were not conducted then as at present. The Puritans and their descendants were reared with full faith in the maxim "Spare the rod and you spoil the child." Their teachers were usually anxious that pupils should not spoil on their hands, and many old men retain a vivid recollection of what school discipline was in their boyhood.

An account of the exercises during a half-day of school in those days would be amusing, though it is a question whether, in some respects, modern customs are great improvements.

Many can remember that when word was passed around "Master's comin'!" a general scramble for seats took place, so that every one was found in his place and order prevailed when the august dispenser of wisdom entered; and if, for any reason, he remained at the house during the intermission at noon it was necessary that he should walk a short distance away and then retrace his steps, in order that he might be "comin'." On entering he took off his hat and bowed to the scholars, a compliment which they arose and returned. He then walked majestically across the room, hung his hat on its accustomed peg, turned around and announced "School's begun!" Then, taking up his book, he called, "First class in the English Reader! arise! attention!" At the word, which was often contracted to "rise," the boys of the class on one side of the room, and the girls on the other, arose as one; and when "'tention" or "'beesance" (obeisance) was called, the boys bowed and the girls "curchied." If these motions were not properly made a short drill ensued. When they had been executed with sufficient precision the reading was proceeded with. The members of the class arose in their places, one by one, and each read his or her verse, prompted or corrected by the master, who, as occasion required, called to inattentive ones, "Look over!" and to the one reading, "Read louder!" or, "Mind the pauses!" or occasionally to the school, "Less noise!" When the class had "read round," at the word "Class dissmissed" they laid aside their books, faced about, and such as chose to do so drew their writing books from under the desk and engaged for a time in a writing exercise; though there was no stated time for this. Writing was then done with quill pens on coarse, unruled paper. Beginners were permitted to rule their paper, which they did with leaden "plummels" and wooden "rulers"; but after a time they were to acquire the art of writing "straight," without ruling. The master wrote or "set" all the copies; and it is a notable fact that when printed copies and ruled paper were first introduced they were looked upon with the utmost contempt. At first only "coarse hand" was permitted, which, as the learner became more proficient, was gradually brought down to "fine hand"; then ruling was dispensed with. Strange as it may appear to those who are instructed according to modern system, a majority of pupils in those days acquired a very good chirography. Next in order, the second class was called. The teacher was usually able to hear this class and at the same time respond to the frequent calls to "mend my pen." Then followed the other classes in order, ending with the children that were called one at a time to the side of the teacher and asked: "What's that?" "A-uh!" "What's that?" "B-uh!" etc. Then followed "Boys mer gwout!" and after they were recalled by vigorous rapping on the window the girls were given a similar recess. Next came the recitations in geography and grammar—if any—one at a time, for there were then no classes except in reading and spelling, and blackboards were unknown. Next came (in the afternoon) parsing, if there were any advanced grammar scholars. Then followed the spelling classes, beginning with the lowest and concluding with the first class. Stated times were set apart for studying the spelling lessons, and the practice of "going up" was adopted by all; and those who were "at the head" the greatest number of times were rewarded with prizes. During all this time the teacher was frequently called to respond to the questions: "M'I speak?" "M'I gwout?" "M'I git some drink?" "Show me how ter do this sum?" "M'I go t' the fire?" "Where does the Missippy rise?" etc.,

etc. Of course the exercises were varied as emergencies arose by practical illustrations of moral suasion—as then practiced—with the ferule and rod. When the scholars filed out of the house at night, after those who were designated to "hand round the things" had discharged that duty, each was required to turn around at the door, make a bow or "curchy," and say, "Good afternoon, sir," which was soon shortened to "'Dart noon sir." Then children were required in going to and returning from school to raise their hats and bow to older persons when they met them. If such a custom were prevalent now the manners of people would not be the worse for it.

It must be admitted that, notwithstanding the miserable text-books then in use, and the—in many respects—awkward methods of teaching which prevailed the schools of that period furnished some excellent scholars; perhaps almost as large a proportion as those of the present time. The early establishment of an efficient common school system in this State was due in a great measure to the eager demand for such a system by New England immigrants.

In 1858 an act was passed by the Legislature dividing the county of Wyoming, which is a single Assembly district, into two districts for the election of school commissioners. The towns of Sheldon, Bennington, Orangeville, Attica, Warsaw, Middlebury, Covington and Perry constitute number 1 of these districts; and the towns of Arcade, Genesee Falls, Java, Eagle, Wethersfield, Pike, Gainesville and Castile, number 2.

It is hardly necessary to call attention to the measures which have been adopted to give greater efficiency to the common schools of the State. In every instance Wyoming county has been among the first to make available the facilities which have been thus provided. In 1835 was passed the first act making provision for school district libraries. About the year 1843, for the purpose of elevating the standard of qualification among teachers, two sagacious men conceived the plan of holding teachers' institutes. These men were the late judges A. S. Stevens, of Attica, and Jacob S. Denman, of Ithaca, Tompkins county, each of whom was in his own county the first county superintendent appointed under the law of 1842. It is a singular fact that each of these men conceived the plan of holding an institute in his own county, and held such institute the same month, without any knowledge of the doings of the other.

From some reports and other documents furnished by E. F. Chaffee it is learned that in the discharge of the duties of his office Judge Stevens, to use his own words, saw "that there was no uniformity of system in the mode or manner of teaching and governing in our schools; that each and all teachers had their own peculiar notions, while but few seemed to have confidence in their own method. In fact, the whole method was without a head. I found many young and not experienced teachers, in small and sparsely settled districts, laboring hard to do something, but having no well digested system of their own, and none borrowed and well arranged, but getting along with detached ideas and forms, often varying them to suit the notions and whims of parents."

To establish the desired uniformity, and to make available for each teacher the best ideas of all the others, he decided to call together the teachers of the county, and to invite the friends of education to meet with and aid them. Accordingly he "issued a circular calling on the teachers to meet and hold an institute at the pleasant little village of Wethersfield Springs, in the center of Wyoming county, in October, 1843." This call was issued "with the concurrence of the following town superintendents": E. Bishop, Attica; N. Tolles, Bennington; A. W. Conklin, Castile; John Smith, China; J. Durfee, Covington; R. Whitney, Gainseville; L. C. Ward, Java; —— ——, Middlebury; P. Merril, Orangeville; C. A. Huntington, Perry; M. A. Hinman, Sheldon; A. Holley, Warsaw; B. Bancroft, Wethersfield.

Seventy-five teachers responded to this call, and so successful was this first experiment that at this session Judge Stevens was appointed a committee to memorialize the Legislature, through Colonel S. Young, the able State superintendent, for future aid in holding similar institutes. In reply to a communication giving an account of this experiment and its results, Colonel Young wrote to Judge Stevens as follows:

"State Superintendent's Office, Albany,
October 26th, 1843.

" * * * I heartily congratulate you and the friends of common school education in your county on the cheering results which have been accomplished and are in the process of accomplishment under your auspices. The continuation of such exertions in such a spirit is all that is needed to make our common schools indeed the nurseries of virtue and the temples of sound knowledge. I trust no obstacles will be permitted to deter or discourage you from the completion of the noble undertaking you have begun. You must rely for your reward, not so much upon the temporary and fleeting popularity of the hour, as upon the approval of your own conscience and the ultimate justice which, in the long run, is sure to be awarded to faithful public servants.

"Yours truly,
S. Young.

"A. S. Stevens, Esq.,
"Supt. of Common Schools, Wyoming County, Attica."

The aid asked was at once granted by the Legislature. From this beginning teachers' institutes have come to be established in most of the States in the Union. Wyoming county, which had the honor of holding the first, has never failed to hold her annual institute since.

A prominent feature in the character of the New England pioneers in this county was the readiness with which they transplanted the religious faith of their fathers in their new home. Religious societies were early established in the new settlements, and these often became the nuclei of prosperous churches. At first meetings were held in private houses and school-houses, but as soon as these societies acquired sufficient strength houses of worship were erected, some of which remain with little change, beyond ordinary repairs, to the present day.

Of pioneer preachers, Rev. Dr Nassau, in an address delivered before the Wyoming County Pioneer Association in 1879, said:

"I hesitate to mention any of these leaders lest I omit some as prominent and worthy as those named. But such ministers as the first bishops and clergy of the Methodist church did a grand work for their generation. There were Bishops Asbury and McKendree, Messrs. Fillmore, Grant, White, Bangs, Laning, Cummins, Paddock, Pearce and a host of kindred spirits. Among the able and successful evangelists and pastors of the Presbyterian and Congregational faith were such worthies as the indefatigable veteran 'Father Spencer,' Zadoc Hunn, John Lindsley, Messrs. Axtell, Higgins, Robbins, Eells, Chapman, Stone, the Hubbards, the Parmelees, the Cottons, Williston, Bushnell, Fulton, Ayer, Harrower, Denoon, Bull, Perrine, Fitch, Richards and Hotchkins. And these were representative of many others. The Baptists, Reformed Dutch, Episcopalians, Friends and other denominations were well and faithfully represented on this ground. Praiseworthy efforts to send the gospel to the destitute were made by several local societies.

"The lives of such Christian leaders were a happy commentary upon their preaching, devoted, enthusiastic and successful. Then, as now, the minister was expected to take part in affairs of local importance, and in times of peril was often looked to as a champion. It has been said, with truth, 'that the office of Christian ministers was no sinecure upon the Holland Purchase in early years. They encountered the roughest features of pioneer life.'"

It is a notable fact that when the descendants of the Puritans brought hither their religious faith they left behind much of the intolerance and bigotry which had disgraced the Puritan character. When, however, it is remembered that most of these were of the younger classes, the fact is no matter of surprise, for they are always the progressive ones.

It is sometimes thought by those who have been reared in what are termed old countries, in the midst of the comforts and luxuries which the industry of several generations has accumulated, with the best of educational facilities, surrounded by refined society, and feeling, in the language of Burns, "not a want but what themselves create," that their more active brothers who have turned their backs to the land of their nativity, and sought homes and fortunes in the untamed wilderness, have become in a measure outcasts from refined society; that their manners have necessarily become uncouth, and their tastes coarse; and that were they to return they would be hardly fit associates for those who have remained among the refinements of what they term civilized life. They think, too, that the active, toilsome life which these pioneers lead, and the privations and hardships to which they subject themselves, are not compatible with the development of that intelligence of which they fancy themselves the sole conservators. They sometimes heave a sigh of pity over the hard fate of these their loved friends, and if, in after years, they visit these companions and playmates of their youth in their distant homes, they do so with the expectation of being put to shame by their roughness and ignorance.

They are surprised to find that though these people are not surrounded by all the luxuries which they enjoyed at home, that though indeed they have limited their wants to very few of these, they are not the rough, uncouth beings they pictured to themselves. They find them in houses that are certainly not built with a view to display architectural taste, for they are formed of logs, with stone fireplaces and stick chimneys; but they shelter the inmates from the rains of summer and autumn, and keep out the chilling blasts of winter. They are not fashionably furnished; for in this respect comfort and convenience, instead of style, have been aimed at. The pioneers' fare is simple, but wholesome. No dainties are set before them to tempt the pampered appetites of slothful, enervated drones, but plain, substantial food, sweetened by the zest and relish which health and industry impart.

The visitors see, perhaps, that in intelligence these more active ones have quite outstripped them, and that they themselves are the objects of pity, because they were not endowed with the energy that might have enabled them to accomplish what these pioneers have done.

They see, too, here and there houses of worship, not with spires pointing skyward, carpeted aisles, cushioned seats, elaborately carved desks and gilded organs, but plain edifices, adapted to the circumstances and wants of the people who meet there for religious instruction and worship, and not to gratify their vanity by a display of stylish finery, or to criticise the display of others. They see all these things, and they awake to the consciousness that, notwithstanding the toils, hardships and privations that these pioneers have endured, they are contented and happy.

They look upon the children that are growing up in this new country, and they see that they have inherited the sterling qualities of their parents; and that not till several generations of their descendants have grown up in luxurious ease will they become degenerated to the level of those who were left behind by the courageous and ambitious ones who struck out into the forest, and instead of avoiding the obstacles which lay in their way battled against them manfully and overcame them.

They look back and remember that their forefathers left their homes, braved the perils of the sea and peopled the rocky hills of New England with a race of which these pioneers are the representatives; and they reluctantly arrive at the conclusion that they are themselves the degenerate offshoots from this stock.

CHAPTER XI.

ORGANIZATION AND SUBDIVISION OF WYOMING COUNTY— CONSTRUCTION OF COUNTY BUILDINGS.

BETWEEN 1772 and 1784 all but the eastern portion of New York was called Tryon county, after the governor of the province, having previously been part of Albany, which was one of the ten original counties formed November 1st, 1683. In 1784 the same territory took the name of Montgomery, in honor of a Revolutionary hero and martyr. In 1789 all the State west of the preemption line, which was a meridian drawn through Seneca lake and extending northward to Lake Ontario and southward to the Pensylvania line, was set off under the title of Ontario county. A single town, called Northampton, swallowed up the entire Holland Purchase.

March 30th, 1802, the county of Genesee was formed from Ontario, and included all that portion of the State west of the Genesee river and a line extending due south from the point where Canaseraga creek and that river unite, to the line between New York and Pennsylvania. The town of Northampton was divided into four; of which Batavia comprised all of the State west from the west transit line—the entire Holland Purchase. The first town meeting in Batavia was held in what is now the town of Clarence, Erie county, about one hundred miles from the farthest extremity of the town.

April 11th, 1804, Batavia was divided into four towns. The one farthest east retained the old name and all the territory east of a meridian from Lake Ontario, which passed just east from the line between Orleans and Niagara counties. The next was Willink, which extended to the west transit line. The next was Erie, which included one tier of townships in the present county of Chautauqua, and the next Chautauqua, which embraced the rest of old Batavia.

Genesee county was first divided in 1806 by the formation from it of Allegany. In 1808 Cattaraugus, Niagara, and Chautauqua were erected, Niagara including the present county of Erie. When Livingston and Monroe were organized, in 1821, the portions of those counties lying west from the Genesee river were taken from Genesee county. In 1824 the county of Orleans was formed, in part from Genesee.

During seventeen years previous to the erection of the county of Wyoming, Genesee county had the form of a parallelogram, thirty-six miles in length from north to south, with a breadth of twenty-six miles from east to west. Batavia, the county seat, was located only nine miles, or one-fourth the length of the county, from its northern boundary.

Previous to the erection of Orleans county from Genesee the project of forming a new county from the southern part of Genesee and the northern towns of Allegany was talked of, and application was made to the Legislature for the formation of such a county. The subject was not seriously agitated again till 1840, when the Legislature enacted a law authorizing the erection of a new court-house and jail in Genesee county, and appointing commissioners to determine the location of these buildings. The decision of these commissioners in favor of Batavia was not satisfactory to the people in the southern part of the county, and at a meeting held for the purpose resolutions were adopted expressive of their disapprobation, and in favor of a more central location of the county seat, or a division of the county.

In 1841 a bill was introduced in the Legislature to divide the county; or, rather, to submit the question of a removal of the county seat to a vote of the people, and to divide the county if it was decided negatively. Rather than risk an affirmative decision by the people, the Batavians instructed their representative to favor a division of the county. On his motion the provision for submission was stricken out; and on the 19th of April, 1841, the bill passed, with only a few negative votes, and became a law. It provided that "all that part of the county of Genesee lying and being on the south side of a line beginning at the northwest corner of the town of Bennington, in the county aforesaid, and running thence east on the north line of the towns of Bennington, Attica and Middlebury, to the west line of the town of Covington; thence south, on the east line of Middlebury, to the southwest corner of the Cragie tract; thence east on the south line of said Cragie tract, and on the south bounds of the Forty-thousand-acre tract, to the east line of said town of Covington—shall be a separate and distinct county of the State of New York, and be known by the name of Wyoming, and entitled to and possessed of all the benefits, rights, privileges, and immunities, and subject to the same duties as the other counties of this State."

The act also provided that the part of the town of Covington lying north from the line that thus ran through it should continue to be a town in Genesee county, and known by the name of Pavilion; and that part south from this line should remain a separate town in the new county, and should retain its name of Covington. It was also provided that such of the officers of the old town as resided in that portion which retained the name of Covington should continue to exercise the duties of their respective offices in this town, and that a town election should be held on the first Tuesday of the next June for the election of such officers as did not reside in said town.

By an act passed April 1st, 1846, "the towns of Eagle, Pike and all that part of the town of Portage in the county of Allegany, lying on the west side of the Genesee river, bounded as follows—on the east by the Genesee river, on the south by a line running due easterly from the south line of the town of Pike until it intersects the Genesee river, and west and north by the original lines of the said town [of Pike]—from and after the passage of this act shall be and the same are hereby annexed to the county of Wyoming." No other change in the boundaries of the county has been made.

When the name of the post-office at Middlebury village was changed, the late Judge Skinner, who was an admirer of Indian names, proposed several, and among them "Osceola" and "Wyoming." The latter was adopted, and afterwards, in 1841, was made the name of the county. The original name in the Delaware tongue was Maughwauwama, and was applied to a region on the Susquehanna river. According to Heckewelder it was compounded of *Maughwau*—large—and *wama*—plains. The Iroquois word with the same meaning is Sghahontowanno. By the early settlers in the Wyoming valley its Indian name was corrupted successively to Wauwama, Wauwamick, Wywamick, Wywaming, and finally Wyoming.

The act of 1841 provided that the first term of the courts of common pleas and general sessions should be held at the public house at East Orangeville; and that the subsequent terms should be held at such places as the judges should direct, till a court-house should be so nearly completed as to be, in the opinion of the judges, suitable for holding such courts; and the temporary county clerk's office was to be kept in such a place as these judges should direct. The circuit courts and courts of oyer and terminer were to be held at the places appointed by the county judges for holding their courts. It was also provided that these judges should determine the form and device for a county seal. Pursuant to this statute the court convened at the place designated on the 21st day of June, 1841. At this session there were present Hon. Paul Richards, first judge; Hon. James Sprague and Hon. Peter Patterson, judges. At this court an order was made that the device for a county seal should be "the figure of an American eagle surrounded by a circle, upon which is engraved in Roman letters, 'Wyoming County Clerk's Office.'" In 1849 this device was changed. It is now the goddess of liberty, surrounded by a circle with the words WYOMING, N. Y., SEAL.

Masonic Hall, in the village of Warsaw, was the place designated for holding the next term of the court. At this hall the sessions of the court were held till the June term in 1843, which was held at the court-house. The first session of the circuit court and court of oyer and terminer was held on the 15th of December, 1841, Hon. N. Dayton presiding.

Until the completion of the clerk's office, the county records were kept in a small building on the east side of Main street, Warsaw, north from the Bingham House.

The commissioners named in the act to determine the location of the court-house, jail and clerk's office, were: Peter R. Reed, of Onondaga; Davis Hurd, of Niagara, and John Thompson, of Steuben county.

As usual in such cases the question of the location of these buildings excited a deep interest in different localities. Warsaw had strong supporters by reason of its accessibility its nearly central location and the business interests that existed or that were springing up there. Wethersfield Springs was advocated because it was more nearly the geographical center of the county. At that time the villages of Warsaw and Perry were more nearly equal in size than they now are, and, as usual in such cases, were rivals. Many of the people in Perry strongly urged the claims of Wethersfield Springs because they foresaw that the location of the county seat there would leave the rival villages with more nearly equal advantages. After visiting the different towns in the county the commissioners, upon due deliberation, decided in favor of Warsaw.

The board of supervisors of Wyoming county were empowered by the act of incorporation to appoint, at a special meeting, three commissioners to superintend the erection of the county buildings. These commissioners were John A. McElwain, of Warsaw; Paul Richards, of Orangeville; and Jonathan Perry, of Middlebury. The lot upon which the court-house and clerk's office were erected was a donation to the county from Hon. Trumbull Cary, of Batavia. The contract for building them was awarded to Josiah Hovey, and the work was superintended by his son-in-law, P. Pixley. The jail was built in 1841 and the court-house in 1842. The act authorized a loan from the State to the new county of $10,000, and prescribed the terms of its payment. The cost of the three buildings did not exceed the amount of this loan.

The court-house is a brick structure, fronting on Main street, just north from the business portion of the village. It has a convenient court-room and the usual jury room. The county judge and surrogate and the sheriff have their offices in this building. The clerk's office, a fire-proof building, also of brick, stands a short distance south from the courthouse, and a finely shaded lawn lies in front of both. The jail is a wooden structure, standing west from the other two. All these are sufficiently distant from each other for safety in case of fire.

The decision of the commissioners in locating the county seat at Warsaw, just and equitable as it was, of course did not give universal satisfaction.

At the annual meeting of the board of supervisors of Wyoming county on the 21st day of November, 1877, the following preamble and resolutions were presented:

"*Whereas*, The county buildings of this county are old and out of repair; and

"*Whereas*, The present site is in an Inaccessible and unhealthy locality; and

"*Whereas*, The people of the county would be greatly accommodated by their removal to a more convenient, accessible and healthy locality; therefore

"Resolved, The county buildings and the county seat of this county be removed from the village of Warsaw to the town of Gainsville; and be located, at or near what is known as East Gainsville, in the said county, somewhere near the junction of the Erie and State Line railroads; and that this resolution be submitted to the people of the several towns on the last Tuesday in February next, the day on which the annual town meetings are to be held in said county; that a separate ballot box shall be kept at each of the polls in the towns of said county for the reception of the ballots on said question; that the ballots on said question shall be printed or written in the following manner, viz.: 'Resolution: For Removing the County Seat,' and 'Resolution: Against Removing the County Seat.' And that the proper town officers shall make a return after canvassing the same to the county clerk of said county, whose duty it shall be to declare the result in the county, and publish the same according to law."

These were adopted by a vote of 12 to 3, the minority not being permitted to delay action. These proceedings fell upon the people like a thunderbolt from an unclouded sky. They were amazed, as no such action had been called for, none had been anticipated. But it was forced upon them, and they must decide the question at their next town meeting. The excitement was intense, and much bitterness and ill feeling was manifested during the canvass of the question by the rival parties. Town meeting was held on the 26th of February, 1878, and the following is the official vote on the question:

TOWNS.	WHOLE NO. OF VOTES.	FOR REMOVAL.	AGAINST REMOVAL.
Arcade	395	184	211
Attica	553	459	94
Bennington	325	136	189
Castile	501	415	86
Covington	195	34	161
Eagle	229	115	114
Gainsville	417	275	142
Genesee Falls	196	184	12
Java	278	125	153
Middlebury	322	34	288
Orangeville	258	14	244
Perry	588	429	159
Pike	421	248	173
Sheldon	474	50	424
Warsaw	831	23	808
Wethersfield	327	262	65
Totals	6,310	2,987	3,323

Here was a majority of 336 *against* removal, while the law requires a vote of two-thirds *for* removal. By the census of 1875 it appears there were 8,685 persons of voting age in the county, so that 2,375 persons did not vote at all on the question; had they all voted for it, and no others against it, the measure would still have lacked several hundred votes of the number necessary for its adoption.

The county poor-house is located in the town of Orangeville. On the 8th of July, 1843, the county purchased from Jonathan Gates sixty acres of land for $720. Additions have since been made to this farm from time to time, till it now includes 280 acres. It is now valued at $25,000.

The first building, erected in 1843, was 24 by 48 feet, one and a half stories in height. It was occupied by the paupers of the county, forty-seven in number, in the autumn of that year. Other buildings were added from time to time, and in 1862 the building for the keeper's dwelling and superintendent's office was erected—a wooden structure, two stories in height, 36 by 40. The original buildings, except one barn, have been removed and commodious ones erected in their stead.

The principal buildings now used are the lunatic asylum—a detached two-story edifice, 36 by 38, erected in 1864; the idiot asylum, also detached, a one-story structure, 24 by 40, erected in 1874, at an expense of $1,200. Each asylum has a large and commodious yard, enclosed by a close, high board fence. A men's building was erected in 1876. It is a wooden structure, two stories in height, 24 by 40, and its cost was about $1,500. The dining hall, erected in 1878, is a two-story building, 24 by 42, the second story of which is divided into sleeping rooms. The lower story is divided into two dining rooms, one for men and the other for women. The women's building, also erected in 1878, is a two-story structure, 28 by 56. It and the dining hall cost $3,000. These are all commodious structures, well ventilated, and substantially and tastefully finished. The women's building and the insane asylum are heated by furnaces, and pure spring water is brought to the grounds and into most of the buildings from a distance of a fourth of a mile.

After the formation of Wyoming county, and previous to the erection of the county buildings, the paupers were kept on the premises of James H. Morse, near East Orangeville. Mr. Morse was appointed the first keeper, at a salary of $200 per year, and he also received a yearly rent of $200 for his farm. Joram Kelsey was the first keeper after the purchase of the farm. The first superintendents after the erection of the county were Job Sherman and Thicol M. Ward. The present superintendents are J. S. Rogers, B. F. Bristol and J. G. Hammond. The present keeper is S. Field. The present number of poor is sixty-two, and of chronic insane, fourteen. Mr. Field has been keeper since 1873. During 1878 the cost of keeping the paupers was $1.10 per week each over and above the products of the farm. The stock on the farm consists of twenty-two cows, four horses and seventeen hogs.

The eastern boundary of Wyoming county is a line six miles east from the transit line or eastern boundary of the Holland Purchase, and running parallel with it from the northeast corner of the county till it strikes the Genesee river, which bounds it on the east from that point to its southeast corner. The area between this boundary and the transit line was included in what was known as the Morris Reserve, which was sold in parcels to different parties after the sale to the Holland Land Company. A portion of the Gardeau reservation was included in this area.

That portion of this reserve which is now known as the Ogden tract includes the towns of Covington and Perry, and a part of Castile. It is, of course, six miles in width from the transit line, and has a length from the south line of the Cragie and Forty-thousand-acre tracts, which is also the north line of Wyoming county, of fourteen miles, one chain and sixty-six links. The Cotringer tract lies next south from the Ogden tract, and is of exactly the same shape and size; each containing fifty thousand acres. A part of Castile and all of Genesee Falls except its western tier of lots lie in this tract.

The western part of the north half of the Ogden tract was conveyed by Samuel Ogden to James Guernsey, and the eastern part to Heman Ely (in trust for Justin Ely and others). Ely and his grantees made an erroneous survey of their tract, and ran their boundary line at a distance east from the east line of the tract conveyed to Guernsey, leaving between these tracts a strip having an average width of more than five chains, which strip has since been known as "the gore." All these tracts have been subdivided and laid out in lots; but not according to any uniform plan.

That portion of the county lying west from this transit line was included in the Holland Purchase. The county is divided into sixteen towns, which are laid out with remarkable regularity. Each town in the two tiers lying next west from the east transit line is six miles square, and is bounded by township and range lines, except Pike, from which the eastern tier of lots was taken in 1846 and added to Genesee Falls. The four western towns have the same breadth from north to south, but their length between east and west is eight miles, except Bennington, which has a length between east and west of nine miles.

The towns lying east from the transit line are less regular. The eastern boundary of Genesee Falls and a part of Castile is the somewhat tortuous Genesee river. The last named town has a length from north to south of seven miles. Perry is six miles square, and Covington six miles from east to west, by four and one-half from north to south. The county contains six hundred square miles, or three hundred and eighty-four thousand acres.

As before stated, the town of Batavia when it was erected was made to include all the State west from the eastern boundary of the Holland Purchase. Warsaw was taken from it March 19th, 1808, and included Gainesville and Middlebury. On the same date Sheldon was formed, and it comprised what are now Arcade, Attica, Bennington, Java, Orangeville and Wethersfield. April 4th, 1811, Attica was taken from Sheldon, and included the present towns of Orangeville and Wethersfield.

Middlebury was erected from Warsaw March 20th, 1812. February 25th, 1814, Gainesville was taken from Warsaw. It was first called *Hebe*. Its present name was given to it April 17th, 1816. Perry was formed from Leicester—one of the towns into which Northampton was divided—March 11th, 1814. It included Castile and a part of Covington. Orangeville was formed from Attica, February 14th, 1816, and included Wethersfield. Covington was formed from Le Roy (Genesee county) and Perry, January 31st, 1817. As before stated, a part of it, under the name of Pavilion, was retained in Genesee county when

Wyoming was set off. China, which included the present town of Java, was formed from Sheldon March 6th, 1818. The name was afterwards changed to Arcade. On the same day Pike, including Eagle and a part of Genesee Falls, was taken from Nunda (Livingston county). On the same day also Bennington was formed from Sheldon. Eagle was taken from Pike, January 21st, 1821. Wethersfield was formed from Orangeville, April 12th, 1823. Java, previously a part of China, was incorporated April 20th, 1832, and Genesee Falls was formed from Portage (Livingston county) and Pike, April 1st, 1846.

CHAPTER XII.

LIST OF THE COUNTY OFFICERS AND LEGISLATIVE REPRESENTATIVES OF WYOMING COUNTY.

BEFORE 1841 the people of this county assisted in the election of the officers of Genesee county, and lived under their administration. The names of these officers are therefore given. Under the first constitution of the State all county officers were appointed by the governor and one senator from each of the four senatorial districts into which the State was then divided, who constituted the council of appointment.

Under the constitution of 1821 sheriffs and county clerks were elected by the people at the November election. In the following lists the year of election or appointment is given:

Sheriffs.—Genesee County:—Richard M. Stoddard, 1803; Benjamin Barton, 1807; Asher Bates, 1808; Nathan Marvin, 1810; Aaron Van Cleve, 1811; Parmenlo Adams, 1815, 1818; William Sheldon, 1816; Worthy L. Churchill, 1821, 1822; R. Thompson, 1825; John A. McElwain, 1831; Nathan Townsend, 1833; Rufus Robinson, 1840. Wyoming County:—William R. Groger, 1841; Roswell Gardner, 1843; Abraham Smith, 1846; Timothy H. Buxton, 1849; Jairus Moffet, 1852; Newcomb Demary, jr., 1855; Mills L. Rice, 1858; William D. Miner, 1861; John Renwick, 1864; William W. Davis, 1867; George W. Sweet, 1870; George M. Wilder, 1873; J. P. Randal, 1875; Albert P. Gage, 1875; Edgar A. Day, 1878.

County Clerks.—Genesee County:—James W. Stevens, 1803; Josiah Babcock, 1810; Simeon Cumings, 1811, 1818; John Z. Rose, 1816; Chauncey L. Sheldon, 1821, 1822; Ralph Coffin, 1825; David C. Miller, 1828; Timothy Fitch, 1831; Horace U. Soper, 1837, 1840. Wyoming County:—Nelson Wolcott, 1841; Walter Howard, 1843; Abel Webster, 1846; Ransom B. Crippen, 1849, 1864; Nathan P. Currier, 1852; John H. Bailey, 1855; Charles O. Shepard, 1858; Charles W.

Bailey, 1861; John P. Robinson, 1867; E. M. Jennings, 1870; Charles J. Gardner, 1873, 1876.

Surrogates.—Previous to 1847 surrogates were appointed in the same manner as were judges. Under the constitution adopted that year they are elected in counties the population of which exceeds 40,000. In counties having a less population the duties of surrogate devolve on the county judge. Genesee County:—Jeremiah Munson, 1804; Richard Smith, 1805, 1812; Andrew A. Ellicott, 1811, 1815; Ebenezer Mix, 1821; Harvey Putnam, 1840; Timothy Fitch, 1841. Wyoming County:—Harvey Putnam, 1841; William Mitchell, 1843.

County Treasurers.—County treasurers were appointed by the boards of supervisors prior to 1846. Under the constitution then adopted they are elected by the people. The first treasurer was elected in 1848. The list for Wyoming county is as follows: Truman Lewis, 1841; William Bingham, 1842, 1843; Roswell Gould, 1844, 1845, 1853; John A. McElwain, 1846, 1847, 1850; Samuel S. Blanchard, 1848; Peter Caner, 1850; Lloyd R. Heyward, 1856, 1859; Leonard W. Smith, 1862, 1865; Harwood A. Dudley, 1868, 1871; Simon D. Lewis, 1874, 1877.

First Judges.—Prior to 1821 all judges were appointed by the council of appointment. Under the constitution of that year, the governor and Senate appointed them for a term of five years. Under the constitution of 1846, a county judge in each county was elected for a term of four years, except in New York county. The term of office has been changed to six years. Genesee county:—Joseph Ellicott, 1806; Ezra Platt, 1807; John H. Jones, 1812; John Z. Ross, 1823: William H. Tisdall, 1827; Isaac Wilson, 1830; Phineas L. Tracy, 1841. Wyoming county:—Paul Richards, 1841; John B. Skinner, 1846; W. Riley Smith, 1847; Marvin Trall, 1851; Harlow L. Comstock, 1855, 1859, 1863; Byron Healy, 1867, 1871, 1877.

Associate Judges.—The constitution of 1821 made the county court to consist of a first judge and four associate judges. These associate judges in Wyoming county were Alonzo B. Rose, Joseph Johnson, Peter Patterson, 1841; Dr. Augustus Frank, 1842 (in place of Johnson, resigned); Nyrum Reynolds, Moseley Stoddard and James Sprague (2nd), 1845.

Justices of Sessions.—The constitution of 1846 abolished the office of associate judge. Under that constitution two justices of sessions are annually chosen from among the justices of the peace of the county. Their duties are similar to those of associate judges. The list for Wyoming follows: P. M. Ward, Uriah Johnson, 1847; H. O. Brown, Cyril Ransom, 1849; Herman Wilson, Orlando Kelly, 1851; V. D. Eastman, Orlando Kelly, 1852; V. D. Eastman, A. W. Blackmer, 1853, 1854; Gorton Bentley, Benjamin J. Bristol, 1855, 1856; Gorton Bentley, A. P. Thompson, 1857; Erastus D. Day, A. P. Thompson, 1858; Erastus D. Day, P. M. Ward, 1859; J. W. Knapp, D. E. Warren, 1860; Martin Hodge, Gorton Bently, 1861; Gorton Bently, H. O. Brown, 1862; M. S. Durfey, H. O. Brown, 1863; L. S. Torry, John M. Webster, 1864; J. M. Webster, Timothy Loomis, 1865; Timothy Loomis, Gorton Bently, 1866; Harvey Stone, L. S. Torry, 1867; Harvey Stone, E. B. Z. Sheeler, 1868; E. P. Randal, William H. Hills, 1869; William H. Hills, J. W. Gould, 1870; L. P. Runnals, William Deeney, 1871; J. W. Gould, Jacob W. Knapp, 1872; Charles E. Thayer, Gideon H. Jenkins, 1873; Guy P. Morgan,

Irving E. Blackmer, 1874, 1875; Byron L. Stearns, Robert J. Shearman, 1876; Daniel Ball, Robert J. Shearman, 1877; Daniel Ball, Denslow D. Davis, 1878.

District Attorneys.—An act passed in 1801 created the office of district attorney. One passed in 1818 made each county a separate district. Under both these acts district attorneys were appointed by the council of appointment. Under the constitution of 1821 they were appointed by the court of General Sessions of each county, and under that of 1846 they are elected by the people. Genesee county:—Daniel D. Brown, 1818; Heman J. Redfield, 1821; Levi Rumsey, 1829; Daniel H. Chandler, 1834; Isaac. A. Verplanck, 1838. Wyoming county:—W. Riley Smith, 1841; James R. Doolittle, 1847; Harlow L. Comstock, 1850; J. C. D. McKay, 1856; Thomas Corlett, 1859; Byron Healy, 1865; Elbert E. Farman, 1868; Andrew J. Knight, 1874; I. Samuel Johnson, 1876.

Superintendents and Commissioners of Common Schools.—In 1842 the office of county superintendent of common schools was created, and after a few years abolished. A. S. Stevens was appointed to this office in 1842, J. S. Denman in 1844, and Leonard Hoskins in 1846. Since the office of Assembly district school commissioner was established the following gentlemen have been elected to the office in this county: Harvey W. Hardy, 1856; Warren S. Brown, 1859; George W. Dunham, Warren S. Brown, 1860; W. Bean, E. F. Chaffee, 1853, 1865; J. B. Smallwood, Richard Langdon, 1859; Edwin S. Smith, Edson S. Quigley, 1872, 1875; E. A. Hall, John B. Smallwood, 1878.

State Senators.—Prior to 1821 the State was divided into four senatorial districts. Under the constitution of 1821 there were eight, and under that of 1846 there are thirty-two, from each of which a senator is chosen every two years. Wyoming county has been represented as follows: 1842, Harvey Putnam, Attica, four years; 1847, J. W. Brownson, Gainesville, two years; 1851, John A. McElwain, Warsaw, two years; 1855, John B. Halstead, Castile, four years; 1865, W. J. Humphrey, Warsaw, four years; 1877, James H. Loomis, Attica.

Members of Assembly.—1841, Eleazer Baldwin, Sheldon; John W. Brownson, Gainesville; 1842, Eleazer Baldwin, Sheldon; Truman Benedict, Perry; 1843, Truman Benedict, Perry; Leverett Spring, China; 1844, Leverett Spring, China; Andrew W. Young, Warsaw; 1845, Andrew W. Young, Warsaw; Arden Woodruff, Sheldon; 1846, Arden Woodruff, Sheldon; 1847, 1848, Paul Richards, Orangeville; 1849, James Sprague, Covington; 1850, 1851, Wolcott J. Humphrey, Sheldon; 1852, 1853, Alonzo B. Rose, Castile; 1854, 1855, John C. Paine, Covington; 1856, 1857, Cyril Rawson, Eagle; 1858, Elias C. Holt, Bennington; 1859, 1864, and 1865 (speaker), George G. Hoskins, Bennington; 1860, John J. Dolittle, Wethersfield; 1861, Lucius Peck, Java; 1862, 1863, Byron Healy, Warsaw; 1866, 1867, William Bristol, Gainesville; 1868, 1869, Marcus A. Hull, Pike; 1870, Henry S. Joy, Java; 1871, 1872, John D. Davidson, Genesee Falls; 1873, 1874, Samuel W. Tewksbury, Perry; 1875, 1876, Arthur Clark, Java; 1877, John E. Lowing, Java; 1878, Orange L. Tozier, Sheldon.

Members of Congress resident in Wyoming county have been elected as follows, a "congress" commencing on the 4th of March following the election, and ending on the 3d of March two years thereafter: 1836, William Patterson, Warsaw; 1846, 1848, Harvey Putnam, Attica; 1858, 1860, 1862, Augustus Frank, Warsaw; 1872, 1874, George G. Hoskins, Attica; 1876, Charles B. Benedict, Attica.

CHAPTER XIII.

THE CONSTRUCTION AND OPENING OF RAILROADS IN WYOMING COUNTY.

UP to the year 1843 the regular mode of public conveyance in this county was the stage coach, but with the completion of the Tonawanda and Rochester Railroad to Attica, and the Buffalo and Attica Railroad, other roads were projected. No others, however, were built until the year 1852, since which time the county of Wyoming will compare favorably with its sister counties in this respect.

WARSAW AND LE ROY RAILROAD.

On the 5th of May, 1834, an act of the Legislature was passed incorporating the Warsaw and Le Roy Railroad Company, and empowering it to build a road from Warsaw through the valley of the Oakta creek to Le Roy, with a capital of not less than $100,000.

The stock was readily subscribed, and a report of the survey and estimate of the cost of the work prepared, which report was submitted to the board of directors on the 12th day of November, 1835. Some delay was occasioned by an endeavor to procure an extension of the route from Le Roy to Bergen, where it would intersect the Tonawanda Railroad from Rochester. This latter line was found to be too expensive and the project was not carried out. In the meantime the directors found they were unable to proceed with the construction of the Warsaw railroad according to the terms of the charter, and, the Legislature refusing to grant them an extension of time, they paid back to the stockholders the amounts of their subscriptions, less the expense, and the company was disbanded.

ERIE RAILWAY.

What constitutes the Buffalo division of the New York, Lake Erie and Western Railroad was originally built as the "Attica and Hornellsville Railroad," and extends southeasterly through the towns of Attica, Middlebury, Warsaw, Gainesville, Castile and Genesee Falls, in this county, crossing the Genesee river near the celebrated falls at Portage, and connecting with the main line at Hornellsville.

In the summer of 1850 this branch of the Erie Railway was projected, and public meetings held at different points along the line to arouse the desired enthusiasm. Surveys of the route were made by William Wallace, C. E., of

Buffalo, the same year, and the required amount of stock was subscribed by persons along the route and at Buffalo. In September an organization was perfected and the following gentlemen were chosen directors: Russell H. Heywood (president), A. D. Patchin, Samuel Swain, jr., H. O. Brown, B. R. Folsom, J. C. Bronson, Hiram Cooley and George B. Chace.

The maps were filed Feburary 27th, 1851, and soon after a contract for building the road was made with Messrs. Lanman, Rockafellow & Moore, who were to furnish all the materials except the iron, and to complete it by the first of May, 1852. Before the road was completed the New York Central Railroad, having built a new line from Batavia to Buffalo, sold to the Attica and Hornellsville Railroad that portion of their road from Attica to Buffalo, and the corporate name of the road was changed to the "Buffalo and New York City Railroad," running from Buffalo to Hornellsville, a distance of ninety-one miles.

On the 26th day of July, 1852, the first train of passenger cars passed over the road, and on the completion of the famous Portage bridge, August 25th, 1852, the entire line was opened for traffic. Portage bridge is said to have been the largest wooden bridge in the world—was eight hundred feet in length, two hundred and thirty-four feet high and contained one million, six hundred thousand feet of timber, one hundred and six thousand, two hundred and eighty pounds of iron and cost $175,000. On the 6th day of May, 1875, this structure was burned. Steps were immediately taken to rebuild the bridge of iron, and the Watson Manufacturing Company, of Patterson, took the contract for $90,000, to be finished on the first of August, 1875. It was completed within the time allotted by the contract, and is eight hundred and twenty feet long by two hundred and thirty-five feet in height. For the past twenty years this road has been owned by the Erie Railway Company; and it is an important factor in the great line of travel between New York and the West.

ATTICA AND ARCADE RAILROAD.

Prior to the completion of the above named road steps were taken to construct a railroad from Attica to Arcade, passing through the towns of Attica, Bennington, Sheldon, Java and Arcade, in this county. The required stock was subscribed along the route, and the line was located in the early part of the year 1852. Work was commenced immediately, and the roadbeds, culverts and superstructure finished in the spring of 1853. Part of the track was laid, but financial embarrassments overtook the project and the work was abandoned. In the year 1870 efforts were made to finish the road, and some work was done, but at the present time it remains unfinished, although a comparatively small sum of money would put it in running order, and its operation would be a great benefit to the localities which it traverses.

SILVER LAKE RAILWAY.

The citizens of the town of Perry, feeling the want of railroad communication, began in the summer of 1869 to agitate the feasibility of a road from East Gainesville, on the Erie Railway, to the village of Perry. A survey of a route was made in the early autumn of that year by Colonel James O. McClure, C. E., and his report was presented at a public meeting held in the village of Perry, October 22nd, 1869. At that meeting great enthusiasm prevailed, and the project grew rapidly in public favor. The town of Perry promptly bonded itself for the sum of $100,000 in aid of the road, and on the 10th of August, 1870, R. C. Moredoff, R. W. Brigham and L. G. Morgan were appointed railroad commissioners.

On the 15th of December, 1870, the contract for the grading and masonry between Perry and East Gainesville, a distance of six and one-quarter miles, was let, to be completed August 1st, 1871. The work was commenced immediately, and the locomotive announced its first arrival in Perry October 20th, 1871. The first regular train left Perry for East Gainesville on the 14th of February, 1872, since which time trains have run regularly, and the road has accumulated a fair surplus.

ROCHESTER AND STATE LINE RAILWAY.

The first meeting held in the interest of this popular thoroughfare was at Wiscoy on the 5th of March, 1869, and was attended by prominent citizens of Rochester and the towns along the proposed route. This meeting was adjourned to convene at Castile on the 17th of March, when a report as to its feasibility was presented. Another meeting in aid of the project was called at Caledonia, March 31st, and subsequently at Rochester on the 8th day of April, 1869, at which time the "Rochester and State Line Railway Company" was duly organized.

The route at first contemplated passed through the towns of Caledonia, Perry and Castile, up the Genesee river into Pennsylvania. Surveys were made on this route by William Wallace, C. E., and subsequently another route was located through Mumford, Le Roy, Pavilion, Warsaw, Gainesville, Pike, Eagle, and thence to Salamanca, at which place it would connect with the Erie and Atlantic and Great Western Railways; thereby forming a trunk line to the Southwest. In aid of this route the town of Wheatland, Monroe county, bonded itself for $70,000; Le Roy, Genesee county, $100,000; Pavilion, $40,000; Covington, Wyoming county, $45,000; Middlebury, $50,000; Warsaw, $120,000; Gainesville, $50,000, and Eagle, $30,000. The city of Rochester was bonded for $600,000. The commissioners appointed by the county judge to issue bonds for the towns in Wyoming were: Warsaw, Augustus Frank, Linus W. Thayer, Simeon D. Lewis; Middlebury, Isaac G. Hammond, Ethel

V. Sherman, Thomas G. Cushing; Covington, Duncan Cameron, Jedediah S. Walker, Hawley Daniels; Gainesville, Benjamin F. Bristol, Charles S. Farman, Robert F. Shearman; Eagle, Freeman S. Marchant, Beckley Howes, Ira Eastman.

The total amount of town and city bonds reached the sum of $1,105,000, and the directors adopted the Warsaw route, as it was called, on the 17th of January, 1870. On the first day of May, 1872, a corps of engineers under the direction of Charles S. Masters, C. E., began the location of the road, and in the spring of 1873 the grading, masonry and superstructure were let to A. M. Slocum & Co. for the whole road. The work progressed rapidly till the latter part of 1873, when this road, in common with many others, succumbed to the panic of that year. The eastern portion of the road, from Rochester to Le Roy, was, however, completed and put into operation on the 15th day of September, 1874. After a series of delays the work was resumed by the contractors, and the road opened to Warsaw August 6th, 1877, and to Salamanca May 16th, 1878.

From its completion the road has been successful, and it is now transporting more petroleum than any other road in the country. The regular and special trains running (in 1879) over this road daily number twenty; comprising one hundred oil tank cars, each of one hundred barrels capacity, and the business is rapidly increasing.

CHAPTER XIV.

WYOMING COUNTY BIBLE SOCIETY, AGRICULTURAL SOCIETY AND INSURANCE COMPANY.

NOVEMBER 22nd, 1841, a meeting of persons favorable to the organization of a county Bible society was held in the session room of the Presbyterian church at Warsaw. Deacon William Buxton was chairman, and Edwin B. Miller secretary. It was resolved that it was expedient to call a meeting of persons in the county favorable to the design and operations of the American Bible Society, to consider the propriety of forming a Wyoming county Bible Society, auxiliary to the former. Rev. Salmon Judd, Rev. Richard Ray, and Edwin B. Miller were appointed a committee to arrange the time and place of the meeting.

Notice of such meeting was published in the *Western New Yorker* November 24th, 1841, calling a meeting for December 2nd of that year, in the Presbyterian church in Warsaw. The meeting was held; Rev. Richard Ray, pastor of the church, presided, and E. B. Miller was the secretary. Rev. J. M. Ballou, of

Gainesville, moved that it was expedient to form such society, and the resolution passed unanimously.

The form of a constitution was presented by Rev. J. J. Aiken and adopted; Dr. Augustus Frank, Rev. Pliny Twitchell, and John Crocker were appointed a committee to nominate officers for the society. The committee recommended as officers: President, John B. Skinner, of Wyoming; vice-presidents, Salmon Judd, of Warsaw, and James C. Ferris, of Wyoming; secretary, Edwin B. Miller, of Warsaw; treasurer, John Crocker, of Warsaw.

May 21st, 1842, the first regular meeting of the society was held, in the session room of the Presbyterian church in Warsaw. The president stated that the Genesee County Bible Society had resolved to place one-third of the Bibles and Testaments in their possession at the disposal of the Wyoming county society, being the just proportion to which the latter would be entitled by its former connection with the Genesee county society. Books were also ordered from the American Bible Society, and a depository of books was opened in the store of the treasurer in Warsaw.

October 19th, 1842, Nelson Wolcott was chosen treasurer. November 27th, 1844, three additional vice-presidents were chosen—A. G. Hammond, of Warsaw, Rev. Joseph R. Page, of Perry; and Rev. Joseph Pearsall, of Warsaw.

Dr. Augustus Frank was afterward chosen treasurer, which position he held until his death, in 1861—succeeded by his son, Augustus Frank.

In 1845 the county was thoroughly canvassed, for the purpose of obtaining funds and supplying the destitute with the Holy Scriptures, by Mr. Amasa Lord. Two thousand four hundred and one dollars were received for books and in free donations, nearly the whole amount being donated. Rev. Gilbert Crawford and Rev. J. H. Wallace were made life members of the American Bible Society, and one thousand dollars were donated to the same society. Town societies were formed in every town in the county during the year 1845. In 1850 Hon. John B. Skinner, and in 1853 Edwin B. Miller were made life directors of the American Bible Society.

In 1854 the county was again thoroughly explored; 5,209 families were visited; a large number of Bibles were sold, destitute families were supplied with the Scriptures, and donations received. April 7th, 1859, Joshua H. Darling, of Warsaw, was chosen treasurer. In 1859 Rev. E. Everett was employed by the society to canvass the county, spending 119 days, and visiting 5,041 families. Destitute families were also supplied with the Scriptures.

January 8th, 1861, the president, Hon. John B. Skinner, declined a further re-election, stating that he had been president nearly twenty years, and felt it a necessity that he be relieved from further duties. Edwin B. Miller was chosen president, and Rev. John Jones secretary in place of Mr. Miller, who had held the office from the organization of the society.

January 27th, 1863, George W. Morris, of Warsaw, was made president. January 7th, 1866, Hon. Augustus Frank was chosen president, Joshua H. Darling treasurer, and L. E. Walker secretary. In 1868 Rev. G. Lane explored the county, visiting 5,947 families, and supplying 419 families that were destitute of the Scriptures. He also received donations, and made sales of Bibles and Testaments. Lloyd A. Hayward was chosen treasurer of the society in place of J. H. Darling, deceased.

The present officers of the society, 1879, are Hon. Augustus Frank, president, with one vice-president in each town. L. A. Hayward is the treasurer and John B. Matthews secretary.

WYOMING COUNTY AGRICULTURAL SOCIETY.

In the month of October, 1843, a meeting of those interested in agricultural pursuits was held at the court-house, pursuant to previous notice, for the purpose of organizing a county agricultural society.

Of this meeting Calvin P. Bailey, of Perry, was chairman, and James L. Hosford, of Castile, secretary. A committee appointed for the purpose, consisting of James L. Hosford, John A. McElwain, John W. Paddock, Uriah Johnson, Seth C. Grosvenor and George B. Chase reported a constitution, which was adopted.

The first officers chosen were James C. Ferris, of Middletown, president; Lyman Brainard, Attica; Philo Durkee, Bennington; Stephen D. Tabor, Castile; James Steele, China; Micha Johnson, Covington; Rufus Conable, Gainesville; Allen Waldo, Java; Job Sherman, Middlebury, Truman Lewis, Orangeville; Rufus H. Smith, Perry; Godfrey Grosvenor, Sheldon; Dr. Augustus Frank, Warsaw; and Reuben Doolittle, Wethersfield, vice-presidents; James L. Hosford, corresponding secretary; Linus W. Thayer, recording secretary; and John A. McElwain, treasurer. One manager and a committee of three were appointed in each town.

The following resolution among others was adopted: "Resolved, that, inasmuch as intelligence is the mainspring of action, every member of this society be earnestly requested to become a subscriber to some agricultural paper of this State."

The annual fairs of the society were held nearly every year at Warsaw. The interest taken in these annual exhibitions was such that it was deemed expedient to establish a permanent place for holding them. On the 27th of September, 1855, a meeting of the society was held in the court-house at Warsaw to elaborate a plan for procuring and fitting up grounds for the fairs of the society. A committee consisting of John A. McElwain, Frank Miller, James C. Ferris, Uriah Johnson, Samuel Fisher (2nd), Newbury Bronson, W. Bristol, jr., and E. C. Skiff, was appointed and authorized to take such action as should be deemed expedient in the premises. At a subsequent meeting this committee reported in favor of purchasing twenty-one acres of land from David McWithy, selecting for the use of the society ten acres and selling the balance. They also presented an estimate of the expense of fencing this ground and building a hall, which they had fixed at $1,000.

In order that the society might have a legal status and be able to hold and convey real estate, it was necessary that it should be reorganized. This reorganization was accomplished and Hugh T. Brooks chosen president; Uriah Johnson; vice-president; H. A. Dudley, recording secretary; John L. Clark, corresponding secretary; and John A. McElwain treasurer. The directors chosen were: for one year—Ezra Bishop, Attica; Norman Howes, Eagle; Newbury Bronson, Warsaw; for two years—Arten Woodruff, Sheldon; A. D. Lucas, Gainesville, E. C. Skiff, Pike; for three years—Welcome Wilcox, Wethersfield; A. S. Patterson, Perry; E. A. Durfee, Middlebury.

Warsaw was designated as the permanent place for holding the fairs of the society, and the officers were empowered to purchase and fit up grounds and make all other necessary arrangements for holding such fairs.

The executive committee finally arranged to purchase from Samuel Fisher (2nd) ten acres of land near the corner of Brooklyn and Liberty streets in the village of Warsaw, and to fence and improve this land for a fair ground; and the officers were authorized to execute the necessary papers.

A driving track of one-third of a mile was laid out on this ground, but in 1866, when the society acquired four acres in addition to the ten originally purchased, and the State at the same time purchased three and one-half acres, which was occupied jointly for a parade ground by the regiment of national guard and by the society for a fair ground, this track was enlarged to half a mile.

After the year 1853 the annual exhibitions were held in a tent, which was purchased that year for that purpose. This having become worn and dilapidated, it was deemed expedient to erect an exhibition hall, which was done in 1874, under the superintendence of the building committee, consisting of J. O. McClure, M. Hatfield and A. F. Chase. The cost of this hall was about $1,500. The society also incurred the expense of erecting cattle pens and rebuilding the grand stand, which had been blown down.

In 1875 an unsuccessful attempt was made to merge the society in a joint stock association.

The position of president of this society has been occupied by the following gentlemen, each having been re-elected till the year of his successor's election: 1843, James C. Ferris, Middlebury; 1847, Mosely Stoddard, Castile; 1849, E. P. Beck, Sheldon; 1851, Newbury Bronson, Warsaw; 1853, Hugh T. Brooks, Covington; 1858, J. A. McElwain, Warsaw; 1862, Duncan Cameron, Covington; 1863, J. Ephraim Wheeler, Orangeville; 1865, Thomas J. Patterson, Warsaw; 1868, J. S. Walker, Covington; 1869, Emory B. Chase, Castile; 1871, Gideon H. Jenkins, Covington; 1873, Charles Brown, Warsaw; 1875, Albert F. Chase, Gainesville; 1876, Ethel C. Sherman, Middlebury; 1878, William Bristoll, Warsaw.

WYOMING COUNTY INSURANCE COMPANY.

In the year 1851 the Wyoming County Mutual Insurance Company was formed and a charter obtained, authorizing a working capital of $100,000. Its founders were among the leading men of Warsaw, possessing probity of character and business capacity. Its principal office was located at Warsaw, and the following persons composed the first board of directors: John A. McElwain, Isaac C. Bronson, Elijah W. Andrews, George Reed, Augustus Frank, Seth M. Gates, F. C. D. McKay, Israel Hodge, Charles J. Judd, Timothy H. Buxton, E. H. Lansing, W. Riley Smith, and Joshua H. Darling.

J. A. McElwain was elected president, Seth M. Gates vice-president, J. H. Darling treasurer, and C. J. Judd secretary. In 1853 Mr. Judd retired from the office of secretary, and was succeeded by L. A. Hayward, who was afterwards also elected treasurer.

The company's field of operations was restricted to the western counties of the State, in which it very soon secured a good position. Its risks for the first few years embraced both a merchants' and farmers' class; but in 1856 the former class was dropped, and all the risks afterwards confined entirely to the latter. Its reputation as a prudently managed and secure company was maintained throughout its entire career.

The following named persons, in addition to the above, were elected directors of the company at different periods during its existence: James G. Hoyt, James C. Ferris, John B. Halsted, W. J. Chapin, Joel S. Smith, L. A. Hayward, Nelson Wolcott, Linus W. Thayer, William Bristol, Ezra Bishop, Peter Patterson, Ira F. Pratt, James H. Loomis, Jedediah S. Walker, Noble Morris, and Alanson Holly.

The company continued to do business until the latter part of 1865, making no assessments, paying all its losses with promptness, steadily accumulating a surplus fund, and gaining year by year in the confidence of the community. In the meantime rival companies had multiplied, and, in the intense competition that had sprung up, the rates of insurance were forced down below the point at which a company could safely do business. The directors therefore prudently resolved to cease the further issue of policies and take measures to close up the affairs of the company. A re-insurance of all the existing risks of the company was accordingly effected with the Home Insurance Company of New York, for the sum of $5,000. This left a surplus in the treasury of the company of something over $5,000. The directors, being at a loss how to dispose of this amount in a legal manner, obtained an act of the Legislature authorizing them to invest it in the stock of the Warsaw Water Works Company. This was accordingly done. The investment having proved unexpectedly remunerative, the directors made sale of the stock, under a further act of the Legislature, and applied the entire proceeds of the sale toward the erection of the Wyoming county soldiers' monument. The risks of the company all expired in the year 1868, and it was left without liability or indebtedness of any kind. Its financial record has but few parallels in the history of insurance in this State.

CHAPTER XV.

ORIGIN AND EARLY INCIDENTS OF THE CIVIL WAR—PATRIOTIC SPIRIT IN WYOMING COUNTY.

THE limits and scope of this work will not permit even an enumeration of all the events that led to the civil war. It is quite proper, however, that a brief mention should be made of some of the more important and immediate antecedents of the contest, in which many of the citizens of this county bore a conspicuous and honorable part, and in which many laid down their lives.

The doctrine which has by some been termed a grand political heresy—that of *State sovereignty*, or, as it was improperly termed at the South, *State rights*, was what led to the civil war. By this is meant the right of a State to set aside any act of Congress which may be deemed unconstitutional by the State authorities. This doctrine was distinctly set forth in the famous Kentucky resolutions of 1798, and was for a long time accepted by many, perhaps by a majority, in all parts of the country. This doctrine involves not the right of nullification alone, but that of secession. South Carolina in 1832 was dissatisfied with the protective tariff which Congress established, and adopted an ordinance of nullification and secession. A compromise was effected, some concessions to the prejudices were made, and she repealed her ordinances.

The question of the introduction of slavery into Kansas arose, and the people of the Northern States evinced a determination to prevent it, in which they were successful. In 1856 threats of secession were freely uttered in case of the success of the Republican party, which in 1855 had been formed on the issue of slavery extension. In 1860 Abraham Lincoln was elected President, and this was regarded by southern statesmen as the finishing stroke to the extension of their institution, and they proceeded to execute their threats. South Carolina took the lead in this, followed by Georgia, Mississippi, Alabama, Virginia, Florida and Louisiana, all of which before the end of November issued calls for State conventions to consider the question of secession. In this they were followed after a time by Tennessee, Texas, Arkansas and North Carolina, all of which adopted ordinances of secession.

South Carolina adopted the ordinance of secession on the first day of December, 1860. Three days later Governor Pickens issued his proclamation, declaring it to be a "separate, sovereign, true and independent State, having a right to levy war, conclude peace, negotiate treaties," etc.

John B. Floyd, of Virginia, was at that time Secretary of War. He had caused 70,000 stands of arms to be placed in the arsenal at Charleston, and had put that arsenal in the care of the governor of South Carolina; and thus when the State decided it was able to possess itself of these arms, it was also found that the northern arsenals generally had been depleted and the arms sent south. Many of the ships of the navy had been sent to distant seas, and the government was left without efficient resources with which to repress a sudden uprising.

The senators from South Carolina were first to resign their seats, followed by others and by members of the Cabinet, and of the House of Representatives. Texas, the last of the seven States which united in forming the "Southern Confederacy," adopted the ordinance of secession February 1st, 1861. On the 4th of the same month the delegates who had been appointed by the conventions for that purpose met at Montgomery, Ala., to form a government. They adopted the constitution of the United States, with some additions and alterations, as the constitution of the confederate States, and chose for provisional President and Vice-President Jefferson Davis and Alexander H. Stevens.

When South Carolina passed the ordinance of secession in December, 1860, Fort Moultrie, in Charleston harbor, was garrisoned by sixty effective men in command of Major Anderson. The fort was not secure against attack, and Major Anderson was denied reinforcements. Accordingly on the night of December 20th he removed his force to Fort Sumter, which had been quietly prepared for his occupation. He had been instructed by the President "not to take up without necessity any position which could be construed into a hostile attitude, but to hold possession of the forts, and if attacked, defend himself." This evacuation of Fort Moultrie therefore surprised the President and aroused the indignation of the South Carolinians, who thought they had a pledge from the President to prevent such removal. He was induced to take this step because he entertained just apprehensions of the occupation of Fort Sumter by the South Carolina troops, and an attack on his small force in the nearly defenseless fort which he was, in which case it would have been impossible for him to hold out a day.

Three commissioners that had been appointed by the South Carolina convention "to treat with the United States" repaired to Washington, and in obedience to their instructions demanded that Major Anderson should be ordered back to Fort Moultrie, and in case of refusal that the forts in Charleston harbor should be unconditionally evacuated. About this time the government offices, forts, etc., were possessed by the State troops, who were supplied with arms and ammunition from the arsenal.

An attempt was made by the government to revictual and reinforce Fort Sumter, and for that purpose the steamer "Star of the West" was sent in January, 1861, with two hundred men, provisions, ammunition, etc. She was fired on from Morris Island, was struck by several shot and compelled to return without landing her troops and cargo.

April 12th, 1861, at 4 A. M., the bombardment of Fort Sumter was commenced from the batteries of Fort Moultrie, Sullivan's Island and elsewhere.

The rebel forces were under command of General Beauregard, who demanded the surrender of the fort. Major Anderson replied that he would only surrender when his supplies were exhausted. The cannonading was kept up with spirit on both sides. The result was the surrender of the fort on the 13th, and on the 14th Major Anderson and his command left on the steamer "Isabel" for New York.

After the attack on Fort Sumter it was feared that the confederate troops would march at once on Washington, and all the available forces were so disposed so as to afford the best protection to the capital possible with the meagre number of troops available. Measures were at once taken to raise troops in several States, and thousands of volunteers at once offered their services. President Lincoln promptly issued his proclamation and call for 75,000 troops for three months, and stated that they would first be used to "repossess the forts, places and property which had been seized from the Union." The proclamation also called a special session of Congress for the next 4th of July, to do whatever might be deemed necessary for the public safety. Another proclamation, declaring a blockade, was soon issued.

To this call for volunteers the people of the loyal States responded with the utmost alacrity. Only two days after Governor Andrew, of Massachusetts, issued orders calling for troops, two regiments were on their way to Washington. In every city and almost every village in the loyal North meetings were held, large sums of money were pledged for the support of the families of volunteer companies, and regiments were raised and sent forward, and a degree of patriotic feeling was aroused the existence of which had by some been doubted.

On the 29th of April the President called for 40,000 volunteers to serve three years, and 25,000 regulars for five years' service. In his message to Congress, which convened in special session in July, he recommended the passage of a law authorizing the raising of 400,000 men and placing $400,000,000 at the disposal of the government, in order to make this contest a short and decisive one. During the nine days of the session acts were passed to legalize the past action of the President to authorize the calling out of 500,000 volunteers, to appropriate some $266,000,000 for the prosecution of the war, and to confiscate property used for insurrectionary purposes.

At the breaking out of the war hardly any one anticipated a struggle of beyond two or three months; but instead of the short, decisive war that was at first anticipated the contest was prolonged through four years, with an expenditure of life and treasure unparalleled in the history of similar wars. During this time the Union forces experienced alternate successes and reverses till the decisive triumphs of Grant and Sheridan, the resistless march of Sherman to the sea, and the complete exhaustion of the enemy's resources, brought the consummation for which the friends of the Union had so long labored and prayed. The tension at which the feelings of the friends of humanity had been held during four years was relaxed, and the world breathed free again.

On Tuesday evening, April 23d, 1861, the first war meeting was held at Warsaw. The *Western New Yorker* of the 25th headed its account of the meeting with

"WARSAW AWAKE!

"Raising the Stars and Stripes—Rousing Union Demonstration—Volunteers Forming—Liberal Subscriptions by our Citizens—Wyoming Sound!

"Tuesday's proceedings show that the people of Warsaw cherish the same Union sentiment that summons so many brave arms and dauntless spirits to the conflict now upon us. Our citizens are in earnest. There is patriotic work to be done, and they will do their share. Wyoming county believes the government should be sustained in its attempt at self-assertion, and her sons are preparing if need be to strike brave blows against the traitors who are striving to prove this last attempt at self-government by the people a miserable failure.

"The loyal men were out on Tuesday. A fine flag-staff was raised at the junction of Main and Buffalo streets, and the national colors are floating from its summit."

A meeting was held at the court-house in the evening, over which General L. W. Thayer was called to preside, and a vice-president was chosen from each town in the county. The court-house did not afford standing room for the crowd, and the meeting adjourned to the lawn in front. There speeches were made by the Hon. Martin Grover, of Angelica, Hon. John B. Skinner, of Buffalo, and Hon. Seth Wakeman, of Batavia.

After the close of the meeting, which broke up reluctantly, the people reassembled in the court-house, where they were addressed by Hon. H. L. Comstock, of Warsaw, C. A. Macomber, of Buffalo, and others. For the raising of funds for the families of volunteers a committee, consisting of Messrs. Buxton, Ferris, Farman, Miller, Blake, Morris and Darling, was appointed. At the close of the meeting this committee reported the following contributions: J. H. Darling, $500; Augustus Frank, $250; C. and T. Buxton, $200; Artemas Blake, $150; James H. Loomis, Amos Otis, Selden C. Allis, F. and E. B. Miller, J. A. McElwain, L. W. Thayer, H. L. Comstock, B. B. Conable, Henry Garretsee, and Morris & Lewis, each $100; C. W. Bailey, George W. Frank, A. B. Lawrence, E. E. Farman, George Duryee, William Bingham, Uriah Johnson. R. H. Miller, Robert R. Munger and Truman Lewis, each $50; C. C. Gates, A. Y. Breck, J. Watts, L. W. Smith, Esek Cook, R. W. Hewett, Walter R. Keith, Alonzo Cleveland, Miles H. Morris and Bryon Healy, each $25; R. A. Crippen, B. F. Homer, E. C. Shattuck and Manlius Gay, each $20; M. L. Rice, $15; and B. F. Fargo, Hiram Stearns, O. A. Shaw, James A. Webster, Edmund Buck, Godfrey Gates, Benjamin Bisby and Simeon Holton, each $10; a total of $3,000. Thirty men were enrolled as volunteers at this meeting.

On Wednesday, the 24th, a similar meeting was held at Pearl Creek, in the town of Covington, and upwards of $2,000 was subscribed for the benefit of the families of volunteers in that town. On the list of subscribers to this fund appeared the names of Selden Allen for $200; J. H. Burroughs, E. Durfee, Major Corey, Rev. D. Morey, M. Weed, C. Burroughs, M. and J. Everes and C. L. Hayden, each $100; and D. Keith, Rev. Dr. Dean, D. Barrett, Walter Keith, Rev. J. Jones and R. Whiteside, each $50. Were the records of similar meetings that were held in other parts of the county accessible, it would he seen that there was nowhere a lack of patriotism. Had the subscriptions of smaller amounts been reported, it would have appeared in many a case, as in that of the widow who gave her mite, that when measured by the ability of the giver the contribution was greater than many which were expressed by larger figures. The poor as well as the rich recognized the danger which menaced the free institutions of the country, and in proportion to their ability they were even more ready to make sacrifices for the preservation of those institutions.

On Friday, the 26th, the thirty who were enrolled at Warsaw on the 23d held a meeting, at which there were patriotic speeches and music, and about forty names were added to the roll. On Monday, the 29th, the enrollment list, including the full complement of names, was forwarded to Albany. The officers named were G. H. Jenkins, captain; H. A. Dudley, first lieutenant; and A. M. Whaley, second lieutenant.

The alacrity with which the call for troops had been answered throughout the country was such that some delay was necessarily experienced in sending forward the companies that were so promptly raised, and organizing them in regiments. In many localities, and in Wyoming county among them, impatience began to be felt at this delay.

On the 20th of May, nearly a month after the company was filled, orders to move forward were received. A collation was served to the men by some kind hearted citizens, a Bible presented to each one by Rev. Dr. Nassau in behalf of the Wyoming County Bible Society, farewells and tearful leave takings were exchanged, and the volunteers moved to the railroad station, whence, in the presence of the thousands who had assembled to witness their departure, they were borne away. After a halt of two days in Albany they were ordered to New York, where they were assigned to the 17th regiment New York volunteers, under command of Colonel Lansing, of Albany.

In this county, as in all parts of the country, the departure of the first company of volunteers was an occasion of peculiar interest. It was the first time in the history of the country that the national existence had been threatened, and the patriotic feelings of every loyal citizen were roused into intense activity. It was the first general call which had been made upon the present generation for volunteers to serve in the field, and of course the first occasion on which the people had been called to bid adieu to fathers, sons or brothers, who took their lives in their hands for the defense of their country. They experienced a higher pride in the patriotism of their kindred and friends, and a more poignant grief at parting, than they felt on similar occasions afterwards; for the acuteness of these feelings was to some extent worn away by frequent exercise, and after the first departure less of idle curiosity was felt.

The brave volunteers of Wyoming county who left the comforts of their homes, their social and domestic pleasures, and who severed for the time the ties which linked them to their families and friends, to rally for the defense of the institutions under which they had been permitted to enjoy these comforts, pleasures, and affections; to face the stern realities of grim visaged war, to endure the hardships and privations of the field, to inhale the pestilential emanations from southern swamps, to languish in sickness and pain on pallets, "with no hand of kindred to smooth their lone pillows," and, too often, to find solitary graves where neither mother nor sister, wife nor children could come to "drop affection's tear," deserve a more minute history than the merits of this work will permit. They constituted parts of organizations the balance of which came from other regions, and their histories are inseparably connected with those of these organizations.

CHAPTER XVI.

HISTORIES OF THE TWENTY-FIRST AND TWENTY-SEVENTH NEW YORK INFANTRY.

THE following sketch of the 21st is compiled mainly from the third annual report of the Bureau of Military Record:

This regiment, called also the "first Buffalo regiment," was organized, accepted into the State service and numbered on the 13th of May, 1861. It was made up mostly from companies recruited from Buffalo, but Wyoming county was represented in it by Horace W. Jones, Arcade; William H. Boorman, Castile; Walter M. Fox, Orangeville; John Bump, James Bump, Job Bump, Charles M. Fox, Sheldon; Charles H. Littlebridge, Pike; George W. Bassett, Edwin P. Fanning, Horace Firman, Warsaw.

The regiment left Elmira on the 18th of June. On the 14th of July it moved into Virginia and was assigned to duty at Fort Runyon. There it was occupied in guard and camp duties and in drilling with the guns of the fort. September 28th it advanced to Upton Hill, where it expected to meet the enemy, but the place was deserted, and the formidable "cannon" on the breastworks were found to consist of a few pump logs and some old stovepipe on wheels—varieties of "quaker" guns. The regiment went into camp and erected a fort, which was named Fort Buffalo. At that place, and on the 15th of December, it went into winter quarters.

At the end of 1861 it was found that the regiment, which left Elmira with 754 men, had lost by discharge 80, and by death 4; and that it had gained by recruits 64, leaving it with a strength of 734.

On the 10th of March, 1862, it was in the reconnoisance in force towards Centreville, where it was found that the enemy had left their fortifications with the (quaker) guns mounted. Here General Patrick assumed command of the brigade, General Wadsworth, who had commanded, having been made military governor of the District of Columbia.

On the 15th the regiment returned to Alexandria, and from there went to what was appropriately termed "Camp Misery," where it enjoyed Virginia mud and Virginia weather during three weeks. On the 18th of April it, with McDowell's command, moved towards Richmond, encountering the enemy occasionally in light skirmishes. On the 19th of May it reached and crossed the Rappahannock and took up camp on Hazel Run, in the rear of Fredericksburg. On the 9th of August the regiment, with the division to which it was attached, left Fredericksburg under orders to join the corps at Culpepper, where the army, under General Pope, was concentrating. On the 14th it crossed Cedar Run and encamped, the army occupying both flanks of Cedar mountain to await the approach of Jackson. Here it remained till the 18th, when General Pope became satisfied that the enemy was preparing to advance in overwhelming numbers, and he determined to withdraw behind the Rappahannock. In the ensuing engagement the 21st regiment became exposed to the enemy's artillery and sharpshooters. The enemy withdrew across the river. The regiment then returned to a former position on the right to oppose an expected attempt of the enemy to cross a second time. Here, in the ravine in which it was stationed, it was exposed to a shower of projectiles. The order soon came to fall back, as it was discovered that the enemy had planted a new battery fully commanding the ravine. The movement of the regiment to the wood was executed in a masterly manner, and the day closed without the loss of a man.

August 26th the regiment reached Warrenton at dark. On the 27th it moved to the Sulphur Springs, encountered the enemy's pickets and lay all day between the contending artillery. On the 28th it moved toward Groveton, and was in the reserve in the engagement at that place in the evening. On the 29th and 30th it took part in the second battle of Bull Run, and formed the right of the line of battle at Chantilly September 1st. It fell back with the army and reached Upton's Hill on the night of the 2nd of September, 1862.

On the 14th the 21st took part in the battle of South Mountain, where it was engaged in the severe contest for the possession of the crest on the left of the ravine. It was deployed as skirmishers in this action, and went straight up the slope, drawing the fire of the enemy and revealing his position. On the 16th and 17th, at Antietam, it was on the right, under General Hooker, and fought valiantly during several hours.

It next took part in the battle of Fredericksburg, and at the end of 1863 was encamped at Cottage Grove, on the left flank of the army.

At the beginning of 1862 the regiment was 734 strong. At the end of the the same year there were present for duty 295.

On the 9th of January, 1863, the 21st was transferred to the command of General M. K. Patrick, for duty as provost guard of the army, and it continued in his command till it was sent home for discharge.

The regiment returned to Buffalo on the 11th of May, 1863. On the 21st a reorganization was authorized, but the authorization was revoked on the 30thof the next September.

TWENTY-SEVENTH REGIMENT INFANTRY.

The 27th regiment was organized at Elmira May 21st, 1861, to serve two years. It was composed of companies recruited in Orleans, Allegany, Livingston, Broome, Monroe, Wayne and Westchester counties. Wyoming county was represented by George Cady, William Fitch, Thomas C. Health, William F. Johnson, J. McDuffy, Atwood Preston, Simon Ray, Charles Rock, Harman Stannard, William E. Smith, Elias Smith and J. L. Smith.

The field officers were: colonel, Henry W. Slocum; lieutenant-colonel, Joseph J. Chambers; major, Joseph J. Bartlett.

The regiment was mustered in July 5th, 1861, at Elmira, and on the next day set out for Washington, where it arrived on the 11th. On the 16th it left Washington, and on the evening of the 18th encamped near Centreville. At 2 o'clock on the morning of Sunday, July 21st, it marched to the field of Bull Run, where it fought well under General Hunter and suffered severely.

It withdrew from the field in order, but when it encountered the rest of the army in a confused retreat it broke up, as did other regiments in the flight to Washington.

August 14th the 27th encamped near Alexandria, Va. There Colonel Slocum was promoted to the position of brigadier-general, Lieutenant-Colonel Chambers resigned, and Major Bartlett was made colonel, Captain Adams lieutenant-colonel, and Captain Gardner major.

September 12th the regiment commenced the work of building Fort Lyon. October 14th it went into winter quarters at Camp Clara, four miles north from Fort Lyon. April 17th, 1862, the division to which the 27th belonged embarked on transports, and on the afternoon of the 23d sailed to Fortress Monroe. On the 24th the regiment camped on a peninsula about seven miles from Yorktown.

May 5th the troops went up to the head of navigation on York river, and landed under cover of the gunboats, from which a few shots were fired, scattering the rebel cavalry and infantry that were skirmishing on the shore.

The 27th was the first to land. The enemy was near, and a line of battle was at once formed. Six companies were sent out as skirmishing pickets, and the other four acted as reserves. Picket firing at once commenced and was kept up during the night. The regiment sustained a loss of several killed and wounded, and succeeded in taking a few prisoners.

On the morning of the 7th of May, while the Union troops were at breakfast, they were surprised by the enemy. A severe engagement followed, in which the fighting was done in the midst of thick bushes. The enemy were finally driven back with the loss of one of their batteries. The Union troops lost between 100 and 200 killed and wounded.

On Thursday, May 22nd, a reconnoisance was made, in which this regiment participated. From that time forward until June 29th it was actively engaged, most of the time in skirmishing. On the afternoon of the 27th it crossed the

Chickahominy and participated in the battle of Gaines's Mills, losing 179 men in killed, wounded and missing.

Near Harrison's Landing the regiment remained some time, throwing up entrenchments. Shortly after began a retrograde movement toward Yorktown, and the regiment on the 21st day of August was at Newport News. There it embarked for Alexandria. From there it moved on to Manassas, and arrived just in time to cover the retreat of General Pope at the second Bull Run battle.

September 14th, the 27th was in an engagement at South Mountain, acting as skirmishers and routing a rebel battery. The regiment was engaged again on the 17th, at Antietam, but suffered no loss. In December the 27th marched to the fight at Fredericksburg, sharing in the terrible sacrifices made by the Union troops, and in the defeat. From this memorable field the regiment returned to camp at White Oak Church.

In the last week in April it was again engaged at Fredericksburg, under General Sedgwick, and soon afterward in the disastrous battle of Chancellorsville. After this the regiment guarded Banks's Ford until its term of service expired. The mustering out order, which was dated May 13th, 1863, and signed by Major-General Sedgwick, contained the following: "The general commanding the corps congratulates the officers and men of the 27th N. Y. volunteers upon their honorable return to civil life. They have enjoyed the respect and confidence of their commanders and companions. They have illustrated their term of service by gallant deeds, and have won for themselves a reputation not surpassed in the Army of the Potomac, and have nobly earned the gratitude of the Republic."

The regiment was mustered out at Elmira.

CHAPTER XVII.

THE NOBLE RECORD OF THE 17TH NEW YORK INFANTRY—THE DEATH OF CHARLES E. BILLS.

THE data for this sketch are gleaned from the report of the chief of the bureau of military record, the files of the *Western New Yorker* and the *Wyoming County Mirror*, from a diary kept by the late Orlando S. Smith, and other sources. This regiment, at first called also the "Westchester Chasseurs," was made up of companies that were recruited in various parts of the State. Westchester county furnished four, New York city two, Rockland, Chenango, and Wayne counties each one, and Company K represented Wyoming county. The following is a roll of this company at its organization:

COMPANY K.

Officers.—Gideon H. Jenkins, captain; H. A. Dudley, first lieutenant; Alvin M Whaley, second lieutenant. Sergeants—Charles V. Jenkins, Warsaw; Edwin H. Beardsley, Warsaw; Adelbert H. Jenkins, Warsaw; Joseph W. Morey, Wyoming. Corporals—Frank S. Austin, Perry; Charles J. Watkins, Warsaw; Lucien H. Post, Perry; Oscar Nicholson, Warsaw.

Privates—Charles H. Agar, George Armstrong, George Baker, Riley R. Baker, Galusha W. Blowers, John R. Brown, Homer C. Curtis, Eugene Edson, William Fisk, Miles P. Fowler, Sumner Gill, Willard L. Hitchcock, Edward Harty, Jason M. Johnson, Frank H. Johnson, Lucien P. Knapp, Thomas E. Knapp, Frank Lamphire, Charles W. Lewis, Ira Lounsbury, Ellis Luther, jr., George F. Martin, Jesse J. Mattocks, Adelbert Mosier, Samuel R. Munger, William Parker, Charles A. Patridge, William Poland, George Reynick, John T. Reynick, Daniel Starks, James A. Smith, Wilber H. Snyder, America M. Turner, James Tyler, William H. Walker, Alfred Watrous, Morris Warren, Romanzo L. Wilkin, William B. Young, Warsaw; Charles Bills, Henry Cronkhite, Thomas Durfee, Henry C. Ferris, William Hodge, Solon G. Ripley, Orlando S. Smith, Walter C. Tillotson, Otto Warner, Middlebury; William P. Bovie, Martin H. Carpenter, Frank Graves, Lafayette K. Hastings, Henry Rice, Devello Sheffield, Arthur E. Thorpe, Edwin R. Wood, Gainesville; George A. Armour, David Jones, Albert Lewis, Augustus Satyr, Henry Stroemer, Henry Schneider, Orangeville; Michael Metzger, Nicholas Smith, Sheldon; Alton P. Beardsley, Oscar Ayres, Perry; Mansor Dunbar, Origen Dunnell, John Etwell, Alson Peet, Wethersfield; William R. Benchley, Dale; Jacob Darrow, York; Giles Gilbert, Pike; William A. Houghton, La Grange; Samuel Houghton, Fredonia.

Henry S. Lansing was appointed colonel of this regiment, Thomas J. Morris lieutenant-colonel, and Charles A. Johnson major. Company K was mustered into the United States service on the 25th of May, 1861, and the regiment was mustered on the 28th.

It is perhaps due to the regiment to speak of the claim which its officers put forth for it: that recruiting for it began on the 16th of April and ended on the 5th of May, 1861; that it was numbered successively 9, 11 and 17, and its organization delayed by the action of the State military board for reasons that were then deemed sufficient; that the headquarters of the regiment was established at the corner of Rector street and Broadway, New York, in a store, the rent of which ($12,000 per annum) was paid by the Union Defense Committee; that it occupied the City Hall barracks during about six weeks without uniforms, and was then moved (June 15th) to Camp Washington, Staten Island.

It left Staten Island on the 21st of June, and proceeded, *via* New Jersey, Harrisburg and Baltimore, to Washington, where it arrived on the 23d. The expenditure by the Union Defense Committee up to August 16th, 1861, was $22,351.58. The State expended for the regiment, exclusive of quarters and subsistence, $41,983.22.

On their arrival at Washington the troops went into camp about two miles west from the city. They remained at that camp, perfecting themselves in military drill, till July 14th, when they went to Alexandria and encamped about two miles above the city, near Fort Ellsworth. At that place Company K was detailed on its first duty—that of guarding military stores on the dock. They were placed temporarily in the second brigade of the fifth division, and shared in the movements of the reserve at the "reconnoisance in force," and battle of Bull Run.

The regiment went to Fairfax Seminary in September, and participated in a reconnoisance to Mason's Hill. It went to Hall's Hill in October, where it went into camp, and there spent the winter of 1861-2. Soon after its arrival at that camp, which was called Camp Butterfield, in honor of General Butterfield, to whose brigade they were assigned, the men received Sibley tents in place of the A tents that were first given to them, and in the following February the smooth-bore muskets that they originally received were exchanged for Springfield rifles.

On the 12th of the following March (1862) the regiment left Camp Butterfield and went with its brigade on a reconnoisance. It stopped at Fairfax Seminary, from which place it moved on the 21st to Alexandria, and went on board the steamer "Knickerbocker." The following entries appear on Smith's diary:

"March 23d, 1862.—In the Chesapeake Bay. Pleasant. Saw the 'Monitor,' the iron gunboat that had a fight with the 'Merrimac.' Left the boat about dark. Passed Old Point Comfort, and we are lying on the ground. 'Knickerbocker' sprung a leak so we had to leave her.

"Monday, March 24th.—Arose and moved about sunrise about one mile and pitched our tents. Had dress parade at 6 P. M. Pleasant day. Passed through the village of Hampton—now in ruins, having been burned by the enemy to prevent the Union men from having winter quarters there."

On the 25th they moved about four miles and camped in the woods. On the 26th they went to Wall's Creek on a reconnoisance, discovered the enemy in force, and returned with one prisoner. On the 27th the force went to Big Bethel on a reconnoisance, which the diary describes thus:

"Thursday, March 27th.— * * * Arrived at Great Bethel at noon. The enemy fled before us. Marched in line of battle across the flat up to the enemy's breast-works, and placed the stars and stripes on the first fortification. Returned to camp, the distance said to be ten miles. The sharpshooters shot two rebels."

April 4th they moved toward Yorktown, and on the 5th marched nine miles and reached the scene of active operations in the siege. Under this date the diary say: "Marched soon after sunrise. Halted about noon to leave our knap-sacks and prepare for a fight. Pitched our tents in sight of the enemy's batteries; exchanging shots freely now, while I write and rest with my knee for a desk."

The regiment remained at this siege, engaged in picket and fatigue duty, with occasional drill, during about a month. On the 3d of May the rebels evacuated Yorktown. The diary says: "Sunday, May 4th. The 44th went out to work and saw our flag on the enemy's parapet. Went over and found our men in possession. Several had been killed by torpedoes that they had stepped on (which had been left by the enemy). Got a good many prisoners. Our flying artillery and cavalry in pursuit."

On the 8th the regiment passed through Yorktown and embarked on the steamer "S. R. Spaulding" for West Point, whence, two or three days afterward, it went to Cumberland. The roads had been obstructed with fallen trees, and the woods set on fire; and during the severe march the men were obliged to remove the obstructions and labor to extinguish the fires. They remained one day at Cumberland and marched to White House. The regiment then moved and made its camp on Gaines's farm, on the Chickahominy. Nothing noteworthy occurred till, on the 27th, the regiment moved with the brigade for the purpose of attacking the enemy at Hanover Court-house. After a tiresome march of about fourteen miles, the enemy was encountered about two miles from the court-house, where the road joins Ashland, with a guideboard marked "To Richmond seven miles—to Port Green Church two miles." There, according to a correspondent, a brilliant charge was made by the 17th, and a howitzer captured and turned on its late possessors. The enemy were completely routed, and after the regiment had spent a short time going through their abandoned camp it proceeded to the court-house. A sharp and vigorous attack on the rear of the division was repulsed, and the victory was complete. The next day the regiment went down the railroad and burned some bridges, and returned to its camp on the Gaines farm on the 29th. It remained in this camp, occupied with the usual details of fatigue and picket duty, till June 22nd, when it moved six miles back.

According to the third report of the bureau of military record the regiment remained in camp until the 26th of June, when it marched to Old Church. While there the battle of Gaines Mills was fought (June 27th). This regiment, being in the rear, was cut off from the main army, and under General Stoneman retreated toward the White House. The distance was twenty-two miles, and the march one of great suffering. Says a correspondent: "History will not record a more hasty, timely, or terrible march than this by such worn out and fatigued men. Many fell fainting by the roadside and recovered at their leisure. The last few miles was positively awful. The colonel, a good brave man, rode bareheaded down the rapidly decimating ranks and exclaimed, 'Men, it is hard, but if you do this to-day your country will not, cannot be ungrateful.' We accomplished it; and as I looked at my blistered and swollen feet, I thought painfully of other days. The result was, as had been anticipated by General McClellan when he ordered Stoneman to fall back to White House if cut off, the movement of the enemy in that direction was anticipated, the stores removed or destroyed, and the regiment and other forces then embarked on the gunboats. On the 30th the gunboats sailed for Fortress Monroe.

"The regiment reached Yorktown on the 1st of July, and there passed from the gunboat to the steamer 'Cattskill,' subsequently to the tugboat 'Adriatic,' and from the latter to the steamer 'Kennebeck,' and sailed for Harrison's Landing, where it arrived on the 2nd. It remained in camp at Harrison's Landing until the evacuation. In this time its camp was exposed to the artillery of the enemy in the attack of the 30th and one man killed; and it was detailed on duty on the opposite bank of the James in cutting down timber and patrolling the country. On the 14th of August it moved at midnight, and reached and crossed the Chickahominy, continued the march on the 15th, and passed Williamsburg; on the 16th reached Yorktown; on the 17th marched seventeen miles, and from thence to Newport News. This was a very severe march, and will be long remembered by those who participated in it."

From Newport News the regiment was transferred by water to Aquia creek. On the morning of the 21st it went to Fredericksburg by railroad, and from thence marched up the Rapidan to Warrenton and Manassas, and opened the fight at Groveton on the 30th. Says a correspondent: "When the enemy made their sudden and powerful advance toward our center on Saturday, Porter's corps was ordered up to meet the attack. Butterfield's brigade was sent forward—the 17th N. Y. having the advance. They marched up the hill amid the fierce leaden hail as if it had been but a pleasant summer shower. On they went, and fiercer and hotter was the fire. First a battery on the right and another on the left opened and poured a devastating fire into their devoted ranks, but they never wavered. Faithfully did they ply their trusty muskets, and held their position. Officers who witnessed the scene describe it as most terrific. Storm upon storm of bullets, grape shot, screaming shell, and pieces of railroad iron were hurled into, through and over them. Thus they stood, their ranks being thinned at every discharge. The enemy suffered too, and quickly sought the cover of the woods. At length came the order to fall back, it having been found impossible to reinforce them. The line was still preserved, and at the command they moved off steadily and coolly, although the dreadful fire of the enemy never ceased for one moment. The colors were shot into shreds, both flagstaffs were shot in pieces by grape shot, and three color bearers were shot down. Out of 350 men that went into this charge, 13 officers and 250 men were killed or wounded. Captains Wilson, Blauvelt and Demarest, and Lieutenant Reid were among the killed; and Major T. C. Grover, at that time in command of the regiment, acting Adjutant Sprague and Captains Burleigh, Martin and Foley, and Lieutenants Green and Morey were among the wounded—Major Grover wounded in four places.

"The regiment fell back with the army to Fairfax, Chain Bridge, Long Bridge and Alexandria; and from thence moved to Fairfax Seminary and Hall's Hill. On the 12th of September it started on the Maryland campaign, passed through Georgetown and Washington, and by railroad to within five miles of Rockville; on the 13th passed through Rockville and took the road to Frederick; on the 14th reached Frederick; on the 15th to the vicinity of South Mountain; on the 16th to the vicinity of the battle ground of Antietam. During this movement Porter's corps was in the reserve and was not engaged, although an occasional shell reached its position. On the 18th the regiment moved to Sharpsburg, and thence to Antietam Iron Works. Here it was engaged in picketing the Potomac and in camp duties until the 30th of October, when it moved in the direction of Harper's Ferry; passed through that place on the 31st to the Blue Mountains; on the 2nd of November moved on the Leesburg turnpike to Woodgrove, and then struck the road to the right in the direction of Snickersville, and came up with and relieved Sumner's corps, who were holding Snicker's Gap; remained at Snicker's Gap until the 6th, and then moved on the Alexandria road toward Middleburg; moved on the 7th, but was compelled to bivouac in consequence of a severe snow-storm: on the 8th followed the Orange and Alexandria railroad to New Baltimore, and from thence to Warrenton Junction, and followed the track toward Fredericksburg; 18th, continued on the march, and also on the 19th, and camped; on the 24th camped a short distance from the railroad at Falmouth."

The regiment remained in camp until the 11th of December, when it moved with the brigade in the advance on Fredericksburg. It crossed the river in the evening, participated in the movements of the brigade, and returned on the 16th with one officer (Adjutant Wilson) killed, and two officers and four men wounded. It remained in camp until the "mud march" on January 20th. From this march it returned on the 24th, and went into permanent winter quarters.

On the 27th of April, 1863, the regiment started on the Chancellorsville campaign. It arrived on the enemy's flank on the 1st of May. On the 2nd it threw up breastworks, and on the 3d was in action, but not heavily engaged; remained in position on the 4th, and at about 2 A. M. on the 5th moved toward United States Ford, covered the retreat and was the last to cross. It reached camp at Falmouth on the 6th. On the 18th it left camp for New York, where it was mustered out on the 22nd.

On the 3d of June Major W. T. C. Grover received authority to reorganize the regiment. Under this authorization a very considerable number of the members who returned with it re-enlisted for three years. The reorganization was finally effected by the consolidation with it of recruits for the 9th regiment, the 38th regiment N. Y. S. V., and the "Union Sharpshooters." It left the State in October, 1863, officered by a majority of its old officers, and by officers formerly of the 9th, and composed almost entirely of veterans. It was ordered to the Department of the Southwest, joined the army under General Sherman, and served under him until it left the field.

The movements of the regiment in the Department of the Southwest may be briefly stated. On the 21st of December, 1863, under A. J. Smith, it began the Tennessee campaign after Forrest, losing, principally by severe frosts, about 200 men (many losing the use of both hands and feet, while there was scarcely an officer or man but was more or less frostbitten), and joining General Sherman at Vicksburg January 24th, 1864. Under that general it made the Mississippi or Meriden campaign, leaving Vicksburg on the 2nd of February and marching more than four hundred and sixty miles. In April it moved to Decatur, Ala., where for thirty-three days it had skirmishes with the forces of General Roddy almost as regularly as reveille call. It subsequently attacked Roddy at Pond Spring, Courtland, etc., routed his forces, and captured the whole of his camp an garrison, equipage, baggage, horses, etc. At Atlanta it was in the trenches. At Jonesboro it charged and fought Clayborne's "invincible" Texas Rangers, who boasted never to have been defeated, but who were then broken, routed, and had their works taken from them. Here Colonel Grover was killed, and 101 of its men left on the field. From Atlanta it participated in the Hood campaign in the rear of the army, and marched more than 600 miles. It returned to Atlanta at night, and started the next morning without preparation on Sherman's grand march to the sea. On the march from Savannah to the Carolinas it engaged the enemy at Averysboro, and had its lieutenant-colonel commanding, James Lake, wounded, and Captain Wm. G. Barnett killed. The last engagement was at Bentonville, where it cut its way through the lines of the enemy when surrounded by the falling back of the first division.

After the surrender of General Johnston the regiment marched to Washington, took part in the review of General Sherman's army, and was soon afterwards mustered out of service. It reached New York on the 16th of June, 1865, bearing with it testimonials from the officers commanding the 1st brigade, the 2nd division, and of the 14th army corps; the first asserting that: "In all the essential qualities which distinguish the heroic citizen-soldier, the 17th New York has been excelled by none. Representatives as you are of the great city of New York, your association with the men of the Northwest, composing the balance of the brigade, has been of the most pleasing and genial kind"; the second, that "the general will always remember with pride its gallant bravery in the charge at Jonesboro, and in the battles of Averysboro and Bentonville"; and the last, that "its soldierly conduct, attention to duty, and invariably gallant conduct in action, has reflected credit upon itself and the corps."

The following was related by a fellow soldier of Charles E. Bills, of the Wyoming company in this regiment. It has been extensively published, but it is worthy of a place here:

"I was in the hospital as nurse for a long time, and assisted in taking off limbs and dressing all sorts of wounds; but the hardest thing I ever did was to take my thumb off a man's leg.

"It was a young man who had a severe wound in the thigh. The ball passed completely through, and amputation was necessary. The limb was cut off close to the body, the arteries taken up, and he seemed to be doing well. Subsequently one of the small arteries sloughed off. An incision was made and it was again taken up. 'It is well it was not the main artery,' said the surgeon as he performed the opertion; 'he might have bled to death before it could be taken up.' But Charley got on finely, and was a favorite with us all.

"I was passing through the ward one night, about midnight, when suddenly, as I was passing Charley's bed, he spoke to me: 'H—, my leg is bleeding again.' I threw back the bed clothes, and the blood spurted in the air. The main artery had sloughed off!

"Fortunately, I knew just what to do, and in an instant I had pressed my thumb on the place and stopped the bleeding. It was so close to the body that there was barely room for my thumb, but I succeeded in keeping it there, and, arousing one of the convalescents, sent him for the surgeon, who came in on the run. 'I am so thankful, H—,' said he as he saw me, 'that you were here and knew what to do, for he must have bled to death before I could have got here.

"But on examination of the case he looked exceedingly serious, and sent out for other surgeons. All came who were within reach, and a consultation was held over the poor fellow. One conclusion was reached by all. There was no place to work save the spot where my thumb was placed; they could not work under my thumb, and if I moved it he would bleed to death before the artery could be taken up. There was no way to save his life.

"Poor Charley! He was very calm when they told him, and requested that his brother, who was in the same hospital, might be called up. He came and sat down by the bedside, and for three hours I stood and by the pressure of my thumb kept up the life of Charley, while the brothers held their last conversation on earth. It was a strange place for me to be in, to feel that I held the life of a fellow mortal in my hands, as it were, and stranger yet to feel that an act of mine must cause that life to depart. Loving the poor fellow as I did, it was a hard thought; but there was no alternative.

"The last words were spoken. Charley had arranged all his business affairs, and sent tender messages to absent ones, who little dreamed how near their loved one stood to the grave. The tears filled my eyes more than once as I listened to those parting words. All were said, and he turned to me. 'Now, H—, I guess you had better take off your thumb! 'O, Charley, how can I? said I. 'But it must be, you know,' he replied, cheerfully. 'I thank you very much for your kindness, and now good-bye.'

"He turned away his head; I raised my thumb; once more the life current gushed forth, and in three minutes poor Charley was dead."

CHAPTER XVIII.

FIFTH NEW YORK CAVALRY, OR "FIRST IRA HARRIS GUARD"— "ELLSWORTH'S AVENGERS."

EARLY in the Rebellion, both in numbers and effectiveness, the cavalry of the rebels was far superior to that of the Union forces. Having been made aware of this deficiency, the military authorities at once set about the work of supplying it. On the 26th of July, 1861, the Secretary of War authorized Colonel Othniel De Forest, of New York city, to raise a regiment of cavalry, and by the last of September of that year he had gathered on Staten Island the nucleus of a cavalry brigade. From his recruits Colonel De Forest organized the 5th N. Y. cavalry, which was called the "First Ira Harris Guard," in honor of Senator Ira Harris, of Albany, under whose patronage the organization was accomplished. The men of this regiment were largely furnished from New York city, though companies and parts of companies were raised in

Wyoming, Allegany, Essex, Tioga and Orange counties, and a few men came from Massachusetts, Connecticut and New Jersey. Wyoming county was represented in this regiment by the men named below:

> Merrit D. Chaffee, G. L. Platt, E. D. Tolles, Luke S. Williams, Attica; George D. Rathbun, Castile; Charles Whitney, Eagle; Wesley Barnard, Thomas Donlin, William E. Briggs, John W. Barnard, Wilson Cummings, Joseph Coggon, Peter Freeman, P. A. Graves, Franklin S. Huestis, William D. Lucas, James H. Rice, Charles B. Thomas, Gainesville; Alfred W. Nourse, Genesee Falls; Horace Aiken, Joseph D. Axtel, Milton Bennet, George W. Dodge, Samuel Falson, Lucius Griffith, Martin Granger, William Pickett, Dwight Patridge, John Smith, George W. Wells, William H. Wells, Willis Washington Wheeler, Pike; William Hutton, Asa A. Luther, Warsaw.

No bounties were then paid to recruits, and a bounty of only $100 was promised to be paid by the government at the expiration of the term of service.

On Staten Island the regiment was quartered in what are termed A tents, and the place was called "Camp Scott," in honor of the veteran who was then closing his active military labors. The first and second battalions received their horses during the month of October, and began to receive instructions in mounted drill. On the 31st of the same month the regiment was inspected for the first time by Lieutenant-Colonel D. B. Sackett, of the United States army. At that time the last company had been mustered in, and the command numbered 1,064 men besides the officers. On this day of inspection the regiment was mustered for pay, and on the 6th of November was paid. That time the men were paid in gold and silver, but they were not again encumbered with the precious metals.

On Monday, November 11th, the regiment was presented with two beautiful flags, one by the Common Council of the city of New York, and the other by Misses Kate Harris and Mary F. Blake. The presentation speech was made by Senator Harris.

The regiment left its rendezvous on the 18th of November and arrived at Baltimore on the 19th. While it was here the 3d battalion drew horses and equipments, and on the 25th the regiment made its first march, from Baltimore to Annapolis. On the 28th it pitched its tents about three miles from the city, at a place which was named, in honor of its patron, Camp Harris. In this camp it remained till the last day of March, 1862, when it broke camp and prepared for the realities of field service.

During the month following it was almost constantly on the move, but was not engaged in any fight. On the 6th of May, about four miles from Harrisonburg, the rebel colonel Turner Ashby was encountered, and a sharp engagement ensued. The rebel force consisted of picked cavalrymen, and the quality of the 5th was tested for the first time. In the conflict one man was killed, two wounded, and one, Sergeant William H. Whitcomb, taken prisoner. He effected his escape, however, before leaving the field.

May 12th the 5th had a skirmish with the enemy at Woodstock, and on the 21st General Hatch, with about 150 of the regiment, made a successful attack on Ashby's forces, driving them many miles, and killing, wounding and capturing several, without the loss of a man.

About this time Company H, which had been in the Luray Valley with General Sullivan, and had been engaged in quite a number of skirmishes, rejoined the regiment.

On the 23d of May, 1862, General Banks received information, through messengers of the 5th, that a sudden attack had been made by Stonewall Jackson on Colonel Kenley's force at Front Royal. Companies B and D of the 5th were sent to Colonel Kenley, and arrived just as the rebels came upon the garrison from the hills and down the valley.

The cavalry charged them in a gallant manner, but were compelled to retire because they were greatly outnumbered, flanked, and almost surrounded. In this charge the gallant young officer Lieutenant Dwyer, of Company B, was mortally wounded, and Captain A. H. White, of Company D, and Adjutant Griffin were taken prisoners.

The valley was at that time cleared of Union troops, and the rebels began to throw their forces across the Blue Ridge to attack the main Union army in front of Washington; leaving only a strong picket line at the foot of the valley opposed to the Union army in Maryland. The 5th regiment, which had been divided in the retreat, advanced from Harper's Ferry and from Williamsport. The former column met the enemy at Charlestown and repulsed them; and the latter advanced on Martinsburg, drove the pickets through the town, captured several prisoners, a wagon, muskets, ammunition and an American flag. They also recaptured several of the officers and men lost at Front Royal, and among them Adjutant Griffin.

This encouraging advance took place May 31st. On the 4th of June the regiment advanced to Winchester, where its fragments were reunited. Companies B and D, however, which had distinguished themselves at Front Royal, were detached from the regiment to serve on a battery.

Nothing noteworthy occurred after that till the 6th of July. On that day a squad of cavalry was encountered at Sperryville, and the 5th was victorious in the fight. July 8th the regiment engaged in a skirmish with the enemy at Culpepper Court-house and drove them through the town, capturing fifteen prisoners. On the 17th the 5th had a skirmish at Orange Court-house, and on the 18th it returned to Rapidan Ford. A large portion of Company A was captured while doing picket duty at Barnett's Ford.

On the 2nd of August the regiment was engaged in a brisk battle at Orange Court-house, under General Crawford. The rebels were driven back with a loss of 50 prisoners, including a major, a chaplain and two lieutenants.

On the 17th of August, 1862, detachments from the 5th N. Y. cavalry and the 1st Michigan, under Colonel Brodhead, went to Louisa Court-house and captured General Stewart's adjutant-general and several important dispatches.

On the 20th of August the regiment advanced to Kelley's Ford, and in a general engagement there acted as support to a battery which was exposed to a terrible fire. On the 24th it participated in a severe engagement at Waterloo bridge, but suffered little loss. On October 20th the regiment was ordered to do picket duty at Chantilly, and it continued to picket and patrol the country till the 28th, when it went to Centreville, and the next day to Manassas Junction and back to Chantilly.

During the month of November the regiment was engaged in picketing and scouting. On the 29th the men of the 5th, in command of Captain Krom, of Company H, went with an expedition under General Stahl into the Shenandoah valley. On their arrival at Snicker's Ferry, on the Shenandoah, the rebels annoyed them by firing from houses beyond the river, but they were soon attacked and defeated with a loss of two lieutenants, thirty-two privates, one stand of colors and several wagons, one of which was laden with tents and provisions. On the 30th the expedition returned to Chantilly. After the close of the campaign of 1862 the 5th made its camp at Germantown, and spent the winter in picketing and scouting. During this time Mosby's guerrillas gave much trouble, and on the 23d of March, 1863, they gave the regiment a lively chase, inflicting on it serious injury. April 21st it received a new and beautiful flag, which was presented by the city of New York. On the 3d of May the 5th engaged in another hand-to-hand fight with the Mosby cavalry, in which it defeated the enemy and captured twenty-three wounded men. May 30th it had a sharp but short contest with Mosby's men again, and took from them a twelve-pound howitzer. June 30th, while the regiment was at Hanover, Va., it met the rebel cavalry under General Stewart, in a hand-to-hand conflict, in which it lost 9 men killed, 31 wounded, and a few prisoners. The rebels were routed with heavy loss. In this engagement Adjutant Gall was killed.

A volume of history would be required to follow this gallant regiment through all its marches, campings and conflicts, until the close of its term of service. Indeed, a history of the regiment was written by Rev. Louis N. Boudrye, chaplain of the regiment, which is in book form. It is but justice to the author to state that this sketch was compiled from his work.

In July, 1863, the regiment won a series of victories over Stewart's cavalry. Its most important engagement in the campaign of that year was on the 11th of October, at Brandy Station.

The regiment had its quarters for the winter of 1863–4 at a point known as "Devil's Leap."

February 28th, 1864, a detachment of the 5th accompanied Colonel Ulric Dahlgren on his raid to Richmond. The purpose of this was to release Union officers and men confined in prisons there, and to destroy the mills, workshops, materials, stores and public property of the rebels in that city and vicinity, and to cut off their railroad communications. In this expedition fifteen of the regiment were captured; the others returned March 12th.

To the 5th was accorded the honor of opening the battle of the Wilderness, May 5th, but it paid dearly for this honor, for it lost heavily. Subsequently it shared the varying fortunes of the Army of the Potomac, until the close of the war.

In the history written by Mr. Boudrye one hundred and seventy-two distinct engagements or fights in which the regiment participated are mentioned. Of these, one hundred and nineteen were termed skirmishes.

The regiment numbered when it left for the war, 1,064 men. While in the service 5 officers were killed, 22 were seriously wounded, 19 were made prisoners, 4 died of disease, 10 were dismissed by court-martial, 5 discharged, and 37 resigned; 75 enlisted men were killed or mortally wounded, 236 were seriously wounded, 517 were captured, 114 died in rebel prisons, and 90 died of disease. Only 167 of the original veterans remained when the regiment was mustered out in July, 1865. The commanders of the regiment during its term of service were Othniel De Forest, John Hammond, and Amos H. White.

FORTY-FOURTH N. Y. VOLUNTEER INFANTRY.

The 44th New York volunteer infantry was organized at Albany early in the autumn of 1861. It was more commonly called "the Ellsworth regiment," or "Ellsworth's Avengers," having been raised by an association which sought in this way to honor the memory of one of the most conspicuous of the early victims of the war for the Union, as well as to powerfully promote the objects of the war. It was also sometimes called "the people's regiment," from its consisting of picked men from all over the State, of exceptional character and physique.

The field and staff officers (nominated by the association's committee) were: Stephen W. Stryker, colonel; James C. Rice, lieutenant-colonel; James McKown, major; William Frothingham, surgeon; Charles L. Bissel, assistant surgeon; Loomis H. Pease, chaplain; Edward B. Knox, adjutant; and Frederick R. Mundy, quartermaster.

After receiving a beautiful flag from Mrs. Erastus Corning, and being reviewed by Governor Morgan and a committee of the Ellsworth Association, the regiment left Albany for the front on the 21st of October, 1,061 strong. A week later it encamped at Hall's Hill, Va., near Washington.

The following winter the 44th did picket duty along the Leesburg turnpike. On the 21st of March, 1862, it sailed from Alexandria for Fortress Monroe, whence on the 1st of April it marched for Yorktown.

After garrisoning Fort Magruder, the 44th left that post on the 15th of May, and a few days after set out for Gaines's Mill, on the expedition to Hanover Court-house. On the 27th it bore a leading part in the sanguinary battle at that place, holding the field with the 2nd Maine against superior numbers, and suffering terrible loss. The 44th, having exhausted its ammunition, was on the point of charging when reinforcements arrived. The regiment lost 30 killed and 70 wounded. Its flag was pierced by more than forty balls and four times shot down. The enemy were finally routed.

During the next month the 44th did picket duty along the Chickahominy, and on the 27th was engaged in the battle of Gaines's Mill. An extemporized earthwork thrown up and defended by this regiment on the Union left proved the salvation of that part of the line.

The Ellsworth men were next in action at Turkey Bend, and next came the battle of Malvern Hill, July 21st. It is recorded that in the charge of the 44th in this action "Colonel Rice halted his men four times under the fire of the enemy, and as carefully 'aligned' them as though they had been on a dress parade. He charged a brigade of rebels, took their colors and more prisoners than he brought men of his own alive out of the charge."

In August, 1862, the 44th fought in the second Bull Run battle, coming out of it only 87 muskets strong. It was held in reserve at Antietam, and was actively engaged at Shepardston Ford. After a variety of camping and marching experiences the regiment found itself in the battle of Fredericksburg, December 13th, under a destructive fire.

On the 30th of April, 1863, the regiment led the advance of the Army of the Potomac to Chancellorsville. After a large part of the line had been driven in by "Stonewall" Jackson in the battle of the 2nd of May, Couch's corps, with the 44th N. Y. on the right, repulsed his repeated assaults, inflicting fearful loss upon the rebels.

The next fighting was at Middleburg, June 21st, and the next at Gettysburg, July 2nd, when the 44th lost 111 killed and wounded, among the former Captain Larrabee and Lieutenant Dunham. In November the regiment fought at Rappahannock Station and Mine Run.

The 44th bore itself gallantly and conspicuously in Grant's Virginia campaign of 1864; beginning with the Wilderness on the 5th of May, where it lost 60 killed and wounded in half an hour, but bravely held the ground. On the 7th it fought at Spottsylvania Court-house, receiving a repulse after a gallant and bloody struggle.

It fought with its accustomed bravery at North Anna, Bethesda Church and Petersburg in May and June, and last on the Weldon Railroad, in August. September 24th it was mustered out and left for home, reaching Albany on the 29th, where it was honored with a brilliant reception, Governor Seymour delivering an address. But 14 officers and 170 enlisted men returned.

CHAPTER XIX.

HISTORY OF THE ONE HUNDRED AND FOURTH NEW YORK INFANTRY.

IN the autumn of 1861 a regiment was recruited, with its rendezvous at Geneseo, Livingston county, N. Y., under Colonel John Rorbach. In this regiment Wyoming county was represented by the following named men:

Ezra Billings, Earl L. Gitchell, Charles Hall, James L. Quackenbush, Hiram L. Wing, Charles Wing, Castile; James William Dow, Alvin Jeffers, Wilson Wolcott, Covington; William Aiken, Andrew Andrus, Daniel Catten, Gilbert Grey, George W. Helmer, Ira Parker, Joseph L. Phillips, Seymour Phillips, Gilbert G. Prey, Austin N. Richardson, James Richardson, Sydney Richardson, Eugene Sparks, John W. Tabor, Levi Van Acker, Nelson J. Wing, Stephen L. Wing, Eagle; L. Brainard, George Flint, Nelson Hicks, John McGure, Gainesville; Charles Barber, William Thomas, George Thomas, Java; John Westbrook, George Westbrook, Orson Wolcott, Perry; George S. Adams, Ortillus Beardesley, Edwin E. Barnes, Lyman Bunnell, Henry O. Besancon, Derrick J. Bush, Frank S. Bates, Ceylon Clarke, Yohst Cain, Rensselaer Dunning, Emery N. Emery, James Farrell, Jasher M. Griggs, Orange C. Gardner, Norval Halstead, Newton Rent, Daniel Russel, Judson A. Rose, Wiley Streeter, Beriah Sparks, Cyrenus Streeter, Henry Spencer, Oliver G. Smith, Sherman Streeter, Cooley H. Thomas, Horace Thomas, David Uter, William Willis, Isaac Whiting, Abram Whiting, Hall Whiting, Pike; and Algeroy Aiken and Sullivan Gibson, Warsaw.

It was first called the Wadsworth Guards, in honor of General James Wadsworth, of Geneseo. On the 26th of February, 1862, it was ordered to Albany, N. Y., to prepare for the field. On its arrival at Albany the ten companies of which it was composed—some of which were mere skeletons—were consolidated into seven; and a skeleton regiment then recruiting at Troy was consolidated into three companies and added to it, making a full regiment, which was numbered the 104th. The lieutenant-colonelcy of the regiment was accorded to the last three companies.

The regimental officers and captains originally were: colonel, John Rorbach; lieutenant-colonel, R. Wells Kenyon; major, L. C. Skinner; adjutant, F. T. Vance; quartermaster, Henry V. Colt; Company A, Captain Tuthill; Company B, Captain Day; Company C, Captain Wing; Company D, Captain Simpson; Company E, Captain Latimer; Company F, Captain Prey; Company G, Captain Gault; Company H, Captain Sellick; Company I, Captain McCaffry.

About the middle of March the regiment was ordered to Washington, D. C., and encamped on Kalorama Hill, just without the city, where it was attached to General Duryea's brigade, General Pickett's division, and soon after ordered to Cloud's Mills, Va., about six miles from Alexandria; thence to Catlett's Station, farther up the valley. From there it was ordered to Thoroughfare Gap, in the Bull Run Mountains, to support General Geary. After doing picket duty and scouting a day or two, General Geary's forces were ordered to Manassas, thence to Waterloo and thence to Slaughter Mountain, to support General Banks. There the regiment was first brought under fire. With the rest of the troops it fell back on Bull Run at the time of the second battle there. On the retreat to Centreville it was engaged in the fight at Chantilly, where General Kearney was killed.

With the rest of the Army of the Potomac it took up its march, after guarding the capital a few days, to intercept the confederate forces on their march toward Pennsylvania. They were engaged in the battles of South Mountain and Antietam, which were fought in September, 1862. After these they remained in camp till the latter part of October, when they resumed march, crossed the river at Berlin, passed through Virginia to Fredericksburg, and took part in the battle at that place on the 12th and 13th of December. They remained and held the ground a few days after the battle, then recrossed the river and went into winter quarters at Belle Plain. During the month of January, 1863, they took a part in General Burnside's celebrated mud campaign, from which they returned and remained in their quarters till the spring campaign opened with a simultaneous attack on Fredericksburg and Chancellorsville.

The 104th, with its division, marched to the river just below Fredericksburg, with the intention of crossing, but they were ordered to Chancellorsville, where the main army had been two days engaged, crossed the river and pushed on to the front. There they advanced on the road leading to Ely's Ford, where the 104th, with a company of skirmishers in front, advanced by moonlight a mile in front of the Union line, threw out a picket and awaited orders. They were soon ordered back to the lines, where they threw up breastworks. The next day they were sent forward to nearly the same position they occupied in the night. Here they remained during the day, and at about sunset had a brisk skirmish with the enemy, whom they repulsed.

The next march of the regiment was to Thoroughfare Gap to prevent the enemy from coming through. He was found in possession of the Gap and an unsuccessful attempt was made to dislodge him. This was the northward movement of the confederate forces for the invasion of Pennsylvania, and soon afterward they were encountered at Gettysburg, where the 104th, with its corps, met and engaged the advance at Sumner's Hill, half a mile west from the town, on the 1st day of July, 1863. In this day's action, which lasted till 5 P. M., the regiment lost in killed and wounded just one-half the number of men it contained in the morning. Seven color bearers were killed. As often as one fell another grasped the flag and kept it floating. Colonel Prey commanded the brigade in this action, he being the senior officer present. During the fighting of the next two days the division to which the 104th belonged was kept marching from point to point to strengthen weak places in the Union lines. At the close of the second day they were marched at double quick to save the cannon of the second corps, all the artillery horses of which were lost. The enemy was driven back and the pieces brought off the field at about dark.

The next march of the 104th was in pursuit of General Lee and his forces to Williamsport, on the upper Potomac, where he was allowed to cross without giving him battle.

The 104th filled the remainder of the season with marches from point to point and an occasional skirmish. They had but one engagement—that at Mine Run. They went into winter quarters at Mitchell's Station, on the Rapidan river, and spent the winter doing picket duty along the river near that point.

On the 4th of May, 1864, they struck tents for the summer campaign, crossed the river at Wilderness Run, and engaged on the 5th in the battle of the Wilderness. They fought all day near Wilderness Run while the rest of the army was crossing at the different fords below. It is unnecessary to detail the several days' fighting which followed, in which the 104th was more or less engaged. They soon afterward crossed the James below Petersburg and had brisk fighting for a few days at that city, with more or less fighting and skirmishing during the month of June. In July the brigade to which the 104th was attached was occupied in building a fort and doing picket duty. This fort was known as Fort Warren, and was situated on the Jerusalem plank road, a short distance from Petersburg. There they remained till the 18th of August, when the 5th corps, to which they belonged, made a detour of six or eight miles and struck the Weldon railroad about three miles from Petersburg, at what was called the Yellow Tavern. Brisk fights occurred on that afternoon and the afternoon of the 19th, and by some mismanagement on the part of the division general, Crawford, nearly the whole division was captured. The 104th was ordered from the line in the midst of the engagement to fill a gap between the 5th and 11th corps, and while moving in a by road in the woods to the designated point, it was surrounded by a brigade of the enemy and captured. It was not liberated till the general exchange of prisoners, February 21st, 1865. After that it took part in the battles at and around Appomattox during the concluding campaign in the spring of 1865.

The regiment participated in the grand review at Washington, and was mustered out at Elmira, July 17th, 1865. From the records in the office of the adjutant-general the following list of the field and staff officers of this regiment is taken:

Colonels.—John Rorbach, Lewis C. Skinner, Gilbert G. Prey, John R. Strang.

Lieutenant-Colonels.—R. Wells Kenyon, Lewis C. Skinner, Gilbert G. Prey, H. G. Tuttle, John R. Strang, H. A. Wiley.

Majors.—Lewis C. Skinner, Gilbert G. Prey, John R. Strang, Henry V. Colt, Henry A. Wiley, William C. Wilson.

Adjutants.—Frederick T. Vance, George L. Synder, John R. Jarvis.

Quartermasters.—Henry V. Colt, Seneca Warner, jr.

Surgeons.—Enos G. Chace, Charles H. Richmond.

Assistant Surgeons.—George S. Rugg, Douglas S. Langdon, Charles H. Richmond.

Chaplains.—Daniel Russel, Alford C. Roe, Ferdinand De W. Ward.

BATTLES.

Cedar Mountain, 2nd Bull Run, Chantilly, South Mountain, Antietam, Fredericksburg, Chancellorsville, Gettysburg, Mine Run, Wilderness, Spottsylvania, North Anna, Bethesda Church, Block House, Tolopotomy, Petersburg, Weldon Railroad, Hatcher's Run, Rappahannock Station, Thoroughfare Gap.

CHAPTER XX.

THE 24TH INDEPENDENT BATTERY—A GLIMPSE AT THE HORRORS OF ANDERSONVILLE.

THERE were few organizations in the service during the late civil war the record of which is sadder than that of this battery.

Those who go forth at the call of their country to do battle in defense of that country's honor, or to offer their lives if necessary for the preservation of its free institutions, do so with the expectation of encountering all the hazards of ordinary civilized warfare; and if they fall in battle, or perish by any of the casualties or exposures incident to life in the field, the grief of their surviving friends is not intensified by the reflection that they lingered through slow tortures, such as untamed savages delight to inflict on defenseless captives.

While the war was in progress, and the feelings which it engendered were active, there was room to hope that the tales of cruelty toward Union captives in southern prisons might be exaggerated; that the common feelings of humanity were not thus outraged, and the usages of civilized peoples thus violated. Fifteen years have passed since then, and time has only brought more damning proof that the horrors were not all told.

The 24thbattery was raised principally in the counties of Wyoming, Monroe and Livingston. Wyoming was represented in it by the men whose names follow:

Henry Chadbourne, William E. Chapin, Timothy E. Shockensy, Arcade; W. E. Bulkley, Charles Bulkley, Castile; John Baker, Covington; William B. Blake, A. L. Culver, Thomas McGuire, James McGuire, Michael McGuire, William Roach, J. E. Lee, George S. Hastings, William Alburty, Francis M. Alburty, Lemuel Andrews, Mark Andrews, George L. Atwood, Roswell Barnes, Hartwell Bartlett, B. Frank Bachelder, Rufus Brayton, Robert Buck, Paul Calteaux, James Calkins, William S. Camp, John Chapman, A. W. Comstock, William W. Crooker, Charles H. Dolbeer, George Duryea, Joseph Duryea, John Filbin, Charles W. Fitch, Thomas Fitzgerald, Jonas E. Galusha, Charles R. Griffith, Albert Griffith,

Thomas Grisewood, Charles Hathaway, Charles H. Homan, George B. Johnson, George W. Keeney, Abram Lee, Abram Lent, John McCrink, James McCrink, Patrick Marren, J. W. Merrit, J. Gile Miner, L. Newcomb, H. C. Page, George W. Piper, A. Piper, Philander Pratt, John Quinn, Sydney S. Rathbone, Porter D. Rawson, Elias Richards, Albert Richards, Le Grande Rood, Pembroke J. Safford, Phares Shirley, Mason C. Smith, Samuel Stoddard, Edward Welch, Oliver Williams, Perry; Marion K. Mosier, Wethersfield; Dennis Finnegan, Hector C. Martin, Warsaw.

The town of Perry was more largely represented in it than any other in the county. The first enlistments were in the latter part of September and in October of 1861. Its place of rendezvous was Fort Porter, Buffalo, where the company remained till the middle of November, when it went forward to Albany. There the men were formed into the rocket battalion, under Major Thomas W. Lion, formerly an English officer, who claimed to be the inventor of a wonderful fire rocket, and who told so plausible a story to the Secretary of War and the chief of artillery that they were induced to incur the expense of a practical test. The battalion when organized consisted of two companies, A and B, each numbering eighty men. They were mustered into the service December 6th, 1861, and the next day left Albany for Washington, where they remained six months experimenting with the new projectile.

The advantages claimed for Lion's rocket were the great distance to which it could be thrown, its capability of setting on fire everything of a combustible nature, and of frightening horses. The results of experiments with this rocket were not satisfactory. It was found that it could not always be relied on to go where it was sent, but like an unskillfully thrown boomerang it would return to hurt the one who threw it. One of the men in a letter giving an account of their experiments with it, stated that their target, which was an army blanket, was stolen by some graceless scamp while they were firing at it.

During the six months in which these experiments were being made there was little to vary the easy daily routine of camp life. As usual in such cases jealousies and animosities arose among the officers and men, for light camp duty is not the most favorable for developing soldierly qualities.

After the rocket project was abandoned the battalion was changed to batteries A and B, light artillery. The men from Wyoming were put in battery B; but were soon made an independent four-gun battery, and ordered to Newport barracks. At this time the battery consisted of but eighty men. The chief officers were Captain Jay E. Lee, First Lieutenant Lester A. Cady, and Second Lieutenant George W. Graham.

In August, 1862, G. S. Hastings was authorized to raise recruits for this battery, and in less than a month about 60 young men from Perry and its vicinity left to join the battery at Newport barracks.

It is worthy of remark that about $6,000 was raised by subscription to pay bounties to these men, for at that time the government had not offered the bounties which it afterwards paid recruits. In due time they arrived at their destination, and on the 19th of October orders were received designating the company the "24th Independent Battery of Light Artillery, New York State Volunteers." George S. Hastings and Fred. Hastings were made respectively additional first and second lieutenants.

The battery remained at Newport barracks about five months, during which time the boys were called out on one scouting expedition, and one trip to Newbern. On the 11th of December two detachments of the battery went with General Foster, and participated in the battles of Kinston, Whitehall and Goldsboro. After their return they remained at Newbern till about the middle of the next March (1863). At that time a feint was made on that place by the rebels, and soon afterward they advanced on Plymouth and Washington, N. C. About the 1st of April the 24th was sent to Plymouth. There it remained almost a year. Stables were built, guns parked, and occasional scouts as cavalry were made.

In June Captain Lee was discharged on a surgeon's certificate, and Lieutenant Cady promoted to the captaincy, J. S. Hastings taking his place, and C. H. Holden receiving a second lieutenant's commission. During this time the older members of the battery whose terms expired re-enlisted; but the numbers were so reduced that two lieutenants (Hastings and Dolbeer) left. The winter of that year passed very pleasantly with the men of the battery, but the spring brought a change.

On the 17th of April, 1864, the cavalry of the rebels attacked the pickets of the garrison, and it soon became evident that something more than a feint or raid was intended. The garrison consisted of 1,900 effective men, under General Wessels. Non-combatants were removed during the following night, and preparations made to resist the attack. Desultory firing was kept up during the night, and the next day it was steadily maintained till about 5 P. M., when an advance was made and earnest fighting commenced. The rebel artillery, consisting of about forty pieces, opened fire on the works, and the artillery of the defenders replied with such terrible precision that it was believed half the artillerymen of the enemy were put out of the fight. Of course a detailed account of this battle cannot be given here. It may be briefly stated that during the night of the 18th the rebel ram "Albermarle" succeeded in driving away the naval supports of the garrison, and taking a position where her guns could be used with effect. During the day and night of the 19th the forces of the enemy assumed more advantageous positions, and on the 20th made a simultaneous assault on the entire Union lines, and at the same time sent a column into the town. It is said that in endeavoring to repel this assault the 24th battery did effective work, "hurling disorder and death into the ranks of the enemy; and not until the rebels seized the muzzles of their guns did the cannoniers fail in their work." The garrison reluctantly surrendered, only when their works were so completely invested and fiercely assailed as to render destruction certain.

The Union loss, notwithstanding their strong breastworks, was about 180. That of the rebels was not positively known, but was stated in the Raleigh papers at 2,200. When it is remembered that the garrison of 1,900 defended the town against a force of 12,000 during four days, and only surrendered when further resistance would have been certain destruction, no suspicion of a want of bravery will be entertained.

Hitherto the 24th had known no hardships. Now, in their first battle, they had fought "vainly but well." Fortune had not favored them, and they were captives in the hands of unpitying foes. One of them, in an account which he gave of the surrender, said:

"Stripped of arms, mortified, sick at heart, we were penned by rebel guards and allowed to take a night's rest on the greensward. As the sun lowered we took a view of our once pleasant and happy camp. How desolate and dreary was it now! Proud in our strength, we had been conquered. How much of passion, hate and revenge rankled in the bosoms of even those who would be Christians. Our comrades killed, the battle lost to us, our friends at home frightened, anxious, full of sorrow, our prospects for freedom from this degrading imprisonment far in the dim, dim future."

A number of the men of the battery were made prisoners during the fight, and were taken to the prisons at Florence and Charleston, from which some never returned.

On the next day those who had surrendered took up their march under rebel guards, who were loaded with the plunder they had taken from the town, much of which they were compelled to throw away. On the 25th of April they arrived at Tarboro, where the officers were separated from the men and taken to Richmond. The men were then taken on platform cars, by way of Wilmington, Charleston, Savannah and Macon, to Andersonville. On their arrival there they had their first sight of Captain Wirz. One of them described him thus: "Suddenly, as if it had been the devil himself, this fiend made his appearance through or nearone of the fires. Short in stature, stooping figure, ill shaped head, awkward limbs and movement, a deep set ugly eye, and a tongue reeking with profanity—such was Captain Wirz."

Andersonville has been so often described and its loathsome horrors so minutely depicted that no recapitulation is needed here. Clara Barton says of it:

"After this, whenever any man who has lain a prisoner within the stockade of Andersonville would tell you of his sufferings—how he fainted, scorched, drenched, hungered, sickened, was scoffed, scourged, hunted and persecuted—though the tale be long and twice told: as you would have your own wrongs appreciated and your own woes pitied, your own cries for mercy heard, I charge you listen and believe him. However definitely he may have spoken, know that he has not told you all. However strongly he may have outlined or deeply he may have colored his picture, know that the reality calls for a better light and a nearer view than your clouded distant gaze will ever get; and your sympathies need not be confined to Andersonville while similar horrors glared in the sunny light, and spotted the flower-girt garden fields of that whole desperate, misguided and bewildered people. Wherever stretched the form of a Union prisoner there rose the signal for cruelty and the cry of agony, and there day by day grew the skeleton graves of the nameless dead."

Father Hamilton, who was there to administer the rites of the Catholic church to the sick and dying, said of what he found there:

"I saw a great many men perfectly naked, walking about through the stockade. They seemed to have lost all regard for delicacy, shame, morality, or anything else. I would frequently have to creep on my hands and knees into the holes the men had burrowed in the ground, and stretch myself out alongside of them to hear their confessions. I found them almost living in vermin in these holes. They could not be in any other condition than a filthy one, because they got no soap and no change of clothing, and were there all huddled together."

Mr. Merril, in his "Record," says of the cruelties inflicted on prisoners there:

"Several times they ceased to issue rations for a day, and even two days; cause—some few of our number had dug a tunnel in order to escape, and to punish these, thousands of starving men were deprived of the morsel that would barely keep the breath of life in them from day to day. They shot men; cause—they had reached over the dead line for water or for a cracker that was a foot beyond it. They chased men with dogs, and these dogs did bite and mutilate them, from the effects of which they died; cause—they were attempting to escape. They put prisoners in chain gangs and in stocks; they whipped them at a whipping-post; they hung them up by the thumbs; cause—these prisoners attempted to escape. They did force prisoners to be vaccinated with poisonous virus, and but few that were vaccinated lived. They beat and kicked sick soldiers who were too ill to keep up in line of march, and last of all, when they had killed by inhuman treatment and cruelties, they buried our friends and comrades in an indecent manner that even barbarians could not have excelled."

During seven months these men were kept in this prison, and in that time famine, pestilence and cruelty accomplished their work. About half their number died there, and of the remainder many returned with broken constitutions and permanently impaired health.

The following are lists of the members of this organization who died while in the service of the United States—taken from Mr. Merril's "Record."

Killed in battle.—Pierce Fitzpatrick, Wilbur M. Hoyt, George F. H. Meade, Robert Turner.

Died of disease while in the U. S. service.—Lemuel Andrews, L. M. Beers, Rufus Brayton, Murray Grant, G. H. Keith, William A. McCrary, Michael McGuire, Darius Monroe, F. D. Otis, O. M. Truair.

Died at their homes while in the service.—Ira Billingham, James McVey.

Died after reaching the Federal lines.—J. E. Galusha, Samuel Nichols, William P. Nichols.

Died at Charleston prison.—William Ainsworth, Porter D. Rawson.

Died at Florence prison.—John Bartley, William Blood, John Brooks, Orren S. McCrary, James McCrink, Henry McNinch, George W. Piper, A. Piper, Stephen Root, George W. Stevens, Samuel Tirrell, Chauncey Wetmore.

Died at Andersonville prison.—William Alburty, William Armstrong, George S. Atwood, John Baker, Roswell Barnes, Hartwell Bartlett, B. F. Bachelder, W. D. Blake, James Button, Paul Calteaux, James Calkins, Charles Carnahan, Henry Chadbourne, H. V. Clute, A. W. Comstock, B. F. Corbin, Morton Crosby, George Crounce, A. L. Culver, Edwin Eastwood, John Filbin, Charles W. Fitch, Thomas Fitzgerald, James Flynn, Charles R. Griffith, Albert Griffith, Charles Hathaway, W. F. Hosford, E. H. Hunter, George W. Keeney, Sylvanus King, L. H. Lapham, Abram Lee, Abram Lent, John McCrink, Archibald McDonald, Charles A. Marean, H. C. Martin, J. Gile Miner, Riley J. Newton, Philander Pratt, Thurmon Rich, Le Grand D. Rood, Pembroke J. Safford, Laban H. Shank, Phares Shirley, Timothy F. Shockensey, Mason C. Smith, Henry Tilton, Edward Welch, Oliver Williams, Emmet Wood, George B. Johnson.

CHAPTER XXI.

HISTORY OF THE NINTH NEW YORK CAVALRY AND FOURTH ARTILLERY.

FIVE companies of the 9th cavalry were raised in the counties of Wyoming, Cattaraugus, and Chautauqua. It was first called "Stoneman Cavalry," in honor of General Stoneman, chief of cavalry in the Army of the Potomac. He was once a resident of Chautauqua, and went from that county to West Point; and among the officers and men of the regiment were many of his old friends and schoolmates. It afterward came to be designated, like other regiments, by its number.

The Wyoming county companies numbered about 225 men, of whom a portion came from Genesee county and elsewhere. The chief company officers were: Company A.—captain, H. R. Stimson; lieutenants, A. B. Merril, and D. W. Lapham. Company H.—captain, W. G. Bentley; lieutenants, P. E. Bailey, and William L. Knapp. Company G.—captain, O. L. Tozier, and lieutenant, W. Carson.

The first place of rendezvous was Camp Seward, at Westfield, Chautauqua county. There the newly raised companies were placed in command of Colonel Porter, an experienced cavalry officer. He soon came to be regarded with disfavor by the line officers. Many of these were men of talent and education, and entertained the opinion that a man might be at the same time "an officer and a gentleman." They could not readily be brought to submit to the insolence of one who looked with contempt upon everything that was not "regular," and who, under the protection of his shoulder straps, gave unbridled license to his domineering spirit and his native churlishness. They were willing to make sacrifices for the cause in which they enlisted, but they could not consent to sacrifice their self respect. Colonel Porter was soon relieved.

The field officers, designated by special order, numbered 511, from general headquarters, State of New York, were: Colonel, John Beardsley; lieutenant-colonel, William B. Hyde; majors, William Sackett, Charles McLean Knox and George S. Nichols.

From Camp Seward they went to Albany, and thence, November 26th, 1861, to Washington. There they made their winter quarters at Camp Fenton, in a grove between Seventh and Fourteenth streets, in the northwest part of the city. Captain Stimson called their camp "a city of white houses among the pines." They remained in this camp during the following winter, discharging the ordinary routine of camp duties and perfecting themselves in the drill.

In the month of March they went out as an escort to some artillery trains, and the opening of the spring campaign found them in the field. There had been frequent rumors of the discharge of this regiment, and these rumors were not wholly without foundation; for at one time such a measure was talked of at the department. From this time forward they were in active service.

Early in July, 1862, they received their horses, and became, in the language of one of their number, what they were enlisted for, "a cavalry regiment." It was then attached to Buford's cavalry brigade, and from that time it was constantly in active service, and its record was as brilliant as that of any cavalry regiment in the service.

It must be remembered that cavalry service is different from that of infantry or artillery—companies and squads of cavalry are frequently sent on reconnoisances, raids, and forays, where celerity of movement is required, and quick, sharp fighting is to be done. The members of cavalry organizations are, of course, more constantly in motion, and oftener in action than those of any other branch of the service.

The 9th was in the campaigns in Virginia and Maryland in the summer of 1862. In the winter of 1862 and 1863 it was in the region about Culpepper. In the summer of 1863 it was with the army in Virginia, Maryland and Pennsylvania. It passed the winter of 1863 and 1864 in Loudon valley, with headquarters at Stephensburg. In the spring and early part of the summer of 1864 it was with General Grant, and afterward with General Sheridan in his campaign in the Shenandoah valley.

Although the record of all the engagements in which all or portions of the 9th participated is not accessible, it is known that the number of these is fifty-seven, and that some among these were very severe actions. The following are recorded: Yorktown, Williamsburg, Cedar Mountain, Brandy Station, Aldie, Upperville, Gainesville, Second Bull Run, Chantilly, Antietam, Gettysburg, Kelly's Ford, Rappahannock Station, Sulphur Springs, Opequan, Wilderness, Cold Harbor, Mechanicsville, Deep Bottom, Winchester, Fisher's Hill, Cedar Creek, Petersburg, Five Forks, Trevillian Station, Beverly Ford, Malvern Hill, Appomattox Court-house, Germantown, Haymarket, Berryville, Middleburg, Spotted Tavern, Goose Creek, Boonsboro, Funktown, Falling Waters, Stevensburg, Culpepper, Bealton and Mine Run, in most of which it suffered in killed, wounded or prisoners.

At the expiration of its term of service the original members, except those who re-enlisted, were mustered out; and the 4th New York cavalry was transferred to this as companies B, E and L, and, thus made up of veterans and recruits, the organization continued in the service till after the close of hostilities. It was mustered out July 17th, 1865.

Among the testimonials which this regiment has received of the confidence which its commanders reposed in it, the following order may be quoted:

{"Headquarters and brigade, 1st cavalry division. * * * June 14th, 1864.
"SPECIAL ORDERS NO. 27.

"The 9th New York cavalry of this brigade having been ordered to the Department of the Shenandoah, the brevet brigadier-general commanding considers it an act of justice to the officers and men of this decimated command to refer to their services during the campaign just ended. Upon them devolved the duty of sustaining the reputation of the fighting 9th upon the brilliant operation upon the enemy's communications north of the James river, and in the campaign that culminated in the suppression of the Rebellion. At the battles of Five Forks, Shiloh Creek, Scott's Crossroads and Appomattox Court-house, their behavior under their gallant leader, Major Dinnan, elicited the highest commendations; and their stubborn valor on more than one occasion assisted materially in the success achieved. Their glorious record will always be one of the brightest chapters in the history of the 2nd brigade.

"CHARLES J. FITZHUGH,
"Brevet Brigadier-General commanding."

THE FOURTH ARTILLERY.

This organization was formed in New York city, and consisted originally of eight companies. Wyoming county was represented in it by Eugene A. Aken, Abner P. Adams, Page Burnell, Lewis Cain, Owen Huntley, John W. Hatch, Samuel S. Mais, John Prill, Albert Pratt, Goodley Puff, William Spicknell, Spencer Thrall, William W. Warner, Joel H. Watson, Darwin Waite, Pike; Francis Davidson, William E. G. Puff, Genesee Falls; William Gregg, Frank Hardens, James Hildrum, William H. Mateson, Perry; and Walter Tallman, Castile.

The regiment was raised in 1861 and 1862. During the summer of 1862 it garrisoned the forts in front of Georgetown. On the 28th of September it was sent to Fort Rumsey, Va., and thence to Fort Ethan Allen, some five or six miles away. This fort it guarded a long time without being in any active engagement. In the month of June, 1863, the maneuvers of the contending armies brought the 4th artillery to the front, although still in charge of Fort Ethan Allen, and likewise garrisoning Fort Rumsey without infantry support. There, at that time, they were constantly liable to cavalry raids.

March 7th, 1863, Colonel Doubleday was discharged, and Colonel De Russey succeeded him. On the 23d of May following DeRussey was promoted to the position of brigadier-general of volunteers, and was succeeded by Colonel Hall, who remained in command until the 6th of the following August, when he resigned. The next colonel was Captain John C. Tidbull, an artillery captain in the regular army, and a thorough fighter; having carried his battery through the principal battles of the war with success.

The regiment remained at Fort Ethan Allen till March 27th, 1864, when it was sent to the front, numbering 2,400. Up to June, 1864, after having participated in the battles of the Wilderness, Spottsylvania, North Anna, Tolopotomy and Cold Harbor, no casualties were reported in it. From a letter written by one of the officers of Battery D in this regiment, the following is copied: "We are working six co-horn mortars. Each throws a 24-pound shell. Much curiosity and great excitement are caused among the infantry by the operation of these pieces. They are so small that four men can pick one up and travel away with it. We can throw a shell from 25 to 1,200 yards with one of them, as we choose. The infantry all declare that the rebels shall never take our battery, and they mean it. We took our present position on the night of June 3d, and we have been under fire ever since three o'clock A. M. of the 4th. As I write the bullets are whistling and shrieking over our heads. On our part we have thrown 150 shells among them. The effect of them has been terrific. They fall directly among the Johnnies, and create great consternation. We have seen two of the poor fellows blown ten feet into the air by one of them,—heads off, and arms and legs shattered. So far, the reb's have injured none of our battery boys, but have killed and wounded quite a number of others."

The position mentioned was before Cold Harbor, and the battery was detached from the regiment. A long period of comparative inaction before Petersburg was brought to a close on the morning of July 30th by the memorable mine explosion. This mine had been constructed under a strong rebel fort in front of Burnside's line. It was a very large one, containing six tons of powder.

The explosion took place about five o'clock in the morning. A shower of dirt was sent up about three hundred feet, completely demolishing the fort, and burying in its ruins the greater part of a South Carolina regiment and six guns. Immediately after the explosion our batteries opened fire, and simultaneously our forces, including the 4th artillery, charged on the works, and a great part of the second line of defenses was taken. Company C of the 4th operated in this engagement with a battery of cohorn mortars, which were served splendidly.

The next engagement in which this regiment participated was at Deep Bottom. Having embarked on the James and dropped down a few miles it returned, and in conjunction with the 10th corps attacked the rebels and won a victory.

The next fight was on the 25th of August, at Ream's Station, on the Weldon railroad, and in that the 4th suffered terrible loss; 900 of the regiment went into the fight, and but 503 came out. Among the losses were 19 officers killed, wounded and missing. Four charges were made by the rebels and bloodily repulsed; but in the fifth they succeeded in breaking the Union line. In this engagement the 4th was supporting two or three four-gun batteries, and fought under Hancock.

After this the regiment encamped on what was known as the Jerusalem plank road, and reorganized, armed recruits, drilled, worked in trenches, etc. It then went to the vicinity of Fort Hell, and thence to the left of the line before Petersburg, and encamped about two miles west from the Weldon railroad, where it remained during the winter.

It was mustered out of the service the next June.

CHAPTER XXII.

A HARD YEAR'S FIGHTING BY THE EIGHTH NEW YORK HEAVY ARTILLERY.

THE history of this regiment is a terrible one. Volumes that will never be written are expressed in the truth that during its services it lost nearly twelve hundred men in killed, wounded and missing. Twenty-two officers and two hundred and eleven men were killed, twenty-nine officers and six hundred and fifty-three men were wounded and fifty men missing.

This regiment was organized in the gloomiest period of the war. The Union troops in front of Richmond had been repulsed, and they awaited help to check the advance northward of the enemy. The demand of the hour was men. In this crisis the President issued a call for 300,000 troops, and it was in response to this that the 8th heavy artillery was organized. It was raised in the counties of Wyoming, Niagara, Orleans and Genesee by Colonel Peter A. Porter, of Niagara Falls under authority granted by Governor Fenton. It was completed and mustered into the service at Camp Church (Lockport) on the 22nd of August, 1862, with the following regimental officers: Colonel, Peter A. Porter, Niagara Falls; lieutenant-colonel, W. W. Bates, Orleans county; major, James M. Willett, Batavia; adjutant, E. L. Blake, Lockport; quartermaster, George B. Wilson, Lockport; surgeon, James M. Leet, Lockport; assistant surgeon, H. C. Hill, Somerset; chaplain, Gilbert De La Matyr. Wyoming county had in this regiment the following representatives:

Elias M. Doty, James Ellis, Lawrence Flynn, Edward Hooper, John Hush, Henry M. Jones, George W. Kendal, Henry McMay, Carl Martin, Frederick Pilgrim, Henry Rush, Augustus Stuby, William Silsal, Marion Buck, Luke White, Attica;

John Amerdick, David Burleigh, Ira Cross, Ervin Ewell, Kirk L. Ewell, N. Ferner, Adam Grill, J. G. Husch, Mart. Lingfield, Andrew Lingfield, S. Dexter Ludden, Stephen Myers, Michael Myers, Charles Rice, Friend Rice, John Shum, H. H. Van Dake, Eugene Plumley, Bennington; Elias Burt, Charles Scribner, William Scribner, Castile; Lyman Bennett, Ezra Flint, George W. Johnson, Hiram Johnson, Gainesville; Charles H. Fuller, J. B. Jewett, Stephen Judd, Middlebury; Thomas Cofield, Perry; Elias Gratton, Sheldon; John Aiken, Charles C. Bishop, Michael Burke, Lewis E. Clement, George Gibson, Alfred W. Hoyt, Milton W. Hurlburt, Abraham Ennis Keeney, L. D. Mapes, Alburtis Sammis, Thomas J. Scribner, Luther J. Spencer, Charles E. Whittam, Warsaw; and H. Z. Owen, Wethersfield.

The regiment served from the time of its muster till the spring of 1864 in the defenses of Baltimore, with the exception of a short campaign to Harper's Ferry and in western Virginia. There it was subjected to none of the privations and to few of the restraints of military life. Officers' balls, company dances, Christmas, New Year and Thanksgiving feasts and merry makings varied the monotony of garrison duty, but none of the hardships of the field were encountered. During nearly two years they "played soldier."

On the morning of May 15th, 1864, the regiment was ordered to the front. About five o'clock in the evening of the 17th it crossed the river on a pontoon. In almost every building were crowded the wounded from the recent battles of the Wilderness and Spottsylvania Court-house. The regiment marched through Fredericksburg and up the heights beyond the town, until at eight o'clock it stopped for rest and supper. At ten o'clock it started on the march again. Soon after two o'clock in the morning the welcome order was given to rest until daylight.

With the first light of morning the dull booming of distant cannon was heard. The 8th regiment had joined the great "battering ram," the Army of the Potomac, and was at the front. After breakfast it started in the direction of the firing, which was not heavy, nor was the engagement general. As the troops neared the scene of action they met numbers of wounded men moving to the rear with mangled limbs and bloody faces, while near the front lines others were waiting for stretchers. On the night of May 18th, 1864, they rested quietly, camped in a lovely spot. They remained there during the next day awaiting orders.

On the night of the 19th the 8th had its first encounter with the enemy. About 4 o'clock in the afternoon of that day the troops heard heavy musketry firing to the northeast of them, and they immediately started in that direction on the double quick. They soon began to meet the wounded and the bullets began to whistle over their heads. The regiment took a strong position in the second line and lay down behind the crest of a ridge. At dusk it advanced across a small stream and through a cornfield and was soon engaged. The first charge was made into the woods, where it was dark. The 8th was there until about 9 o'clock, directing its fire by the flash of the enemy's guns. The loss was light—33 killed, wounded and missing. The wounded were carried to a field hospital and soon all was quiet again. Morning revealed only abandoned positions, for the enemy had fled with the darkness. After burying its dead the regiment returned to its old camp.

At midnight on the night of May 20th the regiment broke camp and went, *via* Bowling Green, to Milford Station, on the Richmond and Potomac Railroad, a distance of twenty-five miles, arriving after a steady march of fifteen hours at 3 P. M. There had been a brisk cavalry fight at Milford Station that day, and some of the wounded, with a few prisoners, were still there. The 8th rested there for dinner and marched again at 10 o'clock that night. About 5 o'clock in the evening of the 23d it arrived at North Anna river in the vicinity of the Chesterfield bridge. The rebels held an ugly fortification, which at 6 P. M., after a vigorous fire from three sections of artillery, was stormed and captured by Pierce's and Egan's brigades, of Birney's division. Thirty of the garrison were captured, and the remainder sent across the river in such haste that they were not able to burn the bridge. The 8th lay on its arms till morning. The rebels sent their compliments with early dawn. The 8th replied and continued to fire all day. From this time until June 2nd the regiment was most of the time on the road to Cold Harbor, meantime engaging in several sharp skirmishes.

About 11 A. M., June 2nd, this regiment took the front at Cold Harbor, relieving other troops. In an eager and confident frame of mind the men received the order to be ready to charge at 4 o'clock; and at that hour they were found sitting behind their breastworks, every man grasping his gun, ready to spring at the command. One of the officers of the regiment says: "We were acting very much unlike the stern and silent soldiers we read of, for we were laughing and chatting, speculating upon the prospect before us as if it were a mere holiday or some bore of a parade." But it began to rain and the order was countermanded. The sun went down under a cloud and thus night settled.

Thousands beheld the dawn on the 3d for the last time. The signal gun was fired at daybreak, when the men were not thinking so much about the order to advance as they were about their coffee.

The distance between the lines of the 8th and the rebel lines has been variously estimated at from seven hundred to one thousand yards. The first battalion, on the left of the regiment, was commanded by Lieutenant-Colonel Bates; the second, in the center, by Captain McGinnis (Major Spaulding being sick); the third, on the extreme right, by Major Willett. The batteries in the rear of the regiment opened a heavy fire simultaneously with the advance of the charging column, and the rebels replied no less vigorously. One after another went down beneath the storm of iron and lead which swept the plain. As the ranks thinned they closed up sternly, and, with arms at a trail and bayonets fixed, they pressed forward on a run without firing a shot. Down went the colors, the staff splintered and broken as well as the hand that held it; brave hands seized them again and bore them onward until the enemy's works were close at hand. Colonel Porter fell, crying, "Close in on the colors, boys!" Major Willett was wounded, a large number of line officers lay dead and dying, one-third of the rank and file was *hors du combat*, a part of the regiment was floundering in the mire, the rebels were pouring in double charges of grape and canister at less than point blank range, sweeping away a score every moment. The line, having lost its momentum, stopped from sheer exhaustion within a stone's throw of the enemy's works.

All this transpired in a short time. The supporting line failed to come up—old soldiers declaring that it was foolhardiness to advance under such a fire; so the brave men of the 8th were compelled to look out for themselves. They began to dig, and every man was working himself into the ground. Every stump, mole hill, bush and tree was a shelter. Thus the regiment lay all day under the very noses of the rebels, and came away in squads, under cover of the darkness. This seemed as hazardous as the charge itself; for no sooner did the rebels detect a movement in their front than they opened a murderous fire of both musketry and artillery. Some were killed in attempting to come out; among them Captain Gardner, of Company I. An officer, describing the fire, says: "It was either more severe than in the morning, or darkness made it seem more terrible."

At 9 that night the regiment was in its old position and had brought away most of the severely wounded, who had been unable to get back during the day. The dead were lying where they fell. Some were buried during the night following, and some lay exposed till the truce of June 6th. No one knew exactly where the body of Colonel Porter lay, and all effort to find it during the night of the 3d proved unavailing. It was discovered the next day midway between the advanced pickets, about twenty yards from either. To recover it during the day was too hazardous to attempt, for the rebel sharpshooters were always on the alert. About midnight on the 4th Le Roy Williams crept stealthily from his picket post, followed by Samuel Traverse, of Company B, and in a few minutes they reached the body without attracting the attention of their vigilant neighbors. But they could not carry the body without rising to their feet, and that they dared not do; so Williams watched the body while Traverse returned to the pit and sent a comrade to the regiment after ropes. In less than an hour they had tent ropes enough to reach the body, and, having fastened one end to the feet of their dead commander, they lay on their faces, one behind the other, and gradually dragged the body to a place of comparative safety. From there it was taken to Colonel Bates's headquarters and then to the hospital, where it arrived about 3 o'clock on the morning of June 5th.

Greeley once said, in speaking of Colonel Porter: "He was but one among thousands actuated by like motives, but none ever volunteered with purer motives, or served with more unselfish devotion than Peter A. Porter." On the evening previous to the battle, he was asked, "Don't you think it very foolish to charge across there? We don't expect that many of us will ever come back alive." The colonel replied, "That has nothing to do with the matter. If I am ordered to go *I* shall go, and I *think* my regiment will follow me."

The following figures tell something of the desperate work the 8th heavy artillery performed in this action: Killed, 9 officers and 146 men; wounded, 14 officers and 323 men; missing, I officer and 12 men; making an aggregate loss of 24 officers and 481 men. The material that composed the regiment was equal to any that went out, and the story of its experience June 3d carried desolation to many once happy homes.

The regiment went from Cold Harbor to Petersburg, under Colonel Willet, engaging in sharp skirmishes on the way. Its services from this time forward, until the close of the war, were in and about Petersburg. Arriving there June 16th it was in the engagement of that day, and took part again on the 18th and 22nd. It fought at Ream's Station, Deep Bottom, Hatcher's Run and Appomattox, doing its full share of duty, and suffering the loss of 13 officers and 65 men killed, 15 officers and 230 men wounded, and 4 officers and 238 men missing.

June 4th, 1865, six companies were transferred to other regiments, and the next day the remaining six were mustered out.

CHAPTER XXIII.

HISTORY OF THE 130TH VOLUNTEERS, OR 1ST NEW YORK DRAGOONS.

IN the month of July, 1862, the disastrous campaign of General McClellan on the Peninsula culminated at Harrison's Landing. A gigantic effort had been put forth, and a signal failure was the result.

A call was made for men to recruit the depleted ranks of the regiments in the field, and to constitute along with these regiments an army that would be able to check the progress of the Rebellion, retrieve the national prestige, and demonstrate to the world the cohesive force of republican institutions. The need of a stronger force was recognized, and in response to this call regiments sprang into existence as if by magic. The 130th N. Y. volunteers was organized at this time. It included in its ranks many of the best citizens of Wyoming, Allegany and Livingston counties.

The governor of New York, at the suggestion of General McClellan, appointed Alfred Gibbs colonel of this regiment. Colonel Gibbs was a classmate with General McClellan at West Point, and he had had the benefit of twenty years' experience in the regular army. Thomas J. Thorpe and Rufus Scott, who were appointed respectively lieutenant-colonel and major, had fought side by side in the Peninsular campaign, and both had received wounds.

Companies A, C and D were from Wyoming county. In point of character and patriotism the men of this regiment were not second to any in the service. Their record of brilliant achievements, untarnished by a single disaster, tells its own story.

September 6th, 1862, the regiment left its rendezvous at Portage for the seat of war, followed by the adieus, the cheers, and the "God speeds" of a throng of friends who had gathered from all parts of the senatorial district to witness its departure. Its route was over the Northern Central railroad through Pennsylvania. It halted a single night at Washington, and was then pushed at once to the front south of the James river, at Suffolk, Va., where it arrived September 13th. From this time till January 29th, 1863, the men were occupied with the usual duties of the soldier in an advanced garrisoned position—picket duty, throwing up entrenchments, building corduroy roads, burying the victims of swamp malaria, turning out at midnight for long roll alarm, usually without cause, and occasionally, to relieve the monotony, going on a reconnoisance to the Blackwater, with no other results than blistered feet and swollen limbs.

On the night of January 29th, 1863, this monotony was relieved by a genuine sensation; and the regiment received its "baptism of fire." At midnight a large force was turned out for an expedition. It consisted of 3,500 infantry; made up of Corcoran's brigade, the 130th, and two other regiments, 12 pieces of artillery and Spears's cavalry in advance. About 4 o'clock on the morning of the 30th, at Deserted Farm, midway between Suffolk and the Blackwater, this force encountered a rebel advance on Suffolk, under General Roger A. Pryor. His force consisted of about 2,500 infantry, 14 pieces of artillery, and the proper ratio of cavalry. Without halting the column, the Union cavalry by a single dash drove the enemy's pickets back upon the main body, which was stationed on the far side of an open field one-quarter to one-half a mile in width. Into this open field on the near side the Union artillery at once debouched and opened fire, with the 130th and the other two regiments of infantry supporting and immediately behind it—Corcoran's brigade being still further in the rear. For two hours, with the forces thus disposed, the action was made an *artillery duel.*

The cannonade was incessant and terrific. Shot and shell went plowing through the ranks of the infantry in rear of the artillery, with terrible effect. Colonel Gibbs, a veteran of the Mexican war, ventured to expostulate with Corcoran at the outset against this disposition, and to suggest that the infantry should be posted on the flanks of the artillery, where they would escape the raking fire, and where they could repel an assault upon it, if made. For his temerity in so doing he was put under arrest by Corcoran and his sword taken from him. But the wisdom of his suggestion was soon demonstrated. Corcoran's own brigade, unused to fire, broke in confusion and disorder, and began a precipitate retreat. He was himself obliged to leave the field and join in the effort to rally them. In this he only partially succeeded.

Meanwhile the fight in front went on without orders or direction. The day was just breaking. Everybody looked the puzzled astonishment that they felt. Were there orders to retreat? No one knew of any orders of any kind—and yet the last of the artillery was filing by. "This is a shame!" began some one. "This is a shame!" echoed all. "Let's go on without orders! let's charge them!" The key note had been struck. "Let's charge them! let's charge them!" went up as from one throat along the whole line. Everybody knew now just what to do. Quicker than it can be told here, three regiments in line of battle moved out from the edge of the wood and charged across the open field. Who that was there can ever forget it? Who that witnessed it will not always remember the thrilling picture of brave Colonel Gibbs, under arrest as he was, swordless and horseless, seizing the colors and bearing them, like the hero that he was, in front of the regiment throughout the whole of that charge? From that hour his kingdom in the regiment was established. There had been doubts, almost murmurings, but now and henceforth every man in the regiment was willing to die for him.

The enemy broke and ran in confusion, leaving many of their dead on the field. The 130th was at once deployed as skirmishers, and pushed into the woods beyond, where they soon developed two pieces of artillery and a force of the enemy covering the retreat. They were forcing them steadily back amidst a shower of grape and canister, and were shooting the gunners at their guns, when General Corcoran arrived on the field and recalled them. After two hours' delay, in which were gathered up the remaining fragments of Corcoran's brigade, the pursuit was resumed, but without success, only a small rear guard being overtaken.

This engagement established on a firm footing that mutual confidence between officers and men so essential to success. Thereafter each felt that they could depend in any emergency upon the other. In this engagement the regiment lost Captain Taylor, Company C, killed, and about 30 men killed and wounded; among the latter E. M. Jennings, who lost an arm. Once afterward during the winter the regiment made a reconnoisance to the Blackwater, and engaged in a brisk skirmish across the river, in which it lost two men killed and several wounded.

April 3d, 1863, Longstreet in force invested the place. The 130th was stationed on the South Quay road, upon which he approached and upon which his main force operated. April 17th a sortie was made by the 130th and two other regiments, for the purpose of developing the enemy's strength. The affair was brilliant and successful beyond expectation. The enemy were driven from their rifle pits and first line of earthworks and compelled to disclose the main body of their forces. The greatest difficulty was experienced by the officers in getting the men to retreat. They were bound to have "another shot," and officers were actually compelled to draw their pistols to force some of them to retreat to save them from capture. In this sortie Major Scott was struck in his sword arm by a ball which sent his sabre flying some feet distant. Picking it up with his other hand he went on as though nothing had happened. The loss was only 8 or 10 killed and wounded. May 1st the siege was abandoned and the 130th regiment joined in the pursuit.

June 19th it embarked for the peninsula, and by way of Norfolk reached Yorktown, and at once joined Keyes's command in the second peninsula advance upon Richmond. The regiment sustained its part in all the minor and insignificant engagements, and on being ordered to join the Army of the Potomac returned to Yorktown July 7th, and proceeded thence by transport to Washington, and thence by rail to Frederick City, Md., which it reached July 13th.

July 19th, by a forced night march, the Army of the Potomac was reached at Berlin, and the Pleasant valley traversed to Warrenton, Va. At this point the regiment was changed to cavalry, given the title of 1st N.Y. Dragoons, and ordered into drilling camp at Manassas, Va. Drill was prosecuted incessantly until late in September, when the regiment was mounted, and after a few days' mounted drill resumed active duty.

This was at the time when Meade was falling back from the Rapidan, hotly pursued by Lee. The first duty of the regiment was a reconnoisance by three companies through Thoroughfare Gap into Pleasant valley, October 12th, to ascertain the truth of the report that a large force of the enemy was advancing through it to repeat the tactics of falling on the Union rear. The reconnoisance pushed through as far as Salem, demonstrating the fact that no force was there. At that point it was recalled and ordered to join the main army near Catlett's Station, the officer in command to report to General Meade. He was found leaning against a stump near Catlett's Station, weary, worn and haggard. When told by the officer, in answer to his inquiries, where he had been and that he found no enemy there, he heaved a sigh of relief, and said: "You don't know how much I am obliged to you; it's a great relief to me."

During the remainder of the retreat to Centreville the regiment was guarding the approaches on the left flank of the army, and between it and the enemy. After reaching Centreville it recrossed Bull Run, on the evening of October 16th, and engaged in a skirmish on its recent camp ground. On the evening of the 17th of October it again crossed, and on the plains of Manassas, single-handed, charged a rebel brigade of cavalry and drove them near to Bristoe Station, with considerable loss in killed and wounded. It was near sunset when the charge began, and night only put a stop to the pursuit. The following day the pursuit was resumed, when the destruction of the Orange and Alexandria railroad was discovered, up to the point to which the enemy had been driven the night before.

The pursuit continued without further engagement to the Rappahannock. After picketing the line for some time, stationed at Morrisville and Bealton, the regiment, November 8th, moved with the cavalry column rapidly to White Sulphur Springs, crossed the Rappahannock, and pushing rapidly forward attacked the enemy in flank as they were retreating through Culpepper on the 9th. In this engagement the regiment suffered no loss, though inflicting severe punishment upon the enemy. The following day Culpepper was occupied, some captures made and the enemy followed across the Rapidan. Captain Knapp, of Company D, was in command of the squadron in this raid. Shortly afterward the regiment went into camp beyond and near Culpepper, from which point it made several important reconnoisances, engaging the enemy, in one of which it captured a signal station on the top of Slaughter Mountain, and in another of which it pushed up to within sixty rods of the rebel works at Rapidan Station, and engaged the forces in them, developing their full strength.

November 23d this regiment, with others, moved rapidly down the river, crossed at Ely's ford, occupied the heights beyond and raided the country to and beyond Chancellorsville, covering the operations of Meade at Mine Run. This position was held until after the withdrawal of Meade. Returning to Culpepper the regiment soon afterward went into winter quarters near Mitchell's Station, and the following winter was occupied in picketing the Rapidan, with occasional raids. In one of these, with 140 men of the regiment, to Sperryville, on the night of January 10th, 1864, two officers and six men of a Virginia regiment were captured, and a barbarous practice of shooting pickets was broken up.

May 4th, 1864, the regiment started out on the campaign of *the* war. Pursuing its route of the previous autumn by Ely's ford to Chancellorsville, it passed thence to the left of Grant's army, engaged in the Wilderness fight, and on the afternoon of May 7th attacked the enemy's line on a small run beyond Todd's Tavern, maintaining the contest until far into the night against greatly superior numbers. Twice was the line broken by the desperate efforts of the enemy. Twice was the front changed and the enemy compelled to relinquish their temporary advantage. Night found them pushed, with great loss, far back into the woods towards Spottsylvania. All night long was spent in burying the dead. In the morning, while yet the fire from belching carbines lit up the darkness, the contest was resumed. Steadily the enemy were forced back until the breastworks, lined with their infantry, were reached. Here the 5th corps relieved the cavalry, which at once prepared for new work; 104 empty saddles was the result of this engagement.

After remaining one day at Aldrich's Tavern to replenish supplies the 1st Dragoons, with Sheridan's cavalry, pushed for Lee's line of communications. On the evening of May 9th, which had been a sultry, dusty day, they were at Beaver Dam Station, where they burned Lee's supplies, captured several trains of cars, sent cannon balls through the locomotives and destroyed the track. The next day the column marched towards Richmond.

The 1st Dragoons had the rear. General Stuart, with his rebel cavalry, was hovering on the left flank and rear, and twice during the day he charged on the rear, but was repulsed with loss each time. The column encamped at night beyond Squirrel Bridge.

At early dawn the next morning an attack was made at the point where the 1st Dragoons was encamped. Leaving horses to be saddled by every fourth man the balance seized their arms and charged the assailants. Although the charge was irresistible, the enemy were stubborn and yielded ground slowly. Major Scott was wounded in the thigh in this charge. After the enemy had been driven far enough to give the necessary time the regiment hastily returned to its horses, mounted and filed out after the main column just as the enemy again got in range, and opened on them without effect. The casualties in these affairs were always slight.

In the afternoon Stuart's cavalry had reached a point so nearly in advance of the column that they commanded the junction of the old Brock road with that over which the column advanced, near Hungary, or Yellow Tavern. To dislodge them, the line was formed with the 1st Dragoons supported on either side by regular regiments. The artillery of the enemy had taken a commanding position, and the plan was formed to swing to the left and envelope it. The 1st Dragoons made an impetuous charge on the enemy, and but for the want of support by the too cautious regulars, would have captured them. In this charge the rebel General Stuart was killed. The result of the fight was the opening of the road to Richmond; but twenty men of the 1st Dragoons did not take it. They had taken the one to eternity.

It was near night when the action ended, yet the troops moved on toward Richmond, crossed the Chickahominy by Russel's bridge, and the command was inside of the first line of the defenses of Richmond. The command turned to the left and moved down the river between the lines. As the day dawned torpedoes began to explode under the tread of the troops, and the advance was soon engaged with the second line of defenses. An effort to recross the river at Meadow Bridge disclosed Stuart's cavalry on the opposite side, disputing the passage. With the enemy in large force in front, and the enemy and the river in the rear, the situation was critical. While the attack in front was kept up, a division was massed to force the passage at Meadow Bridge. A hot, dismounted fight for the control of the bridge ended with Sheridan's troops in possession and occupying the opposite bank. The bridge was repaired, and the 1st Dragoons crossed in advance of the mounted troops, and charged the enemy, who fled in every direction.

The road was thus opened to Mechanicsville, and the 1st Dragoons led in the march thither. At noon pickets were thrown out in all directions during the bivouac for dinner, after which the march in the direction of Cold Harbor was resumed, the brigade to which the 1st was attached taking the lead. The regiment itself was delayed in drawing in its pickets, but it pushed rapidly by the moving column to overtake the advance. The rattle of musketry was heard in front, and an orderly came in haste with orders for the 1st Dragoons to hurry up, which they did at a gallop. As they came abreast of the battery, which stood in column, they met the balance of the brigade retreating in wild confusion, closely pursued by the exultant foe. The bullets were flying thickly, and the battery seemed to be doomed. As the head of the 1st Dragoons came abreast of the battery, Colonel Thorpe, who was in command, shouted the order, "Forward into line! Prepare to fight on foot!" They galloped forward into line, and each man numbered for fighting on foot leaped from his saddle as he reached the line, and ran forward, firing as he went. In ten minutes the enemy were in full flight, and fifty prisoners were taken—nearly all of them found behind entrenchments which were thrown up by the enemy during the Peninsula campaign of 1862. Not a man was lost.

After various movements with Sheridan's command, the 1st Dragoons joined the Army of the Potomac, on its race with Lee to reach Richmond. The regiment wheeled about and took the advance again, and at daylight on the morning of the 26th dashed across the Pamunkey at Hanover Town, and during that and the next day drove the enemy some distance beyond Hawes's

Shop. On the 28th a large rebel force attempted to dislodge this advance by such an impetuous attack that the fight really opened from General Gregg's headquarters. Then ensued, during several hours, one of the most hotly contested fights of the war. Flanking forces were sent to the right, in the advance of which marched the 1st Dragoons. They were met with a shower of grape and canister from a battery across a deep and seemingly impassable gulf. They at once turned it to their advantage by dismounting, sending their horses to the rear, and plunging into it out of harm's way. It was better than a breastwork, for the guns of the enemy could not be depressed to reach them, and when they charged up the opposite bank, under Captain Knapp, the rebels quickly took to flight. They then turned to the left and attacked the remaining force, which fled precipitately, leaving their dead on the field.

On the 30th, at Old Church, a charge by Custer's brigade and the 1st Dragoons drove the enemy back, with considerable loss, on Cold Harbor, before which the Union forces encamped for the night.

The next day the contest was resumed for the possession of that point. During the night the enemy threw up formidable lines of earthworks, and behind them awaited the attack. In the afternoon the assault was made directly in front, openly, boldly, and with full notice. The route of the 1st Dragoons was over an open field, billowed with swells and troughs. From cover to cover of these troughs they charged through showers of bullets, halting in each for a fresh start. In that way they reached the last trough, within five rods of the works. There they paused and made extra preparations for the final assault. Every carbine was charged, every muscle was ready for the word. With a shout they ran to the crest and rushed for the works. The contest was terrible. They pressed to within twenty feet of the rebel line, with ranks constantly becoming thinner. Soon one-third of the line officers had been wounded. It was more than poor human nature could bear. It became evident that the rebel line could never be taken with that force, and doggedly the men fell back to their cover and opened a straggling fire. The general saw the need of the hour. At once was heard on the left the eternal bugle advance of Custer. His line swept up with that of the 1st Dragoons; they rose the crest again together and charged. Another fierce but short conflict ensued. Custer had struck the weak point in the rebel line, and doubling it back, he sent a shower of bullets raking down the line in front of the 1st. The fire in front slackened, and the men leaped upon the works as the enemy ran in confusion from them, and the day was won. They had driven Hoke's division of infantry from their breastworks, and they found that among their prisoners were 300 of the men who captured the 85th N. Y. at Plymouth; 60 of their brave comrades had fallen, but they had gained a victory.

During the next forenoon the 1st Dragoons held the ground against repeated and desperate assaults without the surrender of a foot. At about noon they were relieved by the 6th corps, and moved to near Bottom's Bridge, where they remained two days. They next went to Old Church, and then to Trevillian Station, where, on the 11th and 12th of June, they were again hotly engaged, and where, in the thick of the fight, Colonel Thorpe was wounded and taken prisoner. Returning, they recrossed the James with the main army, and had some rest until July 26th.

On the afternoon of that day, with other cavalry, the regiment crossed the Appomattox at Point of Rocks, marched all night and crossed the James early in the morning at Jones's Neck, passed around to the right of the infantry on the afternoon of the 27th, and charged a force of the enemy at Darbytown, obtaining possession of the Newmarket road and driving the enemy back for miles. The following day the rebel division of Wilcox attempted to dislodge the Union force and recover the position. Hawes's shop was repeated. The enemy gained a temporary advantage, only to be repulsed in the end with terrible slaughter. A squadron of the 1st Dragoons made the charge on the first day, and General Wade Hampton and staff barely escaped capture by them. On the second day the regiment maintained the only unbroken portion of the line, repulsing repeated assaults. On the evening of the 28th it recrossed the James, and on the following evening returned to its position with the army at Petersburg.

On the 1st of August the regiment was ordered to the Shenandoah valley. On the 9th it moved, with other cavalry, up the valley to aid in operations against Early. It turned to the left at Berryville, and on the 10th took part in an encounter with the enemy at White Post, where it charged a rebel force from behind a stone wall in brilliant style, and with but little loss made important captures. On the 11th it was sent to reach Newtown, or demonstrate the presence of Early's forces at that point. Half a mile from Newtown and five miles from the main body of Union forces it encountered both his infantry and cavalry, and during an hour and a half it maintained without aid the fiercest and most desperate contest, never yielding an inch of ground, but gallantly maintaining its position until the arrival of the main force, though too late for operations on that day. In this engagement Sergeant Charles J. Gardner lost a leg, and the regiment suffered severely.

During the night the enemy withdrew, and the hospital records found in their abandoned camp contained a list of wounded men in the previous day's action from thirty-three different regiments. During the following two days the regiment took part in the pursuit to Strasburg, and returned down the valley when the pursuit ended. At Smithfield and Kearnstown on the 25th, 26th and 28th of August, the regiment was hotly engaged and lost heavily—brave Lieutenant Alfred being killed and many officers wounded.

On the 19th of September in the battle of Opequan, or Winchester, as it is sometimes called, the 1st Dragoons bore a conspicuous part, charging the enemy's infantry, after routing their cavalry, capturing twice its number of prisoners and three battle flags. The gallant Captain Thorpe was killed in the charge on the enemy's cavalry. But few of this regiment were killed in this battle, and the bodies of these were found far to the front on the most hotly contested ground and buried there by those who followed for that purpose. During three days succeeding the battle of Opequan skirmishing and picketing in the pursuit occupied the troops. Early fled to Fisher's Hill, from which he was driven on the evening of the 22nd with the loss of 1,300 prisoners and 23 pieces of artillery. During the following night, in the thick darkness, the 1st had the advance in following the retreat of Early.

In the morning of the 24th the enemy was found posted on the bluffs at Mt. Jackson, across the river and flats beyond the town, with their cavalry occupying the open fields and hillside across the river to the left. The 1st Dragoons was sent against this cavalry. The regiment forded the river, and having gained the open country beyond they charged at once. The cavalry soon broke and retired by various roads through broken timber. The main flank of the force of the enemy which was thus exposed abandoned its position and retreated. On the 26th, with the 1st Dragoons again in advance, an unsuccessful attack was made between Port Republic and Brown's Gap. On the 9th of October, at Tom's Brook, the 1st Dragoons was engaged in turning on Early's cavalry and capturing their trains and artillery.

A short period of comparative quiet followed, during which the dragoons remained near Middletown doing picket and scout duty. October 19th was fought the battle of Cedar Creek. In this battle the 1st Dragoons more than sustained its reputation. The rebel army was put to flight, with the loss of 40 guns and a large quantity of stores. During all the demoralized portion of that day the 1st Dragoons maintained its organization intact, and contributed largely to stay the tide and restore the order of battle. When the final charge came it loaded itself with honors and captures.

This practically closed a six months period of constant active service and hardship, such as fell to the lot of few regiments in the army.

In November the regiment participated in an expedition to Loudon valley, which was by common consent styled the "bull raid," from the nature of the captures made.

In December it constituted a portion of the force which advanced from Winchester on Gordonsville; and just at night on the 22nd, at Liberty Mills, it made a gallant charge and captured 2 pieces of artillery and about 30 prisoners. On this raid the regiment suffered greatly from intense cold, many of the men having their feet frozen.

During the month of December, 1864, Captain Jacob W. Knapp, who had often led the 1st Dragoons in action, was promoted to the position of major, and he was in command of the regiment till the close of its term of service. To say that Major Knapp contributed his full share toward the brilliant record of this regiment detracts nothing from the reputation of its excellent colonels, Thorpe and Scott, or from that of its efficient line officers.

After a brief stay at Lovettsville, on the 24th of February, 1865, the brigade to which the 1st Dragoons was attached was ordered to take the field. Sheridan left Winchester with 10,000 cavalry, including this command, and arrived at Staunton in four days, defeated and captured the remnants of Early's forces at Waynesboro, crossed the Blue Ridge at Rockfish Gap, turned and destroyed the Virginia Central railroad from Frederick's Hall to Beaver Dam, and won the memorable and decisive victory at Five Forks, on the 1st of April, 1864. From that time till the 9th the cavalry were daily in action, inflicting on the rebel army the blows which so rapidly crippled it and brought on its final catastrophe.

On the morning of April 9th the dismounted cavalrymen were withdrawn from the skirmish line, and mounted for a charge. Several corps of infantry slowly encircled Lee's army, and a hundred cannon frowned on him from the surrounding heights. The alternative of surrender or annihilation was forced on him.

The cavalry were moving on him, and the fighting became more and more animated, when suddenly the stillness of the Sabbath succeeded the roar of artillery, and an aide-de-camp rode along the line, communicating the joyful news of the surrender of Lee and his entire army.

Thus closed the war of the Rebellion, and the active service of the regiment the history of which has here been sketched. During its term of service it captured 1,533 prisoners, 19 pieces of artillery, 21 caissons, 240 artillery horses, 40 army wagons and ambulances, 160 animals of draught, and 4 battle flags. It lost in killed 4 officers and 155 enlisted men; and in wounded, 24 officers and 204 enlisted men. One officer and 80 enlisted men died of disease. The regiment participated in the following

ENGAGEMENTS:

Deserted House, Va., Jan. 30, 1863.
Siege of Suffolk, Va., April 11 to May 3, 1863.
South Quay, Va., June 12, 1863.
Franklin, Va., June 13, 1863.
Baltimore Cross Roads, Va., June 26, 1863.
Manassas Plains, Va., Oct. 16, 1863.
Culpeper Court-house, Va., Nov. 20, 1863.
Stannardsville, Va., Mch. 1, 1864.
Todd's Tavern, Va., May 7, 1864.
Spottsylvania, Va., May 8, 1864.
Anderson's Ridge, Va., May 10, 1864.
Yellow Tavern, Va., May 11, 1864.
Meadow Bridge, Va., May 12, 1864.
Mechanicsville, Va., May 12, 1864.
Hawes's Shop, Va., May 28, 1864.
Old Church, Va., May 30, 1864.
Cold Harbor, Va., May 31 or June 1, 1864.
Trevillian Station, Va., June 11 and 12, 1864.
Darby Town or Deep Bottom, Va., July 27 and 28, 1864.
White Post, Va., Aug. 10, 1864.
Newtown, Va., Aug. 11, 1864.
Kearneysville, Va., Aug. 25, 1864.
Shepardstown, Va., Aug. 25, 1864.
Smithfield, Va., Aug. 28 and 29, 1864.
Opequan Mills, Va., Sept. 19, 1864.
Winchester, Va., Sept. 19, 1864.

Mount Jackson, Va., Sept. 23, 1864.
New Market, Va., Sept. 25, 1864.
Port Republic, Va., Sept. 25, 1864.
Cross Keys, Va., Sept. 28, 1864.
Tom's Brook, Va., Oct. 8, 1864.
Strasburg, Va., Oct. 14, 1864.
Cedar Creek, Va., Oct. 19, 1864.
Newtown, Va., Nov. 12, 1864.
Bloomfield, Va., Nov 29, 1864.
Liberty Mills, Va., Dec. 22, 1864.
Gordonsville, Va., Dec. 23, 1864.
Dinwiddie Court-house, Va., Mch. 31, 1865.
Five Forks, Va., Apr. 1, 1865.
Sutherland Station, Va., Apr. 2, 1865.
Amelia Court-house, Va., Apr. 4, 1865.
Sailor's Creek, Va., Apr. 6, 1865.
Appomattox Station, Va., Apr. 8, 1865.
Appomattox Court-house (Lee's surrender), Apr. 9, 1865.

ROLL OF THE FIRST DRAGOONS.

REGIMENTAL OFFICERS.

Alfred Gibbs, colonel; appointed Sept. 6, 1862; promoted brigadier-general Dec. 1, 1864; brevet major-general Apr. 1, 1865.

Thomas J. Thorpe, lieutenant-colonel; appointed Aug. 27, 1862; promoted colonel Mch 1, 1865; wounded five times.

Rufus Scott, major; appointed Aug. 27, 1862; promoted lieutenant-colonel Mch. 1, 1865; wounded five times.

George R. Cowee, adjutant; appointed Sept. 3, 1862; resigned Oct. 12, 1862.

Abram B. Lawrence, quartermaster; appointed July 28, 1862; promoted successively captain and quartermaster U.S. volunteers, major and quartermaster 18th army corps, and lieutenant-colonel and quartermaster 29tharmy corps.

Arthur H. Watts, quartermaster; appointed on the promotion of A. B. Lawrence.

George B. Lemans, commissary; appointed on the change of the regiment cavalry.

T. Kneeland, surgeon; appointed July 29, 1862.

John Patterson, assistant surgeon; appointed Sept. 5, 1862; resigned.

James Saunders, assistant surgeon; appointed Sept. 5, 1862; resigned.

Joshua B. Purchase, assistant surgeon; appointed April 1, 1863; resigned.

D. C. Fowler, assistant surgeon; appointed Apr. 1, 1863; resigned.

Robert E. Rae, assistant surgeon; appointed May 1, 1864.

Albert W. Tallman, sergeant-major.

John W. Bonnond, quartermaster-sergeant.

Andrew J. Lorish, commissary-sergeant.

George D. Waldo, hospital steward.

Adelbert J. Worclen, hospital steward.

Walter H. Jackson, chief bugler.
Robert Cameron, saddler.

COMPANY A.

Officers.—James E. Bills, captain; appointed Aug. 7, 1862; resigned Oct. 1, 1862.

John P. Robinson, first lieutenant; appointed Aug. 7, 1862; promoted captain Oct. 1, 1862; wounded.

Charles L. Daily, second lieutenant; appointed Aug. 7, 1862; resigned Oct. 6, 1862.

George T. Hamilton, first lieutenant; appointed Oct. 1, 1862; promoted captain of Co. F Jan. 1, 1865; wounded.

William G. Luther, second lieutenant; appointed Oct. 6, 1862; resigned Feb. 5, 1863.

Thomas J. Burr, second lieutenant; appointed Feb. 5, 1853; twice wounded.

William W. Winegar, first lieutenant; appointed Mch. 31, 1863.

Sergeants—Darius Mattison, East Gainesville; Merrit W. Norton, Castile, wounded at Mt. Jackson; George W. Curtis, Fillmore; Edgar A. Day, East Gainesville; Darius W. Luther, Castile; Silas Dewey, Perry.

Corporals—Benjamin C. Smith, Castile; Isaac Baker, Castile; George Harrington, Gainesville, wounded at Deserted House, Va.; George W. Jones, Cuylersville; Ten Eyck Van Liew, East Gainesville; Simon E. Welch, Castile; George N. Barrell, Gainesville, wounded at Deserted House, Wilderness, and Newtown.

Farrier, William H. Boyd, Dansville.

Blacksmith, Harvey B. Orcutt, Portville.

Wagoner, John M. Hall, Portage.

Buglers—James L. Wade, Castile; Frank C. Needham, Castile.

Privates.—Latham H. Ayer, Moscow. Alfred Bigelow, Castile. John Briggs, Castile. Levi R. Buck, Edgewood, Ill. George W. Burr, Independence, Ia. Michael B. Brennan, Portsmouth, Va. Wilber E. Brainard, Germania; wounded at the Wilderness. Warren M. Brown, Wiscoy. George C. Belden, Castile; wounded at Deserted House. Zaddock Barnes, Perry. Dwight C. Borden, Naples. Charles Callaghan, Hunt's Hollow; wounded at Trevillian Station. Andrew A. Chapman, Castile. Jerry Driscoll, Nunda Station. John Dibley, Hamilton Center. Marcus Granger, Gainesville. Joseph Gilbert, Carlton. Henry M. Hardy, Gainesville. John Haley, Pike. Rufus C. Jefferson, Warsaw. C. Delavan Jackson, Portage. Loren Johnson, North Java. Robert Kershaw, East Gainesville. Parmer R. Karns, Burns. Aaron Karns, Burns. Lewis B. Knox, Redding Center. Cyrus Ketch, Wallace. Daniel Leddick, Perry; wounded and taken prisoner Jan. 22, 1865. Joseph Leggett, Castile. Eugene D. H. Land, Castile. Nyrum Rathbone, Castile. Theodore Strawberger, Schenactady. Lyman G. Simons, Castile. George H. Walker, Gainesville. Elias West, Castile. Lyman A. Campbell, sergeant, Pike. Ansel B. Smith, corporal, Castile; wounded Apr. 2, 1865. Marcus A. Atwell, Castile. Henry L. Cummings, Castile; wounded at Trevillian Station. John Clocharta, ——. Edward P. Hunt, Gainesville; wounded at

Newtown. D. W. Harrington, Castile; wounded at Wilderness. Nelson Pettie, Pike. William J. Sheldon, Castile. William H. Wing, Castile. Charles T. Wolcott, Pike. John A. Wilson, Perry; sent to government insane asylum Oct., 1863. John Duggan, ——; promoted to sergeant May 19, 1865. Lewis Blackman. Charles H. Brooker, wounded at Newton Aug. 11, 1864. Gottlob Brightlop, Charles Beresford, Isaac Barton, John Brenell, Albert Butler, William H. Campbell, Patrick Cary, Marcus Curtis, Daniel Ferguson, John P. Francis, John Hayse, M. Hungerford, Jerry McGuire, Dennis McGuire. John McGuire, taken prisoner Oct. 28, 1864. William Mahanna, Michael Masterson, Nathaniel Royce, Reuben Salsberry, James Smith, Charles H. Starks, E. H. Stanley, William Stratton, John Saterly, George Vanderwalker, John P. Walker, George Wessels, James Williams, Theodore Wasterson.

Discharged.—Frederick E. Howard, sergeant, Castile; wounded at Shepardstown. George W. Clute, sergeant, Moscow; wounded at Wilderness. Frank Robinson, saddler; Pike. Eli C. Bishop, Perry. Lester Blackman, Gainesville. Jered M. Bills, Wyoming. Marcellus B. Card, Gainesville. George W. Fisher, Pike. Albert Gage, corporal, Eagle; Mch. 8, 1865. E. M. Jennings, Portage; May 20, 1863, on account of wounds received Jan. 30, 1863, at Deserted House. George Johnson, Castile; Nov. 20, 1862. Robert Meade, Castile; Jan. 20, 1863. Merrick Weaver, Rock Stream; Apr. 13, 1865.

Transferred.—Hiram B. Covell, Gainesville, to veteran reserve corps Sept 20, 1864. Martin Gitchel, Castile, to veteran reserve corps; wounded at Wilderness. Daniel McGuire, Gainesville, to veteran reserve corps; wounded at Trevillian. Philip M. Payne, Castile, to veteran reserve corps June 13, 1864.

Deceased.—William B. Lawrence, first sergeant, Gainesville, died Nov. 24, 1862. John Parkins, color sergeant, Warsaw, died at Winchester Dec. 7, 1864, of wounds received at Loudon valley. Robert H. Sears, sergeant, Moscow, killed at Newtown. Stephen M. Skiff, corporal, Hume, killed at Blackwater. John Hare, corporal, Perry Center, died at Frederick, Md., May 13, 1864, of wounds received at Wilderness. William E. Patridge, corporal, Pike, killed at Trevillian Station. Isaac M. Allen, Portage, died June 2, 1864, of wounds received May 8, 1864, at Wilderness. E. M. Carpenter, Castile, died of wounds received at Wilderness. Moses Griffith, Pike, died June 3, 1864, at Old Church, of wounds received May 30, 1864, at Cold Harbor. George M. Gearhart, Portage, killed at Cedar Creek. Willard Green, Castile, died May 8, 1864. Sidney Graves, Plattsburg, killed at Newtown, Nov. 12, 1864. Cullin B. Halstead, Pike, died July 2, 1864, of wounds received May 30, 1864, at Cold Harbor. Orvell Hinman. East Pike, died at Suffolk Feb. 26, 1862. Lyman R. Hanks, West Almond, killed at Yellow Tavern. Clarkson Helmer, Eagle, killed at Trevillian Station. Job S. Hicks, Eagle, died May 20, 1865. John Keghan, Portage, killed at Deserted House. L. B. Leddick, Perry, killed at Cold Harbor. Charles H. Leach, Pike, died at Suffolk, Va. James E. Rood, Perry, wounded June 11, 1864, at Trevillian Station; died Sept. 10, 1864. Nelson Rolph, Portage, died Dec. 24, 1863. Edwin M. Slocum, Castile, died Oct. 29, 1863. P. E. Simmons, Portage, died Oct. 20, 1862. Charles H. Sterling, Van Buren, Mich., died Dec. 10, 1864. Charles M. Wood, Portage, killed at Deserted House. Oliver Washburn, Portage, killed at Deserted House. Edward Wickson, Pike, died October 31, 1862. Dan P. Waller, Arcade, died Mch. 17, 1865.

COMPANY C.

Officers.—Rowley P. Taylor, captain; appointed Aug. 14, 1862; killed at Deserted Farm, Jan. 30, 1863.

Oscar R. Cook, first lieutenant; appointed Aug. 14, 1862; resigned in 1863.

S. Upham Waldo, second lieutenant; appointed Aug. 14, 1862; resigned in 1863.

Wyman H. A. Godfrey, captain; appointed Jan 30, 1863.

William H. Emmons, first lieutenant; appointed in 1863; made adjutant Mch. 1, 1863; made assistant adjutant-general, with rank of captain; wounded.

Joel B. Slater, second lieutenant; appointed in 1863; promoted first lieutenant Mch. 1, 1863.

Joseph N. Flint, second lieutenant; appointed Mch. 1, 1863; made first lieutenant Company G in Feb., 1865.

Andrew J. Lorish, second lieutenant; appointed in Feb., 1865.

Sergeants.—Francis S. Godfrey, Attica, wounded June 7, 1864. Lewis Page, Portageville, wounded June 12, 1864. Douglas R. Phelps, Attica, wounded Aug., 1864. Henry E. Thompson, Eagle. William H. Fairfield, Arcade. Peter Ruth, Attica. Henry Matterson, Attica.

Corporals—James W. Harden, Java; William Sanderson, Attica, wounded Sept. 16, 1864; Joseph B. Fellows, Bennington, wounded June 11, 1864; William Griswold, Bennington; Samuel S. Barnes, Eagle.

Blacksmith, Hiram Henshaw, China, wounded Jan. 30, 1863.

Farrier, Evan G. Griffith, Attica.

Wagoner, Orange Gardner, Attica.

Saddler, Edson S. Barber, Attica.

Buglers, Sidney J. Richardson, Eagle; Peter Gilley, Attica.

Privates.—Ferdinand Button, Attica. Azern Bowen, Arcade, taken prisoner Sept. 17, 1863. Daniel Bowen, Yorkshire. Lorenzo Burdick, Bennington, wounded Aug. 11, 1863. Albert G. Burke, Arcade, taken prisoner May 7, 1864. Sidney Case, Sheldon, wounded April 1, 1863. Alfred R. Calkins, Arcade. John F. Cole, Eagle. Henry F. Chase, Rochester. Austin M. Drock, Portageville, wounded April 17, 1863. Willred I. Eastwood, Bennington. Daniel Fish, jr., Sheldon. Julius R. Ford, Rushford. Amos Hopkins, Centreville. Loomis D. Hall, China. William H. Hedger, Portage. Nathan E. Heald, Rushford. George W. Jones, China. G. Wallace Jones, China. William McKerrow, Arcade. George H. Kemball, Centreville. Anson F. Lawton, Rushford. William Langbush, jr., Attica. John Moores, Centreville. William H. Marsten, China. Darwin Nichols, Attica, wounded June 30, 1864. Gaius B. Parker, China. Willis Parker, Attica. James W. Randall, Java, wounded Sept. 19, 1863. Joseph Romlair, Java. George Suitor, Bennington. Velorous Swift, Rushford. Dwight Scott, Rushford. Martin Tuobey, Avon. Randal Taylor, Centreville. Richard Vename, Centreville. Samuel T. Williams, Bennington, wounded June 12, 1864. Leverett H. Waldo, Arcade. Wilber S. Wight, Centreville. Warren D. Withey, Rushford. John Parker, sergeant,

China, taken prisoner May 7, 1964. Artemas H. Jackson, corporal, Java, wounded Oct. 19, 1864. Hiram T. Merville, corporal, Eagle. William S. Avery, Tarrytown, wounded Apr. 1, 1863. George Button, Attica, taken prisoner Sept. 16, 1863. Elijah Bishop, Rushford. Herbert W. Cheeny, Eagle. David D. Chandler, Portageville. George H. Clark, Rochester. George W. Dutton, Eagle, taken prisoner Mch. 30, 1865. Thomas H. Gerand, Arcade. Eugene Griswold, Portage. William Langbush, Attica. Charles A. Maxon, Attica. Madison Merville, Eagle. Sperry A. Merville, Eagle. Matthias Rafter, Portage, wounded Apr. 17, 1863. Parmenius W. Simpson, Bennington, missing in action June 12, 1864. James C. Seely, Portage, missing in action June 12, 1864. George H. Smith, Eagle, wounded April 17, 1863. Andrew A. Williams, Bennington, taken prisoner Sept. 17, 1863. John M. White, Portage. Frank M. Smith, corporal, Friendship. James H. Agen, Wethersfield. Hector A. Arnold, West Almond. Simon Burbee, Wethersfield. Joseph Button, Sheldon. Charles Fairnier, New York city. Richard Hall, Ward. George W. Haynes, Scio. Henry Kelly, Oramel. Le Roy Lowe, Angelica. Dewitt Page, Belfast. Gardner Pratt, Buffalo. Calvin Shurtleff, West Spurtan. John M. Vanderwalker, Wethersfield. Eugene R. Vanderwalker, Gainesville, missing in action Sept. 19, 1864.

Discharged.—Oliver W. Atwood, sergeant, Cowlsville, discharged June, 1863. Charles J. Gardner, Attica, wounded Aug. 11, 1864. John T. Knox, corporal, Attica, wounded Jan. 30, 1863. Horatio T. Austin, Cowlsville, wounded Jan. 30, 1863. Dwight Abrams. Eagle. John H. Bradway, Attica. Lester T. Farrand, Arcade. Horace Nichols, China. Leverett Peck, Attica. Warren M. Reed, Java.

Transferred.—Charles Melvin, sergeant, Attica, to veteran reserve corps Jan., 1865. Walter A. Jackson, bugler, China. Benjamin F. Fairchild, Portage, wounded May 7, 1864; transferred to veteran reserve corps Oct., 1864.

Deceased.—Irving Pratt, sergeant Attica, of wounds received May 7, 1864. Monroe A. Terry, sergeant Attica, of wounds received May 30, 1864. Abel Clough, corporal, China, killed Oct. 10, 1864. Julius R. Fillmore, corporal, Attica, killed Sept. 19, 1864. Benjamin F. Atwood, Attica, of wounds received June 11, 1864. Leman E. Allen, Cowisville, killed May 11, 1864. Silas Armstrong, Portage, killed June 11, 1864. Harvey F. Guile, Attica, of wounds received May 7, 1864. Albert W. Hooper, Portage, of wounds received May 7, 1864. Humphrey M. Jones, Attica, of wounds received May 31, 1864. Frederick W. Knox, Attica, in prison Jan., 1864. Lyman Mead, Bennington, killed Apr. 17, 1863. Seymour L. Robinson, Bennington, of disease Sept., 1864. Michael Redding, Wethersfield, killed May 7, 1864. Jacob Sundraker, Attica, of disease Dec., 1864. Nelson W. Skinner, China, of wounds received June 31, 1864. Robert W. Van Valkenburg, Attica, killed Jan. 30, 1863. Charles Wolf, Portage, killed Oct. 17, 1868. Newton Wells, China, killed June 11, 1864.

COMPANY D.

Officers.—Jacob W. Knapp, captain; appointed Aug. 15, 1862; promoted major Dec. 10, 1864.

Leonard Wilkins, first lieutenant; appointed Aug. 5, 1862; resigned Sept. 13, 1863.

Jared M. Bills, second lieutenant; appointed Aug. 5, 1862; promoted first lieutenant Sept. 13, 1863: resigned Jan. 18, 1864.

William C. Morey, second lieutenant; appointed Aug. 1, 1863; promoted first lieutenant Jan. 18, 1864; made captain Dec. 10, 1864.

A. Hammond Hicks, second lieutenant; appointed Apr. 7, 1864; resigned Aug. 9, 1864.

Charles B. Annabel, second lieutenant; appointed Sept. 14, 1864; wounded.

James R. De Wolf, first lieutenant; appointed Dec. 10, 1864.

Sergeants—Eton D. Humphrey, Wyoming, wounded at Smithfield; Paul P. Draper, Warsaw; Harry Hibbard, North Collins, wounded at Trevillian Station; William H. Clark, La Grange; Joel Cronkite, Wyoming; Randolph Robinson, La Grange; Walter Curtis, Warsaw, wounded at Cold Harbor.

Corporals—Hiram L. Birdsall, La Grange; Sullivan Gibson, Warsaw; James E. Bishop, Warsaw; Edwin F. Newcomb, Pike; John Jones, Dale.

Blacksmith, Andrew Calvin, Castile.

Farrier, Orrin Gill, Warsaw.

Saddler, Charles Crocker, Peoria, wounded at Trevillian Station.

Buglers—Amos W. Austin, Perry Center; Henry Hollenbeck, Perry.

Privates.— Joel N. Austin, Eagle. Job S. Austin, Eagle. Elijah Briggs, Wyoming, George W. Bradley, Wyoming. James M. Barber, Otto. Chauncey W. Bussree, Perry. Edwin L. Chandler, Pike. John A. Cross, Eagle. Smith Dole, Wiscoy. James Dole, Wiscoy. Edwin P. Fanning, Perry. Alexander Granger, Warsaw. Hiram Gilman, Dale. Edward Gilman, Dale. Marquis F. Holton, Warsaw. Homer O. Holley, Warsaw. Charles Holley, Warsaw. William Hawley, Pike. John Herman, Orangeville. Charles Hyde, Lima. Edwin Hodge, Pike. James R. Hitchcock, Rushford. Jerome Kimball, North Collins. Charles O. Law, Perry. Charles D. Mosher, Rivington. Lawrence Mix, Warsaw. John McGinty, Lima. Joseph W. Morey, Delevan, Ill. Lyman Parshall, Leroy. Milo Pixley, Wyoming. Marcellus J. Peck, Pike. Franklin Pinney, Arcade. Olin S. Perkins, Wyoming. William Reynolds, Perry. Theodore Reynolds, Perry. George H. Root, Warsaw. Levi Rouse, Lima. Roselle Rose, Rochester. Ambrose Spencer, Eagle. Augustus F. Steele, Warsaw. Anson J. Smith, Warsaw. George W. Smith, Wiscoy. Anson J. Soules, Dale. George Snyde, Orangeville. Corwin J. Thomas, Pike. Peter Welch, Java Center. James D. Bishop, sergeant, Warsaw; wounded at Trevillian. Mills Marchant, corporal, Warsaw; wounded at Five Forks. Robert Barnett, Warsaw; wounded at Strasburg. Melaothon McWithey, Wethersfield. Charles G. Westlake, Perry. Edwin Bryant, Wethersfield. Henry W. Bleaker, Wyoming. William Baker, Geneseo. Clarence Clough, Almond. Emory F. Crocker, Peoria. Theodore F. Chapin, Wyoming. Arnold De Guile, Auburn. James B. Dubois, Dansville. George G. Eastland, Oswego. J. N. Graham, New York city. Mark Hughes, New York city. Thomas Howard, Mount Morris. Henry Lyon, La Grange; wounded July 19, 1864. Thomas McMann, Wirt. Henry O. Miller, New York city. S. M. Murphy, Geneseo. Thomas McReese, Dansville. William McPecker, Dansville. Thomas Mullen, Dansville. Merrit Raymond, Varysburg. William Redding, Eagle. George E. Reese, Dansville. George F. Robinson, Wirt.

George Reynick, Wyoming. Lawrence G. Russel, York Center. James O. Slayton, Dansville. Frederick Foyle, Dansville. Charles O. Willard, Canadice. Elijah Wilson, New Market.

Discharged—A. Hall Clarkson, Wethersfield. Charles B. Annabel, Bethany Center. Norton C. Bradish, Warsaw. William M. Bartlett, Warsaw. Frank Flint, Pike. William F. Graves, Warsaw. Andrew Gliss, Warsaw. William W. Gray, Portage. David S. Jenks, Orangeville. Porter B. Munger. Warsaw. Jeremiah G. Morgan, Wethersfield. Chauncey Osborne, Wethersfield. Arthur L. Spooner, Warsaw. Hopkins Salisbury, Warsaw. Allen M. Stark, Warsaw. Arthur H. Smith, Fowlerville. Benjamin J. Thompson, Perry.

Transferred.—Jonas Beardsley, Springwater, to U. S. artillery. Patrick Clifford, Dale, to V. R. C. Samuel M. Fisher, Warsaw, to V. R. C. Mace C. Lewis, Warsaw, to V. R. C. George F. Scribner, Warsaw, to V. R. C. Henry A. Tousley, Warsaw, to V. R. C. William Thompson, Warsaw, to 2nd U. S. artillery. Arthur H. Watts, Warsaw, to non-commissioned staff. Sept., 1862.

Deceased.—Charles B. Darling, sergeant, Warsaw, Dec. 14, 1864. L. C. Crittenden, sergeant, Warsaw, killed at Newtown. Bush Adams, corporal, Pike, killed at Port Republic. Charles H. Austin, Perry, Aug. 15, 1864. Ennis Barnes, Warsaw, killed at Trevillian Station. Albion J. Bentley, Covington. Charles Day, Wethersfield, Mch., 1864. Carlos Evans, Portage. Henry M. Gay, Pavillion, killed at Trevillian Station. Stephen A. Hood, Warsaw, July 2, 1864. Alonzo Hodge, Genesee Falls, July 29, 1863. Timothy Peaseley, Warsaw. Tunis Smith, Wyoming, of wounds received at Cedar Creek. Judson A. Spencer, Warsaw. James B. Simons, Perry, Sept. 23, 1864. Henry Spencer, Wethersfield, May 16, 1864. Jared Seymour, Perry, Aug. 26, 1864. Corydon C. Weaver, Castile, killed at Cold Harbor. Sylvester Wilday, Genesee Falls, Jan. 11, 1865.

CHAPTER XXIV.

HISTORY OF THE 136TH REGIMENT NEW YORK STATE VOLUNTEER INFANTRY.

WITHOUT recalling the circumstances of the time, the story of raising and arming volunteers in the late summer and the early autumn of 1862 reads like romance. Five times the ninety days which Seward's hopes had led him to prophesy as the time that would be required to crush the Rebellion had passed; great armies had been put into the field; repeated reverses had overtaken them; the peninsular campaign had ended disastrously; armed opposition to the government had grown into the most formidable revolt of modern times; the Confederate army, flushed with success, a second time menaced Washington.

In August, 1862, the struggle had not continued long enough to exhaust the loyal States, or to seriously tax their resources; it had been sufficiently severe and protracted to arouse their whole people.

The need of soldiers was great; the people felt deeply that their institutions were in peril; the pretensions of the Confederate government had assumed an importance which the loyal North was unwilling to accord them in the spring of 1861, and volunteers answered the call of the government as fast as they could be armed and organized for service.

The 136th regiment of infantry was raised at this time. Its ranks were filled from the counties of Wyoming, Livingston and Allegany, which then constituted the 30th senatorial district of New York. The 130th regiment, recruited from the same localities, had been mustered into the service a few days previous.

Three full companies of the 136th regiment were filled in Wyoming county,—Company D, Captain Augustus Harrington; Company E, Captain Henry B. Jenks; Company H, Captain E. H. Jeffres. Captain Harrington received authority to raise a company of volunteers, and commenced recruiting for the new regiment August 18th; and on the 29th of the same month he reported with a full company at Camp Portage, for muster. This was the first company in camp, and was recruited in about a week. Captain Jenks reported with a full company September 1st; Captain Jeffres's company was filled soon after.

Companies A and K were recruited in Allegany, and Companies B, C, F, G and I in Livingston county.

The 136th regiment was mustered September 25th, 1862, at Portage, Livingston county, with the following field and staff officers: Colonel, James Wood, jr.; lieutenant-colonel, Lester B. Faulkner; major, David C. Hartshorne; adjutant, Campbell H. Young; surgeon, B. L. Hovey; first assistant surgeon, Edwin Amsden; second assistant surgeon, Charles F. Warner.

The regiment left Camp Portage October 2nd. At Elmira its arms and equipments were issued. October 4th it went into Camp Seward, on Arlington Heights, which was its first encampment on rebel territory. From Arlington it moved to Fairfax Court house, Va., where it was attached to the 2nd brigade of the 11th corps, with Von Steinwehr as brigade commander, and Sigel, conspicuous with the recent renown of Pea Ridge, as corps commander. This regiment was occupied in picket duty on the advanced line of the army, and it suffered the hardships incident to changes of food, climate and habits—in short, to the change from civil to military life in time of war. Only three captains in the regiment were on duty November 9th. Company D, which left Portage 94 strong, reported only 45 men for duty November 26th.

The battle of Antietam was nobly won, and Lee hurried across the Potomac September 18th. Yet for more than a month McClellan's army remained in Maryland, and so this victory was rendered barren. Then the Army of the Potomac was reorganized. Burnside was placed in command. Sigel had a grand division, which formed the reserve, in which was the 136th regiment.

December 10th it left camp at Germantown, Va., and marched to the front. The regiment was reduced in numbers, but the men that were left had hardened, and gained the bearing and acquired the habits of soldiers. After the second day's march the sound of cannonading on the Rappahannock told that a battle was in progress; but the regiment reached Falmouth just after the army had recrossed the river from its disastrous attempt to carry the rebel works behind Fredericksburg. It soon moved up the river to Banks Ford, where it did picket duty in face of the enemy. Pontoons and artillery arrived on the 20th of January, 1863, and batteries were placed in position on the 21st; but, in consequence of a severe storm, the projected movement was reluctantly abandoned. Before the army could move the rebels had strengthened their position, and further offensive operations at that point were impracticable.

From Banks Ford the regiment went into camp at Stafford Court-house, Va., where it remained until the last of April, when it crossed the river at Kellogg's farm, and moved to Chancellorsville. There the brigade to which it was attached made a reconnoissance to the right of the 11th corps, under General Barlow, and captured nearly one thousand prisoners. While the 136th was absent on this reconnoissance the 11th corps was driven from the field, and the guards and camp equipage left behind by the regiment fell into the enemy's hands.

The brigade then took position in the rear of General Sickles command, in time for the 136th regiment to witness one of the severest conflicts of the war.

After Chancellorsville the regiment went into its old quarters at Stafford Court-house, where it remained until Lee again assumed the offensive, when it moved at about equal pace with the enemy to Hagerstown, Md., where the regiment remained a short time.

July 1st, at 5 P. M., the 136th regiment left its camp at Hagerstown, and at 11 A. M. July 2nd it reached Gettysburg, making in this time the remarkable march of thirty-eight miles. This regiment was a part of the first brigade that reached the battle field. It was assigned a position fronting Gettysburg from the face of Cemetery hill, where it remained from the morning of the 2nd until the evening of the 4th of July. The battle raged fiercely, but these men did not waver amid the thunder of cannon, the plowing of shot and shell, the rattle of musketry and the groans of the wounded and dying. This decisive victory rolled back the tide of rebel invasion, and struck the army of Virginia a blow from which it never recovered.

The 136th regiment remained with the Army of the Potomac until September 23d, when the 11th and the 12th corps were detached from this army and sent under Hooker to the relief of Rosecrans at Chattanooga.

When Hooker's command reached Lookout Mountain, from its summit the enemy saw his disposition of the Union forces, and their first camp had hardly become quiet at night when the roar of artillery, the screaming of shells and the rattle of small arms opened the grand and awful spectacle of a battle at night. The rebels made a fierce attack on General Geary. They were intrenched on a steep hill, and the 136th New York, the 73d Ohio and the 33d Massachusetts were ordered to charge. Under the lead of Colonel Smith of the 73d Ohio these three regiments drove the enemy from this strong position, and their heavy loss told how gallantly they had borne themselves in the conflict.

After this engagement the regiment, with its brigade, crossed the Chattanooga and joined the command of General Thomas. Every duty assigned it here was successfully done. It was engaged in the battle of November 25th, which terminated the three days' conflict by which Bragg was driven back into Georgia.

The 11th corps was then ordered to the relief of Burnside at Knoxville. The weather was severe. Many of the men marched on the frozen ground, with feet nearly bare. Without rations, haversacks, knapsacks, tents or blankets, the hardships of this march cannot be described. They were severe, probably beyond any other campaign of the war; but there was very little murmuring.

As this re-enforcement approached Knoxville, the rebels fell back without further struggle. The regiment then returned to the Wahatchie valley, and went into comfortable winter quarters.

The army was reorganized for the spring campaign. Hooker had the 20th corps, and the regiment was attached to the 3d brigade of the 3d division. Resaca was the first battle of the campaign, and to the 136th this was the most destructive of all its engagements. The 3d brigade was ordered to storm the rebel works. In making this charge the 136th regiment crossed an open field, exposed to the bullets of rebel sharpshooters, and in face of a murderous fire of artillery and musketry from behind formidable intrenchments. In this charge it suffered a loss of more than one-fourth its effective force, and did all that bravery could, although the works were not carried.

From Resaca the regiment marched with its brigade to Pallas Church, where it met the enemy. The next engagement was the battle of Peach Tree Creek. During this action, while the Union regiments were moving to repel a charge of the enemy, a rebel color bearer advanced in front of his regiment and confronted this. The color bearer of the 136th at once advanced to meet him, and these daring soldiers of the blue and the grey stood defiant in the face of two armies. The bold rebel was instantly shot; his colors were captured and flaunted in the face of the foe. A soldier avenged his comrade by the death of the man who had slain him, and recovered the colors. As this captor was bearing it away a loyal hand slew him, and the thrice captured flag was retaken. It now hangs among the war trophies in the military bureau is Albany, with other captured rebel battle-flags.

The regiment took an active part in the masterly series of maneuvers in northern Georgia by which Sherman outflanked Johnston and beat him in battles, after which he defeated Hood, and forced that Confederate commander to abandon Atlanta.

In that grand march of our army from Atlanta to the sea the 136th regiment sustained its reputation and won fresh laurels. The hardships of that memorable campaign were shared by these now veterans; marching through swamps, fighting and foraging through the Empire State of the south, no force could withstand our brave soldiers, no danger intimidate, no obstacle hinder. From the 15th of November, when Sherman left his base of supplies and turned his back on the ruins of Atlanta, through all that stretch of hostile territory occupying every town on the line of march, overcoming every force sent against him, carrying Fort McAllister by assault instead of besieging that stronghold, to the 21st of December, when our victorious army reached a new base and occupied Savannah, every day had its story of heroic endurance and soldierly achievements, to which the 136th regiment contributed.

And, when the history of that bold anabasis shall be fully written, and the men who fought and established the theory of the genius who planned that dazzling campaign shall receive their share of its glory, no mean place will belong to these loyal men, who left the valleys and hills of Wyoming to take up the musket and the sword in defense of the Union established by the fathers.

From Savannah the regiment moved northward with its brigade. Columbia was captured February 17th, and the evacuation of Charleston by the Confederates then became a military necessity. Hardee was defeated March 16th, and four days later Johnston was conquered. Then came the occupation of Petersburg, and the fall of Richmond and the surrender of Lee, and the great rebellion was ended.

From Richmond the 136th regiment moved over the field of Chancellorsville, and across the territory where it learned its first lessons in war three years before, to Washington; at last freed from danger and no longer menaced by the foe its valor had helped to vanquish. Thence it was transported to Rochester, where the regiment was discharged from the service it had so faithfully performed.

Then came a fresh marvel of history. These men, so long accustomed to the license of camp, returned to the peaceful pursuits of civil life, and without social disturbance were transformed from soldiers into orderly and industrious citizens of the government they bravely fought to save.

CHAPTER XXV.

HISTORY OF THE "GOVERNOR'S GUARD," OR SECOND REGIMENT OF MOUNTED RIFLES.

IN the month of July, 1863, under the head of "GOVERNOR'S GUARD," the following announcement was made in the papers throughout western New York, and circulated through the country in the form of handbills:

"Colonel John Fisk, of Niagara, has been authorized by Governor Seymour to raise a regiment for three years'service in the U. S. Army, to be known as the 'Governor's Guard.' Any person desiring to raise a company to be attached to this regiment can procure authority by applying to Colonel John

Fisk, of Suspension Bridge, or Lieutenant-Colonel Cook, or Captain William P. Warren, late of the 28th New York.

"Captain Warren will act as adjutant in forming the regiment. Headquarters at Lockport."

It was shortly afterward made known that the regiment would do mounted rifle service. Twelve companies were raised, and by February, 1864, the regiment was ready for the field.

The regimental officers were: Colonel, John Fisk, Niagara Falls; lieutenant-colonel, Jasper N. Raymond, New York; lieutenant-colonel, Joseph Wood, 2nd regular cavalry; major, William H. H. Mapes, Lockport; major, John D. Newman, Lockport; major, John H. Fralick, Little Falls; adjutant, William P. Warren, Lockport; adjutant, Franklin Rogers, Buffalo; quartermaster, Henry F. Pierce, Niagara Falls; commissary, Joseph A. Briggs, Buffalo; commissary, John M. Hill, Lockport; surgeon, Robert T. Paine, Lockport; assistant surgeon, Hugh McGregor Wilson, Lockport; assistant surgeon, E. Woodworth, Allegany; chaplain, Washington Stickney.

Wyoming county was represented in this regiment by the men named below:

Frederick Churning, Charles E. Gale, Charles Grabe, Thomas Haley, Norman L. Knox, Edward Lampman, Edward Launt, Michael Martin, Timothy Moronay, Lewis Meuning, Albert Nichols, James H. Phillips, Thomas Rial, Francis Shandal, Stephen B. Sprague, William Weaver, Attica; O. P. French, Bennington; Albert G. Borden, George C. Babcock, Hiram E. Booth, John Fingal, Andrew Frayer, Thomas Gibbons, Nicholas Hannah, Thomas Hannah, Frank Higgins, Francis Hardin, Jonathan Johnson, John Lee, Alexander Mead, Edwin Mosier, P. McMarriman, Ezra Patterson, George P. Pierce, Castile; T. W. Copeland, Joseph M. Hewit, Charles Perkins, Johnson C. Robinson, Francis Shannon, Covington; Abram A. Howell, Gensee Falls; Washington Whitney, Eagle; Phillip Webber, Middlebury; George B. Austin, Engene Besancon, C. E. Cruttenden, John Drake, Abram Ellis, M. F. Horing, George M. Spencer, John W. Kellogg, Charles Lyon, Frank W. Lilybridge, Lester McCollum, Jeremiah P. Morrison (second lieutenant), Henry Pike, William Henry, Russel Henry Runyon, La Fayette Randal, Earl F. Thomas, Charles W. Trail, Martin L. Van Slyke, Henry Vosbnrgh, G. B. Woodworth, Benjamin Waite, Pike; Francis A. Calkins, Perry; Daniel W. Peck, Marvin Preston, John Streamer, Joseph J. Streamer and Morris Warren, Warsaw.

The regiment first rendezvoused at Lockport, but the barracks were insufficient and it was ordered to Fort Porter, Buffalo, which latter barracks were made a recruiting station and camp of instruction. The 2nd remained there from December, 1863, until the March following, when three battalions being completed they were ordered to Camp Stoneman, near Giesboro Point, in the neighborhood of Washington. Here they remained till about May 1st, when they were ordered to the front to reinforce the Army of the Potomac. Instead of being furnished with the cavalry outfit for which they were sent to Camp Stoneman, or receiving instruction in cavalry tactics, which had been promised them, they were assigned to a provisional brigade composed of dismounted cavalry and heavy artillery, commanded by Colonel Marshall, of the 14th heavy artillery, in the 9th army corps, under General Burnside.

On the day following their arrival at Camp Stoneman they participated in the battle of Spottsylvania, suffering but little loss. Their next engagement was at the battle of North Anna, southeast of Spottsylvania. In this their loss was light.

Returning from North Anna, the regiment was placed as rear guard of the 9th corps, when it had a severe engagement at Tolopotomy creek, losing quite a number of men. The next day it was in the fight at Bethesda Church, a few miles from Tolopotomy. At this time the regiment was under command of Lieutenant-Colonel Raymond, of New York. The loss at Bethesda was quite heavy, 50 or 60 killed and wounded. Among those killed was Lieutenant Jeremiah R. Morrison, of Wyoming county.

Hardly had the smoke of this battle cleared away before the 2nd was in the memorable fight at Cold Harbor in early June, but its loss here was not heavy. Among those wounded was Lieutenant Charles W. Flagler. From Cold Harbor the regiment moved with the army of the Potomac and crossed the James river, arriving at Petersburg June 16th—just in time for service again. On the morning of the 17th the 2nd made a charge over the enemy's works and captured a large number of prisoners, who were sent to the rear in charge of Captain W. Fitzer Williams. The regiment was engaged during the entire day, but its loss was light. On the morning of the 18th of June it again advanced on the enemy's works near the Weldon railroad, and toward evening made a gallant charge which resulted in the capture of the railroad, the 2nd, however, suffering a terrible loss—some 200 men, killed and wounded.

From this time until July 29th, 1864, the regiment lay in the rifle pits under a constant fire, losing men day by day, and among them Lieutenant J. L. Atwood, who was killed by a sharpshooter. On the morning of July 30th the mine in front of Petersburg was exploded. A terrible struggle followed, in which the 2nd regiment was engaged under command of Major Mapes. One division was repulsed by the rebels. The division in which the 2nd fought had been held for the final charge, in case those already in the fight did not hold their ground. The order was finally given for them to charge, and they did it nobly, capturing two lines of the enemy's works. They held them about six hours, but as no relief came they were compelled to fail back. In this engagement the regiment lost nearly 150 men killed, wounded and prisoners.

The next battle was at Pegram's Farm, southwest of Petersburg, where Major Mapes, Captain Stebbins, Lieutenant Mansfield, Lieutenant Bush and others, in all 40 or 50, were taken prisoners. The killed and wounded numbered between 50 and 75. The next field was the battle of Hatcher's Run, in October, 1864. The loss was slight. From there the 2nd went back to Pegram's Farm, where it remained until the last of November. It was then ordered to dismounted camp at City Point, where the men received their promised horses, with orders to report to General Charles H. Smith, of the 3d brigade, 2nd cavalry division. The second day after reporting the regiment went on a raid to Stony Creek Station, where, with the rest of the division, it assisted in destroying a large amount of stores and taking many prisoners, sustaining slight loss. It then returned to camp near Fort Stevenson, in the vicinity of South Petersburg, where it remained until December, 1864. The regiment next accompanied the celebrated Warren raiders, and assisted in the destruction of the Weldon railroad, from near Petersburg to Weldon, N. C.

At this time the 2nd was divided, a detachment having been sent back to the second battle of Hatcher's Run, under command of Lieutenant Newman. In this action the 2nd lost about 40 men, among them Captain Watson and Lieutenant Tippling, of Wayne county. It went into camp again and remained until March 29th, 1865, doing picket duty and losing but few men. On this date it started with General Sheridan's corps in the final pursuit of Lee, and March 30th engaged in the battle of Dinwiddie Court-house, southeast of Petersburg.

The next day the 2nd was in the battle of Five Forks, but sustained no loss. Next at Jettysville, it lost a dozen wounded, but none killed. At Sailor's Creek it lost a few men; also at Farmville. It was next engaged at Appomattox Court-house, where Joshua Smith was killed. After doing service at Appomattox, the brigade to which this regiment belonged was detailed as an escort of General Grant from Appomattox to Burkville Junction, Va. It then returned to Petersburg, when, pending negotiations between Johnston and Sherman, it was ordered to North Carolina to reinforce Sherman. There it was learned that Johnston had surrendered, and the 2nd was ordered back to Petersburg, and from there to Buckingham county, Va., where it remained on provost duty until August, 1865.

This closed the eventful career of the regiment, and its next movement was homeward. It arrived in Buffalo August 10th, 1865, and was mustered out. It left home 1,500 strong, and during the service was reinforced by more than 300 recruits; but came back with only between 700 and 800 men. The depleted ranks, and the scars the survivors bore, told the story of their service in their country's defense. They were in the field a little more than a year, and they took part in nineteen distinct engagements, as recorded in this narrative.

CHAPTER XXVI.

THE HISTORY OF POLITICAL OPINION AND PARTY FORTUNES IN WYOMING COUNTY.

AT the commencement of the settlement of this county two great political parties existed—the Federal and the Republican. The opposition of the Federalists to the war of 1812 rendered them so exceedingly unpopular that their name was dropped, and the members of the party in this State sought other affiliations. The Republicans had, by their opponents, been termed in the way of reproach or derision Democrats, a name which they came gradually to adopt. They were also nicknamed "Bucktails," because a club or society of their party adopted as a badge the caudal appendage of a deer. Their opponents were called "Clintonians," after their leader, De Witt Clinton. They were afterward termed National Republicans, which name distinguished them from the Democratic Republicans, or Democrats, as the old Republican party was afterward called.

In 1826 arose the famous Morgan excitement, which had its origin in Batavia. Of this it is only necessary briefly to say that one William Morgan had written for publication a book, purporting to disclose the secrets of free masonry. It was alleged that for this he was abducted and probably murdered by the masons. This gave origin to the Anti-Masonic party, which became fully organized in 1828, and which at once became overwhelmingly strong in western New York, and especially in Genesee county. In 1832 a coalition was formed between the Anti-Masonic and National Republican parties in this State, the objects of which were to elect the Anti-Masonic State ticket and carry the State for Henry Clay, the National Republican candidate for President; but neither was successful. The existence of the Anti-Masonic party terminated with this coalition, which took the name of Whig, and retained it till the present Republican party was formed.

The systematic agitation of the slavery question commenced in the year 1833, during which the American Anti-Slavery Society was formed; and that question has exerted a most potent influence on political affairs, national and local. From time to time the Legislature enacted laws concerning slavery down to the year 1819. A law passed in 1799 provided for the gradual extinction of slavery in the State. "In 1817 a further act was passed, decreeing that there should be no slavery in the State after the 4th of July, 1827. Ten thousand slaves were set free by this act."

In the latter part of 1835, at Utica, "a meeting, convened to form a State anti-slavery society, was broken up by a most respectable committee appointed by a large meeting of citizens. * * * The abolitionists, at Gerrit Smith's invitation, adjourned to his home at Peterboro, Madison county, and there completed their organization." It was afterward learned that a mob had been organized to follow and break up the convention at Peterboro, but desisted from its purpose on learning that the convention had adjourned.

To that convention Dr. Augustus Frank, F. C. D. McKay, Samuel Fisher (2nd), William Buxton and Rev. Abraham Ennis from this county were delegates.

A county anti-slavery society was formed in Genesee county. It held a meeting at Batavia March 16th, 1836. General John D. Landon, of Castile, and William Patterson,of Warsaw, were members of a committee appointed on this occasion to answer an address from the pro-slavery people of Batavia, who threatened to and finally did, break up the meeting. The meeting adjourned to reconvene at Warsaw a week later.

"Pursuant to adjournment the Genesee County Anti-Slavery Society met at Warsaw March 23d, 1836. A series of resolutions and an address were adopted, together with a 'declaration of sentiment,' expressing in brief form the principles of the abolitionists for the information of any who might never have seen a statement of them. Measures were also taken for establishing a free press, and $1,000 was pledged for its support the first year. Such a paper was accordingly established at Warsaw [the *American Citizen*; removed in a year to Perry, and afterward to Rochester].

"A meeting of the Western New York Anti-Slavery Society was held at Warsaw, in the Presbyterian church, November 13th, 1839. The extreme badness of the roads prevented a general attendance. There were present about fifty persons as members, nearly all of them from the southern towns of the county, then Genesee. A proposition was made to nominate candidates for President and Vice-President. It was opposed by a large portion of the members, but its advocates, among whom were Myron Holley and William L. Chaplin, able and eloquent men, who had come for this special purpose, succeeded, after a two days' discussion, in carrying the measure by a small majority. James G. Birney, formerly a slaveholder in Alabama, who had emancipated his slaves and removed to the north, was nominated for President, and Francis J. Lemoyne, of Pennsylvania, for Vice-President.

"The result of this measure was to divide the abolitionists. A large majority in this State and other States refused to join the new party, and continued their connection with the old parties, voting generally, however, for candidates for Congress who were in favor of a respectful reception of anti-slavery petitions, and for abolishing slavery in the District of Columbia, and opposed to its extension into free territory, by which party soever they had been nominated."

The supporters of Birney were called the Liberty party. They generally cast from 300 to 500 votes in this county, and about 15,000 in the State. In 1848 they joined the Free-Soil party.

Party organizations in this State and in this county were greatly disturbed by the Free-Soil movement of 1848. For some years previous to that time a division had existed in the Democratic party, one faction being known as "Hunkers" and the other as "Barnburners," the latter faction being opposed to slavery extension, especially into the territory that had then recently been acquired from Mexico. This schism became an open rupture in 1848. The Barnburners held a convention at Utica, in which they nominated Martin Van Buren for President, and afterward another at Buffalo, which was participated in by delegates from other States, and over which the late Chief Justice Chase presided. At that convention, which adopted what has ever since been known as the Buffalo Platform—the distinctive features of which were the abolition of slavery wherever it existed in territories under the jurisdiction of Congress, and its non-extension into territory under such jurisdiction—the county of Wyoming was fully represented. A State convention was afterward called by this, which was known as the Free-Soil party, and a State ticket nominated, on which John A. Dix was the candidate for governor, and Seth M. Gates, a citizen of this county, for lieutenant-governor. Among the active leaders in this party in the county of Wyoming were: Seth M. Gates, F. C. D. McKay, L. W. Thayer, J. R. Doolittle, W. Riley Smith and A. W. Young, of Warsaw; James H. Loomis and John B. Skinner, 2nd, of Attica; James C. Ferris, of Wyoming; D. L. Gilman and L. A. Haywood, of Perry; E. O. Shepard, of Arcade; A. P. Sherril, of Pike, and William Bristol, of Gainesville. The Free-Soil vote at the ensuing election was drawn from both the Whig and Democratic parties, and of course embraced that of the Liberty party, which was then merged in it.

The Free-Soil party maintained its organization till 1849, but in 1850 the Barnburners and Hunkers united and nominated Horatio Seymour for Governor. About that time a schism came to exist in the Hunker wing of the Democratic party. Those who opposed union with the Barnburners were termed "Hard Shells," or "Hards," and those who favored such union "Softs." About the same time, or during the administration of President Fillmore, the Whig party became divided into the Conservatives, or "Silver Grays," the supporters of the administration, and the Radicals, or "Wooly-Heads," under the leadership of William H. Seward. In Wyoming county the Radicals of the Whig party and the Softs among the Democrats were largely in the majority in their respective parties.

In 1852 the Whig party suffered such an overwhelming defeat that it was practically annihilated, and from its ruins sprang the present Republican party, which embraced many who had belonged to the Barnburner wing of the Democratic party.

About the year 1853, or soon after the defeat of the Whig party, the American party suddenly sprang into existence. The deliberations of the members of this party were conducted in secret, and when questioned concerning things pertaining to the party, its members professed to know nothing of them; hence they acquired the name of the Know-Nothing party. Opposition to the influence of foreigners who had not acquired a sufficient knowledge of the institutions of this country to vote intelligently was the basic idea in the political faith which this party professed; and such a modification of the naturalization laws as would extend the term of probation of immigrants from other countries was the principal measure which was advocated by this party. It was believed that in the unsettled condition of parties at that time, and the weakness of party ties consequent upon that condition, many were induced to become members of that party from curiosity, or a love of novelty, or from a desire to enjoy the sport which arose out of the discomfiture, disappointment and wrath of old party leaders when they found their plans thwarted and their calculations upset by a secret agency, of which they knew nothing. The party had only a brief existence.

The Republican party was organized in 1855. The advocates of slavery had long seen that in the rapid growth of this country their "peculiar institution" would, if left to itself, become impotent, or, in other words, the "balance of power" between the free and slave States would be lost to them in the "irrepressible conflict" between freedom and slavery. They therefore endeavored to extend their institution into the territories of the United States, and in order to accomplish their purpose they sought to remove the barriers that had been established by the compromises previously made, a history of which cannot be given here. Had slavery never assumed this aggressive character, the Republican party would have had no existence; for it was established on the issue of slavery extension. In 1856 were freely uttered by political leaders threats of secession in case of the election of John C. Fremont, the Republican candidate for President. In 1860 the Republican candidate, Abraham Lincoln, was elected. A portion of the slave States enacted ordinances of secession, and the late civil war, with the extinction of slavery, was the result. During the fourteen years that have elapsed since the termination of this war the Republican and Democratic parties have continued to oppose each other on minor and comparatively insignificant issues; and on the approach of each election the old question and its answer seem quite apropos—

> "What is all this wondrous fuss, this war of words, about?
> The outs are trying to get in, the ins to keep them out."

Excepting the anti-slavery sentiment there has been nothing peculiar in the relations of polical parties here. Party lines have been distinctly drawn, and party feeling has run high. A few years since it was related by the late John A. McElwain, in an article published in the *Western New Yorker*, that at an election in Warsaw in 1820, when the Clintonians and the Bucktails were the opposing parties, very forcible arguments were used; and in the rough and tumble work of the election some had their clothes torn from their backs, and it was found necessary to invoke the aid of the sheriff of Genesee county and a corps of deputies to prevent serious disorder.

At the time of the organization of Wyoming county the Whig and Democratic parties were the chief opponents. Among the active members of the former party at that time are remembered Harvey Putnam, James G. Hoyt and W. Riley Smith, of Attica; John B. Halsted and Alonzo B. Rose, Castile; John A. McElwain, Dr. Augustus Frank, John Wilder, Andrew W. Young

Andrew W. Young.

and Roswell Gould, Warsaw; Peter Patterson, Calvin P. Bailey, Isaac N. Stoddard and Robert Patterson, Perry; Eleazer Baldwin and Arden Woodruff, Sheldon; James Sprague, Covington; John W. Brownson, Gainesville; John Head, Truman Lewis and Lyman Babbit, Orangeville; William R. Groger and Abel Webster, Wethersfield; Nelson Wolcott, Java, and others. Of Democrats there are remembered Alden S. Stevens, Attica; John B. Skinner, Middlebury; Nyrum Reynolds, Gainesville; Samuel Smith, Java; Joel S. Smith and James R. Doolittle, Wethersfield; Rufus H. Smith, William Mitchell, Mosely Stoddard and Linus W. Thayer, Perry; Benjamin F. Folsom, Bennington, and others.

The following statement of the number of votes cast for principal candidates at important elections since the organization of the county shows the relative strength of the parties during that time:

At the special election in June, 1841, William R. Groger, the Whig candidate for sheriff, received 1,632 votes; John D. Landon, Democrat, 1,335.

In 1842 Luther Bradish, Whig candidate for governor, received 2,063; William C. Bouck, Democrat, 1,889; Alvan Stewart, Liberty, 335. Subsequent votes, in brief, have been as follows:

In 1844: For governor—Millard Fillmore, Whig, 2,797; Silas Wright, Democrat, 2,110; Alvan Stewart, Liberty, 408. For President—Henry Clay, Whig, 2,754; James K. Polk, 2,102; James G. Birney, Liberty, 442.

In 1846: For governor—John Young, Whig, 2,875; Silas Wright, Democrat, 1,702; Harvey Bradley, Liberty, 326.

In 1848: For governor—Hamilton Fish, Whig, 2,554; Reuben H. Walworth, Democrat, 1,881; John A. Dix, Free Soil, 1,576. For President—Zachary Taylor, Whig, 2,381; Lewis Cass, Democrat, 1,337; Martin Van Buren, Free Soil, 1,630.

In 1850: For governor—Washington Hunt, Whig, 2,788; Horatio Seymour, Democrat, 2,111.

In 1852: For governor—Washington Hunt, Whig, 3,090; Horatio Seymour, Democrat, 2,600; Minthorne Tompkins, Liberty, 510. For President—Winfield Scott, Whig, 3,005; Franklin Pierce, Democrat, 2,471; John P. Hale, Liberty, 727.

In 1854: For governor—Myron H. Clark, Whig, 2,100; Horatio Seymour, Democrat, 1,242; Daniel Ulman, American, 981; Greene C. Bronson, "Hard," 546.

In 1856: For governor—John R. King, Republican, 3,942; Amasa J. Parker, Democrat, 1,969; Erastus Brooks, American, 642. For President—John C. Fremont, Republican, 4,066; James Buchanan, Democrat, 1,911; Millard Fillmore, American, 571.

In 1858: For governor—Edwin D. Morgan, Republican, 3,204; Amasa J. Parker, Democrat, 1,952; Lorenzo Burrows, American, 350.

In 1860: For governor—Edwin D. Morgan, Republican, 4,488; William Kelly, Democrat, 2,349. For President—Abraham Lincoln, Republican, 4,498; Stephen A. Douglas, Democrat, 2,394.

In 1862: For governor—James Wadsworth, Republican, 3,677; Horatio Seymour, Democrat, 2,897.

In 1864: For governor—Reuben E. Fenton, Republican, 4,146; Horatio Seymour, Democrat, 2,563. For President—Abraham Lincoln, Republican, 4,126; George B. McClellan, Democrat, 2,569.

In 1866: For governor—Reuben E. Fenton, Republican, 4,105; John T. Hoffman, Democrat, 2,298.

In 1868: For governor—John A. Griswold, Republican, 4,205; John T. Hoffman, Democrat, 2,620. For President—U. S. Grant, Republican, 4,226; Horatio Seymour, Democrat, 2,591.

In 1870: For governor—Stewart L. Woodford, Republican, 3,584; John T. Hoffman, Democrat, 2,399.

In 1872: For governor—John A. Dix, Republican, 3,945; Francis Kernan, Democrat, 2,363. For President—U. S. Grant, Republican, 3,909; Horace Greeley, Democrat and Liberal Republican, 2,301.

In 1874: For governor—John A. Dix, Republican, 3,438; Samuel J. Tilden, Democrat, 2,416.

In 1876: For governor—Edwin D. Morgan, Republican, 4,404; Lucius Robinson, Democrat, 3,277. For President—R. B. Hayes, Republican, 4,428; Samuel J. Tilden, Democrat, 3,266.

In 1879: For governor—A. B. Cornell, Republican, 3,821; Lucius Robinson, Democrat, 2,494.

CHAPTER XXVII.

WYOMING CO. CONGREGATIONAL CONFERENCE—S. S. TEACHERS' ASSOCIATION & BIBLE SOCIETY—TEMPERANCE REFORM.

IN compliance with a call which had been issued by a committee of the Congregational church in Gainesville, a meeting was held at their church "to consider, and, if deemed expedient, to devise some means of promoting the fellowship and spiritual edification of our churches."

At this meeting there were present from the Congregational church at China, Rev. Lewis P. Frost, R. W. Lyman; Castile—Rev. Charles Machim, Gideon Schofield, William Kellogg; Gainesville—Rev. John Cunningham, Benjamin F. Bristol, Phineas Danforth; Orangeville—Rev. E. H. Stratton,

Marshal B. Crosset; Java—Rev. L. Parker, George W. Wainright, Demetrius Smith; Strykersville—Rev. James R. Bourne, Adin Woodruff; Warsaw—Rev. E. E. Williams, Newberry Bronson, Hanover Bradley.

For the accomplishment of the objects set forth in the call it was deemed expedient to form an association, and a constitution was adopted. It was called the Wyoming County Conference of Congregational Ministers and Churches, the churches being present at meetings by delegates. The officers chosen annually were a moderator and a scribe, to whom was afterward added a statistical secretary, who was also treasurer.

Biennial sessions of the conference were prescribed in the constitution, and one of the articles distinctly stated that no ecclesiastical power should be delegated to or exercised by the body. It was afterward provided that if any minister or church should be guilty of unchristian conduct, or of maintaining any fundamental error, or ot denying any fundamental doctrine of Christianity, the conference should withdraw fellowship from such minister or church.

One article read: "The sessions of the conference shall be devoted to such religious exercises as shall seem best fitted to subserve the end for which it is established; particularly to addresses on the responsibilities of the churches, on family religion, the maintenance of Christian discipline, the interests of Sabbath-schools, the claims of benevolent objects, and whatever bears directly and obviously on the spiritual progress and welfare of the churches."

In the new constitution, which was adopted in 1865, it was provided that "any person applying for approval as a candidate [for the ministry] shall be required to exhibit satisfactory evidence of his good standing in some evangelical church, and to sustain an examination in regard to his literary and scientific attainments, his knowledge of mental and moral philosophy, natural and revealed theology, the evidences of Christianity, ecclesiastical history, church polity, homiletics and the principles of biblical interpretation. He shall also read a sermon, and give an account of his religious experience, and of his motives in entering the ministry. No part shall be omitted, except by special vote. The examination shall be conducted by committees, chosen annually for this purpose."

In its practical working this conference has enabled the churches to keep up an interest in each other—has been a source of encouragement and a means of mutual usefulness, as well as a bond of friendship. Its meetings have always been public. The present officers are: Rev. E. F. Atwood, moderator, and Jeremiah Lamberson, scribe, statistical secretary and treasurer.

WYOMING COUNTY SUNDAY-SCHOOL ASSOCIATION.

At the State convention of Sabbath-school teachers in 1857 at Rochester a resolution was passed recommending such action in each county as should lead to the formation of county associations auxiliary to the State association.

For the purpose of carrying out this object a meeting of the pastors of churches and delegates from their Sunday-schools was called at the court-house in Warsaw on the 17th of November, 1857. At this meeting delegates were present from churches and schools in the towns of Attica, China, Gainesville, Middlebury, Orangeville, Perry and Warsaw. Articles of association were adopted, the first two of which read as follows:

"This association shall be called the Wyoming County Sunday-school Association, and shall consist of such teachers and officers as are hereinafter provided.

"The objects of this association are to obtain statistical information relative to the Sunday-schools of the county; to inquire into and search out the destitutions of this county; to visit and co-operate with every town and neighborhood in the building up and enlarging of schools now existing, and the establishing of new schools where needed, to the end that all children and youth may be gathered into Sunday-school."

The other articles prescribed the usual officers and their duties, and the manner of carrying out the objects of the association. The permanent officers chosen at that meeting were: President, Rev. S. Luckey, D. D., of Gainesville; recording secretary, I. Swift, of Warsaw; corresponding secretary, L. E. Walker, Warsaw. The town secretaries chosen and appointed were: Attica, James Baker; Bennington, Dr. E. C. Holt; Castile, S. Sedgwick; China, R. W. Lyman; Covington, Arnold Green; Eagle, Rev. William Plumb; Gainesville, William Glover; Genesee Falls, Homer Smith; Java, W. S. Brown; Middlebury, H. J. Reddish; Orangeville, George H. Dunham; Perry, Nathan Bills, Pike, Rev. Z. Hurd; Sheldon, Arden Woodbury; Warsaw, N. Jackson Morris; Wethersfield, Daniel Stedman.

The articles provided for stated meetings of the association for the election of officers, the transaction of business, etc. These meetings were held successively at different places in the county.

"The results attained from this association in Wyoming county have been an intelligent co-operative interest in Bible study, and a healthy public opinion on theological subjects without sectarian prejudice. Bible subjects have been found too inexhaustible for mere dogmatic interpretation, and a more intelligent liberal spirit has seemed to manifest itself through the annual and semi-annual comparison of views, methods and results of this special Christian working, in which Wyoming county has ever been at the front.

"The mission work growing out of this association has resulted in elevating the love and standard of morality in outlying districts, repressing evil tendencies and establishing the fact of such association work being a conservation of public morals and good citizenship."

TEMPERANCE.

Octogenarians distinctly remember that in the days of their youth the use of spirituous liquors as a beverage was almost universal. Many of the early settlers of this county and of this entire region were accustomed to take their daily drams, and a failure to treat a visitor was regarded as a breach of hospitality. At logging "bees," raising, etc., the whiskey jug was considered a positive necessity, and the failure of bees by reason of its absence is still remembered by some old people. It was regularly taken into the harvest field, and by many liquor was regularly placed on the breakfast table, where it was used as an appetizer. It was made bitter with tansy, wormwood, or some other herb or drug, and used as a domestic remedy for many real or imaginary ailments.

Distilleries early sprang up in many of the towns, and liquor was easily procured at a cheap rate. Nearly all country merchants kept it for sale, and were in the habit of treating their patrons from decanters kept for that purpose on their counters, as a compliment when they made liberal purchases, or to put them in a tradeable mood.

It was used to keep out the cold and to protect against the heat. Its use was not limited to the vulgar alone, but was sanctioned and adopted by all classes. The physician sought to protect himself against the contagion to which he was often exposed, and to solace himself during his weary nocturnal rides by its use; the jurist sharpened his perceptions, and prepared himself for powerful forensic efforts in the same way; and often the clergyman drank from the glass a portion of the inspiration that enabled him to present divine truth in its clearest light. The words of a modern poet—

"The power enslaved in yonder cask
Shall many burdens bear;
Shall nerve the toiler at his task,
The soul at prayer—"

seem quite apropos concerning alcohol as used in those days.

It is difficult now to learn who commenced the temperance reform or where it originated. It is remembered, however, that temperance societies began to come into existence about the year 1828, 1829 or 1830. Like all important reforms it took shape gradually. The first pledges proscribed only ardent spirits, and left people quite at liberty to use fermented liquors ad libitum. It was found that this did not reach the root of the evil; that persons who had acquired an appetite for stimulants only changed the kind of drink, and indulged these appetites as before; and that intemperate habits were quite as readily acquired by the use of the milder beverages. It was readily seen, therefore, that in order to accomplish the desired good a pledge of abstinence from all that could intoxicate was necessary, and societies generally readily adopted this pledge. The Genesee County Temperance Society, at a meeting held in Warsaw in 1836, adopted this pledge, after having discussed the question during two days, with only two negative votes; and these were given by conservatives, who feared the alienation of the friends of temperance by a too rapid advance.

At the present day it seems hardly credible that the temperance reform could ever have encountered serious opposition from men of intelligence and character; but when the fact is considered that the custom of using stimulants had been handed down through many generations, and that the utility and even the necessity of their moderate use had hardly been questioned; and when the additional fact is considered that men are always slow to adopt new customs or to relinquish old ones, even after the utility of those or the pernicious character of these is demonstrated, it will be less a matter of wonder. It did encounter such opposition, and in 1836 its conservative friends feared the effect of what they deemed too rapid advance.

Among the early and earnest workers in the cause of temperance may be named Dr. Rumsey, Deacon John Munger, Frank Miller, Dr. Augustus Frank, Hon. William Patterson, Hon. Andrew W. Young, James and John Crocker, and soon afterward Joshua H. Darling, Isaac Preston, Deacon William Buxton, George W. Morris, F. C. D. McKay, Charles J. Judd, Alanson Holly, Hon. Seth M. Gates, E. B. Miller and Rev. Richard Kay at the county seat. Hon. John B. Skinner, of Wyoming; Benedict Brooks, of Covington; Alden S. Stevens, Hon. Barney Putnam and James G. Hoyt, of Attica; John B. Halstead and A. B. Rose, of Castile; C. O. Shepard and Mr. Lymans, of Arcade; Willard C. Chapin, Jonah Andrews and the Messrs. Phenix and Thicol M. Ward, of Perry; Nelson Wolcott, of Java; Lyman H. Babbitt, of Orangeville; Arden Woodruff, of Sheldon; and many others whose names cannot now be recalled, were equally earnest and efficient in all parts of the county. The philanthropic labors of these men continued, and much good was accomplished, not only in the reclamation of unfortunate victims of their appetite, but it prevented the acquisition of such appetite in many young men.

So eficient has been the work of temperance men of an early day, together with those since the organization of the county of Wyoming, that whenever opportunity has been given to vote upon the question of license or no license the majorities have always been large for no license. In 1846, when the first local option law allowed a vote to be taken, but *one* of sixteen towns in the county voted for license. Large county meetings have been held at the county seat, and town meetings in the towns, to advance the interest of temperance during the existence of the county.

What is true of almost every movement that has become popular is true of the temperance reform: it has had its revivals or seasons of increased interest. These have almost always been caused or accompanied not by the development of any new truths, but by new methods of advocating and promulgating old ones; and such is man's love of novelty that whenever any such new method has been introduced a wave of excitement has swept over the country, which has kindled in many sanguine friends of temperance the hope that the hour of final triumph was at hand. These periods of excitement have naturally been succeeded by others of depression, during which the less hopeful have been able to see nothing but disaster and impending ruin.

On the whole there is no reason to doubt that much good has been accomplished, especially by the influence which has from time to time been thrown around the young to prevent them from the formation of those habits that would lead them to inevitable ruin. It is, however, thought by many that had the efforts of the advocates of temperance never been misdirected a much larger amount of good might have been accomplished.

The first of these great temperance waves swept over the country about the year 1840. It had its beginning in the city of Baltimore, where a few confirmed drunkards had suddenly resolved to reform and at once carried their resolution into effect. They were encouraged in this, and others soon joined them. They at first took the name of reformed drunkards, and a few men of ability among them assembled some of their old associates, and lectured to them effectively. Thus commenced the mission work which spread over the entire country. Drunkards took the pledge, abandoned their habits of inebriety, and the more able among them became lecturers. They soon took the distinguishing title of Washingtonians, and the societies which they established were called Washingtonian societies.

For a time hardly any other lecturers than these reformed men were in the field, and their success was great. Thousands of drunkards were temporarily reclaimed; many were permanently reformed; many moderate drinkers were arrested in their downward course, and many young people who had been surrounded by influences that would have led them to destruction were saved from ruin, and came to be worthy members of society.

Every undue excitement is certain to be succeeded by a corresponding reaction. In this case the remarkable success of the movement induced many unfit persons to engage in it, and soon or late they brought discredit on it. They were regarded with great popular favor, and their extravagancies were for a time accepted. In the language of an excellent writer, "often was the pulpit surrendered on the Sabbath to men whose vulgar, laughter-provoking stories were wholly unbecoming the place and the occasion." Such exhibitions soon disgusted the more intelligent, and after a time ceased to attract the populace.

In many of the towns in Wyoming county—and notably in the town of Warsaw—the reaction from this excitement was not as disastrous as in many places. Such was the prevalent moral sentiment that there were elected during some years supervisors and magistrates (who then constituted the boards of excise) that refused to grant licenses for the sale of liquor by the dram; and, although to some extent it was sold in violation of the law, drunkenness was greatly diminished, and many who had become occasional tipplers abandoned the habit, and became sober, exemplary men.

It is thought by many that, had the friends of temperance continued to put forth their efforts as at first, the result might have been better than it is. They were not satisfied with the good results which they had wrought, and they sought the accomplishment of the desired end mainly by the aid of restrictive and prohibitory statutes. Their mistake is thought to have consisted not so much in seeking such aid as in relaxing their efforts to educate the public sentiment to the point of sustaining such laws, and thus allowing the good work which they had accomplished to be in part undone.

The first restrictive law went into effect in 1846. It was termed the "License or No License law," and sometimes, from one of its provisions, "the Five-Gallon law." It was a sort of local option law. It was for many reasons not successful in its operation throughout the State, but seemed to be eminently so in Wyoming county.

Eight years later, or in 1855, what was known as the Maine prohibitory law was enacted in this State, and strong hopes were entertained of good results from its operation. It was by the Court of Appeals decided to be unconstitutional. It was followed by a law providing for commissioners of excise for the counties, to be appointed by the county judge. Commissioners were appointed in Wyoming county, who gave licenses in nearly all the towns, and in several, including Warsaw, that had been without any sales of liquor as a beverage for many years.

The temperance workers labored on, hoping to create such a public sentiment that when opportunity again occurred to make their votes effective in opposition to the license of the sale of intoxicating drinks they would be prepared to act. The present local option law gave the opportunity, allowing, as it does, each town to elect excise commissioners, in whose hands rests the whole question of license or no license. Under the operation of this law for several years past many of the towns have been entirely free from the legalized sale of liquor. At the election of excise commissioners in the spring of 1879, but five of the sixteen towns chose commissioners favorable to the granting of licenses. The people of the towns that have been the longest time without license seem to think well of the workings of the law. They claim that it greatly diminishes the sale and use of liquor; that it reduces their taxes, causes their young men to grow up temperate and industrious, and in every way proves beneficial to their interests. Various temperance organizations exist in the county, and it is thought they are efficient in the work they seek to accomplish.

WYOMING COUNTY MEDICAL SOCIETY.

Of the early history of the Wyoming County Medical Society very little is known. The records have been lost or destroyed, and for many years no attempt was made to keep the organization in running order. In August, 1870, a call was issued and an invitation was extended to all medical men in the county to meet at Warsaw, for the purpose of reorganizing the society. The following physicians were present: Drs. T. D. Powell, Milan Baker, J. T. McArthur, S. Chester Smith, G. B. Gilbert, Julius A. Post, C. W. Howe, F. E. Bliss, O. B. Adams, George M. Palmer, W. D. Hunt, Jacob K. Smith, H. P. Merville.

The meeting was a very pleasant one, but for some reason the society continued to languish up to 1874, when new life seemed to be infused into it. It is now prospering finely.

The officers of the society for 1879 were as follows: Z. J. Lusk, president; William N. Martin, vice-president; Julius A. Post, secretary; S. Chester Smith, treasurer; Julius A. Post, William N. Martin, E. G. Harding, S. Chester Smith and Milan Baker, censors; Dr. George M. Palmer, delegate to State Medical Society; Dr. Milan Baker, delegate to American Medical Association; Robert

Rae, Julius A. Post, George M. Palmer, O. B. Adams, Milan Baker, William N. Martin, delegates to Medical Association of Central New York.

TONAWANDA HARMONIC ASSOCIATION.

About the year 1860 a musical association was formed at Varysburg, composed of singers from Attica, Bennington, Orangeville, Java and Sheldon. This organization has maintained its existence until the present time. Its object is improvement in church music. Hon. W. J. Humphrey was its first president, succeeded by David Lewis, F. D. Powell, M. D., A Lyford, J. W. Ives and W. Cheney, who is now acting as president.

David Wilder, the pioneer singing teacher of western New York, was conductor for several years, and is now honorary conductor; Matthew Eastman is conductor, and W. W. Blakely assistant. Three regular meetings of two days each have been held in each year in the different churches with which the members are connected, more frequently in Attica, Varysburg, Johnsonburg, Strykersville, North Java and Java.

Sessions of four days each have been held at different times, conducted by such men as George F. Root, Perkins, Loomis and others.

CHAPTER XXVIII.

THE LETCHWORTH RIFLES—ACTION DURING THE RAILROAD RIOTS—VICTORIES IN SHOOTING MATCHES.

THIS organization was the outgrowth of the veteran element of the county, represented in the membership of Gibbs Post G. A. R., at Warsaw, and was organized on application to the governor of the State of New York by a majority of its subsequent members, who elected both commissioned officers and non-commissioned, mainly from the veterans of the war of 1861–65.

It was organized under orders from general headquarters July 17th, 1876. The commissions of the captain and lieutenant bore date May 18th, 1876. It was inspected and mustered in the presence of the brigade commander and staff July 29th, 1876, from which time the five years enrollment of the company dates; and on the 24th of August the membership numbered 3 commissioned officers and 100 non-commissioned officers and privates, that being the full number allowed under the State authority.

Of the men who compose this organization it is not too much to say that the best elements of society are represented among them, and that as a whole they will compare favorably with any similar organization in the State.

The company was designated the fourth separate company of infantry, 31st brigade, 8th division, N. G. S. N. Y., which name it bore until, in the reorganization of the State forces, December 8th, 1877, the designation was changed to the 19th separate company of infantry, 14th brigade, 8th division, N. G. S. N. Y. The company adopted its local name in honor of the distinguished philanthropist Hon. William P. Letchworth, of Genesee Falls. The part taken by him in the effort to make Warsaw a place of deposit for military stores and a rendezvous and point of training for the infantry of the national guard of the State, as also the interest shown by him in the various public enterprises of the county, rendered the adoption of this name quite appropriate.

This command was among the first organized under the provision of the statute distributing the military equipment of the State in the rural districts, by the organization in counties of separate companies, to be attached to the various brigades and divisions, the boundaries of which are those of the judicial districts; thus locating the reserve force of the government among the intelligent citizens, who must, in a country like this, always be relied on for the maintenance of order and the repression of lawless outbreaks among the class of social parasites who have come to be known as tramps and communists. The history of the efficient services of this command in the suppression of the labor strikes of 1877 illustrates the wisdom of this policy.

When this command was organized the social features which the organization presented were strong attractions, and rendered the work of recruiting the company easy. A year of holiday soldiering followed, during which soldierly education and discipline and thorough tactical drilling were not neglected.

June 30th, 1877, a call was made on this portion of the reserve arm of the government for a guard at Portage. The prompt response to this call, and the valuable services of the company in the discharge of this duty, were recognized in official communication from general headquarters. These prompt and efficient services not only demonstrated the utility and economy of maintaining such an organization, which in this case probably saved the county an outlay far in excess of the expense incurred, but materially changed the views of the members of the command concerning the character and value of their services, and the utility and necessity of exact military discipline. It also demonstrated to lookers on, who admire the beauty and precision of military evolutions, that the drill and discipline by which this precision is acquired have a purpose beyond the display which they admire.

The brief experiences at Portage were more emphatically repeated soon afterward. On the 22nd of July, 1877, orders were received for the entire command to be in readiness for emergent duty on the occasion of that outburst of lawlessness which has passed into history as the great strike. At noon of the next day, in response to orders of not more than three hours, nearly the whole of the command reported from their scattered homes, armed and equipped for duty, and at 5 P. M. the command took train for Buffalo, leaving a guard at Warsaw. At Attica twenty-two men, under orders from Major-General Howard, relieved about four times their number of Buffalo troops in charge of and guarding public property, effectually suppressing riotous demonstrations at that point until July 27th, under command at first of Lieutenant C. T. Watkins, and subsequently of Lieutenant J. M. Smith.

The balance, fifty in number, under command of Captain A. B. Lawrence, proceeded to Buffalo, arriving at about 9 P. M., passed through the blockade of rioters, which a few hours later attacked and destroyed the car containing the Westfield company, similarly en route; remained constantly on duty till the 27th, when, the riotous demonstrations having ceased, the command returned, having received the compliments, congratulations and thanks of the citizens of Buffalo.

They took up the detail at Attica, and were welcomed at Warsaw by the citizens and ladies with a beautiful collation, which had been spread in the armory, in anticipation of their return.

For this service the command was again officially and specially commended from general headquarters. The result of this and similar service confirmed the policy of the distribution of the companies in the rural districts of the State. In his report for that year the adjutant-general said:

"The success which has attended the organization of separate companies of infantry has been greater than was anticipated when authority of law was obtained for that purpose, some three years since. All of those companies were on active duty during the recent campaign, and behaved well; and no difficulty was experienced in uniting several of them and forming a battalion under the command of the senior officer, although the companies came from different counties. * * * There should be at least one of these companies in every county in which there are no regiments or battalions, and then every sheriff in the State would have at his call an organized force to aid him in preserving the peace, which could be almost as readily summoned as the police in the cities. As an evidence of what can be done in this way, and how advantageously the national guard can be thus used, reference is made to the report of Captain A. B. Lawrence, of the action of his command—the fourth separate company of the thirty-first brigade—in aiding the sheriff in quelling a riotous disturbance which occurred in Wyoming county recently."

The services referred to in this report were the suppression of a riot on the State Line railroad in Gainesville, October 18th, 1877, on the requisition of the sheriff of Wyoming county, who, with the county, had been made responsible for the results of that riot by the demands of the railroad anthorities upon him officially. The prompt and efficient action of the command ended the riot with a brief campaign, relieving the county from a heavy bill of damages.

Attached to and a part of this company is a band of more than average musical ability, under the leadership of H. D. Hurlburt, whose value as a citizen has been enhanced by his enlistment as a soldier and his ability as a leader, and to whose efficiency the more than local reputation of this band is largely due.

A principal feature in this command has been, and it still is, its record in military rifle practice. It is largely composed of men who have developed taste and skill in this important branch of military service. The first year of the company's existence three State badges were awarded to its members; the second, seventeen; and the third, fifty-two—the largest number awarded to any similar organization in the State.

The following extract is from the report of the general inspector of rifle practice, in the adjutant-general's report, 1878:

"I enclose also copies of the scores made by the several teams who contested for the State prize September 4th, at which time the prize was won by the team from the 4th separate company of infantry, 31st brigade, at Warsaw. The prize was presented to the company at Warsaw in the presence of a large number of citizens, on Wednesday, September 26th."

This prize was won in a competition with eleven teams. It is a massive silver water cooler, three feet in height, of elegant design, on which is engraved: "Presented by the State of New York as the first prize in the 8th division rifle match, shot at Buffalo September 3d, 1877; won by the team from Warsaw, N. Y."

The career of this company is a source of just pride to the county, whose reputation it so creditably maintains. Its efficiency and its excellent reputation are due not only to the excellent material of which the rank and file is composed, but to the veteran experience of its officers.

Captain A. B. Lawrence was a member of the 130th regiment of infantry—afterward the first dragoons. The qualities of a good officer—ability, ambition and strict discipline—are prominent in him.

First Lieutenant Jacob M. Smith was a most efficient member of the 9th N. Y. cavalry. He resigned, and was honorably discharged April 18th, 1878.

Second Lieutenant Charles T. Watkins was first sergeant of the first company that left Wyoming county—Company K, 17th N. Y. infantry. He was elected to the position of first lieutenant, made vacant by the resignation of Lieutenant Smith.

The position made vacant by the promotion of Lieutenant Watkins was filled by Jacob R. Smith, who was elected and commissioned with rank from May 30th, 1878. Lieutenant Smith was a veteran of the 3d Connecticut infantry. He met a tragic death on the 10th of April, 1879, while in the discharge of his professional duty, universally respected and lamented.

CHAPTER XXIX.

THE WYOMING HISTORICAL PIONEER ASSOCIATION AND ITS LOG CABIN MUSEUM.

THE idea of a gathering at Silver lake of the pioneers of Wyoming county was suggested by Jonathan Sleeper, and notice of such a gathering in the summer of 1872 was circulated by him. The result was a pleasant social gathering and picnic at the lake, far larger than was anticipated.

At this meeting arrangements were made for a similar gathering the next summer. The meeting in 1873 was a still larger one. An address was delivered by General L. W. Thayer, a paper by Amos Otis was read, several impromptu speeches were made, and a good time was had.

At this meeting it was resolved to hold annual gatherings, and a chairman and secretary for the next meeting were appointed. In May, 1874, the secretary, George Tomlinson, of Perry, issued a call, and a meeting was held, at which an executive committee was appointed, also a committee in each town to report statistics of deaths, etc. Mr. W. P. Letchworth, of Portage, was invited to deliver an address, and more thorough preparations were made for the gathering than in previous years. A notable feature of the meeting in that year was the attendance with Mr. Letchworth of Shongo, a descendant of Mary Jemison, and a young Indian girl in the costume worn by her people at the time of Mary Jemison's captivity. The statistical reports of the town committees proved to be a feature of great interest. Similar meetings were held in each succeeding summer, with a constantly increasing interest. Addresses were delivered in 1875 by Hugh T. Brooks, of Covington; in 1876 by Hon. Augustus Frank, of Warsaw, and in 1877 by Norman Seymour, of Mount Morris. At the meeting in 1877 steps were taken toward the formation of a legal association. A resolution was adopted that the association organize under the laws of the State, and be known as "The Wyoming Historical Pioneer Association." The corporators were Jonathan Sleeper, R. W. Brigham, Mason Lock, R. E. Moredoff and George Tomlinson. In the certificate of association the objects were stated to be, "to collect historical facts in relation to the early settlement of this county, gather tools, machinery, manufactured articles and such other things as relate to the pioneers of western New York; also to form a museum of curiosities, and to hold reunions of pioneers, associations and conventions."

William P. Letchworth, H. A. Dudley, F. W. Capwell, Joseph Clark, Augustus Frank, R. B. Moredoff, Jonathan Sleeper, Myron Lock, Robert T. Shearman, O.V. Whitcomb, George Tomlinson, H. N. Page, H. M. Scranton,

Robert Grisewood and Ezra Kelsey were named as trustees for the first year for the management of the affairs of the society.

A. S. Simmons was authorized by this board of trustees to contract with Samuel Sharp for one acre of land at $350. This duty was discharged, and a deed was executed December 5th, 1877. Myron Lock, A. S. Simmons, O. V. Whitcomb, Robert Grisewood and Ezra Kelsey were appointed executive committee, "to grade and fence the grounds, build all buildings and take the general management of the property of the society."

During the spring and summer of 1878 the pioneer cabin was erected, seats and tables were arranged on the grounds of the society and made ready for the annual meeting, which was held August 1st of that year. At that meeting a historical address was delivered by A. N. Cole, of Wellsville, and an oration by Dr. Mills, of Mt. Morris. An address dedicating the cabin was made by the secretary.

This cabin is erected in a pleasant grove of chestnut, maple, oak and hickory trees on the grounds of the society, in the town of Castile, near what was formerly known as "Chapin's Landing," a few rods east from Silver lake. It was built under the superintendence of the executive committee before named, and the expense was defrayed wholly by voluntary contribution. The logs of which this cabin is constructed were contributed by the pioneers of the county, or their descendants in cases of deceased pioneers, and the name of each contributor of a log is recorded on a bulletin board that hangs on the front of the cabin. They are as follows:

S. Armstrong, J. Allen, David Andrus, J. Abbott, I. Allen, H. F. Austin, K. W. Brigham, D. Ball, T. Benedict, A. Bradt, C. F. Benedict, H. Barnes, J. E. Beebe, B. Bradt, J. N. Bolton, G. Benedict, R. Buell, J. P. Buckland, N. Bacon, E. Bathrick, S. Burt, C. P. Bailey, T. Bacheldor, Truman Benedict, L. Bacheldor, J. H. Bolton, George Colburn, F. Cone, J. Cronkhite, George W. Clark, C. A. Chapin, O. Chapman, J. W. Campbell, Dow T. Clute, William Dolbeer, Silas Rawson, E. Edgerly, J. and R. Edgerly, T. Flske, E. Fitch, W. Grove, T. F. Gray, R. Grisewood, W. Granger, D. W. Hough, S. A. Higgins, M. Hull, M. Hathaway, J. Hollister, S. Howard, D. Higgins, H. K. Higgins, George Johnson, J. Jones, H. Karringer, William A. Lacy, J. E. Lowing, E. Lacy, W. P. Lotchworth, M. Locke, T. McEntee, J. Miner, J. Metcalf, Dr. J. Nevens, D. Nevens, A. Otis, J. Olin, P. Olin, W. A. Phillips, H. N. Page, C. Phillips, J. R. Potter, L. Phillips, A. Rapalee, J. Richards, L. Russell, E. Robinson, W. A. Sanger, R. H. Smith, N. Saxton, S. Safford, J. Sayles, G. N. Sherman, C. L. Schenck, N. Seymour, J. Sleeper, P. F. Schenck, I. H. True, E. Tallman, I. True, G. Tabor, Z. Toan, George Tomlinson, J. D. Turrell, D. R. Taylor, S. Utter, F. Williams, D. A. Wallace, J. Walker, Dr. J. Ward, W. Willey, G. H. Wright, R. Watrous, D. Wygant, P. M. Ward, Dr. G. L. Keeney, S. Hatch, R. Harrison, E. A. Kelsey, S. Waldo, C. R. Bradt, M. T. Bristol, J. C. Karringer, J. W. Kingsley, Augustus Frank, A. S. Simmons, Lyman Taylor, Paul Stowell, Thomas Buell, Benjamin Johnson, J. W. Capwell, Samuel Benedict, Walter Gillispie, William Agate, Alanson Lacey, Jehial Glasgow, Ezra Olin, Eleazer Sheldon, Estes M. Nutter, M. Andrews, John Halstead, Daniel W. Mattison, W. J. Chapin and B. Gardner.

The house is twenty-four by forty feet, and the roof has a projection on each side of six feet. It is built exactly in the style of the houses that the pioneers erected when they first came into this region. The doors are hung on wooden hinges, and fastened with wooden latches, which are raised by latch strings as of old. The fire-place has no jambs, has a stone back, and a stick chimney that is plastered inside. In this chimney is a lug pole from which to suspend cooking utensils. It has also the more modern crane, which was used for the same purpose. In the corner, on one side of the fire-place, wooden pins are inserted in the logs, and on these are placed boards. These shelves represent the pioneer pantry. On the other side of the fire-place is the rustic ladder for ascending to the loft. Between the braces which sustain the chimney runs a piece of split timber, the pioneer mantel shelf. In front hooks cut from the limbs of trees are fastened to the rough joists above, and on these are placed poles—young trees cut from the forest; across these are laid pieces of smaller saplings on which to suspend any article. Some strips of dried pumpkins are clinging to one of these—exact representatives of old time domestic economy. Hooks and pegs appear on the logs at the sides of the one room that the house comprises. In some instances these are the antlers of deer. In one comer is a pioneer bedstead, made by inserting the ends of large poles in auger holes, and supporting the comer by a post. In place of a cord strips of elm bark cross each other. Near the head of this bed is the rough shelf for toilet articles, and in the logs over it are driven nails on which to hang the comb case, etc. A larger nail in a higher log is for suspending the looking glass. The shelf for the old fashioned clock has not been forgotten. The loft is exactly what lofts formerly were, except that the larger size of the building makes it more spacious.

The fire-place is furnished with all the utensils for cooking that were formerly used, and many of these are duplicated and even triplicated. From the lug pole and crane are suspended by trammels and hooks every variety of old iron vessels, and by the sides of the andirons stand bake kettles, spiders, skillets, gridirons, toasters, griddles, tin bakers, etc., etc. At the sides of the fire-place are the fire shovels and tongs made for handling the heavy logs and brands of old time fires, waffle irons, etc. Hanging to the chimney braces are bellows, gourds, and other articles, and resting on and hanging in front of the mantel shelf are the lanterns, candlesticks of tin and iron of various fashions, tongs for lighting candles or pipes, kettle hooks, spits or trammeled hooks for roasting meat, etc.

The shelves on the logs at the side of the fire-place are covered with everything which such shelves formerly held, far more and in greater variety than any one cabin was furnished with. On these shelves and in the fire-place may be seen specimens of every utensil used in the culinary department of early settlers' houses. All these have seen actual service among the first inhabitants, and many were old heirlooms in their families. It is impossible, within reasonable limits, to enumerate the articles that may be seen in this corner. Everything, from a bark bread tray and wooden mortar to the minutest articles formerly in use, may be found there.

In the opposite corner, under the ladder, stands an old dye tub; the seat which noisy urchins were sometimes required to occupy, the one where studious youths sat to read or cypher by firelight, and the one where their grandmothers rested, with their elbows on their knees, while the smoke from their pipes ascended the chimney with that from the fire. Near to it stands another obsolete article—the rack used in making tallow dips or candles; and on this lie some of the old candle rods, to which the candles were suspended during the process of dipping.

Suspended on the poles in front of the fire-place are canteens and runlets or water bottles, one of which has two cavities, one for water and one for ——; old fashioned saddle bags, such as pioneer physicians carried into many a log house; and among other articles the identical chair once used by Dehewamis, or "the white woman."

The pegs and hooks on the walls support specimens of almost everything which formerly pertained to pioneer houses. Quaint old bonnets and hats and other articles of apparel, pictures and prints, guns, bayonets, cartridge boxes, powder horns, swords, pistols, etc., etc., some of which did service in the Revolution, and even in the French and Indian war; various inplements of farm and domestic industry, the uses of some of which are hardly known now, warming pans, children's dresses, specimens of domestic linen, etc.

The bedstead is surrounded by tasteful old curtains of spotless white, and over it is spread a coverlet woven in 1698. Standing by the head of the bed is an old tin candle stand. Above the toilet shelf hangs a mirror, which began to cast reflections in 1803. Under this is the comb basket, and on the shelf lies the old pin cushion.

On the shelf at the foot of the bed is "grandfather's clock," which during eighty years, "without slumbering, tick tick-tick," has numbered the passing seconds and struck the hours; and still it ticks and strikes.

In front of the bed stands a cradle, in which the ruddy babies of probably more than one generation have been rocked.

A long board table, seventy years old, stands In the middle of the floor, and on this rests the first show case that was used to display goods in the village of Perry. This case contains many rare and interesting relics.

Standing against the wall is an old secretary and book case, filled with such books as were found in the scanty libraries of pioneers; among which are many specimens of old time school books. Many ancient records and old papers are deposited here. One of these is a copy of No. LV. of "*The New England Weekly Journal*, containing the most remarkable occurrences, foreign and domestic," dated "Monday, April 8th, 1728."

This sheet was published in Boston, "Printed by S. Kneeland & T. Green, at the Printing House in Queen street, where advertisements are taken in."

The sheet measures twelve by six inches, printed on both sides, in two columns. At the head of the first column it is stated:

"There are measures concerting for rendering this paper yet more universally esteemed and useful, in which 'tis hoped the Publick will be gratified, and

by which gentlemen who desire to be improved in History, Philosophy, Poetry &c., will be greatly advantaged. We will take the liberty at this time to insert the following Passage of History":

Then follow the quotation and a story. The next column is filled with communications between "His Excellency Robert Hunter, Esq.," and the council. The third column is filled with items of intelligence from England, bearing various dates from October 28th, 1727, to November 16th of the same year.

At the head of the fourth column appears: "*Burials in the Town of Boston since our last*, Five Whites, One Black—*Baptized in the Several Churches*, Nine."

Then follows: "*Custom House, Boston, April 6th, Entred Inwards*" (names of persons), "*Cleared out*" (names), and "*Outward Bound*" (names).

The remaining space in the column is filled with advertisements of discourses and other publications, one of which was "On the Nature and Necessity of REPENTANCE; Occasioned by the Earthquake."

Arthur Savage advertises "*Choice New Coffee*," at "*Eight shillings per pound.*"

"Mr. *Nath. Pigott* intends to open school on Monday next, for the instruction of Negro's in Reading, Catechizing and Writing, if required; if any are so well inclined as to send their servants to said school near Mr. *Checkley's* Meeting House care will be taken for their instruction as aforesaid."

"*A very likely Negro woman who can do household work and is fit either for Town or Country service, about* 22 *years of age, to be sold. Inquire of the printer hereof.*"

"A very likely Negro girl about 13 or 14 years of age, speaks good English, has been in the Country some years, to be sold. Inquire of the printer hereof."

A copy of the *Ulster County Gazette*, published at Kingston January 4th, 1800, contributed by Mrs. Prindle, of East Bethany, is also here. It contains copious extracts from journals concerning the war then in progress in Europe. The inside is dressed in mourning for the death of George Washington, and contains an account of his obsequies and communications between the Senate and President John Adams, on the occasion of his death. In this paper also is advertised for sale by John Schoonmaker, of the town of Rochester, "A STOUT, HEALTHY, ACTIVE negro wench."

There is also a fac-simile of the first number of the *Boston News Letter*, the first newspaper published in America.

In the loft are deposited several spinning wheels, reels, swifts, quill wheels, and a loom with all its fixtures—all the facilities, in short, for the domestic manufacture of cloth.

In the rear of the building, under the projecting eaves, are old ox yokes, calf yokes, double neck yokes for old Dutch harnesses, a one-handed bull plough, with its wooden mold-board, a three-cornered harrow, corn fans, a flax brake and swingling board and knife; and the logs under the eaves are garnished with bunches of dried herbs.

A short distance from the cabin is a well with a section of a hollow log for a curb, and a primitive sweep for drawing water. At the end of the house are growing bunches of useful and ornamental plants, such as hollyhocks, comfrey, catnip, carraway, smellage, tanzy, etc., and in the top of a partially hollow stump near by flourishes a cluster of live-forever. In front is a small bed in which are cultivated striped grass, sweet clover, *fleur de lis*, etc. These are such manifestations of esthetic taste as the circumstances by which pioneer wives were surrounded would permit. A platform is laid under the projecting roof in front, and on this stand old wagon chairs and primitive benches made of slabs.

In front of the gateway stands a column or post taken from a school-house that was built in 1832. On the top of this is a large wooden ball that was the first school globe ever used in the town of Perry. The rustic arch over the gateway is surmounted by the dried head of an elk, with enormous spreading and branching antlers.

This cabin, with its surroundings and the relics which it contains, is almost a complete pioneer history.

On one portion of the grounds seats and speakers' stands are arranged, and another part is occupied by tables for spreading refreshments for several hundred people at the annual picnics of the association. Squirrels gambol over the grounds and sport among the limbs of the trees almost without fear, and the grove is vocal with the songs of birds.

CHAPTER XXX.

A GEOLOGICAL SKETCH OF WYOMING COUNTY.

BY A. P. CHAPIN.

THIS county presents many interesting features to the geological student, only a few of which can be included in this chapter. Standard works on the subject, and careful observation of the rock formations and water marks as found in the ravines and on the hillsides, will afford ample opportunity to those who desire to pursue the study further than will interest the general reader.

In their lithological character the rocks of this region are much varied in composition and texture. To this fact is due not only those pleasing and beneficial inequalities of surface, but also the origin of some of the streams and waterfalls which beautify and enliven the scenery and encourage agriculture, industry and enterprise among the people. To the same cause to which we owe these prominent features is due also the deep fertile soil prevailing throughout the greater part of the county. The materials excavated from these valleys, in the form of decomposed and disintegrated rocks, have been transported and reduced to the condition of sand, clay and pebbles, which are distributed over the surface of the lower lands. The high hills and deep valleys and gorges indicate the extent of this work. The effects of erosion are seen, first in the imprint of the falling rain drop—a trifling matter to the ordinary observer, but not so to the geologist; for it remains among the earliest as well as the latest strata, and shows that it rained then as now. It teaches what lands at that time were exposed, and what were buried beneath the waters of the ocean. The gathering drops from the rills combine into rivulets, and the rivulets wear pathways down the hillsides. The rivulets unite to form larger streams, and these work with accumulating force and excavate deep gorges. The mist and rains about the higher lands are usually the main source of the water. As the streamlets combine the torrent increases, and thus exercises the greatest force near the base of the declivity. There the valley first takes its shape and size. Examples of this form of erosion may be found among the tributaries of Allan's creek, and in various other parts of the county. As the erosion continues a constantly deepening valley is formed, the head of which slowly but surely travels up the stream. The nature of the rocks causes modifications in these results. If the rocks are of a soft shaly character, as are many of the rocks in this region, the work progresses much more rapidly than among rocks of a dense and compact character. The composition of the rocks may also have much to do in regulating the rate of wear. Many examples are on record where gorges hundreds of feet deep have been cut in the solid rock by the work of only two or three centuries. This, however, is accomplished only under the most favorable circumstances. Although the rocks of Wyoming county are not of the denser varieties, doubtless her precipitous valleys have been undergoing many centuries of formation. The products of erosion are carried down into the valleys, where the speed of the water slackens, and there form the alluvial beds so characteristic of the valleys.

The soil of the entire county rests upon rocks known as the

PORTAGE GROUP.

This group presents an extensive development of shales and flagstones, and some sandstone toward its upper part. It is extremely variable in character at different points. "From its superior development along the banks of the Genesee river in the vicinity of Portage it has received that name to distinguish it from the higher rocks, which possess some differences in lithological characters, but a more striking dissimilarity in organic remains." This group rises sometimes in a gentle slope, and at other times quite abruptly from the softer shales below. The enduring sandstones of the upper part have enabled it to withstand the action of air and water to a considerable degree. These sandstone formations often extend well to the northward on the elevated grounds between the deep valleys, running in a north and south direction, or nearly so. The valleys are generally bounded by steep hills, thinly covered with northern drift. This character of the formation is well illustrated along the Genesee valley for several miles below Portage bridge, and in the valleys of Allan's creek and the Tonawanda creek. On approaching the northern margin of the Portage group the observer finds a gradually increasing elevation of hills and abruptness of slope. These elevations often extend several miles unbroken, except partially by the deep ravines which indent their sides, and which originated in water-courses which took their rise upon the summits of these hills.

The higher sandstones of the group, and in many instances the intermediate ones, have produced falls in the streams which pass over them. Some of the most beautiful cascades in the State are found among the rocks of this group. The highest perpendicular fail of water in the State is found in the rocks of this group, and its grand and picturesque scenery is rarely equaled. The traveler often finds his course impeded by a deep gorge, and in the very bottom of this is the small winding stream, the only representative of the once rushing torrent that has worn so deep a pathway through the rocks. The rocks of this group are generally divided into three parts. The lower of these is known as the

Cashaqua Shale.

This rests upon what is known as the Genesee slate. It differs in its fossils sufficiently from those above to be considered under a separate name. From its more complete development upon the Cashaqua creek the name was originally applied to it, and before the overlapping rocks had been thoroughly examined. This formation consists of a soft, argillaceous rock of a greenish color, which rapidly crumbles on being exposed to the atmosphere and storms, and forms a soft, sticky clay. It is therefore difficult to procure good specimens, and its fossils, not being abundant, are quite apt to be overlooked. Certain species of shells, however, have been found only in this rock, and these are found in the same position to an extent of one hundred and fifty miles. On tracing it west of the Genesee it presents continually the same features as on the Cashaqua creek. The lower part is occasionally darker colored, and in some places is separated from the Genesee slate by a thin band of a species of limestone. It is largely exposed in the numerous streams and ravines situated in the hills bordering on Allan's creek and Tonawanda creek. It appears at the village of Wyoming and at numerous other points in that vicinity. Its greatest thickness at any visible point is on the Genesee river, and is about one hundred and ten feet. It decreases in thickness toward the north, and disappears on a line running through the southern part of Genesee county. Resting upon this is the middle division of the Fortage group, known as the

Gardeau Shale and Flagstones.

Along the Genesee river, above the Cashaqua shale, we find an extensive development of greenish black slaty and sandy shales, of various shades of color between green and black, with thin layers of sandstone, which form beautiful and enduring flagstones. These flagstones are found in the same geological position in several places in this county, and adorn many of the streets of our villages. These rocks form high, almost perpendicular banks on the Genesee and in some of the numerous ravines of this county, only indented as the results of slides or running water. From their extensive exposure along the Gardeau reservation that name was adopted to distinguish this part of the formation. As we ascend the arenaceous matter increases, and the shale forms distinct alternations of black and green, often many times in succession within a perpendicular distance of fifty or sixty feet. The sandstone layers in the upper part of the formation are generally too thick for flagstones, and the shale divides into thicker leaves. These characteristics, however, vary considerably in different localities, and the observer, needs to note carefully the composition of the rocks and the few native fossils, to be sure of his position.

Portage Sandstones.

"The thick-bedded sandstones at Portage form the terminal rocks of the group. These are well exposed in the deep gorge below Portageville, where the perpendicular cliffs rise to the height of three hundred and fifty feet. The upper part consists of thick-bedded sandstone, with little shale; while below the sandy layers become thinner, with more frequent alternations of shale. The character of the sandstones, and the presence of fucoids passing vertically through the strata, induced the separation from the rocks below, where the characteristic species of the same genus lies horizontally upon the surface of the strata. The lithological character of the sandstone, and the presence of the vertical fucoid, hold uniform over a considerable extent; and the presence of the latter alone is often sufficient to decide the position of the rock where it is but slightly exposed."

The preceding description of these three divisions will furnish a correct idea of the group, and will apply to nearly if not quite the entire surface of Wyoming county. The whole series consists of shales and shaly sandstones. Nevertheless, in lithological characters there is no abrupt change, or evidence of very different conditions in the ocean from which they were deposited, from the termination of the Tully limestone to the final deposition of the Chemung group. Shales and sandstones compose the entire assemblage. The Portage group forms the lower part of this great division of rocks.

Fossils.

Throughout the entire thickness of the Portage group, which is not less than one thousand feet, there are but two forms of organic remains, which can be referred to the Brachiopoda; one of these is the Delthyris, and the other the Orthis. Both of these are quite unlike any others which have been seen in the rocks above or below. Shells of this family, though of a different variety, predominate in the Hamilton and Chemung groups, and are much more numerous than in the Portage group. In addition we find the Goniatites, a group of Cephalopods with Nautilus-like shells; the Bellerophon, a genus of Heteropods, with the respiratory and digestive organs forming a kind of nucleus on the posterior part of the back, and with the foot divided into a ventral fin, sucker and terminal fin. They are rapid swimmers, found at the surface in mid-ocean, moving by their fin-shaped foot and tail, and attaching themselves to seaweed by the sucker. They feed on minute pteropods and jelly fishes. These are the animals which lived in the great ocean of waters while all this region was beneath its surface, and while its slow but constant deposition formed the rocks covering a large portion of western New York. The paucity of fossils in this group, when compared with those below and above it, is a marked characteristic. Whole days maybe spent without finding more than a few, and sometimes even no shells. In a few localities some forms have been detected which seem peculiarly typical of the group, and so far as at present known, have never been found elsewhere.

In this absence of fossil shells we find a great abundance of marine vegetation, or fucoids. Scarcely a locality can be examined where one or more species does not occur. The Fucoides Graphica occurs in great numbers, in short, rigid fragments, throughout the central portion of the group, and generally lying on the surface of the thin layers of flagstones. The sidewalks often furnish good specimens of this class of fucoids. They are also often found in profusion in the beds of the ravines, having fallen down in broken fragments of rocks from either side. The Fucoides Verticalis is characteristic of the upper part of the group. It may be at the lower falls of Portage, and in many of the sandstone strata above this; but it is most abundant in the upper sandstone at Portage. The terminating mass of the group may be everywhere recognized by its presence. These constitute the principal fossils of this group of rocks, and they are the only ones that occur with any regularity in this county, though some few others may be occasionally found.

Ripple marks are abundant in the sandy shale, or where the shale becomes interstratified with sandstone; but it is often difficult to obtain good specimens. Many of them have the appearance of being produced by a "chopped sea," or where a current opposed the direction of the wind. The same effect is often visible on sandy beaches where the tide has ebbed; the surface being broken, interrupted and irregular ripples produced either by the tidal current opposing the wind or by some other similar conflict of forces. There is abundant proof among the strata that such circumstances were in operation at the time these rocks were deposited, and that the sea was alternately shallow and again deeper. The dark and green shales bear no evidence of ripple marks, or diagonal lamination, and were probably deposited in deep water; but all the sandy shales and alternations of shale and sandstone furnish evidence of a shallow sea.

"This group throughout presents a great variety of concretionary forms. The strata, however, are all uniform, and rarely give any appearance of concretionary structure in themselves. The concretions are more or less calcareous in different parts of the group and in different shales. The more perfectly spherical, with seams of crystalline matter, are found in the black shale, while the forms varying from this to the very flat or lenticular ones are found in the shales varying from blackish to greenish black and green." The more spherical forms are due to a higher degree of crystallization, which results from a larger proportion of carbonate of lime, while the flattened forms are less crystalline, and consequently less spherical, from the larger amount of argillaceous matter. These forms are too well known to need further description. They sometimes assume fantastic shapes, which cause them to be mistaken for organic bodies. This arises from the seams on the surface, which are fancied to resemble the lines of suture in the shells of the tortoise or turtle, and by these names they are frequently known in localities where they occur plentifully. The more usual form of these bodies is that of a flattened spheroid. They are in some places burned for hydraulic cement, and produce a very good material for this purpose.

Minerals.

The minerals of the Portage group of rocks are as follows, and all are represented in Wyoming county: The concretions contain crystallized carbonate of lime, and sometimes sulphate of baryta. Iron pyrites is freely disseminated through the rock, and from its decomposition the surface of the slaty laminæ and the sides of joints are often stained with iron. It also gives origin to sulphate of lime, or gypsum, which often coats the shaly laminæ, or appears in the form of small crystals in the seams and joints. Carbonaceous matter is disseminated through the black shales, and sometimes appears in seams of half an inch in thickness. Some fragments of large vegetable forms appear, and thin laminæ of coal usually accompany these. From the frequency of these small seams of coal, which are usually of no greater extent than the specimen procured, excavations and borings have been made, in the hope of finding large deposits of coal. It ought to be unnecessary to say that these undertakings in rocks of this period always have failed, and always will fail. If the people could be made to understand that coal does not exist in any valuable quantity in these rocks, useless expenditure of time and money might be prevented. They seem, however, to prefer to learn the lesson at the cost of their own experience in a vain effort to find it.

Springs and Soils.

Numerous never failing springs water well this region of country. Except where the black slaty shale is thick there is no difficulty in procuring water. In these shales the vertical joints seem to be more open and to allow the water to percolate through them. The only remedy for this is to bore through the black to the green shales, which are more impervious to water. In the present condition of this county there is little difficulty in procuring the desired supply with slight labor and expense. If the true origin of springs was generally known, and means taken to protect them, the supply of water would always be plentiful. If, however, the higher lands should be robbed of their shady woods, many of the springs and smaller streams will disappear.

The soil in the northern part of the county is generally a stiff clay, the sand being in too small proportions to produce much perceptible effect. Farther south the arenaceous matter increases, and the broken fragments of the sandy strata become intermixed with the finer materials, giving it the character of a clayey gravel. The valleys and the lower northern slopes are more deeply covered with northern drift and alluvium, and the soil contains a larger proportion of calcareous matter. This calcareous matter is composed chiefly of decomposed limestone and calcareous shales, with a small admixture of sand. This kind of soil is but sparingly spread over the hilltops, and in some of the highest localities is scarcely seen at all. In consequence of this the character and productions of the soil of the hills and valleys are quite different.

In the valleys and on the low northern slopes the soil produces wheat with the same facility as the soil of the formations which come to the surface immediately to the north of the Portage group. As we ascend to the south the wheat crops are less abundant and less certain, and give place largely to the coarser grains and to pasturage. For the latter purpose the soil is superior to that on the north of it, and this fact is fully substantiated by the increasing number of cattle and the product of the dairies.

Town and Village Histories.

THE TOWN OF ARCADE.

ARCADE is the southwest corner town of the county, and before the formation of Wyoming belonged to the county of Genesee.

It was known by the name of China till 1866, when its name was changed to Arcade, in accordance with the name of its principal village.

The area of the town is 29,440 acres. The assessed valuation for 1879 was: real estate, $936,184; personal estate, $63,700; total valuation, $999,884. State, county and town tax, $6,791.15.

The population of the town at the last ten State censuses is given as follows in the Legislative manual: 1830, 2,387; 1835, 1,279; 1840, 1,436; 1845, 1,643; 1850, 1,961; 1855, 2,108; 1860, 2,036; 1865, 1,903; 1870, 1,742; 1875, 2,036.

RESOURCES.

The leading agricultural interest of Arcade is dairying. There are six cheese factories in the town, which in 1878 made 877,207 pounds. The product sold at an average of nine cents per pound, amounting to $78,938.63. Quantities of apples, potatoes and hay are annually sold for shipment. There is but little grain raised, as the soil is better adapted to grass, and the dairying business has afforded such profits for a few years past that many farmers are not even trying to raise their own bread.

In the north and east parts of the town apple trees are thrifty and bear well.

Since the completion of the railroad through the town the farmers have had the benefits of as good a market as is to be found for the sale of their produce. Arcade is the headquarters for cheese buyers in all these western counties, and there is probably more cheese shipped from this station than from any other west of Herkimer and Oneida counties; while butter, apples, potatoes, hay and all other articles of produce find a market at good prices.

SETTLEMENT AND EARLY EVENTS.

The records of the Holland Company contain the following notes of early purchases and purchasers of land in the town:

Range 4.—Abner Bump, 1809, lot 39; Silas Parker, 1809, lot 15; Leonard Parker, 1809, lot 14; Jacob Jackson, 1809, lot 3; Simeon Wells, 1809, lot 7; Samuel

Nichols, 1810, lot 22; Bartholomew Armstrong, 1810, lot 11; Abraham Jackson and Abraham Jackson, jr., 1810, part of lot 12, lots 4, 6, 21, 23, 24, 32, 42 and 43; Israel Kibbe, 1810, lot 25; Alba Carpenter, 1810, part of lot 16; Simon Carpenter, 1810, part of lot 16; Charles Jackson, 1809, lot 5; James W. Stevens, 1810, lot 1; Abner Bump, 1810, lot 40; Joseph Doane, 1809, part of lot 30; Andrew A. Elicott, 1810, part of lot 13; Moses Smith, 1810, lot 8.

Range 3.—John Nichols, 1806, part of lot 20; Silas Meach, 1807, lot 23; Amasa Kilborn, 1806, part of lot 36; Samuel Nichols, 1809, part of lot 35; Abraham Jackson, jr., 1810, part of lot 34; Alfred Kilbourn, 1809, part of lot 36; Peter Belknap, 1810, part of lot 35.

Abraham Jackson, of Mount Holly, Vt., explored this part of the Holland Purchase in 1807. He came by way of Batavia; made arrangements with Joseph Ellicott to make a settlement, and was directed to Cattaraugus lake (now called Java lake). He went through to Lodi (now Gowanda), but finally concluded to commence a settlement in this town, which was called Jackson settlement, and located ten sections of land. He then went back to Vermont, and early in the spring of 1809 returned to this town with his son, Jacob Jackson, and Silas Parker, and their families. The next year he built and moved his family into a log house on what is known as the Burdett Jackson farm.

In 1810 Israel Kibbe came and settled at Kibbe's Corners.

Silas Meach took an article of the first land that was articled in the town, in 1808, but went away and did not return till 1810.

Prominent among the early influences for good in the town were the self-sacrificing labors of Deacon Walter Hinckley, who came, together with D. Rowley, in 1810. We are told by some of the early settlers that it was his custom, especially in the winter, to rise early Sunday morning, build a fire at the log school-house, do his chores, get out his horses and sleigh, and gather in the people. He would then read a sermon, pray with them fervently, and exhort them, often with tears, superintend the Sabbath-school and teach an evening singing school; all without fee or reward, except the reward that proceeds from a consciousness of having done his duty to his fellow man in regard to the present and the long hereafter. But, what would seem paradoxical or very peculiar at the present writing, the deacon at that time kept a hotel and sold liquor. The sentiment of that day did not condemn him as a hypocrite or brand him as a sinner for this dereliction, and doubtless his own conscience did not, so much is conscience the creature of education.

Moses Smith and Simeon Wells came on and settled with their families in 1811. Isaac Saunders and others settled in the east part of the town in 1812.

The northwest part of the town was first settled by William Bennett, Aaron Sillaway and Peter and David Salter, with Isaac H. Salter, a son of Peter Salter, and Asa Fisher. Jonathan Hadley came in 1816, and his family in 1817.

Moses Blood came about 1820. This settlement was known for many years as Hadley's Comers; afterward as the brick school-house. Three or four farms dipping down toward what are called the Sardinia flats are some of the best lands in Arcade. The old farm taken up by Peter Salter is now owned and occupied by his grandson, L. C. Salter. Ruth Hadley, the widow of Jonathan Hadley, is still living on the premises taken up by him over sixty years ago, and John Blood, Esq., owns the homestead of his father, Moses Blood, who died many years ago.

There is a cheese factory near these corners; also a school-house. Years ago they established a Baptist church, but were not sufficiently prospered to build a house of worship.

Charles Beebe, of Vermont, and his wife, who was Elizabeth Train, of Cazenovia, N. Y., started in 1815 for Chautauqua county "on a sled, with a nice yoke of four-year-old oxen with brass buttons on their horns." The snow went off and left them in the mud, and they concluded to settle near Kibbe's Corners. Their furniture consisted of one chair, one bed, and such goods as could be packed in a large chest. It was three years before they had another chair. They had eleven children, six of whom still survive, enjoying a well earned competency.

Israel Friend came from Massachusetts in 1821, on a homemade one-horse sleigh, and was eleven weeks on the road. His first house was a log shanty covered with basswood bark.

Prominent among the pioneers were Elias and Silas Parker. Elias had nine children—five sons and four daughters. Silas had ten sons and four daughters, all of whom grew to maturity.

Sardis Davis came from Canandaigua to Freedom in 1815, and settled in a small log house on the Beebe farm.

Nearly all of the early settlers participated in the battle of Black Rock. Captain Kilbourn was killed, and report says that six others were neither seen or heard from afterward. Among those who were in that engagement Simeon Wells, Silas Parker, Samuel Nichols and three or four others returned; Jacob Jackson was taken prisoner and sent to Halifax, but after a year and a half was exchanged and allowed to return. The war stopped settlement from 1812 to 1815.

The first marriage in the town was that of Silas Meach to Lydia Parker in 1810. Mrs. Meach is still living, the oldest female resident of the town.

The first birth was that of a daughter of Jacob Jackson. The first boy born was a son of Samuel Nichols.

The first burial was that of Mrs. Amasa Kilbourn.

The first preacher of the gospel was the Rev. John Spencer, a Congregational missionary from Connecticut.

The first Sunday-school was established in 1812, in the old log school-house near what is now called the Railroad Block. The first lesson was in the xiv. chapter of St. John.

Colonel D. Rowley built a grist-mill on the north side of the creek, half a mile below the village, in 1811.

At an early day Abner Bump erected a grist-mill at a settlement called Hurdville, on the Cattaraugus creek, in the west part of the town, some fifty rods west of the trestle work and bridge of the B., N. Y. and P. R. R.; the same water power has also been since used for a saw-mill and cheese box factory, both of which were destroyed by fire some years ago. There is another saw-mill in the eastern part of the town, owned and operated by James Dealing, who furnishes considerable hard wood and hemlock lumber for the use of the surrounding vicinity.

CIVIL HISTORY OF ARCADE.

The first town meeting was held, as the record reads, "on the first Tuesday A. D. 1818, pursuant to the law passed March 6th, 1818, to regulate the meetings of a town."

"The meeting called to order by Elias Parker, Esq., the said Elias Parker requested that Abraham Jackson, Walter Hinckley and Salah Jackson preside with him to form a board. Passed by a unanimous vote.

"Voted, that Abraham Jackson serve as moderator of the day; then voted that Ralph Kilbourn serve as clerk; then proceeded the choice of supervisor. On counting the votes it was ascertained that Silas Parker had a majority."

Then followed the choice of town clerk, Walter Hinckley; assessors—Jacob Jackson, Isaac H. Salter and D. H. Wooster; commissioners of schools—Joel Dutton, Lemuel C. Paul and Eliphaz Nicholson; overseers of the poor—Simeon Wells and Thomas W. Colby; commissioners of highways—Samuel Nichols, Moses Wooley and Milo Warren; constable and collector, John Brown; constables—James Francis and John Nichols, jr.; inspectors of common schools—John Brown, David Salter, Joseph Pasco and Silas Parker.

It was voted that pathmasters serve as poundmasters and fence viewers. The following persons were chosen pathmasters: Freedom Lord, Rufus Jewett, Aaron Thomas, Caleb Carpenter, Barney Lockwood, Silas Meach, Talcott Wells, Jacob Jackson, Juda Brown, Ezekiel D. Runals, Jared Witherell, Joseph Hall, David Salter, Abraham Smith, D. H. Wooster and Abner Ward.

It was voted that $75 be raised for common schools; that $80 be levied to build roads and bridges; that $10 be raised for the scalp of each wolf caught in the town by an inhabitant of said town; and that the next annual town meeting be "holden at the house of Abraham Smith, jr."

The gentlemen named below have served as supervisors of the town in the years given:

In 1819, Silas Parker; 1820, 1821, Walter Hinckley; 1822, Elias Parker; 1823, 1824, D. H. Wooster; 1825, 1826, 1828, Abraham Smith; 1827, 1836, Salah Jackson; 1829–33, 1847, 1848, David Calkins; 1834, 1835, 1837, 1840, 1841, John Smith; 1838, James Steele; 1839, 1852, 1857, Leverett H. Spring; 1842, 1843, 1853, Heman Wilson; 1844, 1845, 1855, 1858, Charles O. Shepard; 1846, John C. Paine; 1849, Horatio Hodge; 1850, 1851, 1864, 1865, Horace S. Parker; 1854, 1856, Joseph Currier; 1859, James C. Hooker; 1860, 1861, Alonzo Steele; 1862, 1863, David Steele; 1866, 1867, Ryder Barnes; 1868, Harvey Arnold; 1869, 1870, William H. Wilson; 1871, Andrew Knight; 1877–79, Lucius Peck.

Politically the town votes sometimes one way and sometimes the other, but on a full vote the Democrats have a majority of 60 or 70. The village is quite largely Republican.

In 1865 or 1866 an act was passed by the Legislature cutting off three tiers of lots from the east side of the town, and attaching them to the town of Eagle. This measure was bitterly opposed by so large a portion of the tax payers and residents of the town that in two or three years afterward it was repealed, and the town restored to its original dimensions, although the name of Arcade was retained, which the bill included, and the old name of China from that day became obsolete.

BURIAL PLACES.

The first burial of an adult was that of Mrs. Amasa Kilbourn, in 1810. This was at Jackson's settlement, near the center of the town. It is stated that the coffin was made of planks split and hewed from logs, and stained with a decoction of butternut bark. This story is well authenticated, and no doubt true, as it was before the day of saw-mills, and the luxury of a high priced and fashionable funeral, or the idea of one, had not yet dawned on the imagination of the primitive inhabitants.

Quite a number of burials took place in this vicinity at an early day, but since the rural cemetery, near the village, was established, most of the bodies have been removed to that ground.

Persons were buried on the farm of James Steele, below Arcade village, most of whom have been removed.

A public cemetery, laid out and used many years, on Main street, in the east part of the village of Arcade, has been superseded by and the remains removed to the rural cemetery, the land sold and the proceeds turned over to the trustees of the Rural Cemetery Association.

There have been some burials on the farm of Simeon Wells.

The Roman Catholic cemetery at East Arcade, on the grounds adjacent to St. Mary's Church, has been used for thirty years or more. It is well fenced and well kept.

On the 4th of May, 1852, the citizens of Arcade and vicinity met at the Congregational church, and took steps which resulted, on the 9th of August, 1853, in the organization of the Arcade Rural Cemetery Association under the general law of the State. Nine trustees were elected and classified as follows: First class—A. C. Atwater, Alonzo Steele and Ryder Barnes; second class—Ira Rowley, Leverett Spring and Sanford S. Hooker; third class—H. Price, L. D. Davis and Charles O. Shepard. The board was organized the same day by electing Colonel Charles O. Shepard president, Ryder Barnes vice-president, and Alonzo Steele secretary and treasurer. Five acres of ground had been purchased on a beautiful bluff south of the village, to which eight acres more were subsequently added. This was known as Prospect Hill. After it was properly fenced, and walks and carriage-roads graded, the grounds were publicly dedicated on the 9th day of October, 1855, with religious exercises, including a hymn composed for the occasion by L. A. Haywood, of Warsaw.

The substantial and costly vault, on the north slope of Prospect Hill, was donated to the association by Mrs. Miranda Steele.

ROMAN CATHOLIC CHURCH.

St. Mary's Roman Catholic Church at East Arcade was built in 1846. The site for the church and parsonage was donated to the first Catholic settlers by Heman Wilson, Esq. This church in its initial stages was affiliated with the church at Java under one pastorate; but in a few years the number of Catholics had so increased that the church asked for a pastor, and has since retained the services of a resident priest.

The Roman Catholics numbered about thirty families when they first thought of building a house of worship. Following are the names of the pioneers in this section who were instrumental in building this church: Edward Wales, William Hutchinson, Dennis Casey, Lawrence McGuire, Edward O. Sullivan, Andrew Lenox, Thomas McGloughlin, Bernard Sullivan, John Bennett, John Burns, Felix Gillespie, David Roach, and others.

The building is a wooden structure, and has a capacity for seating four hundred worshipers. It is located on the east bank of the Cattaraugus creek, about five miles from the village of Arcade. The Rev. Mr. Flynn, the first pastor, took charge in 1848. He was succeeded by the Rev. Mr. Miller, who, after a short pastorate, was followed by the Rev. Mr. Stager. Rev. John Fitzpatrick was the next pastor, and after him came Rev. Francis R. Cook. The latter was relieved by Rev. John C. O'Riley, who in turn gave way to the present incumbent, Rev. Edward McShane, who at this writing is building a new parsonage, which, when completed, will have cost $1,500.

RAILROAD COMMUNICATIONS INTRODUCED.

About 1870 the town bonded itself conditionally in aid of what was called the Buffalo and Washington Railroad Company, for the sum of $50,000; one-half of the bonds to be issued and delivered when the railroad was finished to the main road leading from Arcade to Yorkshire, and the other half when it was finished through the town and a depot of certain dimensions finished. The town was to take the stock of the company in exchange for the town bonds. Subsequent to this the town sold its stock to some of the members of the company, and realized $28,000, leaving a debt against the town of $22,000, on which interest has been paid semi-annually, and principal reduced $1,000 each year for the last five years, leaving the present bonded debt $17,000.

This railroad—now called the Buffalo, New York and Philadelphia—has been the source of much profit and convenience to the people of the town.

ARCADE IN DEFENSE OF THE UNION.

The archives of the town do not contain a record of the enlistment of volunteers, but enough has been gathered from well authenticated sources to show that the town did its full share in the suppression of the Rebellion. The following named soldiers enlisted during the war and performed service therein:

Samuel U. Waldo, John W. O'Neil, Wallace Nichols, Henry Fessenden, David Witherell, Hiram A. Williams, Horace W. Jones, D. P. Weller, Henry Chadbone, Timothy Shockeney, Cromwell Magee, Newton Wells (died June 11th, 1864), Abel Clough (died October 19th, 1864), Seaman Cornwell, William Fairfield, Curtis S. Pinney, Charles G. Pinney, Francis J. Eaton, Franklin H. Pinney, John Parker, Alfred R. Calkins, Joel B. Slater, A. B. Bostford, Hiram W. Jackson, John W. Jackson, John Clough, James Clough, George W. Jones, G. Wallace Jones, James W. A. Smith, Leverett H. Waldo, Walker B. Perry, Joseph Eggleston, Milan Jones, William McKenow, William Austin, Nathan Kidder, Levi Van Auker, John Dennis, John Hartigan, John Burlingame, Thomas Rowen, Dennis Rowen, C. A. Woodworth, Benjamin McGee, Dr. Henry S. Day, Dr. Dwight W. Day, Thomas Howard, Charles O. Shepard, Asa Burleson, Rollin Stearns, Patrick Flaherty, Thomas Dillon, James Montgomery, Newton Sage, John Brennon, James Rowen, Owen Whalen, Alonzo H. Jenks, Harrison Waterman, Nelson W. Skinner (died June 30th, 1864), Hiram Henshaw, Marshall Magee, Michael Burns, Patrick Sullivan, Thomas Burrows, John Conner, Frank Conner, A. Sidney Cornwell, Horace Nichols, Thomas Farrond, Loomis D. Hall, Azene Bowen, Daniel Bowen, Gaius Parker, Herman Gerber, Walter H. Jackson, A. G. Whitney, McEhenny Jackson, George Donovan, Nathan Dake, James Brayton, Newland Burns, Carl Whitney, Alexander Dillingham, Perry Morse, Patrick Welch, John Bannon, John Welch, John Roach, William Roach, Dennis Finnegan, Bernard Burns, Michael Redding, Edward Welch, William Simpson, Truman A. Drake, George Vedder, Sheldon J. Merchant, Romanzo B. Drake, Wallace W. Wade, Ira Parker, Cornelius Kibbe, Henry Francis, Porter Francis and William J. Daily.

Quite a proportion of those who went forward to the field never returned, and now fill unknown and unmarked graves in the "sacred soil" of the South—sacred indeed on account of the dust of the heroes that reposes in its bosom.

The town paid liberal bounties to its volunteers, and patriotic citizens not liable to duty furnished substitutes.

RESIDENCE OF Mr JOHN BROWN, TOWN OF WARSAW, WYOMING CO., N.Y.

RESIDENCE OF HARVEY ARNOLD, ARCADE, WYOMING CO., N.Y.

RESIDENCE OF GEO. L. CONE, GAINESVILLE, WYOMING CO., N.Y.

ARCADE VILLAGE.

The village of Arcade is situated at the confluence of Clear creek with the Cattaraugus, in the southwest part of the town. The early settlement and settlers have been traced in the history of the town. The corporate limits embrace one and three-fourths square miles, the western part of which is crossed by the Buffalo, New York and Philadelphia Railroad.

A notice of an election to determine whether this territory should be incorporated as the village of Arcade was published, dated July 12th, 1871; the election to be held at Hamilton's Hotel August 15th, 1871. The notice was signed by S. S. Waldo, C. O. Hitchcock, A. F. Skinner, Sidney Richardson, C. A. Woodworth, C. S. Hamilton, H. N. Waldo, J. S. Bushnell, W. W. Davis, Andrew Seaman, A. A. Spencer, I. Sam. Johnson, B. F. Hurty, E. P. Carter, W. S. Smith, N. Moore, William McKenow, J. D. Nichols, Oliver Wade, J. F. Smith, J. H. Gibson, S. F. Mann, D. B. Shedd, H. S. Parker and John Dillingham.

The whole number of votes cast at this election was 152, of which 104 were in the affirmative and 48 in the negative.

The first election of officers was held at Hamilton's Hotel September 10th, 1871, pursuant to notice signed by Andrew Knight, supervisor, and Silas F. Mann, town clerk. The following officers were elected: J. T. Cummings, president; B. F. Hurty, E. P. Carter and James Perkins, trustees; Silas F. Mann, treasurer, and Sidney Richardson, collector.

The first meeting of the board of trustees was held September 21st, 1871, at the bank of Hurty & Chamberlain, and organized by taking the oath of office, and appointing E. Puzy clerk.

At the annual meeting held March 18th, 1879, the following officers were elected: Dr. Henry L. Day, president; A. L. Moulton and Isaac Smith, trustees for two years, and B. F. Hurty to fill vacancy; A. B. Bishop, treasurer; A. J. Whitney, collector. The board at a subsequent meeting appointed the following: W. W. Wade, clerk; James M. Witherell, street commissioner; I. A. Cornwell, police constable; J. S. Bushnell, chief engineer of the fire department, and L. B. Calkins and A. A. Spencer, fire wardens.

PROFESSIONAL MEN AND BUSINESS ESTABLISHMENTS.

Among the early settlers that tried lawsuits was Silas Parker, although there is no evidence that he ever was admitted as a regular lawyer. His son, Charles R. Parker, studied law, was regularly admitted, and for many years practiced his profession with success. Leverett Spring came into the town from Vermont about forty-five years ago; he is still hale, and in the practice of his profession, doing business in Wyoming and adjoining counties. Byron Healy, now county judge, commenced his practice in Arcade, as also did I. S. Johnson, now district attorney. Andrew J. Knight, ex-district attorney, has an office, and is doing a good business. William H. Nourse has been doing a legal business in Arcade two or three years. Henry M. Hill and Gustavus A. Barnes are younger members of the bar.

The town of Arcade, like all other towns, has no doubt been blessed with all sorts of doctors, good, bad and indifferent, and they all had their friends that were willing to stand by them through evil and through good report. The first one we find mentioned was Dr. Joseph Pasco, but whether he was regular or irregular we have no means of knowing. Then we hear of Dr. Israel Kibbe, who dealt out roots, herbs, etc., for the relief of the sick and afflicted. He was a good, well disposed man, and of course had a great many friends. We hear also of Dr. Kilbourn, but do not know what his medical tenets were. A Dr. Powers and a Dr. Burrows have also had residences here. Dr. Ira Shedd located here probably near fifty years ago. He was a regular physician and a very worthy man, and for a great many years was the only physician in the town. He left here in 1872, then well toward seventy years old, and is living with his son at Grand Rapids, Mich. Dr. Washington W. Day came here from Eagle some twenty years ago, and practiced his profession till his health failed in 1868. He died March 12th, 1873. Since that time Dr. Hanks and Dr. FitzGibbons, allopathic, Dr. Stearns, eclectic, and Dr. Sovereign, homœopathic, have been in Arcade for short periods. The present physicians are Dr. Henry L. Day, son of Dr. Washington W. Day, who has been in successful practice about fifteen years; Dr. Lucius Peck, who moved here from Java in 1869, and has practiced here and in Java and Eagle something over thirty years; and Dr. E. W. Earle, homœopathic physician, who has been in practice in Arcade and Freedom three or four years.

On the 31st of March, 1859, James H. Gibson started a newspaper here, called the *Arcade Enterprise*, which afterward went into the hands of Charles Young. It was published by successive proprietors, with indifferent success for several years, and gave way to the *Arcade Times*, which was published here by S. Wilson Wade three or four years, and then removed to Warsaw, taking the name of the *Wyoming County Times*, where it is still published.

The *Arcade Leader* was commenced in January, 1875, by Wallace W. Wade, and published by him until October 1st, 1879, when he was succeeded by I. Allen Cornwell, who is its present editor and proprietor.

There is at present only one drug store in the place. It is under the management of A. B. Bishop, a graduate of the Philadelphia College of Pharmacy.

About 1828 the site and water privilege for the grist-mill, tannery and saw-mill were deeded by Deacon Walter Hinckley to Harry Jackson, a son of Salah Jackson. The water was taken out of Clear creek by a head race, commencing on the farm of Captain Barrows, now owned by Martin J. Stearns, on the west side of Clear creek. This has proved to be a very valuable water power. The grist-mill was built about 1828 by Harry Jackson; the next year he built a saw-mill. In 1852 the brothers Asahel and John Jackson built a tannery on the same water power. This property is now all owned by Silas F. Clough. The grist-mill and tannery seem to be in a flourishing condition, but the saw-mill has been on the retired list for some time.

There is a small grist-mill on the Cattaraugus creek, about two miles above the village, which is now owned and operated by A. D. Hedges, Esq. This mill has been in use probably for twenty years or more, and still does quite a respectable business.

C. A. Clough owns and operates a saw-mill in the west part of Arcade village, and is doing a respectable business for a section of country like this, nearly destitute of timber.

A cheese box factory, situated in the west part of the village and operated by C. A. Clough and J. H. Howard, is doing a fine business, and employs six or seven hands about eight or nine months in the year.

The planing-mill, together with a sash, door and blind factory, is situated on Clear creek, near its confluence with the Cattaraugus. It is owned and operated by J. S. Bushnell, who employs four or five hands the year round, doing a good business on a small scale in the way of planing, matching, manufacturing siding, brackets, mouldings, etc.

Samuel Upham built the first cloth-dressing and wool-carding factory in 1819. He operated and owned it till 1834, when his son in-law, H. N. Waldo, became the owner. In 1837 the building was enlarged and machinery introduced for the manufacture of cloth, on a small scale. He kept on enlarging and introducing machinery till 1863, when it had a capacity of turning out from seventy-five to one hundred yards of flannels and cassimeres per day. A partnership was organized about this time, under the firm name of Waldo, Steele & Co., who soon afterward pulled down the old building and erected a new one, thirty by eighty feet, with an "L" thirty by fifty feet, with all the modern machinery for spinning, weaving and finishing cloth. The factory now had a capacity for two hundred yards per day, employed about twenty-five hands and was run up to its full capacity till October 30th, 1868, when it was destroyed by fire. The last month was the best month of its existence. It was rebuilt by Waldo & Son in 1871, fifty by eighty feet, of brick, with stone basement, and is now owned and operated by Smith & Wilson as a yarn factory. Under the present management it employs fourteen hands and manufactures about two hundred pounds of yarn per day, worth on an average $1.50 per pound. It is run nine or ten months in the year. The annual income is about $35,000.

Hurty & Chamberlain established a bank here July 1st, 1867, in Carter's building, east of the Clear creek bridge, which was conducted by Mr. Hurty. In 1873 in was reorganized, passing into the hands of the firm of B. F. Hurty & Co., composed of B. F. Hurty, D. C. Beebe and A. Knight. In 1874 the banking company built the three-story brick block known as the Keystone Block, in the upper story of which is Keystone Hall. The east side of the lower story is used as a bank. It is finished in modern style, with a vault of great security.

There are two regular dry goods stores in the village—the old and well known store of D. C. Beebe, who has been successfully engaged in the business

PRESBYTERY. ST MARY'S CHURCH, REV. EDWARD McSHANE, PASTOR, EAST ARCADE, N.Y.

RESIDENCE of S. T. GILBERT, ARCADE, N. Y.

"ARCADE HOUSE" L. B. CALKINS, PROPRIETOR, ARCADE, N.Y.

RESIDENCE of B. F. HURTY, ARCADE, N. Y.

here and in the towns adjoining for twenty years; and that kept by Silas F. Mann, who has followed the business toward twenty years with good success.

Whitney & Guild, Jared F. Smith and Joshua D. Nichols sell groceries and provisions, glassware and notions. W. W. Davis also deals in groceries, provisions, feed, salt, lime, coal, seeds and fruits, etc.

James Perkins & Son, M. T. C. Perkins, manufacture and sell everything in the line of carriages and sleighs but lumber wagons. They have a paint and blacksmith shop connected with their establishment, and turn out a large quantity of work for a town like this. Charles Witherell has a carriage shop on Liberty street.

Louis H. Johnson manufactures gravestones and monuments.

Of resident cheese buyers there are S. Wade, H. D. Barnes, A. S. Moulton, H. M. Holmes, Hiram Steele, Wellington Beebe, V. C. Beebe and L. L. Horton.

The livery business is probably not quite as good as it was fifteen or twenty years ago, but supports three stables in the village, viz.: those of Herbert Allen (the old stable of Spencer & Davis); Judson Bostwick, who occupies the barn of A. A. Spencer, near the Arcade Hotel; and George Green.

There are at least a half dozen blacksmith shops in the village, where horseshoeing, carriage ironing and all kinds of general blacksmithing are carried on. Among the workmen are William McKenow, Henry Kilton, James Mulvey, A. D. Dennison, Mr. Upham and Horatio Hodge.

The only hardware store in Arcade is now kept by Gilbert & Foote, two young men who embarked in the trade within the last six months, by buying out the stock of E. W. Wilcox. They keep everything usually kept in hardware stores except stoves. A. F. Skinner and Chauncey make and sell tinware, and deal in stoves.

English & Carter keep a general assortment of watches, clocks, silverware, cutlery and notions for sale at their store, and repair clocks, watches, etc.

This store and shop was first owned and carried on by E. P. Carter, but two or three years ago passed into the hands of the present proprietors.

There are three hotels within the limits of the corporation of the village. The Arcade Hotel is owned by Levi B. Calkins, and for many years was the only one in the village or in the town. It has had many proprietors, and is now under the superintendence of Mace Lord, a landlord of much experience. Three or four years ago it was thoroughly repaired, and a third story added to the front, making it one of the finest and best managed hotel buildings in the county.

The United States Hotel was founded and has always been kept by Z. Foote, who in 1871 bought out what had been used for a store and dwelling house, and converted it into this hotel. He also built a capacious barn in the rear, and otherwise improved the property.

About 1874 Hyder Barnes built a hotel at the railroad station. It was immediately bought and is now kept by R. H. McReady.

There are two boot and shoe shops, carried on by C. H. Beardsly and H. S. Hubbard.

H. J. Beardsley carries on business as a merchant tailor; is doing quite an extensive business in the clothing trade.

There is at present but one meat market in the village, kept by George W. Jones and E. C. Rogers.

Mrs. John Syke and the Misses Fuller are the milliners of the place, and Mrs. Shalies does an extensive business in dress making.

SCHOOLS.

In 1839 Professor Samuel Sedgwick opened a select school in the basement of the old Congregational church. In 1844 he built Sedgwick Seminary. He was succeeded by D. G. Calkins and others. This building was afterward sold, and made over into a Methodist church.

The original subscription for establishing the Arcade academy was dated October 1st, 1861. The charter was granted in February, 1862, and the school opened in April, 1863, with J. W. Earle as principal. During the eight years of its existence as the Arcade Academy the principals were J. W. Earle, W. M. Benson, Mr. Huzzy, J. W. Snow and E. H. Latimer.

In April, 1870, it was sold to school district No. 1, which includes the whole village of Arcade, and the Arcade Academy and Union School was established under the general law of the State. Since the change the principals have been D. H. Burke, three terms; Miss Mary Wright, three terms; G. M. Forbes, three terms; R. W. Whelan, three terms; G. M. Forbes, again, three terms; A. M. Moss, two terms; J. H. Gibson, seven terms; and A. L. Eastman, who is the present principal. Three assistants are usually employed, and the average attendance is about one hundred and sixty pupils.

ARCADE LODGE, NO. 419, F. & A. M.

was constituted May 19th, 1856 (date of warrant June 16th, 1857), with Ezra Farrington, W. M.; Heman Wilson, S. W.; and Philander Cook, J. W. The charter members were: Ezra Farrington, Heman Wilson, Philander Cook, A. B. Botsford, Silas Parker, Ira Rowley, S. Guild, E. Holmes, John Wade, H. Smith, J. G. Wood and J. S. Colby.

Since its organization the following have been W. M.: Ezra Farrington, Heman Wilson, Reuben Ball, Gideon Bentley, Hiram Smith, David Sill, I. Samuel Johnson, D. J. Woodworth, W. W. Wade and M. T. C. Perkins.

Meetings are held the first and third Fridays of each month. The membership is 94.

Officers for 1879: M. T. C. Perkins, W. M.; I. A. Cornwell, S. W.; Lucius Peck, J. W.; R. Ball, treasurer; J. H. Howard, secretary; A. F. Skinner, S. D.; William C. Ladd, J. D.; H. T. Wade, S. M. C.; J. S. Bushnell, J. M. C.; G. G. Williams, tyler.

FIRES AND FIRE DEPARTMENT.

The first fire of any note was that which destroyed the Arcade Woolen Mills October 30th, 1868. This was a three-story building, and there was not a ladder in town by which the roof could be reached.

December 16th, 1871, a hook and ladder company was organized, with the following officers: J. S. Bushnell, foreman; T. J. Cornwell, assistant foreman; Charles T. Waldo, secretary; other members—George S. Guild, W. B. Perry, J. H. Beardsly, V. C. Beebe, H. E. Kilton, George Green, W. H. Pugh, John Haskell, H. W. Jones, D. Dennison, I. A. Cornwell, L. H. Johnson, Butler Wood, Clark Beardsly and H. S. Mosher.

The present officers are: A. H. Carter, foreman; J. M. Witherell, assistant foreman; and B. F. Hurty, secretary and treasurer.

The Chemical Fire Engine Company was organized April 7th, 187–, with the following officers, viz.: B. F. Lewis, foreman; J. S. Bushnell, assistant foreman; Fremont Knight, secretary; M. A. Hyland, treasurer. At a special meeting called for that purpose the corporation voted $1,000 for the purchase of a Babcock chemical engine.

The present officers are: F. M. Foote, foreman; L. A. Davis, assistant foreman; F. A. Seaman, secretary; and James Crawford, treasurer; other members—F. C. Knight, W. S. Stearns, W. I. Mastin, J. W. Blakely, E. C. Wade, M. A. Hyland, C. A. Moon, H. S. Hubbard, H. O. Shedd, C. H. St. John, A. A. House, S. T. Gilbert, C. H. Beardsly, Allen W. Peck, Chauncey White and Millard Holmes.

The village consists largely of wooden buildings, which in many places stand very compact, and it is remarkable that it has thus far escaped disastrous fires.

CHURCH HISTORY.

Congregational.—The first Congregational church of Arcade was organized on Saturday, July 24th, 1813, at a meeting held in the school-house. Rev. John Spencer was moderator of the meeting, and the original members were Walter Hinckley, Azubah Kibbe and Peggy Dutton. Articles of faith and covenant were adopted, and Walter Hinckley was chosen deacon of the church, also moderator and clerk for future meetings. He was the only deacon until 1832, when two more were chosen to assist him, and he held the office of clerk until 1836. He was also the originator and superintendent of the Sunday-school.

The Lord's Supper was administered the Sunday following the organization, by the Rev. John Spencer, who also served the church more or less regularly for the first ten years of its history, when he was succeeded by the Rev. Edmund Ingalls, who labored in the field successfully another ten years or more.

Revs. Solomon Stevens, Calvin Grey, Caleb E. Fisher, Henry Snyder, Timothy Stow, Ovid Miner, Lewis P. Frost, John Dodd (who died in the

RESIDENCE OF JOHN J. QUACKENBUSH, EAGLE, N.Y.

RESIDENCE OF W. W. DAVIS, ARCADE, N.Y.

pastorate in 1864), William Dewey, W. H. Thomas, Charles Strong and Eugene F. Atwood served the church for a longer or shorter time. The present pastor, Rev. Newton H. Bell, began his ministry with this church in 1877.

Although this church was Congregational in its polity from the beginning, it was connected with the presbytery until 1858, and sent its delegate annually to that body. In 1858 it voted to unite with the Wyoming County Conference of Congregational Churches. April 2nd, 1854, a colony of members was dismissed for the purpose of organizing a church at Currier's Corners, in Java.

During its early history the church enjoyed an unusual degree of prosperity, and hundreds were added by letter and profession of faith; but owing to many causes it became so reduced in strength that in 1879 it had only thirty resident members, and its utter extinction seemed imminent, but since that time a large congregation has been gathered, and its membership more than doubled.

A flourishing Sunday-school of more than a hundred scholars, with an average attendance of seventy-five, is under the efficient management of Mr. L. A. Davis and a good corps of teachers.

The first house of worship was built and dedicated in 1834. It was valued at about $2,500, and the sale of pews fully covered the amount. In 1877 the property was put into the hands of a committee, consisting of Messrs. B. F. Hurty, William W. Davis and Smith Lyon, and they were authorized to erect a new building for the use of the church. The work was finished with such dispatch that on the 5th of December of the same year a beautiful structure, costing about $6,000, was dedicated, free of debt. It is built of wood. The style is gothic. The audience room has a seating capacity of three hundred, and is connected in the rear with a large lecture room, Bible class-room and library. The old bell rings in the new belfry. The whole is tastefully finished and furnished, and is an ornament as well as credit to the village.

Baptist.—Among the early settlers of the town were a few Baptists, who previous to 1816 held meetings, generally in private houses, under the lead of Deacon Caleb Calkins, Deacon John Colby and Stephen Pratt, of Sardinia. After that date Rev. Elias Harmon, who settled in Aurora, Rev. William Merrick, then of Sheldon, and others preached for them occasionally. The first Baptist church was organized October 13th, 1820, and recognized by a council in February, 1821, as a branch of the China and Concord church. In November, 1825, this body assumed the name of the China and Freedom church. Deacon Caleb Calkins, Deacon Samuel Upham and Dr. S. W. Pattison were active members of this body.

In 1825 Rev. Whitman Metcalf settled in Sardinia, and was soon engaged to preach in Arcade one-fourth of the time, and this church became connected as a branch with that of Sardinia, under the name of the Sardinia and China church. Meetings were held in the school-house, which was also occupied by the other denominations. Rev. Clark Carr, a missionary of the Holland Purchase Baptist Association, which had been organized in 1811, preached sometimes in 1831, as did also Rev. E. Loomis, then pastor of Boston and Springville. Rev. Alfred

Handy, who succeeded Elder Metcalf at Sardinia in 1833, also preached till 1836.

The church was organized as a separate and distinct church, by the name of the Baptist Church of Christ in Arcade, August 8th, 1835. The constituted members were: L. D. Davis, James Steele, Calvin R. Davis, Eliakim How, Samuel Upham, Ira Rowley, Lester Withey, Sylvia Withey, Hannah How, Polly Upham, Lucy Upham, Ira Shedd, Hiram Bartow, Hugh Steele, A. D. Warren, Abigail Warren, Francis Eaton, Lyman Carpenter, Chester A. Calkins, Milan Jones, G. Knight, Diana Smith, Maria Nourse, Alzina Gillett, Eurilla Bartow, Lucinda Steele, Susan Warren, Phœbe Warren, Emily Eaton, Susan Rowley, Julia Ann Shedd, Sophronia Crary, Miranda Steele, Mary A. Steele, Pomel Beckwith, Erville Pickard, Harriet Beckwith; six of these now belong to the church.

October 7th, 1835, a council met at the Congregational meeting-house in Arcade, at which the Rev. Elisha Tucker was moderator, and publicly recognized this body as a regular gospel church. Dr. Ira Shedd was the first clerk, and served from that time till he removed to Grand Rapids, Mich., in 1872. He was succeeded by A. J. Knight, the present incumbent.

The first deacons were James Steele, L. D. Davis and Ira Shedd. They have been succeeded by Samuel Upham, Daniel Woodworth and Abel Clough. The present deacons are Chester A. Calkins and Heman Wilson.

Rev. Alfred Handy preached till 1836; Rev. A. Miner, of Rushford, and Rev. Silas Tucker, then a student at Hamilton, in 1836 and 1837; Rev. Sheldon N. Smith and Rev. Steadman Searle, in 1837 and 1838, and Rev. Whitman Metcalf, from 1838 to 1840. Their first resident pastor, Rev. J. M. Purrington, was with them from 1840 to 1845.

In 1839 they commenced building their first house of worship. It was a substantial frame building, forty by fifty feet, cost $2,400, and was dedicated in January, 1841. In 1844 they built a parsonage, at a cost of about $400.

Rev. David Searles was pastor in 1845 and 1846.

The pulpit was supplied for about one year by Rev. S. Tucker, Rev. Z. Smith and others. Rev. E. W. Clark was pastor from 1847 to 1853; Rev. E. W. Bliss from 1853 to 1855; Rev. R. Morey in 1856 and 1857: Rev. A. G. Bowles from 1858 to 1860; Rev. Franklin Kidder from 1860 to 1866; Rev. L. S. Stowell, 1866 and 1867; Rev. Abner Morrill, 1868 to 1874; Rev. A. D. Bush has been pastor since 1874.

In 1874 the church rebuilt and enlarged the parsonage, at a cost of about $800, and in 1875 rebuilt, enlarged and refurnished the meeting-house, at a cost of about $6,400. The present number of members is one hundred and eighteen. Since the erection of the meeting-house in 1840, the members have maintained an efficient Sunday-school. L. Spring was its first superintendent. A. J. Knight is now superintendent. The school has fourteen officers and one hundred and forty pupils, and about one hundred and fifty library books.

Methodist Episcopal.—It has been difficult to obtain information of the early Methodists in the town, but it appears that they began to have preaching here about 1830. They had no house of worship, but held their services, which were at irregular intervals, in the Congregational and Baptist churches. About 1850 they bought of one Sedgwick a building then used as a seminary, and in 1856 repaired it extensively, giving it a much more churchlike appearance.

The church thus repaired was dedicated July 31st, 1856. In 1878 the house was entirely rebuilt, in modern style, with the addition of a lecture-room, and furnace in the basement. The audience room has a seating capacity of three hundred. The society is now in a flourishing condition, the accessions within the last year having been at least one-half of their present membership, which is about seventy. The Sabbath-school numbers about fifty pupils, and is superintended by A. F. Skinner.

The present pastor is Rev. J. A. Smith.

BIOGRAPHICAL.

JESSE AMES was born in Orwell, Vt., in 1814. He was a son of Jacob Ames, also a native of Vermont, who died in Arcade in 1864. Mr. Ames married Jane R. Jackson, of Cherry Valley, Otsego county, in 1844. He came to Arcade in 1845, having lived in Colchester and South Dansville previously. The father of Mrs. Ames was born in Hartford, Conn., and coming to Arcade in 1819, was one of the early settlers of the town.

CHARLES W. ARNOLD was born in China (now Arcade) in 1816. He has been a life-long resident of the town, which he has served as clerk. In 1848 he was married to Dolly Foster Runnells, niece of Silas Meach, prominent in pioneer days. Mr. Arnold contributed liberally to the prosecution of the late war.

GIDEON ARNOLD, deceased, was born July 8th, 1789, at Hampton, Conn., and came to Arcade in 1811. Returning to his native place in 1815, he married Lovina Williams August 20th, and came back and settled on the farm now owned by his son, Harvey Arnold, who was born September 12th, 1826, and married to Susan, daughter of Phineas Stearns, of Arcade, October 19th, 1852. He has served as assessor, and is president of the board of education of Arcade union school.

HYDER BARNES was born at Rutland, Vt., September 11th, 1804, and died December 18th, 1879. He married Daphne B. Palmer, of Orwell, Vt., October 19th, 1828, and resided at Addison, Vt., until he came to Arcade, in 1852. He was active in business, and held local offices. His sons, H. Dana and Gustavus A. Barnes, the former an extensive dealer in butter and cheese, the latter a lawyer, are well known in the town.

D. C. BEEBE was born at Freedom, Cattaraugus county, October 22nd, 1830, and married Azelia A., daughter of Philander Cook, October 18th, 1858. Mr. Beebe, who is a merchant and banker, is a son of Charles Beebe, a settler from Vermont, who came into Arcade in 1815.

V. C. BEEBE, son of Charles Beebe, was born at Freedom, N. Y., February 4th, 1851, and is unmarried. He was educated at the district school and at Arcade Academy. He began his business career as a clerk and salesman at the age of eighteen, and a few years later became a member of the firm of Horton & Beebe in the wholesaler cheese and butter trade; and, though young, has an enviable reputation among the dairymen of western New York.

Judson Bostwick, liveryman, was born in Pike, March 19th, 1830, and was married February 23d, 1854, to Lovina Smith, daughter of William Smith, of Castile. Mr. Bostwick enlisted in September, 1861, in Company F, 5th N. Y. cavalry. He was disabled at Annapolis and discharged in 1862. He lived nine years in Michigan, and located in Arcade in 1878.

Rev. Newton H. Bell, pastor of the Congregational church of Arcade, is a man of exceptional classical, literary and theological erudition. He was born at Kossuth, Iowa, April 22nd, 1841, and married Emma H., daughter of Rev. Erastus Curtiss, of North New Salem, Mass., August 11th, 1868. He is a graduate of Denmark Academy, of Iowa, Amherst College and Princeton and Bangor theological seminaries, and has traveled extensively on both hemispheres, having preached at Stafford Springs, Conn., and Owatanna, Minn., and been a missionary at Mardin, in Turkey. He assumed charge of the Arcade church in November, 1877.

William Bixby was born in 1824, at Freedom, N. Y. He married Salome L. Clough, in 1850. Mr. Bixby's father, Barnes Bixby, was born in Hillsboro county, N. H., in 1785, and was a settler in Arcade in 1817. He died in his ninetieth year.

Levi B. Calkins was born October 18th, 1820, at St. Albans, Vt., and removed with his mother to Aurora, Erie county, in 1833. October 18th, 1840, he was married to Matilda, daughter of Seth Willery, of Cambridge, Vt., and March 12th, 1861, to Emily Farrington Reed, of Olean, N. Y. He has followed the milling business twenty years, been a farmer three years, and has had much experience as a hotel proprietor: in Lockport three years and sixteen years in Arcade.

Egbert P. Carter, jeweler and dealer in clocks, watches and silverware, is a son of Miles Carter, and was born in Ontario county, April 21st, 1825. He married Eliza Ann, daughter of Walter Brooks, of Yorkshire, N. Y., in 1848. He has a store in Eldred, Pa.

Chancey A. Clough, son of Abel Clough, was born April 6th, 1841, in Fabius, Onondaga county. He married Abbie Webber, daughter of Levi Webber, of Farmersville, N. Y., October 14th, 1862. Mr. Clough is a saw and planing-mill proprietor and a leading lumberman and manufacturer.

Irvin Allen Cornwell, son of John Cornwell, was born March 18th, 1852, at Arcade. He is editor and proprietor of the *Arcade Leader*, and has served two years as chief of police, three years as constable and two years as town clerk. His father was a sergeant in the English navy in the war of 1812. His mother was Viletta Seaman, of Dutchess county.

William W. Davis, son of Sardis and grandson of Sylvester Davis, was born in Freedom, N.Y., September 24th, 1825. July 6th, 1851, he was married to Julia A. Maynard, of Arcade. Their son, Lyman, is now engaged with his father in farming, and the purchase, baling and sale of hay and a general merchandise trade. Sylvester Davis, a blacksmith, removed with his family from New Hampshire to Canandaigua, N. Y., about 1798. Sardis Davis came from there to Freedom in 1815, and settled on the Beebe farm. William W. Davis has served one year as under sheriff.

JESSE DENNIS was born at Tioga Lake, Pa., in 1818, and was married to Fannie L. Chaffee, of Boston, Erie county, in 1844. He came with his parents to Arcade when it was called China. His father married Hannah Brown, of Vermont. They were early settlers. Chester Chaffee, father of Mrs. Jesse Dennis, was a native of Vermont. He became a resident of Arcade in 1830. He died in 1876.

DR. E. W. EARLE is a son of Prof. J. W. Earle, widely known in western New York as a teacher. He was born June 16th, 1845, in Centervillo, N. Y., and in 1850 went with his father's family to Minnesota, where his brother was killed and his mother and sister were made captives in the Sioux war. He was married January 31st, 1867, to Hannah Hills, of Yorkshire, N. Y. He graduated at Cincinnati Medical College in April, 1877, and now has a lucrative practice.

Z. FOOTE was born January 6th, 1822, at Hamilton, N. Y., and came to Arcade from Java. He is proprietor of the United States Hotel, which stands on the ground occupied by the pioneer log tavern of the town. He kept a hotel at Java Lake three years. June 6th, 1855, he married Ann Eliza Kingman, of Java.

JOHN FRIEND, a son of Isaac Friend, of Dregget, Mass., was born January 2nd, 1826, in Sheldon (now Java), and married Harriet A. Twiss, daughter of Moses Twiss, of Charlton, Mass., October 7th, 1852. He is a farmer and produce dealer, and lives at Currier's Corners, on the farm where his father settled in 1821. The elder Friend is living. He came from Massachusetts, and was one of the men prominent in the construction of the Attica and Allegany Valley Railroad.

J. H. GIBSON was born at Darien, Genesee county, August 13th, 1834, and came to Arcade from Alexander, Genesee county, in 1856. March 21st, 1859, he married Helen M. Lyon, of Arcade. From 1875 to 1879 he was teacher in the Arcade Academy and Union School, serving three years as principal. He is also a popular lecturer on natural science. He was a member of the first firm in the drug trade and was the first newspaper publisher in Arcade.

SAMUEL T. GILBERT, the senior member of the firm of Gilbert & Foote, general dealers in hardware, paints and oils, was born September 2nd, 1853, in Thorold, Canada, and was married October 27th, 1879, to Ella M. Morris, of Otto, Cattaraugus county. He has been a resident of Arcade since 1876.

HENRY M. HILL, attorney, was educated at Arcade Academy and Syracuse University, and is a graduate of Ann Arbor University, Mich. He has been admitted to practice in the courts of the State of New York and in the United States courts. He has traveled considerably, and for a time had an office at Fort Scott, Kansas. He married Annie Burlew, of Ovid, New York, October 16th, 1873.

OLIVER HODGES, ESQ., who died on the 19th day of June, 1878, came as early as 1805, in company with his parents, when he was only seven years old, to the town of Attica. His father, Eliphalet Hodges, located on the farm where his grandson, Garcy, now resides, and the land has always remained in the title of his father since the decease of his grandparents. When Oliver Hodges came to this town there were only a few pioneer settlers, who had raised three or four log cabins. Hardly any clearings had been made, nor any better roads laid out than footpaths through the woods, between the settlers dwellings. He assisted in clearing the land to which he was heir, became accustomed to hard labor, and identified himself with the growth and business prosperity of the town. When eleven years of age he carried the mall regularly between Attica and Batavia, making the journey on horseback, sometimes requiring his horse to leap over the trees that had fallen across his pathway. He was at home on horseback from childhood. In the days when men were arrested and imprisoned for debt he was constable and collector of this town, and his duties, if not always pleasant, were at least full of excitement. His business habits were such that he was repeatedly appointed deputy sheriff of Genesee county when this part of Wyoming belonged to Genesee. The older inhabitants can recollect the capture of the notorious counterfeiter Law, of his being brought to trial and the murderous assault he made in the court room upon an accomplice, Topliff, who testified against him. It is believed he would have accomplished his purpose if he had not been forcibly prevented. Mr. Hodges and Rue Nelson walked from Brierfield, Mass., to Attica in eight days, a pretty good illustration of the active habits of the young men in those times. Afterward Mr. Hodges used to draw dry goods and groceries from Albany to Attica for $8.25 per hundred. He took a reasonable amount of interest in town politics, and was a Whig until the organization of the Republican party. He was considered a man of excellent judgment, a good citizen, a kind neighbor and pleasant in his social relations.

B. F. HURTY, banker, Arcade, was born December 3d, 1824, at Lowville, Lewis county. In 1849 he married Mary Bailey, of Cuba, Allegany county. His father, John Hurty, was a farmer of German descent, and moved with his family to Bethany in 1836. The later years of his life were spent in Cuba, Allegany county, where he died in 1866. After receiving such educational advantages as were afforded by the district school, young Hurty attended the academy at Alexander two winters, working on the farm during the summer. He began teaching school at Farmersville at $10 per month, "boarding around." He afterward began teaching and attending school until he secured a liberal academic education. He was successful as a teacher in high schools at Cuba, Randolph and other points; was book-keeper for a contractor on public works six years, and spent two years in the South in government employ during the Rebellion.

HON. MARCUS A. HULL, son of Dr. Laurens Hull, of Angelica, N. Y., was born at Bridgewater, N. Y., December 26th, 1819. He settled in Pike in 1856, and for several years had a woolen mill there. From Pike he removed to Arcade, where he is a well known manufacturer. He was elected to the Legislature in 1869, and re-elected in 1870. In 1873 he was appointed inspector of customs for the district of Niagara, port of Suspension Bridge, which position he still occupies. September 5th, 1848, he was married to Susan C. Ackerman, of Allen, N. Y.

JOHN JACKSON, son of Salah Jackson, and great-grandson of Dr. Orville Jackson, who was surgeon in the French army during the French and Indian war, was born in Arcade May 30th, 1817. Mr. Jackson married Mary Knapp, of Lindley, N. Y., in 1845. He is a miller and carpenter. His family were early in the town, his brothers Henry and Salah being well remembered pioneers.

J. WESLEY JACKSON, son of Harry Jackson and grandson of Salah Jackson, was born in Arcade September 3d, 1842, and was married May 29th, 1866, to Henrietta, daughter of Smith Lyon, of Arcade. Mr. Jackson enlisted as second lieutenant of Company H, 78th N. Y. infantry, in November, 1861, served two years and resigned on account

RESIDENCE OF JAMES Mc ELROY, EAGLE, WYOMING CO., N.Y.

RESIDENCE OF ALBERT NEWKIRK, EAGLE, N.Y.

RESIDENCE OF E.P. CARTER, ARCADE, WYOMING CO., N.Y.

RES. OF MRS. L.R. SHERWOOD, ARCADE, WYOMING CO., N.Y.

RES. OF MRS. ELIZA WELLES & SON', ARCADE, WYOMING CO., N.Y.

RES. OF T. F. GRAY, CASTILE, N.Y.

CHURCH OF THE ASSUMPTION OF THE B.V. I. McGRATH, Pastor, PORTAGEVILLE, N.Y.

of sickness. In September, 1864, he re-enlisted, in the 1st N. Y. dragoons, and served until the close of the war. Mr. Jackson has long been a farmer and cattle dealer, and is engaged in the western cattle trade, having large ranches in Kansas.

LOUIS H. JOHNSON, who is engaged in the marble business at Arcade, was born in Rochester, N. Y., October 5th, 1852, and married Genevieve, daughter of Milton Pittenger, of Shiloh, O.

GEORGE W. JONES was born in Arcade June 2nd, 1839, and married Martha Price, of Old Town, O., April 19th, 1860. He served in the war of the Rebellion in Company C, 1st N. Y. dragoons; was wounded in a cavalry charge near Strasburg, Va., and discharged at the close of the war.

HORACE W. JONES was born at Sardinia, Erie county, in 1840. He came from Sardinia to Arcade, where he has since resided, except two years spent in Yorkshire. May 4th, 1861, he enlisted in the 21st N. Y. volunteers. He participated in the 2nd battle of Bull Run, Antietam (where he was wounded), Fredericksburg, South Mountain and in other engagements. In 1864 he married Elizabeth Whitney, widow of Carleton Whitney, and daughter of Benjamin Town, who was born in Vermont in 1799, and has lived in Richfield, Otsego county, and Centreville, Allegany county, before coming to Arcade, where he now resides.

ANDREW J. KNIGHT, attorney, was born June 3d, 1839, at Nunda, Livingston county, where he was a student at the academy until he entered Rochester University. He was principal of the schools at Portage and Castile one year each, during which time he was reading law, and was admitted to the bar in 1864. He was elected district attorney in 1874, but resigned in 1876 on account of an injury which prevented his serving. In June, 1865, he married Althea E. Angler, of Nunda.

MACE LARD is one of the best known men in the county, where he has been a popular landlord and stage proprietor for many years. He has been located at Pike, Warsaw and Arcade. From 1860 to 1864 he was in California, mining, keeping hotels and lumbering, where he experienced many vicissitudes of fortune. He was born October 10th, 1819.

NELSON MOORE was born in Fenner, Madison county, March 4th, 1823. In 1824 he came with his parents to China; they settled near North Java. In 1843 he removed to Arcade, where he married Sarepta Parker in 1847, and has since resided here, engaged in farming. His father, Hiram Moore, went west, and died there in 1877.

ALBERT L. MOULTON was born November 18th, 1826, at Holland, N. Y., December 26th, 1847, he married Betsey Ann Burbank, of Arcade, who was a daughter of Solomon Burbank, and was born October 16th, 1830. Mr. Moulton is a boot and shoe maker by trade, but is now a wholesale dealer in butter and cheese for the New York market, his trade extending through five or six counties of western New York.

COLONEL SAMUEL NICKOLS was born at Francestown, N. H., in 1786, and died at Arcade in 1856. His grandfather, John Nickols, came from Ireland. Colonel Nickols was married at Francestown, N. H., to Sarah Dutton. They raised a family of six children, three of whom are living. The only member of the family now in the town is Mrs. Eurilla Bartow, who was the first white female born in town (May 3d, 1811), and received a liberal education for the early days; taught school two terms, and married Hiram Bartow December 9th, 1832. He was one of six men who formed the first temperance society in town. He died May 20th, 1872. Mrs. Bartow's mother made the first cheese manufactured in the town and sold outside.

MRS. MARIA NOURSE, whose maiden name was Upham, was born in Rushford, Allegany county, in 1817, and was married to Orson F. Nourse in 1834. Mr. Nourse was engaged in the cattle trade, and bought very extensively for eastern markets. He was also a well known farmer. The dye house of Mrs. Nourse's father was one of the early buildings in the town.

WILLIAM H. NOURSE, son of Nelson Nourse, of Hinsdale, Cattaraugus county, was born there June 23d, 1853, and married Idella Robeson, of Franklinville, December 26th, 1877. Mr. Nourse received an academic education at the Franklinville and Friendship academies, read law in the office of Colonel A. G. Rice, of Buffalo, and was admitted to the bar in 1877. The previous year he appeared as a political orator in behalf of the Republican cause in Erie, Niagara and Cattaraugus counties.

HORACE PARKER, deceased, was the third son of Silas Parker, an honored pioneer in the county, and like his father was a successful farmer. He was born April 27th, 1811, and was the first male child born in the town. He was often called to public positions in the town, and served as supervisor. In 1832 he married Betsey Youngs, of Florida, N. Y.

IRA PARKER, a grandson of Silas Parker, who was the first supervisor of the town of China, was born in Arcade April 9th, 1832. He married Alzina E. Pike, daughter of William W. Pike, of Eagle, August 28th, 1851. August 10th, 1861, Mr. Pike enlisted in Company C 104th N. Y. volunteers, and participated in the battles of Slaughter Mountain, Thoroughfare Gap, Rappahannock Station, Haymarket, Second Bull Run, Frederick City, South Mountain, Antietam, the two engagements at Fredericksburg, Chancellorsville and Gettysburg; was under fire ninety-one days in succession; was taken prisoner while tearing up the Weldon Railroad; was confined in Libby prison and Castle Thunder, and was discharged June 17th, 1885.

JAMES PERKINS was born August 24th, 1811, at Enfield, Grafton county, N. H. He married Sophronia Wells, of Danville, Caledonia county, Vt., November 4th, 1832, and came from there to Arcade in October, 1835, but did not become a permanent resident until August, 1839. He is a carriage builder. He has served as town superintendent of schools, justice of the peace, president of the village and in many lees important offices.

SIDNEY RICHARDSON, son of Washington E. Richardson, was born March 31st, 1835, in Arcade. August 26th, 1857, he married Harriet Elizabeth Calton, daughter of John C. Calton. Mr. Richardson is a farmer and dealer in live stock and produce; he has served several years as deputy sheriff, and has been constable and collector and commissioner of highways.

DANIEL P. SHAW was born in Monroe county in 1827, and was married in 1852 to Caroline Woolsey, of Arcade. At the age of two he removed with his parents to Java; thence to Arcade. He has been highway commissioner six years, and assessor for the past nine years. Mr. Shaw's father, Cyrus Shaw, was born in Connecticut in 1796, and died in Arcade in 1860. Harry Woolsey, Mrs. Shaw's father, was born in Hudson, N. Y., and died in Arcade in 1870.

MRS. LUCETTA R. SHERWOOD, daughter of Milo Wells, and granddaughter of Captain Simeon Wells, was born in China (now Arcade), March 27th, 1830, and married

Sherman M. Sherwood, son of Dr. Anson Sherwood, of Michigan, February 26th, 1849. Her husband was of Scotch descent. She owns a farm of two hundred and three acres. Mr. Sherwood died February 23d, 1878.

HON. LEVERETT SPRING, son of Samuel Spring, was born October 19th, 1809, at Grafton, Vt., and came to Arcade in 1836, where he married Lucy Upham in 1837. He is both a lawyer and a farmer. He read law with Daniel Kellogg, of Vermont, where he was admitted to practice in 1835. In the practice of his profession he has not been limited to Wyoming county, but has practiced in adjoining counties, especially Buffalo. In 1837 he was elected magistrate, and served six years. Subsequently he was supervisor. He was a member of the Legislature in 1844 and 1845, and was appointed district attorney in 1876. Although past seventy, he is still actively engaged in a lucrative practice, and is one of three remaining members of the early Wyoming county bar.

PHINEAS STEARNS was born in Waltham, Mass., February 11th, 1795, and married Miriam Armstrong, of Fletcher, Vt., in 1824, having emigrated to that State. In 1835 he removed to Saratoga Springs, N. Y., with his parents. He afterward lived at Collins and at Springville, Erie county. In 1844 he located in Arcade, where he now lives with his son, Martin J. Stearns, on a farm of one hundred and forty acres. He is in receipt of a pension as a veteran of the war of 1812.

JAMES STEELE, deceased, was born May 4th, 1783, at Londonderry, N. H., and married Miranda Parker, daughter of Elias Parker, of Arcade, October 17th, 1818. Mr. Steele came to Arcade in 1811, and died October 8th, 1852. He has had two sons and two daughters. Elias Steele, one of the former, was born December 3d, 1833, and married Martha D., daughter of Hyder Barnes, Esq., January 20th, 1863. He is a successful farmer, and occupies the farm left by his father.

MRS. S. U. R. TILDEN was born October 6th, 1812, in Rushford, Allegany county. She has been twice married—to Ira Rowley, son of Colonel Rowley, and to Samuel Tilden, of Arcade, who is living. Mrs. Tilden is a daughter of Samuel Upham, and is one of a very few persons left in the town who can tell of the experiences of the pioneers from memory.

JONATHAN WADE, deceased, was born February 5th, 1788, in Elizabethtown, N. J. He has been twice married—to Anna Childs and to Abigail Gillett—the second marriage taking place November 11th, 1824. By his first marriage he had seven sons; by his second a son and a daughter. Mr. Childs came from Stafford, Genesee county, and located on the John Lennox farm in 1828. Henry T. Wade, his youngest son, was born August 11th, 1827, at Stafford, Genesee county, and married Harriet, daughter of Heman Wilson, October 8th, 1850. The issue of this marriage has been two children—Nellie A. and Henry McClellan. Mr. Wade is a farmer.

HORATIO N. WALDO, a son of Lyman Waldo, was born at Coventry, Conn., February 21st, 1806, and was married October 8th, 1829, to Eunice, daughter of Samuel Upham, of Arcade. Mr. Waldo came to Arcade from Portage, N. Y., in 1828, and became well known as a woolen manufacturer. Under his management the "Arcade cloth" had an extended and favorable reputation. Mr. Waldo is living retired.

A. WALLACE WADE was born November 9th, 1840, at Farmersville, Cattaraugus county, and was married May 22nd, 1872, to Frances A. Remington, of Stafford, Genesee county. He lived in China, N. Y., from 1841 to 1849. His parents went to Michigan in

1854. He enlisted as a private in the 3d Michigan infantry in 1861, and was discharged in 1863, and soon after re-enlisted in Custer's brigade band, as 1st sergeant, with the Michigan cavalry, and remained until the close of the war. He returned to Arcade in 1867, and has served the village as trustee, a member of the board of education and as village clerk from 1873 to 1879, one year excepted. From 1876 to 1879 he was editor of the *Arcade Leader*, and is at present engaged in the wholesale cheese trade.

CAPTAIN SIMEON WELLES was born in Belton, Conn., August 4th, 1770, and died August 29th, 1845, in Arcade. He was married in 1791 to Rhoda L. Bostwiek, of Connecticut. He came to Arcade in 1819, and settled on the farm now owned by his grandson, Milo B. Welles. Captain Welles had seven children—Bostwick, Talcott, Milo, Lemuel C., Harriet, Phebe and Elmira. Lemuel C. Welles was married to Eliza Miller, daughter of John F. Miller, of Ovid, N. Y., April 27th, 1826, and died April 28th, 1849. He had nine children, eight of whom are living. Mrs. Eliza Welles, with her sons, Y. C. and E. C., owns the old homestead.

JARED WITHERIL located on a farm of three hundred acres on lot No. 41, in the southwest corner of the town, about 1817, and participated in the first town meeting, held the next year. He died about 1848 or 1849.

His son, NELSON WITHERIL, owns and occupies part of the old farm. He was born in Harford, Conn., in 1815; came with his parents to Arcade; and was married December 25th, 1839, to Sarah Ann Wilber, of Arcade. He has been a farmer and contractor, and has, in the latter capacity, built more bridges than any other man in the town.

GEORGE WILLIAMS, son of John Williams, who was born in Danby, Vt., in 1793, and died in Erie county in 1863, was born in Rutland, Vt., October 23d, 1817, and married Lucy Arnold, of Arcade, in 1850. Mr. Williams, who had lived in Vermont, in Erie county and in Yorkshire, came to Arcade in 1864.

RUFUS WOOLSEY was born in Sheldon (now Java), N. Y., September 8th, 1820, and married Hannah Bryant, of Angelica, N. Y., February 13th, 1851. He is a son of Henry Woolsey, of Columbia county, N. Y., who settled on the old Woolsey farm in Java in 1819. Mr. Woolsey has served five years as commissioner of highways.

REV. CHARLES A. WOODWORTH, preacher and furniture dealer, was born in Fenner, Madison county, November 13th, 1838, and was married February 9th, 1864, to Mary L. Smith, of Fredonia, N. Y. He received an academic education at Fredonia and Middlebury academies, and was teaching school in Lexington, Ky., in the fall of 1859. He came north and enlisted in Company H, 44th N. Y. infantry, August 8th, 1861. September 20th he was commissioned first lieutenant. He was appointed recruiting officer for the general service January 1st, 1862, and stationed at Rochester. He rejoined his regiment April 5th, 1862, and was in command of Company E during the siege of Yorktown; was in the battle of Hanover Court-house and the Seven Days Fight; lost his left eye at Malvern Hill; was taken prisoner and confined in Libby prison till July 14th, when he was released and sent home. He was commissioned captain of Company K, 44th N. Y. volunteers, and assumed command January 1st, 1863; was discharged June 30th, 1865. He was commissioned colonel of the 97th regiment of Missouri militia, to suppress the Rebellion against the State government in 1867, and resigned in 1868. For ten years he has been a member of the village board of education. He entered the ministry October 5th, 1878.

THE TOWN OF ATTICA.

THE following list, showing the names of many of the pioneers of this town, and the date and location of their purchases, is taken from the records of the Holland Land Company:

Zerah Phelps, 1802, lots 1–6, section 12; Benjamin Porter, 1802, lots 7, 9 and 11, section 6; Levi Porter, 1802, lots 8, 10 and 12, section 6; Stephen Crow (from whom Crow creek was named), 1802, lots 2, 4 and 6, section 6; Nathaniel Sprout, 1806, lots 9 and 11, section 8; S. Crow and T. Adams, 1806, lots 9–12, section 12; Zerah Phelps, 1804, lots 4 to 6, section 16; Amos Sprout, 1803, lot 12, section 8; Nathaniel Sprout, jr., 1803, part of lots 10 and 12, section 7, and of lots 2, 4 and 6, section 11; John Keen, 1805, part of lots 7 and 9, section 16; Andrew McKlen, 1805, lot 8, section 8; Charles Patterson, 1805, lots 1–3, section 16; Stephen Crow, 1804, part of lots 1, 3 and 5; Abijah Nichols, 1804, part of lots 1, 3 and 5, section 4; Dan Adams, 1805, lot 6, section 8; Joshua B. Bearss, 1805, part of lots 2, 4 and 6, section 3; Lemuel Whaley, 1805, part of lots 2, 4 and 6, section 8; Joseph Munger, 1805, lots 1, 3 and 5, section 2; Reynolds Whaley, 1805, part of lots 1, 3 and 5, section 3; Zadoc Williams, 1804, part of lot 81, section 12; Luther Stanhope, 1805, part of lots 2 and 4, section 11; Justus Walbridge, 1805, lot 5, part of lot 8, section 15; Elihu and David Beckwith, jr., 1806, lots 1 and 3, section 10, and parts of lots 1, 3 and 5, section 5; Parmenio Adams, 1806, parts of lots 7, 8 and 11, section 10; John Grant, 1806, parts of lots 7, 9 and 11, section 10; Archibald Nelson, 1806, lot 1 and part of lot 3, section 15; Daniel Gardner, 1804, lots 2, 4 and 6, section 4; Joel Maxon, 1806, parts of lots 2, 4 and 6, section 14; Nathaniel Eastman, 1805, lots 11–13, section 11; Joseph Chaffee, 1806, lot 10, section 4; Dudley Nichols, 1806, lots 8 and 12, section 4; Nehemiah Osborn, 1805, lot 8, section 4; William Osborn, 1806, lot 5, section 10; Nancy Wood, 1805 part of lots 7, 9 and 11, section 5; Jacob Wood, 1806, lot 7, section 11; John Hassett, 1807, parts of lots 8 and 10, section 3; Aaron Bailey, 1808, parts of lots 2, 4 and 6, section 6; Jonathan Wallingsford, 1808, parts of lots 2, 4 and 6, section 6; Isaac Adams, 1808, lots 1 and 3, section 9; Charles L. Imus, 1806, lot 9, section 11; Thomas Whaley, 1805, parts of lots 1, 3 and 5, section 3; Lemuel Whaley, 1808, lot 2, section 2; Daniel Durkee, 1809, lot 12, section 10; John Burley, 1806, parts of lots 4 and 6, section 10; William Burlingame, 1806, parts of lots 1, 3 and 5, section 4; Timothy Burt, 1808, lot 8, part of lot 10, section 2; Samuel Mott, 1808, parts of lots 10 and 12, section 7; David Fletcher and Frederick H. Swears, 1809, parts of lots 8 and 10, section 5; Amos Muzzy, 1808, lot 9, section 4; Zadoc Williams, 1808, lot 3, section 8; Jesse Ditson, 1808, lot 11, section 4; John Hubbard, 1808, lot 12 and part of lot 10, section 2; Hanford Conger, 1809, lot 1, section 8; John Crowl, 1807, parts of lots 8 and 10, section 5; Elijah Childs, 1807, parts of lots 8 and 10, section 5; Orator

Holcomb, 1805, parts of lots 1, 3 and 5, section 6; Eliphalet Hodges, 1808, lot 8, section 7; Benjamin Potter, 1804, lot 10, section 8; John M. Coughram, 1805, lot 2, section 15; John Chapel, 1810, lot 4, section 2; Adolphus Gardner, 1809, lot 6, section 2; Ebenezer Humphrey, 1809, lot 11, section 9; Reuben Beman, 1809, lot 7, section 13; Nehemiah Baker, lots 3 and 5, section 13; Nathaniel Eastman, 1807, lot 11 and part of lot 9, section 3; Thomas O. Kelley and John Rogers, 1803, lot 7 and part of lot 9, section 3: Joseph Chaffee, 1808, lot 12, section 3; Sargent Jones, 1810, lot 11, section 2; Hutchins Washburn, 1810, lot 9, section 2; Amaziah Randall, 1810, lot 9, section 9.

In 1802 Zerah Phelps, wishing to better his condition and having heard much talk of the land flowing with milk and honey known all over the eastern States as the "Genesee country," bade farewell to kindred and friends in the old "nutmeg State," and pushed out for the headquarters of the Holland Land Company, whose office at that time was at Batavia. He was finally "booked," "articled" and "deeded" a tract of land in what, nine years after, turned out to be the town of Attica. He was accompanied by Deacon Porter, Nathaniel Sprout, Isaac Townsend and Major P. Adams. With a major to command the movements and a deacon to look after the spiritual wants of the little band, they continuously and courageously advanced upon the dense forest that lay before them, and plunged into its very heart. They had to brave the dangers, endure the toil and suffer the hardships incident to pioneer life; but they were born of a stock inured to privations and educated in the school of devotion to principle.

July 25th, 1803, the household of Zerah Phelps rejoiced over the birth of the pioneer baby in their family, who was duly named Harriet Phelps.

The contracting parties to the first wedding in this town were Stephen Crow and Lucy Elwell. The first death in this town after it was first settled by Mr. Phelps was that of Thomas Mather, in the winter of 1803.

It was not long before the little band of first comers received accessions, for we find that in 1804 John Smith, John Richards, Steward Gardner, Daniel Gardner, Daniel Burbank, Nathaniel Sprout, jr., Eli Hayes, Daniel White, Zadoc Williams and Zadoc Whipple bought land in this township. Levi Nelson came in 1804 and settled on the farm now owned by William Nelson, south of Attica village.

The trials, hardships and privations of this colony were not as severe as those of the first, for they benefited by the experience and were sheltered by the cabins of their predecessors while they were building their own houses. Their furniture was of the most primitive kind, to say nothing of the log cabin without floor, door or windows, and the cracks between the logs of the house were unchinked, that the smoke might have a chance to circulate freely. The bedstead was made by driving four crotches in the ground in one corner of the mansion, with poles laid in for side pieces and smaller ones laid across to serve as a bedcord, and on top of them a few spruce boughs laid by way of matress. The table was made in another corner by boring two holes in the side of the house at the proper height, and driving into them sticks projecting enough to hold a sheet of bark. The dishes were wooden or pewter, and the old fashioned long handled frying-pan, the bake-kettle, a dinner-pot and a dish-kettle composed the whole kit of cooking utensils. The old broad fire-place, without chimney or jambs, served the triple purpose of cooking, heating and lighting, and the chairs were blocks or logs.

In 1805 the town received a fresh supply of New England bone and sinew, by the immigration of such families as those of Oliver Hodges, Clark Burlingame, Benjamin Powers, Eliphalet Hodges, Jacob Howe, John M. Coffin, Joseph Munger, Levi Stanhope, Patrick Alvord, Thomas Whaley, Nancy Wood, Samuel Smith, Nathaniel Eastman, Benjamin Nelson, Orator Holcomb, Stephen Crawford, Luther Stanhope, Simeon Porter, Benjamin Moulton, David Beckwith, Joseph Hopkins, Elijah Rice, Elihu Beckwith, Daniel Adams, Joel Bradnor, Francis Rodgers, John Kean, Joseph Munger, Nehemiah Osborn and Lemuel Whaley.

In 1806 Owen Cotton came in from Vermont, and in 1808 and 1809 he was followed by Asher Gardner, John Wilder, Asa Johnson, Joseph Wilder, William Vary and one Fuller.

Charles D. Beman, born in Williamstown, Mass., January 11th, 1797, also located in Attica in 1809, where he still resides. We are indebted to him for much valuable information. He was one of the soldiers of 1812 from this town; others were Abel Baker, Caleb Starkweather and Joel Boughton.

In 1811 Gaius B. Rich and Seymour Brainard came to this town, Brainard locating about three miles east of what is now the village of Attica. He bought his land of Daniel Burbank, and in 1820 built a grist-mill down the Tonawanda creek, a short distance from Attica. He was a farmer, as well as mill owner, and had at one time about twenty acres of wheat, which at that period was considered a very large acreage for this country. In the spring it had the appearance of having been winter killed, and he sowed it again, which resulted in a harvest of over eight hundred bushels of very nice wheat. When he commenced building his grist-mill wheat was worth $2.50 per bushel, but it was worth only about three shillings a bushel when he was ready for converting wheat into flour.

LOCATION AND OCCUPATION OF EARLY SETTLERS.

The farm now owned and occupied by Truman F. Baldwin, three miles east of Attica village, is the spot where Seymour Brainard finally located. He lived two and a half years in a log house a little further east, on the place now owned by Kriegelstein, and finally located on the Baldwin farm, where he lived until his death. He came from Old Haddam, Conn. His team consisted of two yoke of oxen and one horse, all hitched to an ox-cart of his own make. Upon the cart were piled all the goods and chattels possessed by Mr. B. The old cart body was made long, and above the wheels spread out to about ten feet wide. Over the whole was a top or cover, the bows made of saplings cut in the woods, and the covering of cotton cloth. In this "schooner" was loaded not only his furniture, but his family, which consisted of a wife and seven children, and the "spike team" was headed for the Genesee country, where cart and family finally arrived without the loss of a relic. It should not be forgotten that in the bottom of the load, among the blacksmith tools, for Brainard was a blacksmith, were stowed away four thousand dollars in cash, with which he made his purchases, cleared lands, built mills and distilleries, and, in short, became the "farmer prince" of the region. It was nothing unusual for him to fatten from fifty to one hundred head of cattle annually for the Albany and New York markets, and this, too, before there was any means of transportation other than driving them on foot. He would feed them on "still slops," as it was called, through the winter, and start them for market in the spring, after the grass was up enough to feed the drove along the way and keep them in good condition. Thus he managed, and amassed a fortune. He was a large land owner in this town, and as his children were married off they were each provided with a well stocked farm for a "start" in life. Although a blacksmith, Mr. Brainard never worked at his trade after coming to the town. After his distillery was in operation in 1816 he contracted with John Wilder, of Batavia, to deliver at his place ten thousand gallons of rye whiskey, at sixteen cents per gallon, which he made in one season. He built a grist-mill in 1820, on the Tonawanda creek, about a mile and a half below Attica. This was afterward known as the Blodgett mill, and in a few years was destroyed by fire. In 1824 he built a distillery on the farm now owned by Charles Kriegelstein.

Dudley Nichols located in the northeast part of the town in 1808, on the farm now owned and occupied by J. S. Kriegelstein. He was a stonemason by trade. He built a stone house, in which he lived for many years. The house has been taken down, and the stone used for other purposes.

Oliver Hodges, who settled here in 1805, was a farmer by occupation, and lived on the farm now owned by Armenius B. Scoville, a son-in-law of Mr. Hodges.

Parmenio Adams located on the place which Mrs. Mason now owns, in the village of Attica. He was a farmer. He was known as Major Adams, as he had been commissioned as major in the State militia of Connecticut. In 1824 he was elected to Congress over Isaac Wilson by one majority. The result greatly pleased his friends in the town, and a great jubilee was held to celebrate the event.

Orator Holcomb located in this town in 1805, on what is now the Vernal road. He was a millwright by trade, and worked for Mr. Brainard on his distilleries and mills.

Clark Burlingame located up Crow creek, near the center of the town. He was a carpenter by trade, and in 1813 built a frame barn for Seymour Brainard.

Asher Gardner located in 1808 about one mile south of the village, on the farm owned by Mr. Stocky.

Zadoc Williams located here in 1804, on the farm now owned by Hiram Cooley, northeast of the village. He was a farmer.

Deacon Porter was a farmer, and located here in 1802, near Attica Center.

Stewart Gardner located on his purchase near the east line of the town, at what was once the village of Vernal, and Daniel Gardner, who came here the same year, settled southwest of what is now the village of Attica.

Lemuel Whaley, who came in 1805, settled on the east line, near the northeast corner of the town.

Owen Cotton, who came in 1806, was a millwright by trade, and finally located three miles south of Attica village, on the Tonawanda creek.

In 1809 a man by the name of Pierson located where Hiram Cooley now lives, and built a small tannery, which he carried on several years.

The first surveyor who resided in this town was Daniel Adams, who came here in 1805, and located a mile east of Attica village.

The pioneer lawyers in the village were Harvey Putnam, who came here in 1814, and soon afterward Moulton Farnham, who died but a few years ago.

The pioneer tavern was kept in a log house in 1810, on the corner about a mile east of the village of Attica, on the site now occupied by Spann & Andrews's cheese factory. It was indeed a primitive affair. It did not even hang out the old pioneer sign, with the words "entertainment for man and beast." Nevertheless, it was known as *the* place for the weary traveler to rest and refresh himself. Mine host Hezekiah Eastman did the honors of the establishment. The next hostelry was kept by John Wilder, on what is now Market street, in the village of Attica, and in 1808 Erastus Crosby purchased of Dyer Fitch his house on what is now the corner of Main and Exchange streets in the village, and opened what was termed in those days a first class tavern, in a little frame house. As the country was new and sparsely settled, these three taverns were quite sufficient for the accommodation of the traveling public and for what little town custom they received. The same year that Crosby opened his tavern he built a distillery near where William Wilder's carpenter shop now stands, on Washington street.

In 1810 Hezekiah Eastman built a distillery on the cheese factory lot of Spann & Andrews, east of the village, which stood but a few years. Brainard's distillery, built in 1815, is noticed in another place. There was also a distillery at Vernal, a small hamlet in the northeast corner of the town, in 1820; one in the gulf near the cemetery, in the west part of the village, another at Attica Center, another east of where Nelson Reynolds's house now stands, in the village of Attica, one on the west side of the town, and another a little west of the present Attica cemetery grounds, all of which went to decay many years ago.

Hezekiah Eastman was not only landlord and distiller, but a physician as well, having quite a large practice for a new country.

His brother, Nathaniel Eastman, M. D., first settled south of Attica village, and in 1811 located on the farm now owned by Francis M. Wilson, east of the village. As this part of the Holland Purchase became more thickly settled other physicians came, and among the number were Dr. Park, who located at Vernal, and Drs. Crocker and Disbrow, near the Center. On the farm of Orlando Earl, on the north side of the village of Attica, is a sulphur spring, and as long ago as

1811 its waters were applied both externally and internally for the various ills that pioneer life was heir to. A rude building was erected over the spring, in one part of which was a room rudely fitted up for a shower bath. The waters of this spring have not been used for medical purposes for many years.

In 1806 Asa Johnson, John Wilder and Joseph Wilder located in the town, near what is now the village of Attica. They were all carpenters and millwrights, and were engaged in putting up the first mills and other frame buildings in the town. They built the first mills at Attica and Varysburg, and the distilleries throughout this region.

The first weaver here, Reynolds Whaley, came in 1805. He lived a short distance east of the village of Attica. The inhabitants furnished him the raw material, and he returned to them coverlids and blankets of the most approved pattern of the times.

In 1808 George Cooley, with his family, located in the northeast part of the town. Mrs. Cooley had in her younger days learned the tailoress's trade. She soon became the neighborhood tailoress, and such "fits," Ephraim Brainard, Esq., says he has never seen since and never experienced before. However well the clothes *didn't* fit the boy had to "don" them, if his feelings did suffer martyrdom.

William Jenkins, a native of Massachusetts, was the pioneer saddler and harness maker in Attica. He worked here as early as 1816, and a few years ago he returned to Boston, Mass., where he died in January, 1879, aged eighty-four years.

At what is known on the map as "Vernal," in the northeast part of the town, Allen and Cable built a distillery, tavern, store and dwelling as early as 1809, and for many years this was the business part of the town. Now the old well from which the settlers drew water is the only evidence of a once flourishing hamlet.

In 1810 there was a brick yard near the site now occupied by Vosburgh's steam mills, on the east side of Attica village. Charles D. Beman, who now lives in the village, worked in the brick yard that year. The brick were made in the same way as at present; and in those early days but few were used, and those for chimneys only.

FIRST ROADS.

The oldest road in this town crossed it from Vernal, on the east line, to Attica village, and so on west to Bennington. It is known as the Buffalo and Moscow road; constitutes Main street in Attica, and is called the Bennington road west from Attica. There was also a road leading from near the Brainard settlement to Attica Center. The road leading up Tonawanda creek from Attica to Varysburg, in Sheldon, was in use as early as 1806. The one running up Crow creek to Attica Center was also one of the pioneer roads. At this early date, 1806, these roads had not been worked, and in most places were mere paths. The Bennington road, toward Buffalo, was followed by marked trees until after a mail route was established, about 1814. The first road laid out according to law was from Attica to Geneseo.

POLITICAL HISTORY AND STATISTICS.

This town was formed from Sheldon, Genesee county, April 4th, 1811, and originally included the present town of Orangeville, which was taken off in 1816.

The following is a list of the supervisors of the town of Attica from 1812 to 1879, inclusive:

In 1812, John Hubbard; 1813, 1814, 1826, Thomas Cooley; 1815, Asa Johnson, jr.; 1816, 1817, Robert Earle; 1818, 1823, 1824, Thomas Cooley, jr.; 1819, 1820, Hanford Conger; 1821, 1822, 1837, George Cooley; 1825, 1838, David Scott; 1827, 1844, Charlee Chaffey; 1829–31, 1845, 1846, Reuben Benham; 1832, 1834, Hosea B. Sprout; 1883, James Douglas; 1835, Ezra Bishop; 1836, 1839, John S. Billings; 1840, 1841, Oliver Hodges; 1842, 1843, 1847, Roswell Gardner; 1848, 1850, 1855, William Walbridge; 1851–53, William Powers; 1854, Newcomb Demary, jr.; 1856, William B. Goodwin; 1857, 1858, 1864–66, 1872, James H. Loomis; 1859, Lyman Brainard; 1860, 1861, William C. Smith; 1862, 1863, John B. Skinner (second) 1867, 1868, M. C. Bigelow; 1869–71, 1873–75, Charlee B. Benedict; 1876, Augustus A. Smith; 1877, 1878, R. J. Rodgers; 1879, R. H. Farnham.

The following named persons have been town clerks from 1842 to 1879. The record previous to 1842 has been lost or destroyed:

In 1842, Noah Wells; 1843, 1845, 1848, 1856, Jirah A. Pember; 1844, Parmenio N. Adams; 1846, 1847, Horace D. W. Gladding; 1849–51, Hiram T. Beman; 1852, 1853, Timothy Loomis; 1854, 1855, C. C. Pratt; 1857–59, John S. Putnam; 1860, John W. Colton; 1861, 1862, Edward R. West; 1863, Charles Houghton; 1864, 1865, Edward D. Tolles; 1866–68, William Ballsmith; 1869, 1870, 1878, Jacob Algier, jr.; 1871, 1872, James H. Hill; 1873–75, George W. Reynolds; 1876, B. F. Ellison; 1877, 1879, J. D. Evans.

Attica has probably furnished its full share of the public men of this county, not only for home service, but in the legislative halls of the State and nation. The town has been represented in the Assembly by Gaius B. Rich, David Scott and Reuben Benham; and in the Senate by Harvey Putnam for four years, and by Hon. James H. Loomis, the present State Senator. Of the citizens of Attica Parmenio Adams was a member of Congress in 1824, and Harvey Putnam, George G. Hoskins (elected lieutenant-governor in 1879), and (in the last Congress) Charles B. Benedict have held the same position. County judges from this town have been Robert Earll, A. S. Stevens and W. Riley Smith. The county has also selected from this town for sheriffs John Wilder, Parmenio Adams and Newcomb Demary.

In 1875 the census reported 17,453 acres of improved land, and 4,191 acres woodland in Attica, the whole valued by the occupants at $1,191,145; farm buildings, $915,070; stock, $206,472; tools, $53,960, making a grand total of farm property in 1875 of $2,366,647; there were 8,686 acres of pasture land in the town, and 5,270 acres of meadow land, which produced 7,192 tons of hay. The same year there were raised 6,811 bushels of barley, 2,828 of buckwheat, 16,440 of corn, 25,826 of oats, 3,852 of spring wheat, 7,881 of winter wheat, 29,049 of potatoes and 56,638 of apples. There were 28,765 pounds of maple sugar made that year. The clip of wool in 1875 was 13,857 pounds, from 2,118 sheep shorn. Pork made on farms amounted to 122,163 pounds.

The population of Attica at the State census of 1875 was larger than at any previous one, but the growth has not been uniform, as will be seen by the annexed returns: 1830, 2,485; 1835, 2,981; 1840, 2,709; 1845, 2,382; 1850, 2,363; 1855, 2,679; 1860, 2,547; 1865, 2,367; 1870, 2,546; 1875, 3,057.

The assessment on the property of the New York, Lake Erie and Western Railroad Company in 1878 was $44,000, tax $199.09; Central assessment, $10,000, tax $45.25.

The first orchard in this town is the Steven's orchard, in the village of Attica. It was set out by Samuel Sexton, or Saxton, who came here as early as 1810 or 1811. Previous to that, orchards, as such, were unknown. From that time to the present there has been a pretty steady increase in fruit culture until, in 1875, the census showed 33,657 apple trees, besides large numbers of other fruit trees.

THE BRAINARD CEMETERY ASSOCIATION.

The Brainard Cemetery, in the northeast part of the town, contained originally one acre of land, and was bequeathed to the inhabitants of that part of the town for burial purposes by the late Seymour Brainard. For the better preservation of the grounds an association was formed October 11th, 1832, trustees elected, and a committee appointed to raise sixty dollars for building fence and improving the grounds. In this way the grounds were cared for until 1861, when Ephraim Brainard, John S. Kriegelstein and Lucius Austin were elected trustees, and Ephraim Brainard secretary and treasurer. The same condition of affairs continued until on October 19th, 1872, a public meeting was called, at which the Brainard Cemetery Association was formed, and the following persons were elected trustees: For three years, Ephraim Brainard, David Filkins; for two years, Charles Kriegelstein, Elbridge Austin; for one year, Robert Roberts, Jasper J. Brainard. On the 5th of the next month the following officers were elected: President, David Filkins; vice-president, Jasper J. Brainard; treasurer, Charles Kriegelstein; secretary, Ephraim Brainard.

The association subsequently purchased of Charles Austin one and a half acres of land on the east side of the old grounds, at an expense of about $250. Since then the grounds have been kept in a good state of preservation.

The following are the present trustees and officers of the association: Trustees, Jasper J. Brainard, Robert H. Roberts, Charles Kriegelstein, David

Filkins, Elbridge Austin and Francis M. Wilson; president, David Filkins; treasurer, Francis M. Wilson; secretary, Ephraim Brainard.

DAIRY INTERESTS.

Until the advent of cheese factories in this town, in 1866, when the Lindsay factory was built, dairying was considered of much less importance than at the present day, when there are five cheese factories, the smallest of which has a capacity for using the milk of three hundred and fifty cows.

The Andrews factory, three-quarters of a mile east of the village of Attica, was built in the spring of 1870. In 1878 it used the milk from six hundred and fifty cows, and made one hundred and fifty-eight thousand six hundred and fifty pounds of cheese.

The Attica Center factory is located at Attica Center, and in 1878 used the milk of three hundred and fifty cows.

The Town Line factory is located on the east line of the town, a little south of the Vernal road, and made cheese from the milk of two hundred and fifty cows in 1878.

The Madison factory is a mile west of the village of Attica, and in 1878 manufactured the milk of three hundred cows.

The Cowden factory, three miles south of Attica village up Tonawanda creek, made into cheese the milk from four hundred cows during the season of 1878.

It will be seen that in 1878 there was taken to factories the milk of one thousand nine hundred cows.

In 1875 there were ninety-one thousand seven hundred and thirty-six pounds of butter, and forty-seven thousand nine hundred and sixty-five pounds of cheese made in families, and five thousand one hundred and ninety-five gallons of milk sold in market. The average number of cows kept in this town in 1875 was one thousand eight hundred and seventy-eight.

UNION SOLDIERS FROM ATTICA.

The first soldiers to enlist from this town for the suppression of the Rebellion were Nelson Updyke, April 18th, 1861; James Shipard, April 27th, 1861, and George Baars, May 13th, 1861. These men enlisted under the first call for three months, were discharged at the expiration of their time, and re-enlisted.

On the 9th of September, 1861, the following persons left this town to join a company of cavalry, which was organized at Pike by Captain Washington Wheeler, E. D. and R. N. Tolles, Merritt N. Chaffee, Luke S. Williams, William H. Niemann, Gardner L. Pratt, Horton Kimball, Hickson Fowler, W. H. Fowler and Nelson Updyke. So large a number of young men, so well known, leaving at one time, so early in the war, caused great interest, and a large concourse of citizens gathered at the railroad to see them off. Miss Nellie Disbrow, now Mrs. James O. Prescott, presented each of the volunteers with a bouquet on behalf of the scholars of the union school, and Merritt N. Chaffee responded on behalf of the volunters.

The company which they joined was known as Company F, 5th N. Y. cavalry, Colonel O. De Forrest. This regiment served in the Army of the Potomac, and made for itself a very honorable record, Company F doing its full share in securing its good name and reputation.

Only five of the above named volunteers are now alive:—Edward D. Tolles and M. N. Chaffee, both first lieutenants when discharged; Gardner L. Pratt, Nelson Updyke and William H. Fowler.

Early in 1864 it was voted to pay a bounty of $300 to each volunteer who should be credited to Attica on the latest call for 200,000 men.

At a special town meeting held at Doty's hall, in the village of Attica, July 16th, 1864, it was voted to pay a sum not exceeding four hundred dollars to any person who should volunteer for this town on any future call of the President for men.

At a special town meeting held August 19th, 1864, it was resolved that a town bounty of $400, over and above the county bounty, be paid to each person who furnished a substitute to be credited to Attica, under the latest call, and a like sum, not exceeding $400, to each person who should thereafter volunteer on that call, or be drafted and accepted, or furnish a substitute to be credited to the town; and that the town board be authorized to issue and dispose of bonds to raise money for such purpose.

The following list of the men from this town who volunteered and served in the Union armies during the Rebellion gives their regiments and companies, rank, if officers, and date of enlistment, when known. When another date immediately follows it is that of discharge.

160*th Infantry, Company G.*—Nelson Allen, Sept. 5, 1862; 1864. Martin Alien, Sept. 6, 1862. James W. Boyce, Aug. 29, 1862; died in hospital Aug. 6, 1864. Julius Baker, sergeant, Sept. 5, 1862; Nov. 1, 1865. George Baker, Sept. 1, 1862; died Jan. 5, 1865. Gardner Cabel, Aug. 25, 1862; remained in U. S. service. Jacob Conrad, Sept. 3, 1862; discharged with regiment. Casper Flock, Sept. 5, 1862; Aug. 21, 1863. O. D. C. Hammond, Aug. 29, 1862; Nov. 1, 1865. D. Hanifen, Aug. 29, 1862; July 1, 1865. Samuel Kriegelstein, sergeant, Sept. 29, 1862; died Apr. 5, 1865. Morris Kennedy, Sept. 6, 1862. Peter McGrath, Sept. 5, 1862; died Mch. 9, 1863. Philo Myers, Sept. 5, 1862; died Feb. 3, 1863. Samuel R. Merchant, Sept. 6, 1862; June 5, 1865. George Marley, sergeant Aug. 30, 1862; Nov. 1, 1865. Otto Miller, Aug. 30, 1862; Nov. 1, 1865. Charles Nichols, corporal, Sept 6, 1862; Nov. 1, 1865. Edwin A. Nichols, Sept. 6, 1862; died Dec. 17, 1863. Franklin Nelson, Sept, 1862; died Mch. 21, 1863. Albert Nichols, 1862. George Pettouf, Sept. 5, 1862; Nov. 1, 1865. David Ritter, Sept. 6, 1862; deserted Dec. 1, 1862. Andrew J. Starks, Aug. 30. 1862; Nov. 1, 1865. John E. Smith, Sept. 5, 1862; died Sept. 13, 1863. Edwin F. Spink, musician, Aug. 8, 1862; Nov. 1, 1865. Elon P. 8pink, first lieutenant, Aug. 31, 1862; Nov. 1, 1865. Valentine Stark, Sept. 6, 1862; June 4, 1865. Fayette Terry, corporal, Sept. 6, 1862: died in rebel prison Feb. 14, 1865. Nelson Underwood, wagoner, Aug. 30,

1862; May 14, 1865. Frederick Wadka, corporal, Aug, 30, 1862; Nov. 1, 1865. Isaac Williams, Sept 6, 1862; died Apr. 10, 1864. George H. Wood, corporal, Aug. 28, 1862; died Aug. 27, 1863. Henry R. Walbridge, musician, Aug. 29, 1862; Nov. 1, 1865.

1*st Dragoons, Company C* —John H. Bradway, Aug. 8, 1862; Mch. 1, 1864. W. H. A. Godfrey, captain, Aug. 4, 1862; June 30, 1865. F. E. Godfrey, sergeant Aug. 5, 1862; discharged with regiment. Charles J. Gardner, sergeant, Aug. 6, 1862; Apr. 11, 1865. Orange Gardner, wagoner, Aug. 9, 1862; June 30, 1865. Evan G. Griffith, farrier, Aug. 4, 1862; June 30, 1865. Harvey I. Guile, Aug. 7, 1862; died May 18, 1864. William H. Hedger, Aug. 19, 1862; June 30, 1865. John T. Knox, corporal, Aug. 6, 1862; Sept. 12, 1863. Frederick W. Knox, Aug. 3, 1862; died in Libby Prison, Feb. 23, 1864. Andrew J. Lorish, 2nd lieutenant, Aug. 5, 1862; June 30, 1865. Henry Matteson, sergeant, Aug. 6, 1862; June 30, 1865. Norman B. Martin, Aug. 11, 1862. Charles A. Maxon, Aug. 4, 1862. Darwin Nichols, Aug. 9, 1862; June 30, 1865. Irving Pratt, sergeant, Aug. 9, 1862; died May 29, 1864. Leverett H. Peck, Aug. 9, 1862; July 30, 1864. Willis Parker, Aug. 26, 1862; June 30, 1865. Gardner L. Pratt, Feb. 18, 1865; June 30, 1865. Douglas R. Phelps, sergeant, Aug. 5, 1862; June 20, 1865. Peter Ruth, sergeant, Aug. 5, 1862; June 30, 1865. William Sangbush, Aug. 9, 1862; May 31, 1865. William Sangbush, jr., Aug. 9, 1862; June 30, 1865. James Saunders, assistant surgeon, Aug. 1862. William Saunderson, corporal, Aug. 5, 1862; June 30, 1865. Monroe A. Terry, sergeant Aug. 5, 1862; died Oct. 21, 1864. C. S. Pettibone, Aug., 1862; discharged for disability. Jacob Sundricker, Aug. 4, 1862; died in Dec., 1862. R. P. Taylor, captain, organized the company; killed Jan. 30, 1863. Robert Van Volkenburgh, Sept. 3, 1862; killed Jan. 30; 1863.

2*nd Rifles.*—Nelson T. Bent, Dec. 22, 1863; Sept 29, 1865. Jeremiah Brotherton, musician, Jan. 26, 1864. Frederick Churnning, L, Dec. 24, 1863; discharged with regiment. Charles Grabe, C, Dec. 21, 1863; supposed dead. Charles E. Gale, Feb. 15, 1864. Thomas Haley, Feb. 17, 1864. William L. Knox, C, Dec. 28, 1863; Apr. 7, 1865. Edward Lampman, L, musician, Dec. 26, 1863; discharged with regiment. Edward Launt, Dec. 24, 1863. Michael Martin, Jan. 11, 1864. Timothy Maroney, C, Dec. 8, 1863; discharged with regiment. Lewis Menslng, L, Feb. 9, 1864. Albert Nichols, L, Dec. 21, 1863. James W. Phillips, Dec. 28, 1863. Thomas Rial, Dec. 21, 1863. Francis Shandel, Jan. 11, 1864. Stephen T. Sprague, Dec. 21, 1863. Hiram Weaver, Dec. 21, 1863.

8*th Heavy Artillery.*—M. F. Buck, L, Dec. 7, 1863; June 20, 1865. Elias M. Doty, Dec. 22, 1863. James Ellis and Lawrence Flynn, Dec. 21, 1863. Elwin Hooper, corporal, L; discharged with regiment. John Heish, Dec. 21, 1863. George W. Kendall, L, Dec. 7, 1863; discharged in 1864. Mort Lingfield, Dec. 22, 1863. Carl Martin, Jan. 4, 1864. Henry McMay, Sept. 7, 1864. Henry Rush, Jan. 4, 1864. Luke White, G, Dec. 7, 1863; died at Andersonville, Ga.

14*th U. S. Infantry.*—Henry Blake, Dec. 24, 1864. James Bennett, Dec. 28, 1864. William Cook, Dec. 23, 1864. Patrick Dolan and William Gage, Dec. 27, 1864. Ferdinand Hoffman, Dec. 26, 1864. James Leonard. Dec. 21, 1864. Martin Pilgrim, D, May 1st, 1861; discharged with regiment James Roach, Dec. 21, 1864. Peter Van Volkenburgh, D, May 8, 1861; May 17, 1863.

9th Cavalry.—George W. Barrs, H, July 1, 1862; Dec. 12, 1862. Walter Farnham. John J. Gath, Sept. 7, 1864. Howell Jones, corporal, Sept. 20, 1861; killed Oct. 11, 1863. Michael Mulcahay, Sept. 15, 1864. John M. Mader, H, Sept. 7, 1864; July 13, 1865. Franklin Nelson, 1862. John T. Phillips, A, Sept. 23, 1864; discharged with regiment.

5th Cavalry—Merritt N. Chaffee, F, Sept. 10, 1861. Gardner L. Pratt, Sept. 12, 1861; June 18, 1862. Edward D. Tolles, first lieutenant F, Sept. 10, 1861; Oct. 31, 1863. Nelson Updyke, F, Sept. 10, 1861; Feb. 23, 1865. Luke S. Williams, F, bugler, Sept. 10, 1861; Oct. 14, 1864.

136th Infantry—Joseph Burke, Sept. 7, 1864. Nelson Higley, Feb. 13, 1864. Harvey Melven, D, Sept. 5, 1862; April 20, 1863. James L. Southard, Sept. 8, 1864. Thomas Smith, Sept. 7, 1864. John Walter, Sept. 7, 1864. Hiram Weaver, 1862. Jacob Weber, Feb. 15, 1864.

94th Infantry.—Frederick Bannerwait, Jan. 4, 1864. Allen Brewer, first sergeant H, Oct. 17, 1861; Nov. 15, 1864. George A. Benson, H, Jan. 15, 1862; Jan. 14, 1865. Ira L. Egbury, H, Dec., 1861. Noah B. Morse, Dec. 15, 1861; died in 1863. Lorenzo Osborn, Jan. 9, 1862; Feb. 18, 1865.

U. S. C. T.—Edward Blosgin, Sept. 2, 1864. George Bowen (20th), Jan. 9, 1864. Nathan Frazier (100th), Aug. 18, 1864. James Johnson (26th), Feb. 18, 1864. William Jacobs (15th), Dec. 22, 1864. Isaac Still (26th), Feb. 19, 1864. George Wilmer, Sept 9, 1864.

105th Infantry—Jeremiah Brotherton, E, musician. Benjamin Chaddock, A; died in hospital Nov. 30, 1862. Solomon Eighmy, A, Dec. 19, 1861; Oct, 1863. U. N. Harmon. A, Jan. 25, 1862: Feb. 8, 1863. Albert Nichols, A, 1862. Homer and Riley Nichols, A.

8th Cavalry. —Henry H. Jones, Sept. 9, 1864. Frederick Pilgrim, Oct 5, 1861; remained in the service. William Stetsil, H, Oct. 5, 1861. Augustus Stuby, H, Oct. 5, 1861; Nov. 14, 1864.

12th Infantry. —George W. Barrs, K, May 13, 1861; May 3, 1862. James Shepard, K, Apr. 27, 1861; May 22, 1868. Timothy Tierney, May 1, 1861; May 11, 1863.

2nd Arttillery—William Miller, M, Dec. 28, 1863; Sept. 29, 1865. Joseph A. Sleeper, M, Dec. 29, 1863; wounded June 3, 1864.

7th Infantry.—Benjamin Knapp, Sept 14, 1864. Charles Lent, Sept. 9, 1834. Harvey McCormack, September 9, 1864. Lathrop Smith, Sept. 15, 1864.

1st Heavy Artillery.—Duane W. Sewell, M, Sept. 7, 1864. Frank Tisdale, M, Sept. 22, 1864; June 23, 1865.

9th Heavy Artillery—Arthur Z. Godfrey, musician, M, December 28, 1863; Oct 11, 1865: Henry Luth, Jan. 4, 1864. Rial Newland, Dec. 25, 1863.

18th Infantry.—John T. Pace and Emery F. Prichard, Sept. 7, 1864. John Williams, Sept. 14, 1864.

3d Cavalry.—George Munson, Sept. 5, 1864. Elijah Wilson, Sept. 16, 1864.

Independent Company—William Gould and Jerry Sullivan, Sept. 14, 1864.

Miscellaneous.—Frederick Aspinwall, Aug. 19, 1864. Henry Atkinson, Aug. 22, 1864. John Bridmer, July 16, 1864. John M. Bell, 115th infantry, Sept. 10, 1864; went into the navy. Valentine Conners, Aug. 26, 1864. Edgar F. Doty, 18th heavy artillery, Sept. 8, 1864. John M. Denton, seaman, Dec. 28, 1864. George W. Eastman, musician, D, 16th, Feb. 26, 1862; died May 14th, 1862. John Edgell, Dec. 11, 1863. Charles Flessarer and John P. George, Dec. 24, 1864. Reuben B. Heacock, captain, E, 19th, July 1, 1862; killed May 18, 1864. George Henning, 10th cavalry. Daniel Hoon, July 1, 1864. Peter Hollander, Aug. 3, 1864. Henry Hike, 64th infantry, A, Sept. 6, 1864; May 30, 1865. John Johnson, July 13, 1864. Henry Jones, Aug. 12, 1864. Benjamin M. Johnson, Jan. 28, 1864. William Knox, G, 10th, Nov., 1862; transferred to veteran reserve corps. James Sanbonke, Sept. 7, 1864. Charles Melvin, sergeant 18th, G, Aug. 7, 1862; June 30, 1865. Charles A. Over, July 22, 1864. John Offerman, Sept. 6, 1864. James Quinn. Asahel Tobias, corporal, 179th infantry, U, Mch. 24, 1864; killed April 2, 1865; Charles Thomas, Aug, 27, 1864. Charles Thompson, Sept. 2, 1864. Martin Fietzer, Sept. 6, 1864. Nelson Updike, 18th infantry, H, Apr. 18, 1861; Aug. 13, 1861. William A. Wilder, 1st N. J. cavalry, G, Dec. 17, 1863; died in Andersonville, Ga. Charles Williams, July 1st 1864. Charles T. Whitcomb, clerk in the naval service; Dec. 28, 1864.

ATTICA CENTER.

Attica Center is a small hamlet near the center of the town, and about six miles from Attica village. It was settled about 1806 by Stephen Crow. It was once the business center of the town, but as railroads and canals drew the business in other directions, the Center began to decline. There was at that point a flourishing church, which has also had to succumb to the losses occasioned by a change of business center. There are at present a German Baptist church, supplied from other places, a cheese factory, a school-house, two blacksmith shops and six or eight dwellings.

ATTICA VILLAGE.

Less than three-quarters of a century ago this place was known only as Phelps Settlement, for the reason that Zerah Phelps, of Connecticut, had purchased the land upon which the village now stands, and was the first settler at this point. The most vivid imagination of the wisest denizen of the Phelps Settlement of 1802 could not have pictured the Attica of 1879; for then a dense wilderness covered the ground, inhabited only by wild beasts, and in the way of communications there was only a trail leading out to Batavia.

When Mr. Phelps settled here, in 1802, he cleared a spot of ground, and built a double log house on the site now occupied by Mrs. Maxon's millinery shop, on the east side of Market street. In 1803 Mr. Phelps built a grist-mill at this place, which was not only the first one in the town but in the county also. It stood on the east side of the creek, in the rear of where I. H. Torn's blacksmith shop now stands. The mill dam was where it now is. The mill was run by an old fashioned undershot wheel, and the grinding was done with one run of "rock stone." Roswell Munger was the millwright who built the mill. This mill was burned in 1805, by a man who had worked for Mr. Phelps and for good reasons had been discharged. The saw-mill built at or about the same time stood on the west bank of the creek, in the rear of where Barross & Fay's grist-mill now stands. In 1806 Mr. Phelps built another grist-mill, on the west side of the creek and north side of Main street, where S. A. Krauss & Sons' and Smith & Bostwick's brick blocks now stand, on Market street. This mill was supplied with the same kind of stone as the former one, but with a tub wheel. In 1813 this mill was accidentally burnt, and rebuilt the same year by John Peabody, who then owned it. In 1818 it was again destroyed by fire, with about three thousand bushels of wheat. The miller, Abram Andrews, who slept in the mill, escaped by jumping from an upper window. The mill was then owned by Messrs. Wilder, Peabody & Thomas. It was rebuilt in 1819, and in 1827 an addition was made and the flouring facilities increased by Parmenio Adams, who then owned it. In 1847, when owned by David Scott, the establishment was again swept away by fire, and in 1848 the present brick mill was built by B. R. Folsom, with all the modern improvements, making it a first class flouring and custom mill. It is now owned and operated by Barross & Fay.

The first blacksmith shop in the village, and probably in the town, was opened in 1805 by two brothers named Hossington. It stood on the south side of Main street, where R. Rykert's paint shop now stands. The Hossingtons were succeeded by David Wright, who continued the business many years.

The first tannery in the village was built by Elial Piersons, who, having sold the one on the Cooley farm east of the village, came here, and about 1810 built a tannery on the site now occupied by D. H. Pryor's house, at the corner of Washington and Main streets. He sold out to Timothy Loomis in 1816. The first brick building in the village stood where R. J. Rodgers's store now stands, on Market street.

The first store in the village was opened in 1806 by T. Carey, of Batavia, on the corner of Main and Exchange streets, where Dr. Davis's brick house now stands. John Wilder owned the property, and sold it to a Mr. Fitch, and he to Erastus Crosby, who opened a tavern in 1808 or there abouts. Soon after this Fitch opened a store on the site now occupied by C. W. Krauss, on the corner of Market and Bennington streets.

The old carding-mill that stood where Mrs. Pfeinder's block on Market street now stands, was built in 1814 by Messrs. Fuller & Sabin, who carried on the business for quite a number of years.

The pioneer school-house was built, of logs, in 1811, on the site now occupied by the bakery on Water street, just north of Main.

The first postmaster of the place was Gaius B. Rich. He was appointed in 1814. The office was kept in his store, on the site now occupied by Doty Brothers' store, on the east side of Market street. The mail was received once a week from Batavia. It was carried at first by a man named Murphy, and subsequently by Hanford Conger. It was carried on horseback a number of years. At present the mails are received seven times a day, and from all parts of the world, requiring a horse and dray to convey the mail bags from the railroad depot to the post-office, a distance of about one-third of a mile. A. J. Lorish is the present postmaster, and the office occupies a whole floor in thc Loomis block, on Main at the head of Market street.

The first brick store was built where R. J. Rodgers's drug store now stands in 1827, by David Scott. The stores south of the Scott building were built in 1830, by David Collins, Philip Smith, William Jenks and Harry Putnam. The block known as the Loomis block was built in 1833, by Owen Cotton.

The oldest brick dwelling house in the town stands on the corner of Market and Buffalo streets, in the village of Attica, and is now occupied by C. W. Krauss. It was built by Isaac Townsend, in 1827. On the site now occupied by Dr. O. Davis the first frame house in the town was erected, in 1808, by Joseph Wilder.

In 1828 Lewis Drake built a foundry on the west side of Market street east of Buffalo street. He sold it to Dix & Murphy, and Murphy sold to Jirah Chapman, who located where he now lives in 1832. Mr. Chapman conducted the foundry business until 1873, when he took the building down, and the site is now occupied by his garden.

The brick house on the corner of Buffalo and Market streets, now owned and occupied by C. W. Krauss, was built in 1828 by Isaac Townsend, who kept a tavern there for a number of years, and sold it to a man named Rice. Subsequently Gideon Tyrrel occupied it for a tavern till 1859.

In 1828 James Douglas built a threshing machine manufactory, on the site now occupied by Isaac Williams, on the west side of Market street east of Buffalo street.

In 1830 there was a wagon shop standing where Frederick Trummel's furniture store now stands, on Main street. The business was carried on by Timothy Crosby, who also did a cabinet business in 1830, on the site now occupied by V. C. Barross's residence, on Main street.

The pioneer boot and shoe store was opened in 1812 by a Mr. Gray, on the site of the late American Hotel and of the present Loomis block.

PIONEER SINGING SCHOOL.

Among all the cares and trials of pioneer life the early settlers were not unmindful of the cultivation of their musical talent, and in 1805 the first singing school was started at Phelps Settlement, as it was then called. At first the pupils and teachers met at private houses, as there was no school house at the time; but finally a novel idea entered the mind of some one. There was standing between what is now Water street and the creek, near where Mrs. Kearney's dwelling stood, a large, hollow buttonwood tree, about eight feet in diameter. This tree was felled, a section about thirty feet in length cut off, several appertures cut through for windows, seats arranged along the sides, and from this pioneer music hall the voices of the young folks echoed and re-echoed—to their satisfaction at least. The teacher was John Bogart, a Mohawk German. In after years his school room was cut off the right length for a boat, split open, the ends planked up at right angles, and it was launched in the mill pond, and afforded the young folks many a pleasant boating excursion; but in a time of high water it got loose from its moorings, went over the dam and was broken to pieces and carried down stream by the raging Tonawanda.

ATTICA INCORPORATED.

Within the brief space of thirty-five years from the time the first white settler located in this town the village of Attica was incorporated. May 2nd, 1837, a charter was granted. We have no means of ascertaining the names of the first village officers, the date of their election, or, in fact, any of the officers' names until within the last two or three years. As the population increased and the corporate bounds needed enlarging, a new charter, granting the "city fathers" greater power, was found necessary, and the present charter was granted by the Legislature January 22nd, 1853. The village officers consist of five trustees, with large powers, three assessors, a treasurer, constable and collector and village clerk. These are elected on the second Tuesday of March in each year. At the first meeting of the board of trustees subsequent to election they appoint one of their number to act as president of the board for the ensuing year. The village officers for 1879 are as follows: Trustees, A. A. Smith, I. O. Williams, I. E. Jefferson, I. H. Toms and M. C. Shea; assessors, Burley Smith, H. L. Doty and H. Spann; treasurer, G. T. Loomis; constable and collector, H. P. Gardner; clerk of the village, George B. Smith; president of the board of trustees, A. A. Smith. The territory of the corporation is an oblong in the northwest comer of the town, being two hundred and eighty rods north and south, and four hundred and fifty rods east and west.

RAILROAD COMMUNICATIONS—REPAIR SHOPS.

In 1843 the railroad was opened between Attica and Batavia. About the same year a charter was obtained, and work commenced on the "Buffalo and Attica Railroad," thirty-one miles long, which was finished in the spring of 1843, making the last link of a continuous line from Buffalo to Albany. Attica was made one of the principal stopping places, and continued so for many years.

The "Buffalo and New York City Railroad" was chartered to run parallel with the Buffalo and Attica road between these two points, and then to Hornellsville. The links that made up the original New York Central were consolidated, and that portion between Buffalo and Attica sold to A. D. Patchin, who subsequently sold to the Buffalo and New York City Railroad Company, and that company was finally merged in the New York and Erie Railway Company. At the same time the New York Central main line was extended from Batavia to Buffalo, and the Batavia and Attica road retained as a branch, which is still in operation, the depot being removed from Exchange street to grounds near the railroad crossing on East Main street. The Erie soon obtained a charter and laid a track parallel with the Central from this place to Batavia, thus giving Attica the advantage of two roads from the north, of one of which this place is the terminus. Soon the Erie was completed from Buffalo to New York, thus placing Attica on one of the great trunk lines to the West.

There is a projected road surveyed through this village, known as the "Tonawanda Valley and Lockport Railroad," running from Arcade, where it connects with the Buffalo, Philadelphia and New York road to Lockport, thus adding to the already excellent railroad facilities of the village.

Besides the through trains, all of which stop here, there are several trains made up daily at this place for the various points north, east and south, making this perhaps the liveliest railroad village of its size in the State.

The machine and repair shop of the Erie gives regular employment to a large number of men. It is supplied with a steam engine that drives machinery for cutting screws and nuts of all desired sizes; planing and turning iron; drilling and punching, and doing other work pertaining to repairing bridges, track, locomotives and cars. There are in the shop about a dozen blast fires, and repairing "track rail" is one of the many specialties of this shop. Imperfect or worn parts are cut out, or cut off, and when too short two of these trimmed rails are welded together. The best of these "reconstructed" rails are used to replace worn or broken ones in the main track, and are as good as new. All that are unfit for use in any way are sent to the rolling-mill to be made over into new rails. Another large item is the "switch work," and under this head come switch rods, switch guards and turning and signal apparatus, etc., for which the quantity of iron and the amount of labor required are immense.

In short, the Attica shop is the repair shop for the entire Buffalo division and its branches, and all the rail repairs, the smith work, the track work, the bridge work, the frogs and guards, track tools for repairs, repairs of engines and cars are done at this place. The force employed in this shop is of a high mechanical order, and the wages paid range from $1.50 to $3.00 per day. The depot and freight-house of the N. Y., L. E. & W. Rail road is on the east side of Exchange street. The principal railroad men connected with this road residing at this place are Thomas D. Jones, foreman of the repair and machine shop; David Kirkpatrick, superintendent of the Buffalo division, from Buffalo to

Hornellsville; George W. Wells, station agent; George B. Smith, ticket agent; Thomas Fitzgerald, superintendent of telegraph; Edwin Dearborn, night telegraph operator; L. P. Warren, keeper of railroad stores; P. J. Lynch, civil engineer, in charge of laying double track on the whole road; W. W. Dunbar, wood agent on the Buffalo and Rochester division; James R. Ogden, Rollo Benedict and Henry Shilling, railroad engineers, and J. O. Prescott, excursion conductor between Philadelphia and New York.

CEMETERIES—ATTICA CEMETERY ASSOCIATION.

According to probable tradition, the oldest burial place in the town is that in the village of Attica, adjoining the south side of the lands of the Erie railway company, and on the east side of Exchange street. The first death in this town was that of Thomas Mather, in the winter of 1803, less than a year from the time that Zerah Phelps first came here. It is supposed that he came here with Phelps, but this is not known, and it is a mere supposition that he was buried in the old graveyard at Attica.

Soon after the ground at the village was set apart for burial purposes, one was opened at Attica Center, which is still used as such; another, also still used, about half way between Attica village and Attica Center, on Crow creek; and still another, which has been abandoned, on what was known as Cooley street. There were several family burial grounds, but most if not all of them have gone out of use, and the cemeteries cared for by associations organized under the State laws are the only ones used.

In the old grounds, in the rear of the Erie depot at Attica, may be found this epitaph:

ELI BARRS
DIED AUG. 11, 1818,
IN THE 23D YEAR OF HIS AGE.

Hark, my gay friends, the solemn toll
Speaks the departure of the soul;
It's gone, that's all, we know not where,
Or how the unbodied soul doth fare
In that mysterious world; none knows
But God alone, to whom it goes;
To whom departed souls return,
To take their doom—to smile or mourn.

At a meeting of the citizens of Attica held at Doty's Hall, September 29th, 1868, for that purpose, the Attica Cemetery Association was organized. Trustees were chosen as follows: For one year—James H. Loomis, R. G. Bowen, R. J. Rodgers; for two years—L. Stanhope, J. S. Putnam, C. B. Benedict; for three years—A. Krauss, J. G. Doty, R. S. Stevens. The first Tuesday in October of each year was fixed upon as the time of holding annual meetings.

At a meeting of the trustees October 5th, 1868, the following officers were elected: President, James H. Loomis; vice-president, Andrew Krauss; secretary, J. S. Putnam; treasurer, C. B. Benedict.

At a meeting of the trustees in June, 1869, C. B. Benedict, J. H. Doty and J. H. Loomis were appointed a committee to buy land for cemetery purposes, and they contracted with Miss Samantha Gardner for her house and lot of about twelve acres, on High street within the limits of the corporation, for $3, 500.

Previous to the deed being given the house was burned. The insurance, $1,000, was paid to Miss Gardner, leaving the association but $2,500 in debt, which was subsequently paid, and the grounds were laid out in lots of suitable size, with proper walks and roads, making this one of the most beautiful "cities of the dead" in Wyoming county.

The following are the present officers: President, James G. Doty; vice-president, Andrew Krauss; treasurer, James H. Loomis; secretary, Ephraim Brainard. Trustees—James G. Doty, Andrew Krauss, James H. Loomis, Ephraim Brainard, O. S. Thomson, C. W. Krauss, William Wilder, Edward D: Tolles, A. A. Smith.

The following sums were subscribed toward the purchase and improvement of the cemetery grounds:

J. H. Loomis, R. S. Stearns and E. Bishop, each $200; A. Krauss, $150; C. W. Krauss, J. Belden, C. B. Benedict, G. Dorrance, J. S. Putnam, Mrs. D. A. Spink and C. Wilkie, each $100; J. Karcher, R. G. Bowen, F. Trummell, M. E. Potter, J. G. Doty, J. Bane, A. G. Ellenwood, E. P. Spink, J. W. Vincent, R. Benham and William Powers, each $50; H. Spann, Groat & Wilson, F. D. Wilcox, P. Brechsen, W. H. Hill, J. Chapman, E. F. Chaffee, R. Lemon, William M. Walbridge, E. C. Williams, William Walbridge, James Baker, O. Davis, James Dunbar, V. C. Barross, J. H. Backus and E. H. Cotton, each $25; H. Palmer, William Wilder and George Benham, each $20; C. R. Baker, A. Ganter, W, F. Sanborn, H. P. Sanborn, T. Loomis and L. Pfender, each $15; William Ballsmith, N. Bogart, D. Wilder, Wilbor Nelson, J. C. Gardner, L. W. Miles, T. M. Gladding, H. Heath, George Fouth, William Deckleman, F. C. Ballsmith, J. R. Williams, I. H. Toms, F. D. Andrews, C. S. Thomson, Charles King, J. M. Baldolf, F. Thorpe, A. J. Lorish, Isaac Toms, H. L. Doty, S. C. Archer, G. W. Reynolds, B. Reynolds, Lawrence & Norton, M. Godfrey, D. H. Pryor, L. Barrs, William Nelson, F. R. Barross, J. H. Hill, A. Maxon and John Schuman, each $10; R. Newland, L. W. Moody and George Tubbs, each $5; total, $2,920.

EDUCATIONAL.

No sooner had the sturdy New Englanders located in what is now the village of Attica, and got a preaching place established, than they began to look for a place to build a school-house. No other material being at hand, they built of logs, on what is now Water street, a short distance from Main. The first school was taught here, in the summer of 1807, by Miss Sophia Williams. From that time to the present educational interests have continued to prosper.

In 1850 a fine brick building was erected on Prospect street for school purposes. The grounds contained one acre. The building was nearly square, two stories high, and contained three main departments with three recitation rooms. For twenty years it was sufficient for the demands of the village.

In the year 1870, at the time the present principal, Thomas B. Lovell, came, the proposition was discussed to enlarge the building. Hon. Robert S. Stevens, who was a student in this village in 1838 and 1839, offered a donation of $5,000 to the district, if it would raise as much more, for the purpose of putting up a wing on the south side of the old building. This was gladly agreed to; and the building was finished according to contract in September, 1872. During this year a large amount of apparatus was added to the institution.

This building proved insufficient for school purposes in the year 1874. Hon. R. S. Stevens generously offered $1,100 to the district if it would raise sufficient money to build a wing on the north side similar to the one on the south side. This was done; thus adding to the architectural beauty, capacity and convenience of the structure, and making it worthy of the citizens of Attica, and an ornament to the village.

The Attica Union School and Academy was incorporated by the Legislature in 1867, and received under the visitation of the regents of the University of New York. The school now numbers about four hundred pupils attending at one time. There are about seven hundred pupils of school age residing in the district, of whom about five hundred and sixty attend during the year. There are thirty-one graduates of the institution. The present principal, Thomas B. Lovell, A. M., has been in charge of the institution for nine years.

The board of education for the years 1878 and 1879 was as follows: Hon. James H. Loomis, chairman; Edward D. Tolles, secretary; James G. Doty, Andrew Krauss, Noah North and Warren S. Brown.

The school money apportioned to this town for 1879 was $2,282.15, to be distributed among the thirteen districts in this town; more than one-half the amount was drawn by the Attica village district.

THE PRESS OF ATTICA.

The publication of newspapers was commenced in the town in 1833 by David Scott, who began the publication in that year of the *Attica Republican.* The name was soon after changed to the *Attica Republican and Genesee Advertiser.* The paper was subsequently sold to E. A. Cooley, who became publisher, and the name was changed to the *Attica Democrat.* This paper was published until 1846.

In October, 1846, Mr. Abram Dinsmore commenced the publication of the *Attica Telegraph*, and continued it about two years, when newspaper enterprise in this place was for a time abandoned.

April 1st, 1848, R. W. Dibble and W. H. Civer commenced the publication of the *Old Eighth Whig*. At the end of six months Mr. Dibble retired from the concern and the name of the paper was changed to the *Spirit of the Old Eighth* by Mr. Civer, who conducted it until 1850, when this paper was also abandoned.

The next journal here was the *Attica Atlas*, published by Silas Folsom from January 1st, 1851, until the spring of 1872, when the whole establishment was destroyed by fire, together with the American Hotel and a large number of dwellings. Mr. Folsom then retired from the business.

In June, 1872, Charles F. Meloy established the *Attica Weekly News*. He was succeeded in 1874 by C. L. Shepherd, who dropped the word *Weekly* from the heading, leaving the name *Attica News*, by which name it is now, in its seventh volume, published and edited by Addis E. Bishop. The paper is Republican in politics.

Number 1 of volume 1 of the *Attica Argus* was issued Saturday, April 7th, 1877, by George A. Sanders, as editor and proprietor. He continued the publication until September, 1877, when he sold to S. Wilson Wade, of the *Wyoming County Times*, and at the same time the editorial department was placed in charge of D. A. Denison. January 1st, 1878, Mr. Wade sold his interest to Messrs. Denison and Benham, and in July of the same year Mr. Denison purchased Mr. Benham's interest in the paper, since which time he has been publisher and editor. Politically the paper is Democratic.

BANKING IN ATTICA.

Previous to 1838 the business men of Attica were obliged to go to Batavia or Buffalo on banking business. In that year Gaius B. Rich established the Bank of Attica in what is now a part of the Davis house, at the corner of Main and Exchange streets. It stood a little west of the main building, between that and J. D. Turrel's. In 1841 he removed the business to Buffalo, where it is still known as the Bank of Attica.

In 1856 Lonidas Doty and Dean Richmond opened the Farmers' Bank of Attica, and continued it till 1860, when it was removed to Batavia. It was succeeded by Benedict & Doty as individual bankers. They were followed by C. B. Benedict & Son, and later by the Attica National Bank.

In 1863 the First National Bank of Attica was organized, and closed business in 1865, being the first failure of a national bank in the United States.

Thomson & Loomis opened a bank in 1847, and were followed by J. H. Loomis & Son, who are now doing a banking business.

TONAWANDA VALLEY DRIVING PARK AND AGRICULTURAL ASSOCIATION.

This association was organized in 1875, with a capital stock of $10,000, and its first fair was held in September of that year. The officers for 1875 were: President, L. R. Vincent; secretary, Edward Skinner; treasurer, Lewis Benedict. Directors—L. R. Vincent, J. J. Brainard, Ronald McLeod, F. M. Wilson, Andrew Krauss, Reuben Lemon, R. J. Rogers, A. A. Smith, Joseph W. Vincent and Lewis Benedict, Attica; Sanford Riddle, Alexander; Edward Madden, Varysburg; E. R. Yates and Richard Losee, Darien; J. W. Danley, Bennington.

The association bought fifty-three acres from J. J. Brainard and F. M. Wilson, at $100 per acre. The land is beautifully and centrally located on the south side of Main street, and is bounded on the west by the east line of the corporation of Attica, and on the south by the N. Y., L. E. and W. Railroad.

The association has expended a large amount of money to make the grounds the most attractive of their kind in western New York. On the south side, along the railroad, is a beautiful grove, suitable for holding picnics, camp meetings, or military encampments, with most excellent parade grounds in front. On the northeast side of the grove is an artificial lake, which has been made one of the principal attractions of the grounds. The trotting course, in the north west part of the grounds, was constructed by Mr. O. Buell, of Rochester, and is about sixty feet wide, elliptical in form, and by a complete system of drainage is rendered dry, even during the rainy season. It is considered the finest half-mile course in the country.

On the east side of the track, occupying an elevated position, is the grand stand, one hundred and fifty feet in length, with a seating capacity for two thousand people, and directly under it is a dining hall, about forty by one hundred and fifty feet. Horticultural Hall is near the center of the spacious grounds, and contains over ten thousand feet of available room.

Stables, one hundred and fifty feet in length, with a wide awning in front, extending the whole length, are provided for the accommodation of horses. They have all the modern improvements. There are also large and commodious sheds, containing pens for sheep and swine. Buildings ample for the exhibition of carriages, sleighs and agricultural implements occupy their proper place along the east side of the ground.

This fair ground in point of size, beauty of location, accessibility, extent and number of buildings and the substantial manner in which they are constructed, has no superior in the State. The total sum spent on it has been $16,300. The society was in debt January 1st, 1879, $4,000.

The officers for 1879 were: President, Edward Madden, Varysburg; vice-president, Sanford Riddle, Alexander; secretary, James G. Dorrance, Attica; treasurer, C. E. Loomis, Attica. Directors—L. R. Vincent, J. J. Brainard, Ronald McLeod, F. M. Wilson, A. A. Smith, J. G. Dorrance, Dr. H. B. Miller and J. W. Vincent, Attica; Samuel Griswold and Sanford Riddle, Alexander; Edward Madden and Gad C. Parker, Sheldon; J. W. Danley, Bennington; Charles H. Brainard, Alexander.

WILLIAMS, OPERA HOUSE, ATTICA, N.Y.

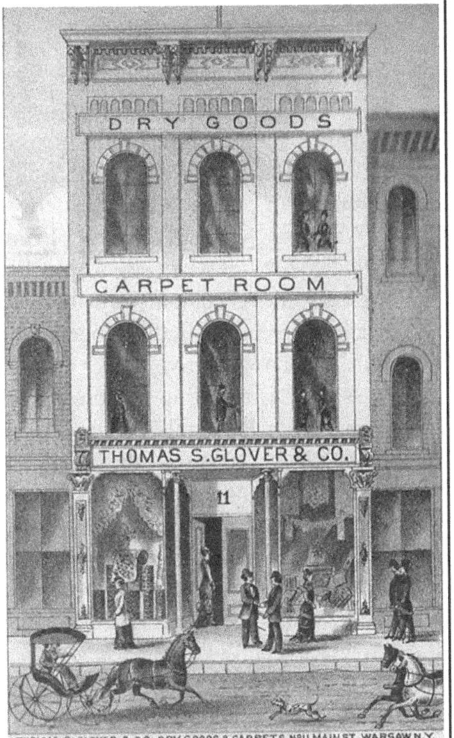

THOMAS S. GLOVER & CO., DRY GOODS & CARPETS, No 11 MAIN ST., WARSAW, N.Y.

RESIDENCE OF H. MUNS, COWLESVILLE, TOWN OF BENNINGTON, WYOMING CO., N.Y.

BUSINESS OF ATTICA IN 1879.

With the advent of the village charter, railroads, telegraphs and other improvements of the age, there seemed to be infused new life and vitality, and Attica was fully embarked on the course of improvement and prosperity to which its present condition is due. Having read the earlier history of the village the reader will find interesting matter for comparison in the following summary of present business interests.

Vosburgh's steam saw and planing mill, located in the eastern part of the village, south of Main street, was built in 1878. It is convenient for receiving logs and delivering lumber. It has a machine attached which finishes staves and heading ready for putting together. There is also a custom grist and flouring mill, receiving motive power from the same forty horse power engine. The saw-mill has a cutting capacity of 1,000 feet per hour, which was a full day's work for Phelps's mill, that stood in the village in 1803.

The Attica grist and flouring mill, built in 1848 by B. R. Folsom, and located on the south side of Main street at the west end of the bridge, is a five-story brick structure forty-five by fifty feet. The present proprietors, Messrs. Barross & Fay, purchased the property in 1855, and put in improved machinery, and are maintaining the reputation of running one of the best custom mills, on the Tonawanda creek, Mr. Barross being an experienced miller, and Mr. Fay an experienced millwright.

There are nine hotels in the village, including the Wyoming, Exchange street, north of the railroad, built in 1878 by D. Filkins; Washburn House, corner of Main and Exchange streets, built in 1825 by Gaius B. Rich; the Berlin House, Exchange street, north of the railroad, built in 1877; the Western, opposite the Erie depot, built in 1835; and the Saint James, Market street, built in 1870.

There are two public halls, besides those used by secret societies—Lemon's Hall, Main street, at the east end of the iron bridge, built in 1840 by one Lemon; and Loomis Hall, Market street, built in 1870 by Hon. J. H. Loomis. Williams Opera House, Exchange street, adjoining the Wyoming House, was built in 1879 by Charles Williams. The building is of brick, sixty-three by one hundred and ten feet, and contains two large stores and a livery stable, besides the Opera House. It has an elevation of sixty feet from the water table and seventy feet from the basement floor. The whole building is warmed by steam and furnished with all the modern improvements, costing over $15,000.

The machine shop owned by Earl Fay is run by the Attica mill water power. It is located in the rear of the Loomis block, on Main street, entrance from High street. This shop is equipped for a variety of work, and is mostly devoted to repairing farm tools and machinery.

The lumber and coal dealers are John Belden, on Washington street, and George S. Drew, Exchange street. The blacksmithing business is carried on by I. H. Toms, on Main street; Isaac Toms, Water street, and Isaacs & Knapp, Exchange street. There are two carriage and sleigh manufacturing establishments here—Charles Morganstern's, Water street, and that of Dauber Brothers, Main street.

The lawyers are A. J. Lorish and O. H. Hopkins, in the Loomis block, Main street, head of Market, and M. Trall and V. C. Peckham, Benedict block, corner of Main and Market streets.

The dentists are A. S. Cheeseman, over Rodgers's drug store, on Market street, and J. Q. Bradt, Main street.

Besides the Attica mills, there are two feed and flour stores—C. S. Thompson's, on Water street, and Henry Seirk & Son's, Main street, opposite Water.

The drug business is carried on by G. Dorrance & Son, east side, and R. J. Rogers and D. P. Steadman, west side of Market street. The jewelry business is conducted by H. T. Bramer, Main street, and George Taylor, Exchange street; and the cabinet and furniture trade by Frederick Trummell, Main street, and H. Groat, in the Loomis block. There are two large hardware houses here—Loomis, Tolles & Co, Main street, head of Market, and Andrews & Ballsmith, Main street, east end of the iron bridge. The dealers in groceries exclusively are J. D. Evans and C. W. Krauss, west side, and M. C. Shea, east side of Market street; L. Sanderson and P. Breicheisen, Main street; Henry Spann and E. L. & G. D. Kenyon, Exchange street. Those dealing in dry goods exclusively are E. B. Wallace, H. L. Doty & Co., and Smith & Bostwick, all on the east side of Market street. The clothing houses are John Karcher's, west side of Market street, and the Philadelphia Clothing House, by I. Whiteson, north side of Main street, west of bridge. Clothing and boots and shoes are sold by Andrew Krauss & Co.; and boots and shoes exclusively by Carl Ganter, Market street, H. Palmer and L. Balduf, Exchange street. A. Krauss & Co., east side of Market street, are wholesale boot and shoe manufacturers. Merchant tailoring is carried on by V. Decot, west side of Market street. The marble business is conducted by Julius Baur, east side of Market street; and wholesale liquor stores are kept by I. E. Jefferson, Exchange street, north of the railroad, and J. E. Noblett, Market street. The cigar manufacturers are Smith & Frey, Sanderson block, Market street, and H. L. Belott, Exchange street. The Attica brewery was built in 1878 by R. H. Farnham, at the east end of Main street. It has a capacity of six thousand barrels of lager beer per annum. There are three meat markets—one on Market, one on Main, and one on Exchange street. There are two barber shops, four paint shops, one cooper shop, three dressmakers, four millinery stores, and various other trades usually carried on in a village of the size of Attica, which has about 2,500 inhabitants.

The resident physicians are Drs. J. A. Post, C. R. Seeley, W. B. Gifford, F. R. Barross, A. G. Ellenwood, S. C. Archer and Orin Davis, the last of whom has for many years resided on the corner of Main and Exchange streets.

Dr. Davis established his Health Institute in Attica in 1854. Its continued success during a quarter of a century has constituted an important item in the history of the village.

The hay trade is a large item of the business interests of this place. T. F. Wilson's steam apparatus for cutting, pressing and baling hay, at the junction of Pearl with Genesee street, can cut, press and bale, and load into cars, a ton of hay in forty minutes. Thomas Cook's hay barn is located near the junction of Main and Pearl streets, by the side of the Central railroad track. He makes a business of buying, packing and shipping hay, to supply the New York Central stock yard at Buffalo. His shipments at times amount to one hundred and fifty tons per month.

The cultivation of flowers and ornamental plants always marks an enlightened stage of civilization. Mrs. A. S. Stevens planted the first flower garden in Attica, many years ago, on Main street, nearly opposite the Presbyterian church, and it is to-day one of the loveliest places in the village. In the fall of 1876, her son, Mr. R. S. Stevens, built the Attica Green House, in the rear of the Erie depot, of which Mr. Frederick Snyder is the lessee. The location, sloping south, is well adapted to plant culture. The buildings and fixtures, exclusive of the plants, cost $3,000. Mr. Snyder has stocked the place with thousands of floral beauties, embracing over five hundred varieties, which include many rich and rare novelties and attractive old favorites. Mr. Snyder is at home in his vocation, and by his taste and skill has built up one of the many paying institutions of Attica. There are many places in this village that might be mentioned for their floricultural beauty, and it is safe to say that there is no place of its size in the State that makes such a floral display as Attica.

THE CHURCHES OF ATTICA.

FIRST BAPTIST.

In a small log house owned by Simeon Williams, about one mile east of what is now Attica, was organized, August 21st, 1806, the first Baptist church on the Holland Purchase, consisting of eight members, Deacon J. Tubbs acting as moderator, and S. Williams clerk, January 30th, 1808, it was publicly recognized, with a membership of thirteen; Rev. Joel Butler, Deacon Reuben Osborn and Nathaniel Groves, of Sangersfield, N. Y., and Peter P. Roots, a missionary, sitting in council.

Its earliest meetings were held in dwellings, school-houses, barns, and sometimes in the fields, as they could best be accommodated, until 1837, when the society became sufficiently prosperous to build a meeting-house, which was erected under the pastorate of Rev. Joel W. Nye; and in 1867, under the energetic labors of Rev. P. J. Williams, then pastor, was remodeled and thoroughly repaired.

This church first joined the Holland Purchase Association, and in 1811 Rev. Reuben Osborn and Deacon Jonas Osborn, the first delegates, were sent to represent it in that body, which met at Willink, Erie county. In 1831, by request, it was dismissed therefrom, and united the same year with the Genesee Baptist

Association. Riley Munger and Jacob Wood were the first delegates to that body. The church seemed to prosper at times until 1845, when difficulties arose of such a character as to distract and divide its members, and on May 24th of that year a resolution was passed to disband.

On January 5th, 1846, through the energetic labors of Deacons William Chaffee, Thomas Beasley, Jacob Wood, James Dunbar and others, it was reorganized, and on the 11th of February following was recognized by an ecclesiastical council.

The first received by baptism were Jacob Wood, Robert Carr and John Stone, February 14th, 1808. Rev. Joel Butler preached the first sermon.

In 1809 Rev. Reuben Osborn became the settled pastor, and continued his labors until 1813, when he died. From that time until 1835 there was preaching a part of the time by Rev. Messrs. Hoxie, Case, Boomer, Herrick, Throop, B. Hill, Braman, I. Brown and Samuel Jones. Under the labors of the latter many were converted, and large accessions made to the church.

From the autumn of 1835 Joel W. Nye was pastor until the fall of 1837, when Rev. Mr. Wilson was called, and settled as pastor one year. Rev. O. D. Taylor next filled the pulpit until 1842; Rev. Mr. Buck until April, 1843, and Rev. Mr. Pickett until September following. Then the pulpit until 1846 was only occasionally supplied. Elder D. Munger was pastor from April 4th, 1846, until 1848; Rev. B. Hill until October, 1849. Then for about one year the pulpit was partially supplied by Elders J. Blain, R. Morey and Reed. Then Rev. C. Miner was pastor until March, 1855, and Rev. C. H. Underhill until his death, July 15th, 1856. Rev. A. Wells next filled the pulpit until March, 1859, when he resigned.

For a short period thereafter the desk was very acceptably supplied by Rev. O. E. Mallory. In August, 1859, Rev. R. C. Palmer became pastor, and in May, 1860, Rev. A. Wade, who continued for one year. Rev. L. Davis remained until May, 1863. From this time until April, 1864, the pulpit was only occasionally supplied. Rev. C. H. James next became pastor; he left in October, 1866, and for about one year Rev. R. T. Smith preached. From October, 1867, Rev. P. J. Williams was pastor until April, 1869. Rev. I. W. Emery then preached two years, and was succeeded by Rev. M. P. Forbes; and he by Rev. B. T. Garfield, who died while here, lamented by all who knew him. Professor T. B. Lovell, of Attica, then supplied the pulpit until April, 1876, when Rev. A. Lindsay, the present pastor, was settled here.

The following is a list of the names of deacons and clerks, in their order:

Deacons—Simeon Williams, J. Tubb, Jonas Osborn, William Osborn, Riley Munger, William Chaffee, David Slyke, Thomas Beasley, Giles Pettibone, James Dunbar, Slyke, Thomas Beasley, Giles Pettibone, James Dunbar, H. C. Wilbur and W. A. Pettibone; clerks—S. Williams, Benjamin Knapp, Jacob Wood, R. Munger, Dr. Walker, W. H. Andrews, Amos D. Munger, J. Hoxie, S. Ewell, Giles Pettibone, L. Austin, W. A. Pettibone and E. F. Chaffee, the present clerk.

This church is in a prosperous condition, with a membership of eighty.

The Sabbath-school connected with this church dates from the year 1832, when Deacon William Chaffee organized and conducted a Sabbath-school in the brick school-house three miles south of the village of Attica, in which vicinity many families connected with the Baptist church then resided. After a short time it was held in the Baptist meeting house in Attica. E. F. Chaffee, a son of Deacon Chaffee, was superintendent some years, under whose care the school prospered and increased. Prof. T. B. Lovel, who has been principal of the academy in Attica since 1869, has superintended the school successfully for the past five years. The average attendance of pupils ranges from eighty to one hundred, and the library contains over four hundred volumes.

A flourishing Sabbath-school is still carried on in the school-house where the Baptist church originated, conducted by Mr. E. F. Chaffee.

PRESBYTERIAN.

The Congregational, now Presbyterian, church in Attica was organized in 1807, by Rev. Royal Phelps, a nephew of Zerah Phelps, who settled in Attica in 1803. The church at that time consisted of five members, viz.: Mr. Green and wife, Stephen Crow and wife and Mrs. Zerah Phelps. A confession of faith and covenant were adopted, the form of which continued in use till a short time since. For the first ten years the church depended for preaching on occasional help from missionaries, or brief temporary supplies; while sometimes the presbytery sent men to minister. Among these were Rev. Dr. Wisner, of Lockport, and Rev. Mr. Crawford, of Leroy.

In 1817 commenced the first regular stated supply of the pulpit, by Rev. Solomon Hebard. He "remained four years, and was followed by Rev. Mr. Page, who was a missionary, but served most of the time until 1823. In February of this year the society voted to unite with the presbytery, and appointed Deacon Solomon Kingsley delegate to the next semi-annual meeting. The design was merely to act with the presbytery under the plan of union. The resolution was carried into effect, and after this the records of the church were carried up and submitted to the presbytery.

On October 20th, 1819, after due notice having been given two Sabbaths to the congregation accustomed to assemble at the village and at the school-house near John Hubbard's, alternately, the society was formed, according to law, under the title of "First Congregational Society of Attica." The church was formed in 1807, the society in 1819. The first trustees elected were Orator Holcomb, Solomon Kingsley and Abner Chittenden.

Next in the service of the ministry appears the name of Rev. A. P. Brown, coming in December, 1822, and continuing to minister for several years—how many is uncertain.

To preserve the names of many of the residents at this time, and to show the spirit and customs of the period in a religious direction, we insert the following record, dated February 22nd, 1823—the first formal provision and subscription for the stated preaching of the gospel:

"We, the undersigned, inhabitants of the town of Attica and towns adjacent, promise to pay to the trustees of the First Congregational Society in the said town of Attica the sums set to our names respectively, yearly for the term of three years from the commencement of the preaching of the gospel by the Rev. Amos P. Brown—being the consideration for said preaching one-half the time at the village of Attica; said sums to be paid one-fourth in cash and three-fourths in produce; provided also that after the first year any person shall have the privilege of withdrawing his name from said subscription on giving said trustees three months' notice and paying all arrears."

The subscribers and sums subscribed were as follows:

G. B. Rich, $20; David Scott, $15; Timothy Loomis, Parmenio Adams and Moses Disbrow, each $10; Abel Wilder and Owen Cotton, each $7; Harvey Putnam, Joseph Solomon. Abner Chittenden, John Newell, each $6; Laban Ainsworth, George Cooley, Ezra Bishop, Joshua Caugran, Isaac Anderson, N. K. Doty, Clark Hubbard, each $5; Hanford Conger, Charles Chaffey, William Jenkins, each $4; Reuben Patrick, George G. Gilbert, Solomon Kingsley, Moses H. Wethee, each $3; Raymond Peck, Allen Woodruff, Alden S. Stevens, Nathan Wight, Stephen Ellis, Lorin Hodges, Jeremiah Peck, Eliab Farnam, Heman Chittenden, Joseph Andrews, Thomas B. Benedict, Simeon Williams, Timothy Crosby, Niles Randall, John C. Melay, Henry Warriner, William Bliton, Gardner Hawes, Pardee Brainard, Ezekiel Woodruff, Thomas Ellis, Robert Simonton, jr., James Hill, Willard Thomson, C. Wilkie, each $2; Orville Woodruff, Lyman Bugbee, $1.50; Oliver Hodges, A. K., Daniel and Oliver C. Hubbard, Zadoc Williams, Alfred Hall, each $1.

"The undersigned agree to pay from November 1st, 1824, in the same way and manner as above mentioned":

William Hayden, $10: Samuel B. Hawes, $4; James B. Palmer, $2.50; David Andrews and Samuel Williams, jr., each $2; Seymour Morton (one year, from Jan. 1, 1826), $1.50; Hiram Richard, Ira Earil, N. H. Rockwell, David Stevens, W. B. Seebert, W. B. Crosby, each $1; David Wright, Alexander Wright and Samuel H. Leonard, from January, 1826, each $1; Obadiah Fuller and Elisha Wood, 50 cents each, from November 1st, 1824.

A subscription paper dated September 1st, 1824, received the signatures below, of persons "desirous of having the Rev. Mr. Brown preach in the south part of the town of Attica one-half of the time for two years; meetings to be held one-fourth of the time at or near the school house in district No. 6, and one-fourth at or near the school-house in district No. 8:"

Adams Gibson, William Potter and Hawley Smith, each $1.50; John T. Sanborn, $5; William Tanner, Lyman Dayton, Seth Melvin, Levi Hebard, William Moses and Erastus Bennett, each $8; Daniel Cooley, Grove Cooley, Aaron Allen, Charles Wilder, Zenas Andrews, Godfrey Bailey, Artemus Wilder, David W. Bagley, Asa

Johnson, jr., each $2; Nancy Sanborn, Thomas Wilder, Alfred Woodruff, Elisha Smith, Freeman Bailey, Moses McIntyre, Asa Wood, each $1.

The first report on the records as to the number of members in the church appears in 1827, when there were 52. In 1828 the first meeting-house was built. There is the following note in the records: "Be it remembered that the meeting-house was erected in the year of 1828 and 1829, at the cost of $3,000 [on the same spot on which the present house now stands], under the superintendence of Harvey Putnam, G. B. Rich and Owen Cotton, building committee. The house was finished in all its parts without the use of ardent spirits, it being the first successful experiment ever had in town for the great moral reform of temperance."

The subscribers and sums contributed toward this church were as follows:

G. B. Rich, $800; O. Cotton, P. Adams, D. Scott, each $150; H. Putnam, T. Loomis, M. Disbrow, W. Hayden, E. S. Salisbury, each $100; H. Conger, $75; A. P. Curtis, William Jenkins, A. Pember, G. Cooley, J. Caughran, C. Chaffey, A. Bishop, each $50; A. S. Stevens, S. Hubbard, N. K. Doty, each $30; W. B. Seebert, A. Wright, J. Circe, D. Wright, A. Chittenden, J. Anderson, J. Hills, D. Andrews, J. Newell, G. Hawes, A. Allen, each $25; F. Finney, N. Bennett, M. Farnham, J. Howe, each $20; A. Woodruff, $16; S. P. Morton, $15; A. Cooley, H. Bement, Walter Burlingame, D. Churchill, C. Clark, C. D. Beman, S. Williams, A. Achilles, G. F. Smith, E. Osborn, Willard Thompson, Ira Eastman, J. Adams, E. Conger, L. Washburne, H. B. Sprout, C. Cornwell, T. B. Benedict, J. M. Morton, T. Powers, T. Cogswell, each $10; one other, $12. Total $2,873.

The builder's contract was for $2,605, the cost of land $100, and we have recorded the following other charges: "Paid M. Hunt for stone and others for work, $166; O. Cotton's bill, $20."

In the ministry of the church next appears the name of Rev. Dexter Clary, who remained less than a year. Then Rev. Lemuel Brooks preached fifteen months, no less than forty-five being added to the church on profession of faith during this time. Then Rev. B. J. Lane ministered a little over a year; Rev. Hiland Hulburd less than a year, and after him the first minister installed as pastor, Rev. James B. Shaw, now of Rochester. He was with the session of the church December 4th, 1834. During his ministry, February 5th, 1835, it was resolved "that this church hereafter conduct its business, discipline and government according to the constitution of the Presbyterian Church in the United States." After a full discussion in two meetings of the session, the vote was taken and decided in the affirmative, though the society continues to bear the name under which it was organized, "First Congregational Society of Attica." The number in-communion at this time was 152. Mr. Shaw continued to serve the church until February, 1839, making a term of four years.

Rev. J. B. Preston was next installed as pastor, and remained with this church five and a half years, until 1845. His ministry was a very successful one. Before he left there were 238 members, the largest number ever in connection with the church at one time, though many of these united with the church under the administration of Mr. Shaw. After Mr. Preston Rev. D. Chichester served less than a year, and Rev. Mr. Kidder a little over a year. From August, 1847, Rev. Charles Morgan served about three years.

In April, 1851, Rev. A. C. Raymond was installed pastor, and September 18th, 1852, Rev. George P. Falsom, who remained until 1859. Rev. Isaac Ely followed, serving less than a year. Rev. Alfred North was called in August, 1860, and remained until July, 1863. Rev. John Wicks commenced his labors February 14th, 1864, and is still the pastor (1879).

The building of the present meeting-house was commenced on the 3d of April, 1872, and it was dedicated April 10th, 1873. It was built by William Wilder, one of the trustees of the church. The total cost of building and furniture was $20,462. The whole amount except $975 was contributed by the members of the church and society. Of the whole cost of the church building $9,000 was contributed by Hon. Robert S. Stevens, of Attica.

The Sunday-school connected with this society was organized in 1820, by Rev. Solomon Hebard and Moses H. Wilder. The school has continued since, and is now in a most prosperous condition.

It has a membership of about 135, with an average attendance of 130. Edward D. Tolles is the superintendent.

METHODIST EPISCOPAL.

From the scanty records we have been able to consult, we learn that the first Methodist minister that found the first Methodist family that crossed the Genesee river as settlers was the Rev. James Mitchell, afterward Dr. Mitchell, of Philadelphia. To him must be ascribed the honor of being the first itinerant who traveled over the territory in which Attica lies. He came into this country in the year 1809. Attica was then a part of the Holland Purchase circuit. The name was changed in 1813 to Clarence circuit.

In 1819 Rev. Zachariah Paddock, still living, was appointed to the Attica circuit. He was present at the 25th anniversary of the dedication of the second church edifice in Attica, in 1878, and related many interesting reminiscences of that early time, which are recorded in the history of Attica Methodism by the present pastor, Rev. W. C. Wilbor. He says: "At that time (1819) there were but three or four little huts—you would hardly call them houses—and a school-house here."

In 1823 the first Methodist Episcopal society in the town of Attica was incorporated. Asa Orcutt was preacher in charge. This interesting instrument of incorporation, now yellow and worn with age, declares that "at a meeting held for the purpose, in a school-house in the town of Attica and county of Genesee, on Wednesday, the 23d day of June, 1824, Tyler D. Featherly, Cyrus Steward and Charles L. Imus, discreet persons of said congregation, were duly elected trustees of the same congregation, to be denominated and known in law by the name of the trustees of the First Methodist Episcopal Society in Attica." This being the first religious society organized in the town of the Methodist denomination, the Holland Company deeded to the trustees of the society fifty acres of land at Attica Center. The original deed, now in possession of J. E. Briggs, Esq., is a document of much interest.

This primitive Methodist society erected a church and flourished for a time, but gradually its numbers decreased, and now not a single family or member of the church remains; the edifice has disappeared and the property has passed into other hands.

The year 1830 witnessed a great revival in Attica. Asa Abell, presiding elder, wrote to the *Christian Advocate* as follows: "In Attica, Buffalo district, early in the winter of this conference year, 1830, there was a gracious outpouring of the Divine spirit, resulting in the conversion of as many as seventy or eighty and perhaps one hundred persons. So that where there had previously been formed a small society of some twelve or fifteen, there were united in church fellowship upwards of eighty."

The following year also saw large numbers added to the church. Rev. S. W. D. Chase was pastor, with Rev. James Durham colleague. As the result of this revival and increase, a fine brick church was erected, and also a parsonage. The church is still standing on Main street, beside the old school-house, and has been occupied for many years by the Society of the Free Will Baptists.

The early members of the church who united to form this society were George Adams and wife, Mrs. S. W. D. Chase, David Wright and wife, Childs and wife, Mrs. Goodell, Mrs. Jane Corlett, William Hayden, class leader, and wife.

Among the one hundred and fifty converts who joined the church at this time were Jireh Pember and wife, Nelson Beman and wife and Mrs. Stephen Ellis, all of whom are now living in Attica.

During the year 1834, with S. W. D. Chase as pastor for a second time, the society in the village was incorporated, having previously been connected with the church at Alexander. The original paper, now in possession of the trustees, certifies that William Hayden, James Hills and Augustus P. Curtis were duly elected trustees, and the society was to be known by the name and title of the Second Society of the Methodist Episcopal Church in Attica. This was recorded with the county clerk February 16th, 1835.

Owing to neglect of the trustees to secure the election of their successors, the society found it necessary to secure a new act of incorporation in the year 1837, with Rev. D. F. Parsons pastor. Stephen A. Knapp, Stephen Ellis, James Hills, Ezra Bishop and Jedediah K. Wood were elected trustees; and it was resolved that the society should be known as "The First Society of the Methodist Episcopal Church in the Village of Attica." This last act of incorporation was recorded June 27th, 1837. Under this organization the church now exists.

During 1837 the ground upon which the old brick church still stands was deeded to the society by David Scott and Maria his wife, in consideration of the sum of one dollar.

The year 1852 was an important one for Methodism in Attica, as it witnessed the building of the present church edifice. It was dedicated to the worship of God on Thanksgiving day, 1853, with Charles Shelling as pastor and Dr. E. Thomas presiding elder. Rev. Moses Crow, D. D., preached the dedicatory sermon. The site upon which this church now stands, conceded by all to be the finest church location in town, was deeded to the trustces, Newcomb Demary and Aaron Colton, by Elias A. Kennedy and Lydia, his wife, and Thomas Corlett, for $200. This deed was executed December 2nd, 1851.

During the years 1864 and 1865 Rev. J. E. Bills was pastor, and through his efforts the bell which still calls the people to prayer was purchased and hung in the tower, at a cost of $413.

During the pastorate of Rev. J. O. Wilsea, in 1868, the pipe organ was purchased. Dr. Orin Davis, the present chorister, raised $750 (contributing a generous portion himself) toward the cost of it, which was $1,500.

The year 1869 brought a period of storms and darkness to the Methodist church in Attica. Difficulties arose between some of the members and the trustees, instigated by vicious and unprincipled men, which resulted in mob violence, which wrested the church from its rightful owners. The trustees quietly sought legal redress, and through five long years, at great private expense, contended for the right in the courts of justice. In 1875 their persevering endeavor was rewarded by the restoration of the church property to their hands, and the payment of $1,800 damages. Great credit is due these faithful guardians of a public trust, but for whose courage and persistency the cause of Methodism must have been entirely destroyed in Attica.

Rev. T. H. Perkins was pastor during the last of these dark days, and during his third year, 1875–6, after recovering possession of the property, the church was put in thorough repair, at a cost of $1,000, and beautified with new carpets throughout, orchestra chairs, new pulpit, kalsomining and painting within and without.

This year also the Sanday-scbool was reorganized and placed in charge of the present superintendent, R. J. Rogers, a man of large experience and success in Sunday-school work. A new library, costing $425, was purchased. The centennial year saw Attica M. E. church enter upon brighter prospects and a new era of prosperity.

The present pastor of the church (1879) is Rev. William C. Wilbor. Under his administration the church enjoys increasing prosperity, and the membership has more than doubled in the three years of his pastorate. The society has just finished an elegant parsonage worth $2,500.

The church trustees at present are: A. H. Van Buren, Charles Adams, Stephen Ellis, A. J. Lorish, R. J. Rogers.

The following is a list of the pastors who have served the church from the beginning, with their years of service:

In 1809, James Mitchell; 1810, John Kimberlin, William Brown; 1811, Loring Graft, E. Metcalf, M. Pierce; 1812, R. M Evarts; 1813, Elijah King, Ebenezer Doolittle; 1814, William Brown, Elijah Warren; 1815, James M. Harris; 1816, Thomas McGee, Robert Minshall; 1817, William Jones, R. Aylesworth; 1818, Aurora Seeger; 1819, Zechariah Paddock, Alba Beckwith; 1820, Zaohariah Paddock, James H. Hall; 1821, James Gilmore, James Bennett; 1822, John Coraart; 1823, Asa Orcutt; 1824, A. Prindall, J. B. Roach; 1825, B. Williams, A. Prlndall; 1826, J. Huestis, B. Williams; 1827, John Coraart; 1828, C. V. Adgate; 1829, 1830, Micah Seager; 1831, S. W. D. Chase, James Durham; 1832, John H. Wallace; 1833, L. B. Casette, Reeder Smith; 1884, S. W. D. Chase; 1885, 1888, De Forrest Parsons, W. Cochran; 1837, David Nutten, C. S. Baker; 1838, S. A. Baker: 1839, Chauncey S. Baker; 1840, 1841, Alpha Wright; 1842, —— Taylor; 1843, 1844, Gershom Benedict; 1845, Henry Ryan Smith; 1846, Allen P. Ripley, D. D.; 1847, 1848, E. E. Chambers, D. D.; 1849, D. F. Parsons; 1850, C. M. Woodward; 1851, 1852, Charles Shelling; 1853, A. W. Luce; 1854, 1855, Jason G. Miller; 1856, A. Kendall; 1857, 1858, D. B. Worthington; 1859, 1860, J. H. Bayliss, D. D.; 1861, Albert N. Fisher; 1862, 1863, E. L. Newman; 1864, 1865, James E. Bills; 1866, R. L. Waite; 1867, F. E. Woods; 1868, J. O. Wilsea; 1869, R. W. Copeland, J. Watts. W. W. Ripley; 1870, 1871, William Jennings; 1872, C. B. Sparrow; 1873–75, J. H. Perkins; 1876–78, William C. Wilbor.

FREE WILL BAPTIST.

The Free Will Baptist society was among the early religious organizations of the village of Attica, but owing to the destruction of the early records of the church, through carelessness of the person having them in charge, we are unable to give anything more than a mere mention of this organization.

The church edifice is on Main street, between Washington and Water streets, and is built of brick. The property was formerly owned by the Methodist society, and sold to this church when the Methodists erected their new edifice on Main street. The present pastor is Rev. Mr. Steele.

ROMAN CATHOLIC.

The Roman Catholic church of Attica was organized as a mission in 1856, and remains a mission, supplied from Batavia. The church building was erected in 1856, at a cost of $750.

At that time there were only about half a dozen members, among whom were Thomas O'Herin, Michael Cornwell, Patrick Conway, Dennis Shea and Daniel Hanefin. They were unable to complete the church, and the interior has been only recently finished. The building is of wood, of plain architectural design.

The priests serving here, in their order, have been Fathers O'Farrel, Brown, Cunningham, Donohoe, McGrath and McDonnel, the present pastor. The membership numbers two hundred. The church property is valued at $2,000. For the past two years V. Decot has been the trustee of the church property.

The Sunday-school connected with the church is under the superintendence of Father McDonnel, with Miss Mary J. McMahan and Miss Sophia Frey as teachers.

UNIVERSALIST SOCIETY.

A ladies' aid society was formed, which culminated in thc formation of this society.

The first Universalist conference in this village was held in the German Lutheran church, on Washington street, February 9th and 10th, 1870. Revs. C. C. Dutton, R. G. Goodenough, S. Crane, G. P. Hubbard and —— Hallcock officiated. There was no preaching from that time until March 27th, when Rev. F. S. Bacon preached for the society in Templars' Hall. By a vote of the Templars, the Universalist society was denied the farther use of the hall, and services were held by Revs. F. S. Bacon and G. P. Hibbard in the Academy building until August 29th, when, by a vote of the authorities having charge of the school building, this society was again deprived of a place of worship. The society then hired Doty's Hall, where services were held until W. B. Goodwin arranged a hall over his store, on Market street. This the society fitted up at an expense of $400, and services were held regularly until the spring of 1878, when financial embarrasments of the principal supporters of the society caused a suspension of preaching for a time. The following are the names of the early members of the society: W. W. Dunbar and wife, Miss D. Dunbar, Mr. E. Jolies and wife, Mrs. W. S. Brown, Mr. V. C. Barross and wife, Mrs. E. C. Williams, Mrs. M. Munger, Mrs. O. Earll, Mrs. M. Earll, C. Morgan and wife, Miss E. Guile, Miss S. Guile, Mrs. L. Shepherd, Mrs. J. Washburn, L. Pratt, W. B. Goodwin, Mrs. L. Lovelace, J. W. Colton, C. McCord and wife, Mrs. J. Richardson, Mrs. Wadsworth, O. Davis and wife.

The society was incorporated in pursuance of action taken at a meeting in St. Paul's church, March 21st, 1877, and named The Universalist Society of Attica.

The present officers are: Trustees—Alvin Starkey, William W. Dunbar and V. C. Barross; secretary and treasurer, Mrs. W. S. Brown; superintendent of Sunday-school, W. W. Dunbar. The society is now without stated preaching.

LODGES AND SOCIETIES.

MASONIC.

Attica Lodge, No. 462, Free and Accepted Masons was instituted during the early part of the summer of 1858, and worked under dispensation for nearly or quite a year, when the present charter was granted, dated June 20th, 1859, with the following named persons constituting the charter members and original officers: Francis C. Cunningham, W. M.; Owen Cotton, S. W.; Henry Spann, J. W.; Jared D. Tuerrel, secretary; Roswell Gardner, treasurer; George Cooley, S. D.; Grove Cooley, J. D.; and Peter Cole, tyler.

At present there are 111 members, and the following named persons were officers for the year 1879: W. Benham, W. M.; H. S. Kriegelstein, S. W., A. S. Cheeseman, J. W.; Henry Spann, treasurer; Jacob Algier, secretary; J. A. Post, S. D.; John Griffith, J. D.; H. W. Pettibone, tyler. The regular meetings of Attica Lodge are held in Masonic Hall, Rogers's block, Market street, on the first and third Wednesday evenings of each month.

Previous to the Morgan excitement, which began in 1826, there was a masonic lodge at this place, but we were unable to obtain either its number, the date of the charter or names of officers.

SAINT PAUL'S BENEVOLENT SOCIETY.

This society was organized June 5th, 1862. The name denotes its object. The membership is composed entirely of Germans. Following is a list of the original members and officers: Matthew Balduff, George Becker, Frederick Derr, George Echtenacker, Johann Eller, Jacob Eller, George Herzog, Johann Klingenmeyer, George Mintz, Adam Rauhut, Frederick Schaffer, Christopher Schuster, George Weihe, Johann Weis, Wilhelm Zoellner. Original officers: President, George Herzog; vice-president, Frederick Derr; secretary, George Weihe; treasurer, Matthew Balduff. The society is in a prosperous condition, although having but 29 members upon the rolls. Their hall is in the upper story of the Reynolds block, on Main street, and the regular meetings are held on the first and third Thursday evenings of each month. The officers for 1879 are: Michael Frey, president; Albert Kreimann, vice-president; Frederick Harder, recording secretary; Christian Duwel, financial secretary; Frederick Trummel, treasurer; Ludwig Kreimann, janitor; Henry Radder, Ludwig Dohse and Johann Reusch, trustees of the society.

ODD FELLOWS.

Citizens' Lodge, No. 309, I. O. of O. F. was instituted February 27th, 1872, by A. F. Lawrence, D. D. G. M., with the following charter members: David Kilpatrick, A. T. Godfrey, W. N. Barrows, L. B. Stanley, J. Godfrey, C. J. Gardner, I. O. Williams, G. B. Smith, E. H. Fillmore, M. A. Phelps and R. McCaw.

The following officers of the lodge were on the same evening installed: David Kirkpatrick, N. G.; C. J. Gardner, V.G.; L. B. Stanley, recording secretary; W. N. Barrows, P. secretary; A. T. Godfrey, treasurer; I. O. Williams, warder; G. B. Smith, conductor; R. McCaw, O. G.; E. Fay, I. G.; J. H. Loomis, R. S. N. G.; J. Godfrey, L. S. N. G.; H. Matteson, L. S. V. G.

The meetings of the lodge are held in Odd Fellows' Hall, on Market street, on Tuesday evening of each week.

Since the institution of this lodge it has been the parent of two other lodges, viz., one at Varysburgh, in this county, and one at Darien, in Genesee county.

The following persons have served as noble grand of Citizens' Lodge: David Kirkpatrick, C. J. Gardner, I. O. Williams, G. B. Smith, J. G. Dorrance, L. B. Stanley, H. Shilling, L. Chaddock, O. A. Clough, M. T. Hills and R. McCaw.

The following named persons were the officers for 1879: W. McNaught, N. G.; A. A. Ford, V. G.; B. Slater, recording secretary; I. O. Williams, P. secretary; J. G. Dorrance, treasurer; B. T. Ellison, warder; I. H. Toms, conductor; Lewis Chaddock, chaplain; G. B. Smith, R. S. N. G.; J. Q. Bradt, L. S. N. G.; J. V. Williams, R. S. V. G; J. D. Evans, L. S. V. G.; George Goodwin, R. S. S.; Samuel Conklin, R. McCaw, O. G.; M. T. Hills, I. G.

The present membership numbers 67.

ANCIENT ORDER OF UNITED WORKMEN.

Attica Lodge, No. 7, A. O. U. W.—The Ancient Order of United Workmen was established in the village of Attica by the institution of Pioneer Lodge, No. 7, October 30th, 1873, by W. H. Comstock, D. S. M. W. of Northeast, Pennsylvania, with the following officers and members, viz.: L. B. Stanley, P. M. W.; Joseph Wilson, M. W.; John E. Neff, G. F.; John Rodgers, O.; Purdy Rodgers, G.; N. S. Salisbury, receiver; L. C. Squires, recorder; Charles Toms, I. W.; Dr. F. R. Barross, medical examiner, together with W. F. Sanborn and Thomas J. Noblett. The name of the lodge was subsequently changed from Pioneer to Attica. The regular meetings of the lodge are held on alternate Monday evenings, in D. O. H. Hall. This lodge has lost two members by death since its institution, viz., Joseph Wilson and Purdy Rodgers The officers for 1879 were: H. C. Webb, P. M. W.; Charles Morganstern, M. W.; Jacob Welker, G. F.; George Fauth, O.; L. C. Streby, recorder; J. G. Bostwick, F.; C. W. Krauss, receiver; J. Fowler, G.; J. Baur, I. W.; H. Hart, O. W.; Dr. W. B. Gifford, medical examiner.

At present the lodge has a membership of fifty-eight.

D. O. H.

Ewigkeit Lodge, No. 336, D. O. H. was organized by authority of the Grand Lodge of the State of New York, March 16th, 1874, with the following as the original members and officers: Philip Brecheisen, E. B.; Peter Schmidt, G. B.; William Ballsmith, U. B.; Frederick C. Ballsmith, Sekr.; C. W. Krauss, Schatzm.; A. Krauss, R. G. O. B.; Frederick Morganstern, L. G. O. B.; Jacob Dietrich, R. G. U. B.; Christian Harder, L. G. U. B.; Carl Morganstern, F.;

Mathaeus Balduf, A.; Michael Baker, I. W.; Carl Sangbush, A. W. This society is an insurance association, similar to the United Workmen. Meetings are held on the second and fourth Tuesday evenings of each month, in Bostwick Hall, Market street. The present membership numbers thirty.

The officers for 1879 were as follows: Edward Volchens, B. B.; Paul Weber, O. B.; Christian Schroeder, U. B.; F. C. Ballsmith, Sekr.; Jacob Dietrich, R. F.; Charles W. Krauss, Schatzm.; Carl Morganstern, R. G. O. B.; John George,.L. G. O. B.; Lewis Schroeder, R. G. U. B.; William Sangbush, L. G. U. B.; Theodore Weinholz, A.; Carl Sangbush, F.; Joseph Weber, I. W.; John Lang, A. W.

JEFFERSON'S SILVER CORNET BAND.

The Jefferson Cornet Band was organized October 14th, 1876, with eighteen members, viz.: I. E. Jefferson, S. B. Benham, Frank Benham, J. E. Noblett, Michael Baker, Edwin Tanner, John Williams, Philip Balduf, H. T. Bramer, L. Shadbolt, Frank Roberts, Cassius Munger, John Salsbury, Frank Thomas, H. M. Norton, P. Lorish, Frederick Hagan, S. Ryckert. The regular meetings of the band are held on Friday evening of each week, in Music Hall, over Doty's store, on Market street. Their instruments are the most improved, costing the band association over $800. The officers of the band are as follows: Leader, E. S. Benham; musical director, I. E. Jefferson; president and financial agent, I. E. Jefferson; treasurer, L. Shadbolt; secretary, J. E. Noblett.

EMPIRE ORDER OF MUTUAL AID.

Wyoming Lodge, No. 1.—This lodge was instituted April 10th, 1878, by George Sanborn, with the following charter members: H. C. Webb, W. F. Sanborn, O. H. Hopkins, William Balduf, J. G. Bostwick, George Fauth, C. Dauber, J. Welker, Otto Spann, Julius Post, M. D., C. Morganstern, J. F. Lorentz, I. H. Toms and A. Krauss.

At the first election the following, officers were chosen: J. H. Toms, P.; O. H. Hopkins, V. P.; William Balduf, R. S.; Jacob Welker, F. S.; C. Morganstern, T.; J. F. Lorentz, conductor; George Fauth, I. G.; C. Dauber, O. G.; H. C. Webb, chaplain:

This lodge was originally instituted as Wyoming Lodge, No. 114, I. O. W. M., and chartered by the Grand Lodge of the State of Pennsylvania. July 10th, 1878, the Grand Lodge of this State was instituted, and December 11th, 1878, this State was set off from Pennsylvania, paying the assessments for deaths in this State, and the name of the order changed to Empire Order of Mutual Aid. Wyoming became lodge number 1 of the new order. The lodge has twenty members, no deaths having occurred in it since its organization. The following were the officers for 1879: L. C. Stuby, P.; Charles Morganstern, V. P.; William Balduf, R. S.; Ira H. Toms, F. S.; George Fauth, T.; J. Welker, chaplain; C. Dauber, I. and O. G.; T. Eastman, conductor.

CATHOLIC MUTUAL BENEFIT ASSOCIATION.

The C. M. B. A. of Attica was instituted April 9th, 1879. The following is the list of original and present officers of the association, as well as of charter members: President, V. Decot; first vice-president, J. J. Cummings; second, T. Cole; marshal, Dennis McMahon; guard, Patrick Slattrey; recording secretary, Thomas Fitzgerald; assistant secretary, B. Kieley; financial secretary, George B. Smith; treasurer, P. Hanifen; directors—Thomas Cole, Dennis and Daniel McMahon, J. J. Cummings, Timothy O'Neal; business committee—Patrick Murray, James Fitzgerald, Patrick Shehan; financial and auditing committee—J. McMahon, B. Kieley and P. Slattrey.

The meetings of the association are held on Wednesday evening of each week in Volcken's Hall, on Main street.

ATTICA FIRE DEPARTMENT.

WYOMING HOSE COMPANY NO. I.

This company was organized under the general laws as an independent volunteer company, with a charter dated July 26th, 1878, at which time the organization was fully completed, with the following officers and members: F. C. Stevens, president; H. C. Walton, vice-president; C. T. McCord, secretary; L. C. Stuby, treasurer; J. R. Whitlock, foreman; J. E. Chase, first assistant; A. F.'Blauvelt, second assistant; Richard Carrick and Michael Darby, pipemen; William Smith, first assistant; A. H. Hills, second assistant; M. T. Hills, C. Whitman, Charles J. Morganstern, Byron H. Backus, John V. Barross, C. E. Toms, Patrick Daly, William G. Colton, J. C. Williams and Charles McCarthy, privates; F. C. Stevens, L. C. Stuby and C. T. McCord were the trustees from July 26th, 1878, until January 1st, 1879.

The company was fully equipped for service, being furnished with a hose cart and nine hundred feet of hose, costing $1,160. The company is very finely uniformed, and its parlors on Market street fitted up in a style of elegance equal to any outside the large cities, with all the conveniences necessary for such an organization. The hose house is on the corner of Main and Water streets. The present number of members is 22.

The officers for 1879 were as follows: President, F. C. Stevens; vice-president, H. C. Walton; secretary, C. T. McCord; financial secretary, George Goodwin; treasurer, L. C. Stuby; foreman, J. R. Whitlock; first assistant, J. E. Chase; second assistant, D. A. Dennison: pipemen, Richard Carrick and Michael Darby; first and second assistant pipemen, William Smith and A. H. Hills; trustees—one year, William G. Cotton; two years, M. T. Hills; three years, C. Whitman.

RESCUE ENGINE COMPANY NO. 1.

This company was organized March 6th, 1878, with the following named members: E. P. Foss, John G. Herzog, Earl Fay, John Corry, V. Decot, J. F. Lorentz, John Scott, Michael Dauber, G. Wolf, A. G. Krauss, Frederick Balduf, Jacob Dietrich, John Timm, George Mentz, jr., H. P. Gardner, Adam Walter, George Snyder, Bartel Weaver, John J. Cummings, Jacob Algeir, jr., Charles Sinclair, Jacob Taylor, Philip Balduf, R. R. Rykert, James Ryan, John M. Leary, John M. Brecheisen, Jacob Hamling, John Torpy, Thomas Isaacs, W. W. Reynolds, E. Volchens, Paul Glor, Frederick Hagan, Michael Baker, James Weaver, George Goodwin and H. Snyder.

The following were the officers elected at the organization of the company: President, E. S. Foss; vice-president, John J. Cummings; secretary, John G. Herzog; treasurer, Jacob Algeir, jr.; foreman, Earl Fay; 1st assistant foreman, Charles Sinclair; 2nd assistant foreman, John Corry.

This is a volunteer company, fully uniformed and equipped for service. Its "machine" was made by Rumsey, of Seneca Falls, and cost $600. The engine house is on Water street.

The number of members is forty, and the officers are: Foreman, Earl Fay; 1st assistant foreman, John Corry; 2nd assistant foreman, E. Volchens; president, E. S. Foss; vice-president, V. Decot; treasurer, J. Algeir, jr.; secretary, A. G. Krauss.

HOOK AND LADDER COMPANY NO. 1.

This company was organized September 13th, 1877, and on the 20th of the same month a constitution and by-laws were adopted.

The original members were; Samuel Daly, F. D. Pryor, William Parker, B. F. Ellison, Carl Ganter, J. G. Bostwick, I. Whiteson, H. T. Bramer, T. D. Jones, M. J. Balliette, Lewis Benedict, T. R. Andrews, J. E. Noblett, E. B. Wallis, Harry Hall, J. E. Briggs, Paul Ganter, Otto Spann, A. E. Bishop, A. McClellin, John Williams, T. Fitzgerald, A. A. Ford, J. B. Reed, J. D. Evans.

The first officers were: Harry Hall, foreman; T. D. Jones, first assistant foreman; M. J. Balliette, second assistant foreman; Lewis Benedict, president; T. R, Andrews, vice-president; F. D. Pryor, second vice-president; B. F. Ellison, secretary; J. G. Bostwick, treasurer; T. D. Jones, T. R. Andrews and Lewis Benedict, trustees.

This is a volunteer company. Their apparatus has the latest improvements, and cost $650. The carriage-house and parlors of the company are on the corner of Main and Water streets. The number of members is 34. The officers last elected are: Foreman, T. D. Jones; first assistant foreman, J. E. Noblett; second assistant foreman, M. J. Balliette; president, E. B. Skinner; first vice-president, Frank Ellison; second vice-president, William Parker; secretary, V. E. Peckham; financial secretary, J. G. Bostwick; treasurer, J. V.Williams; trustees—Dr. A. S. Cheeseman, T. R. Andrews, Lewis Benedict.

BIOGRAPHICAL.

MRS. NEWTON H. ADAMS was born in Bennington September 14th, 1842, and married Dr. Newton H. Adams, a surgeon in the U. S. navy, then of North Java, October 17th, 1860.

ELBRIDGE AUSTIN was born in Attica in 1837. He has always been a farmer. In 1858 he rented his father's farm, and in 1860 that where he now lives, and bought it in 1863. He was married in 1858 to Bertha, daughter of David and Roxy Filkins, of Attica, who died in 1873. In 1877 he married Kittie, daughter of Isaac Phelps, of Le Roy, Genesee county.

BENJAMIN F. BARNETT was born in Kendall, Orleans county, in 1832. In 1867 he married Sylvia Doty, of Attica, of which place he has been a resident since 1840. He is a farmer and an extensive breeder of merino sheep.

VOLNEY C. BARROSS was born in Lynden, N. Y., in 1811. His father, Calvin Barross, was a native of Massachusetts. He came to Genesee county in 1805, settling at Bushville, where he carded the first wool and dressed the first flax on the Holland Purchase. Mr. Barross learned the clothier's trade, and worked at it till 1845, when he engaged in the milling business at Lynden. In 1855 he came to Attica, and continued the same occupation. He married Elvira Richards, daughter of the first judge of Wyoming county; she died in 1852. Mr. Barross's present wife was Ann, daughter of William Lock, of Attica.

CHARLES L. BEMAN was born at Attica February 10th, 1827. He enlisted August 20th, 1861, in Company C, 1st regiment California cavalry volunteers, and served until discharged on the Rio Grande, in New Mexico, September 7th, 1864. He was long a well known railroad man; is now a farmer.

JOHN BELDEN was born in Alexander, N. Y., in 1819, and came to Attica in 1850, establishing himself in the lumber and coal business in 1857, under the firm name of J. Belden & Co. Previous to that time he was in the grocery trade. He has served as U. S. deputy assessor. His father, Kellogg Belden, was a native of Connecticut. His mother's maiden name was McNeil.

HON. C. B. BENEDICT was born in Attica in 1828. He was five years a member of the county board of supervisors; was elected to the 45th Congress in 1874; was a member of the Democratic State committee in 1875, and was a Presidential elector on the Democratic ticket in 1876. He read law, and was admitted to the bar in 1856. In 1860 he engaged in the banking business, in which he continues. His son Lewis was made a member of the firm of C. B. Benedict A Son in 1874.

GEORGE BENHAM was born July 24th, 1811, in Cheshire, Conn., and came to Attica in September, 1815. He is a well known farmer, and has served as assessor and commissioner of highways. He was married November 19th, 1840, to Eliza Ann Bentley, of Attica, and October 12th, 1878, to Ellen H. Spink, of Orangeville.

A. E. BISHOP was born in 1850 in Warsaw, and came from there to Attica in 1875. December 1st of that year he established the *Attica News*. His father, Benjamin Bishop, a native of New Hampshire, was a settler at Warsaw in 1824. His mother, whose maiden name was Lydia Wakefield, was a native of the county.

J. Q. BRADT was born in Genesee county in 1847. He began the practice of dentistry in Buffalo, where for seven years he was a manufacturer of dental materials. In 1877 he established himself in his profession at Attica. His father, Isaac Bradt, and his mother, formerly Miss Becker, were both natives of Schenectady.

EPHRAIM BRAINARD was born February 9th, 1812, at Attica. He is a farmer, and has served as justice of the peace, and school commissioner and superintendent. He married Sophia Wright, of Middlebury, February 19th, 1839.

JASPER J. BRAINARD was born in Attica November 21st, 1836. He was married January 29th, 1868, to Marion M. Page, of Middlebury. He is a farmer and an extensive breeder of American merino sheep.

PHILIP BRECHEISEN was born March 20th, 1838, in Lemboch Unter Elsses (then France), Germany, and came to Attica in 1847, where he is proprietor of a grocery and crockery store. April 17th, 1855, he married Barbara Baker, of Sheldon.

RUFUS BRIGGS was born in Tivoli, Columbia county, December 19th, 1820. October 3d, 1844, he entered the U. S. marine corps, and was discharged October 3d, 1848. He had previously served from June 5th, 1839, to June 5th, 1844, in the 2nd U. S. dragoons. In 1849 he married Caroline Stevens, of Attica. He is a carpenter and joiner by trade.

JOSEPH H. BUTTON, son of Joseph and Salina Button, was born in Sheldon February 14th, 1843, and came to Attica in 1849. Joseph Button was born in Montague, Mass., April 10th, 1806, and died in Attica, N. Y., May 6th, 1879, aged seventy-three years. His early life was spent in the New England cotton factories, where his parents found employment. After his marriage with Salina Adams, April 23d, 1886, he came to western New York and settled in Sheldon. Soon afterward his parents with their entire family followed, and found homes in the vicinity. For the last thirty yean of his life his home was in Attica. Salina Adams Button was born in the town of Brookfield, Mass., November 28d, 1809, and died in Attica, N.Y., October 25th, 1878, aged nearly sixty-nine years. She was descended from Puritan stock, and was one of the Adams family that gave to the United States two Presidents. Mr. and Mrs. Button were married at Brookfield, Mass., April 23d, 1828.

A. S. CHEESEMAN was born in Shelby, N. Y., in 1839. He learned dentistry with Dr. Homer Belding, of Medina, and began to practice in 1860 at East Aurora, Erie county. He removed to Angola, and from there to Attica in 1876. He married Miss Emily Edwards, of Aurora. His father, John Cheeseman, was a native of Schoharie county. His mother's maiden name was Sherwood.

MRS. MOSES P. COGSWELL was born in Buffalo October 14th, 1839, and was married to her deceased husband, then of Brockport, N. Y. October 14th, 1858, and came to Attica in 1864. Mr. Cogswell was killed in the Ashtabula disaster, December 29th, 1876.

PATIENCE COLLINS was born at Exeter, Otsego county, September 28th, 1805, and married Lewis Collins, of Middlebury, June 17th, 1829. She came to Attica in 1867, and is engaged in farming.

HIRAM COOLEY was born in Paris, Oneida county, October 28th, 1808, and came from there to Attica February 28th, 1811. Mr. Cooley is a farmer; he was one of the directors of the Buffalo & New York City Railroad, and acted as a commissioner in settling for the right of way for that road. His first wife, Mrs. B. A. Cooley, was born September 4th,

1811, and died May 16th, 1836. Mrs. Amy H. Housford, who became his second wife, was born February 13th, 1815, and died November 11th, 1878.

ORIN DAVIS, SEN., proprietor and physician of Davis's Health Institute, Attica, was born in York, Livingston county, June 28th, 1823, and was married August 16th, 1848, to Miss Ruth Edson Goddard, of Mt. Morris, Livingston county. He was formerly editor of the *Eclectic Medical and Surgical Journal*, Rochester, N. Y., and professor in the Central Medical College at that place. He came to Attica in 1854.

VAL DECOT was born in Lorraine, France, and was married May 28th, 1878, to Annie B. Clark, of Batavia, Genesee county. He came October 2nd, 1876, from Huntsville, Alabama, to Attica, where he is engaged in business as a merchant tailor.

D. A. DENISON was born at Dodge's Creek, N. Y., in 1850. He came to Attica from Cattaraugus county in 1877, and took charge of the Argus, afterward purchasing the interest of the former proprietor. His father, William A. Denison, was a native of Erie county, as was his mother, whose maiden name was Hicks. Mr. Denison married Miss Emma D. King, a native of Attica.

JAMES G. DORRANCE was born in Attica in 1844, and has since resided there. The drug business of Dorrance & Son was established by Gardner Dorrance in 1843, when he came to Wyoming county. James G. Dorrance was admitted to the firm in 1868. Mr. Dorrance, sen., who was a native of Windsor, Mass., died in Attica in 1874. His wife, whose maiden name was Lee, was a native of Connecticut.

BENJAMIN F. DOTY was born in Bennington, Genesee county, May 17th, 1828, and married Louise Innes, of Batavia, in 1852. He is a clothier.

GEORGE S. DREW was born November 26th, 1831, at Ossipee. N. H., and came to Attica, where he is well known as a coal dealer, from Wakefield, N. Y., in 1860. December 31st, 1862, he married Eveleen A. Churchill, of Attica.

A. G. ELLINWOOD, M. D., was born July 1st, 1834, at Clinton, Oneida county. He entered the medical college at Geneva, N. Y., in 1847, and the Buffalo Medical College in 1848, graduating from that institution the same year. March 15th, 1855, he married Alotta Maria Bass, of Randolph, Mass., and came from Pembroke to Attica in 1862.

MOULTON G. FARNHAM was born August 30th, 1829, at Attica. His father, of the same name, was a native of Shaftesbury, Vt., one of the early settlers at Attica. His mother was formerly of Canton, Conn., and her maiden name was Humphries. Mr. Farnham is extensively engaged in brewing. November 7th, 1861, he married Jennie M. Foster, of Antwerp, N. Y.

R. H. FARNHAM, a brother of the above named, and like him a brewer (their business having been established in 1878), was also born in Attica, in 1827. He served as justice of the peace in 1855–56.

MICHARL FREY, florist, was born September 29th, 1831, in Baden, Germany, his native town being Doggengan. He married Kate Kromer, of Koppel, Baden, February 17th, 1855, and came to Attica from Connecticut in 1856.

GEORGE FULLINGTON was born in Fulton, Schoharie county, April 23d, 1828. He enlisted in the "band of pioneers," the 104th regiment, 28th brigade, N. Y. infantry, September 1st, 1845, but was not called into active service during the Mexican war.

He is a farmer and carpenter and joiner. March 9th, 1851, he married Deborah M. Jillson, of Attica, where he has resided since December 7th of the previous year. Jeremiah and Lydia Jillson, parents of Mrs. Fullington, were born in Albany county, May 22nd, 1804, and April 2nd, 1806, respectively, and died February 2nd, 1872, and April 11th, 1861.

ADOLPHAS GARDENER, son of Adolphas and Mehitable Gardner, was born in Attica, February 12th, 1827; lived at home until he was twenty; boated on the Erie Canal 1849–53; went to California in 1854, and remained there twenty years, mining and driving stage, and returned to Attica in 1873 and purchased the farm where he lives.

HENRY P. GARDENER, deputy sheriff of Wyoming county, was born August 15th, 1851, in this town, and married Cora A. Perry, of Linden, N. Y. December 4th, 1872.

FREDERICK GLOR was born December 6th, 1843, at Orangeville, and came to Attica in 1860, where he has been engaged as a carpenter and joiner. December 31st, 1863, he married Caroline Broadbrooks, of Attica, Both are members of the German Lutheran church.

EVAN G. GRIFFITH was born November 4th, 1836, in Steuben, Oneida county, and came to Attica March 1st, 1850. August 4th, 1862, he enlisted in Company C, 1st N. Y. Dragoons, under Captain Taylor, and served until discharged, July 14th, 1865. March 20th, 1866, he married Harriet C. Smith, of Attica. He is a farmer.

CARL GAUTER was born in Burrentahl, Germany, September 3d, 1848, and came to America with his parents in 1850. After remaining in New York six months they removed to Bennington, and from there to Attica in 1851. Mr. Andrew Gauter, father of Carl, is dead. The latter is engaged in the boot and shoe trade. January 7th, 1879, he married Joanna R. Shea, of Attica.

JACOB HARNLING was born June 22nd, 1810, in Bavaria, and was married June 14th, 1836, to Rosina Elsenrish, of Wisenburg, France, who died July 9th, 1868. He came to America, and in 1850 purchased a mill at Varysburg, which was carried away by a flood in 1851. He subsequently removed to Attica, where he is a hotel keeper.

MARTIN T. HILLS was born in Buffalo in 1848. He came to Attica in 1856. He is a well known photographer.

OLIVER HODGES, ESQ., who died on the 19th day of June, 1878, came as early as 1805, in company with his parents, when he was only seven years old, to the town of Attica. His father, Eliphalet Hodges, located on the farm where his grandson, Garey, now resides, and the land has always remained in the title of his father since the decease of his grandparents. When Oliver Hodges came to this town there were only a few pioneer settlers, who had raised three or four log cabins. Hardly any clearings had been made, nor any better roads laid out than footpaths through the woods, between the settlers' dwellings. He assisted in clearing the land to which he was heir, became accustomed to hard labor, and identified himself with the growth and business prosperity of the town. When eleven years of age he carried the mail regularly between Attica and Batavia, making the journey on horseback, sometimes requiring his horse to leap over the trees that had fallen across his pathway. He was at home on horseback from childhood. In the days when men were arrested and imprisoned for debt he was constable and collector of this town, and his duties, if not always pleasant, were at least full of excitement. His business habits were such that he was repeatedly appointed deputy sheriff of Genesee county when this part of Wyoming belonged to Genesee. The older inhabitants can recollect the capture of the notorious counterfeiter Law, of his being brought to trial and the murderous assault he made in the court room upon an accomplice, Topliff, who testified against him. It is believed he would have accomplished his purpose if ho had not been forcibly prevented. Mr. Hodges and Rue Nelson walked from Brierfield, Mass., to Attica in eight days, a pretty good illustration of the active habits of the young men in those times. Afterward Mr. Hodges used to draw dry goods and groceries from Albany to Attica for $3.25 per hundred. He took a seasonable amount of interest in town politics, and was a Whig until the organization of the Republican party. He was considered a man of excellent judgment, a good citisen, a kind neighbor and pleasant in his social relations.

MRS. OLIVER HODGES was born in Middlebury in 1818, and married Oliver Hodges, of Attica, in October, 1851. Mr. Hodges died June 19th, 1978, and was buried in the Attica Cemetery. He had held the offices of deputy sheriff and supervisor.

NORMAN L. KNOX was born January 25th, 1820, at East Granby, Conn., and was married March 18th, 1840, to Lucinda Childs, of Pembroke, N. Y., where he had removed from Connecticut in August, 1839. He has been a resident of Attica since 1844. He is a farmer and by trade a cooper. At the age of nineteen he was elected lieutenant of a militia company at East Granby, Conn.

ANDRBW KRAUSS was born October 22nd, 1829, at Altlussheim, Baden, Germany, and came from his native land in 1849 to Attica, where he is engaged in the sale of clothing, boots and shoes, hats and caps and gentlemen's furnishing goods generally. September 2nd, 1851, he married Magdalena Foote, formerly of Postdorf, Alsace, France.

CARMI V. LINDSEY, son of Kilian and Eleanor Lindsey, was born in Attica November 24th, 1881, on the farm where he lives; remained at home until twenty-two; taught school three years; in 1854 bought a saw-mill in the southwest part of the town; in 1861 moved to the family homestead and worked the farm on shares; in 1865 built a cheese factory, and managed it four years; in 1869 bought the homestead. He married Lovlca, daughter of Henry and Lydia Smith, of Middlebury, March 20th, 1859.

KILLAB LINDSEY was born in Warren County, N. Y., April 30th, 1783; settled in Attica in 1822, and died June 18th, 1876, at the age of eighty-nine. He was married January 15th, 1807, to Eleanor Loop, who died April 15th, 1869, at the age of eighty-two. Martin Lindsey, son of the above and brother of Carmi V. Lindsey, was born in Warren county, March 3d, 1821. He is a farmer and has held the office of assessor. He married Lovina Smith, daughter of Henry and Lydia Smith, of Middlebury, January 31st, 1844.

WILLIAM LINDSEY, brother of Carmi and Martin, was born in Attica January 18th, 1828; lived at home until he was twenty-six; in 1849 removed to Genesee county; in 1856 bought the farm where he has since lived, and was married to Harriet, daughter of Alpheus and Lydia Holcomb, of Java, in 1859.

JOHN M. LEARY was born March 27th, 1852, in Bennington, Vt. He lived in Massachusetts, and came from Northampton, in that State, to Attica in 1875. He is a painter and paper hanger, and is connected with Reserve Engine Company, No. 1. He was married January 5th, 1879, to Sophia A. King, of Attica.

HON. J. H. LOOMIS was born in Attica in 1823. His father, and his mother, whose maiden name was Collar, were natives of Connecticut. They came to Attica in 1816. The former died in 1841, the latter in 1823, while the subject of this sketch was an infant. Hon. J. H. Loomis established himself in the banking business in Attica in 1867. He has served the town as assessor, and was elected State Senator in 1877.

JULIANA LUBBA was born in France October 28th, 1820, and married Frederick Lubba, of Batavia, Genesee county, October 29th, 1839. She came to Attica in 1835 and is engaged in farming.

CAPTAIN EDWIN S. MCINTYRE was born in Elba, Genesee county, where his father was a pioneer, in 1816, and removed with his parents to Attica in 1825. He subsequently lived in Careyville and Alexander, Genesee county, and returned to Attica in 1860, in which year he married Mrs. Maryetta Royce, widow of Harmon Royce, of Alexander. He is a farmer and the owner of eighty-six acres. He was appointed captain of militia by Governor Washington Hunt, and held the office five years. He is a painter by trade. His father, Captain Moses C. McIntyre, was born in Charlton, Mass., and died in Attica at the age of seventy-two, in 1861.

MRS. ELIZA B. MCLEOD was born March 4th, 1817, in Williamsville, Erie county, and married Ronald McLeod, of St. Lawrence county. She removed to Attica from Mackinaw in 1871, and is engaged in farming.

GORGE MANTZ, hotel keeper, was born in Attica April 8th, 1858, and married Kate M. Shafer, of that place, January 8th, 1880. He is the proprietor of a bakery.

GEORGE D. MILLER was born at Wallkill, Orange county, October 28th, 1828, and came to Attica in 1838. He has been roadmaster on the Buffalo division of the N. Y., L. E. and W. R. R. ten years, and has served as commissioner of highways three years. He married Mary A. Wilson, of Attica, September 3d, 1874.

DAVID (son of Henry and Elinor) NESBITT was born in Gaines, Orleans county, in 1834, and soon afterward removed with his parents to Attica. He was married in 1862 to Jane E., daughter of Asher and Ann Kinney, of Warsaw. Mr. Nesbitt is a farmer and dairyman.

HENRY NESBITT, father of David Nesbitt, was born in County Cavan, Ireland, in 1808. He came to America in 1820, worked by the month in Washington county for a time, and remained there till 1830; removed to Gaines, Orleans county. In 1834 he located in Attica, where he has since lived. In 1831 he married Miss Elinor Smith, of Washington county, who died in 1862. In 1863 he married Miss Sally Underwood, of Attica, his present wife. Mr. Nesbitt has always been frugal and industrious. Two of his sons are graduates of the Buffalo Medical College.

A. E. NICHOLS, son of Edwin A. and Mary R. Nichols, was born in Attica October 17th, 1851. Edwin A. Nichols was born in Attica July 10th, 1833. September 6th, 1862, he enlisted in Company G, 160th regiment N. Y. volunteers, and died at University Hospital, New Orleans, La., December 17th, 1863. Mrs. Nichols was born in Wheatland, Monroe county, September 5th, 1831.

JOHN E. NOBLETT was born in Hackettstown, Ireland, February 26th, 1847. In October, 1868, he came to Attica, where he has been engaged in business as a liquor dealer and builder, and has held the offices of collector, police constable and excise commissioner. He was married December 8th, 1869, to Anna C. Kaiser, of Attica.

NOAH NORTH was born at Alexander, Genesee county, June 27th, 1809. June 6th, 1841, he married Ann C. Williams; she died June 12th, 1872. January 19th, 1876, Mr. North married Caroline Gibson. Both of these ladles were residents of Darien, Genesee county. From that place Mr. North came, May 24th, 1889, to Attica, where he has been employed as farmer, manufaofacturer of lumber, painter and teacher, and has served on the board of education. He was justice of the peace in Darien ten years.

SEYMOUR NORTON was born March 11th, 1785, in Southerton, Hartford county, Conn. In 1810 he married Miss Anna Clark, and soon afterward removed to Greene county. In 1813 he visited western New York, and settled Bennington in 1814. In 1854 he came to Attica and resided wtth his daughter, Miss M. A. Norton, until his death, May 6th, 1874. His wife died in 1867.

OWEN OWENS was born December 25th, 1827, in Wales. He came to Attica from Utica in 1863. He was married March 2nd, 1860, to Mary Meredith, a native of North Wales. He is a farmer.

HENRY PALMER was born March 16th, 1811, at Maryland, Otsego county. He was married June 1st, 1831, to Marsha McKnight, of Batavia, Genesee county, and again in February, 1857, to Abigail Hendrick, of Henrietta, Monroe county. He come to Attica in 1888, and is a boot and shoe maker.

JOHN PORTER was born in County Cavan, Ireland, August 14th, 1828. April 4th, 1852, he married Mary Scally, of Butternuts, Otsego county. He is a farmer. He came to Attica from Tompkins, Delaware county, in 1862.

MRS. HARRIET PRIME was born August 8th, 1819, at Paris, Oneida county, and came to Attica in 1824. June 14th, 1846, she married Joseph Prime, who lived near Philadelphia, Pa.

NELSON REYNOLDS was born May 19th, 1814, in Bethany, Genesee county. He became a resident of Attica in 1856, and has served three years as assessor and five years as highway commissioner. He married Harriet Wales, of Attica, May 23d, 1842.

AARON RICHARDSON was born in Cheshire, Berkshire county. Mass., August 15th, 1804. October 18th, 1827, he married Deidamia C. Whipple, of his native place. In 1834 he removed, with his family, to Trenton, Oneida county, and from there to Attica in 1818. He is a carpenter and joiner by trade, and has served as assessor one term. His father and mother, Rufus and Wally Richardson, were born in Massachusetts, where the former died.

R. J. ROGERS was born in Lime, Conn., in 1829. Ezekiel Rogers, his father, and his mother, whose maiden name was Mary Beckworth, were both natives of Connecticut. Mr. Rogers embarked in the drug trade at Lewiston, Niagara county, in 1860; from there he removed to Niles, Mich., and from Niles to Attica in 1860. He married a daughter of Asa Bishop, M. D., of Oneida county. He has been master of his masonic lodge.

JAMBS SANBORN, son of Warren and Amanda Sanbora, was born in Attica, March 23d, 1860. In 1870 he enlisted at Buffalo in Company G, 8th regiment, U. S. infantry, and joined his regiment in New York that fall and remained there one year; he went to Chicago and from there at the end of six months to Fort Russell, Wyoming Territory, thence to Utah and Arizona. He was promoted to the tank of corporal and afterward to that of sergeant, and was honorably discharged at Camp Lowell, Arizona, in 1876. He is now engaged in railroading.

WARREN F. SANBORN was born at Attica in 1831, and was married to Miss Ellen Norton, of Linden, Genesee county, in 1859. He was a member of the State militia, and was early in the war of the Rebellion, going to Harrisburg, Pa., in 1861. His father, Warren Sanford, was a native of New Hampshire, who came to Wyoming county when a small boy, with his parents, locating in Attica. He was married in 1830 to Miss Amanda M. Eastman. He worked at the cooper's trade until 1840, and from that date until 1876, the year of his death, was engaged in the grocery business.

MRS. MARYETTE SCOVILLE was born September 27th, 1825, at Attica. She married Armenius B. Scoville, of that place, December 10th, 1846.

WHITNEY D. SCOVILLE, son of Ebenezer and Abigail Scoville, was born in Attica in 1818, and married Elizabeth Chambers in 1851. She was a native of Scotland, and came to America in 1842. Mr. Scoville has always lived in the town until the spring of 1879, excepting seven years spent in Wheatland, Monroe county. He commenced life a poor boy, but by perseverance and industry has accumulated a handsome property, and is now one of the most extensive farmers in the town.

MRS. HANNAH SHELDON, widow of Horace Sheldon, of Attica, who died in 1885, was born in Coshocton county, O., in 1832, and was married in 1859; she had one son. She came to this State from Indiana in 1852, and is making and dealing in all kinds of hair work, puffs, curls and switches.

HENRY SIERK was born in Holstein, Germany, December 27th, 1823, and married Elsabe Oldschwager, of his native place, February 8th, 1858, and during the same year came to Attica. He is a farmer, miller and dealer in flour and feed.

A. A. SMITH was born in Manchester, Mass., July 17th, 1839, and has been a resident of Attica since the spring of 1866. He served as supervisor of the town of Attica in 1876, and as president of the village board of trustees 1877–79. He was married September 10th, 1867, to Mary K. Kelham.

HARRY W. SMITH was born October 9th, 1817, in Attica, and married Eliza Austin, of that place, in the spring of 1847. Mr. Smith is a farmer. He has served as commissioner of highways. Mrs. Smith was born January 17th, 1828, and died October 18th, 1882. Elisha Smith, Harry W. Smith's father, was born March 24th, 1787, and came to Attica in 1818. He died June 19th, 1869. His wife, Amy B. Smith, was born February 8d, 1798, and died November 12th, 1885. They were married November 19th, 1816.

LUTHER STANHOPE, drayman and expressman and mail messenger, was born at Attica June 10th, 1810, and married Sibyl Davis, of Attica, October 20th, 1831.

MRS. VALLONIA RICHARDS GARRETSEE TANNER was born in Milton, Saratoga county, N. Y., March 17th. 1797. She was married to Garretsee, of Schenectady, a soldier of 1812, March 25th, 1815, and to Captain William Tanner December 5th, 1831, her first husband having died February 10th, 1821. She came to Attica in 1830, from Salina,

N. Y. Captain Tanner was a postmaster several years, and held other offices. He was an early settler in Orangeville, and came from there to Attica Center, where he died in 1868.

C. S. THOMPSON was born in Le Roy, Genesee county, in 1823. At the age of eleven he went to Lockport, Niagara county, and remained there until he was twenty; removed to Monroe county, and from there in 1846 to Attica. He was of the firm of Thompson & Loomis, bankers, and has been in the milling business since 1876. He married Sarah A., daughter of Isaac Fargo, of Stafford, N. Y. His father, Hazel Thompson, a Scotchman by nativity, came early in life to America, and died in 1826.

DANIEL THOMSON was born in Trenton, Oneida county, March 31st, 1810, and was married January 20th, 1837, to Acheah W. Burlingame, of his native town. They came to Attica in the fall of 1837. Mr. Thomson, who is a gardener and manages a farm near the Centre, is a man noted for his benevolence, and his many benefactions, in which his wife has participated. May 16th, 1874, they deeded a house and lot, valued at $1,400, to the Central Association, a benevolent society, for church extension, education and home and foreign missions; and on the 23d of the same month Mrs. Thomson, with the consent of Mr. Thomson, gave the same association $1,000 to help endow a David Marks professorship in Hillsdale, Michigan. On these amounts they are to receive interest during their natural lives.

EDWARD D. TOLLES, hardware dealer at Attica, was born in Bennington February 20th, 1841, and was married April 22nd, 1865, to Josephine B. Brainard, of Attica. During the civil war he was first lieutenant of Company F, 5th N. Y. cavalry.

FREDRICK TRUMMEL was born in Prussia August 16th, 1834, and came to Atticn, where he is engaged in the manufacture and sale of furniture and coffins, from Buffalo in 1853. October 11th, 1859, he married Kate Ganglaff, of Town Line, Erie county.

ALEXANDER H. VAN BUREN, son of Bernard and Barbara Wood Van Buren, was born at South Trenton, Oneida county, N. Y., November 14th, 1814. In childhood he was adopted by Ebenezer and Phebe Lewis, of Gorham, Ontario county, and he lived there most of the time till he was twenty-five. He then lived at Canandaigua five years and a half, in Aurora, Erie county, six months, in Wales, Erie county, three years, and in Orangeville until May 2nd, 1876, when he came to the village of Attica. At Gorham, September 30th, 1838, he married Nancy Wilson. She died at Attica July 30th, 1875, and on the 3d of September, 1876, Mr. Van Buren married Sarah B. Royce, of Attica, who was born in Moravia, N. Y., December 28th, 1822. He has been a trustee of the M. E. church since the autumn of 1866, and president of the board.

WILLIAM WALBRIDGE, farmer, was born in Attica in 1812, and married Lois Lindsey in 1833. In the military he has held all of the offices from 4th corporal to lieutenant-colonel, and he has served seven years as supervisor, three years as highway commissioner and three years as assessor.

CHARLES WEBER was born in Nassau, Germany, in 1817, and was married to Miss Catharine Hardt, of that place in 1842. They came to America in 1845, and located in Warsaw. Afterward they lived in Middlebury, and came to Attica in 1865. Mr. Weber, who spent eighteen years of his life in the coal and iron mines of Germany, owns a fine farm of two hundred and sixty-one and a half acres, the result of frugality and industry.

RESIDENCE OF HON. JAMES H. LOOMIS, PROSPECT ST., ATTICA, N.Y.

INTERIOR VIEW OF THE LOG CABIN, SILVER LAKE.

SUGAR LOAF ROCK, BELOW PORTAGE.

INTERIOR OF THE OLD INDIAN COUNCIL HOUSE, GLEN IRIS.

William Wilder was born in Madison, N. Y., April 7th, 1816; came from there to Attica in 1826, and is well known as a contractor and builder. January 26th, 1841, he married Adeline M. Seeney, of Canandaigua.

J. O. Williams was born in Attica February 24th, 1845, and is a tanner by occupation. He was married to Emma B. Doty, of Attica, September 27th, 1871. He has served as justice of the peace, and three years as village trustee.

Lebanah Winchester was born at Westmoreland, Chester county, N. H., April 10th, 1796. In 1802 he removed to Marcellus, Onondaga county, with his parents; in 1820 to Batavia, Genesee county; to Orangeville, Genesee county, in 1825, and to Attica in 1847. In 1818 he was married to Miss E. Campbell, a native of Bainbridge, Chenango county, who, with her parents, was living in Marcellus. While a resident of Orangeville, Genesee county, Mr. Winchester served as highway commissioner two years, school commissioner two years, justice of the peace sixteen years and supervisor two years; and he has been for two years assessor of the town of Attica.

THE TOWN OF BENNINGTON.

THIS is the northeast corner town of the county, and contains 33,900 acres. The area of improved land is greater than in any other town in the county, it being 26,149 acres. The cash value of farms in 1875 was $1,322,081, and of farm buildings other than dwellings $149,760. The gross sales from farms in that year were $126,113. The stock on the farms was valued at $201,359. There were 11,997 acres in pasture, and 7,450 acres of meadow land; 2,251 cows were kept, from which was made in families 85,212 pounds of butter and 33,347 pounds of cheese, besides 8,522 gallons of milk sold in market. There were produced 8,865 tons of hay and 3,323 bushels of barley; 20,144 bushels of corn, 55,203 bushels of oats, 3,728 bushels of spring and 5,215 bushels of winter wheat, 56,302 bushels of potatoes, 35,871 bushels of apples and 31,460 pounds of maple sugar. The value of poultry sold was $2,350, and of eggs $3,290. There were 1,576 sheep kept, which produced 7,786 pounds of wool. There were 672 swine slaughtered, which made 162,744 pounds of pork.

The following is an exhibit of the earlier purchases of land from the Holland Company in this town, with the names of purchasers, as entered in the company's records:

John Tolles, 1808, lots 2, 4 and 6, section 3; Jacob Wright, 1806, parts of lots 8, 10 and 12, section 3; John Jones, 1804, lots 1, 3 and 5, section 4; Jabish Warren, 1806, lots 2, 4 and 6, section 5; Almond C. Laire, 1804, parts of lots 1, 3 and 5, section 7, also parts of lots 7, 9 and 11, section 7; Asa Jones, 1804; lots 7, 9 and 11, section 4; Ebenezer Smith, 1804, lots 1, 3 and 5, section 3; Joseph Browning, 1804, parts of lots 2, 4 and 6, section 6; Jacob Wright, 1806, lot 7 and part of lot 9, section 3; Job Mattson, 1805, lots 1, 3 and 5, section 5; Daniel Root, second, 1808, part of lots 11 and 12 section 3; Stephen Wickham, 1806, parts of lots 9 and 11, section 3; William Adams, 1805, lots 8, 10 and 12, section 5; John Toles, 1806, parts of lots 8, 10 and 12, section 3; Almond C. Laire, 1805, lots 2, 4 and 6, section 7; Joseph Bromagham, 1806, parts of lots 1, 3 and 5, section 1; Bartholomew Armstrong, 1805, lots 1, 3 and 5, section 6, also lot 5 and part of lot 6, section 8, also lot 1 and part of lot 3, section 8; Daniel Watkins, 1805, parts of lots 7, 9 and 11, section 7; Chauncey and Justice Loomis, 1806, lots 1–8, section 11; Joseph Browning, 1804, parts of lots 2, 4 and 6, section 8, and parts of lots 1, 3 and 5 section 7; David Ward, 1806, lot 5, section 9; Ichabod Smith, 1804, parts of lots 2, 4 and 6, section 6; Aaron Whitney, 1805, lots 8, 10 and 12, section 7; R. Newell, 1810, parts of lots 2, 4 and 6, section 4; Joel Maxon, 1810, lot 9, section 1; Joshua Lamphier, 1810, parts of lots 7, 9 and 11, section 5; John Green, 1810, parts of lots 7, 9 and 11, section 5; John Jones, 1809, lot 11, section 1; Chauncey and Justice Loomis, 1806, lots 1–9, 13, 21, 23, 29 (5,820 24–100 acres).

PIONEER TIMES.

John Tolles, of the town of Orwell, Vt., in the spring of 1802, with no other outfit than a system inured to labor, an indomitable will, a few necessary articles of apparel, and the means of locomotion furnished by nature, started from his boyhood home, to carve out for himself a home in the far West. He fell in with Jacob Wright at the great bend of the Tonawanda, now Batavia. The latter was also from one of the Eastern States, and a "land looker," as the pioneers were termed. They pursued their journey together, and located in the northeast corner of the present town of Bennington. They were the first settlers of this town.

After looking about a little they built two rude cabins about half a mile apart, covered them with bark, which was a good protection from the storm, and with a fire built outside and burning brightly, they were able to sleep soundly, notwithstanding the howl of the wolf and the occasional scream of the panther. The country was at that time an unbroken wilderness, where no foot but that of the red man had ever trod, excepting the surveyor, who was then in the woods. After building their log cabins the settlers cleared three or four acres of land, and sowed it to wheat, after which they returned to the East for their families. They arrived again at their new homes in February, 1803, and found that another settler had located his family on a part of the same quarter section, and had a good fire burning in his new log cabin to welcome his neighbors to their forest home.

During the summer of 1803 several other persons made a "pitch," as it was familiarly called, in the vicinity of the first settlers, and now commenced the work of opening the forest, the axman plying his ax, the sturdy monarchs of the forest giving way, permitting the sun to shine where it had not for centuries before, and the cereals and esculent plants taking the place of the leek and the brake. The wild animals that gave way before the advancing pioneer were the deer, bear, wolf, panther, fox, wildcat and a large family of squirrels, while the streams were inhabited by the otter, mink and muskrat.

When the first wheat was harvested a "threshing floor" was made by splitting and evening the surface of some basswood logs, and placing them side by side and as close as possible. There was no roof over this floor, for it was usually made near the wheat field, and could be removed to another field when required. The threshing was done with a flail. The winnowing was done in the primitive way of dropping the grain from a platform through a natural current of air. Then, with an ox-team, the grain would be carried twenty miles, to the mill at Buttermilk fall, now Leroy, to be ground; and as some time would elapse before the return of the grist, and provisions got rather short, the good housewife would resort to boiling wheat to satisfy the demands of the hungry juveniles, thus preparing an article of food not much inferior to boiled rice. When the corn crop was harvested, which had been raised among the logs, each settler provided himself with a mortar, which was made by hollowing to the proper depth a sound log or stump, making a pestle with a round face, and

JACOB CLARK

RESIDENCE OF JACOB CLARK, DECEASED, CASTILE, N.Y.

RESIDENCE OF JONAS CLARK, CASTILE, N.Y.

RESIDENCE OF JOHN B. CLARK, CASTILE, N.Y.

with it pounding the corn into meal. A better pestle, and more easily worked, was made by suspending a pole, with a mallet face at the lower end, from a spring pole overhead. In this way hominy was made, which was to the pioneer a saving of time to mill and a big toll.

At the close of the year 1815 wheat was worth two dollars a bushel in Buffalo. Not having the conveniences of the present day for threshing, the pioneer, when he had a barn floor large enough, would place his wheat on the floor, and drive his horses around on it until the grain was out. In this way one of the pioneers of the town commenced one morning in that winter, and threshed until dark; then, by the light of a tallow candle in an old tin lantern, cleaned up the wheat with an old-fashioned hand fan, fitting it for market, and at sunrise he had forty bushels bagged. He then started with it for Buffalo, made the thirty-five miles before sunset, and sold his wheat for eighty silver dollars. Soon after dark he was on his way home, arriving there at breakfast time, having in forty-eight hours threshed and marketed forty bushels of wheat, without aid other than that of his two trusty horses. This is only a sample of what Bennington pioneers could do.

During the summer of 1803 quite a number of homed cattle were brought into the county. For want of fences, and boys to watch, they were allowed to roam where they pleased and with the browse they found they soon became good beef, without expense to the owner. They were kept during the first two or three winters on browse without much difficulty. Early in the winter of 1804, the snow having become deep, the cattle strayed away in search of food. A company of men started in pursuit, and after much search found them on the Tonawanda, about six miles distant, but too late to get them home that night, or perhaps in a day or two. A crisis had come. The snow was deep, the weather cold, and night at hand. The old flint and steel were produced, for that was the only way of starting a fire in those days. But the flint being well worn, and the hand that held it numb with cold, the "punk" would not ignite, and there was a fair prospect of having to camp over night without fire. The flint and steel were passed to Nathan Clapp, who, after a few abortive attempts, in which he brought them within about six inches of each other, handed them back, with the remark, "I must freeze," and began to shiver and prepare to meet his doom. In warmer hands the flint and steel did better execution, and a fire was soon started, when Nathan concluded to help make a fire for the rest before laying down that mortal coil, and, seizing the ax, plied it dexterously for a few moments, when he was warm enough without a fire. The party slept soundly that night, and reached home the next day with their stock.

In the summer of 1804 several more families or young men came into the town. The settlers began to clear away the forest, and supply themselves with teams, cows, sheep and swine, which were allowed to get their living in the woods. But the bears, wolves, and some other beasts of the forest were very destructive of unprotected domestic animals, and for several years it was necessary to guard the sheep to protect them from the wolves.

It was the special duty of every boy of sufficient age to see that the sheep were yarded at night. When James Tolles was about eight years of age he was going for the sheep one night, when he was pleased to hear the tinkle of the sheep bell and to see the sheep coming toward the yard at great speed; but when they had passed him he was surprised to find them followed by a pack of ravenous wolves, the foremost of which came within a few feet of him, when he halloed with such spirit as to halt them, and succeeded in shutting the sheep safely in the yard. He well remembers the circumstances, and the appearance of the large wolf that led the van, which, after running from him a short distance, turned with a malicious look to view the insignificant object that had thwarted his designs on the sheep.

Bears were also very plenty, and very annoying to the pioneer settlers. Every pig that undertook the hazardous task of sleeping beside an old log was pretty sure to pay the penalty by becoming a feast for Mrs. Bruin and her offspring. The bears committed most of their depredations in the night time, and were seldom or never known to molest mankind. After the county was cultivated the bears became very destructive in the wheat and corn fields. Two young men, who had a crop of wheat ready to gather and were leaving it out to dry a few days, slept in their log barn one night; while there a thunder shower came up, and during the flashes of lightning they could see, through the cracks, the bears pulling down and destroying their stacks of wheat, and helping themselves.

It may be presumed that the howlings from the forest were at first alarming to the women and children. Yet after becoming acquainted with them it was amusing rather than otherwise, while sitting around a blazing wood fire of an evening in a log cabin, to hear the howl of a pack of wolves in as many tones as there were individuals among them, and these answered by a pack in another direction, and then another and perhaps another, until the forest seemed alive with wolves.

In October, 1804, Roswell, son of Mr. and Mrs. John Tolles, was born. This was the first birth in the town, and the second on the Holland Purchase South of Batavia. He grew with the growth of the country, and strengthened with its strength, until he saw the wilderness on which his eyes first opened converted into cornfields and meadows, teeming with the life and cultivation of the husbandman. He moved to Raymond, Racine county, Wis., in 1856, and lived there till his death, April 14th, 1878. His days were filled up with usefulness, and his memory is cherished by all who knew him.

The first death of a white adult in what is now Bennington was that of Amos Tolles, who died in the early part of December, 1805.

"Land lookers" began to come in during the latter part of the winter of 1804 and 1805 and the spring of the latter year, and with them came improvement in almost everything pertaining to the town's welfare. Many settlements were the made, log cabins multiplied in sight of the older ones, and the lowing of the ox and the bleating of the sheep began to be heard in place of the snarling of the bear and the howl of the wolf. The corn field was seeded to grass, and the plow for the first time on the "Purchase" had commenced mellowing the soil, on the farm of Jacob Wright. But the thing dignified by the name of "plow" was but a small advance upon the crotch of a tree. The merry ring of the scythe was also heard in the hay field this summer, for the first time. This was also the year in which Jacob Wright had erected for him the first frame barn in the town. A Mr. Bradway was the boss carpenter. He worked by what was then called the "tumble and scribe rule," as mathematical calculations had not then been applied to barn building. When raising day came nearly every man west of the Genesee river was invited to the raising. The old pioneer barn did good service till 1853, when the incendiary's torch reduced it to a heap of smouldering ruins, it being then owned by Leveret Peck, Esq., who owned the farm on which the next barn was erected, which is still standing.

At the commencement of 1806 there were over twenty families located in this town, and the settlements began to present the appearance of an old place. Several incidents of more or less importance occurred during this year. Early in May a boy was lost in the woods, and he was never found. His father, David Tolles, had cleared a piece of ground and sowed it to wheat that year, and, as was customary at that time, had omitted making fence until spring. A neighbor's cow coming into the wheat while the family were at breakfast, Hiram, a lad six years old, was directed to drive the cow out across the brook, which was not ten rods distant from the house. He did not immediately return, and the family, going about their usual work, forgot the circumstance until after noon. Search was then made among the neighbors without success, but not until the next day was much anxiety felt, when the alarm was spread far and wide, and the whole population for forty or fifty miles around, with true backwoods fraternity, commenced the search. Mr. Ellicott, the land agent, graciously sent provisions on pack horses to supply those in search. The Indians were, by the generosity of Mr. Ellicott and others, stimulated by a large reward to aid in the search. But the country was an unbroken wilderness to the west, the direction in which the boy went. His tracks in wet places were several times discovered. Although the search by the main body was continued for twenty days, it had to be abandoned without success.

In 1806 a tannery was set in full operation, and a shoe shop erected, which supplied boots and shoes to all the south part of the Holland Purchase. A blacksmith shop was also erected, and the settlers, through these few improvements, became quite independent of outside assistance. In the fall and winter neighborhood "bees," including pumpkin-paring bees, huskings, sleighrides (sometimes with a pair of oxen), quiltings and balls were the order of the day among the young folks, and some not so very young and none was known to move to "postpone the general order." In 1805 Rev. Peter B. Root and Rev. Mr. Butler, Baptists, came into this town and held a series of meetings, in which nearly all the adults in the settlement participated. In 1806 the society was connected with that at Attica, under the pastorate of Rev. Mr. Osborn, the first preacher in this part of the Holland Purchase.

In 1806 a singing-school was established, under the care and instruction of Mr. John Van Bogart, a German from the Mohawk country. The schools were held in the old log school-house, near what is now Danley's Corners.

Mr. James Tolles says in regard to early religious efforts in this town:

> "Two Methodist brethren, one by the name of Van Nest, came into the town this year and commenced preaching in the school-house soon after it was built, and organized a society. Rev. Messrs. Mitchell and Gatchell followed Van Nest and preached alternatively on this circuit. An incident in one of the sermons of Mr. Mitchell illustrates the powers of his pioneer preaching. The speaker was illustrating what would be the condition of the lost soul, and the utter inability of escape after once being confined in the great prison-house of despair. He said figuratively that the Lord would come down from the abodes of bliss, and having selected his saints the wicked would be driven away from his presence into the abode of the finally impenitent; that the Lord would shut to the great iron door as it creaked on its massive hinges, and taking a great ponderous key would fast lock the door (turning the key round, working out every supposed action with the gesture of great labor). He would then throw away the key, there to lie and rust during endless ages; and, suiting the gesture to the expression, I just as much expected to see some ponderous key fly from the hands of the speaker as to see the motion of his arm, and so did every one in the house, for every eye was turned in the direction of the motion. Such was the simplicity and force with which he delivered his discourses, that notwithstanding that three-quarters of a century have passed, his remarks and gestures are as vivid to my mind as at the time."

Settlements on the "Purchase" generally, and in Bennington particularly, were retarded by the want of roads. The Holland Company had opened one road from Batavia to the northeast corner of the town, thence southwest and south through the town; that is, had cut down and cleared out the timber about one rod wide, bridged the small streams with logs, and corduroyed some of the bad swamps. When they were not corduroyed they were so badly cut up by travel that it was next to impossible to travel over them. This state of roads lasted only through the wet season of spring and fall, but that was nearly half the year. In 1809 Chauncey Loomis, who had moved in here in 1807, had a road built at his own expense from Bennington Centre directly across the Indian Reservation to Buffalo. But the difficulty of making roads through the forests was very great, and made the passage through the country very slow. There was no market yet for the surplus produce that might be raised, and none was required, as the new arrivals in town took about what surplus crops were raised; yet roads were needed for other purposes than marketing produce of that early day. The Buffalo and Moscow road, which was laid out through the town in 1814 and partially opened, was in 1818 opened through. This gave better facilities, and settlements began rapidly to increase.

The season of 1807 brought several conspicuous events. In this year the first school-house in this town was erected, at what is now known as Danley's Corners, in the northeast part of the town. The first school was taught during the summer of 1807, by Miss Rachael Tunsdale. She was not only the first school teacher in this town, but also the first bride, as she was married during the summer to Aaron Whitney. She was the first teacher and this the first wedding in all this part of the "Purchase." The couple remained in this town, and died at a good old age.

During the summer of 1807 Chauncey Loomis moved into this town, and located at what is now Bennington Centre, where he built a saw-mill the next season. The mill was a little south of the corners, down on the creek, on the east side of the road. The remains of the old dam are still to be seen. He also brought with him a small stock of domestic goods to sell to his neighbors, and opened the first store in this town.

This season orchards began to be set out, and John Tolles planted a nursery of young fruit trees, brought from Charlestown (now Lima), Livingston county, N. Y. Mr. Loomis was accompanied by his mother, she being a widow lady, his brother Justin, several hired men and some others, with a train of wagons carrying the household goods, farming implements, store goods and everything for conducting a large business. They came from Connecticut, and Mrs. Loomis, being a woman of energy, drove her own chaise, a two-wheeled vehicle, the whole distance, not allowing any of the party to assist her in the least by guiding the horse over bad roads or through streams. Mr. Loomis had to cut the road for the last two miles. Here he purchased a large tract of land, paying one dollar per acre, and afterward selling portions of it to his former townsmen, who built log cabins, cleared off patches of the woods, and in a short time this was known as the Loomis settlement.

Pelatiah Case, father of Martin Case, came to this town in 1807 from Windsor, Conn., and located south of the Centre.

The pioneer saw-mill was built in the summer of 1807, by David, Elisha and Henry Hoard, on Cayuga creek, near the south line of the town, on the farm now owned by Pomeroy Warren.

During this year there came into the Loomis settlement Ezra Luddon, Pelatiah Case, George Hoskins, George Loomis, Aaron Clapp, Joseph Farnham and a few others, whose descendants form a respectable portion of the inhabitants of that and other sections at the present day.

In 1808 the first frame school-house in the town was built at Bennington Centre. This was the second school-house in the town, and stood until 1855, when it was replaced by the present one at the Centre. This and the one at Danley's Corners, or East Bennington, as it was then called, were the only school-houses in this town until 1818, the year that the town was formed.

In January, 1813, the school in the east part of the town was reorganized under the new law, and James Tolles, now living near where the old school-house stood, was hired to teach three months during the summer. He drew all the money apportioned to the town, as this was the only school in the town that year. This was the first public money ever drawn from the town treasury.

Early in 1809 Chauncey Loomis had been appointed one of the judges of "Genesee Common Pleas," and had become one of the most prominent men in

RES. OF W. L. HAWES, COWLESVILLE, WYOMING CO., N.Y.

W. L. Hawes

JOHN LOOMIS.

RESIDENCE OF JOHN LOOMIS, BENNINGTON, WYOMING CO., N.Y.

RESIDENCE OF GEORGE CHICK, BENNINGTON, WYOMING CO., N.Y

this part of the Holland Purchase. He was married this year to Miss Rachael Evans, a sister of Hon. David E. Evans, of Batavia. By way of wedding tour he moved his estimable bride home, eighteen miles into the wilderness of Bennington, on horseback.

Bears and wolves, apparently invited by the increase in the number of sheep and pigs, became more troublesome than in former years. They would frequently come into the barn yard during the day and carry off a lamb or a pig, and a bear has been known to refuse to give up his pig, though hotly pursued by the farmer, his good wife, loving daughter and dutiful son, all armed with implements of warfare suitable for the occasion, such as axes, old chairs, fire shovel and clubs.

Parties were occasionally made up to watch the corn and wheat fields by night. A few dogs had by this time been obtained which had the courage to "tree" a bear. A party of six or eight had been made up, in the fall of 1809, to watch a corn field, and had provided themselves with two good dogs for the occasion. Among the party was a well built lad of twenty-one summers, of German descent, and familiarly called Jake. Soon after approaching the field they discovered, by the barking of the dogs, that their game was "treed"; and following as well as they could in the dark were soon assembled in a dense grove of hemlocks, near the field. After much "ground" if not "lofty" tumbling, Mr. Bruin's tree was pointed out by the dogs. Some of the party engaged in striking up a fire, intending to lie by until daylight should reveal the position of his bearship, and make a better mark for them to shoot at. Before the fire was lighted, Jake exclaimed: "Dunder! and I'll shoot arter him"; and suiting the action to the word, elevated his old fowling piece, charged with something less than a half pound of powder and half a dozen rifle balls, which served for buckshot, pulled at a venture, and to the astonishment of the whole party, down came a three-year-old bear, so near to Jake as to brush his clothes in the descent.

Ezra Ludden, father of Samuel Ludden, came from East Hampton in 1809.

Elias Gillett, father of Noah D. Gillett, came from Granby, Conn., in 1813, and took up fifty acres of wild land, two miles from the Centre. The journey was made with an ox team and took over a month. He built a log house, cleared the farm, and died October 7th, 1850, aged sixty-eight.

Isaac Pierce, father of the present Isaac Pierce, moved from the vicinity of Caledonia, Livingston county, in 1820, to Bennington, and took up fifty acres of unimproved land, two miles and a half northeast of the Centre. This place he improved, putting up a log house; but in 1830 removed to the farm now called by his name.

Kiliab Lindsay, son of Archibald and father of C. V., William and Martin Lindsay, was born April 30th, 1786, in Warren county, N.Y., and in 1822 settled on the farm where his son C. V. now lives. There he passed the remainder of his life, dying June 16th, 1875. His wife, formerly Eleanor Loop, to whom he was married January 13th, 1807, died April 5th, 1869.

The fluctuations of population in this town in half a century are shown by the following series of census returns, copied from the Manual of the Legislature; 1830, 2,217; 1835, 2,617; 1840, 3,367; 1845, 2,104; 1850, 2,406; 1855, 2,555; 1860, 2,615; 1865, 2,445; 1870, 2,385; 1875, 2,483.

THE INDIANS.

The original lords of the soil in their sale to Robert Morris had reserved various extensive tracts, on which they resided. One of these formed the western boundary of this town, namely the Buffalo Reservation, where the celebrated Red Jacket, with several others of minor note, resided. Here lived Horatio Jones, the interpreter. In passing to and from other tribes on the Genesee river, eastward to the Mohawk, and southward to Pennsylvania, they crossed this town. By the continual tramp of ages the path had become indented in the soil, in some places to the depth of a foot or more. It was slightly serpentine, though following a generally straight course. Although the path was not more than fifteen or eighteen inches wide, it was familiarly known as the "red man's broad highway." It entered the town near the northwest corner, and pursued a course nearly east, through the northern tier of lots and quarter sections, and left the town half a mile south of the northeast corner, crossing the Tonawanda a short distance below Attica, on some driftwood.

The Indians, during the hunting season, frequently built their temporary lodges in the vicinity of the settlers, and remained, one or two families together, hunting and smoking their meats. On one of these visits an old man, who said he had seen one hundred and four winters, and whose general aspect would warrant that conclusion, encamped alone, near one of the settlers, and commenced traffic in articles such as brooms, trays and other Indian manufactures. In offering a lady a tray one day, he said if she would give him his tray full of flour she might have the tray *for nothing.* He was called "Hispaniola." He was a hard featured savage, and had a peculiarly disagreeable scowl on his countenance. Early in the winter of 1804, the deep snow coming on, the old Indian was unable to obtain the means of support. The settlers provided for him awhile; a young Indian, as he was called, though probably seventy years of age, then came to his relief, but the old man died, and was buried near his cabin, on lands afterward owned by Nathaniel K. Doty. It had become an axiom with settlers that untrustworthiness and treachery were synonyms of Indian, but Hispaniola always repelled the slander. Such was the character of the tribe in this vicinity that if any of the settlers' wives or families were to be left alone over night, and a squaw could be found to remain with them, all was supposed to be safe. Several times, when any of the settlers got out of their reckoning in the woods, and could not find the way out, an Indian would pilot him out, or if near night would keep him in his cabin till morning, and send him on his way rejoicing. Thus the settlers and Indians in this town were on the most friendly terms.

HURRICANES.

In June, 1805, this town was visited by a tornado more severe than any before or since. The principal track of the hurricane was nearly due east, entering the town near the northwest corner, pursuing its course on the north tier of lots, and leaving the town near the northeast corner. It prostrated all the trees in its track, which was about half a mile wide, and in the middle of which the trees lay as evenly as a mowing machine lays the grass in the meadows. On the borders of the whirlwind's track the timber fell in every direction. For a part of its course it pursued the Indian trail heretofore mentioned, filling it completely, leaving no alternative but temporarily to go further north; but the Indians returned to the old track as soon as the obstructions were removed.

June 13th, 1872, the town of Bennington was again visited by a tornado such as had not occurred since 1805. It pursued a course almost directly from west to east, about a mile south of the one in 1805, and its path was about half a mile wide. As there were no forests now as then to level, it spent its fury in demolishing buildings and orchards. Amid all the crashing of houses, barns and fences, and the uprooting of trees, not a person or animal was materially injured.

THE MILITIA AND THE WAR OF 1812.

In 1807 the military authorities of the State organized a regiment on the Holland Purchase, and one of the companies was located in Bennington and adjoining towns, this town being honored with the principal officers. John Jones was commissioned as captain, and Jacob Wright was appointed ensign. In the fall of 1808 the first regimental or general training was held at Alexander, and reviewed by Brigadier General Alexander Rhea. The regiment was formed on the ground east of the bridge at Alexander village, and on the north side of the road, the right resting near the site of the present stone church, on a line parallel with the road. Everybody went to general training—men, women, children and dogs. Some went on foot, some on horseback, and some in ox wagons. The young fellows wore new "fine" shirts, about as fine and white as stuff now used for bags, but which cost six shillings a yard, and these were the first fine shirts worn in this town. The misfortune of the occasion was that owners of sheep did not get home in time to yard them at night, and found in the morning that the wolves had made sad havoc among their little flocks.

The troubles occasioned between the British and French by the Berlin and Milan decrees of 1806–8 began in 1810 to affect western New York, and to materially check settlement in this town. The embargo laid in 1807 had the effect rather than otherwise to advance the settlement of the town. In the fall of 1810 a large business sprang up in running property into Canada. Mr. Loomis's road across the Indian reservation afforded a ready and out of the way winter route to Lake Erie, which could be crossed on the ice. Many loads of pork, wheat, corn and whiskey passed through this town on the way to Canada, and

PORTAGE BRIDGE FALLS.

"CLIFFDALE" RES. OF WILLIS H. FULLER, PORTAGEVILLE, N.Y.

RESIDENCE OF PETER V. LUCAS, (DECEASED) CASTILE, N.Y.

RESIDENCE OF LEVI RIDER, CASTILE, N.Y.

HOTEL & CARRIAGE SHOP OF R.L. HANNA, GAINESVILLE, N.Y.

FARM RESIDENCE OF AUGUSTUS DODGE, PIKE, WYOMING CO., N.Y.

almost every house was, during the winters while the embargo continued, converted into a public house for the accommodation of man and beast.

On the breaking out of the war of 1812 some of the settlers left for places of safety and some volunteered to defend their country, enlisting for six months, three years or during the war, and some going into the regular army for five years. Among the latter were Joseph Farnham, Justice Loomis, Alva Wood, Walter Burnham, John Tolles, Abel Baker and some others. So large a number being withdrawn from a new community left but a few to till the soil, in which the women assisted, while the felling of the forest ceased for the time. The war on the frontier continued during 1813 and 1814 to absorb every other interest, and the morning and evening guns at Buffalo could be distinctly heard in Bennington. So many of the settlers were gone to the war or elsewhere that the bears and wolves became very bold in their depredations on the farmers' grain, sheep and swine. Lads of a dozen summers were often obliged to go out at night and drive from the pig sty or sheep fold the hungry bear or ravenous wolf, which they could easily do with a blazing fire brand. In this state of affairs no new settlements were made, and little or no improvement of lots already located. The volunteers were still in the army and the skulkers still remained abroad.

As no new settlers came into the town during the war the people left here began to feel the need of a market. In the absence of all currency business transactions began to be done in kind. A note would be given to be paid in a specified number of bushels of wheat, or payable in live stock or labor. A man would be hired to do work, agreeing to take his pay in stock or grain. The best of cows would not sell for more than $8, and the best yoke of oxen would change owners for $40. All kinds of foreign goods were scarce, prices ruled very high, and the strictest economy had to be practiced; goods of that kind were only bought when necessity or a craving appetite actually demanded them. From the few sheep in the town wool was grown and from the cleared patches of land flax was raised, and the pioneer wife and daughter would spin, weave and make them into clothing for the family. The corn and wheat which the mother and sons raised supplied the bread, and the maple forests the sugar, and for coffee burnt barley, peas and corn were substituted; so that but very little was purchased of the pioneer store keeper, and that little consisted mostly of tea and tobacco. The superabundant herbage in the forest furnished a ready pasturage during the summer.

December 30th, 1813, a British force of about one thousand men landed at Buffalo, captured the place, and spread alarm throughout all western New York. The militia that had been provided to guard Buffalo fled to Bennington, causing consternation among the settlers by their fright, and their wild and extravagant report that the British regulars and the Canadian Indians were but a short distance behind, in full pursuit. A general stampede commenced at once. Every man or woman who had one or more draft animals put them into immediate requisition, with such vehicles as could be had, many of which were improvised for the occasion, and of the rudest sort at that; and the beginning of

1814 saw Bennington nearly depopulated. Some of those who fled remained away all winter, while most of them returned in a few days to their old cabins, and did not allow themselves to be disturbed again by flying reports during the remainder of the war.

With the close of 1814 came the end of the war, and such of Bennington's soldiers as survived the conflict returned to their homes, and their time was again given to clearing off the forests.

HARD TIMES AND RELIEF.

The severity of the season, and the high price of wheat in the fall of 1816, induced every settler to put into wheat during that and the following season every acre of land that could be prepared for it. But when there was a crop for the market there was no market for the crop. The settlers had heretofore required for home consumption all that was raised, or nearly so. But now, in 1818, every one had some to spare. The season was unfavorable for corn, and but very little was raised, consequently but very little pork was made; no money was in circulation, and everything looked rather "blue." But the indomitable will of the pioneer was not to be thwarted, and improvements still went on.

About this time Trumbull Casey, of Batavia, commenced paying cash for black salts, at the rate of $2.50 per hundred pounds. This opportunity the settlers improved in clearing off the forests, as this was the only article of commerce within their reach for which they could get cash. Lands were cleared by the job for little more than the ashes.

Nearly every lot in the town had its log cabin, and yet, except the land purchased by the Loomis family and one or two others, the fee simple still remained in the Holland Land Company, the settlers holding only under an "article."

In 1820, there still being no market, no cash was paid for produce, and all business transactions were done in "barter." Shoemakers, tailors, blacksmiths, school teachers, clergymen and men of all trades and professions were paid in grain, or not paid at all. Even the marriage ceremony was sometimes performed by justices for wheat. But one young man, rather more noble than the rest, carried on his back four bushels of wheat a distance of five miles, and sold it to a new settler for one dollar. He gave a clergyman the dollar the next day to make him a happy husband. The system of the Holland Company in selling their lands on long credit, and not even enforcing the contracts when due, had given rise to carelessness or indifference on the part of the settler, and even the interest on the purchases went unpaid; consequently land purchased at $1.25 per acre had doubled, and the burden of what seemed a great debt became an incubus on the settler. Many began to feel that they could not pay for their lands, but did not like the idea of leaving their homes to others more fortunate, and quite an uneasiness was felt among the early settlers. The Holland Company saw the necessity of doing something to prevent the further accumulation of debt, and in 1823 commenced taking stock and produce on their contracts. This had the effect in many cases of alleviating the anxiety, and many in this way paid for their farms.

In 1822 the work on the Erie Canal in this vicinity gave employment to men and teams from this town at remunerative prices, and brought returns in cash, which restored a circulating medium, and the practice of barter ceased. The completion of the Erie Canal was a god-send to the settlers. Grain, which had heretofore been a drug, now commanded cash at home, and the canal proved of great value to Bennington, although thirty miles distant.

In 1828 and 1829 some of the settlers who had come into the town young and robust, and had gathered around them numerous families, found that the amount yet due the land office was in many instances equal to the price of their land, and that the settler, after spending the prime of his life clearing off the forests, might be left penniless. Feeling that they had made the value of the land by their improvements, they were not willing to leave them without some remuneration. Murmurings began to prevail, which broke into open rebellion, and a mob of several hundred men marched upon the land office at Batavia, as related on page 105; several Bennington pioneers were present.

The Holland Company sold many occupied farms in this town to speculators, who undertook to remove the settlers by legal process. But after a few fruitless attempts, during which one of the speculators and his assistants were treated to a coat of tar and feathers by a mob of settlers, legal proceedings were abandoned.

Yet many of the settlers became discouraged by their indebtedness and failure to perfect their titles, neglected their farms and began selling out. Thus in a very few years an almost new set of inhabitants supplied the place of those settled first, and a better state of things was manifested. The old log cabins, now decaying, gave place to substantial frame or brick dwellings and frame barns. Hay and grain were housed and livestock sheltered. New fences and pens kept domestic animals within bounds. The completion of a continuous line of railroad from Buffalo to Albany gave Bennington the benefit of markets east and west, the want of which had been felt from the earliest settlement of the town.

OFFICERS OF THE TOWN.

This town was formed from Sheldon March 6th, 1818. The first town meeting was held at the house of David Farnham. The meeting "resolved that Jonathan G. Palmer be clerk *Pro tempore*, and adjourned to the school-house near Strong Hayden's, and the following persons were made choice of as town officers: Ezra Ludden, John Newell and Enoch Winslow, school commissioners; William Stedman, George Loomis, Jonathan G. Palmer, James Danley, Johnson Noyes and Seth Pomeroy, inspectors of common schools; George Loomis, supervisor; Jonathan G. Palmer, town clerk; William Washburn, constable and collector; Pelatiah Case and Nathan Clapp, poormasters; Seymour Norton, John Noyes and Hezekiah Lattimer, assessors; Nathan Clapp, Joseph Farnham and Abram Clough, commissioners of highway. It was voted that there be but one constable in town, and that pathmasters be pound keepers and fence viewers. The overseers of highways chosen at this time were Aldrich Freeman, Quartus Clapp, James Diskill, John Jones 2nd, Isaac Anderson, John Tolles, Daniel Root, Joseph Farnham, John Carter, Elias Gillett, Stephen Baker, John Tucker, Bissel Sherman and Allen Matterson. It was voted that there be $50 raised for the support of roads and bridges.

The civil list of Bennington includes the following names:

Supervisors.—1818, George Loomis; 1819–25, 1827, 1830, 1832–36, Strong Hayden; 1826, Benjamin Piper; 1828, 1829, Pelatiah Case, jr.; 1831, Sylvester R. Crane; 1837, 1838, Ira Cross: 1839, Albert Hayden (resigned, and Strong Hayden was elected October 1st, 1839); 1840, 1844–49, B. R. Folsom; 1841, 1842, Isaac Pierce, jr.; 1843, Anthony Potter; 1850–53, 1855, 1860, 1864, 1871, 1872, 1878, John B. Folsom; 1854, 1873, 1874, E. C. Holt; 1856, 1875–77, Isaac Pierce; 1857; Lucien Brown; 1858, 1859, Benajah Griswold; 1861, 1867, G. G. Hoskins; 1862, 1863, 1879, Lucien H. Brown; 1865, 1866, Ami H. Hoskins; 1868, George E. Mattison; 1869, 1870, Milton P. Persons.

Town Clerks.—1818, Jonathan G. Palmer; 1819–21, 1823–29, 1831–34, George Loomis; 1822, 1830, Caleb H. King; 1835, 1838, Henry L. Rowley; 1837, Albert Hayden; 1838–40, Chandler Parsons; 1841, 1842, 1849, Chauncey L. Hayden; 1843, 1844, Marcus L. Vosburgh; 1845, O. F. Fuller; 1846–48, Bissel S. King; 1850, 1851, George L. Hoskins; 1852, 1853, E. L. Woodford; 1854, F. H. Day; 1855, 1856, Edwin Stanley; 1857, 1858, John Dunson; 1859, 1861, 1864, William L. Hawes; 1860, James W. Owen; 1862, 1863, Frank Parsons; 1865, 1866, Andrew Nimme; 1867, Paul Stephens; 1868–71, Peter Muth; 1872, 1873, Martin Fredman; 1874, 1875, S. D. Ludden; 1876–79, Joseph Sellman.

February 25th, 1875, the board of supervisors set off and erected into a new town, to be named "Elmont," all that part of the town lying west of the "mile strip," leaving the town of Bennington a little over five and a quarter miles wide. But through some error in the proceedings the act of the board did net take effect as intended, the project failed, and the old town remains intact, as formed in 1818.

SUICIDES.

The record of suicides in Bennington is so remarkable for a rural community as to deserve notice.

In 1846 German by the name of Straus committed suicide by hanging, in a barn near the Roman Catholic church, in the northeast part of the town.

About 1840 a Mr. Ludden, who lived near the center of the town, hung himself to the limb of a tree.

In 1871 Mr. John F. Maxon, aged about seventy years, who lived in the southeast quarter of the town, hung himself in his own house by fastening one end of a rope through a stove-pipe hole, and the other around his neck, and then stepping off from a chair. In the same year Mrs. Thomas Gillett and Mrs. Martha Cross committed suicide in their own dwellings, in a similar manner; and Mrs. Clapp, then living near the center of the town, committed suicide by poisoning, the same year of the above. In 1871, also, an unknown man was found hung to the limb of a tree, near John Henig's.

In 1874 Mr. Loyal Hawes, who lived at Cowlesville and had resided in this town from his birth, committed suicide at his home while in a state of temporary insanity.

BENNINGTON'S VOLUNTEERS.

The first to volunteer from this town at the call of President Lincoln for soldiers to put down the Rebellion were Ralph N. Tolles and Merritt N. Chaffee. They enlisted in Company F, 5th N. Y. cavalry, September 10th, 1861. This company was organized at Pike, by Captain Washington Wheeler. Ralph N. Tolles was accidentally shot at Newmarket, Va., May 9th, 1862, by a comrade named John B. McMillan. His remains was brought home for burial, and deposited in the Hubbard cemetery. He was the first Bennington soldier who lost his life. Merritt N. Chaffee served through the war, and was several times promoted. After the war he removed to Michigan, and he has represented his district several times in the Legislature of that State.

Bounties to volunteers were offered by the town at several times during the war. At a special town meeting July 12th, 1864, a bounty of $300 was voted to drafted men who served or sent substitutes, and $400 to each volunteer.

Bennington contributed to the Union armies during the Rebellion the men named below, as stated in the records of the Soldiers' Monument Association. They were private soldiers where not otherwise stated. The first date given is that of enlistment.

8*th N. Y. Heavy Artillery.*—John Amerdic, 1863. David Burleigh, 1863. Ira Cross, 1863. Ervin Newell, lieutenant, Dec., 1863. Kirk L. Ewell, corporal, Dec., 1863; died in 1864. H. Ferner, 1863. Adam Grill, Dec., 1863. J. G. Kerach, corporal, Dec., 1863. Mart Lingfield, Dec., 1863; died in Aug., 1864. Andrew Lingfield, Dec., 1863; died in Dec., 1864. Dexter S. Ludden, major, Dec., 1863. Stephen Myers, Dec., 1863. Michael Myers, Dec., 1863. Eugene Plumley, corporal, Dec., 1863. Charles Rice, Aug. 2, 1862. Friend Rice, Aug. 5, 1862. John Shurn, Dec. 23, 1863. H. H. Van Dake, lieutenant, Dec., 1863.

136*th N.Y. Infantry.*—G. G. Atwood, Sept., 1862; died in Dec., 1862. Harlow Dudley, Sept. 12, 1862. Edward D. Kellogg, Charles Maxon, Sept. 12, 1862.

105*th N. Y. Infantry.*—C. M. Rowley, 1863; died in 1863. John Kersch, 1861.

14*th N. Y. Infantry.*—F. O. Barber, 1862; died in 1863. Harry Parsons, sergeant, 1861.

Miscellaneous.—Benjamin Atwood, 1st N. Y. Dragoons, Company C; mortally wounded June 11th, 1864; died July 2. George W. Crossfield, 10th N. Y. cavalry. Harrison V. Day, 48th heavy artillery, Dec. 28, 1863. O. P. French, 9th N. Y. cavalry, Oct., 1864. Charles Green, 10th N. Y. artillery, Aug. 8, 1862. James King, corporal, 16th U.S. volunteers, Aug. 19, 1864. John Muns, sergeant, 187th N. Y. infantry, 1861; died same year. Jacob A. Sohlick, captain, 6th Wisconsin infantry, Apr. 19, 1861.

BENNINGTON CENTRE.

This village was settled in the summer of 1807 by Chauncey Loomis, whose advent is elsewhere described. He purchased a large tract of land, upon which the village was afterward built. The place was known for many years as the Loomis settlement. Loomis opened a store on a small scale for the accommodation of those who settled around him. Through his enterprise and generosity the settlement enlarged, until it spread out over nearly the whole town. At present there are three stores, Peter Muth's, Jacob Hine's and James King's; three churches, Roman Catholic, Baptist and German Lutheran; two wagon shops; an ashery; a grist and cider-mill; a steam saw-mill; a job printing office; two school-houses, Roman Catholic and Protestant; two taverns and two physicians, E. C. Holt and Charles A. Young. The present postmaster is Alonzo Persons, and the post-office is kept at the store of P. Muth. The population is about 200. The first postmaster at this place was Strong Hayden. He was appointed in 1818.

FIRST BAPTIST CHURCH, BENNINGTON CENTRE.

Agreeable to the vote of the Second Baptist Church in Sheldon, passed the Saturday preceding the first Sunday in September, 1812, the members of that church living on lot No. 10, 4th range, and its vicinity, viewing themselves as a distinct branch of that church, agreed to hold conference, covenant and other meetings in their neighborhood, and chose Ezra Ludden to serve as clerk in this branch of the church. They also agreed to choose a moderator to lead in their meetings.

The names of these members were as follows: Pelatiah Case, Darius Cross, Justin Loomis, Ezekiel Harris, Bela Bibbins, Alphea Loomis, Apphia Case, Betsey Cross, Elizabeth Rockwell and Anna Harris. October 15th, 1812, Ezra Ludden, William Washburn, Bathsheba Jennings and Philomela Risley were baptized by Elder Irish. No more were added to the church until June 14th, 1814.

April 10th, 1814, at a covenant meeting Pelatiah Case was chosen the first moderator.

September 1st, 1814, Elder Carr administered the sacrament.

At a church meeting held August 14th, 1817, at which Elder Cyrus Andrews was present, it was voted to apply to the churches of Sheldon and Pembroke for their elders and delegates to meet with this church on the 21st inst. to compose a council to consider the propriety of granting the members living on lot No. 10, 4th range, fellowship as a distinct church. Agreeable to this vote, the following persons met in council on the 21st: From Sheldon, Elder William Hemick and L. Castle; from Pembroke, Elder William Throop. Elder Throop was appointed moderator of the council, and L. Castle clerk. The council found eight male and ten female members, to whom it unanimously agreed to give fellowship as a church in sister relation.

March 19th, 1819, Pelatiah Case was chosen the first deacon of the church. April 11th, 1819, Elder Throop administered the Lord's Supper. The first letter granted by this church was given September 26th, 1819, to Mehitabel King, to join in Oxford, Upper Canada.

Elder Ebenezer Hall was pastor of the church from July 9th, 1836, to February 18th, 1837; January 8th, 1838, Elder Colby commenced his labors, and remained until May 9th, 1842; Elder F. Burr was next pastor from November 1st, 1842, till September 9th, 1843; Elder Nelson Chapin then began his labors here, which ended September 14th, 1845; he was succeeded November 2nd, 1845, by Elder Joel Lyons, who staid until April 9th, 1848; Elder Elisha Sardis Smith was pastor from January 17th, 1849, until January 1st, 1851; and from January 15th, 1851, Elder Samuel J. Olney served to March 10th, 1852; Elder E. S. Smith then came and remained till February, 1853; Elder David Loomis was a supply from April 2nd, 1853, till February 20th, 1854; Elder Ansel Clark came June 6th, 1854, and left April 6th, 1856; Elder A. S. Kneeland supplied the pulpit until April 12th, 1857; Elder S. Kyes, jr., was pastor from June 6th, 1857, until April 30th, 1865; Elder Charles Berry to March 18th, 1866. For three years the church was without stated preaching. June 2nd, 1869, Elder A. H. Tood became the settled pastor; he resigned June 3d, 1871. For nearly three years the church was again without a pastor. Elder W. Martin came in March, 1874, and left October 29th, 1877; Elder E. Owens commenced his labors January 6th, 1878, and closed his engagement April 1st, 1879. The present number of members is twenty-five.

This society was given a "gospel lot" by the Holland Land Company. The first church edifice was built in 1832, by Ezra Ludden, at a contract price of $350. It stood on the site occupied by the present church edifice. In 1856 it was sold to S. D. Ludden. In consideration he was to pay $25 in cash, remove the old church from the lot, and ring the bell on the new church three times a day for one year.

The present church edifice, which is of wood, was built in 1856 by Hawes & Ludden, and cost the society $1,500. It was dedicated February 26th, 1857, by Rev. S. F. Holt.

PRESBYTERIAN CHURCH, BENNINGTON CENTER.

Hotchkin's history says: "Public worship was instituted about 1810, and a Congregational church, consisting of seven members, was organized in 1814 by Rev. John Spencer and Hugh Wallis. This is the church, as the author supposes, which was designated as Sheldon, No. 10, 3d range. It was received under the care of the Presbytery of Niagara February 3d, 1818, and was assigned to the Presbytery of Genesee on the organization of the latter. In 1825 it numbered 14 members, and in 1846 47, the highest number it has ever reported." "In 1842 Rev. Isaac Chichester was employed as a stated supply, and on the 3d day of December, 1844, he was installed pastor of the church. On the same day their new house of worship, which is a well built edifice forty-two feet in length and thirty-four in breadth, was dedicated to the worship of the triune God. Since the settlement of Mr. Chichester there has been a gradual enlargement of the church. The American Home Missionary Society has lent its aid to this church in the support of its pastor." In 1878 the church property was leased to the "German Lutheran Society" for a term of fifteen years, with the privilege of occupying it for one service each Sabbath during that time. The Presbyterians have no preaching, and hold no services in their church. The present membership is about 12.

ROMAN CATHOLIC CHURCHES AND SCHOOLS.

The very first thing which we know in the town of Bennington about Catholicism is that some few families scattered around over a good distance assembled for service in a house on the Allegany road, about a mile north from Bennington Centre, now belonging to Mr. Vincent Ganter. This was about 1847, when a priest from Buffalo visited them as a missionary from time to time.

Occasionally the Catholics also assembled in another farmhouse, which belongs to-day to Mr. Michael Meier, near the actual old Catholic church, and later also in a large public house called Danley's Tavern. There are still some of the Bennington Catholics who have been married in that tavern.

The first baptism recorded in the parochial books was that of John Winter, which was administered by Rev. Father Tshenhens, C. S.S. R., on April 5th, 1848.

It was only in 1848 that some Germans proposed to build a church, and soon they went to work, so that under Rev. Father Kubin they opened a little church, about thirty feet wide by forty feet long, for service in the year 1850. Among the oldest German settlers that erected this church, costing a little over $1,500, we find the following names in the annals of the church: John Schum*, Frank Bauk, John Frisen, Joseph Frauenknecht*, George Mayer, John Diestler, Leonhard Geitner, John Siegert, Wendelin Grail, George Meinwieser, Frank Ailingen, Joseph Syndecus*, Joseph Linssen, John Uhl, Nicholas Stum, John Besold, Mich. Swegler*, John Walter, Joseph Rosenwirth*, George Benedict, Adam Dersam*, George Reichert, Leonhard Henke*, John Engel*, John Lingfelder, Bartholomew Sperl, David Schiller.

The names having an asterisk are those of persons still living in Bennington in the autumn of 1879.

The church, dedicated to St. Mary Help of Christians, was blessed by Rt. Rev. Bishop Timon, of Buffalo. It was rebuilt in 1855. The congregation increased very fast, and counted in 1855 and 1856 already 140 to 150 families.

Bennington, notwithstanding this important Catholic membership, was never the residence of a priest, but has been a station even to this day.

The Catholic school here, under the charge of Prof. Smith is attended by 450 children, and is in a prosperous condition.

From 1850 to 1854 this place was attended from Sheldon, Wyoming county, and from 1854 to 1870 from Aldcn, Erie county.

In 1871, under Rev. Father Kofler, commenced a new period for Bennington. After many struggles and vigorous efforts he resolved to build a new church in Bennington Centre, about four miles distant from the old Bennington church. Naturally this could not but weaken the old Bennington congregation, for a great number of families would join the new one. Under the wise management of Mr. Kofler a nice church of seventy feet by thirty-five was erected at Bennington Centre. The consecration of the new church, dedicated to the Sacred Heart of Jesus, took place October 29th, 1872, and was performed by Rt. Rev. Bishop Ryan, of Buffalo. The new society started with thirty-three families, and numbers to-day eighty-seven families.

The cost of the new building was estimated in the beginning at $3,000, but exceeds at the present moment $7,000. This new church is handsomely fitted up, and will be furnished very soon with stained glass windows.

As real founders of the church are to be remembered Adam Syndecus, Martin Fridmann, Jacob Collein, John Schum, jr., Mary Bleyler, Henri Peyrick, Charles Fridmann, Lewis Fridmann, Bernard Biegler, Nicholas Demuth, Peter Zehler, jr., George Schumann, Joseph Sellmann, Michael Schum and Bernard Geise.

At the east side of the church building there is a Catholic school with about fifty-nine children connected with it, of which Mr. John Ziewers has been the efficient teacher since 1875. At the west side of the church is the pastor's residence, very nicely located and admired by all the priests who have occupied it.

Rev. Gerard H. Gysen, the late pastor of Bennington Centre and Bennington, is a native of Holland, and studied theology at the celebrated university and American college at Louvain, Belgium. In 1876 he came to America, and was stationed in Bennington Centre the following year. In the latter part of 1879 he removed to Alden, Erie county, and was succeeded by Rev. James Schneider.

The priests who have had charge over Bennington and Bennington Centre, with the dates of their service, have been the following, the station having been attended from Buffalo until 1850, then nine years from Sheldon, then from Alden until 1871:

Rev. P. Tshenhens, T. S. S. R., 1848, who was a native of Wurtemberg, and died in Baltimore in 1877, aged seventy-six years.

Rev. J. P. Kromer, 1848, a native of Bavaria.

John B Folsom

Rev. J. G. Shaefer, February 19th, 1849; May 28th, 1849.

Rev. P. Kubin, November 13th, 1849, to January 7th, 1850.

Rev. Sebastian B. Gruber, February 27th, 1850, to June 6th, 1852. He is a native of Bavaria; was one of the most zealous pastors here, and is now stationed in New Oregon, Erie county.

Rev. Carl Kubin, September 13th, 1852, to February 6th, 1854.

Rev. Anthony Rief, August 21st, to October 15th, 1853.

Rev. N. P. Neumann, March 9th, 1854, to June 18th, 1854.

Rev. Mr. Heuberech, July, 1834.

Rev. Sebastian B. Gruber, July 22nd, 1854, to July 29th, 1856.

Rev. Patrick Seibold, August 3d, 1856, to November 21st, 1857; was a native of Wurtemberg.

Rev. Stephen Eicher, January 24th, to May 1st, 1858. He was a native of Switzerland, and died in Sheldon.

Rev. Anthony Saeger, May 17th, 1858, to September, 1858; a native of Wurtemberg.

Rev. Mr. Lochert, October 25th, 1858, to February 21st, 1850; a native of Alsace.

Rev. Michael Rosenbauer, C. S. S. R., 1850; a native of Wurtemberg.

Rev. Philip Poch, June 1st, 1859, to March 7th, 1860.

Rev. M. Schinabeck, April 16th, 1860, to October 4th, 1861.

Rev. F. Heimbucher, November 5th, 1861, to February 10th, 1862; a native of Bavaria; died September 15th, 1875, in Lattnerville, Iowa.

Rev. P. L. Ewald, C. S. S. R., April 27th, 1862, to July 21st, 1862. He was born in Prussia, and is at present in Philadelphia, Pa.

Rev. J. N. Arendt, September 1st, 1862, to June 27th, 1870; is a native of Bavaria, and now pastor in Gardenville, Erie county.

Rev. Charles Wenzierski, September 4th, 1870, to May 25th, 1871; a native of Prussia; is now in Donnelly, Minn.

Rev. F. X. Kofler, August 10th, 1871, to August 25th, 1872. He is a native of Austria, and now pastor of St. Francis Xavier Church, North Buffalo, Erie county.

Rev. Joseph Niebling, December 8th, 1872, to March 20th, 1873; a native of Bavaria; now at Peking, Ill.

Rev. Innocent Sager, May 4th, 1873, to November 15th, 1873; a native of Switzerland; now in Hamburg, Erie county.

Rev. Anthony Adolph, December 24th, 1873, to March 4th, 1876. He is a native of Prussia, and now stationed at Buffalo Plains, Erie county.

Rev. John J. Hamel, March 26th, 1876, to September 24th, 1876; was born in Brooklyn, N. Y., and is now pastor at Olean, Cattaraugus county, N. Y.

Rev. Victor Ritter, October 1st, 1876, to March 14th, 1877; a native of Alsace.

Rev. Gerard H. Gysen, March 14th, 1877; a native of Venloo, Holland.

Rev. James Schneider, born in Silesia, Germany, who has lived in the United States since 1875.

The Catholic school at Bennington was established in 1854 by Rev. Father Gruber, and has had several teachers, among whom were the following: Adam Handel, the first teacher, now in St. Francis Hospital, Pittsburg, Pa.; T. Schneider; Franz Adamberger (twice); Peter Berndt; —— Rothmund; Mrs. Caroline Keller (twice); Zacharias Hangauer; Laurenz Hopfenmuller; Anton Lechner; Henry. Smith, the present teacher.

The Bennington Centre school was established in 1873. The first teacher was Zacharias Hangauer. John Ziewers is the present teacher.

The present trustees of Bennington are Adam Dersam and John Smidt; at Bennington Centre, Jos. Sellmann, Peter Zehler, jr., and Frank Kos.

FOLSOMDALE.

This village is located about two miles southeast from Cowlesville, on the banks of the Cayuga creek, and about three miles southwest from Bennington Centre. It was originally called "West Bennington," then "Scottsville," from the fact that David Scott was the owner of the land upon which the village is located, and an enterprising pioneer of the place. It was named Folsomdale in honor of John B. Folsom, who was the first postmaster at this place, and subsequently owned all the property formerly owned by Scott. He kept the office in the old Scott store, which is still standing and was built by David Scott in 1831. The first mail carrier was a Mr. Cheesebro. The mails were received once a week, if the roads were good. There have been seven postmasters at this place, including the present one, Samuel A. Willard, Esq. In 1831 there was an ashery where the barn now stands, just below the grist-mill.

The first school-house at this place was built where the burying-ground is situated, about three-quarters of a mile above the village.

The first distillery at this place was built by David Scott, in 1831, on the site now occupied by the blacksmith shop, southeast of the mills.

The pioneer blacksmiths at this place were Baxter & Tinker, who were here in 1831. The shop stood opposite where Mrs. Zebulon Meade now lives, on the site occupied by her barn.

In 1832 there was a tannery built near the creek, opposite J. B. Folsom's residence; it was burned in February, 1833. Another was built the same year on the same site, and subsequently went to decay.

Joseph Fitch built a saw and grist-mill about 1823, on the site occupied by the present mills, and it was burned in 1845. He also set out the first orchard here, on the lot now owned by Mr. Robbie, of Buffalo, and he built the first log house here, which stood just north of where the Scott store stands, and near the spring. The lot is now owned by J. B. Folsom.

The first tavern here was built by David Scott, in 1834 or 1835, where Hon. J. B. Folsom now lives, opposite S. A. Willard's store.

The first frame building at this place was the Scott store, built in 1831.

The pioneer carpenters were J. I. Matthews and R. M. Willard. Isaac A. Cushman, who still resides here, worked for them. He has lived here longer than any other person in the place.

The pioneer weaver was Mrs. Zebulon Meade, who still resides here. She is a pensioner of the war of 1812, as her husband was a soldier of that war.

At present there are at Folsomdale two churches, Free Will Baptist and German Baptist, the store of S. A. Willard, an ashery, a saw-mill, a grist-mill, a school-house and about one hundred and fifty inhabitants.

FREE WILL BAPTIST CHURCH OF FOLSOMDALE.

About sixty persons assembled at the Starbird school-house in Folsomdale on the 24th of April, 1856, to consult on the expediency of organizing a church. Deacon I. Hall attended council with Elder H. N. Plumb. After a sermon by Elder Plumb on church building and the doctrine of the Free Will Baptists, the following were admitted as the original members of this church: David Clough, Samuel Willard, Charles Duncomb, Benjamin Willard, Annetta Wilder, Marietta Howard, Angelica Howard, Clarinda Plumb, Almira Duncomb and Emily Duncomb, who were organized into a church.

At a "covenant" meeting held May 3d, 1856, at the parsonage, C. Harrison Wilder was elected clerk of the church, and Elder Plumb and C. H. Wilder were appointed delegates to the Genesee Quarterly Conference to petition that body to receive this church as a part of it. In August, 1856, H. B. Alger was elected the first deacon of this church.

September 14th, 1857, a meeting was held to make arrangements for building a church edifice, at which time R. P. Rice, J. B. Folsom, L. Berry, N. Clough and Isaac A. Cushman were elected trustees, and O. Hall, J. B. Folsom and D. N. Clough were appointed a building committee. The present church edifice was built in 1857, and dedicated in 1858 by Elder Ball, of Buffalo.

The pastors of this church have been as follows: From the organization of the church to March 14th, 1857, Rev. H. N. Plumb; April 11th, 1857, to March, 1859, Rev. Allen Brown; April, 1859, to March, 1860, Rev. H. N. Plumb; March 30th, 1860, to some time in 1861, Elder Hitchcock; from 1861 to April 13th, 1868, was no stated preaching; June 6th, 1868, to April, 1870, Rev. Richard Richardson; April 9th, 1870, to April, 1871, Rev. B. H. Damon; for three months from June 3d, 1871, Elder Smith; September 23d, 1871, to the spring of 1873, Rev. Alexander Dick; May 3d, 1873, to March 6th, 1875, Rev. George W. Knapp. He was followed by Rev. E. W. Crowel. From April 14th, 1877, to April 13th, 1878, Rev. H. N. Plumb was again pastor, and from May 11th, 1878, to January 19th, 1879, Rev. Alexander Striemer; May 1st, 1879, Rev. O. B. Buffum, the present pastor, commenced his labors.

The present membership numbers 24. The church property cost $700, and is valued at that sum. The present trustees are S. A. Willard, D. N. Clough, L. Berry, William Coville and James Scott; church clerk, L. Berry.

The Sabbath-school connected with the society was organized before the church was. The present superintendent is James Scott. There is an average attendance of 30 scholars.

GERMAN BAPTIST CHURCH OF FOLSOMDALE.

This society was formerly a branch of the German Baptist church at Bennington Centre, and was organized as a separate church November 20th, 1867. It occupied the Free Will Baptist church at Folsomdale until July 16th, 1869, when its own church edifice was finished.

The first trustees were Leonard Reilan, Henry Meisner and George Meyers, who were elected in 1869. The original members of the society were: Martin and Carolina Shneckenburger, Mary Meyer, Barbara Kern, Kate and George Steingruper, Leonard Reilan, John, Jacob and Minna Kern, Leonard Meyers and Mary Heintz.

The pastors here have been Revs. Peter Ritter, David Swing, Charles Rantz, Frederick Koehler and Frantz Frederick, the present pastor.

The church edifice is located at Folsomdale, and cost $1,200, and is now valued at $1,200, together with the parsonage, purchased since building the church. The present membership numbers fifty-seven.

The Sabbath-school connected with the society was organized in 1867, with twenty-eight scholars, and John Kern as superintendent. The school at present has an average attendance of forty scholars, with Gotleib Kreuter as superintendent.

COWLESVILLE.

The land upon which the village of Cowlesville is situated was purchased in 1818 by Quartus Clapp, who built a saw-mill the same year, on the site now occupied by the gristmill, at the foot of Mill street. His house stood on the corner of Mill and Main streets. It was a frame house, and is now occupied by Mrs. Crouch.

Mr. Clapp built a grist-mill in 1826, adjoining his saw-mill, both of which were carried away by the high water in 1861. The hamlet was known until 1832 as "Clapp's Mills." In 1862 the present grist-mill was built by Richard Yeomans.

The first school-house in this place was built in 1827, about seven or eight rods west of the Universalist church. Dr. Howe's house stands on the same site.

Gaius B. Rich opened a store here in 1827, in a part of the house where Ira Clapp now lives.

In 1828 Elisha Daggett and Ellis Loomis had a carding-mill where Franklin's saw-mill now stands, in the lower end of the village. In 1835 they put in clothiers' machinery, and subsequently Robinson & Daggett carried on the business. The mills were burned in 1851. William Franklin afterward built the present saw-mill on the same site.

In 1837 John Whitney built a tannery where the Franklin House now stands.

The first blacksmith in the village was Russell Hoag. His shop is now occupied by Mrs. Wilson. Hoag was appointed postmaster in 1832. He kept the office in his house, where Chauncey Baker now lives. The name of "Cowlesville" was given to the village at this time in honor of Hiram Cowles, a clerk for G. B. Rich.

The pioneer physician of the village was Erastus Cross. He lived in the building now used by Mr. Sargent as a cooper shop. It stood near Mrs. Sargent's house, where her barn now stands. The pioneer village tailor was Samuel Starbird.

The first tavern built for that purpose was the present one occupied by Mr. Austin, at the corner of Main and Hill streets, and was erected in 1840.

The Cowlesville Furnace was erected in 1844 by Elisha Daggett, and is now owned and operated by his sons.

The present school-house was built in 1848.

In the summer of 1876 Mr. Adelbert Gillett commenced the publication of a wide-awake newsy little journal, called the *Little Centennial*, and continued it about a year, when the name was changed to *Cowlesville News*. The *News* was issued about six months, when journalism in Cowlesville proved unremunerative, and the enterprise was abandoned. Since then Mr. Orville Millar continues the job printing business.

The present business establishments, etc., of the village are as follows: General stores—Sargent & Hawes, Case & Cushman; hotels—Franklin House, Austin House; furnace, L. Daggett & Brother; hardware and tin store, Milo Westcott; blacksmiths—Chauncey Baker, Alexander McBain, Fred. Matz; wagon makers—George W. Klock, R. B. Millar; painters, Clark & Patterson; cheese factory, C. H. Cummings; tailor, Gail Nichols; physicians—W. N. Martin, C. W. Howe; cooper shop, J. M. Sargeant; shoe shop, Zach. Millar; sawmill, Mrs. W. Franklin; grist mill, Richard Yeomans; printing office, O. Millar. The present postmaster is John M. Sargent.

COWLESVILLE CEMETERY ASSOCIATION.

For nearly sixty years the old "graveyard" on the hill has served well the purposes for which it was anciently fenced off, but the time came when more room was wanted, and on the 13th of April, 1864, the above named association was formed. The following trustees were elected: George E. Mattison, Lysander Cushman and S. P. Barnum for one year; Richard Yeomans, John M. Sargent and Henry C. Sargeant for two years; William Franklin, Robert B. Millar and Isaac Albe for three years.

At a meeting of the trustees April 23d, John M. Sargent was elected president of the association, W. L. Munger secretary and H. C. Sargent treasurer.

The old ground was soon improved, and May 7th, 1870, the association purchased land on the north and east sides of it, paying $75. May 5th, 1873, the trustees bought for $160 one and five-eighths acres from J. M. Sargent, adjoining their former purchases. The whole was immediately properly fenced and surveyed into burial lots, and several hundred dollars spent in improvements. Since then the grounds have been kept in accordance with the laws of the State. At present the trustees are Samuel Starbird, L. H. Brown, W. N. Martin, M. N. Williams, Joseph Hinckley, Zachariah Millar, J. M. Sargent, R. B. Millar and H. C. Fillmore. The officers are: President, J. M. Sargent; treasurer, Samuel Starbird; secretary, W. N. Martin, M. D.

THE FRANKLIN MINERAL SPRING.

Certain oily substances having been noticed for a long time on the surface of the water in the creek and adjacent springs, some of the villagers embraced the idea that oil might be found by sinking a well. In the spring of 1865 an association was formed and money contributed for that purpose. The boring was commenced at the lower end of the village, within about three rods of the north margin of the creek, on the land of Mr. William Franklin, and nearly opposite his house on the bank above. The earth was removed to the slate rock, about six feet, and the drill started into the rock. After drilling three hundred and twenty feet into the rock the drill dropped eighteen inches, and immediately a column of water, accompanied with large quantities of gas, rushed up with great force, and the gas taking fire accidentally the workmen had great trouble in the endeavor to prevent the loss of their derrick by fire. Oil being the object, drilling was continued until the well was seven hundred and fifty feet deep, five inches in diameter, full of water gradually flowing into the creek, and the gas constantly bubbling up. Here the well was abandoned and the association broken up. Two or three years after, as the well was on Mr. Franklin's land and the gas constantly passing away, he made a cistern at the head of the well, placed a tank to gather the gas, and pipes from the tank to his farmhouse, and lighted his house. From that time dates the general knowledge of the astonishing curative effects of the water in various diseases, such as scrofula, diabetes, Bright's disease, all kidney troubles, rheumatism, gout, skin diseases and all impurities of the blood. It is known that it is a very powerful agent in the cure of the diseases named and those of a kindred character, and probably the most effective water known for that class of diseases.

A very singular feature connected with the Franklin Mineral Spring is its periodical rise and fall. Once in ninety days the water is driven to the surface with tremendous force, and continues flowing from two hours to two hours and a half, sending out perhaps a thousand barrels. It then subsides and falls back into the well about two feet; then gradually rising fills the cistern, and flows off slowly as before, until the ninety days come around again.

When the flow is about to commence the tank used for collecting the gas is raised out of the cistern, and after the flow has begun the gas is lighted. If in the evening the display is very fine and attracts crowds from the village and surrounding towns to witness it.

THE COWLESVILLE CHURCHES.

FREE WILL BAPTIST.

This society was first organized in 1842, but from various causes the project of sustaining a society with stated preaching was for a while abandoned. The present organization was effected in 1867, at a meeting called at the house of Lysander Cushman, in Cowlesville, where Rev. Richard Richardson was the presiding officer. The original members joining at that time were Lysander and Elizabeth Cushman, Sevilla Weed and Sabin Jenkins. Lysander Cushman was elected clerk of the organization, and Sabin Jenkins deacon.

The present church edifice, on Church street, Cowlesville, was built in October, 1872, at a cost of $2,000, and dedicated by Rev. Dr. Ball, of Buffalo.

The following are the names of the pastors of this society:

Richard Richardson, —— Dingman, I. B. Smith, Alexander Dick, G. W. Knapp and E. Crowell, who left the society in the spring of 1878, when Rev. O. B. Buffum supplied the pulpit until May, 1879.

The present membership numbers 45. The value of the church property is $2,000. The Sunday-school was organized in October, 1872, with 65 scholars, and W. L. Munger as superintendent. The present membership is about the same, with the same superintendent.

THE FIRST UNIVERSALIST CHURCH,

whose edifice is on Main street, in Cowlesville, was organized September 9th, 1844, when a constitution was adopted and subscribed by the following persons, "desirous of advancing the principles of morality and good works among men": Elisha Daggett, H. Warner, Joab Lister, I. I. Matthews, James Nobles, Gideon Williams, Lebbeus Whitney, Samuel Doolittle, John Eastwood, Edward B. Hunt, Thomas Austin, Mary Lister, Ruth Cleveland, Sarah Eastwood, Elizabeth Angle, Doctor Cross, S. K. Skeele, S. R. Crane, Esq., A. B. Starbird, Benjamin North, Wesley Bicknell, John Whitney, D. Cleveland, I. P. Miller, Thomas L. Robinson, Lewis I. Hunt, Eunice Starbird, Margaret Loomis, Lydia Ann Loomis, Tabitha Daggett, Elvira Starbird, Louisa Warriner, Fanny Winslow, A. Starbird, John Doolittle, Sally Loomis, Lovett Whitney, John L. Hutchinson, Enoch Winslow, J. B. Bass and Zachariah Millar.

September 16th, 1844, John Eastwood was elected treasurer, and E. B. Hunt clerk of the church for the ensuing year, and the following gentlemen trustees: A. B. Starbird and Joab Lister, first class; S. R. Crane and Hiram Warriner, second class; I. P. Miller and Elisha Daggett, third class.

The present church edifice was erected in 1844, at a cost of $2,000. It was dedicated in the spring of 1845, by Rev. S. R. Smith, of Buffalo.

The following ministers, and in the order named, have served as pastors of this church, viz.: Revs. Benjamin Hunt, Gough, Strickland, G. S. Abbott, Benjamin Hunt, E. W. Whitcomb, Gowdy, Benjamin Hunt and Charles Hatch.

The present membership is twenty-nine. The trustees are: Lafayette Daggett, W. I. Eastwood, L. H. Brown, W. N. Martin, Samuel Starbird and Zachariah Millar; treasurer, L. H. Brown; clerk of the church, W. I. Eastwood.

The church property is valued at $2,000.

There is a union Sunday-school connected with the church, of which Henry McBain is superintendent, with an average attendance of sixty scholars.

SOCIETIES.

I. O. OF O. F.

Cowlesville Lodge, No. 332, Independent Order of Odd Fellows was organized January 10th, 1851, with a full complement of officers, and worked until about 1869, when labor was suspended. For lack of records we are unable to give a list of members and officers.

VICTOR COUNCIL, NO. 37, R. T. OF T.

This council of Royal Templars of Temperance was instituted at Cowlesville March 12th, 1878, by A. P. Greene, G. V. C., and A. F. Lawrence, G. S., of the Grand Council of the State of New York, with the following members and officers for 1878, viz.: Earl D. Cushman, William E. Austin, Charles D. Hart, Alexander McBain, Olive R. McBain, Ella J. Cushman, Henry W. Phelps, O. C. Fillmore, Hattie A. McBain, C. W. Tweedie, E. M. Richardson, Solomon Cushman, Francis S. Porter, Mary I. Wescott, C. W. Howe, Milo Wescott, G. H. Austin, A. M. Richardson and H. C. Harrow. The officers for 1878 were: A. McBain, S. C.; Charles D. Hart, V. C.; Solomon Cushman, P. C.; Rev. A. M. Richardson, chaplain; E. D. Cushman, secretary; Henry W. Phelps, treasurer; Henry Austin, sentinel; Milo Wescott, guard; O. C. Fillmore, herald.

The regular meetings are held on Friday evening of each week in Templar Hall, Main street.

The present officers are: E. D. Cushman, S. C; A. McBain, V. C; C. D. Hart, P. C.; A. M. Richardson, chaplain; A. A. Case, secretary; Milo Wescott, treasurer; O. C. Fillman, herald; S. Cushman, sentinel; G. H. Austin, guard.

BIOGRAPHICAL.

Isaac Albee was born in Rutland county, Vt., in 1807. At the age of nineteen he accompanied his parents to Plattsburgh, N. Y., and a few years later to St. Lawrence county. From there he came, in 1832, to Cowlesville, and purchased a farm. He has served some time as highway commissioner and overseer of the poor. In 1827 he married Sophia, daughter of Ellas Lincoln, of Bennington, Vt. (deceased). In 1876 he married Nancy Griswold, of Darien.

GEORGE HENRY AUSTIN was born in Bennington in 1838, and married Josephine, daughter of Arthur O'Neil (a native of Scotland), of Cowlesville, in 1863. Mr. Austin, who is a well known farmer, has served the town as constable several times. His father was born in Massachusetts, and in 1878 died in Bennington, where he settled shortly after the war of 1812–14, in which he served. Mrs. Austin was Miss Harriet Rhodes, of Rhode Island. She was born in 1801, and died in 1866. Mr. Rhodes onlisted in the 14th N. Y. Infantry in 1861, and was killed in the Seven Days' fight before Richmond, Va.

ISAAC W. AUSTIN was born in Rome, Oneida county, October 11th, 1815. He was married in 1836 to Mary Anne Clark, of Darien. His present wife was Margaret Hinck, daughter of Henry and Hannah Smith. Mr. Austin came from Rome to Darien, and in 1837 from there to Cowlesville. His father, John W. Austin, was born in Rhode Island in 1788; removed to Oneida county in 1812; in 1816 to Genesee county, and in 1850 to Wyoming county, where he died at the age of seventy-six. Henry Smith, Mrs. Austin's father, came to Genesee county at an early day from Kinderhook.

J. R. S. AUSTIN was born in Bennington August 12th, 1839. He was formerly a farmer, and is now a hotel keeper. July 4th, 1865, he married Ellen E. Pattingall, of Bennington.

JOHN B. (son of Ebenezer and Sophia) BECK, was born in Dumfries, Scotland, in 1827. He came to America in 1833, and located in Upper Canada. In 1835 he removed to Wheatland, Monroe county; in 1837 to Sheldon, and in 1854 to the southeast part of Bennington. He is engaged principally in dairy farming. March 28th, 1849, he married Phebe L., daughter of Ira and Phebe Thomas, of Sheldon.

LUTHER BERRY, farmer, was born in Concord, N. H., in 1816, and came from there to Folsomdale, where he has since lived, in 1832. He has been twice married, uniting with Sarah Anne Berry in 1848, and with Mrs. Mary Anne Kitsley, whose maiden name was Malcolm, in 1863. Mr. and Mrs. Berry are prominent Free Will Baptists.

LUCY BORDEN was born in Sheldon in 1839, and married Gail Borden, of Wales, N. Y., in 1861. Mr. Borden was born in Wales, N. Y., in 1836. His father, from Worcester county, Mass., was a comparatively early settler there, and was in the military service during the brief but exciting "patriot war." Mrs. Borden's father was born in Massachusetts in 1806; accompanied his sister to Wales, N. Y., at the age of seven, and came to Bennington in 1821. He was a militia captain, and served as assessor and highway commissioner. He died in 1865.

LUCY A. BORR was born in Waterbury, Conn., in 1836, and came from there to Bennington in 1847. In 1864 she married A. J. Borr, a native of Holland, who came with his father, John C. Borr, to America in 1858. Mrs. Borr is engaged in farming. Her father, C. G. Atwood, was born in Litchfield county, Conn., and came to Bennington in 1847, and bought the farm upon which Mrs. Borr resides. He entered the 186th regiment N. Y. volunteers in September, 1863, and died in the following December of a disease of the lungs. Mrs. Borr had a brother in the 1st N. Y. dragoons. He enlisted August 14th, 1862, and participated in all of the engagements in which his regiment took part until his death, which was caused by a wound received at the battle of Spottsylvania Court-house, July 2nd, 1864.

RUFUS G. BOWEN, son of J. G. and Helen Bowen, was born in Pembroke, Genesee county, in 1817, and married Mary, daughter of Walter and Effa Guiles, of Bennington. Mr. Bowen, who has been a farmer most of his life, moved to Attica in 1836, and from there to Bennington in 1879. He was assessor in the town of Attica twelve years.

JOHN BROMLEY, son of John and Elizabeth Bromley, was born in Spatchet, Rhode Island, in 1800; was married to Laura, daughter of Thomas and Sally Weaver, of Genesee county, in 1823, and came to Bennington in 1826 from Alexander, Genesee county. He had removed from Rhode Island in 1810 with his grandfather, who settled at Batavia, Genesee county. He purchased and sold several farms after he came to Bennington. Although very young he saw service in the war of 1812–14. He died May 11th, 1866. An ancestor of Mrs. Bromley came to America with the Pilgrims in 1620.

LUCIEN H. BROWN was born May 15th, 1816, at London, N. H., and came to Cowlesville in 1831. He has been a commercial agent, and has represented his town in the county board of supervisors. November 9th, 1846, he married Caroline E. Lanphear, of Bennington.

R. S. BURDICK, farmer, was born in Bennington November 1st, 1819, and married Lovina Bailey, of Attica, August 29th, 1841. He is a son of Amos Burdick, who was for a time a resident of Bennington. He was a member of the Wyoming county militia, and was promoted from corporal to first lieutenant. For a number of years he served as school trustee. His eldest son, Loronzo D., served in the late war with the 130th N. Y. volunteers, and was wounded in the hand.

JOSEPH, son of Frederick and Charlotte BURR, was born in Mecklenburg, Germany, January 3d, 1840, and in 1862 married Mary Redder, who had come from Germany the previous year. He came to America in 1868, with his parents, who located in Attica. He removed to Bennington in 1869. He has a farm of eighty-eight acres.

LAMBERT CANNON was born in Yorkshire, Eng., in 1830. He came to Cowlesville, where he is a well known farmer, in 1836, from Lockport, Niagara county. In 1870 he purchased his present farm. He married Mary Lamb, of Darien, N. Y., in 1866. He showed his patriotism by sending a substitute to the front in the Rebellion, and otherwise contributed to the prosecution of the war. Elijah Lamb, Mrs. Cannon's father, was early in western New York. His widow (formerly Mary Freeman), was born in 1793.

MARTIN CASE was born in Windsor, Conn., in 1807. At the age of two he accompanied his parents to Bennington. They located south of the Centre. Up to 1878 he was a farmer, but he at that time retired from active business. In 1829 he was married to Lucinda Spreig, who died March 23d, 1879, at the age of seventy. January 1st, 1880, he married the widow of the late Mr. Rowley, of Bennington. Roger E., son of Roger Rowley, was born in 1801 at Bloomfield, Conn. In 1808 he came with his parents to Bennington and located a mile west of the Centre. They were among the early settlers of the town, and his mother was the first white woman who lived in the town west of the Centre. He was a life-long farmer. He was married in 1828 to Hannah S. Osgood. By that marriage there are three children living. Mrs. Rowley died October 7th, 1852, at the age of forty-two. Mr. Rowley was again married, February 6th, 1858, to Carolina S. Hubbard, of Bloomfield, Conn., and died February 6th, 1870, at the age of sixty-seven.

GEORGE CHICK, son of Charlotte and John Chick, was born in Axmore, England, in 1825, and was married in 1851 to Jane Pursey, of Devonshire, Eng., who was born in Somersetshire, Eng., in 1827. He came to America in 1851 and located at Buffalo. In 1872 he came to Bennington and bought the Tracy farm of three hundred and twenty-five acres, in the eastern part of the town, where he has been successful in stock raising.

D. N. CLOUGH was born in Sheldon in 1831, and came to Folsomdale in 1834. He was married in 1857 to Elizabeth, daughter of Theodore and Nancy (formerly Albridge) Noyce, of Bennington. Mr. Clough aided in the prosecution of the late war, and is a temperance man, and a prominent member of the Free Will Baptist church at Folsomdale. His father, David Clough, was born in New Hampshire in 1786. He was one of the pioneers of the county. His wife was Mary Norris, of New Hampshire. He served many years as justice of the peace.

LESTER S. COOPER (son of Sanford and Betsey Ann Cooper) farmer, was born in Bennington in 1836, and married Margaretta D. Kones, daughter of John G. and Ann Kones, of Sheldon, in 1858. They have had two children, only one of whom, Elbert K., is living. He was born August 15th, 1871. In 1858 Mr. Cooper bought his farm in the southwest part of the town.

SYLVESTER K. COX was born at East Otto, Cattaraugus county, in 1842. At the age of nineteen he enlisted in the 64th N. Y. volunteers, and served honorably until discharged, receiving wounds at Chancellorsville and Fredericksburg. He was married to Helen M. Hammond, of East Otto. His present wife was Miss Eva E. Rich, of Wales, Erie county, to whom he was married May 20th, 1877. His father, Ell D. Cox, was born in Clarence, Erie county, in 1806, and died in 1877. Mrs. Eli D. Cox, formerly Eliza S. Williams, is living with her son, Hiram D. Cox, at East Otto, Cattaraugus county. P. Clarke Rich, father of Mrs. Sylvester B. Cox, is a native of Wethersfield, and a prominent resident of Wales, Erie county.

M. DE LAFAYETTE CORNELL was born in Middlebury, in 1844. His father was born at Newcastle, Westchester county, January 18th, 1801. He lived after the age of twenty-four successively in New York city, Seneca county and Middlebury, and came to Bennington in 1849 and bought his present farm. He married Anne H. Dillingham in 1825. This lady, the daughter of Henry Dillingham, of Westchester county (who died in 1818), is a lineal descendant of the Strangs, who fled from France during the Catholic persecution, his mother having been Jerusha Strang. M. de Lafayette Cornell married Edith L. Porter, December 25th, 1879. With the aid of his brother he has invented a useful and ingenious device for mounting window curtains.

FREDERICK CRAM, son of Fred and Fredreca Cram, was born in Wildecar, Prussia, in 1833, and emigrated many years ago; lived in Buffalo and Attica, and removed to Bennington in 1838, and has been engaged in farming. He was married November 4th, 1858, to Lucy, daughter of Bartlett and Lucy Brundage, of Bennington. Mr. and Mrs. Cram own the old Brundage farm. Bartlett Brundage, son of Nathaniel and Anna Brundage, was born at Balstown, Cayuga county, November 4th, 1796, and died August 3d, 1875. He moved with his parents to Bethany, Genesee county, when a small boy, and later lived in Niagara county ten years. In 1838 he came to Bennington, and bought the farm where he lived out his days. December 30th, 1818, he was married to Lucy, daughter of James and Hannah Thomas, from Farmington, Conn., who died April 7th, 1861.

SOLOMON CUSHMAN was born at Tunbridge, Orange county, Vt., in 1819, and came to Bennington in 1819. In 1855 he purchased his farm. In 1849 he was married to Luoy B. Brigham, of Chelsea, Orange county, Vt. Abraham Brigham, father of the latter, was born at Winchester, N. H., in 1788, and married Martha Hayward, of Connecticut.

ELISHA DAGGETT was born in Chenango county in 1806. In 1825 he removed to Newark, and later to Bennington, where he went into business, and afterward built the furnaces now owned and worked by his sons, Lafayette and Elliott. He married Tabitha Loomis, of Bennington, in 1833, who survives him, he having died in 1872.

JEHIEL W. DANLEY was born in 1826 in Bennington, where he has served two years as highway commissioner, and four years as a magistrate. In 1855 he married Helen M., daughter of Daniel P. and Phebe Steadman, of Bennington. He owns a farm of one hundred and four acres. Mr. Danley's parents were Seth and Lydia Danley, who came from Vermont to the Genesee country about 1812, and located at Danley's Corners, where Mr. Danley built a hotel and continued in the hotel business until his death, in 1853. In 1844 he was made an agent for the sale of the lands of the Holland Land Company in Bennington.

HARRISON Y. DAY, son of Volney and Electa Day, was born in Bennington April 28nd, 1840. December 28th, 1863, he enlisted in Company L, 8th N. Y. H. A., joined the army of the James with his regiment, and participated in all of the engagements in which that branch of the forces took part until the battle of Petersburg. October 27th, 1864, he was taken prisoner, and confined in Libby prison until February 17th, 1866. Since the war he has been a farmer. He was married October 23d, 1866, to Eva Peck, who died March 28th, 1871. October 6th, 1878, he married Elisabeth Kilion.

VOLNEY DAY, son of Linus and Lydia Day, was born August 18th, 1809, at Granby, Hartford county, Conn. When young he taught school. He is now a farmer. He has served the town as highway commissioner. February 16th, 1835, he married Electa Oration, of Bennington. Linus Day was born in Connecticut November 18th, 1778, and came to Bennington in 1818. He was a hatter by trade, and after his settlement worked at that occupation in the winter, attending to farming the balance of the year. He was married October 4th, 1808, to Lydia, daughter of Adonijah and Charity Holcomb. Mr. Day died December 29th, 1858; Mrs. Day two days earlier.

ANDREW J. DRISCOLL was born in Bennington in 1816, and married Elizabeth Yeomans, of Leicestershire, Eng., in 1848. He served in the county militia as orderly sergeant and second lieutenant, and gave countenance and aid to the prosecution of the late war. Mrs. Driscoll's father came to America when she was fifteen years old. He settled in Bennington, where he died in 1866. Mr. Driscoll's father, James Driscoll, was born in South Kingston, R. I., in 1788. At the age of thirty-three he removed to Massachusetts, and afterward settled in Bennington. He served five weeks at Beckett's Harbor in the war of 1818–14. He married Susannah Noroott, of Old Plymouth, Mass., who was born in 1784.

HARLOW G. DUDLEY was born in Barre, N. Y., November 6th, 1828, and came to Bennington in the spring of 1830, where he was known as a farmer and mechanic. February 1st, 1848, he married Susan I. Melvin, of Bennington. He enlisted as a private in Company H, 186th regiment, 11th corps and 2nd division, U. S. volunteers, September 10th, 1862.

He was in a number of battles, the first of which was at Gettysburg and the last at Lookout Mountain. He died at Chattanooga, March 1st, 1864.

HIRAM FENTON, farmer, son of Stephen Fenton, was born in Coxsackie, N. Y., in 1841, and removed to Bennington with his parents the next year. They located in the south-east part of the town. In 1872 Mr. Fenton married Laura, daughter of Lydia and Seth Danley, who had previously been married to Junius Cooley. Mr. Fenton died October 16th, 1878.

BURTON FRENCH, son of Ira and Sylvia French, was born January 25th, 1817, at Doster, Bennington county, Vt. In 1826 he removed with the family of his stepfather to Warsaw, and came to Bennington in 1887. September 7th, 1881, he was married to Mary A., daughter of Palmer and Caroline Fargo, of Warsaw. He is a farmer and an extensive dealer in livestock and wool. He has been justice of the peace, and held other offices in the gift of his townsmen.

BURTON F. FRENCH, farmer, was born in Bennington May 2nd, 1846, and married Rilla A., daughter of Chauncey B. and Elisa Dunbar, in 1869. They have one child.

IRA B. FRENCH, son of Burton and Mary A. French, was born in Bennington March 7th, 1839, and was married in 1861 to Huldah M., daughter of Asa L. and Lillias Clapp. They have three children. Mr. French is a farmer.

COLONEL JOHN B. FOLSOM was born January 28th, 1811, in Warsaw. For the past forty years he has been a resident of Bennington. Up to 1870 he was engaged in milling, trade, farming and the manufacture of potash. He has retired from active business. Mr. Folsom was colonel in the N. Y. State militia, 1840–48; brigade inspector, 1841–47; and again colonel, 1853–56. At different times between 1844 and 1878 he served the town as supervisor and justice of the peace. January 4th, 1831, he married Clarinda C. Hamden, of Sheldon.

AMBROSE FULLER, son of Isaac and Jerusha Fuller, was born in Elba, Genesee county, about 1826. There he married, as his second wife, Miss Jerusha Bush. In 1827 he removed to Bennington, and purchased the farm on which he died in 1864. His wife died in 1868. Ambrose Fuller, who is a farmer and owner of one hundred and fifty-three acres, married Miss Elvira Danley, daughter of James and Sylvia Danley, in 1846.

V. GAUTER, son of Ignas and Mary Gauter, was born at Baden, Germany, January 31st, 1824. In 1851 he married Mardgdalina Bleyler and emigrated to America, locating at Buffalo, where he remained until his removal to Bennington, where he purchased his farm of one hundred and ninety-three acres, a mile north of the Centre. Mr. Gauter has seen military service on both hemispheres, having been seven years a soldier in Germany, and drafted into the United States army in 1864.

NOAH D. GILLETT, son of Elias and Flavia Gillett, was born April 12th, 1811, at Granby, Hartford county, Conn., and in 1818 came to Bennington with his parents. His father died October 7th, 1860. Mr. Gillett has been three times married—January 20th, 1838, to Rhoda P. Warren, who died January 6th, 1841; August 15th, 1842, to Flora Day, daughter of Asa and Wealthy Day, of Bennington, who died June 20th, 1849; September 19th, 1850, to Phidelia Peck, daughter of Nathaniel and Tryphena Peck, of Bennington.

PRENTIS GREEN was born in Pennsylvania in 1801, and moved into western New York in 1806 with the family of his stepfather. Before there were any roads in most parts of western New York he traded extensively, frequently sleeping out doors, and at times accepting the hospitality of the Indians. He first owned land in the town of Sheldon. In 1860 he located where he now lives. He was married to Perlina Richardson in 1832. She died in 1852. In 1860 he married Phebe Rowley.

HENRY A. GRISWOLD was born in Byron, Genesee county, in 1829. He went with his parents to Alabama, in the same county, thence to Elba, and at the age of twenty-one to Michigan, and thence to Bennington. In 1881 he purchased the farm on which he now lives. He has served the town as school trustee. He has been twice married—in 1851 to Nancy Dibble, of Elba, Genesee county, and in 1859 to Julia Griswold. Mrs. Griswold's father, Lot K. Griswold, was born in Sangersfield. Conn., in 1791, was an early settler in Bennington, and died in 1870. His wife was Phebe Tucker, of Sangersfield. Henry Griswold, father of Henry A Griswold, was also a native of Sangersfield, and died in 1868. His wife was Louisa Allen.

BARNUM HARNDEN was born in Bethany, Genesee county, in 1820. He remained in his native town until he was eight; then removed to Varysburgh; thence to Springville; thence in 1841 to Bennington, where he owns a farm of two hundred and eighteen acres. He has been overseer of the poor four years and highway commissioner six years. He was married March 17th, 1846, to Hannah Borden, daughter of David Borden, of Bennington. He has always been a staunch advocate of education. His father, Oliver Hamden, was an early settler in western New York.

WARREN L. HAWES is the youngest member of a family of twelve children, five only of whom are now living. His father, Ebenezer Hawes, was one of the early settlers of the town of Darien, Genesee county, having emigrated to that town from Vermont about 1818. He bought and cleared a tract of land near what is now known as Griswold Station, on the Erie Railway, where he resided with his family until about 1830, when he bought and removed to a farm in the northeast corner of the town of Bennington, where Warren L. was born November 11th, 1838. His mother's maiden name was Sarah Howe. She was a lineal descendant of Jemima Howe, who was taken captive by the Indians at Hinsdale, N. H., during the Revolutionary war. The names of the children are as follows: Eleanor, Henry H., Samuel, Jane, Ebenezer, Alexander M., Allen R., Ira, George W., La Fayette, Sarah J. and Warren L. Warren L. in early youth learned the carriage making trade, and with his brothers Allen R. and La Fayette carried on the business quite extensively at Bennington Centre for a number of years. In 1864 he removed to Cowlesville in this town, and engaged in the mercantile business with A. H. Hoskins, brother of the Hon. G. G. Hoskins, present lieutenant-governor of the State. They remained in business together for about nine years, since which time Mr. Hawes has been in company in the same business with J. M. Sargent, under the firm of Sargent A Hawes. Both firms have been successful, and the present one was never in a more flourishing condition than now. September 25th, 1870, Mr. Hawes was married to Harriet M. Lake, youngest daughter of Godfrey Lake, of Pembroke, Genesee county, N. Y., by whom he has one child—a daughter, Lethe Eleanore, born October 24th, 1878. His wife was born March 11th, 1847. He has been three times elected clerk of his town, twice appointed postmaster of Cowlesville, and is now serving the third term as coroner for Wyoming county. He is an ardent Republican in politics, and belongs to the progressive school of thought on all social, scientific and religious questions. With the exception of about ten months' residence near Hammondsport, Steuben county, he has always lived in his native town, and since 1864 in the village of Cowlesville.

NATHANIEL PARKER HEDGES was born in Sheldon in 1815. His father, a native of Morristown, N. J., was born in 1775. At twenty he moved to Phelpstown; from there to Sheldon in 1806. He moved his family back to Phelpstown during the war of 1812–14, in which he served, but became a resident of Sheldon again when peace was restored. In 1841 Nathaniel Parker Hedges married Harriet Foster, who was born in Sugar Grove, Pa., in 1828. He came to Bennington, where he has been a resident for forty years, from Sheldon. He has a fine education, obtained in the common schools, at an academy and in college, and possesses a wide range of general and practical knowledge. He is a surveyor by profession, and has taught school one hundred and three terms in New York, Pennsylvania and Indiana, and has been professor of penmanship in academies in those three States. Three gifted daughters—Violetta M., Virginia M. and Clara J.—also teachers of repute, have died of consumption.

JOHN M., son of Andrew and Margaret HENNIG, was born in Bairen, Germany, in 1833. In 1844 he came to America with his parents, and located in Bennington. Beginning poor, he has by his industry and economy amassed considerable property in the town. In 1871 he was married to Catharine Welker, of Bennington, who died June 16th, 1879.

HON. ELIAS CLEVELAND HOLT was born January 30th, 1823, in Penfield (now Webster), Monroe county. From there he came to Bennington August 7th, 1848. October 2nd of the same year he married Cornelia E. Witter, of Chaplin, Conn. He has served as supervisor of his town, coroner of his county, and, in 1850, represented his district in the Assembly.

AMMI H. HOSKINS, the subject of this sketch, has been one of the leading citizens of this town ever shies attaining his majority. His father, George Hoskins, was one of the pioneers of what was known as the Loomis settlement, at Bennington Centre, having emigrated from Bloomfield, Conn., and settled on a tract of land a short distance west of the Centre in the fall of 1836. His wife's name was Lovley Parsons. She was also a native of Connecticut and both belonged to the old Puritan New England stock. The country at that time was a wilderness, but with strong hands and willing hearts they labored on, and the Hoskins mansion soon became known as one of the most hospitable, and the farm as one of the best managed in all that section. Here were born their three children—Roxey L., George G. and Ammi H.

GEORGE G. HOSKINS, born December 13th, 1824, has gained not only a local and State reputation, but a national one as well. After having been repeatedly elected to every important office in the town, from supervisor down, he was three times elected to the State Legislature, and once its Speaker. He has been twice member of Congress, and is now the lieutenant-governor of the State, having been elected November 4th, 1879, over Clarkson N. Potter, the Democratic candidate, by a majority of 290. Mr. Hoskins was born in Bennington; married Miss L. A. Hollenbeck, of that town, December 30th, 1846; and removed to Attica in 1863. His business has been that of a merchant. His only child, Miss E. Georgie, born June 6th, 1854, was married September 25th, 1878, to R. P. Scott, a lawyer of Butler, Pa.

ROXEY L. became the wife of Caleb A. King, deceased—a prominent man in his day—a farmer and stock dealer. His widow still lives on the original King homestead, near her birthplace.

AMMI H. was born October 21st, 1823, and is still in the prime of life. He remained with his father on the old homestead until the fall of 1849, when he engaged in mercantile pursuits at Bennington Centre with his brother, under the firm name of G. G. & A. H. Hoskins. The firm did a large and successful business, and continued till January 1st, 1864, when A. H. retired, leaving the business in the hands of his brother. In March, 1864, he engaged in trade in the village of Cowlesville, and in June following associated with him Warren L. Hawes, under the firm name of Hoskins & Hawes. They did a successful business for nine years, when Mr. Hoskins bought the interest of Mr. Hawes and continued the business alone for two years. He then sold his stock to H. Case, and retired from mercantile pursuits. Since that time he has been engaged in the banking business in the village of Cowlesville, where he resides. During all this time he has always borne the reputation of an honorable and sagacious business man, and boasts that there has never been a single year in his business life that he has not been moderately successful. In April, 1858, he was commissioned postmaster at Bennington Centre, and in 1869 was the census enumerator for the towns of Bennington and Attica. In 1861 he was commissioned major of the 67th regiment, National Guard, S. N. Y., and in 1864 was promoted lieutenant-colonel. In 1865 he was supervisor of the town, and re-elected in 1866. Mr. Hoskins started out in politics as a Whig, and continued to act with that party till it was merged in the Republican party, when he went with the Democrats, and continued to act with that party till after the close of the Rebellion. He was a war Democrat, member of the committee to raise volunteers for his town, and an active member of the county committee for the same purpose. He is now an influential member of the Republican party. He has always paid liberally toward the support of churches, and although quite tolerant in such matters he has a strong leaning toward the Old School Presbyterians, of which denomination his father and mother were honored members. He is a genial, kindly gentleman, a strong and true friend, and those who know him best appreciate him most. June 2nd, 1852, he was married to Lodema A. Hollenbeck, of this town, but has never had any children.

FRANK R. (son of Frank and Elizabeth) KOS was born in Belgium in 1833. In 1863 he emigrated to America and located in Bergen, Genesee county. In 1870 he came to Bennington, and bought eighteen acres of land three miles south of the Centre. In 1877 he added twenty-seven acres to the original purchase. January 81st, 1870, he married Mary, daughter of John and Kate Victor, of Sheldon, formerly of Belgium.

HENRY LAPP, son of William and Christena Lapp, was born in Hesse Darmstadt, Germany, in 1837, and came to Bennington in 1852. In 1862 he enlisted in the 22nd N. Y. independent battery, and was with the Army of the Potomac to the close of the war, participating in all engagements, and was mustered out of service October 10th, 1865. June 30th, 1866, he married Mary S. Ott, of Buffalo, formerly of France.

JOHN (son of Justin and Polly) LOOMIS was born in Bennington June 19th, 1820. In 1841 he married Julia M. Potter, daughter of Benjamin Potter, of Sheldon. Mr. Loomis is a farmer. Justin Loomis was born in 1785, and came into Bennington in 1831 and took up one thousand acres of land east of the Centre, where he built one of the first houses in the town. The first marriage in Bennington, it is believed, was that of Justin Loomis to Polly Rolf, in 1807.

SAMUEL D. LUDDEN, son of Ezra and Deidama Ludden, was born in East Hampton, Mass., in 1806. He came to Bennington in 1809, and has held several important offices. In 1838 he married Mary Shaffer, who died in 1841, and in 1851 Mr. Ludden married Mrs. Charlotte Van Dake, of Rochester, N. Y. He is by occupation a farmer and carpenter. Samuel D. Ludden, jr., enlisted in Company D, 8th H. A., in 1863, and was in the service until the close of the war. He was a participant in several battles. At the second Bull Run engagement he was captured, and confined in Libby prison, from which he escaped by disguising himself in a rebel uniform. He was promoted to the office of major. Ezra Ludden, father of Samuel D. Ludden, sen., was born in East Hampton, Mass., in 1781, and came to Bennington in 1833 and took up one hundred acres of land. He married Deidama Klapp, of Massachusetts. He was a sergeant in the war of 1812–14, and held several town offices. He died in 1861; his wife in 1842.

WELLINGTON MAXON was born on the farm where he now lives, in Bennington, in 1842. He was married in 1866 to Rulla Cooper, daughter of Sanford and Betsey Ann Cooper, of Bennington. He is a farmer and carpenter and joiner. His father, John F. Maxon, was born in 1804, and came to Bennington from Schoharie county about 1809. In 1840 he bought the farm where his son now lives. He was married in 1841 to Elmira Shook, daughter of Benjamin and Catharine Shook, of Bennington. He died in 1871. He served the town as overseer of the poor.

ROBERT BRUGE MILLAR was born in Bennington, Vt., in 1814. Less than two years later he came with his parents to Pembroke, Genesee county. In 1838 he came to Cowlesville, and was the second man in the town who did wagon making and repairing. He retired from business in May, 1883. His son, Robert H. Bruce, is now in the same line of business. Mr. Millar was formerly a captain in the Wyoming county militia, and he has been elected overseer of the poor, highway commissioner and justice of the peace, having held the last named office two terms. He was married in 1840 to Eliza McBain, of Albany, N. Y. The younger Millar was married in 1885 to Olivia Chesebro, of Erie county.

JAMES MONTGOMERY was born near Petico, County Donegal, Ireland, in 1800. In 1824 he married Betsey Page, of Herkimer county, who died in 1879. He has served as overseer of the poor. His father, Thomas Montgomery, was born near Enneskillen, Ireland, about 1760, and married Miss Mary Johnson, of his native place. In 1812 the family took passage on an American vessel bound for New York, at Warring's Point, in the north of Ireland. After a voyage of four weeks the vessel reached the coast of Newfoundland, where it was taken in charge by a British man-of-war, and all on board were made prisoners of war and taken to St. Johns, where they were detained four weeks. Upon their release the Montgomerys were obliged to make their way to Quebec, British subjects not being allowed to land on American soil during the continuance of the war; and until 1816 they remained in Canada, but came to New York State in the latter year, locating in Westmoreland, Oneida county, and removing from there to Bennington two years later, when Mr. Montgomery purchased one hundred and twenty-five acres of lot 9, section 8, where he died in 1830, at the age of seventy-three, and his wife in 1831, aged seven-one.

HARD MUNS was born in Aver, Cambridgeshire, England, in 1808. In 1832 he married Elizabeth Botting, and the same year came to America. He lived at Lockport, Niagara county, three years; at Niagara Falls fourteen years, and in 1849 came from there to Bennington, where he owns a farm of one hundred and eighty-five acres. He has always been prominent in the Baptist church. He and his wife were among the original members, and he was the first deacon of the first church of that denomination organized at Niagara Falls. He was married a second time in 1852, to Nancy Fairbanks, of Yorkshire, England. Mr. Muns's son, Sergeant John Muns, was a member of the 187th regiment, and was shot through the heart at Dinwiddle Court-house. George Muns, another son, entered the 49th regiment as a private, and was promoted to he sergeant and second lieutenant, serving until mustered out at the close of war.

LEWIS MUTH, son of Conrad and Mary E. Muth, was born in Hesse Darmstadt, Germany, in 1837. The next year he accompanied his parents to America. He lived at Rochester, Geneva and Henrietta, N. Y., and in 1850 came to Bennington, where he is a successful farmer. January 22nd, 1862, he was married to Kate E. Pardy, daughter of Isaac and Caroline Pardy, of Niagara county.

PETER MUTH, brother of Lewis Muth, was born in Germany in 1832, and the record of his coming to America and sojourn at various places before coming to Bennington, in 1850, is the same as above given. Until 1865 he was a farmer. He is now a merchant and deputy postmaster at Bennington Centre. He has held the office of town clerk three years. In 1855 he married Margaret Swyers, of Sheldon.

ALONZO PERSONS was born in Sheldon February 1st, 1811. He came to Bennington in 1847, and has since been a well known farmer in the vicinity of Bennington Centre. He was appointed postmaster by President Grant, and is yet in office. His father, Uriah Persons, was born in New Jersey in 1763. In 1806 he took up a section of land in Sheldon. He was one of the first settlers, and built the first frame house and kept the first tavern in that town. He held several minor town offices. He married Mary Sesion of Connecticut, by whom he had three children. He had been previously married, and by that marriage had nine children. He died March 20th, 1842; Mrs. Persons in 1856.

ISAAC (son of Isaac and Thankful) PIERCE was born December 24th, 1806, in Berkshire county, Massachusetts. In 1807 his parents removed to western New York, and located near Caledonia, Livingston county. In 1820 they came to Bennington, where his father took up fifty acres north of the Centre, where he remained until 1839, when he moved to the Isaac Pierce farm. Mr. Pierce has been supervisor and held other minor offices. He was married December 18th, 1831, to Laura M., daughter of Roger and Rebecca Rowley, of Bennington.

EUGENE PLUMLEY was born in Attica September 19th, 1841. In 1861 he enlisted in Company D, 19th Ohio volunteers, and was discharged four months later. In 1863 he re-enlisted, in Company L, 8th N. T. heavy artillery, and served until discharged, December 22nd, 1864, on account of a wound received at the battle of Petersburg, Va. Since the war he has been a farmer. December 11th, 1865, he married Mary R., daughter of James and Sarah Ann Owen, of Bennington.

WILLIAM B. (son of Joseph and Mary Ann) PERRY was born at Constable, Franklin county, October 22nd, 1823. Up to the age of twenty-seven he divided his time between farming and clerking in his father's store. In 1862 he came from Alexander, Genesee county, to Bennington, and located on a farm belonging to Pomeroy Warren, his father-in-law. In 1863 he engaged in trade in Sheldon. In 1870 he returned to the farm in Bennington, where he lives. He has served as supervisor, town clerk and justice of the peace in Sheldon, and justice of the peace in Bennington. December 31st, 1851, he married Asenath Warren.

GEORGE (son of George and Rickheaney) REDFOOT was born in Ryersbroom, Germany, August 20th, 1834. He came to America in 1855 and located at Town Line, Erie county. In 1867 he came to Bennington, where he owns a farm of fifty acres. At the time of his arrival in this country he had but $1 in money. December 28th, 1856, he married Laney Snyder, daughter of Philip and Kate Snyder, of Erie county, formerly from Germany.

SALLY (daughter of Rufus) MUNGER was born in 1814 in Genesee county, where her father, born in Tolland, Conn., in 1781, was an early settler; and was married in 1842 to Richard Richardson, and came to Cowlesville in 1844. Her husband was the first pastor of the Free Will Baptist church of this village. He died very suddenly, having attended four services the previous day, and was deeply mourned by many.

STEPHEN RINER is a son of Casper and Elizabeth Riner. He was born at Bassihein, Bairen, Germany, in 1822. He came to America in 1851, and located in Erie county, having married, the same year, Margaretta, daughter of Nicholas and Margaretta Fetzer. Philip Riner, their son, was born at Williamsville February 3d, 1852. In 1853 Mr. Riner removed to Bennington, and lived in different parts of the town until 1874, when he bought his present farm of one hundred and eleven acres.

JOHN F. RUDOLPH, son of Louis and Matlina Rudolph, was born in Hesse Darmstadt, Germany, February 13th, 1826. He came to America in 1848, and for a time worked by the month for farmers. He is the owner of a farm of one hundred and thirteen acres, a mile north of Bennington Centre. In 1848 he married Catharine Clinker, of Germany, who died in 1866. Two years later Mr. Rudolph married Henrietta Arendt, of Bennington.

LEWIS C. RUDOLPH, son of John F. and Catharine Rudolph, above mentioned, was born in Bennington in 1854. In 1875 he learned the carpenter and joiner's trade, at which he has since worked in connection with farming. He purchased his farm of thirty-nine acres in 1876. November 27th, 1877, he married Maggie Kilion, daughter of William Kilion, of Bennington.

JULIA A. SARGENT was born in Oneida county in 1810. She moved with her parents to Alexander. Genesee county; thence to Erie county; thence to Bennington in 1849. She has been twice married—in 1832 to Osman B. Wood, of Alexander, Genesee county, and in 1849 to John Sargent, a native of New Hampshire. She has had two children; one, Miss Julia D., born in 1850, is living. Mrs. and Miss Sargent are members of the Free Will Baptist church at Cowlesville. Mr. Sargent came to Bennington from his native State in 1820, and purchased the farm where his widow resides. He was married three times—to Miss Mudgett, of Bennington, to Harriet Fairbanks and to the surviving Mrs. Sargent. He was a member of the Free Will Baptist church, and was baptized on his seventy-ninth birthday; he died in 1874. He was a cooper by trade, and worked as such until within a few years of his death. His son, James, served in the army in the late war, and died of congestion of the lungs.

JOSEPH SELMAN, whose father's name was the same as his, was born in Germany in 1837. He came to America at the age of ten, and located in Lancaster, Erie county. In 1851 he removed to Bennington, where he has been town clerk four years and has held the office of collector. He was married January 21st, 1879, to Elizabeth Denz, of Buffalo.

JOHN SHADBOLT was born in Bennington in 1825, and was married to Sarah Bromley, of this town, in 1850. He has served as overseer of the poor, and was elected justice of the peace in 1877 and still holds the office. In 1872, in company with Burton French, he built the East Bennington cheese factory, which they still own and manage. Rowland Shadbolt, his father, was, as was also his mother, a native of Poughkeepsie, N. Y. They came to the Genesee country in 1818, and stopping north of Portage until the fall of 1819, they came to Bennington, where Mr. Shadbolt purchased sixty acres of lot 12, section 7, and added to his possessions until he bad the farm of one hundred and ninety-seven acres now owned by his son. He died in 1856; his wife in 1874.

JOHN SNYDER, son of George and Elizabeth Snyder, was born in Wellesley, Waterloo county, Canada, March 29th, 1849. He learned the manufacture of woolen goods, and worked at his trade until 1868, since which time he has been a farmer. March 10th, 1874, he married Mary, daughter of Barnard and Margaret Welker, of Bennington, and during the same spring located on the farm where he now lives.

FATHER JAMES SCHNEIDER, pastor of the Church of the Sacred Heart, Bennington, and of the Roman Catholic church at Old Bennington, was born in Prussia, June 11th, 1845; was there ordained to the priesthood, and came to America in 1875, locating at Buffalo. From Buffalo he went to Alden, Erie county, and from there came to Bennington.

DANIEL P. STEADMAN was born in Tirringham, Mass., December 31st, 1804, and came with his parents to Geneseo, Livingston county, in 1808. They were married about 1798, and removed from Rhode Island, their native State, to Massachusetts soon after. At Geneseo Mrs. Steadman died, and her husband, William Steadman, soon re-married and removed to Riga, Monroe county, later to Wheatland, and from Wheatland to Bennington in 1817. Here he purchased one hundred and fifty acres of lot 8, section 7, where he lived until his death, in 1843, when he was almost seventy-three years old. He was a volunteer soldier in the war of 1812–14, and in civil life he held a number of town offices. Daniel P. Steadman married in 1827 Miss Phebe Latson, of Dutchess county, and in 1842 Miss Juliette Fuller, of Bennington. He has served in Bennington more than thirty years as magistrate, as assessor fifteen years, and has held other offices.

NELSON STONE was born at Sand Lake, Rensselaer county, in 1824, and after residing for longer or shorter periods in various localities, came to Bennington in 1875. He was married to Anne Morris, of Gainesville, Wyoming county, in 1852. They have one son, Emmett, born in 1860, who has passed the regent's examination and is now teaching. The family are Free Will Baptists. Mr. Stone's father was born in Vermont. He was twice married, to Hannah Sheppard, and to Mary King, of Oneida county.

CHRISTOPHER J. (son of George and Mary) SWYERS, farmer and butcher, was born in Bennington in 1853. March 8th, 1875, he married Lane R. Redfoot, daughter of George Redfoot, of Bennington. He has been in business for himself since he was nineteen.

WILLIAM SWYERS, hotel keeper, was born in Wales, Erie county, in 1848, and married November 12th, 1871, to Mary, daughter of Nicholas and Catharine Hoffman, He came to Bennington in 1850 from his native place.

JOHN J. TARNISH was born in Mussle, Prussia, in 1819. He came to America in 1840, and lived in Sheldon until his removal to Bennington in 1850, when he bought the farm where he lived until his death, October 18th, 1879. In 1840 he married Caroline, daughter of Plater and Mary Myer, formerly of Prussia, who survives him.

ROSE, widow of Ithia S. THOMSON, whom she married in 1873, was born in Clayton, Jefferson county, in 1833, and at the age of twelve removed to Erie county, and from there to Bennington. She is a farmer and bee keeper. Her deceased husband was born in Oneida county in 1809. He was the first postmaster at Dale, and held many important offices in Middlebury, where he occupied a prominent position.

JAMES S. TOLLES was born in Orwell, Vt., in 1800. He has been three times married—in 1824 to Nancy H. Doty, of Bennington, who died in 1844; in 1846 to Armedia L. Hamferton, of Darien, who died in 1853, and in 1854 to Mrs. Susan Brown, of Buffalo. His parents were John and Catharine Tolles, born respectively in Connecticut in 1770, and in Massachusetts in 1777. Mr. Tolles came on foot from Vermont to Bennington in 1802, and took up two hundred acres of lots 4 and 6, section 8. He cleared some land, planted a crop and erected a cabin that year, and in the fall returned on foot to Vermont bringing back his family with a team of horses as far as Avon, Livingston county, and the rest of the way with oxen. He died in 1847; his wife in 1850. James S. Tolles has held the office of justice of the peace eight years, and as a military man has held every office from ensign to lieutenant-colonel.

JOHN B., son of Barnard and Margaret WELKER, was born in Baden, Germany, in 1835. In 1847 he came to America with his parents and located at Bennington. In 1860 he bought one hundred and thirty-nine acres between two and three miles east of the Centre, where he now lives. He was married in 1860 to Catharine Snyder, who died in 1872. During that year Mr. Welker married her sister, Margaret Snyder.

LEONARD WELKER, brother of the above mentioned, was born in 1837, and came to this country with the rest of his father's family, and has since lived in Bennington. In 1866 he married Mary, daughter of David and Rose Thaler. Mr. Welker was a native of Germany; Miss Thaler of Switzerland.

JOHN WERNER, farmer, was born at Ballne, Germany, in 1819. He came to Bennington in 1849, and purchased the farm upon which he resides. He has been overseer of the poor four years and a trustee in the Presbyterian Church. He married Miss Witherspan, a native of Germany, in 1849.

SAMUEL A. WILLARD, postmaster and dealer in dry goods and general merchandise at Folsomdale, was born in Bennington in 1833, in the first frame house erected (by his father) in Folsomdale; in which village he has since resided, except during six or seven years spent in Erie and Cattaraugus counties. He was married in 1855 to Nancy Newkirk, and in 1869 to Julia Moore, of Cattaraugus county. R. M. Willard, father of Samuel A. Willard, was born in Boston, Mass., in 1806, and came to Folsomdale in 1831, where he worked at his trade, that of carpenter and joiner. He spent a number of years in Indiana, Michigan and Missouri, and returned to Folsomdale in 1879. He was married in 1832 to Julia Olger, and in 1826 to Sophronia Berry.

MAKENDRA N. WILLIAMS was born in Burlington, Otsego county, in 1826. He lived for a time in Darien, and came from that town to Bennington in 1854 (in which year he married Abagail Austin) and engaged in mercantile pursuits. Two years later he purchased the farm where he has since lived. He also owns property in Marilla. His father was born in Rhode Island in 1786 and settled in Darien in 1829. He was a soldier in the war of 1812–14, and was wounded at Lewiston. His wife was Lucy Bardeen, of Burlington, Otsego county.

JOSEPH WILLIAMSON, farmer, was born in Stockport, Cheshire, England, in 1812, and was married to Martha Howard, of his native place, in 1839. He came to America in 1839 and for a time resided in Buffalo. In 1854 he came to Bennington, where he has since lived. Mrs. Williamson died in 1842.

JOHN ZIEEVERS, son of Michael and Anna Zieevers, was born at Biersdorf, Prussia, January 3d, 1854, and came to Bennington in 1874. October 30th, 1874, he married Barbara Meyer. Mr. Zieevers is a teacher.

THE TOWN OF CASTILE.

CASTILE was set off from Perry February 27th, 1821, and has an area of twenty-two thousand eight hundred acres. The land was originally timbered with oak and chestnut, intermixed with pine along the banks of Wolf creek, once employing fourteen saw-mills to cut out lumber for the Rochester market.

The portion of country now embraced in Castile was not settled, except in part, as early as most of the surrounding towns, for the reason that about one-half the town, and the best was occupied by that part of the Indian reservation called the "White Woman's Tract" which was not opened for sale and settlement until 1823, and some one thousand two hundred and eighty acres lying on the Genesee river, called the "White Woman's Reserve," was not on sale until 1830.

As early as 1809 some white families began to build log shanties and log houses in the territory now called Castile. Foremost among these squatters were two Scotch pioneers from Caledonia, on the Genesee river, near Rochester—Robert Whaley and his brother-in-law, Daniel McKay. Whaley built a log tavern about a mile northeast of the site of Castile village, where he continued to keep a tavern until he died, in 1817. McKay built a saw-mill on Wolf creek, near the west line of the Indian reservation, with the intention of getting pine logs from the reservation to stock his mill, intending to raft the boards down the Genesee river. About this time some men from Caledonia or Rochester cut and drew to the river bank from a splendid white pine grove on the reservation of some two hundred acres, near the river, several thousand pine logs, intending, when there came a freshet, to roll them in and run them to Rochester. For some reason they remained there awhile, and in a dry time some one (supposed to be Indians) set fire to them and destroyed them all. McKay soon abandoned his saw-mill. This seemed to check any further extensive depredations.

In 1817 occurred the great land slide near the Indian burying grounds. About twelve or fifteen acres of the West hill, some two hundred feet high, and composed of white clay, after a long rain slid down into the bed of the river and half across the flats, covering twenty-five or thirty acres of land, filling up the river bed and turning the stream across the flats, above the slide and around it to the east bank. A raft of saw logs moored under the slide lies there still.

S. D. TABER.

MRS. S. D. TABER.

F. M. TABER.

RESIDENCE OF S. D. TABER, DECEASED, CASTILE, N. Y.

MRS. F. M. TABER.

RESIDENCE OF F. M. TABER, CASTILE, N. Y.

Conspicuous among the early settlers of Castile west of Silver lake were Rescom Tallman and his three sons (two of them married and with families), Giles, Charles and David. Rescom settled on lot 58 and Giles on lot 59. David remained on the homestead, lot 58 Ogden tract, and Charles located on lot No. 1 Cotringer tract. These men were hardy, energetic and persevering of mind as well as muscle, and they not only made fine farms and residences for themselves and their children, but their moral and religious example has left its impress and influence on the population of that part of the town, including their descendants, to the present time, though over sixty years have passed. They settled on what was then called Oak hill, and were soon followed by Captain William Tripp, Captain Ebenezer Seymour, Eliakim Bottsford, Joseph Abbott and his sons, James and Gurley, Jeremiah Matteson and others.

Prominent among the early settlers in the east part of Castile were Clark Sanford, Esq., and his brother Freeman, who came in 1816, articled wild lands, and made for themselves and families beautiful farms and homes. They distinguished themselves as industrious, exemplary Christian citizens, serving the town many years as magistrate and supervisor.

They were followed and assisted by Dow I. Clute, John W. Boughton, John Bowers, Esq., Captain Rockwood, Gilbert Crist, Aaron D. Truesdell and others, who, having a rich soil to cultivate, soon made the northeast part of the town a beautiful and prosperous settlement of intelligent, moral and Christian people.

The first settlers of Castile, in addition to the difficulties of settling a new country, found themselves almost destitute of a market for their produce or their cattle at remunerative prices. Their wheat would barter for about thirty-one cents per bushel, corn and rye for twelve and a half cents, but there was no cash market. A few individuals went to Canandaigua and prevailed on Mr. Greig, the land agent, to open a lumber yard at Rochester, appoint an agent to receive the lumber there and sell it, giving them lumber receipts to apply on their land. This very favorable arrangement favored all the settlers, for those who chose to remain on their farms could find a market for their wheat, beef, cattle, pork, hay or vegetables, and take lumber receipts, which enabled the holder to pay for his land. We should think it a hard, slow way to pay for land that trebled the cost by adding interest every year to the principal, in lumber, at Rochester, first rate at $10 per thousand, $8 for second rate, and $6 for third rate. Of course those who bought the produce could not afford to pay much for it, and those who made the lumber did not get much for their labor; but a way was opened, and many availed themselves of it who otherwise could never have paid for their land. Some who had labored for years, and found themselves unable to pay even the back interest, and the interest on that, which doubled or trebled the original price of the land, sold out for little or nothing and left the country. But most of the settlers came in the prime of life, with a determination to stay and overcome all obstacles.

In the autumn of 1825 the canal was opened, and that relieved the settlers greatly; since after drawing their grain to York Landing, on the Genesee river, a distance of from sixteen to eighteen miles, it could be boated down the river to the canal, thus enabling the farmer to obtain from eight to ten or twelve shillings per bushel.

The land when the settlers came had for a great many years been burned over by the Indians in autumn and spring, in order to facilitate still hunting. This destroyed all the leaves and vegetable accumulation, and left the land naked and barren. In 1818 the settlers determined to stop this forest burning, and in three or four years they succeeded. The first crop of wheat or grass would be light, but by experimenting with gypsum or plaster the growth of clover would be greatly increased, and the clover in blossom plowed under greatly increased the wheat and other crops.

Dairying is now an important industry. Apples are becoming a staple product. The growers export about sixteen thousand barrels annually, and dry and manufacture into cider about as many more.

In 1814 Robert Whaley rented his tavern to Lemuel Eldridge, and removed his family to his saw-mill on Wolf creek. In 1816 the tavern took fire in the night and burned down, killing two travelers from Leroy.

In 1816 the Cotringer tract in Castile was put in the market, and in 1817 Whaley returned, rebuilt his tavern, and bought lot 38 of that tract, on which it stood. The same year he died, of apoplexy, but his widow continued to keep a tavern there for many years. She sold to C. Needham, and the farm is now owned by George Needham, of Perry.

In the early settlement of Castile grain was plenty, and there being no cash market the distillery offered the best market, paying in whiskey. There were three distilleries in the village of Castile, then called Wolf Creek, and six taverns in the town. A large part of the population consisted of lumbermen, and many of them bought whiskey by the barrel. Every one drank, temperately at first but drunkards multiplied alarmingly. Some few philanthropic men, seconded by a noble band of patriotic temperance women, united in a call for a temperance meeting, and formed a society and circulated a pledge. This was about the year 1825. Many inebriates were reclaimed and young men trained to abstinence from alcoholic drinks, and, as light increased from all intoxicating beverages. Revivals of religion followed, churches were formed, meeting-houses were built, and general prosperity followed. Although intemperance has not been entirely banished, there are now in the town no liquor dealers and no licenses to sell for any purpose, and the inhabitants seem to be practically temperance men from necessity, if not all from principle. In former years there were needed in the town four magistrates and four constables, nearly all actively engaged in their official capacity, to preserve the peace. Now there is very little litigation, and scarcely any use for constables, and poor families have the money they might otherwise pay for intoxicating beverages to buy the necessary comforts of life.

St. Helena, once a place of some note, lying on the west bank of Genesee river, is now only a small hamlet of twelve or fifteen houses.

Gardeau, once occupied by Mary Jemison (whose eventful history is given in Chapter 3 [of the General County History]) and several Indian families, has been changed into a series of pleasant and fruitful farms.

During the last fifty years the population of Castile has ranged as indicated in the following figures from the Legislative "red book": 1830, 2,259: 1835, 2,536; 1840, 2,828; 1845, 2,526; 1850, 2,446; 1855, 2,343; 1860, 2,323; 1865, 2,081; 1870, 2,186; 1875, 2,274.

SUPERVISORS.

The following is a list of supervisors of the town of Castile since its organization, with the years for which they were respectively elected:

Ziba Hurd, 1821–23; James Thompson, 1824, 1825, 1827, 1829, 1832; Rosell M. Curtis, 1826; Charles Tollman, 1828; Clark Sanford, 1830, 1831, 1840, 1841; Stephen D. Taber, 1835–39, 1845–47; John Calkins, 1842; Freeman Sanford, 1843; Joseph Wildman, 1844; Alonso B. Rose, 1848; George B. Chase, 1849–51, 1854; William H. Conklin, 1852; Mosely Stoddard, 1854; Samuel L. Chapin, 1847–60; George F. Pierce, 1861, 1862; William R. Fitch, 1863, 1864; Davis W. Smith, 1865; Socrates N. Hopkins, 1863, 1867, 1873, 1874; Lester B. Crego, 1868–72; James F. Abbott, 1875; Edward A. Pierce, 1876–79;

PATRIOTS OF 1861–65.

From the records of the Soldiers' Monument Association we learn that the men named in the following lists enlisted in the defence of the Union during the Rebellion. The first date given is that of enlistment. These men were private soldiers where not otherwise specified.

1st N. Y. Dragoons.—Marcus A. Atwell, Aug. 4, 1862. Isaac Baker, corporal, Aug. 6, 1862. George W. Burr, Aug. 6, 1862. George C. Belden, Aug. 6, 1862. Thomas J. Burr, second lieutenant, Aug. 2, 1862. Nelson Belden. Andrew Chapman, Sept. 8, 1864. Henry L. Cummings, Aug. 3, 1862. William H. Campbell, sergeant, Mch. 1, 1865. K. M. Carpenter, Aug. 6, 1862. George W. Curtis, Aug. 7, 1862. Andrew Calvin, Aug. 7, 1862. John Duggan, sergeant, Feb. 24, 1864. Simeon E. Felch, corporal, Aug. 6, 1862. Martin Getchell, Aug. 6, 1862. William Gray. Willard Greene, Aug. 7, 1862; died May 8, 1864. John Hare, corporal, Aug. 6, 1862; died May 7, 1864. D. Harrington, Aug. 3, 1862. F. E. Howard, sergeant, Aug. 6, 1862. George Johnson, Aug. 7, 1862. Robert Kershaw, Aug. 6, 1862. Charles Law. Lawrence B. Leddick, Aug. 2, 1862; died May 31, 1864. Daniel Leddick, Aug. 6, 1862. Eugene D. Lord, Sept. 27, 1864. Darius W. Luther, corporal, Aug. 6, 1862. William S. Luther, second lieutenant, Aug. 6, 1862. Henry Clay Lyons, Sept., 1864. Darius Maddison, sergeant, Aug. 6, 1862. Robert Mead. Frank C. Needham, bugler, Aug. 6, 1862. John Perkins, corporal, Aug. 6, 1862; died Dec.

7, 1864. John P. Robinson, major, Aug. 7, 1862. James E. Rood, Feb. 12, 1864; died Sept. 10, 1864. Reuben Salsbury. Edwin W. Slocum, Aug. 7, 1862; died Oct. 29, 1862. Benjamin C. Smith, corporal, Aug. 6, 1862. Lyman G. Simons, Aug. 7, 1862. Ansel B. Smith, corporal, Aug. 4, 1862. William J. Sheldon, Aug. 7, 1862. Albert W. Tallman, sergeant, Aug. 2, 1862. James L. Wade, bugler, Aug. 2, 1862. William H. Wing, Aug. 6, 1862.

2nd N. Y. Mounted Rifles.—Albert G. Borden, Mch., 1863. George C. Babcock. Hiram E. Booth. John Fingall. Thomas Gibbons. Nicholas Hannah. Thomas Hannah. Francis Hardin. Jonathan Johnson. John Lee. Alexander Mead. Edwin Mosier. P. McManiman. Ezra Patterson. George G. Pierce, 1863; died July, 1874. Andrew Trayer.

136*th N. Y. Infantry*—Milton Burknap, Aug. 25, 1862. George Capin. R. G. Dudley. William R. Dudley; died May 15, 1864. —— French, Aug., 1862; died in March, 1863. Elias C. Hoyt. John Lester. Benjamin F. Pond. James D. Smith, corporal, Apr. 27, 1861. Herbert W. Stocking. Franklin Tallman. George Telford. Eugene Wilson, Aug., 1862.

27*th N. Y. Infantry.*—J. McDuffy. Atwood Preston. Simon Ray. Charles Rock. William B. Smith. Elias Smith. J. L. Smith. Harmon Standard.

24*th N. Y. Battery*—Leonard Andrews, Oct. 18, 1862. Charles Bulkey, Feb. 15, 1864. Josiah Fernan. Henry Patterson. Josiah Perrin. George W. Piper. Myron Powell. Joseph B. Smith, 1862. Emmet G. Wood.

104*th N. Y. Infantry.*—Ezra Billings, 1861. Earle L. Gitchell. Charles Hall. James L. Quackenbush. George Westbrook, Nov. 30, 1861. Hiram L. Wing, sergeant. Charles Wing.

9*th N. Y. Cavalry*— Frank S. Barnes. Edwin C. Barlow, 1861. Lamberton Doolittle. Walter Farman. Bela Post.

1*st Mounted Rifles.*—Frank Higgins, Aug. 16, 1862. John Keeton, Aug. 16, 1862. Emerson E. Rogers. Nathan H. Sherwood.

8*th N. Y. Heavy Artillery.*—Elias Burt, Dec. 1, 1863; died Jan. 20, 1864. Charles Scribner, Dec. 18, 1863. William Scribner, Dec. 23, 1863.

Miscellaneous.—Samuel Andrus, Aug., 1861. William H. Borman, 21st N.Y. Infantry. A. Boughton, corporal, 89th N. Y. infantry, Nov. 20, 1861; died July 5, 1862. Horace Brownell. Nichols Baird. James Buck. Ira Burt.

George Cady, 27th N. Y. infantry, 1861. George Crowley, Jan., 1862. Henry Gibbins, 10th N. Y. infantry. John Gregg, 1861. George W. Greene, 1861. William Hamlin. Hark Hurd, 1862. Ezra Higgins, 1862. William Hill, 80th N. Y. infantry. Henry Johnson. Samuel Judd. Isaac Kidney. Philander Merithen, 1861. Eli Nichols, 1862. Edward A. Pierce, 7th Mass, volunteers, May 15, 1861. Wesley Porter. John Piper. George G. Rathbun, 5th N. Y. cavalry. Jacob K. Smith, 3d Conn, infantry, May, 1861. Franklin Steel. Chester S. Smith, surgeon, U. S. navy, 1861. Benjamin Tallman. Walter Tillman, sergeant, 4th N. Y. heavy artillery. Matthew Valmer.

JOHN A. THOMSON.

JOHN A. THOMSON.

John A. Thomson was born October 19th, 1824, m the town of Grove, Allegany county, N. Y. He engaged as clerk in the dry goods store of Oramel Griffin, in the town of Rushford, in the same county, on the 5th of October, 1839, and remained in his employ until January, 1845. He then went to Centerville and bought a dairy farm in company with his brother, A. D. Thomson. In 1848 he bought his brother's interest. June 19th, 1849, he married Jane A., daughter of Rev. Salmon Wheat. In March, 1852, he leased his farm and stock and bought a store and ashery in Centerville village in company with the brother above named. In 1856 he was appointed postmaster. In 1857 he began buying butter and cheese and shipping to New York. At this time he sold his interest in the store to his brother. The latter sold out in 1858, and our subject repaired and stocked the store and took in as a partner Mr. M. D. Hanks. In 1860 he bought out Hanks, and in 1861 the store and contents were burned, involving a clear loss of $3,000. On the day of the fire Mr. Thomson took one of his ashery teams and drove to Warsaw, where he bought a stock of dry goods from Augustus Frank; then hired a small store and commenced selling goods the next day. He immediately increased his stock and built a double store, filling one part with dry goods and groceries and the other with drugs; bought of Peter Cole the other dry goods store in the town and took a partner. He next traded one-half of the store and goods to J. Couch for a farm and two hundred sheep; exchanged the sheep for cows and rented the farm and stock. In 1863 he removed to Castile, bought a house and lot, including a frog pond, at the railroad station; filled up the pond and built a store and storehouse; filled the store with dry goods and groceries; manufactured clothing and continued dealing heavily in butter, cheese and wool. September 17th, 1870, the store was burned, causing a loss, over insurance, of $4,000. Mr. Thomson rebuilt and stocked it on a larger scale, and in 1877 traded it for four cheese factories, and he has bought and built eight other factories. On the 28th of June, 1877, his wife died, aged fifty-one; they had two sons. In 1878 Mr. Thomson made and bought about thirty thousand boxes of cheese, amounting to over $200,000; and in 1879 made and bought about twenty-five thousand boxes, amounting to $150,000. October 20th, 1879, he married Bell Broughton, of Covington. He still lives in Castile, prosecuting business with the same restless energy and activity indicated in the foregoing sketch; but confining himself at present to making and buying cheese and shipping to New York. In all his remarkable business career his rule has been to press forward, keep up good spirits and never say "can't."

CASTILE VILLAGE.

The first effectual blow the white man ever struck within the limits of the present corporation, to banish the desolation of the primeval wilderness, was given by Ziba Hurd, on the premises now owned and occupied by G. A. Davis. It was done on the 19th day of July, 1816. That blow, with its numerous repetitions, leveled and destroyed the forests, converting the places they had hitherto occupied in to, first, luxuriant and fruitful fields, and then village lots that were one after another changed into comfortable and happy homes.

The first building ever erected in the village was on the lot where Dr. Smith now resides. It was of logs, and a shanty at that—the roof all on one side. The next was a framed house, built but a short time after the log shanty and by the same man, but on the site now occupied by the residence of G. A. Davis.

In 1816 Ziba Hurd articled four hundred acres of the Cotringer tract of John Gregg, Esq., of Canandaigua. It was the first purchase ever made of any part of the site of the present village of Castile. The timber was generally beech and maple, along the creek some hemlock, on parts of the site some very heavy pines. The land cleared by Mr. Hurd in 1816 included the site, garden and orchard of the present residence of G. A. Davis. In the following winter he went to Vermont, and on his return, early in the spring, brought with him two yoke of oxen, two cows, two potash kettles, one double wagon and several hundred yards of "fulled cloth." He built the log shanty above referred to, near where Dr. Smith now lives, and the frame house before mentioned on ground nearly opposite.

In 1817, with the help of Gunnel Stanard, Mr. Hurd cleared twenty acres of land, adjoining and north of the three or four acres cleared the year before; built an ashery where Norman Calkins's dwelling-house now is, and began manufacturing potash, the only article the pioneers had to depend on for cash.

In this year Jacob Kellogg articled fifty acres of land where his son Asahel now lives, and commenced clearing it. He built a log house for himself and family, and a log shanty for his shop, he being a blacksmith.

In the autumn of 1817 Sylvester Derby and family moved to the place. Derby was a mason, and occupied Hurd's shanty. In this year also a clearing was commenced on the Jonathan Gilbert place, where Mrs. Crawford now lives. It included some three acres where the buildings are. Daniel W. Bannister built a saw-mill on ground now in the upper and west part of the Hopkins mill pond. Timothy Bannister built a double log house opposite the present "Christian" church. Ziba Hurd was made one of the three road commissioners of the then town of Perry.

J. Gilbert and family joined the settlement early in the spring of 1818. During that year Hurd completed a sawmill on the lot now owned and occupied by D. Pickett, Esq.; Tilly Gilbert came and setted in the village; Hurd and J. Gilbert built the cloth-dressing works, and the former built a barn near where J. D. Lane's ice-house now stands (the barn is now owned and occupied by F. C. Spillman as a joiner's shop and lumber-house); Hurd and the other commissioners of the town of Perry straightened the Allegany road between Castile village and the present town of Perry; J. Gilbert built the west part of the upright of the house where old Mrs. Davison now lives; Elisha Hurlburd joined the settlement and worked for Ziba Hurd, and Nathan Whitman and Joshua Smith came; Elihu Burr commenced building a grist-mill where the Hopkins mill now is, and built a log house near the Hopkins mill, and Ziba Hurd harvested over four hundred bushels of the real Genesee wheat, which he could sell for either six quarts of whiskey, or twenty-five cents in cash, per bushel.

The events of 1819 were as follows: Ziba Hurd and J. Gilbert added a carding machine to their cloth-dressing works. E. Burr completed the mill began the year before. School district No. 1 (village) built its first school-house, on the site now occupied by Mrs. Moshier. Rev. William True, of Covington, organized the first religious society in the village of Castile (the "Christian" church). T. Gilbert commenced building a framed house on the grounds where the Cure now stands.

In 1820 T. Gilbert built a framed house where J. W. True now resides, and T. Bannister converted his log house into a tavern. Laban G. Wheeler started the first store ever in Castile village, in a part of the Bannister tavern; and it is said he transported all the goods from Perry on his back. The brothers David and Heman Merwin located this year in Castile village, and David Merwin built a log house on grounds now included in Miss Greene's lawn. He and George Burr built a distillery just below the said lawn.

February 27th, 1821, the town of Castile was set off from Perry; Z. Hurd was elected the first supervisor, and T. Gilbert the first town clerk. J. Gilbert and Woodruff erected the first store building, on the lot where Mrs. Crawford's yellow house stands, and Sylvester Derby completed the building started by T. Gilbert two years before, and used it as a public house.

In 1822 J. Gilbert built a store on the lot next southwest of Dr. Wright's present residence, and Dyer Walker a framed house on the lot where Dr. Smith resides, which forms the present wing to the upright. H. Merwin commenced building what is now the back part of the house where Mrs. Bowman lives; and he also built an ashery a few roads below Pond's grocery. Lucas Janes built a house and tannery on the grounds originally occupied by Ziba Hurd's ashery; and Isaac Pratt built the saw-mill now owned and worked by Chapman & Son.

In 1823 Lyman Hurd built a framed house on the lot now occupied by the residence of G. F. Lucas, Esq.—the house that J. B. Howard owns, and F. H. Smith occupies. In 1824 the clothing works, nearly opposite the Cure, were burned.

One of the most noteworthy figures in the earlier history of the town was Gershom Welles, M. D., a son of Israel Wyatt and Eunice Lord Welles. He was born in Colchester, Conn., on the 8th of May, 1803, and was graduated in medicine at Yale College about 1826. After practicing a short time at Geneseo he came to Castile. "Dr. Welles, of Castile" soon earned a wide reputation, extending even as far south as Pennsylvania. He accumulated by his profession what in his day was called a fortune, and yet a large percentage of all he booked he never collected. The writer remembers the doctor burning a bundle of some $4,000 of the paper of poor patients, concluding it would embarrass them more to pay than it would himself to give. He was a pioneer and most earnest laborer in the temperance and antislavery enterprises. The doctor's ride was what the physicians in those days called a hard one, being crossed by the deep chasm of the Genesee river. It was not only hard but extensive, and his work never ceasing. He knew no vacations. The territory over which he rode, and the constancy of his practice, made an old man of him before his years called for it; they prematurely wore him out, and he died a little before the completion of his fifty-fifth year, on the 9th of April, 1858, missed and mourned by all who knew him.

The growth of the village from 1824 to 1830 was quite rapid. From 1830 to 1840 it was perhaps somewhat less rapid, and yet it included two new and very respectable public houses, three church edifices and many other substantial improvements. It was during the next decade that some of the best family residences were built. From 1850 to 1864 the growth of the place was remarkably slow, notwithstanding the fact that the branch of the Erie Railroad connecting Buffalo and Hornellsville had been built and put in operation as early as the summer of 1852, and made to pass only a little to the southwest of what had hitherto been the village site. The growth, however, that was realized during the period last named was mostly in the neighborhood of the depot.

In 1864 Miss Greene took charge of the Cure, which had been for some years under the supervision of her father, and so organized and managed it that it soon infused new life and energy into the whole village. The growth of the place from about the time the war closed up to the present has been quite rapid and uniform. The Cure is really the distinguishing feature of the place. It brings in and distributes that which is essential to its financial health and prosperity.

The village was incorporated June 19th, 1877, with a population of 869; and at its first election, July 21st, 1877, the following officers were chosen: H. W. Smith, president; John N. Hoagland, Allen D. Thomson and Walter Shay, trustees.

The village at the present time contains twenty shops for the various departments of mechanical skill and labor; six mills for grinding, flouring, sawing and cider making; seventeen stores for dry goods, groceries, drugs and medicines, hardware, boots and shoes, hats and caps, ready made clothing, ready made carriages, musical instruments and furniture; four factories—cheese, cheese box, shingle and vinegar; an apple dryer, a marble and granite factory, a photograph gallery, a union school-house (graded school), a printing office, a bank, four boarding houses, two public houses, four churches, two parsonages, one lawyer's office, five doctors'offices, two meat markets, three milliners'shops, two liveries, two lumber yards, two coal yards, two apple houses, agricultural works, and

"THE CURE."

In the year 1849 the hotel built and occupied by John D. Landon was fitted up as a hydropathic institution, by Mr. J. Greene. Since his death, in 1864, it has been continued by his daughter. "The Cure" is designed for ladies and children, accommodates about twenty-eight invalids, and is usually full at all seasons of the year. The institution is now under the charge of Cordelia A. Greene, M. D., assisted by Caroline Stevens, M. D. These ladies are graduates from two of our best medical colleges. The system of practice pursued is the choice of that which is well attested as best, not only in the hydropathic, but in all the other methods of medical practice. Although the institution itself will accommodate only about twenty or thirty invalids, yet by aid of boarding and public houses the number is often increased to forty or fifty, and even above the latter figure.

THE CASTILIAN.

In February, 1873, the *Castilian* was started at Castile by A. Gaines, by whom it was published until 1877, when Frank B. Smith bought a half interest. In 1878 Mr. Gaines again assumed entire control, and he is the present editor and proprietor.

THE CASTILE BAPTIST CHURCH.

The nucleus of the Baptist church was formed at the house of Gaius Blowers, on the 28th of April, 1817, when seven male and ten female members of Baptist churches united in the formation of a religious conference. Their names were Joseph Porter, Gaius Blowers, James A. Crawford, James Hale, Charles P. Hyde, Samuel King, Otis Wood, Mehitable Porter, Betsey Blowers, Polly Wiseman, Sally Munger, Lydia Wood, Clarissa Wood, Jerusha Porter, Eunice Hyde, Clarissa Crawford and Polly Hale.

On the 25thof June following these persons were recognized as a regular Baptist church, by a council of delegates from the first and second churches of Middlebury and those of Orangeville, Nunda and Warsaw. Joseph Porter was chosen deacon. Elder Joseph Case was chairman of the council, and preached to the church half the time for two years.

The country was sparsely settled, and the members of the church were necessarily scattered over a wide range, traveling on foot or with ox teams to the log dwelling house or barn appointed for worship, frequently a distance of six or eight miles. The hearers when assembled had ears to hear, and received the Word gladly, and the little church prospered.

In 1818 four were received by baptism and six by letter, including by letter from Saratoga church James Reed, who was chosen a leader in the social meetings. In 1819 five were received by baptism and five by letter. Jacob Mabie was received by letter from the Baptist church in Delhi, Delaware county, N. Y., and appointed deacon. In 1820 nine were received by baptism and seventeen by letter. In 1821 two were received by baptism and ten by letter, and James Reed was licensed to preach, and Charles Tallman was appointed deacon. In 1822 twenty-five were received by baptism and seven by letter. In 1823 two were received by baptism and twenty-eight by letter. A large immigration in these years brought many additions to the church by letters from other churches. In 1824 two were received by baptism and eighteen by letter.

In 1825 Elder James Reed, who had previously been ordained a minister at Friendship, Allegany county, N. Y., returned to Castile and was chosen pastor of the church.

Five were received by baptism in 1825, and twelve by letter, and in 1826 twenty-six by baptism and fourteen by letter; in 1827 five by baptism and seven by letter. This year Amasa Belden and Daniel Herrington were chosen deacons,

CORDELIA A. GREENE M.D. PROPR.

HYDROPATHIC SANITARIUM FOR LADIES.
CASTILE, WYOMING COUNTY, N.Y.

CAROLINE STEVENS, M.D., ASSISTANT.

and fifty-six members were dismissed to help constitute the Baptist church in Pike, and seven to constitute the Baptist church in Gainesville.

In 1828 a tract society was formed in the church, and resolutions adopted advising the members not to have any connection with masonic lodges.

In 1829 an extensive revival of religion prevailed; forty-five were received by baptism; twelve by letter; in December of this year Hosea Fuller, who had been licensed to preach, was ordained.

In 1830 twenty-five were received by baptism, four by letter. Up to this date the church was spread over three or four towns, with two regular places of meeting; one at the head of Silver lake in Castile, at the school-house near Deacon Charles Tallman's, and the other at Portage (now Genesee Falls), at the school-house near Anson Bigelow's, there being at this date no other place of meeting except a dwelling house or barn. The church now having at both places of meeting large congregations, and also having in its membership two very useful and efficient ordained preachers (James Reed, living in Gainesville, near Portage, and Hosea Fuller, living in Castile, near Deacon Taliman's), it was unanimously agreed to divide, and Elder Reed was chosen pastor of the Portage church, and Elder Fuller of the Castile church. During their separate existence of about four years ordinary prosperity attended each church, with accessions to each body, but no extensive revivals in either.

Near the close of 1834, the congregations becoming too large for the school-houses, and Castile village, nearly midway between the two places of meeting, becoming a center of business, the two bodies cordially agreed to form one, with Elder James Reed as pastor. A building lot was purchased in Castile village, and a meeting-house erected and dedicated in 1835, at a cost of about $2,000.

In 1836 thirty were baptized into the church and seventeen added by letter, and in 1838, 1839, 1840 and 1843 extensive revivals occurred and further additions were made. In 1839 Calvin Needham was elected deacon. In 1840 strong anti-slavery resolutions were adopted, and Elias West was appointed a deacon. In 1843 John Lewen was chosen deacon. During this year about thirty members were dismissed to form a Baptist church at Genesee Falls. During the succeeding seven years of the church's history up to the resignation of Elder Reed, in 1850, after a very successful and prosperous pastorate of over twenty-five years, the church enjoyed uninterrupted prosperity and harmony.

From 1851 Elder L. W. Olney was pastor until January, 1853, during which time twenty-eight were added by baptism and thirty-two by letter. In July, 1853, Elder P. R. Palmer became pastor, but remained only eight months. After a vacancy of four months A. R. Tupper became pastor; during his pastorate of about one year twenty were added by baptism and ten by letter. E. W. Bliss became pastor in July, 1855, and remained two years and four months; ninety members were received by him by baptism and thirty-three by letter. In 1851, 1854, 1856 and 1858 extensive revivals occurred. In 1858 Elder L. W. Olney became pastor the second time, and he continued such until April 1st, 1864. During his second pastorate twenty-six were received by baptism and thirty-eight by letter. In March, 1860, Benson Tallman, son of Deacon Charles Tailman, and Charles R. Needham, son of Deacon Calvin Needham, were chosen deacons. From August, 1864, A. L. Farr was pastor until March, 1867, during which time thirty-two new members were received. In March, 1867, Rev. C. A. Votey became pastor, and continued as such until April 1st, 1870; forty-two members were received by him. April 17th, 1870, Rev. L. E. Spafford became pastor, and remained until April 1st, 1872, during which time seventeen were added to the church. September 3d, 1872, Rev. W. P. Decker became pastor. His pastorate ceased May 1st, 1878; sixty one members having been added.

July 1st, 1878, Rev. J. V. Osterhout, the present pastor, began his labors here, which have resulted in an accession of forty members by baptism, while twenty-five have been received by letter.

From the records it appears that the church during its existence of sixty-two years has received by baptism seven hundred and fifty-six, and six hundred and forty-one by letter from other churches, making in all one thousand three hundred and ninety-seven members. At least eight members of this church have been licensed or ordained to the ministry.

The present membership is two hundred and forty-one. Benson and Charles Tallman are deacons, and L. C. Felch is the church clerk.

In 1835 the Sunday-school was organized. Elias West was appointed superintendent; the school prospered and increased, and has continued to be a prolific nursery of the church. During the past year thirty-five members of the Sunday-school have been baptized and received into the church. The school consists of one hundred and forty-nine scholars and twelve teachers; A. H. Felch is the superintendent, Charles Hess assistant, George R. Allen treasurer, E. V. Spelman secretary, G. L. Washburn chorister, and Marcia Washburn organist.

BIOGRAPHICAL.

Gurley F. Abbott, son of Joseph and Betsey Abbott, was born at Shaftsbury, Vt., in 1822, and came to Castile in 1839. In 1845 he married Miss Betsey Ames, daughter of John and Polly Ames, of Castile, by whom he had one child. Mr. Abbott died in 1870. His widow remains upon the homestead.

Nicholas A. Alpaugh, son of Aaron and Sarah Alpaugh, was born in Lebanon, N. J., in 1841. He was married to Miss Elizabeth Crego, daughter of the late Lester B. Crego, of Castile, in 1862. They have one child, a daughter. Mr. Alpaugh settled in Castile in 1865. He is a farmer, and has served as highway commissioner for the last five years.

Barnabas Ames, son of John and Polly Ames, was born in 1823 in Castile, and was married in 1850 to Miss Jerusha J. Lake, daughter of Ralph and Maria Lake, of Castile. He is a farmer and mechanic. His father came on foot to Castile in 1818, articled fifty acres of wild land in section 60, and continued to reside upon it to the time of his death.

JAMES ANDERSON, son of George and Jane Anderson, was born at Sligo, Ireland, in 1802, and came to America in 1808 with his parents; remaining for a time in New York city, and 1814 in Greene county, N. Y., where George Anderson died. James was married in 1819 to Miss Lorinda Hutchinson, daughter of Daniel and Polly Hutchinson, of Dutchess county, N. Y., and had children. In 1820 James Anderson removed to his late residence, on lot 85 of the Gardeau reservation, where he died in 1869, his widow surviving.

A. J. AXTELL was born in 1848 at Pike, N. Y., and was married in 1876 to Miss Laura J. Post, daughter of John and Jane Post, of Castile. He came to Castile in 1869, and is proprietor of Post's Hotel at Castile station. He keeps a first-class house with livery stable attached.

ALFRED BALDWIN, a son of Josiah and Sarah Baldwin, was born in Lime, Grafton county, N. H., in 1809. He was a wagon maker through the more active part of his life. In 1832 he came to Perry, and in 1835 to Castile. He was married to Miss Sibyl Burrows, daughter of Benjamin and Eunice Burrows, of Livonia, Livingston county, N. Y.

ORSON C. BELDEN, son of Paul and Miranda Belden, was born in Castile in 1827, and married Miss Cornelia F., daughter of Rufus and Cornelia Peet, of Castile. They had four children. Mr. Belden died in 1871; he held the office of commissioner of highways.

NELSON S. BELDEN was born in 1839 in Castile, and was married in 1863 to Miss Margaret A. Baker, of Castile. He is a farmer. His parents were Paul and Miranda Belden.

SCHUYLER BLISS, son of Eleazer and Clarissa Bliss, was born in Otsego county, N. Y., in 1810, and in 1830 came to Pike, N. Y. In 1833 he married Miss Marietta Porter, daughter of Joseph and Alice Porter, and has had two children. He came to Castile to reside in 1871, and bought his present farm.

ABRAHAM BRADT, son of John A. and Wilmot Bradt, was born in 1800 in Schenectady county, N. Y., and was married in 1825 to Miss Mary Jane Crawford, daughter of Joseph and Isabel Crawford, of Schenectady. He came to Castile in 1824, and settled on his present place.

GEORGE H. BUSH was born in 1840 in Wethersfield, N. Y., and was married in 1865 to Miss Lucy Gordon, of Pike. He came to Castile village in 1869, and is a partner in the old and successful firm of Wing & Bush, druggists and dealers in toys, fancy goods, books, etc.

ELISHA S. BUCKLAND was born September 21st, 1821, in Perry. He married Christina Beadle in 1854. She died. He married Adelia Johnson May 23d, 1860. He is a farmer, and has been a resident of Castile since 1854.

MORGAN L. CALKINS, son of John and Electa Calkins, was born in 1824 in Cayuga county, N. Y., and in 1850 was married to Miss Lydia I. Needham, of Castile. They have five children. He came to the town with his parents in 1826, and is a farmer.

MORGAN L. CALKINS, son of Captain Daniel and Tabitha Calkins, was born in Aurelius, Cayuga county, N. Y., in 1821, and came to Castile in 1824. In 1844 he was married to Miss Cynthia, daughter of John and Polly Ames, of Castile, who died in 1872, aged fifty-one years. In 1874 Mr. Calkins married Miss Mary, daughter of Robert and May Gregg, of Castile. They have two sons. Mr. Calkins has been justice of the peace since 1876.

ROLLIN N. CALKINS was born in 1835 at Centerville, N. Y. His business is milling and manufacturing cider, vinegar, etc., he being a member of the firm of Lock & Calkins.

HARVEY T. CASTLE, son of Samuel J. and Permelia Castle, was born in Bennington, N. Y., in 1842. He served in Company B 17th Pa. cavalry through the last three years of the civil war. He came to Castile in 1869, where he was married the following year to Miss Eliza B. Potter, of the same place. He is a carpenter and joiner.

ALBERT F. CHACE, the youngest son of George B. and Loretta M. Chace, was born in the town of Castile in 1843. His parents came from Washington county, N. Y., to Castile in 1825. Albert F. was first married in 1868 to Miss Emma P. Stickney, of Fowlerville, Livingston county. Her death occurred the same year, and he was married in 1872 to Miss Frances M. Boughton, of Susquehanna county, Pa. They have two children. Mr. Chace is a farmer, and has been more or less intimately connected with the Wyoming County Agricultural Society. He was four or five years its general superintendent, and has also been its president

OLIVER C. CHAPMAN, son of Jabez and Chloe Chapman, was born in Vermont in 1808, and came with his parents to Wyoming county in 1810. In 1838 he married Miss Maria Whitlock, daughter of Samuel and Polly Whitlock, of Warsaw, by whom he has seven children. From 1866 he has been a resident of Castile, and has been highway commissioner, etc. He is a farmer. His parents came from Vermont with an ox-team to the Genesee country in 1810, being forty days on the road, in the months of October and November.

ROYAL CHASE, son of Darius and Mahala Chase, was born in 1834 in Washington county, N. Y.; was married in 1859 to Miss A. Fuller, of Castile. He has been a farmer since 1846.

DARIUS CHASE, son of Royal and Ruth Chase, was born in Rhode Island in 1804. In childhood he removed with his parents to Washington county, N. Y., and in 1836 to Cayuga county, N. Y. In 1827 he married Miss Mahala Draper, daughter of James and Cynthia Draper. In 1845 he came to Castile and purchased eighty acres of lot 45 Cotringer tract. He has three children living.

LYMAN J. CLARK, born in 1828, in Erie county, N. Y., was married in 1858 to Miss Eliza Fuller, daughter of Elijah and Martha Fuller, of Castile. She died in 1864, and in 1867 he married Miss H. Minerva Belden, daughter of Paul and Miranda Belden, of Castile. He has two children. He is a farmer, and by trade a wagon maker. He came to Castile in 1836.

JOHN B. CLARK, son of Jacob and Nancy Clark, was born in 1826 in Castile, where he has since resided. He was married in 1851 to Miss Margaret Kennedy, who died in 1859. In 1873 he married Miss Elizabeth O'Hara, of Cayuga county. N. Y. He is a farmer.

JONAS CLARK, farmer, son of Jacob and Nancy Clark, was born in 1839 in Castile, and was married in 1861 to Miss Roxana Utter, daughter of Sylvester and Betsey Utter, of

Castile. He has five children. His father, Jacob Clark, enlisted in the war of 1812, at the age of seventeen years, and received a pension.

Dow I. Clute was born in Schenectady in 1813, and was married in 1841 to Miss Sarah B. Sayles, of Castile. They had one child. Mrs. Clute died in 1854, and Mr. Clute married in 1861 Miss Mary Jane Eveland, of Castile. He came to Castile in 1818 with his parents, Dow I. Clute and Ann Clute, who had thirteen children. His father served in the war of 1812, and died at Castile in 1864, aged one hundred years and three months.

Lyman S. Coleman was born August 30th, 1840, in West Haven, Vt., and was married to Miss Lucy A. Bliss, of Genesee Falls, N. Y., December 10th, 1860. He came to Castile Station in October, 1860. He and his partner, Orange Taber, are produce dealers. Mr. C. has held various positions of honor and trust in his town and in the State Legislature.

John W. Cook, son of P. L. and Hannah Cook, of Castile, was born in 1835 at Castile, and was married to Miss Marette Cook, daughter of Edwin E. and Almira Cook, of Cortland county. He has three children. He is an agent of the Empire Oil Company, of Buffalo.

Henry L. Cummins was born in 1838 in Livingston county, N. Y., and in 1870 was married to Miss Emma Telford of Castile. He came to Castile in 1843. He is a member of the firm of Hoagland, Cummins & Co., manufacturers of and wholesale and retail dealers in improved chilled plows, cultivators and other agricultural implements. He enlisted in 1862 in Company A, 1st dragoons; was wounded June 11th, 1864, and in July, 1865, he was discharged.

Hiram Dudley was born in 1810 in Plattsburgh, N. Y., and in 1816 came with his parents, Zina and Susan D., to Castile. In 1832 he was married to Miss Polly Horning, of Pike, daughter of Robert and Elizabeth Horning. Mr. Dudley is a farmer and mechanic. He has one son, Homer, and lost one in the civil war. His father was constable and collector of Castile for twenty years; died in 1871, aged eighty-nine years.

Philip Duryee, son of James and Francis Duryee, was born in Schenectady, N. Y., in 1810, and was married in 1834 to Miss Margaret Sharpsteen, of Leicester, N. Y. She died in 1843, aged twenty-seven years, and he married Miss Rebecca N. Cuykendall, of Skaneateles, N. Y. He has two children. He came here in 1820. He is a farmer.

Porter W. Felch, son of Willis A. and Eunice Felch, was born in 1846 in Castile, and in 1867 was married to Katharine Lock, daughter of Deacon Myron and Elizabeth Lock, of Castile. He has two children. He is a farmer and partner in the True & Felch livery stable of Castile.

John N. Felch, son of John and Eunice Felch, was born in Washington county, N. Y., in 1804 and in 1836 came to Castile and settled on lot 11 Cotringer tract. He married Elizabeth, daughter of Stephen and Amy Sayles, of Castile. In 1877 he died, aged seventy-three years, leaving a widow and three children.

Byron A. Fuller is a son of Lysander W. and Julia Fuller, who came from Livingston county, N. Y., to Castile. Lysander Fuller died at Castile in 1873, aged forty-nine years. His widow resides with her son, Byron A., at Castile. He is a farmer.

Henry J. Fuller, a son of Jeremiah and Hannah Fuller, was born in this town in 1837, and married Miss Betsey Akin, of Genesee Falls, in 1862. They have three children, two

RESIDENCE OF C. S. ROOD, CASTILE, N. Y.

CHESTER S. ROOD,

RESIDENCE OF E. S. BUCKLAND, GAINESVILLE, N. Y.

RESIDENCE OF O. M. TABER, CASTILE STATION, N. Y.

FURNITURE ESTABLISHMENT OF KELLOGG & CRARY, PIKE, N. Y.

RESIDENCE OF HENRY KARIGER, CASTILE, N. Y.

sons and a daughter. Mr. Fuller is a harness maker and general dealer in the specialties pertaining to his line of business.

ALMANZER GAINES, son of Solomon and Sarah Gaines, was born in 1842, and was married to Miss Maggie E. Oliver in 1865. He is by trade a goldsmith, but is proprietor of the *Castilian* newspaper and job printing office at the Castile station.

ASA W. GIFFORD, born in 1796 in Vermont, is a son of Gideon and Betsey Gifford. His father served through the Revolutionary war. Mr. Gifford has been married three times. He came to Castile in 1832.

ISAAC GILLETT, son of Jacob and Polly Gillett, was born in 1822, and was married in 1846 to Miss Sarah G., daughter of Dr. Rufus and Laura Whitney, of Gainesville; he has three children. In 1863 he removed to Perry, and in 1866 bought his present farm. Jacob Gillett, his father, was in the war of 1812.

THEODORE F. GRAY, son of Richard and Mary Gray, was born in Livingston county, N. Y., in 1826, and was married in 1848 to Miss Mary K. Rood, daughter of James and Betsey Rood, of Castile; he has two sons. He is a farmer, owning the old homestead, on lot 10 Gardeau reservation.

REV. ROBERT GRISEWOOD, son of Thomas and Lydia Grisewood, of England, was born in Ontario county, N. Y., in 1807, came with his parents to Castile in 1812 and settled on lot 99 Ogden tract. In 1831 he married Miss Lydia Handly, of Perry; they have four children. He is a superannuated preacher in the M. E. church, having been an active and useful minister until age and infirmity compelled him to retire.

ROBERT E. GRISEWOOD, son of Robert and Lydia Grisewood, was born in Castile in 1847, and was married in 1876 to Miss Ada Vetzy, daughter of Mark and Elvira Vetzy, of Covington; they have one child. Mr. Grisewood is a farmer on one hundred acres, being the farm settled by his grandfather, Thomas Grisewood, on lot 39 Ogden tract.

JOHN HALSTEAD, a son of Lawrence and Hannah Halstead, was born in Fishkill, Cayuga county, N. Y., in 1799. In 1823 he married Miss Jane Wilsey, daughter of Martin and Elizabeth Wilsey. In 1826 he journeyed on foot to Castile and bought his present farm. He, however, retraced his steps as farms the town of Ledyard, Cayuga county, where he worked a farm on shares for nine years before clearing his own. In 1835 he removed to Castile.

WILLIAM M. HART, son of Solomon R. Hart, was born in Niagara county, N.Y., in 1835, and in 1857 removed to Allegany county. In 1867 he came to Castile and purchased one hundred and four acres southeast of and near Perry village. He was married in 1868 to Miss Jennie S. McComber, daughter of Allen and Esther McComber, of Perry. His father, Solomon R. Hart, was born in Berkshire, Mass., in 1804, and now resides in Castile with his son, William, who is a farmer.

MICAH HATHAWAY, son of Royal and Susan Hathaway, was born in Cayuga county, N. Y., in 1835, and was married in 1859 to Miss Cornelia Bottom, daughter of James H. and Alvira Bottom, of Livingston county, N. Y. He is a farmer, and came to reside here in 1856.

GEORGE HESS, son of David and Julietta Hess, was born in Saratoga county, N. Y., in 1822, came to Castile with his parents in 1833, and in 1849 was married to Miss Saloma

Townsend, daughter of Abel and Beulah Townsend, by whom he had two children. He is a farmer on one hundred and sixteen acres near Castile village.

DAVID HESS, son of Peter and Sarah Hess, was born in Saratoga county, N. Y., in 1797, and was married in 1822 to Miss Julietta Kellogg, daughter of Elisha and Sarah Kellogg, of that county. Two of his children are now living. In 1838 he came to Castile and purchased one hundred acres of land. His wife died in 1876, aged seventy-six.

NILES D. HIGGINS, son of Dr. Otis and Hannah Higgins, was born in 1828 in Perry, and was married to Miss Sarah J. Wygant, daughter of Daniel Wygant, of Perry; they have three children. Mr. Higgins is a farmer, and has a village residence.

SANFORD A. HIGGINS, son of Henry R. and Esther A. Higgins, was born in 1849 in Perry, and in 1872 he was married to Miss Emma A. Karrigar, daughter of Henry and Alvira Karrigar, of Castile. He has three children. He came to Castile in 1869 from Perry, and is a farmer.

DANIEL W. HOUGH, son of Daniel and Hannah Hough, was born in 1848 in Covington, and was married in 1869 to Miss Martha Boughton, daughter of James and Abigail Boughton, of Castile. He has four children. He is a farmer, owning one hundred and forty-five acres. He came to reside in Castile in 1849, and has served as town collector two years.

ANSON HOWARD, son of Samuel and Rachel T. Howard, was born in the town of Bolton, Tolland county, Conn., in 1805, and in 1811 with his father's family came to Perry. He located in Castile in 1829, and was married in 1830 to Miss Hannah C. Hurd, daughter of Ziba and Sally Hurd. Only three of his six children are living. Mr. Howard was by trade a hatter. He was constable and collector six years, postmaster twelve years, and justice of the peace a quarter of a century.

WALTER HOWARD, son of Samuel and Rachel Talcott Howard, was born December 14th, 1802, in Bolton, Conn., and came with his parents to Perry in 1811. He located in Castile in 1828, and was married the following year to Miss Ruth Kinney, of Manchester, Conn. His business ever after locating in Castile was merchandising. He, however, was three years county clerk, and was interested several years in the manufacturing of lumber in Allegany county. He had seven sons and one daughter. The eldest son, George M., a lad of great intellectual promise, died in the summer of 1841, when but eleven years old; and the fourth, Frederick E., a member of Company H, 1st dragoons, was wounded on a scouting expedition in Virginia in 1864, from the effects of which he died April 15th, 1878, aged forty-one years. The others are all living. Mr. Howard himself died June 25th, 1867. Mrs. Howard continues to occupy the old homestead.

ZIBA HURD, a son of Daniel and Lucinda Hurd, was born in Tinmouth, Vt., May 22nd, 1785, and married Miss Sally Gilbert, of Bennington, in 1806. Six of their seven children grew to maturity, and three are still living. Mr. Hurd was the founder of Castile village, as elsewhere related. To him belongs the honor of naming the town. He was a justice of the peace many years. His first wife died January 16th, 1841, and he was married the same year to Miss Mary Center, who died January 25th, 1864. Mr. Hurd himself died March 14th, 1854.

NORMAN G. HURD, son of Ziba and Sally Hurd, was born in Tinmouth, Vt., in 1806. He came with his parents to the site of Castile village in the spring of 1816. He was first married in 1829, to Miss Antoinette Curtis, daughter of David and Polly Curtis, of Castile. They had five children, and two are still living. Mr. Hurd moved his family to Illinois in 1841, and thence in 1860 to Kansas. Here Mrs. Hurd died in 1861, and Mr. Hurd in 1871 married Mrs. Roxilian Hurd, of Castile, where he has resided ever since the year 1865.

G. W. JONES, station agent at Castile village, was born in Genesee Falls in 1850, and in 1871 was married to Miss Ermina Briggs, of that town.

MRS. HARRIET JOSLIN, born in 1804 in Otsego county, N. Y., married in 1819 Wilson Willey. He died in 1855, and she was married to Daniel Joslin, an early settler of the town, who died in Castile in 1869.

HENRY KARRIGAR, son of Peter Karrigar, was born in 1817 in Schoharie county, N. Y. In 1821 his parents removed to Otto, Cattaraugus county, N.Y., and in 1840 he went to Livingston county. He was married in 1848 to Miss Alvira Phelps, of Castile, and came to his present place. He is by trade a house joiner, but since 1847 has been a farmer.

JOHN KEETON, farmer, son of John and Sarah Keeton, was born in England in 1836; came to America with his parents in 1839, and settled in Castile in 1862. He served three years in the 1st N. Y. mounted rifles during the Rebellion. He was married in 1873 to Miss Mary I. Johnson, daughter of James and Maria Johnson, of Castile, and has one child. His wife died in 1874, and he was married in 1876 to Miss Eliza Johnson, sister of his first wife.

JOHN P. KELLEY, son of Peter and Deborah Kelley, was born in the city of New York in 1810, and married in 1832 to Miss Clarisea A. Goddard, of Shaftsbury, Vt. They settled in Castile in 1833, where Mr. Kelley was a farmer till 1840. He then moved to Moscow, Livingston county, where he spent twenty years in wheat buying. In 1860 he and his wife went to Oakland, Cal., hoping the change of climate might improve the health of their only son and child. From 1865 they lived at Rochester, N. Y., till the fall of 1871. They then returned to Castile, where Mr. Kelley died in the spring of 1876. His widow still lives here.

ASAHEL KELLOGG, son of Jacob and Susan Kellogg, was born in Saratoga county, N. Y., in 1813, and came with his parents in 1817 to the place where he now lives. He was married in 1847 to Miss Susan Smith, daughter of Deacon Ezra B. and Harriet Smith, of Castile, and he has two sons and two daughters.

EZRA A. KELSEY, son of Charles C. and Sarah Kelsey, was born in Addison county, Vt., in 1819, and was married in 1841 to Miss Jane Kimball, daughter of James and Mary Kimball, of Hague, N. Y. She died in 1845, leaving one daughter. Mr. Kelsey was married in 1848 to Miss Harriet Kimball, of St. Lawrence county, N. Y. They have four children. In 1842 he removed from Vermont to St. Lawrence county, N. Y. In 1868 he bought and removed to his present farm. He is a trustee of the Wyoming County Pioneer Association.

RALPH KENDALL, son of Elijah and Nancy Kendall, was born in Turin, Lewis county, N. Y., in the year 1808, and came with his parents in 1812 to the town of York, Livingston county, and in 1816 to Covington. Here he was married in 1834 to Miss Sallaina Clute. They had three sons and two daughters, all of whom are now living. Mr. Kendall moved to Castile in the spring of 1859, and has now retired from a large to a smaller farm, to enjoy the remnant of life in comparative quietude and comfort.

AMOS KINGSLEY, son of Solomon and Esther Kingsley, was born in 1813 in Attica, and was married in 1838 to Miss Pamelia Bigelow, of Genesee Falls. In 1847 he came to Castile to reside. He is a farmer, and has served as superintendent of common schools, etc. His father served as captain of cavalry at Buffalo in the war of 1812.

JOHN D. LANDON, son of Jeremiah and Rebecca Landon, was born in Williamstown, Berkshire, Mass., January 1st, 1800, and came to Perry about 1821. He rose from captain to brigadier-general of militia. He was married to Miss Eliza Dodge, of Leroy, Genesee county, January 7th, 1827. General Landon came to Castile about 1826, engaging first in the mercantile business, but soon abandoned it for building and hotel keeping. His hotel is now the front of Miss Greene's Cure. The general was not only popular as a landlord, but equally so as a man. He was intuitively a scholar and a gentleman. He was many times elected a justice of the peace, being never defeated. Mrs. Landon died May 29th, 1849, and the general followed her in June, 1855.

RALPH LAKE, son of David and Jerusha Lake, was born in Albany, N. Y., in 1799. In 1826 he married Miss Maria, daughter of Uri and Gedida Doolittle, of Stratford, Conn. They have five living children. He came to Oneida county with his parents, and remained there until 1826, when he removed to Perry, N. Y. In 1833 he came to Castile and settled on lots 57 and 58 Ogden tract, buying seventy acres.

HORACE J. LARY was born in 1844 in Jefferson county, N. Y., and in 1869 was married to Miss Ella J. Brown, daughter of Luther and Hannah Brown, of Wethersfield, N. Y. He came to Castile in 1848, and is proprietor of a restaurant and billiard saloon at the Castile station.

BENJAMIN LUCAS, son of Ralph and Hannah Lucas, was born in 1797 in Washington county, N. Y., and was married to Miss Almira Rich. They have two children. Mr. Lucas came to Castile in 1825, and died in 1862. He was a farmer.

PETER V. LUCAS, son of Ralph and Hannah Lucas, was born in 1802, and was married in 1832 to Miss Mary Thayer, daughter of Willard and Phebe Thayer, of Gainesville. He came to Castile in 1825, and died in 1878. He was a farmer, and held various town offices.

MYRON LUCE was born in 1821 in Seneca county, N. Y., and was married in 1844 to Miss Mary A. Card, of Ossian. His second wife was Mary Adams, his third Mrs. Van Arsdote, of Castile, and his fourth Miss Esther A. Rood, of Castile. He setted in Castile in 1834, and is a farmer.

WILLIAM J. PALMER, son of Alton and Harriet Palmer, was born in Scipio, Cayuga county, in 1827, and came with his parents to Perry in 1830. In 1865 he removed to Castile and purchased part of his present farm. He was married in 1854 to Miss Marilla Toan, daughter of Thomas and Betsey Toan, of Perry, and has four children.

LUTHER E. PELTON, son of Cole and Esther Pelton, was born in 1803 in Franklin county, Mass., and was married in 1828 to Miss Eunice Dodge, daughter of Content and Silas Dodge. He removed to Leicester, N. Y., in 1826, and to Castile in 1844. He is a farmer, and has been an assessor for twenty-five years.

JOHN PENNOCK, Castile, son of Zelah and Lydia Pennock, was born in 1794, in Vermont, and in 1831 was married to Miss Ruth Howard, of Middlebury, N. Y.

E. PALMER PHELPS was born February 17th, 1824, in Leicester, N. Y., and in 1826 came to Castile with his parents, Elam and Eunice Phelps. In 1846 he married Miss Anna Beach, of Castile, and has one child. Mr. Phelps is among the most thrifty and independent farmers of Castile, and devotes part of his spare winter time to teaching vocal music and holding musical conventions.

DANIEL S. PICKETT, son of James R. and Betsey Pickett, was born in Castile in 1827, and in 1851 was married to Eliza I. Graves, daughter of Joseph and Mary Graves, of Castile, formerly of Great Britain. He is a farmer and dealer in labor saving agricultural implements at Castile village. His father, James R. Pickett, married Betsey Cross, and in March, 1818, removed to Castile and articled fifty acres on lot 16 Cotringer tract. He faithfully and honestly served his town in offices of trust.

GEORGE F. PIERCE, son of Benjamin and Lydia Gurley Pierce, was born in Brooklyn, Conn., April 14th, 1802. On leaving his native State he went first to Livonia, Livingston county, N. Y., where he was a clerk for his brothers about a year, in the dry goods trade; then after working several years in Mt. Morris he came to Castile in the fall of 1834, and bought the mill originally built and run by Elijah Burr. In 1836 he built a new mill, which was the beginning of the mill now owned and run by the Messrs Hopkins.

EDWARD A. PIERCE, son of David and Elizabeth Pierce, was born in Brooklyn, Conn., January 12th, 1841, and came with his parents to Castile in the spring of 1844. During the Rebellion he served in Company F, 7th Mass. He was honorably discharged in July, 1864. In March, 1867, he was married to Miss Jane Lynch, of Wyandotte, Kansas. They have two children, a son and daughter. Mr. Pierce was elected supervisor in 1875, and still holds the office.

NORMAN W. POND, a son of Seavy and Prudence Pond, was born in this town in 1831, and was married in 1855 to Miss Louisa J., daughter of Daniel and Lucy Loper, of the same place. Two of his four children are living. Mr. Pond was a Union soldier in 1865. Mrs. Pond died in 1869, aged thirty-six years, and Mr. Pond was married in 1871 to Miss Mary L. Ogden, of Groveland, Livingston county. He is by trade a carpenter and joiner, but is now a grocer.

BELA POST, a son of Aaron and Elizabeth Post, was born in Vershier, Vt., in 1797, and came with his parents to Castile in 1813. In 1823 he was married to Miss Melissa Belden, daughter of Simeon and Calcina Belden, of Castile, another Vermonter by birth. Mr. and Mrs. Post raised thirteen children, all of whom are still living. Aaron D., born in 1850, and the youngest of the thirteen, is still living on the old homestead.

AVERY RAPPELLEE, son of James and Betsy Rappellee, was born in Milo, Yates county, N. Y., in 1808, and was mrrried in 1830 to Miss Marilla Townsend, daughter of Uriah and Fanny Townsend, of Seneca county, N. Y. He has three children living. In 1837 he removed his family to Castile, and bought part of his present farm.

JAMES H. RATHBONE, farmer, son of James Rathbone, was born in the town of Rhinebeck, Dutchess county, N. Y., in 1820; went to Erie county in 1838, and in 1836 came to Castile and settled on lot 71 Ogden tract. He was married in 1858 to Miss

Elizabeth Dildine, daughter of Zachariah and Sarah Dildine, of Dansville, N. Y., and he has two sons.

REV. JAMES REED was born at Saratoga, N. Y., April 20th, 1791. After receiving the rudiments of education in the district school of the early settlement of Saratoga, he engaged as clerk in a store. In 1814 he married Betsy Crawford, and in 1817 emigrated to Gainesville and engaged in surveying and school teaching, together with clearing a new farm. In 1818 he united with the Baptist church. In 1823 he was ordained to the ministry. In 1836 his first wife died, and he married Sina Jones. In 1834 and 1835 he was a missionary in Allegany county. He died November 27th, 1857, aged sixty-six years. Eight hundred persons were baptized and many churches planted by him, and he was regarded as the father of the Castile church.

LEVI RIDER was born in Springwater, N. Y., in 1831, and was married in 1854 to Miss Mary J. Brainard, daughter of Day and Emily Brainard, of Gainesville; they have two children. Mr. Rider carries on a farm of ninety-five acres. He came to Castile in 1867, and his father, Ruggles Rider in 1838. The latter died at Castile in 1846, aged forty years. His widow still lives.

JAMES RIDSDALE, son of Miles and Jane Ridsdale, was born in Perry in 1831. In 1852 he went to Ohio and purchased eighty acres of land. In 1866 he returned to Castile, and bought the homestead of his father, on which he now resides. He was married in 1854 to Miss Laura A. Williams, of Ohio, daughter of Elisha and Hannah Williams. He has five children.

ELIHU ROBINSON, son of John and Hope Robinson, was born in Washington county, N. Y., in 1798; removed with his parents to Scipio, Cayuga county, in 1811, and in 1825 came to Castile. In 1826 he bought eighty acres of wild land in section 6 of the Gardeau reservation. He was married in 1827 to Miss Ann Beardsley, daughter of Jared and Betsey Beardsley, of Cayuga county, N. Y., and has one child, Mrs. Augustus Taber, with whom he now resides. His wife died in 1855, aged fifty four years.

JOHN ROBINSON, son of John and Hope Robinson, was born in Washington county, N. Y., in 1811; removed with his parents to Scipio, N. Y., and in 1850 came to Castile and bought his present farm. He married in 1836 Miss Mary A. Beardsley, daughter of Jared and Betsey Beardsley, of Scipio, and has three children.

CHESTER S. ROOD, son of James and Betsey Rood, was born in Cayuga county, N. Y., in 1811, and came to Castile in 1841. In 1835 he was married to Miss Martha Aram, of Perry, daughter of Mathias and Elizabeth Aram. They have three living children. He is a farmer, owning sixty-five acres. His son, James E, enlisted in 1864 in Company A, 1st N. Y. Dragoons, and was at the battles of the Wilderness, Squirrel Ridge, Beaver Dam, Yellow Tavern and at Deep Bottom, where he was disabled by sun stroke, and died at City Point, Va., from its effects in 1864.

ISAAC ROOD, farmer, son of James and Betsey Rood, was born in Cayuga county, N. Y., in 1823, and came with his parents to Perry and to Castile in 1841. He was married in 1856 to Miss Agnes Skillen, daughter of James and Martha Skillen, and has two children, Rebecca and Frank.

ALONZO B. ROSE was born in the town of Lisle, Broome county, N. Y., February 7th, 1799. In 1818 he came to Castile. Subsequently to his arrival here he devoted a portion of his time to teaching; he was in fact one of the pioneers in Webster, Daboll, Morse and Murray. Mr. Rose was married in 1824 to Miss Faithful Groendycke of Lima, Livingston county. They had six children, three sons and three daughters, all of whom grew to maturity. Two of the daughters still survive. One of the sons was instantly killed near the close of the "Seven Days fight" in front of Richmond. Judge Rose was elected to the office of magistrate the first year the people were trusted with such responsibility, and successively thereafter till 1841, when he was made associate justice. He was, however, still later chosen magistrate from time to time, until he had held that office nearly or quite a quarter of a century, He was elected to the Assembly in 1853 and 1854, serving each term to the entire satisfaction of his constituency. He has held many minor offices, and was one of the stalwarts in the temperance enterprise.

James S. Sanford, son of Clark and Mary A. Sanford, was born in this town in 1821, and was married in 1844 to Miss Caroline A. Gray, daughter of Richard and Polly Gray, of Castile; they had one child. His wife Caroline died in 1860, and in 1862 he married Miss Mary A. Smallwood, daughter of Michael and Elizabeth Smallwood, of Warsaw. Two of their children are now living. Mr. Sanford died in Washington, D. C., in 1875, where he held an office in the post-office department.

Erwin Sanford, son of Freeman and Cynthia Sanford, was born in Castile in 1824, and was married in 1849 to Miss Elizabeth Vanslyke, daughter of Henry and Hannah Vanslyke, of Perry; they had three children. He remained on the homestead until he died, aged fifty-two years. His father, Freeman Sanford, came from Connecticut and settled in Castile in 1816, and married Miss Cynthia Bowers. Erwin was their only child.

Henry D. Sayes was born in 1824 at Pinkney, Lewis county, and came to Castile in 1884. He married Emmerancy T. Minor, of Castile, in 1849. He is a farmer.

John R. Sayles, farmer, son of James and Ruth Sayles, was born in Saratoga county, N. Y., in 1822, and came with his parents to Castile in 1836. In 1849 he married Miss Emeline C., daughter of Russell and Emily Calkins, of Castile, and has one child. He has served nine years successively as commissioner of highways.

Gideon Scofield, son of Gideon and Abigail Scofield, was born in Albany county, N. Y., in 1802, and was married in 1824 to Miss Permelia Wescott, daughter of John and Eunice Wescott, of Saratoga county, N. Y. He came to Castile in 1836 and has followed farming. He has been a magistrate and overseer of the poor, and is elder in the Presbyterian church in Castile. Deacon Scofield has during his long residence in Castile occupied the front rank among the anti-slavery and temperance workers.

Miles Sharpsteen, son of Samuel and Margaret Sharpsteen, was born in 1823 in Cayuga county, N.Y., and was married in 1848 to Miss Julia L. Davis, of Livingston county, who died in 1877, aged forty-eight years, leaving one son. Miles Sharpsteen has been a resident of Castile since 1863, and is a farmer.

Walter Shay was born in Boston, Mass., in 1819; in 1837 he removed to Allegany county, N. Y., and remained there until 1840, when he removed to Eagle, Wyoming county. He was two years supervisor of that town. In 1850 he was married to Miss Caroline F. Gally, of Nunda, N. Y., by whom he had two children. In 1858 he engaged in mercantile business at Eagle Village. He was a United States assistant assessor for the

E. PALMER PHELPS.

MRS. ANNA PHELPS.

RESIDENCE OF E. PALMER PHELPS, CASTILE, N.Y.

ELAM PHELPS

RES. OF ELAM PHELPS, DECEASED, CASTILE, N.Y.

MRS. ELAM PHELPS.

RESIDENCE OF CHAS. TALLMAN, CASTILE, N.Y.

RESIDENCE OF E.G. MATTHEWS, PERRY, N.Y.

29th district for nine years from 1862. In 1873 he removed to Castile village, and was there elected a justice of the peace.

PHILO SHELDON, son of Isaac and Sally Sheldon, was born in the town of Pawlet, Vt., in 1806, and married Miss Henrietta Edgerton, of the same place, in 1830. They have had five children, three of whom are living. Mr. Sheldon came to Cayuga county, N. Y., in 1825, and thence to Castile in 1858. His son William was in the United States service three years during the war of the Rebellion, and was honorably discharged.

NORMAN SIMONS, son of Silas and Hannah Simons, was born in Connecticut in 1807, and in 1829 came to Castile. In 1838 he married Miss Lucinda Phelps, daughter of Eldad and Abigail Phelps, of Castile. They have three children. In 1831 Mr. Simons bought his present farm.

JOSLAH SLADE, son of Joseph and Rhoda Slade, was born in Rensselaer county, N. Y., in 1821. In 1838 he moved to Madison county, N. Y., and in 1846 came to Castile, where he has since 1858 been employed as a dealer in produce and in Scotch and American granite. He was married in 1860 to Miss Martha A. Scott, daughter of Isaac and Mary Scott, of Allegany county, N. Y. Of his five children Mary I. Slade, M. D., is a graduate of the Ann Arbor Medical Institute.

PETER L. SMITH, son of Isaac and Lydia Smith, was born in Genesee Falls in 1844, and was married in 1869 to Miss Mary L., daughter of William B. and P. Wiseman, of Gainesville. He has two children. He came to Castile in 1878, and is a farmer. His parents came west from Dutchess county, and settled on new land in Genesee Falls. His father died in 1875, aged eighty-three years.

DAVIS W. SMITH was born in Vermont in 1815, and in 1835 removed to Troy, N. Y., where he graduated as a law student. In 1838 he came to Castile, and kept a select school until the spring of 1855, when failing health required its close. In 1841 he was married to Miss Emily S. Welles, of Castile, daughter of Israel and Emily S. Welles, of Connecticut. She died in 1872, leaving two sons and a daughter, who are still living. Mr. Smith continues to reside on the spot where he spent the prime of live.

HARRISON W. SMITH was born in 1826 in Livingston county, N. Y., and was married in 1848 to Nancy I. Mills, of that county. He came to Castile in 1857, and is an attorney and counselor at law at the village. Of his six children one son, Frederick, is practicing law on Main street; another, E. C. Smith, is a druggist at Castile, and a third, Charles J. Smith, is a dry goods merchant at Castile.

S. CHESTER SMITH, M. D., a son of Ezra B. and Harriet Smith, was born in Preston, Conn., in 1833, and came with his parents in 1834 to Castile. He graduated in medicine at New York in 1860, and was a surgeon in the navy until 1864, when he resigned. He was married to Miss Lida Van Arsdale, daughter of Abram and Maria Van Arsdale, of Castile, in 1868. They have one child, a boy, about ten years old. Dr. Smith is now practicing at Castile.

REV. WILLIAM HENRY SNYDER, son of Dr. Andrew and Lydia Snyder, was born in the town of Hurley, Ulster county, N. Y., in 1794. About 1829 he became pastor of a Dutch Reformed church in Fayette, Seneca county, N. Y. He was married in 1827 to Miss Harriet Sturtivant, daughter of Zebidee and Jerusha Sturtivant, of Columbia county, N. Y. He has had one son and three daughters. The daughters are still living. After some ten years of professional life, ill health compelled him to abandon the pulpit and go to farming; he died in 1874. Mrs. Snyder still lives at the old homestead.

John Sowerby, son of George and Elizabeth Sowerby, was born in Yorkshire, England, in 1808. In 1828 he came to Geneva, N. Y., and in 1832 to Castile, and settled on lot 48 Ogden tract. He was married in 1832 to Miss Jane Brown, daughter of Thomas and Mary Brown, and has six children. He is a farmer.

Charles Strong, son of Eliphalet and Sally Strong, was born in 1812 in Northampton, Mass. In 1845 he married Miss Christine Eveland, of Livingston county, N. Y. In 1835 he came to Castile, where he is now engaged in farming. In 1861 his first wife died, and in 1864 he married Miss Arminda Stone, of Orangeville, N. Y. They have four children.

Thomas H. and Charles Sutherland, of the firm of T. H. Sutherland A Co., are sons of George and Mary A. Sutherland, and were born in the town of Hamilton, Canada West—Thomas H. February 1st, 1855, and Charles February 28th, 1859. They came with their parents to Castile in 1873. Charles was married to Miss Mary M. Sears, of Caneadea, Allegany county, August, 1878. The brothers are the present proprietors of the Castile Marble and Granite Works, a few doors east of the corner of Main and Water streets.

Harmon E. Taber, son of Colonel Stephen D. and Percy P. Taber, was born in 1840 at Castile, and was married in 1870 to Miss Jennie Pettibone, of Michigan. He owns a first class farm of one hundred and thirty-five acres on the Gardeau reservation.

Francis M. Taber, son of Colonel Stephen D. and Percy P. Taber, was born in 1839 in Castile, and in 1863 was married to Miss Susan D. Robinson, of Castile; they have two children. Mr. Taber is a farmer, having one hundred and fifty acres of the old Gardeau reservation. His father was born at Broadalbin, N.Y., in 1796, and came to Perry in 1817, and from there to Castile in 1832. He was for many years supervisor of Castile, and also a loan commissioner. He died in 1871, aged seventy-three years, honored and respected by all who knew him.

Orange M. Taber, son of Gideon and Elpha Taber, was born in 1825 in Perry, and was married in 1852 to Miss Loretta E. Curtiss, of Geauga county, O. She died in 1854, and in 1856 he married Mrs. Cynthia D. Pettibone, of Warsaw. Mr. Taber is justice of the peace, and a member of the firm of Coleman & Taber, who have a storehouse and are large produce dealers at Castile station. Mr. Taber's father died in Castile in 1861, aged ninety years.

David Taggart, son of David and Sarah Taggart, was born in Washington county, N. Y., in 1802, and in 1827 came to Castile and bought the farm lately occupied by him. He married Miss Betsey Woodruff, of Gainesville, who died in 1874. He died in 1876, leaving to his son and daughter, who still reside on the homestead, one of the most attractive suburban farm residences in Castile.

Charles Tallman, son of Lewis and Julia Tallman, was born in 1831 in Genesee Falls. He married in 1857 Miss Sarah Belden, daughter of Paul and Miranda Belden, of Castile, and has two children. He came to Castile to reside in 1871, and is a farmer. Mr. Tallman is deacon of the Baptist church at Castile, and a grandson of Deacon Charles Tallman, an early settler of this town.

FRANK G. TALLMAN, son of Benson and Sophia Tallman, was born at Castile in 1839, and was married in 1860 to Miss Laverna Allen, of Gainesville. He is a member of the firm of Hoagland, Cummins & Co., manufacturers of and wholesale dealers in plows, harrows, cultivators and other improved farming implements connected with their iron foundry at Castile village.

BENSON TALLMAN, son of Charles and Esther Tallman, was born in Delaware county, N. Y., in 1812, and came with his parents to Castile in 1817, since which time he has resided here. He was married in 1833 to Miss Sophia Carlisle, daughter of William and Nancy Carlisle, of Castile, and they have three children. He has held the office of assessor of the town for twenty years, and has been a deacon of the Baptist church in Castile for thirty years. He is by occupation a farmer. His father came with an ox team, being two weeks on the journey. The father, Charles Tallman, was a deacon of the Baptist church, and held the offices of supervisor and justice of the peace of Castile.

CAPTAIN ELIAS TALLMAN, son of Giles Tallman, was born in Delaware county, N. Y., in 1815, and came with his parents in 1816 to Castile with an ox-team. He settled on lot 59 Ogden tract, and was married in 1839 to Miss Cynthia Mattison, daughter of Jeremiah and Barbara Mattison, who came to Castile in 1822 from Vermont. Captain Tallman has four children, two of whom served in the war of the Rebellion. He was at the age of seventeen at Buffalo with his regiment during the Patriot war, and he afterward became captain of the same artillery company. His father served in the war of 1812 for which his widow still receives a pension. Captain Tallman is a farmer on the old homestead of one hundred acres, and has discharged the duties of various offices of honor and trust in his town.

JOHN A. THOMPSON was born in 1824 in Allegany county, N. Y., and married Miss Jane A. Wheat, of Centerville, N. Y., in 1849. He came to Castile in 1863. He is a retired merchant, and is manufacturing cheese in twelve factories, and buying and shipping butter, cheese and wool at Castile station.

IRA TRUE, son of Samuel and Zeruiah True, was born in Vermont in 1799 and in 1815 came to Wyoming county with his parents and their effects, with two ox-teams and one horse, being forty-two days on a journey of four hundred miles. In October Mr. True arrived in Covington and articled eighty acres of wild land. They slept in their covered wagons until they had erected a log house. In the spring of 1816 they sold out for one hundred dollars, and purchased sixty acres in Perry. In 1826 Ira True was married to Miss Judith Nevins, of Perry, and in 1830 he removed to his late farm in Castile. He died in 1879, aged eighty years, leaving a widow and five children. Dr. Jacob True, his son, residing on the farm, is an electro-theuraputist practitioner, and is successfully treating diseases at his residence.

WILLIAM D. TRUE, son of Stephen D. and Mary True, of Castile, was born in this town in 1836, and in 1861 was married to Miss Ella Bogart, daughter of Dr. Gilbert and Catharine Bogart, of Genesee Falls. He is a farmer and a partner in the True & Felch livery business.

JOSEPH W. TRUE, a son of William and Sally True, was born in Hardwick, Vt., in 1811, and came with his parents to Covington in 1814. The trip took twenty-five days, an ox team being the motor. Mr. True left Covington and settled in Castile in 1833, and was married to Miss Dorcas Gilbert, of the latter place, in 1836. The more active part of his life was very successfully spent in the undertaking and the furniture business, from which he has retired.

HORACE WADSWORTH, former, was born in 1832 in Farmersville, N. Y., and in 1857 was married to Miss Martha Brainard, daughter of David and Emily Brainard, of Gainesville. He has one child.

FRANCIS M. WARNER was born in Windsor, N. Y., in 1845, and was married in 1867 to Miss Sarah L. Nash, of Perry. He came to Castile in 1868, and bought a farm of eighty-one acres on lot 55, Cotringer tract.

WHEELER R. WARRINER, son of Chester and Drusilla Warriner, was born in Gainesville in 1812, and was married in 1835 to Miss Angeline Willcox, daughter of Robert and Sally Willcox, of Castile. She died in 1855, and he married, in 1856, Mrs. Jane Lucas, of Castile, daughter of Conrad and Magdalena Vanliew, of Gainesville. Mr. Warriner has been assessor of Castile for twelve years, and has lived in the town since 1856. He is a farmer. Post-office, Gainesville.

DAVID A. WALLACE was born in this town in 1821, and is the son of David D. and Hannah Wallace. In 1843 he married Sarah Ely, daughter of John B. and Jane Ely, of Gainesville; and of his nine children eight are living. Mr. Wallace has always been a farmer and a resident of this town, excepting eight years in Michigan—1850–58. His father was born in 1792 in Massachusetts, and in 1816 settled in Castile. His first wife was Hannah Moon, of Scipio, N. Y., by whom he had four children, three of whom are living. She died in 1831, and in 1832 Mr. Wallace married Elizabeth Grisewood, who bore him one child. On her death, in 1848, he married Permella Sanford, who died in 1874. Mr. Wallace died in 1870.

GEORGE WHEELER, son of Jesse and Polly Wheeler, was born in Keene, N. H., November 8th, 1790. He learned the trade of wool carding and cloth dressing at Littleton, N. H., and on coming of age engaged in the business for himself at that place. In 1815 he removed to Paris, Oneida county, N. Y,, and in 1818 to Lisle, Broome county, where he prosecuted his original business twenty-two years. He next pursued milling for eight years. In 1848 he located at East Pike, owning and running the stone mill at that place. He moved to Castile in 1855. Farming, sawing, planing and lath and shingle-making have come in for a share of his attention. Mr. Wheeler was first married to Miss Betsy Sartwell, of Littleton, N. H., in 1823. They had four children, two of whom survive. Mrs. Betsy Wheeler died in Castile in 1861, aged sixty-seven years. Mr Wheeler was married in 1862 to Mrs. Tursey Gould, of Nunda, Livingston county. She died in Castile October 14th, 1873, aged seventy-six years. He was justice of the peace in Lisle sixteen years, and was one of the associate judges of Broome county, and one of the commissioners for building the court-house and jail of that county. He became a brigadier-general of militia, was a member of the Legislature, and postmaster at Upper Lisle twenty years.

ANSON WILLIAMS, born in 1808 in Otsego county, N. Y., married in 1828 Miss Urminda Lamman, of Orangeville, N. Y. He came here in 1816, and is a shoemaker at Castile.

JOHN WRIGHT, son of John and Tamar Wright, was born in Dutchess county, N. Y., in 1801. In 1825 he came to Castile and bought a portion of his present farm. In 1826 he married Miss Lovica Wixon, daughter of John and Phebe Wixon, and has six living children.

RESIDENCE OF Wm J. PALMER, WEST SIDE OF SILVER LAKE, CASTILE, N.Y.

THE TOWN OF COVINGTON.

EIGHTEEN hundred and six found Covington a wilderness without inhabitants. Its gently rolling surface, varied here and there by a plain, a gorge, a rugged rise, was densely covered with tall maples, beech, basswood, black cherry, spreading elms and sturdy oaks—beech and maple predominating.

The paths of men, gently trod by moccasined feet, were there, leading from wigwams on the Genesee toward the council fires of Buffalo and Tonawanda. Bronze-faced travelers, with strong bow and well-aimed arrow, stopped the timid deer in its flight, brought the agile squirrel from the top of nut-bearing beech, and with rod and line jerked speckled fish from the crystal pools of Pearl brook and from the quiet spring-fed waters of the Oatka (Allen's) creek. Reaching the "Big spring" (at Waldron's, formerly Judge Sprague's mill) they kindled fires, rested awhile on the sloping banks of the stream, and cooked and ate with more than civilized relish what vulgar moderns call a "square meal." Crossing the Oatka, pursuing their trail westward up the ravine, they pass to other hunting grounds, to perish miserably from the earth, sadly conscious that savages have no rights Christians are bound to respect.

PIONEER ARRIVALS AND ENTERPRISES.

In the panorama of events a new scene opened. The Indian trail was trod by one of a different race, precursor of a marvelous change Tall, muscular, thoughtful, reserved, bred at the base of the Green mountains, firm in his tread, firmer in his purpose, Jairus Cruttenden followed the paths so often trod by Red Jacket, Tall Chief, Cornplanter and their tribes, carefully scrutinizing timber, soil and situations till he came to the "Big spring," a few rods south of where Pearl creek empties into the Oatka. Here the deep, strong soil, magnificent timber and the expanse of level land greatly impressed him. He at once resolved to make his home there. As he decided, a strange darkness came over the land, the stars were visible at midday, birds and beasts sought their resting places, the wild men of the woods were sore afraid—it was the "great eclipse of 1806"!

Adventurers, three or four years before, had built their cabins at Buttermilk Falls (Le Roy), ten miles southwest of there at Wright's, and at Warsaw, but between these places and eastward to the Genesee river was no white inhabitant. Mr. Cruttenden went to work at once cutting trees, putting up a log house and clearing two or three acres of land, which he sowed to wheat the same season. He lived alone, changing works occasionally with his five or six neighbors at "Wright's Corners," two miles west, where his bread was baked. For the rest he extemporized his own cooking. We may well believe that he went back to Pultney, Vt., for his wife and child as soon as he could get ready for them. Returning in October he pushed forward his improvements; but soon a serious unpleasantness occurred. During his absence a brother of Jemima Wilkinson, "the prophetess," or, as she styled herself, "the universal friend," who founded a sect or community on Seneca lake, had bought the premises from the Holland Company, and so he duly notified the occupant. The land was not surveyed when Cruttenden came, but he was assured that he could choose his place and it would be reserved for him—a promise not kept, so he had to begin anew. He went half a mile to the northwest and commenced again. Soon after his brothers-in-law, William and John Sprague, settled east of him on the same lot. William Sprague, a hatter, built a shop to make and sell hats, and erected a log house where Mrs. Cameron now lives. His brother John started the pioneer tannery a little east of him, and close to where Gurdon Miller built soon after, it being the east part of the Gorton farm. He ground his bark by rolling a huge stone, like a grind stone with a shaft through it, round a platform with a horse, removing the fine bark and putting the coarse in the track of the wheel.

In 1810 William Miller came from Sherburne and settled three-fourths of a mile north of Pearl Creek, on the Warsaw and LeRoy road. He entertained travelers, sold goods, made potash (the first in the neighborhood), sold it for $175 per ton in Caledonia, and subsequently ran a line of stages.

Dr. Daniel White, the first physician in the town, settled north and adjoining Mr. Miller. He was a surgeon in the war of 1812, was skillful, had a large practice, gave calomel and used whiskey freely, as the fashion was, and was more companionable than constant as his wife believed. He was a leading member and champion of the masonic order. While leading a grand masonic procession on "St. John's day," at Pavilion, arrayed in royal robes, his wife, who had more temper than self respect and frequently gave her husband the benefit of it, brought up the rear clad in the most slatternly garments imaginable. Their daughter Volina was the first child born in the town. The family moved west about 1826.

The first settler east of the Warsaw and Le Roy road was Captain Levi Beardsley, who in 1810 or 1811 took up six hundred acres where John C. Taine now lives. His sons Dyer, Jesse, Elisha, Levi and William took farms, and were industrious and enterprising citizens. Amenzo Beardsley, a grandson of Captain Beardsley, lives in Middlebury, and his daughter married Charles B. Matthews.

Captain Beardsley is gratefully remembered for the kindly welcome and generous aid he extended to many early comers. He removed with most of his sons to Chautauqua county, N. Y.

In 1811 Marshall Davis, from Vermont, settled at Pearl Creek, where Chauncey Pond now lives, and a year or two later he sold to Timothy Cruttenden (father of Jairus) and his son Julius, who came from Pultney, Vt., and Mr. Davis moved east about a mile, where he resided till his death. Soon after his removal he was joined by his mother and his brothers Calvin, Jonathan, Edward and

Lewis. Edward was a farmer, a preacher and a school teacher, whom the writer remembers gratefully as a kind and faithful teacher. He married his brother Marshall's widow for his second wife, and is now living in Macomb county, Mich., about ninety years of age.

Calvin Davis married Captain Beardsley's daughter Sylvia, in 1814, it being the first marriage in the town.

About this time William Cruttenden, cousin to Jairus, settled three-fourths of a mile south of Pearl Creek, on the Warsaw road. He sold to Ethel Cushman and his son Joseph T. Cushman, who sold to Joseph Burleigh, whose son Edward sold to Mr. Boyce.

Luke Keith built on the east side of Allen's creek. Shortly after Salmon and David Hurlburt, Mr. Raymond, a cooper, Orin and Elnathan Scranton and Jonathan Peterson settled on the creek near Captain Sprague's saw-mill and woolen-mill, which stood a little above where William Croman's sawmill now stands. This was the most popular part of the town. Captain James Sprague came in 1812. His house was on the west side of Alien's creek, where Messrs. Henry and George Eastman now live, and nearly opposite his sawmill.

James C. Ferris, a leading business man of Middlebury, built a store at Pearl Creek, where T. G. Miller's grocery now is, and which was moved by N. B. Miller, and is now occupied by Norman Shepard. Mr. Ferris also owned and lived on the farm east of Wyoming where Mr. Thayer resides. He built and occupied a house on the Samuel Webb farm, and sold to Mr. Squires, its present owner. Mr. Ferris came from Albany in 1817, and long conducted a very large mercantile business at Wyoming; also farming to a considerable extent. He made potash extensively, and after the completion of the Erie Canal shipped it at Brockport.

South of the Samuel Webb farm lived Thomas Tygart, who was taken prisoner in the war of 1812 and sent to Halifax, suffering great hardships; he died in Wisconsin. While in Covington his three-year-old boy Merrit was lost in the woods, and only found the day after by a general turnout of the inhabitants.

Deacon Daniel Judd, living on the Warsaw road, came in 1817, and the Presbyterians held their meetings at his house. Abijah Owen, Elisha Palmer, David Beebe, on the E. Murry place, and Mr. Locke and four sons on the Havens place, all came between 1820 and 1830.

In 1825 Jedediah Walker moved with his son, Jedediah S. Walker, from Rutland, Vt., and bought Deacon Nathaniel Brown's place, adjoining William Miller's. Deacon Brown had resided there several years, and William Miller married his daughter.

Jacob Lemley, a skillful blacksmith, opened a shop at Pearl Creek in 1825, and his son has continued the business since. The same year Daniel Sprague, of Livonia, exchanged his farm with William Sprague, the hatter, and he came on with his sons James 2nd and Chauncey. James Sprague 2nd, afterward appointed judge, also purchased the mill then recently erected by Erastus Bailey, of Le Roy (afterward owned by Duncan Cameron, and later by O. D. Waldron). About 1826 John Doty, who had married a sister of J. S. Walker, bought a farm on the Pavilion road, a part of it having belonged to Jonathan Petersen.

About the same time Joshua Dean bought a farm at Pearl Creek; he died at that place a few years after. The farm is now owned and occupied by Chauncey Pond. Chester Moulton, from Vermont, owns the house built by George Partridge, a manufacturer of spinning wheels, whose wife was a sister of Jairus Cruttenden.

S. O. and Beaumont Parks, near Pearl Creek, live on a farm formerly owned by Hiram Brooks, who sold it to Esquire Bowers; the next farm east was taken up by Lazarus Green, a seceder from the Shakers; the writer remembers his collecting a large number of men to plant his potatoes before the change of the moon.

The Davises and Peter Knapp, deputy postmaster of Covington under Benedict Brooks, lived west of the Norris hill, on land now owned by Harry Sprague.

Daniel Balcom built, at a very early day, the first gristmill in the town; it was small, of the Grahamitish order, having no bolt, and was used mainly to grind feed and "samp"; it stood where Mr. Mather lives, west of Harry Sprague, on Pond creek. It was converted into a carding machine by Mr. Hough. Timothy and Julius Cruttenden, Hurlburt, Patridge, Church, Norton, Crocker and others all made spinning wheels, "big" and "little," and all the women used them.

David Norris came to Covington Centre in 1812, and "took out an article" of a farm. Returning to Vermont he came back with his family March 14th, 1813. He stopped over night at Levi McWethey's, on the corners north of Covington Centre.

Isaiah Phelps was living near the present school-house, on the west side of the road, and Captain Beardsley at what is now called "Paine's Corners"; these were the only. settlers on the road until Perry Centre was reached; there was no inhabitant east of this

The next year Thatcher Beardsley and William Norris settled a little east of him; and the next year (1815) Edward Norris bought land south of him, lying near Captain Beardsley. Rev. William True came with him from Vermont; they were twenty-six days on the road, with ox teams.

The first frame tavern, with barn, bar-room, ball-room and beds, was erected and installed at Covington Centre by Daniel Balcom, in 1817. There pleasure seekers "tripped the light fantastic toe" in rather heavy boots, while on Sunday in the same assembly room Elders William True, Millard and Badger exhorted sinners to repentance. Daniel Balcom was succeeded by James Norris, brother of Mark, in the tavern. Some years later Enos Newman and Colonel Miller kept open house where William Bryon now lives.

In 1817 Mark Norris came to Covington; he was born in 1796 in Peacham, Vt.; taught school in Lima, N. Y., and married Roccina B. Vail, sister of Benjamin Vail. He opened a store and an ashery; did a large business for some years, then sold to B. Vail & Compton, who had been clerks in his employ, and went to Ypsilanti, Mich.

MAJOR, H. T. BROOKS.

C. T. DEYO.

WALTER M. HATCH.

Yours truly
Gerard H. Gysen

Henry Hoyt

DANIEL HOWARD,
FATHER OF JONATHAN HOWARD.

JUDGE M. TRALL.

Alonzo Persons

Oliver Hodges

In 1817 John Nobles and his brother came to this town, and settled on "No. six." John married Mary, daughter of Captain Sprague, attended his grist-mill for many years, and afterward bought a farm in Pavilion, where he is still living, at the age of eighty-two years; his wife died in 1878; two sons and two daughters are in Pavilion.

Mark Norris was succeeded by Vail & Compton, who married daughters of Dr. Derby. They did a large mercantile business until Vail was succeeded by Samuel B. Peck, a nephew of Benedict Brooks, who eventually bought Compton's interest in the store, and for several years kept a large assortment of goods and did a good business. Since that time much of the trade of Covington Centre has been diverted to other places.

About 1830 the Genesee road was moved a third of a mile further north for a better grade, and public buildings were then erected on their present sites.

Enos Newman settled in 1811 on the Leicester or Elicott road, leading from Cuylerville through Pavilion to Tonawanda. This road was surveyed by Joseph Elicott, and opened by Sylvenus Young, father of Mr. S. Young, of Geneseo, who had settled on Alien's creek (Oatka) in 1810.

In 1814 Joseph Perry settled on the Leicester road, where Harrison McWethey now lives. The Carrs and Crowfoots came about 1816, and settled on the same road.

Deacon David Fowler came from Ulster county, N, Y., in 1824, and settled a little east of Covington Centre; his daughter married Dr. Eben Warner, who practiced medicine successfully at Covington Centre.

Alexander Boyd, born near Glasgow, Scotland, came to Saratoga county, N. Y., in 1811, and to Covington in 1824, taking a part of Gilbert Lang's place, who came in 1822. Mr. B. was a very industrious farmer, who improved his cattle and sheep, and for fifty years was never absent from the communion table of his church. He brought from the church in Scotland this significant testimonial: "We have known him from infancy, and he has always behaved soberly and honestly." His sons are James, Samuel and Alexander; his daughters Margaret and Jane. Mr. Boyd died in 1874, aged eighty-four.

James McQueen came in 1825. Mordecai Brownell came in 1825, and settled just west of the Scott or Orr farm. He, together with his son, Lorenzo Brownell, living on the Orin Scranton place, took much interest in the improvement of sheep and cattle. Peter Forbes and Alexander Douglass came in 1827.

On the eastern borders of Covington, just west of the United Presbyterian church, is a farm that deserves special mention. About 1819 Captain Scott and Captain Mow took up six hundred acres of land, which they divided, Captain Scott taking the south part. They both pushed their improvements vigorously, Captain Scott performing a feat unparalleled in pioneer annals. He chopped, cleared, fenced into ten-acre lots, and sowed to winter wheat, one hundred acres in one year, and all in the most thorough manner. He got the enormous yield of fifty bushels of wheat to the acre.

It was cut with sickles, Mr. John Nobles, of Pavilion, being one of the reapers; they were divided into three squads, of five men each, and at once entered into a vigorous competition for the lead; so much so that before night on the first day half the men were "under the fence," being helped there in some cases by the barrel of whiskey, with a faucet and tin cup, kept in the harvest field and in the woods while the land was being cleared. This crop of wheat was threshed with flails, drawn to Albany on wagons, and sold for two dollars a bushel, the teams loading back with goods. Elated with his success, Captain Scott, socially inclined, spent the following season in Washington, having sold his farm to James Gilmore. A year or two later he went West, and died without becoming rich. Mr. Gilmore sold the farm to Mr. Sturtevant, and he to John Orr, who came from Scotland with his father to Caledonia when he was four years old. His father, while at a chopping bee, was killed with an ax by a comrade frenzied with drink. McLean, the murderer, fled to the woods, where he was fed several days by his mother. He was afterward arrested on the road while leaving the country and hung at Batavia in 1807—the first execution in Genesee county. John Orr was a man of great industry and perseverance; while young he assisted his widowed mother, whose labors, trials and achievements seem almost incredible. His wife and two sons occupy the Scott farm.

Peoria, a village of twenty-five or thirty residences, with shops, hotel and store, was not settled till the close of the war of 1812. About that time Deacon Butler located a little west and Mr. Mills a little southeast of the present village. Subsequently Deacon James Wells opened a store and his son a hotel at the "Corners," and about 1827 Mr. James Gordon established himself in business, with his sons. He kept a full assortment, had a good trade and still continues it. His eldest son is actively employed elsewhere, and his son Thomas collects the farm produce and ships it at Pavilion, on the State Line railroad. One of Mr. Gordon's daughters is the wife of Rev. Mr. Gilfillin, the eloquent and popular pastor of the United Presbyterian church.

A joint stock company, aided by subsidies, built a substantial steam flouring-mill, but finding the cost of running greater than of water-mills, it was abandoned as a mill.

Mr. Fiero for several years manufactured the diamond toothed cultivator, that perhaps has never been excelled for stirring the soil in corn fields and cutting up weeds and grass. The tooth is a diamond shaped steel plate attached to an iron shank.

Mr. Guthrie, of Peoria, has invented an iron fence post of undoubted value—a large stone is drilled and the post, an inch bar, inserted in it.

Elijah Kendall came to the southeast part of Covington in 1817; his brother-in-law, Jonathan Cooley, about the same time; they were from Springfield, Mass., and were the first settlers in that part of the town. Mr. Cooley's wife survives him, at the age of ninety-six. Of his sons, Frederick, Gilbert, Alonzo, Ashley and Carlton, the last occupies the homestead. Elijah Kendall's sons are Franklin, Ralph, Alfred, William and Lawson. Theodore, his grandson, lives on the homestead.

Mr. Barr took up the farm where Leicester Rood now lives. Elijah Lamb was an early settler. James Armstrong settled further west. Isaac Wellman moved in 1821 from Vermont to Friendship, and the year following to the "State road" in Covington, where Mr. Morrow now lives; he died in 1847. John, Andrew and David Morrow came with their mother from Saratoga county and settled on the State road, at the source of Pearl creek, in 1821. John went to Michigan, where he died. Joseph Durfle came from Rhode Island in 1822, and settled at Paine's Corners.

Jasher Taylor, son of Jasher Taylor of Ashfield, Mass., came with his family in 1827 and bought Elisha Beardsle's place, adjoining Captain Beardsley's farm. Mr. Taylor died in 1872.

David Wylie came in 1814, and bought Mr. Fosgate's "chance" to a farm on the Perry road, half a mile south of Captain Beardsley's; and Hardin Bradly settled the same year a little further south, toward La Grange. In 1813 Daniel Howard came to La Grange, where he built a house on the northeast corner. Samuel Russell and James Miller, who had married his sisters, built on the northwest corner, and Mr. Armstrong on the southeast corner. There was no settlement east short of Moscow, near the Genesee river.

Asaph White, commonly called Bachelor White, came from the town of Heath, Mass., in 1815, and bought a farm west of La Grange; cleared twelve acres with the help of Calvin Lewis and Samuel Hatch, and sowed it to wheat. Being disappointed in receiving money from the east which was due to him, he sold in the spring of 1817 to William Alton, who harvested forty-five bushels to the acre. Wheat being scarce after the cold season of 1816, Alton sold it for $2 per bushel. Mr. Alton died, and his son William succeeded to the place, which is now owned by Deacon Austin Lane, who was an early settler. John Howard lived east of his brother Deacon Howard, and sold in 1819 to John Boughton. Captain Gillett bought the place now owned by Mark Vebyg.

Captain James Sprague, one of the prominent farmers and business men of Covington, was born in Connecticut in 1766, and was living with his mother, brothers and sisters near New London, Conn., when that town was burned by Benedict Arnold in September; 1781, the most valuable of their goods were burned. In 1798 he married Abiah Carpenter, and they lived in New Marlborough, Mass., where all his children were born. In 1812 he removed to Covington, and immediately built a saw-mill on the Oatka, in company with Aaron Spaulding, it being the first saw-mill in the neighborhood and a very great convenience to the settlers. Soon afterward he erected a carding and cloth dressing establishment. In 1826 he built the grist-mill now owned by William Crossman. He subsequently established his sons in business in Pavilion; James in cloth dressing, Daniel and William as merchants, while Paul took charge of the grist and saw-mills, and Erastus of the farm of four hundred acres. William on retiring from mercantile business practiced medicine successfully at Pavilion for several years.

Captain Sprague was respected as a man of energy and integrity, of much public spirit. For a long time he stood first in wealth and enterprise in the town of Covington. He died in Pavilion in October, 1849.

Daniel Howard, the son of Elisha Howard and Patty Williams, was born in West Rockingham, Windsor county, Vt. After living awhile in Middlebury, Vt., he removed to Oswego county, N. Y., and married Patty Sherman. He selected a farm in 1813 on the northeast corner at La Grange. His brother and brothers-in-law settled at La Grange about the same time, being the first settlers in the south part of the town. Mr. Howard and his wife were soon taken down with fever, and lay at the point of death for eight weeks. Day after day and week after week women came three or four miles on horseback to minister to Mrs. Howard's necessities during each night, and then returned to severe labors at their own homes. She is still living. Mr. Howard bought his farm for $4 per acre, and sold it in 1816 for $13. He bought another, one and a-half miles west of La Grange, where his son Jonathan now lives, for $5 per acre, and cleared it. He was a staunch Democrat, a Baptist, a deacon, an efficient highway commissioner when the duties were arduous, and in all respects a good citizen. He died in 1856.

Mr. Howard frankly acknowledged that his wife "did as much to pay for the farm" as himself, and many other men could say as much if they would. The labors of pioneer women are almost incredible. Mrs. Howard, while rearing her family, cut and made clothes for the people round about, did the housework, boarded the hired man, boarded "Bachelor" White and his men, wove cloth for the neighborhood, kept a ministers', pedlars' and land-lookers' tavern, and made butter and cheese to buy groceries and store goods.

Her son, Austin A., who died in 1879, attained distinction as a lawyer in Buffalo. From the time he left home to attend Williams College, to his death, forty years afterward, he never failed on his mother's birthday to write her a good letter and to accompany it with a substantial token of regard.

Thomas Fisher came to Covington in 1817 from Stafford, Genesee county, where he had cleared up a farm. He came to Stafford from the town of Pompey, Onondaga county, N. Y. He was the son of Jacob Fisher, of Sharon, Mass., and came to this State when fourteen years old. He married Desire Pratt, sister of Webster Pratt, who also came to Covington in 1817. Mr. Pratt's father, Noah, served through the Revolutionary war, and died about 1830. Thomas Fisher purchased a large farm on lot 4, of Stephen Wilkinson, and cleared it up, performing a great amount of hard labor; he was an upright and respected citizen.

Duncan Cameron was prominent among the business men of Covington and, indeed, of western New York. Born in Saratoga county, N. Y., of Scotch ancestors, he came, about 1820, with his parents, two brothers and two sisters, to York, Livingston county. He then bought the Lazarus Green farm of John Gilmore, whose sister he had married. He exchanged farms with Chauncey Sprague, taking one at the mouth of Pearl creek, first occupied by William Sprague. He purchased the grist-mill now owned by O. D. Waldron. From about 1840 he speculated in grain and wool. He was a decided and active Whig and Republican; was very public spirited; active as a supervisor in getting soldiers to put down the Rebellion, and in all respects a good citizen. He died in 1874, aged 65, of over-work.

Benedict Brooks came from Cheshire, Conn., to Bloomfield, Ontario county, N. Y., where his brother General Micah Brooks then resided, who represented a large part of western New York in Congress. Remaining at his brother's during the winter, he taught the district school, and in May, 1812, married Maria, daughter of Judge Hugh McNair, clerk of Ontario county, and returned with his wife to Cheshire. He soon sold his farm, a part of the ancestral estate, and moved to what is now Livingston county, N.Y., and immediately enlisted in the cavalry service and took part in the war of 1812. At the close of the war he bought of Stephen Wilkinson two hundred and sixty-seven acres of land at Pearl Creek, at $7 per acre. He subsequently enlarged his farm to six hundred acres, and dealt more or less in other lands. He kept a large share of his land in timber, and always seemed to mourn when a fine tree must be cut. He

RESIDENCE OF J. S. WALKER, PEARL CREEK, WYOMING CO., N. Y.

employed a good many men, helping many in time of need. He was industrious, frugal and obliging. He was a staunch Democrat, and was never known to ask for an office. He was several years supervisor of the town, still longer a justice of the peace,—being always known as 'Squire Brooks,— and in 1821 represented Genesee county in the Legislature. He brought the first merino sheep west of Genesee river, purchasing them of James and General William Wadsworth. They were the immediate descendants of merinos imported by General Humphrey from Spain, and were considered a great curiosity, on account of their dark color and the superabundant wool on their faces and legs. They were extensively crossed with light-wooled natives, and effected great improvement. He also brought from Batavia an "English" (Durham) bull, from stock introduced from Philadelphia by the Holland Land Company, which improved the scrawny cattle of the period. While others impoverished their farms he constantly improved his, by scrupulous care of manure and frequent seeding down to grass. He deprecated slavery, and warmly advocated colonization. He prophesied civil war as the result of anti-slavery agitation. His wife died in 1848. She was a woman of rare energy, industry, fortitude, perseverance and discrimination. She was charitable, warm in her friendships, steadfast, well-balanced, and a Christian in faith and practice.

It is recorded in the Brooks family Bible that "Benedict Brooks was born in Cheshire, Conn., March 9th, 1797. He was the son of David, who was the son of Enos, who was the son of Thomas, who was the son of Henry Brooks, who came from Cheshire in England to New Haven in Connecticut. He had fought under Oliver Cromwell, and the restoration of Charles the Second was offensive to him, which caused him to remove to America. His son Thomas removed fourteen miles north from New Haven and the town to which he removed was called Cheshire, after the place of his father's nativity."

The mother of Benedict Brooks was Elizabeth Doolittle, of Wallingford, Conn., daughter of Daniel Doolittle, the son of David, who was the son of Abram Doolittle, who came from England with the first New Haven colonists.

Of the children of Benedict and Maria Brooks, Elizabeth, wife of Hiram McCollum, of Lockport, died without issue.

Phebe Ann, wife of I. V. Mathews, born February 17th, 1815, died January 31st, 1859, leaving Martha, Henry, Charles B, and Hugh V. Martha married Edward Wheeler, and lives in Kansas.

Hugh Torbert Brooks, born April 12th, 1817, resides at the Pearl Creek homestead. He married Mary D., daughter of Dr. William Cecil Dwight, of Moscow, N. Y., and they have three children—Mary D., wife of Henry B. Ellwanger, (Mt. Hope, Rochester), Charlotte Wilmerding and Benedict Martha, Mary, Henrietta and Grace, daughters of Benedict Brooks, died early in life, beloved by all who knew them. Alice Catherine, his youngest daughter, lives at Pearl Creek.

Unreliable and incomplete is any history that fails to notice that numerous, laborious and unfortunate portion of the population who took up land, cleared and fenced it, but failed to perfect their titles, and after years of agonizing labor sold for what they could get, or were sold out by the sheriff without getting anything.

Farms cleared up and partly paid for by those who were obliged to leave them make a melancholy and voluminous catalogue. Abel Warren and his partner in business sold to Joseph Durfee in 1822 a farm on Pearl creek, for eight dollars an acre. The buildings and improvements cost more than the land sold for, to say nothing about the money they had advanced, which was about half the original price.

Captain Beardsly, to whom Covington owes so much, brought seventeen hundred dollars—then a very large sum—into the town, and invested it in land, leaving a part of the price unpaid. In a currency collapse that followed he was obliged, after clearing the land, putting up buildings and planting orchards, to sell out, and, as Mr. Durfee expressed it, "he went up the Wylie hill in his old age, on his way to Chautauqua, with only $150 in his pockets."

We should belie the truth of history if we did not acknowledge that the fortunes of the republic and the fortunes of many of the fortunate were largely made by hired men. Through the whole history of the country men working by the month brought to their tasks judgment, energy and application of the highest order, consequential factors in the country's development. Fortis Tower, who chopped many years for Thomas Fisher and others as few can chop, did more for the State than some Congressmen.

Benedict Brooks, sitting a long time in a musing mood, finally said: "Ansel Warren split and drew the rails and laid up half a mile of fence for me in a month, and I think I ought to have acknowledged my obligations to him more distinctly than I did." This was said forty years after the fence was built.

CHANGES SEVENTY-FIVE YEARS HAVE WROUGHT.

Perhaps the most noticeable feature of this country, or of any country, is the marvelous growth of labor-saving appliances. In 1818 Covington had no plows except the "bull plow," made of wood, with an iron point, sharpened and put on by the blacksmith. It turned the soil very imperfectly, and the dirt adhered to it persistently. The steel plow, the chilled plow, the sulky plow, leave little room for improvement this side of the steam plow, which is on trial. Grain cradles (the other kind was plenty enough) had scarcely been seen. Slow moving sickles were honored and cherished instruments in 1820. The reaper, as a successful instrument, is not fifty years old. Ira Maher brought the Hussey machine to Covington about 1840. It was able to contend with stones and stumps, and had a good many to contend with. A man followed and raked off the grain behind, which must be removed before the machine could go round again. It had to be driven fast to get up sufficient motion. McCormick's reaper, which took the premium at the first world's fair, succeeded it. About the same time Job Sherman introduced a Ketchum mower, strong and heavy, with a stiff cutting bar; it was exceptional, being made of good iron. The hand rake held its place till 1830, and the raking of hay was a tedious process. The "revolver" helped a good deal, and the steel tooth wheel rake leaves little to be hoped for. The dung fork "of the daddies" was distress to thousands who used it. The spade of 1812 and the spade of 1880 appear to be ten centuries apart. Carts and carriages seem to be a new creation. There was not a threshing machine in western New York in 1820. Grain was pounded out with a stick, and as there was neither canal or railroad it was carted to Albany on wagons, and sent down the Hudson on sloops. Friction matches came in with Paris millinery, about 1830; the early inhabitants covered up wood fires, and if they went out went a mile, more or less, and "borrowed" some, or with flint and steel drew from the source of supply. Broadcloth was confined to ministers and merchants; the son of a well-to do Covington farmer borrowed a "factory made" coat to be married in, but "home spun" and "home made" held the fort. There was no gaslight in western New York till after 1825; tallow candles, dipped at home, were supplemented and supplanted by fish oil, then lard oil, and twenty years ago by kerosene.

There was not a coal fire or a cook-stove in any house in western New York in 1820, nor a marriageable girl that knew how to play the pianoforte, or one who didn't know how to make johnny cakes and bake good bread.

Nobody rode on elliptic springs till after 1825, and Mrs. Warren, a pious Methodist sister, remarked in the hearing of the writer when he was a little boy that she felt very thankful that she could now "go to meeting in a *wagon*" (it was a lumber wagon, without springs or paint); "it is so much *easier* and *nicer* than the old cart—the cart made the whole jolt at once, the wagon divides it"; jolts were the rule, not the exception, when our grandmothers went to meeting.

The first settlers of Covington, coming mostly from New England, had been accustomed to fruit. The absence of it in the new settlements was a serious grievance. Even the blackberry and raspberry did not grow in the dense woods, but they promptly followed the openings westward. The first settlers frequently gathered crab apples and wild plums on the Genesee river, which the good housewives made into preserves for state occasions. The Indians of Gardeau sold "huckleberries," and those who could afford it went "over the river" every fall and brought back a wagon load of apples, which were carefully looked after. The children were occasionally allowed one for good behavior; as a significant testimonial a *red* one was given. Nurseries were started as soon as clearings were made. Isaac Andrus, on the Warsaw road, Lazarus Green and David Norris grew trees for sale, but nothing was grafted till 1825, when the Spitzenberg, Yellow Bellflower, Roxbury Russet, Rhode Island Greening, and subsequently the Northern Spy and Baldwin were introduced. The first trees came from beyond the Genesee river. Stephen Wilkinson brought from Rhode Island a small, very sweet and rich fall apple, and two or three orchards were planted with *sprouts* from these trees. About 1850 the market demand for apples induced the planting of large orchards. Apples are fast becoming a leading product of the town. Small fruits are neglected; few farmers provide an adequate supply for their families.

During the war of 1812, still called by the old people "the last war," Gurdon Miller, Dr. Daniel White, William Cruttenden, Abel Norris, William Norris and others went into the service from this town, led by Captain Jairus Cruttenden and Benedict Brooks, and Thomas Tygart and Webster Pratt also enlisted, though not then living in Covington. Families suffered in the absence of their head. The fear that "the British and Indians would come on" and burn and plunder the settlements caused great anxiety.

Disputed land titles were a great annoyance. Many writs of ejectment were served. Gideon Granger and others, who sold the land, refused to defend against the claimants. The settlers organized, with Benedict Brooks at their head, employed Miles P. Hopkins and Abram Van Vechten, of Albany, to manage their suit, and were finally successful. Roxana, daughter of David Norris, still living at Covington Centre, said, very pathetically, "I never saw my mother so distressed as when the officer came and said we must leave the place; we had paid in all we had."

The first settlers in Covington went to Caledonia to mill, also to Bosly's mill, beyond Geneseo, and later to Hawsly's mill at Perry. It took Captain Cruttenden three days to get his first grists ground and get home with them, and for several years more than one day was required. People generally went to mill on horseback, and more than one instance is recorded where men have carried two bushels of corn and wheat two or three miles to mill on their backs. Mrs. Orr, at Caledonia, after the murder of her husband, carried two bushels of wheat to mill on her back. Before saw-mills, house floors were made of split and hewed logs. Jairus Cruttenden's barn rafters and braces are hewn.

Mrs. Daniel Howard describes the destitution in the "cold season,"—1816. She had given to a poor family till her husband told her they could spare nothing more. Mr. Howard coming in the next day to his supper found his wife in tears; he asked the cause. "I was thinking of Mrs. ——, who has a young baby and not a morsel of bread in the house." "Take her something," he replied. She prepared what she could, and conveyed it to the poor woman. Putting it on the table she sat and wept; they both wept. Mrs. Howard rose and departed; neither of them said a word. There was no county poor-house to go to. Paupers were then "bid off" by those who would keep them the cheapest, and the towns paid the bill.

Spirituous liquors were much used in all the pioneer settlements. A friend hardly considered himself well received, or properly entertained, if "something to drink" was not offered.

Manufacturing whiskey was an important business enterprise, as it made a market for the corn, and few stopped to inquire whether the whiskey damaged more than the corn came to. John Nobles speaks of the chopping and logging bees, where whiskey was indispensable and freely used. His brother Lemuel remarked one day that liquor was getting the better of many of the best choppers. John said: "When you think I have drunk enough touch me slightly, and I will do the same by you." "Agreed," said Lemuel, and the brothers watched each other and escaped ruin, which fell on too many.

RESIDENCE of JOEL C. CLARK, TOWN of COVINGTON.

RESIDENCE of E. C. SHERMAN, MIDDLEBURY, N. Y.

SILVER LAKE

GLEN IRIS

WYOMING COUNTY SCENERY, NEW YORK.

O. G. WARREN

Covington never had but one distillery. It was where Nicholas Chilson now lives, and was carried on by Judson Lewis, and afterwards by Mr. Culver. Covington has granted no licenses for about twenty-five years, and no town in the county has so little litigation or disturbance of the peace. The writer was justice of the peace for twelve years, and in his half of the town there were but two complaints made, and not a single case went to trial in that time. At first it was feared that temperance men could not get their work done nor their buildings raised. J. S. Walker relates: "The liquor men said if I didn't furnish whiskey my barn frame would never go up. I mounted my horse and took a wide circle, gave out my invitations, explained the situation to the temperance men, and had plenty of help; all seemed satisfied with cake and coffee."

Recently Mr. Wright, of Covington, a respectable and industrious man, who sometimes drank to excess, was made drunk by legalized rumsellers in Pavilion; in returning home he fell from his wagon, cracked his skull, and died instantly.

About 1850 a "union store" was established at Peoria. Persons wishing to become stockholders took shares— generally to the amount of $50 or $100— and were then entitled to goods at ten per cent above cost. A good assortment was kept, the trade was brisk, customers declared they got their goods much cheaper than before; but being allowed to trade out their stock, they did so, and the store soon passed into private hands.

The population of Covington has long been decreasing, as appears from the following State census returns: 1830, 2,716; 1835, 3,514; 1840, 2,438; 1845, 1,427; 1850, 1,385; 1855, 1,330; 1860, 1,286; 1865, 1,233; 1870, 1,189; 1875, 1,130.

Hon. Augustus Frank, of Warsaw, in a well-considered address delivered at a large gathering at Silver Lake, commented appropriately on the decline of population in the rural districts of Wyoming county. In subsequent conversations with the writer Mr. Frank suggested that fruit growing gives much larger returns from the same land than ordinary farming, and, since it gives employment to more laborers, it is obvious that the increase of fruit culture would be the increase of population.

The neglect of farmers who employ hired help to provide houses for their workmen is one cause of the decline of the rural population. Men with families are driven into the cities and villages to find shelter, when they would be glad to live in the country if they could find a place to live. Thus it becomes necessary for farmers, however inconvenient, to board their hired help, which is the prevailing practice.

TOWN ORGANIZED.

Covington was formed from Perry and Le Roy, January 31st, 1817. It was divided in 1840, and Pavilion formed from the north part of Covington and south part of Le Roy. It was named after General Leonard Covington. A town meeting was held April 7th, 1817; called to order by Dr. Daniel White, justice of the peace by appointment, when Jairus Cruttenden was elected supervisor; Rufus Partridge, town clerk; Jonathan E. Davis, Mosely Stoddard and Marshall Smead, assessors; Benedict Brooks and Henry Bond, jr., overseers of the poor; Enos Newman, Benedict Brooks and William Markham, commissioner of highways. The next year Benedict Brooks was elected supervisor. John C. Paine, Duncan Cameron, Lorenzo Wylie and Harry Sprague have each served several terms as supervisor; Mark Norris, Benjamin Vail, Samuel B. Peck, Charles Taylor and others as clerk.

SCHOOLS.

In 1815 Thatcher Beardsley taught the first school, near Captain Beardsley's, and Lucy Sleeper taught at La Grange the same year.

A school was opened about this time near Scranton's, where C. Kane now lives. Shortly after this the "brick school-house" was built, a mile east of Pearl creek (since taken down), and it became a great religious as well as literary center. Women taught in the summer, seldom receiving more than a dollar a week. They were not without those useful implements the ferule and rod; and they used them as freely as they could afford to for the wages they got. "Uncle Ned" (Edward Davis) was the best known teacher in the town.

RELIGIOUS PRIVILEGES.

Rev. Mark Norris, from Vermont, a brother of David Norris, preached the first sermon in the town, at Covington Centre, in 1815. Rev. William True settled and preached at Covington the same year.

A religious revival followed their labors, Polly Norris being the first one baptized. She was immersed in Pearl creek.

A church of "Christians" was organized. They held meetings at La Grange and other places, and their "two days meeting" was attended by the brethren from long distances. On one of these occasions David Norris invited all not otherwise provided for to come to his house; fifty came and staid over night; before the meeting was over the flour from his grist of ten bushels of wheat, provided for the occasion, was consumed.

Shortly afterward, when the Methodists held a quarterly meeting in the brick school-house, the presiding elder asked who would keep strangers over night. A zealous brother arose and said, with emphasis: "I will keep as many as there are boards in my floor." We do not know how many accepted this invitation. The Methodists, through their "circuit" arrangement, had preaching at an early day. The first circuits embraced all of the State west of the Genesee river, and a circuit-rider, as the minister was called, was about a month getting round; having preached during that time thirty or forty sermons, wherever he could find hearers.

"The brick school-house," a mile east of Pearl Creek, was a favorite place for Methodist gatherings; their camp meetings in the Jacob Passage (now

Chauncey Sprague's) woods were largely attended. Plain dressing was insisted on by the early Methodists. When they held their "love feasts" a person at the entrance was required to exclude every one who wore ornaments. Boys of fifteen came to meeting bare-footed. Women wore handkerchiefs on their heads.

A meeting-house was built near the "brick school-house" about 1830, which is now in Pavilion and used as a Methodist church. Ebenezer and Abel Warren, the Sheffields, Knapps, Passages, Lemuel Nobles, Guerdon and William Miller, and indeed a large share of the Covington settlers, were Methodists. Elders Millard, Church, Anson, Badger, Segar, Story, May, Hamilton, Davis, Wait and Comfort were preachers. As early as 1810 the Genesee Conference, covering a large part of the State of New York, was organized. The preachers were zealous, self-denying and illiterate, were never allowed to read their sermons, and it is not supposed they wrote them. Single men were allowed $80 per year. Any member who should attend theatres, ball-rooms, or horse-races "must make confession of the same, and promise to desist from such nefarious practices in the future."

October 25th, 1817, Rev. John F. Bliss, missionary, organized a Congregational church in Covington, composed of the following members: Nathaniel Brown, Hannah Brown, Benedict Brooks, Maria Brooks, Samuel Pelton, Hannah, Joyce Bradley, Elizabeth Miller and Anne Warren. Subsequently David J. Fowler, John C. Paine, Henry B. Watkins, George W. Whitney, Deacon Alvah Whitney and Ira Townsend became active and prominent members.

They erected a substantial meeting-house in 1832, but in 1840 a large proportion of the members withdrew and organized a church in the Oatka valley, in Pavilion. The weakened church dissolved in 1840, and gave the building for a "town house." It is now a convenient assembly-room for general purposes. Rev. Mr. Griswold, Rev. Mr. Hart, of Bethany, Rev. Mr. Flagler and others were the different pastors; Mr. Littlejohn, a noted but eccentric revivalist, also conducted services here.

The United Presbyterian Church of Covington and York was organized in 1827, as an Associate Presbyterian church. James Balfour, who died at the age of one hundred and four, Hugh Innis, William Stewart and James Renlie, elders in the Associate Reformed church of York, withdrew, and were joined by ten other families, and formed the organization. For two years they met in the houses and barns of J. Balfour and H. Innis, and in 1829 built their present house of worship, a substantial wooden building on the borders of Covington and York. Their church numbers 150 members; Sabbath-school, 100. Rev. David Strang, D. S. McHenry and A. B. Gilfillin, all very able preachers, have ministered to the church. Mr. Strang, a very studious man, took prizes for scholarship at St. Andrew's University, Scotland. After preaching nineteen years to this church he removed to Monmouth, III., where he died, and where his daughters engaged in teaching, and where his widow still resides. The Covington church, it is said, left the York church because the latter neglected to observe rigorously the appointed fasts.

The Methodist church in the Kendall neighborhood was erected in 1832. The society has regular services, and numbers about 40 members.

The first Sunday-school was started by Clarissa Starr, a relative of Frederick Starr, of Rochester, widely known as a business man and a Christian gentleman. He furnished Miss Starr with books, and called her attention to Sunday-schools as an instrument of good. She organized the school at Pavilion while it was a part of Covington, and was assisted by Captain Betts, who was a good singer, and others. The people on the north, west and south sides of Covington attend churches and Sunday-schools just over the line, in adjoining towns.

BIOGRAPHICAL.

HARRIET B. CAMERON came to Covington about 1825 with her father, Hon. James Sprague, who was born in 1792. On his arrival Mr. Sprague purchased a mill privilege. During the latter part of his life, which closed at the age of seventy-two, he resided in Warsaw. He was during his active life supervisor for several years, county judge, and for two terms member of Assembly. Mrs. Cameron's deceased husband, Duncan Cameron, came with his father's family from Inverness, Scotland. He was prominent in the vicinity, was an active business man and interested in public affairs, holding the office of supervisor in his town, and exerting considerable influence toward the construction of the State Line railroad. At one time he dealt extensively in wool. Mrs. Cameron's son, James G. Cameron, was a captain in the 136th N. Y. volunteers.

FLORENCE CLARKE, daughter of William Covell, of Middlebury, was born in Pavilion, Genesee county, March 26th, 1849. Her father and Miss Eliza Tufts were married in 1847. Mr. Covell was born in Chautauqua county in 1818; Mrs. Covell in 1824. Before her marriage Mrs. Clarke was a successful teacher. She married Henry C., son of Joseph Clarke, a settler in Covington in 1837, October 23d, 1870. Mrs. Clarke is a Baptist.

MRS. JOEL C. CLARKE was born in Covington February 20th, 1818. In 1840 she married Joel C. Clarke, and resides in Covington, where her father, Daniel Howard, was an early settler, first locating at La Grange, and two years later removing to the Howard homestead, where his widow, whose maiden name was Pattie Sherman, is now living.

JOSEPH CLARKE was born in South Hadley, Mass., in 1815. He lived in Pittsfield four years, at Perry ten years, and came to Covington in 1832. He has served the town as assessor. In 1837 he was married to Esther Harvey, of Herkimer county. He gave liberally toward the suppression of the Rebellion. His father, Joel Clarke, was born in Massachusetts in 1774. He was of English descent. He was three times married, and he died in Covington April 15th, 1861. Mr. Clarke's grandfather was one of the earliest settlers in Wyoming county.

THOMAS W. COPELAND was born in Covington October 28th, 1840, and has been a resident of the town since, except during three years spent in California and in the army. He was with the 33d N. Y. infantry, and participated in all its battles from Bull Run to Chancellorsville, both inclusive. He married Maggie E. Dow in 1873. Mr. Copeland's father, James Copeland, was born in Antrim, Ireland, in 1801, and came from his native country to the town of York, Livingston county, and from York to Covington.

His wife was Margaret Johnson, of Antrim, Ireland. John Dow, Mrs. Copeland's father, is a native of Glasgow, Scotland, and at the age of eleven removed to York, Livingston county, where he now resides. He married Mary Wooster in 1842.

EMERSON CORNWELL was born in Mt. Morris, Livingston county, in 1834, and moved from there to Perry with his parents when two months old. He resided on the old Cronkhite farm until he was twenty-two, when he came to Covington, where he owns a farm of one hundred and eighty-two acres. He gave largely of his means to aid the Northern cause during the Rebellion. In 1855 he married Mary, daughter of Lester and Mary Rude. Mr. Cornwell's father was born in Kings county in 1772, removed to Dutchess county, thence to Cayuga county, thence to Livingston county and thence to Covington. He married Margaret Hunt in 1828.

SAMUEL P. COVERT, blacksmith, was born in Newburgh, N. Y., in 1814. In 1836 he married Eliza A. Hallett, and in 1864 Dorcas Doane. He came from Newburgh to La Grange in 1841. James Covert, son of Samuel P. Covert, served during the Rebellion in the 9th N. Y. cavalry until discharged on account of sickness. Mr. Covert's father was born in White Plains, N. Y., in 1781, and removed from there to Newburgh, where he died in 1868. The present Mrs. Covert, daughter of Mr. and Mrs. (formerly Abigail Bristol) Jabes Ball, was born in Perry in 1829; her mother at New Marlborough, Mass., in 1791.

EDGAR E. CRONKHITE, farmer, was born at Hoosic, Rensselaer county, in 1851, and was married in 1872 to Ellen Fancher, daughter of Rufus and Lucy Fancher, of La Grange. Tunis Cronkhite, his father, was born at Hoosic, and moved from there to Washington county, and from there to Covington, where he lived until his death in 1877. He was three times married, the last time in 1878, to Esther Tripp, whose father, Anthony Tripp, was born in New Bedford, in 1796, and was married in 1828 to Polly Sprague, daughter of Benjamin Sprague.

LEWIS, son of Charles and Polly CRONKHITE, was born in Covington February 7th, 1860, and was married in 1876 to Haidee M. Wheeldon, of Belise, Central America. Polly Cronkhite, who is still living, was born in Rensselaer county in 1818. She was married in 1885 to Charles Cronkhite, who died in 1878.

WILLIAM CROSMAN was born in Pavilion in 1822, and came to Covington in 1854. He has been engaged in business as a farmer and miller, and has served the town as tax collector and highway commissioner for some years. He married Della Shepard in 1865. Mr. Crosman contributed to the prosecution of the late war. He and his brother and an employee were all drafted at the same time. His father, Peter Crosman, was born in 1780, and married Hannah Bowen, of Saratoga. He served in the war of 1812–14, and Mrs. Crosman is the recipient of a pension on account of said service.

C. T. DEYO was born in Columbia in 1817. In 1844 he married Diantha Palmer, who died in 1860. In 1862 he married Matilda Meserve. He removed from his native place to Prattsville, Greene county, and from there to Covington in 1843. He is the owner of one hundred and three acres of land. His father, Richard Deyo, served in the war of 1812. Mr. and Mrs. Deyo are earnest workers in the Baptist church, Mr. Deyo having given much time and attention to the duties of a colporteur.

W. L. FARR was born in Le Roy, Genesee county, in 1844, and married Sarah Freeman, of Wyoming village, in 1866. In 1867 he came to Covington, where he is a farmer. Mr. Farr's father, Chauncey Farr, was born in New York, and lived in Genesee and Orleans

RESIDENCE OF A. D. THOMSON, CASTILE STATION WYOMING CO., N.Y.

RESIDENCE OF PETER L. SMITH, CASTILE WYOMING CO., N.Y.

RESIDENCE OF L. S. COLEMAN CASTILE STATION, WYOMING CO., N.Y.

RESIDENCE OF S. A. HIGGINS, CASTILE, WYOMING CO., N.Y.

RESIDENCE OF H. L. CUMMING, WATER STREET, CASTILE, WYOMING CO., N.Y.

RESIDENCE & OFFICE OF DR. E. WRIGHT, CASTILE, WYOMING CO., N.Y.

counties. His wife was Mary Ann Gray, of Pavilion. Mr. Farr is path master, and also holds the office of trustee of the Baptist church, of which he and Mrs. Farr are members.

THOMAS FISHER, farmer, was born in Covington, December 4th, 1854, and was married in 1875 to Imogene Avery. His father, Noah J. Fisher, was born in Covington in 1828, and has since resided there. In 1849 he married Philena B. Keith, daughter of Daniel Keith, of Wyoming. Both are members of the Presbyterian church.

JOHN H. GORTON was born in 1827, has lived one year in California, and has been a resident of Covington forty-eight years. His father is Samuel Gorton. His mother was formerly Betsey Hamilton. Both were born in Edinburgh, Saratoga county, the former in 1796. Mr. Gorton has held the offices of assessor and justice of the peace. Mr. Hamilton, Mrs. Gorton's father, was prominent in Saratoga county, holding the offices of supervisor, justice of the peace and member of the Legislature. After their marriage they removed to Onondaga county, and ten years later to Covington.

FRANKLIN GRIFFITH was born in Pike in 1835, and married Mary Barlow, of Covington, in 1868. His father, Amos Griffith, was born in Vermont about 1789, and removed to Washington county, N.Y., and from there to Pike, where he died in 1845. Mrs. Griffith's father was born in Vermont; at the age of twelve removed to Washington county, N. Y., and in 1887 to Covington, where he lived until about three months prior to his death. He died at the residence of his daughter in Batavia, at the age of seventy-three.

JONATHAN HOWARD, farmer, was born in Covington in 1824, and in 1850 married Harriett E. Mendell. Mr. Howard's mother was Pattie Sherman, who was born in New Haven, Vt., in 1791, lived later in Essex county, N. Y., and came to Covington in 1814, and whose father, Amasa Sherman, married Hannah Douglas. Daniel Howard was born in 1789, and was an early settler in the Genesee country.

MORTIMER E. JUDSON was born in Friendship, Allegany county, in 1827. In 1855 he married Sabra A. Moore, of Batavia, by whom he has had two children, one of whom is living. He came from his native place to Pavilion with his father, Monsieur D. Judson, who was born in Sunderland, Bennington county Vt.; married Phebe Calkins, by whom he had two children, of whom Mortimer E. is the only one living; was, with his wife, a member of the Methodist church; moved to Covington in 1880, and held the offices of highway commissioner and overseer of the poor many years. Mr. Judson was not liable to duty in the late war, but was liberal with his time and means in securing volunteers. He has been excise commissioner live years. Mrs. Judson is a member of the Methodist church.

AUSTIN LANK was born in Cayuga county in 1815, and was married in 1845 to Lucinda Witter, who was born in 1828. He went from Cayuga county to Oswego county, and from there to Covington, where he has lived for the past fifty years. He has been a member of the Baptist church at La Grange thirty-six years, Sunday-school superintendent twenty-four years and secretary of the Baptist society twenty-one years. His father, Luzman Lane, was born in Connecticut in 1771, and married Sarah Austin, of Hartford, Conn. They were pioneers in several different sections successively.

WINDSOR LAPHAM was born in Scipio, Cayuga county, in 1800. In 1824 he married Elmima Dunham. At the age of twenty-seven he removed to Chautauqua county, and from there to Covington. Mr. Lapham's parents were both natives of Rhode Island. His mother's maiden name was Thankful Smith. His father was born in 1760; his mother four years later. They removed to Cayuga county, and from there to the locality of their present residence.

JOHN C. LEWIS was born at Brinkworth, Wiltshire, England, in 1836. In 1875 he married Wealthy, daughter of Joseph and Rosetta Billings. After his arrival in America he worked by the month for a time, and later purchased his present farm. Mrs. Lewis's brother, Ezra Billings, served until discharged in the 104th regiment, and subsequently re-enlisted and was in active service until the close of the Rebellion. Another brother enlisted in the regular army.

MORGAN L. MATHEW was born in Washington county in 1830, and after living in Onondaga and Cayuga counties came to Covington thirty-two years ago, where he is known as a carpenter and farmer. In 1862 he enlisted in the 136th N. Y. volunteers, and was wounded at Gettysburg. From that time until the close of the war he was in detached service. He married Eliza Noonan, of Wyoming county, in 1852, and Mrs. Phebe A. Doan, widow of John Doan and daughter of Samuel Covert, at a later date. Gilbert B. Mayhew was born in Dutchess county in 1793, and while a resident there married Phebe Holmes.

EDWARD J. MURRAY was born September 22nd, 1821, in Ludbury, Rutland county, Vt. June 11th, 1845, he married Mary E. Beebe. He lived in Boston, Lockport, Niagara county, and Middlebury, and came to Covington in 1852. For twelve years he was in the mercantile business at Wyoming, where he was postmaster. He has been town clerk. His grandfather fought in the Revolutionary war, and until his death received a pension of $12 per month. His father, Ebor R. Murray, was born in 1793 and died in 1841. Mrs. Murray's father, John Beebe, was born September 4th, 1794, at Litchfield, N. Y., and married Aurilla Paddock April 22nd, 1819. At the age of thirty-one he came to Covington, where he died November 17th, 1845.

BENJAMIN SQUIRES was born in Sheffield, Mass., in 1813. He settled first in Middlebury. In 1866 he moved to his present farm. His father, Manasseh Squires, was born in Connecticut (as was also his grandfather), and removed to Massachusetts. He was killed by a falling tree. Mr. Squires married Olive Robins January 31st, 1838. She died in 1868. January 31st, 1872, he married Electa A. Miller, daughter of Dewey Miller, an early comer in Genesee county.

WILLIAM A. THAYER was born in Gainesville in 1819, and was married in 1854 to Mary E. Brownell. He removed from his native place to Warsaw in 1865, and to Covington in 1868, and purchased the farm of ninety acres where he has since lived. Willard Thayer, his father, came from Lima, Livingston county, in 1812, and was a pioneer there. Gideon Thayer, brother of the latter, served in the war of 1812–14.

MARK N. VELZY was born in Covington November 15th, 1825. At the age of twenty-two he removed to Perry, remained there twenty years and returned to Covington, where he has a farm of one hundred and twenty-five acres. While in Perry he was assessor and held other offices. His father, John Velzy, was born in Stephentown, Westchester county; resided in Saratoga county, and removed to Covington in 1814; thence to Perry with his son, and died there in January, 1863. Mr. Velzy's grandfather, who died in 1813, at the age of seventy-three, served during the Revolutionary war, and was at one time a prisoner-of-war in New York. Mr. Velzy married Elvira Barlow May 12th, 1847. She died in 1858, and October 27th, 1859, he married Catharine E. Boyce, of Saratoga county.

J. S. WALKER, farmer, was born January 9th, 1809, at Rutland, Vt., and came to Covington from that place in 1825. He has served for thirty-two years either as assessor, highway commissioner or superintendent of the poor. He held the office of notary public, and since the organization of the company has been commissioner of the State Line railroad. January 20th, 1833, he married Sophia M. Tilletson, of Berkshire county, Mass. Jedediah Tilletson, Mrs. Walker's father, was born in Rehoboth, R. I., in 1762. He fought in the Revolution, in Captain Amidown's company from Rehoboth. Mr. and Mrs. Walker are members of the Pavilion Baptist church.

LORENZO WYLIE was born in Covington June 10th, 1817. He is a farmer and surveyor. For forty-three years he has been a member of the Methodist church. Until the abolition of that office in 1856 he was town superintendent; was town clerk 1857–59; was elected supervisor in 1859, and served six terms, and for the past nine years he has held the office of justice of the peace.

THE TOWN OF EAGLE.

EAGLE was formed from Pike, January 21st, 1823. It lies on the summit of western New York. Its watercourses are tributary to streams which reach Lakes Ontario and Erie and the Gulf of Mexico. The brooks in the town were at an early day filled with trout. Timothy Buckland often put grain bag into one of the streams at the head of Spring glen and caught half a bushel at once.

No relics of forts or battle fields of the aborigines are to be found in Eagle. Near the center of the town, a short distance east of what is now Bliss station on the Rochester & State Line Railroad, was one of their camping grounds. The last time they were here in any great numbers was about 1842, on the occasion of vast numbers of pigeons nesting here. The woods on both sides of the valley were filled with pigeons raising their young, and the Indians from all quarters gathered here to get the young pigeons or squabs. A great many came from the Cattaraugus and Tonawanda reservations and camped here during the stay of the pigeons, catching and smoking the squabs, tons of which were taken away by them.

DEALINGS WITH THE HOLLAND COMPANY.

Eagle is a part of the Holland Purchase, and was under the control of a Mr. Devereau as agent for the company, with his office for many years at Batavia, Genesee county. Having disposed of a good share of this part of the tract he removed to Ellicottville, Cattaraugus county, where for many years the people of this section had to go yearly to make the payments upon their farms, often having nothing to pay with, and hard and perhaps vain work to raise the interest. But they would go to Ellicottville, talk the matter over, and come home well pleased that the company would allow the interest to run a while longer. This of course made the matter still worse the next year, and so it went from year to year, until either some other person bought the place from under them, or they would be obliged to give it up to the company, or sell their improvements for a trifle and start again. None of the land was deeded until paid for, every one holding his land by a written article guaranteeing a deed when paid in full. A large share of the lands were bought by speculators, and sold out as they could find purchasers; consequently it is hard to tell who the first settler was on each lot. The following, from the books of the Holland Company, will give the names of early buyers, and show what purchases they made:

Chauncey Loomis 1807, lots 32, 36 and 40; Chauncey and Justin Loomis, 1807, lots 30 and 38; Justin Loomis, 1808, lots 6, 31 and 69; Chauncey Loomis,1808, lot 27; Silas Hudges, 1814, part of lot 8; Amos Smith, 1816, part of lot 7; Seneca Baker, 1816, part of lot 7; Silas Hodges, 1818, part of lot 8; Dan Beach, 1818, part of lot 45; David Sturges, 1826, part of lot 25; Phineas Graves, 1829, part of lot 25; Ambrose Clark, 1829, part of lot 26; Anson Hinman, 1831, part of lot 14; William Van Dyke, 1832, part of lot 18; Jacob Newman, 1833, part of lot 50; Timothy Buckland, 1833, part of lot 59; Josiah Sanford, 1333, part of lot 2; Moses Smith, 1834, 61, 62 and part of 4; Barzilla Hurlburt, 1834, part of lot 14; William Van Dyke, 1834, part of lot 18; Justus Lyon, 1834, lot 22; David Dane, 1834; part of lot 59; Chandius Randall, 1834, part of lot 59; Nicholas Devereux and others, 1835, parts of lots 4, 9, 11, 13, 19, 20, 21, 23, 24, 29, 33, 34, 41. 42, 43, 46, 52, 53, 54, 55, 57, 58, 60, 63 and lots 38, 61, 62 and 63; Smith Lyon, 1835, part of lot 14; Cyrus Brooks, 1835, part of lot 14; Seneca Baker, 1835, part of lot 15; Amos Otis, 1835, part of lot 16; Jethro Grover, 1835, part of lot 16; Jonathan and Stephen Wyley, 1835, part of lot 17; Milo Metcalf, 1835, part of lot 19; William Watkins, 1835, parts of 42 and 50; Gideon H. Austin, 1835, part of 44; Anson Hills, 1835, part of 44; Aaron Van Cleve, lot 28; Joseph Sadgebar, 1831, part of lots 9, 41, 42, 50 and 58; these lands were sold from under settlers who failed in their payments; also most of those taken by Devereux and others.

Elias Loomis, James J. Jackson, Kilborn D. Smith, Isaac Hunt and Abraham Ward were among the early settlers on the west town line, on lots 62, 63 and 64.

SETTLEMENT AND EARLY EVENTS.

The first settlers in the town were William and Silas Hodges. William ran away from his home in Massachusetts when nineteen years of age; Silas bought his time. Both went to Herkimer county, N. Y. William was married to Miss Abigail Howard, of that county, on the last day of February, 1808. Soon afterward William and Silas came to this town and took up a quarter section of land designated as lot 8, range 2, township 7 Holland Company's land; built a log house, and had some timber felled by a man named Smith, who came with them—the first trees cut by a white man in the town. Both returned to Herkimer county, and in April, 1809, Silas, with an ox-team, and William, hiring his brother-in-law to move him and his effects with his horse team, returned. They fell in on the route with a company going to Ischua, Cattaraugus county, and traveled with them for a number of days. When they left for the east for their effects they closed their house and covered the chimney. When they returned in the spring they found that the house had been occupied by the Indians, who, not understanding chimneys, did not take the cover off the top, and the house was thoroughly smoked. In a few days all was made right, and the brothers went to work clearing for a spring crop. The roof of the house was made of bark; the floors and doors of split basswood logs. In 1817 William planted an orchard of fifty apple trees, over half of which are now standing. On their arrival in the spring of 1809 they planted some apple seeds, from which they raised a few trees, three of which are still standing and bearing.

Dan Beach, of Montgomery county, N. Y., hired two teams to move him, and settled on lot 45 in August, 1810; his brother-in-law, Seth Wetmore, on lot 52 in 1811; Demarkus Rathbone on the northwest part of lot 45 in 1811.

Nathaniel Hills and his brother, A. Hills, came in from Montgomery county in the spring of 1810. Both families lived in one room. When Dan Beach came, in the fall, he stopped with the Hillses a few days—three families in one room. During the first week following these three men erected a log house for A. Hills. The next week they built one for Beach. A portion of this was covered with bark, the remainder open for the smoke to escape, as the fire was built on the ground. Elm logs were split and laid side by side for the floor. Hemlock boughs on the floor formed the bedstead. Beach's was the fifth family in the town. The Hodges and Hills families preceded him. The outside door of Beach's house at first was a bed quilt. The opening in the roof and the spaces between the logs gave sufficient light for the room without windows. These settlers were at first without roads or teams, twelve miles from a mill where lumber could be got, and thirty-one miles from Geneseo, the nearest point where other building material could be obtained. On arriving at this desolate spot, and paying the men who had brought him and his, Mr. Beach had $104, a hoe, an ax and a shovel, unfamiliar implements, as he was not a farmer but a saddler by trade. In eight years he had paid for his farm, and was in possession of a comfortable home. Simeon Baker came in 1815 with a yoke of oxen, and settled on lot 7 in 1814. A Mr. Foster, from Vermont, located in 1815 on lot 12. Peter Keyes came from Vermont in 1816, with a yoke of cattle and a horse hitched forward of them, and settled on lot 16. Joseph Barnhart in 1819 bought Eber Benton's farm on lot 24, for a yoke of oxen and a rifle, Benton having been on the place since 1816. Jethro Grover, from Vermont, in 1820 settled on lot 7. Robert Hamilton came west from Vermont in 1820 with a horse team, and located on lot 32. The winter of 1820 and 1821 was very severe. The snow was two feet deep in April, fodder all used up, and the settlers were obliged to cut browse for their stock. Maple and basswood timber appeared to relish with the cattle, and they thrived very well on the boughs of those trees. In May of that year there was a hard snow storm, lasting three days, after the settlers had made up their minds that winter was over and all was coming out right. Early herbs and leeks were up enough to have helped the cattle; but this snow covered everything green, and cattle could get nothing to eat. The writer has heard Timothy Buckland often tell that he fed out the straw from his straw beds, and when the last bed was emptied he lay all day between two feather beds, in order not to hear the bawling of his cows.

Philip Baker came from Vermont late in March, 1821, and settled on lot 7. He was accompanied by his brother Elisha. They together had a horse team. Elisha staid until the roads became settled, when he moved on to Chautauqua county. Ebenezer Dutton also came in 1821 from Vermont with a horse team, and settled on lot 24. The Bakers, Grovers, Duttons and Hamiltons were all connected by marriage. Nicholas Severance, from Vermont, settled on lot 15 in 1817, built a log house and barn, cleared a number of acres of land, dwelt there a number of years and removed to Castile, where he kept tavern for a long time. His only child was born in this town. She became the wife of William S. Agett.

Barzilla Bedee settled on lot 15 in 1815. A Mr. Foster came in from Vermont in 1815 with an ox-team, and settled on lot 16. Elijah Poole in April, 1821, settled on lot 8. Urocalton Geary in 1822 settled on lot 31. Joseph Crocker, from Vermont, settled on lot 23 in 1822. He built the first hewed log house in town, and taught a singing-school. Jedediah Dutton, another Vermonter, in 1831 settled on lot 15. Joseph Rawson was an early settler on lot 32. William Hodges built the first framed barn in the town in 1817, and first framed house on the North road in 1823. William and Silas Hodges sowed the first wheat in the town, procuring the seed in the town of Gainesville. They worked together for a number of years.

In 1816 a log school-house was built on the North road. Mrs. Arnold (a widow) was the first teacher. Mrs. Gage, Mrs. Stevens, Cyrus Beeman, Simeon Hodges and John Hodges are surviving pupils of that school.

Among the early settlers in the south part of the town, on Wing street, were Jonathan Wing, Jonathan, William and David Van Dyke, John Allen, John Davis, Abraham Wade, Ralph Graves, Wooster Randal, a Mr. Wilcox, Ebenezer Pitty and Ira Millin.

In the west part of the town Elijah Hodges settled in 1818; Stephen Jones in 1820, and Timothy Buckland in 1822, all on lot 59. Other settlers thereabouts were Ezekiel Randal, George W. Knapp, George Galey, Dr. Hewit, Benjamin F. Tiffany, Ardon Tabor and a Mr. Olds.

Among the first settlers in the east part of the town were Amos Huntly, about 1815 or 1816; soon after, Barzilla Hurlburt and Alvin Howes.

Among the early settlers on the Center road, known as the Telegraph road, were Milo Sawyer, Jefferson Metcalf and Richard Slusson. Previous to these, however, Hezekiah Bedee, the first settler on the Telegraph road, settled on lot 12; Daniel Johnston, the next settler, located on lot 20.

The first child born in the town was Alanson Hodges, son of Silas Hodges. The first marriage in the town was that of Mr. Hubbard Starkweather to a Miss Hancock. Among the early marriages were those of Samuel Robinson and a Mr. Conkey.

The first death was that of a Mr. Malory, a traveler from the South, stopping at Amos Huntly's inn. He died of yellow fever, and was buried in what is now Lyonsburg Cemetery, in the east part of the town. His was the first grave in that ground, which was afterward established as a graveyard. Mr. Huntly soon after lost two children, who were buried there.

Soon after a graveyard was established near the inn of Dan Beach. The first grave in this ground was that of Elijah Hills, son of Adam, who came to his death by an injury received while logging.

A few years afterward there was opened north of Hydeville a burying ground, which is now known as the Eagle Village Cemetery. The one at Lyonsburg and that at Eagle Village are in a fair condition, with an appropriate number of evergreen and shade trees. The one near the old Dan Beach stand has been abandoned for years. The first burial in the Eagle Village graveyard was that of Andrew Jackson, son of Timothy and Lorinda Buckland, in February, 1829. The next burial followed in May, of the same year, that of John Anderson, his brother. The age of the first was ten months; that of the other two years and one month.

Timothy Buckland, whose name has occurred several times, was a successful hunter. He came from Vermont in 1816 to Centerville, Allegany county, for the purpose of hunting. Having lost the sight of his right eye by smallpox at Liverpool (he was a sailor in early life), he shot left handed, and a truer shot never lived in the town. The writer has seen him center a snowball ten rods distant, off hand, when seventy years of age. During his residence in Centerville and in this town (to which he came in 1822), he killed twenty-four bears, seventy-five wolves (on which the bounty amounted to $10 a head), and deer past counting. He also caught a great deal of smaller game by trapping, such as otter, mink, sable, foxes, raccoon, etc. He caught a number of foxes in his wolf traps, setting the traps in a spring. During his voyages at sea he and others would save their rations of whiskey or rum during the week and keep it in a large can until Saturday night. when, if the state of the weather was such that duty was light, they would bring on the can and have a jolly time drinking, telling yarns and singing songs, as Buckland could sing songs all night and not repeat one. This habit became so strong that he practiced it occasionally during his whole life. Each one of these Saturday night cans would last from two to three days. The last day he would be asleep an hour or two, get up and take a drink or two, sing awhile, go out and shin up the sign post to show how the sailors climbed, all this time wearing nothing on him but a shirt.

As a general thing he would tan the skins of the deer he killed. His wife made the skins up into gloves, mittens, occasionally a pair of moccasins, and a vest sometimes, when she was working a light, thin skin.

During the residence of Buckland and his wife in Centerville, two miles from any neighbor, with the wolves howling on every side, Mrs. Buckland would go on horseback two miles through the forest visiting the neighbors, very often alone, and enjoy not only the visit but the ride. The route was where the Rochester and State Line Railroad now runs through the corner of Centerville and into the town of Freedom. Those she visited resided not far from Freedom Station on that road. Uncle Tim. had a horse, yet he has often been heard to say that when he set foot on the Holland Purchase he had but eighteen pence and a chew of tobacco. He delighted in playing tricks on the tavern keepers, who were well acquainted with him for miles around. He sent Dan Burrows, then keeping in the town of Castile, a quarter of a wolf for venison. Dan returned his thanks, accompanied with a paper of choice lettuce seed, with particular directions how to prepare the soil and sow the seed. The directions were all carried out, and in due time Uncle Tim. had a fine bed of luxuriant bull thistles.

There was a great amount of very nice black cherry timber in a portion of the town. From 1840 to 1845 it was in good demand for shipping east. A man named Green, as shipper, staid here a portion of the season for three or four years, directing how to manufacture the timber to secure the best market. He would even go into the forest and show how he would like to have the trees cut into logs, etc. A great many thousand feet were cut and shipped from this town, the price ranging according to the width of the lumber; boards thirty inches wide would bring $30; twenty inches wide, $20 per thousand, etc. A great many of the logs were sawed without squaring, as the lumber would then average wider and bring more per thousand.

When the timber became rather scarce Colonel G. G. Prey and a brother-in-law went out in search of a few trees. They found an old stub some fifty feet high, the top having been blown off, which had been passed by as good for nothing. They bought and felled it, and got five splendid logs, about four feet in diameter. Two miles south lived Jesse Dutton, who weighed four hundred and forty pounds. It was jocularly proposed to "save a few boards out of one of these logs for Uncle Dutton's coffin," and it was but a short time before those same boards were actually so used.

POLITICAL HISTORY.

The first town meeting was held at the house of Seth Wetmore, agreeable to an act of the Legislature, on the 11th of February, 1823. Dan Beach was chosen moderator of the meeting, and the following persons were elected to office: Lorey Buckley, supervisor; Demarkus Rathbone, town clerk; Joseph Crocker, Amos Huntly and Jonathan Wing, assessors; Philip Baker, collector; Daniel Johnston and Barzilla Bedee, overseers of poor; Ralph Graves, Joseph Rawson and Seth Wetmore; commissioners of highways; Benjamin Tiffany. Seth Wetmore and Philip Baker, commissioners of common schools; John Pierce and Hezekiah Bedee, constables.

The following were appointed overseers of the different road districts: No. 1, Daniel McMartin; No. 2, Daniel Johnston; No. 3, Richard Bedee; No. 4, Peter Keyes; No. 5, Stephen Jones; No. 6, Dan Beach; No. 7, Demarkus Rathbone; No. 8, Ira Millin.

The following provisions were carried by vote at this town meeting: That double the amount of money be raised for the support of common schools that was drawn from the State; that $250 be raised for highway purposes, "to be distributed in such a manner that every man may have his share of it if he will do his share of the work"; that hogs are not free commoners; that a bounty of $5 be paid on every wolf caught in the town by an inhabitant thereof; that the meeting be adjourned to the house of Amos Huntly, the following year, the first Tuesday in April.

This first town meeting was a jolly affair. In the room where the votes were polled, good authority says, there was a barrel of whiskey, and on the table where the ballot box sat, and which was surrounded by the official board, were a decanter and glasses.

On the 1st day of July, 1828, was made the first survey of a road after the organization of the town. The record of it is as follows: "Survey of a road, beginning at a cherry stump on a road leading from the forks of the Cattaraugus to Ezekiel Randal's; running thence south 75° west 28 chains; thence south 60° west 20 chains and 50 links; thence south 10° west 11 chains, to intersect a road near the house of Elijah Hyde. Seth Wetmore, Surveyor."

This road was taken up so long ago that hardly a person now remembers it. The same day a road was surveyed by the same party, beginning near Elijah Hyde's saw-mill, running thence north 15° west 35 chains to intersect the old Cattaraugus road east of the house of Timothy Buckland. This Cattaraugus road is now known as the old State road (the survey having been authorized by the Legislature of 1828), running from Fredonia, Chautauqua county, through the town of Eagle to the transit line at or near the village of Perry.

In the survey of roads through the town Seth Wetmore took a prominent part, he being the Holland Company's surveyor for a number of years, dividing up the lots of the original survey by Joseph Ellicott into parcels as dictated by the company. A. Forbs, Joseph Miller, William A. Perry, Timothy Buckland, I. E. Wheeden, Simeon Capson, D. Smith and V. D. Beach also surveyed some of the roads in the town, in company and assisted by the highway commissioners.

There are but three bridges in the town worthy the name—one over the stream at Eagle Village, one near the junction at the center of the town, or Bliss, and one over the stream in the east part of the town. Neither of these three is over thirty feet long. There are other cheap structures of from four to ten feet span, the building of which would hardly come under the head of bridging.

On the first of March, 1823, the commissioners of common schools met for the purpose of dividing the towns into school districts. They made seven school districts, as follows: No. 1, lots 1, 2, 9, 10, 17, 18, 25, 26, 33, 34; No. 2, lots 3, 4, 11, 12, 19, 20: No. 3, lots 5, 6, 13, 14, 21, 22, 29, 30; No. 4, lots 7, 8, 15, 16; No. 5, lots 41, 42, 49, 50, 57, 58, 59; No. 6, lots 27, 28, 35, 36, 37, 38, 43, 44, 45, 46, 51, 52, 53, 54, 60, 61, 62; No. 7, lots 23, 24, 31, 32, 39, 40, 47, 48, 55, 63, 64.

The first school in the town was taught in Mr. Barzilla Hurlburt's barn on lot 1; Miss Orilla Blackman was the first teacher. The next year a log school-house was erected in the same neighborhood. Mrs. Norman Howes and two of her brothers, Barzilla and Gideon Hurlburt, are survivors of the first school.

At the town meeting held on the 6th of April, 1830, a resolution was passed changing the day of meeting from April to the first Tuesday in March. The town meeting was held on that day until 1846, when the time was changed to the last Tuesday in February, on which day it has been held ever since.

On the 19th of May, 1846, a special town meeting was held on the question of licensing the sale of spirituous liquors; 107 votes were cast in favor of license and 58 for no license.

Cyril Rawson was the only person who has represented the town in the Legislature. It has furnished one sheriff, Albert Gage, elected in 1874. The supervisors of the town have been as follows:

Lorey Buckley, 1828–26, 1836; Benjamin F. Tiffany, 1827–30, 1833, 1834; Jonathan Wing, 1831, 1832, 1835; Norman Howes, 1836 (to fill vacancy caused by the removal of Mr. Buckley; votes cast, 49)–41, 1849–51, 1853, 1856, 1857; Cyril Rawson, 1842, 1843 (the election of 1843 resulting in no choice), 1848; Ebenezer Pitee, 1844, 1845, Samuel Tucker, 1846, 1847; Oliver Phelps, 1852; William S. Agett, 1854, 1855 (the only Democrat ever elected); Oliver H. P. Griggs, 1857, 1858; Walter Shay, 1859, 1860; Ira Eastman, 1861, 1862, 1871, 1872; P. D. Lyon, 1863–66; Beckley Howes, 1868, 1869; Austin N. Richardson, 1870; Albert P. Gage, 1873, 1874; Gilbert G. Prey, 1875; Marcena Drake, 1876–79.

The State census returns from Eagle for the last fifty years exhibit a slow but uninterrupted growth in population up to 1855, and since then a gradual decline. They are as follows: 1830, 892; 1835, 1,149; 1840, 1,222; 1845, 1,314; 1850, 1,381; 1855, 1,390; 1860, 1,312; 1865, 1,211; 1870, 1,040; 1875, 1,041.

THE DEVELOPMENT AND COURSE OF BUSINESS.

The first flouring-mill was erected by Dexter Brothers, at what is now Eagle Village, then called Hydeville. These Dexters were in an early day residents of Centerville, and were among the first carpenters who worked in the town, though they were not residents until 1823 or 1824. James Baker was the first carpenter residing in the town. There were four of the Dexters—Knight, Chauncey, Harrison and Antipas. Their father, Delno Dexter, sometimes worked with them. They came in from Centerville to work at their trade years before they came to live here. Among the first framed buildings erected in the town by the Dexters were the mill, Timothy Buckland's inn, Stephen Jones's dwelling, and one or two dwellings and a store at Hydeville.

Mr. Wart's tavern stand was on lot 45. The house was enclosed when the log house was destroyed by fire, and the family was obliged to move in. Hubbard Thompson, son-in-law of Delno Dexter, worked on the Wart inn in its erection.

The above mentioned mill was operated by different individuals until 1845 or 1846. The last person who occupied it for grinding purposes was Charles H. Denman. A portion of it was purchased by William S. Agett, and moved some twenty rods to the north, an addition put to it, and it has been occupied for different purposes—part of the time for a barn, store-house, paint shop, school-room, town hall—and it is now used as a barn, standing as an ornament to Pearl street, Eagle Village.

The second grist-mill was built by Aaron Sevey, near the east line of the town. It is now occupied by Vernon Wineger, and is the only flouring-mill in the town. A few years ago Mr. Wineger and his brother were running the mill together. His brother, doing something about the dam at the time of a freshet, was accidentally drowned. Vernon has since worked the mill.

The first saw-mill was built by Amos Huntly, at what is called Lyonsburg, in the eastern part of the town, on the west branch of the Wiscoy. At the same point other manufactures were carried on at different times, such as turning broom handles, dressing flax, making lath and boring and fitting pump logs, which is now done.

There was another saw-mill built at Hydeville soon after Huntly's by Dexter Brothers, using the old flutter waterwheel. It was worn out and another erected near the same place, which did more or less business until within four or five years, when it was abandoned, and it is now in a dilapidated condition, leaving a fine little water power wasting away.

About 1840 Mr. Elisha Whipple built a saw-mill on the east branch of the Wiscoy, about a mile west of the Huntly mill. It continued to run until 1878, when Martin, son of Elisha Whipple, who was then running it, died. Previous to his death for a year or two he had a feed mill attached. Since then it has done but little business, yet it is still in working order.

Mr. Collins Thomas built and has operated a steam sawmill and planer a little east of Eagle Village for a few years past.

The first clothiery in the town was erected by V. D. Beach and his brother Emmet on lot 59, at the head of Spring glen, in 1834. They worked the factory until 1846 or 1847, and for the last year or two of their occupancy put in and operated machinery for dressing flax. In 1846 or 1847 they disposed of the premises to Mr. Griffith, of Rushford, Allegany county. James Thompson carried on the business for Griffith, or rented the establishment a few years; became proprietor and carried on the factory until 1853, when he sold to Messrs. John Mitchell and William Taylor. They built a saw-mill with a breast water wheel thirty feet in diameter. It stood some twenty rods north of the old factory site. They carried on the mill until 1868. In the meantime Mr. Taylor sold his share to John G., son of John Mitchell. The firm of Mitchell & Son abandoned the saw-mill, it being nearly worn out, and erected a feed-mill across the road from the old factory site. They operated it in connection with a turning lathe, added to it a cider mill, and are now running all together, the springs around the head of the glen furnishing sufficient water, with but a small reservoir, to do considerable business. Hundreds of barrels of cider are made every autumn, besides the grinding of feed and turning of almost every description.

The first wagon maker in the town was Quartus Clark, who came from Freedom, Cattaraugus county, about 1846; located at Eagle Village, and carried on the business until about 1868, when he went to farming, in the town of Arcade.

The first tannery was erected by Samuel Watson and Walter Shay, in 1844 or 1845, at Eagle Village. They ran it in connection with boot and shoe making. Watson attended to the tannery part. They carried on the business in company for a number of years, when Mr. Watson removed to Philipsburg, now Belmont, Allegany county, leaving the entire business in the hands of Shay.

The latter operated the works a few years. During the war he was appointed government assessor. He slackened up in the tanning business, put in a stock of dry goods and groceries, and finally, at the close of the war or soon after, sold out his tannery to James Dempsey and his store to S. N. Naramore, and removed to Castile. Dempsey carried on the tannery until the spring of 1877, when it was destroyed by fire; and also the manufacture of harnesses. Since the loss of the tannery he has done a large business in boots and shoes and harnesses for a country place, having as good a show of his kind of goods as will be seen outside of the cities. At all of these points the manufacture of sawed shingles has been more or less extensively carried on.

The soil of the town is much better adapted of late years to grazing than grain growing, yet when the country was new and before the soil became exhausted by continued tillage good crops of nearly all grains were realized. Thirty to thirty-five bushels of wheat, fifty to seventy-five bushels of oats, fifty bushels of shelled corn, two hundred to three hundred bushels of potatoes, or one and a half to two and a half tons of hay per acre were not an uncommon yield. Good crops of barley, peas and millet were also raised, together with flax.

For a few years before and during the war farmers kept all the cows they could, made and packed butter, and sold it to shippers or shipped it themselves to eastern markets.

In 1865 or 1866 the first cheese factory in the town was built just south of Eagle Village, by Luther Cummins, who worked it one year, when Austin N. Richardson came into possession. He carried it on a few years, working up the milk of about eight hundred cows. In 1871 Asa C. Hubbard purchased it, and operated it directly or indirectly until 1879, when it was sold to Mr. Lewis Safford, and during the season of 1879 it was carried on by him.

About the time this factory was built one was put in operation on the North road, known as the Hunn factory. After a few years it was removed to the State road, a short distance west of Lyonsburg, enlarged, and has done a large business each year since. One year this factory made butter and skimmed milk cheese. Since then cheese has been made exclusively.

Mr. Jerome Lewis, of the town of Freedom, Cattaraugus county, an adept at cheese making, a few years since built a factory at Husted's Corners, in the southwest corner of Eagle, and one at Eagle Center. Another has been built on Wing street near the south line of the town, on the Center road, within the past few years. Two years ago one was built on the North road, about three miles west of the site of the old Hunn factory, making five cheese factories in the town, each working up the milk of from three hundred to five hundred cows, and making from ten to twenty cheese per day during most of the season, each cheese weighing about fifty-six to sixty pounds. Besides these cheese factories, there is a creamery about two miles east of the center of the town, on the old Telegraph road, which makes butter exclusively, feeding the buttermilk to calves and hogs. It has been in operation some three or four years; Mr. Adelbert Lathrop proprietor. This creamery receives the milk of nearly the same number of cows as one of the cheese factories.

While the principal feature in the agriculture of the town for fifteen or twenty years has been butter and cheese making, the raising of fruits, especially apples, has for the past few years taken some of the attention of the farming public. In an early day peaches grew and fruited finely here, but of late years scarcely any have been raised.

The first store in the town was located at Hydesville (now Eagle Village), and kept by Elijah Hyde. In connection with his store he manufactured potash, running an ashery containing two potash kettles of one hundred and twenty gallons capacity, keeping a team on the road constantly gathering ashes, which were plenty in those days, as the settlers were clearing the land and burning a great deal of timber. He also carded wool and dressed cloth before the Beach brothers operated their clothiery. The mode of trade was barter, almost everything being taken in exchange for goods, from a yoke of cattle to a barrel of soap. Some of the settlers chose to work up their own ashes into "black salts," which passed current for all kinds of goods at a regular price. Hyde sold goods some six years, commencing about 1818; George W. Knapp succeeded him, being in trade a year or two; Samuel Curtis next carried on the business as much longer; Benjamin Coddington succeeded him, and sold goods about a year. From the time he closed out until 1842 there was no store kept at this place. Henry Martin then opened a store, and sold goods until 1843. In that year William S. Agett, a young widower, came as agent for a house in Perry, and took the place of Martin. He became proprietor in a short time, and has continued in business ever since. During a great share of the time he has sold dry goods in connection with groceries and provisions; but for a few years past has given up dry goods, and has been and is now dealing in groceries, provisions, Yankee notions, etc. The trade for a number of years was carried on by barter. The time has been when black salts, ashes and stags were legal tender, the latter at forty dollars a yoke, ten yoke having passed through the hands of Captain Agett at that price in exchange for goods, without a word of banter, more than there would be over a silver dollar or a dollar greenback.

A Mr. Geer sold goods in an early day at Lyonsburg. For a year or two, about 1840, Cyril Rawson kept a store at Lyonsburg, running an ashery in connection. He afterward turned his attention to the manufacture of wooden articles, such as broom handles and other turned work, lath, etc. At Eagle Village, from about 1847 or 1848, a dry goods and grocery store was kept, first by a young man named Rufus Scott, who after a few years went to Michigan. Joseph W. Gledhill followed him, and was in trade until about 1870, when he removed to Castile, leaving his son Albert in the store. The latter, after two or three years, removed from the town. A Mr. Kimble was then the merchant for a year. Since then the store has been kept as a hardware establishment. Mr. William W. Merrill is the present occupant and tradesman. Since W. Shay sold to Mr. Naramore the latter has continued in trade, sometimes with a partner, and is now dealing in dry goods, groceries, Yankee notions and clothing. His last partner, Jeff Bliss, on the dissolution of the firm in the spring of 1879 removed to Bliss Station, on the Rochester and State Line Railroad, and opened a store, and is doing business in the firm of Bliss Bros.

Every person in an early day had to open his house to travelers; the roads were so bad that they were obliged to stop at almost every house, and the people began to prepare for entertaining them. The first tavern in the town regularly opened was kept by Dan Beach, who was among the first settlers. It was kept in a log house. He had accommodations for about six or eight persons and stabling for three or four teams. After his death Jacob Wart married his widow, put up a frame building, and kept tavern until about 1850. In 1822 Timothy Buckland built a frame house on the State road, on the north line of lot 59, and opened a tavern with about the same accommodations as Mr. Beach. He kept the inn until 1848 or 1849, when his son Timothy W. built a more commodious house across the road, and took upon himself to entertain the traveling public. Amos Huntly kept tavern at Lyonsburg at an early day. About 1830 Justice Lyon opened a hotel at Lyonsburg, and a tavern was kept there for fifteen or twenty years thereafter. About 1848 the first genuine hotel at Eagle Village was built by Lyman Scott, who kept it until his death. He dropped dead while playing a game of checkers. Previous to this a tavern as kept a few years by a Mr. Perry on the same site, in an old dwelling fitted up for that purpose by William S. Agett and rented by Perry. Scott's tavern was continued by John Cole, his son-in-law, until 1864, when he was followed by S. N. Naramore, who kept it until 1867. He then sold to George B. McCraley, who kept the house until 1875, when he died. His widow has kept it from that time to the present.

One Fitch was the first blacksmith in Eagle. He carried on the business in the eastern part of the town. Among the early blacksmiths was a Mr. Crosby, who carried on the business at Hydeville, having his shop partly over the mill race. It was afterward occupied by Tubal Bascomb, after whom Joshua Nichols worked at the business until the shop was burned. It was rebuilt, and is now occupied by Jasper Smith. In 1845 James Yule came from the town of Freedom, Cattaraugus county, built a shop and carried on black smithing until about 1858. This shop was afterward run by Mr. Markham and Mr. Fisher. S. N. Naramore purchased it in 1861, kept it three years, and sold to James Rossney, who now carries it on.

Amos Huntly operated the first distillery, located in the eastern part of the town. He commenced about 1820. His distillery had quite a patronage from the Indians. Richard Pardy next went into the business of distilling, at Lyon's farm. Soon afterward P. T. Beardsley began it a short distance east of Bliss Station. Martin Whipple, between Bliss and Lyon's, was the next distiller. None of these did a very heavy business. Part of the time from 1845 to 1850 Elijah Godfrey distilled oils and essences a mile north of Eagle Village, from herbs and boughs.

Harrington Hewett was the first physician in the town. He resided about a mile and a half east of Hydeville, in a log house. He lost the use of an arm by being thrown from a horse while racing on the causeway, or corduroy road, just east of the inn kept by Timothy Buckland. Washington W. Day was the next physician. He settled on the southwest corner lot in the town, now occupied by Milton Husted. He came in 1836 or 1837. He practiced there about two years, and removed to Hydeville; remained there until about 1860, when he removed to Arcade. Dr. Bogart came and stayed about a year; Dr. McArthur a few years. He was succeeded by Dr. Eli Woodworth, who still remains. In the spring of 1875 Dr. Z. J. Lusk came from Clarence, Erie county. He practiced three years, and re moved to Warsaw. Dr. Ballou has taken his place.

The early preachers were Messrs. Kendal, Cady, Harvey and Nathaniel Hills.

The first post route was established from Pike Hollow to Arcade, about 1820. G. W. Knapp was the first postmaster. He was followed by James Baker. The next was Oliver Phelps. The post-offices were kept in different parts of the town, in the postmaster's dwelling. About 1843 the second post-office was given to the town, namely, the Eagle Village post-office. The first was located at or near the center of the town, or at Bliss.

The first post rider was Harlow Huntly, who continued for a number of years. Morris Walradt followed him.

VILLAGES OF THE TOWN.

EAGLE VILLAGE is located in the southwest part of the town, at the mouth of Spring glen. It contains a church edifice (Methodist Episcopal)—a wooden structure, thirty by fifty-two feet, with moderate sized spire and belfry; a school-house with two departments-a wooden building, fifty by twenty-eight feet, with vestibule eight by fourteen feet, with belfry and bell, situated near the church on Pearl street, a short distance from Main; a dry goods store, a grocery, a hardware store, a millinery establishment, a wagon shop, two custom blacksmith shops, a boot, shoe and harness shop and store, a hotel and a cheese factory.

The first owner of land where the village now stands was Elijah Hyde. The place contains twenty-nine dwellings. It has a good, durable water power, unused at present; a steam saw-mill, with planer, in the eastern suburbs; a feed and cider mill a short distance south.

BLISS STATION, on the Rochester and State Line Railroad, near the center of the town, is a hamlet built since the State Line road was located. It consists of a dry goods and grocery store, a blacksmith shop, a wagon shop, a hotel, erected during the past season, a steam saw-mill nearly completed, nine dwellings and a station house, with a school-house near. The first owner of the land where Bliss Station now stands was Justin Loomis, who owned four quarter sections. He became insane, and the Court of Chancery appointed Strong Hayden to sell the land for the support of the Loomis family. Sylvester Bliss bought the land where the station now stands, and it is now occupied by his son Stephen, except such portion as he has sold for railroad purposes and building lots.

LYONSBURG is a hamlet. It contains a manufactory of wooden articles, such as broom handles, pump logs, etc., a saw-mill, and about ten dwellings. Its condition is nearly the same as thirty years ago. It has a school-house near by, and a chair factory within half a mile. The first owner of land at Lyonsburg was Amos Huntly.

CHURCHES.

The first church organization in the town was at Eagle Village, and of the Free Will Baptist denomination. Among the leading members were Deacon Ephraim Dennis, Martin and Marvin Shepherd, Calvin Chamberlin, Ralph Graves, two or three brothers named Campbell, and a Mr. Holt. Elders Jackson, Chaffee and Carter were the first preachers, followed by Elders Kellogg, Ward, Strickland, Rycart and Campbell. Elders Kellogg and Ward became unsound in doctrine, and preached Universalism. About 1853 most of the members removed to Pike, built a school, and have been successful in sustaining it.

The real estate upon which this church edifice was built was deeded to them by Charles H. Denman, on condition that if they ceased to be a society the property should fall to any other denomination having evangelical views. Accordingly it fell into the hands of the Methodist Episcopal church. The edifice was built in 1842—a wooden structure, thirty by forty feet, and thirteen feet high inside, with no steeple or belfry. It was built by the community at large, irrespective of religious views. In 1870 the Methodists moved the house from its first location into the village, added twelve feet to its height, put on a belfry and spire, reseated the audience room, and raised it to sixteen feet inside.

About the time the Free Will Baptist church was formed the Congregationalists organized a church; but they were unable to sustain preaching, and disbanded after a year or two. Rev. Mr. Danforth was pastor. A portion of its members joined the Methodists on the organization about 1854.

At Eagle Valley is a church edifice belonging to a Methodist society with a considerable membership.

The first Sunday-school was held in the east part of the town, near Lyonsburg. Alvin Howes was the superintendent. This school was held in 1825. The next was kept in 1829 or 1830, south of Eagle Village, near the southwest corner of the town, in a barn near Eagle lake. Elder Cady was the superintendent. None of these schools have existed to the present, yet most of the time Sunday-schools have been kept in the town. There were five in the summer of 1879; one at Eagle Village, one at Eagle Valley, one at Lyonsburg, one at the center of the town and one on Wing street. These are summer schools, except that at Eagle Village, which is kept up summer and winter.

SOCIETIES.

A division of the Sons of Temperance was organized 1852. Among the prominent active members were John J. Watson, Joseph W. Gledhill, Walter Shay, Gilbert G. Prey, Albert P. Watson, Hiram Beach, Stephen Jones, J. H. Bailey, D. L. Shields, Rhinaldo Jones and others.

After a number of years the Sons of Temperance were followed by the Good Templars, who maintained their organization several years. They disbanded for a time and reorganized, but for only a short time.

Since then there has been no secret organization until the autumn of 1879, when a lodge of the "Ancient" Order United Workmen was instituted, which has a membership of about 30, and is gaining. James Dempsey holds the highest office in the lodge.

EAGLE'S MILITARY RECORD.

Philip Baker and Jether Grover were soldiers of 1812 while residing in Vermont, previous to becoming residents of this town. Ebenezer Dutton was also a soldier of 1812. William S. Agett has a commission as captain in the State militia at a later day.

We give below records of the soldiers of 1861–65 from this town:

Alvah Lard; wounded twice; captured once; discharged; promoted lieutenant. Austin N. Richardson; promoted captain; discharged. John Tabor; captured; discharged. Levi Vanauken; lost foot. Captain Stephen Wing; resigned. Lieutenant Nelson Wing; promoted captain; resigned. Andrew Andrews; killed. Joseph Phillips; lost foot. Ira Parker, Harvey Pike and Eugene Sparks, discharged. William Akin; discharged in the spring of 1862. Harvey Akin; discharged in April, 1862. Clark and Stephen Helmer, killed. Washington Helmer; discharged. Charles Cathin and Frank Lincoln; killed. Anson Clement, Stanly Merrell, Albert True, Albert P. Watson, Robert Watson, Richard Jackson, George Ross, Gideon Hurlburt, Reuben Hamasor, William Walt, James Walt, Darwin Walt and C. P. Dutton, discharged. Henry J. Spencer; died. Job S. Hicks, jr., and Charles Lyon; discharged. Seymour Sykes; died in prison. Job and Joel Austin; discharged, P. Metcalf; died. George Metcalf and Eugene Pratt; discharged, Nicholas Zola; died. Ennis Barnes; killed. Samuel Barnes, Hiram Merville, Herbert Cheney, Frank Cheney and George W. Dutton; discharged. George H. Smith, lost a finger; discharged. Dwight Abrams, Henry Thompson and Tyler Cole; discharged. John Campbell; killed. Madison Merville, Ambrose Spencer, Vertulan Baker, John F. Dutton, James Maher and Avery Eager; discharged. Thomas Nelson. Henry Wing; died. Aaron Walker; discharged. William Rouse; died. John Cummings, Daniel Wood, William Bracy, Elisha Bracy, John Walton, Washington Whitney, Riley Hurtlburt and Henry Hurlburt; discharged. Lyman Hurlburt; killed. Philex Gillespie, James Gillespie, Edwin D. Morgan, John Ward, John Drake, Sidney Richardson and Albert Gage; discharged; Augustus Sisson; killed. Silas Atwood; killed. Timothy W. Buckland; died in prison. Colonel Gilbert G. Prey, 104th infantry. Norman Patridge, Lyman Crowley, Harvey Pierce, Stephen Pierce, Samuel Taylor, Charles Wing, Austin Wing, Judson Metcalf and Eugene Grover; discharged. Charles Whitney; killed. Carlton Whitney, killed at Buffalo before leaving the state. George Brainard and Ornon Houghton; discharged. Michael Redding; killed. William Redding; discharged. Sperry Merville; killed. Butler Wood, James Eager, Chauncey Osborn, Henry Rugg, James Letson, Monroe Zimmer, Albert French, Herman Lawson and Jonas Grover; discharged.

ROCHESTER AND STATE LINE RAILROAD.

In 1872 the Rochester and State Line Railroad was located through the town. The financial depression of 1873 suspended operations on the road, and nothing was done until 1877, when work was resumed, and in February, 1878, track laying was completed. The two gangs of hands, one working from the north, the other from the south, met and joined rails in this town, just south of Eagle Village station, on Mitchell's dump; so called. The road has done a thriving business. Over two hundred car loads of different articles have been shipped yearly from this town.

BIOGRAPHICAL.

WILLIAM AKIN was born in Delhi, Delaware county, December 24th, 1821. He was married June 14th, 1845, to Miss Lucetta, daughter of James H. Rawson, an early settler and prominent man in Nunda, Livingston county, where he died in 1879. His father, Lewis Akin, settled in Genesee Falls in 1823, became well known there, and died in 1864 on the farm now owned by his son Charles. His mother, who died in Genesee Falls in 1865, was a daughter of R. Taliman, an early settler in Castile. Her christian name was Lydia. Mr. Akin enlisted in the 5th N. Y. cavalry in September, 1861; was transferred to Company C, 104th infantry, and served in the quartermaster's department one year. His sons Harvey and Eugene were also in the service. The former enlisted in 1861 in Company C, 104th infantry, and was discharged for disability; the latter in 1864 in Company B, 2nd mounted rifles; was present at Lee's surrender, and was discharged from the service in 1865.

E. H. BALLOU, M. D., was born August 23d, 1858, at Gainesville Creek. He is a son of Rev. John M. Ballou. In 1878 he graduated at Parker Institute, at Clarence, Erie county. He then read medicine with Dr. Lapp, of that place, and attended lectures at the Cincinnati and Buffalo medical colleges, and took the degree of M. D. in the spring of 1878. He immediately entered upon an independent practice at Gardensville, Erie county. July 1st, 1879, he located at Eagle Village.

JAMES DEMPSEY, manufacturer of boots and shoes and dealer in the same at Eagle Village, was born November 17th, 1844, in Waverly, Cattaraugus county, and was married November 17th, 1865, to Miss A. Donovan, daughter of John Donovan, of Arcade.

NORMAN HOWES, son of Alvin and Wealthy Howes, was born at Richfield, Otsego county, April 2nd, 1806. In 1817 he removed with his parents to Covington. In 1824 they came to Eagle and bought a farm of fifty acres. At the age of twenty-one Mr. Howes was elected school commissioner. He has been supervisor twelve years, and was at one time county superintendent of the poor of Allegany county, besides holding the offices of assessor, highway commissioner and justice of the peace. At the taking of the census of 1855 he was census enumerator for the town of Eagle. He was married in 1827 to Cornelia Hulbert, daughter of Barzilla and Lovina Hulbert, of Wethersfield, Conn.

LEWIS M. HUSTED was born in Western, Oneida county, May 16th, 1837. He was married December 24th, 1862, to Miss Desdemona F. Crane, daughter of Ulysses P. Crane, of Freedom, Cattaraugus county, who died May 20th, 1867. October 20th, 1869, he married his present wife, Miss Louisa J. Fox, daughter of Charles M. Fox, of Sheldon, who died March 21st, 1864. Mr. Husted came to Eagle in 1840 with his father, Silas Husted, a native of Halfmoon, Saratoga county, and located on the farm he now owns.

STEPHEN JONES was born January 23d, 1823, in Eagle, and died May 22nd, 1868. He was married March 21st, 1847, to Charlotte Fox, who has two children, William S. and Ada C., the latter being the wife of Edward W. Kellogg.

JAMES MCELROY was born in Albany county June 22nd, 1820, and was married June 22nd, 1848, to Serene D. Beach, daughter of Dan. Beach, of Eagle. The latter came to the town in 1810, and kept tavern in a log house. Mr. McElroy is a well known farmer, and has served four years as town clerk, three as highway commissioner and now holds the office of excise commissioner.

S. N. NARAMORE was born in Coeymans, Albany county, October 10th, 1829, and was married in 1852 to Miss T. D. Moorey, daughter of Joseph Moorey, an early resident of Warsaw, who died in September, 1862. Mr. Naramore's father, Elihu Naramore, of English descent, was a native of Albany county. He came to Eagle in 1832, and engaged in the dry goods and grocery trade. From 1864 to 1867 Mr. Naramore was the proprietor of a hotel at Eagle. In the fall of the latter year he purchased the store where he now does business. He has been notary public for twelve years, and has held the office of supervisor and other positions of trust and responsibility.

ALBERT NEWKIRK, farmer, was born in Ashford, Cattaraugue county, January 17th, 1828. His father, Francis Newkirk, a Schoharie county farmer (born in 1799), had located there at an early day, and died in 1847. He married Maria Alden in 1849. Mrs. Newkirk's father was Moses W. Alden, deceased, of Freedom, Cattaraugus county. Her mother, whose malden name was Amanda Borden, now lives with Mr. and Mrs. Newkirk, at the age of seventy-seven.

ZALMON PLATT was born in Bredport, Vt., June 16th, 1813. September 3d, 1834, he married Sarah Bemis, daughter of Silas Bemis, a native of Vermont and a settler in Pike in 1817, now living at the age of ninety-one in Cuba, Allegany county. Mr. Platt's father, Eljlah Platt, was a native of Peru, N. Y. He was a soldier in the war of 1812–14. He removed to Eagle, accompanied by his family, from Palmyra, Wayne county, in 1832, and died in Michigan in 1865. Mr. Platt is a farmer, and has worked at his trade of carpenter many years. He moved on to his present farm in 1865.

BYRON POWELL, son of Israel Powell, who came from Locke, Cayuga county, to Arcade was born April 27th, 1833. July 3d, 1861, he married Sarah Husted, daughter of Silas Husted, deceased, an early and well known resident of the town, and came from Centerville and located where he now lives during that year. He is a farmer.

COLONEL G. G. PREY was born in St. Andrews, New Brunswick, in 1823. March 19th, 1843, he married Jane Ann Buckland, daughter of Timothy Buckland, a native of Connecticut and a settler in 1816 in Centerville, Allegany county, who removed to Eagle subsequently and engaged in hotel keeping and farming, and died at the age of eighty-four, February 4th, 1856. Colonel Prey came to Eagle with his father, John Prey, a native of Scotland, in 1839. He is a carpenter and joiner.

JOHN QUACKENBUSH was born in Ashford, Cattaraugus county, in 1844, and was married July 4th, 1867, to Miss Lucinda Willis. His father, John Quackenbush, sen., is a native of Herkimer county, and was an early settler at Ashford, Cattaraugus county. At the time of their marriage Mr. Walter D. Willis, father of Mrs. Lucinda Quackenbush, was a resident of Ashford, Cattaraugus county. He died in Hume, Allegany county, in 1871. Mr. Quackenbush, who is a farmer, came from Ashford, Cattaraugus county, to Eagle March 20th, 1875.

DAVID VAN DYKE was born in Otsego county, November 12th, 1805, and died September 10th, 1872. His father, William Van Dyke, was of German descent and was born in 1763. He came to Eagle from Otsego county in 1813, accompanied by his sons William, John, David and Lewis, all of whom lived out their lives in the town, where the family lived for many years, identified with leading interests. January 1st, 1833, Mr. Van Dyke was married to Lucinda Griggs. Her father, Philip Griggs, was a native of Vermont. He settled in Pike in 1816, and lived there until his death, in 1863. Mr. Van Dyke has held positions of importance.

WILLIAM W. VAN DYKE, farmer, was born on the old Van Dyke homestead, in Eagle, January 20th, 1851. He was married March 19th, 1876, to Miss Libbie Cross, daughter of Alonzo Cross, a farmer well and favorably known in the town.

ALBERT P. WATSON was born at New Baltimore. Greene county, in 1830. He was married March 4th, 1860, to Miss Clarissa Guilds, daughter of the late Thomas Guilds, of Perry. She died March 21st, 1869. September 12th, 1869, he married Amelia Pratt, daughter of Alanson Pratt, in his time an influential farmer and leading citizen of Centerville, Allegany county. His father, John J. Watson, a native of Allegany county, came to Eagle in 1848, and located at the village. He died at Cowlesville November 11th, 1864. Mr. Watson was the first volunteer for military service in the Rebellion from the town of Eagle. He enlisted May 6th, 1861, and was mustered into Company F, 33d N. Y. volunteers, May 22nd. He participated in all engagements in which the regiment took part, and was wounded at Chancellorsville. He was discharged June 2nd, 1863, and enlisted January 6th, 1864, in Company B, 2nd N. Y. mounded riflies. He was captured by the enemy after receiving a wound at Popular Spring Grove, October 14th, 1864, and confined four months in Libby prison. He was promoted to the office of commissary, and discharged in August, 1865.

WASHINGTON W. WHITNEY was born in Eagle November 18th, 1827. November 2nd, 1852, he married Miss Susan Clement, daughter of Sewell Clement, from Vermont, who located in Eagle in 1837 and died there. Joshua Whitney, a Revolutionary soldier and a native of Massachusetta, grandfather of Washington W. Whitney, and Joshua Whitney, jr., a native of New Hampshire, son of Joshua Whitney, and father of Washington W. Whitney, located in this section in 1812. In 1834 Joshua Whitney, jr., moved on to the farm where Washington W. Whitney now lives, and died there in 1869. He was a man of prominence in town affairs, and served as assessor and overseer of the poor. Washington W. Whitney enlisted in Company B of the 2nd N. Y. mounted rifles January 4th, 1864, and after participating in fourteen engagements, including the battles of Spottsylvania, the Wilderness and Cold Harbor (where he was wounded), was discharged in June, 1865.

E. D. WOODWORTH, M. D, was born in Fenner, Madison county, in March, 1833. He was educated at the academies of Rushford, Allegany county, and Fredonia, Chautauqua county; began studying medicine in 1857; attended lectures at the University of Michigan in 1858, and at the University of New York, where he was a student of Dr. T. Gaillard, in 1860–61, graduating in the spring of the latter year. In December, 1861, he enlisted in Company K of the 105th N. Y. infantry, as second lieutenant, and July 10th, 1862, was promoted to first lieutenant. In March, 1864, he was discharged and appointed assistant surgeon of the 2nd N. Y. mounted rifles, which office he held until discharged in the fall of 1865, when he was brevetted major by Governor Reuben E. Fenton. He came to Eagle Village, in 1868, from Yorkshire, Cattaraugus county, where he lived for twenty-five years. In 1870 he was married to Miss Jennie W. Shields, of English descent, daughter of Mrs. D. F. Shields, of Eagle Village.

THE TOWN OF GAINESVILLE.

THE original name of this town was Hebe. It was formed from Warsaw, February 25th, 1814, and took its present name from General Edmund Pendleton Gaines. It is township 8, range 1, of the Holland Purchase.

There are three cheese factories; one at Gainesville, one at East Gainesville, and one near Rock Glen. The annual sales of cheese aggregate about $50,000. Very few sheep are kept. Cattle are the principal stock raised. These are mostly native breeds crossed with Durham. Neither horses nor hogs are raised, except to supply the wants of the people. Next after dairy products, potatoes are the leading product.

An extensive bed of yellow ochre has been opened some two miles north-west of the Centre. It is now owned by a company organized in Rochester.

At Rock Glen are extensive and valuable quarries of the famous Gainesville sandstone. This stone has been extensively introduced, and has come to be prominent among building materials.

SETTLEMENT AND GROWTH.

Within the memory of men now living the agents of the Amsterdam merchants first offered for sale this portion of the three million six hundred thousand acres they purchased of Robert Morris July 20th, 1793. Three years after the land office was opened at Batavia, William Bristol, in the year 1805, an unmarried man from Columbia county, N. Y., joined a surveying party in charge of William Peacock, and engaged in surveying this town. After a journey of twenty-nine miles he reached the O-is-ki. The primeval forest of deciduous trees, with patches of pine and hemlock, was unbroken. The graceful elm, the towering maple, the stately beech, here attained enormous size. Indian trails were the only paths. Bears, wolves and deer roamed at will.

The rich bottom land was inviting, and Mr. Bristol selected a tract on both sides of the creek, on which he lived more than half a century, and where his remains were deposited in 1859.

His brothers, Richard and Charles, from Columbia county, and Elnathan George, from Vermont, also settled here in 1805. James Cravath and John Patterson settled here in 1806; Willard Thayer in 1807; William Broughton in 1810.

Solomon Morris and James Reed surveyed the highways of the town.

The following is a statement, from the original books of the Holland Company, of the names of the original purchasers of lands in this town, the dates of their contracts, with the numbers of the lots and parts of lots purchased by each during the first five years after its survey:

1805.—William Bristol, lots 16, 26, 27 and 85; Elnathan George, lot 52; James Cravath, lots 57, 59, 60, 61; Benjamin Morse, lot 40; David Hardy, part of lot 53.

1806.—John Patterson, part of lot 53; Reuben Orris, part of lot 42; John Grant, lot 18; Barzilla Yates, lot 23; Pearl Flower, lot 48; Dwight Noble, part of lot 8; Stephen Perkins, part of lot 8; Russell Post, part of lot 31; Hosea Sheffield, part of lot 81; William Blanchard, part of lot 81; Ebeneser West, part of lot 81; William Fuller, part of lot 22; Wheelock Wood, part of lot 22; William Thayer, part of lot 7; Lewis Wood, lot 32.

1807.—Nehemiah Park, lot 47; Appleton Bailey, lot 28; Ithuriel Flower, part of lot 49; Manton Davis, part of lot 44; Willard Thayer, part of lot 15; Daniel W. Bannister, lot 5.

1808.—Archelaus Price, lot 36; Benjamin Cole, part of lot 3.

1809.—Bezaleel Beede, part of lot 45; Jedediah Green, part of lot 62; Francis Ellingwood, part of lot 19; Samuel Fuller, part of lot 1; Jared Money, part of lot 87.

1810.—Noah Wiseman, part of lot 48; Gaius Blowers, part of lot 48; Joseph Parker, lot 30; Daniel Cargill, part of lot 3; Leonard and Ethan Cooley, part of lot 45; Joab Wetherbee, part of lot 46; William Broughton, part of lot 14; John B. Eggleston, part of lot 55; John Hoxie, part of lot 55; Simeon Gibson, lot 56; Davis Wood, part of lot 21; Otis Wood, part of lot 21; Philip Reed, lot 6; Stephen Potter, part of lot 44.

Pamelia Patterson was the first child born, in 1807. The first school was at the Centre, taught by Benjamin Cole. The first public house was at the Centre, kept by Charles Bristol in 1815, and the first store was Lewis Wood's, in the "Yates Settlement," in 1816. Wheelock Wood built the first saw-mill in 1809, on Oatka creek; Tilly Parker the first tannery, in 1815, just south of the creek; Sylvester Lathrop the first establishment for wool carding, dyeing and cloth dressing, in 1820, at "the Creek"; John Card and Benjamin Mallory the first grist-mill, in 1825, also at "the creek"; William and John Coon the first blacksmith shop, in 1817, at the Centre, which they carried on till 1819, when Chauncey Smith succeeded them; Daniel Wheeler built the first distillery in the north part of the town, and Abel Moore the first at "the Creek." These were the only distilleries ever built in the town.

The first log house was built by William Bristol and his brothers Charles and Richard, in 1805, on the south bank of the creek, east of and near the Centre road. William Bristol afterward erected the first frame house, which stood where the hotel now stands.

The first brick building was a school-house in district No. 9, near "Pike" station, built in 1818. The first grounds used for the burial of the dead were on lot 28, on the east side of the Centre road, at the intersection of the street opened in 1879; in the southeast part of the town, on lot 2; on Delhi street, on lot 53: in the northeast part of the town, on lot 7; at East Gainesville and at North Gainesville, on the present sites. The land for the present cemetery at Gainesville was afterward donated by William Bristol and dedicated to this use.

C. D. FARMAN.
MRS. C. D. FARMAN.
SPRING AND HYDRAULIC RAM
TROUT POND. STOCK BARNS. TROUT POND.
FLAX MILL.
TENEMENT HOUSE.
RESIDENCE.
HORSE BARN.
LOWER TROUT POND.
RESIDENCE OF C. D. FARMAN GAINESVILLE WYOMING, CO., N.Y.

David Beardsley and Daniel Fuller were the first carpenters.

The earliest school-houses were on or near the Centre road, two on the east side and one on the west; one in the northwest corner of lot 26, about forty rods from the Centre road; one nearly opposite the Congregational church, and one on the hill north of the Female Seminary.

Among the early stores were Mr. Grummond's, on Delhi street, near the west line of the town; Ira N. Pratt's, at the creek, and Pearl Flower's, just east of Pike station. All trade was barter in those early days. The merchants exchanged their goods for ashes, black salts and potashes, which the early settlers obtained in large quantities by cutting and burning the heavy deciduous timber in the process of clearing their lands. For a time the settlers had little else to pay for such necessaries as the merchants supplied.

The taverns of that day were mostly log buildings, and there were as many as six in the town at one time. Whiskey was sold in all, and was the chief source of their revenue. William Bristol, Charles Bristol, Frederick A. Moore, William Patterson, Nyrum Reynolds, John D. Gillett and Gideon Tyrrel were the early tavern keepers.

Among the early marriages were those of William Fuller, James Gates, John D. Gillett, Joseph Williams, Pearl Flower and John F. Howell.

Among the early deaths were those of Noah Wiseman, in 1812, Mrs. Hosea Sheffield, in 1815, and Seth Griswold.

The early physicians were John W. Brownson and Rufus Whitney, at the Creek; Elihu and Joel Amsden, at East Gainesville, and James Kelley.

The early postmasters were William Bristol, John Russell, Hiram Wright and John. D. Gillett. For many years there was a daily stage route passing through the town, from Le Roy to Angelica, and a postrider weekly from Perry to Fredonia.

Though the town has never had a resident lawyer, its justices' courts have never been idle. Nyrum Reynolds for many years was retained on one side of nearly every case litigated in these courts. His keen perceptions, retentive memory, energy and sturdy common sense contributed to his remarkable success in these cases. He was appointed associate judge of Wyoming county in 1845. His literary attainments were small. On one occasion, when ridiculed on account of his bad spelling, he is said to have retorted: "It isn't much of a man who can't spell a word more than one way." After Judge Reynolds probably B. F. Bristol has tried more cases before a justice's court than any other man who ever lived in town.

The early settlers were generally poor, and their farms small. William Bristol sold his interest in lot 16 for a horse, in lot 26 for a pair of oxen, and made his first payment on lot 27 in services rendered the company. There were exceptions; notably, James Cravath, who came from Preble, N. Y., in 1805, and had the first deed of lands in town. It is related that, soon after Mr. Bristol built his log house, Mr. Cravath examined and selected about fifteen hundred acres in the west tier of lots. He then went to the land office and asked the price of these lands. The agent advised him to "article" a small piece. Persisting in his request a price was named for the tract, and Mr. Cravath poured gold upon the table from his leather saddle bags to pay for the whole.

The work of clearing was great, but it was substantially accomplished in the first twenty-five years. In 1830 the town supported a larger population than in 1855 or 1880. The maximum population was reached in 1840. The following figures show the number of inhabitants in the years named: 1830, 1,934; 1835, 2,097; 1840, 2,367; 1845, 1,897; 1850, 1,760; 1855, 1,753; 1860, 1,732; 1865, 1,635; 1870, 1,612; 1875, 1,710.

CHURCHES.

There are six churches in the town—one Congregational, two Methodist Episcopal, one Free Methodist, one Universalist and one Roman Catholic.

Congregational.—The first church was Congregational, located in the east part of the town, organized March nth, 1815. In January, 1816, this church united with the presbytery at Mount Morris. In September, 1835, it united with the second Congregational church, at Gainesville, under the sanction of the presbytery; since which time the united body has been known as the First Congregational Church of Gainesville.

The second Congregational church was organized September 14th, 1818, with the following members of the session: Stephen B. Bell, Andrew Brunson, Calvin Colton and Moses Bull. The following persons constituted the church: Samuel Olcott, Elisha Osborn, Sheffield Burdick, Joel Smith, Abigail Bristol, Esther Potter, Phebe P. Burdick, Edith Smith, R. L. Cravath, Elizabeth Murray and Polly Trowbridge.

The following ministers of the gospel have officiated as pastors of this church: Rev. Messrs. Ashley, John F. Bliss, Sullivan Halliday, Noah Cook, Conrad Ten Eyck, John M. Ballou, James Henry, John Cunningham, John L. Jenkins, J. Hunter Clark, David Henderson and T. H. Quigley.

Rev. John M. Ballou commenced his labors as pastor of this church in 1835. Resigning in 1856, he removed to Clarence, Erie county, where he now resides. He is a graduate of Auburn Theological Seminary and a member of the presbytery. After twenty years of unremitting toil as an able and faithful pastor, he left a record of Christian life, both public and private, upon which no one has ever found a stain.

Rev. John Cunningham was paster nine years. He was educated at Oberlin, Ohio, and is an able and faithful minister.

The present membership of the church is about fifty.

Baptist.—There was formerly a Baptist church at the Centre, but no records are to be found. Elder Patterson was the first Baptist minister in the town, and Rev. Mr. Pierce the last. They have had no service for the past twenty-five years. The church and its edifice long since ceased to exist. Deacons William Wiseman, S. Porter, Daniel Nichols, Gaius Blowers and Eber Hastings were early members of the church.

Methodist.—Somewhere between 1815 and 1825 there existed a Methodist Episcopal class on Delhi street. They worshiped in the school-house ordinarily, but used a barn for quarterly meetings. Among their ministers were Rev. Samuel Wooster and Rev. Mr. Cozort. There was also a class organized in the West part of the town. No records of these churches or classes have been preserved. The first Methodist Episcopal church in the town, was organized on Delhi street in the year 1827. It embraced the whole town. The first minister was Rev. Ira Brunson. The first trustees were Joel Pratt, Thomas Wiseman, jr., Samuel P. Russell, Joseph Olds, Samuel Warren, James Wiseman, Elijah Benedict, Luther Jennison and Nicholas Cleveland. The first clerk was James Wiseman.

The North Gainesville M. E. church was the next formed.

The M. E. church on Delhi street was merged in that at the Creek, which was organized April 28th, 1827, as the First M. E. Church of Gainesville. The first trustees of the latter were John Card, Horatio M. Gere, Elijah Benedict, William S. Knapp, Day Brainerd and Elisha Brainerd, jr. The first class at the Creek consisted of Milton Foote and wife, John Card and wife, Mrs. Day Brainerd and Miss Hall.

The following are the names of the ministers who have been stationed over this church since its organization:

1829, Rev. Messrs Willey and Anderson; 1830, Cozort and Stanton; 1831, Castle and P. E. Brown: 1832, Samuel Wooster and William Buck; 1833, Samuel Wooster, Fuller Atchinson; 1834, Parker and Castle; 1835, Alva Waller, H. M. Seaver; 1836, Alvah Waller and Benjamin Knapp; 1837, W. D. Hewitt, Wooster Wright; 1838, D. J. B. Hoyt, Mason Brownell; 1839, John Shaw, Charles D. Burlington, Thomas D. Hudson; 1841, A. Anderson; 1842, M. Preston, J. B. Jenkins; 1842–45, Gershom Benedict; 1846, 1847, Jacob Hager; 1848, John Wallace; 1849, Ephraim Herrick; 1850, 1851, Jason G. Miller; 1852, 1853, George W. Terry; 1854, 1855, Alfred Kendall; 1855, 1856, Mr. Ripley; 1857, Samuel Luckey, J. M. Simpkinss; 1858, W. B. Buck; 1859, 1860, R. E. Thomas; 1861, James E. Bills; 1862, Albert Plumley; 1863, William Barrett; 1864, 1865, William Blake; 1866–68, Enos Smith; 1871, 1872, C. G. Stevens; 1873, O. S. Chamberlayne; 1874–6, J. Hurd; A. W. Staples, 1877–80.

The church is in a flourishing condition, and has about 80 members. A new parsonage was built in 1879.

Free Methodist.—The first Free Methodist church was organized at Gainesville Centre, by Rev. Asa Abell. The church consisted of Rev. M. E. Brown, preacher, and the following named persons: John Sherwood and Mary Sherwood, Betsey Sherwood, John and Jane Handyside, Mary Willis, Caroline Freeman, Mary Freeman, Emeline Johnson, Mrs. Lent and William Zech.

During the year 1866 the church edifice at Gainesville Creek was built and dedicated.

The following named clergymen have been regular ministers to this church: M. E. Brown, William Cusack, Phillips, William Jackson, J. C. White, Curley Oaks, Joseph Henning and James McAlpine. The membership has numbered 40.

The *Universalist* church has had no regular service for fifteen years past. The clergymen officiating in this church have been Rev. William E. Manley, Stephen Miles, Hiram Van Campen, U. M. Fish, B. N. Wile6, Alfred Peck, Alanson Kelsey, E. W. Locke, C. Dodge, A. B. Raymond, S. Crane, W. Hand, Mr. Sanford.

A *Roman Catholic* church was organized and a church edifice erected at East Gainesville in 1879. Rev. Father Berkery is the pastor.

SCHOOLS.

In 1855 Miss C. A. Eldridge and Miss Maryette Hardy founded at "the Creek" Gainesville Female Seminary. The inhabitants subscribed $2,000 toward the erection of the building, which was burned in 1861, and rebuilt in 1862 by Joel G. Davis for $4,000. The inhabitants also subscribed $2,000 toward the second building. It consists of a main part forty feet square, three stories high, and two wings two stories high. The school was on the plan of the seminary at South Hadley, Mass. (Mt. Holyoke). It was prosperous for ten years, until the adoption of the present free school system, when it went down. The building has been used for a hotel, and is now occupied for residences. The largest number of students at any time was one hundred and fifty. The founders of this institution were offered superior advantages in larger places, but having a desire to benefit their native town they located here, and no one thing ever benefited the town more than this school. The intellectual endowments, earnestness, labor and zeal, and the high Christian character of its founders and teachers made the school a power for good.

Miss Hardy married in 1858 Rev. Mr. Freeland, of the Free Methodist denomination. She occasionally preaches, very acceptably. Miss Eldridge in 1878 married Benjamin Burlingham, of Castile, N. Y., where she now resides. Misses Hardy and Eldridge were educated at Cary Collegiate Institute, in Genesee county, and at Genesee Wesleyan Seminary, at Lima, N. Y.

This town has eleven school districts, which with two or three exceptions have comfortable school-houses. The best of these is at Gainesville. It is a new two-story building, with a wing. Next to this is the new one at East Gainesville, which is also two stories. Most of the people of the town manifest a commendable interest in the cause of education, and the town has furnished its share of the teachers and scholars for the county.

TEMPERANCE.

In the briefest historical sketch of Gainesville mention must be made of the part it bore in the temperance reformation. The first total abstinence society was formed in this country in 1826. About the year 1835 the movement may be said to have commenced in this town. Among the early workers in the cause were John W. Brownson, William Broughton, Joel Davis, George Harrington, B. F. Bristol, E. Z. Stowe, Jehiel Tanner and M. B. Spafford. At first only spirituous

Wm Bristol

liquors were proscribed, but soon after pledges were circulated requiring abstinence from all intoxicating drinks. With the progress of the temperance cause the manufacture of domestic distilled spirits rapidly declined, and soon the distilleries in the town were stopped. The Washingtonian movement, that great temperance revival of 1840, swept over this town, and the cause gained a new impulse. The temperance men, "tee-totalers" in the cant of the opposition, were thoroughly earnest, and soon raised the question of "license or no license." At this time the board of excise consisted of the supervisor and the four justices of the peace. The issues thus raised were well fought. In this town a majority of the men elected to these offices for many years were opposed to granting licenses. So complete was the reformation that, with the exception of six months, no license has been granted in this town for the sale of intoxicating liquors for about forty years. The exception referred to was the year 1848. A majority of the board of excise had been elected by the no-license party. In the absence of B. F. Bristol, one of the justices opposed to license, the board was convened and Adrian Tenant licensed for the final six months of that year. This violation of the moral sentiment of the town has never been repeated.

POLITICAL.

Prior to 1848 the vote of the town was usually Democratic, with a strong anti-slavery sentiment. In that year the Van Buren and Adams electors received a plurality of the votes cast. In 1852 in Gainesville, as elsewhere in this State, nearly all the Whigs and Democrats who had joined the Free-Soil movement four years before returned to their former parties for the time, and the vote of the town was cast for Pierce.

But the old leaven was at work, and the sentiment which culminated in the war spirit of 1861 wrought a radical change here.

In 1856 the Republican ticket received the unprecedented majority of 196 in a total vote of less than 400, and that party has ever since carried the town upon political issues.

At the first town meeting, in 1814, William Bristol was elected supervisor, and Nehemiah Park town clerk.

The following list shows the supervisors of Gainesville, and their years of service, from its organization:

William Bristol, 1814, 1816, 1819–21; James Cravath, 1815; Daniel Kellogg, 1817; Richard Bristol, 1818, 1825; Elisha Brainerd, 1822–24; Nyrum Reynolds, 1826–28, 1836, 1838, 1843, 1847, 1850–53; Gideon Tyrrel, 1829; Willard Thayer, 1830–33, Ira F. Pratt, 1834, 1835, 1841, 1842, 1849; E. Z. Stowe, 1837; Daniel Wheeler, 1839, 1840; John W. Brownson, 1844, 1845; Cheney Wood, 1846; Christopher Post, 1848; John E. Lowing, 1854, 1868–70; William Bristol, jr., 1855, 1863–66; Cyrus Jefferson, 1856; Edwin Amsden, 1857, 1858; B. F. Bristol, 1859, 1860; John Howell, 1861, 1862; Charles D. Farman, 1867, 1871; James Bristol, 1872, 1873; Merritt W. Broughton, 1874, 1875; George L. Cone, 1876–78; Nyrum R. Tiffany, 1879, 1880.

This town has furnished the member of the Assembly for the county seven years, viz., William Bristol, 1823; John W. Brownson, 1840–42; William Bristol, jr., 1867, 1868; John E. Lowing, 1877. It has furnished the senator for the 30th district two years, viz., John M. Brownson, 1848 and 1849; and sheriff one term, viz., E. A. Day, 1879. The school commissioner for the county has three times been taken from this town, viz., Harvey W. Hardy, elected in 1857, one term, and Edson J. Quigley, 1872–78, two terms. Hon. William Bristol was chosen Presidential elector and was secretary of the electoral college in 1864.

VILLAGES OF THE TOWN.

Gainesville, sometimes called Gainesville Creek, is the largest village, situated a little south of the center of the town. It contains about one hundred houses and is growing quite rapidly. It has four churches, Congregational, Methodist Episcopal, Universalist and Free Methodist; three stores, a grist-mill, a saw-mill, two blacksmith and two wagon shops, a harness shop, a planing-mill, a cheese factory, a hotel, a fine school-house, the Gainesville Bank, owned and managed by Seth P. Allen, and a depot of the Rochester and State Line Railroad. The village is pleasantly and healthily situated. The people are thrifty and enterprising, and they manifest an interest in religious and educational matters which promises well for the future of the town.

East Gainesville, situated in the east part of the town on Wolf creek, contains about forty houses, three stores, a hotel, a cheese factory, a blacksmith shop, a Catholic church, a depot on the N. Y., L. E. and W. Railroad, which is also used as a terminus of the Silver Lake Railroad, a depot on the R. and S. L. Railroad, and a new school-house.

Pike Station is situated in the southwestern part of the town, on the R. and S. L. Railroad. It contains a hotel and a few houses. It has recently been started, and may become a village of some importance.

Rock Glen is situated in the northern part of the town, on Oatka creek, on the R. and S. L. Railroad. It is surrounded by picturesque scenery. It contains a depot building, a grocery, a post-office, a saw-mill and a blacksmith shop. It has a good water power, which at present is not extensively used. At this place are extensive and valuable quarries of gray sandstone.

The factory of the Warsaw Furniture Company, a joint stock company with a capital stock nominally of $50,000, was located at Rock Glen. The main building was of stone, three stories in height, heated with steam and filled with excellent machinery. It was burned in 1877.

RAILROADS.

This town has three railroads, the N. Y., L. E. and W., the Rochester and State Line and the Silver Lake. The first named crosses the northeastern portion of the town, runs five miles within the town and has one station, which is located at East Gainesville. Several citizens of the town subscribed liberally toward its construction. The Silver Lake Railroad is a short road between Perry and East Gainesville.

The Rochester and State Line Railroad extends diagonally through the town from northeast to southwest, having eleven miles of road in the town and four depots, Rock Glen, East Gainesville, Gainesville and Pike. The town was bonded in the sum of $50,000 to aid in its construction. B. F. Bristol, Robert F. Shearman and Charles D. Farman were appointed commissioners to issue the bonds of the town, and represent its interests in the road. The commissioners issued the bonds and exchanged with the railroad company for first mortgage bonds of the road. These bonds were afterward exchanged for railroad stock, in order to enable the company to complete the road. September 18th, 1877, the track was laid to Main street, Gainesville, and the first locomotive passed to that point. The event was celebrated by a public meeting and festival. The first survey for the road was made in 1870.

The citizens of Gainesville raised by subscription one half the cost of the depot at that village, and persons residing near Rock Glen were equally public spirited in contributing to build the depot at that station. The depot known as Pike station was built mainly by the contribution of people residing in the adjacent towns of Pike and Wethersfield, to secure a station at that point.

WAR HISTORY.

As the town of Gainesville was organized during the war of 1812, it is difficult, if not impossible, to give a complete list of all who enlisted in that war from this town. Isaac Wilson, of Middlebury, afterward first judge of Genesee county, was captain of a company of cavalry, in which William Bristol was lieutenant; Chester Warriner was a sergeant. Daniel W. Bannister, Noah Wiseman, who died during the war and was buried at Gainesville with military honors, and Ezra B. Warriner, and perhaps some others, were members of a company of light infantry. The five persons named were from that part of the original town of Warsaw now known as Gainesville.

War of the Rebellion.

No sketch of Gainesville would deserve the name historical without an account of the part borne by her citizens in the suppression of the great Rebellion. The first rebel gun was fired at Fort Sumter April 12th, 1861. Three days later President Lincoln issued his call for seventy-five thousand volunteers. The 17th N. Y. infantry, with the first company from this county in its ranks, went to the front in May, 1861, with eleven enlisted men from this town. Four months later the 5th N. Y. cavalry was organized, and Gainesville furnished thirteen enlisted men for that regiment. A year later the 130th N. Y. infantry, with thirty-three, and the 136th N. Y. infantry, with twenty-four enlisted men from this town, went forward. Others went in various organizations, which were mainly recruited elsewhere. The names of 130 men enlisted from this town, with a population of 1,732, are given below, six of whom are sons of Dennis McGuire.

In the summer of 1863 thirty-nine men were required from Gainesville under the call for 300,000. Volunteering and substitution made up the number, so that there are no records of any drafted men going to the war from this town.

In the autumn of 1863 came the call for 500,000 men. At a special town meeting it was voted to pay a town bounty at the discretion of the supervisor. Only three votes were cast against the proposition. Recruiting was kept up steadily for the old regiments in the field, and before the draft was made the quota of Gainesville (of forty-three) was filled.

July 18th, 1864, 500,000 more volunteers were called for. Before the day set for the draft the town's quota of forty-three was again filled.

To the last call for 300,000 men, for one year, Gainesville was not required to contribute. The average term of the enlistments of the men so far exceeded that of the enlistments in other localities that she was exempt from further requisition.

Every call of the government upon this town was answered; the required bounties were paid by her patriotic citizens by tax and voluntary contribution.

The following sums were levied upon the taxable property of the town: 1864, May, special county bounty tax, $5,278.50; 1864, November, annual county bounty tax, $3,795.07; 1864, November, town war bonds, $3,242.00; 1865, May, special county $9,568.00; 1865, November, annual county bounty, $8,746.07; 1866, May, special county bounty, $2,973.79; total amount raised by taxation, $33,603.43.

In addition to this large sum, the town paid $16,600 as town bounties, which the State ultimately refunded.

Considerable sums for bounties, and for the support of volunteers' families, were also paid by voluntary subscriptions.

Through all these years Hon. William Bristol was supervisor of the town, and to his activity and devotion to this patriotic work it is due in no small degree that the town had no war debt at the close of the war.

The following list contains the names, so far as they can be obtained, of all who at the time of their enlistment were residents of Gainesville, though some enlisted elsewhere. Further information will be found in the histories of various regiments:

1*st N. Y. Dragoons*—James A. Brown, Lewis Blackman, Lester Blackman, James C. Bills, John W. Briggs, Wilbur E. Brainard, George Barrell, M. B. Card, Marcus Curtis, Walter Curtis, Hiram B. Coville, E. A. Day, Silas Dewey, George S. Harrington, Edward E. Hunt, O. Hinman, Henry F. Hardy, Rufus Jefferson, William B. Lawrence, Jerry McGuire, Dennis McGuire, Daniel McGuire, William Mahony, Merritt Norton, William C. Partridge, George Reynolds, Allen Starks, Augustus Steel, Henry Towsley, Ten Eyck Van Liew, George H. Walker.

136*th N. Y. Infantry*—Edwin Amsden, William Altoft, John H. Bowen, George Capin, James Culver, Harvey Carpenter, C. W. Card, James Decker, Charles

Hickey, Franklin Henrietta, Charles M. Hawley, John Jewett, D. N. Jenks, John Johnson, George D. Knapp, Chester Kinney, Henry S. Lucas, John Leffingwell, James Mix, George Moore, Wilbur Phillips, Francis Rowland, Hosea Webster, John Ward.

5th N. Y. Cavalry.—Wesley Barnard, William E. Briggs, John W. Barnard, Nelson Cummings, Joseph Coggen, Thomas Denham, Peter Freeman, P. A. Graves, Charles H. Harrington, Francis S. Huestis, G. D. Lawrence, William D. Lucas, James Rice, Charles B. Thomas.

17th N. Y. Infantry.—William P. Bovee, Samuel D. Barnard, M. H. Carpenter, Franklin Graves, Lafayette Hastings, H. Kent, Charles Lewis, Henry Rice, Devello Sheffield, A. Thorp, Edmund K. Wood.

11th Pa. Cavalry.—Charles Barnard, O. Bancroft, Joseph Broadbent, George Bigford, Henry Draper, H. Dunning, Albert Inglesby, Charles H. Starks, Andrew J. Stone, George Suidam, Thomas H. Wiseman.

27th Wis. Infantry.—Abram Allen, George Dunshie, James Lacock, Harrison J. Moore, Calvin Rice, Wells Reynolds, S. B. Sheffield, Calvin Wing, W. Worden, George Zurhorst.

24th N. Y. Battery—William D. Blake, A. L. Culver, James McGuire, Thomas McGuire, Michael McGuire, William Roach.

8th N. Y. Heavy Artillery.—Lyman Bennett, Ezra Flint, George W. Johnson, Hiram Johnson.

9th N. Y. Cavalry.—A. M. Danforth, William and James Freeman, Asa M. Foote, Homer Inglesbee, Crandall Willis.

104th N. Y. Infantry—Lorenzo Brainard, George Flint, Nelson Hickey, John McGuire.

U. S. Navy (1861).—Judson Bennett, William Henrietta, James Lester and Morton Older.

Miscellaneous.—Thomas C. Heath, 1862, 33d N. Y. infantry; James Breslin, George Carvey, Wilbur Olds.

BIOGRAPHICAL.

ELIHU AMSDEN, M. D., was born in Conway, Mass., October 14th, 1791; came to Gainesville in 1816, and practiced medicine there fifty-three years. He was school commissioner of the town, and always prominent in all local educational movements. He took an active part in building up East Gainesville, known years ago as "Amsden's Corners." The first frame house there was built by Dr. Amsden, who was the first practicing physician of East Gainesville, and for many years a leading medical and surgical practitioner in Wyoming county. He died in 1870. His daughter Janette was for a long time a successful teacher in the schools of the town. She and her sister Ellen still reside in Gainesville. Edwin Amsden, M. D., son of Elihu, was a practicing physician and

RESIDENCE OF WALTER H. CUMMINGS EAST GAINESVILLE, N. Y.

STORE & RESIDENCE OF L.E PELTON Jr., EAST GAINESVILLE, N.Y.

RESIDENCE OF PARKER J. WILSON, GAINESVILLE, N.Y.

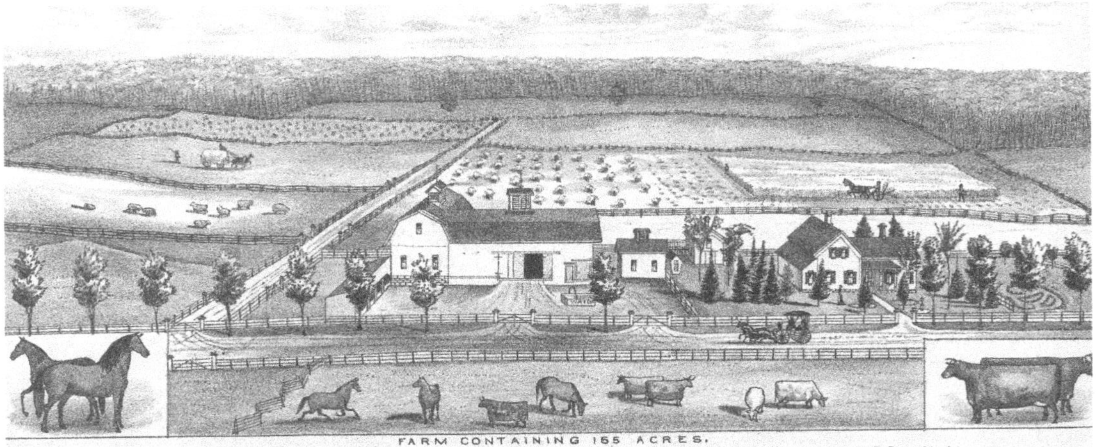

FARM CONTAINING 165 ACRES.
BIRDS-EYE VIEW OF WALTER H. CUMMING'S FARM, EAST GAINESVILLE, WYOMING CO., N.Y.

surgeon in the town, and in 1882 he went with the 136th N. Y. volunteer infantry as assistant surgeon of the regiment. He was supervisor of the town two terms, 1857 and 1858. He now resides at Allegan, Mich.

JACOB BOGART, farmer, was born in Livingston county in 1823, and in 1851 married Ann E. Smith, of Genesee Falls. Gilbert Bogart, his father, was born in New Jersey in 1798. He became a physician of note, practicing his profession fifty-eight years, for a long time in the town of Castile. Mr. Bogart had two brothers in the late war. One was a surgeon; the other, a private soldier, died in the service.

JAMES M. BRAINERD was born in Gainesville in 1842. He is engaged with John Hickey in milling at Gainesville, as proprietor of the custom and flouring and saw mills. In 1865 he married Sarah J. Gibson, of Michigan, and in 1875 Delord Higgins, of Gainesville. He has served the town as collector. His father, Elisha Brainerd, Jr., was born in Madison county, N. Y., in 1801, and came to Gainesville in 1816 with his father, Elisha Brainerd. He was married to Hannah Patterson in 1825. She died in 1838, and during that year Mr. Brainerd married Mary Miller.

WILLIAM BRISTOL was born in Canaan, Columbia county, N. Y., August 19th, 1775, and settled at "the Creek" in 1805, on the land which he occupied fifty-four years. He came to this town, then Batavia, as a member of William Peacock's party, which was surveying the township for the Holland Land Company. Availing himself of the opportunities thus afforded, he located about 1,500 acres of land. Of this he selected lot No. 27, made a clearing, put up a log house, and set about the task of making a home in the forest. He married Martha Stevens, of Lima, N. Y., February 22nd, 1807; he was born in Worcester, Mass., September 1st, 1786. He cut the Centre road through the town, from north to south, for the Holland Company. In 1800, and again in 1811, he was made a justice of the peace by the council of appointment. He served as a lieutenant in Captain Isaac Wilson's company of cavalry in the war of 1818. Upon its incorporation he was elected a trustee of the Warsaw Union Society, which was the first incorporated religious society in the town, January 14th, 1818. The second Congregational church of Gainesville was formed September 14th, 1818, and he was interested in its prosperity from the first. He donated the site for this church, contributed one-eighth of the cost of its erection, and donated the land for a cemetery, which is the only burial place now in use except one at East Gainesville and one at North Gainesville. He also gave the site for the school-house in district No. 9. He was elected the first supervisor of Gainesville, in 1814, again in 1816, and in 1819–21 he held the same office. In 1828 he represented Genesee county in the Assembly. Mr. Bristol died January 4th, 1865. They had six children, of whom Francis S., born March 22nd, 1806, married Merab Stone April 5th, 1882, and died in Warsaw July 25th, 1845. Benjamin F. is noticed below. Mary S., born March 20th, 1818, married John M. Lawrence April 7th, 1881. Their children were William B., who died in the army in 1868, and George D. She died September 1st 1876. Lamira married George Harrington. William is mentioned below. Laura, born March 3d, 1824, married Corydon Doolittle December 7th, 1848, and died April 19th, 1853.

WILLIAM BRISTOL, son of William and Martha Bristol, was born in Gainesville March 7th, 1821. Until 1867 he resided on his father's homestead, his principal business being terming. He was justice of the peace, also postmaster several years. He was supervisor of the town in 1865, and again four years during the war. As a member of the committee appointed by Governor Morgan to promote enlistment in the 30th senatorial district, Mr. Bristol did efficient service. His patriotic course, his careful seal and his expenditure of time and money in those years made him a central figure in the local history of the town during the war period. A considerable portion of his large income was devoted to this work, and by and through his efforts, sustained by the loyal sentiment of his townsmen, Gainesville filled every quota promptly and came out of the war without debt. He was under sheriff of the county in 1842; presidential elector and secretary of the electoral college in 1864; member of Assembly in 1867 and 1868. He contributed materially to establish and sustain Gainesville Female Seminary. A director of the Rochester and State Line Railway Company from its organization, no one in Wyoming county has a larger share in the responsibility of the location of its line through Gainesville than Mr. Bristol. He moved to Warsaw in 1868, where he has since resided. He married Adelia M. Lockwood January 12th, 1843, and had three children, Laura B., who married Major John P. Robinson; Belle, who married M. A. Hunts, and Caroline, who married Nathan S. Beardslee. Mrs. Bristol died November 2nd, 1865, and he married Martha J. Jewett January 8th, 1867, by whom he has three children, William, Millie and Henry R.

BENJAMIN F. BRISTOL was born in Gainesville June 17th, 1811. He married Margaret A., daughter of Joel Davis (see sketch), March 4th, 1835. He is a farmer, and has served in various public positions in the town and county. He has been justice of the peace twenty-five years, supervisor two years, superintendent of the poor for Wyoming county seventeen years, justice of sessions, and for the past nine years a railroad commissioner. Formerly a Whig, he voted for Van Buren in 1848, for Hale in 1862, for Fremont in 1866, and since he has been a prominent member of the Republican party. A Whig in a Democratic town, he was elected three times justice of the peace as a no-license candidate. His life embraces the whole period of the history of the town as a separate organization. Mr. and Mrs. Bristol have six children: Joel W., who is postmaster and a merchant; James, who has been supervisor two terms; Theodore, Corydon and Benjamin F., all living in Gainesville, and Martin F., who resides in Indianapolis, Ind.

WILLIAM BROUGHTON was born in Canton, Conn., June 4th, 1785. He married Sally, daughter of David Blakely, of Pawlet, Vt., November 11th, 1810, and the same year settled in the east part of Gainesville, at "the end of the road," on lot 14. From the place he had selected for his future home he followed an Indian trail to Batavia, and procured a deed of the land which he occupied till his death. The log house hastily thrown up was the home into which he brought his young wife. In 1812 he was interested with his father-in-law in the purchase of lot 28. In the log house were born to him seven daughters, five of whom are now living. The youngest married Isaac W. Quick, a manufacturer, of Auburn, N. Y. Sophronia, one of the youngest daughters, formerly connected with a prominent school for young ladies in Batavia, and for some time engaged in educational interests in Berlin, is now the accomplished head of Clare Place, a boarding and day school for young ladies at Warsaw, N. Y. Colonel Broughton's tastes were scholarly, he early accumulated a library extensive for the time, which contributed to benefit and build the character, not only of his own family, but of young men who to-day honor his memory. He was a Christian gentleman, whose influence was felt for good in the political, temperance and social forces of his day. He voted with the Whig party. He died March 6th, 1888. Mrs. Broughton died in Warsaw October 27th, 1866.

Charles K. Brown was born in Genesee county in 1811, and came, to Gainesville in 1875. He was captain of cavalry in 1838. He has been twice married.

John D. Brownell was born in Westport, Mass., in 1814, and married Elizabeth Little, of that place. He came from Westport to East Gainesville in 1851, and has since been a merchant and a builder. He has served as justice of the peace.

John W. Brownson was a son of John W. Brownson, M. D., who came from New England with his family and commenced practice at Gainesville in 1814, being probably the first resident physician in town. John W. Brownson, jr., was born in Sunderland, Bennington county, Vt., March 12th, 1807. At the age of seven years he came with his father's family to this town, of which he was an honored citizen about forty years. He married Frances L. Cole, February 27th, 1832. He was a man of good judgment and varied information. He was interested in the cause of education, and a pioneer in the temperance move. The Whig party had in him one of its trusted members. In 1840 and 1841 he represented Genesee county, and in 1848 he represented Wyoming county in the Assembly. He was supervisor of the town in 1844 and 1845. In 1848 and 1849 he was senator of the 80th district. He occupied other places of trust, and was prominently identified with public affairs for many years. In 1858 he removed to Sharon, Wis., where he died September 5th, 1860. His widow and his daughter, Mrs. Ellen B. Treat, still reside at Sharon.

The Calkins Family.—Elisha D. Calkins settled on lot number 3 in this town in the spring of 1815. He was born in Sharon, Litchfield county, Conn., November 11th, 1781. When he was about seven years of age his father moved to Saratoga county, N.Y. Elisha D. married Abigail Lockwood in Greenfield, Saratoga county, N. Y., April 22nd, 1810. She was born in New Canaan, Fairfield county, Conn., October 13th, 1792. He died in Gainesville, June 24th, 1849. His widow, Abigail, died in Gainesville, March 18th, 1859. The children of Elisha D. and Abigail Calkins were: Sarah Elizabeth, born June 84th, 1811, died September 24th, 1818; David Lockwood, born December 24th, 1818, in Amsterdam, N. Y.; William Henry, born January 18th, 1816, in Gainesville, N. Y.; Norman A., born September 9th, 1828, in Gainesville, N.Y.; Charles, born April 30th, 1886, died August 22nd, 1848; James Hervey, born March 1st, 1828; Hiram, born December 28th, 1830; Franklin Augustus, born August 11th, 1835. David L. Calkins resides upon the original farm on which his father settled; William H. in Castile; Norman A., Hiram and Franklin A. in the city of New York; James H. in Galesburg, III. Hugh Calkins, the ancestor of all bearing this family name in America, came from Monmouthshire, England; landed at Plymouth, Mass., in 1610, and subsequently settled at New London, Conn. He represented that town in the General Court of Connecticut for twelve terms. He represented that town also in the Legislative Court of Connecticut. The following names show the line of ancestors to Elisha D. Calkins: 1, Hugh; 2, John; 3, Samuel; 4, Stephen; 5, David; 6, Elisha D. Norman A. was for several years a successful teacher in the schools of his native town. He has been a devoted and industrious worker in the cause of education. For seventeen years past he has been one of the superintendents of public schools in the city of New York, and for about twenty-three years treasurer of a society for church building. He has edited several works of an educational character, and his name is extensively known among friends of education throughout the country. Hiram was formerly engaged upon the *New York Herald*, but for some time he has been an assistant editor of the *New York World.* As the Albany correspondent of these journals he is known throughout the State. His intimate acquaintance with New York politics admirably fits him for his present position, while his personal qualities gain him friends in all parties, and thus contribute to his efficiency. Franklin A. is an engineer on the Central Park, where he has been engaged some fifteen years. James H. is a justice of the peace in Galesburg, Ill. He was at one time mayor of that city.

GEORGE L. CONE was born in Gainesville in August, 1882, and married Frances A. Lucas, of Gainesville, in November, 1856. Mr. Cone has always been a farmer. He has been supervisor three years; chairman of the county board of supervisors one year; highway commissioner and assessor. Thomas Cone, his father, came to Gainesville about fifty years ago, and remained there until his death.

WALTER H. CUMMINGS was born May 18th, 1852, in Warsaw. He was married June 22nd, 1875, to Grace A. Woodruff, of East Gainesville. Mrs. Cummings was the only child of the late Merritt Woodruff, Esq., of East Gainesville, and since Mr. Woodruff's death Mr. Cummings has had charge of his large estate. Mr. Cummings is a member of the Congregational church of Warsaw, and has served on its board of trustees two years.

DE LEDROIT COOK, farmer, was born in Pavilion in 1820. He married Harriet J. Stowe, of Warsaw, in 1844.

JOEL DAVIS was born at Winchester, Conn., in 1783. With his father's family he came to Paris, and afterward to Preble, Oneida county, N. Y., where he resided until 1827, when he removed to Gainesville and engaged in farming. He married Resign Hinman, of Torringford, Conn., in 1804. Their children were Joel G., who is engaged in milling, and resides at Rochester, N. Y.; Margaret A., who married B. F. Bristol, Esq. (see sketch); Amanda, who died in Gainesville, unmarried; Giles A., now a banker, residing in Castile, N.Y.; Esther, who married R. Burchard, and died in Minnesota; Emily, who married James Cravath, and afterward married F. Kinney, and died in Oberlin, O. Mr. and Mrs. Davis were members of the Congregational church of the town. He voted with the Whig party, was interested in temperance, and a substantial citizen of the town until 1864, when he went to Castile, where he died in 1875.

MICHAEL DUNNING was born in Saratoga county, May 19th, 1828, and came to Gainesville in 1835. He is a farmer, drover and butcher. He has been town clerk.

SIMEON E. FELCH was born in Washington county, in September, 1848. He married Mary J. Mattice, of York, Livingston county, in December, 1866, and came to Gainesville from Castile in 1867. He is a dealer in lumber and builders' supplies. He is serving his third term as justice of the peace.

GEORGE HARRINGTON was born September 17th, 1808, in Norwich, Chenango county, N. Y. Both his parents came from Smithfield, R. I., in 1790. He has resided in Gainesville since March 31st, 1830. He married Lamira, daughter of Hon. William Bristol, November 19th, 1834. From this marriage were born four sons—Augustus, a lawyer at Warsaw; George S., who resides in Chicago; Charles H. and Francis B., both of whom have resided at Grafton, Neb., since June, 1874. Francis B. was less than eighteen years old at the beginning of the Rebellion. Augustus raised Company D and was a captain in the 136th N. Y. volunteer infantry. George S. was a sergeant in Company

A, 130th regiment N. Y. volunteer infantry, afterward the 1st N. Y. dragoons, and was wounded in the battle of Deserted House, Va. Charles H., after efficient service in the ranks of the 5th N. Y. cavalry, known as the Ira Harris guards, was commissioned lieutenant by Governor Morgan. Lamira Bristol was born in Gainesville, June 27th, 1815; she died September 14th, 1849, and Mr. Harrington married Sarah A. Johnson June 17th, 1851. None of the children of this marriage—Edgar, Ella, Clara and Carrie—are living, except Carrie, the youngest, who is now a successful teacher in the schools of her native town. For thirty years of his active life he was a prominent builder. From the beginning of the movement in the town he was always an earnest advocate of the temperance cause. A Democrat of the school of Silas Wright, he voted for Van Buren and Adams in 1848, for Fremont in 1856, and he has since been attached to the Republican party. He was ever an ardent friend of the cause of education, serving as a trustee his school district for twelve years; and that the schools of his village were long exceptionally good was, in no small degree, due to his zealous and intelligent devotion to their interests. He has been an industrious, upright and public spirited citizen of the town for more than half a century.

CLARKSON A. HALL was a member of Company D, 130th regiment N. Y. State volunteers, in which he was first sergeant. He was in the battle of Deserted House, and was with his regiment at the siege of Suffolk. His father, David Hall, was born in Rhode Island, in 1802, and came to Wethersfield about 1826. He was commissioner of highways, and in the pioneer days assisted in laying out the roads in that town. Mr. Hall was born in Wethersfield, in 1839, and married Laura A. Brainerd, of his native town. He has served as school commissioner.

RICHARD L. HANNA was born in Bath, Steuben county, in 1831, and came from there to Gainesville in 1869. In 1871 he married Mrs. Adelia S. Flint, of Gainesville. Mr. Hanna served in the war in Company C, 18th regiment N. Y. State volunteers; has been engaged in farming and blacksmithing, and is at present keeping hotel. Mrs. Hanna's father was born in Pennsylvania, in 1790, and came to Gainesville in 1866. By her former marriage Mrs. Hanna has a son, who was born in Gainesville, in 1855.

CAROLINE B. HILL was born May 30th, 1823, in Orangeville, N. Y., and married Lewis A. Hill August 3d, 1851. Amasai Briggs, Mrs. Hill's father, was born in Belchertown, Mass., December 26th, 1787, and was married June 5th, 1815, to Abigail Shumway, of Amherst, Mass., who was born November 18th, 1790. They removed to Eaton soon after their marriage. In 1818 they came to Orangeville, N. Y. Mr. Briggs was a physician, and practiced his profession nearly fifty years. He was an early settler in Wyoming county. During a severe storm, while Dr. Briggs was absent and his wife was alone with their children, the roof of their house was blown off at night, and Mrs. Briggs was obliged to wade a deep stream with them, one by one, in order to reach a place of safety. Prof. Horace Briggs, of Buffalo, is a son of Dr. Briggs.

LEVI MADISON was born in Hebron, Washington county, in January, 1810, and came to Gainesville with his father's family in 1816. They were three weeks on the road. In September, 1844, he married Ida Post, of East Gainesville. He has been a farmer.

NEHEMIAH PARK, JR., was born in Tyringham, Mass., in 1779. His father, Nehemiah Park, sen., became an early resident of South Warsaw, where for many years he kept a public house, and where he died March 11th, 1838, aged eighty-five years. Nehemiah

Park, jr., married for his second wife Miss Hill, of Canaan, N. Y. He purchased land in Gainesville in 1806, settled there in 1809, and was elected town clerk at the first town meeting. He removed to South Warsaw in 1814. Nehemiah, son of the above, born in Warsaw, November 2nd, 1816, married Ann Janett Doolittle, of Wethersfield. He was engaged in mercantile business in Gainesville from 1839 to 1848. In 1861 he removed to Warsaw, where he now resides. They have one daughter, Ellen A., who married Elijah P. Harris, a professor in Amherst College.

LUTHER E. PELTON, grocer and dealer in boots, shoes and notions, and postmaster at East Gainesville, was born in 1835. He married Betsey E. Helmer, of Eagle, in 1863.

JONATHAN E. PIERCE, farmer and justice of the peace, was born April 17th, 1832, in Washington county. February 22nd, 1852, he married Elizabeth A. Henderson, of Johnsburgh, N. Y., who died December 21st, 1854. April 22nd, 1855, he married Eliza A. Lake, of Chester, N. Y.

CHRISTOPHER POST was born November 20th, 1794, in New Jersey. In June, 1815, he married Maria Yan Liew. Mr. Post has always been a farmer. He has served the town as supervisor, superintendent of common schools, highway commissioner, and seven years as assessor. His father married the daughter of Captain Schenck, who served in the Revolutionary war, and came from New Jersey with an ox team, the journey consuming three weeks. Mr. Post lived two years under the administration of President Washington. At an early day he articled one hundred and fifty acres of land, and has owned two hundred and forty acres at one time. His name was on the petition to have the name of the town changed from Hebe to Gainesville. Years ago his house was often visited by Mary Jemison, the celebrated "white woman." Mr. and Mrs. Post are the only survivors of the pioneer period of the town.

E. J. QUIGLEY was born in Gainesville, in 1840. He was educated in the common schools and in Pike Seminary. He is a teacher by profession; was principal of the Yorkville public school, of Kendall county, Ill., for six years, and of Castile union school three years. He held the office of county commissioner of schools for the second district of Wyoming for six years, ending December 31st, 1878, and has been justice of the peace for the past eight years.

REBEKA SHATTUCK was born October 28th, 1820, in Leyden, Mass., and married Samuel H. Shattuck, of that place, September 22nd, 1842. Mr. Shattuck was born October 28th, 1808, and died January 5th, 1873. He came into the town in 1842, and was engaged in farming until 1870, when he retired from active life and removed to Gainesville. He was a prominent member of the Methodist church, with which Mrs. Shattuck is also connected.

ROBERT F. SHEARMAN was born in Perry, August 22nd, 1828, and was married March 1st, 1854, to Sarah L. Norton, of Gainesville, where he has lived since 1855. He has served as assessor three years, justice of the peace four years, inspector of elections, justice of sessions two years, and loan commissioner three years. Gideon Shearman, father of Robert F. Shearman, was born in Rhode Island in 1781, and was colonel of a regiment in the war of 1812–14. His wife drove a horse from their former place of residence to western New York, carrying a child in her arms at the same time.

DEVELLO Z. SHEFFIELD was born in this town, in 1840. He obtained a good academic education at Warsaw and taught school winters until 1861, when he enlisted in the 17th N. Y. infantry. After the civil war he was principal of Castile union school. He subsequently attended the Auburn Theological Seminary, and upon his graduation he married Miss Ella Sherril, of Pike, and went as a missionary to China, where he has resided the past ten years.

N. R. TIFFANY was born, in Eagle, in 1886, and married Mary D. Gile, of Gainesville. He is a farmer. He has served the town as supervisor and collector, and has been assessor six years. Benjamin F. Tiffany, his father, was born in Oneida county, in 1800.

MRS. SUSAN M. WARRINER was born in Vershire, Vt., August 18th, 1828, and was married to James L. Warriner, of Gainesville, April 3d, 1843. He was born in 1824. She came from Vermont to East Gainesville in 1834.

WILLIAM WEBSTER, farmer, was born in Warsaw, December 15th, 1818, and was married in April, 1842, to Calista Keeney, of his native town. That year he came to Gainesville, where he has served as assessor four years, and as overseer of the poor. Mr. Webster was a member of a stock company which built a large stone building near Rock Glen for the manufacture of furniture. It was 75 by 40 feet, with a drying-house 22 by 20 feet. It was burned about 1876. William Webster, father of the above mentioned, was born in Washington county, in 1787, and came to Warsaw in 1808. He and his wife both lived until past ninety.

PARKER WILSON was born in Gainesville, in 1827, and married Delina Snyder, of York, in 1851. Mr. and Mrs. Wilson have three children, Mary, Charles and Frank, born respectively in 1853, 1855 and 1857.

MERRITT WOODRUFF was born in Washington, Litchfield county, Conn., November 25th, 1798, and emigrated with his parents to Gainesville in 1816, where he resided until his death, December 13th, 1873. Mr. Woodruff was one of the solid Yankee pioneers of Gainesville; he had the confidence of the people, and never betrayed them. It seemed to be his aim to do right. Right and justice were the ruling principles of his life from youth to old age. He was honest from principle, and loved truth and right with as much ardor as Horace Greeley; was quiet and unobtrusive in his manners, of a reflective mind, and always thought before he spoke or answered a question. He held the office of justice of the peace many years, and important lawsuits were tried before him, and the sharpest lawyers could not swerve him from what he thought was right. He was one of the first abolitionists in town, and voted that ticket for several years all alone. He was a good neighbor, friend, husband and father; and by good judgment, economy and industry accumulated a handsome property. He married Elizabeth Tinker, of Monroe county, and they had one child, Grace A., who married Walter H. Cummings of Warsaw.

RESIDENCE OF NORMAN SCHENCK, WYOMING CO., N. Y.

'POST'S HOTEL', A. J. AXTELL, PROPRIETOR, CASTILE, N. Y.

SAMUEL H. SHATTUCK.

RESIDENCE OF REBEKAH SHATTUCK, GAINESVILLE, N. Y.

THE TOWN OF GENESEE FALLS

THE original town of Portage was taken from Nunda, Allegany county, and incorporated in 1827. On the 1st of April, 1846, the Legislature enacted as follows:

"Section 1.—The towns of Eagle, Pike and all that part of Portage in the county of Allegany lying on the west side of the Genesee river, and bounded as follows:— On the east by the Genesee river, on the south by a line running due easterly from the south line of the town of Pike until it intersects the Genesee river, and west and north by the original lines of said town—from and after the passage of this act shall be, and the same are hereby annexed to the county of Wyoming."

"Section 2.—The territory hereby taken from the said town of Portage and three-quarters of a mile of territory, being one tier of lots as surveyed by the Holland Land Company, from the east side of said town of Pike, shall from and after the passage of this act be a separate town by the name of the town of Genesee Falls; and the first meeting therein shall be held at the house of Anson Tinkham on the second Tuesday of April next, to commence at ten o'clock in the forenoon, for the purpose of electing all necessary town officers for the said town of Genesee Falls."

"Section 4.—All the residue of the town of Portage lying west of the Genesee river shall, from and after the passage of this act, be annexed to the town of Hume, in the county of Allegany."

The original name, Portage, which means a carrying place, was derived from the portage around the falls in the river, over which the canoes of the Indians, the boats of early white navigators, and the lumber rafts which in later years descended the river, were carried. The derivation of Genesee Falls, from the falls in the neighborhood, is evident.

Except the tier of lots taken from Pike, the town is included in the Cotringer tract, elsewhere described, through which lumber was conveyed to market.

SETTLEMENT.

The land on that portion of this town which was included in the Cotringer tract came into market about the year 1816. Previous to that time what were termed squatters had come in and established themselves along the river. Most of these left when the land came into market. Of those who became permanent settlers the names are remembered of Joseph Dixon, Benjamin B. Earl, Increase Hawley, Aaron Davis, Zachariah Van Buskirk, George Brown, Thomas Mc-Clenathan, David Handy, Anson Bigelow, Jacob Mabie, Orrin

Goodell, Truman Blood, John Robinson, Elisha Leach, Albert Langdon, —— Carpenter and Thomas Buckman. Of these Anson Bigelow and Truman Blood, both between eighty and ninety years of age, remain on the farms where they first settled.

At the time this town was settled John Hornby owned most of this portion of the Cotringer tract. The settlers usually took "articles," on which they paid small sums. These articles ran four years, but lenity was given beyond that time. The price at which these lands were sold was $5.50 per acre,—more than double the price of the Holland Land Company's lands,—and of course the Holland Purchase was more rapidly settled.

The hills along the valley of the river were originally covered with pine, oak and chestnut timber, and during many years after the first settlement of the town the chief business of the settlers was to cut and convert this timber into lumber, which at an early time was rafted down the river. Rafts were constructed below the falls, and taken down during high water. The logs that were cut a few miles above Portageville were floated to the mill at that place, where they were sawed and the lumber drawn down the carrying place during the winter, ready for rafting in the spring. After the completion of the Genesee Valley Canal it was the avenue. Probably a majority of the earliest settlers sold their "betterments" after a few years and went elsewhere.

Several saw-mills were erected at an early period on the small affluents of the river; but with the disappearance of the pine timber these have gone to decay.

Six State censuses taken during the existence of Genesee Falls show an almost uninterrupted decrease in the population of the town. The figures are appended: 1850, 1,322; 1855, 1,098; 1860, 1,020; 1865, 1,070; 1870, 979; 1875, 906.

ROADS.

An Indian trail led from Wiscoy to Mt. Morris through this town. It followed the course of the river till it reached the village of Portageville, where it wound over the hill and crossed the river at a ford, near where the iron bridge now is.

The river road was laid out about the year 1822. It followed nearly the line of marked trees which had previously guided the few settlers, and in its general course adapted itself to the windings of the river. A man named Spencer was the commissioner who laid it. Another road was laid through the tier of lots next west from the transit line, and another runs through the north half of the town just east from that line. Another crosses the town diagonally on a course southwest from Portageville. These are the principal roads in the town, but there are numerous cross-roads among them.

MATTER FROM THE TOWN RECORDS.

In accordance with the provisions of the act of incorporation, the first town meeting was held on the 14th of April, 1846. At this meeting Robert Flint was chosen supervisor; Nathan Platt, town clerk; Henry O. Brown and Ephraim Smith, justices of the peace; Laban Hassett, superintendent of common schools; Leman W. Dyer, collector; Ephraim Smith, Lewis Wood and Perry Jones, assessors; William Davidson, Homer Smith and Jared B. Smith, commissioners of highways; Joshua Abbott, overseer of the poor; William Kendal, Josiah Mosher and Leman W. Dyer, constables; Samuel Shaw, Leonard Hoskins and Miles Moffatt, inspectors of elections; and James M. Knowlton, sealer of weights and measures.

The following is a list of the supervisors in this town, with the years of their election. Each one named was re-elected each year till his successor was chosen:

1846, Robert Flint; 1849, Henry O. Brown; 1851, Peter Dunn; 1853, Levi Trueedell; 1856, Levi Bond; 1857, Miles Moffat; 1858, Nathan Platt; 1859, George Fox; 1861, Marcus W. Wilner, 1863, Joseph Ingham; 1866, Samuel Shaw; 1867, Isaac V. Matthews; 1868, Oscar Adams; 1870, Horace Green; 1871, Luke Smith; 1872, Oscar Adams; 1873, Peter Dunn; 1875, Augustus Bradley; 1877, John L. Davidson.

It appears from the town record that here, as in some other towns, the operation of the first local option law was not satisfactory. May 19th, 1846, ninety-two votes were cast for no license, and forty-two for license. A year later the vote was seventy-nine for to forty against license.

In 1857 a bounty of fifty cents was voted on each fox, and six and a quarter cents on each crow killed in the town.

The records show that prompt action was taken to fill the quota of men in this town under the different calls of the President during the war of the Rebellion. They also show that the loyal sentiment increased in intensity, and became more widely prevalent as the war progressed.

On the 30th of December, 1863, a special town meeting voted in favor of a tax to raise $1,722 as bounties for fourteen volunteers needed from this town on the latest call of the President. In August, 1864, a bounty of $250 was voted to each man who should go or send a substitute under a recent call for volunteers, and in March, 1865, a bounty of $100 was voted (sixty-three to four) as an inducement for volunteers under the latest requisition of the President.

CEMETERIES.

The first cemetery in Genesee Falls was used very early, near Fort hill, on lot 107, northwest from and close by the hill. During several years all the interments, especially in the south part of the town, were at this place. About 1826 or 1827 burials here ceased, and afterward a private road, which is still in use, was opened across it. No monuments were erected here, and a few depressions alone mark the sites of graves.

Soon after the above was first used interments commenced on lot 86, near the transit line. This cemetery is still used. Another was early used near the Genesee river, just below the middle falls. Another, which was at first a private burial place, was on lot 102, near the transit.

The old village cemetery was commenced in 1827. The first interment there was that of Lot Griffith, who was killed in August of that year by a fall from a load of hay.

At one time the owner of the land which included this cemetery proposed to remove the bodies entombed there, and use the ground for other purposes. The people became highly indignant at this, which they considered a profanation, and he abandoned his purpose, after receiving strong hints that if he persisted a small space might be required for him.

Not long previous to the occupancy of this cemetery two bodies were, buried a short distance north from it. They were those of a daughter of Seth Smith and her grandfather, Mr. Bangs, the father of the late Nathan Bangs, D. D. Their bodies have never been removed. The ground where they lie is now used for a barn yard. None of these cemeteries are known to have been under the control of legally organized associations.

About seven years since a lot of some four acres was purchased from the estate of H. O. Brown by the village of Portageville for a cemetery. This ground was grubbed, partially graded and seeded. Some lots were disposed of, and a number of interments have taken place there. The relinquishment of the village charter in 1874 left this cemetery in a somewhat uncertain state.

GLEN IRIS.

The scenery along the Genesee river, from the lower falls to Portage bridge, has been many times described, and its banks portrayed from almost every point of view, and an elaborate description of it cannot be given here. It is, however, a portion of Wyoming—probably no portion of this county has been seen and admired by a greater number of people.

To the student of geology it presents features of peculiar interest. Although there is no portion of the earth's surface where the foot of man has ever trod or where it can tread that is not replete with interest, and has not a history extending back through unnumbered aeons of ages, there are regions where, as here, a portion of this history is more plainly legible than it is on a plain, where only gentle undulations, covered with vegetation, are visible, and where only evidences are seen of a long succession of forests which have sprung up, matured and fallen.

When the escarpment of the chasm which has been excavated from the lower falls to the bridge is examined, and the character of the strata through which it is cut is noted the nature of the process by which this immense work has been accomplished will be comprehended; though the mind will fail to grasp the vast stretch of time during which it has been in progress.

These strata, which were of course submarine deposits, are seen to be of greatly varying degrees of hardness. Many of these are so soft that were they not protected by the harder ones that overlie them the wall of the gorge would weather away, and become the sloping side of a valley instead of the perpendicular wall which it now is. The edges of these strata, which are from a fraction of an inch to several inches in thickness, project beyond the softer ones beneath them, and thus prevent the weathering down of this wall.

When the slowness with which the deposit of these strata took place, according to the estimates of geologists, is considered, some faint and imperfect idea can be formed of the lapse of time requisite for their formation.

At a period away back in the past, the river, which ran over the surface of this formation upon a hard stratum of rock, and shifted its bed from time to time as it now does above and below this gorge, found a point where the continuity of this stratum was broken; and it poured over this broken edge and cut away the edges of the softer strata beneath more rapidly than the edge of this hard stratum wore away. Thus left to project without support beneath, its edge was broken off from time to time by the weight of the water when it was high, or by heavy bodies which it brought down with it, and the soft rock beneath it was again more rapidly eroded. The edges of thinner hard strata beneath the brink of the fall were in like manner left to project, and were broken off by the falling water, and thus the fall went on to recede up the stream.

The bed of the stream below the fall was a hard stratum of greater thickness, which did not wear away by the falling of the water on it and the passage of the current over it. In the lapse of immense time, however, its continuity was in like manner broken, and another fall commenced to follow its predecessor, and so on. There are three of these falls now in existence, and above the upper fall are evidences of the former existence of another that cut through the rock which apparently constituted a barrier between the valley above and the gorge below.

At the middle fall are evidences of a comparatively recent change in the course of the river above, which changed the direction of the channel below; then of a return of the river to near its old bed; and along the course of the gorge, between the middle and lower falls, are evidences of similar changes in past time.

A survey of this gorge, and of the surface of the ground on each side of it, reveals the fact that when the middle fall had reached a point some distance down the stream from where it now is, a point where the surface on each side is higher than it is up or down the stream from it, it was many feet higher than it now is, and the upper wall had no existence, for the strata over which the water now runs were buried many feet beneath what was then the surface. A fall, however, was in existence near or a short distance above where the bridge now is, and was cutting through the barrier of some two hundred feet in height which then existed there. Of the condition of things above that barrier, and between it and the point where the middle fall then was, it is only necessary to

RESIDENCE OF DAVID P. STOWELL, WEST PERRY, N. Y.

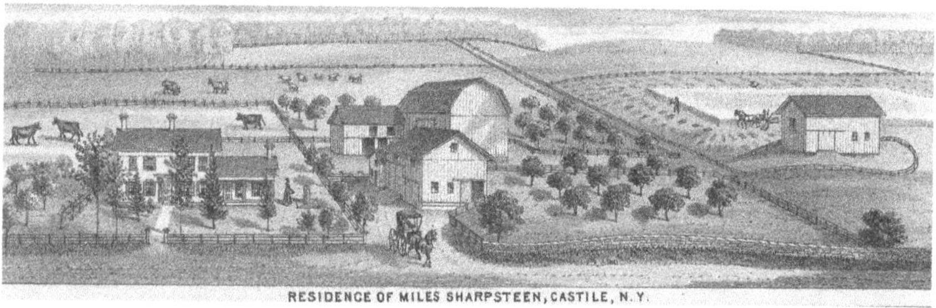

RESIDENCE OF MILES SHARPSTEEN, CASTILE, N. Y.

RESIDENCE OF JOHN KEETON, CASTILE, N. Y.

RESIDENCE OF T. G. WALLACE, GENESEE FALLS, N. Y.

say that there were no lakes there, because there were no depressions to contain them. The valley has been excavated since.

Such, briefly, is the history of these glens, as it is written on their walls and at the falls, where they are steadily though slowly extending up the stream. Of the scenery along the two or three miles of this river between the lower and upper falls it is hardly necessary to speak. It has been many times ably described. It is not too much to say of it, however, that it is not excelled in grandeur by that of any region in this part of the country.

As one stands at the brink of one of these falls, and watches the mist which comes up from below and rises many yards above his head, the question readily arises, what force brings up this spray and carries it to such a height, and what determines its course? That the water in its descent should be broken into small particles is no matter of surprise; but that the law of gravity should be reversed with reference to it seems strange.

It is well known that the air has a weight of fifteen pounds on every square inch of the water as it descends. By reason of this it is constantly carried downward with the falling stream and sent forward, and reflected upward from the bed of the river below. This upward movement is more abrupt and violent because the walls of the gulf prevent the air from passing off laterally. The direction of the rising column is influenced by the form and course of these walls.

The mist into which the falling water is divided is carried upward by this reflex current of air, and becomes the sport of the winds, or falls in a gentle shower in the vicinity. The rays from the sun passing through this mist are decomposed and reflected, so that a rainbow is constantly visible. This suggested the name of the glen, and the history of the rainbow is thus briefly told.

Glen Iris, which includes that portion of the valley between the high point of the sides of the gorge spoken of and Portage bridge, gives evidence of many mutations during the long period that has elapsed since the middle fall was at that point. The river has doubtless changed its bed many times within that period, and accumulations of drift may have been frequently deposited in the same place and carried away again.

A plateau of drift several acres in extent lies just opposite to and below the middle fall. The surface of this plateau is more than forty feet higher than that of the valley farther up the river, and the ascent to it is very steep. In that portion of the glen the evidences may still be traced of a former river bed, close to the hills and the edge of this plateau on the west side, and the fall and the chasm just below it show that during a long period it poured over the precipice from that side. It has run in its present bed only a short time compared with its course there. Down the river from this plateau are a series of undulations, a portion of which are drift, but which blend with the original hills west from the glen.

Many years since the project of utilizing the water power from above the upper fall and building up a manufacturing village in the glen was entertained, but it was never executed. About twenty years since the glen was purchased by Hon. William P. Letchworth, of Buffalo, for the purpose of converting it into a pleasant summer retreat. The improvements which he has made here have all been of a character to restore and heighten the original beauties of the glen. Some eight or nine thousand trees have been planted here, and in planting these so closely has nature been imitated that most of them are mistaken for original growths. A plain but tasteful residence, surrounded by pleasant lawns, stands on the plateau some sixty yards from the middle fall. This is the summer residence where Hon. William P. Letchworth each year seeks a brief season of rest from his severe self-imposed labors.

Of him it is quite proper to say in this connection that since his retirement from business he has devoted his time and energies to the work of improving the administration of the public charities, especially so far as relates to children and the chronic insane, seeking no reward for his philanthropic labors beyond the consciousness of having benefited humanity. From his labors as president of the State Board of Charities he comes here each year for a season of partial respite and retirement, in the midst of the scenery which he has done much to beautify.

On a hill which overlooks the glen the council-house grounds are arranged. This council-house originally stood at Caneadea, in Allegany county, N. Y. When it was erected is not known. It has doubtless been the scene of many grave discussions among the Senecas. Its walls have echoed the eloquence of Brant, of Cornplanter, of Red Jacket, and other Indian orators. Councils have been held in it to deliberate upon and arrange plans for hostile excursions against nations to the south and east, as well as west, against whom the Senecas warred. Here, it is believed, arrangements were made for the massacre in the Wyoming valley; and here the savages met to rejoice on their return from that expedition. It was at Caneadea, in the spring of 1782, that Moses Van Campen and his companions were compelled to run the gauntlet for the amusement of the warriors and squaws, and the council-house was the goal that they were to reach. Van Campen ran against and pitched headlong to the earth two young squaws who stood in the road, and in the merriment which this caused all reached the council-house in safety.

Here, doubtless, the Protestant missionaries, and among them Rev. Samuel Kirkland, who visited the Senecas in 1765, taught their faith; and the neat carving of a Latin cross on one of its logs gives reason for the belief that it had been previously visited by those earnest propagandists of their faith, the Jesuits. Some Indian carvings may be seen on the walls.

The rude carving of a "square and compass" on the outside of a log has led many to the belief that in very early times it may have been visited by some Indian who had been made a mason in the lodge which Sir William Johnson established at his castle among the Mohawks. After it had ceased to be used by the Indians it became the dwelling of white settlers, and was finally abandoned by them.

Some years since, prompted by a laudable desire to rescue this building from decay and oblivion, Mr. Letchworth caused it to be carefully taken down, and the material of' which it was constructed removed to its present site at that place and re-erected exactly in its original form, each timber having been marked as it was taken down and replaced in just the same relation as it was originally. By reason of this removal and careful re-erection, the old council-house may, by the care which will be given to it, endure for another century. As it was, it would have passed away in a few years.

On the first of October, 1872, a council assembled in the old council-house at Glen Iris. About a score of Indians were present, and several of their women. They were plumed and dressed in Indian costume, and some of them were painted and armed in ancient style. Among those present were the descendants of some prominent historic characters. The Mohawks were represented by Colonel Simcoe Kerr, a grandson of the Mohawk chief Joseph Brant and great grandson of Sir William Johnson. His sister, Mrs. Kate Osborne, was also present. Of the Senecas there were present John Jacket, a grandson of the celebrated Red Jacket; Cornplanter, a grandson of the great chief of that name; Thomas Jemison, a grandson of the "white woman" and son of the babe which she brought on her back from Ohio to this valley; Nicholson H. Parker, brother of General Ely S. Parker; William and Jesse Tallchief, grandsons of a sachem of that name; William Blacksnake, grandson of old "Governor Blacksnake"; James Shongo, son of Colonel Shongo, who is said to have led the Senecas in the expedition to Wyoming, and George Jones, grandson of Tommy Jemmy, a sachem who officiated as executioner at what was probably the last capital punishment for witchcraft in this country. After the lighting of the fire, speeches were made in the Indian tongue and in their peculiar style of eloquence by several of the chiefs present. That of Cornplanter was said to be peculiarly affecting. Ex-President Fillmore, the poet Hosmer and other distinguished persons were present at this council.

It will be remembered that in the war of 1812 the Mohawks were the allies of the English, and thus became estranged from the Senecas, who adhered to the cause of the Americans. In his speech Cornplanter said:

> "In the last war with England the Mohawks met us as foes on the warpath. For seventy-five years their place has been vacant at our council fires. They left us when we were strong, a nation of warriors, and they left us in anger.
>
> "Brothers, we are now poor and weak. There are none who fear us or court our Influence. We are reduced to a handful, and have scarce a place to spread our blankets in the vast territory owned by our fathers. But in our poverty and desolation our long estranged brothers, the Mohawks, have come back to us. The vacant seats are filled again. Although the council fire of our nation is little more than a heap of ashes, let us stir its dying embers, that by their light we may see the faces of our brothers once more.
>
> "Brothers, my heart is gladdened by seeing a grandson of that great chief Thayen-dan-ega-onh (Captain Brant) at our council-fire. His grandfather often met our fathers in council when the Six Nations were one people and were happy and strong.

"In grateful remembrance of that nation, and that great warrior, and in token of buried enmity, I will extend my hand to our Mohawk brother. May he feel that he is our brother, and that we are brethren."

It is stated elsewhere that a tree was planted near the foot of Mary Jemison's grave by Thomas Jemison. On the occasion of this council John Jacket, a grandson of the Seneca orator, planted a tree near the west door of the council-house; and Mrs. Kate Osborne, granddaughter of the Mohawk chief Joseph Brant, assisted by ex-President Fillmore, planted another near the east door. It will be remembered that of the Ho-de-no-sau-nee, or people of the long house, the Senecas were the keepers of the west door, and the Mohawks of the east; hence the planting of these trees in their respective positions by the representatives of these nations. The grounds have been visited by two grandsons of Sir William Johnson, one of whom, who is a baronet and captain in the royal navy, planted a tree there. Another tree has been planted by Charles Jones, son of Captain Horatio Jones, the Indian interpreter.

A short distance from the council-house stands a section of the famous oak tree which is said by some historians to have suggested the name of the Seneca chief Big Tree, as well as of the Indian village near it which bore the same name, and which has been made memorable by the important treaty which was made there in 1797. The tree was blown down some years since, and this piece of it has been brought here and placed under a roof, to be preserved as an ancient landmark.

The council-house now contains quite a number of Indian relics, and Mr. Letchworth has in contemplation the erection of a fire-proof building for a museum in which to place these and some 3,000 others that are now collected, with such others as may be deposited there for exhibition.

All parts of the glen and its surroundings, which have at a large expense been thus tastefully fitted up, have always been freely open to pleasure-seekers and the public, and Mr. Letchworth feels a pride in saying that, though thousands have visited these grounds, not an instance of malicious trespass has occurred.

PORTAGEVILLE.

The village of Portageville was originally named Schuyler, in honor of General Philip Schuyler. This name was dropped about 1829 in favor of Portage, which was changed to Portageville in 1846, on the division of the town.

Among the very early settlers was Seth Smith, a Canadian, who was compelled, for political reasons, to fly from Canada. His wife and three children followed—she and the youngest child on horseback, and the other two children, a boy and girl, in a canoe. After suffering severe hardships they all arrived in this State, and ultimately settled here. When Mr. Smith came here he was one of a company consisting of Mumford, Hubbard, McKay and Smith. This company purchased from the proprietor of the tract the land which now includes the village of Portageville, and Mr. Smith, who was a millwright, at once commenced the work of erecting mills here. He built the dam across the river, a portion of which still remains, though other parts have been several times carried away. He erected a saw-mill and a grist-mill. The sawmill was carried away in a flood in 1835, was rebuilt, and afterward, with the grist-mill and a sash factory, burned. It was again rebuilt, but is now nearly gone to decay. The grist-mill stood some twenty rods below the dam. Above it was the saw-mill, and above this a clothiery, which Mr. Ezra Smith erected. This clothiery was carried away with the saw-mill.

This company laid out the village, very nearly as it is now. Smith and McKay, of this firm, sold their share of the property to Elijah Elmer and Colonel George Williams. Mr. Williams purchased the interest of Mr. Elmer, and then of Mumford and Hubbard, and thus became the sole owner. This ownership he retained till his death in 1876.

About the year 1837 work was commenced here on the Genesee Valley Canal, and in the next three years a large influx of laborers took place, and the village presented a lively aspect. About 1849 work was resumed on the canal after a stoppage of some eight years, and within two years from that time the Attica and Hornellsville railroad was commenced. While these works were in progress the village displayed great activity; but on their completion the population diminished and business became stagnant.

The first framed buildings in the town were the mills spoken of. The next was a house built by Ezra Smith, which, after many repairs and alterations, is still standing, between Hamilton street and the river, nearly opposite the dam. It is the oldest building now in the town. This house was the first tavern in the town. Liquors were dispensed there, and entertainment could be furnished for a guest or two at a time. Soon afterward a tavern was erected by Lewis Wood, Esq., on the corner of Hamilton and Main streets. Additions were from time to time made to this, as increasing patronage demanded, till it assumed quite large proportions. It was burned in 1843 or 1844.

The first blacksmith was Samuel Kingsley. The first resident carpenter was B. Shaw. The first distillery stood just south from the Hamilton street canal bridge, on ground that was afterward excavated for the canal. It was built by John Gibbs and Robert Graham, and first carried on by them. Alexander Martin and Lucius C. Foote, under the firm name of Foote & Martin, kept the first store, in a small building near the river bridge. The first physician was Dr. E. D. Moses. The first attorney was Lucius C. Foote. The first postmaster was E. D. Moses, appointed about 1823. The first school was taught about the year 1826, by Eliza Tanner, in a plank school-house half a mile up the river from Portageville. Miss Tanner afterward became Mrs. Rood.

Portageville was incorporated under the general act in 1806. The first president was Henry O. Brown. By a vote of the people the charter was relinquished in 1874. Dr. Robert Rae was president when the village ceased to be a corporation.

CHURCHES IN PORTAGEVILLE.

METHODIST EPISCOPAL SOCIETY.

The records of this society were burned a few years since, and it is therefore necessary to rely on the memory of old members for facts concerning its history. Allowance must therefore be made for possible errors of recollection.

In 1825 there was one Methodist in the town—Mrs. Sarah Smith, a sister of Dr. Nathan Bangs. About that time a Methodist clergyman named Richardson preached occasionally in a school-house half a mile up the river from Portageville. Among the earliest Methodists are remembered Jotham Tower, Lot Griffith, Sarah Smith, John Sloan, Peter Van Buskirk, Mrs. Elijah Elmer, Alvah Green, Mrs. Alvah Green and Mrs. Amelia Jackson. The first class was formed about 1826, with Jotham Tower as class leader, and a society was organized soon afterward.

The first quarterly meeting here was held in Seth Smith's born, in 1828. It was conducted by Presiding Elder Grant, and Bishop Hedding and Rev. Dr. Bangs were present. Meetings were often held in barns and private houses then.

In 1852 the church edifice was erected. It is a wooden structure about forty by sixty feet, standing on Pike street

The society has never been an independent station, but has been connected with other societies in the vicinity.

The names of preachers who are remembered to have officiated on the circuits or charges of which this society has constituted a part are Shepardson, Castle, Cosart, Philo E. Brown, Dow, Buck, Harker, Seaver, Waller, Burlingham, Hudson, Stiles, Stainton, Grisewood, Cooley, Holmes, Jason Miller, Rollin Miller, H. Ripley, Rollin Welch, Alfred Abell, Wooley, Alfred Kendal, J. P. Kent, E. Sears, George W. Coe, John Smallwood, J. H. Rogers, Wilson, T. H. Bell, Joseph. Wayne, T. F. Parker, King, John Spinks, E. F. Bacheldor and J. O. Jarman.

The present number of members is forty.

FIRST PRESBYTERIAN CHURCH.

The Presbyterian Church of Portageville was organized originally as a Congregational church, June 26th, 1827, by Rev. Silas Hubbard, at the house of Joseph Waldo, in the village of Portageville (then Schuyler). At its organization it consisted of the following eighteen members: Joseph Waldo, Mary Waldo, Bezaleel Shaw, Molly Shaw, Elizabeth Van Buskirk, Richard W. Robinson,

Eunice Smith, Lovina Inman, Henry Smith, Cornelia Smith, Lydia Smith, Homer Smith, Rebekah Foot, Bezaleel Shaw, jr., Persis Shaw, Elizabeth Shaw, Charlotte Robinson and Nancy Spencer. The church elected Joseph Waldo deacon, and Richard W. Robinson clerk.

Articles of faith and a covenant were adopted at the organization, which are still used in substance, being orthodox according to the Westminster confession of faith.

For the two succeeding years no records were made in the book. On the 5th of October, 1829, a meeting was held, and "The First Congregational Society of Portage" was organized. Richard W. Robinson, Homer Smith and Joseph Waldo were elected trustees.

For four or five years the meetings were held in the village school-house. The church was connected with Angelica Presbytery on the "accommodation plan." It is said that there was occasional preaching by Rev. Horatio Waldo, Messrs. Smith, Spicer, Mason, King and others.

December 7th, 1832, the society resolved to build a meeting-house "like the one in Pike," and that the slips be annually sold to supply the pulpit. Orson Waldo, Homer Smith and Ephraim Smith were appointed a building committee. It is believed that the church was built within a year. This house was sold to George Williams, and a new one erected about the year 1859, at a cost of more than $3,500. It is located at the eastern end of Main street.

The following is a list of the pastors, with the period of their pastorate: Revs. Horatio Waldo, 1826–31; E. King, 1831–34; J. B. Wilcox, 1834–37; A. Caldwell, 1838, 1839; —— Leonard, 1839–49; Jesse Edwards, 1850–54; William Jackson, 1856–60; E. W. Kellogg, 1861–63; J. S. Bingham, 1863–66; C. W. McCarthy; 1866–75; F. Billsby, 1875, 1876; R. H. Dexter, 1876, present pastor.

Deacons have been elected as follows: Joseph Waldo, 1826; Comfort Hamilton and Homer Smith, 1837; Emmons Manly, 1843; Chester Clark, 1844. Elders elected—Nathan Platt, Ephraim Smith, Dwight Waldo, Allen Payne, Latham H. Agar and Homer Smith, 1844; Horace Smith, 1863; Elisha Town, John L. Waldo and A. F. Kinney, 1868; Homer Smith, Horace Smith, John L. Waldo and A. F. Kinney are the present elders. The present trustees are Horace Smith, R. T. Spencer, Judson Stock well, Nathaniel Wilder, A. F. Kinney and Fitch Robinson.

At one time there were 92 members, but in 1876 there were only 40. The present membership is 50. Homer Smith and Charlotte Robinson are the only original members left.

In 1845 the church united with the Presbytery of Buffalo.

The first superintendent of the Sunday-school was Nathan Platt, with Ephraim Smith assistant; elected at a meeting of the session April 9th, 1845. Horace Smith is the present superintendent. The school numbers about 60 scholars and teachers.

BAPTIST CHURCH.

The First Baptist Church of Portageville was organized on the 5th of December, 1838, with Dexter Carpenter, Artemas Tucker, Lewis A. Tallman, Benjamin C. Colby, Anson Bigelow, Noah Payne, jr., and George Williams as trustees.

In 1841 the society erected a house of worship, thirty-eight by fifty feet, at an expense of $2,000. The church record states that the house was built by James & Son, builders, "on lots No. 1 and 2 in block G, given by George Williams for that purpose to the society."

In 1852 a bell was placed in the tower of this house, at an expense of $183.96.

July 4th, 1877, the house was partially unroofed by a tornado. A new roof was put on and other needed repairs were made, and the whole completed by the 14th of the same month.

The following are the recorded names of pastors, with the dates of the commencement of their pastorates: Revs. Thomas Theal, 1847; G. W. Huntley, 1849; James Reed, 1852; D. De Lano, 1853; A. L. L. Potter, 1855; —— Sabin, 1858; J. H. Green, 1867; —— Stowell, 1868; J. H. Green, 1869; W. Martin, 1871; E. Owen, 1876; J. V. Osterhout, 1879.

It is recorded November 1st, 1871, that a committee was appointed to petition for admission as a branch of the Castile church.

UNIVERSALIST CHURCH.

The first Universalist church and society of Portageville was organized February 9th, 1841. Among the original members were the following:

> Dr. E. D. Moses, the first Universalist who lived in the town, Henry O. Brown, Mrs. Henry O. Brown. Aaron Davis, George Bliss, Samuel Shaw, —— Page, Abner Adams, Mrs. Abner Adams, Mrs. Samuel Shaw, Mrs. George Bliss, Mrs. Page, James S. Taylor, Mrs. James S. Taylor, J. D. Shuart, Mrs. J. D. Shuart, William C. Norton, Levi Truesdell, Amos Truesdell, Lewis Wood, sen., Mrs. Lewis Wood, sen., Marvin Wood, Mrs. Marvin Wood, Otis Wood, Mrs. Otis Wood, Lewis Wood, Mrs. Lewis Wood, Alanson Ward, Mrs. Alan son Ward, —— Nelson, Truman Blood, Rodney Day, John Van Slyck, —— Gordon, George Wilner, Mrs. George Wilner, Jerry Chandler, Lyman Church, Jared Smith, Nicholas Andrus, J. P. Hart and George Hopkins.

Of these, Mr. and Mrs. Marvin Wood, Mr. and Mrs. Samuel Shaw and Mrs. Henry O. Brown are known to be still living.

The society at first met in the school-house that stood on Pike street. The church edifice was built in 1841. It is a wooden structure, thirty-four by forty-four feet, standing on the corner of Pike and Wood streets. Marvin Wood, one of the building committee, was the builder. Rev. A. Kelsey preached the dedication sermon. The seats, desk, etc., were rearranged in 1857. Aside from this, the house has had only ordinary repairs.

The first Universalist minister who preached in Portageville was Rev. Mr. Saddler. The first preacher who officiated regularly was Rev. Judah Babcock, in 1838 and 1839, before the formation of a society.

The first pastor of the society, Rev. A. Kelsey, came in 1840. He continued with the society three years, and was followed by Rev. H. Van Campen, who remained three years, when Mr. Kelsey was recalled, and continued till 1850. Rev. O. F. Brayton was pastor during 1851 and 1852; Rev. O. Roberts the three following years. The next pastor was Rev. S. R. Ward, who labored faithfully till 1859. The following are the names of the pastors from 1859 to the present time: Revs. A. B. Harvey, one year; A. B. Raymond, three years; D. C. Tomlinson, two years; W. O. Delong, two years; U. M. Fisk, two years; G. P. Hibbard, one year; O. B. Clark, three years; J. A. Dobson, one year; S. Crane, two years; L. T. Aldrich, three years; and William Sisson, the present pastor.

In 1848 Ebenezer Watson, of Genesee Falls, died, and left to the society a fund of about $5,000, the income from which was to be applied to the support of preaching.

CHURCH OF THE ASSUMPTION OF THE BLESSED VIRGIN.

The mission of Portageville was established about 1848, among the laborers on the Genesee Valley Canal and the Erie Railway.

The first priest who came among the Catholics of this place was Rev. Father McEvoy, then of Rochester. Having become the resident pastor of Java mission, and Portageville like many others being a dependent to Java, he built in the year 1848 the present church, and had it dedicated in the same year by Bishop Timon, of Buffalo, under the patronage of the Blessed Virgin. The dimensions of this building are sixty by forty feet.

Father McEvoy attended the mission until 1851, when Rev. Daniel Dolan became the first resident pastor. He was succeeded by Fathers Moore, Ryan, Deane, McConnell, Purcell, Gregg, Lawton, McGinnis, Cook, Donaghue and McGrath—the present pastor.

A number of outside stations now, as in the past, comprise the mission of Portageville. Mount Morris, Warsaw and Perry were for many years attended from Portage, but each has now a resident pastor.

The Catholics have a cemetery, pleasantly situated, on the hillside a short distance from their church. This was the gift of the late Colonel Williams.

BIOGRAPHICAL.

Henry O. Brown was born in Westchester county, N. Y., on the 7th of March, 1808. He removed to Portageville in 1824, and established the manufacture of leather, harness, saddles, boots and shoes, in which business he continued till 1842. From that time until his death he resided on and cultivated his farm. He held office almost continually from 1842 till the time of his decease. In politics he was a staunch Democrat during his entire life. He was quite active, as far as in his power, in obtaining the grant for the Genesee Valley Canal, and he was one of the organizers and original directors of the Attica A Hornellsville Railroad Company, now the Buffalo division of the New York, Lake Erie & Western Railroad Company. He was married in September, 1827, to Olive Everest, of Pike, in this county. He died January 20th, 1868, at Portageville, where he had lived since 1824.

Isaac V. Matthews was born in Hampton, Washington county, in 1810. He came to Genesee Falls in 1866, from Wyoming village, Middlebury, where he had lived twenty years. He is a farmer and a retired merchant. While a resident of Middlebury he held the offices of justice of the peace (fourteen years) and assessor; he was justice of the peace in Covington, and in Genesee Falls has been supervisor, and he was appointed loan commissioner of Wyoming county by Governor Washington Hunt, and held the office three years.

William Redner, constable, was born in Steuben, Oneida county, August 7th, 1824. His father was Abram Redner, a native of Rensselaer county, of Dutch descent, who died in Genesee Falls in December, 1872. His mother, formerly Betsey Hayden, now lives with him, at the age of seventy. In 1847 he married Mary Ann Stocker, daughter of George Stocker, grocer, formerly of Geneva, and who died at Syracuse, N. Y. During the same year he came to Genesee Falls from Weedsport, Cayuga county, and engaged in lumbering. He is a farmer, and carries the mail between Portage and Caneadea, Allegany county.

Charles Stroud was born in Dorsetshire, England, July 28th, 1821. He came from England to Vermont in 1866 and four months later to Nunda, Livingston county. He purchased the farm upon which he lives in 1866. In 1848 he married Jane Lambert, daughter of David Lambert, of Dorsetshire, England, by whom he has had children as follows: Elizabeth (died in 1868), Anna (died in 1868), William (in California), George (died in 1876), Priscilla (died in 1862), Anna Emily and Rose. His father was Thomas Stroud.

A. E. Tallmam was born in Genesee Falls, Juno 8th, 1834. He lived in Castile eight years and returned to Genesee Falls. In 1867 he married Mary E. Howe, daughter of Calvin Howe, of Vermont. He is a farmer.

THE TOWN OF JAVA

THE town of Java comprises township 8 in the 3d and 4th ranges of the Holland Purchase, and has an area of 29,750 acres. Most of the cereals are cultivated to some extent; stock raising and dairying are among the chief pursuits of the inhabitants. There are five cheese factories in the town, each producing from 75,000 to 200,000 pounds of cheese annually.

The Manual of the Legislature contains the following census returns in regard to the population of this town for the last forty-five years: 1835, 1,972; 1840, 2,332; 1845, 2,331; 1850, 2,245; 1860, 2,358; 1865, 2,142; 1870, 1,956; 1875, 1,946.

Fully one-half the inhabitants of the town are natives of Ireland or of Irish parentage.

ORGANIZATION AND CIVIL HISTORY.

Java was originally embraced within the limits of the town of China, now Arcade, from which it was set off by an act of the Legislature passed April 20th, 1832. This act was ratified and the organization of the town fully completed at a town meeting held at the house of Abner Currier, of Currier's Corners, on the first Tuesday in March, 1833, at which meeting Esquires Damon Bryant and Charles Bell presided and Moses Twiss served as clerk, and the following first officers of the town were elected: Moses Twiss, supervisor; Nelson Wolcott, town clerk; Nahum Thompson and Seth Lewis, justices of the peace; Allen Twiss, Lyman Wood and Rufus Jewell, assessors; Jarvis Young and James McGinnis, overseers of the poor; James Francis, Asa Hall and Ezekiel Brown, commissioners of highways; Nelson Wolcott, Everet Wilson and Hylon Martin,'commissioners of common schools; Samuel Clark, William W. Crane and Milo Warner, inspectors of common schools; Harry Harrington, collector; Harry Harrington, Levi Spencer, John Thompson and Seymour Jones, constables; David Chase, sealer of weights and measures; Stephen Carson, Jarvis Young, Heman Harrington and Samuel W. Pattison, pound keepers. There were also forty-one overseers of highways appointed.

The following persons have served as supervisors and clerks since the organization of the town:

Supervisors.—Moses Twin, 1833–37; John Parish, 1838; Nelson Wolcott, 1839; Samuel Clark, 1840, 1845–53, 1855; Joseph Currier, 1841, 1844; Ebeneser Jackson, 1842, 1843; Merritt B. Lewis, 1854; Samuel Woodworth, 1856; John S. Rogers, 1857, 1858; Denalow D. Davis, 1859, 1860; Amos Stevens, 1861; William W. Blakeley, 1862, 1863; Ira B. Healy, 1864, 1865; Samuel Smith, 1866,

1867, 1871, 1872, 1873; William Lewis, 1806; Henry S. Joy, 1869, 1870; James W. Ives, 1874, 1875; Walter S. Joy, 1876–78; Augustus Lyford, 1879.

Town Clerks.—Nelson Wolcott, 1833, 1834, 1837; Samuel Clark, 1835, 1836; Joseph Currier, 1838, 1839; Moses Twiss, 1840–43, 1846; Nathan P. Currier, 1844; Obed R. Marston, 1845; Thomas B. Ring, 1847, 1848; Milton R. Brown, 1849; A. R. Bevler, 1860; Patrick O'Connor, 1861, 1858, 1886–78; Philo W. Potter, 1862; Linus Peck, 1864; James H. Moore, 1874; James A. McCluskey, 1875–80.

PIONEER SETTLERS.

No permanent settlements were begun in this town previous to 1809. In that year the Holland Land Company issued the first articles to land in township number 8, range 3. The first six articles were taken by Samuel Coleman, Joshua Gates, David Wolcott, Erastus Wells, Guy Morgan and Abraham C. Hollenbeck, but there is no evidence that either of these ever located on his land. The first six who "articled" land in range 4 (1811) were Timothy Kerby, Daniel H. Wooster, Amasa Joslin, James Hall, Lemuel J. Paul and Orren Waters.

Timothy Kerby, from Massachusetts, is said to have been the pioneer settler of the town, locating on lot 32, range 4, about 1812. A few years later he removed to Currier's Corners, where he soon after died. It is impossible to give the names of the pioneers in the order of their settlement, but among those who located in the northwest part of the town during the war of 1812 were William and Josiah Richardson, Daniel H. Wooster, Milo Warner, Daniel Smith, Elijah Smith and Lemuel J. Paul. In 1817 settlements were begun in the vicinity of Currier's Corners. In the fall of that year Moses and Allen Twiss located on lot 17. They were soon after followed by John Brown, Henry Woolsey, Rodney Day, Cyrus McClure, B. Dickerson, Charles Fox and others.

John Eddy was the first settler between Java Village and Currier's Corners. He came in the spring of 1818. He is a native of Rhode Island, born in 1795, came in 1815 to Sheldon, where he was married in December, 1817, to Caroline Ward, whose parents located in Sheldon in 1811. Mr. Eddy located on lot 20, and is still living near the site of his first pioneer shanty. His wife, a native of New Hampshire, born in January, 1799, is also living, and was the pioneer female in the western portion of the town. They are the oldest living couple in the town.

Samuel Woodworth, from Vermont, located on lot 32, range 4, in 1819, and remained a resident of the town until his death, in 1869. Henry Woolsey, from Columbia county, located in 1819 on lot 23, range 4, where he died in 1870.

The first settlements in township 8, range 3, were made in the vicinity of North Java. Rufus Jewell located on lot 16 in the spring of 1816; Barney Lockwood and his son Squire Lockwood on lot 7 in the spring of 1817; Elijah Bassett on. the same lot in 1819.

Moses Twiss and his brother Allen were the pioneer settlers in the south-western part of the town. They were born in Charlton, Worcester county, Mass., the former January 17th, 1793, and the latter May 11th, 1795. In the spring of 1817 they came on foot to this county, arriving at Strykersville on May 11th, having been seventeen days on the road. They immediately "articled" land on lot 17, range 4, and the following fall constructed a log cabin and commenced improvements. For the first few months they were obliged to go to Strykersville, six miles away, for their baking, there not being a house between that place and their shanty. Moses Twiss was married April 25th, 1810, to Louisa Woodworth, of Rutland county, Vt., where she was born July 27th, 1798. He continued to reside on and improve the farm upon which he first located until October, 1836, when he removed to one on lot 18, where he remained until his death, January 29th, 1868. He was an active and successful business man, and an influential citizen, being prominently identified with the political history of the town While Java was yet a part of China he held several town offices, serving as town clerk a number of years. He was instrumental in the formation of the town of Java, was elected its first supervisor, and held that office five consecutive years. He reared ten children, most of whom are still residents of the county. His wife is living with her son on the old homestead.

Allen Twiss is still living where he first located, one of the oldest residents of the town. He was married May 25th, 1823, to Jeannette M. Russell, of Arcade. She died February 1st, 1854. Mr. Twiss has always had the confidence and respect of the community, who have honored him with offices of trust. He has held the office of assessor for thirty years.

Milo Warner became a resident of Java in March, 1814, removing his family and effects from Vermont with an ox team, occupying twenty-six days on the journey. He located in the forest, on lot 32, range 4, where he carved out a home and remained until his death, May 1st, 1873. He was born in Rutland county, Vt., June 11th, 1791, and was married in November, 1812, to Lucina K. Sykes, of the same county. She died in Java July 20th, 1843. Mr.Warner was foremost in educational, temperance, religious and all other efforts for the improvement and advancement of society, and was first to abandon liquor in the harvest field. He was one of the first school teachers in that section, was instrumental in the organization of the Congregational church at Strykersville, was chosen its first deacon, and served as such until his death. He was kind, generous and hospitable, influential and respected. He reared a large family, many of whom are still residents of the county. He was a soldier in the war of 1812.

Daniel H. Wooster was one of the first settlers in the town. In 1811 he articled the tract of land upon which Java village is now situated, where he located as early as 1812 or 1813. He was a native of this State, and came from Canandaigua to Sheldon about 1808, where he was soon after married to Anna Gillett. He was the pioneer millwright and miller of the town, and remained a resident until about 1826, when he removed to Strykersville, where he died in 1873, aged ninety-two years. Soon after his advent in this town he came very near losing his life in a combat with a huge buck which he surprised in the woods asleep. As the buck sprang up to run, his horns caught in some bushes for a moment, and Mr. Wooster thought to make him his prey; but the buck soon released himself, and turned upon his antagonist A large club lying providentially at hand dispatched the buck and saved Mr. Wooster's life, but not until his clothes were nearly all torn from his body.

Lemuel J. Paul, from Vermont, took up one hundred and fifty acres just north of Java village in 1811, and settled in the spring of 1814 where James W. Ives now resides, where he remained until his death.

Jonas Brown, a native of New Hampshire, came to Java village in June, 1829, where he remained until his death in March, 1876. He was a soldier in the war of 1812. His wife is still a resident of the place, in her eighty-sixth year.

Daniel Smith took up three hundred acres of land on lot 39, upon which he located in the spring of 1814. He lived here until July, 1823, when he sold and removed.

Among the Irish population the first to locate in Java were three brothers— Lawrence, Owen and Richard McGwyer— who came in the spring of 1829. They were all unmarried, but became permanent residents here. They were followed the same year by James McGinnis, James Conroy, Patrick Corcoran and John King.

JAVA VILLAGE.

This enterprising little village contains a grist-mill and two saw-mills, in connection with one of which is a cheese-box and barrel factory; a hotel, two general stores, a hardware store and tin shop, a tannery, a cheese factory, one wagon and two blacksmith shops, a cabinetware and undertaking establishment, besides several other shops. The present population is about 200.

HISTORY OF BUSINESS AT JAVA VILLAGE.

The first grist-mill in the town of Java was built, at this place, in 1816, by Samuel H. Wooster. It stood not far from the east bank of Buffalo creek, from which the water was conveyed through pump logs to the overshot water wheel. The stones used were chiseled from native rocks, and moose wood bark constituted most of the belting and fastenings. Many laughable stories are yet told of the capacity and workings of this mill. It continued to do execution for two or three years, when Mr. Wooster built another, near the site of the present one. It was a square building of hewed logs, and the power and machinery were sufficient for the demand for a time: This mill he operated until about 1822, when he sold it to Goumey & Whitney. They were succeeded by Joseph Barber and Charles Richardson. The construction of the present grist-mill was begun by Barber & Richardson in 1835, and completed by Mr. Richardson in 1836.

Harry Eddy built a saw-mill at this place as early as 1820, which he operated several years. It was afterward owned by D. W. Hall, and still later by L. Cleft, on whose hands it burned down.

Lyman D. Wood located here about 1825, and soon after built a mill for wool carding and cloth dressing, which he carried on many years. The building was converted into a saw-mill by Peter G. Clark, and is now owned and operated by Richardson Howard as a saw-mill and cheese-box factory.

The first stock of goods was brought in about 1824 by H. J. Comstock, who occupied a portion of the hewed log gristmill as a store. His successor in trade was Levi Smith, who sold at the same place. Lyman D. Wood built the first store, which he stocked about 1828 or 1829. The building is the one now occupied by Nichols & Conrad for the same purposes. Among the other early merchants at this place were Sheffield Herrington, George Baldwin, George Farwell, Schuyler Gough, Porter and Lyndorf Potter, Timothy G. Clark and his son Timothy G. Clark, jr., Barnard C. Ring, Charles H. Richardson and Sylvester Griggs.

William Brooks, who located here about 1826, built the first tannery soon after. He was followed by John Fry, Gilbert Winegar and Obadiah Green. This establishment was burned about 1848; but eight or ten years previous to this John Fry had built a second tannery. In 1852 Elijah Smith built one on a more extensive scale than his predecessors, and he conducted the business several years. He was followed in ownership by Andrew J. Taylor, Amos Stevens and Dr. Green. The building was burned in 1871. The present tannery was built in 1873 by Patrick Hogan.

Wood & Nelson built a distillery here about 1829.

Palmer Whitney came here about 1823, and soon after opened the first hotel. Joseph Barber opened the first shoe shop, in 1823, and Jacob Fancher the first blacksmith shop, in 1825.

A post-office was established here about 1826, under the name of Gurney's Mills. Lyman D. Wood was the first postmaster. The name of the office was a few years later changed to Java Village.

A school-house was built about 1818, and was the first frame building in the village.

The first and present cemetery was established about 1827. A child of Harry Eddy was the first person buried in it.

GOOD TEMPLARS' LODGE.

Java Village Lodge, No. 574, I. O. G. T. was instituted April 3d, 1868, by R. L. Hurlburt, with thirty-two members. The first leading officers were: G. B. Clark, W. C. T.; Mrs. Howard M. Clark, W. V. T.; Joseph Cooper, W. C.; J. W. Ives, W. S.; James Barnes, W. T.; Henry B. Hogan, P. W, C.T. This lodge has sustained its organization without intermission from its commencement, and has lately built a two-story building for its accommodation. Regular meetings are held on Saturday evenings.

NORTH JAVA.

But few inland villages in Wyoming county do a more flourishing business, in proportion to the number of occupations represented, than does North Java. It is situated in the northeast part of the town, and contains 160 inhabitants, with two general stores, one hardware store, two churches, a hotel, three blacksmith and two wagon shops, two millinery and dressmaking shops, a patent medicine establishment, one harness and two shoe shops, a photograph gallery and two resident physicians. A saw and shingle mill and a cheese factory are located within a convenient distance of the village.

Among the first settlers on the site of the village were Rufus Jewell, —— Watson, —— Ingraham, Stephen Carson, —— Grover and Levi Mann, locating from 1816 to 1820.

About 1823 James Mann, who had previously located near the site of the present M. E. church, converted his log dwelling into a tavern, and immediately after put up a frame addition to it, which was the first frame structure erected in this part of the town. Though removed from its original site, it is still in existence, and is occupied as part of a large dwelling. Mr. Mann continued. to accommodate the public at his original place until 1829, when he erected the present hotel on the corners, which he kept for several years, and was succeeded by A. C. Williams. It was subsequently owned and kept by Merrit B. Lewis until 1855, when it was bought by the present proprietor, O. G. Warren.

The first store was built and opened in 1832, by Ormus Doolittle and David McWethy as proprietors. Elijah Bassett did the carpenter and joiner work, Doolittle and McWethy furnished the stock and Seth Lewis managed the business. The latter subsequently became sole proprietor.

Among the other early merchants at this point were James Bronson, Jotham D. Tower and Alpheus Baldwin.

Elijah Bassett opened the first shoe shop here, about 1820, and Abram Fancher the first blacksmith shop about 1830.

Dr. Benjamin Potter, of Sheldon, was the first physician to practice in this vicinity, and Dr. Isaac Garvin the first to locate at North Java.

The first school-house in the district was built of logs, about 1823, and stood three-fourths of a mile south of the village. About 1830 the first school-house (frame) was built at North Java.

CHURCHES OF NORTH JAVA.

Free Will Baptist.—A church of this denomination was organized at the Gulf school-house, on the east line of the town, about 1828. The constituent members were few, but a revival soon increased their number to over forty. Their services were at first held at the Gulf school-house and at North Java. Among the first pastors were Revs. H. Jenkins, Hitchcock, Moses, Tanner, Brown and Miner. The society began the construction of a meeting-house within a few years after its organization, but the church having become reduced in 1836 to but few members, it was disbanded before the building was finished. About 1847 a reorganization of the church was effected, and by uniting with the Congregational society, which was organized the same year, the church building was completed, and was used by both societies alternately for a few years, when the former became extinct as an organization, and the latter society became sole owner of the church property by mutual consent.

First Congregational.—This church was constituted August 14th, 1847, under the direction of Rev. W. C. Childs, with fifteen members, viz.: Deacon S. B. Joy, Deacon M. C. Humphrey, M. M. Childs, Dr. J. C. Tibbetts, H. M. Humphrey, John R. Mills, C. Lovell, Nathan R. Clark, Mrs. E. Joy, Mrs. Sarah Lovell, Mrs. Charity Mills, Mrs. Lydia Humphrey, Mrs. L. Chipman, Mrs. S. Humphrey and Miss Sophia Joy.

Rev. W. C. Childs became the first pastor of the church, and remained until 1851. His successors were Rev. N. T. Yeomans, from June, 1852, until June, 1855; Rev. C. C. Crossfield, from 1855 to 1857; Rev. T. J. Quigley, for three years from April, 1858; Rev. D. Powell, one year; Rev. William Hall, one year from October 1st, 1862. After this the church was Supplied at stated intervals for a time by Rev. Messrs. Smith and Dewey.

This church had seasons of increase and prosperity, but deaths and removals at length diminished the membership, until in 1874 only two members remained, Mrs. E. Joy and Sophia Joy.

In October, 1874, a reorganization of this church was effected, under the direction of Rev. J. C. Caswell, with sixteen members. The church building was repaired and refitted at an expense of $700, and was afterward supplied with a bell, an organ and commodious sheds.'

Mr. Caswell remained as pastor until the spring of 1878, and was succeeded the same year by the present pastor, Rev. D. Dunham.

The church now numbers forty-two members.

LODGES AT NORTH JAVA.

Mount Vernon Lodge, No. 263, *F. & A. M.*, of North Java, was chartered June 17th, 1852, and is the oldest lodge of this order now in existence in the county. Among its charter members were John C. Tibbetts, George A. Johnson, Calvin Rogers, John Curtis, John Parish, Amasa Briggs, Justus Blakely, James Case and Ebenezer Jackson. The first leading officers were John C. Tibbetts, W. M.; George A. Johnson, S. W.; and Calvin Rogers, J. W. Its meetings were continued quite regularly until 1869, when they were neglected, and the charter was at length arrested by the grand lodge. In June, 1871, Charles D. Wolcott, Nelson E. Torrey and Dr. T. D. Powell were sent as delegates to the meeting of the grand lodge in New York, and succeeded in securing the restoration of the charter, since which time the lodge has been in a flourishing condition. In 1873 it erected a two-story frame building at North Java, at a cost of about $1,000, the upper part of which is used for lodge purposes. The present membership is 46.

North Java Lodge, No. 126, *A. O. U. W.* was instituted at North Java January 25th, 1878, by–Webb, with fourteen charter members. The following were among the first officers elected: Master Workman, Walter S. Joy; P. M. W., D. C. Blakely; recorder, William W. Boddy; general foreman, Nelson E. Torrey; Overseer, E. R. Fox; financier, Leonard Blakely. Regular meetings are held on Friday evenings, in Masonic Hall.

CURRIER'S CORNERS (JAVA POST-OFFICE).

This locality was originally know as Fox's Comers, but was subsequently called Currier's Corners, by which name it is still known throughout this part of the country, although the name of the post-office is Java, and has been since its establishment.

The first settler here was John Brown, who came from Vermont in the winter of 1817 and 1818. He was followed in the spring of 1819 by Charles Fox, who in 1822 built a tavern on one of the four comers. He was succeeded in 1827 by Nahum Thompson, and he two years later by Edgar Camp, who soon after removed the original building, and built the present hotel on the same site. About 1831 this property came into the possession of Abner Currier. The business was continued by Mr. Currier and his two sons, Ulricks and Joseph, successively for many years, from which fact the village derived its present name. In 1829 Nahum Thompson built a hotel. He kept it about three years, when it was converted into a private dwelling.

The first stock of merchandise was brought to this place in 1828, by Daniel and William Jackman, who built and occupied the store now occupied by Lyford & Kent. They also built an ashery here about the same time, which they carried on in connection with store keeping. Among the other early merchants were Edgar Camp, Abner Currier, Watson Miller and Colonel Abraham Smith.

A saw mill was built in this vicinity in 1831, by Blake Howard. It was subsequently owned and worked by Gordin D. Fox, and afterward by Dan Dickerson. It was eventually destroyed by fire, and rebuilt by Mr. Dickerson, but finally abandoned as unprofitable.

The village now contains two general stores, a hotel, a church, a steam saw-mill, a cheese factory, one wagon shop and two blacksmith shops.

CONGREGATIONAL CHURCH AT CURRIER'S CORNERS.

This church was organized in the school-house at Currier's Comers in May, 1854, by Revs. J. S. Northrup and L. A. Skinner, with thirty-one constituent members, among whom were Ira Kibbe, Ephraim Fisk, Moses Smith, Luke Smith, Hiram Moore and George Wainwright. Ira Kibbe and Ephraim Fisk were chosen as the first deacons.

The society was legally incorporated January 11th, 1855, under the name of the "First Congregational Society of West Java." The first trustees were Ephraim Fisk, jr., Ira Kibbe and Gordin D. Fox. A building committee, consisting of

Moses Smith, John B. Gillett and Lucius Thompson was appointed at the same time, and the society soon after built a frame church edifice, which was completed and dedicated early in 1856 by Rev. G. S. Northrup. It cost, including ground and sheds, about $2,000.

Rev. G. S. Northrup served as the first pastor, and was followed by Revs. L. Parker, Gregg, Frost and others.

The present membership is 35.

WILLIAMSVILLE,

situated three-fourths of a mile south of North Java, contains a few mechanics'shops and about a dozen dwellings, and is identified with North Java in all its interests. The locality takes its name from Hiram Williams, who settled here about 1838, and for many years did quite an extensive business in a mechanical line. The mercantile business, which was begun at this point by James Bronson in 1852, has long since been absorbed by North Java.

EAST JAVA.

East Java, situated in the southeasterly part of the town, is a hamlet containing a store, a hotel, a cheese factory and half a dozen dwellings. The place is more familiarly known as Java Lake, being situated near the outlet of Cattaraugus lake. Levi Stearns was the first settler in this locality, about 1816. Freedom Lord located near here in 1820, and about 1825 opened a tavern in a two-story log house, the upper part of which was used by a masonic lodge, which became extinct soon after the abduction of Morgan. James Barton built and worked an ashery here about 1821, and a few years later opened a log tavern on one ot the present four corners. Henry Rice built and kept the first frame hotel, about 1829; the building is still standing, and known as "the red house." The present hotel was built in 1832, by Joseph Fuller, who kept it several years.

A man named Wright built a store here and brought in the first stock of goods about 1824. Andelusha Pyer acted as his agent. Nelson Wolcott was also an early merchant here.

JAVA CENTRE

has one of the largest and most costly churches in this part of the State, recently erected by the Catholic society of the town. The hamlet also contains the priest's residence, a hotel, a cheese factory and five or six dwellings.

James McGinnis, who was the first settler here, located in 1829, and soon after opened his new home as a tavern, continuing the business until his death in 1852. This was, in early times, quite a trading point. Benjamin Gardner, Booth and Denio were among the first to sell goods here, but the business has long since been abandoned.

BIOGRAPHICAL.

BENJAMIN C. BARBER, cabinet maker and undertaker since 1836, and before that a miller, was born in Franklin county, Mass., December 9th, 1812, and came to Java Village in October, 1823, where he has since resided. He was married September 29th 1833, to Eliza Carroll, of Fitswiiliam, N. H., a native of Massachusetts. He has been a deacon of the Baptist church of Strykersville many years. His father, Joseph Barber, came from Massachusetts—where he was born in 1700—to Java Village in 1883, bringing with him a large family. He opened the first shoe shop at Java Village, and continued that business until his death, March 3d, 1839.

CHARLES BARBER, son of Joseph Barber, is a native of Java, born February 6th, 1821, and was married August 8th, 1847, to Fidelia Stockwell, a native of Jefferson county, N. Y. Excepting seven years spent in Illinois he has remained a resident of this town. He located on his present farm in 1876. He enlisted October 8th, 1861, in Company A, 101th N. Y. Infantry; was wounded at the Wilderness, and honorably discharged October 30th, 1864.

JAMES S. BARNES, a native and life-long resident of Java, was born April 15th, 1845. In the spring of 1853 he located at Java Village, where he has since been blacksmithing. He was married in July, 1867, to Mary A. Murther, of Java. His father, Michael Barnes, emigrated from Ireland to Connecticut in his youth, and came to Java about 1833, where he died in February, 1879.

SAMUEL THORNE BROWER is descended from ancestors who emigrated from Holland to this State in 1630. He was born in Dutchess county. N. Y., December 30th, 1810. He is a tinsmith, and was at one time extensively engaged in the hardware business in Syracuse. For about seven years he kept hotels in Otsego and Greene counties, and was deputy sheriff several terms. He spent several years at his trade in Buffalo. He located at Java Village in 1878. He was married in 1838 to Sarah S. Wood, of Otsego, and has six children.

THOMAS BURNHAM came to Java Village in 1840. He was born in Upper Canada December 16th, 1812, and was married January 18th, 1843, to Philena, daughter of Joseph Barber, of Java Village. He is a carpenter and joiner.

JAMES L. BASSETT was born in Pittston, Albany county, N. Y., July 17th, 1817, and came to Java with his parents in the fall of 1810, where he afterward followed shoemaking for a time. In 1845 he removed to Madison county, N. Y., and the following spring was married to Abbie J. Cook, of Connecticut, who died March 31st, 1856. In April, 1868, he located at North Java. He was married to Clorinda Warren, his present wife, July 31st, 1836. She is a daughter of Ami Warren, and was born in Sheldon, October 19th, 1819. Mr. Bassett's father, Elijah, was born in Connecticut in December, 1791, and was married about 1818, to Lydia Warren, of Bristol, R. I. in 1815 he removed to Albany county, N. Y., and in 1819 to Java. His wife died in March, 1830. He soon after located at North Java, where he was the first to engage in shoemaking. In 1848 he removed to Warsaw, where he died in November, 1871.

THOMAS BUCK was born in Worthington, Hampshire county, Mass., February 16th, 1780, and was married in 1797 to Mary Wharton, of Plymouth, Mass. She was born

August 25th, 1779. Mr. Buck was a tanner and shoemaker. In the spring of 1821 he came from Massachusetts to Erie county, N. Y., bringing his family and household effects on two sleds, drawn by oxen, being twenty-two days in performing the journey. In the spring of 1822 he settled on lot 2, range 4, in Java. He was a justice of the peace many years, and was a leading mason. He died at his homestead in Java July 29th, 1868. His wife died June 20th, 1868.

Martin F. Buck, son of Thomas Buck, was born in Worthington, Mass., May 80th, 1809, and came to Java with his parents in the spring of 1823. He was married December 2nd, 1831, to Delilah Russell, a native of Gainesville, Wyoming county, born July 7th, 1818. Soon after becoming of age Mr. Buck bought his father's farm, to which he has added one hundred acres. He has been inspector of elections and collector of the town of Java. He has reared seven children, all of whom still live in the county.

Justus Blakeley was born in Jericho, Chittenden county, Vt., April 1st, 1802; removed to Bethany, Genesee county, N. Y., in 1816, and in December, 1826, came to Java, having bought his present farm. He was married December 9th, 1827, to Susan Curtis, of Wethersfield, who was born in Cortland county, N. Y., October 6th, 1806. They have eight sons and one daughter. Mr. Blakeley has been a Methodist class-leader for thirty-five consecutive years. He was ensign, lieutenant and captain under the old militia law, and has been assessor of the town twenty-two years. His father, Moses Blakeley, was a native of Massachusetts, born in 1767, and was married in 1790 to Mrs. Phebe Kibby Atchison, of Connecticut He lived in Java from the spring of 1821 until his death, in April, 1847; his wife died in I860. He was one of the members of the first Methodist class formed in Java.

Jambs Conroy was born in County Louth, Ireland, in 1801, and was married to Rose Kelley, of the same county, in 1826. In 1827 he emigrated to New Jersey, and in 1829 settled in Java on a new farm, where he remained until his death, February 3d, 1879. He was a successful business man and an influential citizen, and served during his lifetime in many official capacities.

Lawrence E. Conroy, son of James Conroy, is a native and life-long resident of Java, born November 10th, 1849, and now owns and carries on the homestead farm of his father, on lot 5, range 4.

Albert Cooper has lived at Java Village since 1835. He was born in Erie county December 27th, 1820. He was a carriage maker until 1875, when he began farming and raising Ayreshires and Jerseys. He was married June 29th, 1848, to Clarissa Parsons, daughter of Pelatiah Parsons, an early settler in Bennington. His father, Joseph Cooper, was born in New Haven March 7th, 1790; came to Erie county in 1809, and to Java in June, 1835, remaining a resident until his death, September 28th, 1836. He was married in 1818 to Lydia Dustin, who is still living on the old homestead at Java Village.

John P. Cooper, son of Joseph Cooper, was born in Erie county February 11th, 1825, and came to Java with his parents in 1835. He was married October 16th, 1851, to Olive Parsons, of Bennington. He has always been a farmer. He located on a portion of his present large farm soon after marriage. He has one son, Frank S., born October 7th, 1852, who married Harriet G. Bowen, of East Aurora, June 10th, 1874.

Jacob C. Conrad was born in Sheldon June 4th, 1855. He made cheese at Java Village four seasons from 1872; then he served as clerk in a dry goods store at Strykersville.

In December, 1878, he embarked in trade at Java Village, in company with E. M. Nichols, which he still follows. His father was born in Germany in 1817, and in 1839 came with his parents to Sheldon, where he still resides.

ARTHUR CLARK, a native and lifelong resident of Java, was born February 14th, 1839, and was reared on his present farm, which was his father's. He has twice represented Wyoming county in the Legislature. His father, Samuel Clark, was born in Andover, Vt., June 8th, 1805, and came from there on foot to Java in 1831, locating on lot 8, range 4, where he lived until his death, April 5th, 1870. He held offices almost constantly, being justice of the peace nearly twenty years, and supervisor eleven terms.

JUDGE DENSLOW D. DAVIS has always lived at Currier's Corners, where he was born May 30th, 1826. He has taught successfully twenty-seven terms in the public schools. He is a carpenter and joiner. He was married April 19th, 1856, to Ann E. Bavor, a native of Erie county, born October 19th, 1830. He is now serving his fourth term as justice of the peace, and was elected session justice of the county in the fall of 1878. His father, Abram Davis, was one of the first settlers of Currior's Corners, locating as early as 1822. He was born in Saratoga county in 1803, and was married in 1824 to Flavilla Buck, of Java. In 1849 he removed to the town of Arcade, where he died February 15th, 1859.

CORMICK DOUGAN was born in county Donegal, Ireland. In 1882 he came to America with his father and two brothers, all of whom located in Java the following year. Mr. Dougan was married to Mary O'Neil, of Buffalo, January 29th, 1840. He is a farmer and dairyman, and has served in official capacities. His father remained a resident of the town until his death, in November, 1850.

HIRAM FANCHER was born in Smithfield, Schoharie county, N. Y., October 18th, 1815. In 1819 his parents removed to Sheldon, and in 1829, to Java Village, where his mother died April 11th, 1831. Soon after he learned the blacksmith's trade, and followed it many years. He was married October 18th, 1834, to Milly A. Brown, daughter of Jonas Brown, of Java. From 1861 he was farming on lot 38 until 1836, when he removed to Java Village. His father died here in 1851.

CHARLES FRANCIS has always lived in Java. His father, James Francis, was a native of Rutland county, Vt., born in 1795, and married to Sophrona Woodworth, of the same county, in 1814. In 1818 he removed to Java Village, and soon after located permanently on one hundred acres of wild land on lot 21, range 4, being one of the first settlers in that part of the town; where he remained until his death, June 29th, 1820. His wife survived until January 19th, 1852. He was an influential and respected citizen, generous and philanthropic, and is still kindly remembered by many of the older inhabitants for his friendly advice and timely assistance. Charles was born May 24th, 1819, and was married January 3d, 1850, to Eliza, daughter of Henry Woolsey, of Java. He succeeded his father in the possession of the old homestead, where he still resides.

CHARLES FOX, a native of Dutchess county, N. Y., was a pioneer of what is now Currier's Corners, and the first inn keeper in the town. He was born February 15th, 1780, and married Mrs. Silvia Davis, a daughter of William Bump, of Dutchess county. She was born July 22nd, 1779. Mr. Fox removed to Darien, Genesee county, previous to 1812. In the spring of 1819 he came to Currier's Corners, "articled" a tract of land on lot 18, made a small improvement, built a framed house, and planted a nursery with apple seeds which he brought with him, from which many of the older orchards in that vicinity sprung. In the spring of 1820 he brought on his family, and from 1822 kept tavern a few years. He subsequently removed to Chautauqua county, where he died August 2nd, 1869; his wife died June 22nd, 1868. He served for a time in the war of 1812 as baggage master, using his own team.

GORDIN D. FOX, son of Charles Fox, was born in Darien, Genesee county, December 11th, 1812, and came with his parents to Currier's Corners in 1820, where he still resides. He was married February 15th, 1838, to Irene G. Woolley, a native of Perry, Wyoming county, born August 18th, 1818. He was a farmer until 1875, when he retired.

THOMAS GILLETT, hotel proprietor and farmer at Currier's Corners, was born in Gainesville, October 12th, 1820, and came to Currier's Corners in 1844, where he was married September 24th, 1848, to Emily A., daughter of Moses Twiss, of Java. She was born July 11th, 1822. They have two sons and two daughters. Mr. Gillett followed farming exclusively until 1862, when he purchased his present hotel property. His father, John D. Gillett, was born in Delhi, Delaware county, N. Y., in 1798, and came with his parents to Gainesville in 1808, where he subsequently held the office of postmaster. Ho was married to Cornelia Bronson in 1815, and in 1838 removed to Batavia and engaged in hotel keeping. In 1845 he came to Currier's Corners, and was engaged in the same business for a few years. In 1860 he located at Pavilion, where he still resides, and where he was for many years postmaster. He has held commissions as lieutenant, captain, and major under the old military law.

EBENIZER F. HENSHAW was born in New Bedford, Mass., May 15th, 1808, and in 1825 came with his father's family from Cayuga county to Java, locating on lot 5, range 3. He was married to Polly Lisk, of Java, January 28th, 1830, after which he cleared up a farm in Wethersfield, and remained there until about 1845, when he removed to North Java, and thence to Williamsville, where he still resides, engaged in blacksmithing.

CHARLES HALE has lived in Java since 1888, and followed farming. He was born in Nashua, N. H., December 28th, 1826, and was married January 2nd, 1862, to Celia Woodworth, of Java. He is an only son of Benning Hale, who was born in Corinth, Vt., January 6th, 1797, removed with his family to Java in August, 1838, and lived here until 1876, when he removed to Erie county, where he still resides.

DR. JAMES IVES, son of James and Lucy Brower Ives, was born in Middletown, Rutland county, Vt., August 31st, 1819, and came with his parents to Erie county, N. Y. in 1824. In early life he served as store clerk until 1832, when he began the study of medicine, receiving his diploma from the Fairfield (Herkimer county) Medical College. He continued the practice and study of medicine with Dr. Colgrove in Sardinia until the fall of 1836, when he located at Strykersville, where he practiced most of the time until his death, in June, 1879. He was connected with and deeply interested in all moral and educational movements of his day and place, and an active worker in the Interests of temperance, Sabbath-schools, music and religion. He was a member of the Strykersville Baptist church thirty-nine years, and served as its deacon twenty-nine years.

JAMES W. IVES, son of Dr. James Ives, was born in Strykersville, December 30th, 1837, and has lived in Java since 1848. He was educated at Middlebury Academy and Rochester University. After leaving college he was a dry goods clerk a year or more, when he opened a store at Java Village. He has been salesman and treasurer of the large cheese factory at Java Village a number of years. In 1863 he engaged in milling, which, in connection with farming, he still continues. He was married in July, 1861, to Helen F., daughter of Charles Richardson, of Java. She died in 1871, and he married in 1873 Frank A., daughter of Charles H. Richardson, of Java. He has been twice elected supervisor of his town, and is at present postmaster at Java Village.

ASAPH JEWELL was born in Java, April 29th, 1822, and has always lived here, generally farming. In October, 1877, in company with Edgar K. Field, he embarked in the mercantile business at North Java, which he still follows. He served in the 98d N. Y. infantry during the Rebellion. He married Phebe, daughter of Ami Warren, of Sheldon, and has two children.

RUFUS JEWELL was among the first settlers in the town. He was born in Otsego County, N. Y. September 14th, 1792. He came to Java in the spring of 1817, and settled on lot 16, range 3. On February 22nd, 1821, he was married to Rebecca Potter, of Otsego county, who still survives, one of the oldest living pioneers of the town. Mr. Jewell died September 7th, 1879. He was one of three assessors first elected in the town.

SILAS A. KIMBALL was born in Wlliiamstown, Orange county, Vt., September 21st, 1800. In 1825 he came to Darien, Genesee county, where he was married April 2nd, 1823, to Mary Murphy, of that place, and immediately after removed to his present farm. He has reared nine children, six of whom are still living. One son, John H. Kimball, died in the war of the Rebellion, of typhoid fever, at Newtown, Va., May 29th, 1860.

ULRICH KREUTTER was born in Wurtemburg, Germany, December 24th, 1834, and came to America in 1852, first locating at Attica. In 1853 he came to Strykersville, and in 1858 settled in Java Village, where he still remains, engaged in blacksmithing and wagon making. In 1861 he returned to Germany on a visit, where he was married March 2nd, 1862, to Anna B. Schweitzer, of Wurtemburg.

PATRICK LACY was born in county Wexford, Ireland, in 1793, and in early manhood came to Newfoundland, where he was engaged in cod fishing for several years. From thence he went to Boston, where he married Margaret Murphy. About 1846 he removed to Java, where he still resides, engaged in farming. His son, James Lacy, was born in Boston, in 1837, and came to Java with his parents. He spent two years in the war of the Rebellion with the 71st N. Y. Infantry, since which he has been engaged most of the time in the oil regions of Pennsylvania.

BARNEY LOCKWOOD was one of the first settlers in the west half of the town. He was born in Weston, Fairfield connty, Conn., August 19th, 1776, and was married in 1796, to Elizabeth Squire, of the same county. In April, 1817, he came to Java and bought one hundred acres on lot 7, range 8, which he cleared, and on which he lived until his death, November 30th, 1863. His wife died December 9th, 1853.

SQUIRE LOCKWOOD, son of Barney Lockwood, was born in Weston, Fairfield county, Conn., July 27th, 1797; came with his father to Java in the spring of 1817, and bought one hundred acres of his present farm, which now consists of two hundred and fifty-seven acres. He was married May 18th, 1822, to Aseneth Jewell, of Java, who was born in Otsego county, February 15th, 1796, and died April 30th, 1878.

AUGUSTUS LYFORD, of the firm of Lyford A Kent, merchants at Currier's Corners, was born in Cabot, Vt., January 3d, 1832, and came with his parents to Holland, Erie county, in 1886. In 1852 he opened a store at Protection, where he was the first postmaster. In

March, 1861, he located at Currier's Corners. He married in 1853 Emily S. Hubbard, of Eigin, Ill., who died April 25th, 1858. He was married in June, 1861, to Frances A. Lyford, of Cabot, Vt. He was elected supervisor of Java in the spring of 1889.

ANDREW J. MCCUTCHEON was born in county Down, Ireland, April 10th, 1847, and came to this country in 1849 with his parents. He was married August 12th, 1875, to Libbie E„ only daughter of John B. Gillett, of Java. She was born in Lewiston, Niagara county, August 5th, 1850. Soon after marriage Mr. McCutcheon located on his present farm. He has one son, Henry Gillett, born May 18th, 1879. Mrs. McCutcheon's father was a native of Connecticut, born March 31st, 1809. He came to western New York in his youth, residing in various places until 1848, when he located in Java, where he lived until his death, February 11th, 1875.

RICHARD MCCORMIC was born in county Leinster, Ireland, in 1793, and came to America about 1824, suffering shipwreck on the passage and being obliged to subsist on horseflesh for three weeks. After traveling extensively in the United States he located in Java in 1835, and remained until his death, December 29th, 1846. He was married in 1831 to Ann Ham, who is still living. He was a successful business man, an influential citizen and held several town officers. His oldest son, Richard, who was born in Java, March 27th, 1837, now occupies the old homestead with his mother, and is engaged in farming and dairying.

JOHN E. MASON, of Mason & Crahan, hardware merchants at North Java, and son of Thomas Mason, was born in Wethersfield, October 25th, 1848. From 1870 he spent about seven years in the bakery and confectionery business at Chicago, where he was married April 25th, 1876, to Eva K. Bald, a native of Chicago, born August 12th, 1859. In the spring of 1877 he located at North Java.

JOHN MARKEY, farmer, was born in Java, April 27th, 1847, and excepting eight years spent in the oil regions of Pennsylvania, he has lived in this town. He was married February 9th, 1869, to Anna E. Tuite, of Java. He settled on his present farm in July, 1875. He is the present collector of Java. His father, James Markey, came from Ireland in 1887, and located in Java in 1842, where he died July 10th, 1873.

THOMAS MARKEY, son of James Markey, was born in Java, November 7th, 1842. Leaving home when about twenty years of age, he spent several years in the Pennsylvania oil regions. He was married September 7th, 1869, to Anna L. Conroy, daughter of James Conroy, one of the first Irish settlers in Java. Soon after his marriage Mr. Markey located at Java Center.

DENIS MOLONEY, hotel proprietor at Java Village, was born in county Clare, Ireland, May 15th, 1839, and emigrated to America in 1861, spending the next seven yean in the coal regions of Pennsylvania. He was married February 22nd, 1865, to Margaret Russell, of Java, where she was born October 22nd, 1845. In March, 1868, Mr. Moloney located at Java Village, and was in the grocery trade until 1872, when he built the hotel or which he has since been proprietor.

GEORGE W. NICHOLS was born December 28th, 1806, in Amherst, N. H., where was married to Sarah Wiley in October, 1827. In 1836 he removed to Springfield, Mass., and about 1850 to Java, where he has since been farming. He located on his present farm in October, 1867. His first wife died in February, 1831, and he was married in May, 1838, to Mary Robinson, of Lowell, Mass. She died in May, 1850. In February, 1851, he married Laura Eddy, daughter of John Eddy, one of the pioneers of Java.

EDWIN M. NICHOLS, of the firm of Nichols A Conrad, merchants at Java Village, was born in Springfield, Mass, December 18th, 1818; came to Java with his father's family in 1850 and has since lived in the town. He was married December 10th, 1875, to Helen M. Sill, of South Wales, N. Y. He made cheese from 1870 until 1878. In December, 1878, he begin merchandising at Java Village.

JOSEPH O'CONNOR, youngest son of Patrick O'Connor, whose former homestead he now owns, has always lived in Java, and followed farming. He was born here December 31st, 1848, and was married January 20th, 1875, to Mary Ham, of Java, where she was born in 1850. His father was born in county Westmeath, Ireland, where he was married to Catharine Hackett. He came to New York about 1830, and about 1833 located on a farm at Java Center. He was a shoemaker, following that business in connection with farming several years after locating here. For nineteen consecutive years previous to his death (which occurred in March, 1874), he had held the office of town clerk.

ASAHEL POTTER, son of Windsor Potter, was born in Sheldon, April 13th, 1819, and in childhood removed with his parents to Java, where he has since remained. He was married December 10th, 1843, to Betsey, daughter of Jonas Brown, of Java. She was born in New Hampshire, February 9th, 1820. Mr. Potter is a farmer on the old homestead of his father.

WINDSOR POTTER was a pioneer in this part of the county. He was born in Scituate, Mass., July 20th, 1790, and was married March 22nd, 1812, to Deborah Eddy, of the same place. In 1815 he came to Sheldon, locating near Strykersville. About 1823 he became a permanent resident of Java, first clearing a farm on lot 13, range 4. This he sold, and removed to 38, the present farm of Asahel Potter. Here he died November 24th, 1875. He was a successful business man, an influential citizen, and a consistent member of the Strykersville Baptist church. His wife died March 25th, 1870, aged seventy-eight years.

JAMES H. POTTER was born in Mt. Morris, N. Y., January 22nd, 1835. The following spring his parents removed to Sheldon, where his youthful days were spent. He was educated at the Aurora Academy, and taught several years, principally in Minnesota and Illinois. He was sergeant major in the 133d Illinois volunteer infantry during the Rebellion. He was married November 1st, 1865, to Lucina, daughter of Charles Reed, of Java. Since 1871 he has been farming in Java. His father, Zebina Potter, a native of Massachusetts, born in 1790, lived in Sheldon most of the time from 1835 until his death, in June, 1876.

ALLEN RAMSEY was born in Pleasant Valley, Dutchess county, N. Y., October 29th, 1821, and came with his parents from Erie county to Sheldon in the spring of 1839. He was married January 24th, 1849, to Betsey Briggs, of Sheldon, where she was born March 1st, 1827. Mr. Ramsey has lived on his present farm since August, 1856. Excepting eight seasons spent in boating on the Erie Canal, he has always followed farming. He has been postmaster since 1871. His father, Samuel Ramsey, was born in county Antrim, Ireland, in December, 1780, and was a weaver. In the spring of 1811 he married Elizabeth Laughlin, and emigrated to this State. He located in Sheldon in 1830, and in 1856 in Java, where he died in May, 1858.

HORACE D. REEVES, farmer and stock raiser, was born at Riverhead, Long Island, November 4th, 1826, and came to Java with his parents in the fall of 1837. He was married April 2nd, 1851, to Lucinda Lewis, daughter of Evin K. Lewis, an early settler in Wethersfield. She was born in Wethersfield, September 10th, 1833. His father, David Reeves, is also a native of Long Island, bora in 1792, and for many years was engaged in boating on the Sound. In 1835 he removed with his family to Java, locating on lot 8, where he remained until 1850, when he sold his homestead to his son Horace, and returned to Long Island, where he still resides.

CHARLES REED was born in Newport, Herkimer county, N. Y., April 5th, 1802, and in 1810 came to Erie county with his parents. His father was a soldier in the war of 1812, and lost his life at the burning of Buffalo. In 1821 Mr. Reed married Katie Stryker, and in February, 1823, removed to Java. His wife died May 3d, 1825. September 16th, 1827, he married Eveline Sykes, a native of Rutland county, Vt., who was born July 30th, 1808, and came with her parents to Sheldon in 1816, and thence to Java in 1819. Mr. Reed was a prominent and influential citizen, possessed of sound Judgment, a fluent speaker and a successful business man. He was a member of the Baptist church at Strykersville from 1827 until his death, and served many years as deacon. He died February 12th, 1833. His wife still resides upon the old homestead, in unusual health and vigor.

ADDISON REED, son of Charles Reed, was born in Erie county, September 15th, 1823, and moved to Java in February, 1828. He was married September 18th 1846, to Rosetta, daughter of Jonas Brown, of Java. She was born in New Haven, February 9th, 1824. Soon after his marriage Mr. Reed located on lot 87, buying a new farm, which he cleared up and improved, and where he remained until March, 1871, when he removed to the old homestead of Jonas Brown, near Java Village.

JOHN S. ROGERS was born in Sheldon, March 29th, 1818. From seventeen years of age he was a clerk in the dry goods store of Buell & Gates, at Sheldon Center, five years. In 1840 he embarked in trade with his uncle, and was subsequently associated with W. J. Humphrey in the same business until 1846, when he turned his attention to farming. In 1858 he located at North Java, where he was a successful merchant eighteen years, when he sold his business and retired. Possessed of excellent business qualifications and strict integrity, he has often been called upon to serve in official capacities. He held the offices of highway commissioner, town clerk and supervisor in Sheldon, has been twice elected supervisor of Java, and is serving his third three-year term as county superintendent of the poor. He was married July 19th, 1840, to Eliza, daughter of Gideon Warren, of Sheldon, who died December 6th, 1859, leaving three children. September 17th, 1860, he married Altie A., daughter of M. C. Humphrey, of Java. She died July 22nd, 1867, leaving two children. On December 25th, 1883, Mr. Rogers married his present wife, Mrs. Minerva W. Hewett, daughter of Eli Merrell, of Warsaw. His father, James A. Rogers, was born in New London county, Conn., in 1792, and came to Sheldon in 1815, where he lived on the same farm fifty years. He died in North Java February 27th, 1869.

HORATIO B. ROGERS, son of James A. Rogers, was born in Sheldon, July 9th, 1833. From 1849 he was employed as dry goods clerk at Buffalo ten years. From 1860 he was in trade at North Java until thé fall of 1877, when he sold out and engaged in farming. He has been postmaster at North Java fifteen years. He was married September 24th,

1861, to Mary A. Clake, of North Java, who died August 13th, 1863. April 1st, 1864, he married Wealthy W. Cole, of Lyons, N. Y.

SIMEON BOYCE, proprietor of the Boyce saw-mill, was born in Cayuga county, October 5th, 1831, and came to Wethersfield with his parents in the spring of 1837. In 1852 he located where he now resides. His principal occupation has been that of a sawyer and lumberman. He was married October 6th, 1846, to Sarah E. Balcom, of Sheidon, who died March 6th, 1852. March 17th, 1859, he married Nancy C. Propper, of Java. She is a native of Groveland, Livingston county, N. Y., born January 1st, 1842.

CHARLES RICHARDSON was among the first permanent residents in the northwestern part of the town. He was born in Dracott, Mass., in 1788, and was married in 1819 to Sally E. Parker, of the same place, immediately after which he settled on lot 32, range 4, in Java. He was for many years the leading member and most liberal supporter of the Strykersville Baptist church. He also lent his aid and influence to many other religious institutions and societies. He donated $1,000 to the Rochester University, and his will provided for the distribution of $2,500 among the different charitable institutions connected with the Baptist denomination.

CHARLES H. RICHARDSON, oldest son of Charles Richardson, now owns and occupies the old homestead of his father, where he was born November 5th, 1828. During his early manhood he spent some time in teaching. He was married to Mary B. Balcom in 1844. From 1846 he was in trade at Java Village until 1859, since when he has been farming. He has been postmaster at Strykersville for the past six years.

FAYETTE O. RICHARDSON, son of Charles H. Richardson, was born in Java Village, December 28th, 1848, and was married October 28th, 1874, to Maria Rogers, of Holland, Erie county. Mr. Richardson, in company with John Howard, is now extensively engaged in the manufacture and sale of cheese boxes and barrels at Java Village, having begun this business in January, 1874, which now amounts to from $7,000 to $10,000 annually.

ALFRED SHAW, farmer, dairyman and stockdealer, was born in Java, February 8th, 1825. He was married about 1852 to Sophia Thurston, of Java, soon after which he bought a farm on lot 35. In March, 1855, he removed to his present farm. His father, Cyrus, a native of Massachusetts, came to Java as early as 1833, first locating near Currier's Corners, but subsequently settled on lot 36, where he remained until his death, about 1860. He was married in 1824 to Martha Woodworth, of Java, who still resides on the old homestead in her 77th year.

ELIJAH SMITH was one of the earliest settlers in Java. He was born in Hadley, Mass., March 15th, 1795, and became a permanent resident of Java on lot 89 in March, 1815. He married Olive Dickerson May 21st, 1817. Commencing in the wilderness with only a rude shanty for a covering, he succeeded, by perseverance and hard labor, in improving and paying for a large farm, erecting fine frame buildings and surrounding himself with numerous comforts and conveniences, which he lived many years to enjoy. He was a consistent and useful member of the Congregational church from its organization until his death, which occurred January 22nd, 1869. His wife died April 20th, 1870. He was a soldier in the war of 1812.

ROWLAND H. SMITH, youngest son of Elijah Smith, has always lived in Java. He was born here July 6th, 1834, on the old homestead farm which he now owns and works.

He was married December 18th, 1866, to Susan Crawford, of Java. He has three children—Edwin E., born September 12th, 1869; Alice M., born October 22nd, 1871, and Olive E., born December 16th, 1874.

LUCIUS THOMPSON, farmer and dairyman, was born in Darien, Genesee county, May 7th, 1811, and came with his parents in 1826 to Currier's Corners, where he has since resided. He was married January 18th, 1833, to Samantha H. Smith, of Arcade, a native of Vermont, born July 7th, 1816. From 1861 until 1865 Mr. Thompson was a merchant at Currier's Corners, and subsequently a cheese maker for six years. He was a captain of militia. His wife died June 19th, 1879. His father, Nahum Thompson, was born in Shaftsbury, Vt., May 7th, 1777, where he was married September 12th, 1808, to Mary Little. In 1807 he removed to Darien, Genesee county, and from there to Currier's Corner in 1885, where he kept a hotel a few year, and subsequently farmed until his death, September 22nd, 1838. His wife died May 30th, 1844. He commanded a company under Colonel Mattison in the war of 1812.

JAMES TUITE, only son of Nicholas Tuite, was born in Java, July 28th, 1832, and has always lived in the town. He was a carpenter and joiner until about 1861, when the old homestead of his father came into his possession, since which he has been successfully engaged in farming and dairying, having enlarged the original farm of sixty acres to two hundred and twenty acres. He was married January 27th, 1868, to Margaret Murrey, of Java. His father emigrated from county Louth, Ireland, in 1831, and located in Java in 1832, where he died in 1861, aged sixty-one years.

DANIEL S. TWISS, oldest son of Allen Twiss, was born in Java, March 28th, 1824. After he was twenty-one he spent three years in Genesee county. April 22nd, 1847, he married Adeline Baird, of Java, born in Middlebury October 28th, 1824. Soon afterward he located on a farm in Arcade. In 1870 he bought his present farm, the old homestead of his father. His wife died August 12th, 1874, leaving six children. Mr. Twiss has been assessor for the past nine years.

ADDISON TWISS, son of Moses Twiss, is a native and lifelong resident of Java, born May 6th, 1828. He learned the business of carpenter and joiner, and followed it until 1872, when he located on the old homestead. He was married September 11th, 1877, to Mrs. Amanda Buck land, daughter of John Smith, of Arcade, and has one child, Mary Louise, born Juno 11th, 1878.

MYRON WARNER, oldest son of Milo Warner, is a native and a lifelong resident of Java. He now owns and works the homestead farm, where he was born July 25th, 1814, and where he has resided most of his life. He was married June 1st, 1837, to Sophia Morse, a native of Pembroke, N. H., born October 14th, 1811. In early life he taught several years. He has reared five children. His son, O. Corydon Warner, served three years during the Rebellion from September, 1861, in Company H, 44th N. Y. volunteer infantry.

DAVID C. WOOLLBY was born in the town of Arcade, June 12th, 1818. He was married August 24th, 1844, to Minerva Woodworth, of Java, and soon afterward located on his present farm. He has been assessor six years. His father, Moses Woolley, was born in Vermont, August 16th, 1787, and settled in the town of Perry in 1812. In 1830 he removed to Java, where he remained most of the time until his death, October 20th, 1862.

JOSEPH WESTOVER, born in Sheldon, March 2nd, 1818, came to Java in 1832. In 1834 his stepfather's family located on part of Mr. Westover's present farm, which has been increased to two hundred and fourteen acres. Mr. Westover was married in November, 1848, to Betsey C. Paul, of Java Village, who died November 27th, 1861. January 11th, 1866, he married Mrs. Phebe J. Haskins, daughter of Edmund Brasted, and a native of Steuben county, N. Y. His father, Leman Westover, early came from Connecticut to Sheldon, where he was married in 1818 to Mrs. Tamzan Tichner Miller. He located in the southeast part of the town, where he died in 1827.

PATRICK WELCH was born in county Kilkenny, Ireland, in 1828, and came to Java with his parents about 1836. He owns and carries on the homestead farm. He was married in 1845 to Jane Rimmer, of Java, and has seven children, all still residents of the county. Patrick James Welch, a grandson whom he has adopted, was born January 28th, 1878. Mr. Welch's father, Michael Welch, was born in Ireland, about 1786, where he married Mary Butler, and emigrated to Java about 1836, where he remained until his death, in 1861.

AMI WARREN, son of Colonel Gideon Warren, was born in Hampton, Washington county, N. Y., July 12th, 1790. In 1808 he came to Warsaw, and was for some time in the employ of Judge Elizur Webster, his brother-inlaw. As early as 1810 he bought one hundred acres of land on lot 1 in Sheldon, soon after which he returned to Washington county, and was married in 1811 to Clarissa Ruggles, of that county. In February, 1816, he removed to Sheldon, remaining there until 1886, when he sold out. He soon after located on lot 24, range 8, in Java, where he died October 18th, 1869. His wife died in Java, December 23d, 1878.

DENNISON C. WARREN, oldest son of Ami Warren, was born in Washington county, April 28th, 1812, and came to Sheldon with his parents in 1816. He learned the trades of tanner and currier and shoemaker, and from 1834 until 1839 he carried on that business, in company with Darius Baker, at Strykersville. From May, 1842, he was engaged in shoemaking twenty-two years, at North Java; then in farming in Sheldon until 1876, when he returned to North Java and retired. He was for many years a justice of the peace in Java, and has also been twice elected session justice of the county. He was married April 28th, 1839, to Philena A. Booth, of Orangeville, a native of Massachusetts, born September 12th, 1813, with whom he still lives.

GIDEON WARREN, ESQ., son of Colonel Gideon Warren, was born in Washington county, N. Y., March 9th, 1792. When about sixteen years of age he came to Richmond, Ontario county, and resided with Judge Lemuel Chipman until he became of age. He was married in the spring of 1816 to Sally Boyd, who had been reared in the family of Judge Chipman, and immediately thereafter removed to and located in Sheldon, on lot 1, range 8, where he carved out a home from the wilderness, and remained until 1835, when he sold out and removed to another farm near Sheldon Centre. His wife died July 28th, 1846. About 1866 he removed with his son to North Java, where he died March 17th, 1876. He participated in a three months campaign on the frontier in the war of 1812. He served for many years as justice of the peace, and held other offices of trust.

OSCAR G. WARREN, son of Gideon Warren, ESQ., was born in Sheldon, January 8th, 1826, and was married February 3d, 1847, to Sally Mann, daughter of Alva Mann, an early settler in Java. He bought the homestead, and lived there until 1866, when he sold the farm and purchased his hotel at North Java. He has been constantly engaged in farming, and owns and manages two or three well stocked farms near North Java.

Frank Warren, farmer, son of Oscar G. Warren, was born in Sheldon, January 26th, 1851, and came with his parents in 1856 to North Java, of which place he has since been a resident. He was married in September, 1871, to Flora Munger, of Darien city, Genesee county, a native of Attica.

Joab H. Wooster, son of Daniel H. Wooster, is said to have been the first white child born in Java. He was born at Java Village, March 12th, 1816. At twelve years of age he left home and was for two years employed by William Coughran, of Attica, in making spinning wheels. He subsequently learned the carpenter's and millwright's trade. He has lived at Strykersville most of the time since 1825. He was first married December 14th, 1838, to Eveline Stryker, who died August 16th, 1846. November 30th, 1846, he married Mahala Rogers. She died July 18th, 1852, and October 6th, 1852, he married Laura Clark, who died December 28d, 1856. Miss Eveline Spencer became his wife February 12th, 1862. Mr. Wooster has been exclusively engaged in mill wrighting since 1840, erecting some of the most important mills in this section of the State. He has been a deacon of the Baptist church of Strykersville for twenty-five years or more.

THE TOWN OF MIDDLEBURY.

THE beginning of history in all the towns of the Holland Purchase was the buying of or contracting for the company's lands by the settlers. We cannot, therefore, more appropriately introduce the history of Middlebury than with the following list of such early purchases and buyers, taken from the records of the company:

J. Selleck, May 1, 1802, lots 1, 3 and 5, section 8; Starin Stearns, May 1, 1802, lots 2, 4 and 6, section 8; Jabish Warren, May 31, 1802, lots 8, 10 and 12, section 8, and 7, 9 and 11, section 4; Frederick Gilbert, 1802, lot 8, and part of lot 10, section 4; Israel M. Dewey, 1802, lots 8, 10 and 12, section 8; Jabish Warren, October 1, 1802, lots 8, 10 and 12, section 12; Samuel Ewell, 1802, lots 7, 9 and 11, section 8; John Hill, 1803, lot 1 and part of lot 10, section 4; Robert Berry, 1803, lots 7, 9 and 11, section 7; Samuel Jolls, 1803, lots 1 and 2, section 16; Jotham Curtiss, 1803, lots 3, 5, 7, 4, 6 and 8, section 15; Charles Shrief, 1802, lots 8, 10 and 12, section 6; Parmenio Adams, 1804, lots 8 and 10, section 16; Benjamin Vannorman, 1806, part of lots 2, 4 and 6 and lot 8, section 2; Daniel Vannorman, 1808, part of lots 2, 4 and 6, section 2; Jesse Vannorman, 1803, part of lots 2, 4 and 6, section 2; Edmund Curtis, 1804, lots 4 and 6, section 14; Gideon Burdick, 1804, lot 6, section 4; John Roberts, 1805, lot 8, section 8; Marshall Davis, 1805, part of lots 8, 10 and 12, section 1; Ward Davis, 1805, part of lots 8, 10 and 12, section 1; William White, 1805, part of lots 8, 10 and 12, section 1; Oziel Smith, 1803, lots 2, 4 and 6, section 12; Henry Ewell, 1805, lots 8, 10 and 12. section 7; Samuel Bartlett, 1805, part of lots 7, 9 and 11, section 1; John White, 1805, lot 6, section 8; Daniel Terrel, 1805, lot 6, section 7; William Lacore, 1805, lot 8, section 8; Edmund Curtis, 1805, lots 2, 4 and 6, section 18; Wyllard Chaddock, 1806, lot 8, section 12; John Smith, 1806, lot 1, section 13; Abraham Thomas, 1805, lots 4 and 6, section 8; Elihu Hall, 1805, lots 7 and 9, section 16; James Hall, 1805, lots 7 and 9, section 10; David Morgan, 1805, lot 2, section 16; Jonathan Thompson, 1805, lots 1, 8 and 5, section 6; David Thompson, 1806, lots 1, 8 and 5, section 5; Eliphalet Owens, 1806, part of lots 1, 8 and 6, section 5; Timothy Mallison, 1806, part of lots 8, 5 and 7, section 15; Jonathan Curtis, 1806, part of lots 8, 5, 7, 4, 6 and 8, section 15; Edmund Curtis, 1806, part of lots 4 and 16, section 14; James Ward, 1805, part of lots 2, 4 and 6, section 5; Zina Dunbar, 1805, part of lots 2, 4 and 6, section 5; Edmund Curtis. 1806, part of lots 1 and 8, section 14; Edmund Curtis, 1806, lots 10 and 12, section 9; Joseph Bettes, 1806, lots 7, 9 and 11, section 7; Solomon and John Prindle, 1806, lots 7, 9, 10 and 11, section 2; Elijah Smith, 1806, lot 6, section 16; Joseph Smith, 1806, lot 8, section 2; Marsena Munn, 1806, lot 1, section 6; Moses Hurlbert, 1805, lot 9, section 15; David Thompson, 1806, lot 7, section 6; Walter Underwood, 1806, lot 6, section 10; Elias Munger, 1806, lot 4, section 16; Daniel Hoyt, 1806, lot 7, section 15; Daniel Hoyt, 1806, lot 8, section 16; Stewart Gardner, 1806, lot 10, section 10; Edmund Curtis, 1806, lots 7 and 9, section 18; Horace Dewey, 1808, lot 10, section 8; Israel Dewey, 1808, part of lot 8, section 8; Israel Dewey, 1808, lot 12, section 8; Thomas Williams, 1804, lot 8, section 10; Alven Caddook, part of lot 8, section 18: Isaac Wilson, 1808, lots 10 and 18 and part of lot 8, section 18; William and Micajah Brotherton, 1807, lots 2, 4 and 6, section 10; Gurdin Miller, 1806, lot 2, section 7; George Fox, 1808, lots 1, 8 and 5, section 4; Ebenezer Wilson, 1809, lot 8, section 11; Alven Chaddook, 1807, lot 4, section 7; Walter M. Davis, 1809, lot 6, section 1; Samuel Hannum, 1806, lots 10 and 18, section 6; Ebenezer Wilson, 1806, lot 1, section 18; Elijah Marsh, 1806, lots 7, 9 and 12, section 6; Asa Folsom, 1809, lots 7 and 9, section 7: Ebenezer Wilson, 1809, lot 8, section 18; Caleb Healy, 1809, lot 11, section 11; Elijah 8mtth, 1809, lot 6, section 18; Seymour Ensign, 1810, lot 11, section 8; Michael Hopson, 1810, lot 1, section 7; William Calkins, 1809, lot 6, section 10; James Duel, 1809, lots 1 and 8, section 10; Ebenezer Wilson, 1810, part of lots 7 and 9.

The pioneer settler of this town was Jabez Warren. He located here in 1802, at what is known as Wright's Corners, in the northwest part of the town. In 1805 he sold his lot, with a small clearing and a log house, to Amzi Wright. Mr. Warren had raised a crop the year or two previous, the first raised in what is now Middlebury.

Mr. Wright also purchased of Sterling Stearns the farm upon which his son, Allen E. Wright, now resides, at Wright's Corners. Jonas Sellick came about the same time with Mr. Warren. He located where the village of Wyoming now stands, in the rear of Nicholas Sherman's place. Reuben Chamberlain located a mile northwest of the village, where Mr. Dodson now lives. He died on the same place. Frederick Gilbert located on the hill above the village. He was the "pioneer Yankee peddler and music teacher." He lived here a number of years, and was one of the "useful" men of the town. Israel M. Dewey was one of the early settlers of 1802.

The above named settlers were from Middlebury, Vt., and when a name was wanted for the new town the pioneers were not long in deciding upon it, and showing that they had not forgotten the place of their nativity.

Among the settlers in 1803 were J. Sellick, who located on the farm now owned by Chauncey L. Hayden, northwest from the village; Thomas Cahoon, James Fay, Elijah Cutting and David Torrey, who settled west of the village of Wyoming; Job Hill, on the east side of the creek, on the Warsaw road; Zophar Evans, where Mr, Bills now lives, on the Bethany road; Daniel Vanorman, on the east road, to Warsaw; Jonathan Curtis, at Wright's Corners; Asahel Wright, on the farm now owned by Alexander Smith; Samuel Ewell, where Babbit now lives; Reuben Hall, on the east road, to Warsaw, where William Hodge now lives; and Edmund Curtis, also on the Warsaw road.

There were three of the Curtis brothers—Edmund, Calvin and Comfort. Of the Ewell family there were seven brothers—Samuel, Eli, John, Peleg, James, Henry and William. Samuel and Henry came from Massachusetts in 1803, chopped and cleared twenty acres of land, and sowed to wheat ten acres, which was more than all the others had cleared up to this time. This was included in the lot taken by Sylvanus Howe and now owned by James A. Ewell. It was known by the name of "Old Field" by the pioneer settlers, but is at present a fine grove of timber. The Ewells bought a barrel of pork and half a bushel of potatoes at Bloomfield, when on the way to their wilderness home. They put up a rude log cabin, in which they lived while clearing their land. They were somewhat annoyed by the earlier inhabitants of the forest—the historic bear and wolf. They seldom left their work in the daytime, but did their "store trading" and marketing in the evening. The Sellick family had preceded them in the forest, and they got baking done at Sellick's. One evening, as was his custom, Henry went after some bread that Mrs. Sellick had ready baked, and on his return he heard the wolves fiercely howling. Being somewhat nervous about the matter, he concluded that he would be a little safer if he had company; and as Mrs. Sellick's cow was close by, and had on a large bell such as was used in those days, he thought best to take her along, which he did, and she proved to be a protection against the wild beasts. As the wolves approached and their howls became fiercer, the smell of the warm bread the while sharpening their appetites, he would step up to the cow and give the old bell a violent shake, which served for a time to alarm the beasts. Soon they would gather again, but by repeating the operation several times he reached his cabin in safety, and ever after, no doubt, went to the "pioneer baking" by daylight, when there was no danger from wolves. The Ewells returned to Massachusetts, a journey of three hundred miles, which they performed in ten days. After spending the winter in their native State, and Henry in the meantime getting married, they returned to this town in the spring of 1804, fully equipped for all the duties of pioneer life. Their wheat field was on the road north of Babbit's Corners, in the north part of the town, on the east side of the road. Three of the Ewell brothers served in the war of 1812. Their father, James Ewell, followed them to this town in 1816.

Among the other early settlers were John Roberts, Job Hill, Samuel Tolles, Abner Bacon, Jonathan Whitney and Elihu Hall.

"They built log houses, amid forests in which never before had been heard the sound of the woodman's ax. With incredible toil the early settlers subdued the heavily timbered lands, fitting them for the plough. Few had efficient tools or teams. The ownership of a good lumber wagon argued wealth. Money was very scarce. Nearly all buying and selling was by exchange of produce. A gentleman of comparative wealth found difficulty in borrowing the small sum of five shillings for a few days; and being called upon to pay, was able to do it only by doing a hard day's work for one shilling, and another for a peck of salt, which he succeeded in selling for four shillings. Wheat was carried by teams all the way to Albany, subsequently to Rochester, and sold there for two shillings per bushel. In 1808 Mr. James Quail, father of Mrs. Jairus Miller, settled on a part of the farm now owned by his son-in-law."

Deacon Eliphalet Owen came to this town in 1806 and located on Oatka creek, where his descendants now reside, in the south part of the town, when the whole region was an unbroken wilderness. Before cutting the first tree he kneeled at its roots and committed himself and his interests to God in prayer. He interested himself in establishing a Baptist church, and became an efficient officer of the same, making it a principle to attend all its meetings. He was never known to remain at home upon the Sabbath, excepting one instance. He was one of the founders of Middlebury Academy, and one of its trustees during his life. He died in 1856, aged seventy-three.

Moses Gleason came in about the same time, and settled near Owen. In 1812 Moses Moon settled on the farm where he died in 1868 or 1869, aged ninety years.

During the war of 1812 the people were frequently alarmed by rumors of Indians coming to lay waste the country. They had burned Buffalo and devastated several places in the vicinity. Some of the inhabitants fled to the east, where they remained until they thought the danger was over. On one occasion the alarm was spread that the Indians were coming. Some left their houses and went into the dense forest. One man moved his pork barrel into the woods and drove his cattle into a swamp. Most of the inhabitants concealed themselves in some place; some of them fled to the gulf through which Red brook runs, thinking that neither Indian nor white man could find them or would think of looking in such a rugged, dark and dismal place. Mrs. Miller relates that she often heard her grandmother, Mrs. Moses Gleason, tell of that terrible night when they all fled. She alone remained, and after covering up the fire, not daring to let it burn, she sat alone through the whole night. Aaron Miller and his family remained in their house. Mrs. Miller said she would not run until she saw some danger. When peace was declared most of the inhabitants returned to their homes.

Among the other and prominent settlers was General Stanton, who went from this town to the war of 1812; was captured by the British, taken to Halifax, and in 1815, after the close of the war, returned to this town, where he died, honored and respected.

Stephen Miller located in this town in 1814, coming from Massachusetts. He was a soldier of the Revolution; enlisted under General Gates; was in the battle of Saratoga and at the surrender of Burgoyne. He came to this town with a team consisting of two spans of horses, attached to a sleigh. His family consisted of a wife and seven children.

Among the other prominent early settlers of the northwest part of the town were Ebenezer Wilson and his sons, Ira, Isaac, Amos, Heman and Orsamus, all of whom lived on farms in the vicinity. Several families of Smiths lived near the Wilsons.

Three persons in the town have lived to exceed the age of one hundred years: Mrs. Gould lived to the age of one hundred and three; Mrs. Peck died in March, 1863, aged one hundred years and three months; Mrs. Sarah Peterson, who came here in 1814, died December 9th, 1865, aged one hundred and two years and three months. A performance occurred in May, 1817, that for nerve and endurance has seldom, if ever, been equaled. Mr. Artemus Shattuck, a citizen of the town, went to the woods on the farm now owned by Hiram Miller, to do some chopping, and while cutting off a tree that had fallen and partially split open, his foot was caught in the crack, and he hung for a long time suspended by it and partially supported by one arm. His ax in the meantime had fallen beyond his reach. Despairing of receiving aid, and entirely unable to extricate himself, he finally cut off his foot at the ankle with his jackknife, made a crutch of a crooked stick, and started for home, having previously crawled to his dinner basket, wrapped his maimed limb in a napkin and used his garter for a ligature. Having fainted before reaching home, he was found about dark and carried to the house of Mr. Aaron Miller, where Dr. Seaver attended him. He recovered, became a Baptist and lived to preach many years.

Amzi Wright, Esq., was born in Lenox, Mass., October 24th, 1781, and in the spring of 1804 came to Middlebury, then Warsaw, and located at what is known as Wright's Corners. His farm was articled the previous year by Mr. Stearns, and is now owned by one of Mr. Wright's sons. Mr. Wright built a log house and had the usual trials and struggles of the early settlers: The herculean task of clearing away the forest he performed with patient and unremitting industry. He did his first milling at Caledonia, making his way through the woods with an ox sled and team. To answer the pressing demand of "land lookers," he opened his log house for their accommodation in 1806. Frequently several families stopped over night, covering the floor with beds, which they generally brought with them. This primitive tavern had but one room, one corner of which was the kitchen, another the pantry, another the bed-room, and another the bar; yet Mrs. Persis Cushing stated that on the 4th of July, 1815, she sat down to dinner at Mr. Wright's with three hundred persons, the cooking being done and the tables set in a neighboring grove. After a while Mr. Wright added another room at the rear.

The first saw-mill was built in 1809, at West Middlebury, now Dale village, by A. Worden.

The first store in the town was opened by Edward Putnam, at Wright's Comers, in 1810.

In 1816 Amzi Wright built his brick hotel, which is still standing, at Wright's Corners, and is owned by his son, Enos K. Wright.

In 1817 there was not a single church building in the town, but seven distilleries were at work. One was near the North Baptist church; one on Mr. Moon's place; one near E. C. Sherman's; one in the gulf, and one near the Warsaw line. The moral status of the distillery was regarded differently at that day from what it is with us. These distilleries reduced the bulk of farm produce in proportion to its value, thus lessening the difficulty and expense of transportation; but the moral influence of the distillery can be only evil. To-day there is not one distillery in the town, not one place where intoxicating drinks can legally be sold. In their place there are five flourishing churches, an academy and many schools.

The pioneer shoemaker was "Squire Abel," as he was familiarly called. It was customary in those days to "whip the cat," as it was called; that is, go from house to house in the autumn or early winter, and make up shoes for such of the family as were large enough to wear them. A pair of "cow hides" for a young man, or a pair of "kip skins" for the average girl of sixteen summers, were calculated to last two years, as they wore them only on extra occasions, such as goin' to meetin' and the like o' that.

The first hatter was a Mr. Howell, a queer genius, who would take the measure of his customer's head and in a few weeks return with a genuine "beaver," with "bell" crown. The price would vary according to the size of one's cranium.

The great Indian trail from Squawkie Hill, or from Buffalo to the Genesee river, passed through this town a little north of where E. C. Sherman now lives, thence on westerly about forty rods north of Amzi Wright's house at Wright's Corners, and east by the spring near Cameron's. Mr. Wright had many of the Indians visit him, among them Red Jacket. The Indians would come from a distance and build rude huts near Wright's Corners in the winter, and kill deer and other game, which they exchanged for flour and other necessaries. Allen's creek, in this town, was a famous place for the Indians to fish for trout.

In the earlier settlement of this town the principal products were wheat and corn; but as the country became cleared up the climate changed, and was not as favorable for the old staples, and others had to be resorted to. We find from the census for 1875 that the area of improved farms was 18,711 acres, valued at $1,444,489; stock was valued at $178,423; the gross sales for that year were $137,626. There were 4,557 acres under cultivation and $5,009 acres in meadow, which produced 6,818 tons of hay. There were raised that year 8,560 bushels of barley; 1,142 of buckwheat; 18,664 of corn; 19,830 of oats; 19,386 of wheat; 18,619 of beans; 21,423 of potatoes; 63,136 of apples; 11,170 pounds of grapes; 27,398 pounds of maple sugar; value of poultry sold during the year, $2,923; eggs, $2,345. There were kept 696 cows, from which were made 69,121 pounds of butter, in families. The number of sheep shorn in that year was 6,816, producing 42,087 pounds of wool. There were also made upon farms 97,380 pounds of pork.

The general decline in the population of Middlebury during the last half century, until the census of 1875, is shown by the following State census returns: 1830, 2,415; 1835, 2518; 1840, 2,447; 1845, 2,022; 1850, 1,799; 1855, 1,787; 1860, 1,708; 1865, 1,724: 1870, 1,620; 1875, 1,732.

TOWN MEETINGS AND THEIR RESULTS.

Middlebury was formed from Warsaw, March 20th, 1812. At the first town meeting of which there is any record, held at Alvin Chaddock's on the first Tuesday of March, 1819, the following officers were elected for the ensuing year: G. W. Fox, supervisor; H. G. Walker, town clerk; Luther Smith, William Mitchell and Russell Abel, assessors; Alexander Tackles and Ebenezer Wilson, overseers of the poor; Horace Healy, collector; William Collins, Oliver Smith and Martin Choate, commissioners of highways; Thomas Healy and Amos Bond, constables; Russell Abel, Paul Hawes and Asahel Perry, commissioners of common schools; William B. Collar, Anson Root, William Mitchel, Robert Seaver, Joseph Gary and John F. Cary, inspectors of common schools; thirty-one path masters and fence viewers; Levi Hillogg and Amzi Wright, pound masters; Augustin Belknap, sealer of weights and measures.

It was "voted that the next annual town meeting be held at the Academy in said town."

At an annual election on the 27th, 28th and 29th of April, 1819, the following votes for member of Assembly were given: For Robert McKay, 145; Joseph Sibley, 141; Chauncey L. Sheldon, 115; Fitch Chipman, 73; Gideon T. Jenkins, 58; John H. Bushnell, 6; Abram Matterson, 3; Thomas Tufts and R. McKay, each 1. The canvass is certified by George W. Fox, William Mitchell, Henry G. Walker, Luther Smith and Russell Abel, inspectors of election.

At the same time an election was held for State senators, with the following result: For Philetus Swift, 133; Nathaniel Garrow,132; Gideon Granger, 53; Lyman Payne, 54.

In 1820 it was voted that Amzi Wright, Jonathan Perry and Ebenezer Wilson be inspectors of spirituous liquors.

In 1822 it was voted that the collector's office be set up to the highest bidder. Silas Newell bid $24.75, and got it.

It was also "voted that there be two pounds in town, one near Allen's creek and one near Tontawanta creek," to be built for $9.50 each. Aaron Bailey and David W. Phillips were made pound masters, and constituted a committee to build the pounds.

In 1823: it was voted that the fees for collecting the taxes of the town be reduced to three per cent.

At a special town meeting held April 27th, 1847, 278 votes were cast, of which 73 were for and 205 against licenses to sell liquor, and none have been granted in this town since then.

The assessment roll for 1814 contains one hundred and thirty-eight names, including those of many of the early and prominent settlers of this town, and the assessment for that year amounts to $49,616, besides three thousand three hundred and twenty-eight acres assessed to Joseph Ellicott, the valuation of which is not carried out. There were only three persons in the town whose valuation of taxable property exceeded $1,000, viz.: Timothy Mallison, $1,462; Silas Newell, $1,973; Ebenezer Wilson, $2,185. The lowest assessment was $39, that of Moses Rowe. The assessors that year were Luther Smith, Nathan Wilson and Alexander Tackles.

Below are lists of the successive supervisors and clerks of Middlebury, as supplied by the town records:

Supervisors.—1819, 1820, George W. Fox; 1821, William Mitchell; 1822, 1823, Russell Abel; 1824–26, Henry G. Walker; 1827–29, 1836, Horace Healey; 1830, 1881, James C. Ferris; 1832, 1834, 1835, Robert Paddock; 1836, 1837, 1839, 1842, William C. Collar; 1838, 1847, 1848, 1856, 1857, Aury H. Cronkhite; 1840, 1841, 1845, 1846, Thomas Durfee; 1843, 1844, 1862, Jonathan Perry; 1840, 1850, 1853, Joseph L. Foster; 1851, Isaac V. Matthews; 1854, 1866, Abner W. Blackmer; 1856, 1859, Philander Choat; 1860, 1861, 1871, Ebenezer Webster; 1862, 1863, Orlando Kelley; 1864–70, Isaac G. Hammond; 1871, John M. Webster; 1873, 1874, David Cox; 1875, James B. Burleigh; 1876–79, Merritt R. Bailey.

STORE OF MASON & CRAHAN.
Dealers in Hardware, Iron and Stoves, Paints, Oils, Glass, Agricultural Implements, Silver-Plated Ware and Guns. Manufacturers of Copper, Tin and Sheet Iron Ware.
NORTH JAVA, N.Y.

RESIDENCE OF EDWARD BARBER, MIDDLEBURY, N.Y.

RESIDENCE OF J. B. WELKER, BENNINGTON, N.Y.

BARTLETT BLOCK, WARSAW, N.Y.

RESIDENCE OF NATHAN BABBITT, MIDDLEBURY, N.Y.

Town Clerks.—1810, 1821, H. G. Walker; 1820, 1822–26, William B. Collar; 1827, 1828, Knowlton Rich; 1829, Lyman Phillips; 1830–36, Seth Cushing, jr.; 1837, 1838, 1845, Ransom B. Crippin; 1839, Gideon H. Jenkins; 1840, 1841, 1844, 1846–48, Lewis W. Pray; 1842, 1843, Smith Chapman; 1849–51, E. J. Murray; 1852, 1853, 1855, William Tillotson; 1854, William Collins; 1856, 1858, Isaac H. Gould; 1857, W. Cheny elected, and I. H. Gould appointed; 1859, 1860, William W. Keith; 1861, Eugene Thompson; 1862, Horace G. Cushing; 1863, Charles Fancher; 1864–70, Charles H. Fancher; 1871, 1872, Otis H. Keith; 1873–79, Charles H. Buel.

Several special town meetings were held during the spring and summer of 1864 relative to securing recruits for the armies then engaged in putting down the Rebellion. At one held "at the house of Joseph Newell," in Wyoming village, on the 20th of March, I. H. Gould presiding, it was resolved that the town pay a bounty of $300 to each person who should enlist to fill the quota of the town under the latest call of the President, for two hundred thousand men.

At a special meeting held at the same place on the 16th of June, it was voted to empower the supervisor to pay $100 for procuring each volunteer who should be accepted to fill any quota of the town. At another meeting held at the same place, on the 27th of July, it was unanimously voted that a tax be levied sufficient, in addition to the county bounty of $400, to pay each volunteer credited to the town for one or two or three years the sum of $1,000, unless such volunteer could be secured for a less sum; also that the supervisor and town clerk be authorized to issue town bonds accordingly, and to refund to I. G. Hammond $400 for money expended in procuring two substitutes.

SECOND BAPTIST CHURCH.

Prominent among the pioneer Baptists of West Middlebury were Ebenezer Wilson and several of his numerous family, who settled in the wilds of western New York in 1808. Mr. Wilson soon gathered about him a company of kindred spirits, which was gradually increased by the arrival of other Baptists among the new settlers. March 11th 1811, the little band was organized, under the name of the Third Baptist Church of Warsaw. This name it retained till the town of Middlebury was formed, in 1815, after which it became the Second Baptist church of the town.

The names of the constituent members were Ebenezer Wilson, Joseph Brundage, Elias Munger, Isaac Wilson, Ichabod Cummins, Heman Brundage, Lydia Mallison, Lydia Wilson, Hannah Darling, Rachel Bowers, Mercy Wilson, Catherine Munger, Susannah Wilson, Lydia Smith, Rachel Hill, Bebe Cummins and Keziah Darling, in all seventeen.

Owing to the disturbances of the war of 1812, and hindrances incident to a new country, the little flock thus gathered had only occasional preaching for over six years by different ministers and missionaries, among whom were Elders Jeremiah Irons, William Troop, Joy Hands and Jabez Boomer. When not thus supplied sermons were read, or warm hearted, stirring exhortations given by the veteran leader, Ebenezer Wilson, and others, which went far toward supplying the deficiency. The success which attended these earnest efforts to maintain the ordinances of the church may be inferred from the fact that in eight years sixty-one were added to its number by baptism, and twenty by letter. During the latter part of this period the church enjoyed the labors of Rev. William Patterson, the first settled pastor; but he came among them a licentiate, and left soon after his ordination.

In 1812 Bartimeus Braman became the second pastor. During his pastorate of six years fifteen members were added by baptism and twenty-four by letter. From his resignation in October, 1825, to July, 1830, the church was again without a settled pastor, though supplied occasionally by Elders Boomer and Harmon, and suffered a period of coldness and distraction.

In the spring of 1830 Elder Joseph Elliot, so widely known for his eloquence and piety, took charge of this church and the one at Wyoming. Then for two years a revival continued, till ninety persons were baptized into the west church and twenty-six added by letter; while in the east or Warming church, in the same period, one hundred and fifty-three were baptized and thirty-nine added by letter. These were times of the highest prosperity to both churches, as were also the six following years to the Wyoming society, while Elder Elliot devoted his exclusive labors to that people. He did not retire from the charge of the west church until he had brought to its notice his successor, B. N. Leach, and had seen begun the building of the present neat and commodious house of worship, the rededication of which took place June 21st, 1832, Elder Elliot preaching the sermon.

Elder Leach entered upon his charge in September, 1832, and baptized twenty-eight the first year and twenty-seven the two succeeding years. It was during his labors that the parsonage was built. The members in Bethany were dismissed to form a separate organization, and soon set in a sweeping tide of emigration, mostly westward, which took with it nearly all the pillars of the church. For twenty years the removals and separations from the church continued, until the membership was reduced from 210 to 49.

The first pastor during these twenty years was Rev. Mead Bailey, who succeeded Elder Leach March 1st, 1839. He had previously been licensed by the church, and was ordained May 3d, 1837, near the close of his pastorate. Under his labors five persons were baptized and three added to the church by letter, but thirty-six were lost through emigration. The next pastor was Elder Joel Johnson, who entered upon his labors May 5th, 1838, and remained until 1841. During his pastorate ten were baptized and eighteen were added by letter, but there was a further decrease of 44 in the membership.

During 1841 this church was supplied by Elder Amasa Buck. June 4th, 1842, Elder R. C. Palmer became pastor, and he remained one year. Twenty-six persons were baptized, thirteen added by letter, one restored and eleven dismissed, increasing the membership to 101. May 6th, 1843, Elder G. N. Roe began a five-years pastorate, during which there were thirteen baptized, thirty-one added by letter and thirty-nine dismissed. He soon after died. Elder H. Levenworth next took the pastorate, in March, 1848, but at the end of six months his health failed, and his successor filled out the labors of the year. During this time thirty-five members were lost. Elder S. Olney became pastor in March, 1849, and remained two years, baptizing two, adding by letter thirteen, dismissing five and excluding two. Elder A. S. Jones followed in August, 1851, and labored one year, baptizing four, adding by letter two and dismissing five. He was succeeded by Elder C. Purrett, who served for one year, baptizing one, adding by letter four and dismissing five. The church was next supplied by Elders D. Munger and R. Morey till May, 1854. During this time one was baptized, four added by letter and seven dismissed. The next pastor was Elder Samuel Gilbert, who settled with the church in May, 1854, and remained two years, baptizing three, adding by letter one, dismissing twelve and excluding four.

Under the succeeding pastor, Elder Charles Berry, commenced a gradual improvement. He began his labors August 1st, 1856, baptizing thirteen the first year and sixteen the next, while eleven were dismissed. He was succeeded September 1st, 1858, by Elder W. S. Crane, who made a useful pastorate of six years, baptizing thirty-three in all; added by letter twenty-one, dismissed twenty-one, dropped eight, excluded three, and closed with a membership of one hundred and one. The next pastor was Elder J. W. Hammond, who began his labors September 1st, 1864, to continue them four years. Thirty-four were baptized, nine were added by letter, twenty-four dismissed by letter, nine excluded and two restored. The church was next supplied one year by Elder James Mallory. He baptized one, six were dismissed and five excluded. September 19th, 1862, Elder Lucius Atwater became pastor, and continued for four years and six months. During his pastorate sixteen were added to the church, fifteen dismissed and five excluded.

May 24th, 1874, Elder R: C. Palmer took the pastorate, and he remained two years. During this time the church remodeled the house of worship and parsonage. This brings the history of the church down to the time of the present pastor, Rev. J. M. Durby, who commenced his labors April 1st, 1876, since which time twenty-two have been baptized and twelve dismissed by letter.

The deacons of this church have been Ebenezer Wilson, Henry Ewell, Isaac Wilson, Peter Capwell, Heman Wilson, Hanford Conger, Aaron Bailey, Abel Barns, Alvey Bentley, Simeon Covill, Stephen Ewell, James M. Quale, Cornelius Ewell, Charles Snell and Myron C. Bailey.

The clerks of the church have been Isaac Wilson, Heman Wilson, Alvin Conger, L. P. Smith, Stephen Ewell and M. R. Bailey.

The following members have been licensed by the church to preach: Mead Bailey, Anson Root, H. B. Ewell and Orin Munger. William Patterson and Mead Bailey were ordained.

The number of pastors has been 19; of deacons, 15; of clerks, 6; of licenses, 4; of ordinations, 2; constituent members, 17; highest number of members, 210; whole number baptized, 412.

WYOMING.

The tract of land upon which most of Wyoming is situated was purchased in 1809 by Silas Newell, who located here in that year and built a double log house, or, in other words, one with two rooms, on the corner of Church and Academy streets, where the brick block known as "Union Hall" now stands. He soon after put up a frame addition, making the first log and the first frame building in the village. Mr. Newell came from Hoosick, Rensselaer county, this State, and was one of those enterprising men fitted for the development of a new country. Coming from the flats of the Hoosick river, he was not afraid, like other early settlers, to locate on the flats in the wilderness, which were then covered with a heavy growth of timber. The next frame building at this place was built by Mr. Newell in 1811, on the site now occupied by Newell's Hotel, at the crossing of Academy and Church streets. The building is now used by John Gaffin for a barn. In 1812 Mr. Newell opened the pioneer store, in a small frame building, where William Roberts now lives, on Hill street. At that time he had a large sugar orchard on the south side of Academy street.

Soon others began to see the fertility of the soil on the flats, and that disease did not infest that neighborhood any more than it did the upland; and new "land lookers" would settle here, instead of in the hill country.

The scarcity of fruit was being realized, when Mr. Newell cleared about five acres of that part of the village lying south of Academy and east of Church street, and set out apple and pear trees. This was the "pioneer orchard" of the town.

The pioneer furnace was built by William Hall, about 1816. It was a small frame building, and stood where the west sheds of the Presbyterian church now stand. It was removed to make room for the sheds in 1830, when they were built.

William B. Collar was the pioneer physician. He was also the first postmaster at Wyoming. He first lived in the house next south of the Methodist church; afterward where William Durfee now lives, on Church street. He married a daughter of Elder Joshua Bradley.

The first lawyer who located in the village was Hon. John B. Skinner, who attained in after years a State reputation as one of the ablest jurists of western New York. He was also a prominent politician of the Democratic faith.

In 1816 Silas Newell built a woolen factory and carding mill on the site now occupied by William Reddish's house, on Church street. He built a grist-mill in 1817, on the site now occupied by the stone blacksmith shop on Gulf street. The building is now used for a wagon shop, and stands at the south side of the blacksmith shop.

The academy, erected in 1817, was the first brick building in the village. The brick were made by Silas Newell, on the lot now owned by Mr. Reddish, on Church street.

The pioneer tannery was built in 1817, by Moses Rowe, where Alvin Keith now lives, on Academy street. The first blacksmiths in the village were the

SARAH DURFEE.

THOMAS DURFEE.

RESIDENCE OF E. A. DURFEE, NEAR WYOMING VILLAGE, N.Y.

RESIDENCE OF WM. F. THAYER. COVINGTON, N.Y.

firm of Phillips & Dixon. The shop stood where the Presbyterian church now stands; it is now used for a bam.

The present hotel building, the Newell House, kept by Joseph Newell, a son of the pioneer, was built in 1840 by Thomas Paddock. Mr. Newell has kept it as a hotel for the last thirty-five years.

Previous to the establishment of the post-office at this place the hamlet was known as "Newell's Settlement," and afterward as "Middlebury Post-office"; until, in 1829, through the influence of Hon. John B. Skinner, the name was changed to Wyoming.

The place now contains the honored old academy and the school-house of district No. 2. A furniture establishment is carried on by S. Hawley; dry goods and groceries are sold by O. H. Keith; drug and groceries by Cushing Brothers; hardware by C. H. Buel; heading and staves by Nathan Page; notions and groceries by S. W. Lincoln; a steam planing-mill is carried on by Z. C. Cowley; two blacksmith shops, by William Roberts and W. Tillotson & Son; two wagon and sleigh shops, by C. W. Durfee and H. J. Reddish; two grist-mills, by C. W. Durfee and Robert Y. McConnell; there are three churches—Methodist Episcopal, Baptist and Presbyterian; a circulating library, a printing office and a cornet band. "Union Hall," on the corner of Academy and junction of Church, Hill and Gulf streets, was built in 1870, by a stock company, at a cost of $3,000. There are two physicians—Drs. E. G. Harding and R. Wadsworth; the dentist is V. H. Jackson. The depot of the Rochester and State Line Railroad is located about half a mile southeast of the village, at the end of Church street; R. S. Muir is station agent and telegraph operator. The present postmaster is C. H. Buel, and the mail carrier between depot and post-office is Dexter Gould, Esq. The mail is received at this office twice per day, morning and evening. The village contains about six hundred inhabitants.

MIDDLEBURY ACADEMY.

Newell's Settlement, afterward Middlebury village, afterward Wyoming, in 1816 had three frame houses and about a dozen log ones. Silas Newell, a man six feet high and well-proportioned, had moved there in 1809, riding a horse and carrying a child, while his wife rode another horse, carrying another child. He took up four hundred acres of land, covering the entire area of Wyoming village. He started a subscription to build an academy, himself subscribing six hundred dollars. Four thousand dollars were subscribed, and Mr. Newell contracted to build a suitable brick building, forty feet by fifty, two stories high, for that sum. He promptly filled his contract, making the brick, excellent in quality, and erecting the building in the summer of 1817. Some subscribers failed to pay their subscriptions, and the loss fell upon Mr. Newell.

An endowment fund had to be created before a charter could be obtained. For this purpose $25, $50 and $100 notes were given, running twenty years, interest payable annually. The makers of the $100 notes were entitled to schooling for one pupil till the notes were due. These notes, amounting to over

$4,000, were subsequently collected, and the funds invested in other securities for the benefit of the institution. Mr. Newell also mortgaged his farm for $3,600 for the benefit of the institution.

A building erected and an endowment secured, application was made to the Regents of the New York University, composed of the governor, lieutenant-governor, secretary of state, and eighteen other persons appointed by the Legislature to supervise the schools of the State, for a charter, which was granted January 26th, 1819.

The trustees named in the instrument are Ebenezer Wilson, Isaac Wilson, William Patterson, William B. Collar, Jabish Warren, Samuel Ewell, Joseph Alma, William Bond, Silas Allen, Paul Howes, Russel Abel, Augustin Belknap, Silas Newell, Isaac Andrus, William Mitchell, Eliphalet Owens, Major Evans, Gaius Thomas, Peleg Ewell, Archibald Hotchkiss, Joseph Eastland, Moses Rowe and David Knowlton.

The institution was made subject to the "visitation" of the regents, and has ever since received a portion of the "literature fund" of the State.

John F. Carey, who had married a sister of Major General Stanton, had already opened a select school in the building. He was a fine scholar; he graduated at Dartmouth College, in the same class with Webster, delivering the "valedictory," while Daniel sat demurely in his seat, resolving to come out ahead next time. Soon after this, Mr. Carey remarked prophetically to Captain Waldron: "Daniel Webster will distinguish himself; he will be talked of for President of the United States."

The irrepressibles of 1818 were an overmatch for the learned and amiable Professor Carey. The boys of the period (not to speak of the girls) considered going to school a sort of pastime, and they improved it as such. Professor Carey failed to govern them, and resigned his charge, a good deal disheartened. Soon after, while in a shoe shop, he looked thoughtfully for some time at the pegging process, and sadly remarked to the cobbler, "I would be glad to exchange my education for yours." In saying this he did not disparage science—he exalted art!

To secure a competent presiding officer for the first and only classical school of western New York was a matter of great solicitude. Judge Isaac Wilson, member of Assembly from Genesee county, who had been active in obtaining the charter, had formed acquaintance with Rev. Joshua Bradley, the active, eloquent and aggressive pastor of one of the Albany churches. Mr. Bradley was offered the presidency, and, after considering the matter, accepted it. A brick house, elaborately finished, was prepared for him, and he left the city of Albany with his family in the fall of 1819 for the hamlet on the Oatka. He proved to be the right man in the right place. He was a full match for the boys. Sometimes he took the truants into his room, and spent a long time with them in exhortation and prayer; if that didn't cure the rogues, he was sure to fetch them with beech sprouts, vigorously applied.

The school was a great success, averaging one hundred and fifty scholars, and rising as high as two hundred. They were from the very first families of western New York. The Rochesters, Fitzhughs, Redfields, Evanses and Careys of Batavia were represented. Seven presidents of colleges began their academic studies at Middlebury Academy. Seth M. Gates, M. C., William A Howard, M. C., of Michigan, now governor of Dakota, Senator Doolittle, of Wisconsin, Dr. James P. White, of Buffalo, Professor Henry A. Ward, of Rochester, and many others with a national reputation, were pupils there.

Seth Cushing, A. M., of Massachusetts, taught the languages and higher mathematics, remaining at his post till his death, in 1837. He was a thorough scholar, very orderly in his habits and greatly respected. Mr. Tuttle taught under Mr. Bradley, and was succeeded by Rev. Eliphalet Spencer, a brother of Joshua A. Spencer, a distinguished lawyer residing at Utica, N. Y.

The five years for which Mr. Bradley was elected having expired, he went west, where he founded several collegiate institutions, and died at St. Paul, Minn., in 1855. He is widely known for the active part he took in the anti-masonic excitement. His work on "Masonry" had a wide circulation. He was succeeded by his assistant, Rev. Eliphalet Spencer, who conducted the academy with marked ability, assisted by Mr. Cushing, Mr. Gillet and others.

Few at this day can conceive of the immense excitement that attended the abduction of William Morgan for his attempted revelation of the secrets of masonry. All the masonic lodges were held responsible for the alleged murder of Morgan, and many churches required their members to renounce masonry on pain of excommunication. The Baptists were in the ascendant at Middlebury. A majority of the trustees of the academy were of that denomination. It was expected that they would continue to control it, though there is nothing to that effect in the charter, and all contributed to its funds. Mr. Spencer, principal of the academy, Mr. Gillet, teacher, General Stanton, trustee, and several other Baptists, refused to renounce masonry when required by their church to do so; they joined the Presbyterians, who were more accommodating in such matters. This threw the Baptists into a minority, and Rev. Eli S. Hunter, D. D., pastor of the Presbyterian church at Middlebury, was made principal of the academy. The institution still continued to prosper, having no formidable competitor west of Genesee river. In 1827 Colonel Wales Cheney, graduate of a military school at the east, took charge of the English department, and drilled the students in military exercises, continuing for several years, when he turned his attention to horticulture. He is widely known as the originator of the "Colonel Cheney" strawberry, and is still residing at Wyoming. He was secretary of the first temperance society in this vicinity, founded about 1830.

Dr. Hunter was succeeded by Rev. Norris Bull, D. D., of Geneseo, a very eminent preacher and a Presbyterian. He was elected by a close vote. Mr. Warren, a Baptist trustee, was engaged in earnest conversation when the votes were cast, asserting vigorously that a Presbyterian principal "was a violation of the understanding—a fraudand while demobstrating this to one of the opposite party, who had voted, and who listened to him very quietly, *the hat was turned*, and Mr. Warren found to his horror that he had forgotten to vote, and the Presbyterian was elected by one majority! The history of this period should not fail to note that sectarian disputes ran very high. The contentions for mastery in the academy continued for several years, and were a part of the denominational controversies that many remember, but which fortunately have given, place to a more tolerant spirit.

During Dr. Bull's administration the Presbyterian board of education sent large numbers of divinity students to the academy to prepare for college. He was succeeded by Rev. Joseph Elliot, pastor of the Baptist church in Wyoming, a popular preacher, who sustained the high reputation of the school, and was succeeded in 1838 by Rev. Mr. Buck, who was followed by Rev. Beriah Leach. During this period Professor Whitlock, afterward teacher at Lima; Professor Houghton, brother of the noted Boston publisher; Professor Paddock, afterward professor at Willoughby, O., and many other eminent teachers were employed, and with uniform success.

Mr. Joel Whiting, a graduate of Hamilton College, a scholar and a Christian gentleman, assisted by Professor Joseph Brown, Mr. Albert Capwell and Miss Aurelia Whitney, of Le Roy, conducted the school till they were succeeded, in 1846, by Professor David Burbank, a graduate of Brown University, who was assisted by Professor H. K. Sanford, Miss Lucia A. K. Waldo, and Miss Jane Thompson as teacher of music.

July 28th, 1852, Monroe Weed, a graduate of Madison University, was elected principal, and filled the office for fourteen years. Without disparaging the eminent and worthy educators who preceded and succeeded Mr. Weed, it will be admitted that a more faithful or a more competent instructor has seldom or never presided over an institution of learning. He resigned his place, and was called to a similar institution at the east, where he died. He was assisted by his father-in-law, the learned and venerated Professor Morse, formerly of Hamilton; by his wife, and by Miss Mary Chapman and several other very competent instructors.

Rev. J. M. Scarff succeeded Mr. Weed as principal, followed by Mr. Eugene Saterlee, who was succeeded by Rev. Irvin Smith in 1868. He was followed by Professor F. W. Forbes, of Rochester University, and he by the present principal, Professor H. G. Davis.

Among the accomplished lady teachers not mentioned above were Miss Dency Cook, now Mrs. S. B. Peck, of Michigan; Miss Reynolds; Miss Elizabeth Cook, of Homer, N. Y.; Miss Look, now Mrs. A. B. Capwell, of Brooklyn; Mrs. Mary S. Squires, of Wyoming; Miss Rose Forbes, now teaching in the institution; and Mrs. Davis, wife of the principal.

Judge Isaac Wilson was the first president of the board of trustees. His successors were Hon. Hanford Conger, Hon. John B. Skinner, who always took a lively interest in the institution, Rev. Charles Ray and Major Hugh T. Brooks.

Among the later trustees (the original board are all long since dead) who have been fast friends of the school were Peter Capwell, Henry, G. Walker, Benedict Brooks, Rufus H. Main, Smith Chapman, Daniel and Abijah Bradley, A. Blackman, Rev. William Dean, D. D., Rev. Harrison Daniels, Rev. Jesse Elliot, Lewis Prey and Major-General Phineas Stanton. The present secretary is Ebenezer Webster.

HENRY W. SMITH.

A. B. Rose

CARLOS LEONARD STEBBINS.

MERRITT C. PAGE.

A. H. CRONKHITE.

S. W. TEWKSBURY.

Reubon Stone

Julia Stone

JAS. L. WARRINER.

The *exhibitions* of Middlebury Academy at an early day were the chief entertainments of the period. People came from every quarter, and tragedies and comedies were acted in the highest style of histrionic art. The masonic lodge furnished the costumes.

About all the families took boarders at Middlebury village, but there was no boarding house connected with the institution. Board at first was a dollar a week, then $1.25, $1.50, $2.00 and finally $2.50, illustrating the great law of progress.

The chief service of history is to show the progress of ideas. For many years no female teachers were employed in Middlebury Academy, though young women as well as young men were always instructed there. That ladies can instruct as well and better in some departments than men is a somewhat modern discovery. The treasurer's books show a gratifying increase in "women's wages"; beginning with $150 a year the preceptresses attained to $400.

"Corporeal punishment" is a problem of the ages. "Flogging in the navy" found stout defenders in the middle of the nineteenth century. Ropes' ends were specifies for marine emergencies. "Elder" Bradley, our pioneer principal, was an *eclectic;* he tried all sorts of remedies for insubordination, and he always cured! The last thorough-going flogging in Middlebury Academy antedates 1830; the beneficiary was a clergyman's son. "Moral suasion" did not become very popular in common schools till a later day.

The domestic arts were not "lost" till after November 14th, 1826. At that time Joseph Woodhull conferred on Middlebury Academy "the right to make, vend and use" an improved instrument for spinning and reeling cotton and wool; whether the pupils were instructed in that art does not appear—there is abundant evidence that their mothers understood and practiced it, and weaving, too.

The coarse yellow writing paper used in 1819 by the treasurer of Middlebury Academy, and that used by treasurer Isaac G. Hammond in 1879, illustrate the general smoothing off of ruder methods.

Baptists have a clear majority in the board of trustees, but for several years there have been no sectarian controversies, and principals and teachers have been chosen with little or no reference to their ecclesiastical connections. Here also we learn the spirit of the age.

Two or three thousand dollars, raised by subscription, was expended recently in improving the Academy buildings and in enlarging the endowment fund, and the facilities for obtaining a classical education at this pioneer academy are believed to be unsurpassed.

WYOMING SALT WELL.

The project of drilling a test well for oil in the Wyoming valley was determined upon in February, 1878, by the Vacuum Oil Company, of Rochester. H. B. Everest, secretary and general manager of the company, and formerly a citizen of Wyoming, and J. D. Helmer, of Pike, president of the company, offered, if land could be leased, to drill a well, and allow the owners of the land one-eighth of any valuable mineral obtained. A tract of considerable extent was leased, and a well sunk on the farm of C. B. Matthews after the manner of those in the Pennsylvania oil regions. In the course of the drilling, on the 19th of June, a bed of rock salt was struck at a depth of one thousand two hundred and sixty-five feet, which proved to be seventy feet thick. Sulphur water being struck below this, further boring was given up and the well was plugged at the bottom of the salt bed. A three-inch iron pipe was put in. Pure water from an adjacent brook being admitted outside the tube forms brine, which is pumped out through the tubing. An analysis of the brine by Prof. S. A. Latimore gave the following percentages of components: Salt, 97.919; gypsum, 1.26; chloride of lime, 1.02; chloride of magnesium, 001; aluminum, traces; pounds of salt in one U. S. gallon, 2.36, or a bushfel to twenty-four gallons of brine. As yet the well has not been extensively utilized.

CHURCHES OF WYOMING.

PRESBYTERIAN.

On the 14th of June, 1817, at the frame school-house at Newell's Settlement, now Wyoming, the First Congregational Church of Middlebury was organized by Rev. John F. Bliss, a missionary.

Daniel C. Judd was chosen deacon, and Philetus Sprague, M. D., clerk. Of the original members none remain. They were Daniel C. Judd, Ebenezer Rich, Teresa Rich, Alexander Tackles, Philene Tackles, Asa Hill, Sarah Hill, Philetus Sprague, Laura Sprague, Elizabeth Knowlton, Henry Reid, Mary Bennett, Etsey Nelson, Desire Fisher and Huldah Wright.

It would seem that the first organization was short lived, for July 15th, 1819, the members of the Presbyterian or Congregational order met and resolved that the society should be known as the First Congregational Society of Middlebury, and elected Alexander Tackles, D. C. Judd, Ebenezer Rich, H. G. Walker, Philetus Sprague and Henry Wighteman the first trustees. The annual meeting of the society was fixed on the 1st Monday of July. In 1820 J. Eastland and Jedediah Palmer were elected trustees, and in 1821 Mr. Eastland was chosen deacon. Under date of August 8th is found the following record: "That D. C. Judd and J. Eastman be a committee to settle with Elder J. Bradley relative to an arrangement entered into with him for his supplying us with ministerial labors of our own order the past year." Elder Bradley was partly supported by this society, and in return was to exchange with Presbyterian ministers. An excellent feeling seems to have existed between Christians of various orders, all meeting together for Sabbath service in the academy. February 3d, 1822, it was voted to make application for admission to the Genesee Presbytery. March 23d Daniel C. Judd, Joseph Eastland and Timothy Judd were elected the first elders, and constituted the session. In the records of the society, under date of July 3d, is the following minute: "Voted unanimously that this society hereafter shall be known by the name of the First Presbyterian Society of Middlebury, N. Y."

In 1825 Joseph Gillett and H. G. Walker were elected elders. This year Rev. Eli Hunter, D. D., commenced his labors with this church, as their first stated supply, July 17th.

In 1826 the names of James C. Ferris and John B. Skinner first appeared as trustees, and the records of the session were first approved in presbytery.

On the 21st of March, 1829, the society met in the academy, and it was resolved unanimously to build a house of worship. Joel Harrison, H. G. Walker and Russel Abel were appointed a building committee. Deeds of the land for the site were drawn in favor of the society by Benedict Brooks and wife, for $450, and by Sylvester Wood and wife, for $125. The contract for building was let to Mr. Chester Hurd, of Warsaw; the foreman was Mr. John S. Culver. The raising of the frame was completed September 19th, and it was left partially unenclosed during the winter. In the spring of 1830 the work on the church was resumed. The church, when completed, was justly regarded as a beautiful edifice, fully equal to the best rural churches of that day. It was dedicated on the 9th of September. The pastor, Rev. Eli S. Hunter, preached the sermon. Jedediah Palmer was the regular leader of the choir, but in the dedicatory services Thomas Hastings, then of Geneseo, took charge of the music. D. C. Judd, Joseph Eastland, Timothy Judd, Joseph Gillet and H. G. Walker constituted the session. The trustees of the society were D. C. Judd, H. G. Walker, James C. Ferris, John B. Skinner, Russel Abel and Phineas Stanton.

On the 4th of June, 1832, the church made a call for the pastoral services of Norris Bull, D. D. Dr. Bull accepted, and became the first regularly called and installed pastor of the church. His pastorate continued about four years.

For about two years the church had occasional supplies. Rev. Messrs. Parten, Schaffer, Colton and Birge officiated during this time.

July 28th, 1838, the society called the Rev. Pliny Twitchell to be the pastor. Mr. Twitchell accepted, and entered at once on his labors.

February 7th, 1842, the church resolved to connect itself with the new Caledonia (old school) Presbytery.

In June of 1839 organ was placed in the church, chiefly by the instrumentality of General Stanton. It was made by Mr. Camp, of Warsaw.

Mr. Twitchell's pastorate continued till 1852, between fourteen and fifteen years. August 14th, 1852, Rev. John W. Wood was engaged as stated supply, and he continued his labors between six and seven years.

In 1858 Otis G. Keith was elected an elder, and Wales Cheney a deacon.

In 1859 the Rev. John Jones was installed pastor by the Presbytery of Genesee River. His pastorate continued three years. Rev. Charles Ray commenced his labors on the first Sabbath of September, 1862, and was installed October 30th. October 26th, 1870, Rev. Mr. Ray, on account of ill health, tendered to the session his resignation of the pastorate. During his eight years ministry seventy were added to the church on examination, and thirty-three on certificate. February 6th, 1871, a call was given to Rev. A. B. Morse, who, accepting, began work March 12th.

In 1867 the church edifice at the junction of Academy street and Hill road was remodeled and repaired at an expense of $7,000, anid it was rededicated January 2nd, 1868, Rev. Charles Ray, the pastor, preaching the dedicatory sermon.

The pastors from the organization of the society until the present time have been: John F. Bliss, 1817; Samuel Fuller, 1819; Salmon Hebard, 1820; E. J. Chapman, 1820, and Mr. Fitch, 1820; J. Bradley, 1821; Eli S. Hunter, 1825–32; Norris Bull, 1832–36; Pliny Twitchell, 1838–52; John W. Wood, 1852–58; John Jones, 1859–62; Charles Ray, 1862–70; and Andrew B. Morse, 1871, who still retains the pastorate.

The present board of elders consists of Otis G. Keith, chosen January 24th, 1858; Allen Wright, November 16th, 1862; Hugh T. Brooks, November 16th, 1862; John C. Paine, December 24th, 1871; Ethel C. Sherman, November 16th, 1862; Henry T. Strong, January 5th, 1878. Clerk of session, O. G. Keith. Deacons—Alexander Smith, November 16th, 1862; Edwin Stanley, December 17th, 1871; Thomas S. Cushing, December 17th, 1871. Trustees (elected first Monday in 1879)—Alexander Smith, Russel Barber, O. G. Keith, N. H. Gillet, John Ridge, E. C. Sherman. Clerk of society, T. S. Cushing. Treasurer, O. G. Keith.

The Sabbath-school connected with the church was organized in 1830. The officers for 1879 were: Superintendent, C. B. Matthews; assistant superintendent, T. S. Cushing; secretary and treasurer, H. S. Strong; librarian, E. C. Hayden, and an assistant secretary, a chorister and organist, together with 186 scholars.

During the present pastorate to date there have been added to the church seventy-nine on examination, and twenty-one on certificate; one hundred in all.

The whole number of members of the church from the beginning is 530. Of these 415 united by confession, and 115 by letter. The present membership is 195.

FIRST BAPTIST.

Among the early settlers were several Baptists. They often assembled for worship, and received several accessions about the year 1809.

On the 18th of September, 1810, a Baptist church was organized, under the name of "The First Baptist Church of Middlebury." A delegation was present from the church in Attica, Elder Reuben Osborne pastor, at that time the only Baptist church in all this region.

Seventeen persons constituted the church, viz.: Thomas Stetson, Eliphalet Owen, Francis Curtis, Jonathan Thompson, Salmon Smith, David Thompson, Oliver Curtis, Isaac Andrus, Abigail Owen, Betsey Curtis, Sally Thompson, Polly Curtis, Mrs. Geer, Clark Andrus, Theresa Smith, Sally Thompson, jr., and Hannah Curtis. In 1815 the church united with the "Holland Purchase Conference," having at that time thirty-nine members.

Elder Joseph Case was pastor during a portion of the period up to 1820. Thus far no very reliable records were kept. From 1820 to 1825 Elder Joshua Bradley labored with the church. In 1822 the Baptist church in Perry became a branch of this church, which relation was dissolved at the end of three years.

Elder Bradley was succeeded by Elder E. M. Spencer in 1825. As a result of the anti-masonic controversy which arose in 1827 the latter joined the Presbyterians, and his church suffered a decrease in membership of sixty-four.

In 1827 the church withdrew from the Holland Purchase Conference and united with the Genesee Baptist Association. For the next three years the desk was supplied wholly or in part by Elder David Bernard. In 1830 Elder Joseph Elliott began his labors as pastor of this church, and for two years divided his time between this and the West Middlebury, then known as the second Middlebury church.

In the summer of 1831 the society built a church edifice on what is now Main street, in the village of Wyoming, which was dedicated toward the close of the same year. From 1832 to 1838 Elder Elliot confined his labors to the church in Wyoming village. During his pastorate the church reached its highest membership, viz., 314. In 1838 Elder B. N. Leach became pastor of the church. He was followed in 1841 by Elder Jesse Elliot, who remained eight years. In 1849 Elder R. Morey commenced his labors with this people, and he remained three years.

His successor was Elder R. C. Palmer, in 1852, who staid two and a half years. In 1856 Elder H. Daniels assumed the pastorate, which he held for nearly four years. Elder A. A. Russell became pastor in 1860, and remained three years. In October, 1863, Elder William C. McCarthy became pastor, and remained until July, 1865. Elder J. Maloy preached as a supply from December 1st, 1865, to April 1st, 1866. Rev. Ebenezer Packwood commenced his pastorate with this people October 6th, 1866, and remained until January, 1869. From April, 1869, till July 8th, 1877, the pastor was Rev. M. Forbes. During his pastorate, Saturday evening December 9th, 1876, the church edifice was burned. September 22nd, 1878, a call was extended to Rev. I. N. Earl, who is the present pastor; he united with this church by letter May 31st.

After the burning of the church edifice services were held in the academy building until the erection of the new church, in the summer of 1879; which was built of brick, upon the site of the old church, at a cost of $7,500. In 1867 the society bought a parsonage for $1,000.

The first deacons were Eliphalet Owen, supposed to have been appointed when the church was first organized; Amasa Curtis, —— Hoyt, Daniel Brady, James M. Wallace, appointed in December, 1831.

The Sabbath-school connected with this church was organized about 1831. The present superintendent is Rev. I. N. Earl; assistant superintendent, L. D. Gould; secretary, Miss C. N. Wheeldon; treasurer, L. S. Gould; number of scholars, 100; average attendance, 82; number of teachers, 12.

METHODIST EPISCOPAL.

There having been little or no record kept of the official doings of this church, we are enabled to give only such facts of its history as can be gleaned from the "History of the Genesee Conference," which are very meagre, and others from tradition and from the memory of some of the pioneer members of the society.

John White was first a member of the society formed in Middlebury, across the creek, a little south from the present village of Wyoming, where he settled about 1808. "Jesse Van Norman was the leader, and Cyrus Storey, then a local preacher, was a member of the society, at the time a part of the Holland Purchase Mission. In 1808 to 1810 George Lane, James Mitchell, Joseph Gatchell, John Kimberlin and William Brown were the missionaries on that ground."

The society was incorporated January 9th, 1835, when the following trustees were elected: James C. Ferris, Horace Healy, Abner Corey, Stephen Panner, John Ewell and Philip Perkins.

During that year the society built a church edifice, of wood, on the site now occupied by the Methodist parsonage, at the crossing of Church and Mill streets. In 1849 the church was removed to its present location, and repaired and improved to correspond with the architectural ideas of that day. The society soon after built the present parsonage. The following clergymen have been appointed to this church by the annual conference: Revs. Peter Smith, 1835; John G. Jenkins, 1840; L. L. Waite, David Fellows, J. B. Hoyt, H. Hines, John C. Nobles, W. D. Buck, G. De LaMatyr (1856), C. S. Baker, Samuel Smith, L. S. Newman, E. K. Freeman, T. F. Parker, C. Eddy, J. F. Derr, R. E. Thomas, E. Beebe, L. S. Atkins, A. Staples and E. J. Batchelder, the present pastor.

The church property is valued at $7,000, and is free from debt. The church membership at present numbers fifty-five.

The Sabbath-school connected with this church was organized as early as 1835. The present superintendent is J. H. Reddish; average number of scholars, 45.

CEMETERY ASSOCIATION.

As it was the custom in the early settlement of the town to fence off neighborhood lots for burial purposes, without any one in particular to look after and care for them, so it continued to be until about 1847, when a general law was passed by the Legislature for the organization of "rural cemetery associations," for the better protection and preservation of burial grounds; and under such law was organized the Wyoming Cemetery Association, at Union Hall in the village of Wyoming, June 15th, 1878. The following named persons were elected trustees: S. Hawley, E. C. Sherman, C. J. Shaw, H. S. Strong, Thomas Cushing, H. C. Eastman, George Hammond, E. A. Durfee and David Keith. At a meeting of the trustees at Union Hall, on the 17th of June, 1878, the following officers were elected for the ensuing year: President, E. C. Sherman; vice-president, C.

J. Shaw; secretary, Thomas S. Cushing; treasurer, S. Hawley; auditing committee, Henry Eastman, David Keith.

The grounds of the association are located on a rise of ground west of and overlooking the village. They are richly ornamented with beautiful trees and evergreen shrubbery, and contain about two acres.

CORNET BAND.

The Wyoming Comet Band was organized June 1st, 1877, with the following named persons as original members: Charles Lamb, Robert E. Muir, Jesse Wright, Levi Gould, Lewis Burleigh, Myron Kelly, Frederick Webster, Howard Clark, Frederick Cushing, George Smith, Wilson Rice, Merrit Howard, Frank Childs, Dr. V. H. Jackson, Mark Freeman, John Boyce.

The regular meetings of the band are held on Saturday evening of each week, in Union Hall.

The present officers are as follows: Leader and musical director, Prof. H. G. Davis; second, Charles Lamb; president, Myron Kelly; treasurer and secretary, Frederick Cushing. The instruments are the property of the band association.

"THE VALLEY ERA."

October 28th, 1878, Frank B. Smith, a young typo and native of Warsaw, who had learned the printer's trade there, established weekly paper at this place, called the *Valley Era*, which he is still publishing.

DALE.

This village was settled as early as 1825, in which year Archibald Worden built a saw-mill where Loomis's steam saw-mill now stands, in the south part of the village.

The first frame house was built by Horace Hewett, on the site now occupied by H. K. Faunice's house, on the corner opposite the church. The old house is now used as a cooper shop, and stands in the rear of Faunce's store.

The first tannery at this place was built by Solomon Kinney, where John Babbitt now lives. He subsequently built two others here, but they have all gone to decay.

The first store at this place was opened in 1830 by Enos and Harry Wright, in the old building now standing opposite the grocery, and owned by S. S. Monroe.

The first tavern at this place was opened in 1831, by Amos Whiting, in the old building now standing opposite Faunce's store.

The first ashery was built by E. and H. Wright in 1832, near where the railroad depot now stands. A large heap of ashes still marks the spot where the old ashery stood.

The first physician at this place was George Angel, who located here in 1844.

The first farm settled near the village was that taken up by Jonathan Curtis, where Albertus Ewell now lives.

Ephraim Whaley built a saw-mill in 1816 on the town line, near Dale. Mr. Whaley is still living. He was born in Petersburgh, N. Y., in 1800, came with his father to this town in 1805 and located on the town line road.

Work on the railroad was commenced here in the fall of 1849, and the track laid in 1851, the workmen commencing both at Hornellsville and Attica, and connecting the rails on the farm now owned by Alanson Miller, just north of the village. There are now at this place a church, a schoolhouse, two stores, a blacksmith shop, a steam saw-mill and stave factory and feed mill carried on by J. M. Loomis, two cooper shops and a shoe shop. There are 150 inhabitants.

Ithar Thompson was the first postmaster in this part of the town. He lived two and a half miles southwest from the village, where Charles Thompson now lives. He was succeeded by Daniel Smith, who kept the office in his shoe shop, in one corner of his tannery, that stood on the corner near the depot. S. S. Monroe was appointed in 1846. He kept the office in his store, in the old building that stands opposite Vader's store on Main street. H. K. Faunce is the present postmaster.

FREE-WILL BAPTIST CHURCH OF DALE.

This society was organized May 8th, 1824, by Elder Herman Jenkins. Michael Simmons was elected clerk, and the second Saturday in each succeeding month was designated as a day to be observed for covenant meeting.

It was unanimously agreed that if any member neglect to attend monthly meetings for three successive times, such neglect should be a cause of trial.

The following are the names of members admitted to fellowship at that time:

> Michael Simmons, Peter S. Vader, Tobias Vader, Thomas West, Horace Hewett, James Prescott, John Malllson, Caty Vader, Sally Brotherton, Sarah Hewett, Joannah Hewett. Anna Vader, Huldah Mallison, Sarah Kent, Lydia Chapman, Levi Smith, Dorothy Prescott, Philinda Whaley, Elizabeth Curtis, Tacy Darling, Sarah Brockett, Pellna Smith Hewett, Almira Curtis, Oliver Perry, Caleb Hewett, Nathaniel Jenkins, Elnathan Baker, Lydia Mallison, John Bean, Hannah Hogle, Gideon Brainard, Lucina Ritter, Rezina Baker, Levi Brockett and Scutt Brocket.

March 12th, 1825, it was agreed to hold the monthly meetings alternately "at the school house near Micajah Brotherton's, at the school-house near Belah Butler's and at the school-house near William Chaffee's."

Curtis Vader and Nicholas Vader are believed to have been the first deacons.

In 1840 the society, having become quite strong, and feeling the necessity of a regular place of meeting other than the school-houses, resolved to build a meeting-house, and the present large and substantial church edifice was built. It was dedicated in February, 1841.

The following list of pastors have served this people, and for the time named, as near as can be ascertained: Rev. Jeremiah Folsom, who preached here in 1816, and occasionally for several succeeding years; from 1824 to 1840, Rev. Hermon Jenkins; May 9th, 1840, to November 16th, 1844, Rev. D. M. L. Rollins; January 11th, 1845, till November 18th, 1846, Rev. H. N. Plumb, whose salary was fixed at $200 per year; January 9th, 1847, to November 18th, 1847, Rev. O. Johnson; January 10th, 1848, to March 15th, 1849, Rev. Mr. Hitchcock; August 11th, 1849, to March, 1852, Rev. H. Blackman; March 28th, 1852, to January, 1854, Rev. L. I. Madden. Next followed Rev. Mr. Perry, who supplied the pulpit for a while, when he was succeeded by Rev. William A. Lighthead, who resigned his pastorate May 3d, 1860. The pulpit was supplied by Rev. Messrs. Perry and Madden until January, 1861, when Rev. H. Gilman was installed as pastor, who remained until January, 1868; from May 3d, 1868, to January 7th, 1871, Rev. S. B. Andrews was pastor; Rev. L. B. Starr was installed May 6th, 1871, and remained until the pastorate of Rev. G. W. Knapp commenced, April 1st, 1876. The latter remains the pastor. The present membership is 181; value of church property, $3,000.

The present trustees are Alanson Miller, elected December 25th, 1876; John Jones, elected November 24th, 1877; and Isaac Chase, elected November 30th, 1878. W. H. P. Smith is the present church clerk.

The Sunday-school was organized as early as 1830. At present there is a flourishing school of 175 scholars, with 50 scholars in the primary department, under Mrs. Knapp, and the whole under the superintendence of Edwin Smith, Esq.

DALE CEMETERY ASSOCIATION.

At a meeting of the citizens of Dale and vicinity at the Free-Will Baptist church, November 29th, 1873, Isaac Chase, Zadoc Nichols, Horace Jones, Charles D. Thompson, E. S. Smith and Orin Smith were elected trustees of the above named association. It was decided to hold the annual meetings of the association on the last Saturday in November of each year. Upon the adjournment of the general meeting, the trustees elected the following officers of the association, to serve for one year: President, Zadoc Nichols; vice-president, Charles D. Thompson; secretary, E. S. Smith; treasurer, H. R. Farmer.

The trustees subsequently purchased three acres and a quarter north of the village from George Jenks and wife, for $323, and of Orin Smith and wife, for $50, the right of way from the Gulf road along the west side of their farm to the cemetery grounds—a strip twenty feet wide; also, of P. Mallison and wife, for $3, a small corner of a lot adjoining the cemetery grounds.

The grounds were surveyed into burial lots of suitable size, which are held at $10 each for those outside of the center circle, and $20 each for those inside the circle.

The officers elected November 30th, 1878, were: Zadoc Nichols, president; J. M. Smith, treasurer; E. S. Smith, secretary; trustees—Z. Nichols, J. M. Smith, O. Smith, E. S. Smith, Charles D. Thompson and Charles Weber.

Eng^d by Geo E. Perine N York.

John B. Skinner

BIOGRAPHICAL.

JUDGE JOHN B. SKINNER

Judge John B. Skinner. This eminent citizen of western New York, long a resident of the village of Wyoming, died June 6th, 1871, at the home of his later years, No. 155 North street, Buffalo. The following biographical sketch, originally published in the Buffalo *Courier*, is extracted from a memorial volume containing the tributes of the pulpit and the press, statesmen and corporations to the memory of its illustrious subject.

John B. Skinner, son of Benjamin Skinner, of Williamstown, Berkshire county, Mass., was born July 23d, 1790, in a house erected by Colonel Simonds, his maternal grandfather, on the bank of the Hoosack river. His paternal grandfather was the Rev. Thomas Skinner, a graduate of Harvard University, and during his whole ministerial life pastor of the Congregational church at Westchester, Conn. His father was one of the first settlers of Williamstown; assisted in the erection of Williams College, and was ever liberal and efficient in support of the interests of the church and every Christian and benevolent enterprise. John B. graduated from Williams in 1818; read law with the Hon. David Buel, of Troy, and after attending a course of lectures at the law school of Judges Reeves and Gould, at Litchfield. Conn., we understand that he spent some time in Governor Marcy's office, but whether before or after his admission to the bar we do not learn. Between young Skinner and the governor there existed a warm friendship, which only terminated with the death of the latter. He was admitted to the Supreme Court of the State of New York in August, 1821. His advantages were of the highest order; the young student knew how to use them for what they were worth, and with a thorough knowledge of his profession, high aspirations and a determination to succeed, he entered upon his career as a lawyer. He commenced practice in the town of Middlebury, near the center of the old county of Genesee, at present known as the village of Wyoming, in the county of the same name—both named by him.

His thorough knowledge of the law, his indefatigable industry, his enthusiasm and eloquence, and genial manners soon attracted attention, and business flowed in upon him from the neighboring counties, which continued and increased until he retired from the practice. In the year 1826, when the two political parties were under the great leaders De Witt Clinton and Martin Van Buren, without his solicitation he was nominated for the Assembly; and although the opposing party had been in the ascendancy for years, he was elected by an overwhelming majority. He was re-elected the two succeeding years, without opposition, a compliment which had never before, and has never since, been paid to any individual in the district. As a member of the Legislature he was among the most prominent He was chairman of the committee upon literature, and of many important select committees; and the journals of the House and the political history of the period supply ample evidence as to how admirably he discharged his duties. In the year 1838 he was, at the solicitation of the bar, nominated by Governor Marcy and unanimously confirmed by the Senate circuit judge and vice-chancellor of the eighth district. In 1846 he was appointed district judge of the Court of Common Pleas, which office he held until the change of the constitution abolished the office. In 1852 he was, with the Hon. Horatio Seymour, appointed State delegate to the Baltimore convention which nominated General Pierce for President; and the next year one of the Presidential electors to cast for him the vote of the State. In 1858 he was appointed attorney of the United States for the northern district of New York, an office of much responsibility and greatly sought for, but which, owing to his business in the State courts, he respectfully declined.

In 1830 Mr. Skinner was married to Catharine, only daughter of Richard M. Stoddard, one of the most prominent of the early settlers of western New York. This amiable and accomplished lady died in 1838. He was again married in 1867, to Sarah A., daughter of Henry G. Walker, of Wyoming, who bore him one daughter, his only child, the late Mrs. Josiah Letchworth.

At an early period of his residence at Wyoming Judge Skinner united with the Presbyterian church, of which he was soon appointed an elder, and his liberal and active efforts contributed much to raise this church from a feeble beginning to a position of influence in that community. He identified himself with the moral and religious progress of an active and earnest people, and at the time of his removal from the county was president of the Bible, temperance and colonization societies; and it may be truly said of him that few men have been more widely known or have exerted a more salutary influence.

In the year 1860 he removed to this city, having previously secured one of the finest locations here; and since that time he has enjoyed, in comparative retiracy, the fruits of an active and laborious life. At the time of his death he was a member of the board of education of the Presbyterian church; president of the board of trustees of the New York State Asylum for the Blind, an institution recently established at Batavia, and one of the noblest charities of the age; president of the State normal school, in this city; vice-president of the reformatory at Warsaw, a member of the board of trustees of the Buffalo Female Acadamy, and also a member of the board of trustees of the Buffalo City Savings Bank.

His broad and active benevolence invited the manifold responsibilities of a charitable and humane order which pressed upon him; and in the discharge of the duties incident to them he was gratifying his very highest ambition.

As an advocate few men in the State enjoyed a higher reputation than Judge Skinner. The known purity and uprightness of his character, his comprehensive knowledge of men, his great readiness and self-command, combined with an earnest and impressive manner, enchained the attention while it enlisted the sympathies of a jury, and he very rarely failed to carry them with him. As a judge he was clear, quick in apprehension and prompt in decision, and these characteristics rendered him useful, reliable and popular on the bench. Indeed, there were no qualities wanting in Judge Skinner to make him the consummate lawyer and the able jurist. His mind eminently fitted him for statesmanship, but he fairly shrank from public life, and whatever of political prominence he had he owed first to an ardent devotion to the principles of the Democratic party, and secondly to an intense desire on the part of those who knew him to compel him to act in public life. Undoubtedly the most reasonable explanation of his avoidance of everything that could be interpreted to mean political ambition was his great love for his profession and his undying attachment to persons, places and things. It is said of him that if he owned an old horse it was to him the best horse in the world and worthy of his kindest and most thoughtful attentions, and he never wished to part with it. The same constancy was expressed toward everything he loved, and such men out of their habitat are never truly themselves. He was a man of the very strongest convictions; and as a Democrat of the old school, and a communicant in the Presbyterian church, his faith was unqualified and unwavering. The religious element of his character was largely unfolded, and with an active and profound benevolence, he was a thoroughly Christian gentleman. He was catholic and liberal in his views; was decidedly an optimist, and. viewed human nature, with all its shortcomings, with the kindliest eyes; and his masculine will and power were so blended with exquisite tenderness as to present him as the incarnation of strength and delicacy. He has always been known for his fine sensibilities, and equally well for the irresistible power he exerted when arrayed against a bad man or a great wrong. Whenever he was compelled to apply the lash he threw the whole strength of his nature into the business and was merciless; but no appeal to his heart was ever made in vain. Through the iron of his character ran a vein of silver, and he was known of men to be as truly good as he was nobly strong. In his later years he filled the term "venerable" to perfection, and the radiance of his pure and lofty life, his fidelity to principle, his genuine manliness, his large, benevolence and his loving and lovable nature, should keep his memory green forever.

JOHN QUINCY ADAMS was born March 17th, 1836, in Stafford, Genesee county, and came to this town in 1858 from the place of his nativity. He was married November 8th, 1850, to Frances M. Cox, of Middlebury. Mr. Adams is a well known farmer, and is noted for his public spirit. He has always lent his aid in the erection of bridges and churches, and in other public improvements. Mr. and Mrs. Adams are members of the Baptist church. The former has long held the office of trustee; the latter has for years been a teacher in the Sunday-school.

SELDEN ALLEN was born October 27th, 1808, and died October 6th, 1871. He came to Middlebury from Minden, Conn., in 1815. February 27th, 1841, he married Miss Eunice C. French, of Pavilion, who was born July 15th, 1819. Mr. Allen was influential in measures looking to the construction of the State Line Railroad. His father, Silas Allen, was born in Minden, Conn., and came to Middlebury in 1815. He assisted materially in building Middlebury Academy and the Baptist church. Mr. Alien's mother, formerly Esther Bradley, was also a native of Connecticut. Sherman French and wife (formerly Charity Beach), father and mother of Mrs. Selden Allen, were born in Connecticut. Two of Mrs. Allen's brothers were soldiers during the Rebellion.

NATHAN BABBITT was born in Massachusetts, October 18th, 1808, and married Sophronia Holloway (born March 10th, 1810), of Middleborough, Mass., June 22nd, 1832. They have three children. The family removed to Middlebury in August, 1835. Mr. Babbitt, who owns a farm of one hundred and sixty-eight acres, has served the town as commissioner of highways two years. Mr. and Mrs. Babbitt are members of the Presbyterian church, and Mr. Babbitt helped to build the Free-Will Baptist church. Mrs. Babbitt has had charge of the Sabbath-schools in Dale.

MERITT R. BAILEY, farmer, was born May 22nd, 1829, in Middlebury, and was married November 28th, 1850, to Rosella Wilson, of that town. He has served as supervisor of the town four years; also as collector, and assisted materially in repairing the Baptist church at Middlebury. He has been clerk of the church of which his wife is a member twenty-one years. His father, Aaron Bailey, was born in Westmoreland county, Pa., in December, 1801, and came to Warsaw in 1806, locating west of the village, and spending his first night there in a cabin without doors or floor. He was deacon in the Baptist church forty years. He died in 1876. Mrs. Bailey's father, Ira Wilson, saw service as a captain in the war of 1812–14, and was afterwards appointed colonel of militia.

Mr. Bailey had two brothers in the late war, one of whom was a captain; the other is judge of the Court of Appeals in Chicago.

MYRON C. BAILEY was born in Middlebury, October 28th, 1842. November 14th, 1866, he married Rosetta M. Choate, of this town. He has served as constable and collector; is now assessor. He was a soldier in the late war. He is a member and deacon of the Middlebury Baptist church, and has been for five years teacher in the Bible class. Mrs. Bailey is also a Sunday-school teacher.

EDWARD BARBER was born in Washington county, August 17th, 1843. June 13th, 1871, he married Ella Miller, of Middlebury, who was born December 8th, 1847, the year in which Mr. Barber came to Middlebury from Washington county. They have two children. Mr. Barber is a farmer, and the owner of one hundred and forty acres of land. Mr. and Mrs. Barber are members of the Presbyterian church, and Mrs. Barber instructs a class in the Sunday-school.

RUSSEL BARBER was born in Vermont in 1810, came to Middlebury in 1846, and in 1849 married Parmella Fisher, of Covington, where her father, Thomas Fisher, was a settler in 1817, having previously lived for a time in Stafford, Genesee county. Mr. Barber has been twice married. He has three children by the first and two by the present wife. The family are members of the Presbyterian church. Charles Barber, their youngest son, is a graduate of Rochester University, and is preparing for the medical profession.

SPENCER H. BRADLEY was born in Middlebury, April 19th, 1819. He is a farmer and the owner of one hundred and ten acres. December 9th, 1863, he married Sally P. Smith, of York, Livingston county. His father, Abijah Bradley, was born in Connecticut, August 28th, 1796, and came to Middlebury in 1811, accompanied by his wife. They made the journey with a wagon, and were eighteen days on the road. The family have for many years been connected with the Baptist church. Abljah helped to build the first Baptist church at Wyoming and the academy at Middlebury. Allen Smith, father of Mrs. Bradley, was born in Connecticut, September 18th, 1780, and came to York, Livingston county, in 1818, accompanied by his wife, formerly Patience Graham. There were seven children in the family.

FRANKLIN W. CAPWELL was born in Middlebury, April 21st, 1823. January 1st, 1850, he married Ellen C. Cory, of Middlebury. He is an insurance agent. He has served fifteen years as justice of the peace, ten years as president of the Genesee Baptist Sunday-school Association, and twenty-one years as secretary of the Wyoming Sabbath-school Teachers' Association. Mrs. Capwell has been a teacher in the Baptist Sunday-school. Peter Capwell came to Middlebury from Albany county in 1808. Two families, consisting of fourteen persons, and all their earthly possessions were conveyed to their future home in a covered wagon, camping out in the woods nights, and being guided on their journey, which consumed two weeks, by blazed trees. Upon their arrival the first few meals of which Mr. Capwell partook were spread on the cover of a chest. The first table in use in the family in their new home was made of lumber which Mr. Capwell brought a distance of twelve miles on his back and on horseback. On the way he was chased by a panther. He received his education after his marriage, at the common schools, which he attended with his oldest son. He was one of the originators of the old Middlebury Academy, of which he was treasurer for many years, and is remembered as an ex-soldier of the war of 1812–14. He was a deacon in the Baptist church and a militia captain. Abner Cory, Mrs. Capwell's father, came from Rhode Island in 1817, and returned to his native State three times on horseback.

ISAAC CHASE was born in Orangeville, May 12th, 1811, and came to Middlebury from Attica in 1855. He is a farmer, and has served the town as justice of the peace and highway commissioner, and the Free-Will Baptist church as trustee. He was married March 26th, 1835, to Sally Benham, of Attica, who died December 27th, 1865. December 16th, 1869, he married Mrs. Miranda Ellis, of Parma. He has eight children living, seven of whom are the issue of his first marriage.

OSCAR CHABB was born in Attica, October 31st, 1838, and was married October 5th, 1870, to Miss Mary A. Benchley, of Middlebury. He came to the town in January, 1866, and is a school teacher, station agent and telegraph operator. He has served as collector two years and has been elected town clerk.

SAMUBL A. COX was born February 11th, 1833, in Middlebury. He was married May 19th, 1859, to Amanda Owen, of Middlebury. They have six children. He has been a blacksmith and carpenter, and for twenty year a farmer. Mr. and Mrs. Cox are members of the Baptist church, and Mrs. Cox has long been a Sabbath-school teacher.

HENRY CRONKHITE was born December 81st, 1836, in Middlebury. He was married September 9th, 1866, to Jenny L. Barrett, of this town. He served as a soldier in the late war, and is now a farmer. He has been chosen to the offices of inspector of elections and excise commissioner, and is a trustee of Middlebury Academy. He is a member of the Baptist church. His father, A. H. Cronkhite was born in Rensselaer county, November 1st, 1804, and came to Middlebury, of which town he was the first supervisor in 1831. The maiden name of Mr. Cronkhite's mother was Matilda Baldwin. Mr. and Mrs. Cronkhite were Baptists. Dyer Barrett, Mrs. Cronkhite's father, was born in Rutland, Vt., December 10th, 1814. He was supervisor of Middlebury when it formed a part of Genesee. Her mother, formerly Louisa Clark, was born May 6th, 1825.

HORACE G. CUSHING was born in Wyoming, January 29th, 1832. He was married January 12th, 1860, to Miss Mary Miller, of his native place, who is a member of the Baptist church. Mr. Cushing is a member of the firm of Cushing Brothers, dealers in drugs, medicines, books, stationery, groceries, etc., at Wyoming. The records show that he has served the town as clerk. He is a member of the Masonic fraternity, and belongs to Warsaw Lodge, No. 549. He states that the Brothers of the Mystic Tie held communications in Middlebury at an early day. Hezekiah Miller, Mrs. Cushing's father, was born in Massachusetts in 1797.

THOMAS S. CUSHING, senior member of the firm of Cushing Brothers, was born January 5th, 1829, in Wyoming, and married Miss Lavinia Pratt, of Syracuse, in 1859. Mr. Cushing was appointed postmaster by President Pierce, and held the office nine years. He is now notary public. He owns sixteen acres of land in the village of Wyoming. The Cushing brick block is one of the finest in the section. Mr. and Mrs. Cushing, who have four children, are members of the Presbyterian church, of which the former is clerk, and toward the building of the house of worship Mr. Cushing was a liberal contributor. Seth Cushing, father of Thomas S. and Horace G. Cushing, was born in Hingham, Mass., in 1795. He came to Wyoming some time previous to 1820, and was the first classical teacher in Middlebury Academy, and continued his services in that capacity for twenty years. In consideration of his valuable services his children were educated at the academy free of expense. He died in February, 1837. His wife, formerly Persia Stanton, sister to General Phineas Stanton, was born in Woodstock, Vt. She died August 29th, 1878.

MATTHEW DODDS was born in Yorkshire, England, May 1st, 1848. February 27th, 1878, he married Harriet D. Warren, of Warsaw, by whom he has had two children. He came to America from Yorkshire, England, in the fall of 1865, and is one of the most successful bee keepers in western New York, keeping fifty swarms. Russell Warren, Mrs. Dodd's father, was born in Washington county, October 28th, 1808, and settled in Wyoming county in 1826. Emily Thompson, afterward Mrs. Russell Warren, was also a native of Washington county. She came to Wyoming county in 1824, traveling with an ox team and consuming twenty-two days in the journey. She died March 21st, 1876. Mr. and Mrs. Warren had nine children. The latter was a member of the Methodist church thirty-five years.

ERNEST A. DURFEE was born in Massachusetts, July 29th, 1826, and came to Middlebury in 1831. He is a leading farmer, owns three hundred and twenty acres of land, and has been prominently identified with the best interests of the town. His father, Thomas Durfee, was born in 1804, and brought his family to the town at the date above given. He owned at one time nearly four hundred acres of land in the States of New York and Michigan. He was supervisor and held other town offices. Mr. Durfee's grandmother lived in Rhode Island during the Revolutionary war. One day, when she was about twelve years old, some British officers entered the house, and in a scuffle which ensued she was thrown on her face and her nose was broken by the concussion.

LEANDER EASTMAN was born in Genesee county, October 9th, 1815, and has been twice married; the last time, September 14th, 1865, to Harriet Cox, of Middlebury, who was born July 23d, 1830. By his first wife he has two children; by his second, one. Nathaniel Eastman, his father, came to Middlebury in 1817, and lived for fifty years on the farm he then took up. Mr. Eastman is a teacher and farmer, and Mrs. Eastman is a member of the Methodist church and has been a teacher of common and Sunday-schools.

Miss M. P. EWELL was born in Middlebury, May 12th, 1818. She was educated at the Middlebury Academy, under the instruction of Joseph Elliott, and has been a teacher in the common schools. She manifests a great interest in Sunday-schools and Bible classes, and has long been a teacher of the same. She is a member of the Middlebury Baptist church. Her home is with her brother, Hiram Ewell. Her mother taught, in a log school-house, the first school in the neighborhood of Wyoming. She was a woman of great religious influence, and was known as a Christian guide at an early day.

WILLIAM H. EWELL was born in Middlebury, December 1st, 1830. October 20th, 1852, he married Miss Emerancy J. Miller, of Middlebury, by whom he has eight children. He is a farmer, and owns one hundred and forty-six acres of land. He has served as assessor. Mrs. Ewell is a member of the Presbyterian church.

ELISHA GAT was born in Middlebury, December 15th, 1835. May 25th, 1857, he married Harriet Smith, of Middlebury. Mr. Gay built a cheese factory, which has been in successful operation for ten years. He gave $500 toward the endowment fund of Pike Seminary. His father was born in 1790, and came to Wyoming county from Oneida county penniless, but in time became the owner of seven hundred acres of land. His grandfather was a Revolutionary soldier.

SIMEON HOWARD was born in Attica, January 25th, 1837, and came to Middlebury in 1854. He is a farmer, and for the past ten years has dealt in produce. He has helped to lay out roads, and interested himself in public affairs. He is a member of the Ancient Order of United Workmen. At present he holds the office of assessor. He was married January 3d, 1867, to Ellen Dodson, and March 18th, 1879, to Loeza Taber, both of Middlebury.

ORTAVILLE R. HOWES was born September 14th, 1844, in Middlebury. January 29th, 1888, he married Mias Mary J. Dodson, of Friendship, Allegany county. He is a farmer, and has been chosen assessor. He is a member of the Free-Will Baptist church, and of Warsaw Lodge, No. 547, F. & A. M. Mrs. Howes is a member of the Baptist church. William Howes, his father, served in the war of 1812–14. He came on foot from Massachusetts to Middlebury, his total wealth consisting of eighteen Spanish dollars. Subsequently he amassed a fine property. The father of William Howes and grandfather of Ortaville R. Howes was a Revolutionary soldier. Elmer Dodson, Mrs. Howes's brother, was a soldier in the late war and died in Andersonville prison.

HIRAM HUNT was born in Newstead, Erie county, and married Hattie Cox, of Middlebury, and came from Erie county to this town, where he is a farmer, March 25th, 1855. David Cox, Mrs. Hunt's father, was born in Vermont, in 1814. He came to Middlebury empty-handed, and by the exercise of perseverance and industry paid for over seven hundred acres of land. He was formerly a teacher in the common schools, and for two terms served the town as supervisor. He died April 10th, 1874. He married Aurelia Dow (born February 1st, 1818,) in 1846. Her father came from Vermont in 1840 and is living, at the age of ninety-two.

NELSON W. HUNTINGTON was born in New Haven, Vt., October 23d, 1821, and came from there to Middlebury in 1864. November 18th, 1849, he was married to Mary Conklin, and February 26th, 1861, he married Rosanna Wilson. The present Mrs. Huntington's father was an early settler in the town, and among other pioneer experiences often related that of the loss of his only porker by the bold descent of a bear upon his sty. Mr. and Mrs. Huntington are members of the Free-Will Baptist church.

OTIS H. KEITH was born in Easton, Mass., in 1842, and married Miss Taylor, of Perry, December 25th, 1861. He has since 1844 been a resident of Wyoming, where he is a leading dealer in dry goods, groceries, hats and caps, boots and shoes and general merchandise. He has been town clerk two years. Mr. and Mrs. Keith have for fourteen years been members of the Presbyterian church, and Mrs. Keith renders efficient service in the Sunday-school. Mr. Keith's father, Otis G. Keith, was born in Easton, Maas.

GIORGE M. MILLER was born in Middlebury, August 23d, 1834, and married Mary Bradley, of Middlebury, by whom he has a son and a daughter. He is a farmer, and has assisted in laying out roads in the town. Mr. and Mrs. Miller are Baptists, and in the erection of the Wyoming Baptist church he rendered valuable aid.

HENDERSON MILLER was born August 3d, 1834, in Middlebury. January 1st, 1864, he married Laura E. Decker, of Ohio, who was born August 18th, 1835. Mr. and Mrs; Miller are prominent in the Presbyterian church, which they assisted in rebuilding. They have five children. Mr. Miller has helped to lay out roads in the town. He is a farmer and owns two hundred and fifty acres. The tree in which Shattuck caught his foot grew upon H. Miller's farm. He saved his life by severing the foot at the ankle joint with a jack knife.

HEZEKIAH MILLER was born in Williamsburgh, Mass., March 25th, 1798, and arrived in Middlebury February 12th, 1814, having journeyed from his native town on foot in fourteen days He is a farmer, and has served the town as commissioner of highways six years, assessor six years, and as overseer of the poor six or eight years, and was trustee of the Middlebury Academy. Mr. Miller has helped to build all of the churches in Middlebury, and is a liberal contributor toward the erection of the now unfinished Baptist church of Wyoming. Charles F. Miller, his son, served in the late war, and was for a time a prisoner of war at Belle Isle. Mr. Miller has been twice married—the first time May 31st, 1882, to Rosa L. Newton, of Iowa, by whom he had four children. His present wife, Lucy, had been previously married and had four children. Mr. and Mrs. Miller have been members of the Baptist church forty and forty-five years respectively. The former has been trustee.

JOHN S. MILLER was born May 12th, 1819, in Middlebury, and was married November 18th, 1849, to Sarah G. Smith, of Middlebury. He is a farmer, and has been instrumental in laying out roads and building school-houses and churches. His father, Aaron Miller, was born in Williamsburgh, Mass., February 8th, 1782, and came with an ox team (the journey consuming three weeks) to Middlebury in 1812, and cleared the farm where John S. Miller now lives. In the pioneer days the nearest store was at Batavia, and Mr. Miller was obliged to go twenty miles to mill. Seth Smith, Mrs. Miller's father, saw service in the war of 1812, and received a land warrant from the government. Mr. Miller's grandmother died at the age of ninety-seven; Mrs. Miller's at one hundred and two.

SIDNEY S. MONROE, farmer and owner of one hundred and seventy-five acres, was born in Hoosac, N.Y.,, January 30th, 1804, and was married October 18th, 1832, to Harriet Kemp, who was born September 10th, 1811, and who has borne him six children. He came to Middlebury in 1842 from Genesee county. He served as constable in Onondaga county eight years, and for the same length of time in Genesee county. Mr. Monroe's father, Samuel Monroe, was a soldier in the last war with England, and died of an epidemic soon after the battle of Queenston Heights. Mrs. Monroe's father, John Kemp, was a machinist, and by industry amassed a competency. He owned at one time one hundred and eighty acres of land, and served the town as highway, commissioner.

AMBROSE P. MOSHER was born in Schoharie county, February 8th, 1824, and came to Middlebury in 1845, having married, July 3d of that year, Mahala Cronkhite, of Otsego county. Mr. Mosher has been a blacksmith and a merchant and is now a farmer. Mrs. Mosher's father helped to haul the materials for Middlebury Academy. Mr. and Mrs. Mosher are members and the former a trustee of the Baptist church.

ZADOC NICHOLS was born in Attica, March 16th, 1824, and married Julia Hinman, of Warsaw, October 3d, 1850. Mr. Nichols's birthplace was over the town line, in Attica, but in the school district in which he lives. He is a farmer, and owns one hundred and ninety-eight and one-half acres. His father, Zadoc, sen., was an early settler. His only means of obtaining the necessaries of life was by the manufacture and sale of potash, which he was obliged to haul to Rochester to market with an ox team. His pioneer experiences were many. Mr. and Mrs. Nichols are members of the Free-Will Baptist church. Mr. Nichols is president of the new cemetery association.

JOSEPH NEWELL was born April 9th, 1807, in Rensselaer county, and came to Middlebury with his parents. He married Anna Warren, of Geneseo, Livingston county, June 20th, 1838. His father, Silas Newell, came to Wyoming county in 1809 from Rensselaer county with a team, requiring about seventeen days to perform the journey. He purchased four hundred acres of land, on which the village of Wyoming is located. He kept the first hotel there, which stood in the center of the road in front of the present town hall. It was a double log house with a frame addition. He next put up a barn on the site of the present hotel. At that time the nearest neighbors were a mile distent each way. He next built and opened a store. His next enterprise was a clothiery, which was operated by a man by the name of Carmible. Later he built the old Mansion House, on the site of the town hall, which was burned about eight years ago. In 1817 he built Middlebury Academy and also the first grist-mill, employing that year about fifty men. Joseph's mother bought the bell for the academy, which was the first ever hung west of the Genesee river. Joseph was the oldest son, and was a farmer from the age of fourteen up to thirty-one. From that time he has been the proprietor of Newell's Hotel. He has been a member of the Presbyterian church forty-five years and his wife forty-two years. Mr. Newell has always manifested a lively interest in the elevation of society, and has been a consistent and ardent advocate of temperance.

CHARLES F. NEWTON was born in Covington, August 8th, 1852. Orville H. Newton, his father, was born in Jefferson county, in 1826, and came to Perry in 1837. He returned to Jefferson county and enlisted as a soldier in the late war. While in the service he was afflicted with erysipelas and it was necessary to amputate his leg three times. He survived the last operation only two days. At the time of his death he had been two years in the service. Mr. Newton's mother (formerly Chloe Carlisle) was born in Warsaw, January 19th, 1828, and was married to Mr. Newton July 24th. 1851. They had five children. Mr. Charles F. Newton's grandfather was a soldier in the war of 1812 and died in the service. His great grandfather on his mother's side was on duty in the Revolutionary war.

ZENAS H. OWEN was born in Middlebury, February 23d, 1810, and was married January 29th, 1838, to Miss C. Ludden, of Bennington. They have twelve living children. The family are Baptists. He has served the public as constable, school inspector and trustee of Middlebury Academy. Mr. Owen's father, Eliphalet Owen, was born in Windham, Conn, May 9th, 1784, and came to Middlebury in June, 1806, settling on the farm now owned by his son. He was viewing this place with an idea of locating here at the time of the great eclipse of that year. Zenas Owen had two sons in the late war. After his settlement the nearest grist-mill was twenty-five miles away, and he was often obliged to crack his grain with a stump and pole mortar and pestle. He was many years a deacon in the Baptist church. One of his sons is a Baptist preacher. Mrs. Owen's parents were natives of Easthampton, Mass., and located in Bennington in 1808, where Mr. Ludden built the first framed house. They were two weeks on the journey, traveling with an ox sled. He was a member and for forty years clerk of the Baptist church, with which his wife was also connected. He was for years a teacher of vocal music.

SOLON PAGE was born in Addison county, Vt., November 17th, 1801. September 5th, 1821, he married Nancy Garfield, of Schroon, Essex county, where his father, Timothy Page (who died in 1810), was a well known physician; and came to Middlebury in 1844, where he has been a carpenter, a mill-wright, and for thirty-five years a farmer. His sons, Selieucius and James W. Page, enlisted in Company B, 2nd Iowa volunteers. The former was a color bearer and died with his country's flag in his hand, while participating in a gallant charge on Fort Dohelson, under command of General Grant. James W. served his term of three years; was discharged and re-enlisted, and served until the close of the war. Mrs. Page's brother, Caleb C. Garfield, was a soldier in the war of 1812–14, and took part in the battle of Plattsburgh.

TIMOTHY PAGE was born in Vermont, May 24th, 1797, and came to Middlebury in July, 1830. January 29th, 1835, he married Lydia Wilson, of Middlebury, by whom he has a son and a daughter. He is a farmer. Coming to Wyoming at a comparatively early day, Mr. Page has seen the village grow up, and has himself erected some of the best buildings there. Merritt C. Page, son of Timothy Page, was a graduate of Yale College. He was appointed attorney-general of Montana by President Grant, and died while fording a river in 1877. Ira Wilson, Mrs. Pages's father, was born in Vermont, in 1789, and came to Middlebury in 1808. He served in the war of 1812–14, and held a colonel's commission. He was justice of the peace a number of terms. His death occurred in 1875.

JOHN RIDGE was born in Devonshire, England, June 22nd, 1819. At the age of seventeen he came to America and located in Le Roy, Genesee county; and three years later came to Middlebury, where for thirty years he has successfully engaged in blacksmithing and the manufacture of carriages. During his long business career he was never sued and never sued but one man, and never sold a customer's note. At one time he owned three hundred acres of land, but retains only his home farm of fifty acres. May 18th, 1843, he married Miss Nancy Perkins, of Middlebury, daughter of Philip Perkins, a native of Rutland, Vt., who came to the town at an early day; by her he had four children. He held the office of highway commissioner. Mrs. Ridge's mother, formerly Cynthia Woodworth, was born in Canada, in 1799. Mr. and Mrs. Perkins were familiar with the hardships and vicissitudes of pioneer life. Mr. Ridge has served nine years as assessor, and is trustee of the Presbyterian church, of which Mrs. Ridge is also a member.

JOE SHERMAN was born February 13th, 1795, in Lanesborough, Mass, and came to Middlebury in 1818, locating where his son, Ethiel C. Sherman, now lives. He was superintendent of the poor in Genesee county before Wyoming was organized; was one of the commissioners to locate the site for the Wyoming county almshouse; laid out the "Gulf road" from Wyoming to Dale; assisted in building the Presbyterian church, and at his death (October 7th, 1882) left a legacy of 11,000 to that church, in which while living he had been a trustee and elder. Ethiel C. Sherman was born October 11th, 1818, the year of his father's advent in Middlebury, and was married March 6th, 1844, to Elizabeth E. Fargo, of Stafford, Genesee county, a native of Montville, Conn. He has served as commissioner of the R. and S. L. Railroad; was one of the building commitee of the Presbyterian church, and assisted in the erection of the town hail and the depot.

ANNA SMITH was born in Ireland, where her father died, and came to Middlebury with her mother in 1845. She married Orlando S. Smith, of Middlebury, May 17th, 1872, who died March 30th, 1876. Mr. Smith was a soldier during the war for the Union, and was in the battle of Bull Run and other engagements.

EDWIN S. SMITH was born in China, N. Y., April 25th, 1835. Hawley Smith, his father, came to Attica while yet a youth, from Otsego county, and for a time was captain of a militia company. Mr. Smith, who has been a carpenter and joiner, teacher and farmer, was married April 23d, 1856, to Elizabeth Perry, of Middlebury. He has served as school commissioner six years. Mr. and Mrs. Smith are members of the Free-Will Baptist church. The latter has been superintendent and teacher in Sabbath-schools.

FRANK B. SMITH, editor and proprietor of the *Wyoming Valley Era* and job printing office, was born in Warsaw, February 6th, 1854, and married Miss Belle Wisner, of Mount Morris, Livingston county, September 10th, 1878, and came to Wyoming the following month. He is a member of the Letchworth Rifles Band, and is identified with the Warsaw Episcopal church.

J. Monroe Smith was born in Attica, February 12th, 1831, and came to Middlebury in 1847. In 1814 Henry Smith, father of J. Monroe Smith, came to Middlebury, where he was highway commissioner. He also held commissions as lieutenant and captain of militia. Mr. Smith was married to Frances Johnson, of Bennington, September 5th, 1855. He has held the offices of assessor and inspector of elections, and is prominently identified with the Free-Will Baptist church.

William H. Smith was born in Henrietta, N. Y., October 31st, 1824. He is a farmer, owning one hundred and four acres of land, and has been a resident of Middlebury since the spring of 1848. Henry W. Smith, his father, was born in Montgomery county, in 1795, and removed early to western New York, and in 1831 to Warsaw. He was a member of the Dutch Reformed church, and held the offices of assessor and overseer of the poor. His mother, Clarinda Smith, was born in Connecticut, in 1786; was a member of the Methodist church, and died in 1858. Mr. Smith has two sisters—Mary A., a Congregationalist, and Miranda, a Methodist.

Henry S. Strong was born in Middlebury, August 18th, 1834. He is elder, teacher, treasurer and secretary in the Presbyterian church and Sunday-school, a member of the Wyoming County Sabbath-school Association, and of the executive committee. He is identified with Batavia Lodge, No. 475, F. & A. M. His father, Joshua Strong, was a soldier tn the war of 1812. March 17th, 1869, Mr. Strong married Miss M. Francena Bond, born July 10th, 1836, in Cattaraugus county; then of McKean county, where her father was one of the first to recognize the possibilities of the subsequent great coal developments. Mr. Strong served honorably in the Rebellion, in Company A., 9th N. Y. cavalry.

Nathan B. Strong was born June 22nd, 1823, in Pavilion, and was married September 11th, 1854, to Amanda Taggart. Thomas Taggart, her father, was born in Pennsylvania, and came to Livingston county when about six years old. He served in the war of 1812–14, and was taken prisoner and confined at Halifax. He was a comparatively early settler in Covington, and died in Wisconsin. Mr. Strong was a resident of Middlebury from 1831 until his death, May 12th, 1876. He was and Mrs. Strong is connected with the Presbyterian church. His widow and his son, William T. Strong, live on the homestead, a farm of one hundred and eight acres.

Charles D. Thomson was born in Middlebury, February 12th, 1837. January 6th, 1850, he married Miss A. E. Spring, of Attica. They have two children—Edward E., born in October, 1859 (who married Isabel Miller, in November, 1877), and a daughter. Athai Thomson, father of Charles D. Thomson, was born in Oneida county, in 1805, and came to Middlebury, where the son is a leading farmer and dairyman, in December, 1836. He was the first postmaster at West Middlebury.

David Vanderhayden was born in Schenectady, April 21st, 1800. October 12th, 1826, he married Eve Van Ess, of Middlebury, who died September 18th, 1850, and by whom he had eight children. September 23d, 1860, he married the widow of Charles Van Epps, of Saratoga. N. Y. (who died September 24th, 1854, and to whom Mrs. Vanderhayden was married December 15th, 1830). Mrs. Vanderhayden's maiden name was Betsy Wilson. By her first husband she had seven children, four of whom are living.

Her great-grandfather was a cooper, and worked at his trade after he was ninety years old. He died aged ninety-eight.

EBENEZER WEBSTER, who has circumnavigated the globe, was born in Dryden, Tompkins county, December 20th, 1824, and came from there to Middlebury in 1840 or 1841. He was for a time a member of the crew of a whaling vessel. In less hazardous occupation he has been a farmer and teacher, and has served the town as superintendent of common schools, as justice of the peace two terms and part of a third, and as supervisor three terms. He married Miss Lucinda Higgins, of Middlebury, July 6th, 1848. Both are members of the Baptist church, and have contributed to the up building of society, and have assisted in building school-houses and churches. Henry Higgins, father of Mrs. Webster, was born in Otsego county, in 1801, and came to Wyoming county in 1817. He was justice of the peace four years, assessor twelve or thirteen years, and for a time school commissioner. He also served as captain of militia. His wife was born in Pompey, N. Y., December 24th, 1807, and died November 23d, 1879. They were the oldest members of the Free-Will Baptist church of Dale. Constant Webster, Mr. Webster's father, came to Orangevillein 1887, and was highway commissioner.

ROLLIN R. WEBSTER was born in South Warsaw, December 20th, 1824. December 24th, 1846, he married Miss Laura Baker, of Warsaw, by whom he had seven children, four of whom are living. In April, 1869, he came to Middlebury, where he is a farmer and the owner of one hundred and fifty acres. He has been overseer of the poor six years, and is a member of and has been class leader in the Methodist church. His father, William Webster, was born in Vermont, May 4th, 1787, and came to Warsaw in 1808; and during his residence there he filled every office within the gift of his townsmen. His mother, formerly Charlotte Phelps, was born in Connecticut, April 28th, 1788. His uncle, Elizur Webster, was judge of Genesee county. John Baker and wife, Mrs. Webster's parents, were born in Vermont, and came to this county in 1822. Mrs. Baker's maiden name was Ruth Doan.

THE TOWN OF ORANGEVILLE.

THE first individual titles to lands lying in the present town of Orangeville were granted by the Holland Land Company, in 1803. In that year the following persons "took up" land, located principally in the eastern part of the town, the articles being issued in the order named: Elnathan Finch, James Sayer, John Place, Joseph Ethridge, Christopher Sly, Benjamin Sly and Benjamin Spencer. In the following year the only purchases made were by Solomon West and John Ames. In 1805 the number of sales increased to fourteen, the purchasers being: Seth Sherman, jr., Lemuel Chase, Seth Sherwood, Adial Sherwood, Ebenezer Tyrrill, James Coates. Samuel Wilson, Enos Smith, John Wilcox, James Duncan, Gideon Sly, Noah Willis, Elisha Doty and John Grover. During 1806 articles were taken by Aaron Kinsman, Silas Beckwith, Isaac Gardner, Truman Lewis, John Grover, Stephen King, Seth Sherwood, Jacob Howe, Reuben Morse, Ahaz Allen, Shubael Atkins, Lyman Cady and Levi Atkins.

The foregoing is a complete list of those who had taken articles to land in this town previous to January 1st, 1807, two of whom, John Grover and Seth Sherwood made two purchases of land each.

The following record of early deeds of land in this town is from the books of the Holland Land Company:

James Sayer, 1806, part of lot 14; Daniel Kelly, 1807, part of lot 13; Adial Sherwood, 1809, part of lot 21; Joshua Mitchell, 1809, part of lot 40; Daniel Tupper, 1810, part of lot 7; Nathaniel Tupper, 1816, part of lot 10; John Grover, 1810, part of lot 29; Ephraim Durfee, 1810, part of lot 34; Samuel Ward, 1812, part of lot 14; Peter White, 1812, part of lot 50; Rial J. Merryfield, 1813, part of lot 13; Adial Sherwood, 1813, lot 22; Amasa Smith, 1818, part of lot 39; John Grover, 1814, part of lot 37; Jerry Merrell, 1814, part of lot 37; James Coats, 1814, part of lot 62; Elizur Webster, 1815, lot 9; Elizabeth Merryfield, 1815, part of lot 21; Ryal J. Merryfield, 1815, part of lot 21; Lemuel Chase, 1815, part of lot 28: Anson Sherwood, 1815, part of lot 30; Noah and Harvey Merrill, 1815, part of lot 38; Truman Lewis, 1816, part of lot 28; Reuben Stone, 1816, part of lot 28; Silas Grover, 1816, part of lot 29; S. Wheeler and W. Farmer, 1816, part of lot 30; John Tilton, 1817, part of lot 26; Jotham Butler, 1817, part of lot 26; Ephraim Durfee, 1817, part of lot 34; Alanson Curtiss, 1817, lot 45; Peter White, 1818, part of lot 63; John S. Cowden, 1818, part of lot 54; J. D. M. Collins, 1819, part of lot 7; Joseph Duncan, 1819, part of lot 7; Oliver Lee, 1819, part of lot 28; Jeremiah Butler, 1820, part of lot 10; Elizur Webster, 1821, part of lot 1; William R. Bartlett, 1822, part of lot 15; Phineas Butler, 1822, part of lot 9; Jerry Merrell, 1823, part of lot 29; Joshua Mitchell, 1822, parts of lots 31 and 32: Phineas Butler, 1824, part of lot 2; George A. Johnson, 1825, part of lot 61; Jane Ferguson, 1827, part of lot 3; Giles Benson, 1827, part of lot 2; John Head, 1827, part of lot 17; Jeremiah Butler, 1828, part of lot 10; Calvin Baptist church, 1828, part of lot 20; Phineas Butler, 1829, part of lot 2; Jonathan and Joseph Head, 1829, part of lot 18.

John Duncan and James Sayer, relatives by marriage, were the pioneer settlers of the town. They were immediately followed by Elisha Doty and Lemuel Chase. Duncan came, with his family from Orange county, N. Y., and located on the south part of lot 13 in the winter or spring of 1805, cutting his way through to his land as best he could; a few years later he removed from the town. Elisha Doty settled the same spring on lot 12, nearly opposite Mr. Duncan. Each of these pioneers owned a small amount of stock, which browsed in the woods during the summer months, and was hunted and driven home evenings, generally by the women. Mrs. Duncan once in search of the cows lost her way, and had to pass a restless and perilous night in the forest.

James Sayer was born in the town of Warwick, Orange county, N. Y., November 26th, 1768. He took an article to a tract of land on lot 14 in 1803, and in the first months of 1805 came from Ontario county, bringing his family with him, and permanently located on the southwest corner of the lot, where he carved out a home, planted the first orchard, and continued to reside most of the time until his death, January 29th, 1843. His first wife was Abigail Duncan, of Dutchess county, to whom he was married several years previous to locating in Orangeville. She died in 1807. For his second wife he married Mrs. Rebecca Adair. His son, Benjamin Sayer, was born in Dutchess county, N. Y., May 22nd, 1799, and came to Orangeville with the family in 1805, where his entire after life was spent. He died September 29th, 1847.

Adial Sherwood and his brother, Seth Sherwood, came from Cayuga county and secured articles to unusually large tracts of land in 1805. The former located on lot 22. After several years he removed westward, and became the founder of the "Sherwood tavern stand," a few miles east of Buffalo. He was married in Orangeville in 1809, to a Miss Wood, a native of Maryland. Seth Sherwood also left the town.

Silas Merrifield emigrated from Massachusetts to Cayuga county, N. Y., in 1805, and to Orangeville in 1806. He subsequently bought and located on lot 21—three hundred and sixty acres. He was married in 1808 to Elizabeth Peacock, a native of Maryland, and died in February, 1814. The farm continued in the possession of his family, and is now occupied by his son, William Merrifield.

Truman Lewis, born November 5th, 1784, in Farmington, Conn., set out for Oneida county, N. Y., in 1806, on foot, with an ax, a little bundle of clothing and a pillow. He came to Orangeville, and located on part of lot 28. Here he won an enviable competence. He represented Genesee county in the Legislature in 1835 and 1836, and was appointed the first treasurer of Wyoming county. He was an ensign in the war of 1812. He was one of the founders and supporters of the Presbyterian church of Orangeville. He lived on the farm of his own making most of the time until his death, which occurred September 15th, 1865.

A large and enterprising family named Merrell located near the center of the town from 1807 to 1811. Noah Merrell, the father, was born in Litchfield county, Conn., in 1758, and was married in 1780 to Hepsey Pettibone, of Norfolk, Conn. They reared a family of nine children, all born in Connecticut. In 1802 Mr. Merrell emigrated to Addison county, Vt.; thence to Westmoreland, Oneida county, N. Y., in 1804; and in October, 1811, he came to Orangeville, and took up sixty acres on lot 38. Here he spent the remainder of his life, dying August 26th, 1839. His wife died February 9th, 1840. Mr. Merrell was a soldier in the Revolution under General Poor, volunteering at the age of sixteen. He was present at the surrender of Burgoyne, and participated in several engagements.

Noah Merrell, jr., his eldest son, was born February 24th, 1781. He settled on lot 37, in Orangeville, in 1810. He was a shoemaker and tanner, and tanned the first leather in this town in 1811. His first tannery consisted of rude vats out of door and covered with bark. He subsequently built and operated one on the north part of lot 29. He engaged in the mercantile business about 1817, at Orangeville Center. He was the first supervisor of the town. In 1835 he sold out here and removed to Ohio, where he died.

Jeremiah Merrell, the third son of Noah, was born May 30th, 1785, and came to Orangeville from Oneida county in February, 1811, settling on the northeast corner of lot 37. About 1816 he built a frame tavern at Orangeville Center, of which he was many years proprietor. He was the first postmaster there, which office he held nearly thirty years. He continued a resident of this place until his death.

Harvey Merrell, the fourth son, was born July 28th, 1789. He came from Oneida county to Orangeville in October, 1809, and subdued and improved a tract on lot 38. He assisted in making the first road from Warsaw to Orangeville Center. On February 13th, 1816, he was married to Mary Hoxsie, of Rensselaer county, N. Y. She died October 22nd, 1878. They had nine children, all born on the homestead. Mr. Merrell died here June 19th, 1879.

Ephraim Durfee was born in Tiverton, Rhode Island, June 12th, 1785, and in 1801 removed with his parents to Broadalbin, Fulton county, N. Y. There he remained until 1810, when he married Polly Clawson, of that county, and immediately emigrated to Orangeville. He bought lot 34 (three hundred and sixty acres) and spent his life on the place. He died January 15th, 1879. He had nine children, all of whom were cradled in an ordinary sap trough. Mr. Durfee gave to most of his children well arranged farms in the vicinity of his own house. He was an exemplary member of the Society of Friends for over sixty years, and an industrious and respected citizen.

John S. Cowdin, born in Fitchburg, Mass., in 1785, emigrated thence to Orangeville in February, 1811, purchasing a farm on lot 54, upon which a log house had been built and a small clearing made. Here he lived until his death in 1861. His brother, Putnam Cowdin, was born in 1783, and in the spring of 1811 located on lot 46. In 1851 he removed to Strykersville, where he died in 1857.

Craig Cowdin was born in Fitchburg, Mass., in 1781. He came to Orangeville in 1813, and lived on lot 38 until his death, in 1847.

John Tilton was born in Martha's Vineyard, Mass., December 20th, 1785. In 1787 his father, Cornelius Tilton, removed to Kennebec county, Me., where John remained until twenty one years of age, when he came to New York, staying in Albany county one season. In 1811 he came to Orangeville and bought a farm of one hundred and fifty acres on lot 26. He was first married in 1814 to Elizabeth Butler, of Washington county; afterward (October 22nd, 1824) to Amarilla Doty, of Orangeville, who was born in Scipio, Cayuga county, N. Y., February 11th, 1801, and died in Orangeville June 5th, 1862. Mr. Tilton was a sergeant in the war of 1812. He lived where he first settled until his death, November 3d, 1868.

Jonathan Coburn was born in Connecticut, in 1785. He came with his family from Vermont to Essex county, N. Y., in 1805, and thence to Orangeville in July, 1812. He bought part of lot 52, and cut his own road through the forest from the Orangeville Centre road to his land, upon which he settled and where he spent the remainder of his life. He died in August, 1830.

Simeon Morse was born in Guilford, Conn., in October, 1781. When he was nine years old his parents removed to Greene county, N. Y., where he was married to Catharine Norton in February, 1801. In February, 1814, he removed to Orangeville and settled on lot 42, where he died in July, 1867. His wife died in July, 1849, aged sixty-three.

Reuben Stone was born in Hancock, Berkshire county, Mass., January 26th, 1790. In 1808 he removed with his parents to Greene county, N. Y., thence to Livingston county, and in 1813 to Orangeville, where he bought one hundred acres on lot 28 from the Holland Land Company. He was married in 1815 to Almira, a daughter of Noah Merrell. She died December 22nd, 1831, and in 1832 he married Mrs. Julia Dunham, of Orangeville, a native of Connecticut. Mr. Stone was an orderly sergeant in the war of 1812. He lived on his first farm until his death, April 11th, 1869. His father, Russell Stone, was born in Guilford, Conn., January 26th, 1759. He was a soldier of the Revolution, and was present at the surrender of Burgoyne. He was wounded in the hand at the battle of Stillwater.

Phineas Butler, with a large family of grown up children, became an early settler in the southern part of the town. His resident descendants are probably more numerous at the present time than those of any other pioneer family. Mr. Butler was born of English parents, in Maine, in April, 1760, and was married to Chloe Hammond, of the same State, also of English descent. He removed to Washington county, N. Y., thence to Orangeville in 1815, and settled on sixty acres on lot 19, where he remained until his death in August, 1836. His wife died in the spring of 1822. They reared eight children, all of whom came to Orangeville at an early day. Their names were Ansel, Obadiah, Jeduthun, Elizabeth, Phear, Benjamin, Chloe and Anna. Jeduthun Butler was born in Maine, October 15th, 1786. He was married to Ruth Benson, of Washington county, in 1812, and in 1814 settled on lot 26 in Orangeville, buying at first eighty acres. His first wife died September 29th, 1818, and he was married in November, 1819, to Martha Freeman, of Saratoga county, who died in February, 1858. Mr. Butler lived in the town until his death, May 25th, 1853. Jeremiah Butler settled on lot 10 in 1815. He was born in Maine in October, 1755, and was married to Hannah Robinson, a native of the same State, who died in Orangeville in 1845. He died in the spring of 1850.

John Head was born in Saratoga county, N. Y., November 13th, 1795, and came to Orangeville in the spring of 1816, locating on lot 18. About 1827 he sold out here and removed to Madison county, where, in 1832, he was elected to the Assembly. He returned to Orangeville, and in 1839 was elected member of Assembly from Genesee county. He also held several offices of trust and responsibility in his town and county. He was married November 30th, 1819, to Ruth Head, of Little Compton, R. I., where she was born February 10th, 1796. She died in Orangeville May 2nd, 1877. Mr. Head died at his residence in Orangeville September 17th, 1864. His only surviving child, Mrs. E. M. Benson, now owns and occupies the homestead.

Artemus Benson was born in Easton, Washington county, N. Y., November 30th, 1789. He came to Orangeville in 1814, and bought and cleared one hundred acres on lot 10. In 1840 he sold to John Head, and removed to a farm on lot 2, residing there until his death, August 20th, 1859. He was first married to Lydia Bassett, of Washington county, who died in 1823, leaving two children. In 1825 he married Harriet Vary, of Dutchess county, N. Y., who still resides on the homestead. Two of Mr. Benson's brothers, Giles and Elihu Benson, came from Washington county to Orangeville about the same time with him, the former locating on lot 2 and the latter on lot 18. Giles remained where he first settled until 1840, when he returned to his early home in Washington county, where he died in 1844. Elihu lived in this county till his death, in 1878.

Seth Porter came from Colbrook, Conn., to Orangeville in 1807, and settled on lot 28. He lived in the town until his death.

Levi Johnson was among the first to settle at Johnsonsburg. He was born in Connecticut, in 1766. About the year 1806 he removed with his family to Madison county, N. Y., and in March, 1819, to Orangeville, locating at what is now Johnsonsburg. He first bought thirty acres of land on the east side of Tonawanda creek, upon which a man named Martin had begun building a saw-mill. This mill Mr. Johnson finished, and the same year built a grist-mill at the same place. He continued an active and useful resident of the place until his death, March 6th, 1833. He had four sons—Levi, jr., Harvey, James and George—all of whom except the eldest came to Orangeville with their father, became permanent residents at Johnsonsburg, and were during their lives among the leading business men of the place.

Levi Johnson, jr., was born in Connecticut, in 1795. He came in 1816 from Madison county to Johnsonsburg, where he remained two or three years, and then removed from the county.

MR. O. TILTON

RESIDENCE of OBADIAH TILTON, TOWN of ORANGEVILLE,

MRS. O. TILTON

LEWIS J. MORGAN

MRS. LEWIS J. MORGAN

Erastus Morgan Celestia P. Morgan

Among the pioneers were Aaron Kinsman, on lot 38; Ebenezer Tyrrell, on lot 30; Lemuel Chase, John Grover, Joshua Mitchell, Asahel Ward, Paul Richards, Oliver Lee, Zoar Blackmer, Nicholas Reddish, Job Whiting, Israel Branch, Samuel Mehan, Jonathan Teil, William Buxton, Jacob Crossett, Robert Hopkins and Isaac Moore, all of whom located as early as 1811. There were in that year between forty and fifty families in the town.

Mrs. Dolly Moulton, although not a pioneer, was for many years a resident of the town, and at her death was undoubtedly the oldest person who ever lived in Orangeville. She was born in Ashby, Mass., November 2nd, 1780, and came to Attica in 1830, and from there to Orangeville in 1834. From 1842 until 1870 she resided in Genesee county, when she returned to Orangeville, and spent the remainder of her life at the home of her daughter, Mrs. John L. Lewis, where she died May 10th, 1879, in the ninety-ninth year of her age. She was three times married; her first two husbands were soldiers in the war of 1812. Her last marriage, to Royal Moulton, occurred in 1842. He died in 1870.

The only instance upon the Holland Purchase where an attempt was made to introduce slave labor occurred in this town. Joshua Mitchell and his mother-in-law, Mrs. Wood, from Maryland, came to Orangeville about 1809, bringing with them ten slaves. Soon after their settlement here Adial Sherwood married another daughter of Mrs. Wood, and received a part of the slaves. Turner, in his history of the Holland Purchase, says that "in the end most of the slaves liberated themselves," and "one of the last of the lot was sold to William Keyes, of Batavia." One faithful old servant, named George, remained with Mr. Mitchell until the death of the latter and the dissolution of the family.

INITIAL EVENTS IN ORANGEVILLE.

The first article to land in this town was taken by Elnathan Finch, in the early part of 1803.

The first orchard was planted by James Sayer, on lot 14, in 1805.

The first child born was a son of Seth Sherwood, born in 1807.

The first death was that of Mrs. Abigail, wife of James Sayer, in 1807. She was buried on Mr. Sayer's farm, on lot 14.

The first marriage was that of Adial Sherwood and a Miss Wood, from Maryland, in 1809.

The first saw-mill was built in 1810, by Robert Hopkins on the west side of lot 47, on Stony brook.

The first inn was kept in a log building at Orangeville Center, by Isaac Moore, in 1811. The first frame hotel was built and kept by Jeremiah Merrell, in 1816, at the same place.

The first tannery was built on lot 30, by Spalding Wheeler and Captain William Tanner, in 1814.

The first frame barn was built by Silas Merrifield, on lot 21. Truman Lewis built one about the same time on lot 28. It is said that his neighbors for some distance drew their grain to his barn to thresh it on his barn floor with a flail.

The first store was kept by Silas Hubbard, at the center of the town in 1814.

The first post-office was established as early as 1814, at the center of the town; Jeremiah Merrell was the first postmaster.

Dr. Kelly was the first physician to locate in the town.

The first schools were taught by Miss Corinna Lewis, near the center of the town, and Miss Mary McKnight, on lot 21, each commencing May 1st, 1811. The former occupied a log building erected for religious meetings and day school purposes, on lot 37.

The first school-house was built at the Center, about 1817.

The first grist-mill was built by Levi Johnson, on Tonawanda creek, in 1819.

The first cider-mill was built by Isaac Boardman, on lot 21, about 1820.

The first distillery was built and operated by Benjamin Peck, on lot 4, in 1823. A second distillery was built by Alanson Center on the same lot, in 1831.

TOWN ORGANIZATION AND OFFICERS—STATISTICS.

Orangeville was created by act of Legislature February 14th, 1816. It was taken from Attica, and at that time included Wethersfield, which was set off in April, 1823. Its organization was completed at the first town meeting, held April 2nd, 1816, "at the school-house near the house of John Grover, at which time Zoar Blackmer presided," and the following officers were elected: Noah Merrell, jr., supervisor; Zoar Blackmer, town clerk; James Sayer, John Grover and Manasseh Grover, assessors; Jeremiah Merrell, constable and collector; Samuel Chase and Silas Grover, overseers of the poor; James Coates, Ephraim Durfee and Nicholas Reddish, commissioners of highways; Miner Kelly, Oliver Lee and Luther Briggs, commissioners of common schools; James Kelly, James Richards and William Chase, inspectors of common schools; Peter White, Ephraim Durfee, Elijah Hammond and Samuel Nery, fence viewers; Reuben Stone and Daniel Wolcott, pound keepers; Alpha Rose, constable, and seventeen overseers of highways.

The following are complete lists of supervisors and town clerks from the organization of the town, together with the years in which they served:

Supervisors.—Noah Merrell, jr., 1816, 1817; Truman Lewis, 1818–21, 1848, 1844; James Richards, 1822–26, 1828-30; Jeremiah Merrell, 1826; John Head, 1827, 1835, 1836, appointed to fill vacancy in 1844; Peter Richards, 1831, 1832; Paul Richards 1833, 1834, 1837, 1838; Lebanah Winchester, 1839, 1840; Harvey Case, 1841, 1842; Seth C. Grosvener, 1845; Lyman C. Babbitt, 1846, 1847; Peter White, 1848; Ephraim Wheeler, 1849; Thomas Buell, 1850, 1851; David McWethey, 1852; Charles Richards, 1853, 1854, 1861; Harvey Stone, 1855; Alfred S. Wilcox, 1856, 1864, 1865; Augustus Cowdin, 1857; James H. Webster, 1858, 1859, 1862, 1863; George Peck, 1860; Frank Lewis, 1866, 1867; John Hawley, 1868, 1869; Obadiah Tilton, 1870, 1871: Chauncey Wolcott, 1872, 1873; Ephraim J. Johnson, 1874, 1875, 1876; Eugene Peck, 1877; David Hall, 1878, 1879.

Town Clerks.—Zoar Blackmer, 1816, 1818; Spaulding Wheeler, 1817, 1819; Lewis Blodgett, 1820, 1821; Joel J. Smith, 1822; Paul Richards, 1823, 1824, 1833, 1845; Luther Briggs, 1825, 1826; Charles Jemison, 1827–31, 1834, 1835, 1837–44; David Westworth, 1832, 1833; Theodore S. Barrett, 1846, 1847; Amasa Barrett, jr. 1848, 1849; James Morse, appointed to fill vacancy in 1849; Alonzo Hutchinson, 1850-53, 1856-60, 1872-76, 1878, 1879; John T. Lewis, 1854, 1855; W. D. Richardson, 1861, 1868; A. D. Hutchinson, 1867, 1877; John Holly, 1864–67; Andrew J. Sayer, 1868–71.The town is located in the central part of the county, and for a time was a formidable rival of Warsaw for the location of the county seat. The first courts and meetings of the supervisors were held in a public house at East Orangeville.

The town is six miles square, and contains about 22,500 acres. The census report of 1875 shows that at that time there were 16,574 acres improved and 5,434 acres of wood land, valued at $746,150. The valuation of buildings other than dwellings was $80,520, of stock, $122,868, and of farm tools and implements, $30,982. The gross amount of sales from farms in 1874 was $89,274. The number of tons of hay produced that year was 5,671. The number of acres of pasture in 1875 was 6,915, and of meadow, 4,915.

A quite uniform loss in the population of the town since 1845 is exhibited by the State census returns of half a century, which are annexed: 1830, 1,525; 1835, 1,791; 1840, 1,949; 1845, 1,410; 1850, 1,438; 1855, 1,441; 1860, 1,419; 1865, 1,322; 1870, 1,217; 1875, 1,160.

SCHOOLS OF THE TOWN.

The first school-house in district No. 2 was built, of logs, about 1813. It stood in the present highway, on the south part of lot 56, and was occupied for school purposes until 1824, when a frame building was put up on the southeast comer of the same lot, near the site of the present schoolhouse. Among the early teachers in this district were Ralph Williams and Susan Joslin.

The first school taught in district No. 5 was in a log building standing on lot 37, which was used for this purpose and for religious meetings for several seasons. The first teacher here was Corina Lewis, a sister of Truman Lewis. She was followed by Almira Merrell, afterward Mrs. Reuben Stone. Among other early teachers here were Esther Smith, Adams Gibson, Isaac Bronson and Cyrus and Thomas Tanner.

A log school-house was built in district No. 6 as early as 1814. It stood about twenty-five rods south of the present one, and was used for day-schools until 1824, when a new frame building was erected on the site of the present one. The present school-house was built in 1848. Among the early teachers here were Jane McLaughlin, Louisa Cowdin and Phebe Foster.

The town at one time was divided into thirteen districts and parts of districts, but a decrease in the school population necessitated the consolidation of districts from time to time, until at present there are but six school districts in the town, with as many frame school-houses. The amount of school money divided among these six districts in 1879 was $636.29.

POST-OFFICES AND MAIL ROUTES.

A post-office was established at Orangeville Center as early as 1814. Jeremiah Merrell received the appointment of postmaster, which office he held until 1841. The mail route was from Aurora, in Erie county, through the town of Orangeville to Warsaw. The mail was carried through semi-weekly on horse back; Chipman P. Turner was the postboy. About 1836 this route became a daily one, and a line of four-horse coaches, running from Canandaigua, through Warsaw and Orangeville, to Ellicottville, was put upon the route and run until the completion and opening of the Erie railroad through the county.

The first post-office at Johnsonsburg was established about 1828. George A. Johnson was the first postmaster. The office was kept in his store on the east side of Tonawanda creek.

The post-office at East Orangeville was established about 1850. Marshall B. Crossett was appointed the first postmaster here, but was soon after superseded by Francis Fullington.

The only mail route into the town now is a tri-weekly one from Warsaw, *via* East Orangeville, to Orangeville Center.

THE ORANGEVILLE PIONEER ASSOCIATION

was formed for the purpose of perpetuating the memory of the pioneers and prominent residents of the town, and for social intercourse and amusement. The original movers in its organization were Ephraim Wheeler, Chauncey and Chester L. Wolcott, George H. Dunham and Harvey Stone. It was organized in June, 1876, by the election of Ephraim Wheeler president, and George H. Dunham secretary, who are still retained in the same capacity. Its official meetings occur annually in June, and thus far a general meeting and pioneer picnic has been held on the 4th of July of each year, at Wolcott's grove, on lot 34. These annual gatherings have increased in interest and popularity, being attended by thousands of people from the country.

DAIRY INTERESTS AND CHEESE FACTORIES.

Dairying was initiated here by Reuben Stone, who, in 1823, having come into possession of two farms adjoining his own on lot 28, purchased about twenty cows and commenced the manufacture of butter and cheese. During the following five years Truman Lewis, Spaulding Wheeler, Jerry Merrell, Lyman H. Babbitt and a few others embarked in the same business, which has become the chief industry in the town. Cheese factories were introduced in 1864. There are now six in the town.

BURDEN DURFEE. EPHRAIM DURFEE. MRS. POLLY DURFEE. ELIJAH SMITH.

RESIDENCE OF M^r. BURDEN DURFEE, TOWN OF ORANGEVILLE.

Chauncy Wolcott. Mrs Lydia Wolcott. MRS. OLIVE SMITH.

HOMESTEAD OF EPHRAIM DURFEE – BUILT ABOUT 1820.
RES. OF CHAUNCEY WOLCOTT, TOWN OF ORANGEVILLE.

The *Johnsonsburg Cheese Factory* was built in April, 1864, and was the first establishment of the kind erected in the town. It is a frame structure, sixty by one hundred feet in size, and two stories high. It is on lot 61, near Johnsonsburg, and contains three vats and twenty-four presses. It made in 1878 about 185,000 pounds of cheese. It is still owned and managed by George Hoy, its builder.

Orangeville Center Cheese Factory.—This factory, on lot 30, near Orangeville Center, was built in May, 1864, by James C. Wilcox and Monroe Ferry. It is a frame two-story building, thirty by one hundred feet in size, and contains two vats and eleven presses. The amount of cheese made here in 1878 was 95,000 pounds. This factory, after changing hands several times, was purchased in February, 1878, by George Hoy, the present owner.

The *Orangeville Center Branch Factory* was built in 1870, by Wilder & Hutchinson, on lot 48. The main part is thirty by forty-eight feet, two stories high; the workroom and dwelling attached is twenty-eight by forty-eight feet, and one story high. It contains two vats and eleven presses, and made in 1878 90,000 pounds of cheese. This factory is now owned and managed by George Hoy.

The *East Orangeville Cheese Factory* was erected in 1865, on lot 5, by Crossett, Peck & Eisenbart. It is thirty-six by one hundred feet, two stories high, and contains four vats and twenty-seven presses. It manufactured in 1878 195,000 pounds of cheese. It is owned by Charles A. Green.

The Boler Cheese Factory.—This factory was built in 1870, on lot 15, by R. Boler, and was worked by him until 1876, when it was sold to George Hoy, who still owns and manages it. It is a frame, two-story, thirty-six by one hundred feet structure, containing two vats and fourteen presses, and in 1878 made 85,000 pounds of cheese.

The sixth cheese factory in the town was built on lot 49, in the spring of 1879, by Obadiah Tilton and Peter Eisenbart, and contains two vats and thirteen presses.

ORANGEVILLE,

located three-fourths of a mile north of the geographical center of the town, contains a grocery store and hotel combined, a steam saw-mill, a tannery, a cheese factory, a blacksmith shop, a shoe shop, two churches, a school-house, and twelve or fifteen dwellings, occupied principally by farmers. Settlements were begun here as early as 1807 by Jeremiah Merrell, Ebenezer Tyrrell, and perhaps one or two others. In 1811 Isaac Moore opened a tavern in a log building on the southeast corner of the two streets, which he kept until 1816, when it was removed and a frame hotel built on the same site by Jeremiah Mitchell, who continued the business until 1834. Silas Hubbard opened a store in this vicinity about 1814; three years later he was succeeded by Noah Merrell, jr. Among other early merchants were Charles Jennison and William and Sanger Marsh. A tannery was built here in 1814 by Spaulding Wheeler and Captain William Tanner. It was located about twenty rods north of the present tannery, and was built before the road from Warsaw to Orangeville was established. Tanner came from Otsego county in 1814, and was a tanner and currier by occupation. He remained in company with Mr. Wheeler about ten years, when he sold out, and the business was continued by Wheeler & Briggs until 1828. Mr. Briggs then retired from the firm, and the tannery was owned and opened thereafter by Spaulding Wheeler and his sons, Schuyler and Ephraim Wheeler, successively, until 1848, when the latter erected a new tannery on the same lot and abandoned the first one. The present establishment is a two and a half story frame building, fifty by sixty feet in size, with a stone basement, and has a capacity of tanning seven thousand hides per annum.

JOHNSONSBURG.

Johnsonsburg contains two stores, a hotel, a grist-mill, two saw-mills, a map roller factory, a cheese factory, two blacksmith, one wagon and two harness shops, two churches, and about 250 inhabitants. A man named Martin is supposed to have been the first settler at this place, as early as 1816. He located on the east side of the creek, where he commenced to build a saw mill. In 1819 he sold to Levi Johnson and removed. Mr. Johnson completed the sawmill, and the same year built a grist-mill at the same place, which was operated by him and his sons until 1834, when the present one was built by George and James Johnson sons of Levi Johnson. The saw-mill continued in use until it was worn out. A second saw-mill was put up on the east side of the creek, by Alfred Jones, about 1830, which is still standing. A cloth-dressing establishment was constructed in a part of the grist-mill about 1820, and operated by Levi Johnson and Artemus Mehan. Levi Johnson and Harvey Johnson built a distillery about 1824, on the east side of the creek, which was kept running ten or twelve years.

The first store at this place was built and kept by George Johnson, on the east side, about 1827. Jonas Gates built and opened the first hotel, about 1828, on the site of the present hotel on the west side of the creek. Joseph Lewis built and kept a hotel on the west side about 1830.

John Foote built a tannery on the east side in 1853, which he operated until 1865, when it was sold to Horace Thayer, who converted the building into a map roller factory, for which purpose it is still used. Mr. Thayer was drowned in the mill pond near this factory March 15th, 1875, while attempting to clear the ice from the dam.

Dr. Barber was the first physician to locate at Johnsonsburg.

JOHNSONSBURG SOCIETIES.

Sons of Temperance.—A lodge of this order was organized at Johnsonsburg on the 15th of August, 1869, under the name of Tonawanda Division, No. 4, S. of T., by Mr. Boughton, of New York. The first officers were: Horace. Thayer, W. P.; Augusta Rudd, W. A.; J. E. Lewis, R. S.;Mrs. L. H. Jones, A. R. S.; E.

J. Johnson, F. S.; George A. Blair, treasurer; James Tilton, conductor; Jennie Dunham, A. C; Alfreda Patterson, I. S.; Willie Lewis, O. S.; Alonzo Dunham, chaplain; A. Dunham, P. W. P.; George W. Blair, deputy G. W. P. This organization maintained an existence until February, 1873, when it was disbanded and the Good Templars lodge formed.

West Star Lodge, No. 107, *Good Templars* was constituted February 15th, 1873, by county deputy E. W. Hatch, with sixty-two members. The first officers elected were: C. F. Bentley, lodge deputy; Obadiah Tilton, W. C. T.; Miss Augusta P. Rudd, W. V. T.; Edward Reeves, W. S.; J. J. Head, W. F. S.; Mrs. Harriet A. Head, W. T.; Chester E. Head, W. M.; Miss Angeline Dodge, I. G.; Joseph Head, O. G.; F. L. Gladding, P. W. C. T. The lodge now numbers thirty members, and meets every Friday evening in Tozier's Hall.

Johnsonsburg Lodge, No. 3, *Empire Order of Mutual Aid* was organized April 15th, 1878, by George Sanborn, of Attica, with fifteen charter members. The first officers were: W. J. Standish, past president; J. W. Jones, president; D. R. Munger, vice-president; L. H. Tozier, secretary; E. D. Tuttle, financial secretary; Joseph Ward, treasurer; George West, conductor; H. J. Conger, chaplain; Horace Patrick, inside guardian; Dr. J. C. Van Pelt, outside guardian. The present membership is 15.

The Johnsonsburg Cornet Band was organized in the spring of 1878, with twelve members. The first officers were: Ephraim J. Johnson, president; Truman L. Stone, secretary; William Lewis, treasurer. Emery W. Chase served as leader until his sudden death, November 10th, 1878. The same day H. D. Bentley, another member, also died. T. L. Stone was then chosen leader, which position he still holds. The instruments and equipments so far have cost about $250.

CHURCH HISTORIES.

BAPTIST CHURCH OF ORANGEVILLE.

The first religious organization in the town of Orangeville was Baptist. It was constituted a church in the early part of 1812, with seven constituent members, among whom was James Sayer, who was the first church clerk. William Chase and his wife, John Grover, Nicholas Reddish, William De Voe, Job Whitting, and Elisha Doty and wife were early members. The first addition to the church by baptism was Mrs. Elizabeth Merrifield. This church was given fifty acres of lot 20 by the Holland Land Company.

Among the preachers previous to 1833 were Rev. Messrs. Butler and Case, who were probably the first pastors, followed by Elders Jonas Tuttle, Stutson, Anson and Jabez Boomer. The latter became a resident of the town as early as 1823, and remained several years. He was then in Ohio a few years, but returned.

This church was duly incorporated under the name of "The First Calvinistic Baptist Society of the Town of Orangeville," January 11th, 1823, at a meeting held at the school-house in district No. 4. The trustees elected at that time were James Sayer, John Grover, John W. Meddick, Festus Pettibone, Isaac Boardman, Eli Rood and Oliver Hoisington. This society was reincorporated March 16th, 1842, under the same title, at which time Ephraim Wheeler, Alfred S. Wilcox, Amos Winslow, John Chapin, Charles J. Blackmer, Darius Stone and Hiram Jones were elected trustees. The religious and business meetings of the church and society were held at various places, principally in school-houses in the central and northern portions of the town, until 1852, when the present frame meeting-house was built at Orangeville Center, on ground donated by Ephraim Wheeler. The structure is thirty-two by forty feet in size, and cost about $1,200.

Elder Jabez Boomer closed a pastorate here in the beginning of 1833, and was soon followed by Rev. Peter Freeman, who remained one year or a little more. On July 12th, 1834, the church granted a license to one of its members, Chester Coe, to preach.

The deacons in 1833 were James Sayer and Ezra Olin, and Ira Jones was chosen clerk in October of the same year. Chester Coe was ordained and installed pastor of this church March 18th, 1835, and continued until September 3d, 1836, when he was deposed from the ministry. In May, 1837, Rev. Jabez Boomer returned from. Newbury, O., and again assumed the pastorate of the church. He remained until 1840, and was followed in April of that year by Rev. Alba Thorp, who continued until January 1st, 1842. Rev. Moses Pickett preached a year from March, 1842; Rev. Thomas Phillips one year from May, 1843; Rev. P. Nichols one year.

Alvin Plumley, a licentiate from Hume, Allegany county, became a member of this church November 7th, 1845, and supplied the pulpit for a time. He was ordained here September 30th, 1846, and continued as pastor until the spring of 1857. Rev. William Baxton, from Bethany, preached two years from April, 1858, after whom Rev. Russell T. Smith was pastor one or two years. During the year 1867 Rev. D. B. Morgan labored here, after which the pulpit was supplied for a time by Elder W. I. Crane, of Warsaw, since which the church has had no regular minister and only occasional preaching.

In 1854 the church numbered 45 members, and 34 in 1867, since which time it has been gradually decreasing until there are very few left.

PRESBYTERIAN CHURCH OF ORANGEVILLE.

This church was organized by Rev. John Alexander, at Orangeville Center, July 11th, 1812, with nine constituent members, viz.: Israel Branch, Samuel Mehan, Samuel H. Smith, Noah Merrell, Mary Branch, Hepzibah Merrell, Amanda Teil, Betsey Smith and Anna Mehan. Israel Branch was elected the first deacon, and Noah Merrell first clerk. Rev. James H. Hotchkin, in his history of the Presbyterian church of western New York, says: "The present church of Orangeville was, as the writer supposes, named Attica, and was organized a Congregational church. It was received under the care of the Presbytery of Geneva, on the 'accommodating' plan, September 21st, 1813. From that presbytery it was transferred to Niagara, and from Niagara to Genesee, on the establishment of those presbyteries. In 1825 it consisted of twenty-two members; in 1834 of ninety-eight, and in 1846 of one hundred and two."

The first additions to the church were on July 12th, 1812, when Daniel Easton and Amanda Teil, were baptized by Rev. John Alexander. In the spring of 1813 the pulpit was supplied by Rev. F. Miller. He was followed in July of that year by Rev. Silas Hubbard, who preached here and at Warsaw two years and a half. Rev. Hippocrates Rowe came in September, 1816, and was installed as pastor of this and the Warsaw church December 4th, 1816, and continued two years probably. Mr. Hotchkin says that "in 1819 the church was vacant, and from that period down to 1834 was for the principal part of the time reported vacant." The church was favored, however, with preaching during that time by Rev. Hugh Wallace for four years from September, 1818; Rev. Abiel Parmele during the year 1825; followed by Rev. Hugh Wallace again; Rev. Warren Day, under the patronage of the American Home Missionary Society, preached a year, from April, 1829; Rev. John C. Morganthen preached three years, and Rev. Justin Marsh from 1833 until 1836. "Rev. William C. Kniffin was installed pastor of this church January 7th, 1836. He continued a little more than one year, and was dismissed February 16th, 1837." The preachers since that time have been Rev. Messrs. Isaac Chichester, as stated supply from 1837 to 1841; Nathaniel T. Yeomans from 1841 to 1846; R. H. Conklin as stated supply in 1846; William Platt one year from 1849; —— Baldwin during the years 1850 and 1851; Warren Day four years from 1851; E. H. Stratton four years from 1855; John A. Allen for the year 1860; Martin B. Gregg from 1861 to 1865; J. W. Hunt from 1865 to 1867; —— Quigley in 1868; —— Dewey in 1869 and 1870; A. G. Wilcox in 1876 and 1877, and F. Billsby in 1879. For several years past the church has had preaching only at irregular intervals. The number of members is five. In 1844 the session consisted of Elders Jeremiah Merrell, James Webster, Truman Lewis, Harvey Case and Marshall B. Crossett; the deacons were Harvey Case and Gurdon Armstrong.

In 1826 the society built a large frame meeting-house at Orangeville. The site was opposite the present Presbyterian church, and was donated to the society for church purposes by Jeremiah Merrell. This structure was never completed, and in 1848 it was taken down and removed to East Orangeville, where it was converted into a hotel and occupied as such for many years. The present church edifice was built in 1848, at a cost of about $1,800. It is a frame structure, about thirty-four by fifty feet in size, and was completed and dedicated in 1849.

THE ORANGEVILLE SOCIETY OF FRIENDS.

This society was formed in the southeastern part of the town, and existed as an "indulged meeting," according to the usage of that denomination, as early as 1816. Five or six years later it was formally organized or established at the house of Jeremiah Butler, on lot 10. The leading constituent members were: Jeremiah, Phineas and Jeduthan Butler, Ephraim Durfee, John Head, Samuel Coon, Daniel Freeman and John S. Carr. The society built a meeting-house on lot 10 about 1819, which, though for many years unoccupied, is still standing, a small, unpretending frame structure, without dome or spire. The early recommended ministers of this society were Daniel Freeman and Joseph Head. About 1828 there was a general division of the society throughout the country. After this division the "orthodox" branch of this society held their meetings at the house of Phineas Butler, on lot 19, and the "Hicksites" continued to occupy the meeting-house. These branches long since ceased to exist as a society. There are at present only three persons living who were members of either branch. They are Joseph Head and his wife and William Hall, and are among the oldest inhabitants of the town.

UNION EVANGELICAL CHURCH.

This society was organized in the north part 6f the town in 1831, with twenty-nine members, among whom were Michael Glor, Christian Broadbrooks, Louis Bauer, Jacob Meder, Peter West, Henry Rummage and Michael Warner. The first pastor was Rev. William Feil, followed by Revs. Henry Hohnhulz, T. A. Bayer, —— Schembadius, John Keller, William Brombacher, Christian Hilderbrand, Charles Siebenpfeifer, —— Schmit, George Wiehe and John Althouse, who came in 1849. Rev. Henry Lausterer came in 1864 and remained three years, followed by Rev. Julius Tennessen for one year. Rev. George J. Long preached from March 4th, 1869, to October 4th, 1870. In 1843 the society built a church on lot 48, which was afterward blown down. It was rebuilt on the same spot, at a cost of about $2,000. In 1870 the society erected a new church on lot 40, opposite the first one, on a lot donated by Henry Glor. It is of wood, fifty by forty feet in size, and cost $3,700. It was completed and dedicated by Rev. George J. Long in November, 1870, at which time a division took place between the Lutherans and Dutch Reformed, of which the union was originally formed, the Lutherans withdrawing from the Union Evangelical Society to the number of about fifty. They, however, retained possession of the new Church, and were ministered to by Rev. Mr. Long for about a year, when it was legally decided by the courts that they had no title to the church property as a society, and they were obliged to surrender it. The adherents to the name of Union Evangelical Society took possession of the new edifice, and have since held meetings there. Rev. Charles R. Beyer became their pastor January 1st, 1872, and remained until January 1st, 1878, when he was followed by the present pastor, Rev. T. Huber. The present membership is about forty.

The Lutheran branch of this society returned to the old church, which they still occupy. With the exception of about one year's absence, during which time Rev. Otto Schroeder supplied the pulpit, Rev. Mr. Long has had charge of this church to the present. The membership numbers about thirty-five.

METHODIST EPISCOPAL CHURCH.

A Methodist Episcopal class was formed in the northeast part of the town, as a branch of the Warsaw charge, about 1850. Among its original members were Chester Perkins and wife, Moses Perkins, Silas Snyder, Roswell Warren and wife, and Lucius Byam and wife. Chester Perkins was chosen the first class leader. In 1853 the class was set off to the Wethersfield circuit, and Rev. Ephraim Herrick became pastor. Among the ministers who followed him were Revs. John P. Kent, Newell Newton, Samuel Hopkins, —— Gould, Elam Jeffers, Joseph Terry (who was twice on this circuit), Joseph Latham, jr., John Hills and John W. Vaughn.

In 1861 the society built a meeting-house on lot 7, on ground donated by Lucius Byam. The building is of wood, twenty-eight by forty feet in size, and cost $900. It was dedicated in December, 1861. At this time the church numbered 40 members. After the pastorate of Mr. Vaughn the church was disbanded, and most of the remaining members united with the Warsaw society. The church building is now the property of Samuel W. Perkins, of Warsaw.

FIRST FREE METHODIST CHURCH.

This church was organized in Johnsonsburg, by Ephraim Herrick, in 1862. Elder A. H. Green was the first pastor. Meetings were held in the school-house at Johnsonsburg the first year. In 1863 the society built a meeting-house at that place, which was completed and dedicated in January, 1864, by Rev. D. W. Thurston. The following pastors have ministered to this church, coming in the order named, and remaining one year, unless otherwise mentioned.

A. H. Green, P. Butterfield, O. O. Bacon, P. Butterfield, second time; G. W. Humphrey, two years; H. Hornsby; W. Jackson, two years; A. H. Green, second time; A. A. Burgess, two years; J. Walton; A. B. Mathewson, two years; and the present pastor, who came in 1877. The present number of members is 16.

A well-attended Sunday-school has been kept up in connection with this church most of the time since its organization.

BIOGRAPHICAL

George Ahl was born in Orangeville, June 16th, 1856. January 1st, 1878, he married Ella Wood, born at Warsaw, September, 27th, 1857. Mr. Ahl has been a farmer and cheesemaker. He has been superintendent of the Orangeville cheese factory since 1877. His father, John Ahl, was born near Strasburg, France, in 1817, and emigrated to this State in 1835. He was a tailor, and first located in Buffalo. From 1837 he lived on his farm on lot 30 in Orangeville. He died January 28th, 1872.

HENRY V. BENSON, son of Artemus Benson, was born August 28th, 1826, on the same farm where he now resides, and has always lived in the town. He was married January 7th, 1846, to Esther M. Head, a daughter of Hon. John Head, of Orangeville. She was born in Orangeville, December 21st, 1827. They have two children—Helen M., born April 7th, 1848, and Frank H., born November 18th, 1859.

WILLIAM BUCKEL was born in Hitchin, Hertfordshire, England, July 22nd, 1777. He came to America at the age of nineteen, and remained in New York city a few years; then emigrated to Genesee county (now Wyoming) and settled in the town of Orangeville. He resided there until about a year previous to his death, which occurred at Bedford, Mich., February 19th, 1856, while he was on a visit to his daughter. He was then seventy-nine years of age. He was twice married—first to Persis Ray, June 22nd, 1798; she bore him one daughter (Jane) and died July 24th, 1806. His second wife was Mary Coburn. They were married October 26th, 1806, and both lived many years, surrounded by a family of seven children, three boys and four girls, vis.: William, Thomas, Ezsekiel, Persis, Susan, Esther and Mary. All of these are living except Thomas, who died July 19th, 1884, and Esther, who died February 18th, 1878. Mr. Buckel was among the earliest settlers in the part of Genesee county which is now Wyoming. He was a member of the M. E. church of Orangeville many years, which connection was only severed by his death.

CYRUS COBURN was born in Vermont, March 28th, 1800. His parents removed from Essex county, N. Y., in July, 1812, to lot 52, Orangeville, then an unbroken wilderness. When a young man Mr. Coburn bought and cleared a farm on lot 52, where he lived until his death, July 18th, 1878. In 1867 he built a shingle-mill and turning lathe on his farm, which is still worked part of the time. He was a leading member of the Presbyterian church of Orangeville nearly fifty years. He was married January 6th, 1825, to Hannah, a daughter of Simeon Morse, of Orangeville. She was born in Greene county, N. Y., November 19th, 1806, and came with her parents to Orangeville in 1816. She still, with the assistance of her sons Clifford and Franklin, carries on the homestead farm. Mr. Coburn's children were Calvin L., born November 5th, 1825, who died March 28th, 1854; Clifford M., born July 31st, 1828; James F., born December 8th, 1830; Lucy, born July 16th, 1836, the wife of William F. Walker, of Catarast, Wis.; Norton, born May 27th, 1839, died March 28th, 1867; Mary, born April 6th, 1841, died September 6th, 1844.

WILLIAM H. CORY was born in Orangeville, March 28th, 1841, and was married February 4th, 1864, to Uretta D., daughter of Marshall Hutchinson, of Orangeville. He served in Company G, 9th N. Y. cavalry, the last nine months of the civil war. After marriage he lived several years in Illinois and Iowa. He is a builder and contractor.

HENRY DIXON was born in Chatham, Conn., May 9th, 1811. From 1816 he was on a farm in Bethany, Geneses county, N. Y., until 1867, when he located on a farm on lot 58, Orangeville. In 1869 he removed to Johnsonsburg. His father, Charles Dixon, was a native of Connecticut, and previous to his removal to Genesee county was a seafaring man. Mr. Dixon was married May 27th, 1858, to Mrs. Harriet A. Dixon, a daughter of Hiram Porter and born in Connecticut, March 10th, 1823. Hiram Porter was born in Colebrook, Conn., December 18th, 1797, and in 1839 came with his family to Johnsonsburg. From 1847 he lived on a farm on lot 66 until 1802, when he returned to

Johnsonsburg where, he died May 6th, 1876. He had spent much of his life in mechanical pursuits. He was married October 10th, 1819, to Nancy Francis, a native of Durham, Conn. She was born November 1st, 1796, and is still living with her daughter, Mrs. H. Dixon, of Johnsonsburg. Mr. Porter reared nine children, all of whom came with him from Connecticut to Orangeville.

CONRAD H. DIVERS was born December 26th, 1811, in Stillwater, Sussex county, N. J. There he learned the tailor's trade. In 1834 he came to Batavia, and in 1847 to his present farm on lot 27, Orangeville. He was married October 6th, 1844, to Sarah Butler, a daughter of Jeduthun Butler, of Orangeville. They have two children, Allen B. and Martha O.; the latter the wife of Lyman Blakely, of North Java.

ALLEN B. DIVERS was born in Wethersfield, this county, July 16th, 1845, but has lived in Orangeville since 1847. He was married October 30th, 1877, to Mary Chaddock, of Pike. He was a teacher several years, but since his marriage has been a farmer. For the last four years he has been deputy sheriff.

GEORGE HALL DUNHAM has always lived in Orangeville, where he was born November 14th, 1828. In September, 1847, he graduated at the State normal school at Albany, and he was a teacher many years. He was town superintendent of common schools from 1849 to 1858, and from 1857 was school commissioner for the county seven years. He has also been farming and dairying on lot 50, where he has lived since 1850. He is now in the insurance business, his farm and dairy of thirty-five cows being managed by his two sons. Mr. Dunham was married in April, 1860, to Louisa T. Virgin, of Warsaw. She was born in Waterford, Saratoga county, N. Y., September 20th, 1834, and is the eldest daughter of John and Betsey Virgin, who settled in Warsaw in 1827. They have three children—Gennifrede D., born January 6th, 1851, married November 30th, 1871, to Eli T. Cleveland, of Rockford, Ill., and died April 10th, 1880, aged twenty-nine years; Frank S., born March 23d, 1864, and married February 23d, 1876, to Clara A. North, of Attica, N. Y.; and Fred. H., born October 20th, 1861. Mr. Dunham's father, Simeon, jr., came from Hebron, Conn., to Orangeville with his father, Simeon, in 1816, and located on lot 44. He was married in 1818 to Julia Porter. He died of a cancer in January, 1829, aged thirty-five years. His widow married Reuben Stone, and died (also of cancer) in January, 1859. Julia Porter, who became the wife of Simeon Dunham and the mother of George Hall Dunham, was born in Colebrook, Conn., in December, 1796, and came to Orangeville in 1809. George H. was their second child, their first being Alonso, who was born in October, 1819, and died in October, 1869. Their only other child, Franklin, was born in June 1828, and died in April, 1853.

BURDEN DURFEE, son of Ephraim Durfee, was born in Orangeville, May 21st, 1814. He married Clara D. Pease, of Orangeville, a native of Washington county, N. Y,, May 6th, 1839. Since then he has lived on lot 88, his farm consisting of one hundred and fifty-six acres. His first wife died April 17th, 1847, and on July 18th, 1848, he was married to Alvera Truesdell, of Warsaw, who died March 14th, 1857. September 3d, 1857, Mr. Durfee married Mrs. Mary Moore« a native of Orangeville. He has always been a farmer. Nelson J. Durfee, his only child, was born August 12th, 1840, and is now in Illinois.

EARL DURFEE was born in Orangeville, January 26th, 1819, and married Roxana Potter January 28th, 1844. She died March 2nd, 1856, and Mr. Durfee was married to

Louisa Jane Potter June 22nd, 1856. The children (all born in Orangeville) were Mary J. Durfee, born March 29th, 1857; George W. Durfee, April 24th, 1860, and Lydia Cora Durfee, June 10th, 1863. Mr. Durfee moved on to his homestead in 1844, where he lived up to the time of his death, March 3d, 1860.

MARVIN N. FARGO was born in Warsaw village, January 26th, 1827, and was married May 4th, 1848, to Hannah Devings, who was born in Collins, Erie county, N. Y., December 22nd, 1828. In 1849 Mr. Fargo began farming on lot 4, in Orangeville. He sold out, bought a farm on lot 29, and lived on it from April, 1866, until his death, May 26th, 1867. A portion of his time latterly was spent in making electro-magnetic machines. Mrs. Fargo now carries on the farm with the assistance of her son. Her children are Albert A., born July 19th, 1849; Edwin, born June 29th, 1852, and Mary J. born July 22nd, 1860, the wife of Martin Spink, of Orangeville.

SYLVESTER FIELD was born in Springfield, Sullivan county, N. H,, May 29th, 1827. In 1848, with his father's family, he emigrated to Sheldon, Wyoming county. He was married to Margaret Allen, of Pembroke, Genesee county, N. Y., July 6th, 1858, and in 1856 removed to Hillsdale county, Mich. Six years later he returned, and has since lived in this county. His early life was principally spent in wagon-making. He served in Company H., 136th N. Y. volunteer infantry, the last three yean of the Rebellion. He has been keeper of the Wyoming county alms-house since December, 1878. His father, John Field, was born in New Hampshire, March 28th, 1794, and was a farmer in Sheldon from 1848 until 1871. He then retired from active business, and has since lived with his son Sylvester.

SYDNEY FOSTER was born in Warsaw, September 24th, 1848, and has always lived in the county. He was married to Mrs. Hannah A. Coburn, of Orangeville, May 14th, 1878. Since 1874 he has been a farmer and mechanic in Orangeville.

HENRY GRIFFEN, the oldest son of Jacob T. Griffen, was born in Elba, Genesee county, N. Y., June 16th, 1826. He was married April 11th, 1849, to Rachel E. Crawford, of Orangeville, a native of Saratoga county. Since May, 1850, he has been farming on lot 19 in Orangeville. He owns a steam saw-mill and in connection grinds coarse grain. This mill was built by Mr. Griffin and others in 1852, and in 1874 became the property of the former. Mr. Griffin has been a justice of the peace over twenty years, and has held other offices. His children are: Hannah M., born January 11th, 1850, the wife of William D. Wolcott, of Wethersfield: Hortensie E., born July 3d, 1853; Charles E., born July 2nd, 1857, and Henry R., born February 5th, 1868.

ISAAC GRIFFEN was born in Eiba, Genesee county, N. Y., September 29th, 1831, but since infancy has lived in Orangeville. He was married May 16th, 1855, to Hannah Hand, of Hartland, Niagara county, N. Y., who died July 14th, 1874. He has always been a farmer, and occupies the old homestead on lot 10. He has two children, Oren A., born July 7th, 1856, and Mary L., born October 29th, 1858. Mr. Griffen's father, Jacob T. Griffen, born in Dutchess county, N. Y., August 9th, 1799, came, when nineteen, to Elba, Genesee county. He was married to Bathsheba Butler, of Orangeville, June 5th, 1824. She was born May 17th, 1800, and died April 14th, 1874. In November, 1831, Mr. Griffon removed to lot 10, Orangeville, where he has since remained. He has reared seven children, all of whom are still living. He has been assessor of his town for six years.

RESIDENCE of MR. L. D. MORGAN, WETHERSFIELD SPRINGS, N.Y.

JOHN TILTON

MRS. AMARILA TILTON

OLIVER C. TILTON

RESIDENCE of MR. OLIVER C. TILTON, TOWN of ORANGEVILLE, N.Y.

DAVID HALL was born February 24th, 1834, and reared on the same farm which he now owns and occupies, on lot 19. He has always been a farmer and dairyman, and has held the offices of assessor, collector and supervisor. He was married November 1st, 1860, to Rebecca A., youngest daughter of Joseph Head, of Orangeville. She was born in Orangeville, May 10th, 1836. Their children are Carrie, Maud, Anna and Burton.

WILLIAM HALL, the father of David, was born in Portsmouth, R. I., July 31st, 1798, and at the age of five years removed with his parents to Madison county, N. Y. In 1823 he came to Orangeville. December 4th, 1824, he married Anna Butler, and continued to work on the farm of her father, Phineas Butler, until the latter's death, in 1836. He then had possession of the farm until he transferred it to his son David, with whom he is now living.

GEORGE HOY was born in the county of Monaghan, Ireland, March 1st, 1832, and emigrated to this State in 1849. He lived three years each in East Bloomfield, Ontario county, and Pittsford, Monroe county. In 1866 he located on lot 44, Orangeville, and remained nine years, when he rented his farm of two hundred and twelve acres, and removed to Johnsonsburg. In the spring of 1864 he built a cheese factory there, and began making cheese. He now owns and superintends eight cheese factories in this county, and several dairy farms in Orangeville. He was married March 26th, 1853, to Lucy C. Stone, of Orangeville.

ALONZO HUTCHINSON was born in Ware, Hampshire county, Mass., April 18th, 1815, where he was married June 25th, 1840, to Sophia Babbitt, of the same place. In October, 1839, he removed to Orangeville, where he has since lived. He has been making cheese several years, and has charge of the Orangeville Center branch factory. He was postmaster at Orangeville Center from 1862 to 1876, aud has been town clerk sixteen years. He has one daughter, Ellen M., born March 25th, 1842, the wife of Erotas H. Wilder, of Wethersfield.

MARSHALL HUTCHINSON was born in Ware, Hampshire county, Mass., January 12th, 1812. In 1835 he abandoned the shoemakers' trade, and became a farmer on lot 83, Orangeville. After several purchases and sales of real estate in this town, he settled permanently on a farm of two hundred and sixty acres on lot 54. There he died April 3d, 1873. He was one of the most successful dairymen of Orangeville. He often held town offices, and was an esteemed member of the Presbyterian church of Orangeville. He was married April 3d, 1835, to Lucinda W. Babbitt, of Ware, Mass. She was born March 9th, 1816, and died in Orangeville February 2nd, 1875.

EPHRAIM J. JOHNSON was born in Johnsonsburg, January 15th, 1824, and has always lived there. He is a grandson of Levi Johnson, the founder of the village. Mr. Johnson was a mechanic until 1857, since which date he has been engaged in general merchandising at Johnsonsburg. He has been three times supervisor. His father, Harvey Johnson, was born in Connecticut, in 1798, and was in business at Johnsonsburg from 1819 to his death, July 1st, 1869. He was married to Susan Jackson, of Madison county, N. Y., about 1819. She died March 29th, 1852.

JOHN L. LAWN was born in Exeter, Kent county, R. I., May 1st, 1811, and at the age of seven came with his parents to Orangeville. He was married January 1st, 1839, to Lois Squire, of Orangeville, and in 1856 bought one hundred acres on lot 36, where he has since been farming and dairying. He has been town clerk two terms.

He has six children—Beda O., born January 2nd, 1840, the wife of G. W. Spring, of Orangeville; Mary E., born October 17th, 1841, the wife of Myron D. Palmer, of Wellsville, N. Y.; Ladd J., born December 22nd, 1845, now at Grand Rapids, Mich.; Frank E., born June 16th, 1853; William H., born July 30th, 1856, and George H., born July 4th, 1862. His father, Moses Lewis, was born in Exeter, Kent county, R. I., September 20th, 1779. In 1818 he located on lot 56, Orangeville, and was a farmer in this town until his death, September 25th, 1860.

WAKEMAN LOCKWOOD was born in Java, this county, June 27th, 1827. In March, 1852, he bought and removed to his present farm on lot 57, which he has since carried on. He was married February 19th, 1850, to Lydia Eddie, who died July 13th, 1874. In the spring of 1875 he married Mrs. Rosetta Tuttle, who was born in Orangeville, December 7th, 1841. Mr. Lockwood's children are Florence, born August 22nd, 1858, and Hattie, born September 30th, 1861.

ASA PECK, the oldest son of Benjamin Peck, was born in the town of Milton, Saratoga county, N. Y., January 16th, 1816, and came with his parents to Wyoming county in 1818. In March, 1822, they located on lot 4 in Orangeville, where Mr. Peck carries on farming and dairying. He was married July 28th, 1844, to Betsey McKinsey, of Orangeville, who was born in Essex county, N. Y., August 29th, 1814. Their children are Benjamin A., born November 21st, 1848, and John A., born March 14th, 1850.

BENJAMIN PECK was born in Connecticut, April 14th, 1791. In his youth his parents removed to Saratoga county, where he learned the distilling business, and where he was married to Urana Bouton, May 27th, 1815. In 1818 he removed to Perry, Wyoming county, and afterward to Warsaw. In the spring of 1822 he bought and removed to a farm on lot 4, Orangeville, where he remained until his death, June 23d, 1843. His wife died June 28th 1862.

WILLIAM A. SPINK, son of Whitman Spink, was born in Shaftsbury, Vt., October 22nd, 1816. In 1831 he, with the family, removed to lot 47, Orangeville. He was married January 22nd, 1839, to Eliza J. Johnson, and in 1847 he bought and permanently located on a farm of one hundred acres on lot 46. His wife was born in Attica, February 28th, 1819, and died September 30th, 1874. His children are Euphemia H., born May 22nd, 1843, and married to Amos Otes 2nd, of Warsaw, March 17th, 1864; Daniel W.; Zemira M., born September 24th, 1848, and married to John Q. Lindsey, of Attica, December 8th, 1868; Frances M., born December 27th, 1849, and married November 9th, 1869, to Austin W. Lathrop, of Warsaw.

DANIEL W. SPINK, 2nd, the only son of William A. Spink, was born in the town of Attica, July 1st, 1845, but has lived in Orangeville since he was two years old. He was married February 9th, 1871, to Ella M. Lawrence, of Orangeville, who was born in Hartland, Niagara county, N. Y., May 21st, 1851. Mr. Spink carries on the homestead farm on lot 46. He has been deputy sheriff, and was a lieutenant in the 61st regiment, national guards.

JONATHAN O. SPINK was born in Orangeville, February 18th, 1833. His father, Allen Spink, came from Vermont to Perry, Wyoming county, about 1827, married a few months later, located on lot 47 in Orangeville, and has since lived in the town most of the time. Jonathan O. was married November 22nd, 1860, to Lovina, daughter of Alfred

S. Wilcox, of Orangeville. He was a farmer until May, 1877, when he began store and hotel keeping at Orangeville Center, where he still continues. He a justice of the peace and postmaster.

REUBEN STONE was born in Hancock, Mass., January 26th, 1790. His father, Russel Stone, born in Guilford, Conn., January, 1759, died in Greenville, N. Y., December, 1802, aged forty-three. His mother, Lois Stone, born in April, 1760, at the same place, died in Livonia, N. Y. Russel Stone, the father, was in the war of the Revolution with the Connecticut militia. At the battle of Stillwater he was wounded. Reuben Stone left Hancock, Mass., in 1790 or 1791, with his father's family, and settled in Greenville, N. Y. He, with his brother Joel, came to Livonia in 1809 or 1810. In September, 1813, he came to Orangeville and settled on lot No. 28, a parcel of the farm of nearly four hundred acres on which he lived more than fifty-five years, and where he died April 11th, 1869, aged seventy-nine years. In September, 1815, he married Miss Almira Merrill, daughter of Noah Merrill, of Orangeville, a soldier of the Revolution. She was born in Colebrook, Conn., June 13th, 1792, and died December 22nd, 1831, aged thirty-nine years. Their children were seven. Two died in infancy. Lois, born July 18th, 1816, is now the wife of Obadiah Tilton, of Orangeville; Harvey, born February 14th, 1818, is now living in Orangeville; Sarah, born October 28th, 1820, married Lester Sparks, of North Plains, Mich., April, 1854, and died in January, 1873, at Portland, Mich.; Lucinda, born September 28th, 1826, married Hiram Smith, of Orangeville, in 1851, and died in 1862; Caroline, born December 22nd, 1828, is now living in Wabaunsee, Kansas. In April, 1832, Mr. Stone married Mrs. Julia Dunham, of Orangeville. To them two children were born—Edwin, born April 17th, 1833, now owner and occupant of the homestead, and Lucy, born January 22nd, 1838, now the wife of George Hoy, of Orangeville, of cheese factory fame. Mr. Stone was a leader and worker in the organization of the town, the placing of public roads and schools, and in the organization of the first Presbyterian church in the town, of which he afterward became a useful member. He was one of the earliest dairymen in the town, selling home manufactured cheese as early as 1823. He spent his declining years with mental faculties unclouded, among firm friends, and at home on the old farm.

HARVEY STONE, a son of Reuben Stone, was born at the geographica center of Orangeville, February 14th, 1818, and was married February 20th, 1840, to Eliza Lewis, daughter of Truman Lewis, of Orangeville. He then bought and settled on part of the old homestead on lot 28. In 1844 he sold out here and bought a farm on lot 58, where he still lives. He has always been a farmer and dairyman. He was twelve years justice of the peace, supervisor in 1855, and was elected session justice of the county two terms. His children are: Almira A., born August 20th, 1841, the wife of George L. Parker, of Auburn, N. Y.; Morris L., now of Kansas, born August 8th, 1843, and married to Frances E. Stanley February 1st, 1867; Truman L., born July 1st, 1836, and married to Helen Lewis, December 1st, 1875.

EDWIN STONE, the youngest son of Reuben Stone, has always lived on his present farm. He was born April 17th, 1838, and was married January 1st, 1856, to Emma Crawford, of Wethersfield, who was born in Ontario county, September 11th, 1837. Mr. Stone has always been engaged in farming and dairying, and owns two hundred and sixty acres—the old homestead—which he purchased after the death of his father, in 1869. He has two daughters— Julia, born March 18th, 1863, and Bessie L., born October 10th, 1872.

OBADIAH TILTON, son of the pioneer, John Tilton, was born in Orangeville, January 27th, 1817, and excepting about five years has spent his entire life here, following farming and dairying. He was married to Lois, a daughter of Reuben Stone, June 2nd, 1841, and located on the south part of lot 52, but since 1858 has lived on the north part of it. In company with Peter Eisenbart he owns a cheese factory on lot 49. He has been assessor nine years in succession, and was supervisor in 1870 and 1871.

OLIVER C. TILTON, the youngest son of John and Amarilla Tilton, was born in Orangeville, July 10th, 1833, on his present farm. He was married October 30th, 1862, to Jane N. Johnson, of Orangeville. She was born in Gainesville, Wyoming county, September 10th, 1840. They have three children—Mary, born August 12th, 1866; Altie, born January 8th, 1874; and Owen B., born November 1st, 1878. Mr. Tilton has always been engaged in terming and dairying.

THEODORE WARREN was born at North Java, November 7th, 1847. He lived there until sixteen years old; two years in Cattaraugus county, and since then in this county. He was married January 30th, 1874, to Helen Calkins, who was born in Sheldon, May 7th, 1852. Mr. Warren has been a practical cheese-maker since the spring of 1867, and now superintends the Boler factory, on lot 15, where he has been employed since 1875. His father, Orson Warren, was born in Sheldon, December 1st, 1816, and excepting two years has always lived in this county. He was married in 1844 to Julia A. Martin, of Warsaw, a native of Onondaga county, where she was born February 13th, 1820. Mr. Warren was a shoemaker until 1864, since which time he has been making cheese.

HENRY WEEKS was born in Kennebec county, Maine, November 4th, 1829. For several years after 1832 the family lived on lot 17, Orangeville, after which they returned to Maine; but about 1847 Henry came back to Orangeville, and worked several years with William Eddie as a mason. In 1860 he bought and occupied his present term. Besides farming he worked at his trade part of the time. He was married July 1st, 1852, to Harriet Head, oldest daughter of Joseph Head, of Orangeville. She was born March 16th, 1831. They have one son—Charles E., born December 6th, 1856.

EPHRAIM WHEELER was born in the town of Hartwick, Otsego county, N. Y., October 4th, 1810. His father, Spaulding Wheeler, came with his family to Orangeville in March, 1816, locating on lots 29 and 30, where he early engaged in the tanning business, which he followed for many years. Ephraim Wheeler has always lived in the town since 1815, carrying on the tanner and currier's trade in connection with farming, succeeding his father in the former business in 1836. He was married in March, 1831, to Margaret Lammon, of Orangeville, a native of Otsego county. He has frequently been chosen to positions of honor and responsibility.

JEFFREY H. WILCOX removed from Exeter, R. I., to Warsaw in 1816. In the spring of 1818 he bought and removed to a farm in the northwest part of Orangeville, one of the lint settlers in that part of the town. There he lived the rest of his life, dying May 3d, 1870, aged eighty-seven years.

ALFRED S. WILCOX, son of Jeffrey H. Wilcox, was born in West Greenwich, R. I., April 24th, 1813, and came with his parents to Warsaw in 1816, and in 1818 to Orangeville, where he has since lived. He bought of his father the old homestead on lot 56, and lived there until 1852, when he bought two hundred and fifteen acres on lot 55, on which he has since resided. He now owns three hundred and sixty acres, upon which he keeps a large dairy. He has been justice of the peace sixteen years, overseer of the poor over twenty years, assessor, and supervisor for six terms. He did all the recruiting for Orangeville from the spring of 1868 to the close of the Rebellion. He was a captain in the old militia seven years.

JAMES C. WILCOX, son of Jeffrey Wilcox, has always lived in Orangeville, where he was born July 7th, 1818. He was married February 1st, 1842, to Orpha J. Spink, of Orangeville, who was born in Shaftsbury, Vt., March 1st, 1823, and came with her parents to Orangeville in 1888. From 1845 Mr. Wilcox lived eight years on a farm on lot 55. This he sold, and in 1855 bought one hundred and fifty acres on lots 45 and 37, where he has since lived. He has held town offices many years. His children are: Mary M., born March 2nd, 1844, married Aaron Jones, of Orangeville, October 20th, 1863; Thomas B., born August 18th, 1846, and married to Rosa B. Winchester April 30th, 1868; Cordelia D., born May 16th, 1850, and married to Orlin Lawrence, of Sheldon, March 14th, 1873; Emma J., born November 7th, 1852, and married to David H. Edwards, of Attica, March 2nd, 1875; Clara E., born April 19th, 1856, and married to J. Frank Peck, of Warsaw, June 6th, 1873; Edward J., born April 9th, 1861.

CHAUNCEY WOLCOTT, son of Daniel Wolcott, was born in Wethersfield, January 4th, 1823. In 1855 he removed to his present place, on lot 34, Orangeville. He has always been a farmer and dairyman. Mr. Wolcott has served two terms as supervisor and held other town offices. He was married February 1st, 1844, to Lydia, second daughter of Ephraim Durfee; who was born in Orangeville, April 18th, 1824. They have one son, William D., born in Wethersfield, June 22nd, 1848, and married to Hannah M. Griffen April 12th, 1871.

CHESTER L. WOLCOTT, son of Daniel Wolcott, was born in Wethersfield, August 14th, 1825, and was married February 18th, 1846, to Eliza, daughter of Ephraim Durfee, of Orangeville, where she was born March 25th, 1824. March 1st, 1847, he removed from Wethersfield to Orangeville, and in May, 1852, located permanently on his present term on lot 34. He has always been engaged in farming, dairying and sheep husbandry. He has had four children—Elpha, born June 2nd, 1849, and died November 7th, 1876; Edmund C., born June 3d, 1852, and died October 26th, 1869; Earl D., born June 19th, 1855, and Ella V., born May 4th, 1859.

DANIEL WOLCOTT. CHAS. D. WOLCOTT. MRS. MARIA WOLCOTT.

THE WOLCOTT HOMESTEAD AT POPLAR TREE CORNERS, BUILT ABOUT 1825.
RESIDENCE OF CHARLES D. WOLCOTT, TOWN OF WETHERSFIELD.

Chester L. Wolcott   Mrs Eliza Wolcott

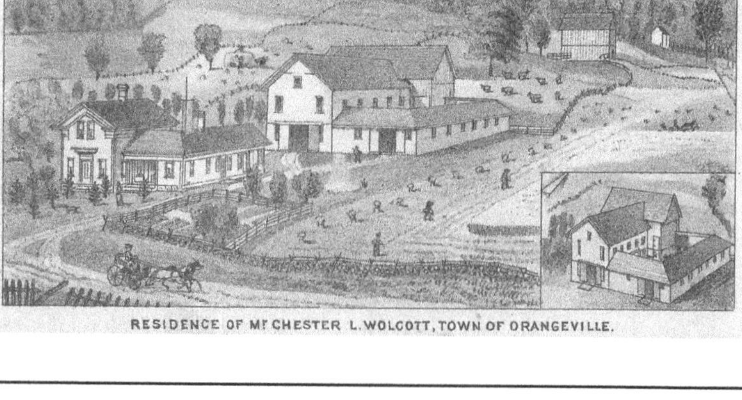

RESIDENCE OF Mr. CHESTER L. WOLCOTT, TOWN OF ORANGEVILLE.

RESIDENCE OF Wm O. NEWCOMB, PERRY CENTRE, WYOMING CO., N. Y.

RESIDENCE OF DAVID ANDRUS, PERRY, WYOMING CO., N. Y.

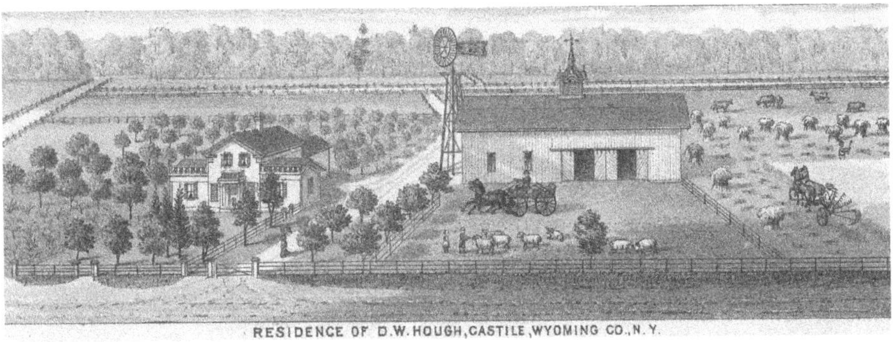

RESIDENCE OF D.W. HOUGH, CASTILE, WYOMING CO., N. Y.

CASTILE AGRICULTURAL WORKS, HOAGLAND CUMMING & CO., PROPRIETORS.
(CHILLED PLOWS A SPECIALTY) WATER STREET, CASTILE, N.Y.

RES. OF J. N. HOAGLAND.

THE TOWN OF PERRY.

THE town of Perry was named in honor of Commodore Oliver H. Perry. It was taken from Leicester and incorporated March 11th, 1814, and at the time of its formation it included Castile and a part of Covington.

The town is included in a tract of fifty thousand acres which was sold by Robert Morris to Samuel Ogden, and which has always been known as the Ogden tract. The north half of this tract, which included about one-third of the town, was sold by Mr. Ogden in two parcels—that on the east to Mr. Ely and others, and that on the west to Mr. Guernsey—and was by them subdivided. Between these, by reason of a discrepancy in the surveys, was what has been known as the gore. The south half, which is called the south Ogden tract, and sometimes the Lake tract, included the balance of the town.

Four principal highways were opened through the town in an early day. The Allegany road, which intersected the Big Tree road near Moscow and led to Olean, crossed the southeast corner of the town. It was laid about 1806. The old Buffalo road, as it was called, was opened across the north part of the town very early, but was not worked, and it never became a thoroughfare because of the impracticable ravines which it crossed. The Big Tree road, which led from Geneseo to Buffalo, crossed the town near the middle, and became the main avenue west, as the Allegany road was south. A road was laid in 1813 from Perry village north through the villages of Perry Center, La Grange, Covington Center and Pavilion to Le Roy, then called Buttermilk Falls. Over these road the first settlers came into the town, and the regions in their vicinity were first settled.

PERRY'S PIONEERS.

Of those here named as having settled on the lots into which the tract was subdivided, some are remembered as original grantees, and others as very early settlers. On the north side of the Big Tree road, on lot No. I, were a Mr. Ensign, Caleb and Nahum Phillips, Samuel Waldo and Elisha Smith; on lot No. 2, Phillips Sparling and Almond Hart; No. 3, Charles Leonard, Gamaliel Leonard, —— Campbell, —— Voorhees, Elkanah Bates; No. 4, east half, Mr. Smith; west half, Ralph and Jabez Ward, who came from New Maltby, Mass., on a cart, and Abram Avery; No. 5, Lemuel Blackmar, Peter Beebe; No. 6, Peter Atwood, who built a hotel on the east part in 1817, Noah D. Sanger, a noted wit and story teller, William True, Graham Benedict and John Squiers; No. 7, Norman Blakeslee and afterward Alexander Kinner (on this lot the first town meetings were held, and the first framed school-house was built);

No. 8, Henry Bush, chiefly known because of his relation to Jack Bush, a slave; No. 9, Buckland, father of J. Buckland, and one Ferris; No. 10, Cassander Watrous, Mark Andrews; No. 11, David Moss, Jesse Moss; on the north side: No. 13, Amos Smith, Gershom Waldo, Gideon Tabor, M. Burt; No 15, Eleazer Sheldon; No. 16, Horace Sheldon; No. 17, Orrin Sheldon, Samuel Howard; No. 18, Nathaniel Howard, Jacob Reed, Pettis brothers; No. 19, John D. Taylor, who was an original grantee in 1814; No. 20, James Taylor; No. 21, Daniel Calkins; No. 22, —— Silver, who had a hotel; No. 24, —— Foskett, father of Daniel Foskett, —— Bills, father of E. O. Bills; No. 27, Elnathan Lacy, who had a tavern on the north end of the lot; No. 28, Josiah Williams; No. 32, Amos Otis, Abram Hamsley, —— Fairchild, Daniel Richards; No. 33, —— Dickerson, Noah Bacon, Freeman Gates, Moses Wooley, Samuel Gates; No. 34, the Kingsleys.

The old Leicester and Buffalo Indian trail crossed lots 31, 32, 33, 34, etc.

In the northeast and north parts of the town settled Richard Alverson and his father, Truman; Samuel Benedict, —— Rudgers (successor to Samuel Gates), Jehiel Glasgow and his father, Hugh; —— Edgerly, at what was Edgerly's Corners. Aaron Hosford, now living at the age of about ninety-seven, and his father, Samuel, settled at Buffalo Corners in 1815. —— Thompson, Bills, Carpenter and others were very early settlers.

The following sketch of pioneer times is gleaned from the recollections of a few of the surviving pioneers of the town:

In 1807 the south half of the Ogden tract, which includes more than half of the town of Perry, was surveyed by William Shepard, of Canandaigua, and soon afterward put in market under the agency of John Greig. As early as 1803 four or five settlements had been commenced on the Holland Purchase west of this tract, a road having been made from Leicester, on the Genesee river, through it. Elizur Webster had settled on the present site of the village of Warsaw, on Oatka, then called Allen's creek. Roswell Turner had gone to North Sheldon, and near the village of Aurora, thirteen miles beyond, Joel Adams, Phineas Stephens, Jabez Warren and others had made a settlement. Considerable settlements had been made in these and other localities on what was called the Big Tree road before any one had located on the Ogden tract.

As early as 1806 the Allegany road from Leicester to Olean was surveyed, and soon afterward opened. A short time after the survey of the tract a road was opened from Leicester to Warsaw through near the center of the town. In 1809 Josiah Williams settled and opened a tavern on this road, about half a mile east from Perry village. In the year 1808 or 1809, a few months previous to the advent of Mr. Williams, Samuel Gates settled on the road between Perry village and South Warsaw, near Silver lake inlet.

Mr. Gates was born in Colchester, Conn., in 1752. When about twenty-four years of age he enlisted in the Revolutionary army under General Gates. He was at Saratoga at the taking of Burgoyne, and in several other battles in the course of the war. After its close he made a voyage to the West Indies, in the course of which a violent storm was encountered, which thoroughly cured him of all desire for a seafaring life. The next spring he shouldered his knapsack and started for the far west. On his arrival at Canajoharie, on the Mohawk, he hired to John and Archibald Kane, farmers and merchants, with whom he remained four years. He then left their service, and was married to a girl sixteen years of age, he being thirty-five. He then engaged for a time in boating on the Mohawk, through Oneida lake, etc., to the foot of Seneca lake. He made several voyages to the head of this lake, when the only whites to be supplied there were Indian traders. He was so well pleased with the country at the head of the lake that he moved his family to the place when there were no whites there. He remained about eight years, then sold his improvements and removed to Caneadea, where he remained about six years. When he went to Caneadea there were but two white families there, those of a father and son named Sanford. On learning that what is now Perry was being surveyed, and hearing good reports of the country, he went there to see it. He was so well pleased with its appearance that he built a house and removed his family there, as before stated, in 1808 or 1809, being then fifty-six years of age. He was the first settler by a few months, cleared the first land, raised the first wheat, and the first white child born in the town was his daughter Nancy, who was afterward married in Bloomfield.

Mrs. Gates died in August, 1812 from the rupture of a blood vessel as she was assisting her husband to roll up a log heap. She was buried near the center of the old cemetery in Perry village. In January, 1813, Mr. Gates died of an epidemic which prevailed that year, after an illness of only about three days. He was buried by the side of his wife. Some three years after his death Mr. Otis discovered an oak sprout, three feet in height growing over their graves. This he trimmed with his pocket knife, and during several years he watched its growth, and occasionally trimmed it till it had reached the height of about twelve feet. It has now grown to be a stately tree, about twenty inches in diameter near the ground. It should be remembered and preserved as nature's monument over the graves of the pioneers of Perry. Mr. Gates passed thirty years of his life on the extreme borders of civilization. His entire life was one of severe labor and hardship.

As before stated, Josiah Williams came in 1809. The death of his daughter Nancy, in 1811, was the first that occurred among the settlers. Mr. Williams died where he settled.

The third settler in the town was Amos Otis, who arrived in February, 1810, and built a log house on the west side of Silver lake inlet, on lot 32, at what is now West Perry. He was born in Colchester, Conn., in 1787. He was kept at school till he was seventeen years of age. He early resolved to be a printer, and on leaving school he applied to Colonel Green, of New London, for a situation as an apprentice. After examining him Mr. Green advised him to accept a position in a drug store, which he offered to procure for him. He went home to consult his parents, and there a friend requested him to accompany him to the Genesee country. He came to Bloomfield, where an uncle resided, and there engaged in teaching. He speaks with pride of his success in his first attempt as a teacher. During a term of five months he did not once administer corporal punishment, though this was near the commencement of the present century. He then went to Lima, where he engaged in teaching for a year and a half. He then alternately worked by the month at farming, and taught during the winter season for a time. While there he was married to Lovisa Davidson, the first white child that was born in the Genesee country. After two or three years they came to Perry and settled, as before stated, on lot 28. His wife died in 1852, since which time he has been twice married. Though he never learned a trade he has worked at the business of a millwright, and has built many mills of different kinds. He has passed through all the phases of pioneer life, and seen the wilderness into which he penetrated when a young man give place to the thriving towns and prosperous rural districts of the present time. He retains vivid recollections of Mary Jemison, who, he says, has often told him of events connected with the Sullivan invasion, which history records incorrectly. In 1867 he removed to Warsaw, where he still resides, at the age of ninety-two.

Elisha M. Smith settled near the inlet, on the Center road, in 1810, built and opened a log tavern, and built a framed barn (the first framed building in town) the same year. It is worthy of note that at the raising of this barn help was so scarce five or six women were called on to assist, which they did. In 1810 Cornelius Anable, Amos Smith, Justus Lyon and Joshua Clark came.

During 1811 Seth Canfield, Julius Curtiss, John Hammersly, James Edgerly and family, Jonathan Atwood, Peter Atwood, Elijah Atwood and Aaron Pond arrived. At the close of this year there were seventeen families in town. Mr. Curtiss purchased a log house that had during the previous year been built but not occupied, on the outlet, near the present Main street bridge, by a man names Palmer. He and Mr. Canfield commenced the erection of a saw-mill that year. John Hammersly, during the year, built a saw-mill and grist-mill at the upper dam, on the outlet. James Thompson was his mill-wright and afterward his son-in-law. James Edgerly erected the first framed house, on the hill at the south end of the village, and kept a tavern there. His son, James E., kept a few dry goods and groceries in the same house. During 1812 settlers came in more rapidly. The war was then in progress, and many chose to stop here rather than go nearer the frontier. In the course of this year David Stannard built a Public house, and William Gould a shoe-shop. Two school-houses were erected in 1812—one at Perry village, the other at West Perry. In the latter Ann Cutting taught the first school that was kept in the town of Perry. She was a sister of Jonas Cutting, of Warsaw. In 1813 Canfield and Curtiss both died of an epidemic which prevailed, and their mills were sold to Levi Benton and in 1817 they were sold to William Wiles, and the same year Jonathan Childs and Benjamin Gardner became the owners of the Hammersly mills.

John H., father of Benjamin H. Hollister, was born April 17th, 1795, in Berkshire, Mass. March 1st, 1816, he arrived in Perry, having driven a team all the way from Massachusetts, and settled on lot 19 in the woods, part of which he had to cut down to get to his place, and more to build a house.

He had married Polly Hart December 31st, 1815. Six of their eleven children are now living.

Wild animals abounded in those days here as elsewhere. In seasons of scarcity, like that of 1816–17, wild game, such as deer, etc., and fish from the lake, were welcome additions to the supplies of the hungry settlers. Bears, as well as wolves, were a pest to the settlers. Mr. Otis states that of five swine which he brought to the country the bears killed four, with their families, though he had the satisfaction of killing an equal number of bears. Bounties were offered for the scalps of wolves, and they were soon thinned out.

Rattlesnakes abounded here at an early day. It is remembered that several people were bitten by them, and were successfully treated by Tallchief, an Indian doctor. They were soon mostly destroyed, though occasionally a solitary pair are still seen.

Almost every pioneer has his stories of encounters with wild animals, and especially with bears, which he delights to relate. It has been said of the plots of romance writers that in the end in almost every case the hero and heroine "got married or else they didn't"; and the similar remark may be made of these bear stories—the bear was killed or escaped.

Among the pioneers of this town was one of whom special mention should be made, because of the uniqueness of his condition here.

Jack Bush, the only slave known to have been brought into Perry, came with his owner, Henry Bush, whose family name he bore, about the year 1811. He was then twenty years of age, and according to the law then in existence he would be free at twenty-eight.

Although his legal status was that of a slave, his servile condition was merely nominal. He was highly esteemed by those who knew him. He was a man of almost gigantic stature and immense physical strength, and although quite peaceable, he was a formidable antagonist when irritated beyond endurance.

A noted bully and bruiser in an adjoining county, having heard of Jack, visited him for the purpose of testing his physical powers. He found him engaged in building fence, and at once made known the object of his visit. Seeing no reason for fighting Jack declined, upon which the man insulted him. Jack at once seized him by the nape of the neck and another convenient part, pitched him over the fence and landed him sprawling on the other side. He arose, rubbed his bruises, declared himself satisfied, and departed. Jack removed to Attica, where he died a few years since.

DEVELOPMENT OF INDUSTRIES.

The first settlers of this town, like those of other parts of this region, manufactured crude potash or black salts from the ashes that remained after burning the timber on their lands. Asheries soon sprang into existence, however. At an early day one was carried on nearly opposite the present residence of Dr. Crichton, at Perry Center, by Landon, Leonard & Sanger. Another was established by Jason Lathrop on the north side of the highway, just east from the cross roads at the same place. Potash was manufactured during many years at this ashery. Another was carried on in the northwest part of the town.

Distilleries sprang up early. The transportation of coarse grain was tedious and expensive, while the spirit into which these distilieries converted it could be taken to market more cheaply. About 1820 one was established at Perry Center by Samuel Howard, and another at West Perry between that year and 1830.

From the first the settlers in Perry, as well as in other towns in this county, engaged in mixed farming. The fertile virgin soil was well adapted to the growth of the cereals which are produced in the latitude, and the protection which the timber of the forest afforded to crops growing in isolated clearings was such that failures were rare.

A saw-mill was built on Beard's creek, near where that stream crosses the county line, by Mr. Fields, about the year 1817. A few years afterward another was erected by Hart & Buell on this creek, farther up, and another on Little Beard's creek, in the northeast part of the town, called the Alverson mill. All these are gone to ruin, and the water of these creeks, since the forest is cleared away, is quite insufficient to propel machinery, except during small portions of each year.

On Silver lake inlet, some two miles west from Perry Center, and about the same distance from West Perry, was also a saw-mill, built by a Mr. Goodell, about 1823. This also has gone to decay.

The first mill erected on the outlet of Silver lake was known as the Hammersly mill, after its builder, John Hammersly. It was erected by him in 1811, and became the property of Childs & Gardner in 1817, and subsequently of Mr. Gardner. It was used as a grist-mill till about 1828. It was converted into a pail factory, and used as such a few years. It fell into disuse, decayed and was finally torn away.

At about the same time Mr. Hammersly built a saw-mill on the north side of the stream. It was propelled by water from the same dam. About the year 1834 James N. Sherman erected a new saw-mill on the site of this. It was used some years, but after a time it was converted into a pump factory, and finally went to decay.

In 1818 William Wiles erected a mill on what is now the fourth dam—where the wheel is now located that propels the machinery of Wyckoff, Tuttle & Olin's large rope factory. The gearing or machinery in this mill was made wholly of wood. The mill was abandoned, and after standing idle a short time, was, in 1860, burned.

About 1823 what is now the fifth dam was thrown across the stream, and a foundry was built there by Harvey Prichard. In this foundry the iron was at first melted in a potash kettle lined with clay, and dipped with ladles by the workmen. A few sleigh shoes that were thus cast are still in the county, and their quality is thought to be superior to that of any that have been manufactured since. A flax-mill took its place about 1860, and it is now operated by William T. Hamlin.

A clothier was built here about 1827, and conducted by Wheeler & Buddington. It was converted into a flouring mill in 1841 by Severance, Palmer & Atwood, and it is now owned by J. Richmond.

About the same time (1823) a clothiery and a saw-mill were built at what is now the third dam. The saw-mill has been rebuilt, repaired and enlarged, and it is now the flourishing lumber and planing-mill and factory of Messrs. Reed & Andrus. The clothiery was, about 1856, converted into a woollen factory, and has since been known as the Perry Woolen-mill. The change was made by John Post. He was succeeded by H. N. Page, then Wylie & Morton, and then the present proprietor, James Wylie.

What is now the second dam was built about 1826. A destillery was first erected on the north side of the stream at this dam, and in 1828 the present grist-mill of George Tomlinson, by Benjamin Gardner. Mr. Gardner had previously built a distillery below the first grist-mill.

About 1830 Bailey & Hatch erected an oil-mill a short distance below the foundry, and oil was manufactured there till about 1848, when the mill fell into disuse.

It was purchased by Robert Grisewood and used as a reservoir for the mill next below, but it finally ceased to be useful even for that purpose.

A short distance below this oil mill a lighter dam was built at a point where the fall in the stream is repid, and a grist-mill was erected by a man named Bailey, from Le Roy. This mill was owned successively by Bailey & Hatch, Bailey, Brown & Grisewood, Robert Grisewood, Bailey, Brown & Frost, G. Taylor, A D. Smith, R. Grisewood. Grisewood & Bradfield, Bradfield & Bolton, Bradfield & Loomis, White & Harrington, and Cornish & Chace.

A tannery was erected about a quarter of a mile below this grist-mill by Samuel and Henry Phenix, and business was carried on there during a series of years; but it finally declined, and the tannery was converted into a spoke factory.

Near the county line, on this stream, a saw-mill was built at an early day. It went down years since. About the year 1864 the dam was rebuilt, and machinery was constructed with which to drill for oil. This was done to a depth of about eight hundred feet, but no oil was found. Gas discharged from the Well for a time profusely.

THE PIONEER PHYSICIAN.

Dr. Otis Higgins was, if not the first, one of the earliest practitioners in the town, and when the difference between then and now is recollected, it will not for a moment be imagined that a physician led a life of greater case than the pioneer who subdued the forest.

There were then no centers of population, like the present large villages which are found in almost every town, but the sparse population was spread over a wide extent of territory. Instead of the smooth roads over which the physicians at the present day ride in their easy carriages, here and there a way was cut through the forest and the stumps left standing; or perhaps the way was only marked, to obviate the danger of being lost. Over such roads Dr. H. could only go on horseback, or in some cases on foot.

Physicians then were more like angels' visits, few and far between, than now. If the husband, wife or child in a distant solitary pioneer cabin languished on a sick bed, the aid of the doctor was invoked; and perhaps the place was only accessible by leaving the horse that had borne him a portion of the distance tied to a sapling, crossing a swollen, unfordable stream on a log, and threading his way through the forest, guided by marked trees, with his saddle bags on his arm. On his return, overtaken perhaps by the darkness, he was compelled to listen to the howling of the wolves; not sufficiently famished to embolden them to making an attack, but hungry enough to prompt such an expression of a desire to pick his bones as to make him think of his fireside and wish himself there. Neither he nor the settlers whom he served enjoyed the facilities which everywhere abound now for procuring medicines. A few common drugs were kept at the pioneer store, and the merchant took with him on his annual or biennial visits to Albany the doctor's memorandum, and brought back the medicines ordered; but he was compelled to rely to some extent on the roots, braks and plants which he gathered in the woods and prepared in his homely office, and thus he kept himself familiar with the medical properties of many indigenous plants of which physicians are now wholly ignorant.

SCHOOLS IN THE TOWN.

About the year 1819 the first school that is remembered was taught in the town of Perry, near the Center, by Samuel Waldo, in a house that stood on the corner just west from S. W. Tewksbury's residence.

Under the school law of 1811 there were commissioners elected, and a division of the town into districts was made in accordance with then existing circumstances. About 1820 the town was redistricted, and the districts then established were changed from time to time, as changing circumstances required.

Latterly, as the rural population has decreased, and fewer children are living in these districts, the number of districts diminishes. This diminution is due both to the decrease of population and to the practice which has come of late to prevail of consolidating districts in order to make the schools larger, extend the curriculum of study in them, and render them more efficient. In this respect the schools of Perry are like those of other towns. The school district at Perry Center embraces a territory some three miles in extent each way, and two teachers are employed in the school.

FARM RESIDENCE OF R.W. BRIGHAM, PERRY, N.Y.

RESIDENCE OF B.H. HOLLISTER, PERRY, N.Y.

RES. OF S.L. CHAPIN, PERRY, N.Y.

RESIDENCE OF JAMES WYLIE, PERRY, N.Y.

THE SILVER LAKE SERPENT.

Some twenty-three years since a very successful canard was circulated here, and afterward, by the connivance of certain editors, it spread through the entire county.

From time immemorial a tradition had existed among the Indians of a monstrous serpent that inhabited Silver lake. This tradition was known to many of the inhabitants in the vicinity, and by some few was credited. A man who was gathering flags between the inlet and the outlet of the Lake, saw suddenly rise before him something which so frightened him that he left in haste and could not be induced to return. Not long afterward several men, who were entirely credible, saw something which they took to be an enormous serpent. These men verified their statement by an affidavit which was published, and many visited the lake and watched for his snakeship. A journalist from Buffalo wrote a glowing account of the serpent, which was illustrated by its likeness, and was republished in all parts of the county. An observatory was erected at a place commanding a view of the entire lake, and in this people watched "from morn till night." An intrepid whaleman, armed with a harpoon and the other of his office, cruised daily in search of the monster. It afterward "leaked out" that a certain fun loving Boniface had hired him to do this, and it was whispered that an attempt was made to manufacture an india-rubber serpent in order to meet an evident demand for a humbug. The journals continued to publish extravagant implements stories of the matter, and the excitement was kept up for some time, greatly to the advantage of railroad companies, stage proprietors advertised than it could have been by any other process. It is doubted, however, whether any snake larger than those which, under certain circumstances, infest people's boots, was ever seen.

POLITICAL HISTORY AND STATISTICS.

As has been stated, Perry was incorporated in 1814. In that year the first town meeting was held at the house of Peter Beebe, at Perry Center; Jairus Cruttenden was chosen supervisor, Warren Buckland town clerk, and Salmon Preston constable and collector. Levi Benton, Pardon Tabor, James Symonds and Robert Moore were the first justices chosen by the supervisors and judges under the constitution of 1821.

The records of the town were burnt on the first of February, 1866. The names of the supervisors previous to that time were obtained from the records of the counties of Genesee and Wyoming. In 1814 Jairus Cruttenden was elected; in 1815 and 1818, Levi Benton; 1817, John Bowers; 1821, Oren Sheldon; 1823 and 1850, Rufus H. Smith; 1827, Robert Moore; 1830 and 1834, James Symonds; 1831, Phicol M. Ward; 1835, Truman Benedict; 1844, Samuel Benedict; 1848, Lewis H. Parsons; 1849, Jason Lathrop; 1851, John Coleman; 1856, Dennis R. Taylor; 1866 and 1873, Samuel W. Tewksbury; 1871, Randall W. Brigham; 1874, William Crichton; 1876, Henry N. Page.

Perry, like several other towns of the county, has suffered a serious loss of population during the last forty years. The State census returns since 1825 furnish the following figures: 1830, 2,792; 1835, 2,984; 1840, 3,087; 1845, 2,952; 1850, 2,832; 1855, 2,560; 1860, 2,452; 1865, 2,366; 1870, 2,342; 1875, 2,416.

WEST PERRY.

West Perry is a hamlet near the foot of Silver lake, about a mile and a half from Perry village.

About the year 1824 the cemetery at West Perry was established, by a voluntary association, of which Dan Dickinson, Nathaniel Otis and Arad Stilwell were trustees. These trustees bought from Charles P. Jewett an acre of ground for $7. This they enclosed with a rail fence, and divided it into lots of a convenient size.

PERRY CENTER.

This village is a place of some forty houses. The first postmaster was Talcott Howard, and he was followed in succession by Jason Lathrop, Henry Cleveland, Charles McEntee and Daniel Ball; but the dates of their appointment are lost.

In 1816 a store was established by a Mr. Pierce, of Avon, with John D. London as his agent. This store was a small building that stood on the present garden of Dr. William Crichton. It was long since moved away, and converted successively into a tailor's shop, dwelling-house, barn, and finally into a hop house, for which it is used by its present owner, William O. Newcomb.

Clough and Howe were the first blacksmiths.

The first tavern at Perry Center was built by Peter Beebe. It, was a log house, and it stood on ground now occupied by Daniel Ball's house. Mr. Beebe settled here in 1810 or 1811, and built this house soon afterward. He occupied it as a tavern a few years, and then erected a framed building on the same site, which he used many years as a hotel. It was afterward moved away, and it is now the principal part of the residence of William O. Newcomb.

On the northwest corner a large framed building was erected for a hotel in 1817, by one Atwood. It was occupied as a hotel by various parties till 1858. It is now the residence of William H. Hawley.

Mrs. Polly Higgins, whose maiden name was Taylor, and who was born in Berkshire county, Mass, in 1800, came to Perry Center in 1813. She is now living at Perry. She remembers that when she came, with her parents, twenty days were consumed on the road, with two teams and some household goods. They brought the second barrel of pork that came into the town. At the time she came there were but two settlers between Moscow and Perry Center. They were a Mr. Smith and a Mr. Blackmore, near the Center. In addition to those already spoken of, she remembers Ralph Ward, Hervey Butler, Orren Sheldon, Mr. Howard and his children, Captain Atwood, Mr. Pettis, Mr. Macklin, Horace Bingham and Noah D. Sanger; north were Thomas McEntee and his brother and others; west were Mr. Buckland, Alexander Kinney and Henry Bush; south were Hollister, Brigham and Gould.

CEMETERY, PERRY CENTER.

The cemetery at Perry Center is under the management of an incorporated association, formed in 1818, with Samuel Howard, Phicol M. Ward and Orren Sheldon as trustees. They bought half an acre from Lemuel Blackmer for $40, and the ground has since been enlarged to two acres. The original divisions was into lots of a square rod each, which were sold at fifty cents apiece. Improvements have been made by voluntary contributions.

CONGREGATIONAL CHURCH, PERRY CENTER.

The first church organization in the town of Perry, and one of the oldest Congregational churches in the county, was organized at Perry Center on the 28th of June, 1814, by Rev. Oliver Ayer and Rev. Silas Hubbard, who had been sent out from the Connecticut Missionary Society. The original members were Samuel Howard, Ralph Ward, Mrs. Lorain Ward, Miss Catey Ward. Hervey Butler, Mrs. Sally Butler and Miss Roxa Carpenter.

The ecclesiastical society was formed and trustees were chosen July 21st, 1817; and the society and reorganized December 6th 1825. The first house of worship was commenced in 1828, and dedicated March 4th, 1830; Rev. Julius Steele, of Warsaw, officiating. It was repaired in 1856, and rededicated on the 29th of December of that year; Rev. J. E. Nassau, of Warsaw, preaching the sermon. It was again repaired in 1867.

In 1816 the church united with the Presbytery of Geneva, but retained the Congregational form of government. This was called union on the "accommodation plan." In 1817, by a division of the Presbytery of Geneva, this church became a part of the Presbytery of Ontario; and by another division, in 1819, of that of Genesee, which connection was retained till 1831, when the church unanimously resolved to dissolve its union with the presbytery, and was regularly dismissed. Since that time its government has been Congregational. In 1865 this church became a member of the Wyoming County Conference of Congregational Ministers and Churches, and advisory body, possessing no ecclesiastical authority.

Since 1824 there has existed among the female members of this church a missionary society, which has been at different times auxiliary to the Foreign Missionary Society, the Home Missionary Society and the Bethel Society. In 1846 the Female Benevolent Society was formed for various benevolent purposes.

The pastors of this church have been:

Revs. Edmund Ingalls, jr., 1816; Elihu Mason, 1817, 1820; Edward Andrews, 1819; Samuel T. Mills, 1821–24; Eli S. Hunter, 1825, 1826; Jonathan Sheldon,

1826, 1827; Lot B. Sullivan, 1827, 1828; Dexter Cary, 1829; William P. Jackson, 1829; Samuel H. Gridley, D. D., 1830–36; Oren Brown, 1836; Caleb Burge, 1837, 1838; George W. Newcomb, 1838-40; John Scott, 1840, 1841; George W. Gridley, 1842; Wales Tileston, 1843, 1844; Philo Canfield, 1845–48; Watson Mearsmith, 1848; Thomas Morey Hodgman, 1848–58; George J. Means, 1859–63; Isaac N. Ely, 1863; Claudius B. Lord, 1864–66; James Pierce Root, 1866–74; W. C. Sexton, 1875–77; Edgar Perkins, the present pastor, came in 1877.

Of these pastors three, S. H. Gridley, D. D., Rev. T. M. Hodgman, and Rev. George J. Means were installed at the beginning of their pastorates. Rev. C. Burge, during his ministry in this church, died because of being thrown from his carriage descending Warsaw hill on his way to conduct the exercises at a funeral.

The following have been elected deacons of this church: Jabez Ward and Hervey Butler in 1814, Horace Sheldon, 1817, Samuel Howard, 1843, Simeon R. Barber, 1854, John M. Butler, 1854.

Of the former members of this church Messrs. Stewart Sheldon, C. A. Huntington and Joseph Ward have become clergymen.

In 1822 a number of the members of this organization established a Presbyterian church in the village of Perry, but in 1831 this organization became extinct. It was revived in 1835, since which time it has been successful.

A Sabbath-school was established and a Bible class formed by Deacon H. Sheldon about 1829. Captain P. McEntee, Deacons S. R. Barber and John S. Butler, Thomas McEntee, George Keeney, George K. Sheldon, Andrew Sheldon, Joseph Buckland and J. L. Wygant have been superintendents.

PERRY VILLAGE.

This place began to give promise of becoming a village soon after the first settlement of the town. A grist-mill and saw-mill were built here in 1811, and within two or three years a small store was established. It was first called by the people of the town Shacksburg, then Columbia, and afterward Nineveh; but it finally, as well as the town, took the name of the hero of Lake Erie.

The first store was kept on the hill near where the railroad depot now stands, but as time went on and the village grew, the center of business came to be where it is now. The village never had any periods of spasmodic growth, but increased steadily in size and activity till about 1842, since which its growth has been less rapid. The location of the county seat at Warsaw induced many to become residents of that village who would otherwise have settled at Perry, and thus its growth was retarded. The general introduction of steam as a motive power has, by facilitating the establishment of manufactories wherever the raw material exists, prevented the utilization of water power; and for this reason Perry is less of a manufacturing village than it might otherwise have become.

Nine years since a railroad was built, by the enterprise of the citizens of the town and village, from this place to Gainesville, where it connects with the

N. Y., L. E. & W. Railroad, thus affording facilities for travel and transportation fully equal to those of any village in this part of the county. Within a few years the beautiful shores of Silver lake have attracted many hither during the summer season, and this of course increases the activity of the place; and this increase is likely to continue, for Silver lake is rapidly becoming more and more of a summer resort. The population of the village in 1870 was 867, and now (1879) it is probably about 1,000.

PERRY VILLAGE POLITICAL HISTORY.

Perry was incorporated by an act of the Legislature in the year 1830. The act of incorporation created the usual municipal officers, and invested these officers with the powers ordinarily conferred for the administration and regulation of village affairs.

It is true of many villages that the inhabitants, who are largely composed of mechanics, tradesmen and retired business men, who own places of business and village residences, are anxious to extend the limits of these corporations, and include sometimes an unreasonable area of real estate in order that their burden of taxation may be lighter. That such was not the case here in shown by the thirteenth section of the act, which reads thus:

> "The lands comprehended within the bounds of the village, and which are reserved as woodlands, meadow lands, pastures, orchards, and in general all such lands as are kept and improved as farming lands, with their appurtenances (dwelling-houses, mills and buildings excepted), shall not, as long as they are so reserved, kept or used, be taxed for the benefit of the village."

This charter was revised and amended, or rather a new one was granted, by a special act in 1864 to meet the wants which changed circumstances had created. The same provision above quoted is a part of this charter.

The records of the village are said to have been destroyed by fire, as were those of the town, in 1866. The charter provides that the president shall be chosen each year by the board of trustees from among their number. Since 1866 the following citizens have held the office of president and trustee:

Presidents.—In 1867, Mortimer Sharpsteen; 1868, John S. Thompson; 1869, 1870, Samuel L. Chapin; 1871, Lyman G. Morgan; 1872, R. C. Moredoff; 1873, 1874, Jerome Allen; 1875, H. N. Page; 1876, 1877, R. C. Smith; 1878, 1879, H. C. Loomis.

Trustees.—J. Beardsley, E. H. Wygant, A. Hershey, James Wylie, Alexander Cole, J. W. Bolton, E. G. Matthews, Hugh M. Scranton, David Andrus, Charles W. G. Nobles, William T. Hamlin, M. C. Williams, D. C. White, M. E. Benedict, M. G. Davis, Alanson King, Horace A. Brigham, George Tomlinson, F. O. Bullard, William Keeton, R. H. Sherman, R. T. Tuttle, Charles H. Homan, S. A. Hatch, G. B. Westlake and John Richmond.

FARM RESIDENCE OF PARIS OLIN, NEAR PERRY CENTRE, N.Y.

FARM RESIDENCE OF A. W. TOAN, PERRY N.Y.

RESIDENCE OF M. C. WILLIAMS, PERRY N.Y.

CEMETERIES IN PERRY VILLAGE.

At a very early day Selden, Ebenezer and Dr. Otis Higgins purchased from William Wiles the land on lot 29 that included the old cemetery, which is now on the east side of Main street. At this time there were two graves there. Interments continued to be made there, and the ground was enclosed by picket fence, planted with trees and more systematically arranged. It originally extended across what is now Main street, and even included a strip of ground on the opposite side, between the Presbyterian and Bapist churches. Main street had no existence then, and the cemetery fronted on the road southeast from it.

This ground became nearly filled with graves, and a voluntary association was formed and arrangements made for a second cemetery. An acre and three-fourths was bought of Calvin P. Bailey and Samuel Hatch by Elnathan Lacy, William Dolbeer and Willard Chapin, October 3d, 1833. In 1857 additional land on the same lot was conveyed to William Dolbeer, and this was the village cemetery from 1833 till 1876.

All this was conveyed to the Hope Cemetery Association, which was organized in the spring of 1876. The corporation were David Andrus, Ann Kinney, Mrs. C. P. Andrus, Edward G. Matthews, Mrs. R. T. Tuttle and G. B. Olin. At their first meeting, May 5th, 1876, David Andrus was chosen president, and G. B. Olin secretary and superintendent of the grounds.

An addition was made to the cemetery lot, and the whole includes five acres. The grounds were laid out by H. B. Allen, surveyor, of Arcade.

Mr. Andrus and Mr. Olin remain president and secretary. The trustees are the same as at first, except Alanson King in place of Mr. Matthews.

BUSINESS MEN OF PERRY.

The following list of the business men in the village of Perry is derived from the memory of citizens, and it is not probably given in the exact order in which they engaged in business, and probably it does not embrace the names of all the business men of the place:

General Merchants:—T. & J. C. Edgerly, Bailey & Hatch, Benjamin Gardner, —— De Zang, Richard Bayley, William Wiles, R. H. Smith, Orris Gardner, Phœnix & Brother, Armitage & Faulkner, L. B. Parsons & Son, Parsons & Clark, Smith & Graves, D. Graves, Cleveland & Graves, C. P. Bailey & Son, Corydon Weed, S. W. Merrill & Sons, George L. Davis, A. D. Smith, H. N. Page, S. P. Clark, J. H. Bailey, H. W. Barton, J. H. & C. W. Bailey, Robert Grisewood, Cook & Currier, N. P. Currier, F. O. Bullard, Moredoff & Higgins, Eugene Andrus, R. C. Moredoff, M. C. Williams, A. H. Sleeper, Robert Stainton.

Grocers:—Walter Little, H.W. Barton, Jirah Higgins, Hicks & Bailey, R. B. Hicks, —— Stratton, E. W. Frost, Williams & Stedman, George Pritchard, C. P. Andrus, Wheeler & Garrison, Billings & Ring, F. O. Bullard, Mark Smith, R. H. Stedman, John Garrison, Hatch & Co.

Hardware Merchants:—E. P. Clark, Wyckoff, Tuttle & Olin.

Druggists:—Joseph Lamberson, D. Mitchell, S. & D. B. Higgins, Wright & Allen, J. H. Terry, W.J. Chaplin, James H. Owen.

Booksellers, Stationers, etc.:—E. M. Tompkins, H. N. Page, E. H. Wygant.

Clothiers:—J. S. Westlake, J. S. Brayton. S. N. May, Alexander Morton, M. Duryee.

Boot and Shoe Dealers:—W. J. Chaplin & Son, Moffat & Brown, R. C. Smith, A. C. Barras, J. B. Sherman, Alexander Cole.

Furniture Dealers:—A. S. Horton, Hooper & Butree, N. Edgerly, W. T. Butree, G. H. Westlake.

Musical Instruments:—German Sweet.

Hotel Keepers:—R. Watrous, J. H. Kermott, —— Livingston, —— Taylor, B. Harford, —— Cole, A. B. Walker.

Foundries and Machine Shops:—Hicks & Bailey, Bacheller & Higgins, suoceeded by many firms, and finally Royce Reaper Manufactory.

Tanneries:—The first tannery was built just at the north end of Andrus's store by Willard J. Chapin, and owned by him till it rotted down. The tannery of the Phoenix Brothers has been elsewhere spoken of.

Physicians:—Otis Higgins, Mason G. Smith, Jacob Nevins, Jabez Ward, George L. Keeney, Jones Huntington, E. Z. Joslyn, Jonathan Howard, R. A. Patchen, C. A. Dake, J. W. Post, M. G. Davis, Charles R. Pearce, T. R. Huntington, G. R. Traver, L. L. Rockafellow, J. H. Wheeldon, L. W. Hunt.

Attorneys:—Robert Moore, Calvin Pepper, M. C. Hough, I. N. Stoddard, L.W. Thayer, Levi Gibbs, J. J. Pettit, William Pettit, L. A. Hayward, William Mitchell, —— Blannerhasset, A. A. Hendee, D. L. Gilman, A. Lent, E. B. Fiske, G. L. Walker, M. A. Lovejoy, Owen Harris.

At the time when hats were manufactured by hand a hatter's shop was to be found in every considerable village, and the making and repairing of hats was a regular branch of industry. Of those who carried on this business in Perry, Alanson O. Buddington, Harmon Skidmore and R. C. Moredoff are remembered. Thomas Brown, George Brown and —— Sleight are spoken of as early tailors; Houghton & Torry, cabinet makers; Antonio Willard, one of the earliest among wagon makers, and B. Townly, the first tinsmith who worked in the village.

SMITH'S BANK

This was organized in 1855 as a State bank, with a capital of $50,000, by R. H. Smith (president) and A. D. Smith, his son (cashier). On the death of R. H. Smith, in 1858, A. D. Smith became president, and Charles W. Hendee cashier. In 1862 H. N. Page became cashier.

A. D. Smith died in 1866, and his widow became sole proprietress of the bank. Mr. Page since had sole charge. When the national banking system went into operation this bank ceased to circulate notes, and it has since been a private bank.

LODGES.

Constellation Lodge, No. 404, *F. & A. M.* was constituted by a charter from the grand lodge of New York, which charter bore date July 5th, 1846. The officers named in this charter were Charles W. Hendee, W. M.; Henry E. Daniels, S. W.; Joseph B. Wycoff, J. W.

The charter was surrendered in 1862, and during ten years the sound of the gavel was not heard. It was restored in 1872.

The present officers are E. M. Reed, W. M.; M. S. Nobles, S. W.; M. Hathaway, J. W.; C. Homan, treasurer; J. J. Martin, secretary; L. E. Chapin, S. D.; H. L. Birdsall, J. D.; R. F. Bullard, tyler. The present membership is 44.

Oriental Lodge, No. 173, *A. O. U. W.* was instituted September 20th, 1878, with thirteen charter members.

The first officers were Robert Stainton, P. M. W.; G. R. Traver, M. W.; F. C. Green recorder; F. E. Cole, F.; M. Duryee, receiver. The trustees were G. R. Smith, A. S. Whitcomb and G. H. Westlake. Since its commencement the lodge has received eleven new members, and has lost one by removal; none have died.

The present officers are the same as at first, except that G. R. Traver is the P. M. W.; Robert Stainton, M. W.; M. E. Williams, G. F.; nd A. S. Whitcomb, recorder. The place of meeting is at their hall, corner of Main and Covington streets, Perry village.

PERRY ACADEMY AND UNION SCHOOL.

Perry Academy was established in 1854. The corner stone of the academy building was laid July 4th, 1853. The expense of the building was defrayed by voluntary contribution of the citizens of the town of Perry, and the school was conducted as a union or non-sectarian academy for three years. During the remainder of its existence as an academy it was controlled by the Methodist denomination.

The building was constructed at a cost of $14,000, eighty-seven by fifty-eight feet, and three stories high above the basement, which was subsequently fitted up for a boarding hall; and having a spacious chapel in the third story and containing thirty study and recitation rooms. The site procured was an eminence in a retired part of the village. The library and apparatus cost $600. The library now consists of over a thousand well selected volumes, and additions are yearly made to the apparatus.

The first principal was Charles H. Dann, now of Warsaw; and there were seven subordinate teachers. During the first year the aggregate number of students was 324. The course of study embraced all the branches usually taught in an academy, and the success of the institution was equal to the average of similar schools.

Previous to 1872 the public school of Perry was held in the old schoolhouse near the Methodist church. The building having become unfit for school purposes, the project of erecting a new one was agitated in several school meetings called for that purpose. At a meeting held April 12th, 1872, it was finally resolved to appropriate $5,500 for the purchase of a new site and the erection of a new building. During the following the week the project of purchasing the Perry Academy instead of putting up a new building was privately discussed, and at a special meeting called for the 23d a committee, consisting of H. H. Brigham, William Chamberlin and George Tomlinson, was appointed to confer with the trustees of the academy, The result of their negotiations was the transfer of the academy property to the district for $4,500.

A meeting was held in August, at which it was voted to organize a union free school, adopting the academy as the academic department. A board of trustees was elected, consisting of E. M. Read, R. C. Mordoff, William Chamberlin, E. G. Matthews, H. A. Brigham, M. C. Williams and H. M. Scranton.

The school opened in October, with the following faculty: Principal, Professor Wildman; preceptress, Miss E. S. Calligan; assistant, Miss E. E. Ames; intermediate, Miss Ellen Smallwood; primary, Miss —— Chamberlin; music, Mrs. A. D. Howland; drawing, Miss Mary Brigham.

The following year Miss Calligan was elected to the principalship, which position she held down to 1878. Under her management the school made excellent progress, improving in scholarship and increasing in numbers. During the last year of her stay the school was carefully regraded to conform to a wider and more thorough course of study. A disagreement arising between her and the board in regard to the number of teachers necessary to carry out the new course of study, she resigned, and Mr. I. P. Bishop was chosen in her place, which he holds at the present date.

The course of study extends over three years in the primary department, three in the intermediate, and three in the grammar school. In the academic department students are allowed the choice of three courses: the English, extending over three years, and the scientific and classical, each extending over four years. The school is now in a flourishing condition and is considered inferior to none in the county in point of thoroughness and efficiency.

The following is the composition of the present faculty and school board: Principal, Irving P. Bishop; preceptress, Miss E. May Skiff; assistants, Miss Minnie F. Wheelock and Miss Hattie Kellog; music, Miss Flora Elliot; drawing, Miss Flora Bradley; intermediate, Miss Cora B. Percival; primary, Mrs. Ida M. Smith; board of education—E. G. Matthews (president), E. H. Wygant (secretary), Willard Chapin, Anson Sleeper, T. B. Catton and Hiram Wright.

THE PRESS OF PERRY.

The *Genesee Recorder* was commenced at Perry by George M. Shipper in 1834, and continued for two years.

In 1841 Peter Lawrence commenced the publication of the *Perry Democrat.* In 1848 it passed into the hands of C. C. Britt, who continued it until 1853.

The *Countryman* was started at Perry in 1843 by N. S. Woodward. Soon after it was purchased by Daniel S. Curtis, who changed its name to the *Impartial Countryman,* and continued it until August, 1864, when it passed to Ansel Warren, who again changed its name to the *Free Citizen*, and issued it until August, 1847.

The *Christian Investigator* was published at the office of the *Free Citizen*, in Perry, for one year, and was edited by William Goodell.

The *Wyoming Advertiser* was commenced December 22nd, 1853, published one year by Horace Wilcox.

The *Wyoming Times* was commenced at Perry in May, 1855, by T. S. Giilett. In 1856 it was destroyed by fire, and was revived soon after. Its publication ceased, however, in the year 1863.

The *Silver Lake Sun* was started at Perry in December, 1865, by George A. Sanders, by whom it was published till 1877.

The *Wyoming County Herald* was established in July, 1877, by Lewis E. Chapin, and published at Perry. The name was changed in 1878 to *The Herald,* and it is still issued.

CHURCHES OF PERRY VILLAGE.

BAPTIST.

As early as 1816 there were a few families of Baptists in Perry and Castile.

On the 25th of October, 1818, the following persons organized themselves into a Baptist Church: Solomon Squiers, John Bowen, Beriah Bowers, David Carlisle, Thomas E. Parmerly, Peter Clark, Samuel Waldo, Martha Barlett, Hannah Finch, Betsey Leonard, Anna Squiers, Sarah Parmerly, Clarinda Bowers and Nancy Bowers. Of these Samuel Waldo alone remained a member of the church in 1879. November 5th, 1818, the church was recognized by a council, convened at the house of John Bowers, at which the sermon was preached by Rev. Daniel McBride.

Rev. Mr. Wisner was the first pastor. He labored about one year, receiving for his salary only such donations as the people were able to offer. He was succeeded in 1820 by Rev. Jesse Brown, who also continued about one year, after which the church was supplied by Rev. Joshua Bradley and others till August 25th, 1822, when it became a branch of the church at Middlebury.

On the first of October, 1825, the church was reorganized and recognized as an independent church, with thirty-three members. In 1826 Rev. Richard H. Benedict became pastor, and he remained two years. Rev. Noah Barell became

REAPER WORKS OF WYCKOFF, TUTTLE & OLIN, PERRY, N.Y.

FARM RESIDENCE OF PHILIP DURYEE, CASTILE, N.Y.

pastor in 1828, and his pastorate continued more than a year, during which intense feeling arose in the church on the subject of masonry. Several members of the masonic fraternity severed their connection with the institution, and a resolution was adopted refusing fellowship with masons.

Rev. Daniel Eldridge became pastor in 1830. In 1833 Rev. Absalaom Miner; 1834, Rev. William Arthur; 1837, Rev. Elon Galusha; 1841, Rev. Daniel Eldridge; 1843, Rev. J. W. Spoor; 1846, Rev. F. Glanville; 1849, Rev. Walter R. Brooks; 1857, Rev. Chauncey W. Wardener; 1859, Rev. Roswell Cheney; 1875, Rev. Charles Ayer; 1877, the present pastor, Rev. J. W. Harris, son of Rev. Norman Harris, who has been during thirty-three years a missionary in burmah.

The society worshiped in school-houses, etc., till 1830, when a church edifice was erected at a cost of $3,000. It has been enlarged to about double its original capacity.

During the pastorate of Mr. Galusha the church took positive ground against American slavery, and the members resolved that "as a church of Christ they could not fellowship slaveholders or their apologists." From this position the church never receded.

In 1850, at the annual meeting, the church resolved "that we deem it the duty of all Christians to abstain from the sale and use of all intoxicating drinks or liquors as a beverage, strong beer not excepted, and we cannot fellowship the conduct of any brother who will not thus abstain."

In July, 1844, it was voted to have no fellowship with members of a secret society. In February, 1861, it was voted a duty to aid in the circulation of such publications as expose free masonry. A resolution was subsequently passed not to require any tests as to society membership. A portion of the members were dissatisfied with this action and withdrew their support. It is therefore difficult to ascertain the present number of members.

PRESBYTERIAN.

The first Presbyterian church organized in Perry was established July 22nd, 1822. Revs. Samuel T. Mills, of Moscow, and Norris Bull, of Geneseo, were present at the organization, and it is remembered that Ebenezer Higgins was chosen clerk. The first organization never numbered more than twenty-seven and never had a settled minister.

On the 14th of July, 1835, this church was reorganized, and soon afterward a house of worship was erected.

Rev. Samuel Gridley, now of Waterloo, N. Y., was active in the second church organization, which consisted of twenty-three members, of whom Mrs. Polly Higgins alone survives. A society had been organized September 13th, 1834, with Merrick Hough, Otis Higgins, Edmund Birdsall, James R. Webster,—now of Waterloo, N. Y.,—Orris D. Gardner and Harvey E. Homans as trustees. In 1838 Rev. S. Haynes—now of Rome—became the supply of this church, and it was determined to build a house of worship. This was done, and on the 1st of January, 1839, it was dedicated; Revs. Erastus Gillett, of Batavia, Joseph Ladd, W. Stratton and S. Haynes Participating in the dedicatory services. Rev. Mr. Haynes was, in February, 1840, succeeded by James R. Page, D. D., now of Brighton, N. Y., who, with the exception of several short intervals, continued to be pastor during twenty-seven years. Revs. J. W. Ray and William Patingill supplied the pulpit for short periods during that time. In 1868 Dr. Page was succeeded by Rev. H. M. Hazeltine, who was pastor till 1870. When he was succeeded by Rev. Mr. Gardner, and he, in 1872, by the present pastor, Rev. E. H. Dibble.

Temporary repairs have been made in the church edifice from time to time. In 1852 a lecture room was built, and a bell was presented to the society by E. P. Clark. In 1875 extensive repairs were made, costing, including an organ, about $6,700. The society owns a parsonage. The present membership of the church is 145; that of the Sunday-school is 150.

METHODIST EPISCOPAL.

The data for this sketch of the M. E. church in Perry down to about 1840 are gleaned from a series of articles written by Rev. John Stainton, who came to this town in 1819, at the age of twenty one.

Henry Wallace, who in June, 1816, settled on the east side of the outlet of Silver lake, about half a mile from Perry village, was a Methodist, and induced Rev. Robert Winchell to visit Perry and preach in his house. Mr. Winchell formed a class of six members—Henry Wallace, leader; Sabra Walace, his wife, Hannah Wallace, his daughter-in-law, Miles Rhoads and wife, and a Mrs. Dow, who had located a mile or two farther south about the same time with Mr. Wallace. Mr. Winchell and his associates, Rev. William Jones and Rev. Thomas Magee, visited and preached to this class occasionally. Of this first class Hannah Wallace died in 1831, Henry Wallace in 1840, at the age of eighty-two, and Sabra Wallace in 1844, aged eighty.

In February, 1817, Rev. William Wiles, with his own and two other families of Methodists, came. Thomas Bachelor, an exhorter, settled near this place about the same time, and in 1818 Thomas Grisewood, three of whose sons were afterward preachers. Mr. Wallace, on becoming deaf, was succeeded as class leader by Story Wiles, and he, in 1819, by Thomas Grisewood.

The class by 1822 numbered thirty or forty. November 23d of that year a society was incorporated, with Samuel Gilman, Thomas Grisewood, William Dolbeer, Daniel Wiles, Thomas Bachelor and Rev. William Wiles as trustees.

Measures were at once instituted and prosecuted for the erection of a house of worship, and in the autumn of 1823 the first church edifice in this part of the country, except at Warsaw, was erected and enclosed. It was finished in 1824, and dedicated that year by Rev. Goodwin Stoddard, presiding elder of the district. In 1826 the Genesee conference sat in this church. It stood on the site of the present residence of Richard Smith, just north from where the present edifice stands.

In 1832 or 1833 this building was found too small, and it was sold, removed and used several years by the Universalist society. It was then converted into a dwelling or boarding-house for the accommodation of the academy, and a more capacious church erected. It was dedicated by Rev. Samuel Lucky, D.D.

In 1839 this house was burned. A chapel was soon erected in which the congregation worshiped about two years, till the completion of the present church edifice. The new and more capacious edifice was completed, and dedicated by Rev. Schuyler Seager, D. D., in the autumn of 1840. This building at one time required extensive repairs after a fire. In January, 1836, a parsonage was bought on Leicester street, a few rods west from where the academy stands. April 19th, 1877, this was burned. A lot was purchased on the corner of Center and Leicester streets, on which was erected one of the most substantial, commodious and beautiful parsonages to be found in western New York. To this enterprise Mr. M. P. Andrews and wife contributed the generous sum of $2,200.

Perry was once a circuit, embracing a large surrounding territory that has since been divided into several distinct pastoral charges. It was set off by itself as a station in 1831, Rev. Philo Woodworth pastor. During its history there have been three sessions of the Genesee Annual Conference in this place—the sessions of 1829, 1837 and 1858. At the session of 1829 action was taken which resulted in the founding of the seminary at Lima.

After the conference of 1858 the Free Methodist church of Perry was formed, by a secession from this one, and in 1861 it was legally organized.

From an early period a Sabbath-school has been sustained in the M. E. church of this place. Among the earliest superintendents were Rev. J. Stainton and Mr. Gilbert Mitchel; in later times Prof. M. R. Atkins, A. B. Cooley, D. P. Stowell and others have filled this office.

Among the pastors here have been Rev. Drs. F. G. Hibbard, Seth Mattison, S. Hunt, J. H. Bayliss, J. B. Wentworth and others widely known through the connection. The society has always contributed liberally to deserving causes. With a membership having an average of about 170 for the last twenty years, the society gave to the cause of missions in the decade ending with 1870, $1,540; during the eight years between 1870 and 1878, $1,279, and to other causes in proportion.

UNIVERSALIST

Universalism was preached in Perry at a very early day; how early it is very difficult now to ascertain. A congregation had worshiped here previous to the formation of a society. At a meeting of that congregation on the 8th of October, 1831, a constitution and profession of faith were adopted, to which the following, as constituent members, subscribed:

Dan Dickerson, Robert Matison, Arvin Olin, Moses Wollen, Eliakim Botsford. Noah Bacon, Joseph Williams, James H. Bolton, Amos Otis, John Griffith, Isaiah T. Gore, Jonas Wood, William Tripp, Homer Bingham, Nathan Chitester,

Oliver Goodspeed, Samuel Marsh, Joseph Wilson, James Calkins, Jacob Ashdin, Rodney Atwood, Stephen D. Tabor, Talmon T. Carver. Hiram Austin, Titus Howe, Ann Dickerson, Betsey Ayers, Betsey Olin, Densa Burnham, Dolly Botsford, Margaret Bacon, Lovina Otis, Deborah Waterman, Mary Patchin, Nancy Wood, Sally Tripp, Polly Bingham, Laura Goodspeed, Harriet Collins, Lucy Ann Collins, Mary Collins.

Josiah Williams, James H. Bolton and Dan Dickerson were chosen trustees. The church organization was effected June 18th, 1843.

At a meeting of the society in 1833 the trustees were authorized to purchase the old Methodist meeting-house. This was used till the erection of the present building, then sold, removed and converted into a dwelling-house, and afterward burned. The present church edifice was completed in the summer of 1852, and dedicated February 9th, 1853, Rev. D. Skinner, of Utica, N. Y., preaching the dedication sermon. It is a wooden structure, sixty by forty-five feet, with a lecture room adjoining; and its cost, including site, was $4,000. An organ has been placed in it at an expense of $800.

According to the record, since the ecclesiastical organization the pastors have been: Daniel Ackley. Stephen Miles, J. S. Brown, Eben Francis, A. B. Grosh, D. C. Tomlinson, Stephen Crane, W. B. Randolph, George Adams and W. Sisson, the present pastor. The records of the society previous to the church organization do not give the names of either pastors or occasional preachers. The following are remembered: Revs. Sampson Skeele, W. T. Reese, Alfred Peck, —— Moreton, John Flagler, Benjamin Luther, L. L. Saddler, T. P. Abell, Seth Barnes, Jacob Chase, Orren Roberts, Alanson Kelsey and B. G. Bennett.

The society has maintained preaching with scarcely an intermission since its organization, and has enjoyed uniform prosperity. The present number of members is 116.

ST. JOSEPH'S ROMAN CATHOLIC.

In 1848 the only Catholic families in Perry were those of Dennis Kennedy, Bernard Smith, Joseph Malone and Thomas Farrell. During that year mass was celebrated for the first time in the town, at the house of Mr. Kennedy, on Watrous street, by Rev. Father McEvoy. During eight or nine years afterward mass was celebrated monthly by Fathers Lawton, Ryan and McEvoy.

About the year 1858 a building on Covington street, which had been used for a private school and for the session room of the Presbyterian society, was purchased from E. P. Clark for $300. This was used as a house of worship till 1872, when a new house was erected and this was sold. The new church was located a short distance east from the academy. It was eighty by forty-five feet, and it cost, with the site, $5,000.

Though from the first the society has steadily increased in numbers, it continued to be a mission till 1879. This mission was attended by Fathers McConnell, Purcell, McGuiness, Gregg, Cook and Fitzpatrick—the last of whom built the present church edifice in 1872; then Father O. Dwyer, who was succeeded in

FARM RESIDENCE OF J. W. DALRYMPLE, NEAR PERRY VILLAGE, WYOMING CO, N.Y.

1879 by Father Berkery. The last also attends a church which he has erected in Gainesville. The parish numbers about 500 members.

In 1851 this parish was first visited by Bishop Timon, who lectured in the Universalist church. Bishop Ryan has several times visited this church.

FREE METHODIST.

Early in the fall of 1859 Jonathan Handley and nineteen other members of the M. E. church were expelled for ecclesiastical reasons similar to those for which Revs. B. T. Roberts and Joseph McCreery had been expelled from the Genesee conference and M. E. church. They procured Smith's Hall, and held regular services in it until they could secure a permanent place of worship. The following summers they built a church of Main and Gardeau streets. This church was dedicated on the 20th of July, 1861, by Revs. Asa Abell and Loren Stiles.

The church organization was effected at Smith's Hall, the following persons constituting the membership: Jonathan Handley, Mary Handley, John Grisewood, Hannah Grisewood, James R. Johnson, Rhoda M. Johnson, Mark Johnson, William Rudd, Sarah Rudd, Thomas B. Catton, Sarah H. Page No. 247 Catton, James Purdy, Sarah Purdy, Wright Mason, Mary Clark Sanford, Hannah Sanford, Lydia Grisewood, Ann Smith and Elizabeth Hare, twenty in all.

A Sunday-school was organized, with T. B. Catton as superintendent.

In the autumn of 1862 the class of twenty-five at Burke Hill withdrew from the M. E. church and united with the Free Methodist; and since that time the two societies have been known as the "Perry and Burke Hill circuit."

The following clergyman have served as pastor of the circuit since the organization of the class at Perry:

> From May to October, 1861, Rev. William Manning; 1861 to 1862, Rev. Asa Abell; Rev. C. Hudson was appointed by the conference of 1862, but dying soon after, the circuit was supplied till the next session of the conference; from 1863 to 1864, Rev. S. H. Lowe; 1864 to 1866, Rev. J. W. Reddy; 1866 to 1868, Rev. Henry Hornsby; 1868 to 1870, Rev. G. W. Humphrey; 1870 to 1872, Rev. F. J. Ewell; 1872 to 1873, Rev. G. W. Humphrey; 1873 to 1875, Rev. M. B. C. Burritt; 1875 to 1877, Rev. G. W. Marcellus; 1877 to 1878, Rev. G. W. Coleman; 1878 to 1879, Rev. W. Manning, the present pastor.

The society owns a parsonage on Watrous street.

J. D. Handley is superintendent of the Sunday-school at Perry village, and Eugene Jeffers of that at Burke Hill.

BIOGRAPHICAL.

G. W. Abrams was born in Rochester, N. Y., in 1850, and was married in 1878 to Jennie N. Olin, daughter of Philip and Maria Olin, of Perry. Mr. Abrams is a farmer. His father, Joseph Abrams, was born in Massachusetts, in 1808. After living for a time in Genesee county he removed with his family to Perry in 1840, and after working at the carpenter's trade purchased the farm where the family now live about fifteen years ago. His wife, Diana Hotchkiss, whom he married in 1836, was a daughter of Ira Hotchkiss, a native of Vermont, who moved to Gainesville, and from there to Warsaw, where he died. Mr. Abram's brother, William Abrams, served in the late war in the 9th N. Y. cavalry and the 9th Michigan volunteers. He was in the battle of Bull Run, and other engagements.

JEROME ALLEN, son of Earl and Eunice Allen, was born in Pavilion, Genesee county, in 1832. January 1st, 1855, he married Cornelia A., daughter of Lemuel Cornish, of Covington. He is a carpenter and joiner and contractor and builder, and has been a resident of Perry since 1863, when he removed from Le Roy, Genesee county.

THOMAS J. ALTON was born in Covington, in 1836, and married Sarah T. Cronkhite, daughter of John and Eunice W. Cronkhite, in 1858. Mrs. Alton was also born in 1836. Mr. Alton is a farmer. He has served the town as constable and collector. John Cronkhite was born in Argyle, Washington county, in 1794. He came to Perry, after living in various localities, and was a resident of the town until his death, in 1877. He was married in 1825 to Eunice Wigans, of Stillwater, Saratoga county, who is still living. He was a member of the Congregational church, with which Mrs. Cronkhite and Mr. and Mrs. Alton are identified. For some years Mr. Cronkhite served his town as assessor and commissioner of highways.

DAVID ANDRUS, son of David and Mary Andrus, was born in Shaftsbury, Vt., in 1825, and removed to western New York with his parents in 1834 and located in Castile. He spent several years in Virginia and California, and returned to Castile in 1863. From Castile he removed to Perry in 1865. He was married in 1854 to Miss Harriet A. Palmer, daughter of Alton and Harriet Palmer, who died in 1863. In 1866 he married her sister, Martha Jane Palmer.

MARTIN ANDRUS, brother of David Andrus, was born in Shaftsbury, Vt., in 1812, and married Clarissa Huntington, of Castile, in 1830. His father, who is mentioned above as a settler in Castile in 1834, died at the residence of Martin Andrus, in Perry village, in 1861, at the age of eighty-two. The latter has been a resident of Perry since 1882.

MARK ANDREWS was born in Turner, Maine, in 1786, and came to Perry in 1816, having just married Dolly McIntyre at Augusta, Maine. They settled on one hundred and twenty acres of partially improved land west of Perry Canter, and Mr. Andrews was a resident of the town until his death, May 19th, 1856. Martin P. Andrews, his son, was born in Perry, August 17th, 1817. November 8th, 1843, he married Mary Hunt, daughter of Elijah and Eunice Hunt, who died July 31st, 1855. March 21st, 1857, he married Mrs. Diana Norton, widow of Isaac Norton, of Livingston county. Paris Andrews, son of Martin P. Andrews, was born in Perry in February, 1845, and married Lydia, daughter of Alfred and Abigail Abell, of Perry, March 21st, 1867. They have one child.

SANFORD ARMSTRONG was born in Connecticut, in 1788, and was married October 5th, 1849, to Marilda, daughter of John and Sophia Wilcox, of Warsaw. Mr. Armstrong was a resident of Perry from 1815 until his death, May 18th, 1866. He held the office of justice of the peace. His son, Sanford Armstrong, was born in July, 1851, and was married in March, 1873, to Emma C., daughter of Ebenezer and Corinda Burt, of Perry, by whom he has three children—Gertie, born August 26th, 1875; Florence, born November 13th, 1876; and Burt, born August 20th, 1879.

AARON AXTELL was born in Grafton, Vt., in 1807; came to Pike in 1822, and to Perry in 1834; was married to Sarah Maria Canfield, of Pike, in 1835, and died in 1877. He was a member of the Baptist church, as is his widow, who lives with her daughter, Mrs. M. A. Ward, milliner, at Perry village. His son, Abner Axtell, enlisted in Company H of the Cameron dragoons in 1861, and died of smallpox at Georgetown in 1862.

ABISHAI G. BACON was born at Mt. Morris, in 1823, and came to Perry with his parents in childhood. In 1856 he married Charlotte M. Macomber. His father, Noah Bacon, was born in Massachusetts, in 1793. In 1808 he accompanied his parents to Windham county, Conn. In 1816 he came to Perry and took up one hundred and thirty-six acres of lot 45, and after six or seven years removed to Mt. Morris, where he engaged in distilling until 1827, when he returned to Perry and purchased the farm where he now resides with his son. He married Anna Dickerson, of Perry, in 1821. She died in 1869.

HON. CALVIN P. BAILEY, son of Charles and Martha Bailey, was born in Newbury, Vt., in 1792. In 1814 he married Sybil, daughter of John and Waitsell Hatch, of Hardwick, Vt. They had eight children, of whom five are living. Mr. Bailey came to Perry in 1816, bringing his family and a stock of goods, with which, in partnership with his brother-in-law, Samuel Hatch, he opened a store on the site of the store of Hatch & Cole, at the corner of Main and Covington streets, in Perry village. Bailey & Hatch soon after engaged in the manufacture of linseed oil. Later they purchased a gristmill which had been built by one Bailey, of Le Roy, Genesee county, about 1826. Mr. Bailey continued in mercantile and general business until his retirement from active pursuits. In 1828 he was elected to represent his district in the Assembly, and in 1840 he was chosen a delegate to the national convention which placed the name of William Henry Harrison in nomination for the Presidency; on which occasion Mr. Bailey proposed the name of Henry Clay for the nomination, but was defeated by the friends of Harrison. Mr. Bailey died at his residence in Perry September 8th, 1860. His wife died in 1872. She was a Presbyterian.

WILLIAM R. BATHRICK was born in Perry in 1842, and married Mancie C., daughter of Andrew Pratt, in 1862. Mr. and Mrs. Bathrick are members of the Congregational church. He is a farmer and owns one hundred and six acres. Mr. Bathrick's father was born in Litchfield, Herkimer county, came to Perry at the age of twenty-four, and died in 1877. His wife was Clarissa Ward. They were Congregationalists. His grandfather served in the Revolutionary war.

CHARLES J. BENEDICT was born in Perry, March 20th, 1823, and was married in 1850 to Florilla Hurd, daughter of Samuel and Orilla Canfield. They have three children—Frank C., born in 1851; Harriet E., born in 1856, and Frederick Graham, born in 1868. Mr. Benedict has been highway commissioner three years. During the war, unable to go to the front, he furnished a substitute. His father, Graham Benedict, whose ancestors came from England, was born in Woodbury, Conn., in 1785; married Luka Hicks in 1814; settled in Perry, where he cleared land and lived in a log cabin, in 1814; and died January 18th, 1862. He was a member of the Episcopal church. Mrs. Benedict's father, Samuel Canfield, was born in Arlington, Vt., in 1798, and was married in 1827 to Aurelia, daughter of Albert and Salome Canfield. His father died at seventy-six, and his mother at seventy-nine. She died in 1870.

MILTON E. BENEDICT was born in Pavilion, Genesee county, in 1836. He removed to Covington in 1854, to Castile in 1862, and to Perry in 1867, where he purchased an interest in the Perry Iron Works, which were operated seven years by Benedict & Co. In 1875 the establishment was sold to M. H. Olin, and Mr. Benedict became and continues to be foreman in the shops of Wyckoff, Tuttle & Olin. He married Emma, daughter of Richard and Mary Gray, of Castile, in 1862. Mrs. Benedict is a member of the Methodist church.

R. Walter Benedict was born in Covington, November 25th, 1838, and came to Perry in 1864, and the next year bought the farm on which he lives. November 24th, 1865, he married Miranda Batchelor, of Perry. Mr. Benedict was educated at the common schools, at Genesee College, Lima, and at Bryant & Stratton's Commercial College, Poughkeepsie, and was in the west for a time, engaged as civil engineer. His father, Gershom, son of Elijah and Lois Benedict, was born in Norfolk, Conn., in 1805; he came to western New York at an early age, and in 1831 he was ordained a minister of the Methodist Episcopal church. He has preached in many places in the Genesee Conference. He came to Wyoming county in 1850. He married Eliza Kendall in 1833, and now lives in Perry.

William Benedict was born in Perry, in 1827. He is now a farmer. For three and a half years he was manager of a union store at Perry Center, and for two years he conducted a store of his own. He was married to Cynthia L. Buell in 1856, and in 1859 to Dorleske Andrews, daughter of Reuben and Mary Copeland. He has three children—Esther Ann, born in 1861; Edith, born in 1863, and Charles Sumner, born in 1869. Mrs. Benedict and her oldest daughter are members of the Universalist church. His father, Hon. Truman Benedict, was born in Manchester, Vt., in 1793, moved to Perry in 1822, and died in 1855. He was member of Assembly two terms, and served as supervisor, assessor and justice of the peace. He was an Episcopalian by choice, but belonged to no cburch organization. He contributed liberally toward the erection of the churches in Perry. Mrs, Benedict's father, Reuben Andrews, was born in Connecticut in 1779, and married Elizabeth Thompson in 1800, and Mary Copeland in 1826.

Rachel Birdsall, widow of James Birdsall, was born in Essex county, N.J., in 1811, and was married in 1831. She has been a resident of Perry since November 15th, 1838, and she and her husband have been identified with the Baptist church. Her father, John Meeker Littell, and her mother, Catharine Bedell, were natives of New Jersey. Her husband was a native of Connecticut. He was born in 1797 and died in 1867. His parents were James and Sarah Birdsall. He removed to Ulster county, afterward lived in New York, and came from there to Perry and bought the farm of one hundred and seventeen acres on which his widow lives. Mr. and Mrs. Birdsall had seven children, three of whom are living. Their son, Hiram L. Birdsall, was a member of the 130th regiment N. Y, cavalry, and participated with the regiment in all its engagements, having three horses shot under him.

Luther B. Bliss was born in Scipio, Cayuga County, in 1830, and came to Perry in 1838. In 1854 he was married to Elizabeth Coleby. He is a cooper and father and has served as constable. His father, Dillon Bliss, was born in Connecticut, in 1801, and in 1827 maried Clarissa Bryan, whose parents were Luther and Rhoda Ticknor. They had three children, Rhoda, Luther and Clarissa, all of whom are living. They were members of the Baptist church.

John C., son of James and Elizabeth Blythe, was born in Yorkshire, England, in 1833. He came to America in 1840, and to Perry in 1850, from Cuylerville, Livingston county.

He is a miller. About 1856 he was married to Miss Adeline Marsh, of Cuylerville, and in 1870 to Miss Ella Grisewood, of Castle.

ALBERT G., son of Samuel and Hannah Borden, was born in Fall River, Mass., in 1817. In 1838 he married Miss Abbey Garner, of Milan, Cayuga county, by whom he had seven children, four of whom are living. In 1866 he married Caroline Simmons, whose parents came from Oneida county to Castile in 1837, by whom he has four children. Mr. Borden removed from Cayuga county to Warsaw in 1841, and to Perry in 1843. He is a carpenter and joiner, and has held the office of street commissioner two years.

HORACE A. BRIGHAM was born in Madison county, in 1817, and came from Leicester, Livingston county, to Perry in 1858. He is a farmer. In 1845 he married Julia Perry, who died in 1870, and in 1872 he married Cora Haskins. Mr. and Mrs. Brigham, and Mrs. Brigham deceased, have been prominent in the Baptist church.

RANDALL W. BRIGHAM, son of J. H. and Elizabeth Brigham, was born in Perry, July 4th, 1826, and was married November 5th, 1851, to Annette, daughter of Edward and Sarah Richards, of Perry. They have two children. Mr. Brigham, who is a farmer, has held the office of highway commissioner nine years, was supervisor in 1871–72, and has served as railroad commissioner. His father, J. H. Brigham, was born May 28th, 1791, at New Marlboro, Mass. He located in Perry, on lot 30, about 1816. He was married September 25th, 1811, to Elizabeth, daughter of Solomon and Jerusha Hart, of New Merlboro, Mass. They have had seven children, four of whom are living. Mr. Brigham died in September, 1827.

SULLIVAN, son of Alpheus BURT, was born in Huntington, Vt., in 1797, and came to Perry in 1818. In 1823 he married Hannah Lacy, daughter of Elnathan and Nancy Lacy, Perry. They had two children, both of whom are now dead. Mrs. Burt died November 30th, 1876, at the age of seventy five. Mr. Burt has been a lifelong farmer.

JOHN M. BUTLER, farmer, was born in Perry, in 1821, and married Clarinda M., daughter of Norman and Selina White, in 1845. They have had five children, four of whom are living. Milton W., born in 1850; Henry C., born in 1853; Laura S., born in 1856; and Elveretta, born in 1861. Mr. and Mrs. Butler are members of the Congregational church, of which the former has been deacon for some years. Mr. Butler has been the principal surveyor in his section for forty years, and has the instruments he has used during that time. He has taught district school four successive winters. Mrs. Butler has taught two summers. William Butler, father of John M. Butler, was born at Clinton, Oneida county, in 1796, and married Laura Curtis, of that place. He purchased his farm in 1814, and worked at the clothiers' trade until 1817 in order to pay for it, as he would not go into debt. In 1817 he settled on it. He cleared the land himself, and erected a log house.

WILLIAM T. BUTTRE, son of William and Mary Buttre, was born in New York city, in 1806, and was married about 1827 to Miss Mary Parsons, of Auburn, N.Y., by whom he had five children, only one of whom is living. Mrs. Buttre died in 1840, and in 1842 Mr. Buttre married Miss Lorain B. Dutcher, of Auburn. Mr. Buttre came to Perry from Auburn in 1841. He is a cabinet maker and dealer in furniture.

PHEBE C. CATE was born in Middlebury, in 1832, and was married in 1853. She has three children, Clarence, born in 1856; Clara M., 1859, and Annie E., 1860. All three are graduates of Middlebury Academy, and the two daughters are school teachers. Mrs. Cate and her children are all members of the La Grange Baptist church. Her husband,

Virgil H. Cate, was born in Rockingham, N. H., in 1833. In 1861 he enlisted in the 7th New Hampshire Volunteers, and held the office of first lieutenant, participating in all of the battles in which his regiment was engaged, until taken prisoner and held four months. He was the officer who was refused an exchange by an official order issued by Jefferson Davis, who threatened to hand him over to the local authorities for trial and punishment for the alleged incitement of negroes to insurrection. After his release he was killed in the battle of Fort Wagner, South Carolina. This was the first engagement in which negro troops participated, and on this occasion the rebels manifested a greater degree of ferocity than is usually witnessed in civilized warfare. Mr. Cate's father, Joseph Cate, married Elizabeth Burbank, a member of a family occupying a high social position in New Hampshire. Mrs. Cate's father was Avery H. Cronkhite, who was born in Rensselaer county in 1804, and married Mathilda Baldwin, of that county, by whom he had eight children, Mrs. Cate being the oldest. Six are living. Mr. Cronkhite was a supervisor in Middlebury before and after the division of the county. Mrs. Cate has been a resident of Perry since 1866.

LEWIS E. CHAPIN was born in Livonia, Livingston county, March 3d, 1855, and came to Perry, where he is publisher of the *Wyoming County Herald,* from Livonia in June, 1877.

SAMUEL L., son of Luther and Charity Chapin, was born in Aurelius, Cayuga county, in 1814; removed to Conesus, Livingston County, in 1822; to Michigan in 1845, returned to Conesus three years later; removed to Castile in 1854 and purchased eighty-five acres of land on the Gardeau reservation, and removed to Perry village in 1863, where he has since resided. He is a produce dealer. He held the office of supervisor in Castile four years, and since the organization of the Perry and Silver Lake Railroad Company he has been its president. Mr. Chapin has been married four times: in 1836 to Miss Sarah Calhoon, of Livonia, Livingston county, by whom he had four children, two of whom are living (Mrs. Chapin died in Michigan in 1847); in 1849 to Elizabeth Nelson, of Livonia, by whom he had one child, and who died in 1856; in 1856 to Miss Priscilla Ackerman, of Pike, who died in 1864, and to Mrs. Louisa P. Hamilton, of Perry, his present wife.

RICHARD CHILDS, son of Oliver Childs, originally from Holden, Mass, and Sally Childs, originally from Rockingham, N. H., was born in Deerfield, Chenango county, May 28th, 1814, and came to Perry in 1821. In 1840 he married Irene Bacon, by whom he had three children, and who died at the age of thirty in 1851. In 1852 he married Loretta Humphrey, daughter of David and Catharine Humphrey, natives, respectively, of Herkimer county and Otsego county, who bore him a son, and who was born in Sweden, Monroe county, in 1820. In 1862 one of Mr. Childs's sons enlisted in Company H., 130th N. Y. volunteers, and served until the close of the war. In 1840 Mr. Childs bought a blacksmith shop at West Perry. In 1842 he purchased and moved to the farm where he now lives, a mile and a half west of West Perry.

EDWARD S. CLARK, son of Greenleaf and Betsey Clark, was born in New Hampshire, February 22nd, 1810, and came with his father's family to Perry. In 1853 he married Sarepta, daughter of Joseph and Margaret Edgerly, of Perry, formerly of Vermont. They have two children. Greenleaf Clark was born April 16th, 1772, in New Hampshire, and came to Perry, then in Genesee county, in 1815. He made the journey from New Hampshire with two two-horse teams, and was six weeks on the road. He bought fifty acres of lot 30, now within the village of Perry, four acres of which had been cleared.

A log house and the frame of a frame house stood in this clearing. The latter when finished was one of the first of its kind erected in the town. Mr. Clark was married in New Hampshire to Betsey Stevens, who bore him eleven children, nine of whom accompanied them to Perry. Mr. Clark died December 22nd, 1853, at the age of eighty-one. Mrs. Clark was born in New Hampshire, September 4th, 1773, and died in Perry, March 30th, 1857, at the age of eighty-four.

GEORGE W., son of Greenleaf and Betsey CLARK, was born in Stafford county, N. H., February 17th, 1814, and accompanied his parents to Perry in 1815. He was married July 16th, 1851, to Louisa, daughter of John and Sally Ann Garrison, of Newburg, Orange county. They have two children. Mr. Clark is a farmer.

HENRY CLEAVELAND was born in Berkshire county, Mass., in 1805. His parents were Lewis and Lydia Cleaveland. In 1839 he married Miss Charlotte A. Dixon, daughter of Andrew and Laura Dixon, of Perry, by whom he had four children, three of whom are living. He came to Wyoming county from Berkshire county, Mass., in 1832, and established himself in the mercantile business at Perry Center; from there he removed to Perry village in 1839. He became interested in western lands, most of which were in Michigan, and after 1846 his time was devoted almost exclusively to their improvement. He died at Lansing, Mich., in 1852.

ALEXANDER, son of Thomas and Mary COLE, was born in Burrington, Devonshire, England, in 1828. He came to America in 1849, and located at Rochester, N. Y. In 1852 he came to Perry, and engaged in the manufacture and sale of boots and shoes as one of the firm of A. Cole & Son. The establishment was burned in 1852, at a loss of $1,500. During that year Mr. Cole married Miss Agnes Richardson, of Rochester. With characteristic energy he soon re-established his business, which he continues at the corner of Main and Covington streets.

NATHAN CRONKHITE was born in Rensselaer county, in 1818. He removed to Washington county, and from there to Covington, from which place he came to Perry, where he is a farmer. He was married in 1846 to Caroline E. Sherman, who has borne him four children, two of whom are living—Angelina Violetta, born November 22nd, 1853, and Ruth H., born March 10th, 1856. Mr. and Mrs. Cronkhite are members of the Congregational church at Perry Center. On the arrival of Mr. Cronkhite in Perry he purchased an improved farm of one hundred acres, upon which he lives. His father, Henry Cronkhite, was born at Hoosac, Rensselaer county, in 1784, and remained there until his death. He married Hannah Suidam, of that place. Mrs. Cronkhite's father, Stephen L. Sherman, married Rude Sisson. Both were members of the Methodist Episcopal church.

JOHN M. DAILEY was born in Ulster county, March 16th, 1821. He removed from there to Scipio, Cayuga county; from there to Mount Morris, Livingston county; from there forty-nine years ago to Leicester, that county, where he remained thirteen years; from there to Covington, and from Covington to Perry, where he owns a farm of two hundred and forty-three acres. He was married October 14th, 1848, to Mary Lauderdale, daughter of Edward Lauderdale and wife (formerly Janette Elliott), of Moscow, Livingston county. His father Henry Dailey, was born in Ulster county, in 1769, and was married about 1818 to Margaret Mastin, a native of the same county. They had eight children, of whom five are living. John M. is the oldest son. Mrs. Dailey was a member of the Presbyterian church. Henry Dailey and family were early settlers in western New York, and were called upon to encounter the various hardships incident to pioneer life.

FRUIT DRYING ESTABLISHMENT OF WHITE & CALKINS, RES. OF D.C. WHITE, PERRY, N.Y.

RESIDENCE OF JOHN S. THOMPSON, PERRY, N.Y.

RESIDENCE OF HOSEA ROBINSON, PIKE, N.Y.

RESIDENCE & OFFICE OF G.R. TRAVER, M.D., PERRY, N.Y.

FARM RESIDENCE OF A. R. HULL, PERRY, N.Y.

RESIDENCE OF H.A. BRIGHAM, PERRY, N.Y.

JOHN W. DALRYMPLE, son of Asa and Elinor Dalrymple, was born in Ammal, N. J., in 1823. In 1826 he removed to Mount Morris, Livingston county, and from there to Geneseo, that county, in 1852. In 1866 he bought a farm in Perry, one and a half miles northeast of the village. In 1851 he was married to Caroline Gladding, of Windham,. Greene county. They have two children living—Emma and John.

WILLIAM, son of Nicholas and Mary DOLBEER, was born in Epsom, N. H., in 1788. In 1816 he married Hannah, daughter of Asa and Betsey Kimball, of Haver, N. H., by whom he had five children. Three daughters are living. In the spring of 1818 Mr. Dolbeer left his native State on horseback in search of a locality for a future home. After a few weeks' ride, in the course of which he visited various localities, he arrived at the village of Perry, then a mere hamlet, where he purchased a village lot of two acres, on which stood a dilapidated house, for which he paid $700. He built a blacksmith shop (he had previously learned and worked at the blacksmith's trade), and became the first regular blacksmith in the town (there had previously been a so-called puddling shop of small account). He worked until fall and then returned to New Hampshire and brought back his family, arriving at Perry November 26th. He was a blacksmith and carriage maker during his business career. He declined all proffered honors in the way of public offices, preferring the quiet of his home to political notoriety; and retired from business in 1860, and died at his residence in 1878, at the age of eighty-four. He and his widow, now living at the age of eighty-seven, were both early identified with the Methodist Episcopal church, with which the latter is yet connected.

EDMOND EDGERLY, son of James and Hannah Edgerly, was born in Danville, Vt., May 17th, 1794, and has been a former and resident in Perry since 1811. In 1819 he bought forty-five acres (seven of which were cleared) of lot 30. He afterward added forty-two acres to this property. He was married in 1834 to Amanda, daughter of Ephraim and Louisa Judson, originally from Vermont, who was born at Fabius, N. Y., July 8th, 1801. They had eight children. Seven are living, three on the old homestead with their mother, who is a member of the Baptist church of Perry. Mr. Edgerly died November 22nd, 1868, at the age of seventy-four.

OSCAR S. EDGERLY was born in Perry, in 1820, and married Charlotte, daughter of Josiah and Elsie Kinsley, of Perry, in 1840. They have had three children, only one of whom lives. Thomas and Sally Edgerley came from New Hampshire in 1814, and took up a farm, which is now within the corporate limits of Perry village. In 1818 he helped to build the first hotel in the village, and kept it four years. He was also the first post-master. He engaged in mercantile business, purchasing his goods in Utica, N. Y., and bringing them to Perry with four-horse teams. He died in 1837, at the age of forty-eight.

WILLIAM ELLSWORTH, son of John and Sally Ellsworth, was born in Cazenovia, Madison county. In 1804. In 1830 he married Miss Susanah Sprague, of Saratoga, N. Y. In 1831 he came to Wyoming county, and located two miles east of La Grange; in 1834 he removed to Castile, and from Castile to Perry in 1855. He was a farmer until his retirement from active life. Mr. and Mrs. Ellsworth are members of the Baptist church.

CALVIN FANNING, son of Charles and Anna Fanning, was born in Chenango county, in 1807, and married Hannah M. Lacy, of Avon, Livingston county, in 1837. They have had four children, two of whom are living. In 1846 Mr Fanning came to Perry from Avon. Mr. and Mrs. Fanning are members of the Presbyterian church. Mr. Fanning, at the age of seventy-three, works daily at his trade of cooper, and says he can turn out twenty apple barrels per day.

JEROME FERGUSON was born in Perry, in 1822, and has been a life-long resident of the town, except three years spent in Illinois. He was married in 1852 to Maria Chappell, daughter of Lyman and Betsy Chappell, of Avon, Livingston county. For three years he has served the town as assessor. He contributed largely of his means and time toward the prosecution of the war. Mrs. Ferguson is a member of the Perry Center Congregational church. Samuel Ferguson, father of the above mentioned, was born in Connecticut, in 1785, and removed from there to Benton, Yates county; thence to Perry, where he was an early settler, taking up unimproved land. His wife was Abigail Powell, a native of New Jersey. Mrs. Jerome Ferguson's father was born in Connecticut, in 1798. He removed to Avon, Livingston county; thence to Perry, where he died. His wife was Betsy Miller, of Massachusetts. They had eleven children; eight are living. Mrs. Ferguson was the third born.

WALTER GILLESPIE, son of Robert and Grace Gillespie, was born in Rhode Island, in 1806. In 1829 he married Miss Mary Agate, whose parents were natives of England, and who came to America in 1814 and located at Perry, where Mr. Agate was a shoemaker. Mr. Gillespie removed to Castile in 1827, from Geneva, Ontario county (where his parents had settled while he was a child), and bought the farm on the old Allegany road now owned by Ezra Kelsie, on which there was at that time standing a log house, and a small portion of which, west of the road, was cleared. This place he improved, and sold in 1868 to Mr. Kelsie, removing to Perry village, where he died April 25th, 1879. He was a member of the Presbyterian church, with which his widow, living at Perry village, is identified.

ALPHONSO R. HULL, son of John and Eliza Hull, was born in Leicester, Livingston county, in 1834, and was married in 1854 to Julia Barnes, daughter of Samuel and Mary Barnes, by whom he has two children—Mary E. and Charles N. Hull. In 1871 he removed from Leicester, Livingston county, to Perry, where he is a farmer, owning two hundred and fifty-one acres of land, located two miles northeast of Perry village. Samuel Barnes, son of Cornelius and Esther Barnes, was born in Cayuga county, in 1801, and came to what was then Genesee county in 1829. After living a short time in Warsaw he removed to Perry, where he remained fifteen years, and went to Leicester, Livingston county, where he lived twenty-five years. In 1871 he returned to Perry, where he has lived with his son-in-law. In 1832 he married Mary, daughter of Daniel and Deborah Sleight. Mrs. Hull was their only child.

EDWARD B. HARRISON was born in Perry, March 7th, 1832, and was married January 1st, 1861, to Caroline Howcraft, whose father and mother were named George and Sarah. They have had four children; two are living. Mr. and Mrs. Harrison are members of the Baptist church of Perry. Edward B. Harrison's father, Robert Harrison, was born in England, in 1789. His parents were John and Rachel Harrison. He came to America and settled at Perry about 1830, in which year he married Elizabeth, daughter of William and Abigail Welds, who had emigrated from England, in 1804. He had been previously married in England, but his first wife died soon after his arrival here. By his second marriage he had two children, one of whom is living. He died August 28th, 1863. His widow, now about ninety, lives with her son.

SAMUEL A. HATCH, son of Samuel and Matilda Hatch, was born in Perry, in 1853. He has served one term on the board of village trustees of Perry village, where, as a member of the firm of Hatch & Cole, at the corner of Main and Covington streets, he is a dealer in groceries and provisions.

WILLIAM HENRY HERRINGTON was born at Hoosac, Rensselaer county, in 1836. In 1860 he married Alche F., daughter of David and Sylvia Case. They have had six children, born as follows: Bertha F., 1861; Arthur C., 1864; Grace, 1871; infant son, 1872; Frank B., 1874, and Lucie E., 1878. Mr. and Mrs. Herrington suffered a severe loss, which they bore with Christian fortitude, in the death, by malignant diphtheria, of three children, Arthur C., Grace and Frank B., in 1877; the infant son mentioned also dying in that year. They are members of the Baptist church at La Grange. Mr. Herrington came to Perry from White Creek, Washington county.

MRS. ABIGAIL B. HIGGINS, formerly Miss Abigail Bailey, daughter of Enoch and Susan Bailey, was born in Hardwick, Caledonia county, Vt., in 1806. At the age of eighteen she began teaching school, and continued in that avocation six years. In 1836 she accompanied her brother, Charles Bailey, from Vermont to Perry, and engaged in teaching at Perry Center. In 1841 she married Mason G. Smith, M. D., who practiced medicine from 1820 until his death, in 1857. He served twenty-two years as school commissioner and several years as justice of the peace. After a widowhood of about five years Mrs. Smith married Henry Higgins, a native of Cayuga county, who located in Perry at an early date and died there in 1872, at the age of seventy-eight. He was a member and for a time a deacon of the Presbyterian church, with which his widow is connected. Mason C. Smith, a son of Dr. Mason G. Smith, then in Hamilton College, enlisted in 1862 in the northern army. He was taken prisoner in North Carolina, and died in the prison pen at Andersonville in 1864.

JOHN H., son of Benjamin and Sarah HOLLISTER, was born in New Marlboro, Mass., April 7th, 1815. December 31st, 1815, he married Polly, daughter of Solomon and Jerusha Hart, of his native place. He arrived in Perry from Massachusetts March 1st, 1816, locating in the woods on lot 19. Mrs. Hollister died August 26th, 1869, at the age of seventy-three. Mr. and Mrs. Hollister had seven children, six of whom are living.

BENJAMIN H. HOLLISTER son of the above mentioned, was born in Perry, in 1839, on the farm where he has since lived. He served in the 24th N.Y. battery from September, 1862, until the close of the war. He was captured at Plymouth, N. C., in April, 1864, and was confined in rebel prisons at Andersonville and Charleston. He was married in 1867 to Alice Macken, daughter of Joseph and Olive Macken, of Wellsville, Allegany county. They have one child.

ELIZA A. HOSFORD was born in Wallingford, Vt., in 1821. Her father was Micajah Kells, a native of Bolton, Mass., who was born in 1796. He was married in 1819 to Betsy Gifford, and they removed to Perry in 1831, after living in several other places. Mr. Kells is still living. Miss Kells was married in 1844 to Almer B. Hosford, a native of Perry, who was born on the farm on which Mrs. Hosford lives. He was a member of the Baptist church, with which his widow is identified. They had two children—Mary L., born in 1848, and Sarah Elizabeth, born in 1852. Amos Hosford Mr. Hosford's father, was born in Massachusetts, in 1787; moved from there to Richmond, Ontario county, and thence to Perry, where he bought of Mr. Granger part of the Phelps purchase. With the assistance of his father he cleared the land and erected a log house. He was in the war of 1812–14, and participated in several battles. He is living.

JAMES HUNT was born in Gorham, Ontario county, February 17th, 1805. In 1831 he married Harriet, daughter of Joseph and Mary Havens, of Benton, Yates county. In 1832 he came to Perry from Gorham, Ontario county, and purchased the Franklin House, which he managed three years. He died at his residence in Perry in 1856. Mrs. Hunt married Edward Richards, a native of Massachusetts, who came to Perry in 1820 and took up eighty acres of land near West Perry, and who died in 1876. Mrs. Richards has two sons by her first marriage living—James W. Hunt, of Terre Haute, Ind., and Frank G. Hunt, of Buffalo. Another son, George D. Hunt, enlisted at Perry in 1861, in Company G., 27th N. Y. volunteers, and died that year at Mill Creek, Va. Sergeant Mayratt Hunt enlisted at Brockport, Monroe county, in 1862, in the 140th N. Y. volunteers, and died that year in the hospital at Washington, D. C. He was in the engagement at Fredericksburg.

LUMAN W. HUNT, M. D., was born in Herkimer county, in 1836. In the spring of 1861 he went to California, where he remained seven years. He returned to Gainesville, and in 1870 married Miss Chloe Stone, of that place. He removed to Perry in 1872.

CHARLES B. HUNTINGTON was born December 23d, 1820, in Greensboro, Vt. He came to Perry in company with Mr. and Mrs. Sanborn, making the journey in a wagon, to live with his sister, Mrs. C. Hetch, and learn the harness-maker's trade. Whatever education he possesses he has obtained by his own exertion, having attended school only three of four months, in the old yellow school-house in Perry. The harness-maker who employed him sold out his business about 1837, and young Huntington was without job; but soon found work at his trade, at which he continued about a year, after which he was associated in business for two years with A. T. Alpin. Since 1842 he has been a farmer. He has been twice married. His first wife was Lucy Jane Olin, who died May 6th, 1842. November 19th, 1846, he married Mary Buell, and soon afterward began housekeeping in an old house near his present comfortable home, which he was won by industry and economy. Mr. Huntington states that he has always avoided the use of whiskey and tobacco, and he has never sought nor accepted office, being content with his home life and the company of his wife, whom he emphatically pronounces his "better half." He has reared a family of six children. His second daughter is a graduate of the Geneseo Normal School. Mr. Huntington's father, a farmer at Greensboro, Vt., was a man honored for his intelligence and social worth, his temperate and industrious habits, and his overflowing benevolence. He died October 1st, 1840.

W. H. JENKINS was born in Warsaw, in 1847, and came from Covington to Perry in 1865. In 1873 he married Aristene, daughter of Thomas and Rebecca Dodson. Mrs. Jenkins is a member of the Methodist Episcopal church at Wyoming.

JAMES C. KARIGER, son of Peter and Mary Kariger, was born October 13th, 1819, in Schoharie county. He worked on his father's farm until 1833, when he went to Carraraugus county. In 1839 he removed to Livingston county, and began to work at his trade (that of a cooper) in 1846. In 1852 he came to Perry, where he has since lived. He was married in 1849 to Clarice, daughter of Joseph and Amanda Thompson, of Bethany, Genesee county. Mr. and Mrs. Kariger and members of the Methodist Episcopal church of Perry. They have two children. Mrs. Kariger's father was originally from Vermont; her mother from Whitehall, N. Y.

ABRAM B., son of Lewis and Mary KING, was born in Greenville, Greene county, in 1824. In 1846 he married Catharine Jaquett, of Fleming, Cayuga county. Four children have been born to them. Mr. King came to Perry from Scipio, Cayuga county, in 1864, and has been a farmer most of the time since. In 1871, under the supervision of Hon. William P. Letchworth, he had charge of the removal of the Caneadea council-house from the Caneadea reservation, and the re-erection of the same at Glen Iris. He also had supervision, under Mr. Letchworth's direction, of the burial of the remains of Mary Jemison in their final resting place. Mr. and Mrs. King are members of the Presbyterian church.

ELIAS, son of Vail and Esther KINGSLEY, was born in Scipio, Cayuga county, in 1805. He was married November 24th, 1822, to Nancy, daughter of Baxter and Florina How, by whom he had fourteen children, five of whom are living, two at home. Mrs. Kingsley died March 2nd, 1879 and Mr. Kingsley married her sister, Electa Bishop, widow of the late Simon Bishop, of Perry, November 4th following.

GEORGE W., son of Elias and Nancy KINGSLEY, was born in Perry, in 1838. He married Clarissa, daughter of George H. and Mercy Wright, of Perry, October 17th, 1865. They have had four children, three of whom were born at the following dates: Gerty M., February 18th, 1868; Willie W., December 18th, 1870, and Edna A., March 18th, 1873. Mr. Kingsley is a farmer and dealer in agricultural implements.

JOSIAH W. KINGSLEY, son of William and Esther Kingsley, was born in Owego, Tioga county, in 1797. In 1815 he married Eliza, daughter of John Burrows, of Aurelius, Cayuga county, by whom he had six children, three of whom are living. His second marriage was to Miss Sally Clark, of Perry. He came to Perry in 1825 from Scipio, Cayuga county, and is a retired farmer and owner of one hundred and ninety-three acres. His first purchase was one hundred acres (twenty-five acres cleared) of Thomas Burrows. It was in section 34 and there was a log house on it. The balance of his tract was a later purchase. He retired from active life in 1870, and removed to Perry village. He is a member of the Universalist church, his wife of the Presbyterian.

GEORGE L. KEENEY, M. D., was a son of Josiah and Phebe Keeney. He was born in 1809 and died in 1867. His parents were natives of Connecticut, and located in Wyoming county, Pa., in the latter part of the 18th century. The doctor graduated at Yale College in 1832, and during that year entered upon the practice of his profession in Perry, where, in 1835, he married Anna, daughter of William and Hannah Dolbeer, who survives him.

WILLIAM, son of Thomas and Maria KEETON, was born in Lincolnshire, England, in 1811. In 1813 he married Fanny, daughter of Charles and Mary Bryant, of Huntington, England, by whom he has had seven children, one of whom is dead. He came to Castile in 1844, and to Perry village in 1858, where he lives retired. He was notary public for several years. Mr. and Mrs. Keeton are of the Baptist faith.

ROBERT KERSHAW was born September 4th, 1836, in Le Roy, Genesee county, and was married in August, 1879, to Libbie M. Kniffin, of Perry, where he has been in business for the past four years as a jeweler and repairer of clocks of watches. He formerly lived in Castile village, and served as town clerk of Castile. August 6th, 1862, he enlisted in Company A, 1st N. Y. dragoons, and was in the battles of Suffolk and Culpepper Court-house, and in all of the other engagements in which the regiment participated. He was discharged at Cloud's Mills, Va., in 1865.

ALANSON LACY, son of Elnathan and Nancy Lacy, was born in Manlius, Onondaga county, September 1st, 1810, and has been a resident of Perry since 1817, and a lifelong farmer. He was married May 29th, 1839, to Sarah Ann Knowlton, daughter of John and Esther Knowlton, of Portage. They have had two children, one of whom is living. James M. Lacy, their oldest son, enlisted in Company K, 1st N. Y. mounted rifles, and died in the hospital at Williamsburg, Va., February 19th, 1863, at the age of twenty-four. Elnathan Lacy, son of Samuel Lacy, was born in Connecticut, June 10th, 1773, and in 1780 accompanied his parents to Milton, Saratoga county. March 17th, 1817, he came with his father from Manlius, Onondaga county, to Perry, and located on lot 21, a mile northeast of the village, the place he afterward cleared and always occupied. He kept a public house twenty-three years. He was married in 1800 to Nancy, daughter of Ebenezer Horton, of Connecticut, and in 1828 to Zilpha Frost, who died November 18th, 1877, aged ninety-two. Mr. Lacy died June 17th, 1862; Samuel Lacy, his father, January 8th, 1820, aged seventy-eight. By his first wife Elnathan Lacy had nine children, six of whom grew up, viz.: Hannah, who married Sullivan Burt; Edward, who died at the age of twenty-four; Martha, who married N. S. Benton; Clarence, the only one now living, and who occupied the old homestead; Aurelia, who married Martin Sweet, and Alvah.

DAVID, son of David and Polly LACY, was born April 3d, 1811, in Columbus, N. Y., and came to Perry in 1818. He is a farmer. January 9th, 1840, he married Miss L. D. Lapham, who died May 30th, 1848. Two children by that marriage are living. October 10th, 1848, he married Susan, daughter of Nathan and Elizabeth Bullard. They have one child living. Mr. and Mrs. Lacy are members of the Baptist church.

WILLIAM A. LACY, farmer, is a son of David and Polly Lacy, and was born in 1809, at Columbus, Chenango county. He has been a resident of Perry since 1818. In 1832 he married Eliza M. Cleveland, by whom he had three children, one of who is living. Mrs. Lacy died at the age of forty-four, in 1853. In 1857 Mr. Lacy married Mary Jane Eggleston, daughter of Moses and Clarinda Eggleston, of Avon, Livingston county. They have one child. Both are Baptists. David Lacy was born in Connecticut, September 31st, 1778; came to Perry in 1818, and died August 16th, 1863. His wife was born January 22nd, 1787, and died February 24th, 1874.

J. B. LAMB was born in Covington, in 1847, and married Mary Frances Jenkins, of Gainesville, in 1864. They have one child—Melville Alverson, born in 1875. Mr. and Mrs. Lamb are members of the Methodist Episcopal church. Mr. Lamb's father, Hiram Lamb, was born in Massachusetts, in 1800, and was an early settler in Covington, where he cleared land and erected a log house, which was destroyed by fire and replaced by a frame dwelling. Mrs. Lamb's father, John B. Jenkins, was born in 1810. He was a Methodist preacher twenty years. He married Sophia Kendall. Mr. Lamb's mother was a native of Pennsylvania. Early in life she removed to Ontario County. At the age of twenty-one she married David Alverson. Several years after his death she married Hiram Lamb, and is living, at eighty-three. Her mother died at eighty-four. Mr. Lamb's grandfather and grandmother were respectively eighty-six and eighty-four at their death.

SIDNEY LAPHAM, son of Thomas and Thankful Lapham, was born in Ledyard, Cayuga county, in 1802, and died in Perry in 1851. In 1825 he married Miss Jane Macomber, daughter of Zebidee and Rebecca Macomber, of Ledyard, Cayuga county, and came to Perry in 1830. Mr. and Mrs. Lapham had two children. Mr. Lapham was a farmer. He was a practical supporter of the Baptist church; politically he was a believer in the principles endorsed at a later day by the Republican party. Mrs. Lapham is a Presbyterian.

MRS. CATHARINE M. LENT is the widow of Abram Lent, who enlisted in the 124th N. Y. Battery in 1862; was taken prisoner at Plymouth, and died in Andersonville prison in 1864. He was a lawyer by profession, and a Democrat politically. He was for several years postmaster at the village of Perry.

ALLEN MACOMBER was born in Kinderbook, N. Y. in 1807. He married Esther Howe, of Castile, in 1821, and in 1825 came from Saratoga county to Perry, where he has served three years as assessor, and owns one hundred and fifty seven acres of land.

EDWARD G. MATTHEWS was born in Leicester, Livingston county, in 1824. He came to Perry from Centreville, Allegany county, in 1852, and during that year married Miss Mary L. Lapham. Mr. Matthews is superintendent, manager and conductor of the Perry & Silver Lake Railroad. He and his wife are members of the Baptist church. His father was John Matthews, a native of Wales, and was brought by his parents to America in childhood. He married Susannah Taber, daughter of Gideon Taber, a native of Vermont and one of the early settlers of Perry. He had nine children, five of whom are living. He came from Pittsford, Monroe county, to Leicester, Livingston county, and took up eighty acres of land on the Gardeau reservation, in 1822; four or five years later he located on the Allegany road, north of Perry village, and in 1840 removed to Allegany county, where he died in 1862.

THOMAS MCCALL, farmer, was born in Washington county, December 15th, 1827, and came to Perry with his parents. In 1857 he married Phelina, daughter of Nathan and Eunice Nolton. He is a member and for twelve years has been trustee of the Congregational church. His father, John McCall, was born in Monaghan county, Ireland, in 1777. He came to America and located for a time in Washington county. About 1830 he came to Wyoming county, where he died in 1837. Nathan Nolton was born in 1792, and married Eunice Randall. He was a cabinet maker by trade.

MARTIN A. MCINTIRE, farmer, was born in Perry, June 1st, 1838, and married Emily, daughter of Oliver C. and Maria Chapman, March 24th, 1864, by whom he has three children. John McIntire, his father, was born February 12th, 1797, at Augusta, Maine, and came to Perry in 1808, locating on the Warsaw road, midway between Perry and Warsaw. In August, 1826, he married Kesiah Wheat, daughter of Samuel and Isabel Wheat. They had nine children; six are living. Calvin H. McIntire, their second son, enlisted in an Iowa regiment, as lieutenant. He was taken sick and died in the south, and his remains were brought to Perry Center for burial. Mr. John McIntire died December 31st, 1872; Mrs. McIntire June 22nd, 1865.

ICHABOD MINOR, farmer, was born in Sandgate, Vt., in 1801, and came to Perry in 1817. In 1829 he married Miss L. Cooley, daughter of Noah and Sabrey (formerly Wells) Cooley, of Perry Center. They have two children—Caroline, born in 1830, and Mary, born in 1833. Joelah Minor, father of the above mentioned, was born in Roxbury, Conn., in 1768. After living in Vermont and Oneida county, he came to Perry in 1817, and bought wild land, cleared it and built a log house thereon, which he occupied during the pioneer period of the town's history. He was a member of the Congregational church. His wife was Keziah Sherman.

RESIDENCE OF C.B. HUNTINGTON, PERRY, WYOMING CO., N.Y.

RESIDENCE OF R.E. ALVERSON, PERRY, WYOMING CO., N.Y.

ST JOSEPH'S CHURCH, PERRY, WYOMING CO., N.Y.

RES. OF BENSON TALLMAN, CASTILE, WYOMING CO., N.Y.

RESIDENCE AND GROCERY STORE OF N. W. POND, CASTILE, WYOMING CO., N.Y.

ST MARYS CHURCH, EAST GAINESVILLE, WYOMING CO., N.Y.

RUSSEL C. MORDOFF, son of James and Lois Mordoff, was born in Chenango county, in 1816. His father was a settler, in 1818, on the west bank of Silver lake, in Castile. In 1841 Mr. Mordoff married Miss Amanda Lord, of Le Roy, Genesee county, by whom he has one daughter. He has held the office of town clerk many years, and for the past nine years that of justice of the peace. He is a self-made man, his father, a native of Scotland, having died when he was five years old. He learned the hatter's trade, and worked at it fifteen years. Gradually he engaged in mercantile pursuits, and is now sole proprietor of one of the finest stores in Perry village, and a leading merchant and produce dealer. His first wife died in 1846, and in 1848 he married Miss Olive McBride, of Castile. Mr. and Mrs. Mordoff are members of the Presbyterian church.

CHAUNCEY NASH, son of Shubal and Sibyl Nash, was born in North Adams, Mass., July 17th, 1798. In 1824 he removed to Pendleton, Niagara county, and in 1846 to Perry, locating two miles west of West Perry. In 1824 he married Ann Young, who died November 1st, 1830, at the age of thirty-five. June 20th, 1831, he married Dorotha Patterson. who bore him eight children, four of whom are living, and died January 6th, 1845, aged forty-two. June 23d, 1845, he married Sarah M. Board, who bore him two children. Mr. Nash died February 21st, 1876, aged seventy-eight. He was a member of the Free-will Baptist church.

WILLIAM S., son of Chauncey and Sarah Nash, was born in Perry, in 1849, and has been a farmer since he was old enough to work. January 30th, 1874, he married Ellen Adela Jenks, daughter of Johnson and Sabrina Jenks, of Perry. They have one child.

MRS. EVELINE E. NEVINS, daughter of Cornelius R. and Amanda (Strong) Nevins, was born in Oneida county, and came to Perry with her parents, who are residents of the town, in 1839. In 1848 she married Dr. Jacob Nevins, of Perry, by whom she had two children, one of whom is living. Dr. Nevins died at his residence in Perry, in 1872.

WILLIAM ORSON NEWCOMB was born in Bridgewater, Oneida county, February 14th, 1820. Losing his father by death when he was a little more than two years old, he became a member of the family of his uncle, William Newcomb, and lived with these friends till he was sixteen. September 9th, 1840, he married Eliza P. Bathrick, of Perry. He lived in East Gainesville and Castile, and became a resident of Perry in 1850. He and his wife are members of the Presbyterian church. He owns a good farm at Perry Center, and is known as an industrious, honest and worthy man.

LUCIUS STEPHEN, son of W. O. NEWCOMB, enlisted as a bugler, being too young for the ranks, in the 24th N. Y. independent battery. In 1964 he reenlisted as a veteran, and was commissioned 2nd lieutenant January 10th, 1865, and 1st lieutenant in July following. In the four-days' fight at Plymouth, N.C., he was captured and sent to Andersonville prison. He was also confined in the prisons at Charleston and Florence, and was in the hands of the rebels ten months and six days. He was in many engagements, several times volunteered for dangerous special service, and on various occasions manifested much coolness and bravery.

WILLIAM NOXON, son of Robert and Letitia Noxon, was born in Beekman, Dutchess county, in 1791, and in 1818, married Ruth, daughter of Samuel and Mary Brownell, of his native place. He removed from Dutchess county of Fleming, Cayuga county, and from there to Castile in 1848, where he purchased one hundred and twenty acres of land, and died in 1867. He held the office of superintendent of the State prison at

Auburn six years, was many years a magistrate, and was known as a useful, energetic business man. His widow removed to Perry village in 1869.

PHILIP, son of Philip and Clarissa OLIN, was born in Canada, in 1837. His father died when he was young, and he was adopted by his uncle. He has been a resident of Perry since 1838. In 1857 he married Maria, daughter of Willard and Lucretia Guld, of Leicester, Livingston county, by whom he had five children, four of whom are living. Mrs. Olin died in 1868, and during that year Mr. Olin married Hattie, daughter of Truman and Mary Ann Madison, of Castile, who has borne him two children; one is living.

THOMAS OLIN, son of Paris and Sophia Olin, was born in Perry, January 9th, 1833. In 1855 he married Miss Emeline Compton, who bore him a son, and died in 1866, at the age of thirty-three. His present wife was Miss Catharine B. McEntee, daughter of Patrick and Mary McEntee, of Perry. During the year of his birth Mr. Olin's father moved to Leicester, Livingston county, where the latter resided until 1871, when he removed to Castile, locating just outside the corporate limits of Perry. He owns one hundred and fifty acres of land, nineteen of which is in Castile and the balance in Leicester, Livingston county. Mr. and Mrs. Olin are Presbyterians, and Mr. Olin has been church clerk for a number of years. Patrick McEntee, Mrs. Olin's father, was a native of Ireland. He came with his parents to Perry in 1814, and his father took up eighty acres of lot 3.

TRUMAN OLIN was born in Shaftsbury, Bennington county, Vt., 1810, and came to Perry from Rutland, Vt., in 1824, with his father, Ezra Olin, and his brothers, Paris and Heman, making the journey with a team, and locating on land taken up by his brother Philip, who was a settler in 1822. Mr. Olin had left his wife and four children to follow him to Perry, They proceeded to Rochester by canal, and walked from Rochester to Perry, except six miles of the distance. Mrs. Olin was at that time fifty, but she preferred to make the journey in this manner rather than wait for a team to come from Perry. In 1825 Mr. Olin, sen., purchased one hundred and five acres from Mr. Bates, on the Perry Center road. A year later he exchanged this farm for one belonging to his son Philip, further east on the same road, where he died in 1858, at the age of eighty-six. Truman Olin was married in 1834 to Betsy, daughter of Daniel and Hannah Hoyt, of Perry, by whom he has two sons. He is a farmer and the owner of one hundred and ninety-one acres of land.

MRS. ELIZA OLNEY is a daughter of John H. and Sarah Hollister, who came from New Marlborough, Mass., in 1816, and took up sixty-eight acres of lot 19, where Mr. Hollister is still living, at eighty-four. His first house in Perry was constructed of slabs. It was soon superseded by a log structure. Miss Eliza Hollister was married at the age of twenty-four to Daniel Richards, a wagon maker, who came from New Hampshire in 1841 and soon afterward engaged in the clothing business. By this marriage Mrs. Olney has had two children, one of whom (Mrs. S. Phillips, of Perry) is living. Mr. Richards died in 1852, at the age of twenty-eight. In 1856 his widow married Frederick T. Olney, of La Grange, a farmer, who died in 1870, at the age of seventy-seven.

HENRY N. PAGE, banker, was born in Harland, Vt., July 18th, 1823, and came from New York to Perry October 1st, 1843. October 7th, 1850, he married Eliza Dolbeer, of Perry. He was one of the projectors of the Silver Lake Railroad, and has been treasurer of the company since its organization. He was supervisor of Perry in 1876–79.

GEORGE F. PECK was born in Vermont, in 1802. In 1824 he married Eliza Page, of Sweden, Monroe county, by whom he had five children, four of whom are living. His second wife, who, as his widow, survives him, was Miss Philinda Hamlin, whose parents came from Vermont to Warsaw in 1814. By this marriage one daughter was born to him. Mr. Peck was the owner of a farm of ninety acres in Castile, where he came in 1841, from Sweden, Monroe county, and died in 1861. He early identified himself with the Methodist church, of which his widow is a devout member.

LYMAN PHILLIPS was born in Perry, on the farm where he now lives, in 1832. His father, Nahum Phillips, was born in New England, in 1793. In 1816 he walked from Dover, Vt., to his future home in Perry, carrying his baggage in a pack strapped to his back. He cleared a farm, and died on it in 1867. His wife was Polly Nevins, of Danville, Vt. They had five children, of whom the above named is the only one living. Mr. and Mrs. Phillips were both members of the Baptist church.

J. D. POLLARD, farmer, was born in Batavia, Genesee county, in 1832. He removed from there to Wales, Erie county; from Wales to Wyoming, and from Wyoming to Perry in 1855. He was married in 1879 to Amelia Goodell, daughter of Charles and Minerva Burt. His father, Sidney Pollard, was born in Clinton, Oneida county, in 1791. After living in different places he settled in Wyoming. He was one of the first settlers in Wales, Erie county, where he located in 1813. He was drafted nine times during the war of 1812–14, and was present at the battle of Black Rock. In 1815 he married Sarah Dustin, by whom he had nine children, of whom J. D. Pollard was the eighth born. Mrs. Pollards's father served three years during the Revolutionary war, and was present at the battle of Trenton, N. J.

MARTIN POST, cabinet maker, son of Jacob and Jane Post, was born in Fleming, Cayuga county, in 1818, and came to Perry from Auburn, Cayuga county, in 1836. In 1838 he married Delia E., daughter to Thomas and Sally Edgerly, of Perry. They have one son, Thomas Post, now of New York city, who served in the late war. He enlisted at Auburn in Company A, 19th N. Y. volunteers (afterward 3d light artillery), and was discharged at Auburn in 1863.

RALPH B. PRATT, owner of a farm of eighty-five acres, was born in Perry, in 1841. In 1858 he married Harriet E., daughter of John and Ruth Bushnell. He contributed toward the prosecution of the late war. His father, Jabesh Pratt, was born in Manchester, Vt., in 1797, and removed from there to Perry, where he purchased a farm and became prominent in public affairs, serving several years as supervisor, assessor and highway commissioner, and doing much toward the development of the town. Mrs. Pratt's father, John Bushnell, was born in Litchfield, Conn., in 1800, and moved to Arcade, and from there to Perry. He married Ruth Hill, by whom he had four children, all of whom are living, and of whom Mrs. Pratt was the third.

JOHN RICHMOND was born in Staffordshire, England, in 1821. He came to America in 1841, and for three years was engaged in milling at Oswego, Baldwinsville and Syracuse, N. Y. In 1846 he married Mary, daughter of John and Susan Payne, of Worcestershire, England, by whom he has three children, his marriage having occurred after his return to England in 1844. He came to America a second time in 1863, locating in Oswego, N. Y. In 1867 he purchased the Geneseo grist and flouring mills at Perry, of which he is proprietor and manager.

MIRANDA G. RICHARDSON, daughter of Hector M. Goodall, married J. Clarke Richardson, of Connecticut, in 1857. Mr. Richardson was a Congregational clergyman, and labored in Kentucky and at Oramel, Allegany county. He died in Livingston county in 1865, leaving three children, Hector G., born in 1859; Amelia M., born in 1861, and Riley Clarke, born in 1864. Mrs. Richardson's father, Hector M. Goodall, married Eliza Silver, who came to Perry with her father in 1815. On his arrival in the town Mr. Goodall took up some wild land, on which he erected a log house and which he cleared. He was a quiet, unobtrusive man, much respected by all who knew him. He died in 1850; his widow, August, 21st, 1877. They had three daughters, Hannah, born in 1827; Miranda, born in 1830, and Mary, born in 1834. Miranda is a member of the Congregational church of Perry Center; her two sisters are Methodists.

CHARLES S. READ, son of Moses and Harriet Read, was born in Seneca, Ontario county, September 24th, 1834. May 7th, 1873, he married Martha, daughter of John and Esther Martin, of Perry, by whom he has two sons. Mr. Read came to Perry from Seneca, Ontario county, in 1863, and engaged in the hardware trade. In 1872 he removed to Lincoln, Neb., where he was in the grocery trade until 1874, when he returned to Perry. In 1875 he purchased a farm in the north part of the town, and in 1879 again came to Perry village and engaged in the hardware business. He has served the town of collector of taxes.

NATHANIEL C. ROBINSON was born in Saratoga county, August 5th, 1797, and married Roxa Mendell, of Massachusetts, in 1828. He moved from Saratoga county to Allegany county; thence to Perry, in 1829, when he purchased his present farm, seventy acres of which was improved. Peleg Robinson, his father, was born in Massachusetts, in 1771. At the age of twenty-five he removed to Saratoga county, where he was an early settler and lived in a log house of his own construction. His wife, formerly Kepsy Coffin, was born in Maine, in 1771. The Robinson family are of English descent. Mr. and Mrs. Robinson were Quakers. Nathaniel C. Robinson has had nine children, seven of whom are living. Of these may be mentioned William, Randolph, Jonathan, Hannah and Eliza.

LYDIA ANNE SAFFORD was born in Manchester, Bennington Co., Vt., in 1818, and married Amos B. Safford, who was born in Connecticut in 1814. Her father, Moses Johnson Sperry, was born in Connecticut, and came to Perry in 1827. His wife was Martha Odell, of Vermont. He removed from Perry to Ohio, where he died in 1839. Mrs. Safford's children are as follows: Laura E., born in 1838; Sperry, born in 1840; Lydia E., born in 1846; Carlton A., born in 1847; Antha D., born in 1848, and William Craydon, born in 1850.

ANDREW SHELDON was born in Perry, in 1836. In 1857 he married Mary Jane Olin, daughter of Paris and Sophia Olin, of Perry. Mr. Sheldon, who is a well-known farmer, was born in the house in which he lives, and has been a life-long resident of the town. He contributed $400 toward the suppression of the Rebellion. Horace Sheldon, father of the above mentioned, was born in Massachusetts, in 1795, and found a woodland home in Perry many years ago. He filled the office of school inspector, and was a member of and a deacon in the Congregational church. He was an ardent advocate of temperance, as is his son, and circulated the first temperance pledge ever offered for signatures in Perry. His wife was Philene Ward, a native of Massachusetts. They had seven children, of whom Andrew Sheldon was the fourth born.

MARCUS D. SMITH, son of Septimus and Clarissa Smith, was born in Wells, Rutland county, Vt., in 1817, and came to Perry in infancy with his parents. He was married in 1841, to Caroline O. Graham, of Perry, formerly of New York city, by whom he had four children, three of whom are living. Mr. Smith built the first hotel at Silver Lake (now a part of N. Saxton's hotel), in 1860, and managed it two years. 1850–54 he was in the employ of the New York Central Railroad Company, as conductor and timekeeper in their shops. He has been a produce dealer and general speculator, but has never aspired to hold any office.

MARVIN SMITH, brother of the above mentioned, was born in Perry, in 1827. In 1849 he married Minerva Andrus, of Castile, who died in 1851. In 1854 he married Miranda Millspaugh, of Perry, by whom he has four children. Mr. Smith has always regarded Perry as his home, though he has been absent some years in business. He is a blacksmith and machinist, and was for five years master mechanic in the shop of Hudnut Metcalf, of Geneseo. Mr. Smith and his wife are members of the Universalist church of Perry. Septimus Smith, father of Marcus D. and Marvin Smith, was born in Pultney, Vt., in 1794. He married Clarissa Goodspeed, of Wells, Rutland county, Vt., by whom he had ten children, six of whom are living. In 1817 he came with a team, in company with Ira Wilson, from Vermont to Perry village, where he located. The journey consumed eighteen days. He worked until the fall of 1818 at the carpenter's trade, and then returned to Vermont and brought back his family, arriving in November. He died in 1835, at the age of forty-two; his wife in 1878. They were members of the Universalist church.

JEBEZ SOWERBY was born in the city of Hull, England, November 18th, 1818, and came to America in 1833, locating at Canandaigua, N. Y.; thence to Perry in 1837. He bought sixty-two acres of land two miles west of west Perry. When a boy, in England, he was apprenticed to learn the carpenter's trade. July 4th, 1840, he married Jane, daughter to Thomas and Elizabeth Blanchard, of Perry, by whom he had two sons and four daughters. He died April 15th, 1875. Mrs. Sowerby was born in England, December 3d, 1818, and came to America with her parents in 1831.

ROBERT STAINTON was born in Castile, April 26th, 1837. January 1st, 1863, he married Martha Green, of Mount Morris, Livingston county. October 26th, 1878, he married M. Ella Smallwood, of Warsaw. Mr. Stainton is a dry goods merchant, and came to Perry in 1868, from the homestead of his father, Rev. John Stainton, in Castile. Mr. and Mrs. Stainton are members, and the former is steward, of the Methodist church of Perry. John Stainton was born in Yorkshire, England, in 1796. His mother died there in 1807, and in 1819 he came to America with his father and only sister, in company with William Smallwood, landing at Alexandria, Virginia, where the party remained a month; when, purchasing a horse and cart, they started for the Genesee country, where a friend from England named Watson had located about two years previously. They were four weeks making the journey from Alexandria to Perry, Miss Stainton occupying the cart while the men walked. On his arrival Mr. Stainton purchased an improvement of fifty acres two miles southeast of Perry, in Castile. This improvement consisted in the "girdling" of about half an acre. To this tract he afterward added eighty acres, on which he made his home forty-four years. He was married in 1830, to Miss Lydia Grisewood, of Castile (whose parents had come from England in 1804 to Geneva, Ontario county, and to Castile in 1818), by whom he has had ten children, four of whom are living. In 1825 Mr. Stainton united with the Methodist church, and a few years later was ordained to the ministry, to the duties of which he devoted much of his time in after life. Mr. and Mrs.

Stainton are living in Perry village, surrounded by friends, ripe in years, and awaiting the call from the earthly life.

AMBROSE H. STOUT, son of Charles E. and Ure Stout, was born in Amity, Allegany county, in 1844, and came to Perry in 1875. He was married June 9th, 1873, to Susan Winslow, daughter of Hezekiah and Marium Winslow, of Potsdam, St. Lawrence county.

MARTIN SWEET, son of Rufus and Ann Sweet, was born in Shaftsbury, Vt., in 1815. He came from his native place in company with his uncle, Simeon Wright, to Leicester, Livingston county, in 1834; thence in 1835 to Perry. In the fall of 1834 his father's family came to Leicester, and after a short time to Perry, where Mr. Sweet, sen., purchased of Freeman Williams ninety acres of land on the Allegany road, which was the family home for many years. In 1844 Martin Sweet married Miss Aurelia Lacy, daughter of Elnathan and Nancy Lacy, of Perry, by whom he had two children, and who died in 1869. In 1870 he married Electa, daughter of Daniel and Polly Lacy, also of Perry. Mr. Sweet is a farmer.

GERMAN SWEET, son of Rufus and Ann Sweet, and brother of Martin Sweet, was born in Shaftsbury, Vt., in 1823, and came to Perry with his parents. Mr. Sweet is a fire, life and accident insurance agent, and a dealer in pianos, organs and other musical instruments. He established his business in Perry in 1851. Much of his time has been devoted to teaching music. In 1852 he married Emily W., daughter of Harvey and Polly Riggs, of Perry Center, by whom he has three children. Mr. and Mrs. Sweet are members of the Baptist church, of which he has been clerk twenty years. He has officiated as leader of the choir thirty years.

HIRAM TAYLOR was born in Perry, in 1823, and has been a life-long resident of the town, where he is a well known farmer. In 1845 he married Miss C. D. R., daughter of Ebenezer Witter. Mr. Taylor served the town nine years as assessor, and contributed liberally of his time and means toward the suppression of the Rebellion. The family are members of the Baptist church at La Grange, of which he has for some years been one of the trustees. Job Taylor, his father, was born in Rensselaer county, in 1794, and settled in Covington fifty years ago and purchased and cleared wild land. He died at the age of eighty-three.

REUBEN A. TAYLOR was born in Washington county, in 1837, and when he was old enough began to work by the month, and continued until twelve years ago, when he purchased a farm of seventy-five acres. He came to Perry from Sheldon. During the late war he was drafted, but paid $300 for a substitute. His father, John R. Taylor, was born in 1799, and married Sarah Oatman, of Vermont. Mr. Taylor was married in 1856 to Julia E. Kinney, daughter of Asher Kinney, who was born in Oneida county, in 1805, and married Anne Armstrong, of that county, in 1886.

JOHN H. TERRY is a son of John Terry. He was five years proprietor of the Perry drug store, since which time he has been engaged in the newspaper business either as reporter or editor. He was an apprentice in the *Wyoming Times* office during the Silver lake snake excitement. In 1869 he was editor of the Adrian, Mich., *Journal;* since that has been local editor of the Ottumwa, Ia., *Democrat*, the Brockport *Democrat* and Perry *Herald*, and is now manager of the Perry department of the *Wyoming County Times*, and special correspondent of the Rochester daily *Democrat* and *Chronicle, Syracuse* daily *Standard*, Elmira daily *Gazette,* New York *Mercury,* Olean *Times*, Nunda *News*, Hornellsville *Times*, and *Castilian*, of Castile. Mr. Terry was born April 15th, 1844, and ranks as a

ELNATHAN LACY.

MRS. ELNATHAN LACY.

FARM RESIDENCE OF ALANSON LACY, ONE MILE EAST OF PERRY VILLAGE, N.Y.

MARTIN P. ANDREWS.

WALTER GILLESPIE.

thorough newspaper man. John Terry, his father, was born in Dutchess county, July 3d, 1798. For many years he was a resident of Perry, where he was engaged in banking. He married Catharine M. Johnson, of Perry, and died in that place July 30th, 1844.

HON. S. W TEWKSBURY was born in Leicester, Genesee county, July 23d, 1820. He came to Perry in 1834, and December 22nd, 1842, married Mary, only daughter of Hon. Truman Benedict, of Perry. Mr. Tewksbury, who is a well known farmer, represented his district in the Assembly of 1874–75; has been superintendent of schools eleven years, justice of the peace about twenty years and assistant assessor two years.

JOHN S. THOMPSON, son of John G. and Mary Thompson, was born in Onondaga, Onondaga county, in 1815, and came with his parents to Perry in 1817. He is a farmer and the owner of nearly five hundred acres of land. He was married in 1839 to Hannah, daughter of Deacon Daniel and Martha Howard, of Covington, For nine years he served as justice of the peace. Captain John S. Thompson was born Cherry Valley, N.Y., in 1790, and married Miss Mary A. Turner about 1810 or 1811, by whom he had seven children, five of whom are living. In the spring of 1817 he brought his family and some necessary portable property from Onondaga county to Pavilion by means of an ox team and a wagon. Unable to get the wagon to Perry, he conveyed his effects to the latter place by means of the oft-described "drag" of pioneer days. He had previously purchased one hundred and fifty acres and made a small clearing. Here he rolled up a rude log cabin, floorless and roofed with elm bark, and the family were soon house-keeping. In the fall he laid a floor of basswood slabs. Captain Thompson and wife were members of the Baptist church at La Grange from its organization to their deaths, which occurred in 1834 and 1864 respectively; the former living to be forty-four and the latter seventy-three.

JOSEPH R. TOAL was born in Covington, in 1855. In 1877 he married Lydia A. Pennock, daughter of Ira and Jane (Campbell) Pennock, and came to Perry, where he is a farmer and a member of the Presbyterian church, His father, David Toal, was born in Ireland, in 1829. He came to Covington in 1830, married Mary Anne Noble, and still resides there. Mr. Toal's grandfather on his mother's side came to Wyoming county in 1815 from Vermont, making the journey with an ox-team and being twenty-one days on the road. He was one of the early settlers in his neighborhood, lived in a log cabin, and helped open the roads through the woods. Ira P. Pennock, Mrs. Toal's father, was born in Perry, in 1838, and after a time removed to Canada, where he lives. In 1856 he married Jane Campbell, who was born in Dublin, Ireland in 1833.

AUSTIN W., son of Thomas and Betsey TOAN, was born in Scipio, Cayuga county, March 29th, 1822. He came to Perry in 1826, and December 8th, 1853, married Elizabeth daughter of Reuben and Sarah Compton, of Perry, by whom he has had two children, one of whom, Charles H., is living. In 1854 Mr. Toan bought the farm on which he now lives. He is a trustee of the Methodist church of Perry, and for the past five years he has been a director of the Silver Lake Railroad Company. Thomas Toan was born in New Jersey, in 1798. In 1826 he came to Perry, and rented the farm now owned by Daniel Stowell, of West Perry. In 1827 he bought one hundred acres of lot 33. In 1821 he married Batsy Harney, by whom he had five children, four of whom are living. Mr. Toan, who served his country in the war of 1812–14, died June 18th, 1862, sixty-nine; his wife November 3d, 1872, aged seventy-five.

GEORGE TOMLINSON, son of George and Hepsibah Tomlinson, was born in Le Roy, Genesee county, in 1822. In 1845 he married Marion B., daughter of James and Martha Sprague, of Pavilion, Genesee county. He came to Perry in 1870. He served as justice of the peace in Genesee county eighteen years and as school commissioner fourteen years. In 1851 he built a flouring mill at Port Washington, Wis., where he remained but a short time. Returning to his native town he engaged in cloth dressing and the manufacture of woollen goods, at which he early served an apprenticeship. He next engaged in trade in company with Samuel J. Lewis, and later with J. S. Noble. In 1861 their store was burned, and Mr. Tomlinson turned his attention to farming until 1870, when George Tomlinson & Son became proprietors of the Silver Lake Flouring Mills.

G. RYERSON TRAVER, M. D., son of Frederick Traver, was born in Westminister, Middlesex county, Ontario, Canada West, in 1844. In 1869 he graduated from the Homœopathic Medical College of New York city. Returning to Canada he became a member of the College of Physicians and Surgeons of Ontario, and practiced his profession four years at St. Catharine's. Later he was associated for a time with Dr. H. M. Dayfoot, of Mount Morris, Livingston county, and came from that place to Perry, where he enjoys the confidence and respect of the public. In 1875 he married Rose, daughter of William H. and Frances Bennett, of Canandaigua, N.Y.

RICHARD T. TUTTLE was born in Seneca, Ontario county, September 18th, 1830, and in December, 1854, came to Perry, and is a member of the firm of Wyokoff, Tuttle & Olin, manufacturers of reapers and dealers in hardware. He formerly resided in Canandaigua, Ontario county, and in April, 1866, married Emma H. Wyckoff, of Hopewell, that county.

SIMON UTTER, son of Abraham and Marilda Utter, was born in Hartford, N. Y., in 1811. He removed to Castile in 1830; to Leicester, Livingston county, in 1852, and to Perry in 1865, where he purchased one hundred acres two miles northeast of the village. In 1835 he married Angeline, daughter of John and Saphira Wiloox, of Warsaw, by whom he has had three children, all of whom are dead.

SAMUEL WALDO was born in Rome, Oneida county, in 1795. At the age of four he removed with his parents to Verona; subsequently returned to Rome; removed to Shaftsbury, Vermont; thence to Perry, where he has lived sixty-three years. He has been five times married, his present wife having been Maria T. (formerly Shaw), widow of William Crooker. Mr. Waldo has been school commissioner and inspector and assessor. He is a member and the clerk of the Baptist church; Mrs. Waldo is identified with the Congregational church. Mr. Waldo's father was born in Connecticut, in 1767, and came to Perry in 1826, where he lived until he died. Mrs. Waldo's father was born in Connecticut, in 1774; removed from there to Chenango county, and thence to Naples, Ontario county, where he purchased a farm in the south part of the town. Her father and mother were member of the Baptist church at Naples.

ARTEMAS B., son of Billings and Hannah WALKER, was born in Windsor county, Vt., in 1813. In 1841 he married Adeline Willey, of Castile. In 1873 he built Walker's Hotel at Silver Lake, and fitted up the grounds for the reception of visitors, and he has since been the proprietor of that favorite resort.

DEACON JOHN S. WESTLAKE, son of Adam and Elizabeth Westlake, was born in Somersetshire, England, in 1811, and married Louisa, daughter of Thomas Hancock, of his native place. He came to America in 1837, and located at Skaneateles, Onondaga county, where he remained one year, removing thence to Venice, Cayuga county, and thence to Perry in 1847. He is a tallor by trade, but is now a dealer in ready-made clothing. He is a member and for ten years has been deacon of the Baptist church, with which his wife is also identified. In 1856 his dwelling was burned, but by his own efforts and friendly aid he was soon the possessor of a new one.

DANIEL C., son of Norman and Tabitha WHITE, was born in Aurelius, Cayuga county, in 1823. He is a retired farmer and produce dealer. He came to Perry in childhood. In 1846 he married Sarah Gale Butler, daughter of William and Laura Butler, of Perry. Norman White was born in Connecticut, and came to Perry from Aurelius, Cayuga county, in 1824, locating on fifty acres of land a mile east of Perry village, where he died in 1857, at the age of sixty-two. He was twice married. His first wife was a daughter of Daniel and Tabitha Calkins, of Aurelius, Cayuga county, by whom he had two children. His second wife was Laura Simmons, of Connecticut, by whom he had one child.

LUTHER C., son of Cyrus and Melissa Willard, was born in Pike, in 1847. In 1875 he married Hattie, daughter of Samuel and Ruth Allen, of Gainesville. In 1878 he came to Perry, where he is engaged in business as a harness maker and dealer in harnesses, robes, blankets, whips, etc.

MOSES C. WILLIAMS was born in Perry, in 1829. He is a merchant tailor and dealer in dry goods. In 1869 he married Helen A. Bullard, daughter of S. C. and Helen D. Bullard, of Perry. His parents were Freeman and Anna Williams, who came from Chenango county to Covington with an ox team in the spring of 1828, and in the following February to Perry, locating a mile and a half northeast of the village, where he had purchased forty acres of land. He purchased seventy acres on the creek road, to which he removed about 1835. In 1853 he retired from active life and removed to Perry village, where he died at the age of seventy-two. His widow survives him. The family have long been identified with the Universalist church, of which the late Freeman Williams was long a trustee, and his widow and Mr. and Mrs. Moses C. Williams are members.

EBENEZER WITTER was born in Scipio, Cayuga county, April 4th, 1815. February 23d, 1837, he married Eliza Ellsworth, daughter of Daniel C. and Eunice (Jones) Ellsworth, who died March 6th, 1878. He removed from Cayuga county to Livonia, Livingston county, to La Grange, to Burke Hill and to his present location. He is a well known farmer, and a member of the Baptist church of La Grange, with which his late wife was also identified. Of six children which have been born to him only three are living—Ebenezer D., born in 1839; Volney S., born in 1842; and William Ellsworth, born in 1853. Mr. Witter's father was born in Preston, Conn., May 7th, 1788, and in 1813 married Lovisa Reed. He came with his father to Cayuga county, where he took up a mile square of land and erected a log house. Ebenezer Witter, his grandfather, enlisted in the company of his father, who was a captain, and served during the greater part of the Revolutionary war. He was also an active supporter of missions among the heathen. Volney S. Witter, one of Mr. Witter's above mentioned sons, served in the 9th N. Y. volunteer cavalry, under Captain H. K. Stimpson, during a portion of the late war.

JAMES WYCKOFF, son of James and Esther Wyckoff, was born in Hopewell, Ontario county, in 1820. In 1843 he married Caroline, daughter of Joseph and Anna Tuttle, of Seneca, Ontario county, and came from Hopewell to Perry in 1857. He is one of the partners in the firm of Wyckoff, Tuttle & Olin, hardware dealers, proprietors of the

Perry foundry, and manufacturers of the Royce reaper and other agricultural implements. This establishment affords employment to sixty-five to seventy men, and turns out about $200,000 worth of manufactures annually.

JAMES, son of Henry and Agnes WYLIE, was born in Elderslie, Scotland, in 1826. Having learned the trade of spinner, he emigrated to America and located at Waterloo, Seneca county, and he was employed two years in the Waterloo shawl factory, where he learned the manufacture of woolen goods, and in 1857 located at Milltown, Pa., whence he removed, in 1865, to Perry, where he is the proprietor of the Perry woolen mills, which turn out ten thousand yards annually, and give employment to eight skilled workmen. In 1859 he married Mary S. Thompson, of Athens, Pa., by whom he has six children. Mr. and Mrs. Wylie are members of the Baptist church.

THE TOWN OF PIKE.

THIS town formed a component part of Albany county from November 1st, 1683, to March 12th, 1772; Tryon county from March, 1772, to April 2nd, 1784; Montgomery county April 2nd, 1784, to January 27th, 1789; Ontario county January 27th, 1789, to March 30th, 1802; Genesee county, town of Batavia, from March 30th, 1802, to April 7th, 1806; Allegany county, town of Angelica, from April 7th, 1806, to March 11th, 1808; town of Nunda from March 11th, 1808, to March 6th, 1818, when it was set off as a separate town, including also the territory of the present towns of Eagle, Centerville and Hume.

The Legislature on the 18th of March, 1818, passed an act dividing the town of Nunda and organizing the four western townships (now Pike, Eagle, Hume and Centerville) into a new town, which they named Pike, after General Zebulon Montgomery Pike, who was killed by the explosion of a mine at the capture of Toronto May 13th, 1813. This action was taken on the request of the people of Nunda, who, in a town meeting at the village of Pike, December 18th, 1817, appointed Dan Beach, Thomas Dole, Asahel Trowbridge, Asahel Newcomb and Seth Wetmore a committee to petition the Legislature in their behalf.

A town meeting for the election of officers for the new town was held at the inn of Benjamin G. Chamberlain, at Pike, on the 7th of April, 1818, when the following were elected: Thomas Dole, supervisor; Asahel Newcomb, town clerk; Dan Beach, Jesse Bullock and Bailey Clough, assessors; Samuel Wolcott, collector; Thomas Dole and Dan Beach, overseers of the poor; Jonathan Barlow, Daniel Coldwell and Jesse Bullock, commissioners of highways; Caleb Powers, Salmon N. Griffiths, Samuel Wolcott, Zaccheus Spencer and Job Bonney, constables; Thomas Dole, Perkins B. Woodward and Seth Wetmore, commissioners of common schools, and George Flint, Salmon Newcomb and Jesse Bullock were elected inspectors of common schools.

It was voted that each overseer of highways should be a fenceviewer and poundmaster, and each fenceviewer's yard a legal pound, and that horned cattle should be free commoners.

At an election in April, 1821, Benjamin Ellicott had 131 votes and Albert H. Tracy 48 votes for member of Congress from the 22nd district. For senators for the western district James McCall received 155 votes and Henry Seymour 152. For Assemblyman to represent the counties of Steuben and Allegany Grattan H. Wheeler had 136 votes, Amos Peabody 159, Asa Davison 64 and William Wood 32 votes. For a convention to amend the constitution there were 133 votes; against convention 61.

At an election held in June, 1821, to elect a delegate to the State convention, James McCall had 108 votes, Alvin Burr 26, and Cornelius Younglove 24. At a special election held in January, 1822, to vote on the amended constitution, 84 votes were given for and 139 against.

The following votes were passed at the annual town meeting held in April, 1827, together with others restraining vagrant live stock.

"Voted, that hogs shall not be free commoners at no times.

"Voted, that geese shall not run at large at no time on the penalty of having their necks rung whenever cetched."

The vote of Pike in November, 1828, for Presidential elector was: for Clark Crandall, Democrat, 150 votes; for John Lloyd, Whig, 139. Since that time, however, the Democrats have been but a feeble minority in presidential elections. They polled but 121 votes to 359 Republican in 1876.

Supervisors and town clerks of the town of Pike have been elected as follows:

Supervisors.—1818, Thomas Dole; 1821, Joshua Skiff; 1822, 1827, George Barlow; 1824, Abner Adams; 1825, William Hyslop; 1826, Ebenezer Griffith; 1830, Hiram Bond; 1832, Luther C. Peck; 1837, Benjamin Burlington; 1840, Timothy Rockwell; 1842, Norman N. Olin; 1846, John V. W. Abbott; 1848, 1854, 1857, 1862, 1873, Orace V. Whitcomb; 1849, John Renwick; 1851, Hiram Watkins; 1852, Cyrenus M. Fuller, jr.; 1855, 1865, 1872. Marcus A. Hull; 1859, A. P. Sherrill; 1863, Henry M. Jackson; 1869, Martin Hodge; 1871, Marvin Trall; 1876. George M. Palmer; 1880, Jesse H. Ward.

Town Clerks.—1818, Asahel Newcomb; 1821, Abner Adams; 1824, Benjamin Packard; 1826, 1829, Asher P. Hickox; 1823, Moses Smith; 1830, 1834, William Windsor; 1833, Jonathan Emery; 1837, James G. Sprague; 1839, 1846, A. M. Huntting; 1848, Alvin Peck; 1849, Delano P. Gordon; 1851, 1854, A. Spencer Huntting; 1853, 1856, Artemus C Bacon; 1855, George S. Huntting; 1861, M. P. Skiff; 1867, N. T. Parker; 1869, A. P. Sherrill; 1878, G. S. Van Gorder.

Of those who have held prominent civil offices from this town, Moses Smith was elected sheriff in 1834, and held the office three years; Luther C. Peck was elected member of Congress in 1837, and held the office for two terms; Ezra Smith was superintendent of the poor three years, and William Windsor was county clerk from 1841 to 1847; Marvin Trall was elected county judge in 1851, and held the office four years; Mills L. Rice, elected sheriff in 1858, held the office for one term; John Renwick, elected in 1864, was sheriff three years; Marcus A. Hull was member of Assembly in 1869 and 1870; Hiram P. Melville is serving his second term as coroner.

The following statistics were taken from the State census of 1875: Number of inhabitants, 1,726—males, 850, females, 876; males of voting age, 511; persons of school age, 385; number of families, 420; inhabited houses, 382; improved land, 14,198 acres; woodland, etc., 4,599; number of farms, 256; cash value of farms, $954,332; acres mown, 3,792; tons of hay, 4,613; acres of barley, 207; number of bushels, 3,600; acres of corn, 227; number of bushels, 8,096; acres of oats, 1,663; number of bushels, 39,832; acres of winter wheat, 448; number of bushels, 5,889; acres of potatoes, 256; number of bushels, 25,500.

We are obliged to remark in the case of Pike, as in reference to so many other towns, the almost constant decrease in population during the last half century. The following interesting figures showing this fact are quoted from the "red book" of the Legislature: 1830, 2,016; 1835, 2,179; 1840, 2,181; 1845, 2,172; 1850, 2,063; 1855, 1,887; 1860, 1,824; 1865, 1,805; 1870, 1,730; 1875, 1,726.

SETTLEMENT AND FIRST EVENTS.

Pike is township 7, range 1, of the Holland Purchase. The first settlers took "articles" from the Holland Company for their lands, and received deeds upon the payment of a stipulated price. Those who took the first articles were:

Peter Granger, Isaac Granger, Eli Griffith and Philip Fuller in 1805; and Azel Lyon, Ashahel Newcomb, Micah Griffith, Joshua Powers, Alanson Landon, Oliver Stacy, Arunah Cooley, Amos Bill, Aaron Fuller, jr., Eli Griffith, jr., Thomas Worden, Christopher Olin, Thomas Dole, Asahel Trowbridge, John Stewart, Eli Stewart, John Willard, Alexander Axtell, David Hoyt and Roger Mills in 1806.

The following were among the first to receive their deeds:

> Benjamin Wakeman, lot 9, 1816; Jonathan Barlow, lot 19, 1814; Ebenezer Harvey, lot 11, 1811; Arnold Sykes, lot 12, 1815; Samuel Flint, lot 15, 1815: Edmund Skiff, lot 17, 1819; Jellis Clute and Elihu Griffith, lot 20, 1816; Amos Griffith, lot 20, 1816; Christopher Olin, lot 22, 1808; Eli Stewart, lot 23, 1809; Benjamin Skiff, lot 25, 1815; Thomas Dole, lot 27, 1811; Salmon and Asahel Newcomb, lot 23, 1816: Josiah Metcalf, lot 36, 1815; Asa Emery, lot 36, 1816; Ezra Willard, lot 41, 1817; Christopher Olin, lot 48, 1816; Eli Griffith, south part of lot 44, 1811; Abner Runnals. northwest part of lot 44, Calvin N. Griffith, north part of lot 44, 1829; Thurston Clark, lot 49, 1817; Timothy Rockwell, lot 49, 1804; John Willard, lot 51, 1815; Jonathan Willard, lot 52, 1816; W. Trowbridge, lot 55, 1817; Russell H. Benton, lot 61, 1809; John Ressique, lot 61, 1812; Calvin Le Gare, lot 62, 1815; Reuben Doty, lot 62, 1816; Silas Hodges, lot 64, 1816.

The oldest deed was given to Russell H. Benton, for the lot No. 61, in 1809. He died December 29th, 1814. There is but one tombstone in the village cemetery older than this, that of Eli Griffith. Esq., who died December 11th, 1812.

The first permanent settlement in Pike was made in 1806, by Asahel Newcomb, Eli Griffith, Peter Granger, Caleb Powers and Phineas Harvey, all from Whitehall, N. Y.

Captain Newcomb settled on lot No. 28, and occupied it till his death. He was justice of the peace, coroner, captain of militia, and was appointed judge of Allegany county by Governor Clinton, but declined the honor. He died May 5th, 1862, aged eighty-two years. Eli Griffith settled on lot 44, which is now Pike village, where he kept the first tavern, in 1808, and built the first saw-mill in 1809, and the first grist-mill in 1810, about three-quarters of a mile north of the village. John Wilder, of Warsaw, was the boss builder. Caleb Powers also settled on lot 44, and Peter Granger near Metcalf's Corners, on the Center road, where he afterward kept a tavern several years.

The first child born was Louisa, daughter of Captain Asahel Newcomb, born in August, 1806. The first marriage was that of Russell H. Benton to Susannah Olin, February 23d, 1809, and the first deaths were those of twin children of Phineas Harvey, in the spring of 1807, which were followed by his death the ensuing autumn.

The first school was taught by Miss Beulah Abel, from Washington county, in the summer of 1809. She afterward married Abel Townsend, who settled on lot 22 in 1808.

Tilly Parker kept the first store, in 1810, in Pike village.

The first carding and fulling mill was built by Ezra Smith and J. Ganson, in 1823–4, upon the site of the present woolen factory. It was burned in December, 1840, and a woolen factory erected the ensuing season by Ezra Smith & Co. M. A. Hull bought a share in the factory in 1843. This building was burned December 28th, 1855, and a larger one was built the next spring. Harvey Smith and Martin M. Smith subsequently owned shares in the factory; but it is now owned and operated by Messrs. G. A., J. F. and D. E. Greene, and is making large quantities of first class woolen cloths, flannels, yarns, etc.

The grist-mill in the village was built by Ezra Smith and J. Ganson in 1821, and subsequently owned by J. G. Sprague, G. C. Sprague, Samuel Hatch, A. C. Bacon and Elijah F. Durfey, who sold it to Allen Clark. The last named reconstructed it and put in new machinery in 1872. It is now owned and run by A. & H. A. Clark.

A furnace was built in 1823 by J. Ganson, on the bank of the Wiscoy creek, where Frank Lyon's barn now stands; after being owned by several persons it was purchased by Albert B. Smith, who added a machine shop and made threshing machines. The establishment was burned down July 1st, 1849, and rebuilt the following year. C. B. Lyon was the owner when it was again burned in May, 1869. It has not been rebuilt.

The following are the dates of the erection of the more prominent buildings in the village of Pike: Baptist church on the hill, 1829; the present building in 1850; Methodist and Presbyterian churches, 1832; the present building of the latter, 1841; Pike Seminary, 1856; Eagle Hotel, 1832; Smith's mill, 1829; present woolen factory, 1856; J. Emory's stone store, 1833; Hatch's stone store, 1839; A. Adams's stone tannery, 1842 (now occupied by William & E. L. Powers for a saw and planing-mill and box factory); red school-house, 1822; new school-house, 1877; grist-mill, 1819 (remodeled to a flouring-mill in 1872); Kerr's hotel, 1839; Skiff's store, 1831; Besancon's, 1832; Adams's yellow tannery, 1830; Kellogg's furniture store, 1856; A. P. Sherrill's store, 1842; the sills and plates of this building were from old trees which were cut down on the transit line when it was run by the Holland Land Company, in 1798.

POST-OFFICES AND MAIL ROUTES.

For a number of years after the first settlement of the town the people went to Geneseo for their mail. The first post-office was established July 4th, 1818; Russell G. Hurd was the first postmaster. A mail route to Warsaw was established, and a few years later a tri-weekly mail route from Canandaigua, Geneseo, Perry and Pike, on to Ellicottville and Jamestown. The following named persons have been appointed postmasters in the years mentioned: Thomas Dole, March, 1819; Justin Otis, 1839; Abraham P. Sherrill, 1840, 1861; Horace Hatch, 1841; Ira Barnes, 1843; Delano P. Gordon, 1845, 1853; Samuel Windsor, 1849.

A post-office was established at East Pike as early as 1827; Henry Burt was the postmaster. His successors have been Daniel Flint, Spencer S. Hammond, Zina Baker, O. B. Van Deusen and Marion R. Mosier.

The office at East Koy was established about 1843; Isaac Quackenbush was the first postmaster. It was discontinued in 1862, but re-established a few years since. James N. Dowd is the postmaster.

SCHOOLS AND SCHOOL BUILDINGS.

From its earliest settlement the citizens of Pike have taken a lively interest in the cause of education. Under the common school system their schools are above the average grade. At first they were kept in private houses or log school-houses, with an open fire-place at one end, with a stick and mud chimney. The seats were of slabs, with auger holes bored through them for the legs. In 1822 the old red school-house was built. It was two stories high, the upper room being for many years used for a masonic lodge. In this house many persons who have since become eminent as ministers, lawyers, doctors, teachers, etc., have received the rudiments of their education.

The first school of a higher grade than the district school, and in which the higher branches were taught, was commenced by Tracy Scott in 1833–34, and continued about three years. It was kept in the old Packard building, near the spot where L. M. Chaffee's house now stands, and was well patronized by students from other towns.

In 1844 the two school districts in the village were consolidated, the school-house in the upper district was removed and annexed to the red school-house, and the district organized under the union school plan. In 1877 the "old red" was sold, removed to the corner of F. D. Chandler's lot, and reconstructed into a dwelling, and it is now owned by Mrs. M. Kendall. The same year a neat new school-house was erected in the village, a few rods nearer the Wiscoy creek than the old one, at a cost of $1,200. The grading and furnishing cost $400 more. Collins W. Thomas was the contractor, and Henry C. Lathrop was the trustee at the time.

PROFESSIONAL AND BUSINESS MEN.

William Hyslop was the first lawyer who settled in the town. He came from Otsego county after the war of 1812. He was supervisor, also justice of the peace for a number of years.

Luther C. Peck came from Orleans county in 1826 or 1827; was supervisor six years, and justice of the peace ten years. In 1836 he was elected to Congress, and re-elected in 1838. While at Washington he married Miss Cynthia Fletcher, a native of that city. He subsequently (1841) removed to Nunda and pursued his profession, in which he held high rank. He died February 5th, 1876.

Benson Owen came in 1830 or 1831, and practiced two or three years. Alvin Peck studied with his brother, Luther, and was admitted to the bar in 1836. He was justice of the peace from 1841 till he removed in May, 1853. Marvin Trall commenced practice in 1837. He was justice of the peace until elected county judge in 1851. In 1874 he removed to Attica. James Harvey Windsor began to practice about 1849. He died in October, 1858. Almon P. Russell came here in the autumn of 1862, and died in October, 1867. Edwin Spencer was in practice here about two years preceding 1869. Francis M. Buck came in 1874, and practiced for about three years, when he removed to Eagle, and was in 1877 succeeded by Greenfield Scott Van Gorder, who is now practicing here. Homer E. Dean has lately been licensed to practice law.

Dr. Andrew Dutton was the first resident physician. He came here soon after the war of 1812, from Vermont.

Simeon Capron, also from Vermont, came in 1817. He was a skillful surgeon, and had an extensive practice. He was surgeon of the 204th regiment N. Y. militia, and as a land surveyor he laid out many of the roads in the town. He died in 1862, aged seventy.

Dr. Isaac Minard came from Vermont, and first settled on the East street, in 1831. He was held in high repute as a practitioner in pulmonary and chronic complaints. He died in 1875.

The names and dates of settlement in the town of the other physicians are nearly as follows: Clifford C. Chaffee, 1837; John V. W. Abbott, 1839; Dr. Wheeler, 1840; Dr. Russell, 1850; George Hutchinson, 1849; Edgar A. Finn, 1852; William W. Fenno, 1856; Horatio Spencer (a native of the town, has practiced over twenty-five years); George M. Palmer, 1856; Hiram P. Merville, 1874; William M. McFarlin, 1878; John J. Van Slyke was a physician of the eclectic school, and resided at East Pike.

Seth Wetmore was the first surveyor. After him were Simeon Capron, Asa Morse, James Reed, Joseph E. Weeden, Allen Nourse, Samuel Burroughs, Carlos Stebbins and C. Butler Ryder. Eli Griffith laid out a road to Leicester in 1806 and 1807. He was a soldier in the war of 1812, and was ordered to Buffalo under Smyth's proclamation, as were Chandler Benton and Jonathan Couch. They all died of disease in the service.

The following have been merchants in the town:

Tilly Parker, Thomas Dole & A. P. Hinman, Russell G. Hurd, John Parker, Lyman Ayrault, Daniel L. Gilman, L. and L. W. Whitcomb, Horace Hatch, Benjamin Packard, Ezra S. Winslow. Abraham M. Huntting, William and August Windsor, Asher P. Hecox, William Sherman, C. L. Dautremont, Abraham P. Sherrill, Albert B. Smith, John Renwick, Rufus Robinson, N. N. Olin, Thomas & Barnes, John C. Gillispie, Amos Brunson, Fuller & Huntting, William E. Hammond, Fuller & Kelly, A. S. Gordon & Co., A. C. Bacon, O. T. Higgins, Samuel Blodgett, James L. Platt, James W. Lloyd, Jonathan Gates, H. G. Rogers, Edmund C. Skiff, John S. Newcomb, William Eggleston, Orman Houghton, Royal Adams, Adams & Bush, Guilford Meacham, M. P. Skiff, Parker & Coons, Wing & Bush, Benjamin Knapp, Horace Blodget, Royal H. Adams, A. J. Beebe, A. C. Thompson, H. C. Lathrop, F. D. Chandler, Powell & Lewis, Curtis A. Prentice, A. O. & S. L. Skiff, John W. Brownson &Co., Charles S. Dean, Beebe & Norris.

PIKE'S MILITARY REPRESENTATIVES.

The following named persons served in the war of the Revolution, and afterward became residents of Pike: Joshua Whitney, Ephraim Patch, John Bostwick, Henry Bennett, William Van Slyke, James Smith and Thomas Griffith.

The following persons held military commissions from the governor, under the old militia system, from 1808 to the close of the war of 1812:

Eli Griffith and Asahel Newcomb, captains; Samuel Wolcott, Joshua Skiff and Bazaleel Beede, lieutenants. In 1822 Thomas Dole was brigadier-general; Anson Hinman, colonel; Amos Griffith, lieutenant-colonel; Simeon Heath, major, and Jacob H. Olin, lieutenant. At later dates Daniel L. Gilman was colonel and George W. Merrill lieutenant-colonel; Abram M. Huntting and Delano P. Gordon were majors; John Comstock and Amos Griffith, captains; Simeon Capron, regimental surgeon; Lewis Graves, lieutenant-colonel of artillery; William Eggleston, captain, and Stephen L. Wing and Lyman Ellithorp, lieutenants.

Eli Griffith, Chandler Benton and Jonathan Couch went from this town in the war of 1812. The following persons served in that war and removed to this town afterward: John I. Helmer, Benjamin Wakeman, Lewis Akin, Smith Ellis, Robert Flint. Samuel Hays, Timothy Rockwell, John Stewart, Martin Van Alst, Joshua Abbott, Sherman Kimberly, Uriah Rose, Asaph Griffith, Abel Spencer, Timothy Brooks, Eliphalet Metcalf, John Gleason, Abraham M. Huntting, Jonathan F. Hibbard, Jacob R. Horning, Calvin Lewis.

The four last named are now living in the town.

John Gurnsey, drum major, John P. Hodges, corporal, and Erastus Bates, private, were soldiers from this town in the Mexican war.

The following citizens of this town were soldiers in the Patriot war: Lewis Graves, lieutenant-colonel; William Eggleston, captain; Stephen L. Wing

Rev. JOHN STAINTON. Mrs. LYDIA STAINTON. Dr. E. C. HOLT.

(Eagle), first lieutenant; Lyman Ellithorp, second lieutenant; Paul S. Newcomb, first sergeant; John F. Ellinwood, second; Samuel Marsh, drummer; Ambrose Spencer, Morris S. Holt, Lewis Holt, Nathaniel Gowan, Hezekiah Metcalf, Simeon Hodges, William P. Smith, George C. Flint.

Pike was not dilatory in responding to the call for volunteers to put down the Rebellion. Among those most prominent in procuring enlistments in the early stages of the war were Major Washington Wheeler, Captain Henry Runyan, Rev. Daniel Russell, Hon. M. A. Hull and Carlos Stebbins. For the records of the soldiers from this town we must refer the reader to the histories of regiments in an earlier portion of the work.

PIKE VILLAGE.

Pike village was incorporated on the 23d of June, 1848, embracing one square mile. The population was 616. The following first officers were elected at the Eagle Tavern on the 11th of September, 1848: Moses Smith, Abner Adams, Marcus A. Hull, A. P. Sherrill and Dr. J. V. W. Abbott, trustees; Ezra Smith, C. M. Fuller, jr., N. N. Olin, assessors; Delano P. Gordon, clerk; Lyman Ayrault, treasurer; Mills L. Rice, collector; Edwin L. Smith, pound master. Moses Smith was chosen president of the board of trustees.

Pursuant to a law of 1870, Pike was incorporated under its provisions on the 23d of March, 1871, when Marvin Trall was unanimously elected president; Silas Newcomb, Horace Blodget and Allen Clark were elected trustees; R. H. Adams treasurer, and Collins W. Thomas collector.

NEWSPAPERS.

In 1837 Thomas Carrier published a paper in Pike, called the *Pike Whig*, which was soon after changed to the *Pike Gazette*; but after being here about a year he removed his press to Angelica, and published the *Allegany Gazette*.

In May, 1876, the *Farmers' Gazette* was established by B. H. Randolph, of Warsaw, and after six months the concern was purchased by H. Besancon, of Pike, and removed thither, the name being changed to *Wyoming County Gazette*. In a few months the name was again changed, to the *Pike Gazette*, and the paper is still published. Mr. Besancon's industry and perseverance have created a paper comparing favorably with many published in larger villages of older growth, and fairly entitling him to a patronage worthy of its merits.

FIRES.

The brick house of John Whiting, on Spencer street, was the first building of much value that was burned.

In September, 1836, the hotel at the east end of the village, occupied by John Bellinger, was burned. The furniture, clothing, etc., were saved.

Ezra Smith's carding and cloth dressing works were burned in February, 1840, and the woolen factory built on the site was burned December 2nd, 1855. The loss in both instances was nearly total, but partially covered by insurance.

A small house of Abner Adams, on Water street, was burned in 1845; and the blacksmith shop of J. M. Stafford, on Main street, in 1849.

The furnace and machine shop of A. B. Smith was burned July 1st, 1850, rebuilt, and again burned in May, 1869, when it was owned by C. B. Lyon. Brownson's building, occupied by F. D. Chandler for a store and H. Blodget for a banking office, was burned May 25th, 1877. The building was insured, and the goods partially.

The paper mill at East Pike was burned in 1858 or 1859, and again in 1877. The buildings and contents were a total loss, but well insured.

PIKE SEMINARY.

Pike Seminary was incorporated by the Regents of the University of the State of New York, February 1st, 1856, under the name of "Genesee Conference Seminary." The first trustees were Samuel Hough, Daniel Russell, Zenas Hurd, Norman N. Olin, Cyrenius M. Fuller, jr., Abner Adams, Abraham P. Sherrill, Marvin Trall, Isaac Minard, Carlos Stebbins, Jason Miller, Andrew Cole, Barnabas Graves, Milo Metcalf, Robert Grisewood, William S. Tuttle, Milo Scott, Jeremiah G. Whitbeck and Ezra M. Hopkins. March 17th, 1856, Norman N. Olin was chosen president, Abraham P. Sherrill secretary, and Marvin Trall treasurer. Committees were appointed to buy a site, report an estimate and plan for the building, and solicit subscriptions. Abner Adams, Isaac Minard and Carlos Stebbins were chosen as a building committee. The frame was made under the direction of Mr. Spafford, of Gainesville; Silas Newcomb superintended the carpenter and joiner work; B. F. & U. W. Wolcott did the mason work, D. P. & A. Gordon the glazing, and W. Kimberly and N. Halstead the painting.

The seminary lot was early occupied by a tavern, which was kept by Benjamin Chamberlain at the time the town was organized, in 1818, and afterward by Russell G. Hurd, Moses Smith, Asa Pratt, Timothy Wells, Jonathan Gates, Alonzo Hopson and several others, and finally was bought by N. N. Olin, who sold the ground for the seminary lot.

The building is three stories high, sixty by sixty-five feet. The corner stone was laid July 22nd, 1856, with appropriate ceremonies. August 2nd and 3d the building was raised, under the direction of Jacob I. Hiller. James O. Gordon (son of Albert Gordon) was a workman on the building, and when the ball on the cupola was hoisted in its place he mounted upon it, and standing erect waved his hat and gave three cheers for Fremont. The cost of the building was about $8,500; of the ground, $600; of bell, library, seats, &c., &c., about $1,200 more, while the subscriptions and available funds were about $7,800, leaving a debt upon the hands of the trustees of about $2,500.

The first term of the school commenced September 16th, 1856. The walls and painting of the seminary not being sufficiently dried, the basement of the Methodist church was occupied for the school a short time. Rev. Zenas Hurd was the principal, and Mrs. S. F. Hurd preceptress; W. W. Bean, professor of mathematics, &c.; Carlos Stebbins, of painting and drawing; and Miss L. H. Pettingall, teacher of music. The number of students for some portion of the first year was 248.

Owing to the financial condition of the seminary, and an unfavorable feeling prevailing in the community, the Genesee Conference abandoned the supervision of the seminary, and it passed into the hands of the Free-Will Baptists on the 1st of April, 1859. The corporate name of the seminary was changed by the regents of the university to Pike Seminary. On the 25th of June, 1859, Prof. Hurd resigned his position as principal, and Rev. Charles Putnam succeeded him, with Prof. Bean as associate principal, and Mrs. M. E. Bowman preceptress. The following named persons have since been appointed principals: Granville C. Waterman, 1862; Rev. D. N. Stuart, November 1st, 1867; Prof. W. W. Bean, August 13th, 1869; Edwin S. Smith, October, 1870; George Porter, the fall term of 1871; William P. Morgan, December, 1871, with Miss Alice W. Vose as preceptress. It was through the efforts of Prof. Morgan that the endowment fund of $20,000 was raised and funds for building a two-story piazza. Rev. Irving B. Smith has been principal since about the close of 1873. The school is steadily advancing in public favor, and its literary standing already exceeds that of the majority of the older academies and seminaries in the State.

CHURCHES AND MINISTERS.

PRESBYTERIAN CHURCH OF PIKE.

The Baptist and Presbyterian societies in Pike each received from the Holland Company a deed of fifty acres on lot No. 27. A Presbyterian church was first formed at East Koy, and was received under the care of the Presbytery of Ontario July 19th, 1819. For several years meetings were held at that place by missionaries, including Rev. Messrs. Hubbard, Ordway, Hunter and Galpin. But this location was not central for the population, and at a meeting on the 9th of September, 1831, a Presbyterian church was formed by the Rev. Messrs. Moses Ordway and Horace Galpin, the following members being received: By letter—Asahel Trowbridge, Roxana Patridge, John Patridge, Francis Hardy, Dorcas Hardy, Hannah Gordon, Diantha Smith, Ezra Smith, Bezaleel Shaw, Lucy Nourse, Darius W. Maples, Diantha Maples, Mary Smith, Amanda Boggs, Esther Gilman, Elizabeth Shaw; on profession—Orson Sheldon, Roswell L. Gordon, Chauncey Bingham, Levaretta Hurd, Rebecca Hurd, Almira Huntting. At the two subsequent meetings there were received on profession: Titus H. Dwight, Benui Shaw, Sparrow Smith, Eliza Ann Shaw and Lucius Post; by letter—Mary Wing, Charles Gordon, Sarah Gordon, Mary Patch, William Lawrence, Elizabeth Lawrence, Elenor Everest, Hannah Axtell, Stephen Skiff, Ada Skiff, David Abell and Sally Lowe.

December 1st, 1831, the "accommodation plan" was adopted, including the confession of faith and discipline of the Presbyterian church. At this meeting Ezra Smith and Sparrow Smith were elected deacons.

In the spring of 1832 a church building (now owned and occupied by Mr. Albert Gordon) was built. February 18th, 1832, the first trustees were elected, viz.: Francis Hardy and David Nourse for one year; Benui Shaw and Adolphus Dwight for two years; Ezra Smith and A. M. Huntting for three years.

Rev. Robert H. Conkling was the minister till the spring of 1834, when there were one hundred and fourteen members. Rev. William P. Kendrick next supplied the church for a few months. Rev. William J. Wilcox was pastor two years, from April, 1835, during which about thirty members were added. Rev. J. B. Taylor preached a few months in the summer of 1837. Rev. Eli Hyde preached two years from about the 1st of November, 1837, and forty-two members were added. Rev. R. H. Conkling became the next pastor during the winter and spring of 1840. As the result of a revival, about fifty were added to the church.

In the winter of 1841 it was resolved to build a new church. The present lot was bought for $300. Deacon Ezra Smith, Dr. J. V. W. Abbott and N. W. Brown were appointed a building committee, and contracted with Jacob I. Hiller to build the church above the foundation wall for $2,000, toward which he was to receive a deed of the "Gospel lot" of fifty acres, from the trustees of the church at East Koy, the lot being valued at $1,000.

The church at East Koy had agreed to donate this lot, and to give up its society organization, inasmuch as most of ts members had united with the village society. The church was dedicated by a committee of the Angelica Presbytery, in February, 1842. Rev. Leverett Hull preached the dedicatory sermon.

From this time to the close of Mr. Conkling's ministry there were from thirty-five to forty more additions to the church. He remained with the church over three years at this time. He was succeeded in August, 1843, by Rev. Henry Snyder, who preached about fifteen months. From December, 1844, Rev. Claudius B. Lord preached about nine years, and received forty-six new members. This church united with the Presbytery of Genesee in the summer of 1845.

In March, 1849, Daniel Lawrence, A. M. Huntting, Jabez Green and S. L. Wing were elected deacons. Rev. R. H. Dexter preached three months in the summer of 1854. Rev. Daniel Russell succeeded him. December 1st, 1855, the society voted to elect ruling elders. Deacon Ezra Smith, J.W. Kelly, Stephen L. Wing and A. P. Sherrill were elected elders, and Hezekiah Metcalf deacon. November 5th, 1865, Jeremiah G. Whitbeck and Isaac V. Matthews were elected elders, and Harvey Smith and Joseph Frank Greene deacons. During Mr. Russell's ministry, which closed in September, 1866, about 120 were received into membership.

October 5th, 1867, Rev. Thomas S. Dewing became pastor. During his ministry some additions were made to the church, but as many or more were dismissed. He resigned in April, 1870, and was succeeded July 2nd, 1871, by Rev. Charles A. Conant, who staid about one year. June 20th, 1872, Milton Miller and R. C. Walker were elected elders of the church, and Asaph Adams deacon.

Rev. Charles Simpson began his labors as pastor February 9th, 1873. During his stay of two years several additions were made to the membership. Rev. F. Byllesby supplied the pulpit for a year from October, 1875. Rev. W. D. McKinley was installed pastor October 24th, 1878. About twenty five members have united with the church during his ministry. Deacon Ezra Smith, the last of the original male members and one of the first elders, died October 5th, 1865. Nearly 700 persons have been members of this church. The present number is 85.

PIKE BAPTIST CHURCH.

The Baptists had meetings in private houses and the school-house for several years, and were supplied by different ministers.

The Baptist church of Pike was organized May 5th, 1827, with Rev. Anson Tuthill for its first pastor. He remained two years, and was succeeded by Elder Oliver Reed, May 10th, 1829.

The first Baptist church was built in 1829 and 1830. It stood on the left hand side of the road leading to the cemetery, on the hill a little east of Mrs. Shepard's house. The building was raised November 2nd, 1829, and the master workman, Mr. James C. Thomas, was killed by the fall of a stick of timber which was being raised. The church had slips on the sides, and a gallery, and a seating capacity of over four hundred. On the erection of the new church in 1850 the old one was sold to Rufus Robinson, who had it moved to the center of the village and remodeled into stores. It is now partly owned by A. J. Beebe, and occupied for a dry goods and grocery store, and D. A. Powell and T. P. Lewis own and occupy one-half for a drug store. The third story is occupied for a masons' lodge. Elder Reed's patorate lasted three years. The church in 1832 was supplied half of the time by Elder John Bostwick. He was a Revolutionary soldier, and died October 21st, 1848, aged eighty-six. Elder James Reed was pastor in 1833, and Elder G. G. Woolley in 1834. Elder Sangster was pastor three years from August, 1835. During the fall and winter of 1835 and 1836 many persons were added to the church. Rev. Cyrenius M. Fuller became pastor in October, 1838, and a large number united with the church during his ministry, which continued five years. He was succeeded in 1843 by his son-in-law, Rev. E. L. Harris, who remained two years. The Rev. Hany Smith began his labors in December, 1845, and resigned in the fall of 1850. From November, 1850, Rev. Ira Bennett occupied the pulpit over two years.

The present church was built in 1850 and 1851. Silas Newcomb was the master builder.

The Rev. Samuel Hough was pastor from June, 1853, eight years. Under his charge many members were added. Elder Alanson Latham became pastor in 1862; Elder Byron P. Russell in 1865; Elder William J. Crane in 1867, and Elder S. N. Calkins in 1869; he was succeeded in 1871 by the Rev. Cyrus R. Negus, who, after a successful ministry of seven years, resigned; Rev. G. S. Clevenger, now the pastor, was ordained and installed August 27th, 1878.

METHODIST CHURCH OF PIKE.

At an early day the Methodist itinerants visited the Holland Purchase and held meetings in log dwellings and barns. A class was formed in Pike village about 1823 or 1824. Among the ministers who had preached here were Revs. Loring Grant, Micah Seager, E. Boardman, James Wiley, Reeder Smith and W. T. Buck.

The church building was put up in 1832, and occupied by the society which had been formed a few years before, and was thereafter supplied by a stated ministry. The following is believed to be very nearly the order of their service here—the period of their ministry being from one to three years:

> 1883–35, De Forest Parsons and Samuel Parker; 1835–37, Philo Woodworth, J. L. Parish, (local); 1838, 1839, Gustavus Hines (while filling his appointment here he was appointed a missionary to Oregon, together with A. F. Waller and J. L. Parish); 1840, 1841, Fuller Atchinson; 1841, A. N. Fillmore; 1842, 1843, J. Durham; 1844, Earl F. Fuller; 1845, E. Latimer; 1846, J. Bowman; 1847, O. Trowbridge; 1848, G. Hines; 1850, Titus Roberts; 1851, W. C. Kendall; 1858, William S. Tuttle; 1854, Zenas Hurd; 1856, G. De La Matyr; 1858, W. C. Willing; 1860, Sanford Parker; 1862, W. Barrett; 1864, R. E. Thomas; 1866, J. B. Lankton; 1807, J. H. Rodgers; 1869, Enos Smith; 1872, Joseph Wayne; 1874, H. M. Osburn; 1876, E. S. Furman; 1877, Samuel Milward; 1879, W. C. Wilbor.

The church is in a prosperous condition.

A class was formed at East Pike, and a church organized under the name of the First Methodist Episcopal Church of East Pike. The meetings were first held in the school-house, but in the summer of 1852 a neat and commodious chapel was built. They have generally been supplied by the minister at Pike or Portageville, who holds one service there each Sunday.

Among the first church members and those who gave liberally toward the building were Asa Sartwell, John Comstock, William Holmes, George Flint, George Wheeler, Carlton Fuller, O. B. Van Deusen, Ira P. Hinman and others.

THE FREE-WILL BAPTIST CHURCH OF PIKE

had its beginning in Eagle Valley, and was organized as the Second Free-Will Baptist church in Eagle, on the 23d day of February, 1852, with twenty members. They chose Rev. Robert Hunt as their pastor, Thomas Pratt clerk, and Sylvester Campbell and Seymour Rugg deacons. They held their meetings for about three years at the house of David Eddy; afterward at Bliss Corners two years (Rev. H. H. Strickland officiating), when they were removed to Lyonsburgh, as being more central and the school-house more commodious. The pulpit was supplied for nearly two years by Rev. Horatio N. Plumb.

At a meeting of the church on the 13th of August, 1859, it was voted to change the name to the First Free-Will Baptist Church of Pike; and as their numbers and influence had greatly increased it was voted to hold the meetings in the village of Pike, as being more central. Accordingly, on the 10th of September, 1859, they met for the first time in one of the large halls of the seminary, which is their present place of worship. Rev. Charles Putnam was chosen pastor of the church, and Rev. Calvin Dodge, Rev. Joel Roberts and Thomas Pratt, licentiates. June 14th, 1862, Elder Putnam was succeeded by Prof. G. C. Waterman, who supplied the church till November following, when the Rev. B. P. Russell was employed. He officiated till July 11th, 1863; Prof. Waterman till May 14th, 1864; Rev. Gorham P. Ramsey till March 9th, 1867; Rev. D. M. Stuart till October 9th, 1869; Rev. Irving B. Smith till March 18th, 1870; Rev. Daniel Jackson until September 13th, 1873; Rev. I. B. Smith for the succeeding year; Rev. D. M. Stuart till June 14th, 1879; since which time Rev. I. B. Smith has temporarily supplied the church.

The records show an accession of over 300 members since its organization, and a present membership of 204.

BIOGRAPHICAL.

ASAPH ADAMS was born in Pike, May 17th, 1821, and was married September 27th, 1848, to Sarah Ann Smith, whose father, James Smith, was of Dutch descent, and was a farmer of Hume, Allegany county, where he died in September, 1881. He has been a shoemaker for many years; has served as village trustee, and held school offices, and is, as is also his wife, a member of the Presbyterian church. His son, George S. Adams, enlisted as bugler in Company C, 104th N. Y. volunteer infantry; took part in the second battle of Bull Run, in the battle of Antietam and other engagements, and was discharged in December, 1862. Abner Adams, father of Asaph, was born in Pittstown, Rensselaer county, in 1794. He was of English descent, and of the John Quincy stock. He learned the trade of tanner and currier, and came to Pike in 1815, bringing his portable valuables in a knapsack on his back. In 1818 he opened a shoe shop, and became the pioneer shoemaker in the village. During the same year he married Lucinda, daughter of Fuller Hubbard, a pioneer and farmer of Hume, Allegany county, who died November 16th, 1878. In time he became a prosperous and influential citizen, and held the offices of justice of the peace, county superintendent of poor, and others of responsibility.

NELSON ARNOLD was born in Berlin, Rensselaer county, February 8th, 1808, and was married December 25th, 1834, to Polly, daughter of Nathaniel Baker, deceased. Mr. Arnold, who is now a retired farmer, came with his father, James Arnold, from Rensselaer county to Sheldon in 1812, where the latter was for many years a leading farmer. In 1866 he removed to Pike, where he has since lived. His son, Nathaniel, served in the late war.

H. Blodget, banker, was born in Gainesville, September 9th, 1817. September 9th, 1844, he married Angeline Bush, of Pike. He has served as justice of the peace and president of the board of village trustees, and is now (1879) corporation treasurer.

Edmund G. E. Bragdon was born in Manlius Center, Onondaga county, September 18th, 1838. In 1867 he married Louie Sherman, whose father, Andrew Sherman, was an early resident and well-known boat builder at Lockport, N. Y., where he died in 1870. In 1868 Mr. Bragdon removed from Lockport to Suspension Bridge, N. Y., and later to Buffalo, where for two years he was engaged at his trade of cooper. From Buffalo he came to Pike village in 1872, where he is employed at his trade and in selling the new Home sewing machine. He enlisted April 27th, 1861, as a private in Company F, 28th N. Y. infantry.

William N. Carpenter was born at Nunda, Livingston county, July 12th, 1838, and came from Nunda to Pike in 1858. In 1860 he married Miss Arilla Walker. Levi Walker, Mrs. Carpenter's father, was born in eastern New York, and came to Pike in 1837, locating on the farm now occupied by Mr. Carpenter, where he died in 1868. In 1862 Mr. Carpenter enlisted in Company D, 136th N. Y. infantry; was promoted to the office of corporal; was twice wounded in the breast; was in the battles of Gettysburg and Chancellorsville and all other engagements in which his regiment took part, and was discharged in June, 1865. Mr. Carpenter's family is descended from the Puritans. His grandfather was an early settler in Livingston county.

William A. Caswell was born in Barnard, Windsor county, Vt., October 23d, 1832, and was married June 3d, 1852, to Miss Eveline Pratt, daughter of Otis Pratt, deceased. Mr. Pratt was a native of Vermont; he settled half a mile south of the Center, in Eagle, in 1885. He became an influential farmer, and died in 1861. Mr. Caswell is a son of Seth Caswell, a farmer of Windham county, Vt. He came to Eagle in 1862, and from Eagle to Pike in March, 1876. Eugene Pratt enlisted in Company F, 5th N. Y. cavalry, September 20th, 1861, and was promoted to the office of orderly sergeant. He was imprisoned in Libby prison seven times, and was discharged with the regiment in July, 1865.

Elihu D. Cruttenden was born April 27th, 1817, and died April 9th, 1877. His native place was Pittsford, Monroe county. He came to Pike in 1834, and with the exception of two years passed in York, Livingston county, resided there until his death. He was a saddler and harness-maker, and carried on a prosperous business in the shop now occupied by his son Frank. He served as trustee of the village. September 15th, 1839, he married Lucretia, daughter of Thomas W. Willard, of Pike, who was born April 24th, 1817, and died February 8th, 1848. His second wife was Lorana, daughter of John Cable, a native and resident farmer of Otsego county.

Harrison Cumins was born in Sweden, Monroe county, January 15th, 1813, and died at West Bethany, Genesee county, January 3d, 1874. He was married April 6th, 1837, to Miss Lucinda Kendall, daughter of Charles Kendall, a farmer of Ledyard, Cayuga county, who died June 24th, 1864. They had two children—Charles K. and Lucy A. The former died September 29th, 1865; the latter is the wife of Irwin H. Baldwin, of Southfield, Berkshire county, Mass. August 23d, 1865, he married Miss Rhoda C. Hardy, a daughter of William Hardy (died October 19th, 1876), a native of Pennsylvania, whose father was one of the original settlers of Pierpont, Ashtabula county, O. By his second marriage he had two children—Rhoda E., born in 1871, and Harrison H., born in 1873. Mrs. Cumins, who is a member of the Free-Will Baptist church, came to Pike, where she has since lived, from West Bethany, Genesee county, April 3d, 1874.

CHARLES DAGGETT was born in Freedom, Cattaraugus county, December 6th, 1825. His father, Loren Daggett, a descendant of the Puritans of New England, and a settler in Freedom in 1819, was born in Westmoreland, Pa. In 1838 he removed to Genesee county. In 1846 Charles Daggett removed from Genesee county to Arcade; in 1859 to Eagle, and in 1864 to Pike, where he has been highway commissioner and held other town offices. January 21st, 1848, he married Lucy E. Dennis, whose father, Ephraim Dennis, deceased, was an early settler and well-known farmer of Arcade.

ISAAC N. DENNIS was born in Arcade, March 17th, 1827. His father, Isaac Dennis, a native of Vermont and a descendant of the pilgrims, located in Arcade in 1812, and, beginning life empty handed in an unbroken wilderness, by industry and frugality accumulated a fine property. He died March 30th, 1861, at the age of eighty-two. His wife was Miss Hannah Brown, of Welsh descent, also a native of Vermont, who died, aged seventy-three, April 3d, 1863. Isaac N. Dennis came to Pike from Arcade in 1861. He married Clarinda Chandler, October 23d, 1844. Her father was Abijah Chandler, deceased, of Erie county, a mechanic, and a native of St. Lawrence county. Mrs. Dennis died May 2nd, 1871; and August 2nd, 1871, Mr. Dennis married Miss L. M. Potter, daughter of Alexander Potter, a farmer of Hinsdale, Cattaraugus county, who died December 25th, 1870.

ABRAHAM W. ELLIS was born in Pike. His father, Smith Ellis, of English descent, a native of Cherry Valley, Otsego county, was a settler in the northwest part of the town, and died in 1875. His mother was formerly Mrs. Christiana Helmer. Mr. Ellis enlisted in the 18tb light battery in 1864; was transferred to the 26th, and was discharged from service in August, 1865. January 1st, 1866, he married Marian A., daughter of Charles C. Phelps, of English descent, who settled in 1830 on the farm now occupied by his son Frank, and died in 1872.

COLONEL JAMES FLENAGIN was born in Chansford, York county, Pa., April 24th, 1808. As early as 1817 his father, a native of Ireland (also named James), took up and began improvements on the farm in Hume, Allegany county, now in possession of his descendants, and became a prosperous and influential citizen. Colonel Flenagin began life for himself at the age of twenty-four, and by industry, economy, honesty and perseverance secured a competency in Hume, where he resided until his removal to Pike, in 1871. September 30th, 1831, he married Julia N. Perkins, daughter of Ichabod Perkins, a native of Otsego county, and a farmer in Hume. By this marriage were born Margaret W., Ichabod and Charles N. Flenagin. Ichabod enlisted in 1862 in the 204th N. Y. volunteers; was promoted to the office of second lieutenant, and was killed August 25th, 1864, at Ream's Station on the Weldon Railroad. Charles N. studied law, and is district attorney of Allegany county, which he has represented in the Assembly. Mrs. Flenagin died January 14th, 1860, and on the 19th of September following Colonel Flenagin married Mary S., daughter of Samuel Nye, a farmer of Hume, who died in February, 1876. Years ago he commanded a regiment of State militia, and in civil life he has been the recipient of many offices at the hands of his townsmen.

DANIEL FLINT was born in Pike, May 1st, 1814. His father was Samuel Flint, of Dutch descent, a native of Montgomery county. He settled in Pike in 1808, on the Captain Murphy farm; took up five hundred acres, improved it and lived on it until his death, May 1st, 1859. He was a wealthy and influential man, and a Republican firm and prominent His father, Robert Flint, a resident of Montgomery county, was a Revolutionary soldier. In 1886 Mr. Flint married Elizabeth, daughter of Lot Griffith, who settled in Genesee Falls in 1818, and died there ten years later. She was born in Vermont.

GEORGE W. FLINT was born at Bonn's creek, Montgomery county, May 4th, 1814. Mr. Flint is a farmer, and came to Pike when a year old (1815) with his father, Joshua Flint, of Dutch-English origin and a native of Montgomery county. His father located on a farm on East street, and beginning with nothing except industry and frugality succeeded well in life, and died March 20th, 1873; his wife, Jane Aikins, a native of Connecticut, January 18th, 1868. The only survivor of the family is George W. Flint, who married Jane Ann Hiller in 1847. Her father was Jacob I. Hiller, a native of Schoharie county, of Dutch origin, who located in East Pike in 1837, and died in Castile in 1877. He was a carpenter and joiner.

RALPH GRAVES was born in Windsor, Windham county, Vt., February 17th, 1796, and died in May, 1875. He began life for himself in Castile in 1819, and by his own unaided exertions became a prosperous and influential farmer of that town, where he died. His widow retains possession of the old homestead, but removed to Pike village, where she has since lived, in 1877. October 30th, 1827, Mr. Graves married Emily Tolles, daughter of Samuel L. Tolles, of Welsh descent and a native of New Haven, Conn, who came to Marcellus, Onondaga county, in 1808, and in 1820 to Centreville, Allegany county, where he took up the farm now owned by Andrew McFarlan. In 1835 he removed from Centreville, and died in Dunkirk, Chautauqua county, in 1866.

GEORGE A. GREEN was born in Lyons, Wayne county, August 5th, 1836. In 1858 he married Anna S. Taft, of Mendon, Worcester county, Mass., and in 1868 came to Pike from Blackstone, Mass. He is a member of the firm of Green Brothers, manufacturers of woolen cloths for men's wear. This business was established on a limited scale in 1816 or 1820, by Ezra Smith. It came into the possession of the present proprietors, George A., J. Frank and David Green, in 1860. They have largely increased the capacity of the mills, which rank high among the manufacturing establishments of this section. Thirty-five men are employed, and 50,000 to 60,000 yards made annually.

JEROME R. GRIFFITH, farmer, was born in Pike, in 1828. October 4th, 1862, he married Angelina M. Nourse, daughter of David Nourse, a native of Vermont and for many years a resident of East street, on the farm owned by J. Parker, where he died August 18th, 1860. His father was Solomon N. Griffith, who was born in Whitehall, Washington county, and accompanied his father, Micah Griffith, from that county to Pike in 1806. Micah Griffith took up lot 12, made improvements thereon, and became influential in the town, where he died in 1881. Solomon N. Griffith, now living with his son Jerome, began life independently at the age of twenty-one, and by honesty, industry and economy secured a competency. His wife was Ann M. Lawrence, daughter of Daniel Lawrence, deceased, of Pike. They had four children—Jerome R., Vernon W. and Roxie R., and Augustus, deceased.

SIMEON HODGES was born in Nunda (now Eagle), in 1810, and has been a veterinary surgeon forty-four years. His father was William Hodges, of English-Irish origin, born in Savoy, Berkshire county. Mass. He came from Herkimer county in 1808, and located on lot 8 in Eagle, which was articled by him and his brother Silas conjointly, and erected a log house without boards or nails, on the Charles Van Hoesen farm. They became leading men in that section of the county, where they both died at the age of sixty-six—William August 12th, 1860, and Silas August 18th, 1868. The former served the town as highway commissioner. Simeon Hodges served in the 14th regiment 5th brigade heavy artillery during the patriot war. In 1849 he married Clara, daughter of Solomon Smith, who settled on Campbell Hill in 1824 and died there in 1826. February 9th, 1867, his first wife died, and February 21st, 1886, he married Lucinda, daughter of Henry Zimmer, who located in Eagle Village in 1888, and is now living in Genesee county.

Oscar Jones was born in Pike, November 27th, 1828. His father, John Jones, of Puritan stock, was born in Massachusetts. He located on the "old Jones place," on Spencer street south of Pike village, and lived there until his death. He gained a competency and became an influential citizen He married Betsy, daughter of Yost Cain, an Eagle farmer of Dutch descent, by whom he had eight children—Lafayette, Jerome, Oscar, George (deceased), George W., Martin (deceased), Charlotte and John. January 10th, 1856, he married Phebe A., daughter of Moses Smith, of English descent, born in Chesterfield, N. H., in 1789. His other children were Albert (died 1865), Elvira and Angelina. Mr. Jones is a farmer, and lives at Perry village.

William W. Martin was born in Poultney, Rutland county, Vermont, September 15th, 1811. Samuel Martin, his father, was born in Scotland, in 1768, and came to America with his father and two brothers in 1775, locating in Massachusetts. He married Lucy Warner, of Onondaga county, and died in Rutland, Vermont, in 1830; his wife in 1849. They had five children—Maria, Augusta G., Alfredia G., William W. and Albert W. In 1882 William W. Martin married Anna Webster. Her father, Walt Webster, was of English descent, was born in Hartford, Conn., and was a farmer in Hampton, Washington county. He died September 29th, 1849. Mr. Martin came to East Pike in 1888 from Washington county, and worked at the blacksmith's trade until I860, when he purchased his present farm.

Captain Francis Murphy was born in Tyrone county, Ireland, March 17th, 1829, and at the age of twenty-one joined his brother James in America, and with little assistance began farming, and continued successfully until the outbreak of the Rebellion. In September, 1861, he obtained permission from Governor Morgan to raise a company for service in the war, recruited a company of 110 men, which, as Company G, was mustered into the 97th N. Y. infantry, commanded by Colonel Charles Wheeler, J. P. Spafford, lieutenant-colonel, October 16th following. They rendesvoused and drilled at Booneville, Oneida county, and started for the front March 12th, 1862, stopping at Arlington Heights two weeks, and at Fort Calkern. The company participated in the battles of Cedar Mountain, Rappahannock Station, Thoroughfare Gap, Bull Run, Chantilly, South Mountain, Antietam, Fredericksburg, Chancellorsville and Gettysburg. Mr. Murphy was first lieutenant of the company until August 28th, 1863, when he was commissioned captain. He was wounded in the groin August 30th, 1862, at the second battle of Bull Run. and in the knee at Gettysburg, where, with many others, he was taken prisoner; was in the hands of the enemy twenty months and twenty days, in Libby prison eleven months, at Macon and Oglethorpe, Ga., three months, at Charleston. S. C., three months, at Columbia, S. C., three months, and at Raleigh, N. C., whence he made a successful escape, having been ten times recaptured in making previous attempts. He was mustered out of service, with the company, at the close of the war. February 8th, 1866, he married Mary, daughter of Thomas McSherry (deceased, of Fermanagh, Ireland), at Salisbury, Herkimer county. He came to Pike October 2nd, 1867, from that place, where he had been engaged in farming since 1850, the year of his emigration from Ireland. They have six children—James F., Thomas H., Charles, Francis. Mary and Margaret.

SILAS NEWCOMB was born in Kingsbury, Washington county, January 4th, 1815. His father, Salmon Newcomb, was born in Columbia, Conn., in 1786, and was of English descent. In 1816 he came from Kingsbury, Washington county, and purchased the farm which was in possession of members of his family until sold recently to L. Robinson, and where he died in 1885. He began life poor, was a school teacher many years, and afterward became a prosperous farmer. He married Miss Abigail Finch, who died November 18th, 1865. Their children were Paul S., Silas, Zala, Sally Ann, Phebe, Jeremiah and Abigail. Silas, Sally Ann and Abigail are living. At the age of fifteen Silas Newcomb began to learn the trade of carpenter and joiner and cabinet maker. He learned carriage making, and in 1865 succeeded S. G. Blanchard in business at Pike village. He increased the facilities for manufacture, and admitted his son, Edwin F., to partnership. They employ ten hands, and are making carriages of a superior grade. Mr. Newcomb was married May 31st, 1838, to Roxanna, daughter of Simon and Mary Lathrop (natives of Vermont and descended from the Puritans), who located in the town in 1832. Mrs. Newcomb died September 6th, 1850. Mr. Newcomb's son, Edwin F. Newcomb, enlisted in August, 1862, in Company D. 130th N. Y. volunteers. He held the office of corporal, and participated in twenty-one general engagements with the Southern forces in Virginia in 1863–64. He was discharged in June, 1865. Paul Newcomb, grandfather of Silas Newcomb, was born in Connecticut, in March, 1752.

ZALA NEWCOMB was born in Lebanon, Windsor county, Conn., December 30th, 1790, and came to Pike in 1816 and purchased seventy-five acres of lot 28 of his brother Salmon. He had previously been seven years /engaged at the hatter's trade at Glen's Falls, N.Y. In 1857 he located at Griffith's Corners, where he now lives. From a poor pioneer he grew to be a well-to-do and respected farmer and business man. Years ago he was identified with the Federal party and he has long been a member of the Methodist church. His father was Paul Newcomb, who was born in Connecticut, in March, 1752. His mother's maiden name was Martha Woodward. His wife was Lydia Manchester, of Kingsbury, Washington county, to whom he was married September 12th, 1822. They had two children—Angeline and Luman (died April 13th, 1846).

HARRISON E. OSBORN, farmer, was born in Centreville, Allegany county, October 8th, 1855, and came from Eagle to Pike in 1869 with his father, Oramel Osborn, of whose family he is the only surviving male member. His brother, Jefferson Osborn, enlisted in Company F, 64th N. Y. volunteers, in 1861; was promoted to the office of sergeant, and was killed at the battle of Fair Oaks, June 1st, 1862.

ORAMEL OSBORN was born in Brattleboro, Vt., December 11th, 1802. In 1818 he came with his father, John Osborn, to Centreville, Allegany county, where he took up wild land and improved it, and remained there until 1868, when he removed to Eagle and from there to the farm on which his son Harrison E. lives, in 1869. He was honest and industrious and acquired a competency. He died February 12th, 1875. He was three times married—first in 1880, to Caroline Potter (daughter of John Potter, a native of Vermont and an early settler in Centreville, Allegany county), who died in 1846. In 1847 he married Sarah Gilman, daughter of George Gilman, who died in 1849. His third wife was Mrs. Lydia Ann Frary, daughter of John Warren, an early settler of Linden, Cattaraugus county.

GEORGE M. PALMER, M. D., was born in Angelica, Allegany county, October 4th, 1827. He came to Pike in 1855 from Hinsdale, Cattaraugus county, and married Hannah O. Wilson, of Pike, May 24th, 1860. He is serving his fourth term as supervisor of the town.

LEONARD PARTRIDGE was born in Worthington, Hampshire county, Mass., April 6th, 1797. In November, 1816, he married Lydia Taylor, of his native place. In 1839 he came to Eagle; thence to Pike in 1876. His first wife having died, he married Mrs. Rosanna Stowe (widow of Alanson Stowe, deceased, of Portage, and daughter of Hesekiah Wilton, a native of Connectiout and a pioneer of Sheldon), who was born in Rome, Oneida county, January 3d, 1807. Mr. Partridge has held the office of poormaster in Eagle. He was a farmer during his active life.

AMOS PRATT was born in Warsaw, in 1821, and came from there to Pike in March, 1852, and the following year located on his present farm. His father was Thomas Pratt, of English descent, who was born in Foster, R. I., in 1780. Early in life he removed to Bolton, Washington county; thence, in 1805, to Warsaw, where he died December 20th, 1830. He married Hannah Perkins, who was born in Hampshire, Mass., in 1782, and died in 1855. The following are the names of their children: Charles (died in 1878), Amasa (in Minnesota), Randall (in Warsaw), Jedediah (died in 1826), Milo (died in 1878), Job and Joel (in Omaha), Thomas (in Eagle), Hannah (in Hinsdale, Cattaraugus county), Maria (in Ohio), Catharine (died in 1878), and Amos, mentioned above. He was married in April, 1848, to Joanna Perkins, daughter of Elisha Perkins, a descendant of the Puritans and. long a resident and prominent farmer in Persia, Cattaraugus county, where he died in 1843. He has in his possession a Bible printed in England in 1765.

E. L. POWERS was born in Pike, June 10th, 1849.

WILLIAM POWERS is a native of Pike.

DANIEL ROCKWELL was born in Hartwick, Otsego county, September 17th, 1815. In 1817 he came to Pike with his father, Timothy Rockwell, who was born in Connecticut in 1786 and died in Pike in 1854, and located on the Harvey Banks farm. His mother was Betsy Kendall, daughter of Peter Kendall, a resident of Otsego county and later of Wyoming. She died in 1827. Mr. Rockwell was married March 26th, 1840, to Mercy, daughter of Solomon Burton, who was born in Massachusetts in 1796, and died there in 1888. Miss Burton came to Perry in 1887, and joined other members of their family. Her grandfather, Jubal Metcalf, was an early settler in Pike. The children born to Mr. and Mrs. Daniel Rockwell are named as follows: Betsy E., Julia A., Daniel W., Mary B., John S. and George H. Daniel W. enlisted in Company D, 136th N. Y. volunteers, in August, 1862, and served with the regiment until discharged in June, 1865. He is now living in Nebraska.

MARTIN B. SHEPARD was born in Otsego county, February 3d, 1815, and died June 13th, 1877. Early in life he came to western New York. He removed from Batavia, Genesee county, to Wethersfield with his brother, Marvin E. Shepard, in 1887. He was there engaged in farming until his removal to Pike, in 1875, and was known there as a self-made man, a prosperous farmer and an influential citizen. His father, John Shepard, of English descent, was a native of Schoharie county. Mr. Shepard was married in 1840 to Elvira Green, who was born in Attica, in 1819. Her father, James Green, lives with her in Pike.

ABRAHAM P. SHERRILL was born at East Hampton, Suffolk county (Long Island), N.Y., September 3d, 1808. After pursuing the studies usually taught in the district schools of those days he studied the higher branches at Clinton Academy (the oldest academy in the State) and was assistant principal of that institution for three years. He afterward taught select schools in Quogue, N. Y., and Middletown, N. J., and in October, 1828, he went to Smithtown, N. Y., to engage in the same business. In 1832 he acted as the special messenger to receive from the clerks of the several counties on Long Island, the city of New York and the counties east of the Hudson the official canvasses of the electoral vote of those counties, and deliver them to the secretary of State at Albany. He remained in Smithtown, and was deputy county clerk till May, 1835, when he moved to the town of Pike, and kept a store of general merchandise. In April, 1837, he took charge of the post-office as deputy under Judge Thomas Dole, and was afterward postmaster until April, 1841, and was subsequently appointed again by President Lincoln. Soon after he sold off his goods and devoted the time he had to spare from official duties to the pension claim and insurance business. Mr. Sherrill is a member of the Presbyterian church; has been clerk of the session nearly forty years, and one of the elders over twenty years. He was a Democrat until alienated from that party by its support of slavery. He joined the Republican party in the support of Fremont in 1856 and Lincoln in 1860. He has been elected supervisor of the town three times, town clerk ten times and is now serving his twentieth year as postmaster. He was married to Elizabeth, daughter of John Saxton, at Smithtown, N. Y., on the 15th of October, 1832. They have had six children, viz.: Anna, born in Smithtown, N.Y. in July, 1833, died March 30th, 1839; Mary Elizabeth, who married the Rev. Charles Simpson, resides at Sherman, N. Y., and has two children, Ella S. and Clarence E.; John Saxton, who married Julia Parsons, of East Hampton, N. Y., is a Presbyterian minister at Litchfield, Minn., and has one child, Bessie; Eleanor W., who married Rev. D. Z. Sheffield, missionary in China, and has four children, Alfred D., Mary E., Flora A., born in China, and Caroline Louisa, born in Pike, N. Y.; Abraham P., jr., an accountant in Detroit, and Edwin Stanton, a graduate of Michigan University, formerly a teacher in Detroit Female Seminary and now studying medicine.

EDMUND SKIFF was born in Hume, Allegany county, June 17th, 1827. His father was Myron Skiff, a native of Otsego county and one of six brothers who located on a farm now owned by Mr. Skiff, a mile north of Mills's Mills, in Hume, Allegany county, where he died in August, 1865, deeply regretted. September 12th, 1855, Mr. Skiff married Fannie P. Goodrich, who died May 8th, 1865. She was a daughter of Michael Goodrich, a native of Delaware county and after 1830 a resident mechanic of Hume, Allegany county. In October, 1871, Mr. Skiff removed to Pike, where he is a well-known farmer. His mother, formerly Mary Morse, a native and at the time of her marriage a resident of Otsego county, lives with him in Pike, aged 84.

MICAJAH P. SKIFF was born in Hartwick, Otsego county, January 1st, 1816, and married Mary S. Hopkins, daughter of Alfred Hopkins, of New England birth and a resident farmer of Pike, April 16th, 1835. Mr. Skiff came with his father, B. Skiff, to Pike in August, 1816. He is a retired merchant, having been succeeded in business by his sons Albert and Samuel L. Skiff in the spring of 1878. During his active life Mr. Skiff was justice of the peace, town clerk and collector, and held other positions of trust and responsibility. His father was one of six brothers who settled in Hume, Allegany county, at an early day. Stephen Skiff, his grandfather, was a Revolutionary soldier, and was a son of Joseph and Elizabeth Skiff, descendants of the Puritans. Mr. Skiff's mother lives with him, aged 91.

HARVEY SMITH was born in Pawlet, Vt., May 15th, 1817, and died July 15th, 1871. His father, Whiting Smith, was of English origin. He came with his family at an early day to Portage; thence in 1826 to Pike. At the age of twenty-one he associated himself with his brother, Ezra, who had early established himself in the milling and wool-carding business. He continued in this line, part of the time in company with his nephew, until 1869, when the establishment was sold to Greene Brothers, doing an extensive and prosperous business. He was married in February, 1840, to Almira Halstead. Her father, George W. Halstead, who served in the war of 1812–14, came to Perry in 1813, and to Pike in 1836. Mrs. Smith lives at Pike village.

MOSES L. SMITH was born in Bethel, Windsor county, Vt., January 8th, 1792. A t the age of twenty-six he married Polly Gibbs, a native and resident of the same place. They then emigrated to what is now Pike, the journey taking twenty days. Mr. Smith bought a farm from the Holland Company, and had to go to Ellicottville to make his payments, which he never failed to meet promptly. As soon as convenient he opened a hotel on what is now called the Allegany road, a mile southwest of the village, which then contained but a few houses. He kept the hotel till 1883, when he sold to Petty & Minard, and built another house, on the farm where he always lived. About the year 1825 his parents came here to live with him. His father, Moses Smith, died December 27th, 1889, at the age of eighty-one. His mother, Bethiah, died August 8th, 1848, at the age of eighty-four. M. L. Smith had three children, two daughters and a son. The daughters are both living. The youngest, Mrs. Wallace Kimberly, who was born April 15th, 1834, lives on the farm, and took care of her parents in their declining years. Moses L. Smith died July 19th, 1875, at the age of eighty-three years. Polly, his wife, died January 7th, 1869, at the age of seventy-two years. His son, Oliver, lived on the home farm until he went into the army in 1861 with Company C of the 104th regiment. He died July 16th, 1862, at Fairfax Seminary, Va., at the age of thirty-two, leaving a wife and two daughters. His wife was Susan Kimberly, sister of Mrs. Kimberly's husband, whose parents came to Pike at an early day, when it was all woods. Moses L. Smith's oldest daughter was born March 24th, 1824. In 1846 she married Charles Willard, who was born August 30th, 1820, and is a son of Jonathan Willard. They now live on the farm where his father first settled about 1816.

HORATIO SPENCER, M. D, was born in Pike, June 8th, 1825. His father was John Spencer, a native of Clarendon, Vt., and a settler in Pike in 1816. He located on Spencer street, cleared and improved the farm on which Dr. Spencer was born, became a well-to-do and an influential citizen, and died in April, 1868. He was of English descent. Doctor Spencer graduated from the Albany Medical College in the class of 1854, and since that time, with the exception of four years, has been engaged in the practice of his profession in his native town. He is a member of the Wyoming County Medical Society. He was married October 3d, 1854, to Frances Rider, daughter of Curtis Rider, a native of New Hampshire and a pioneer and subsequent prosperous farmer and influential citizen of Pike, where he died in 1869.

CARLOS LEONARD STEBBINS was born at York, Livingston county, N. Y., in 1824, and was educated at Pike, where he has lived forty-five years. His father's ancestors were English, of London and Wieset, county of Suffolk. The family crest and arms, with the motto "*Virtus Summa Felicitas*" are recorded in the Herald's office at London. Mr. Stebbins's first names are derived from his mother's ancestors, who were of Italian origin, named Leonardo. The original names were Carlo Leonardo, but have become

Anglicized as above. He has been a farmer, and has developed some artistic and mechanical tendencies. He has been connected with the educational and business interests of the county.

NORMAN VAN SLYKE was born in Sharon, Schoharie county, December 22nd, 1824. After living with his uncle, John Mincklen, in Cherry Valley, Otsego county, he came to Pike in October, 1849, and bought one hundred acres of land of William Van Slyke, his grandfather, who had fought in the Revolutionary war, was a noted man in the town, and died in 1850, at the age of ninety-six. Mr. Van Slyke's father is Peter Van Slyke, who at the age of eighty lives with his son D. N. Van Slyke. His mother was formerly Elizabeth Mincklen, of Otsego county. Mr. Van Slyke, who is a self-made man and a well known farmer, was married December 24th, 1857, to Angenette, daughter of Isaac Quackenbush, a native of Otsego county. Her father was of Dutch descent, was born in 1800, came to Pike in 1836, became a leading man, held many offices of responsibility, and died in 1873. Mrs. Van Slyke's mother was Patty Alger, daughter of Abner Alger, of Vermont. Mr. and Mrs. Van Slyke's children are named Horace D., Jesse M., Maurice G., Martin M., George M., William R., Emmett E. and Lloyd M.

WILLIAM WATSON was born on the family homestead in 1845. He learned the trade of carpenter and joiner. He was married in 1864 to Orilla, daughter of the late John Hayden, of Genesee Falls, and who died in Weedsport, N. Y., in 1876. In 1864 Mr. Watson enlisted in the 18th battery. He was transferred to the 26th, was in the engagement at Spanish Fort, and was discharged in June, 1865.

HIRAM WHEELER was born in Arcadia, Wayne county, July 26th, 1816. In 1820 his father. Henry Wheeler, came from Attica, where he had settled in 1818, and located on East street. Left to shift for himself at eleven, he became a prosperous farmer and an influential citizen. For twelve years he was a shoemaker, and for eight years was postmaster at Mills's Mills, Allegany county. February 3d, 1842, he married Laura F. Skiff, daughter of Myron Skiff, one of the six brothers of that name who came from Otsego county and settled early in Hume, Allegany county. He died in 1865; his widow is living, at the age of eighty-four.

EDWARD WOLCOTT was born in Pike, on the homestead farm, now owned and managed by him, December 16th, 1835. He has been assessor but has never sought office. He was married October 24th, 1859, to Miss L. A. Martin daughter of William W. Martin, a native of Washington county and a farmer of Pike, well and favorably known. Mr. Wolcott's father, George W. Wolcott, was born in Sandersfield, Berkshire county, Mass., and was of English descent, his great grandfather and two brothers having emigrated from England to America at an early day. In 1829 he came from Massachusetts with an ox-team, bought the farm where his son lives, became prosperous and respected, and died May 15th, 1874. aged seventy-eight, leaving a family, all of whom have been highly esteemed and prominently identified with the advancement of the best interests of the town. Mr. Wolcott's mother was also of English origin; was born in Sandersfield, Mass., and died, aged seventy, November 24th, 1869. Her mother's maiden name was Ann Bush.

THE TOWN OF SHELDON.

THIS town was formed from Batavia, Genesee county, March 19th, 1808. Attica was taken off in 1811, and Bennington and China in 1818. Chauncey Loomis was judge and State senator, and lived at Bennington Center. His mother's maiden name was Sheldon, and in honor of that lady the town was named. It extends eight miles east and west, and six miles north and south.

This town reached its maximum population much more recently than most of the other towns of the county, but, like them, has latterly suffered a decrease. This will appear from the following figures published by the State: 1830, 1,731; 1835, 2,186; 1840, 2,366; 1845, 2,435; 1850, 2,527; 1855, 2,666; 1860, 2,794; 1865, 2,591; 1870, 2,258; 1875, 2,273.

EARLY HISTORY.

The whole of this town was deeded by the Holland Land Company to Oliver Phelps and Lemuel Chipman, December 22nd, 1804. Oliver Phelps and wife conveyed all their interest to Lemuel Chipman January 1st, 1807.

It appears from the records and from the books of the company that these grantees conveyed lots and parts of lots to individuals by deeds, and received as security for the payment of a portion of the purchase money mortgages, which they afterward turned over to the company. By reason of the non-payment of some of these, portions of the land reverted to the company.

The following is a list of some of the early purchasers, with years of purchase and number of lots or parts:

Range 3.—William Vary, 1805, lots 4, 6, 7, 8 and 15; George Grinell, 1805, lot 14; Samuel Hinckley, 1805, lot 22; Robert Carr, 1805, part of lot 81; Jotham Godfrey, 1805, lot 32; John Mann, 1805, lot 36; Abijah Scovill, 1805, part of lot 87; William Hadley, 1805, part of lot 39; David Hoard, 1805, part of lot 40; James Case, 1805, part of lot 42; Roswell Turner, 1805, lots 47 and 48; Charles Thomas, 1809, lot 23; Joshua Gates, 1806, part of lots 33 and 41; Seth Gates, 1806, lot 46; Roswell Barber, 1807, lots 13 and 21; Ira Pearl, 1809, part of lot 26; Elijah Woodruff, lot 45, 1808; William Warren, 1809, part of lot 37; Ziba Hamilton, 1809, part of lot 44; John Casey, 1810, part of lot 16; Horace Adams, 1810, part of lot 16; Jared Barber, 1810, part of lot 20; Lemuel Chipman, jr., lot 25; John Minor, 1810, lot 23; Bentley D. Curtis and others, 1810, part of lot 33; Pardon Briggs, 1811, parts of lots 11 and 19; John Briggs, 1811, parts of lots 11 and 19; Roswell Barber, 1811, part of lot 12; Nathan Stone, 1811, part of lot 16; Lemuel Chipman, jr., 1811, part of lot 18; Wheaton A. Briggs, 1811, part of lot

19; Jared Barber, 1811, part of lot 20; George Goff, 1811, part of lot 31; Stephen Sherman, 1811, part of lot 34; Rebecca Mann, 1811, part of lot 34; Gilbert L. Harrison, 1811, part of lot 34; Peter Waters, 1811, part of lot 34; Mary Ann Porter, 1811, part of lot 35; Robert Waters, 1811, part of lot 43; Adrin Merrill, 1811, part of lot 44; Jonah Smith, 1811, part of lot 44; Gideon Warren, 1813, part of lot 9; Ammi Warren, 1814, part of lot 1; Robert Welch, 1815, part of lot 27.

Range 4.—Marvin Brace, 1805, lots 7 and 26; Orange Brace, 1805, lots 8 and 34; Lemuel Castle, 1805, lots 13 and 23; Festus De Wolf, 1805, part of lot 15; Joel Tillotson, 1805, part of lot 16; William Bevens, 1805, lot 20; Jonathan Burrit, 1805, lot 24; John Rolph, 1805, lots 29 and 30, and parts of lots 28 and 36; Joseph Sears, 1805, lots 31 and 39; Stephen Bates, 1805, lot 40, and part of lot 42; Roswell Turner, 1805, part of lot 38; Samuel Crocker, 1806, part of lot 14; William Parsons, 1806, part of lot 32; Ziba Hamilton, 1807, lot 22; Jacob Harwood, 1806, part of lot 12; John Parsons, 1806, part of lot 16; Israel Smith Geer, 1809, lot 11; Simeon Hoard, 1809, part of lot 21; Roswell Platt, 1810, part of lot 16; Joshua Bentley, 1810, parts of lots 19 and 21; Jeremiah Waterman, 1810, part of lot 25; Garrett Stryker, 1810, lot 33; Edward Brace, 1811, part of lot 6; Solomon Dolittle, 1811, part of lot 10; Samuel Lenox, 1811, part of lot 12; Nathan N. Kellogg, 1811, part of lot 12; Ziba Hamilton, 1811, part of lot 14; Elisha Hollister, 1811, part of lot 19; Philo Stevens, 1811, part of lot 25; Ezra Fisk, 1811, parts of lots 27 and 35; James Ward, 1811, part of lot 28.

Roswell Turner was the first settler in Sheldon. He came from Pittston (now Honeoye), Ontario county, in March, 1804, and took up two half lots at North Sheldon. David Hoard, from Rensselaer county, came next, in June following, and located half a mile east of Turner's. He paid eleven shillings per acre for his land. The next settlers were Orange and Marvin Brace, who came from Litchfield, Herkimer county, and settled at North Sheldon. William Vary came next, from Rensselaer county, and settled at Varysburgh. Lodowick Thomas, from the same county, settled three miles east of Turner's Settlement (as it was then called), on Godfrey's Hill. Uriah Persons, Jotham Godfrey, Robert Carr, George Grinold, Joshua Gates and Simeon Hoard soon followed and were known as early settlers.

In 1833 the Germans began to settle in the town. Peter Zittle, Jacob Zittle, John Hausower and John Schmidt were among the first, and settled near Dutch Hollow. After 1835 they settled more rapidly, and now probably three-fourths of the population of the town are German, with a small admixture of French and Belgians.

The town was surveyed by Elijah Warner, assisted by Roswell Turner, Joseph Sears and Tabor Earl.

The first log house was built by Roswell Turner at Turner's Settlement. He also raised the first crop of grain.

The first framed house was built by Colonel Lemuel Castle, one and a half miles west of Turner's Settlement.

The first orchard was planted by Seth Gates, one and a half miles south of the Settlement; the trees were brought from Big Tree (Geneseo).

Orange Brace set out the next orchard, at the "Settlement." The trees were brought from Canandaigua, and many of them are still standing.

The first road was laid out in 1803. It ran from Big Tree (Geneseo) through the north part of the town to Lake Erie, about eight miles above Buffalo, and was called the Big Tree road. It was an old Indian trail, running from the Gardeau to the Buffalo reservation. Every stream west of and including the Genesee had to be forded. The early settlers used to cut a sapling and tie the top to the hind end of their wagons for a brake in going down hill, and piles of these accumulated at the foot of the steep hills.

One Rolph was the first preacher and doctor. He preached the first sermon at the "Settlement" that was preached in the town. He announced in his first sermon that he did not allow himself to preach for a less sum than $5 per day, and he was not invited to continue his labors in that field. His services as doctor were also soon dispensed with. The next minister was the Rev. Mr. Spencer, a Scotchman, noted for preaching many *different* sermons *all alike*, and from the same text.

The first marriage was that of Justin Loomis and Polly Rolph, in 1807 or 1808. The first birth was that of Chipman P. Turner, brother of the author of the "History of the Holland Purchase."

The first school was taught by Polly Rolph, at the Settlement, in 1807. It was taught in a building erected by Mr. Turner for a blacksmith shop, and which was afterward used for that purpose. The first school-house was built in 1810, half a mile west of the Settlement. The first saw-mill was built in 1807, and the first grist-mill in 1808; both by William Vary, of Varysburgh. The first leather was tanned at the Settlement, by Seneca Reed. The first cloth was dressed at Varysburgh, and the first liquor distilled at Strykersville. The first blacksmith shop was at the Settlement. The first store was opened at Sheldon Center by Messrs. Potter & Wilson, in 1816. The first tavern was kept at the Settlement, by the widow of Roswell Turner and her son Horace. It was the first opened west of the "Frontier House," which stood one and a half miles west of the Genesee river, on the Big Tree road.

The first post-office was established at Sheldon Center, in 1810 or 1811; the postmaster was Fitch Chipman. The first mail route started eight miles above Buffalo, at the terminus of the Big Tree road. The first post-office east was Willink, the next Sheldon Center, next Warsaw, then Leicester. Another route took the mail farther east. The mail was carried on horseback by Levi Street. The trip had to be made in a week, and was usually performed in four days. The route was established in 1812. It cost eighteen cents to send a letter from Sheldon to Canandaigua, and the route did not pay, and the people made up the deficiency by subscription. The weekly visits of the old *Ontario Repository* are still remembered by some of the old inhabitants.

There is now a daily line of stages running through the east part of the town, the route from Attica to Arcade. The mail is carried from Johnsonsburg to Sheldon Center every Wednesday and Saturday. There is also a daily line of stages running from Strykersville to East Aurora.

The first blacksmith shop was built by driving down four crotches. Poles were laid across and covered with bark. The first coffin was made of elm bark. The first graveyard was half a mile south of Turner's Settlement.

The pioneer houses were built of logs and covered with bark. Doors were sometimes made out of boxes in which the pioneers had moved their goods. A window consisted of a hole cut through the logs, with a sliding board to close it when the weather was inclement.

The graveyard west of North Sheldon was probably the first opened in the town. It is little used. At Humphrey's Hollow many of the early settlers were buried.

INCIDENTS OF EARLY TIMES.

About the first of April, 1807, occurred one of the most dreadful snow storms on record. Hay and grain were very scarce. Browse was brought to the cattle in baskets, as the snow was too deep to drive the cattle to the woods. That spring the people went to town meeting to Batavia, and the snow averaged four feet deep.

In the month of August, 1806, Walter Welch was killed by the falling of a limb from a tree. French and Child both state in their gazetteers that it was David Hoard who was thus killed. David Hoard died of bilious colic. His son Henry, still living (though nearly ninety years old) on the farm which his father took up, is supposed to know. The death of David Hoard was the first in the town. He was the first settler who followed Roswell Turner. He came from Rensselaer county in June, 1804. In the fall he went back after his family. In December he loaded his effects on two sleighs and started for Sheldon. A little west of Utica the snow went off, and he bought a wagon and pursued his journey as far as the town of Bristol, in Ontario county. The going became so intolerable that he took a piece of land for his boys to work, left his family in Bristol, and came on to Sheldon. He was taken sick soon after, and died June 16th, 1805.

In 1806 the Indian chief Little Beard died. All the Indians of the tribe met at Beardstown (now Cuylerville) to elect a new chief. Many of the settlers were alarmed and fled to places of security, leaving behind them everything which could not be conveniently carried away. A few sought to heighten the excitement by telling stories of bloodshed and plunder, hoping to become the possessors of whatever might be left behind by the fugitives.

When Buffalo was burned there was another general stampede. Houses, furniture, cattle—everything was left behind. The people thought of nothing but saving their scalps.

Seneca Reed, who tanned the first leather in the town of Sheldon, was known as a Tory. In 1813 a lot of soldiers had assembled to go to Buffalo the next day. Reed drank a toast in which he expressed a desire that they all might be taken prisoners; whereon Linas Brace dealt him a blow which crippled him for life. Reed was ultimately compelled to leave the town.

Lyman Tuttle related that his father, John Tuttle, came from Essex county, N. Y., in 1814, with ten young children, and settled near Johnsonsburgh. They were twenty-two days on the road, the family and all their effects on one wagon. The father began life here with ten shillings. He was a cooper, and had to work at Rochester. The provisions he sent home were more than doubled in price by the transportation. The family lived in a shanty without floor, door, window or chimney. Neighbors felled trees for them, which the boy Lyman helped to burn. Corn, potatoes and beans were planted around among the stumps, but before anything could be raised the family became utterly destitute. A neighbor brought a few potatoes, which were too small to plant. These were carefully roasted in the ashes. When they were gone the family dug roots in the woods, and ate basswood buds and slippery elm bark. There was joy in the cabin when the green stalks yielded their first ears of rich, sweet corn, and the potato hills gave up their buried treasure to the famishing ones who had suffered and waited so long and so patiently.

After Garrett Stryker had a piece of land ready for sowing wheat he was taken sick, and Mrs. Stryker did both the sowing and reaping, and threshed the crop on blankets, with such a flail as she was able to cut from the woods.

STRAUB'S CORNERS.

At Straub's Corners there are two hotels, a store, a shoe shop, a carpenter shop, a Catholic church, cemetery and school-house, a public school-house and twenty dwellings.

In January, 1840, the first Roman Catholic church was built, about a quarter of a mile south of Straub's Comers, by about twenty families, who were mostly Germans. The Rev. Father Neuman (who became bishop of Philadelphia in March, 1852), then stationed at Lancaster, N. Y., attended the little congregation once during the first year. From this time until 1847 this mission was visited by the Redemptorist Father Noethan, of Williamsville, once in three months.

In the meantime the primitive building became too small, as the membership had now increased to about a hundred families. Ten acres of land were bought of Nicholas Straub for two hundred dollars, and by the first of August, 1848, a new church was so far completed as to be serviceable. It was dedicated by Bishop Timon, who at the same time appointed Father Schaefer as the first settled priest. February 20th, 1850, he appointed Rev. Bartholomew Gruber as his successor. In June, 1852, Father Gruber was succeeded by Rev. Charles Knemin, who remained until August 1st, 1859. From the 20th of March, 1860, Rev. Stephen Eicher was pastor until April 2nd, 1862, when he suddenly died of heart disease. During his administration a select school was established and kept in the basement of the church by John Schneider, of Lancaster. Rev. Chrysostomus Wagner was the next priest. Under his administration an organ was bought for $800. Joseph Rengel was employed as teacher and organist. In January, 1865, Rev. Edward Baenzinger became pastor, and was succeeded by Rev. M. Winands. Under his administration the church was thoroughly repaired. The old school-house was sold, and a new one built which cost about $1,400. Rev. William Riszewski was the next priest.

The first teacher of St. Cæcilia's school, John Schneider, of Lancaster, who was employed in 1861, continued teaching until October 1st, 1863. Joseph Rengel, first organist, was engaged March 1st, 1864, and remained until April 1st, 1867. E. Breitung was then teacher until November 22nd, 1870; Z. Hangauer until March 1st, 1871; Albert Rengel until April 1st, 1872; John T. Metzger until October 1st, 1875; Miss Mary Kimm organist, and Miss Mary Ess teacher, until March 15th, 1876; Charles Raab until March 12th, 1877; and John T. Metzger, again, until the present time. The number of scholars is from 150 to 160.

The branches taught are reading (German and English), writing, spelling, geography, grammar (English, German and Latin), arithmetic (mental and written), algebra and geometry.

The first church trustees were Nicholas George, 2nd, Perry George, Martin Kihm and Peter Meiers. The present ones are Joseph Becker Cash, John Yungers, Peter Kehl and Frank Amherst.

St. Cæcilias Catholic Cemetery was opened about 1836. The first interment was that of Margaret Pope. After the new Catholic church was built at Straub's Corners a new ground was opened, containing about an acre of land, a little north of the church. It was opened in 1848.

SHELDON CENTER.

There is a road running east and west and another north and south midway through the town. The crossing marks the geographical center of the town and the location of Sheldon Center. The first church was built and the first store opened here. One or two small stores, a hotel, a post office and a few shops and houses are all that remains of Sheldon Center. The town business is still transacted here.

The Episcopal church at Sheldon Center was the first church built in the town. The society dwindled away and the church was burned down. Ebenezer Jackson and Fitch Chipman helped to organize this church in 1814.

At Sheldon Center one of the first burial grounds was opened, but the ploughshare has long since broken the soil over the sleeping dead. Fitch Chipman, one of the original proprietors of the town, was buried here in 1827. In 1849 his remains were taken up and found to be in a tolerable state of preservation.

Many years ago a masonic lodge was instituted at Sheldon Center.

DUTCH HOLLOW.

There are here a church, a cemetery, a school-house, a hotel, a saw-mill, a cider-mill and a few dwellings.

St. John's Lutheran church, whose house of worship is at Dutch Hollow, was organized soon after the Germans began to settle in the town, in 1835 or 1836. Among the early members may be mentioned Michael Hansower, Peter and Jacob Zittle, John Garhard, Michael Copp, John Haverly, Frederick Zath and others, numbering about thirty. Meetings were first held at private dwellings and at the schoolhouse. The meeting-house was completed in 1840 or 1841, having been long building. Members brought boards on their backs long distances to add their mite to the undertaking. The society has always been small, now numbering not more than forty members.

At Dutch Hollow there is a cemetery which was opened in the year 1846. The Lutheran society caused the ground to be laid out four or five years after their church building was erected. The first interment was that of Catharine Haverly.

VARYSBURGH.

Varysburgh (named after William Vary, who purchased 400 acres of land on which the village is located) contains a post-office, grist-mill, saw-mill, cheese-box factory, planning-mill, carding machine, cheese factory, two dry goods stores, hardware store, two blacksmiths'shops, wagon shop, two shoe shops, tin shop, cabinet shop, tailor shop, grocery store, two churches, cemetery, masonic and odd fellows' lodges, and about 200 inhabitants.

The first school in Varysburgh was taught by one Crow, in a log house built in 1814 where William Kettle's house now stands. Miss Anna Grinold, of Varysburgh, attended this school.

It was to the grist-mill at Varysburgh that Tunis White carried three bushels of wheat on his back a distance of over two miles to get it ground.

CHURCHES.

The First Free-Will Baptist Church of Sheldon.—A Free-Will Baptist society was formed as early as 1816. Molbon Godfrey, Eunice Godfrey, George Grinold and Jotham Godfrey may be regarded as the nucleus of the society.

February 1st, 1836, the "First Free-Will Baptist Church of Varysburgh" was legally organized. George Grinold was chosen chairman, and Rev. Benjamin McKoon clerk. The society commenced building a church February 8th, 1836. September 27th, 1837, the pews were sold, and in November the church was dedicated, having cost $1,800.

Rev. Daniel D. Jackson is the pastor. The membership is 38.

The Sabbath-school was organized in May or June, 1835. The number of scholars is 130, with an average attendance of 60. The first superintendent was Sidney B. Joy. The present one is A. G. Thomas.

Methodist Episcopal Church of Varysburgh.—Although an organization had been recognized for many years no record was kept until July 28th, 1836. At that date was organized the "First Society of the M. E. Church of Varysburgh."

Cyrus Haughton, Samuel Parker, Davis Knapp, Almon Perry, Peter White, Jonathan Gates and Leonard Parker were elected trustees.

On the 18th of the following November another meeting was called, in the minutes of which a partial description of a "house suitable for the worship of God" is given. It is expressly stated in the old subscription for raising money to build a house, that other Christian denominations are to have the privilege of using the house when not occupied by the Methodist society. The building was finally completed in 1837. It has recently undergone thorough repairs, and a good bell has been hung in the steeple. Meetings are kept up regularly every Sabbath, although there are but three members remaining in the church.

The Sabbath-school in Varysburgh was originally supported by a union of the Free-Will Baptist and Methodist societies. A separation took place in May, 1876, since which time the Methodists have kept up the organization under the old title. John C. Watson was superintendent at the time, and was followed by W. W. White. John Raab succeeded Mr. White, and is the present superintendent. There are about 80 scholars.

CEMETERIES.

The original ground of the Varysburgh cemetery consisted of half an acre given by William Tompkins in 1814 or 1815. One-fourth of an acre has since been added.

July 3d, 1877, the Varysburgh Cemetery Association was formed. The cemetery now comprises two and a-half acres.

The first interments were those of two infants. The first interment of an adult was that of William Tompkins, who died October 25th, 1816. Two large wild cherry trees are growing out of the grave.

LODGES.

West Star Lodge, No. 413. *F. & A. M.*, at Varysburgh, has 68 members in good standing, with a fund of $500.

The charter bears date June 5th, 1857. The first officers were Eli Williamson, W. M.; George A. Johnson, S. W.; Joshua Coughran, J. W. Charter members: H G. Parker, Chauncey Beebe, Owen Cotton, Roswell Gardner, William Tanner, Amasa Barret, Harvey Johnson, Lindorf Potter, M.D.

The present officers are Edward Madden, W. M.; Sylvester Field, S. W.; Eugene Peck, J. W.; G. C. Parker, secretary: J. B. Beck, treasurer; A. G. Thomas, chaplain; G. H. Parker, S. D.; G. W. Wolf, J. D.; George M. Curry, S. M. C.; Adam Embt, J.M. C.; J. M. Johnson, tyler.

Regular communications are held on the first and third Saturday in each month.

Paola Lodge, Independent Order of Odd Fellows, was instituted at Varysburgh, March 20th, 1863. The charter was resigned in 1863.

Sheldon Lodge, No. 418, at Varysburgh, was chartered August 20th, 1875.

The charter members were H. H. Persons, J. A. Godfrey, H. M. Kittle, E. W. Spencer, H. E. Patrick, G. C. Parker.

The first officers were H. H. Persons, N. G.; J. A. Godfrey, V. G.; G. C. Parker, R. S.; H. M. Kittle, P. S.; E. S. Patrick, treasurer.

The present officers are William Libby, N. G.; Frederick C. Ford, V. G.; S. J. Godfrey, secretary; John Coughran, treasurer.

Regular meetings every Friday night. Number of members 39.

STRYKERSVILLE.

This village is nearly a mile long, and consists principally of one street, running north and south. It derived its name from Garrett Stryker, who, with William Richardson and Philo Stephens, purchased the site of Strykersville about 1808.

There are a hardware store, two dry goods stores, a saloon, two blacksmith shops, two shoe shops, four wagon shops, two harness shops, marble works, a hotel, two churches, a brewery, a cabinet shop, a sash and blind factory, a tin shop, a post-office, a cemetery, a cheese factory, two saw-mills, a grist-mill, a cider-mill and a dealer in agricultural implements.

Calvin Rogers came to Strykersville in 1811. Garrett Stryker, Philo Stephens, Timothy Kirby and William Richardson were the only ones then here. Stryker's house was a quarter of a mile north of the Congregational church. Stephens's house was opposite on the west side of the road. Kirby's was a quarter of a mile south of the Baptist church, on the west side of the road. Richardson's house stood where Charles Richardson's house now stands.

The first grist-mill was built by James Arnold, Calvin Kelsey and one Wires in 1820. The first saw-mill was built in 1814, by Calvin Rogers and Jacob Turner.

The first store was opened in 1825, by Isaac C. Bronson. The post-office was established in 1827. The first distillery was started in 1823, opposite where Charles Richardson now lives, about twenty rods from the road.

CHURCHES OF STRYKERSVILLE.

Baptist.—This is probably one of the oldest Baptist churches of western New York. It is claimed that the nucleus of this church was formed as early as 1808. Meetings were first held at Sheldon Center and Wales. Deacon Tilton Eastman is spoken of as the originator of the first Baptist worship in the vicinity. Worship was held in private houses and barns. Garrett Stryker's barn, on the west side of Buffalo creek, was used for some time.

In 1816 Rev. Elias Harmon and Rev. Mr. Goodrich were employed to preach regularly. The good work done by Elder Harmon is still remembered by the people. In 1819 Rev. David Wooster began to labor in the field, alternating with Elder Harmon.

Many of the Baptists were living at inconvenient distances from each other and from the places of meeting, and it was deemed advisable to organize a church. A council met at the school-house in Sheldon (now Strykersville) September 26th, 1827, and voted to recognize the church as the "Baptist Church of Wales and Sheldon." On the 14th of October, 1833, the name was changed to the Baptist Church of Strykersville. In 1834 the church was without a pastor. Rev. James Reed, the next pastor, preached every alternate Sabbath for $100 a year. Edward Coval, a licentiate, followed in 1836. In 1835 a female "Domestic and Foreign Mission Society" was organized.

A church edifice, costing $2,200, was finished in the spring of 1839, and dedicated April 18th. Charles Richardson donated a lot. At this time 119 members belonged to the church.

Rev. Dexter Smith, who commenced his labors in 1839, is spoken of with great favor. During his pastorate of six years 132 persons were baptized. In 1851 a new bell was procured for the church. Rev. A. S. Kneeland preached thirteen years, from 1852. During his services 158 were baptized and received into the church.

So many Germans settled in and around Strykersville that in 1852 Anton Hausler, a young licentiate, was induced to labor among them in their own language as colporteur. In the spring of 1863 the "Holland German Church" was recognized. In 1856 half an acre of land was purchased and a parsonage built, valued at $1,000. Rev. S. Keys died while pastor of this church, in 1858. Forty-six persons were added to the church under his ministry, and the church was changed and refitted at an expense of $2,000.

July 29th, 1874, M. C. Mason, a recent graduate of Hamilton College, was ordained, and he is now a missionary in Assam.

Rev. R. H. Colby was pastor from November, 1874, until July 1st, 1877. His successor is the present pastor, Rev. Thomas Seyes.

There have been eleven ministers ordained in this church, viz.: Edward Coval, Darius H. Paul, Daniel Reed, D. D., Charles B. Reed, A. L. L. Potter, J. Harrington, A. Hausler, Charles H. Wood, Alfred Saterlee, M. C. Mason and William Barber.

Alfred Saterlee died in a foreign mission.

September 26th, 1877, the church held a grand semi-centennial jubilee at Strykersville. Rev.Whitman Metcalf, who, as a missionary from New England, preached when the church was organized fifty years before, preached the sermon at this jubilee.

The average membership for forty years has been one hundred and eighty-eight, and the present is one hundred and eighty. The present officers are: J. W. Ives, clerk; J. H. Wooster and D. C. Barber, deacons.

The Sabbath-school was organized in 1836. James Ives was the first superintendent. A. L. Stryker was the next, and held the position until 1872. He was succeeded by Joseph Cooper, the present superintendent. There are sixteen teachers and one hundred and fifty scholars, with an average attendance of one hundred. This school furnishes to Rev. M. C. Mason, missionary in Assam, $50 per year, through which means a native missionary is constantly employed.

Congregational Church of Strykersville.—This church was formed from a society which formerly held its meetings at Barber's Hill, about half way between Johnsonsburgh and Humphrey's Hollow, having been organized by the Rev. Hugh Wallace October 3d, 1825. The original members were 17, including Deacon Butrick, Deacon Sad and The ophilus Humphrey. Milo Warner was a deacon in this early church, which office he held until his death, in 1874.

The ministers who have labored in this church have been Revs. R. H. Conklin, H. G. Ward, J. A. Allen, Coleman Blanchard, G. Northrop, Oscar Smith, Ward Child, N. Cobb, William Dewey, J. R. Bourne, J. C. Caswell, O. M. Smith and —— Ballard. The church is at present without a pastor.

The meeting-house was dedicated in January, 1836, and cost $2,500. Calvin Rogers was the architect. The church owns a parsonage valued at $800, and has a fund of $1,000.

The present membership is 40. At no time has it been more than 80. Weekly prayer meetings have always been kept up, and a good degree of zeal manifested by those who have sustained this church.

In 1824 a Sabbath-school was organized, as the "Strykersville Union Sabbath-school." It was made up of the Baptist and Congregational societies. About the time the church was built a separation took place, since which time it has been known as the Congregational Sabbath-school.

This school has been kept up winter and summer since its organization. There is an average attendance of 50 scholars. The first superintendent was Milo Warner; the present one is John Spooncer.

Four young men have gone out from this church and Sabbath-school and proved acceptable ministers.

STRYKERSVILLE CEMETERY ASSOCIATION.

The "old graveyard" of Strykersville is in the north part of the village. The remains of those who died in the the early days of Strykersville probably repose here. Garrett Stryker, one of the original owners of the site of the village, is buried in this ground.

The old ground was used until 1867. The first interment was that of an adopted daughter of Lemuel J. Paul.

On February 18th, 1867, the Strykersville Cemetery Association was organized.

The first trustees and officers were Melancthon Abbott, president; Benjamin Whaley, vice-president; Myron Warner, secretary; Eli Balcom, treasurer; Curtis S. Plant, Charles W. Mason.

The present board is as follows: Charles H. Richardson, president; Myron Warner, vice-president; L. M. Fox, secretary, J. W. Ives, treasurer; B. M. Warner, Amos H. Castle.

The first interment was that of Joseph Willett.

TEMPERANCE SOCIETIES.

Evening Star Lodge, No. 549, *I. O. of G. T.*—A lodge of the Sons and Daughters of Temperance was instituted at Strykersville about twelve years ago. March 15th, 1877, it was merged in the Independent Order of Good Templars.

The charter members were fourteen in number. The first officers were: B. M. Warner, W. C. T.; Hattie Warner, W.V. T.; E. C. Hinckley, W. chaplain; William Spooner, W. S.; Nellie Ring, W. A. S; J. D. Barron, W. F. S.; Mrs. Barron, W. T.; Warren Richardson, W. M.; Lottie Shearing, Asst. M.; Emma Ring, W. I. G.; C. G. Webber, W. O. G.; P. D. Barron, P. W. C. T.; Mrs. Putnam, W. R. S.; Mrs. Jones, W. L. S.

The present officers are: Hiram Cobleigh, W. C. T.; Carrie Fox, W. V. T.; William Spooncer, W. S.; Seward Ames, W. A. S.; J. D. Barron, W. F. S.; L. M. Fox, P. W. C. T.; Charles Shearing, W. O. G.; Carrie Richardson, W. I. G.; L. M. Fox, W. L. D.; Hattie Felt, W. R. S.; Ida Waterman, W. T.; Adelbert Sanders, W. M.; Louisa Thompson, W. L. S.; Myron Warner, W. C.

There are 36 members. Regular meetings occur every Tuesday evening.

Strykersville Anti-Treat Society.—June 16th, 1879, a meeting was held at Benion's Court-room, and an organization effected opposed to the pernicious custom of "treating." Ceremonies were instituted, and grips, signs, salutes and pass-words were improvised. Any member violating his pledge may be fined not less than $1. Officers are elected semi-annually.

The first officers were: Owen Benion, president; Eugene Richardson, vice-president; Frank Marzolf, secretary; A. J. Custer, treasurer; Horatio Castle, assistant secretary; Frank Ambrist and John Metzger, wardens; Michael Thamish, sentinel; Peter Kihm, master of ceremonies; Nathaniel Kellogg, O. S. G.

The present officers are: Owen Benion, president; Peter Hymen, vice-president; Conrad Hymen, jr., secretary; Eugene Richardson, assistant secretary; Andrew J. Custer, treasurer; Charles Cobleigh, M. of C.; Michael Thamish, sen.; John Brevot, A. S. G.; Frank M. Metzger and Peter Kinsinger, wardens.

JOHNSONSBURGH.

This village was named after George Johnson, who caused the first post-office to be established here, and who opened the first store. The village is partly in Orangeville and is treated of in the history of that town.

Lyman Tuttle came to Johnsonsburgh in 1814. At that time there were "five log houses and a shanty." The first store was opened in 1827. The first school was taught in 1821, by Trumbull Hurlbut, in a log dwelling house. Lyman and Ransom Tuttle attended this school. In 1824 the first school-house (framed) was built. Isaac Lamb built the first framed house. One Martin built the first grist-mill.

CHURCHES OF JOHNSONSBURGH.

Methodist Episcopal.—The first class was formed in 1823. Revs. William Jones and John Cosort were the first preachers. Among the first members may be mentioned Lewis, Laura and Sally Colburn, Stephen Colburn and wife, Eber, Peter and Eliza White, Alva and Susan Wilson and Simon Van Cise. It was at his house that the early meetings were principally held. The church was legally organized March 6th, 1858. The first trustees were: G. C. Crippen, Jabez Rudd, John Standish, Jonathan Head, Alexander H. Van Buren, Orville Crawford and Harlan A. Jones.

The church was dedicated February 4th, 1859, with a sermon by Rev. Sanford E. Hunt.

About 1829 Miss L. A. Morse (now Mrs. Lyman Tuttle) organized a Sabbath-school. The children of all classes were invited to come. It is now a union Methodist and Congregational school, and known as the Johnsonsburgh Union Sabbath-school.

There are 130 scholars, with an average attendance of 75. J. W. Jones is the superintendent.

Congregational Church of Johnsonsburgh.—In 1859 the first Congregational sermons were preached in Johnsonsburgh. Meetings were held and the nucleus of the present organization was formed. In the spring of 1860 the society was legally organized. Jabez Rudd, Amasa Barrett and Martin Colburn were the first trustees. The first minister was the Rev. Mr. Stratton. The present pastor is the Rev. Mr. Dunham. The trustees are Jabez Rudd, Obadiah Tilton and George Hoy.

The society is a joint owner with the Methodist society, and occupies the meeting-house half the time. The church was built by both societies and cost about $1,500. The ground, half an acre, on which it stands was donated by Jonathan Head. John Coughran and wife, Jabez Rudd and wife, Mr. Colburn and wife, David Lewis and wife were among the first members. The present membership is about 40.

The Sabbath-school is a union school, supported by the Congregational and Methodist societies.

CEMETERIES.

In an early day there was a public burying ground opened in Orangeville near Johnsonsburgh. No deed, however, was ever given for the land. The farm containing it changed hands and the ground was not preserved. About the year 1830 Isaac Lamb opened to the public half an acre of land nearly half a mile southwest from the village for burial purposes, but retained the ownership. Jonathan Head bought the land, and on May 14th, 1864, deeded the original half acre, with an additional half acre, to the First Methodist Episcopal Society of Johnsonsburgh. On the 26th of March, 1879, he added one and a half acres, and the society deeded the ground to the Johnsonsburgh Cemetery Association.

The following are the names of the first and present officers, as they have not been changed since the association was formed: Obadiah Tilton, president; A. D. Keeney, vice-president; L. H. Tozier, secretary; Wilbur Bentley, treasurer. The first interment was that of Mrs. Isaac Lamb. In the year 1830 most of the bodies in the old Orangeville graveyard were transferred to this.

BIOGRAPHICAL AND BUSINESS NOTICES.

FRANK AMBRIST was born in Germany, May 16th, 1844. He married Clara George November 22nd, 1871. He is a farmer.

C. H. BEAN, of the firm of W. W. Bean & Son, is a general merchant at Varysburgh. He was born in Livingston county, N. Y., November 3d, 1865.

THOMAS BETTENDORF, Strykersville, is a brewer and farmer. He has been commissioner of highways and of excise. He was born in France, February 2nd, 1837, and married Mary C. Faber November 6th, 1865.

ERI BOLKOOM is a native of Bristol county, Mass., and was born March 10th, 1821. He married Matilda Emery in January, 1846 His business is farming.

B. M. BOLOOM, farmer, was born April 28th, 1844, and married Etta Hotchkiss January 7th, 1968.

WILLIAM BOYCE was born in England, in 1839. He has served as justice of the peace. He is a farmer by occupation.

J. M. BRYSON, proprietor of a hardware store and tinshop at Varysburgh, was born September 28th, 1864.

BELUS CALKINS, JR., born September 6th, 1840, married Nettie Wilcox November 6th, 1875. He is engaged in blacksmithing and wagon making at Varysburgh.

AMOS H. CASTLE was born in Ontario county, N.Y., August 12th, 1806, and was married to Ann Phillips March 3d, 1829. He came to Sheldon in 1806. He is a farmer, and has been a justice of the peace many years.

C. W. DAVIS, dealer in general merchandise, Strykersville, was born September 6th, 1837, and married Etta Watterman July 2nd, 1878.

D. S. DAVIS has been postmaster at Varysburgh sixteen years. He is a dealer in general merchandise. He was born June 5th, 1841, and married Alice B. Parker December 18th, 1870.

JOHN ESS was born in France, February 28th, 1835, and came to Sheldon in 1840. He is a farmer, carpenter and joiner.

JAMES H. FILLMORE is a manufacturer of boots and shoes at Varysburgh. He was born in Franklin county, N. Y., August 17th, 1812.

FRARK GLASER is the proprietor of Strykersville Brewery and Hotel, and engaged in farming. He married Margaret Metzger January 16th, 1886. He served in the war of the Rebellion and was honorably discharged.

HENRY HOARD served in the war of 1812. He was born in Rensselaer county, N. Y., July 4th, 1701, and came to Sheldon in 1806.

CONRAD HYMAN is a farmer and proprietor of grist and saw-mills. He was born in Germany, January 28th, 1824. He has served as commissioner of highways.

JOHN W. JONES served in the war of the Rebellion. He is now engaged in the manufacture of carriages and in blacksmithing at Johnsonsburgh. He was born June 23d, 1846.

DOMINICK JUNGERS was born in France, April 18th, 1842. He came to Sheldon in 1861, and is now engaged in farming.

SAMUEL SMITH KENNEDY, physician and surgeon, Johnsonsburgh, graduated from the University of Vermont; studied with Dr. Berry, of Spring Brook, N. Y., and with Dr. Havens, of East Aurora, N. Y., and attended lectures at Buffalo, Ann Arbor, Detroit and in Vermont.

H. M. KITTLE is engaged in the harness business at Varysburgh. He has served as justice of the peace. He was born December 24th, 1848.

GEORGE KNAB was born in Germany, June 16th, 1827, and married Mary Schlanker, September 17th, 1848. His business is farming.

EDWARD MADDEN, manufacturer of cheese boxes and lumber at Varysburgh, was born in Ireland, March 4th, 1822. He married Helen L. Davis, March 1st, 1869.

D. R. MUNGER, carpenter and joiner at Varysburgh, was born May 18th, 1835, and married Ann D. Nichols, January 6th, 1853.

JOHN OBERTEN was taken prisoner in the civil war. He was born in France, October 14th, 1836, and came to America in 1848. He is a farmer.

CHARLES PARKER was born in Onondaga county, N. Y., September 26th, 1802. April 21st, 1825, he married Miss Sarah Libolt, and in March, 1860, Mrs. Mary Barnum. He is a farmer; has served as commissioner of highways and overseer of the poor.

EUGENE PECK was born August 8th, 1860. He is engaged in the cabinet and undertaking business at Varysburg.

MICHAEL REDING, who is a farmer, was born in Germany, August 16th, 1830, and came to America in 1848.

REV. W. RISZEWSKIE, pastor of Sheldon Catholic church, was born in Prussia, August 6th, 1838. He came to America in 1870, and from East Eden, Erie county, to Sheldon in 1876.

JABEZ RUDD was born in Massachusetts, December 6th, 1808, and married Sylvia Butler, September 12th, 1830. He is a member of the Congregational church of Johnsonsburgh, and has been deacon nineteen years and ruling elder twelve years.

JOHN SCHWAB, farmer, was born in Germany, December 20th, 1818, and came to this country in 1849.

LOTT SHAW is the proprietor of Shaw's Hotel, Varysburgh. He is a member of the national guard, 67th regiment.

JOHN SMITH was born in Germany, September 27th, 1830, and came to this country in 1840. His father was a soldier under Napoleon I, and participated in the battle of Waterloo.

JOSEPH STANTON, merchant at Strykersville, has been supervisor and superintendent of schools.

NICHOLAS STRAUB is a farmer, merchant and hotel keeper at Sheldon Center. He has served as commissioner of highways and overseer of the poor. He was born in Germany, May 1st, 1811.

ANDREW STREICKER, born in France, August 27th, 1827, married Elizabeth Kibler, July 6th, 1851. His business is farming.

MARTIN L., son of Garrett STRYKER, after whom the village of Strykersville was named, was born March 28th, 1810, and married Chloe Sykes, October 26th, 1835. He was formerly a teacher of music; is now a farmer.

LESTER H. TOZIER is engaged in the mercantile business at Johnsonsburgh. He has been a notary public, and assistant door keeper in the House of Representatives, and is now an acting justice of the peace.

HON. O. L. TOZIER, a lawyer by profession, served as captain in the civil war, and is now extensively engaged in farming. He has been justice of the peace, supervisor, and member of the Legislature. He was born in Jefferson county, N. Y., December 2nd, 1826. He came to the town of Sheldon in 1841, and married Miss Harriet Humphrey, July 26th, 1847.

EUGENE D. TUTTLE, farmer, was born in Sheldon, N.Y., February 9th, 1834. He married Lucy A. Wilder, April 24th, 1862.

FREDERICK WEBER was born in Germany, November 27th, 1815. He is a farmer. Post-office Wales, Erie county, N. Y.

JOHN WOCKENER, physician and surgeon, Strykersville, was born in Germany, June 28th, 1850; studied medicine with Dr. Holt, of Bennington, and graduated at Buffalo Medical College, in 1874.

THE TOWN OF WARSAW.

A "History of Warsaw" was written by Andrew W. Young, and published in 1869. It is a volume of four hundred pages, beautifully printed, and illustrated with forty steel plate and lithographic portraits of residents of Warsaw at some period of its history. It has also views of residences, churches and scenery in the town. Family sketches and biographical notes, in which about four thousand names appear, fill a large space in the volume. The whole book is filled with interesting matter connected with the history of the town from its settlement to the time when the work was published. Mr. Young was a careful, accurate and excellent historian, and, having resided in Warsaw nearly fifty years, was able to give facts and information that no other could as well. One thousand copies of the book were printed and bound, nearly all of which were taken at once by residents of the town and their relatives and friends elsewhere. It is hardly necessary to say that this work has been made largely available in the preparation of the following history of this town.

FIRST LAND BUYERS AND PURCHASES.

The books of the Holland Land Company contain the following records of purchases in the company's township composing the present town of Warsaw:

Elizur Webster, 1803, lots 25, 27, 32, 35, 36, 37, 38 and 43; Jabish Warren, 1803, lots 26 and 28; Daniel Curtis, 1803, lot 30; Elijah Cutting, 1803, lot 20; Josiah Hovey, jr., 1806, part of lot 24; Sterling Stearns, 1804, part of lot 2; Josiah Boardman, 1804, part of lot 1; Josiah Hovey, sen., 1804, part of lot 81; Josiah Jewett, 1804, part of lot 81; Linus Warner, 1804, part of lot 9; Nehemiah Fargo, 1805, part of lot 30; Parley Chapman and Alden Keith, 1805, part of lot 6; Lot Marchant, 1805, part of lot 21; Giles Parker, 1805, part of lot 22; Elizur Webster, 1806, lots 53, 10 and part of lot 18; Gideon T. Jenkins, lots 5 and 18; Isaiah Jaycox, 1806, part of lot 1; Gideon Thayer, 1806, part of lot 1; Daniel Ferguson, 1806, lot 52; Philip Salisbury, 1806, lot 59; Ephraim Gates, 1806, lot 11; Daniel Knapp, 1806, part of lot 34; Elkanah Day, 1806, lot 61; Aaron Dailey, 1806, lot 54; Micha Marchant, 1806, part of lot 45; Peter W. Harris, 1806, part of lot 60; Curtis Edgerton, 1806, part of lot 60; Nathan Pierce, 1806, lot 62; Stephen James, 1806, parts of lots 46, 47 and 55; John Utter, 1806, part of lot 2; Shubael Morris, 1806, part of lot 84; Gideon R. Truesdell, 1806, part of lot 88: Nehemiah Fargo, 1806, part of lot 19; George Densmore, 1807, part of lot 38; Silas Wethy, 1807, part of lot 60; Lot Marchant, 1807, part of lot 21; Eliphalet Parker, 1807, part of lot 22; Solomon Morris, jr., 1807, part of lot 84; Chester Richards, 1807, part of lot 17; Solomon Morris, sen., 1807, part of lot 26; David Keeler, 1807, lot 44; Daniel Wing, 1807, lot 56; Ebenezer Munger, 1807, part of lot 42; Simeon

Gibson, 1807, lot 41 and part of lot 42; Elkanah Day, 1808, lot 51; Nathan Pierce, 1808, part of lot 46; Flavel Kingsley, 1808, lot 58; Suel Hovey, 1808, part of lot 8; Ziba Hovey, 1808, part of lot 16; Linus Giddings, 1806, part of lot 14; Thomas Sherman, 1808, part of lot 14; Hiram Hoyt, 1806, part of lot 49; Hervey Gibson, 1808, part of lot 49; William S. Stone, 1808, lot 57; Daniel Fuller, 1808, part of lot 18; Noah Willis, 1809, lot 7; Jonathan Miller, 1809, lot 15; James Hitchcock, 1809, part of lot 20; Chester Richards, 1809, part of lot 20; Thomas Morris, 1809, lot 60; Stephen James, 1810, part of lot 64; Abraham W. Brown, 1810, part of lot 4; Stephen G. Brown, 1810, part of lot 4; Silas C. Fargo, 1810, part of lot 19.

SETTLEMENT AND PIONEER LIFE.

Mr. Young in his history of Warsaw gave an excellent account of its settlement and of the experiences of the early settlers, from which the following is copied with but little alteration.

The settlement of Warsaw was commenced by Elizur Webster, of Hampton, Washington county, N. Y., in 1803. Having examined the township with a view to the selection of a location, he determined to settle within its limits. It had not yet been subdivided into lots, and in order to find the center of the township he made a line of bark, and with this determined the middle point in the line between townships 9 and 10, from which point he ran due south by a compass three miles, with such accuracy as to vary but a few rods from what was afterward found by actual survey to be the center. He then repaired to the land office to negotiate a purchase; but the agent, Mr. Ellicott, refused to order a survey to be made for his accommodation, saying there were plenty of good lands already surveyed.

Among the early settlers there were but few who could pay down any portion of the price of their lands. When Mr. Ellicott learned that the applicant whose importunities he had for one or two days resisted could command about one thousand dollars, of which he was ready to pay one-half or more on the execution of a contract, he readily consented and at once ordered the desired survey.

Mr. Webster's purchase included nine or ten lots, aggregating more than 3,000 acres, lying mostly along and in the valley of the Oatka creek. The price at which Mr. Webster purchased these was $1.50 per acre. Mr. Ellicott had not been well informed concerning the lands in this township, and he was deeply chagrined when he learned that he had unwittingly disposed of a large portion of the best land in the township at the lowest price. Most of Mr. Webster's purchases were made on credit; or, as was sometimes done, the land was "booked" to him for a trifling sum, not more than a dollar a lot, for a given time, during which he might sell to other parties at an advance. He sold most of these lands to other settlers at an advance of fifty cents per acre, and they usually assumed his contract at the land office, by taking articles as original purchasers and paying him his advance. His purchase was made June 20th, 1803.

He immediately entered upon his purchase, made a small opening in the forest and built a log house a few rods west from the present site of the Baptist church. He was the only settler, and he must have gone some distance for help to raise his cabin. The nearest settlement was at Wright's Corners, in what is now Middlebury. It is said that the choppers then at work on the "old Buffalo road," which passes east and west through Warsaw, a mile and a half north from the village, assisted. The house was one of the rudest of its kind. As usual the fire place was without jambs, and the aperture for the passage of the smoke was of sufficient capacity to give the house a tolerable lighting from above. The roof was of elm bark, and the floor of split basswood plank, hewn on one side. There was neither board nor nail in the whole structure.

Mr. Webster returned to Hampton, and in October removed to Warsaw with his family, consisting of a wife and five children. He came with two teams, one a horse team driven by himself, the other, two yoke of oxen driven by Shubael Morris and Amos Keeny who came to seek homes. Lyman Morris, also from Hampton, came at the same time or soon afterwards. They came by way of Le Roy and Wright's Corners.

During several years the settlers of Warsaw procured their supplies from a distance. The nearest grist-mill was at Le Roy, a journey to and from which required two or three days with an ox team, by way of Wright's Corners over the half opened roads.

Another was at Conesus, six miles east from Geneseo. Many of the settlers had spent all their means on their journey of three hundred miles hither, and were subjected to many privations. The experience of Mr. Keeny, though extraordinarily severe, may be taken as an example.

As already stated, Mr. Keeny came with Judge Webster to Warsaw in October, 1803, and drove one of his teams. He contracted with Mr. Webster for fifty acres of land, which he was to pay for by clearing ten acres for him. The condition of his domestic affairs prevented him from remaining to build a house, and he traveled back to Hampton on foot with Lyman Morris, who had also bargained for a farm. He returned in March, built his log house, chopped two acres for Mr. Webster, between what is now Main street and the creek north from Buffalo street, in Warsaw village, and started again for Hampton with his provisions in a knapsack. In attempting to ford the Genesee river he came near being drowned. He had but ten shillings in money, and he could not afford to pay the ferriage of a shilling. His brother in Oneida county replenished his knapsack, and he reached Hampton after paying his last sixpence on the morning of the last day for a lodging.

In October he and Lyman Morris came with their families; Mr. Keeny having a wife and three children, and Mr. Morris a wife and two children. They had one wagon, which carried the effects of both families, with the women and children. The wagon and team of two yoke of oxen belonged to Mr. Morris, who had also three cows and Mr. Keeny one. The king-bolt of the wagon broke when they were ten miles from Warsaw, and they were compelled to pass a night in a camp in the woods. The next morning, after vainly trying a wooden bolt, they started on foot, leaving the wagon with the goods in the woods. Mr. Morris drove the oxen and carried Jonathan, then two years old. Stephen Perkins drove the cows and carried George, then nearly five years of age. Mr. Keeny turned up the bottom of his overcoat and formed a kind of sack, in which he carried his two eldest children, Betsey and Harry, and his wife carried the baby, about six months old. This is probably the only instance known of ten immigrants entering a town five of them being carried by four of the other five. Mr. Morris arrived first, and made the situation of the others known to Mr. Webster, who met them at the foot of the hill a mile and a half north, on the old Buffalo road, which had just been opened. He relieved Mrs. Keeny of her burden, and escorted the party to his hospitable cabin.

Mr. Keeny's hardships had but just begun. He owed ten dollars or more for the transportation of his goods. His stock of provisions was reduced, on his arrival, to a few pounds of flour and a part of a salt fish. His house was a rude one of its kind. It had no other chimney than a wide opening. The fireplace had not even a stone back wall, the fire being kept at a safe distance from the wooden wall. Their first night's sleep in their new house was disturbed by the howling of the wolves, with which the wilderness abounded.

Scanty as was Mrs. Keeny's wardrobe, a flannel skirt was sold to Sterling Stearns, for some wheat or flour, and a chintz dress to Josiah Hovey, sen., for twelve bushels of corn, delivered at Geneseo, where Mr. Hovey had in the preceding summer raised it. He hired an ox-team and went for his corn. He took it to Bosley's mill, six miles from Geneseo, and had it ground. He had then a tolerable supply of breadstuff, and in order to store it he cut from a hollow basswood tree several sections some three feet in length, shaved off the bark and smoothed them inside. Into these he put the meal in layers about two inches deep, separated by clean, flat stones. In this way it was kept, and, with the flour previously purchased, lasted nearly a year. One of these vessels is still in use for other purposes, and it will probably descend to "the third and fourth generations" as a memorial of pioneer life on the Holland Purchase.

Their meat during the first winter was chiefly venison, furnished by Judge Webster, who was skillful in the use of the rifle. He killed the deer and half dressed them, which was done by loosening the skin from the fore part of the animal and taking out the entrails. The carcass was then divided crosswise, and the parts were fastened to a sapling bent down, or to the limb of a tree, which, springing back, would raise them beyond the reach of the wolves. Mr. Keeny, guided by the tracks in the snow, found and brought in the meat, taking the fore-quarters for his share. During part of one or two seasons Judge Webster supplied some of the settlers with pigeons, which he caught in a net, and they returned to him the feathers.

In 1804 a number of families and several young men settled in the town. Three named Hovey came early in the spring, and they were followed in a few months by their father with five younger sons, most of them minors. Elijah Cutting, Josiah Jewett, Nehemiah Fargo, Josiah Boardman, Jonas Cutting, William Knapp, Amos Keeny, Lyman Morris, Sterling Stearns and others settled in the course of the season. Mr. Steams was one of the first settlers at Wright's Corners, but he came from there in the spring of 1804. He stopped on his way at Mr. Webster's, where one of his children, a son two years of age, died of croup. It was buried by Amos Keeny, Elijah Cutting and William Webster, the last a youth of seventeen, living with his brother Elizur. They cut away a few trees on the hill half a mile south from Mr. Webster's, and dug a grave; and as the water was high in the creek they crossed it single file, on a large log, a short distance north from the hill, one of them carrying under his arm the coffin, which was made of a portion of a wagon box—the only boards that could be found. This was the old cemetery. There was no one to conduct any religious service. Mr. Stearns was a Revolutionary soldier, a volunteer in the war of 1812, and was killed in the battle of Queenston. The second death in the town was that of a son of Nehemiah Fargo, who was drowned in the Oatka, in the autumn of 1804.

In 1805 no more than three additional settlers are known to have been added to the list—Giles Parker, Lot Marchant and Hezekiah Wakefield.

In 1806 it appears from the number of recorded land sales that the population more than doubled.

The first marriage in Warsaw was that of Silas C. Fargo to Catharine Whiting, March 2nd, 1806. They were married by Elizur Webster, Esq., the first magistrate as well as the first settler.

The first saw-mill in the town was built by Judge Webster; and it supplied a serious want that had been felt before. French's Gazetteer dates the erection of this mill 1804, which must be a mistake; for a portion of the gearing was made by Mr. Simeon Hovey in his kitchen in the winter, and he did not come to Warsaw till the spring of 1804. It could not therefore have been running earlier than 1805. It was built near the point where the Oatka creek is crossed by the first road north from South Warsaw.

The first grist-mill was built near this saw-mill by Joseph Morley, or Manley, as nearly as can be ascertained, in 1806, and sold the same year to Mr. Morris, who completed it in 1807.

According to the Gazetteer the first store was established by Absalom Green and Daniel Shaw, in 1809. It is said that although these men brought some goods with them when they came, they had not a general assortment, and made no purchases afterward. The first regular store was kept by Almon Stevens, agent for John Dixon, a merchant of Richmond, Ontario county. He came in 1813, and at first occupied the bar-room of the tavern which Judge Webster built and discontinued when another had been built capable of accommodating the public. At that time, and during many years afterward, goods were, by reason of the expense of transportation, very dear; especially many articles such as groceries, iron, nails, etc. They were brought in wagons from Albany, and a trip required three or four weeks.

The town had no physician previous to the advent of Dr. Chauncey L. Sheldon, in 1808, and people were obliged to go for one to Attica or Geneseo, the nearest places where there were any.

At first the transaction of public business was attended with much inconvenience. It was all done at Batavia, where it was necessary to go to attend town meetings, which the people did not often do. Attendance on the courts as jurors was, however, obligatory, and burdensome to the poor settlers. Amos Keeny and Peter W. Harris were the first jurors summoned from Warsaw. They were absent five days, two of which were consumed in going and returning. They tried three causes, received seventy-five cents each in fees, and paid two dollars each for board.

THOROUGHFARES.

The old stage road to Buffalo passes east and west nearly through the center of the town, and the road which runs along the valley of the Oatka creek passes north and south through almost the exact center of the town in that direction. These roads were formerly the main avenues of travel and transportation, but became comparatively unused on the construction of railroads. Previous to the completion of the Buffalo and Homellsville Railroad heavy merchandise and produce was transported by way of the Genesee Valley Canal, which was completed to a point opposite to this town, some sixteen miles distant. Two years since the Rochester and State Line Railroad, which also passes through this town, was completed, giving the town facilities for transportation and travel fully equal to those of any other.

The principal road which entered the town from the east—the old Buffalo road—originally crossed the valley and town on the line of lots about a mile north from the present village of Warsaw, which was then the principal settlement in the town. Another road into the valley was opened three-fourths of a mile further south, soon afterward. In accordance with Legislative action, providing for a survey of a road from Canandaigua to Lake Erie, Lemuel Foster made such survey in 1816. The road is the one which now leads from the transit line to the western bounds of the town, through the village of Warsaw. When first established it deflected to the left, near the old residence of Judge Webster at the foot of the gulf, where the road now runs; ascended the hill by a circuitous route, and returned to the present line near the head of the gulf or ravine through which it now passes. This was the route of entrance to and exit from the valley at this point during more than thirty years. In 1834 the present road through the ravine was constructed, and the town record of that year shows that upon the application of Elizur Webster the old road was discontinued.

The contract for the construction bore date June 7th, 1834, and was made by Noah Fisk and Isaac N. Phelps, commissioners of highways, and Samuel McWhorter, of Warsaw, contractor. The contract specified a minimum width of sixteen feet, and an average of twenty; and stipulated that the road should be completed by January 1st, 1835, and warranted for a term of ten years. For this work Mr. McWhorter was to receive $1,000 in installments, and in addition such highway labor as the overseers of any road districts might see fit to bestow on the road.

The great importance of this improvement was at once seen; and when, some twenty years later, the Buffalo and Homellsville Railroad was completed, and a depot established near the head of this ravine, its utility was more than ever before apparent. A plank walk, with a railing at the side of it, is built quite through the ravine for the accommodation of foot passengers, and the road is kept in fine condition.

On the 25th of March, 1814, about a month after the town of Gainesville was set off, the commissioners of highways divided the town into thirty-three road districts; there are now more than fifty.

Previous to the formation of Gainesville some twenty surveys of roads in what is now Warsaw were made by Solomon Morris, jr., and within the next ten years as many more, most of them by him, but a few by P. F. Kellogg and Thomas F. Palmer.

The wooden bridges over the Oatka creek were often so injured by freshets as to require large sums for their repair, and some of them have given place to stone arches.

POLITICAL HISTORY OF WARSAW.

It is said that shortly before the incorporation of this town a list of names was presented to some of the citizens from which to select, and that Warsaw was the one selected.

Warsaw was taken from Batavia, and incorporated on the 11th of March, 1808, and then included the present towns of Middlebury and Gainesville, or a strip six miles in width by eighteen in length along the transit line or eastern boundary of the Holland Purchase. It embraced townships 8, 9 and 10 and range 1 of the purchase. Middlebury, on the north, was set off from it in 1812; and Gainesville, on the south, in 1814, leaving Warsaw in township 9, range 1.

The first town meeting was held at the house of Elizur Webster, April 5th, 1808. The officers chosen at this meeting were: Elizur Webster, supervisor; Samuel McWhorter, town clerk; Richard Bristol, Gideon T. Jenkins, Ebenezer Wilson, jr., assessors; Jonathan Curtis, Solomon Morris, poor-masters; Israel M. Dewey, William Knapp, Barzillai Yates, commissioners of highways; George W. Fox, Daniel Knapp, constables; George W. Fox, collector. Resolutions were then passed defining a "good and lawful fence," etc.

Several pages of the early record are devoted to the records of ear marks, which were quite necessary at a period when cattle and sheep necessarily ran at large in the woods. They were described as slits, half crops, slanting crops, square crops, holes, half pennies, swallow tails, etc., or combinations of them, in one or both ears.

Several pages also are devoted to records of strays, which of course were common in those days, when a large proportion of the town was a wilderness and a common pasture. At the town meeting in 1809 it was "voted that when persons belonging to other counties shall drive cattle in this town for the purpose of feeding in our woods they shall, after having been notified of such offence, forfeit the sum of one dollar per head for every week they neglect taking such cattle away."

The practice of suffering animals to go at large in the woods, which was at first necessary, subsequently came to be a source of annoyance, and the people sought protection against it by providing for the impounding of animals. In 1811 it was "voted that the east part of Elizur Webster's barn yard shall serve as a pound," and other places were afterwards from time to time designated.

In 1821 it was "resolved that it shall not be lawful for swine to run at large in the town of Warsaw, in the highways or commons of said town"; and "that there be hogwards appointed, whose duty it shall be, on finding any swine running at large as aforesaid, to drive or convey them the same to the common pound, the keeper whereof shall receive and impound the same, and to keep and dispose of the same."

In 1810 it was "voted that a bounty of five dollars be raised on wolves' scalps killed in this town, restricted only to the inhabitants of this town, except the inhabitants of such towns as shall raise a bounty of not less than five dollars."

With a wise prevision the following was enacted in 1811: "That a fine of five dollars shall be imposed on any person who shall suffer any Canada thistles to grow on their improvements."

Warsaw, unlike most of the towns of the county, is seeing its best days in regard to population, which has been as follows at the State census dates for the last fifty years: 1830, 2,474; 1835, 2,686; 1840, 2,852; 1845, 2,659; 1850, 2,624; 1855, 2,794: 1860, 2,958; 1865, 2,824; 1870, 3,143; 1875, 3,437.

COMMON SCHOOLS IN THE TOWN OF WARSAW.

Mr. Young, in his excellent history of Warsaw, has given facts of interest concerning the early schools in this town. According to him the first school in the town was taught by Samuel McWhorter, about the year 1807, in a log house which Amos Keeny had built in 1804, and which he occupied as a dwelling until 1806. This house stood in what is now the south part of the village of Warsaw. With all the fitting up which it could have it was still exceedingly rude, and it would now be considered scarcely comfortable. No subsequent record is given of any of the scholars in this school. Mr. McWhorter, during his residence of more than seventy-five years in Warsaw, held many offices in the town, and was during one term an associate judge of Genesee county. He also represented the county in the Assembly.

In the winter of 1807 and 1808 a school was taught in a vacant log house on the east road, about half a mile north from the junction of the roads from Le Roy and Wyoming, north from Warsaw village. A house was built at the junction of these roads in 1817, on land which was leased gratuitously for school purposes by Josiah Jewett.

About the year 1807 a log school-house was built at the cross roads directly west from the village, on lot No. 60. A framed school-house was afterward built further east, and subsequently the present house was erected.

At South Warsaw a school was kept about 1808, in a log house on the east side of the road. About 1811 a framed house was built, which was burned during the first term of school in it. Another was erected, which in a few years was burned and was succeeded by the present house.

A log school-house was built in 1811 at the forks of the road a mile and a half east from the village of Warsaw. Ten years later it was burned, and the present house was erected on its site.

In 1816 Amy Martin, afterward Mrs. Clark, taught a school in a log house which had been the residence of Samuel Salisbury, on lot 41, some three miles southeast from Warsaw village. A year or two later a log schoolhouse was built near where the present house stands. About 1824 a framed house succeeded this, and when a few years later that was burned, the present one was erected in its place.

On the 11th of November, 1813, Elizur Webster, John W. Brownson and Samuel McWhorter were appointed commissioners of common schools, and Russel Noble, Richard Bristol, Chester Warren and Samuel Hough trustees of common schools for the town of Warsaw. The commissioners a few days afterward divided the town into school districts, as follows:

> No. 1. "Beginning at the southeast corner of township No. 9, first range, thence running west two miles, thence north two miles, thence east two miles, thence south two miles."
>
> No. 2. "Beginning at the northeast corner of district No. 1, thence west two miles and a quarter, thence north two miles, thence east two miles and a quarter, thence south to the place of beginning."
>
> No. 3. "Beginning at the northeast corner of district No. 2, thence west two miles, thence north two miles, thence east two miles, thence south two miles."
>
> No. 4. "Beginning at the southwest corner of district No. 1, thence west two miles, thence north two miles and a quarter, thence east two miles, thence south two miles and a quarter."
>
> No. 5. "Beginning at the northwest corner of district No. 4, thence north one hundred and sixty chains, thence east one mile and three-quarters, thence south one hundred and sixty chains, thence west one mile and three-quarters."
>
> No. 6. "Beginning at the northwest corner of district No. 5, thence north two miles, thence east two miles and a half, thence south two miles, thence west two miles and a half."
>
> No. 7. "Beginning at the southwest corner of district No. 4, thence west two miles, to the town line; thence north, on said line, one hundred and fifty chains; thence east two miles, to the northwest corner of district No. 4; thence south, on the said district, to the place of beginning."
>
> No. 8. "Beginning at the northeast corner of district No. 7, thence west on the north line of that district two miles, to the town line; thence north on said line to the northwest corner of lot No. 61, thence east on the north line of said lot two miles, thence south on the west line of district No. 5, to the place of beginning."

No. 9. "Beginning at the northeast corner of district No. 8, thence west on the north line of said district two miles, to the town line; thence north on said line two miles and a quarter, to the northwest corner of the town; thence east on the north line of the town two miles, thence south two miles and a quarter, to the place of beginning."

At the town meeting in 1814 a resolution was adopted requiring the commissioners of schools to serve without fee or reward. At the same meeting, as well as at that of 1815, six trustees of common schools were chosen, to transact the business that was afterward done by the trustees of each district. In the year 1816, and in several of the following years, six inspectors of common schools were chosen.

"UNDERGROUND RAILROAD" INCIDENT.

In 1851 there occurred an incident worthy of record, as illustrating the fame of Warsaw as an anti-slavery region. It is related in Young's History of Warsaw as follows:

"About the year 1848 there removed to the District of Columbia two brothers from Connecticut, who had previously become acquainted with some of our citizens who had a 'perfect hatred' of the Fugitive Slave Law. They engaged in market gardening, and among their help was one very competent female servant, owned in the district and hired out by her master. This slave had two children, one son, whose services were also sold, and a little daughter about seven years of age. She was very intelligent and faithful, and became a favorite with her employers. One day she came to them with tearful eyes, and told them the old story—she was to be sold 'down south,' away from her children and friends. Our freedom-loving Yankees, acting on the 'higher law' some years in advance of Mr. Seward's proclamation of it, resolved to save her from the fate she so dreaded. One of them caused to be made a large box just the size of the broad market wagon in which they took their vegetables to the city. Putting into this some bedding, a jug of water and a supply of food, and leaving at the sides near the bottom holes for ventilation, he nailed the cover down over the slave woman and her little child, and one fine night drove leisurely by the national capitol, intent on giving practical effect in one more instance to the 'self-evident truth' proclaimed by its founders: 'that all men are endowed by their Creator with the inalienable right to life, liberty and the pursuit of happiness.' The morning found him forty miles away in Maryland. He left his wagon in front of a village tavern to prevent suspicion, and fed and rested his horses. On and on he went, following the Northern star, whose light was guide and compass to many fleeing fugitives in southern swamps and friendly forests. In the solitude of night he would attend to the wants of his passengers, and at stopping places by day evade curious questions, correct answers to which would have brought down upon him a United States marshal, with the penitentiary for his reward. Across Maryland and Pennsylvania he drove, over the difficult mountain roads of the Alleghenies, into New York. On the evening of the twenty-second day be reached his journey's end at Warsaw. Driving to the residence of his acquaintance Mr. Isaac N. Phelps, an earnest friend of the slave, the box was quietly opened, and for the first time the poor woman was taken out of quarters so cramped that she could scarcely straighten her form therein. Mother and child were found to be enfeebled, but in good spirits; indeed, nothing but the instinct of liberty would have sustained the courage of the mother, and restrained the betraying prattle of the child through that long, dark ride of three weeks. They were secreted a few days, a part of the time in Arcade, until it was found that their whereabouts were not known, when, by the assistance of a few citizens, who were privy to their history, the mother began to live on her own services, and proved valuable help. In three or four months she gave birth to a son, and in about a year thereafter she died of quick consumption. The little girl was taken and carefully reared in the family of Allen Y. Breck, becoming a skillful worker and exemplary young woman. She is now the wife of a well-to-do colored citizen, William Burghardt, and is mistress of a nice house. The babe was taken and cared for by the family of D. C. Martin, of this town, and has repaid the kindness by growing up an industrious, faithful farmer boy. Many other fugitives from slavery found here a helping hand in their flight to Canada; but few episodes occurred so purely local as the escape and harboring of the woman who was known here by the name of Mrs. Jones."

WARSAW IN THE WAR OF THE REBELLION.

The promptness with which the people of Wyoming county responded to the first call for troops has been spoken of. It has been shown that in the first company that went to the field Warsaw was fully represented.

In the summer of 1862 another call was made for troops, under which the quota for this town was ninety-three men. In addition to the county, state, and national bounties, the citizens of Warsaw raised by subscription a sum sufficient to offer a bounty of $60 for each recruit. Meetings were held to promote enlistments, and the quota of the town was soon filled.

In their sphere the women labored with an enthusiasm fully equal to the men's; and the hospital stores and comforts for the sick and wounded in the field, which they prepared and sent to the seat of war, solaced and assuaged the sufferings of many a poor soldier. During the entire period of the war the ladies of Warsaw were active in this good work.

Early in 1864 the ladies and gentlemen, by a festival in aid of the Sanitary Commission, held in the carriage salesrooms of the Messrs. Buxton, opposite the Presbyterian church, raised $150.

During the summer of 1863 a call was issued for 300,000 more men, and a draft was ordered. Warsaw's quota, however, was made up by volunteers.

At a special town meeting held June 21st, 1864, the town voted a bounty of from $300 to $500 per man, as might be found necessary, to secure recruits; the amount to be raised by a tax. This action was repeated July 12th, and similar action taken August 17th, by which a draft was avoided.

By reason of the large proportion of men from Warsaw who enlisted for three years, the town was not required to furnish any under the last call for 300,000.

The aggregate of taxes to which the town was subjected by reason of the war was $60,810, besides voluntary contributions. All this was paid within a short time after the close of the war and the town left free from debt. Few towns in the state have a more honorable record than this.

WARSAW VILLAGE.

Previous to 1816 Warsaw had very little the appearance of a village. Of framed buildings there were the tavern built by Judge Webster, on the corner of Buffalo and Main streets; a school-house on the site of the present Baptist church; a small house near it—the residence of Nehemiah Fargo—on the opposite side of the street, at the comer of Main and Livingston; Almon Stevens's residence, where the Congregational church now stands; the house of Dr. Sheldon, just north of it; a small house a few feet north from where the Bartlett block now is; the tavern of Russell Noble, on the corner of Main and Genesee streets. Just north from where the Presbyterian church stands was a small building in which Almon Stevens kept a store, and another, used for the same purpose by C. L. Sheldon & Co. On the north side of Buffalo street, just west from the creek, Calvin Rumsey had a tannery and shoe shop, in a part of which he lived.

Warsaw began to assume more the appearance of a village in 1816. In 1815 Simeon Cummings, of Batavia, bought of Judge Webster forty acres of land lying in nearly a square body, north from Buffalo street and west from Main. The primary object of this purchase was the erection of a gristmill, which was put in operation in 1816. An oil-mill was also built, near where the race crosses Water street, a year or two later. The construction of the race and the building of these mills gave to the growth of the place an impetus which it had not before had. Water street and Court street were laid out, and the land contiguous to them and to Main and Buffalo streets was divided into village lots. The first lots sold were on Buffalo street, and among the first buildings erected was the dwelling on the north side of Buffalo street, nearest Main.

Among the first buildings erected on Main street were a dwelling on the west side, by Dr. Augustus Frank, about a quarter of the way from Buffalo to Court street, and two or three others near the corner of Court and Main.

It is not possible within reasonable limits to designate the location, time of erection, and builders of the early buildings here, or to follow their history.

From 1816 to 1836 the village continued gradually to improve without any period of rapid growth. In all this time there were but two houses on Buffalo street west from the bridge. One of these was on the north side of the street near the bridge, and the other was the residence of Judge Webster, near the foot

Augustus Harrington

of the hill, at the comer of Buffalo and Wyoming streets. Mr. Webster was the owner of the land on both sides of the street, and by refusing to sell it in small parcels he prevented the growth of the village in that direction. In 1836 F. C. D. McKay became the owner of this land, and he pursued a different policy. He laid out streets, and subdivided the land into village lots, which he offered for sale. For five years subsequent to that the village gradually increased, and many of these lots were sold, but usually to laboring men, who were only able to build small houses. In 1841, however, the county seat was located here. This gave such an impetus to the growth of the village as it had never before received, and business and population have more than quadrupled.

About ten years since several acres of ground east from the lots on Main street, and north from those on Genesee street, were purchased by George W. Frank and E. E. Farman, and subdivided into village lots with streets running among them. Some fine residences have been erected there, and within two years the area south and east from the Presbyterian church has been similarly improved.

When it is remembered that in 1841 there were but two brick buildings in the village, and the present number of elegant structures of that material is considered, and when the fact is recognized that in all respects the change from then to now is equally great, the progress which the village has made will be more fully appreciated than it is by those who have only noted these changes from year to year.

The population of Warsaw (town) in 1865 was 2,824; in 1870, 3,143; in 1875, 3,437. Of the village in 1865, 1,305; 1870, 1,631; 1875, 2,017.

DEVELOPMENT OF TRADE, MANUFACTURING AND PROFESSIONS.

MERCHANTS.

Mr. Young in his history of Warsaw, from which this is mainly taken, industriously and carefully worked up the subject of mercantile establishments at Warsaw, and furnished the following facts:

The first regular storekeeper was Almon Stevens, who in 1813 opened a store of goods as agent for John Dixon, in the bar-room of the old Webster tavern. The goods were soon removed to a small building on or near the site of the Presbyterian church. Almon and Henry Stevens purchased the stock and continued the business till 1817 or 1818. As a matter of history it may be stated that in the building named, Mr. Young, so distinguished afterward as an author, published the first edition of his "Science of Government" in 1836. The book was printed and bound in this building. Mr. Young in his history of Warsaw says: "The building was removed a few years ago to Liberty street, and now it stands opposite the fair grounds, where it is used for a dwelling. The original printing of the sign, John Dixon, can still be seen on the clapboards."

In 1815 Simeon Cummings, Mr. Brigham and Dr. Sheldon established a store under the firm name of C. L. Sheldon & Co. The business was discontinued in 1816.

In 1816 Erastus Beach, of Mt. Morris, commenced selling goods on the west side of Main street, nearly opposite Genesee street. The business continued less than a year.

Elisha Parmelee commenced trade in 1817, and closed in 1824.

About 1818 Drs. C. L. Sheldon and Augustus Frank commenced on a small scale in a small building on the east side of Main, where E. Buffalo street now runs. A larger store was afterward erected on the same side of the street farther north, and occupied by that firm, by Dr. Sheldon, and by Sheldon & Bascom.

Homer and Ebenezer C. Kimberly commenced in the old Stevens store in 1818, afterward on the comer of Main and Buffalo streets. They dissolved in 1822, and E. C. Kimberly continued the business till 1828.

In 1822 Dr. Augustus Frank commenced on the west side of Main street, and continued in the same place nearly thirty years.

Elias R. Bascom became the partner of Dr. Sheldon, and after the latter's death in 1828 continued the business in a new store till his death, in 1847 or 1848. About 1825 John McWhorter began trade, and continued a year or two.

In 1828 A. W. Young removed goods from Wethersfield and commenced business here. In 1830 J. H. Darling became his partner; then Mr. Young withdrew, then Young & Webster succeeded, then Mr. Darling succeeded them.

In 1831 Isaac C. Bronson became Dr. Frank's partner, retired in 1836, and went into business in 1837 with Chauncey C. Gates, who in 1843 sold his interest to Andrew G. Hammond. Mr. Hammond came as agent of John Dixon in 1833 or 1834, left with goods in about a year, and in 1843 returned and became the partner of Isaac C. Bronson. In 1836 Judd & Masley established themselves in trade here; about 1837 Alanson Holly and James L. Darling; in 1838 Raymond Patterson & Co.; in 1839 W. Raymond & Co., for two years; in 1839 Darling & Patterson (J. H. Darling and John D. Patterson), for two years; about 1842 Morrison & Faulkner, a year; then John H. Morrison alone for two years.

Roswell Gould, who had traded at South Warsaw fifteen years, came to Warsaw village in 1843, and remained till 1851. He afterward engaged largely in the produce business. In 1845 the firm of R. O. Comstock & Co. was established; then followed in 1848 Comstock, Andrews & Co.; in 1851, Watson Murray & Co.; in 1856, S. A. Murray; 1857, Albert Purdy, burned out in 1867; in 1859, Abel Webster.

In 1845 Alonzo Choate succeeded Roswell Gould at South Warsaw; came to Warsaw in 1854, and continued one year.

From 1847 Augustus Frank, jr., was a merchant here until 1855; afterward A. & G. W. Frank, until 1869.

J. M. Darling, A. Y. Breck, Seth M. Gates, Chester Hurd & Son, under different firm names, were in business some years. From 1848 to 1857 Benjamin F. Francis, jr., John M. David and Allen Fargo were in trade under different firms. Erastus D. Day and Ransom A. Crippen were also engaged in trade about this time. In 1862 George L. Foote, R. O. Holden and Thomas S. Glover, as the firm of G. L. Foote & Co., commenced business. In 1864 Mr. Glover succeeded the firm. The business is continued by Thomas S. Glover & Co. In 1865 George L. Foote established a dry goods store, and continued two years. In 1867 A. Miner opened a store. It was discontinued in about a year. In 1868 Green & Co. commenced, and continued about a year. From 1874 Eugene H. Andrews was in trade two years.

The first shoe merchant was J. W. Montgomery, who commenced about the year 1852. Previous to that time merchants had kept, among other articles, ready made boots and shoes, much to the disgust of shoemakers. As time has gone on stores for the sale of boots and shoes exclusively have come into existence. The names of the many shoe dealers who have done business here cannot now be ascertained.

In like manner the sale of ready made clothing has come to be a distinct branch of trade. The names of prominent clothing merchants who have done business here are Funchenstein & Strauss, Elias Weisenbeck, L. Israel, A. Openheimer, Oettinger & Levi.

As has elsewhere been stated, a merchant in early times kept everything which the people required, as is now done to some extent in country stores. Of course the pioneer storekeepers were the pioneer grocers, druggists, booksellers, stationers, etc., etc.

Of hardware merchants the following are remembered: John Windsor, Joshua H. and J. Madison Darling, Seth M. Gates, Henry Garretsee, Chauncey E. Gates, Miles H. Morris, Perry and Israel Hodge, Noble Morris, Otis S. Buxton, C. & T. Buxton, Simeon D. Lewis, N. R. Stedman and Charles R. Williams.

The pioneer drug store was that of Dr. Chauncey L. Sheldon, about 1817; afterward Sheldon & Frank. It was a building no more than twelve by sixteen feet. This building, in which also was kept the post-office, has been twice removed, and it is now the wing of a house on the west side of Water street. The word post-office may still be seen on the frieze, partially covered by an old coat of white paint. From that time the principal stock of drugs and medicines was kept by Dr. Augustus Frank, in connection with his stock of general merchandise, until about 1850, when Edwin H. Lansing commenced the first separate drug business The druggists since have been Charles J. Judd, James C. Ferris, George Reed, Artemas Blake, George Duryee, Josiah S. and John B. Matthews, Dr. Merrick Baker, E. D. Day, Alanson Holly, James O. McClure, Chauncey C. Buxton, Frank Lewis, Frank Wilson, Jacob K. Smith, James A. Bishop.

Charles J. Judd and E. L. Fuller are believed to have been the earliest booksellers. They were succeeded in 1851 by Nehemiah Park, and he in 1854 by Lewis E. Walker, who still continues. Dr. John L. Clark was, about 1852, a bookseller for a few years.

MANUFACTORIES.

The pioneer saw-mill of the town and village was that of Judge Webster, completed in 1805 or 1806. Another was built near the site of this, and it is still running. On the west branch of the Oatka creek four saw-mills were built, and some of them several times rebuilt, but they are all among the things that were. One or more stood on Mill brook, and one on lot No. 7 in the northeast part of the town. The one near South Warsaw and one in Warsaw village are all that are in existence in the town now.

The pioneer grist-mill was the one near South Warsaw. Mills were subsequently built at the head of the gulf, by Cyrus Webster, in 1814 or 1815 (afterward burned), and in the village by Simeon Cummings, as before stated, in 1816. This mill is still running, and is owned by John W. Sprague. One was built near South Warsaw in 1826 by Abiel Lathrop. A few years later one was built on the west branch of the Oatka by Dr. Augustus Frank. In the south part of the village a woolen factory was converted into a grist-mill some years since.

The saw mills in this town furnished only coarse lumber. Pine lumber, which was brought from the pine region south and exchanged for goods and produce, constituted quite a branch of trade. It was dressed and worked up by hand until at a comparatively recent period. In 1833 the first planing-mill was erected by Hurd & Son, in the rear of the Baptist church, on the west side of Main street, opposite Livingston. This was burned in 1859, rebuilt, and again burned in 1865.

The Patterson Manufacturing Company was established in 1866, and its name was changed to the Warsaw Manufacturing Company. Its mill and shops were located on Center street, just south from Buffalo. They were burned in 1871 and immediately rebuilt. The manufacture of sash, blinds, and all kinds of dressed lumber is carried on here, and the company engages largely in building.

The first clothiery, or wool-carding and cloth-dressing-mill was built at South Warsaw, by Seymour Ensign, and another soon afterward by S. R. Glazier. In 1816 one was established near Cummings's grist-mill, by Samuel Hough and Elijah Norton. It was removed to the south part of the village, and afterward converted, first into a tannery, then into a foundry and machine shop. One of the clothieries at South Warsaw was in 1825 enlarged to a woolen factory. A few years later the manufacture of cloth was curtailed and a machine shop added. It was soon afterward burned. In 1841 a woolen-mill was established in the south part of the village, and afterward, as before stated, converted into a grist-mill.

Previous to 1824 Ephraim Beebe conducted the business of repairing wagons and making sleighs. In that year Horace Hollister established a carriage and sleigh shop on Water street. In 1836 the Buxton brothers purchased this establishment, and commenced the business, which they enlarged and prosecuted very successfully, with some slight changes in the firm, during about thirty years. They were succeeded by Crippen & Williams, who discontinued the business in 1874. Fullington, Dibble & Co. commenced in 1870. The firm became Fullington & Brown, and discontinued in 1878. At present there are three or four shops in operation.

It is believed that Deacon John Munger built the first tannery in town, probably soon after he came here, in 1806. He prosecuted the business during twenty years. In 1814 Calvin Rumsey established a tannery on the north side of Buffalo street, just west from the creek. Mr. Frank Miller carried on this tannery for many years. A small one was built in the east part of the town by Abraham W. Brown, and one in the south part by Solomon Truesdell. Truesdell & Clark commenced one at South Warsaw about 1830. A tannery was established in the west part of the village by H. B. Jenks and H. A. Metcalf, and it has since been conducted by different firms.

A map roller factory was established in 1853 by Weaver Martin & Brother, just south of the village, on the Oatka. The business has become a large one, and their rollers are sent to all parts of the United States. The present firm is Martin & Co.

The pioneer foundry was that of Dr. Augustus Frank and Benjamin L. Watkins, established about 1824, on the north side of Buffalo street, between the bridge and the corner of Water street. Mr. Watkins soon retired, and the business was continued by Dr. Augustus Frank, either alone or with partners, till 1837. About that time the business was removed by Gates & Garretsee, into whose hands it came, to its present location in the south part of the village. An extensive business has been done at this foundry, especially in the manufacture of stoves. Business is continued in this establishment by Mavor Martin & Co.

From 1837 to 1846 a foundry was carried on north from the north grist-mill by A. A. Wilder, and afterward by Hodge & Co. It was discontinued.

A brick furnace was erected on Genesee street in 1860 by William Robinson, jr., and the business prosecuted by different parties about three years and discontinued.

The pioneer cabinet shop was established in 1817, by Fitch & Bosworth, on Buffalo street. George D. Farnham, P. Penelleton, Alanson Bartlett, Moses Osgood, L. Stedman, J. Spencer Bartlett and E. E. Shattuck have at different times carried on shops here.

The Warsaw Furniture Company was organized in 1869. It erected an extensive manufactory in the town of Gainesville, and built the block on the comer of Main and Buffalo streets for a warehouse and salesroom. The company is still in existence, but it ceased business in 1875.

PHYSICIANS.

The following list of the medical practitioners of Warsaw, with the years of practice, is believed to be nearly correct:

Chauncey L. Sheldon, from 1808 until his last illness. He died in 1828.

Augustus Frank commenced in 1817. He was engaged regularly in practice during a few years, but afterward, by reason of mercantile and other extensive business, he only practiced occasionally. He resided in Warsaw until his death in 1851.

Daniel Rumsey practiced about two years from 1817, then removed to Alexander. He returned about the year 1823, and after several years' practice removed to Silver Creek and engaged in trade.

Cyrus Rumsey, a brother of Daniel, commenced in 1822, and after six years removed to Medina, Orleans county, thence to Ohio, where he died.

Peter Caner practiced from 1827 until his last sickness. He died in 1854.

Thomas P. Baldwin commenced soon after Dr. Caner, continued about two years, removed to Ogden, returned and practiced during two intervals.

Seth S. Ransom came in 1831, and after practicing about eight years removed to Burlington, Iowa.

Ethan E. Bartlett practiced here three years from 1831, resumed in 1848, practiced regularly during a number of years, and occasionally afterward.

Jonathan Hurlburt commenced in 1834 and continued about two years; Lindorf Potter about two years from 1842; N. D. Stebbins from 1842 a year or more, and removed to Detroit. From 1849 or 1850 Dr. House practiced about a year. John G. Meachem practiced from about 1860 until 1862, and removed to Racine, Wis. From about 1850 to 1855 Charles W. Belden, who had previously been here, practiced in Warsaw. Charles A. Dake practiced most of the time from 1850 until 1867. Dr. Blanchard was here about six months in 1852 or 1853. Dr. Day practiced a few months in 1853. Dr. Gardner commenced in 1854, and practiced about two years. In 1854 Dr. Wells was with C. A. Dake a few months. Dr. West practiced in C. A. Dake's office one year (1854). In 1859 C. M. Dake succeeded his brother, and continued in town about six years. In 1862 Milan Baker succeeded John G. Meachem, and he continues. Dr. E. W. Jenks was here one year (1862). In 1863 Dr. R. B. Roberts came and he continues in practice. Dr. F. C. Pitts came in 1866 and stayed about two years. Dr. Phelan remained one year (1867). In 1868 Dr. Miller & Son discontinued after a practice of one or two years. In 1868 Dr. Maynard commenced, and continued about two years. In 1871 Dr. O. B. Adams located here; he continues in practice. Dr. J. R. Smith, who came in 1872, continued until his death, in 1879. Dr. Evarts was here one year (1876) and left. In 1878 Dr. Wheeler practiced six months and left. In 1879 Drs. Denton and Lusk opened offices here and are still in practice. Dr. Tibbets has been here many years and continues in practice.

LAWYERS.

The following is a list of the attorneys who have practiced in Warsaw, with the years in which they commenced practice:

> Robert Moore, 1817; Mahew Safford, 1817; Warren Loomis, 1817 or 1818; Theophilus Capen, 1818 or 1819; James Crocker, 1821 or 1822; Ferdinand C. D. McKay, 1828; Thomas J. Sutherland, 1834 or 1835; James R. Doolittle and Linus W. Thayer, 1841; W. Riley Smith, 1847; William S. Crozier, 1847; Leonard

W. Smith, 1848; Charles W. Bailey, 1850; Harlow L. Comstock, 1850; Charles Henshaw, 1853; Alonzo W. Wood, 1853; Lloyd A. Hayward, 1854; Byron Healy, 1857; Henry C. Page, 1858; Elbert E. Farman, 1858; Myron E. Bartlett, 1860; I. Samuel Johnson, 1861; Augustus Harrington, 1864; Beriah N. Pierce, L. Lockwood Thayer, 1867; Robert Snow, 1869; C. T. Bartlett, 1870; S. B. Bartlett, 1873; R. B. Farman, 2nd, 1875; B. M. Bartlett, 1879; John S. Rockwell, 1879.

POST-OFFICES IN WARSAW.

Only three post-offices have been established in this town—one at South Warsaw in 1850, with Alonzo Choate postmaster; another, named East Warsaw, in the southeast part of the town, Evans postmaster. Both were discontinued after a few years.

The office in Warsaw village was established in 1811. The postmasters, with the dates of their appointments, have been Chauncey L. Sheldon, April 12th, 1811, January 24th, 1826; Elias R. Bascom, March 3d, 1828; Isaac C. Bronson, August 20th, 1841; William K. Crooks, March 10th, 1843; Edwin L. Fuller, July 5th, 1845; Charles W. Bailey, May 3d, 1849; Jacob W. Knapp, February 28th, 1853; Seth M. Gates, May 28th, 1861, June 3d, 1865; W. H. Merril, July 9th, 1870, June 7th, 1874; William D. Miner, July 21st, 1874, December 14th, 1874.

Previous to 1811 the mail matter for the people here was received and sent at the office in Batavia. Shortly after the establishment of an office here a post route was established from Geneseo to Lake Erie, connecting with a route already established between Geneseo and Canandaigua. Over this route Levi Street, of Sheldon, was the mail carrier during many years; and as late as 1816 he carried it in saddlebags on horseback when the roads were in a bad condition.

Before the adoption of the three-cent letter rate a letter written on one piece of paper was charged—for 30 miles or less, 6¼ cents; from 30 to 80, 10 cents; from 80 to 150, 12½ cents; from 150 to 400, 18¾ cents; and for more than 400, 25 cents.

NEWSPAPERS.

The first newspaper published within the territory comprised in the county of Wyoming was established in Warsaw, in 1828. It was called the *Genesee Register*, and was published by Levi and Warham Walker. For three months it was neutral in politics, after which time it espoused the cause of anti-masonry, which caused the withdrawal of patronage to such an extent as to compel the publishers to relinquish its publication at the end of six months.

In May, 1830, Andrew W. Young commenced the *Warsaw Sentinel*, which was continued until December, 1831, when it was merged in the *Republican Advocate*, of Batavia.

In 1836 the *American Citizen* was commenced by J. A. Hadley, at Warsaw. It was published here one year, and then removed to Perry, where it was published by Mitchell & Warren. The publication was continued until 1841, when the concern was removed to Rochester.

The *Watch Tower*, a Baptist paper, was issued from the office of the *American Citizen* at Warsaw in 1839, by Ansel Warren, and published about one year.

A campaign paper, called the *Register*, was published in 1840, by Isaac N. Stoddart and John H. Bailey.

In 1844 E. L. Fuller started the *Wyoming Republican* at Warsaw, and continued it until March, 1847.

The *Western New Yorker* was commenced at Perry in January, 1841, by John H. Bailey. Shortly afterward it passed into the hands of Barlow & Woodward, who removed it to Warsaw. It was successively published by Barlow & Blanchard, S. S. Blanchard, and, after his death, by H. A. Dudley until April 1st, 1858; subsequently by E. W. Andrews, Andrews & Harrington, Harrington & Farman, Morse & Merrill and W. H. Merrill, who continued its publication until October, 1864, when it was united with the *Wyoming Mirror*, and was published by Dudley & Merrill till August, 1875, since which time it has been published by H. A. Dudley.

The *Wyoming County Mirror* was started at Warsaw in March, 1848; Alanson Holley, publisher. From October, 1849, H. A. Dudley was a partner until September, 1850, when he retired. Mr. Holley continued publication until 1855, when he sold out to E. L. Babbitt and R. S. Lewis. In March, 1857, Mr. Lewis became sole proprietor, and he continued such until March, 1858, when W. H. Merrill became a partner with Lewis. January 1st, 1859, H. A. Dudley purchased the *Mirror*, and published it until October, 1864, when it was merged in the *Western New Yorker.*

The *Arcade Times* was started in November, 1869, by S. W. Wade, and published at Arcade until January, 1876, when it was removed to Warsaw, and in October, 1876, the name was changed to the *Wyoming County Times*, by which it is now known.

The *Wyoming Democrat* was commenced at Warsaw in March, 1863, by John Ransom, and published till August, 1870, when it was purchased by B. H. Randolph, who changed its name to the *Wyoming County Democrat*, and by whom it is now published.

The *Masonic Tidings* was commenced in 1865, as a semimonthly, at Warsaw, by John Ransom. In 1870 it was removed to Lockport and published for one year, when it suspended.

CEMETERIES IN WARSAW.

The first cemetery in the town was that which is now known as the "old burying ground," on the east side of Main street. In the spring of 1804 a two-year-old son of Sterling Stearns died at Mr. Webster's. "Amos Keeny, William

Webster and Elijah Cutting," says Mr. Young, "cut away a few trees, dug a grave and buried the child. A son of Nehemiah Fargo, five years of age, drowned in the Oatka creek the ensuing fall, was next buried in that ground. The third burial was that of Dwight Noble, the first adult person who died in this town, January, 1807. In due time definite bounds were fixed and the lot enclosed."

As nearly as can be learned the only title to this ground that was ever acquired was given by the owners of the land to individuals purchasing lots. It appears from the town records that it was treated as public property, and during many years sextons were appointed at the annual town meeting.

Two other burial grounds were opened in the east part of the town, and one on the West hill near the "Hatch farm"; but they were given up, and not being public property they have been plowed over and effaced.

It soon became necessary to enlarge the old ground, and in March, 1850, the Warsaw Cemetery Association was formed, and the following officers were elected: Elijah Norton, Edwin B. Miller, George H. Morris, Abel Webster, Alanson Holley, John A. McElwain, Joshua H. Darling, Timothy H. Buxton and Allen Fargo. The trustees bought and laid out the lot of R. R. Munger, on the west side of the road, opposite the old burying ground. The cemetery was dedicated with appropriate ceremonies on the 7th of September, 1850, the clergymen of the village taking part. The address was delivered by Judge W. Riley Smith, and original odes prepared for the occasion were sung. In April, 1876, a committee consisting of Augustus Frank, Timothy H. Buxton and Simeon D. Lewis was appointed to buy additional ground. In October, 1877, this committee bought about eight acres just south of the "old burying ground" belonging to the Renwick estate, lying on the east side of Main street and nearly opposite the present cemetery.

The present trustees of the association are Augustus Frank, Wolcott J. Humphrey, Noble Morris, Simeon D. Lewis, James O. McClure, Joseph H. Brown, Norman R. Stedman, Lloyd A. Hayward and Abram B. Lawrence, of whom the following are the officers: President, Hon. Augustus Frank; vice-president, Joseph H. Brown; secretary, James O. McClure; treasurer, Simeon D. Lewis; executive committee—W. J. Humphrey, Noble Morris, Norman R. Stedman.

FIRE DEPARTMENT—GREAT FIRE—WATER WORKS.

About 1834 the citizens of Warsaw bought a fire engine and hose. A fire company was organized, embracing many of the prominent men of the town. The engine house stood on the south side of Genesee street, just in the rear of the tavern on the corner of Main and Genesee streets. The organization continued many years, but was finally allowed to disband.

What has been known in Warsaw as the great fire occurred on the night of February 19th, 1867. It broke out about midnight in a photographic gallery on the west side of Main street, where L. E. Walker's book store now stands. From the corner of Buffalo and Main streets all the buildings on the east side of Main street to a point opposite Genesee street were burned. The value of the property destroyed was about $150,000. The final result was favorable, for the "burnt district" was rebuilt in vastly superior style.

In October, 1868, within the limits of the district before burnt, two grocery stores and a clothing store were destroyed, involving a loss of about $30,000.

This fire (the last serious one in the village) awakened people to the necessity of providing suitable protection. A public meeting was at once called. The formation of a joint stock company, to utilize the supply of water which was known to exist in the vicinity, was resolved on. A charter was granted by the Legislature in 1869, naming as corporators John A. McElwain, William Bristol, Ransom A. Crippen, Thomas S. Glover, Augustus Frank, William D. Miner and Timothy H. Buxton. The capital stock was fixed at $20,000, with the privilege of an increase to $25,000. During the summer of 1869 surveys and estimates were made by James O. McClure, and in the spring of 1870 the entire work was let by contract to Messrs. Michellon & Sexton, of Philadelphia, who completed it in the autumn of that year. The reservoir on the East hill is fed by numerous springs, and has an elevation above Main street of two hundred and sixty-five feet. The water was let into the pipes on the 26th of November, 1870, and since that time the supply has never failed.

Although the only object of these works was to furnish a supply of water for protection against fire, the water came to be used for domestic purposes to such an extent that it was deemed expedient to increase the supply. For this purpose a reservoir was constructed on the West hill, about two miles southwest from the village, at an elevation of three hundred and twenty feet, and connected by pipes with the works already constructed. This reservoir has an abundant supply of water, and there are facilities for increasing this supply to any necessary extent. The expense was defrayed from the income of the company without increase of the capital stock. More than four miles of supply mains are laid in the principal streets, and five hydrants are placed at proper intervals. The reservoirs are so high that no engines are needed. The water is also utilized to some extent for the propulsion of light machinery.

The fire department of Warsaw was established in 1871. During that year Cataract hose company was organized, with W. W. Moody as foreman and twenty-four members.

In 1877 Warsaw hook and ladder company was organized, with twenty-four members, and John Hanigan foreman. In that year both companies acquired a legal status under the general act of incorporation. Both are provided with carts, hose, ladders, etc., at the expense of the village.

George M. Jennings and Charles Klein are the foremen respectively of the hose and hook and ladder companies.

The chief engineers of the fire department have been the following: William Bristol, 1871, 1872: James O. McClure, 1873, 1874, 1879; Simeon D. Lewis, 1875–77; Spencer Cronkhite, 1878.

LIBRARY AND READING-ROOMS.

In 1823 a library was established under the act of April 1st, 1796. The following were the subscribers:

James Crocker, Chauncey L. Sheldon, Theophilus Capen, Benjamin L. Watkins, John Crocker, Howard Bosworth, Daniel Rockwell, Henry Woodward, John A. McElwain, Jonas Cutting, Aaron Rumsey, Lyman Morris, Josiah Hovey, Eli Dibble, jr., William G. Whitney, Hiram Giddings, Allen Fargo, Silas Kidder, Oliver Lee, Elisha W. Soovel, Solomon Morris, jr., John Feagles, Augustus Frank, Cyrus Rice, Elijah Norton, E. C. Kimberly, John Wilder, Francis Newton, Samuel McWhorter, Mayhew Safford, Nehemiah Park, jr., Elizur Webster, Samuel Barnard, John Truesdell, Francis Yates, Matthew Hoffman, Augustine U. Baldwin, Edward Putnam and John R. Knapp.

In 1841 a "Mechanics' Reading-room" was fitted up in an upper room of a wooden building on the west side of Main street, about where the Bank of Warsaw now stands. The room was well supplied with papers, and particularly those of scientific interest. Although it was conducted by the mechanics of the village, it was open to others.

In 1868 a reading-room was opened over the Bank of Warsaw, well filled with papers, magazines and quite a number of valuable books. The number of visitors has been large.

TOWN CLOCKS.

About the year 1835 or 1836 a clock was placed in the tower of the old Presbyterian church. It was bought and mostly paid for by Dr. Frank and a few others. It kept good time, and continued in use until the old church was removed in 1864, to make way for the present beautiful brick structure.

The following transcript from the town record for 1866 gives a sufficient history of the purchase and setting up of the second clock:

"*Whereas* the town of Warsaw has provided $500, and the village of Warsaw has provided $300, to purchase a town clock to be put up in the tower of the Presbyterian church in Warsaw, and said town and village have appointed John A. McElwain and Jeremiah Watts a committee to purchase said clock and make arrangements with the trustees of Union Society for erecting said clock in said tower, and have full power in the premises; now, therefore, the said McElwain and Watts, as such committee, agree to purchase and provide such clock ae shall be satisfactory to the trustees of said society, and to pay for the same not exceeding the sum of $700; and if the same shall cost anymore than that sum said trustees shall be responsible for the excess over $700, and permit the same to be put up in said tower and remain there as long as said trustees or their successors in office shall comply with the terms of the following agreement, viz.:

"Said trustees agree that said clock may be put up and kept up in said tower, and to furnish a suitable bell for the same to strike upon; and that any person appointed by the trustees of said village shall have the right and privilege of entering said church at all proper times for the purpose of repairing and taking care of said dock, and keeping the same running and in running order."

This agreement was signed by J. A. McElwain and Jeremiah Watts, committee, and by T. H. Buxton, Samuel Fisher, 2nd, Augustus Frank, Ransom A. Crippen and H. A. Dudley as trustees of Union Society.

BANKING.

During many years after the first settlement of this town what little banking business was necessary was done at Canandaigua, and later at Geneseo and Batavia, especially at the Bank of Genesee at Batavia.

In 1851 Joshua H. Darling established an individual bank at Warsaw, with a capital of $50,000. It was termed the Wyoming County Bank, and was a well managed institution. It closed in 1865 as an individual concern. Mr. Darling was president up to that time. The cashiers were E. Maynard, Charles Mosher, H. A. Metcalf, J. Darling and Henry B. Jenks.

The *Wyoming County National Bank* was organized in 1865 with a capital of $100,000. The directors were Joshua H. Darling, Augustus Frank, Henry B. Jenks, Lloyd A. Hayward and Artemas Blake.

The present directors are W. J. Humphrey, L. H. Humphrey, jr., Lloyd A. Hayward, George G. Hoskins and Simeon D. Lewis.

The presidents have been Joshua H. Darling, Lloyd A. Hayward and Wolcott J. Humphrey. L. Hayden Humphrey, jr., was chosen vice-president in 1873, and continues in that position. The cashiers have been H. B. Jenks and H. A. Metcalf.

The *Bank of Warsaw* commenced business February 1st, 1871. The *Western New Yorker* noticed the opening of the bank as follows:

"This institution opened under very favorable circumstances last week. The growth of our village, its increasing business in manufactures and trade, and the wealth of the country around render Warsaw a good point for additional banking business. It seems almost a necessity, and there is a general expression of satisfaction at the opening of so promising an institution and under such excellent management. The building has been under construction for some months past, and it is safe to say there is not a more convenient or tasteful bank building in this part of the State. Nothing has been left undone to make the building a model for banking business, and all that skill could produce or money purchase to guarantee perfect protection has been freely supplied. The bank is owned and will be controlled by Hon. Augustus Frank, one of the most sagacious, prudent, public-spirited and sound business men in the State, and one whose character will inspire confidence in the public mind. He has been uniformly successful in all his varied business enterprises hitherto, watchful of all public and private interests committed to his care, and his complete success now is well assured."

The bank is located on Main street, in a beautiful brick building erected for the purpose. From its commencement it has been a successful, popular and well managed bank.

George T. Loomis was its first cashier, for one year.

Eben O. McNair succeeded Mr. Loomis as cashier, and still remains as such, with Edward T. Buxton as assistant cashier.

WARSAW GAS WORKS.

In 1859 measures were taken to light the places of business and the dwellings on the principal streets with gas. Messrs. Lawrence and Metcalf, under the name of the "Warsaw Gaslight Company," erected works, and about a mile of mains were laid on Main and Buffalo streets. The gas was made from resin, and this being a product of the south, when the Rebellion broke out the price so advanced as to stop the manufacture of gas. Prior to this, however, the proprietors had been obliged to close their works.

Immediately after the close of the war in 1865 these works were bought by Messrs. Jeffres & Garlock, of Rochester, who had acquired the right to manufacture petroleum gas, which was then a new discovery. The works was fitted up for this purpose, and in the spring of 1867 gas was again sent through the mains. They operated successfully about three years, under the superintendence of Colonel J. O. McClure. They were then sold to Messrs. Hulett & Pettibone, of Niagara Falls, who changed them so as to manufacture the gas from naphtha. In 1871 the buildings were entirely consumed.

Immediately afterward the Citizens' Gaslight Company of Warsaw was formed, with a capital of $15,000. New and enlarged works were built, and the street mains were extended. There are now about four miles of mains, and the number of consumers averages about two hundred. The price per thousand feet is $3, and the annual consumption is about one million feet. The gas is excellent, giving a light excelled by none.

The directors are Hon. Augustus Frank, Wolcott J. Humphrey, Byron Healy, Simeon D. Lewis, Lanson C. Woodruff, Thaddeus G. Hulett, Stoughton Pettibone, Benjamin F. Fargo and Norman D. Stedman.

The president of the board is Simeon D. Lewis; secretary and treasurer, Benjamin F. Fargo; superintendent, Spencer Cronkhite.

SCHOOLS AT WARSAW.

The first select school was commenced about 1835, and continued some two years. Rev. Anson Tuthill, who had taught in the Middlebury Academy, was the teacher.

Another select school was established by Rev. Julius Steele, pastor of the Presbyterian church, about 1825, and continued till the time of his removal, in 1831.

Rev. Stephen Parker, of Geneva, established an academic school in 1835 and continued it till 1837. Similar schools, the dates of which are not remembered, were taught by Mr. Paddock, Charles J. Judd and Josiah Hurty.

In 1822 a select school for young ladies was taught by Maria Clark, of Le Roy, and subsequently another by Lucinda Gregg, of Londonderry, N. H., who became the wife of Hon. William Patterson, a much esteemed citizen of Warsaw and a member of Congress.

A similar school was established in 1844, and continued several years by Anna P. Sill, afterward the founder of the well known female seminary at Rockford, Ill.

Miss Sophronia Broughton commenced a select school for young ladies on Livingston street, with assistant teachers Miss Quick, of Auburn, and Miss Arnot, of Pennsylvania. Miss Broughton is one of the most accomplished teachers in the United States.

Miss Emeline Monroe, afterward Mrs. Eli Rood, of Wethersfield, was a teacher of common and select schools some seven years, between 1830 and 1840. About this time what were termed infant schools became very popular, and such a school was established in Warsaw by Catharine W. Blanchard, who married Hon. John Fisher, now of Batavia.

In 1877 Miss A. A. Bartlett, who had been a successful teacher of adults, established a kindergarten—a form of primary school introduced in this country about ten years since. At first the number of children received was limited to ten, but the success of the undertaking was such that it became necessary to remove that limit.

As the population of the village increased the district school house, which was sufficient for all the needs of the district when erected, was found to be too small, and a more capacious house was erected on Genesee street. The second story was used for select schools, public meetings and various other purposes for twenty years. It was used as a masonic lodge room till the anti-masonic excitement in 1826, when it was given up by the masons. In the second story of this building was held the first county court. After it ceased to be used for school purposes it became the property of Isaac C. Bronson, who removed it to the west side of Main street and converted it into stores. In the fire of 1867 it was burned.

Soon after the organization of the county the proposition was made and carried out to consolidate the school districts in the village and its immediate vicinity, and to establish a union graded school. Several districts were consolidated and new school buildings were erected in 1846, on the west side of Main street, just south from the Baptist church and nearly opposite the residence of Allen Fargo. Other small buildings were afterward erected in different parts of the village, on Genesee, Brooklyn and other streets, and used principally for primary scholars. The principal edifice, on Main street, was of cobblestone, thirty-seven by thirty-five feet, and two stories in height. Its cost was $1,500, which at that time was considered a large expenditure for a school house.

The first school in this building was taught by C. J. Judd, assisted by Misses Merrill and Stevens. It had one hundred and seventy pupils during the first term. This was a district school, and was subject to all the rules and regulations which governed other district schools. It was soon found that though this was a great improvement on the pre-existing condition it did not yet meet the wants of the people; and the idea of adding to it an academic department was conceived. Necessary legislation was procured, and a meeting was held on the 13th of September, 1853, "for the purpose of determining by vote of the district whether a union free school shall be established therein, in conformity with the provisions of the act passed June 18th, 1853," providing for the organization of the academic department.

It was determined to establish a union free school in accordance with the provisions of the law, and John A. McElwain, Joshua H. Darling, Alanson Holly, Sanford L. Boughton, Charles W. Belden and Lloyd A. Hayward were chosen members of the board of education. Subsequently all the necessary legal steps were taken.

At the time of the change Horace Briggs was principal of the school. The following have been employed since: in 1853, Richard K. Sanford, since State senator from another district, and Horace Briggs, assistant; 1834, Prof. H. F. Wright (since of the Cortland Normal School), with S. D. Lewis as assistant; 1855 and 1856, Profs. Sykes and Brigham; 1857, Prof. H. F. Wright again and Miss Kate Leland. During several years Miss Juliette Cooley, an accomplished teacher, was an assistant. In 1858 Prof. E. P. Harris (since of Amherst College) was employed; 1860, Prof. Joseph Gile and his sister, Mary; 1861, Prof. O. H. Stevens and Miss Mary Gile; 1862, Winslow Schofield and Miss Gile; 1863 to 1871, Prof. C. H. Dann, with Miss Gile, Miss Lizzie Gates, Miss Jennie Ferris and Miss Belle Bristol, successively, as assistants; in 1871, Prof. Peck, during a term or two, then Prof. T. C. Selden, till the new school building was erected, except during the spring term of 1873, when Mrs. Jennie Ferris Martin was principal.

In 1871 and 1872 meetings of the citizens were held in the union school building to discuss the question of disposing of all the outlying primary school premises, and bringing all the departments into one central school building. In January, 1872, at a very large meeting, plans of a building were presented, and after discussion, by a vote of 104 to 52, it was "resolved that it is the sense of this meeting that the central union school system is best for this district"; and by 109 to 7 "that there should be an entire new school building in this school district." Augustus Frank, Thomas S. Glover, W. J. Humphrey, S. D. Lewis and E. E. Farman were appointed a committee to examine and procure estimates of the cost of different sites for the new building.

The edifice was erected in 1872 and 1873, by the Warsaw Manufacturing Company, at a cost, including grounds, of about $40,000. It was dedicated September 16th, 1873, and the school opened with Prof. S. M. Dodge as principal, and Mrs. Jennie F. Martin preceptress. In 1875 Prof. A. P. Chapin became the principal. The faculty in 1879 consisted of A. P. Chapin, principal; Mrs.

Jennie F. Martin, preceptress, and William H. Dexter, Henry B. Haw, Misses Hettie Spink, Libbie Hain and Mary E. Dann, assistants.

The board of education for 1879 were L. A. Hayward, president; O. W. Bailey, secretary; H. A. Dudley, N. R. Stedman, S. D. Purdy, N. D. Fisher.

CHURCH HISTORIES.

METHODIST EPISCOPAL CHURCH OF WARSAW.

Rev. Mr. Van Nest formed a class in the south part of the town in 1807, and Revs. Joseph Gatchell and James Mitchell visited the town in 1809.

The members of the first class were Solomon Morris, sen., and John Morris, with their wives, and others, whose names cannot be learned. In 1810 Revs. William Brown and John Kimberlin organized a class or society in the north part of the town, and of this Josiah Hovey, sen., Simeon Hovey and Josiah Hovey, jr., and their wives, with others, are remembered as members. Simeon Hovey, Josiah Hovey and Shubael Morris were the first class leaders.

Among the first regular preachers on the circuit which included this town was Rev. Loring Grant. It is said that Mrs. Grant sometimes accompanied her husband on horseback on his circuit of near three hundred miles.

The "First Methodist Episcopal Society of Warsaw" was legally organized in 1820. The one hundred-acre lot promised by the Holland Company to the first church in a town was divided between this society and the Union Society.

The first trustees of this society were Simeon Hovey, Chester Hurd, John Morris, Anson A. Perkins, Nathan B. Miller, Lyman Parker, Josiah Hovey, Roderic Chapin, jr., and Eleazer Smith.

The first church edifice was built three-quarters of a mile north from the center of the village, in 1824. It was removed to the site of the present one in 1835. In 1853 it was sold to Rev. J. W. Hines, removed to the south side of Buffalo street, near the bridge, and arranged for dwellings. The new church, which was finished in 1854, was improved, repainted, and frescoed in 1868, at an expense of $1,300.

Strong resolutions were adopted at the quarterly conference of which this society formed a part in 1836, on the subject of temperance, and in 1845 and 1848 against the order of Odd Fellows.

The following is a list of the preachers for each year on the circuit which has included Warsaw. Districts have often, and circuits oftener, been changed since the formation of a society here:

> In 1809, James Mitchell, Joseph Gatchell; 1810, John Kimberlin, William Brown; 1811, Loring Grant, Elijah Metcalf; 1812, Renaldo Everts; 1813, Elijah King, Ebenezer Dolittle; 1814, William Brown, Elijah Warren; 1815, James H. Harris; 1816, Robert Menshall, Thomas McGee; 1817, James Hall; 1818, Aurora Seager, Fetas Foster; 1819, Ava Williams; 1820, James Hall, Zachariah Paddock; 1821, James Gilmore, Jasper Bennett; 1822, John Arnold, Asa Orcutt; 1823, Asa Orcutt, John Beggarly; 1824, Andrew Prindle, J. B. Roach: 1825, Benjamin

Williams, Andrew Prindle; 1826, Benajah Williams, Asa Abel, Jonathan Huestis; 1827, Morgan Sherman, Robert Parker; 1828, Glezen Fillmore, Micha Seager, Chester N. Adgate; 1829, John Cosart, Joseph Atwood; 1830, Hiram May, Joseph Atwood; 1831, Mifflin Harker, George Wilkinson; 1832, Mifflin Harker, Sheldon Dolittle; 1833, Sheldon Dolittle, Merritt Preston; 1834, 1835, Reeder Smith; 1836, Richard Wright, A. O. Hall; 1837, Richard Wright; 1838, James Hall; 1839, Hiram May; 1840, Nelson Hoag; 1841, Salmon Judd; 1842 Salmon Judd; 1843, Chauncey S. Baker; 1844, Joseph Pearsall; 1845, John B. Jenkins; 1846, John B. Jenkins; 1847, Charles D. Burlingham; 1848, David Nichols; 1849, 1850, King David Nettleton; 1851, J. W. Hines; 1852, J. W. Hines; 1853, Zenas Hurd; 1854, B. F. McNeil; 1855, Griffin Smith; 1856, 1857, William C. Willing; 1858, Sumner C. Smith; 1859, 1860, E. M. Buck; 1861, 1862, Schuyler Parker; 1863, 1864, J. H. Baylias; 1865, Rollin C. Welch; 1866, H. H. Lyman; 1867, M. H. Rice; 1868, 1869, O. S. Cbamberlayn; 1870–72, E. T. Green; 1873, D. Leisenring; 1874, J. T. Brownell; 1875, J. Copeland; 1876, T. Cardus; 1877, 1878, William S. Tuttle.

The present number of members is 130.

PRESBYTERIAN CHURCH OF WARSAW.

The first religious society formed in Warsaw was termed the Union Society. It was composed mainly of Presbyterians and Baptists, and it continued to be supported by people of both denominations from the time of its origin, in 1808, and its legal incorporation, in 1812, to 1819, when the Presbyterians purchased the interest of the Baptists in the meeting-house which had been built by the Union Society, and the latter organization was dissolved or lapsed. During the existence of the Union Society both the Presbyterians and Baptists had organizations. The Presbyterians date their organization at the same time with that of the Union Society.

The Presbyterian church was organized July 14th, 1808, by Rev. John Lindsley, a missionary. The names of the members at its organization are Edward Goodspeed, Eliphalet Parker, Luther Parker, Ezra Walker, Abraham Reed, Israel Branch, Polly Day, Prudence A. Walker, Martha Parker and Rhoda Parker. The first deacons were Eliphalet Parker and Israel Branch.

During several years the church was supplied by missionaries and occasional ministers, among whom Rev. Messrs. Lindsley, Phelps, Parmelee, Spencer and Ayer are remembered.

At first the form of government of this church was Congregational, but about the year 1813 the record seems to show that it "formed a relation" with the presbytery, though it retained the Congregational form of government.

In 1813 Rev. Silas Hubbard was installed as pastor, but by reason of failing health he resigned in. 1814. He was succeeded in 1816 by Rev. Hippocrates Rowe, who preached alternately here and at Orangeville. His pastorate terminated at his death, two years later.

In 1817 the first church edifice was erected and enclosed by the Presbyterians and Baptists. It was said by some to be the first erected west from the Genesee river in the State of New York. It was used in the summer season during several years, and in 1821 the Presbyterians purchased the interest of the Baptists and completed the building.

In 1818 the church organized the first Sunday-school, one of the first in the State.

After the death of Mr. Rowe the church was supplied by different clergymen, and among them Rev. Norris Bull, who labored with them during two periods of about a year each, the last terminating in the spring of 1821. It was afterward supplied occasionally by Revs. Calvin Colton, E. Chapin, Samuel T. Mills, Amos Brown and others.

From 1826 Rev. Abial Parmelee supplied the church about four years, and during two years the supply cannot be ascertained. From 1828 to 1831 Rev. Julius Steele was the minister; then for a year Rev. Isaac Oakes. Rev. Ezra Scovel was installed pastor in 1833.

In 1834 the session passed resolutions disapproving of slavery and commending efforts looking toward its abolition.

During 1837 and a portion of 1838 the church was supplied by Revs. O. S. Powel, H. A. Sackett, William Bridgman and others. In 1838 Rev. Daniel Waterbury became pastor, but died after a pastorate of a few weeks.

In 1839 Rev. Ralph S. Crampton was installed. During the following winter the church was divided, a number leaving and forming the Congregational chureh, and Rev. Mr. Crampton exchanged pastorates with Rev. Richard Kay, of Holly, who remained till 1845, and was succeeded by Rev. A. C. McClelland, and he within a year by Rev. Hugh Mair, D. D., who continued a year.

In 1847 Rev. Abraham T. Young became pastor, and he supplied the church three years. During his pastorate a parochial school was established, which continued during twelve or fourteen years. Rev. John R. Cornin supplied the church for a year after Mr. Young, and Rev. Edward Wall during a few weeks.

In 1852 Rev. Stuart Mitchell was ordained and installed; he closed his pastorate in the spring of 1855. In the same year the Rev. Joseph E. Nassau was unanimously called, and on the 24th of October was ordained and installed. The present number of members is 191.

The semi-centenary of this church was celebrated on the grounds of Frank and Edwin B. Miller by the parochial school, Sunday-school and congregation, by appropriate exercises.

In 1864 the erection of a new church edifice was commenced. The building committee consisted of Augustus Frank, Timothy H. Buxton and Samuel Fisher 2nd. Four thousand dollars had been previously pledged by Deacon John Munger, and other liberal subscriptions were made. Contracts were entered into with Ambrose J. Armstrong, of Warsaw, for the brickwork, and James E. Ketchum, of Phelps, as superintendent of the joiner work. The corner stone was laid July 14th, 1864 with appropriate ceremonies. The house was dedicated

September 21st, 1865, by the pastor, Rev. Joseph E. Nassau, assisted by several clergymen. Rev. P. D. Gurley, of Washington, D.C., preached on the occasion.

In 1867 a superior and costly organ was placed in the church. In a 1875 chapel connected with the church was built. Augustus Frank, T. H. Buxton and Cyrus Jefferson were the building committee. It was dedicated with public exercises July 1st, 1875; Rev. Joseph E. Nassau, D. D., the pastor; Rev. Joseph R. Page, D. D., Hon. Augustus Frank, Rev. W. D. McKinley and Rev. A. D. Morse taking part and making remarks on the occasion. The entire expense, including the furniture, was about $5,000.

The first church bell in Warsaw was placed in the belfry of the old church, in 1825. Previous to that for a short time the people had been apprised of the hour by the notes of a bugle. At last, to remind the people that his services had been thus far unrequited, and to give them a hint for the future, the bugler played from the tower a secular tune. The result was his dismissal and a movement for the purchase of a bell. The old bell failed, after doing service thirty-five years, and was replaced by the present one.

WARSAW BAPTIST CHURCH.

The history of this church must of necessity be brief and imperfect because of the loss of a large part of the records. The data for the present sketch were gathered from the recollections of surviving old members, and from a history of this church, written by one of its pastors, Rev. A. Morrill, for presentation at the session of the Baptist Association of Genesee, in 1867.

According to this sketch, the first preacher who visited the Baptists in this vicinity was Rev. Mr. Irish, a missionary, who, on the 25th of November, 1810, organized a church. One authority says there were fourteen, another eighteen, as follows: Joseph Porter and wife, Josiah Boardman and wife and daughter, Noah Wiseman, John Truesdell, Levi Stearns, Hannah Stearns, John Brown, William Brown, Miriam Brown, Levi Rice, Hannah Rice, Jeremiah Truesdell, Elijah Hammond, Rhoda Reed and Joanna Beardsley. It was first named the Second Baptist Church of Warsaw, because a church had already been organized in Middlebury, then a part of Warsaw.

For several years meetings were held in the southern and southwestern portion of the town; often in the barn of John Truesdell. The first house of worship was half a mile south of the village. Some twenty years later the present church edifice was built. The old church was taken down, removed to the village and converted into a dwelling-house.

The first pastor was Rev. Jeremiah Irons, who commenced his pastorate in the autumn of 1811, and preached during a year one-fourth of the time. Rev. David Hurlburt next ministered to the church one year; then Rev. Jabez Boomer, who was the first settled pastor. Mr. Boomer was ordained August 19th, 1816, and continued with the church till 1818.

In 1817 a house of worship was built and enclosed by the Baptists and Presbyterians jointly. In 1821 the Baptists sold their interest in this house to the Presbyterians, who completed it.

Rev. William Pattison became pastor in 1818, and served the church for several years, during which there was a large increase in the number of members. After him came Rev. Leonard Anson for a short time, succeeded by Rev. Anson Tuthill, who remained several years.

From 1827 to 1830 Rev. David Bernard was pastor. During his pastorate a large number were dismissed to form a church at Gainesville, and the first house of worship was dedicated. The subject of freemasonry agitated the church greatly during this period in its history.

In 1828 the church effected a legal organization under the corporate name of the "Baptist Church and Society of Warsaw," and David Fargo, Samuel Salisbury and Seth Higgins were chosen trustees.

Rev. Peter Freeman became the pastor in 1830, and continued three years. After him Rev. Ahraham Ennis was pastor till 1837, then Rev. G. B. Walling a year. From 1838 to 1840 Rev. Joseph Elliott was pastor; succeeded by Rev. B. Wilcox, who continued one year. From 1841 to 1845 Rev. H. K. Stimson was pastor; in this time Hon. James R. Doolittle united with this church. From 1845 to 1848 Rev. J. L. Richmond was pastor; then Rev. A. C. Barell till 1850, then Rev. H. Leavenworth one year. During the next two years Mr. W. C. Hubbard supplied the pulpit a part of the time. In 1853 and 1854 Rev. Philander Shedd was pastor; and in 1855 and 1856 Rev. H. Smith. Rev. William Cormac served the church in 1857 and 1858, and during 1859 the church was without a pastor. It was again agitated during this year on the subject of secret societies. In 1860 Rev. H. K. Stimson was again pastor, but left the pulpit for the "tented field," as a captain of cavalry. Revs. J. B. Pitman and J. Hough were pastors during the next four years, and Rev. J. W. Crane supplied the church one year thereafter. In 1865 Rev. Abner Morill commenced his pastorate, and continued till 1867. A. C. Williams was pastor till 1870, C. M. Booth till 1875, B. H. Damon till 1876 and J. B. Ewell is the present pastor.

TRINITY CHURCH (EPISCOPAL).

From a report made by Rev. Richard Salmon to the New York Convention in 1826, it is learned that he had a conditional engagement to preach at Warsaw and Wethersfield, alternately for half the time during the year 1827. Again, in 1828 it appears by his report that he had become a resident of Warsaw, and had labored there a portion of the time during that year; "that the service was performed with great zeal and propriety," and the number of communicants had increased. During the next year Mr. Salmon was residing elsewhere, but reported concerning this congregation that it was flourishing, and that the Sunday-school had increased from twenty-five to between eighty and ninety. Six were confirmed that year by Bishop Hobart.

In 1831 Mr. Salmon was again a missionary at Warsaw, preaching half the time there, and dividing the other half equally between Sheldon and Wethersfield. There were eleven confirmations in 1832 by Bishop Onderdonk. The Rev. Alexander Frazer, missionary at Warsaw, gave a good report of matters in Warsaw in 1834, and in 1835 Rev. Isaac Garvin reported that he had labored half the time there.

It does not appear that from that time till 1852 there was any other than occasional preaching, though there were some Episcopalians there. Services had sometimes been held in the meeting-houses of other societies, and Bishop De Lancy conducted one of these and baptized one child.

May 12th, 1852, the society was organized, with John A. McElwain, John G. Meachem, Noble Morris, Ransom S. Watson, Nehemiah Park, jr., Richard M. Tunks, Alonzo W. Wood and Charles W. Bailey as corporators. John A. McElwain and John G. Meachem were chosen wardens, and Alonzo W. Wood, Nehemiah Park, jr., Linus W. Thayer, Noble Morris, Ransom S. Watson, Charles W. Bailey, Richard Tunks and Abel Webster elected vestrymen.

In 1853 John G. Meachem, N. Park and A. W. Wood were appointed a building committee, and on the 25th of May, 1854, a church was consecrated by the name of Trinity Church.

By the will of Mrs. Laura S. Watson this church has become the owner of a house and lot for a rectory.

From 1852 to 1855 Rev. A. D. Benedict was rector; 1856 to 1858, Rev. William White Montgomery; 1858 to 1859, Rev. Thomas Applegate; 1859 to 1862, Rev. William O. Gorham; 1862, 1863, Rev. Noble Palmer; 1863 to 1865, Rev. Robert Harwood; 1866 to 1877, Rev. John V. Stryker. Rev. E. Jay Cooke became rector January 1st, 1878, and continues in charge.

FREE-WILL BAPTIST CHURCH OF WARSAW.

This little church was organized in 1833, with only four members. During the year 1834 there was a revival, and some thirty were added. Elder H. Jenkins was the officiating minister at that time, and may properly be called the father of the church. Emery D. Albro and Alden Keith were chosen deacons. October 13th, 1834, the sum of $457 was obtained by subscription to build a house of worship. The timber was furnished by contribution, and the frame was erected by volunteer labor, superintended by Deacon Albro and other leading members of the church. The completion of the house was let to John Blighton, and it was finished and dedicated in 1835, Rev. H. N. Plumb preaching the dedication sermon. Deacon Albro was in truth a father to the church.

Revs. Jared Miner and William Moses supplied the pulpit till 1836; Rev. Mr. Reed became pastor, succeeded in 1837 by Rev. Hiram Whicher, who was pastor two years. He was followed by Rev. H. N. Plumb, who was succeeded by Rev. Silas Davis. Rev. William Moses became pastor in 1843, and remained two years, followed by Rev. A. Hopkins two years, Rev. N. Abbey one, Rev. Luke Hitchcock two, Rev. B. H. Damon one, Rev. Mr. Fessenden one, Rev. I.

Wood one, Rev. H. H. Strickland one, Rev. D. R. Evans two, Rev. Levi Kellogg two, Rev. John Lister, formerly a slave in Virginia, six months in 1859 and 1860; Rev. H. N. Plumb one year, Rev. W. W. Holt three, Rev. Mr. Rollins one, Rev. J. C. Steele two. From 1867 to 1870 the church had no pastor; then Rev. Levi Kellogg served one year; another vacancy of about four years occurred, followed by Rev. M. H. Blackman's pastorate of one year; then another vacancy of about two and one-half years; then the pastorate of the present incumbent, Rev. Benjamin Morey, commenced.

A Sabbath-school has usually been maintained during the summer season. The first recorded name of a superintendent is that of D. R. Norris, who was appointed May 12th, 1838. The present superintendent is Charles Lathrop. The average attendance has been about twenty.

The salary paid to clergymen has ranged from $100 to $500 per year. The church was always opposed to slavery, and has on its records strong resolutions against the institution. It has contributed freely in support of benevolent objects. Some years since a few of its members gave $100 each toward the endowment of a Free-Will Baptist college at Hillsdale, Mich., and in 1867 about $330 was raised by the church to aid in the establishment of a normal school at Harper's Ferry, for the instruction of pupils without regard to color. The seminary at Pike, Wyoming county, has received from this church more than $500 toward an endowment of $25,000. It has assisted other feeble and destitute churches frequently by larger or smaller contributions.

CONGREGATIONAL CHURCH AT WARSAW.

On the 16th of February, 1840, this church was organized and constituted by Rev. Samuel Griswold. At its organization it consisted of thirty-four members, who had withdrawn from the Presbyterian church for the purpose of establishing this. At the end of the first year the church numbered fifty-six members. The constitution forbade the admission of any person to membership who did not wholly refrain from the use of all intoxicating drinks as a beverage, or who countenanced their manufacture or sale; also of any slave holder.

In 1841 a "Declaration of Sentiment" was adopted, refusing all Christain fellowship with slave holders—denouncing all apologists for slavery, and refusing to mingle "religious contributions" with societies that received contributions from slave holders.

At first this society met in a small building over the mill race, on the south side of Buffalo street, but the site of the present church edifice was immediately purchased, and a building completed early in 1841. It was thirty-six by forty-five feet, and cost about $3,000. It was dedicated on the 13th of January, 1841, Rev. Mr. Ward, of Bergen, officiating. It was enlarged five years afterward, and again a few years later. It was furnished with an organ and remodeled in the interior in 1855.

In 1866 a building committee, consisting of Artemas Blake, Joshua H. Darling, Lloyd A. Hayward, Wolcott J. Humphrey, William D. Miner, Simeon

D. Lewis, Lewis E. Walker and Elisha S. Hillman was appointed. The old church, organ and bell were sold; and the corner stone of a new edifice was laid, with appropriate ceremonies, on the 6th of July, 1866, by the pastor, Rev. E. E. Williams. The architect was A. T. Warner, of Rochester, and the builders were Ambrose J. Armstrong, of Warsaw, of the masonry, and Hodge & Son, of Buffalo, of the wood work. Joshua H. Darling, Esq., presented a $2,000 organ. The house was dedicated, free from debt, by Rev. Mr. Williams, August 7th, 1867; the dedication sermon being preached by Rev. Dr. Vermilyea, of Hartford, Conn.

The pastors of this church, in the order of their pastorates, have been Revs. Lyman Huntington, Lyman P. Judson, Reuben H. Conklin, P. H. Myers, Corban Kidder, N. T. Yeomans, Zachary Eddy, John Vincent, Edwin E. Williams and H. F. Dudley.

F. C D. McKay was the first superintendent of the Sunday-school, and held the position about four years. Charles J. Judd, one year; Lloyd A. Hayward, one year; Seth M. Gates, fourteen years, till 1864; then Simeon D. Lewis, till 1877; since which the present superintendent, L. H. Humphrey, jr., has held the position.

The deacons have been Ezra Walker, Peter Young, Hanover Bradley, Charles J. Judd, Lloyd A. Hayward, Stephen Hurd, Edward O. Shattuck, John Matthews, Elisha S. Hillman, H. A. Metcalf, Humphrey W. Snow, Lewis Martin and James Hurd.

The present number of members is 298.

ST. MICHAEL'S CHURCH (CATHOLIC).

This was during many years a station, and afterward a mission. No records were kept, and the few facts concerning it given are drawn from memory. Perfect accuracy cannot be vouched for, therefore, though in the main the sketch is believed to be correct.

About the year 1850 Rev. Father McConnell established a station here and built a church. He was succeeded by a priest whose name cannot be recalled, and he by Rev. F. Cook, who remained in charge about eight years. Mr. Cook was succeeded by Rev. T. Fitzpatrick, the first resident pastor, who was in charge about four years. March 19th, 1874, Rev. M. O'Dwyer, the present pastor, was placed in charge by Bishop Ryan, of the diocese of Buffalo.

The building erected by Father McConnell was not of sufficient capacity to meet the growing wants of the congregation, and Rev. Mr. Fitzpatrick enlarged it to about double its former capacity.

A parsonage was purchased about 1870. At the time Father O'Dwyer came there were many debts, and the real estate was heavily encumbered. This burden of indebtedness has become lighter, and the prospect is brighter than ever before.

A tract of about five acres has been purchased for a cemetery, but it has not yet been consecrated.

LODGE HISTORIES.

MASONIC.

Olive Branch Lodge, F. & A. M.—In October, 1813, John W. Brownson, Almon Stevens, Chauncey L. Sheldon, Zerah Tanner, Samuel Hough, William Knapp, jr., Daniel White, Gurdin Miller, Alanson Curtiss, Adial Sherwood, Ebenezer Turril, Salmon Preston, Seth Porter, Russell Noble, Gideon Jenkins, M. Evans Chester, James Ganson, Jacob Cook, Nathaniel Beecher and Aaron Wing petitioned the grand lodge for a dispensation or warrant for a lodge, to be located in the town of Warsaw, Genesee county, to be called Olive Branch Lodge, which petition was recommended by West Star Lodge, No. 205, at Sheldon.

De Witt Clinton, then grand master, on March 15th, 1814, granted them a dispensation for eighteen months, naming Samuel Hough as master, Zerah Tanner as senior warden, and Chauncey L. Sheldon as junior warden. On the 9th day of June, 1815, a warrant was granted by the grand lodge to the said Olive Branch Lodge, numbered 244. This warrant was surrendered to the grand lodge in 1819; but afterward, on the petition of Samuel Hough, Daniel Knapp, James Webster, Jonas Cutting, Zerah Tanner, Nathan P. Lee, Calvin Rumsey and Chauncey L. Sheldon, recommended by West Star Lodge, No. 205, was restored by the grand lodge December 24th, 1823, with Daniel Knapp as master, Jonas Cutting as senior warden, and Calvin Rumsey as junior warden. The average membership was about 20. For a considerable length of time after the lodge commenced business it was retarded in its labors from the want of a convenient place at which to hold its meetings. During the summer of 1826 the lodge, in connection with Western Luminary Chapter, No. 89, procured a suitable hall, but soon after it ceased to exist.

Warsaw Lodge, No. 549, was constituted by a dispensation granted on the petition of Jabez Warren, N. A. Stedman, John A. Hubbell, John Ransom, Guy P. Morgan, D. L. Cook. William Webster, jr., Norman J. Perry, John Windsor, Hopkins Salisbury, W. Ely, Charles W. Fuller, Mason Hatfield, William E. Murray, John P. Randall, Wallace Wolcott, Chester Wolcott, Jasper Keeny, Charles A. Dake, M. E. Jenkins, Alphonso Brown, A. J. Wheeler, William Lewis, Calvin Ely and A. R. Torrey in the spring of 1864. The charter bore date June 21st of the same year. The first principal officers were John Ransom, W. M.; W. R. Stedman, S. W.; and John A. Hubbell, J. W. The office of W. M. has since been held by Gideon H. Jenkins, Delos A. Crippen, C. L. Fuller, Milan Baker, Asa A. Luther, W. J. Service, D. A. Crippen and John Hannigan, the present master. The other present officers are M. R. Quackenbush, S. W.; A. A. Andrews, J. W.; George Lemon, treasurer; and B. Munger, secretary.

BAXTER
UNIVERSITY OF MUSIC.

This is a full educational institution in every department of musical learning—voice and instrument—from simplest beginnings to finished musician.

Regular school formulæ, graded courses of study, daily instructions, and all instruments for practice in its own buildings.

Its educational plan recognizes music as a form of language addressed to all, and places it in the plain light of common sense, that all may understand.

Yours truly
James Baxter

SCHOLASTIC
MUSICAL GRADUATION.

There are four of these courses, qualifying the learner in reading, writing and rendering musical sense, thought and idea in the music of the church, the parlor, the orchestra and the band respectively.

There are also schools of special virtuosity in the rendition of classic and other elaborate works in solo performance.

With comprehensive understanding of the situation, and soliciting investigation, the institution is confidently offered as the most perfect organization of musical learning ever opened to public opportunity.

JAMES BAXTER, *Pres't.*

Residence of JAMES BAXTER, *BAXTER UNIVERSITY of MUSIC, Founded 1853.*

FRIENDSHIP, N. Y.

Augustus Frank

GRAND ARMY OF THE REPUBLIC.

Gibbs Post, No. 130, G. A. R., was instituted July 29th, 1871, under a charter granted July 24th. 1871.

The charter members were fourteen in number.

The first officers chosen were A. B. Lawrence, commander; A. A. Luther, senior vice-commander; J. A. Stowe, junior vice-commander; Wilson Agar, quartermaster; E. M. Jennings, adjutant; J. K. Smith, surgeon; Rev. C. M. Booth, chaplain; W. D. Martin, sergeant major; A. W. Hough, officer of the day; G. D. Lawrence, officer of the guard.

It was named Gibbs Post in honor of Colonel Gibbs, of the 1st Dragoons. Since its organization it has had seventy-seven members, of whom forty are now members in good standing. One comrade, Jacob K. Smith, has died. The commanders since its organization have been A. B. Lawrence, Asa A. Luther, J. K. Smith and E. M. Jennings. The present officers are E. M. Jennings, commander; Robert Barnett, senior vice-commander; Norton C. Bradish, junior vice-commander; George W. Bradley, quartermaster; John Duggan, adjutant; John Barry, surgeon; Luther E. Spencer, chaplain; A. C. Manson, sergeant major; Charles Holley, quartermaster sergeant; Mills Merchant, officer of the day; —— Brewer, officer of the guard.

UNITED WORKMEN.

Oatka Lodge, No. 110, A. O. U. W. was instituted October 5th, 1877, with twenty-two charter members.

The first officers were: P. M. W., John B. Matthews; M. W., Charles H. Agar; F., Jacob K. Smith; O., Albert A. Andrews; R., George W. Cadman; F., William W. Smallwood; Rc., Frank Bingham; Guide, Humphrey D. Snow; I. W., Charles H. Crocker; O. W., Francis Rebbetoy. One death has occurred among the members of this lodge, that of Dr. Jacob K. Smith, who was drowned April 10th, 1879. The benefit of $2,000 was paid to his daughter, Anna L. Smith.

The present officers are: M. W., Horace A. Metcalf; F., George D. Ellis; O., William H. Luce; R., George W. Cadman; F., William D. Martin; Rc., Charles H. Agar; Guide, Albert A. Andrews; I. W., Ashley McCulloch; O. W., Humphrey D. Snow. The present membership is fifty-one.

BIOGRAPHICAL.

DR. AUGUSTUS FRANK was born January 12th, 1792, in Canaan, Litchfield county, Conn. His father, Andrew Frank, was of German birth, having come to America with his widowed mother and an older sister in 1756, when seven years of age. The family had for generations in Germany been distinguished for learning and philanthrophy, and the name was connectod with eminent professors and men of position and influence.

The name was originally written Francke but many branches of the family have adopted the shorter method of spelling.

The aim of the mother, who sought a home and a future for her young children in the New World, was to rear them in such a manner as to make them useful oltlsens in the land of their adoption. In their young minds she instilled the principles of truth and duty, which, as they grew, developed into patriotism and devotion to the public good.

Their arrival in this country being before the formation of the Federal government, the young son grew up under the colonial rule of Connecticut, imbibing its early spirit, characterised as it was by strict morals and habits of industry. The daughter, Catharine, was married to Oliver Mildeburger, of the city of New York. The mother resided in New York city, making her home with her daughter, Mrs. Mildeburger, until her death. She was remembered by her descendants for her many strong and excellent traits of character and for her deep-toned piety. The son Andrew remained in Connecticut, becoming an agriculturist and manufacturer, which occupations were continued during his life with increasing prosperity. He married Miss Elizabeth Shipman, daughter of Nathaniel Shipman, of Norwich, Conn., a lady of line presence and sterling worth, and of a family distinguished then, as now, in that State. Their home for many years was at Canaan, where Mr. Francke died, leaving four sons and two daughters. He was a man of great firmness, decided ability and strict probity, such a character as might be expected from his ancestry and early training.

The care and guidance of the family now devolved with double responsibility upon the mother. Most faithfully did she devote herself to her trust, moulding the characters of her children in accordance with the principles of true worth, and with rare wisdom directing her sons in paths which led to upright and honorable manhood. She lived until the subject of this sketch. Dr. Augustus Frank, had arrived at years of maturity. He was the youngest of the children, and but eight years of age at the time of his father's death. The training he received from her he remembered during his whole life with gratitude and commendation. It was to her loving counsels and faithful restraints in good measure that he owed the tender conscientiousness and moral purity that early shone in his character, and made him in after years a strong support for others to lean upon. Four years after the death of the father the family removed from Canaan, Conn., to Granville, Washington county, N. Y. The older sons engaged in business and the younger members of the family continued their studies. Augustus, after completing his education, was for a time engaged as a teacher. He decided upon the profession of medicine, studied at the medical school of Dorset, Vt,, and was graduated from that institution. It was during these years that he enlisted as a volunteer in the war of 1812, between this country and Great Britain. He removed in 1814 to Victor, Ontario county, N. Y., where he commenced the practice of medicine, remaining there three years. From that place he moved to Warsaw (then in Genesee county) in 1817, and immediately formed a partnership in professional practice with Dr. Cbauncey L. Sheldon. He was the second physician residing at Warsaw, Dr. Sheldon alone preceding him. Their ride extended long distances over the surrounding country. At that time Western New York was the "far west," and Dr. Frank found the locality of his choice quite primitive in all its characteristics and surroundings, the town having been settled but fourteen years. The whole country was but sparsely populated; even Rochester was but a hamlet and Buffalo a small village. The dwellings were plain and the roads new and rough. There were very few school buildings or church edifices. It is said that the first church building in the State west of the Genesee river was built at Warsaw in the year 1817, in which enterprise Dr. Frank took a deep and active interest. Although but twenty-five years of age when he made Warsaw his home, he immediately engaged in everything that could further the moral intellectual and material interests of the community, and no one was more active and efficient than he in the building up of the place; none more forward in promoting social order, religious privileges and the education of the young. This beautiful and fertile region was already filling up with substantial families, principally from New England, Throughout the whole region his decided character, skill and worth soon secured him a large practice and the warmest friendship of the best people, with whom he continued in the kindest relations during his whole life.

Soon after the formation of the professional partnership between Doctors Sheldon and Frank they engaged also in the mercantile business. There were few stores in the country adjacent, and the firm became widely known as merchants. The chief supervision of the trade department devolved upon Dr. Frank. In 1822 the firm dissolved. Dr. Frank engaged alone in mercantile and kindred transactions, gradually discontinuing his practice as a physician. As such, however, his skill was always valued, and he was frequently called in consultation. From that time on he became eminently a man of business. He purchased lots on the west side of Main street, and erected his store and dwelling. The whole purchase of several hundred feet on Main street was made for fifty dollars, its present value being estimated by thousands. His trade grew and became profitable, extending over several of the adjoining counties. In addition he erected flouring mills, woolen factories, iron foundries and other manufacturing or mechanical establishments. He purchased village lots, and erected on them buildings for trade, manufacturing or dwelling purposes, either for sale or rent. Probably so large an amount of village property passed through the hands of no other citizen. No one employed so many men or did so much to build up the business and increase the population of the town. He was also a partner with others in trade and manufacturing in other towns. He was thorough, systematic and practical in his business operations, an honest dealer, and with all his numerous and large transactions, was never accused of wronging any man. He continued in trade until his death, always maintaining the character of an honorable merchant. His labors and responsibilites were divided with his numerous partners and persons in his employ.

While not a politician in the ordinary sense of that term he was an active member of the party with which he was connected. He was identified with the Whig party from its organization, except as he supported the Free Soil candidate in 1848. He was appointed by his political and personal friend, Governor Seward, associate judge of Wyoming county, which position he held until the office was abolished by the constitution of 1848. In the erection of the county of Wyoming he rendered efficient aid, spending considerable time with others at Albany to effect the division of Genesee and the organization of the new county.

He was much interested in agriculture, owning and cultivating several farms. He assisted in organizing the county agricultural society, and was one of its officers. All matters pertaining to the public good found him ever ready with support and encouragement, and he was foremost among the public spirited men of that time.

Dr. Frank acting, as he always did, from convictions of duty, was an early and efficient opponent of American slavery. Perceiving the cruelty and injustice of the system, without hesitation he took a decided stand against it. This required personal sacrifice that few were prepared to make and the extent of which very few can now appreciate Slavery was so interwoven with political, social, religious, educational and business interests and institutions, and was so thoroughly intrenched, that most people hesitated to avow their opposition to it.

Dr. Frank, in this matter, as in all others, spoke as he thought. To him and those who acted with him millions of freemen are indebted for the liberty they now enjoy. While he was always decided in the expression of his opinion he was able to enforce them by clear and cogent reasons.

The American Anti-Slavery Society was formed in 1833, and was followed immediately by State, county and town societies. The Warsaw Anti Slavery Society was formed the same or the following year. Dr. Frank took part in its organization and subsequent operations.

The first annual meeting of the State Society was held in Utica in 1835. By a mob instigated by leading citizens, and embracing some of them, the meeting was dispersed, and the delegates were compelled to flee to a neighboring county to transact their business. To that meeting the town of Warsaw sent Dr. Frank as one of its delegates.

The first annual meeting of the Genesee County Anti-Slavery Society, held at Batavia March 16th, 1836, was treated in a similar manner. Dr. Frank was also a delegate to this convention. The meeting at Batavia adjourned to meet at Warsaw March 23d, 1836. There a series of resolutions and an address were adopted, together with a "Declaration of Sentiments," expressing. In brief form, the principles of the abolitionists, for the information of any who might never have seen a statement of them. Measures were also taken for establishing a free press, and $1,000 were pledged for its support the first year. Dr. Frank aided largely in furnishing the funds.

In all these labors he took an earnest interest, sparing neither time nor money. His influence during these and subsequent years helped to give the Whig party in western New York its anti-slavery character.

Dr. Frank was among the first to see the necessity of vigorous efforts for the suppression of intemperance. Drinking customs and usages were fearfully prevalent. In this, as in other matters, he took counsel of his sense of duty, and became an uncompromising advocate of temperance. From nature and necessity he was a leader. He spared neither time nor money to forward the great reform. He aided in the formation of the early temperance societies in his town, county and State, and was an active member and supporter of each. Few at the present day know how muoh hard work was done by the early temperance men. His efforts and labors in the cause were unremitting to the last, and he contributed largely to its advancement, not only in his own town and county, but over the whole State.

Education had no firmer friend. His vigorous common sense and clear discrimination led him to see that knowledge is power; and especially did he perceive that self-knowledge, acquaintance with the human organism, is indispensible to its development and efficiency.

From his first residence in Warsaw, N. Y., he was untiring in his efforts to promote popular education. He counselled and encouraged teachers, assisted and organised sohools and cheerfully paid his proportion and more than his proportion for their support. His efforts and contributions were not confined to his immediate locality.

Dr. Frank's religious character and principles were known and respected by everyone. Descended from pious ancestors he early learned to revere the doctrines and institutions of religion. Enjoying the benefit of Christian training and instruction he led an exemplary life; and in 1827 publicly made profession of his faith, uniting with the Presbyterian church at Warsaw. He was well grounded in his beliefs. Like all efficient men he had strong convictions and was always true to them. He never made his religious duties matter of convenience, but faithfully performed them at whatever cost. He took delight in the services of religion, and they became increasingly important in his esteem. He attended to the instruction of his household. The morning and evening knew their appointed services.

He possessed a vigorous mind, and was firm alike in his principles and his purposes. He pursued an object with unwearied assiduity until it was attained or its attalnment was found impracticable. Although not indifferent to the good opinion of others, his conduct was uninfluenced by desire for popular applause. In public as well as private discussion he spoke his sentiments frankly and fearlessly, and although they often conflicted with those of the majority he ever retained the respect of those with whom he differed.

Though a member of the Presbyterian church, which shared in large measure his fostering care, his charities were not circumscribed by its interest. He contributed liberally by personal effort and pecuniary means to the support of religious and benevolent institutions in general.

Dr. Frank was a man of commanding presence, medium height, weighing over two hundred pounds, dark hair and eyes, erect figure, dignified in manner, combining gravity and cheerfulness.

DR. AUGUSTUS FRANK was married to Miss Jerusha H. Baldwin, of Dorset, Vt., September 12th, 1816. She was a lady of refinement, gentleness and force of character, who, although physically delicate, with a brave heart shared with her husband the first years of pioneer life. They had three children—two sons who died young, and one daughter, Henriette, who survived the mother.

Henriette was born September 12th, 1817. She received her education at Ingham University, Le Roy. She married Edward A. McKay, a lawyer, and connected for many years before his death with the National Bank Department at Washington, D. C. Mrs. McKay died at Warsaw in 1877. Three children survive them.

Dr. Frank was married the second time to Miss Jane Patterson, of Londonderry, N. H., August 25th, 1825. She was the youngest daughter of Deacon Thomas Patterson, and was born August 30th, 1795.

Mrs. Frank was a lady of superior mental gifts, and attractive graces of person and heart. In early life she was surrounded in her cultivated Christian home and society by those influences and associations which tend to refine and ennoble character, and by which she was prepared for the wider sphere she was afterward called to fill.

Before her marriage Mrs. Frank was a very successful and acceptable teacher; and when called in the providence of God to preside over a home of her own and lead in many social and Christian activities, her fine mind and noble heart appeared to great advantage.

Though not one of those usually termed "old settlers," Mrs. Frank was an early inhabitant of Warsaw. It was during her sojourn with her brother, Hon. William Patterson, in this town, that she was married to Dr. Augustus Frank. From that time until her death, on the 19th of February, 1867, she resided in the village of Warsaw. Here the greater part of her useful, beautiful and happy life was spent, and it is believed that among the great number who during this long period made her acquaintance there are none who do not delight to cherish her memory.

For more than forty years she was a valued member of the Presbyterian church, and her constant aim was to glorify her Saviour and show by her daily life not only the reality but the beauty of the religion she professed. She was a safe and wise counselor, and her sweet influence was acknowledged in every circle in which she moved. She dispensed her hospitality with a genuine cordiality that will not be forgotten by those who shared it. Possessing a highly social nature, and a mild and cheerful temper, her presence was welcome by persons of all ages and condition. No class was forgotten; the poor widow, the sick, the aged were all remembered, not only by a kind word, but by many a generous gift so delicately bestowed that none could tell which was the happier, the giver or the receiver. She sought opportunities to do good. No trait in her character was more conspicuous than her large hearted benevolence.

In appearance Mrs. Frank was tall and well proportioned, possessing a pleasing countenance, easy manners and an attractive presence. She died in the midst of her usefulness. Her death made a great void in the church and community.

Augustus was born July 17th, 1826. He has always resided at Warsaw. His early life was spent in mercantile pursuits, but for many years past he has been engaged in the business of banking. He married Agnes, daughter of the late William W. McNair, of Groveland, Livingston county, N. Y. Their only son died in August, 1871. They have one daughter, Mary L. (See sketch).

Elizabeth W. married Rev. Joseph B. Nassau, D. D., pastor of the Presbyterian church at Warsaw during the past twenty-five years. They have two children. (See sketch.)

George W. Frank was born November 29th, 1830. He early became actively engaged in mercantile pursuits as a member of the firm of A. & G. W. Frank. The business was carried on extensively for several years, and the firm became widely known throughout the western part of the State as successful and prosperous merchants. Mr. Frank was an energetic business man and a useful and valuable citizen, taking a lively interest in everything that promoted the growth, prosperity and welfare of his town and country.

His removal from Warsaw to Iowa with his family in 1869 was regretted by everyone. In his case, as many others the west offered great inducements to the best business men of the east. He at once in that State became largely and successfully engaged in the real estate business. Shortly after he organized the banking house of George W. Frank & Darrow. They added to their business the negotiation of loans for eastern capitalists. The transactions became so numerous that millions of dollars have been loaned by them.

The care exercised in the conduct of their affairs has given them an enviable reputation through the eastern and western States for prudence and reliability.

Mr. Frank has been the means of establishing numerous villages and cities, not only in his own section, but for long distances around. He engages with untiring energy in the public enterprises in his part of the State, as well as in the adjoining State of Nebraska, that are so rapidly developing that part of the west. He aids largely in the erection of churches and school buildings, and through his generosity many churches and schools are successfully established that save for his labors would not have been erected. The business of the firm increasing so rapidly made it necessary to establish a branch office in New York city, which has been under Mr. Frank's personal supervision for the past four years. He has during the present year, 1880, returned with his family to Corning. Ia., and erected a large and beautiful residence. Mr. Frank married Phoebe T., daughter of the late William W. McNair, Esq., of Groveland, Livingston county, N. T. They have three children; the eldest, Augustus Frank 2nd, is in business.

Jennie P. married Edward K. Greene, a very prominent and influential citizen and business man of Montreal. Their residence has been at Montreal since their marriage, in 1855. They have three children,

Mary A. married Philo D. Browne, a banker of Montreal, Canada. They removed from that city to San Francisco, Cal., where Mr. Browne engaged in the same business. They have two daughters.

Dr. Augustus Frank died January 26th, 1861, aged fifty-nine years. Augustus Frank, eldest son of Dr. Augustus Frank and Mrs. Jane Patterson Frank, was born in Warsaw, N. Y., July 17th, 1826. An account of his parents and ancestry may be found in the preceding sketch.

Upon the completion of his education he took an active part in the management of the mercantile and other branches of his father's extensive business.

Upon attaining his majority, in 1847, he commenced business as a merchant for himself. By energy, persevering industry, and courtesy in the prosecution of his business he achieved unusual success, acquiring in a few years a large and prosperous trade.

While his business was pursued with assiduity he took a deep interest and active part in matters of public concern, and gave a ready support to measures designed to promote the general good. His practical knowledge of affairs brought him early into favorable notice. He was chosen to aid in the organization and management of several chartered business associations, one of which was the Buffalo & New Tork City Railway Company (now the Buffalo division of the New York, Lake Erie & Western Railway), of which he was a director and vice-president.

In political affairs he took an active part in support of the Whig party, casting his first presidential vote for General Taylor in 1848, and delivering his first public political speeches during that campaign.

He labored faithfully for the election in 1862 of the Whig candidate for the Presidency.

He early foresaw the struggle that must occur between the friends of freedom and those who supported the continuance and extension of slavery, and in 1855 was among the first to organize the Republican party. In 1866 he was chosen a delegate to the first national convention of the Republican party, held in Philadelphia, at which General Fremont was nominated for the Presidency. Returning home he engaged vigorously in the campaign, aiding in the thorough organization of the party, and by speeches in his own and other countries as well as through the press, did very much to arouse public sentiment in behalf of the principles involved.

In 1858 he received the Republican nomination for Congress, and was elected, from the district then comprising the counties of Allegany, Wyoming and Genesee, the first political office he ever held. Having, however, for many years directed his attention to questions of State and national policy, he was not unprepared for the responsible trust assigned him, and he soon attained an influential position in the House.

In 1860 he was unanimously renominated, and returned to the 37th Congress by a majority of nearly eight thousand. During the campaign of that year he devoted much of his time to the election of Mr. Lincoln, advocating it in many public addresses and in other effective ways. In 1862 he was elected to the 38th Congress, the district being then composed of the counties of Wyoming, Genesee and Niagara. He closed his third term in March, 1865.

His Congressional career was in every view an honorable one. Though never making himself prominent as a speaker, his readiness of utterance, and the candor of his statements, secured a degree of attention which many of the leaders in debate failed to receive. His propositions commended themselves to the judgment of the House, and were generally adopted.

He was in Congress previous to and during the whole period of the civil war, and while there was an earnest advocate of all measures necessary to sustain the public credit and uphold the government in its efforts to preserve the life of the nation. He gave a hearty and unwavering support to every measure for suppressing the Rebellion.

During these years he also rendered efficient aid in his own State, and particularly his district, by constant and untiring efforts to recruit the army and sustain the honor and prosperity of the government.

Although while at Washington he was deeply engrossed with matters of public importance, and his time largely occupied by Congressional duties, he never failed to look after the interests of the soldiers, whether in the tent or on the field, in hospital or prison.

They were not neglected, and everything in his power necessary for their comfort was cheerfully and promptly done. Thousands of soldiers remembered with gratitude his kindness during the years of the war.

In Congress Mr. Frank participated in all the legislation relating to the abolition of slavery in the District of Columbia and the slave States, faithfully representing the strong anti-slavery sentiments of his district.

On no question did he render more important service than in securing the passage by Congress of the constitutional amendments forever prohibiting slavery in the United States.

The efficiency of his efforts on that occasion were conceded by the press throughout the country. The New York *Tribune* pronounced the passage of this amendment the "Grandest act since the Declaration of Independence," and said, "It was an immense work that was done in securing the passage of this bill by the majority which to-day so delighted the friends of freedom and humanity, and so astounded the allies of slavery. To two Republicans in particular does the nation owe a debt of gratitude." It named one of them as Augustus Frank, of Warsaw, N. Y.

In 1867 he was nominated by a Republican State Convention and elected by the people of the State one of the thirty-two delegates-at-large to the convention for revising the Constitution of the State of New York.

In 1870 he was appointed as one of the managers of the Buffalo State Asylum for the Insane. He was subsequently reappointed to the same position in 1874, which office he still holds. His name was inserted in the original bill as one of the commissioners for the erection of the present State Capitol, but the position was declined.

He is one of the commissioners of the Auburn Theological Seminary, also a councilor of Ingham University, Le Roy; trustee of the Geneseo Academy, and a member of the Prison Association of New York.

Mr. Frank assisted in organizing the Wyoming County Mutual Insurance Co. in 1851, and was a director during its entire existence. He was one of the five who organized the Wyoming County National Bank, and was chosen one of the directors. He is a director of the Rochester and State Line Railway Company, and took a leading and efficient part in carrying forward tbe enterprise from its inception to its completion.

Mr. Frank at home takes an earnest interest in all moral questions designed to promote tbe welfare of the community. His means are freely given for all objects identified with the social and material improvements of the place of his residence. No worthy object fails to receive from him pecuniary aid. His village owes much of its beauty to his culture and liberality.

He was largely instrumental in the erection of tbe handsome brick edifice of the Presbyterian church.

He built the beautiful business block since purchased and now occupied by Mr. Glover, and also the Bank of Warsaw and other public and private buildings. He is president of the Wyoming County Bible Society, president of the Warsaw Manufacturing Company president of the Warsaw Cemetery Association, director in the Warsaw Water Works Company, and director in the Warsaw Gas Works Company.

As previously stated, Mr. Frank was for many years of his early life a merchant.

He has also for years past invested largely in real estate, mostly in the States of Iowa. Minnesota and Nebraska, which investments have proved largely profitable. In 1871 he established the Bank of Warsaw, a private banking institution, which he still continues. In all business affairs he has been eminently successful.

Mr. Frank's public addresses on various subjects have been uniformly favorably received, and many of them have been published.

Mr. Frank married Miss Agnes McNair, daughter of William W. McNair, Esq. Their only son died in 1871. They have one daughter, Mary L., living.

Charles W. Bailey is a son of Calvin P. and Sybil Bailey, natives respectively of Vermont and New Hampshire, who settled in Perry and reared a family of eight

Augustus Frank

children, of whom Charles W., born in Perry March 9th, 1820, was the third. In 1840 Mr. Bailey removed to Warsaw; in 1841 began the study of law, and was admitted in 1849 and began practice in 1872. In 1849 he was appointed postmaster, and held the office until 1853, when he resigned and returned to Perry. In December, 1855, he returned to Warsaw as county clerk, and for three years was clerk and for nine years deputy clerk. In 1872 he entered into partnership with Judge Healy, and has practiced law since. He was married June 30th, 1849, to Jane M., daughter of Almond and Tammy Stevens, of Warsaw. He has held the office of justice of the peace several years, and is a member of the board of education.

MILAN BAKER, M. D., son of Asa and Phoebe Baker, natives of New Hampshire, was born June 2lst, 1827, in West Henrietta, Monroe county, where he remained until 1850, when he began reading medicine with Drs. Tobey and Briggs, of Rochester, and in 1851 entered the Buffalo Medical College, and graduated February 21st, 1855. He soon began the practice of his profession in Caledonia, Livingston county. In the fall of 1861 he came to Warsaw, where he has since lived. He was married in Caledonia, August 5th, 1857, to Jennie A., daughter of Thomas Brown, now of Buffalo. They have two children. Mrs. Baker is a member of the First Presbyterian Church of Warsaw. Dr. Baker has been coroner one term, president of the village two years, and excise commissioner three years. He was one of the number appointed by the governor to locate the State insane asylum, which was located at Buffalo. He also served as examining surgeon for Wyoming county in the draft of 1862. Residence, 84 North Main street.

JAMES N. BARNETT, son of Robert and Sally Barnett, was born in Londonderry, N. H., November 9th, 1820, and came to Warsaw with his parents in 1824. In 1852 he bought a farm in the western part of Warsaw, and was a farmer until his death, June 8th, 1872. February 15th, 1858, he married Miss Sarah, daughter of Edwin and Hannah Painter, of Warsaw, who bore him two children—Sarah R., who died September 30th, 1871, aged eighteen, and Edwin Painter, born March 26th, 1857, who lives with his mother in Warsaw village.

FREDERICK F. BARTLETT was born May 9th, 1854, in Warsaw. He is a law student with R. R. Farman 2nd, and has charge of the rental of buildings.

J. SPENCER BARTLETT, son of Alanson and Maria Bartlett, natives of New Hampshire, was born February 9th, 1828, in the house where he now lives in Warsaw village. He is a cabinet-maker, as was his father before him. He was married August 23d, 1859, to Mary, daughter of Orange and Mercy Hitchcock, of Arcade, by whom he has had five children, two of whom, Charles A. and Lynn E., are living. Mr. and Mrs. Bartlett are members of the Baptist church of Warsaw.

MYRON E. BARTLETT is a son of William and Elmlna Bartlett, natives respectively of New Hampshire and Vermont, who came to Wyoming county in 1820 and settled in Orangeville, and in 1846 removed to Warsaw. They had a family of eight children, of whom Myron E. (born in Orangeville May 7th, 1831) was the fourth. At twenty-one he began to study law with L. W. Smith, and attended school until 1858, when he went to Ohio, and remained there until 1857. Returning to Warsaw he resumed his law studies with Thayer A Smith, and was admitted to the bar in May, 1860. He practiced his profession until October, 1862, when he enlisted as first lieutenant in Company D, 136th N. Y. volunteers, and served until discharged, when he returned to Warsaw. He was married November 23d, 1858, to Cordelia E., daughter of Harvey and Polly McFarlin, of Twinsburgb, O. They have four children. Mr. Bartlett has held the office of justice of the peace.

S. Bonaparte Bartlett, brother of Myron E. Bartlett, was born April 1st, 1849. He began studying law in 1867, and was admitted to the bar in February, 1873. He began to practice in Warsaw. April 1st, 1876, the firm of Bartlett & Farman was formed, and existed one year. In July, 1877, Mr. Bartlett entered into partnership with I. Sam Johnson. He was married August 4th, 1875, to Cora J., daughter of Elijah and Betsey T. Chamberlin, of Warsaw. They have one child, a son named William McKay Bartlett.

Samuel N. Bassett, son of Dan C. and Abigail Bassett, was born in Dayton, Cattaraugus county, January 18th, 1829. In 1861 he came to Warsaw with Lauman Rockafellow & Moor, contractors on the Buffalo & New York City Railroad, and assisted in building that road from Attica to Hornellsville. He was with this company when the first train went over the roads August 26th, 1862. In January, 1867, he went to Illinois, where he had charge of the track of the Illinois Central Railroad from Warren to Dunleith. In 1868 he again had charge of the track of the Erie Railroad; in 1878 he became road master of the New York & Oswego Midland Railroad, and held the position till the spring of 1879. Since then he has been engaged in building a railroad out of Chicago. Mr. Bassett was married August 26th, 1858, to Melissa J. Gay, daughter of Daniel and Betsey Gay, of Warsaw. They have three children. Mr. Bassett has always been a working member of the Democratic party. Mrs. Bassett and her daughter are members of the Presbyterian church.

Andrew J. Beardslee, son of Augustus and Betsey Beardslee, was born November 18th, 1834, in Caneadea, Allegany county. He lived at home till he was twenty-one. In 1865 he bought a farm in Gainesville, and in 1866 that in Warsaw where he lives. He was married November 14th, 1869, to Maria Smith, daughter of Hiram and Polly Smith, of Gainesville. They have had three children, one of whom, Ella B., is living.

Daniel B. Beck, son of John M. and Abigail Beck, was born at Lyme, New London county, Conn., May 23d, 1807. In 1828 he emigrated to East Bethany, Genesee county. In 1844 he came to Middlebury, and in 1859 bought the place in Warsaw where he lives. He was married August 29th, 1839, to Elizabeth Odiorne, daughter of William and Lucinda Odiorne. Her parents were among the first settlers in their locality. By this marriage there were eleven children, ten of whom are living. Mrs. Beck died December 4th, 1861, aged fifty-one. July 31st, 1862, Mr. Beck married Emeline Martin, daughter of David and Elizabeth Martin, of Middlebury. They have one child. Two of Mr. Beck's children, John F. and Anna E., live at home. Mr. and Mrs. Beck are members of the Presbyterian church.

Benjamin Bishop, son of Enos and Mary Bishop, was born November 25th, 1806, at Lancaster, Coos county, N. H. In 1817 he moved with his uncle to Ithaca, Tompkins county; in 1819 to Tioga county, and in 1824 to Warsaw, settling about two and a half miles west of the village. In 1826 he worked for his uncle. In 1826 he taught school in the winter and worked on a farm in the summer, and continued so doing for three years. In 1831 he bought a small farm half a mile south of the Evangelical church, which he sold in 1841 and bought sixty acres on the Buffalo road. In 1866 he bought one hundred and seventeen acres west of the Erie depot, where he lives. In 1841 he was school commissioner. He has also been assessor and justice of the peace. He was married in 1829 to Lydia Wakefield, of Warsaw, by whom he had eleven children, seven of whom are living. Mrs. Bishop died September 10th, 1878, aged sixty-nine. Two of Mr. Bishop's sons were in the army during the late war and one of them was killed at the battle of Cold Harbor.

WILLIAM BINGHAM was born in Lempster, N. H., August 7th, 1799, and died in Warsaw, June 25th, 1869. His first wife was Elizabeth Roe, and his second Betsey Knapp, who survives him. He came to Warsaw from Livingston county, in 1830. In 1838–39 he removed to Buffalo and opened the Commercial Hotel, then a leading house in that city. In 1845 he removed to Portage; thence to Pike and Dansville, returning to Warsaw in 1850, where he opened the Bingham House and kept it until he retired from business, January 1st, 1866, having served the public successively for thirty-six years, with the best reputation for honorable dealing. He was collector of the town of Warsaw in 1832; treasurer of this county in 1842 and 1843, and deputy marshal from 1856 to 1861. He was commissioned second lieutenant in the 7th regiment 4th brigade of artillery in 1826, and colonel of the same regiment in 1831. Colonel Bingham had by his first wife two children—Mortimer, who died in infancy, and Matilda M., who married Daniel A. Knapp and died September 2nd, 1864. His children by his second wife are William M., Lucien W., Huldah, who married Colonel James O. McClure, and Maryette, all of whom are living.

MARTIN W. BRADISH was born in Monroe, Mich., November 23d, 1821. He removed to Monroe county, and from there, in 1858, to Warsaw. He was a farmer until 1862, when he enlisted, August 11th, in Company D, 130th N. Y. volunteers, and served until discharged in 1863. He is now a lumber salesman. October 15th, 1843, he married Mary, daughter of Daniel and Maria Shattuck, of Monroe, Mich., who has borne him three children.

JACOB J. BRINNINSTOOL is a son of Orrin D. and Anna Brinninstool, of Monroe county. Mrs. Brinninstool moved to Michigan about 1870. Orrin D. Brinninstool's family consisted of two children, the first being Jaoob J. Brinninstool, who was born December 4th, 1840, in Brighton, Monroe county. When eighteen years old he began business life as a dry goods clerk in Batavia, remaining there four years. In 1868 he came to Warsaw and, with A. W. Palmer, opened a grocery store. In "the second fire," five years later, the establishment was burned, and Mr. Palmer went west and is engaged in the wholesale business. Mr. Brinninstool then opened and conducted a store four years, when J. Frank McElwain became his partner and continued so until Mr. Brinninstool purchased his interest in the business, six years later. Mr. McElwain went west and Mr. Brinninstool is sole proprietor of tbe store at 25 Main street. Mr. Brinninstool was married December 12th, 1865, to Mrs. Ellen S. Scott, daughter of Isaac B. and Anna H. Blossom, of Batavia. They have had four children, three of whom are living. Arthur B. died June 1st, 1874. The others are Sidney O., Earl A. and Frank M. Mr. and Mrs. Brinnistool are members of the Baptist church.

WILLIAM BRISTOL, son of William and Martha Bristol, was born in Gainesville, N. Y., in 1821. His father was a native of this State, a soldier of 1812, and his grandfather a hero of the Revolution. With a common school education he began life for himself at the old family home in Gainesville, and to his business as a farmer he added that of wool buying, which he followed for over twenty years. A man of quick feeling, of fine address, of business ability and integrity and great energy, Mr. Bristol early became a man of mark in his town. As a business man large interests have been at different times committed to him. He has hardly been what would be called a politician, though a man with his characteristics could not well be left out of public affairs during the stormy period in which he has lived. He was born and bred a Democrat, but becoming dissatisfied with the position his party assumed in regard to certain moral questions, particularly slavery, he abandoned it, and became one of the founders of the Republican party; being a delegate to the historical "Anti-Nebraska" convention held at Saratoga in 1854, and one of the few representatives from this part of the State to the famous "Barn-Burner" convention at Syracuse in 1856, which endorsed Fremont. He was supervisor of his town in 1855, and again four years during the war; was under-sheriff of the county in 1842, presidential elector and secretary of the electoral college in 1864, member of Assembly in 1867 and 1868. He contributed materially to establish and sustain Gainesville Female Seminary. As a member of the committee appointed by Governor Morgan, to promote enlistment in the 30th senatorial district Mr. Bristol did efficient service. His patriotic course, his careful zeal and his expenditure of time and money in those years, made him a central figure in the local history of the town during the war period. A considerable portion of his large income was devoted to this work, and by and through his efforts, sustained by the loyal sentiment of his townsmen, Gainesville filled every quota promptly, and came out of the war without debt. A director of the Rochester and State Line Railway Company from its organization, no one in Wyoming county has a larger share in the responsibility of the location of its line than Mr. Bristol. He moved to Warsaw in 1868, where he has since resided. He married Adella M. Lockwood January 12th, 1843, and had three children: Laura L., who married Major John P. Robinson; Belle, who married M. A. Kurtz, and Caroline, who married Nathan S. Beardslee. Mrs. Bristol died in 1855, and he married Martha J. Jewett in 1857, by whom he has three children, William, Millie J. and Henry R.

JOHN BROWN, whose father bore the same name, was born in Gainesville, May 10th, 1830. Until he was twenty-one he "worked out" summers and lived at home and attended school winters. After he became of age he worked several different farms on shares and was also an extensive stock buyer. In 1856 he went to Wisconsin, where he remained a year and a half, returning in 1858 to Gainesville, where, in 1859, he bought a farm. During the war he bought horses for government use. In 1867 he bought the Jewett farm in Warsaw, on which he lives. He was married June 28th, 1857, to Betsey Norton, daughter of Edward and Lucinda Norton, of Gainesville, by whom he had three children, one of whom is living. The house in which Mr. Brown lives was built nearly seventy years ago, and was one of the first frame houses erected in this section.

JOSEPH C. BUXTON, son of Timothy and Julia Buxton, was born May 10th, 1850, in Warsaw, and has been a life-long resident there. April 10th, 1863, he entered the hardware store of Morris & Lewis, and remained in the capacity of clerk for seven years. He was in the coal trade from that time until 1878, when he became the local agent of the State Line Railroad Company, and still holds the position. He was married December 16th, 1874, to Alice F., daughter of Mr. Gould, of Warsaw. Mr. and Mrs. Buxton have two children.

GEORGE S. CAPWELL, son of Peter and Olive Capwell, was born November 14th, 1815, in MIddlebury. He received a common school education, and was a man of strong and active mind, and showed great energy in all his undertakings. About 1838 he went into the dry goods trade at Wyoming, and remained in that business about twelve years. He then went to New York, and was employed in the custom house twelve years, after which he lived six years in Michigan, returning to Warsaw in 1872. He was married September 12th, 1837, to Phelina, daughter of Joseph and Betsy Weels, of Darien. By that marriage there were three children, only one of whom, Frank W. Capwell, is living. Mr. Capwell was a lifelong supporter of the Democratic party. He died September 17th, 1876, while in Michigan, and his remains were brought to Warsaw for burial.

MARTIN D. CHACE is a son ef George B. and Loretta Chace, natives of Saratoga county, who settled about 1824 near the head of the lake, in the town of Castile. Their family consisted of ten children, eight of whom are living, and of whom Martin D. Chace, born September 12th, 1836, was the oldest son. George B. Chace died in 1858. His widow lives on the old homestead. Martin D. Chace remained at home until April, 1869; then came to Warsaw and bought the Premium Custom and Flouring Mills, which he still owns and manages. He was married November 25th, 1859, to Mary A., daughter of Thomas and Sarah Durfee, of MIddlebury. They have had seven children, four of whom are living.

THOMAS CHASE, son of Stephen and Lois Chase, was born in New Hampshire, in 1784. In 1817 he came to Warsaw with his father and brother, settling on a partly improved farm in the northwest part of the town. He married Rhoda Smith, of New Hampshire, by whom he had five children, three of whom are living. Mr. Chase died in 1858, aged seventy-five. Mrs. Chase died in 1850, aged sixty-six. John S. Chase, their son, was born in New Hampshire, June 9th, 1815, and came to Warsaw with his parents; in 1842–52 he worked by the month and managed farms on shares in Middlebury, Warsaw and Castile. In 1852 he bought the farm in Warsawwhere he lives. He was married January 9th, 1840, to Bathsheba Marsh, of Covington, who died February 3d, 1842. In September, 1843, Mr. Chase married Mrs. Marsh, widow of the late Jonathan Marsh, of Middlebury, who died November 30th, 1859. September 6th, 1860, Mr. Chase married Mrs. Alvina Smead, widow of the late George Smead, of Bethany, N. Y. By his second marriage there were two children, one of whom, D. M., born in Castile, November 14th, 1846, is living. He married Minnie Grosbeck, of Groveland, by whom he has one child, John A., born June 10th, 1878.

DELOSS A. CRIPPEN is a son of Alva and Mary Crippen, natives of Columbia county. The family consisted of nine children, of whom Deloss A. was the fourth born (June 26th, 1828). He is a native of Columbia county. At the age of twenty-two he went to Monroe county, and learned the trade of a carriage-ironer and blacksmith. He then went to Cowlesville, and worked about a year; thence to Attica; in 1853 to Knowlesville, where he opened a carriage shop. In 1867 he came to Warsaw and formed a partnership with F. H. Buxton, which continued two years. At its expiration C. P. Williams and Mr. Crippen formed a partnership, which continued five years. January 1st, 1876, Mr. Crippen opened his present shop, of which he is sole proprietor. He was married July 31st, 1855, to Miss M. Adelia, daughter of John E. and Abigail Smith, of Attica. They have three children—Frank, May and Ina. Mr. and Mrs. Crippen are members of the Congregational church. Mr. Crippen has held the offices of town auditor, assessor (one term), and village trustee (three years).

SPENCER CRONKHITE is a son of Tunis and Caroline Cronkhlte. He was born in MIddlebury, February 3d, 1833, and except eleven years spent in Chautauqua county has lived in Wyoming county. In 1851 he moved to the town of Warsaw and bought land, and followed the occupation of farmer until 1857, when he moved to Warsaw village and was an engineer until 1861, when he enlisted in Company A, 9th N. Y. cavalry, and served until discharged, October 27th, 1864. He was wounded at the battle of Beverly Ford, June 9th, 1863, and confined in the hospital until December. January 24th, 1865, he married Ruth A., daughter of Daniel and Susan Pierce, of Reboboth, Mass., by whom he had two children—Federick P. and Grace. He is superintendent of the Warsaw Citizens' Gaslight Company, and a stockholder in the same.

EDGAR A. DAY, son of Abner O. and Almira Day, who came to Wyoming county in 1834, was born in Gainesville, June 10th, 1842. August 6th, 1862, he enlisted in Company A., 130th N. Y. volunteers. He was afterward transferred to a cavalry regiment, and served three years. He was the fourth child born of his father's family, and was by occupation a farmer until 1878, when he was elected sheriff of Wyoming county. He removed to Warsaw in January, 1879. He was married June 4th, 1868, to Eliza P., daughter of Wheeler and Sarah Bishop, of Genesee Falls. They have one child, Satie F. Mr. Day held the office of highway commissioner eight years in Gainesville.

WILLIAM H. DEXTER, son of Rev. R. H. and Mary J. Dexter, was born March 4th, 1858, at Corfu, Genesee county. In 1868 he came to Wyoming village with his parents. In 1874 he entered the University at Rochester, and graduated from there in 1878. In September, 1878, he came to Warsaw as assistant in the academic department of the union school. He was married April 2nd, 1876, to Miss Kitty Cuningham, daughter of Mrs. Mary Mathers, of Rochester. By this marriage they have one child, Mary E., born August 22nd, 1877. Mr. and Mrs. Dexter are members of the Presbyterian church.

ORACE W. EMERY is a son of Jonathan and Abigail Emery, natives of Vermont, who came to Wyoming county in 1818 and settled in Pike, where Orace W. was born April 8th, 1834. Until April 3d, 1867, he remained in Pike. In 1862 he began reading law, and continued two years, during which time he was acting justice of the peace. Previous to this and from the age of nineteen he taught school winters till 1867, when he came to Warsaw and was in the employ of T. S. Grover until February 27th, 1878, when the firm of T. S. Grover & Co. was formed, Mr. Emery being one of the partners. He was married September 3d, 1869, to Kate, daughter of James Kellogg, of Pike. They have two children.

EDWARD B. EVERINGHAM is a son of John Everingham, who was born in England, April 2nd, 1828, and came to America in 1832, and who since 1876 has been a member of the Warsaw Furnace Company. The former was born in Warsaw, November 1st, 1858, and has been a life-long resident of that place. He is in the employ of the Warsaw Furnace Company. He was married December 31st, 1878, to Fannie P., daughter of Luther and Calista Foster, of Warsaw.

REV. J. B. EWELL, son of Henry B. Ewell, the oldest Baptist pastor in the State (having held one pulpit forty-one years), was born in Genesee county, March 29th, 1853. He is a graduate of Cornell University, Ithaca, and completed his studies in Rochester. He came to Warsaw in 1877, and began his labors with the Baptist church as its pastor. He was married March 13th, 1878, to Florine Mallory, of Wyoming.

BENJAMIN F. FARGO, son of David and Phebe Fargo, was born in Warsaw, in 1817. In 1835 he learned the wool-carding and cloth-dressing trade in the woolen factory of Howard & Kimball, and worked for them at his trade four years. In 1839 he went to Springville, Erie county, and engaged in the same business, forming a partnership with

Mr. E. W. Cook, under the firm name of E. W. Cook & Co., and remained there ten years. In the fall of 1848 he returned to Warsaw and engaged in thé dry goods trade with his brother, under the firm name of F. F. Fargo & Co. The style of the firm was changed in 1851 to B. F. Fargo & Co. He continued in this business until 1857, when he engaged in the produce trade and continued in it four years. In 1870 he built on Main street what is known as the Fargo block, in which is the store he now occupies. In 1876 he opened a grocery store, and has since been engaged in that line of business. Mr. Fargo is an active worker in the Republican party, and has held the office of town clerk six years. He is secretary and treasurer of the Warsaw Citizens' Gaslight Company, and of the Warsaw Water Works Company. In 1841 Mr. Fargo married Marian Bloomfield, of Springville, Erie county, by whom he had three children, two of whom are living. Mrs. Fargo died in 1857. In 1879 Mr. Fargo married Mrs. Calista Blowers, of Warsaw.

Palmer Fargo, son of Nehemiah and Mary Fargo, was born in Connecticut, June 10th, 1796. In 1804 he came to the forest site of what is now the village of Warsaw, where his father built the first log house large enough for the accommodation of strangers, opposite to the site of the Baptist church. Here strangers always found a welcome until they were able to provide a shelter for themselves. In 1818 he took up eighty acres of unimproved land on lot 39. He cleared this place with his own hands, and lived at his original location longer than any other man in town. He was a public spirited man and was always willing to help along any interest that promised to in any way benefit his fellow man. He was a strong anti-slavery man. He was assessor and highway commissioner many years. He was married January 10th, 1818, to Caroline, daughter of Hezekiah and Amy Scovel, of Warsaw, by whom he had twelve children, seven of whom are living. Mr. Fargo died May 21st, 1878, at the age of seventy-seven; Mrs. Fargo November, 26th, 1849, aged forty-seven.

Palmer C. Fargo, son of Palmer and Caroline Fargo, was born January 31st, 1835, in the town of Warsaw, and has always lived on the home farm. He has been inspector of elections thirteen years. He was married September 16th, 1858, to Sarah M. Coburn, daughter of William and Caroline Coburn, by whom he has had two children, one of whom, Ida C., is living. Mr. and Mrs. Fargo are members of the Methodist Episcopal church of Warsaw.

Elbert Eli Farman, United States Agent and Consul-General at Cairo, Egypt, was born at New Haven, Oswego county, N. Y., April 23d, 1831. In the early part of the eighteenth century a planter named Farm an resided near Annapolis, Md. In 1765 his son, John, who had been a soldier under Wolfe at the storming of Quebec, went to the colony of New Hampshire, and settled on the Connecticut river in the township of Bath. Here he married and had eight sons, from whom are descended all persons bearing the family name of Farman tn the northern States. He died in 1782. His oldest son, Roswell, had eight children, among them a son Zadok, born in 1791. Roswell Farman removed with his family in 1805 from New Hampshire to Oneida county, N. Y. and a year later settled in the adjoining county of Oswego. Zadok Farman married Martha Dix, who was born in Wethersfield, Conn., where her family and that of her kinsman, the late General John A. Dix, long resided. They had six children, of whom the fifth is the subject of this sketch.

At the age of seventeen he left home for the residence of an older brother in Gainesville, N. Y. After teaching a district school one winter he entered Genesee Wesleyan Seminary

E. E. Farman

at Lima, N. Y., where he pursued his preparatory studies, and in July, 1851, entered Genesee College, then under the presidency of B. F. Tefft, LL. D. At the beginning of junior year he entered Amherst College, of which Edward Hitchcock, LL. D., was then president, and there took his first degree in 1855. He received the honors of an "oration" at commencement, and an election to Phi Beta Kappa. Soon after leaving college Mr. Farman married Lois Parker, of Gainesville, N. Y., a niece of the late Joel Parker, D. D., of New York city, and became a law student in the office of F. C. D. McKay, then district attorney of Wyoming county. In the Fremont campaign of 1856 he addressed fifty political meetings in Northern New York, and on the hustings developed oratorical powers which contributed to his success before juries. On his admission to the bar in 1858 he accepted Mr. McKay's offer of a partnership, and entered at once upon a desirable practice. His labors, however, were not engrossed by his profession. From 1859 to 1861 Mr. Farman and Augustus Harrington, also an alumnus of Amherst, now a lawyer at Warsaw, were the proprietors of the *Western New Yorker*, a newspaper published at Warsaw, of which Mr. Harrington was editor. As one of its publishers Mr. Farman superintended the business department of the paper, besides attending to his law practice. Under this management it quadrupled its circulation, and soon became, as it since has been, the leading Republican journal in its section of the State.

Mr. McKay removed to Iowa in 1860. During the next five years Mr. Farman devoted himself to his profession, and extended his practice until it became exceptionally lucrative and successful. Determined to enlarge his field of observation, and extend his studies beyond his opportunities, either in college or at a rural county seat, he sailed for Europe in 1865, where he spent two years in travel and study. He attended the universities of Heidelberg in summer and Berlin in winter, and heard lectures on criminal, international and civil law. He also acquired French and German. He then traveled through Italy, Holland and Switserland, and contributed to the *Western New Yorker* accounts of the lands and peoples he visited, which the New York *Observer* and the Utica *Herald* copied and commended.

January, 1868, Governor Fenton appointed him district attorney of Wyoming county to fill a vacancy. The following autumn he was nominated by the Republicans and elected for three years. At the expiration of this term he was elected for another. The fact that during the seven years of his official service no indictment drawn by him was quashed, attests his professional fidelity and careful learning.

March 27th, 1876, Mr. Farman was confirmed agent and consul-general of the United States at Cairo, Egypt, and on the 18th of April he sailed. He has since attended to his duties at Cairo, finding opportunity, however, for trips up the Nile, to Sinai, and through Palestine. In the summers of 1878 and 1879 he visited the United States, returning each year about the middle of October. The duties of his position are chiefly diplomatic. He has received the approval of the home government and also of the Americans who reside in or have visited Cairo. His personal relations with the Khedive and the members of his government have been friendly. During his absence in the autumn of 1878 an American, who then held a high position in Egypt, wrote of him in the following terms: "Every American here hopes Mr. Farman will return. He understands this country and its people. Always efficient in protecting every interest confided to his care, he has done great service to his countrymen here." The New York *Times*, August 11th, 1878, referred to Mr. Farman in flattering terms. Its correspondent at Cairo said: "It will be gratifying to all Americans to know that so competent and excellent an officer as Mr. Farman is in the service of his country." Among the negotiations successfully conducted by Mr. Farman are those for the increase of the number of American judges in the International Tribunal of Egypt, by and through which the United States were permitted to send a third judge. Mr. Farman naturally took a prominent part in the reception of General Grant at Cairo. He presented the general to the Khedive, and acted as interpreter of their speeches. He also gave a reception and state dinner on that occasion. His felicitous speech as host at the dinner was published in this country. Mr. Farman's ability to speak French is a qualification for his position at a court where that is the language of official intercourse. Few of our representatives in Egypt have been more fortunate in their conduct of state affairs than the present consul-general. Mr. Farman's official reports, published at Washington, show that he has taken an active interest in the welfare of the people of the country to which he is accredited. His conviction of the divine equality of all men in privilege drew him into the Fremont campaign and leads him to help the oppressed in Egypt. Eight slaves have been freed through his efforts. The first was a negro boy brought by a slave trader from Soudan. The slave was brutally treated, and an American lady brought him to the notice of the consul-general. He at once interested himself in the case, and in June, 1877, secured an order from the Egyptian government freeing the slave. He obtained another order freeing three slave girls. The most meager sketch would be incomplete without mention of Mr. Farman's services in securing the obelisk known as Cleopatra's Needle, which was erected in Heliopolis about sixteen centuries before Christ, and brought to Alexandria B. C. 22. The city of New York is greatly indebted to Mr. Farman for this interesting monument of one of the oldest civilizations. He has been complimented by the Secretary of State upon his success in this delicate matter. Mr. Farman's professional training is an important qualification for his present position, as the Consular Court over which he presides is the only tribunal in Egypt authorized to try an American citizen for crime committed in that country. Mirzan, an Armenian, naturalized in Boston, assassinated Daban Bey, a legal adviser of the Khedive, in Alexandria, July 17th, 1879. He was arrested by the Egyptian officers, and turned over to our authorities for punishment. He can only be tried by the U. S. Consular Court of Egypt, with the consul-general as presiding judge. This court has also jurisdiction in other cases not infrequently arising there.

Elbert E. Farman, 2nd, is a son of Charles D. and Lydia Farman, who settled in Gainesville, where he was born August 20th, 1848. He remained with his parents until he attained his majority; then went to Missouri and taught school one winter. He returned to Alexander, Genesee county, in 1870, where he was married to Sarah J., daughter of Darius N. Spring, April 6th, 1870. He worked Mr. Spring's farm until February, 1874, when he came to. Warsaw and began to read law with Judge Healy. He attended the Albany Law School, from which he graduated in May, 1875, and was admitted to the bar. Returning to Warsaw he began the practice of his profession. He was appointed justice of the peace to fill a vacancy in December, 1877; elected in February, 1878, for a short term, and in February, 1879, re-elected for a long term.

Albert P. Gage is a son of Platt and Adelaide Gage, natives of Vermont. Mrs. Gage came to Eagle in 1814, and until 1876 lived on the farm where she first located. She is now living with her son. Platt Gage died April 19th, 1860. They had a family of five children, of whom Albert P. was the fourth born (March 17th, 1838). He lived at home until August 7th, 1862, when he enlisted in Company A, 130th N. Y. volunteers, and served until discharged, March 8th, 1865. He returned to Eagle and followed farming till January, 1876, when he came to Warsaw as sheriff of Wyoming county. He is now under-sheriff. He was married April 7th, 1865, to Mary, daughter of Philip and Betsy Baker, of Eagle. They have two children—Bert and Cora Belle. He was supervisor of Eagle two years, assessor two years, and is now trustee of the village of Warsaw.

DR. EDWARD D. GARDINER, son of Charles and Malvina Gardiner, was born at Hamilton, Madison county, in 1851. He graduated at the Madison University in 1873, and eame to Warsaw in 1874 and succeeded W. C. Barrett in the practice of dentistry.

CHARLES J. GARDNER, son of Patrick R. and Janet E. Gardner, was born in Attica, May 12th, 1843, and lived there until the war, when he enlisted as a soldier, August 6th, 1862, and served under Sheridan two years and one month, when he was wounded at the battle of Newtown, in the Shenandoah valley. He was discharged April 28th, 1865, when he returned to Attica, where he remained until January 1st, 1874. When in the hospital after being wounded, and unknown to himself, Mr. Gardner was elected collector of the town of Attica. Likewise in 1865 he was appointed to take the census of the town of Attica. In 1869 he was appointed assistant assessor of internal revenue for five towns. In April, 1870, he was appointed postal clerk between Hornellsville and Attica. He held the position till 1874, when he was elected county clerk of Wyoming county. He was married July 30th, 1865, to Miss Annette R., daughter of William M. and Orinda A. Terry, of Batavia, N. Y. They have three children.

ALBERT HATCH, son of Walter M. and Sally Hatch, was born in Warsaw, April 26th, 1846. He attended the union school of Warsaw until he was twenty. Since then he has lived at home with his parents, and is at present engaged in managing his father's farm.

LYMAN HATCH, son of Walter M. and Sally Hatch, was born May 12th, 1836, in Warsaw. When a young man he lived at home and worked on his father's farm. At the age of twenty-five he became desirous of seeing something of the country, and took an extensive western trip, in which he spent about three years. In 1862 he purchased a tract of land in Kansas, which he sold in 1864. Returning to Warsaw he engaged in the produce trade, and continued in that business until 1870, when he engaged in farming where he now lives. He was married November 17th, 1870, to Susan Pierce, widow of the late Allen Pierce, of Warsaw. She died September 9th, 1869. By this marriage he has one child—Munson L., born March 27th, 1875.

WALTER HATCH, son of Walter M. and Sally Hatch, was born in Warsaw, November 16th, 1839. He lived at home and worked on his father's farm until 1864. In the fall of 1863 he bought a farm of Erastus Day just east of his father's place. He was married March 24th, 1864, to Lois Bently, daughter of Johnson and Clarinda Bently, of Orangeville. By this marriage they have three children—Eddy W., Ernest J. and Lulu B.

WALTER M. HATCH, son of William C. and Jerusha Hatch, was born August 10th, 1802, at Glastonbury, Hartford county, Conn. In February, 1814, he came to Warsaw with his parents, who bought one hundred and fifty acres of land, thirty acres of which were cleared. A log house was built on lot 55. Mr. Hatch's father came the previous year and bought two hundred and fifty acres of unimproved land just west of this farm, and returned to Connecticut in the winter for his family. After Mr. Hatch attained his majority he worked a part of his father's farm on shares. In 1887 his father deeded to him one hundred acres in lot 57, just east of where he now lives, and which forms a part of his present farm. Mr. Hatch has held the offices of commissioner of highways and assessor. He was married November 15th, 1832, to Sally Sherwin, daughter of Bissell and Experience Sherwin, of Warsaw, formerly from Vermont. They have seven children.

LLOYD A. HAYWARD, son of Aloin and Melicent P. Hayward, natives of Maine, and now residents of York, Livingston county, at the ages respectively of ninety and eighty-six, was born in Maine, December 6th, 1816, and settled in Perry in 1841. In 1838 Lloyd A. Hayward began studying law at Amherst College, Massachusetts, where he graduated, and in 1846 was admitted to the bar at Rochester, N. Y. He began the practice of his profession in Perry, and in 1858 came to Warsaw, where he has since resided. He was married October 8tb, 1844, to Mary I., daughter of Edward and Martha Dudley, of Perry. Mrs. Hayward died March 9th, 1878. His family consisted of a daughter, Melicent, the eldest, who died in 1855, and Edward D. and Mary Kate, now living. Mr. Hayward has filled the office of treasurer two terms, and for several years has held the office of president of the board of trustees for the institute for the blind at Batavia. For many years he was president of the board of education of Warsaw, and he served as president of the Wyoming County National Bank in 1869 and 1870.

JOHN HANIGAN, son of John and Elizabeth Hanigan, natives of Ireland, was born June 15th, 1840. In 1850 he came to America and located in Buffalo, where he remained six years, learning the marble cutter's trade and working at the same. He then went to Ohio and remained two years; thence to Pennsylvania, remaining one year. In 1860 he came to Warsaw and established himself as a marble dealer. He enlisted in the Wadsworth guard in 1861, and served six months. He keeps constantly on hand and makes to order American and foreign marble and granite monuments of all kinds at his establishment on Main street, Warsaw. He is overseer of the poor. He was married May 15th, 1862, to Mary, daughter of James and Elizabeth Diven, of Eagle. They have six children.

HON. BYRON HEALY, county judge, is a son of Joshua and Lucy Healy, natives of Vermont, who settled at an early period in Dansville, Steuben county, when nothing but a vast forest surrounded their home, and came to Warsaw. January 10th, 1830, Byron Healy was born, and, save the time spent in school, remained with his parents until he attained his majority. He was educated in the common schools, and spent a short time in the National Law School at Ballston Springs. Saratoga county, from which he graduated in 1853, with the degree of LL. B. He was admitted to the bar in 1852, and in the fall of 1853 began the practice of law at Arcade, where he remained until October, 1857, when he came to Warsaw and formed a partnership with H. L. Comstock, then county judge, which existed until 1866. Mr. Healy was a member of Assembly in 1863 and 1864. In the former year he was chairman of the committee on railroads and was a member of the judiciary committee. In 1864 he was chairman of the committee on insurance and a member of the ways and means committee. In the fall of 1865 he was elected district attorney and served one term. In 1867 he was elected county judge, and re-elected in 1871 and 1877. He was married April 8th, 1868, to Mary C., daughter of Timothy H. and Julia Buxton, of Warsaw. They have two children, I. May, born May 12th, 1869, and Maud, June 12th, 1873.

SMITH HIGGINS, son of Dwight and Rebecca Higgins, residents of Genesee county, was born in MIddlebury, May 7th, 1824, and except during five years lived with his parents until his marriage, April 26th, 1849, to Sarah Bump, who died February 18th, 1854. February 7th, 1858, he married Adell R., daughter of Sidney S. and Harriet Monroe, of Middlebury. He has one child by his first marriage and two by his second. He worked at his trade, that of carpenter and joiner, until 1868. He built and managed the Monroe House, near the depot, five years. In 1874 he moved to the village of Warsaw, and was connected with N. Ottinger in the clothing business over two years. He owns a farm of eighty acres and two village lots, and is identified with the general produce trade.

HORACE HOLLISTER, son of Ashbel and Mary Hollister, natives of Connecticut, was born January 10th, 1798, and came to Wyoming (then Genesee county) in 1824, locating in Warsaw village. He was the fifth-born of a family of nine children, and by trade a wagon-maker. He opened the first wagon shop in Warsaw village. In 1830 he removed to Chautauqua county, where he remained twenty-five years. In 1865 he returned to Warsaw, where he died. He was married November 24th, 1824, and September 17th, 1838, the last time to E. Caroline, daughter of Samuel McWhorter, of Chautauqua county, by whom he had six children, five of whom are living. He also had five children by the first marriage, one of whom is living. The fifth child by the second marriage, Mary B., now lives with her mother, and is a member of the Congregational church.

WILLIAM W. HOLMES (son of Thomas and Mary Holmes, natives of England, who came to America in 1851) was born in York, England, March 17th, 1829, and came to America in 1850, locating in Warsaw. He is by trade a tailor, and except five years, while employed by A. W. Frank, has been in business as a merchant tailor. He was married May 1st, 1856, to Mrs. Elizabeth E., daughter of John and Jane Coddington, of Ithaca, N. Y. They have one child, Miss Annie R. Holmes, born June 20 h, 1860. They are members of the Presbyterian church.

JOHN HOLTON, son of Joseph and Rhoda Holton, was born at Piscataway, N. J., March 10th, 1784, and learned the blacksmith's trade. He came to Attica in 1848. He was married in 1806 to Isabella Runyon, daughter of Renne and Anna Runyon, of Piscataway, N. J. By that marriage there were twelve children, five of whom are living. He died December 3d, 1860. His son, Deacon Simeon Holton, was born at Piscataway, N. J., in 1810. He moved to Le Roy in 1830, to Attica in 1842, and to Warsaw in 1843. At the age of twenty he began to work at the trade of mason and brick layer. In 1843 he had charge of the erection of the brick hotel, and in 1872 he built the union school-house. He has also superintended the erection of many other of the prominent business blocks and private residences of the village. He joined the Baptist church in 1832, and has ever since been an active member, serving as deacon twenty-five years. Mr. Holton was married June 17th, 1834, to Miss Olive Spring, daughter of Mr. A. Spring, of Le Roy, Genesee county. Mr. and Mrs. Holton have had ten children, six of whom are living.

SIMEON HOVEY was born July 6th, 1776, in Lebanon, N. H. He came to Warsaw in 1804, and settled on a farm of one hundred acres, building the third log house erected in the town. August 31st, 1800, he married Jerusha, daughter of Gad and Jerusha Lamb, of Pennsylvania. He died April 25th, 1862, aged eighty-six. His mother died in March, 1855, nearly one hundred years of age. Henry Hovey, son of Simeon and Jerusha, was born in Warsaw, September 1st, 1804, and was the first white child born in the town. In his younger days he was a school teacher, and taught fifteen schools in the county and vicinity. In 1835 he removed to the village of Warsaw, and was town school inspector in 1837–40, after which date he went back to his farm. In 1869 he returned to Warsaw, where he lives. Mr. Hovey was married October 17th, 1838, to Lydia Ann Maher, daughter of William and Zilpha Maher, of Covington, by whom he had five children, four of whom are living.

L. Hayden Humphrey, jr., is a son of Lester H. and Hannah B. Humphrey, natives of Connecticut, who were born respectively December 28th, 1799, and October 25th, 1807, and came to Wyoming county in 1818, settling in Sheldon, where they remained until 1866, when they came to Warsaw. L. Hayden Humphrey was born in Sheldon, January 22nd, 1850, and came to Warsaw August 27th, 1865, and attended school. He was married May 18th, 1875, to Maud Wilton, daughter of Judge O. C. and Sarah Wilton Skinner, of Quincy, Ill. They have two children—O. Skinner and Mary B. Humphrey. At the age of nineteen Mr. Humphrey and his brother, Samuel B. Humphrey, engaged in the tanning and leather business, and in April, 1872, the former became connected with the Wyoming County National Bank; in January, 1873, he was elected vice-president, and since 1874 has been its managing officer.

Wolcott J. Humphrey was the sixth son of Theophilus Humphrey, whose father bore the same name, and whose grandfather was Samuel Humphrey, all natives of Canton, Conn. His mother, whose maiden name was Cynthia Hayden, was a native of Torringford, Conn. Wolcott J. was born at Canton, November 11th, 1817. In 1818 his father removed to Sheldon, Genesee county (now Wyoming), where he engaged in farming, tanning, shoemaking and harness making, in all of which branches of business the son was also engaged till he arrived at the age of twenty-three. His education was derived from the common schools of this town, and from a brief course of instruction by a Congregational clergyman of his neighborhood. Extensive travel and acute observation have supplied the lack of early instruction, and in sound practical knowledge he is excelled by few. At the age of twenty-three he engaged in mercantile business, which he continued during twenty-four years at Varysburg, Sheldon Center, North Java, Bloomington, Ill., and North Java again. During his residence in the West he was largely engaged in successful land speculations. In 1864 he removed to Warsaw and engaged in the business of tanning, which he followed till 1869. He became a stockholder in the Wyoming County National Bank in the latter part of 1869, and in 1871 he was made president of this bank, in which position he still continues. He is also president of the Warsaw Water Works Company, of the stock of which he owns about one-third. Large financial ability, indomitable energy and unbending integrity have made him a man of wealth, but his native good sense has prevented the development of that vanity which too often tarnishes financial success. Mr. Humphrey has always been an active and efficient political worker. He was a Whig till that party ceased to exist, and he has since been a Republican. He was several times chosen supervisor of his town by large majorities; was appointed postmaster in 1849, 1853 and 1860, and was marshal for taking the census of several towns in this county in 1850. He had the honor of being mobbed by the foreign opponents of the draft during the late civil war while in the discharge of his duties as enrolling officer. He was elected to the Assembly in 1850 and again in 1851. During the latter term he was chairman of the committee on railroads, and reported, with its restrictions, the bill for consolidating the Central railroad. He also had charge of the prohibitory liquor law that was passed during that session. He was elected to the Senate in 1865, and again in 1867, from the thirtieth district (Wyoming, Livingston and Allegany) by majorities of more than 5,000.

During his service in tbe Senate he was chairman of the committee on roads and bridges, and of that on commerce and navigation, and was a member of the committees on internal affairs, printing, finance and banks. He has been a member of the Republican county committee for fifteen years, during about ten of which he was its chairman. He

W. J. Humphrey

has also been during the last twenty years a delegate in more than half the Republican State conventions that have been held, and he was a member of the national Republican convention in 1876. March 30th, 1841, he married Amanda B., daughter of William S. Martindale, of Dorset, Vt., who died at Sonora, Cal., June 17th, 1873. He was again married, July 8th, 1874, to Hannah, daughter of Hugh Mulholland, of Parma, Monroe county, N. Y. By his present wife he has two children, Annabel and Wolcott Julius. His first wife bore him no children. He is a liberal contributor to the support of the church and society with which he is associated. In his social relations he is genial and companionable, and his cheerful disposition renders his home the abode of happiness.

CYRUS JEFFERSON.—The grandfather of Cyrus Jefferson, subject of this sketch, was Aaron Jefferson, a soldier in the Revolution. He reared eight sons and four daughters. His father, Job Jefferson, was born in Douglass, Worcester county, Mass., in March, 1780, and died in Wisconsin, August 5th, 1870. His mother, who was the daughter of Peter Read, was born about the year 1788, and died in 1841. They had six daughters and three sons, of whom Cyrus was the oldest. His eldest sister was born November 16th, 1802. She and her husband, Elijah Gile, to whom she was married in Gainesville, are still living in Walworth county, Wisconsin. They have twelve living children, about sixty grandchildren and many great-grandchildren. His sister, Prudy Ann, married Jacob Frayer, son of Deacon John Frayer, of Gainesville. She died in Wisconsin in 1864. Another sister, Lucy, married Samuel Chase, formerly of Gainesville. His brother Charles resides in Iowa. His brother Russel died at the age of twenty, and three sisters died after they had come to be young ladies. In 1817 his father removed to Gainesville. During several years they suffered all the privations and hardships of indigent pioneers. The early opportunities for obtaining an education which Cyrus enjoyed were about equal to those of Abraham Lincoln. He labored on his father's farm till he married, at the age of twenty-one, after which he worked on his own account at anything he could find to do, by the month, day or job, and thus accumulated a small sum of money. In 1829 and 1830 he, in company with Mr. Rufus Conable, carried on a small mercantile busness. During the ten years following 1845 he purchased in Wyoming and the adjoining counties about one million pounds of wool, on which he realised a satisfactory profit. During the last twenty-nine years his principal business has been loaning money in the States of Illinois, Wisconsin and Minnesota, and in this business he has visited these States more than thirty times. He never received a gift of a dollar. He says though he has been fifty-three years a voter he has never voted for a Legislative candidate that was elected. The great wealth which Mr. Jefferson has, by his own exertions, acquired is an evidence of his financial ability. October 25th, 1838, he married Eunice, daughter of Rufus and Sophia Conable, of Gainesville. They had four children—Sophia, who married James Bristol, of Gainesville, and whose two children were Eunice, who died at the age of eighteen, and Charles, now living at sixteen; Willard, who died at three; Isadore, deceased at twenty, and his son Rufus C., who resides at Woodstock, Ill., married Genevieve, daughter of L. S. Church, Esq., and has four children— Cyrus, Rufus, Lawrence and Dora. Mr. Jefferson's first wife died July 16th, 1847. July 12th, 1848, he married Gracia D., her sister, who died January 10th, 1854. September 30th, 1858, he married Elizabeth, daughter of Benjamin and Elizabeth McCluer, of Franklinville, N.Y.

EDWARD M. JENNINGS is a son of James H. and Mary J. Jennings, who settled in Genesee Falls in 1852. They had a family of four children, of whom Edward M. Jennings is the oldest. He was born in Buffalo, November 22nd, 1842. August 4th, 1862, he enlisted in

Company A, 130th N. Y. volunteers. January 30th, 1863, at the battle of Deserted Farm, Va., he was wounded, and in consequence lost his right arm. He was discharged in June following, and returned to Genesee Falls, where he remained until 1869, when he was elected county clerk, and moved to Warsaw, where he lives. In 1874 he was elected clerk of the board of supervisors, and held the office till the fall of 1879, when he was re-elected county clerk. He has also served as clerk of the village of Warsaw. He was married August 18th, 1869, to Miss Mary E., daughter of Richard and Mary Robbins, of Cattaraugus county. They have two children—Milton R. and J. E. Jennings.

I. Sam Johnson is a son of Hiram and Jane S. Johnson. His father was a native of Connecticut, and came to Wyoming county in 1861. I. Sam Johnson was born October 24th, 1810, in Centerfield, Ontario county. He began the study of law with Colonel Thayer in May, 1860, and in August, enlisted in the 186th N. Y. volunteers; was promoted to first lieutenant February 7th, 1863, and discharged January 6th, 1864, on account of physical disability. In May, 1864, he was admitted to the bar, and except ten years spent in Arcade has practiced his profession in Warsaw ever since. He was married May 6th, 1865, to Mary E., daughter of Horace and Polly McFarlin, of Twinsburgh, O. Mr. Johnson has held the office of trustee in Arcade village. He was elected district attorney in 1876, and re-elected in 1879 by 1,978 majority, the largest ever given in the county.

Perry Jones is a son of Dyer and Lana Jones, formerly of Cayuga county, who came to Genesee Falls at an early date and reared a family of six children, of whom Perry was the third (born February 2nd, 1837). At the age of twenty he bought his time and worked by the month at farm labor until 1867, when he purchased a farm in Gainesville, which he now owns. In 1879 he came to Warsaw and opened an eating-house. While a resident of Arcade he held the office of highway commissioner two years. He was married October 27th, 1867, to Mary Jane, daughter of Thomas and Almira Cone, of Gainesville. They have three children.

Sheldon C. Keeney, son of Amos and Polly Keeney, was born in Warsaw, March 1st, 1815, and except five and a half years spent in Pennsylvania, has lived there all his life. He is a farmer. In 1877 he moved to his present location on East Hill, where, in partnership with his son-in-law, he owns ninety-four acres of land. He was married March 31st, 1836, to Ann H., daughter of Abraham and Mary Ennis, of Warsaw, by whom he had three children, two of whom are living. They are J. K. L. Keeney, now in Mattison, Ind.; and Mary B., who was married April 6th, 1872, to Asa A. Luther, a son of Lymas C. and Caroline P. Luther, of Castile. Luther was born November 21st, 1842. He enlisted in September, 1861, in Company F, 6th N. Y. cavalry, and served three years and a half. He was confined in rebel prisons nine months. He holds the office of highway commissioner. Mr. and Mrs. Luther have two sons—Kendrick A. and Ralph E. Luther.

Washington F. Kingsbury, son of Ransom and Marla Kingsbury, was born December 16th, 1815, at Hampton, Conn. In 1830 he learned the carpenter and millwright's trade. In 1810 he removed to Buffalo, and worked in the Buffalo Steam Engine Works until 1851, when he went to Warren, Pa., where he built the Warren Iron Works. In 1859 he set up and operated the first engine that was operated in the oil country, and he was the inventor of the oil-well torpedo. In 1867 he came to Warsaw, and has since been engaged in the oil and lumber business. Mr. Kingsbury was married March 6th, 1846, to Mary A. Brown, daughter of Thomas and Alice Brown, of Perry, by whom he has two children.

JACOB W. KNAPP was born in Warsaw, Genesee (now Wyoming) county, N. Y., August 20th, 1818. His parents, John R. and Melinda Knapp, moved from Orwell, Vt., in 1812. He served as apprentice to Peter Lyon, blacksmith at Canandaigua, N. Y., beginning at the age of fifteen. In August, 1836, he married Elvira Putnam, of Warsaw, and he has since lived in Warsaw village. He has been a justice of the peace nearly all the time since 1842. He was postmaster from 1852 to 1861. He raised a company for the volunteer service in 1862, served as captain to January, 1865, and then as major to July 19th, 1865, when he was mustered out with the regiment—1st N. Y. dragoons—having participated in many battles and skirmishes.

COLONEL ABRAM B. LAWRENCE.—The subject of this sketch was born in Warsaw, May 18th, 1834, of New England parentage, upon his father's side a descendant of John Lawrence, one of the company which came from England with Governor Winthrop in 1680, and upon his mother's side a descendant of French and Welsh families, resident in New England. Colonel Lawrence received a high school education, and was an advanced scholar at twelve years of age, when he was placed in a book store in Warsaw, which afforded him an opportunity, which he did not miss, to add to his store of knowledge. At the age of nineteen he was engaged as accountant in an extensive publishing house in Buffalo, increasing his business education and reputation. In 1856, purchasing a drug business at Niagara Falls, he removed thither, and March 26th, 1857, married Miss Elizabeth Faulkner, of Wheatland, Monroe county, N. Y., by whom he has two children—George M., born June 16th, 1858, at Niagara Falls, and S. Virginia, born February 25th, 1861, in Warsaw. Returning to Warsaw in 1858 he was for a time engaged in mercantile business, meantime projecting and in 1859 building the "Warsaw Gas Light Works" in company with others. He carried on the foundry and machine building business until the war of the Rebellion broke out. He was selected by the senatorial district committee to represent Wyoming county in the staff department as quartermaster of the 30th senatorial district regiment, subsequently known as the 1st N. Y. dragoons. His untiring business energy largely aided in raising and placing this famous regiment early at the front. Soon after arriving in Virginia with his command, in 1862, he was placed on detached service in the commissary and quartermaster's department, Peck's division, 7th army corps. Subsequently he was assigned to duty in Sheridan's cavalry corps, promoted captain and assistant quartermaster U. S. A., with commission from and bearing the autograph of President Lincoln, and with orders to report to General Grant, was assigned to duty at the headquarters of the 18th army corps. July 4th, 1864, he was made chief quartermaster of that corps, and in recognition of his service was soon after promoted to the rank of major in the quartermaster's department, serving thus with the 10th, 18th and 25th corps. Upon the reorganization and consolidation of troops of the 9th, 10th and 18th corps, constituting the 24th army corps, he was assigned by President Lincoln as its chief quartermaster, with rank of lieutenant colonel. During the memorable campaign which ended with the surrender of Lee he was appointed by General Grant "chief quartermaster of the Army of the James," with which the geueral made his headquarters at that time. This army, by the untiring energy of Colonel Lawrence, was kept supplied with commissary stores and ammunition in the ever memorable final race between Grant and Lee, and Colonel Lawrence secured the credit in military circles of having been largely and directly instrumental by his efficiency in the capture of Lee's army. In recognition of this service he was assigned by order of General Grant to receive the surrender and make disposition of the property of the army of Northern Virginia, and to act as the chief quartermaster of the U. S. forces at Appomattox Court-house, Va. The original field order to this effect is preserved by Colonel Lawrence as a valuable memento of those times and scenes. This duty completed he removed the army property to Richmond, Va., after distributing, under the personal orders of General Grant, horses, mules, wagons, etc., to the peaceably disposed farmers; and remained on duty in Richmond during the mustering out of troops, disposition of the surplus property of the army, and the establishment of the work of the Freedmen's Bureau, which he declined to be permanently engaged in. By order of Secretary Stanton he was assigned to duty in the vicinity of the Rooky Mountains in the fall of 1865. While on duty among the Indians of the plains he aided materially in exposing and stopping the frauds then perpetrated by government agents. In the spring of 1866, upon application for "muster out," he returned to Warsaw, where he received an honorable discharge with life brevets, upon nomination by the President and confirmation by the Senate, "for faithful and meritorious services during the war a well earned and honorable distinction. Soon after Colonel Lawrence's return to Warsaw he engaged with Buffalo capitalists in the development of the slate interests in the province of Quebec in connection with Lord Aylmer and his brother; organized the business, formed and put in operation a stock company of $150,000 capital, disposed of his interests and returned to Buffalo and engaged in the lumber and planing mill business, which after a successful term he was induced to sell and return to Warsaw and engage in the furniture trade, which he is now successfully prosecuting. In 1876, upon the organization of the Letchworth Rifles, Colonel Lawrence was commissioned by Governor Tilden as the commandant. In the face of many obstacles this company was placed among the first and best in the State, and its commander was brevetted by Governor Robinson as "lieutenant-colonel National Guard State of New York." In the Grand Army of the Republic Colonel Lawrence has been an active and influential member, for several years commander of Gibbs Post, Warsaw, which he organized; vice department commander State of New York, and repeatedly a State delegate to the national encampment. In 1876 he was unanimously chosen as the delegate at large for the State of New York to the centennial encampment at Philadelphia, and in this connection became the secretary of the Wyoming County Soldiers' Monument Association, whose work has resulted in the erection of the beautiful county monument in Warsaw. Colonel Lawrence united with the Congregational church in Warsaw April 15th, 1864, of which his wife and children are also members. In Buffalo and Niagara Falls he was an active member of the Presbyterian church. Since nineteen years of age he has been an active worker and liberal promoter of Sunday-schools, home and mission. He has always been an energetic man, of indomitable pluck, and thoroughly doing whatever he undertakes; persistent and fearless in maintaining any position he is called upon by duty to take when convinced that he is right; kind, forgiving and charitable to opponents, conscientious and humble as a Christian, soldierly in his instincts and qualities, methodical and systematic in all his business relations and operations.

Simeon D. Lewis, son of Truman and Lucy Lewis, was born in Orangeville, September 8th, 1830. His father was a native of Farmington, Conn. He came to Wyoming county in 1807, and settled in Orangeville. He was one of the first settlers of that section. He died in 1865, aged eighty. Simeon D. Lewis lived with his parents until he was twenty-one, when he entered the Genesee and Wyoming Seminary, at Alexander, Genesee county, as a teacher, remaining there two years. He then taught the union school at Warsaw one year. August 2nd, 1853, Mr Lewis married Miss Sarah L. Canfield, of Alexander, who was born July 21st, 1832. They had two children, one of whom, George A. Lewis, is connected with his father in the boot and shoe store of S. D. Lewis & Co. He was born April 19th, 1856. In that year Mr. Simeon D. Lewis began his mercantile career as a grocer, and continued in that line three years. Then, with Noble Morris, he established himself in the hardware trade, in which he continued nineteen years. In 1878, in company with his son and W. C. Gates, he established his present business. He was elected supervisor of Warsaw in 1871, and served three years. In 1874 he was chosen county treasurer, and was re-elected in 1877. He is president of the Citizens Gas Light Company of Warsaw, and for many years has been secretary and trustee of the cemetery association.

ZERA J. LUSK, M. D., son of William H. and Lovina Lusk, of Erie county, was born April 27th, 1851. At the age of nineteen he began the study of medicine in New York city, and graduated later from the Medical College of Buffalo. He began the practice of his profession in Eagle Village, where he remained four years. April 18th, 1879, he came to Warsaw and formed a partnership, now existing, with Dr. O. B. Adams. He was married October 21st, 1875, to Ida M., daughter of Henry and Huldah Rice, of Clarence, Erie county. They have one child, a son, William R. Lusk. Dr. Lusk is president of the Wyoming County Medical Association.

ALVAH C. MANSON is a son of Oliver and Elizabeth D. Manson, natives of Maine and later residents of New Hampshire. He was born December 27th, 1841, in Portsmouth, N. H. In 1857 he went before the mast on a seven months' voyage to sea. Later he learned the painter's trade, at which he has generally been employed since. April 20th, 1861, he enlisted in the 1st regiment N. H. volunteers. In June he re-enlisted in Company K, 2nd N. H. volunteers, and served until discharged, June 29th, 1864, returning to Portsmouth, and in April, 1865, went to New York and worked at his trade till June, 1872, when he came to Warsaw, where he has since lived. He was married December 17th, 1866, to Eva, daughter of Charles H. Knapp. They have had four children, two of whom are living. Mr. Manson is a member of Gibbs Post G. A. R., and is, as is also his wife, a member of the Episcopal church.

WILLIAM D. MARTIN, dentist, was born in Warsaw, in 1838. In 1871 he married Anna Janette Farriss, of Warsaw. He enlisted in 1862 in Company G, 37th N. Y. volunteers. He re-enlisted in 1863 as orderly sergeant in the 8th N. Y. heavy artillery, and was the only man of two hundred and five on the roll of his company who did not miss a day's service from the time of enlisting until mustered out, June 15th, 1865.

JAMES O. MCCLURE was born in Jordan, Onondaga county, November 16th, 1828. He received his education in the select schools and the Jordan Academic Institute, graduating as civil engineer and surveyor. In 1847 he removed to Syracuse; in 1850 was employed on the Rochester & Syracuse Railroad, and in 1851 on the New York and Erie Railway. From 1852 to 1864, inclusive, he was employed as engineer on the New York State canals. From the Spring of 1865 he carried on the drug trade at Warsaw until 1872, since which time he has followed his profession and the business of fire insurance. In 1870 he was engineer of the Warsaw Water Works Company, and its secretary and superintendent for eight years succeeding. He was village clerk of Warsaw from 1869 to 1878, superintendent of the Warsaw Gas Light Company from 1867 to 1873, secretary of the Warsaw Cemetery Association from 1873 to the present time, and is secretary of the Wyoming County Agricultural Society, to which position he was elected in 1878. He was chief engineer of the fire department of Warsaw in 1873, 1874 and 1879, and engineer in charge of the erection of the Wyoming County Soldiers Monument in 1877. In 1848 he became a member of the Syracuse Citizens' Corps. In 1856 he was lieutenant of the Lockport Light Dragoons. From 1857 he commanded the "Washington Hunt Guards" in that city until the Rebellion of 1861, when the company enlisted in the 28th N. Y. volunteer infantry, which he helped to recruit. In 1863 he was commissioned colonel of the 75th regiment N. G., which he had recruited, and he remained in the State service until September, 1866. Colonel McClure was married April 20th, 1854, to Huldah, daughter of Colonel William Bingham, of Warsaw, by whom he has two children —Ida and Frederic William McClure.

JOHN A. MCELWAIN was born in the town of Palmer, Mass., September 21st, 1794, of Scotch-Irish descent. He resided at home until he was sixteen years old. From that time until he was twenty-one he worked out summers by the month, and winters attended school. October, 1815, with $30 in cash, he put his pack on his back and started for the "Genesee Country." He stopped a few weeks in Otsego county, and arrived at Batavia the last of December at the house of his brother-in-law. The day after his arrival he started off on foot ten miles, to the town of Alexander, to see the trustees, and made a contract to teach their school—borrowing a horse to ride back—and on Monday, the first of January, 1816, he commenced teaching in a log school-house, and boarded with the families whose children attended the school. The next day after his term of school expired he engaged for one year (1816) in the service of Judge Cummings, of Batavia. In the summer of 1817 he first came to Warsaw, still in the employment of Judge Cummings, who had erected a flouring and an oil-mill, which Mr. McElwain and a brother of Judge Cummings had the management of for some years. During that time he enlisted in all the enterprises that were calculated to benefit the county or town, and that he continued to do through life. His first effort was in organizing a Young Men's Library Association, which was carried into effect, and was very useful for some years. He identified himself in 1820 with the Clintonian party, in opposition to D. D. Tompkins. After Clinton's day he was identified with the Anti-Masons, who elected him sheriff of Genesee county in 1831. From that time he was recognized as a Whig, and was elected to the Assembly in 1837, and to the Senate in 1852 and 1858, serving in both places with honor and usefulness. After the disorganization of the Whig party he was independent in politics, and voted for such persons as he thought best qualified for the offices. He was county treasurer five years; was State appraiser of lands to be mortgaged for banking purposes, and was assignee for Wyoming county under the national State bankrupt law as long as it was in force. He was president of the remarkably successful Wyoming County Mutual Insurance Company twelve or fourteen years. He was one of the first subscribers to and a director in the new cemetery association, and was for four years its president. He was a director and the treasurer of the old Warsaw and Le Roy Railroad Company, and one of the party who surveyed it, and was for a time a director in the Buffalo and New York City Railroad Company in 1852. At the first organization of the Episcopal Church he was elected warden, and remained so through life, and was a liberal supporter of that church. He was confirmed about twelve years before his death, and lived in the faithful observance of all the ordinances of the church. It was more, perhaps, by his exertions than any one else's that Wyoming county was formed and the public buildings located at Warsaw. He spent in 1840 and 1841 six months time in Albany on the subject, and when it was effected the supervisors of the new county appointed him one of the commissioners to erect the new public buildings. In 1843 he built the large brick hotel on the corner of Main and Genesee streets—then an ornament to the village, and the first brick building put up after the court-house. General McElwain was one of the first to organize the Wyoming County Agricultural Society, and was made one of its managers and elected its treasurer, and remained such until the grounds were purchased and all the improvements made. Afterward he was for some years president of the society, and during the whole time he had control of its finances. One of the last public services he performed was aiding in the erection of an exhibition hall, the summer before his death, which was changed to a two-story building largely through his exertions. While in the Senate in 1852 and 1853 he procured the passage of the law that abolished the old district school system in Warsaw, and adopted the union free school plan. He was one of the board of education nearly twenty years, being president of the board during the time the stone school-house lot was purchased and the house built, and the lots in different parts of the village for primary schools were secured and buildings procured to put on them, and all in successful operation. Mr. McElwaln's business after he left the grist and oil-mills, aside from his public duties, was keeping a public house, running the early stage lines and farming. His integrity, prudence, energy and strong native common sense won him success in all these callings, and secured for him the confidence and esteem of his fellow citizens. He was a fine type of the resolute and public-spirited citizens who subdued the wilderness of weetern New York, and were worthy pioneers of the present enlightened and prosperous community. He died on the 2nd of March, 1875.

THOMAS MCENTEE, father of Mrs. S. Menton Howard, was of Scotch descent. He came to America in 1794, and was a resident of Perry until 1872, when he moved to Warsaw, where he died in 1877. He reared a family of four children, of whom Mrs. Mary Ann Howard was the second born. She was born in Perry, May 12th, 1828, and married S. Menton Howard, of Perry, October 31st, 1848. He was a son of Samuel and Boxy Howard, natives of Connecticut, and was born April 5th, 1828. He spent four years during the war in the custom house at New York. In 1872 he came to Warsaw, and was connected with the Warsaw Manufacturing Company until January, 1874. He died January 6th, 1874, leaving a family of four children well provided for. He was deeply interested in educational interests, and served as superintendent of schools many years.

EBEN O. MCNAIR, son of David A. and Julia W. McNair, was born in Kalamazoo, Mich., January 1st, 1850, and came to Wyoming county in May, 1871. Previous to this time Mr. McNair was a resident of Washington, D. C., ten years, having been connected with the banking house of Jay Cooke & Co. as paying teller. Since 1872 he has been cashier of the bank at Warsaw. Mr. McNair is a member of the Episcopal church, and has been vestryman for several years. He is treasurer of the Warsaw union school board.

HORACE A. METCALF, son of Hubbard and Marcia Metcalf, was born in Cherry Valley, Otsego county, February 6th, 1834. In the fall of 1854 he went to Buffalo and entered the bank of White & Co. as clerk, and was afterward cashier. In the fall of 1856 he came to Warsaw, and was connected with the Wyoming County Bank a year. He spent the winter of 1856-57 in New Orleans, and in the spring of 1857 returned to White's bank in Buffalo, where he was employed until 1859, when he again came to Warsaw, and in connection with A. B. Lawrence built the first gas works, under the title of the Warsaw Gas Light Company, which made gas from resin. In 1865 they disposed of the property, which was afterward burned. Mr. Metcalf, in company with Mr. H. B. Jenks, built a tannery and managed it until 1864, when Mr. Metcalf sold out and again entered the Wyoming County Bank as clerk and book keeper. In 1869 he was elected cashier, which office he still holds. He has been one of the trustees of Warsaw village three years, and a member of the excise board one year. He was married May 31st, 1859, in Minnesota, to Miss Ellen L., daughter of Porter E. and Sarah Walker. They have two daughters—Louise, born August 4th, 1868, and Virginia B., born March 17th, 1871. Mr. and Mrs. Metcalf are members of the Congregational church.

CYRUS B. MERCHANT is a son of Lot and Tabitha Merchant, natives of Massachusetts, who came to Warsaw in 1806 and reared a family of nine children, six of whom are living, of whom Cyrus B. Merchant was the youngest. He was born July 9th, 1826, in Warsaw, where he has since lived. In October, 1877, he came to his present location on East Hill. He is a farmer and the owner of two hundred and forty-five acres. He was married January 1st, 1849, to Mary E., daughter of Martin and Rhoda Bryant, of Vermont. They have five sons; Frederick, the youngest, now lives with his father. Mrs. Merchant is a member of the Baptist church.

WARRRN S. MERCHANT, son of Cyrus and Mary B. Merchant, was born in Warsaw, May 5th, 1855. He attended the union school until 1875. In 1877 he took one of his father's farms to work on shares, and is now living on the same. He was married February 27th, 1877, to Lura A. Wood, daughter of Daniel and Ann Wood, of East Rushford, Allegany county. They have two children—Edna and Earl. Mr. and Mrs. Merchant are members of the Baptist church.

WILLIAM D. MINER is a son of Isaac and Survilla Miner, who were born respectively April 12th, 1792, and August 18th, 1798, in Stonlngton, Conn. Both are living and are in perfect health and active in mind and body. William D. Miner was born in Cayuga county, October 3d, 1824, and came to Wyoming county in 1826. He lived in Castile twenty-five years, and in Perry ten years. In 1861 be was elected sheriff of Wyoming county, and came to Warsaw, where he has since resided. Mr. Miner was married December 26th, 1848, to Mice Elizabeth S., daughter of James and Ruth M. Sayles, of Castile, Wyoming county. They have three sons, named respectively E. Fay, William D., jr. and John R. E. Fay, a member of the Frank Banking Association, of Corning, la., married Miss Lottie S., daughter of Otis S. Buxton, who for many years was doorkeeper of the House of Representatives, Washington, D. C. The youngest son, William D., jr., is also married, and is in business with his brother in Corning, Ia. John R. is assistant postmaster under his father, who was appointed postmaster to fill a vacancy in July, 1875, and reappointed in December, 1875. He also held the office of supervisor of the town of Warsaw in 1866. Residence, 63 Main street.

JOHN W. MONTGOMERY, son of James and Elizabeth Montgomery, was born in Ireland, May 4th, 1827. His father was born in 1783, and died in 1866. Mr. Montgomery came to America in 1850 and settled in Warsaw, where in 1858 he opened a boot and shoe store. He has been in the same line of trade since. His store was at 29 Main street, but was removed in June, 1880, to 17 Main street, which store he had recently bought. He was married in Warsaw, February 9th, 1860, to Miss Anna Crawford, daughter of Malcom and Elizabeth Crawford, by whom he has had seven children, six of whom are living. Mr. and Mrs. Montgomery are members of the Presbyterian church, and Mr.

Montgomery has held the office of elder since December 8th, 1971, and was ordained December 24th, 1871. Residence on East Court street.

William W. Moody was born in Le Boy, Genesee county, in 1860. In 1870 he came from his native town to Warsaw, where he is a produce merchant. He has been town clerk two years, and clerk of the village of Warsaw one year. June 14th, 1877, he married Elizabeth, daughter of Henry and Elizabeth Garretsee, of Warsaw.

Noble Morris is a son of Solomon and Olive Morris. Solomon Morris was born in Hampton, N. Y., in 1787, and Olive Morris in Orwell, Vt. They came to Wyoming county in 1806. Noble Morris was born March 21st, 1817, in Warsaw. When twenty-two years of age he went to Gainesville, where he remained three years, and returned to South Warsaw and ran a mill one year, which he had previously purchased. Going back to Gainesville he went into partnership with N. Park in the dry goods trade. In November, 1845, he came to Warsaw, and the firm of Hodge & Morris, hardware dealers, was formed. In 1852 Mr. Hodge sold his interest to O. S. Buxton, and the firm was Morris & Buxton until C. & T. Buxton bought a one-third interest and the style of the firm became Morris, Buxton & Co. Three years later Mr. Morris sold out his interest to the other partners, and three years later he and S. D. Lewis purchased the business of Buxton & Co. Morris & Lewis continued business until February, 1878, when Edward H., son of Noble Morris, bought the interest of Mr. Lewis, and the firm is known as N. Morris & Son. Noble Morris was married September 1st, 1842, and again February 22nd, 1866, to Mrs. Helen L., widow of George Benedict. He had two children by the first wife—Edward H. and Lottie. Mr. Morris has been trustee of the village several years.

Solomon Morris, son of Solomon Morris, was born August 9th, 1787, in Washington county. He came to Warsaw about 1808, and located on a farm a mile and a half south of the village. He was married August 23d, 1810, to Mrs. Nobles, widow of Dwight Nobles, by whom he had seven children, five of whom are living. He held the office of supervisor fifteen years, and was county superintendent of the poor a number of years. He was a surveyor, and for some time did the surveying of the town. He died November 20th, 1839; Mrs. Morris died September 22nd, 1852, aged sixty-nine. Luther M. Morris, son of Solomon and Olive Morris, was born at Warsaw, January 3d, 1815. In 1836 he worked for his father by the month. In 1837 he rented his father's farm for three years. After his father's death he took the farm and settled with the other heirs. He was married May 2nd, 1844, to Lucy F. Bradley, daughter of Daniel and Eunice Bradley, by whom he has had a son—Charles L. Morris, born at Warsaw, February 16th, 1845. He has always lived with his father. He was married October 11th, 1866, to Emma Truesdell, daughter of Philander and Eliza Truesdell, of Warsaw. They have one child, Frank L. Morris.

De Witt Munger is a son of Raymond R. and Eliza Munger, natives of Connecticut, who came to Wyoming county in 1816 and settled in Warsaw. Raymond R. Munger was married three times, De Witt being the second son by the second marriage. He was born October 15th, 1842, in Warsaw, and lived at home until he was twenty-three. He then worked a farm three years. In 1868, in partnership with "Mat" Keeney, he opened a livery stable in Warsaw village. The firm existed four years; then Mr. Munger was in partnership with Mr. Andrews one year, and has since been sole proprietor. He was married in January, 1864, to Fanny A., daughter of Willis and Elizabeth Felch, of Castile. They have had four children, two of whom are living—Fannie and Charlie.

PORTER B. MUNGER is a son of Morgan M. and Parnel E. Munger, natives of Connecticut, who came to Warsaw in 1816 and settled on West Hill, where Mrs. Munger still resides, Mr. Munger having died in 1858, leaving a family of ten children, of whom Porter B. Munger was the third. He was born September 15th, 1839. He lived at home until August, 1862, when he enlisted in Company D, 130th N. Y. volunteers (afterward 1st N. Y. dragoons), and served until discharged, May 22nd, 1865. Returning to Warsaw, he worked at farming for a time. He was married to Maria B. Hoisington, who died April 18th, 1876. October 23d, 1878, he married Agnes F., daughter of Harvey and Esther Tuttle, of Warsaw. He worked on the Erie Railway ten years. March 1st, 1875, he was elected constable and collector, and has since held those offices. He has two daughters by his first wife, named Blanch P. and Lilian F. Munger. Mr. and Mrs. Munger and Lilian are members of the Congregational church.

SAMUEL J. MUNGER, son of R. R. and Eliza Munger, was born at Warsaw, November 24th, 1838. He lived at home and worked on his father's farm until he was eighteen years old. In 1856 he worked at the miller's trade in the old Warsaw Mills, now known as the Premium Mills. In 1859 he worked at his trade in Wisconsin. In 1860 he returned to Warsaw, and was engaged in farming three years. In 1863 he bought the South Warsaw Mills, and is the present owner and operator of the same. He was married June 11th, 1863, to Nancy Judd, daughter of David and Jane Judd, by whom he had two children, one of whom, Carrie Bell, is living. Mrs. Munger died August 22nd, 1868, aged twenty-six. Mr. Munger was married April 29th, 1869, to Henrietta M. Felch, by whom he had three children. Mrs. Munger is a member of the Baptist church.

GEORGE C. OTIS, son of Amos and Emeline Otis, was born at Wethersfield, March 24th, 1841. At the age of seventeen he worked a part of his father's farm on shares. Becoming aware of the necessity of an education, at the age of nineteen he entered school at Brockport, Monroe county, where he remained two years. In 1862 he resumed farming, and in 1864 bought what is known as the Stanton farm, in the Wyoming valley, three miles north of the village of Warsaw. In 1878 he rented his farm and moved to the village, where he now resides. He was married December 18th, 1867, to E. Rose Warren, daughter of Jabez and Mary Warren, of Warsaw. They have one daughter, Carrie D. Mrs. Otis is a member of the Presbyterian church.

WARREN F. PECK, son of William B. and Permelia Peck, was born March 31st, 1839, in Covington, and moved to Middlebury with his parents in 1841. In 1873 he came to the town of Warsaw, where he now lives. He was married September 18th, 1873, to Emily Hatch, daughter of Milton D. Hatch, of Warsaw. They have two children, Eva Bell, born June 29th, 1875, and Cassius B., born June 1st, 1879.

REV. JOSEPH EASTBURN NASSAU, D. D., was born in Norristown, Pa., March 12th, 1827. He is the son of the Rev. Charles W. Nassau, D. D., who graduated from the University of Pennsylvania when he was seventeen years of age, and was licensed to preach before ho had attained his majority; became pastor at Norristown, and subsequently a successful educator as professor and president of Lafayette College, Easton, Pa., and later still as principal of the female seminary in Lawrenceville, N. J. Dr. C. W. Nassau died in Trenton, N. J., August 6th, 1878. The son, Dr. Joseph E. Nassau, made a profession of religion while a student in Lafayette College, Easton, Pa., and in his sixteenth year united with the Presbyterian church in that place. He graduated from Lafayette in 1846, with the first honors of his class, and was immediately chosen tutor in the college. This position, after two years, he resigned, to become classical professor in the high school and seminary in Lawrenceville, N. J. He entered the theological seminary at Princeton, N. J., in 1849, and taking the full course graduated in 1852. He had been licensed to preach by the Presbytery of Newton in 1851. In 1853 and 1854 he was principal of the female institute in Wilkes-Barre, Pa. This position he resigned early in 1855, desiring to enter more fully on the work of the ministry. During the summer of that year he supplied successively the Presbyterian churches in Fagg's Manor, Pa., and Warsaw, N. Y. While supplying the latter church he was in September unanimously chosen pastor, and October 24th, 1855, was installed by the Presbytery of Genesee River. Dr. Nassau's pastorate at Warsaw still remains unbroken, and has been much blessed. Under his ministry the church has prospered and steadily grown in numbers and usefulness. It has enjoyed several special revivals, and has uniformly exerted a widespread Christian influence, and been distinguished for the zeal and harmony of its members. He received the honorary degree of Doctor of Divinity, in 1872, from his alma mater, Lafayette College. For more than twenty years he has been the stated clerk of his presbytery, often moderator of presbytery, twice moderator of synod, and several times a commissioner to the general assembly. He has always taken an active interest in the causes of temperance and education, and is a trustee in several literary institutions. Dr. Nassau is eminently a scholarly divine. His sermons show a critical power of analysis of his subject, and a keen acumen in dissecting the motives which dominate men of different modes of thought. He is clear and logical in reasoning, and polished and concise in diction. He is frank and fearless in his denunciations of evil, whether in state or church, at home or abroad; but never censorious, and his reproofs are always taken in the spirit in which they are administered—as a part of the explicit duty of a faithful pastor and friend.

Samuel W. Perkins, son of Elam and Lydia Perkins, was born at Hampton, Washington county, January 22nd, 1809. In February, 1814, he came with his parenta to Warsaw, and lived with them until he was twenty-two. In 1836 he drove stage from Warsaw to Moscow, and the same year he bought fifty-five acres of partly improved land on lot 63. He has since added to it two hundred and eighty-five acres. When he made the first purchase he did not have a cent, and borrowed money to pay for having the papers made out. He has held the office of assessor. He was married March 23d, 1832, to Mary Densmore, daughter of Ephraim and Sarah Densmore, of Warsaw, by whom he had six children, five of whom are living. Mrs. Perkins died July 12th, 1879, aged sixty-eight. Mr. Perkins is a member of the church of United Brethren. His father took up a farm of eighty-three acres when he came to Warsaw, and lived on it until he died. He was married in 1805 to Lydia Wheat, by whom he had nine children, of whom eight lived to be men and women. He was born in Cheshire, Conn., December 4th, 1782, and died April 18th, 1862. His wife died December 18th, 1865, aged seventy-seven.

Samuel D. Purdy (son of Albert and Sarah Purdy, natives of Vermont, who came to Wyoming county in 1830 and settled in Perry) was born July 11th, 1828, in Manchester, Vt., and came with his parents to Wyoming county. Albert Purdy was a merchant, and Samuel D., after he was old enough, assisted his father in the store. They traded in Perry until September, 1854, when they came to Warsaw. Samuel D. Purdy was in the grocery trade in 1855, and in 1856–61 was employed in S. A. Murray's dry goods store. He then bought Mr. Murray out, and traded on his own account until December, 1868, when he sold his stock, and for ten years rented his store. In April, 1879, he again occupied the store, and in July, 1879, the firm of Samuel Purdy & Sons was formed. Mr. Purdy was married August 31st, 1858, to Frances M., daughter of Edmond and Dorcas Bainbridge, of Warsaw. They have three children—Mary Eva, Albert Edmond and Charles Gridley Purdy.

MAURICE R. QUACKENBUSH, son of Isaac and Patty Quackenbush and twin brother of Paul Quackenbush, was born January 31st, 1837, in Pike (then in Allegany county). He had one sister. His father's family came to Wyoming county in 1836, but Mr. Quackenbush remained in Pike, attending school, and afterward entered Union College. March 4th, 1863, he came to Warsaw and entered the county clerk's office, and except during three years has since been employed there as deputy clerk and notary public. He was married in February, 1879, to Miss Mary L., daughter of John and Nancy Ridge, of Middlebury. Mrs. Quackenbush is a member of the First Presbyterian church of Warsaw.

GEORGE C. SHATTUCK was born in Attica, in 1849. He is a grocer, and has long been a resident of Warsaw. In 1878 he married Miss M. Dunham, daughter of Alonzo and Harriet Dunham, of Warsaw. He was a charter member of Cataract Hose Company, of Warsaw, and has since been its foreman, assistant foreman and treasurer.

JOHN H. SLOCUM (son of Peleg, jr., and Catharine Slocum, natives of Rhode Island, who settled in Warsaw in 1880, and reared a family of seven children, of whom John H. was the oldest) was born in Rhode Island, April 14th, 1812, and came to the town with his parents. April 19th, 1837, he removed to his present location, in the eastern part of the town, where he owns sixty-nine and a half acres of land. He has been a carpenter and joiner and a farmer. He was married August 27th, 1837, to Mary Ann, daughter of John and Esther Cottrell, of Ontario county. They have three children—William C., George D. and Mary E. Mrs. Slocum is a member of the Methodist Episcopal church. Mr. Slocum is a Republican politically.

JOHN B. SMALLWOOD, son of Michael and Elizabeth Smallwood, was born at Warsaw, July 19th, 1838. He graduated from Genesee College, at Lima, in 1865. In 1865–66 he was professor of mathematics at the Perry Academy. From the latter year to 1873 he was a farmer. In the fall of 1869 he was elected school superintendent of Wyoming county, and served three years. In 1878 he was re-elected to the same office. He was married December 7th, 1865, to Octavia J. Atkinson, daughter of Martin and Amanda Atkinson, by whom he has five children—Mabel R., aged twelve; Grace A., aged ten; Ruth, aged eight; William T., aged six; Charles B., aged four.

WILLIAM W. SMALLWOOD is a son of Michael and Elizabeth Smallwood, natives of England, who came to America in 1819 and settled in York, Livingston county. In 1828 they came to Warsaw and built a log cabin in the woods, where the Smallwood homestead now stands. They had a family of seven children, of whom William W. was the fourth. He was born December 18th, 1847, and lived at home until he was twenty-five. He was married December 28th, 1871, to Eloise, daughter of Henry and Nancy Martin, of Orleans county. They have three sons and one daughter. Mr. Smallwood holds the office of assessor. Mr. and Mrs. Smallwood are members of the Methodist Episcopal church.

JACOB M. SMITH is a son of Reuben and Eliza Smith, who settled in Orangeville in 1848 and reared a family of eleven children, of whom Jacob M. was the sixth. He was burn July 23d, 1840, in Seneca county, and came to Wyoming county with his parents. At the age of thirteen he went to Java, where he remained eighteen months. In 1869 he removed to Warsaw, and worked at the carpenter's trade until April, 1879, when he established a lumber yard, which he manages in connection with his other business. He was married January 16th, 1866, to Helen G. daughter of Alexander and Agnes Patterson, of Utica, N.Y. They have four children. Mr. Smith enlisted in Company A., 9th N. Y. cavalry, September 20th, 1861, and served until discharged (having been promoted to sergeant), July 24th, 1865. He was elected collector of taxes in 1879. Mr. and Mrs. Smith are members of the Episcopal church.

PAUL P. STEPHENS was born in Germany, July 20th, 1844. He has been a resident of Wyoming county since 1846, and of Warsaw, where he is known as a farmer, since 1869, in which year he removed from Bennington July 12th, 1862, he enlisted in Company H., 129th N. Y. volunteers, and served until discharged, April 14th, 1865. While a resident of Bennington Mr. Stephens served the town as clerk, and was collector in Warsaw in 1878.

H. L. TABOR, son of Gideon and Polly Tabor, was born in Scipio, Cayuga county, March 31st, 1808. In 1817 he moved with his parents to Perry. At the age of seventeen he drove stage from Buffalo to Albany, and continued in that occupation five years. At the age of twenty-two he entered school and devoted the following three years to educating himself. From 1883 to 1887 he taught school at Wyoming. In 1889 he bought a farm on the West hill in Warsaw, and in 1851 the farm in the valley, one mile south of the village, where he now lives. He was married in 1834 to Cornelia Allen, daughter of Silas and Esther Allen, by whom he has had six children, four of whom are living. Henry Tabor was born September 3d, 1845, and lives with his father. He was married September 26th, 1867, to Ellen Webster, daughter of James and Caroline Webster, of Warsaw. They have three children—Carrie, born November 25th, 1871; Charles, born June 11th, 1874, and Jennie, born November 3d, 1878.

LIEUTENANT ZERAH LUTHER TANNER, U. S. Navy, was born December 5th, 1835, at Warsaw, and is a son of Zerah Tanner, who was also a native of Warsaw, born August 9th, 1810, and died in November, 1886. Lieutenant Tanner's mother, still living, was Ruth Emeline Foster, born in Danby, N.Y., May 23d, 1818. He lived at Warsaw until 1865, except two years in Towanda, Penn. He was in the employ of Gales & Garretsee, machinists, from 1852 to 1855, when he went to England, in connection with an invention he had patented there. In October, 1855, he entered on his seafaring career, originally for the improvement of his health. He sailed three times to the East Indies before the Rebellion. He was in the employ of the government through the Rebellion, first in the transport and later in the naval service. His first command was of the captured British blockade-runner "Vixen." In the "Augusta" he made a voyage to Russia in the summer of 1866. He spent three years from June, 1867, in voyaging to and in Chinese waters, receiving command of the "Aroostook" February 25th, 1870. Two years from the spring of 1871 were spent in a voyage among the South Sea Islands, and the summer of 1873 in surveying in Lower California. In the autumn of 1874 Lieutenant Tanner entered the service of the Pacific Mail Steamship Company, and commanded vessels of that company four years. He commanded the U. S. steamer "Speedwell" in scientific operations on the New England coast in 1979, and later in that year was employed in

superintendint the construction of the U. S. Steamer "Fish Hawk" at Wilmington, Del. He was commissioned ensign March 12th, 1968; master January 3d, 1869, and lieutenant March 21st, 1870.

LINUS W. THAYER.—Ferdinando Thayer, the English ancestor of the subject of this sketch, came from Braintree, Essex county, Eng., with his father, Thomas Thayer, about the year 1630, and settled in Braintree in the colony of Massachusetts. He was married to Huldah Hayward, of Braintree, January 14th, 1652. He resided at Braintree until after his father's death, when he and others removed to a new plantation, first called Nipmug, which was changed to Mendon. He was one of the largest proprietors of the township, and then regarded as a man of wealth. He gave a farm to each of eight sons, some of whom became extensive land owners. He held many offices of honor in his town and commonwealth. He died the 28th of March, 1718, at nearly ninety years of age.

Thomas Thayer, a son of Ferdinando and Huldah Thayer, married Mary Adams, and resided in Mendon until his death, in 1788. He died at the age of seventy-six.

Thomas Thayer, jr., his eldest son, was married to Ruth Darling, of Dedham, Mass. He resided at Mendon until his death. He held judicial and other important offices. The second son of Thomas and Ruth Thayer, of the same name, was married to Susannah Blake, and removed to Smithfield, in the colony of Rhode Island.

Gideon Thayer, his eldest son, the grandfather of General L. W. Thayer, was born at Smithfield, R. I., November 5th, 1752; was married to Meribah Wilcox, of the same place, June 10th, 1778, and removed to Mendon, Mass. He was a soldier of the Revolution, serving through the war, and was among the first to receive a pension from the government. Afterward, so intense was his hatred of tories, that at the age of eighty he could hardly be restrained from caning a man whom he suspected of having been one. After the close of the war he removed to Owego, Tioga county, N. Y., and afterward to Lima, Livingston county, where he resided until his death, at eighty-four years of age.

Willard Thayer, the eldest son of Gideon Thayer, was born in Mendon, Mass., March 1st, 1784. Before his marriage he purchased some land upon the "Holland Purchase," then in the town of Batavia, Genesee county (now Gainesville, Wyoming county); cleared a portion of it, and erected a log house. He was married to Phebe Harris, the only daughter of Isaac and Mercy Harris, of Owego, February 7th, 1809. He was one of the earliest settlers of the town of Gainesville. He was the supervisor of the town when a part of Genesee county several consecutive years, and held other important offices. His fellow citizens, having the fullest confidence in his judgment and integrity, often sought his advice, and frequently made him the arbitrator of any disputes between them. Mrs. Phebe Thayer died on the 12th of March, 1817, at the early age of twenty-eight years, and Willard Thayer the 23d day of March 1862, at the advanced age of seventy-eight years.

Linus Warner Thayer, second son of Willard and Phebe Thayer, was born in Gainesville (then Warsaw) May 23d, 1811. Until he reached the age of seventeen he labored on his father's farm, and availed himself of the educational facilities which the common schools at that time afforded. During the succeeding ten years he engaged in teaching in the winter season of each year, and for a portion of that time he assisted his father on his farm during the summer season. Two of these summers were passed at school, one at a select school in Lima, and the other at the Lima Semlnary. During this time, while teaching and laboring, he studied the French and Latin languages, mostly without the aid of teachers. He had early formed the design of obtaining a collegiate education and becoming a lawyer; and in furtherance of this design he not only pursued his linguistic studies, but purchased Blackstone's commentaries and Cowan's treatise. and spent his leisure time in preparation for his subsequent career. At about the age of twenty-one he received from his father a present of a piece of land, the care of which interfered for a time with his purposes; but at the age of twenty-seven he entered the office of I. N. Stoddard, Esq., of Perry, as a student. Some months afterward, and at the close of the school which he was then teaching, he entered into a law partnership with Levi Gibbs, which continued about two and one-half years. He was admitted as an attorney in the Court of Common Pleas of Genesee county in 1839. Upon the organisation of Wyoming county in 1841 he removed to Warsaw, and entered into a partnership with J. R. Doolittle, now of Wisconsin. This partnership terminated about four years afterward. He has continued in the practice of his profession at Warsaw till the present time. In 1865 his son, Linus L. Thayer, became his partner, in which relation he still continues. In politics Mr. Thayer was a Democrat till 1878, except during the existence of the Free Soil Party, of which he was a member. In 1876 he supported Hayes in opposition to Samuel J. Tilden, for reasons which he then made public. He has since been independent. He has never sought office, but in 1867 he was nominated for justice of the Supreme Court for the eighth judicial district. His opponent on the Republican ticket was the late distinguished lawyer Martin Grover; and although the Democrats were 20,000 in the minority in the district Mr. Grover was elected by a majority of only 600. In Erie county Mr. Thayer received a majority of 6,000. He was subsequently nominated for the same position, but declined. In the winter of 1872 he was without his knowledge nominated by Governor Hoffman for judge on the commission of appeals; and though there was a large majority of the adverse party in the Senate there was only a majority of two against him; every Senator from the western half of the State voting for his confirmation. In 1836 he was commissioned by Governor Marcy a major in the 26th regiment of cavalry of this State. In 1839 he was commissioned colonel of the same regiment by Governor Seward, and in 1841, by the same governor, a brigadier-general. October 28th, 1840, he married Caroline M. Lockwood, who was born January 12th, 1823. Their children living are Linus Lockwood, who married Emma A. Hurlburt; Carrie M., who married J. W. Chace, and Florence Louisa; Luella died at the age of sixteen; Clara, at six; Gertrude, at three, and Lillie in infancy. Mr. Thayer stands among the first in his profession. As a citizen his useful and blameless life has won for him universal respect.

SAMUEL D. TUTHILL, son of Louis and Phebe Tuthill, was born at Goshen, Orange county, October 4th, 1805, and came to Warsaw with his father about 1828. In early life he worked by the month for farmers and others. In 1833 he bought a farm of sixty acres just west of where he now lives. In 1847 he added eighty acres to this term. He was married December 30th, 1832, to Charlotte Albright, daughter of Joseph and Nancy Albright, of Ross county, O. Her father was descended from a Pennsylvania Dutch family; her mother was of Scotch descent. Mr. and Mrs. Tuthill have had nine children, six of whom, four boys and two girls, are living.

ALF. WADSWORTH, son of John and Harriet Wadsworth, was born at Brookport, N. Y., in 1844. In 1868 he engaged in business as a baker at Brockport. In 1871 he moved to Warsaw and engaged in the same business. In 1869 he was married to Florence A.

Miller, daughter of Aaron and Abigail Miller, of Brookport, N. Y. They have four children, and are members of the Methodist Episcopal church.

GEORGE W. WARREN is a son of James R. and Theodosia B. Warren, natives of New York and now residents of Canandaigua, N. Y., who were born respectively April 12th, 1819, and August 26th, 1823. Their family consisted of a daughter and two sons, of whom George W. was the second born. He was born in Canandaigua, April 3d, 1849, and remained there until January, 1870, when he came to Warsaw and entered the employ of T. S. Glover, and continued there as book-keeper until February 27th, 1878, when a partnership was formed under the title of T. S. Glover & Co., of which Mr. Warren is a member. He is a member of the Episcopal church.

CHARLES T. WATKINS, son of Warren K. and Minerva Watkins, of Genesee county, was born in Kalamazoo county, Mich., May 10th, 1837, and when thirteen years of age came to Pavilion and lived four years; then came to Warsaw, and learned the blacksmith and wagon-ironer's trade with C. T. Buxton & Co., with whom he worked three years; then removed to Attica, and worked at his trade until May 24th, 1861, when he enlisted in Company K, 17th N. Y. infantry, and served till June 2nd, 1863; then he returned to Warsaw, and worked at his trade till 1869, when he opened a billiard hall, which he has since managed. August 27th, 1863, he married Lucy C., daughter of Silence Bennet, of Pike. Mr. Watkins has held the position of first lieutenant of the S. N. G. and was captain of the rifle team that won the State prize at Bay View, September 17th, 1879.

FRANK WILSON, son of William J. and Mary Wilson, was born in Geneseo, Livingston county, July 28th, 1846, and remained with his parents until 1866, when he came to Warsaw, and for five years was employed as a clerk. In 1871 he opened a drug and grocery store in partnership with —— Smith, at 8 Main street. April 10th, 1879, Mr. Smith died, and Mr. Wilson became sole proprietor. He was married September 5th, 1871, to Fanny J., daughter of T. H. and Julia Buxton, of Warsaw. They have one daughter, Mary F. Wilson. Mr. Wilson has held the office of trustee of the village three years, and is now village treasurer, having been elected In April, 1879. He is president of the E. O. M. A., of Warsaw.

ANDREW W. YOUNG, the well known author of works on the science of government, and of several local histories, was born in Carlisle, Schoharie County, N. Y., March 2nd, 1802. His ancestry on the paternal side is traceable to Holland. His mother was of Scotch-Irish parentage, though her life was spent in this country. His educational opportunities comprised a few years' instruction at the common schools, and a half term in Middlebury Academy at the age of nineteen. Half a dozen years earlier he had taught a term of school, and teaching, with farm labor, was the employment of his youth. From the age of twenty-one he was in the mercantile business several years. In May, 1830, he started the Warsaw *Sentinel*, and January 1st, 1832, consolidated it with the *Republican Advocate*, at Batavia, which he had bought. Three years later he sold out and entered on his labors for the diffusion of a knowledge of governmental administration. His works of this nature were "Science of Government," published at Warsaw, October, 1835; "First Lessons in Civil Government," published in 1848, for use in this State, and a similar work two years later for circulation in Ohio; "The American Statesman," a political history of the United States, published in 1855; the "Citizen's Manual," in 1858; "Government Class Report," in 1860; "National Economy," in 1860, and "First Book on Civil Government," in 1867. Mr. Young was elected to the Assembly in 1845 and 1846, and a delegate to the constitutional convention in the latter year. He came to Warsaw in 1816, and after spending nearly the whole of forty years here removed in 1855 to Ripley, Chautauqua county, and in 1868 to Red Wing, Minn. At the last named place his wife died, and he soon after returned to Warsaw, establishing himself here about a year before his death, which occurred February 17th, 1877. His local historical works above referred to are histories of Chautauqua county, N. Y., and Wayne county, Ind., and the valuable History of Warsaw, from which we have been permitted to draw so largely in the preparation of this work. Many a reader of this notice can, from personal knowledge, supply the deserved eulogy of Mr. Young for which we have here insufficient space.

We have been unable to obtain data for similar notices of the following, who are among the leading citizens of Warsaw: S. Broughton, Charles W. Buell, Leander L. Chafey, A. P. Chapin, E. J. Cooke, Clara B. Darling, H. P. and H. A. Dudley, M. O. Dwyer, Mrs. S. S. M. Howard. James E. Ketchum, G. M. Lawrence, S. Virginia Lawrence, Frank Miller, D. C. Munger, D. B. Peck, B. H. Randolph, C. L. Shattuck, George A. Sweet, S. Wilson Wade, L. E. Walker and C. A. Williams.

THE TOWN OF WETHERSFIELD.

THE town of Wethersfield in its present limits was taken from Orangeville, and organized April 12th, 1823. It was named after the town of Wethersfield in Hartford county, Conn., the native place of many of the early settlers. It embraces all of township 8 in the second range of town-ships of the Holland Purchase, and has an area of 22,572 acres.

The old records of the Holland Land Company show that no articles to land in this town were granted before 1809. In that year Erastus Richards, Jason Smith, Joel S. Smith, Peter Lott, Ebenezer Tyrrell, Gideon Bentley and perhaps a few others obtained articles.

No attempt at a settlement was made until 1809, when James Cravath put up a log house on lot 4, which was immediately occupied by his brother, Ezekiel Cravath, and his family, the latter thus becoming the first residents of the town, and, so far as is known, the only ones in that year. The following year settlements were begun in other portions of the town by Lewis Hancock, Calvin Clifford, John W. Perry and one or two others. The two former came from Jefferson county, N. Y., and first located on lot 11. John W. Perry and his brother Theron came from Oneida county in the fall of 1810, and settled on the site of Wethersfield Springs. The former lived here about forty years, and the latter until his death, about 1827.

But few settlers located during the year 1811, among whom were Reuben Briggs and Jonathan King. Mr. Briggs was a native of New England. He came from Oneida county in the fall of 1811, and took up one hundred acres on lot 15, to which he removed his family the following spring. Here he lived until his death, in the spring of 1829, aged fifty-six years. Jonathan King, from Trenton, Oneida county, bought one hundred acres on lot 32 about the same time. Samuel and Daniel Teal came with him, and assisted him in clearing and building. The following winter he brought his family and effects, and became the first pioneer in the northern part of the town. In a few years, however, he sold out and removed. Samuel and Daniel Teal remained residents of the town until the death of the former, in 1816, when the latter returned to Oneida county.

Daniel Wolcott and Erastus and Manning Wells, from Wethersfield, Conn., located on lot 31 in 1812. Erastus Richards settled on lot 3 about the same time. In 1813 Ebenezer French settled on lot 2, and Amos P. Randall, from Oswego county, on lot 13. Guy Morgan, from Wethersfield, Conn., located on lot 39 in October, 1814. Those who located in 1815 were Samuel and Israel Reed, on lot 18; Samuel and Bliss Charles, from Maine, on lot 35; Amasa and Daniel Belden, on lot 10, Timothy W. Charles on lot 34, Amos Harriman and Joseph Charles on lot 36, and Abram Allen on lot 17. Joshua Parish, from Otsego county, settled on lot 63 in 1816, and remained until his death, and David Randall, from Oneida county, came in October, 1816. Jesse Howe, from Madison county, located on lot 1 in 1817. He built and occupied the first blacksmith shop in the town, and lived here until his death, in 1866, aged ninety-three years. In the autumn of 1816 Alexander Robinson and his son Samuel, from Maine, settled on lot 20, and John Copwell, from Albany county, on lot 58. The first settlers on lot 12 were Thomas Loveland in 1817, and James Warren, jr., in 1818. The former was one of the first to work at shoemaking in the town. William Palmer, from Connecticut, was the first to locate on lot 55, in 1818, and Henry Colwell on lot 56, in 1817.

The population of Wethersfield was less at the last State census than at most preceding ones, as shown by the following returns since 1825: 1830, 1,179; 1835, 1,623; 1840, 1,731; 1845,1,417; 1850, 1,489; 1855, 1,462; 1860, 1,583; 1865, 1,314; 1870, 1,219; 1875, 1,255.

First Town Meeting—Supervisors and Clerks.

The first official town meeting was held at the house of Joel S. Smith, March 5th, 1824. Lewis Blodget was chosen moderator, and the following persons were elected to serve as the first officers of the town: Lewis Blodget, supervisor; Joel S. Smith, town clerk; Ebenezer French, Bliss Charles and Guy Morgan, assessors; Daniel Stowe, Alfred Francis and Erastus Richards, commissioners of highways; Reuben Doolittle and William Hatfield, overseers of the poor; Amos P. Randall, Joel S. Smith and Arden Woodruff, commissioners of common schools; Abel W. Potter, Lewis Blodget and Eugene Z. Stowe, inspectors of common schools; Abel W. Potter and William R. Groger, constables; William R. Groger, collector. There were also appointed fourteen overseers of highways. It was voted to raise fifty dollars for the support of the poor of the town.

The following are complete lists of the supervisors and clerks of the town from its organization to the present, with the years in which each served:

Supervisors.—Lewis Blodget, 1824, 1830, 1831; Joel S. Smith, 1826, 1834–36, 1843, 1848; Ormus Doolittle, 1827, 1832, 1838; Arden Woodruff, 1826, 1829; Daniel Wolcott, 1839–41, 1847, 1848; Abel Webster, 1844–46; Justus Morgan, 1849, 1850; John J. Doolittle, 1851; Joseph A. Chandler, 1852, 1853; Welcom Wilcox, 1854–56; William H. Page, 1857, 1858, 1865, 1866; James L. Blodget, 1859, 1860; John R. Potter, 1861, 1862; William Wolcott, 1826, 1864; John P. Randall, 1867, 1868; Mason Hatfield, 1869, 1870; Daniel P. Joiner, 1871, 1872; Frank H Wilson, 1873, 1874; Alfred G Neely, 1875, 1876;William Body, 1877, 1878; Theodore·J. Hubbard, 1879.

Town Clerks.—Joel S. Smith, 1824, 1829; Bliss Charles, 1825–29, 1835; Eugene Z. Stowe, 1830, 1831; Daniel Wolcott, 1830, 1834, 1843; Ormus Doolittle, 1836–38; Chauncey Doolittle, 1840, 1843, 1850; Abel Webster, 1841; Croydon

Doolittle, 1844; Horace Blodget, 1845, 1848; Richard L. Charies, 1847, 1876, 1877; Joseph A. Chandler, 1848, 1849; James Rood, 1850: Dan Doan, 1851; Jacob Hibbard, 1852 1853; Daniel M. Wolcott, 1854, 1855; Alexander H. Baker, 1856; John R. Potter, 1857–59: Luther Brown, 1861, 1863; Alphonso Brown, 1863–65; Lorenzo D. Cleveland, 1826, 1837; William Body, 1868, 1869; Alfred G. Neely, 1870, 1871; Seth P. Allen, 1872, 1873; Eli Chandler, 1874, 1875; Russell S. Wheeler, 1878, 1879.

First Schools and School-Houses.

The first school taught in the town was opened in the fall of 1813 by Erastus Wells, in his log dwelling on lot 31. It consisted of the children of three families only.

In the spring of 1815 the first school-house in the town was built, of logs, on the northwest corner of lot 32, near the locality known as "the poplar trees," and the following summer Orpha Martin—afterward Mrs. Erastus Wells— taught a school here. In the fall of 1816 John A. Potter caused the second school-house to be built, of logs, near the line between lots 11 and 12—now in school district No. 7; and the next winter a school was taught here by Alpha Omega Rose, followed by Eliza Loveland in the summer of 1817. Among other early teachers here were Oliver Reed and Diantha Potter. This structure sufficed for school purposes in this locality until the spring of 1823, when a frame school-house was built at Hermitage, and Roxie Cravath was employed to teach in it the next summer and winter.

A log school-house was built in the southeast part of the town—now district No. 1—about 1818.

At the organization of the town in 1823 there were seven organized school districts, with as many school-houses, and about 220 school children between the ages of five and sixteen years. In 1835 the latter had increased to 505. The present number is 412. The total amount of public school money appropriated to the several districts in 1825 was $100.09. In 1835 it was $181.06, and in 1879, $1,067.28.

First Post-Offices, Post Routes and Post Riders.

The first post-office in this town was established in 1823, under the name of Wethersfield, at "Smith's Corners." Joel S. Smith, who was instrumental in its creation, was postmaster for many years after its establishment. The post route was from Fredonia to Perry, and mail was carried on horseback once in two weeks by William Hutchins. Weekly trips began in 1824, and in 1826 a line of four horse coaches was put on the route, which, however, were unprofitable, and soon withdrawn. The post-office here now receives a daily mail from Warsaw.

The post-office at Wethersfield Springs was established about 1829, through the instrumentality of Ormus and Reuben Doolittle, the former serving as postmaster. The route extended from the Wethersfield office to the Springs, and mail was carried on horseback by Eli P. Doolittle, a young son of the postmaster.

The post-office at Hermitage was established May 3d, 1837, the office receiving its name from General Jackson's country seat in Tennessee. Sidney Stowe was appointed first postmaster.

A post-office was established at North Wethersfield as early as 1848, and William Lewis appointed postmaster. It was discontinued in 1872.

Dairy Interests.

The Wethersfield farmers began dairying as early as 1826, and the business has become coextensive with grain raising throughout the town. The dairyman usually made butter and cheese on his own premises until 1864, when the erection of cheese factories began.

The West Star Factory, at Hermitage, was one of the first in the county. It was built by John Starks and S. A. Farnam, and commenced operations in April, 1864. It is one of the largest in the county, and made in 1878 218,300 pounds of cheese. It is owned and superintended by Mrs. Mary A. Weeks.

The Wethersfield Springs Factory was built in the spring of 1865 by Ira Granger, and operated by him for seven years. This factory was purchased from George Williams in the spring of 1877 by George Ahl and his sister, Mary A. Weeks, who are the present owners. It manufactured in 1878 127,000 pounds of cheese.

The Star Factory, at Wethersfield (Smith's Corners) was built in the spring of 1867, by A. C. and T. J. Hubbard, who still own it. The product of this factory in 1878 was 200,000 pounds of cheese. Theodore J. Hubbard has been superintendent from the first.

Hermitage

is the largest and most important village in the town. In 1809 James Cravath bought several hundred acresand built a log dwelling upon its site, and in 1812 he built a gristmill. Lewis Blodget was the millwright and director in the construction of this mill, making all the gearing and cutting out the first run of stones from a large boulder near by. Lewis Hancock is credited with being the first miller here, and occupied the above mentioned log house at the same time.

Lewis Blodget contributed largely to the growth and prosperity of this village, as well as of the town. He was a man of force, both mental and physical, a most capable mechanic, able to make almost any implement or machine. He was also distinguished for his sympathy and generosity. In 1830 he built the hotel here, not knowing who would occupy it, and in 1837 he aided materially in building the "Christian" chapel and procuring the bell. He also purchased and set up the town clock, which is still keeping time in the tower of this chapel. He was born in Massachusetts, in 1790; emigrated to this State before

1810, and to Wethersfield as early as 1812, and was married in 1816 to the daughter and only child of James Cravath. The death of his father-in-law in 1826 left Mr. Blodget in possession of a large property, which enabled him to extend his usefulness and manifest his financial ability. Soon after his marriage he located on lot 5, about half a mile north of the grist-mill, and was for many years engaged in lumbering, and farming. In 1840 he built the present grist-mill at Hermitage. In 1861 he removed to the village, where he died September 2nd, 1870. His widow is living, in her eighty-fourth year.

In 1810 Calvin Clifford built a saw-mill above the gristmill; the site is within the limits of the village. This mill was burned after three or four years'service, and about 1816 was rebuilt by James Cravath—Lewis Blodget being the master mechanic; at which time the water was raised, overflowing more than one hundred acres of land, which has since been known as the "Blodget pond." This mill subsequently came into Mr. Blodget's possession, but was also destroyed by fire. Mr. Blodget soon after built the third mill here, which remained in use until April, 1865, when a sudden flood carried away the dam and swept the mill from its foundation. The fourth mill on this site, which includes several different kinds of machinery and is now owned by Charles Whittam, was built in 1867 by John Starks, and operated by him until June 30th, 1869, when he was instantly killed while working a lath cutting machine. Mr. Starks was a native of Rome, N. Y. He was born October 19th, 1812, and married to Louisa L. Spring in 1834. He located in this county in 1843, residing in Orangeville, Warsaw and Gainesville, near Hermitage, until December, 1866, when he removed to the scene of his death. He was for several years a member and a deacon of the Hermitage Baptist church.

The first store at Hermitage was built and stocked in the fall of 1828 by Eugene Z. and Sidney Stowe, on the east side of the creek. The following year this firm built a more commodious building, and increased their stock of merchandise, which was soon after transferred to W. R. and D. L. Groger, who connected with the store an ashery and distillery, carrying on a successful business for several years.

Sidney Stowe built the first two-story dwelling here in 1830, and soon after started a tannery in company with Augustus Hurlburt, to which business was immediately added a shoe shop and leather store. This business afforded employment for ten or twelve men several years.

The first store on the west side of the creek was built and. opened in 1838 by Hall & Benedict. This building has been occupied for mercantile purposes most of the time since. Hall & Benedict were succeeded by Sidney Stowe in 1845, and he by W. H. Page, about 1850. The latter subsequently built and removed to a store opposite, now occupied by his son, Frank A. Page. Other stores, occupied for various branches of trade, have since been built by John P. Randall, Guy P. Morgan, Milo P. Brown and George Beardsley.

Hermitage now contains a hotel, two dry goods stores, a hardware store, two churches, a steam saw-mill, a cheese box and barrel factory, a grist-mill, a cheese factory, a cabinet and machine shop, two millinery stores, two wagon and two blacksmith shops, a harness shop, a shoe shop, and about 200 inhabitants. Whittam's saw-mill and Farman's flax-mills are also included in the suburbs.

On April 13th, 1865, a sudden freshet in East Coy creek swept away the dam at the "Blodgett pond," the saw-mill and the frame bridge at the village, which was carried forty rods down stream. The bridge was replaced, and remained in use until 1877, when the town built a new iron bridge in its stead. S. A. Farman, then town auditor, was actively instrumental in securing the appropriation.

Early in the morning of September 4th, 1875, three masked burglars entered James L. Blodget's dwelling through a window, overpowered, bound and gagged him, intimidated his aged mother to silence (the only two occupants), robbed his safe of $12,000 or $15,000, and departed, leaving Mr. Blodget almost suffocated and entirely helpless. No trace of the money or burglars has yet been found.

Wethersfield Springs.

This village owes it early existence mainly to Ormus and Reuben Doolittle, brothers, who came here from Washington county, N. Y., in 1819. An immense business, comparatively, was at one time done here, and in 1841 the place was a formidable competitor with Warsaw for the location of the county seat. It is noted as the birth-place and early home of Hon. James R. Doolittle, ex-senator from Wisconsin.

Ormus Doolittle was a blacksmith and his brother, Reuben, a cloth dresser. They were partners in all business transactions until the death of the latter, August 22nd, 1846. They purchased a large tract of land on lots 7, 8 and 16, which they improved and cultivated. Soon after locating here they put up a blacksmith shop, and Ormus worked at his trade for a time as occasion required. In 1820 they built the first saw-mill here, bringing the water from East Coy creek, one hundred and eighty rods through a race. About 1825 they built an ashery, which they operated several years, and about this time they built the first store here, which they leased to Andrew W. Young, who was the first to embark in general merchandising. He was succeeded in two or three years by the Doolittles, who continued the business many years. About the year 1827 they put up a wool carding and cloth dressing establishment, which they operated until the death of Reuben, when it was converted into a tannery by Bush & Edwards.

The first tavern at Wethersfield Springs was built and kept by Munson Doolittle as early as 1824. The present hotel was built about 1830 by Peter and Jerry Chandler, from Maine, who kept it several years. Ormus and Reuben Doolittle gave the land upon which it stands, as they did the sites of all the churches and some other buildings. Dr. Benjamin Bancroft, a native of Massachusetts and a graduate of Dartmouth College, was the first physician. He practiced here from 1825 until his death, May 3d, 1864. The first dwelling at this place was built by John W. Perry in 1810. The village now has two stores, two churches, the Doolittle Institute, a hotel, a cheese factory, a saw-mill, a resident physician and a corresponding number of mechanics and tradesmen. Its population is about 150.

Doolittle Institute was founded in 1860 by Ormus Doolittle, who erected three building, one for the principal's dwelling, and fenced and improved the grounds at an expense of about $19,000. He subsequently deeded the property to the Episcopal church and society for school purposes, subject to reversion after a certain time if not occupied as stipulated. It is still under the auspices of that denomination, and at one time was a popular and flourishing institution. Rev. H. V. Gardner first had charge of the institute as principal, succeeded by Rev. Messrs. Faust, Gibbs and others. For several years past the institute has been closed most of the time.

UNITED BRETHREN CHURCH AT WETHERSFIELD SPRINGS.

This society was organized. November 5th, 1876, with twenty-three members. In February, 1879, the society bought for $300 the Methodist church building and grounds at Wethersfield Springs, which it has occupied since its organization.

The pastors of this church have been H. Wiser, James Andrews, H. Thomas and William Robinson, each serving one year.

The Sunday-school was organized in June, 1877. Charles Dresher was the first superintendent.

WETHERSFIELD,

locally known as Smith's Corners, contains a store, a hotel, a cheese factory, a school-house, a blacksmith shop and ten or twelve families. Joel S. Smith, from Vermont, was the first settler here, coming in 1819. He soon after opened a tavern, and in 1830 built the present hotel. About 1827 he opened the first store. He was an enterprising and valuable citizen, a tavern keeper, merchant, drover and farmer. In 1856 he removed to Nebraska, where he died about 1870.

Odd Fellows' Lodge.—Center Lodge, No. 236, I. O. O. F. of Wethersfield, was instituted at Smith's Corners in June, 1850, by Marcus Hull, of Pike, with five charter members. The leading first officers were: Dan Doan, N. G.; V. D. Eastman, V. G.; F. B. Neely, treasurer. This lodge flourished for a time, but died out.

NORTH WETHERSFIELD

contains a saw and shingle-mill and the grist-mill of N. E. Torrey. David Witherell was the first settler here, locating in 1818, and soon after built a small mill for grinding coarse grain. The mill stones he chiseled out of native rocks and the belts were made of moose wood bark. A few years later he built a more substantial mill, containing two runs of stones, and also built a distillery, both of which he subsequently sold to Stephen Royce. The latter did milling here until about 1855, building the present grist-mill about 1841. He also engaged in the grocery trade at this point as early as 1845, which business he soon enlarged to general merchandising. He was followed in the mercantile trade by Jackson, Bronson and others, until 1873, when the business was abandoned.

John Goodspeed built a saw-mill here about 1824 and worked it several years, when he sold it to Stephen Royce, who soon after put up a new one in its stead. The present saw and shingle-mill was built about 1867 by P. W. Potter.

CHURCHES IN WETHERSFIELD.

BAPTIST.

The first religious organization was effected at the house of Daniel Belden in 1817 by Rev. Joseph Case, who became the first pastor. It was received under the care of the Holland Purchase Baptist Association previous to 1821, and in that year reported thirty-six members. The society was legally incorporated under the name of the "First Calvinist Baptist society of Orangeville ánd China, No. 8.," May 14th, 1822, at the house of Daniel Belden, which had been the usual place of meeting. Rev. William Patterson served as moderator and Amos P. Randall as clerk of this meeting, and Daniel Belden, Amos Randall and Amos P. Randall were chosen trustees of the society.

Elder Case was succeeded in 1822 by Oliver Reed, who was ordained and remained pastor until 1826. Henry Stone, Parley Cady and Samuel Ackerly are reported as deacons in 1825.

In June, 1830, the church was divided, and a new organization effected at Hermitage, under the name of the "First Baptist Church of Wethersfield," with seventeen members. The same month they were received into the Genesee River Baptist Association. The other pastors who had served the church up to this time were: Elders Worcester, James Reed, Harvey, Roswell Palmer (ordained by this church) and Jesse Palmer. In November, 1831, John Trowbridge, from Holland, was ordained by this church, and was its pastor a short time. In 1832 Augustus Hurlburt, a licentiate, supplied the pulpit. In June, 1836, Rev. Jesse Palmer is reported as pastor, and his death announced to the association in 1837.

In 1837 the society built its first meeting-house, at Hermitage, which was occupied until 1851, when the church voted to remove the place of worship to Smith's Corners. This was not done until 1853, and caused the members residing in the vicinity of Hermitage to organize a new church there May 19th, 1853, consisting of Rev. T. T. Horton and 29 members, under the name of "The Baptist Church of Christ in Hermitage."

The old Wethersfield church disbanded in 1860, each member being furnished a letter by J. Cross, the church clerk. The pastors who ministered to this church from 1837 to 1860 were Revs. R. C. Palmer, 1839–42; John

Trowbridge, 1842–44; E. J. Scott, 1845; S. Ackerly, 1846; Lewis Ellingwood, licentiate, 1854; G. Jones, 1856; M. M. Coleman, 1859.

The new organization at Hermitage occupied the old meeting-house until 1871, when the building was sold, removed and converted into a cabinet shop. The society built the present brick edifice in 1871, at a cost of $7,300. It was dedicated by the Rev. Mr. Mallory, of Batavia, February 28th, 1872. The pastors of this church since its organization have been Revs. T. T. Horton, four years from May, 1853; A. Plumley, four months; Charles Smith, supply; R. Sabin, two years from the spring of 1859; S. Hough, two years; William Storrs, one year; E. A. Russell, from January 1st, 1865, to July 1st, 1867; S. T. Dean, two years; A. P. Mead, from August, 1869, to April 1st, 1875; T. T. Horton, recalled for one year: J. R. Hutchins, who commenced his labors in July, 1876, was ordained in February, 1877, and remained as pastor until August, 1879.

A parsonage and six acres of land were bought by the society in 1865 for $885.

In May, 1879, Mrs. Maria Stedman left to the church by will a large house and lot in Hermitage and other property of considerable value.

The present membership is about 60.

"CHRISTIAN" CHURCH OF WETHERSFIELD.

A church of this denomination was organized at Hermitage in 1836 by Rev. Messrs. Burgess and Adams. Among the constituent members were David L. Groger, Ebenezer French, Sidney Stowe, Eugene Z. Stowe, Erastus Richards and Daniel Green. It was legally incorporated, as the "First Christian Society of Wethersfield," February 14th, 1837, when David Green, Ebenezer French, Sidney Stowe, David L. Groger and Erastus Richards were elected trustees. The same year the society built a frame church at Hermitage, at a cost of $1,600, which was dedicated in the spring of 1838 by Rev. Joseph Badger, of Mendon, N. Y. Rev. Reuben A. Burgess was the first pastor, followed by Elders Augustus Hurlburt, C. A. Havens, —— Fish and others. The society, owing to the death and removal of most of its members, after many years became extinct.

ST. CLEMENT'S (EPISCOPAL) CHURCH.

An Episcopal society under the above name was organized in the school-house at Wethersfield Springs January 9th, 1826, by the Rev. R. Salmon, at which time Rev. Almon Stevens and Reuben Doolittle were elected wardens, and John W. Perry, Ormus Doolittle, Hiram Welch, Elizur Webster, John A. McElwain, James Rood, William R. Groger and Chauncey Doolittle, vestry-men. A second organization of the church under the same name occurred at the same place April 4th, 1836, Rev. Isaac Garvin presiding, when the following officers were elected: Reuben Doolittle, jr., and Horace Hollister, wardens; Ormus Doolittle, David E. Shader, Samuel R. Braman, John Wilder, John W. Perry, John A. McElwain, Chauncey Doolittle and Joshua H. Darling, vestrymen.

In 1836 a brick edifice was erected for the society at a cost of $5,000, contributed by Ormus and Reuben Doolittle. Rev. Thomas Meacham officiated at the laying of the corner stone, and Rev. Messrs. Bowles and Metcalf at the consecration.

Rev. Isaac Garvin remained rector until April, 1839, and was followed by Rev. Henry Tullage, who was rector two years. Rev. Thomas Meacham was then called, and remained until his death, October 21st, 1849. A tablet in the church and cemetery adjoining was erected to his memory. His successors have been Rev. A. D. Benedict, for four years from May, 1852; Rev. William White Montgomery, June, 1856, to April, 1858; Rev. H. V. Gardner, two years; Rev. Noble Palmer, November, 1862, to November, 1869; Rev. L. H. Strycker, November, 1869, to April, 1872. The present incumbent, Rev. J. E. Batten, commenced his labors here May 1st, 1873.

The present number of members is about 30.

On October 16th, 1865, an endowment was made to this church by Ormus Doolittle for its maintenance.

PRESBYTERIAN CHURCH.

A church of this denomination was organized at Wethersfield Springs by Rev. Abijah Blanchard in the early part of 1832, and was received under the care of the Presbytery of Genesee February 14th of that year. The same year the society built an appropriate house of worship, and in 1834 numbered fifty-six members. Rev. A. Blanchard remained as stated supply three years or more, and was followed by Rev. Conrad Ten Eyck in 1836, under commission from the American Home Missionary Society. In 1841 Rev. Ward Childs labored a part of the time under the same patronage. This church about 1850 became extinct, and the building was converted to mechanical uses.

METHODIST EPISCOPAL CHURCH.

An M. E. class was organized at Wethersfield Springs in 1832, and on November 12th of that year the society was legally incorporated under the name of the "First Society of the Methodist Episcopal Church in the town of Wethersfield." Benjamin Bancroft, Hiram Welch, James Wiseman, Horace Webster and E. H. Mix were elected trustees, and in 1833 the society built a church. In 1857 this society was reorganized, with nearly one hundred members, and continued until 1872. It then disbanded, and in December, 1878, the church property was sold to the United Brethren Society.

BIOGRAPHICAL.

ISAAC E. ALLEN, always a resident of Wethersfield, was born here February 2nd, 1822. He was married June 25th, 1850, to Catharine Walt, who died June 2nd, 1852, leaving one son. July 4th, 1858, Mr. Allen married Lozana Blodget, of Wethersfield, who was born in Warsaw, June 6th, 1832. He located on his present farm of two hundred and forty acres on lot 13 in 1858, and has since put up large and commodious farm buildings, and made many other permanent improvements. He is one of the leading dairy farmers in the town. He is a trustee of the Baptist church of Hermitage, of which he has been a member since 1836. His father, Abraham Allen, one of the first settlers in Wethersfield, was born in Mayfield, Fulton county, N. Y., July 8th, 1794, where he was married to Deborah Akeley, in 1814. In 1815 he came to Wethersfield and bought a farm on lot 17, to which he removed his family in the spring of 1816, cutting his own road for over a mile to his new home. In 1855 he removed to Eagle, where he died May 6th, 1857. His wife died June 27th, 1861.

JOHN ANDREWS, a farmer and dairyman, was born in Westborough, Mass., March 18th, 1828, and came from Washington county, N. Y., with his parents to Wyoming county in 1848. After two years in Genesee Falls they located on the farm of three hundred and twenty acres, on lots 8 and 16, which Mr. Andrews now owns and occupies. He was married July 4th, 1858, to Sylvia E. Rogers, of Warsaw, who was born in Vermont, March 30th, 1826. His father, John Andrews, sen., was born in Massachusetts, November 29th, 1791, and was married about 1826, to Clarissa H. Newton, who died in Washington county in 1835. He was married in 1836 to Charity Locke, of Washington county, who died in Wethersfield, August 7th, 1878. He was a blacksmith until he came to Wethersfield, where he was engaged in farming until his death, May 31st, 1869.

AMASA BARRETT was born in Victor, Ontario county, N. Y., May 15th, 1817. In February, 1828, his parents removed to Orangeville, where he was married October 16th, 1839, to Rebecca S. Head, daughter of Jonathan Head, who was born March 28th, 1818, in Sheldon. Mr. Barrett remained on the old homestead on lot 45 in Orangeville until the fall of 1858, when he removed to Johnsonsburg. In the fall of 1874 he bought and located on a farm on lot 64 in Wethersfield, where he still resides. While in Orangeville he was town clerk five years, and held various other town offices. His father, Amasa Barrett, was born in Massachusetts, April 19th, 1787, and was married to Esther Jackson, of that State, October 6th, 1808. She died in Orangeville, May 11th, 1824, and in 1826 he married Martha Sedgwick, of Massachusetts, who died in Wethersfield, April 10th, 1876, aged ninety. Mr. Barrett lived in Orangeville from 1828 until his death, April 17th, 1856.

GEORGE J. BEARDSLEY, son of Delos Beardsley, was born in Springville, Erie county, N. Y., July 20th, 1844. In early life he was a marble cutter, and a carpenter and joiner. After living at Springville, Eagle, Yorkshire and Arcade, he located in 1870 near Hermitage. In August, 1873, he bought the hotel which he owns at Hermitage. He married, June 29th, 1869, Sarah L. Lacy, of Warsaw, who was born in Henderson, Jefferson county, N. Y., June 5th, 1842. His grandfather, Partridge T. Beardsley, was among the first settlers in Covington.

BENONI B. BELDEN was born in Gainesville, May 23d, 1811. From 1815 his parents lived on lot 10 in Wethersfield until 1825, when they removed to Castile, where he was married November 15th, 1835, to Silvia Fuller, a native of Bennington county, Vt., born December 7th, 1812. Soon after marriage Mr. Belden returned to Wethersfield and cleared his present farm on lot 17. He donated $600 toward building the Hermitage Baptist church.

AMASA BELDEN, the father of Benoni B. Belden, and his brother Daniel were pioneers in the south part of Wethersfield. The former was born in Vermont, January 23d, 1784, and was married December 30th, 1806, to Amy Banister, of the same State. He settled in Wethersfield in the fall of 1815, and remained a resident of the county until his death, April 29th, 1848. His wife died in Genesee Falls, October 25th, 1852.

MILO P. BROWN, the oldest son of Luther Brown, Esq., was born in Gainesville, November 19th, 1846, and in 1850 removed with his parents to Hermitage. He was married November 1st, 1870, to Emma Shader, of Wethersfield. She died September 12th, 1876, leaving two children, Clayton M. and Blanche L. Mr. Brown was married February 5th, 1878, to Eila Shader, of Orangeville, where she was born November 15th, 1852. For the past thirteen years Mr. Brown has been foreman in the flax-mill of C. D. Farman, near Hermitage. He has been collector of Wethersfield two terms. Both Mr. and Mrs. Brown are musicians of considerable note in their locality.

Luther Brown was a native of Gainesville, and the oldest son of Nehemiah Brown. His wife, Hannah, was a daughter of John Russell. a prominent settler of Gainesville. He was at Hermitage in the grocery trade nearly eighteen years from 1860, and was justice of the peace for several years. About 1866 he removed to a farm in Eagle, where he died November 19th, 1875.

NEHEMIAH BROWN, jr., was born in Gainesville, July 15th, 1836. He was engaged in farming, teaching, cheese making, etc., until the spring of 1876, when he located on his present farm. He was married October 21st, 1861, to Sarah A. Wilder, of Farmersville, Cattaraugus county, where she was born March 11th, 1829. His father, Nehemiah Brown, was born in Tyringham, Mass., September 26th, 1796, removed to Onondaga county, N. Y., in 1807, and since 1815 has lived in Gainesville. He was married in 1819 to Ursula Jemison, of Tyringham, Mass. She was born March 26th, 1800, and died in Gainesville, March 22nd, 1867.

JAMES L. BLODGET, son of Lewis Blodget, has always lived in Wethersfield. He was born in September, 1822, and graduated at Yale College. He is a civil engineer, but is now banking and dealing in real estate at Hermitage. He has been postmaster at that place since the early part of President Lincoln's administration. He and his only brother, Horace Blodget, of Pike, are administrators of their father's large estate.

RICHARD LANGDON CHARLES was born in Fryeburg, Maine, September 1st, 1808. His father, Samuel Charles, and family removed to Orangeville in July, 1815, and soon after to Wethersfield, where he resided until his death. His mother was a daughter of Paul Langdon, who graduated at Cambridge, and settled in Wethersfield about 1818. The early life of R. L. Charles was spent in farming and teaching. He was married April 4th, 1827, to Sabina M., daughter of Daniel Stowe, who came to Wethersfield in 1818, where he died in 1842. Mr. Charles was engaged in tanning and shoemaking with his brother-in-law, Sidney Stowe, at Hermitage, from 1841 until 1845, when the latter business came into his hands, which he still follows at the same place. He has been school commissioner, town clerk and justice of the peace.

WILLARD CHAMPLIN was born in Willing, Allegany county, N. Y., August 30th, 1837. In 1856 he removed to Wisconsin, and in 1859 began farming, lumbering and trading in Oceana county, Mich. He was the first merchant and business man at the present thriving village of Hesperior, where he secured the establishment of the post-office. He served six months in the 3d Michigan infantry in 1864. He was superintendent of iron works in the car department of the Pacific Railroad three years. He returned to this State, and was married November 1st, 1871, to Mrs. Jerusha M. Foster, of Wethersfield, where he has since resided, engaged in farming. Mrs. Champlin was born in Wethersfield, May 16th, 1835, and is a daughter of William H. Mead, a native of Morristown, N. Y., who located on lot 55, Wethersfield, in 1838, where he died March 17th, 1870, aged sixty-six years.

JONATHAN COLLINS was born at Warehouse Point, Conn., November 9th, 1813, and soon after removed with his parents to Springfield, Mass. In 1838 he located on a new farm in China, this county. He was married April 5th, 1840, to Julia Parker, born in Arcade, March 9th, 1820. In 1856 Mr. Collins removed to Alexander, Genesee county, and in June, 1879, to his present farm of one hundred and seventy-five acres on lots 9 and 10 in Wethersfield. He has followed bee keeping more or less for the past forty years.

JOHN J. DOOLITTLE, son of Ormus Doolittle, was born in Wethersfield, February 5th, 1825. For several years he followed merchandising at Wethersfield Springs, in connection with farming. Since 1860 he has been speculating and dealing in real estate. He has has been supervisor of Wethersfield, and held most other town offices, and was Assemblyman in 1860. He was married October 9th, 1849, to Jane A. Thompson, a native of Manchester, Eng., and in 1869 removed to Geneva, where he was three times elected supervisor.

CHARLES DRESHER was born in Nassau, Germany, September 22nd, 1822, where he was six years in the army. He was married July 18th, 1858, to Catharine New, and the same year came to Warsaw. He served the last three years of the Rebellion in Company E, 136th N. Y. infantry, and participated in twenty-one engagements, receiving one wound. In 1867 he removed to Wethersfield, and in the fall of 1875 he located on his present farm of one hundred acres on lot 27. Mr. Dresher has been a class leader of the United Brethren Church at Wethersfield Springs two years.

VENSON D. EASTMAN was born in Middlebury, February 17th, 1814, and April 19th, 1836, married Clarissa P. Shattuck, of that town, who was born December 22nd, 1817. Immediately afterward he settled where he now lives. He has been a successful farmer and dairyman, and justice of the peace twenty-six years, and associate judge of the county three years. He was instrumental in establishing his school district in 1848, and the Odd Fellows lodge at Smith's Corners, of which he was a leading member. His father, Nathaniel H. Eastman, a native of Connecticut, lived in Middlebury from 1812 until his death, July 30th, 1868. He was a soldier in the war of 1812.

CHARLES D. FARMAN was born in New Haven, Oswego county, N. Y., November 20th, 1820, and married Lydia Wright, of that place, January 28th, 1838. Soon afterward he removed to Genesee county, and in 1844 engaged in rope making in Gainesville. In 1852 he bought part of his present beautiful homestead, which has been increased to one hundred and ninety acres. In 1861 the rope making gave way to dressing tow for upholstering purposes, which business amounts to $20,000 annually. Mr. Farman has held several town offices, and has twice been supervisor.

SAMUEL A. FARMAN is a native of New Haven, Oswego county, N. Y., born December 6th, 1835. In early life he was a dry goods clerk. From 1856 he was at Fillmore, Allegany county, until August, 1862, when he enlisted as 1st lieutenant in Company F, 130th N. Y. volunteer infantry. He was discharged in 1863 on account of disability. He was married April 19th, 1859, to Sarah A. D'Autremont, a native of Friendship, Allegany county, N. Y., born December 16th, 1835. Soon after leaving the army Mr. Farman located at Hermitage. In 1865 he bought the "Benedict store," enlarged and remodeled it, and carried it on for fourteen years. The stock, though not the building, was transferred to other parties in the spring of 1879.

CHARLES C. FORNCROOK was born in Lysander, Onandaga county, N. Y., February 3d, 1824. In 1848 he came to Pike, where he was employed several years in threshing machine manufactories. He was married April 4th, 1850, to Mary E. Willey, of Eagle, and since the spring of 1854 has carried on blacksmithing at Hermitage; has been a deacon of the Baptist church since 1866.

AUGUSTUS GETTY was born in Pembroke, Genesee county, N. Y., April 16th, 1821, and removed to Attica in 1832, where he was married April 1st, 1845, to Lucy Smith, a native of Batavia, born May 6th, 1825. In 1853 he removed to Granger, Allegany county, and in the spring of 1858 to his present farm of one hundred and thirty acres. He has reared five children, four of whom are still living. His father, William Getty, died in 1821, and in 1822 his mother married Asa Farman. He was born in Vermont, in December, 1788, and was a soldier in the war of 1812, soon after which he came to the Holland Purchase, and is still living at Attica. Mrs. Getty's mother died in June, 1862.

HUDSON GLEASON was born in Byron, Genesee county, N. Y., November 20th, 1809, where his father, Daniel Gleason, was an early settler. In 1832 he came to Orangeville, and was married to Diantha Brady, of Castile, May 9th, 1837. In the spring of 1839 he bought one hundred and seventy-eight acres on lot 55 in Wethersfield, which he has since improved and occupied.

IRA GRANGER was born in Salem, Washington county, N. Y., October 25th, 1819, and came with his parents to Warsaw in 1822. In 1828 the family settled on a new farm in Gainesville, where Mr. Granger was married February 20th, 1844, to Hannah, daughter of Nehemiah Brown, of the same town. In the fall of 1845 he located at Wethersfield Springs, where he was successively grocer, saw-mill proprietor and cheese maker until December, 1871, when he bought his present farm. His father, Ephraim Granger, was born in Vermont, in 1796, married Sally Granger in 1814, and was a resident of Gainesville from 1828 until his death, in 1868.

ANSEL HAMMOND was born in Elba, Genesee county, N. Y., January 25th, 1824. In 1836 his parents removed to Carlton, Orleans county, and in 1839 he came to Gainesville, where he was married to Nancy Reynolds February 18th, 1847. The next spring he located on lot 51 in Wethersfield. Farming and stock dealing has been his principal occupation. He has held several town offices, being assessor fifteen years. His father, Stephen Hammond, was born in Massachusetts in 1781, and was a sailor eleven years. He married Huldah Russell, of Vermont, about 1808, and thereafter lived in Genesee and Orleans counties until his death, in 1889. His wife died in Michigan in 1873.

CALVIN F. HAMMOND, proprietor of the Sodom saw-mill, was born in Springfield, Essex county, N. Y., September 10th, 1827. In 1834 his parents removed to Genesee county, and in 1836 to Sheldon, where Mr. Hammond was married December 24th, 1850, to Rexaville C. Putnam, of Orangeville. In 1853 he settled in Wethersfield, and in 1874 where he now lives. His principal occupation has been that of a millwright and sawyer. He has been a justice of the peace for the past sixteen years.

JOHN HOMER was born October 15th, 1834, in Germany. In 1853 he emigrated to Sheldon, and two years later to his present place. He was a farmer until 1865, since which time, with the exception of three years spent in the grist-mill at Johnsonsburg, he has been constantly employed in the North Wethersfield Mills. He was married October 16th, 1856, to Laura Dayton, adopted daughter of John Bundle, of Wethersfield. She was born in Potter county. Pa., May 8th, 1832. They have six children.

CHARLES A. MASON has always lived on his present place, where he was born August 20th, 1855. He was married September 19th, 1876, to Teresa F. Cusack, of Java. She was born January 29th, 1858, and for several years previous to marriage was a teacher. Mr. Mason is assessor. His father, Thomas Mason, came from Ireland, where he was born in 1809, and for several years was engaged in lead mining at Galena, Ill. In 1840 he married Mary Kavanagh, of Ireland, and located on lot 60, Wethersfield. There he died January 31st, 1863. His wife died December 28th, 1872.

CHARLES A. MEAD was born in Morristown, Morris county, N. J., January 30th, 1808, and removed with his parents to Warren county, N. Y., in 1815, where he was married December 3d, 1834, to Clarissa Lake, of that county. She was born in Vermont, May 7th, 1801. In the fall of 1848 Mr. Mead removed to Wethersfield, and in the spring of 1866 to his present farm. He has always been a farmer. His wife died June 1st, 1878.

GUY MORGAN, Esq., came from Wethersfield, Hartford county, Conn., to lot 39 of this town in October, 1814. He married Nancy Griswold, of Connecticut, in 1806, by whom he had nine sons. She died in Waterford, Conn., in 1852. He was a magistrate several years. About 1883 he removed to Ohio, where he was elected county judge.

JUSTUS MORGAN, the eldest son of Guy Morgan, was born in Wethersfield, Conn., May 2nd, 1807, and has been a resident of Wethersfield, Wyoming county, since October, 1814. He was married February 28th, 1827, to Celestia Picket, of this town. He has held several town offices, serving two terms as supervisor. He lives where he located in 1852. His wife died September 30th, 1878, in her seventy-third year.

LEWIS J. MORGAN, son of Justus Morgan, was born in this town, November 19th, 1836, and was married December 30th, 1862, to Clarissa, daughter of Vinson D. Eastman, of Wethersfield, where she was born December 8th, 1846. Mr. Morgan has lived on the old homestead of three hundred and fifteen acres since 1852, and now owns it. He has been collector and assessor. His children are Belle, Frank, Vinson, Mary and Maria.

GUY P. MORGAN, the eldest son of Justus Morgan, was born in Wethersfield, September 14th, 1830, and was married February 7th, 1854, to Sophia, daughter of William Wolcott, of Wethersfield. She was born September 24th, 1836. In the spring of 1854 he bought and located on his present farm, which now consists of two hundred and ninety-five acres, and is managed by Mr. Morgan and his son Augustus. Since 1872, when he built a large store in Hermitage, he has also been engaged in the hardware trade. He has two children—Augustus W., born November 19th, 1854, and Flora A., born January 2nd, 1862. He has been collector, assessor, justice of the peace for the past eight years, and session justice two terms.

LUCIUS D. MORGAN, also a son of Justus Morgan, was born in Wethersfield, July 24th, 1837, and has always lived in the town. He was married January 3d, 1860, to Mary A. Eastman, of the same town, and in 1861 located on lot 39. In the spring of 1867 he bought his present farm. His wife died November 18th, 1873, and on February 4th, 1875, he was married to Augusta J., daughter of George Peck, of Orangeville.

ALFRED G. NEELY, son of Franklin B. Neely, is a native and life long resident of Wethersfield. He was born December 7th, 1838. He served in Company H, 136th N. Y. volunteer infantry, the last three years of the civil war. He was married July 26th, 1865, to Maria E. Wolcott, of Wethersfield, where she was born May 22nd, 1841. Since the spring of 1867 Mr. Neely has lived in Hermitage, connected with the firm of Neely, Wolcott & Co. in the manufacture of lumber, cheese boxes, barrels, etc. He was elected town clerk in 1870 and 1871, and supervisor in 1875 and 1876, and has held other offices.

WILLIAM H. PAGE, second son of William Page, was born in Chester, Warren county, N. Y., February 22nd, 1817, and at the age of seven years, came to Wethersfield with his parents. He was married January 30th, 1837, to Hannah Parish, of Java, and soon after he located on a farm at Wethersfield Springs. About 1849 he removed to Hermitage, and was engaged in general trade a quarter of a century, and succeeded by his son, Frank A. Page. As supervisor of the town he disbursed nearly $12,000 for military bounties. He was a captain under the old military law for many years. His wife died September 1st, 1848, and he was married December 8th, 1852, to Mary E. Herrick, of Watertown, N. Y. She was born in Fairfield, Herkimer county, February 18th, 1819. William Page was born near Greenwich, Conn., August 19th, 1784, and was married in 1813 to Ruth Mead, of Connecticut. In 1824 he removed with his family from Warren county, N. Y., to lot 14, Wethersfield. He died November 15th, 1871. His wife died April 10th, 1863. He was a soldier in the war of 1812, and subsequently had command of a company of militia.

ALBERT PARISH was born in Java, October, 1st, 1836, and was married January 1st, 1861, to Lucy A. Skinner, of Wethersfield, where she was born February 11th, 1837. He remained in Java, farming, until the spring of 1871, when he removed to Wethersfield, and two years later located on his present farm on lot 47. He is now constable and collector. His father, John Parish, settled on the east line of Java in 1816. He was born in Connecticut, October 18th, 1795, and was married to Mary Teft September 22nd, 1816. He lived in Java half acentury. In 1867 he removed to Hornellsville, where he died May 21st, 1869.

JOHN R. POTTER, dairy farmer, was born in Galway, Saratoga county, N. Y., January 14th, 1814, and came to Wethersfield with his father's family when two years of age. He was married February 16th, 1835, to Mary M. Cookson, of Chautauqua county, who was born February 3d, 1814. Mr. Potter was supervisor in 1860 and 1861; has served as assessor nearly twenty years and held other offices. He has been salesman of the Hermitage cheese factory since 1866. His father, John A. Potter, was born in Rhode Island in 1771, and removed to Saratoga county, N. Y., in his youth, where he was married to Esther Sweet. In June, 1815, he came to Wethersfield, and bought and improved a farm on lot 12, now owned by J. R. Potter. Here he lived until his death, October 31st, 1822. His wife died here in 1840.

JOHN PALMER RANDALL was born in Wethersfield, in 1834, and has always lived here. His wife is a daughter of Stephen I. Mosher, an early settler in Wethersfield, and was born in 1839. Mr. Randall was a farmer several years after his marriage; then traded at

Hermitage about four years. In 1867 he erected a fine two-story building on the corner opposite the present hotel, where he sold clothing, boots and shoes, etc., for a few years, when he sold the business and stock to Martin Grover, but retained the building, the upper story of which is occupied by the Good Templars. Mr. Randall has been twice supervisor, and was appointed sheriff on the death of Sheriff George Wilder. His father, David Randall, was a native of Voluntown, Conn., born April 11th, 1796, and located in Wethersfield in October, 1816. He married Emma Palmer, of Bridgewater, Oneida county, N. Y., February 11th, 1830. He lived in the town until his death, January 20th, 1877. His wife died February 25th, 1869.

MORGAN L. REED, a lifelong resident of Wethersfield, was born March 6th, 1817, and was married October 8th, 1837, to Margaret Sherman, of the same place. She was born in New Jersey, August 29th, 1822. Soon after his marriage Mr. Reed bought and settled on part of his father's farm, where he still lives. He has been a deacon of the Baptist church since 1853. His father, Israel Reed, was born in Saratoga county, N. Y., May 17th, 1796, and in the spring of 1815 located on lot 18, Wethersfield. He was married May 18th, 1816, to Sally Cure, of Saratoga county. He died here April 15th, 1847. His widow is still living in the town, in her eightieth year.

ALEXANDER R. RICHARDS, wagon maker at Hermitage, was born in Lima, Livingston county, N. Y., December 10th, 1831, and came to Wethersfield with his parents in March, 1839. He was married October 27th, 1861, to Jeannette B. Kimball, of Java, where she was born December 6th, 1843. Mr. Richards located in Hermitage about 1864. His father Alpheus Richards, was born in Lima, January 2nd, 1809, and was married February 14th, 1831, to Mary Chapman, of Warsaw. He located on lot 39 in Wethersfield in 1839; was a shoemaker at Wethersfield Springs from 1860 until 1878, since which time he has resided with his son in Hermitage. His wife died August 29th, 1875, aged sixty-four years.

LE ROY SMITH was born in Sidney, Delaware county, N. Y., July 12th, 1843. His father, Solomon Smith, was born in Bennington, Vt., in 1770, and was married in 1805 to Betsey Palmer, of the same place, where she was born August 5th, 1785. He removed to Delaware county, N. Y., in 1812, and thence to Pike, Wyoming county, in 1824, where he died March 12th, 1826. His wife died in Wethersfield, March 8th, 1871. Le Roy Smith located in Wethersfield in 1840, and on his present farm in the spring of 1872. He was married September 14th, 1866, to Mary Johnson, of Wethersfield. She was born in Gainesville, September 21st, 1846. Their children were John D., born October 12th, 1867; Ray L., born May 5th, 1869; Palmer L., born August 6th, 1873; Clayton, born December 30th, 1876, died September 16th, 1878; Hattie, born April 30th, 1879.

ALLEN M. STARKS, son of Deacon John Starks, was born in Batavia, N. Y., September 17th, 1843, soon after which his parents removed to Orangeville. He was married January 30th, 1867, to Emily L. Murray, of Steuben county, where she was born December 11th, 1844. He enlisted August 15th, 1862, in Company D., 130th N. Y. volunteer infantry, and served through the war. In December, 1866, he came to Wethersfield, and in the spring of 1875 located on his present farm. His children are John M., born August 12th, 1869; Earl R., born January 9th, 1874; George S., born June 30th, 1877.

NELSON E. TORREY was born in Java, March 1st, 1832. At the age of eighteen he removed with his parents to Wethersfield, and worked at farming thirteen years. He was married March 7th, 1858, to Laura J. Blakeley, of Concord, Erie county. She was born in Java,

July 20th, 1834. From 1863 until the fall of 1869 he kept hotels at Wethersfield Springs and North Java, after which he was farming again until January, 1877, when he became proprietor of the grist-mill at North Wethersfield, which he still owns and operates. His father, Alvenus Torrey, was born in Vermont, January 5th, 1798, and located in Java in 1824; removed to Wethersfield in 1849, and soon to Mt. Morris, where he died in October, 1862.

PLINY A. WARREN, youngest son of Ammi Warren, was born in Sheldon, June 9th, 1831, and was engaged principally at farming in that town and Java until the spring of 1875, when he purchased the hotel stand at Wethersfield (Smith's Corners), of which he is still the popular host. He was married November 23d, 1857, to Martha Carson, of North Java. She died in March, 1872, and he was married January 4th, 1873, to Kate M. Garrety, of Java. She was born in Trenton, Pa., November 3d, 1845. Mr. Warren served in the 9th N. Y. cavalry from September 27th, 1864, until June, 1865.

ALLEN W. WEEKS was born in Orangeville, March 31st, 1844. He served from August, 1862, in Company H, 136th N. Y. volunteer infantry, till the close of the Rebellion, and was honorably discharged June 20th, 1865. He was married March 26th, 1879, to Mary Ahl, daughter of John Ahl, of Orangeville, since which time he has been making cheese at Hermitage.

DANIEL B. WHIPPLE was born in Orangeville, May 27th, 1843, and in youth was a teacher. From August 18th, 1862, he served in Company H 136th N. Y. volunteer infantry through the civil war. He was married May 25th, 1866, to Harriet E. Butler, of Wethersfield. She was born in Sheldon, March 15th, 1844. Soon after marriage Mr. Whipple removed to his present farm.

FRANK H. WILSON, son of Herman Wilson, was born in Middlebury, April 11th, 1837, soon after which his parents removed to Arcade, where he was married to Ellen A. Jenkins, April 10th, 1859. Soon afterward he removed to Perry, and two years later to Wethersfield. He located on his present farm in 1869. Since youth he has been a butcher and drover, and has for several years been the largest stock dealer in Wyoming county. He has been supervisor, and held the office of town auditor during its entire existence.

DANIEL WOLCOTT, ESQ., was one of the first settlers and most prominent men of the town. He was a son of Elisha Wolcott; was born in Wethersfield, Conn., January 29th, 1790, and was married in 1809 to Maria Morgan, of the same place, where she was born August 15th, 1788. In 1810 Mr. Wolcott came to Wethersfield and "booked" one hundred and fifty acres on lots 31 and 39, and in the spring of 1812 removed his family to this place, cutting his way for a long distance through the forest to his land. He died about 1860. By appointment from the governor he was commissioner of deeds for a few years; was several times assessor, town clerk and supervisor, and was justice of the peace fifteen years. He reared eight sons and two daughters, most of whom are still living in the vicinity Mrs. Wolcott still lives in the town, and was ninety-one years old on the 10th of August, 1879, when nearly one hundred of her descendants, including the fourth generation, were present.

DANIEL M. WOLCOTT, the second son of David Wolcott, Esq., was born in Wethersfield, Conn., October 20th, 1811, but has lived in Wethersfield, N.Y., since infancy. He was married October 24th, 1833, to Mary Willard, of Wethersfield Conn., where she was born April 19th, 1809. She died July 19th, 1840, and on June 22nd, 1848, he married Lucinda

O. Wells, daughter of Deacon Origen Wells, of Newington, Conn., born November 23d, 1814. Mr. Wolcott has carried on his present farm since about 1834. No man living has resided in the town longer than he. He has held several town offices. He has had six children, viz.: Mary E., born December 11th, 1834, married Truman A. Hill November 90th, 1856, and died May 7th, 1870; Hannah M., born September 18th, 1839, married Lucius L. Cory December 26th, 1860; Daniel W., born August 6th, 1839, died April 21st, 1841; Laura, born April 20th, 1842, died September 1st, 1842; Sarah L. born May 16th, 1844, married Truman A. Hill January 21st, 1878; Emma A., born August 24th, 1845, married to Harrison H. Devinney, of Wethersfield, November 26th, 1868.

CHARLES D. WOLCOTT, the youngest son of Daniel Wolcott, Esq., was born in Wethersfield, in 1830, and has always lived here, most of the time on the old homestead, which he purchased soon after the death of his father. He was married in 1851 to Sarah M. Morrell, of Orangeville. They have one daughter, Florence C., the wife of Henry S. Fargo. Mr. Wolcott has frequently represented the Democratic party in State, senatorial and county conventions, and has held several town and government offices.

CHARLES WHITTAM was born near Leeds, England, April 2nd, 1810, and was married to Ann Burnes, of the same place, August 28th, 1830. He is by trade a carpenter and joiner and cabinet maker. He emigrated in 1842 to Warsaw, and in October, 1876, bought the mill property which he now operates.

LUCIUS WOLCOTT, son of Daniel Wolcott, is a native of Wethersfield, born February 6th, 1816, and was married June 2nd, 1840, to Olive W. Chandler, a native of New Hampshire, born October 2nd, 1822. He lived in Wethersfield until 1842, when he removed to Burlington, Ia; thence in 1846 to Monroe, Wis., where he still resides.

JAMES YORK is one of the few surviving pioneers of the town. He was born in Stonington, Conn., September 28th, 1796, where he was married to Sila Palmer in 1814, and in June, 1819, removed to his present farm.

JAMES H. YORK, son of James York, was born in Connecticut, December 2nd, 1815, and came with his parents to Wethersfield in 1819, where he has since remained. He was a carpenter and joiner several years. He was married January 1st, 1837, to Maryetta Hall, of Java, born in New London county, Conn., September 8th, 1820. Mr. York carries on the homestead farm, bought about 1850. He has reared ten children, all of whom are still living.

JONAS H. YOUMANS was born in Albany county, N. Y., November 29th, 1814. In June, 1818, his father, John Youmans, removed with his family to lot 59 in Wethersfield, where he made the first improvements and erected the first log house. After a few years he sold to Benjamin Stevers, a blacksmith, taking one hundred and seventy pitchforks in payment. He then located on lot 1 in Java, where he built and operated a grist-mill for a few years, but eventually turned his attention to farming. About 1860 he removed to Gainesville, where he died July 10th, 1877. He was born in Albany county, August 28th, 1792, and was married February 22nd, 1814, to Almira Hamilton. She died July 14th, 1874, aged seventy-seven years, four months and twenty-four days. Jonas H. was married November 1st, 1840, to Luracy Randall, of Wethersfield. She was born where she now resides, November 22nd, 1818. Mr. Youmans has always followed farming and dairying. He located on his present farm in 1867.

JOHN W. ZEAK was born in Winsted, Conn., June 16th, 1829. His father, John Zeak, was born in Byrum, Sussex county, N. J., September 3d, 1790, and was married August 24th, 1817, to Lucy Austen, of Connecticut, born July 3d, 1789. In the spring of 1834 he came to Hermitage, contracted with Lewis Blodget for a farm on lot 60 in Gainesville, and returned to Connecticut for his family, but died before reaching his new home. His wife and family located in Hermitage in May, 1884, where she remained until her death, September 1st, 1861. John W., her youngest son, learned the shoemaker's trade, and was married August 4th, 1850, to Emily E. Parker, of Arcade. He served from August, 1862, in Company H., 136th N. Y. infantry through the Rebellion. He soon after engaged in harness making at Hermitage, which business he still follows. He has one son, Nelson J., born September 24th, 1851, now a resident of Pennsylvania.

Received too late to come in its alphabetical order:

F. E. Bliss, M, D,, is the resident physician of the village of Wethersfield Springe, Wyoming county, N. Y. He was born in the adjoining town of Eagle in April, 1846. His parents were Harvey and Charlotte Bliss. His father as well as his grandfather, Sylvester Bliss, where both prosperous farmers of that town, and the grandfather was one of its pioneers. The subject of this sketch was therefore brought up a farmer, but at the age of sixteen he acted in the capacity of a teacher, and continued thus employed until he attained his nineteenth year, when he entered the office of Dr. McArthur, of Eagle, under whose direction and supervision he studied three years. Immediately after he entered the Medical University of Buffalo, where he remained during the term of 1867 and 1868. On the 22nd of February of the last year mentioned, he graduated and at once entered into partnership with Dr. O. B. Adams, of Wethersfield Springs, They continued in company until January, 1860, when the partnership was dissolved, Dr. Adams disposing of his interest to Dr. Bliss. From that time onward to the present he has continued to be the resident physician of the village. In that capacity he has brought to his aid the vigor of manhood, and by close application to study his record stands fair with the profession and with those with whom he is brought in daily contact as their medical adviser and family physician. He has been a member of the vestry of St. Clement's church for the past ten years, and has served that corporation in an official capacity ever since his connection with it. On the 22nd of June, 1870, he was joined in marriage to Miss Helen E. Bancroft, daughter of Dr. Benjamin and Eunice Bancroft, and granddaughter of Mrs. O. Doolittle, all residents of Wethersfield Spa. The marriage tie was solemnized in St. Clement's church by the rector of the parish, the Rev. L. H. Stryker. On the 17th of November, 1877, Dr. Bliss was made the happy father of a daughter, who was baptized in the same church by the present rector, Rev. J. E. Battin, on Sunday, September 3d, 1879, receiving then and there the Christian name Maud.

RESIDENCE OF GUY P. MORGAN ESQ., HERMITAGE, N.Y.

Appendix.

The following pages consist almost entirely of items received too late to be printed in the proper connection. Some of the biographical notices are only more adequate sketches of persons merely mentioned in the body of this work.

ATTICA.

MARVIN TRALL, son of Russell and Tirzah Trail, was born in Vernon, Conn., July 20th, 1811. In 1812 he removed with his parents to what is now Centreville, Allegany county, N.Y. The country was then largely a wilderness, inhabited by Indians and wild beasts. For several years afterward cattle were mostly pastured in the woods. It was on an occasion of seeking his father's cows there that he, when twelve years old, and a brother four years younger, became lost, and remained all night in the woods, lying on the ground covered with bark gathered from a fallen tree. The night was dark and accompanied by a thunder shower, and added to this the boys heard approaching them slowly the steps of some beast, which seemed to stop and stand with its head right over them for a time, then walked around them for a considerable time and then moved off. The people were rallied and searched through the night; their horns were heard by the boys, but too far off for relief. The next day they found their own way out all safe. Marvin Trail commenced the study of law with Dudley C. Bryan at Centreville, N. Y., but was afterward a law student for several years in the law offices of Hon. L. C. Peck, at Pike, and Hon. J. B. Skinner, at Wyoming, N. Y. In 1836 he was admitted to the bar of the Court of Common Pleas, Cattaraugus county, and the same year opened a law office at Randolph, in that county, the first law office ever there, and was a few months after joined with Joseph E. Weeden, as a law partner, at that place. Upon the election of L. C. Peck to Congress he soon after returned to Pike; was admitted to the bar of the 8upreme Court and Court of Chancery in January, 1838, and afterward continued the practice of law there for about thirty years, holding in the meantime various positions of trust and town offices, including those of supervisor and justice of the peace, holding the latter about fourteen years in succession. During the administration of Governor Seward he was appointed master and examiner in chancery for Allegany county, and by reappointment held the office two terms. He was afterward twice appointed town commissioner for Wyoming county, holding the office four years. In 1861 he was elected county judge and surrogate of Wyoming county, holding the place for four years. For the last twenty-five years he has been largely engaged in the trial of cases referred to him for trial by the supreme, county and surrogate's courts. He was married in 1836 to Cornelia A. Huntting, at Pike, and by her had three children, all daughters, one of whom, Elmira A., married Edwin D. Fiske, a graduate of the University of Michigan; one, Ellen F., married Elbert F. McCall, a merchant, and the other died in infancy. In 1873 he removed to Attica, N. Y., his present place of residence.

BENNINGTON.

COLONEL JOHN B. FOLSOM was born in the town of Middlebury, Wyoming county, N. Y., January 28th, 1811. His father, Asa Folsom, was one of the early pioneers of Wyoming county. He removed from Orange county, Vt., to the town of Warsaw in 1810. He was with General Wayne in his expedition against the Indians in the northwest. He died in 1813. Mrs. Asa Folsom moved to Attica in 1814, when the subject of this biography was only three years old. There they continued to reside till 1828. Mr. Folsom's early life was a hard and bitter struggle against poverty, and he is to-day an illustration of what may be accomplished by perseverance and integrity. He married Miss Clarinda C. Harnden in 1831, and took up his residence at Varysburg, where he remained until 1834. He then moved to Michigan, but failing to realize his expectations he returned to his native Wyoming, and organized the little hamlet named from him "Folsomdale." Colonel Folsom is truly a self-made man. Deprived of a father at an early age, single handed and alone he has fought the battle of life to a successful issue, and to-day he is one of the solid men of the county of Wyoming. Besides being an extensive real estate owner in Wyoming county he owns a large real estate interest at Omaha, Neb., where he spends a portion of his time every year. He was commissioned colonel in 1840 by Governor W. H. Seward; was appointed brigade-inspector in 1844 by Governor W. C. Bouck, and was again commissioned colonel under the new organization in 1858 by Horatio Seymour.

Colonel Folsom has been a life-long Democrat, and has represented his town as supervisor and Justice of the peace for a long term of years.

In the summer of 1873 he made an extended tour through England, Ireland, Scotland, France and Belgium. He visited the birthplace of Robert Burns, also Kirk Alloway, where the poet's family lies buried. He also visited the battle ground of Waterloo and many other places of classic interest. Mr. Folsom had three children, B. Franklin, Oscar and Mary Augusta. His wife died January 18th, 1873. His son B. Franklin died January 27th, 1873; his daughter, Mary A., February 18th, 1873. He was thus bereft of wife, son and daughter in three brief weeks.

His son Oscar graduated at Rochester University in the class of '59. He at once began the practice of law at Buffalo, N. Y. His success was brilliant from the beginning. He could always be relied on as a man, as a lawyer and as a friend; and after his death, which occurred July 23d, 1875, the bar of Erie county and the different societies of which he was a member paid him the noblest tribute that could be paid to man. The Hon. Judge Clinton, speaking of him, said he was the soul of honor, that his wit knew no sting and his humor was always wholesome. He was kind to all men.

His bosom friend and companion, George S. Wardwell, spoke of him as follows:

"I shall not endeavor to analyze his intellectual qualities or speak of his professional acquirements. These are subjects which should be left to a more impartial tongue than mine. It is in the character of a frank, open hearted, generous, sincere, constant and cordial friend that I prefer now to remember him. I cannot forget the brilliancy of his conversation, the keen edge of his wit, the overflowing humor which nothing could suppress, his shrewd criticisms of men and things, which surprised and delighted all who heard him and were the most admirable to those who knew him best; but more than all else beside was the gentle and magnanimous heart that beat within his bosom—its kindness included everybody. I don't know that he had an enemy in the world, and if by chance the poignancy of his wit at any time offended, some graceful or kindly remark, more efficient but lees conspicuous than a direct apology, suppressed the mortification or healed the wound. We have lost a brilliant member of our profession, an esteemed and honored member of society, a cordial friend; his family an affectionate husband, a loving father and a noble son."

CASTILE.

The *Christian Church*, the first formed in the town (1819), was organized by Elder William True, on the basis of the Bible as a "guide in faith and practice, disregarding the doctrines of men," and Christian character as the only test of fellowship.

Elder True was the pastor about twenty years, other ministers officiating as circumstances required.

Aaron Post was elected deacon at the organization, and Aaron Post, jr., succeeded him in that office. The church elected William H. Luther and Richard Smith deacons, and George Green church clerk, and chose Elder Ezra Smith for pastor. The church numbered at that time forty-nine members, who were earnest workers in the cause of Christ.

This church has had the services of the following pastors, in the order given: William True, Ezra Smith, Joseph Weeks, Elisha Ney, W. Skeels, John Ellis, Thomas Garbutt, Samuel Salisbury, J. W. Noble, A. C. Parker, P. R. Sullon, F. R. Wade, D. L. Pendell and Joseph Weeks, above mentioned, who is also the present pastor, it being his fourth pastorate.

In 1852 the church numbered about one hundred and thirty members. It has a convenient chapel, in which it has worshiped over forty years. It has had a succession of officers from 1819, and has sustained a pastor all that time, with the exception of a very few years. The present officers are as fallows: Trustees—E. P. Phelps, John Pennock and Lewis Finch; deacons—Charles Chittenden and William Post; church clerk, George W. Smith. Several young men who were members of this church are now preaching successfully in different States. The present number of active members is sixty-eight.

A Sunday-school was organized in the spring of 1843, and it has been kept up to the present. The average attendance is about fifty. There are seven teachers, all members of the church. Almanzer Gaines is superintendent, and E. P. Phelps secretary and treasurer.

WILLIS F. GRAVES.

MRS. W. F. GRAVES.

RESIDENCE AND WARE-ROOMS OF W. F. GRAVES, DEALER IN MUSICAL INSTRUMENTS, CASTILE, WYOMING CO., N. Y.

W. F. GRAVES, Castile, N. Y., the widely known dealer in musical instruments, was born January 14th, 1831, in the town of Eagle, Wyoming county, N. Y., where his father, Ralph Graves, a native of Vermont, settled in 1819, and resided (on the same farm) for about sixty years. The subject of this sketch was reared to hard labor, industry and economy. A few weeks each year at the district school, and the books of the school library, constituted nearly all the advantages for mental improvement accessible. By the faithful use of these limited means, and a few weeks spent at a private seminary in Arcade in 1819, he fitted himself for school teaching, which avocation he followed for many years, beginning near home in Eagle. His vacations were passed at Arcade Seminary, or in farm labor or book selling. In 1854 he received an appointment to the State normal school in Albany, where, besides attending the school, he spent some hours each day at work in a piano factory.

He was principal of the following union schools: Sandusky, Cattaraugus county, 1852; Pike, 1853; Centerville, 1854; Portageville, 1855; Attica, 1858–59; Arcade, 1860-62. His vacations and leisure hours were occupied in selling pianos and organs, or at work on farms, which he bought at the commencement of the civil war and managed and sold at great profit. Soon after disposing of these he began to devote his whole time and attention to the music trade, in which he has been very successful; for, besides doing a very extensive trade in western New York, he sends large numbers of instruments to almost every State in the Union. His extensive warerooms in Castile are filled with the choicest instruments of the most celebrated makers, and are continually thronged by customers from the surrounding country. The great manufacturers often visit the rooms of Mr. Graves to solicit his contracts for large numbers of instruments. Everybody knows his slightest word to be as good as a bond. Commercial integrity and the highest degree of honor are the corner stones of his successful business career. Musicians find in him a kind and accommodating friend. Honest people find in him a lenient creditor. The dishonest and indolent he boldly rebukes in severe terms, telling them that industry, economy and integrity can never come to want. Still in the prime of life, with almost faultless physical strength and health, he seems destined to accomplish all he undertakes.

Jennie Colton Graves, wife of W. F. Graves and only daughter of Addison Colton, Esq., of Arcade, N. Y., was born in Vergennes, Vt., April 22nd, 1833, and removed to Arcade in 1835, where she was reared with the best opportunities for schooling and the highest culture in music. She was married to Mr. Graves July 7th, 1858. Although always of frail health and strength, she has acted a very important part in assisting to build the eminent fortune of her husband.

JOHN B. HALSTED was born in the town of Plttston, Luzerne county, Pa., November 7th, 1798. In 1816, when but eighteen years of age, he left his native State for western New York, where he has ever since resided. He came first to Livonia, then Ontario, now Livingston county, and remained there some ten years. In 1826 he took a clerkship in the store of Walter Howard, of Perry. In 1828 Mr. Howard transferred his business and his clerk along with it to Castile. After clerking a short time in the latter place Mr. Halsted set up in business on his own account, and was so prosperous that he was soon able to take to himself a wife, being married October 28th, 1832, to Miss Eunice Talcott, of the town of

Vernon, Tolland county, Conn. Matrimony was then, as now, often spoken of as having more or less of the lottery in it, and Mr. Halstead drew a prise. He continued in business in Castile some thirty years. He represented the people of the 30th senatorial district in the State Legislature in the years 1856-59. In 1862 he was appointed revenue collector of the 29th district in this State, which office he held till 1866. For the last fourteen years his principal business has been loaning money, as agent for corporations and individuals, on bond mortgages. In 1864 he left Castile and located in Batavia, where he still lives. Mr. H., now among the eighties, has always held his life by what might with propriety be called an invalid's title, and yet by constant abstemiousness he has outlasted many among his old-time associates, who were really robust, while he was apparently only a hand's breadth from the grave.

ELI WRIGHT, son of John and Lovicy Wright, was born at Castile, in 1836, and in 1872 was married to Phebe Butts, of Stamford, Dutchess county, N. Y. He resides in Castile village, on Main street; is a practicing physician and dentist, and keeps a medical collection of hygienic remedies, and a boarding-house for patients and others, a view of which may be seen on another page.

COVINGTON.

The children of Mrs. Joel C. Clarke (of whom a notice appears on page 373) were William H., Charles, George C., Mary A., Martha A., Hattie E., Fannie L., Howard and Frederick W. All are living except the son Charles, who died March 12th, 1853.

JOEL T. PRATT, farmer, was born in Perry, in 1838, and married, in 1865, Melodia A. Onley, who died in 1876, since which time his only child, Ida E., born March 16th, 1868, has been his chief dependence as a house keeper. Mr. Pratt is a member of the Baptist church, as was also his late wife. He rendered signal assistance, contributing largely of his means, toward the suppression of the Rebellion. He purchased his farm six years ago. Owing to the loss of his dwelling by fire he was obliged to live in his barn for a time. His father, Rudolphus Wooster Pratt, was born in Manchester, Vt., in 1806, and was for many years a resident of Perry. He and his wife (born in 1818 and still living) long since identified themselves with the Baptist church.

EAGLE.

THEODORE J. HUBBARD was born in Centerville, Allegany county, N. Y., June 4th, 1845. Since the spring of 1867, when he and his father built the Star cheese factory, he has been employed in it, and he is now owner and superintendent. He was supervisor in 1879. His father, Asa C. Hubbard, was born in Champion, Jefferson county, N. Y., November 8th, 1818. About 1840 he moved to a farm in Centerville, Allegany county, and the next year married Fanny Woodard, of Jefferson county. From 1865 he was a cheese maker in Centerville, Wethersfield and Eagle until 1878. Since 1872 he has lived at Eagle Village, where he is now justice of the peace.

GAINESVILLE.

SUPPLEMENTARY.—The writer of the history of Gainesville sent in the following items after the history of that town had been printed: "Please add to the figures given on page 399 the following returns of population: 1815, 586; 1820, 1,088; 1825, 1,482. Add to the county officers from this town named on page 403: Superintendent of the poor seventeen years, Benjamin F. Bristol; commissioners U. S. Deposit Fund, Ira F. Pratt and Robert F. Shearman; Nyrum Reynolds, appointed associate judge of Wyoming county in 1845.

MIDDLEBURY.

MERRITT C. PAGE, son of Timothy and Lydia Page, was born at Wyoming, N. Y., June 12th, 1840. He early evinced a desire for intellectual culture, and while his comrades were engaged in sports incident to childhood and youth he employed his time in acquiring knowledge. He was an indefatigable student. His leisure hours were devoted to the study of music, in which art he greatly excelled. At the age of ten years he commenced his studies at the Middlebury Academy. Nothing of note occurred during those years of study, though he was regarded as a brilliant scholar and a fine elocutionist, being often awarded the prize. At the age of twelve years he united with the M. E. church at Wyoming, and always remained a consistent Christian. At the age of sixteen he left "Old Middlebury," and entered the grammar school at New Haven, Conn., which school he attended one year. He then entered Yale College, and graduated with the highest honors in 1862. He was held in the highest esteem by the members of his class, and was the author of the parting ode, of which we subjoin the last verse:

"Farewell, farewell! the sacred spell of parting closes 'round,
With fettered tear that tells how dear this cloister home we've found.
Then, brothers, up, and pledge the cup of friendship strong and true,
Through all our days to bless and praise old Yale and Sixty-two.

At the close of his collegiate course he went to New York dty, and commenced the study of law in the office of Judge Edmonds, in whom he found a warm, true friend, who took great interest in his welfare and often intrusted him with important commissions, which Mr. Page faithfully executed. While pursuing his studies he sustained himself by teaching mathematics at the Cooper Institute. He remained in the office of Judge Edmonds two years. He then received an appointment in the ordnance office at Chattanooga, Tenn., as clerk, in which place he remained till the close of the war. He then entered into partnership with A. A. Hyde, attorney-general of that circuit, and began the practice of his profession, the firm name being Hyde & Page. He remained at Chattanooga until May, 1868, when, the population of the city having decreased so rapidly that all business became prostrated, and financial ruin and despondency seized upon all, he concluded to abandon an extensive but not lucrative practice. He therefore took up his line of march for the far west, and arrived at Laramie city, Wyoming Territory, the terminus of the Union Pacific Railroad. Finding no immediate business in the way of his profession heengaged in various pursuits through the summer until he was taken dangerously ill with the mountain fever, brought on by fatigue and exposure. After his recovery he opened an office at Laramie, and did an active business in the line of conveyancing. About this time the Legislature of Dakota passed an act creating a new county, and appointing temporarily a set of officers, among whom Mr. Page was appointed probate judge. Soon after he was appointed Mayor of Laramie, and his administration proved a success. It was "the right man in the right place." He had some severe enoounters with roughs and desperadoes that then infested the city. His life was often in danger, but by his indomitable firmness he succeeded in maintaining law and order. In June, 1869, he resigned his office as Mayor, and started out to try his fortunes in the new Eldorado, "Sweet Water Mining Camp." But there disaster overtook him, and all of his hard earned accumulations were swept away. Nothing daunted, however, but with a determined will, be resolved to win. He therefore procured two horses, blankets, provisions and "outfit," as the miners say, and on January 1st, 1871, he joined a small pack train often and started for Montana. His taste for romance and adventure was amply satisfied during this trip. On one occasion he came near being captured by a band of treacherous Sioux. On another the party became lost, and for four days wandered through the mountain fastnesses in search of the trail. But after two months of hardship and danger they arrived at Montana. Mr. Page soon established himself in business, and on the 17th of May, 1872, was appointed United States district attorney of Montana, which office he filled with marked ability for four years. He was reappointed, and continued in the office until his death. He possessed an extensive mining interest, and it was while away attending to a suit involving that interest that he met an untimely death. On his return from Boseman, in company with an attorney named Sanders, they attempted to cross the Madison river, then swollen by the mountain torrent; the wagon was overturned, and himself and companion were at the mercy of the flood. Mr. Sanders escaped, but Mr. Page was drowned. Thus ended the career of one who by indomitable energy and perseverance had mounted step by step to fame and fortune.

OTHER LEADING CITIZENS.

Besides the persons who are the subjects of biographical notices in this work the following may be mentioned as at one time or another among the prominent residents of the respective towns:

C. H. Ames, Mrs. B. Bartow, M. A. Fisk, Charles Gillespie, Rev. E. McShane, Lucius Peck, Leonard C. Salter and W. W. Wade, of Arcade; Henry and Julius Baker, W. Beeran, W. W. Blakely, F. D. Cady, E. F. Chaffee, G. Colton, A. Gowdin, James Dealer, W. W. Fonda, N. A. Gardener, W. B. Gifford, F. and J. Glor, M. W. Granger, Daniel and George Honifore, Albert Lemon, G. Linsey, J. Marley, Charles Morganstern, A. Morther, Rev. J. B. Quigley, J. W. H. Shipler, W. Smith, E. P. Spink, J. C. Stevens, Charles A. Struley, A. H. Van Buren, J. W. and S. R. Vincent, C. F. and E. C. Williams and Joseph Wolf, of Attica; W. B. Austin, G. W. Crossfield, D. B. Herald, Emma D. Hunt, Loren M. Kittsley, Winfield C. Mapes, W. N. Martin, James and John D. Sanborn, W. T. Seville, S. D. Sudden and Milo Westcott, of Bennington; Mrs. H. Fosdick, George L. Harrison, C. S. Jones, H. A.

Pierce, J. W. Price, H. J. Sarz, Norman Schenck, J. R. Slade and Charles Stroud, of Castile; Carlton Cooley, C. E. S. Deyo, James W. Dow, R. A. Forbes, C. R. Isham, J. C. Newman, A. G. Orr, Joel T. Pratt, C. Mendel Robinson, Esther Ann Robinson, Lester Rude, Hiram Taylor and L. F. Wood, of Covington; S. Bliss, Smith Flint, Mrs. H. C. Jones, Mrs. Kate McCraley J. McElroy, W. Redner, of Eagle; Truman Blood, G. W. Botsford, jr., J. N. Davidson, Peter Dunn, Willis H. Fuller, Mrs. M. G. Ingham, Rev. J. McGrath and Robert Rae, of Genesee Falls; George Bemis, Maria Brown, Elisha S. Buckland, O. L. Colton and L. W. Watrous, of Gainesville; Charles Gillespie, W. S. Joy and Alonzo Lane, of Java; Miss G. Chamberlain, Mrs. David Cox, Mrs. D. C. Howes and L. H. Owen, of Mlddlebury; John Holly, of Orangeville; Elias Babbitt, George S. Baker, H. Besancon, E. E. Bragdon, W. A. Brownson, Campbell brothers, Smith G. Clute, Albert B. Crary, Hannah Dodge, J. W. Doud, A. Gordon, Edwin Hodge, A. Hopson, Robert J. Horning, George P. Kellogg, John W. Kellogg, W. Kimberley, Mrs. Knowlton, H. C. Lathrop, Frank Lillibridge, Frank Lyon, Mrs. L. Minard, George W. More, A. L. Partridge, John A. Phillips, Amos Pratt, H. M. Quackenbush, Valentine Ringo, Frank P., Hoses, L. C. and Orin Robinson, Elvira Shepard, A. O. Skiff, Irving B. Smith, C. Stebbins, Mrs. H. Streeter, B. P. and L. Sweet, Mrs. Myra Taylor, Hiram Watkins and Miles W. Wells, of Pike; R. C. Alverson, Aurora Bailey, Rev. P. Birkey, Mrs. R. W. Crabbe, Edgar B. Cronkhite, R. W. Bdgerly, A. D. Keeney, D. Kingsley, Paris Olin, W. N. Pool, Mrs. H. Richards, D. P. Stowel, B. A. Thompson, D. A. Wallace, M. A. Ward and E. H. Wygant, of Perry; F. E. Bliss and William H. Wilcox, of Wethersfield; Mrs. John B. Matthews, Warsaw.

Augustus Hauhinoton was born in Gainesville, Wyoming county, N. Y., August 14th. 1835.

Elenzer Harrington was born in Smithfield, R. I., about 1772. At the age of nineteen he went to Norwich, N. Y., in company with George King, who moved from Smithfield to Norwich at this time. Eleazer Harrington married Dirveras, (daughter of George King. George, the seventh of their eight children, was born in Norwich, September 17th, 1808. At the age of twenty-one he went to Gainesville, where he has since resided.

Amos Bristol and Lois, his wife, removed from New Milford, Conn., to Fort Edward, N. Y., before the Revolution. About the same time William Warner, born July 4th, 1717, and Rebecca, his wife, born July 15th, 1721, removed from West Milford to Canaan, N. Y. Benjamin Bristol, son of Amos and Lois, was married to Abigail, daughter of William and Rebecca Warner, at Canaan, by Rev. John Richards, November 24th, 1774. William, born August 19th, 1775, was the oldest of their eleven children. Benjamin Bristol served under Arnold, in the Army of the North. He fought at Still-water and at Saratoga October 17th, 1777, when Burgoyne surrendered. William Bristol was the first white settler in Gainesville.

Francis Stevens removed from Worcester, Mass., to Lima, N. Y., where his daughter, Martha. married William Bristol, February 22nd, 1807. George Harrington married Lamira. their fourth child, November 19th, 1834. The oldest of their four sons is the subject of this sketch.

Already master of the instruction of its schools and familiar with the volumes in the Franklin and the school district libraries of his native village, at the age of fifteen he attended Genesee Wesleyan Seminary, at Lima, N. Y., then in its most flourishing period, where be pursued his preparatory classical studies. July 10th, 1851, he entered Genesee College, then under the presidency of B. F. Tefft, LL. D., afterward U. S. Minister to Sweden. The following winter, at Wiscoy, N. Y., he successfully conducted a school of over seventy pupils, some or whom were seven years his senior. He returned to Genesee College in the autumn of 1852, and pursued the course to the end of the first term sophomore year, when he entered Amherst College, or which Edward Hitchcock, LL.D., was then president, and there received the degree of A. B. in course, August 14th, 1856.

His recitations at Amherst were creditable, and he found opportunity to delve in society and college libraries among rare volumes till then unknown to him. Here he spent the long vacations in labors that bore fruit which the routine of lecture and recitation rooms could not develop. The pages of *Amherst Collegiate Magazine*, 1855-6, evidence his literary work on a wide range of subjects.

The Sweetzer (rhetorical) prizes were offered to the junior class in 1855, for the two bent essays on subjects selected by the writers. The first prize, of $25, was awarded young Harrington for his essay on "The Philosophy and Character of Franklin." The following year Mr. George Montague, of Montgomery, Ala., offered (metaphysical) prizes to the senior class for the two best essays on assigned subjects. Young Harrington again received the first prize, of $80, for his essay on "The Imagination; its Nature and Province, with its Influence on Life and Character." This essay appeared August, 1856, in *The American Journal of Education and College Review*, published in New York. A foot note by Dr. Peters, the editor, called attention to the surpassing excellence and maturity of this youthful production. The second Montague prize was awarded to William H. Ward, now editor of the N. Y. *Independent*.

Mr. Harrington's industry and force of character gave him position in a class, many of whoso members are positive forces in society; leaders in pulpit, press, law, politics and affairs. He was valedictorian of his societies, Psi Upsilon and Athenian, and received the honors of an "oration" at commencement, and an election to Phi Beta Kappa. His oration on "Enthusiasm" at commencement received complimentary notice in the Springfield *Republican*, then edited by Dr. Holland. It was an impassioned plea for earnest men in literature, politics and the church, as "from these come all that motion and ferment which form the vital feature of modern civilization." This appeared November, 1856, in *The Student*, published in New York, as the monthly selection by the editor of that magazine from the speeches of the time.

During senior year he occasionally accepted invitations to address literary societies in neighboring towns of western Massachusetts.

In the autumn of 1856 he was put at the head of a scientific and classical academy at Millville, N. Y., which he conducted successfully three terms. Here he wrote for various publications, contributing the leading article in the *College Review* for April, 1857, on "The Prospects of American Literature." In 1857 he resigned his position, and began the study of the law at Warsaw, in the office of General L. W. Thayer, a leading practitioner in the courts of western New York.

He formed an editorial connection in October, 1858, with the *Western New Yorker*, a newspaper established in 1840. Whig at first, it had lapsed into Americanism, and did not accord with the political sentiment of the county. He became sole editor and one of the publishers the following May. In assuming editorial charge of this newspaper be said:

"Our aim is to make this, as a newspaper, as a literary journal, as a fearless and outspoken supporter of good morals and sound policy in public affairs; in short, as a high-toned country newspaper, inferior to none. * * * Politically, we are thoroughly Republican. The success of the cause in 1860 is dear to us, and we shall labor with might and main to secure a Republican triumph in the ensuing struggle."

Introducing its twentieth volume to the patrons of the *New Yorker*, Mr. Harrington said:

"We have striven to be faithful to the obligations which lie upon every Journalist, to work in his sphere, whether narrow or conspicuous, as the faithfully of healthy public sentiment and the conscientious advocate of the public interest. We scorn to prostitute the influence of our position to the ministry of a 'party, right or wrong;' and we hope we shall never so far forget ourselves as to follow the lure of political tricksters, where obligations to you and proper respect for ourselves would confront us. * * * So far as is consistent with the nature of the field we work in we shall endeavor to make the *New Yorker* a complete family newspaper, * * * a judicious digest of the occurrences of the day, and a frank, fearless and independent journal."

Mr. Harrington worked industriously and wrote much in every department of his journal; current events, literature, politics, all received attention. The demands of party journalism were not neglected; earnest and timely political articles appeared, local interests were carefully written up, literary and book notices were prepared, the social interests had a place, a corps of local correspondents, at various points, was organized, then an unusual feature of country journalism.

During this time he also prepared a new lecture for a literary society, which he repeated in a large hall in the place it was first delivered, upon request of prominent citizens, and afterward he repeated it in various places.

Family traditions and his study of politics inclined him to the political school of Jefferson, Jackson and Silas Wright; and Mr. Harrington came into the Republican party with the sympathies of a Free-Soll Democrat, although his first presidential vote was cast for Lincoln electors. The *New Yorker*, from 1858 to 1801, gave no uncertain sound in the political strife which culminated in the Rebellion. In its first 'issue after the State convention of 1800 he says:

"The ticket presented to the electors of New York deserves the best services of every Republican. We do not fear any faltering in its support. * * *A hostile party is ringing charges on the 'Jobbing, robbing and corruption of the Republican legislation of the State.' That party could have defeated every corrupt measure in both houses it is true. So their rebuke of Legislative corruption is wretched charlatanry. But the Republican party was in power. Judas and Esau were both in our camp. If we endorse the legislation of last winter as a party, we are responsible for the abomination. Shall the party thus debase itself? * * * If a man can show a clean record, all honor to him say we. But the sentence of political death should be pronounced when the day for renomination comes, against every man who sold himself at Albany. If nominating conventions disregard this, we do not say the Republican party will be defeated, but we do say its triumph would no longer be desirable."

The Republican ticket not only enlisted his best service with his pen, but on the hustings. In addition to editorial work, he addressed a large number of political meetings in that memorable canvass; and on the hustings developed oratorieal powers, which afterward contributed to his power before juries.

Under this management the *New Yorker* quadrupled its circulation, and soon became, as it since has been, the leading Republican journal in its section of the State.

What he construed as a public demand for an emergency summoned Mr. Harrington to this editorial work. His service had extended three years, and he was not satisfied to relinquish his law studies, so he retired from the *New Yorker* in 1861, although its prospects were never better, and its circulation had never been reached by any newspaper in Wyoming county.

Mr. Harrington received authority from Governor Morgan to raise a company of volunteers August 18th, 1862. On the 27th of that month he reported at Camp Portage with a full company for muster. This was the first company in camp. It was mustered as D company, 136th regiment N. Y. volunteer Infantry September 25th, and Mr. Harrington was commissioned captain in the regiment with rank from September 2nd. The regiment left Camp Portage October 2nd, and went into camp on Arlington Heights the second day after. Only three captains in the regiment, of whom Captain Harrington was one, were on duty November 9th; and D company, which left New York ninety-four strong, reported only forty-five men for duty November 26th. After the Fredericksburg disaster and Burnside's failure of January 21st, at Bank's Ford, the army of the Potomac went into winter quarters, and remained inactive till the last of April.

Captain Harrington tendered his resignation, received an honorable discharge and came home with the purpose of entering another branch of the service. Circumstances afterward rendered this impracticable, and, without being drafted, he procured a substitute for three years at his own expense.

September 16th, 1862, Mr. Harrington married Martha Barnett, who was born in Warsaw, September 4th, 1839 and graduated with honors at Elmira Female College July 6th, 1861. She had no children and died October 4th, 1871. She was a member of the Congregational church of Warsaw.

Mr. Harrington married Sarah Alice Earle, eldest daughter of the late Justus E. Earle, of New York, in that city, May 20th, 1874. They have three children: Earle, born May 9th, 1875; George, born May 13th, 1877, and Alice Earle, born August 20th, 1879. Mrs. Harrington was a member of the University Place Presbyterian church in New York. She is now a member of the Presbyterian church of Warsaw.

Mr. Harrington was admitted to the bar May 4th, 1864, and he soon found himself entering upon a desirable practice, He has mainly devoted himself to his profession, extending his practice until it became lucrative and satisfactory, although his labors have not been engrossed by its growing demands. His reading has embraced a wide range, and his pen has been active during a busy life, as in school and college days. Volumes might be selected from his published writings. The cause of education has ever had in him an active friend, and he has traveled extensively and has a large acquaintance in various parts of the country. Occasional addresses, editorial writing in various journals on questions of the hour, discussion of topics of special interest to the community he lived in, have in part satisfied the duty, appreciated by every right minded citizen, of using his best powers to promote the general weal. Matters of local importance have not seldom enlisted his active support.

Accepting an invitation to deliver the annual Decoration Day address at Warsaw in 1872, Mr. Harrington availed himself of that opportunity to make the first public appeal for, and to help inaugurate the first movement to erect, a soldiers' monument for Wyoming county. He labored zealously to promote this object. In its behalf, as chairman of the executive committee of the association, he visited every town in the county, and addressed the people of different localities from the platform and through numerous reports, resolutions and addresses prepared by direction of the association, organized May 30th, 1872, to build this monument, which now stands as a proud memorial of the brave men who volunteered to uphold the flag, and also of the gratitude of our citizens for their splendid donation.

While he has shrunk from no duty which his relations to society imposed, Mr. Harrington has never been an applicant for place or a candidate for office in caucus, convention or before the people; and he has evinced no desire or purpose of being a professional politician. In 1858 Governor Morgan appointed him a commissioner for loaning the U. S. deposit fund in Wyoming county, and he performed the duties of this office creditably during his term. In 1857 a county convention at Warsaw, without his knowledge or consent, nominated him for the office of school commissioner, but he declined to be a candidate.

The same interest in humanity, the same conviction of the equality of men in natural rights, which drew him into the Lincoln campaign of I860, and characterized his political course through the civil war, have interested him in the political issues that have divided the country. He has uniformly voted with the Republican party, and used his time, money and influence to support its measures and maintain its principles.

Such a career is ordinarily tranquil and uneventful so far as the public interest goes, deficient in incident, and lacking what might be called the dramatic quality. Its satisfaction, however, may be in this very fact. The citizen who lives primarily in his domestic affections, faithful in the performance of his social and civic duties, conscientious in the obligations that rest upon him, patient in reverses, considerate of others in success, acts well his part in any community or time.

THE PATTERSON FAMILY.

Of four brothers, born in Londonderry, N. H.—Hon. William Patterson, ex-member of Congress, Hon. George W. Patterson, Judge Peter Patterson and Colonel Robert Patterson—the first two came to western New York in 1818, and the other two a little later.

PETER PATTERSON was born in Londonderry, N. H., November 14th, 1779. In 1806 he engaged in the mercantile business. He held various town offices, and served several years in the Legislature of his native State. In 1829 he removed to Warsaw, and the next year to Perry. After the organization of Wyoming county he was appointed one of its associate judges. In 1852, after a few years' residence in Leicester, he again made Warsaw his home. Mr. Patterson married Mary Wallace, November 8th, 1814. They had five children, three of whom are living. Judge Patterson died February 17th, 1865, aged eighty-five years. Mrs. Patterson died in 1878, aged eighty-six years.

COLONEL ROBERT PATTERSON, one of the brothers mentioned above, removed to Perry, then to Genesee county in 1829. He was a man of decided ability, liberally educated, seeking no position, accepting no office, but quietly attending to the duties devolving upon him as a husband, and father of eight sons and two daughters. He was an agriculturalist, and took pride in every thing that developed his favorite business. He died at Westfield, aged eighty-two years.

Among his sons now living are Colonel James M. Patterson, of California; Alfred S. Patterson, Esq., of Westfield, N. Y. (senior member of the firm of Patterson, Bros., extensive manufacturers of agricultural implements at Patterson, Ontario); John D. Patterson, Esq, the eminent agriculturalist, residing at Geneva, N. Y.; Hon. Reuben S. Patterson, mayor of Belleville, Canada, and Hon. Peter Patterson, of Patterson, Ontario, who is at present and has been for many years past a member of the Canadian parliament.

WILLIAM PATTERSON was born June 4th, 1789. In the winter of 1821-22 be purchased a farm in Warsaw. He remained there, conducting the farming and mill-making business until 1837, when he removed to the village of Warsaw, occupying premises on Genesee street. In September, 1837, he took his seat in Congress at an extra session, and attended also the first regular session, which closed in July, 1838. He returned somewhat indisposed, and died August 14th, 1838. William Patterson was married February 5th, 1828, to Lucinda Gregg, of Derry, N. H. She was ill at the time of his death, and died a week after, suddenly, while seated at the breakfast table. They left three children.

HON. GEORGE W. PATTERSON was born in Londonderry, N. H., November 11th, 1799. He removed to western New York in 1818. He resided in Warsaw, N. Y., for a time in 1821, but soon after removed into Livingston county, N. Y., where he engaged in farming and the manufacture of agricultural implements.

He was eight times elected to the Assembly from Livingston county by the Whigs (in 1832-31 34-35-36-37-38-39 and 40), and was twice made speaker of that body while representing that county. He was elected lieutenant-governor in

1848 on the Whig ticket, headed by Hamilton Fish, and presided over the sessions of 1849 and 1850 with remarkable dignity and fairness.

In February, 1825, he married Hannah Whiting Dickey, daughter of John Dickey, of Leicester. Governor Patterson died at Westfield, N. Y., October 15th, 1879, in his eightieth year, leaving two children, one son and a daughter.

John D. Patterson, a son of Colonel Robert Patterson, was born in 1816. He removed to Warsaw in June, 1829, and in 1830 engaged with Dr. Augustus Frank until March, 1835. when he engaged as clerk in the store of Joshua H. Darling. September 1st, 1838, he formed a copartnership with Mr. Darling, which continued three years. Mr. Patterson married Caroline Glover, of Syracuse, and now resides at Geneva, Ontario county, N. Y.

Joshua H. Darling is a native of Henniker, N. H. In 1830 he left New Hampshire, and calling on the Hon. G. W. Patterson, then residing in Leicester, with whom he visited Warsaw, he made a temporary engagement as a clerk for Dr. Augustus Frank. In the fall of that year he became a partner with A. W. Young for about twenty years. He maintained the reputation of an honest dealer. Mr. Darling established, as an Individual banker, the Wyoming County Bank, under the general banking law of New York, and managed its operations during its existence as a State institution. He was associated with the earliest friends of the temperance and anti-slavery causes, and steadily co-operated in efforts for the promotion of good morals and the interests of education and religion. He was born September 5th, 1808, and died March 21st, 1869.

THE SOLDIERS' MONUMENT.

After the close of the war of the Rebellion a number of the patriotic citizens of Wyoming county, desirous of commemorating in a public manner the devotion of many citizens of the county to the perpetuation of the Union, determined to erect a soldiers' monument or memorial as a fitting tribute. The monumental shaft stands at Warsaw, as a testimonial to all who bore arms in defence of the country.

On the 30th day of May, 1872, an association was organized, called the "Wyoming County Soldiers' Monument Association." The following gentlemen were chosen officers: President, Hon. William P. Letch worth; vice-president, Hon. Augustus Frank; secretary, Colonel Abram B. Lawrence; treasurer, Lloyd A. Hayward, Esq.

An address was issued to the citizens of the county, setting forth the objects of this association, and committees were appointed to solicit funds for carrying forward the enterprise.

During the year 1872 meetings were held in different parts of the county, on which occasions the claims of the soldiers for a suitable testimonial were presented. An effort was made to raise funds for the purchase of a monument by life-membership subscriptions of five dollars each. The amount of subscriptions made and donations pledged was not sufficient, the records of the secretary on July 3d, 1875, showing $206.78 in his hands.

On March 3d, 1873, an act was passed by Congress appropriating captured confederate bronze cannon and 16 iron balls for the use of the association.

By an act of the Legislature of the State of New York, passed May 9th, 1873, the Wyoming County Mutual Insurance Company was authorized to "sell and dispose of one hundred and ten shares of the stock of the Warsaw Water Works Company, * * * and to pay over the same or the proceeds thereof to the treasurer of the Wyoming County Soldiers' Monument Association, to be used and employed by said association for the erection of a monument to the soldiers of Wyoming county who fell in the war of the Rebellion."

A meeting was held in Warsaw May 30th, 1876, to report at an adjourned meeting a plan for raising funds to erect the monument. At an adjourned meeting Hon. Augustus Frank recommended the appointment of a finance committee, who should be empowered to adopt such measures as would be best calculated to secure the early erection of the monument. At a meeting of the association, held at Warsaw on September 8th, 1877, a committee was appointed to select a site for the monument within the limits of the county. The committee decided that the monument should be erected in the village of Warsaw. The trustees of the village of Warsaw passed a resolution granting to the Wyoming County Monument Association the privilege of erecting the monument at the place selected by the committee.

The memorial chosen comprised the beautiful granite shaft which was on exhibition at the Centennial Exposition at Philadelphia, Pa., in 1876, and is of beautiful design. The column is of the Corinthian order, surmounted by a bronze statue of an American soldier, of heroic size. The shaft rests upon a fortress shaped base of nearly twenty feet, with salient angles, upon which are laid as trophies the four captured cannon donated by Congress. Under the principal granite base, resting upon the parapet of the monument, the records, consisting of a roll of 1,575 names of Wyoming county soldiers, with other valuable records, are deposited. The bronze statue that surmounts the monument is beautifully conceived, representing a private soldier with his musket "at rest," while he is looking intently toward the rising sun. In face and general bearing the figure is a striking representation of an intelligent young American soldier. The monument is surrounded by a beautiful granite curbing.

Want of space forbids stating each individual subscription made for the erection of the monument. The total amount given by individuals and towns was $4.147.61. The remainder of the money necessary for the completion of the monument was received from the donation made by the Wyoming County Mutual Insurance Company.

The monument ranks among the finest of the land, and while many vary from it in design and are more costly, none surpass it in perfectness of proportion and beauty of design.

The fundamental principles of free government are inscribed in relief upon four sides of the freize above the die—LIBERY, UNION, LAW, PEACE—under which are these inscriptions on the main block or die, conveying in appropriate terms the homage paid by the donors to the heroes of Wyoming county:—

THEY WERE CITIZENS WHO BECAME
SOLDIERS NOT FROM AMBITION OR LUST OF WAR,
BUT FROM DEVOTION TO THEIR COUNTRY,
AND TO ASSERT THE SOVEREIGNTY OF HER LAWS.

BY VALOR AND BY SACRIFICE, THROUGH
UNMEASURED SUFFERING AND DEATH, THEY PRESERVED
THE HONOR AND INTEGRITY OF THE NATION,
AND MAINTAINED THE PRINCIPLES OF FREE GOVERNMENT IN
AMERICA.

IN MEMORY OF THE DEFENDERS OF OUR COUNTRY.
1861-1865.

THE COUNTY OF WYOMING RENDERS HOMAGE TO HER
PATRIOT DEAD; A RESCUED PEOPLE HOLD THEM IN GRATEFUL
REMEMBRANCE.
A. D. 1876.

Index.

A

B

D

E

F

G

I

J

K

L

M

O

P

S

T

U

V

W

CPSIA information can be obtained
at www.ICGtesting.com
Printed in the USA
BVHW070908060123
655718BV00007B/456

9 781438 487823